Developmental Psychology

Childhood and Adolescence

SEVENTH EDITION

David R. Shaffer

University of Georgia

Katherine Kipp

University of Georgia

THOMSON
WADSWORTH™

Australia • Brazil • Canada • Mexico • Singapore • Spain • United Kingdom • United States

THOMSON

WADSWORTH

Developmental Psychology: Childhood and Adolescence, Seventh Edition

David R. Shaffer, Katherine Kipp

Publisher: Vicki Knight
Executive Editor: Michele Sordi
Development Editor: Jeremy Judson
Managing Assistant Editor: Jennifer Alexander
Editorial Assistant: Kara Warren
Technology Project Manager: Adrian Paz
Marketing Assistant: Natasha Coats
Marketing Communications Manager: Kelley McAllister
Project Manager, Editorial Production: Mary Noel
Creative Director: Rob Hugel
Art Director: Vernon Boes
Print Buyer: Rebecca Cross
Permissions Editor: Sarah D'Stair
Production Service: Carol O'Connell, Graphic World Publishing Services
Text Designer: Lisa Buckley
Photo Researcher: Roman Barnes
Illustrator: Graphic World Illustration Studio
Cover Designer: Larry Didona
Cover Image: Mark Tomalty / Masterfile
Compositor: Graphic World Inc.
Printer: CTPS

Printed in China
2 3 4 5 6 7 10 09 08 07

For more information about our products, contact us at:
Thomson Learning Academic Resource Center
1-800-423-0563
For permission to use material from this text or product, submit a request online at **http://www.thomsonrights.com.**
Any additional questions about permissions can be submitted by e-mail to **thomsonrights@thomson.com.**

Thomson Higher Education
10 Davis Drive
Belmont, CA 94002-3098
USA

Library of Congress Control Number: 0534632521

Student Edition: ISBN-13 978-0-534-63252-6
ISBN-10 0-534-63252-1

International student Edition: ISBN-13 978-0-495-18678-6
ISBN-10 0-495-18678-3

Loose-leaf Edition: ISBN-13 978-0-495-18679-3
ISBN-10 0-495-18679-1

Dedicated to
David F. Bjorklund, PhD

Brief Contents

Contents

PART I INTRODUCTION TO DEVELOPMENTAL PSYCHOLOGY 1

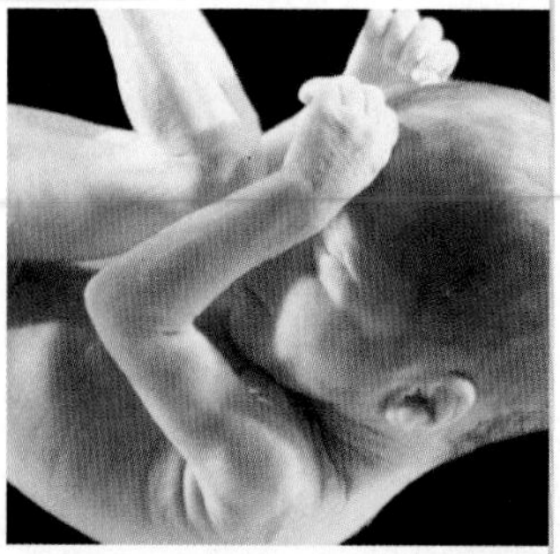

Chapter 6

PART III COGNITIVE DEVELOPMENT 243

Chapter 7

Chapter 12

Development of the Self and Social Cognition 467

Chapter 13

Sex Differences and Gender-Role Development 509

Preface

Our purpose in writing this book has been to produce a current and comprehensive overview of child and adolescent development that reflects the best theories, research, and practical advice that developmentalists have to offer. Throughout our many years of teaching, we had longed for a substantive developmental text that was also interesting, accurate, up to date, and written in clear, concise language that an introductory student could easily understand. At this level, a good text should talk "to" rather than "at" its readers, anticipating their interests, questions, and concerns and treating them as active participants in the learning process. In the field of human development, a good text should also stress the processes that underlie developmental change so that students come away from the course with a firm understanding of the causes and complexities of development. Last but not least, a good text is a relevant text—one that shows how the theory and the research that students are asked to digest can be applied to a number of real-life settings.

The present volume represents our attempt to accomplish all of these objectives. We have tried to write a book that is both rigorous and applied—one that challenges students to think about the fascinating process of human development, to share in the excitement of our young and dynamic discipline, and to acquire a knowledge of developmental principles that will serve them well in their roles as parents, teachers, nurses, day-care workers, pediatricians, psychologists, or in any other capacity by which they may one day influence the lives of developing persons.

Philosophy

Certain philosophical views underlie any systematic treatment of a field as broad as human development. Our philosophy can be summarized as follows:

We Believe in Theoretical Eclecticism

There are many theories that have contributed to what we know about developing persons, and this theoretical diversity is a strength rather than a weakness. Although some theories may do a better job than others of explaining particular aspects of development, we will see—time and time again—that *different theories emphasize different aspects of development* and that knowledge of many theories is necessary to explain the course and complexities of human development. So this book does not attempt to convince its readers that any one theoretical viewpoint is "best." The psychoanalytic, behavioristic, cognitive-developmental, ecological, sociocultural, information-processing, ethological, and behavioral genetic viewpoints (as well as several less-encompassing theories that address selected aspects of development) are all treated with respect.

The Best Information about Human Development Comes from Systematic Research

To teach this course effectively, we believe that one must convince students of the value of theory and systematic research. Although there are many ways to achieve these objectives, we have chosen to contrast the modern developmental sciences with their "prescientific" origins and then to discuss and illustrate the many methodological approaches that researchers use to test their theories and answer important questions about developing children and adolescents. We've taken care to explain why there is no one "best method" for studying developing persons, and we've repeatedly stressed that our most reliable findings are those that can be replicated using a variety of methods.

A Strong "Process" Orientation

A major complaint with many developmental texts (including some best sellers) is that they describe human development without adequately explaining why it occurs. In recent years investigators have become increasingly concerned about identifying and understanding developmental processes—the biological and environmental factors that cause us to change—and this book clearly reflects this emphasis. Our own process orientation is based on the belief that students are more likely to remember what develops and when if they know and understand the reasons *why* these developments take place.

A Strong "Contextual" Orientation

One of the more important lessons that developmentalists have learned is that children and adolescents live in historical eras and sociocultural contexts that affect every aspect of their development. We have chosen to highlight these contextual influences in three major ways. First, *cross-cultural comparisons* are discussed throughout the text. Not only do students enjoy learning about the development of people in other cultures and ethnically diverse subcultures, but cross-cultural research also helps them to see how human beings can be so much alike, and at the same time so different from one another. In addition, the impacts of such immediate contextual influences as our families, neighborhoods, schools, and peer groups are considered throughout the first 14 chapters as we discuss each aspect of human development and again in Chapters 15 and 16 as important topics in their own right.

Human Development Is a Holistic Process

Although individual researchers may concentrate on particular topics such as physical development, cognitive development, or the development of moral reasoning, development is not piecemeal but *holistic:* human beings are at once physical, cognitive, social, and emotional creatures, and each of these components of "self" depends, in part, on the changes that are taking place in other areas of development. This holistic perspective is a central theme in the modern developmental sciences—and one that is emphasized throughout the text.

A Developmental Text Should Be a Resource Book for Students—One That Reflects Current Knowledge

We have chosen to cite more than 800 new studies and reviews (most of which have been published since the fifth edition) to ensure that our coverage (and any outside readings that students may undertake) will represent our current understanding of a topic or topics. However, we have avoided the tendency, common in textbooks, to ignore older research simply because it is older. In fact, many of the "classics" of our discipline are prominently displayed throughout the text to illustrate important breakthroughs and to show how our knowledge about developing persons gradually builds on these earlier findings and insights.

Organization

There are two traditional ways of presenting human development. In the *chronological,* or "ages and stages," approach, the coverage begins at conception and proceeds through the life span, using ages or chronological periods as the organizing principle. By contrast, the *topical* approach is organized around areas of development and follows each from its origins to its mature forms. Each of these presentations has its advantages and disadvantages. On the one hand, a chronological focus highlights the holistic character of development but may obscure the links between early and later events within each developmental domain. On the other hand, a topical approach highlights developmental sequences and processes, but at the risk of failing to convey that development as a holistic enterprise.

We've chosen to organize this book topically to focus intently on developmental processes and to provide the student with an uninterrupted view of the sequences of change that children and adolescents experience within each developmental domain. In our opinion, this topical approach best allows the reader to appreciate the flow of development—the systematic, and often truly dramatic, transformations that take place over the course of childhood and adolescence, as well as the developmental continuities that make each individual a reflection of his or her past self. At the same time, we consider it essential to paint a holistic portrait of the developing person. To accomplish this aim, we've stressed the fundamental interplay among biological, cognitive, social, and cultural influences in our coverage of *every aspect of development.* So even though this text is topically organized, students will not lose sight of the whole person and the holistic character of human development.

Content

We have made an effort to retain in this edition the major qualities that students and professors have said that they like. One such quality is a division of the book into five general parts.

- **Part I: Introduction to Developmental Psychology.** This first part presents an orientation to the discipline and the tools of the trade, including a thorough discussion and illustration of *research methodologies* in **Chapter 1** and a succinct review of the major *theories of human development* in **Chapter 2.** These chapters illustrate why research methods and theories are so important for understanding human development. The coverage also analyzes the contributions and the limitations of each research method and each major theory. In addition, this section introduces four major themes in developmental psychology that will be revisited in each of the remaining chapters of the book. They include nature vs. nurture, the active child, qualitative and quantitative changes in development, and the holistic nature of development.
- **Part II: Biological Foundations of Development.** Chapters 3 through 6 address foundations of development heavily influenced by biological factors. **Chapter 3** focuses on *hereditary contributions* to human development and illustrates how genes and environments interact to influence most human characteristics. **Chapter 4** focuses on *prenatal development* and on the many prenatal environmental factors that influence development. **Chapter 5** examines a newborn's health and readiness for adapting to the world outside the womb. **Chapter 6** is devoted to *physical growth,* including the *development of the brain* and *motor skills.* Connections between physical growth and psychological development are emphasized.
- **Part III: Cognitive Development.** The five chapters of Part III address the many theories and voluminous research pertaining to the development of language, learning capabilities, and intellectual development. **Chapter 7** is devoted to two major viewpoints of intellectual growth: Piaget's *cognitive-developmental*

theory and Vygotsky's *sociocultural theory.* These two theories are covered in detail, because each is important to understand the social, emotional, and language developments that are covered in the later chapters. **Chapter 8** explores perhaps the dominant model of intellectual development today—the *information-processing viewpoint.* Highlighted in this chapter are the many contributions information-processing researchers have made in assisting children to master academic lessons. **Chapter 9** focuses on individual differences in intellectual performance. Here we review the *intelligence testing* movement, the many factors that influence children's IQ scores, and the merits of compensatory interventions designed to improve intellectual performance. The chapter then concludes with a discussion of *creative abilities* and their development. Finally, **Chapter 10** explores the fascinating topic of *language development,* addressing such intriguing issues as: Are children inherently linguistic? Do children acquire language easier than adults? Is sign language a true language? And does bilingualism promote or inhibit linguistic proficiency and cognitive development?

- **Part IV: Social and Personality Development.** The next four chapters focus on crucial aspects of social and personality development. **Chapter 11** examines the process of *emotional development,* the developmental significance of individual differences in *temperament,* and the growth and implications for later development of the *emotional attachments* that children form with their close companions. **Chapter 12,** on the *self,* traces the development of the *self-concept* and children's emerging sense of *self-esteem,* the establishment of an *interpersonal identity* (including a sense of ethnic identity) in adolescence, and the growth of *social cognition* and *interpersonal understanding.* **Chapter 13** focuses on sex differences and on how biological factors, social forces, and intellectual growth interact to steer males and females toward different gender roles. The chapter also examines the utility (or lack thereof) of traditional gender roles and discusses ways in which we might be more successful at combating unfounded gender stereotypes. **Chapter 14** examines three interrelated aspects of social development that people often consider when making judgments about one's character: *aggression, altruism,* and *moral development.*
- **Part V: The Context of Development.** The final section of the text concentrates on the settings or contexts in which people develop, or the "ecology" of development. **Chapter 15** is devoted to *family influences,* focusing on the functions that families serve, patterns of childrearing that foster adaptive or maladaptive outcomes, the impacts of siblings on developing children, and the effects of family diversities and family transitions on child and adolescent development. **Chapter 16** concludes the text with an in-depth examination of four extrafamilial influences on developing children and adolescents: *television, computers, schools,* and the *society of one's peers.*

New to This Edition

This seventh edition has been thoroghly updated and revised to reflect the ever changing field of developmental psychology as well as to provide a fresh new approach to make the text more accessible to a larger audience. A few general updates that cut across all the chapters include: (1) streamlining the text to make the book shorter so that it fits more seamlessly into a single-semester course format; (2) rewriting much of the text to keep the writing style familiar, yet more accessible to a wide audience, including readers in introductory courses; (3) thoroughly updating the concept checks to include a variety of question types and placing the concept checks at each major topical transition so that readers can check their understanding at frequent intervals; (4) reducing the number and type of text boxes to combat the common problem of readers considering those boxes as irrelevant material to their understanding of the main text; (5) bringing emphasis and attention to issues of diversity and cross-cultural development by increasing the use of diverse examples, art, research, and reflection; (6) streamlining the focus on normative development and reducing the emphasis on individual differences in development to provide a more coherent picture of the processes of developmental change; (7) increasing the use of specific examples to highlight research findings and provide applications to real-life situations; and (8) of course, thoroughly updating the research and theory to reflect current thinking in developmental psychology.

In addition to these general changes that cut across all chapters, numerous changes have been made in each chapter. The following are some examples:

Chapter 1 Introduction to Developmental Psychology and Its Research Strategies

- Added photos of a single child depicting each stage of her development to illustrate the developmentalists' conceptualization of stages of development.
- Moved discussion of adolescence and cross-cultural issues into the main text (and out of a boxed discussion).
- Added discussion of Thelen's research methods investigating infants' stepping reflex.
- Reorganized research strategies section to clearly delineate basic methods from basic research designs and both as distinct from purely developmental designs.
- Added discussion of Fuligni and Pedersen's cross-cultural research on familial obligations of adolescents.
- Added discussion of Tronich et al.'s research on cocaine-exposed babies' interactions with their mothers.
- Added discussion of Bamburg's research on identity development in late childhood and early adolescence.
- Added discussion of Posada et al.'s ethnographical research of mother–child interactions.
- Included the field experiment as a basic research design within the main text.
- Included the cross-cultural design as a basic research design in the main text.
- Added discussion of Souza et al.'s cross-cultural research on ADHD.
- Included discussion of the microgenetic design as an example of developmental methods.
- Added discussion of Courage et al.'s microgenetic and cross-cultural research on infant visual self-recognition.
- Moved "Becoming a Wise Consumer of Developmental Research" discussion to an "Applying Research to Your Life" box.

Chapter 2 Theories of Human Development

- More focused and explicit discussion of the "Themes in the Study of Human Development," introducing them here in preparation for a discussion of them in each of the remaining chapters.
- Added the "holistic nature of development" to the major themes section.
- Updated theories and theorists with dynamic photos throughout.
- Updated table reflecting summaries of the major theoretical viewpoints and tied them back to the discussion of themes at the beginning of the chapter.

Chapter 3 Hereditary Influences on Development

- Removed references to genetic blueprints or code to drive home the idea that genes do not have a single direct link to behavior.
- Added "Focus on Research" box on "Crossing Over and Chromosome Segregation During Meiosis," which includes recent research and theory and is illustrated with two new figures.
- Added a new table identifying different levels of gene-environment interaction that influence genetic expression.

- Updated and clarified the figure depicting the sex-linked inheritance of colorblindness.
- Added discussion and a figure depicting additive gene effects in polygenic inheritance.
- Updated the section on hereditary disorders and added a flowchart depicting sources of congenital defects.
- Revised sections on predicting, detecting, and treating hereditary disorders to clarify and illuminate the differences among these aspects of genetic disorders.
- Added a table depicting concordance rates for a variety of personality characteristics, psychological disorders, and cognitive abilities.
- Added a section about myths of heritability estimates (brought it out of a box and into the main text) to highlight and clarify the use of these estimates.
- Added summary section "Applying Developmental Themes to Hereditary Influences on Development" that provides specific expamples from the chapter to illustrate the four main themes of the text.

Chapter 4 Prenatal Development and Birth

- Streamlined this chapter, saving discussion of life after birth for the next chapter on infancy.
- Emphasized the distinctions between the development of the fetus and the pregnant woman's experience by clearly differentiating between the ways these developmental phases are measured and marked.
- Carefully distinguished between the "pregnant woman" and "mother," to emphasize the difference between these life stages.
- Moved discussion of the effects of sexually transmitted diseases out of a box feature and into the main text to emphasize the importance of this issue and provide continuity in the discussion.
- Updated research discussion of the effects of cigarette smoking, the use of illicit drugs, and environmental pollutants on prenatal development with much recent research and examples.
- Added "Focus on Research" box on "Fetal Programming Theory."
- Updated research on the effects of the pregnant woman's stress and reactions to that stress on prenatal and postnatal development.
- Updated research on postpartum depression.
- Updated research on the consequences of low birth weight.
- Added summary section "Applying Developmental Themes to Prenatal Development and Birth" that provides specific examples from the chapter to illustrate the four main themes of the text.

Chapter 5 Infancy

- New chapter that continues the biological theme from heredity and prenatal development in the previous chapters.
- New emphasis on application by moving text information into a new "Applying Research to Your Life" on "Methods of Soothing a Fussy Baby."
- New research on the habituation method of studying infant perception.
- New photos to depict the method of evoked potentials and the high-amplitude sucking method of studying infant perception.
- New figure to display results of habituation method.
- New "Focus on Research" box on the "Causes and Consequences of Hearing Loss."
- New research on visual perception.
- Steamlined coverage of infant sensation, perception, and learning.

Chapter 6 Physical Development: The Brain, Body, Motor Skills, and Sexual Development

- New research and examples to illustrate the psychological impacts of motor development.
- New text section on adolescent body image and unhealthy weight control strategies.
- New "Focus on Research" box on "The Origins of Sexual Orientation."

Chapter 7 Cognitive Development: Piaget's Theory and Vygotsky's Sociocultural Viewpoint

- New "Focus on Research" box on "Cognitive Development and Children's Humor."
- New section on "The Development of Theory of Mind."
- New "Focus on Research" box on "Is Theory of Mind Biologically Programmed?"
- New table to illustrate cultural differences in tools of intellectual adaptation.
- New text section (instead of a box) on cultural differences in cognition.

Chapter 8 Cognitive Development: Information-Processing Perspectives

- Expanded discussions of executive functions, information processing capacity, and short-term memory.
- Added section on infant memory.
- Reorganized sections for improved flow to simplify for students' comprehension.
- More examples and comprehensive treatment of utilization deficiencies, including complete discussion of an experiment with a corresponding illustrative figure.
- Added discussion of strategy use in school settings.
- Recent research examples to illustrate metacognition.
- Added research example illustrating toddler's attention strategies.

Chapter 9 Intelligence: Measuring Mental Performance

- Many new and recent citations supporting the entire chapter.
- Changed emphasis on "factor analysis" to "multicomponent views of intelligence" to put emphasis on theories of intelligence rather than statistical methods.
- New table describing the Bayley scales of infant development.
- Moved discussion of mental retardation and developmental outcome from a box into the main text.
- Deleted the box on stereotypes influencing intellectual performance.

Chapter 10 Development of Language and Communication Skills

- Added updated references to support discussion of the basic components of language (e.g., Diesendruck & Markson, 2001; Kelley, Jones, & Fein, 2004).
- Updated the section on theories of language development (e.g., Lidz, Gleitman, & Gleitman, 2003; Wilson, 2003; Yang, 2004; among others).
- Updated the section on the sensitive period hypothesis and the evaluation of the nativist approach to language acquisition (e.g., Francis, 2005; Goldberg, 2004; Steward, 2004; Tomasello, 2003; among others).
- Updated the section on the interactionist perspective of language acquisition (e.g., Adamson, Bakeman, & Decknew, 2004; Callanan & Sabbagh, 2004; Hoff & Naigles, 2002; McKee & McDaniel, 2004; among others).
- The headings have been redone to make the process of language acquisition clearer.

- Updated references to support the sections on language acquisition (e.g., Anthony & Francis, 2005; Bochner & Jones, 2004; Bornstein et al., 2004; Dominey, 2005; Iverson & Fagon, 2004; Mandler, 2004; Oller, 2005; Wilkinson & Mazzitelli, 2003; among others).
- Updated references to support sections on language learning during the preschool period and throughout childhood (e.g., Anthony & Francis, 2005; Clahsen, Hadler, & Weyerts, 2004; Fielding-Barnsley & Purdie, 2005; Rodriguez-Fornells, Munte, & Clahsen, 2002).
- Updated references to support the sections on bilingualism (e.g., Francis, 2004; Pena, Bedore, & Rappazzo, 2003; among others).

Chapter 11 Emotional Development, Temperament, and Attachment

- New research and examples of negative emotionality and of regulating emotions from infancy to adolescence.
- New research and examples on recognizing and interpreting emotions and on emotions and prosocial development.
- Moved "Cultural Variations in Temperament" from a box to the main text to emphasize the centrality of cultural differences.
- New research and examples on interactional synchrony and the formation of attachments.
- New chapter title to clearly communicate topics to be covered.
- Discussion of current debate in the literature about whether attachment classification would better be understood as an attachment continuum.
- Examples of using attachment classifications to understand parent–child relationships and marital relationships.
- Discussion of research on attachment in twins.
- New research and emphasis on effects of day care on children's attachment and development.
- For emphasis on diversity, the examples, art program, and text have been updated to reflect diversity.
- Moved material on "Fathers and Attachment" from box into main text.
- Added section on the infant mental health field.
- Added discussion of current controversy in the research about emotional regulation.
- Added "Focus on Research" box on a recent research program to assess emotional competence in children.

Chapter 12 Development of the Self and Social Cognition

- To increase focus on diversity, the examples and art program were revamped to reflect diversity.
- The boxes on "Identity Formation in Minority Youth" and "Cultural Influences on Self-Concept" were blended into the main text.
- A section on cultural differences in self-esteem was added to the text.
- Added discussions of recent research and theory throughout, including age trends in self-recognition; parental influences on self-concept; changes in self-esteem; peer influences on self-esteem; culture, ethnicity, and self-esteem; and identity formation in minority youth.

Chapter 13 Sex Differences and Gender-Role Development

- For increased attention to diverstiy, the art program and examples were updated to reflect diversity. In addition, sections were added on "Subcultural Variations in Gender Typing" and "Sex Differences in Gender Typing."
- Added updated research examples throughout.
- Added section on "Evolutionary Theory of Gender Typing."

- Added chapter-opening vignette in personal voice to catch readers' interest and give authenticity to the material in the chapter.

Chapter 14 Aggression, Altruism, and Moral Development

- Changed organization to focus on three main themes: aggression, altruism, and morality.
- Added table depicting mother-rated aggression from 2 to 9 years.
- Added details on bullying.
- Added section on popularity and aggression.
- Cut down on some of the details to reduce chapter length.
- Moved information on cultural differences in thinking about prosocial conduct from a box into the main text.
- Changed organization of the morality section to focus on different aspects of morality (e.g., affective, cognitive, and behavioral) instead of focusing on theories of moral development in the organization.
- Added a box on updating Piaget's theory of moral development.
- Added figure and discussion depicting a social-information-processing model of moral behavior.

Chapter 15 The Context of Development I: The Family

- To increase attention to diversity, updated art program and examples to reflect diversity. In addition, changed the focus on cultural and ethnic differences in parenting to make it more prominent in the chapter.
- Updated references to support sections on the family systems model of development (e.g., Belsky & Fearon 2004; Frascarolo et al., 2004; Leary & Katz, 2004; McHale et al., 2004; Parke, 2004; U.S. Census, 2006; among others).
- A new table depicting recent changes in U.S. family systems.
- Updated references to support discussion of parental socialization during childhood and adolescence (e.g., Kochanska, 2002; Scaramella et al., 2002; among others).
- A new box on parenting styles and developmental outcomes.
- A new box on renegotiating the parent–child relationship during adolescence, including new references (e.g., Barber & Harmon, 2002; Laird et al., 2003; Smetana & Daddis, 2002; Yau & Smetana, in press).
- New references supporting discussions on ethnic variations in child rearing (e.g., Fuligni, Yip, & Tseng, 2002; Hill, Bush, & Roosa, 2003; Ispa et al., 2004; among others).
- New box about development in affluent families, supported by recent research on the topic and including a table describing characteristics of affluent families.
- New focus on diversity in family life, including sections on adoption, donor insemination, and gay and lesbian families.

Chapter 16 The Context of Development II: Television, Computers, School, and Peers

- New section on television viewing and children's health.
- New box on aggression and television viewing.
- Updated effective schooling section.
- Added section on peer sociability.
- New box on parents and peers.

Writing Style

Our goal has been to write a book that speaks directly to its readers and treats them as active participants in an ongoing discussion. We have tried to be relatively informal and down to earth in our writing style and to rely heavily on questions, thought problems, concept checks, and a number of other exercises to stimulate students' interest and involvement. Most of the chapters were "pretested" on our own students, who redpenciled whatever wasn't clear to them and suggested several of the concrete examples, analogies, and occasional anecdotes that we've used when introducing and explaining complex ideas. So, with the valuable assistance of our student-critics, we have attempted to prepare a manuscript that is substantive and challenging but that reads more like a dialogue or a story than like an encyclopedia.

Special Features

The pedagogical features of the text have been greatly expanded in this seventh edition. Among the more important features that are included to encourage student interest and involvement and make the material easier to learn are the following:

- **Four-color design.** An attractive four-color design brightens the book and makes photographs, drawings, and other illustrations come alive.
- **Outlines and chapter summaries.** An outline and brief introductory section at the beginning of each chapter provide the student with a preview of what will be covered. Each chapter concludes with a comprehensive summary, organized according to the major subdivisions of each chapter and highlighting key terms, that allows one to quickly review the chapter's major themes.
- **Subheadings.** Subheadings are employed very frequently to keep the material well organized and to divide the coverage into manageable bites.
- **Vocabulary/key terms.** More than 600 key terms appear in boldface type to alert the student that these are important concepts to learn.
- **Running glossary, key term lists, and comprehensive end-of-book glossary.** A running glossary provides on-the-spot definitions of boldfaced key terms as they appear in the text. At the end of each chapter is a list of key terms that appeared in the narrative, as well as the page number on which each term is defined. A complete glossary of key terms for the entire text appears at the end of the book.
- **Boxes.** Each chapter contains two to three boxes that call attention to important ideas, processes, issues, or applications. The aim of these boxes is to permit a closer or more personal examination of selected topics while stimulating the reader to think about the questions, controversies, practices, and policies under scrutiny. The boxes fall into two categories: **Focus on Research,** which discusses a classic study or set of studies that have been highly influential in illuminating the causes of development ("How Girls Are More Aggressive than Boys"), and **Applying Research to Your Life,** which focuses on applying what we know to optimize developmental outcomes ("Combating Gender Stereotypes with Cognitive Interventions"). All of these boxes are carefully woven into the chapter narrative and were selected to reinforce central themes in the text.
- **Illustrations.** Photographs, tables, and figures are used extensively. Although the illustrations are designed, in part, to provide visual relief and to maintain student interest, they are not merely decorations. All visual aids, including the occasional cartoons, were selected to illustrate important principles and concepts and thereby enhance the educational goals of the text.
- **Concept checks.** The concept checks, introduced in the fourth edition, became an immediate hit. Many, many student comment cards indicated that these brief exercises (three or four per chapter) were having the intended effects of being engaging, challenging, and permitting an active assessment of one's mastery of important concepts and developmental processes. Several students explicitly stated that concept checks helped them far more than the typical "brief summary" sections appearing in their other texts (which were perceived as too brief

and too general to be of much use). The concept checks have been totally rewritten or substantially revised to incorporate more of the kinds of questions students found most useful and to reflect the new concepts and new understandings included in this edition. Answers to all concept checks can be found in the Appendix at the back of the book.

Supplementary Aids

Study Guide 0-534-63258-0

Prepared by S. A. Hensch, University of Wisconsin Colleges, and correlated chapter by chapter with this textbook, the *Study Guide* includes learning objectives, chapter outlines and summaries, vocabulary self-tests, multiple-choice self-tests, short-answer study questions, and a variety of activities for each textbook chapter (including activities using media, self-report activities that personalize the material, activities with children, and activities that ask student to interview or describe other people). The guide also includes answers to the vocabulary self-tests and multiple-choice self-tests with rationales for correct answers and explanations of why wrong answers are wrong.

Instructor's Resource Manual 0-534-63254-8

Written by Jody S. Fournier, Capital University. You'll prepare for class more quickly and effectively with this manual's chapter outlines, learning objectives, lecture suggestions, student activities and projects, application and discussion questions, and film and video suggestions. Also included in this manual is the Resource Integration Guide, a uniquely effective teaching tool that links each chapter in this book to instructional ideas and corresponding supplement resources. At a glance, you'll see which PowerPoint® slides, test questions, and lecture suggestions are appropriate for each key chapter topic.

Test Bank 0-534-63255-6

Written by Lysandra Perez-Strumolo, Ramapo College of New Jersey, and featuring hundreds of text-specific questions for every chapter, this comprehensive resource helps you to easily create tests that target your course objectives. Includes multiple-choice, short-answer, and essay varieties.

ExamView® Computerized Testing 0-534-63256-4

Preloaded with all questions from the Shaffer/Kipp's *Test Bank,* ExamView helps you create, customize, and deliver tests and study guides (both print and online) in minutes. Using ExamView's complete word processing capabilities, you can enter an unlimited number of new questions or edit existing questions.

Multimedia Manager Instructor's Resource CD-ROM 0-534-53257-2

Prepared by Peter Green, Barton College, this one-stop lecture preparation tool—with its ready-to-go Microsoft® PowerPoint® lecture images—makes it easy to present engaging lectures for the course. The images include illustrations and photos from Thomson Wadsworth's developmental psychology texts. The CD-ROM also contains the *Instructor's Manual* and *Test Bank* in Microsoft Word® files.

JoinIn™ on TurningPoint™ 0-495-18671-6

JoinIn on TurningPoint is the easiest way to turn your PowerPoint software into a powerful audience response vehicle. With just a click on a handheld device, your students can respond to multiple-choice questions, short polls, interactive exercises, and peer review questions. You can take attendance, collect student demographics to better assess student needs, and even administer quizzes without collecting paper or grading. Please consult your local Thomson Wadsworth representative for details or visit **www.thomsonedu.com/thomsontechnology** for a demonstration.

NEW! ThomsonNOW™... *Just What You Need to Do NOW!*

Available packaged with each copy of the textbook, this dynamic, online study system features a series of diagnostic tests and *Personalized Study Plans* with learning modules and other media that enable students to discover those areas of the text where they need to focus their efforts. Also includes an instructor grade book. *Turn to the front inside cover of this book for details. Quizzes written by Belinda Blevins-Knabe, University of Arkansas, Little Rock.*

Current Perspectives: Readings from InfoTrac® College Edition on Social Policy and Developmental Psychology 0-495-17062-3

Compiled by Camille Odell, Utah State University, this current collection of topically organized readings from the InfoTrac College Edition library is an excellent way to enrich your course with up-to-date material. Available for packaging with each copy of this book.

Wadsworth Film and Video Library for Developmental Psychology

Qualified adopters can choose from a great variety of continually updated DVD and video options, including selections from Insight Media, Films for the Humanities and Sciences, The Pennsylvania State University's PCR: Films and Videos in the Behavioral Sciences, and more.

Due to contractual reasons, certain ancillaries are available only in higher education or U.S. domestic markets. Minimum purchase may apply to receive the ancillaries at no charge.

Child and Adolescent Development CD-ROM 0-495-09741-1

Perfect for your topically organized course! This multimedia learning tool, by Michie O. Swartwood and Kathy H. Trotter and designed to increase students' understanding of major theories of development, draws powerful connections between the text and your lecture by using video, simulations, quizzing, and the Web.

Observing Children and Adolescents: Student Workbook (with CD-ROM) 0-534-62272-0

Contains 230 minutes of observational video! Enriching students' understanding of major developmental milestones, this four-CD-ROM set with an accompanying workbook by Michie O. Swartwood and Kathy H. Trotter focuses on observable behavior and features segments of children interacting with peers, parents, and teachers.

Acknowledgments

As is always the case with projects as large and as long-lasting as this one, there are many, many individuals whose assistance was invaluable in the planning and production of this book. The quality of any volume about human development depends to a large extent on the quality of the prepublication reviews from developmentalists around the world. Many colleagues (including several dozen or so interested and unpaid volunteers) have influenced this book by contributing constructive criticisms, as well as useful suggestions, references, and a whole lot of encouragement. Each of those experts has helped to make the final product a better one, and we thank them all.

The reviewers of this edition were Elizabeth M. Blunk, Southwest Texas State University; Adam Brown, St. Bonaventure University; Robert Cohen, University of Memphis; K. Laurie Dickson, Northern Arizona University; Rebecca Foushée Eaton, The University of Alabama in Huntsville; William Fabricius, Arizona State University; Jody S. Fournier, Capital University; Fred Grote, Western Washington University; Catherine L. Harris, Boston University; Marité Rodriguez Haynes, Clarion University; Joseph Horton, Grove City College; Gloria Karin, State University of New York at New Paltz; Marianna Footo Linz, Marshall University; Lori N. Marks, University of Maryland; Claire Novosad, Southern Connecticut State University; Lauretta Reeves, University of Texas at Austin; Cosby Steele Rogers, Virginia Polytechnic Institute and State University; Spencer K. Thompson, University of Texas of the Permian Basin.

The reviewers of the first edition were Martin Banks, University of California at Berkeley; Don Baucum, Birmingham-Southern College; Jay Belsky, Pennsylvania State University; Keith Berg, University of Florida; Marvin Berkowitz, Marquette University; Dana Birnbaum, University of Maine at Orono; Kathryn Black, Purdue University; Robert Bohlander, Wilkes College; Cathryn Booth, University of Washington; Yvonne Brackbill, University of Florida; Cheryl Bradley, Central Virginia Community College; John Condry, Cornell University; David Crowell, University of Hawaii; Connie Hamm Duncanson, Northern Michigan University; Mary Ellen Durrett, University of Texas at Austin; Beverly Eubank, Lansing Community College; Beverly Fagot, University of Oregon; Larry Fenson, San Diego State University; Harold Goldsmith, University of Oregon; Charles Halverson, University of Georgia; Lillian Hix, Houston Community College; Frank Laycock, Oberlin College; Patricia Leonhard, University of Illinois at Champaign-Urbana; Mark Lepper, Stanford University; John Ludeman, Stephens College; Phillip J. Mohan, University of Idaho; Robert Plomin, Pennsylvania State University; Judith Powell, University of Wyoming; Daniel Richards, Houston Community College; Peter Scharf, University of Seattle; and Rob Woodson, University of Texas.

The reviewers of the second edition were Kathryn Black, Purdue University; Thomas J. Brendt, Purdue University; Mary Courage, Memorial University of Newfoundland; Donald N. Cousins, Rhode Island College; Mark L. Howe, Memorial University of Newfoundland; Gerald L. Larson, Kent State University; David Liberman, University of Houston; Sharon Nelson-Le Gall, University of Pittsburgh; Richard Newman, University of California at Riverside; Scott Paris, University of Michigan; Thomas S. Parish, Kansas State University; Frederick M. Schwantes, Northern Illinois University; Renuka R. Sethi, California State College at Bakersfield; Faye B. Steuer, College of Charleston; Donald Tyrell, Franklin and Marshall College; and Joachim K. Wohlwill, Pennsylvania State University.

The reviewers of the third edition were David K. Carson, University of Wyoming; Marcia Z. Lippman, Western Washington University; Philip J. Mohan, University of Idaho; Gary Novak, California State University, Stanislaus; Elizabeth Rider, Elizabethtown College; James O. Rust, Middle Tennessee State University; Mark Shatz, Ohio University; and Linda K. Swindell, University of Mississippi.

The reviewers of the fourth edition were M. Kay Alderman, University of Akron, Peggy A. DeCooke, Purchase College, State University of New York; David Dodd, University of Utah; Beverly Fagot, University of Oregon; Rebecca Glover, University of Arkansas; Paul A. Miller, Arizona State University; Amy Needam, Duke University; Spencer Thompson, University of Texas of the Permian Basin; and Albert Yonas, University of Minnesota.

The reviewers of the fifth edition were Mark Alcorn, University of Northern Colorado; AnnJanette Alejano-Steele, Metropolitan State College of Denver; Cynthia Berg, University of Utah; Kathleen Brown, California State University, Fullerton; Gary Creasey, Illinois State University; Teresa Davis, Middle Tennessee State University; Laurie Dickson, Northern Arizona University; Daniel Fasko, Morehead State University; John Felton, University of Evansville; Cynthia Frosch, University of North Carolina; John Gaa, University of Houston; Judith Hudson, Rutgers University; Kimberly Kinsler, Hunter College; Lacy Barnes-Mileham, Reedley College; Sandra Pipp-Siegel, University of Colorado at Boulder; Robert Russell, University of Michigan-Flint; and Frank Sinkavich, York College.

The reviewers of the sixth edition were Mark Alcorn, University of Northern Colorado; AnnJanette Alejano-Steele, Metropolitan State College of Denver; Cynthia Berg, University of Utah; Kathleen Brown, California State University, Fullerton; Mari Clements, Pennsylvania State University; Gary Creasey, Illinois State University; Teresa Davis, Middle Tennessee State University; Laurie Dickson, Northern Arizona University; William Fabricius, Arizona State University; Daniel Fasko, Morehead State University; John Felton, University of Evansville; Cynthia Frosh, University of Illinois; John Gaa, University of Houston; Harvey Ginsburg, Southwest Texas State University; Judith Hudson, Rutgers University; Kevin Keating, Broward Community College; Wallace Kennedy, Florida State University; Kimberly Kinsler, Hunter College; Kristen Kirby-Merritte, Tulane University; Carmelita Lomeo, Mohawk Valley Community College; Lacy Mileham, Kings River Community College; Derek Montgomery, Bradley University; Richard Passman, University of Wisconsin-Milwaukee; Sandra Pipp-Siegel, University of Colorado at Boulder; Frank Sinkavich, York College; Kathy H. Trotter, Chattanooga State; Suzanne Valentine-French, College of Lake County; and Gretchen Van de Walle, Rutgers University.

David F. Bjorklund, of Florida Atlantic University, provided experience and expertise that was invaluable in revising portions of the book dealing with cognitive development. Many developmentalists are familiar with Dave's empirical research and his excellent text, *Children's Thinking: Developmental Function and Individual Differences.* We are also indeed fortunate to have had a scientist and a writer of Dave's caliber to coauthor Chapters 7 and 8.

Katherine Kipp extends special thanks to Julia Cline, research assistant, who provided extensive help in every aspect of the production of this edition. Katherine also thanks her family (John, Rachel, and Debby) and Gary and Jenny, whose immense support allowed her to contemplate and complete such a huge project.

Last, but not least, we owe especially important debts of gratitude to our past and present sponsoring editors. C. Deborah Laughton conceived this project many years ago, and was always there throughout the first and most of the second edition, answering questions, solving problems, and finding ways to get more work out of me than we believed was possible. Vicki Knight came on board for the third edition, and her dedication to the project would make one think that she had conceived it herself. Jim Brace-Thompson skillfully sheparded me through the fourth and fifth editions and is responsible for many of the improvements in the book's design and content. Ms. EB2, Edith Beard Brady, presided over the sixth edition. And last but not least, Michele Sordi, whose unending guidance, support, and enthusiasm made this edition into what we believe is the best edition to date. Although different in their "styles," each of these persons is a splendid editor who has taught us so much about the preparation of effective educational materials. We are indeed fortunate to have had their counsel over the years, and we wish to thank them sincerely for their many, many efforts on our behalf.

We also wish to thank the individuals at Wadsworth who so generously shared their knowledge and talents over the past year. These are the people who made it happen: Jeremy Judson, Vernon Boes, Mary Noel, Jennifer Alexander, Adrian Paz, and Kara Warren.

David R. Shaffer and Katherine Kipp

About the Authors

DAVID R. SHAFFER is a professor of psychology, chair of the Undergraduate program, and past chair of the Life-Span Developmental Psychology program and the Social Psychology program at the University of Georgia, where he has taught courses in human development to graduate and undergraduate students for the past 33 years. His many research articles have concerned such topics as altruism, attitudes and persuasion, moral development, sex roles and social behavior, self-disclosure, and social psychology and the law. He has also served as associate editor for the *Journal of Personality and Social Psychology, Personality and Social Bulletin,* and *Journal of Personality.* In 1990 Dr. Shaffer received the Josiah Meigs Award for Excellence in Instruction, the University of Georgia's highest instructional honor.

KATHERINE KIPP is an associate professor of psychology in the Life-Span Developmental Psychology program and the Cognitive/Experimental Psychology program at the University of Georgia, where she has taught courses in human development to graduate and undergraduate students for the past 15 years. Her research publications cover topics in cognitive development, such as memory development, cognitive inhibition, and attention; individual differences in cognitive development, such as differences in attention-deficit hyperactivity disorder and giftedness in children; and research on the teaching of psychology. She is a member of the Society for Research in Child Development, the American Psychological Association, the American Psychological Society, and the Society for the Teaching of Psychology. She is the recipient of numerous teaching and mentoring awards and fellowships at the University of Georgia. She is also the mother of twin 19-year-old daughters, who have shared their developmental journey with her.

Nicholas Prior/Getty Images

CHAPTER

1 Introduction to Developmental Psychology and Its Research Strategies

One afternoon as I cycled home after attempting to bike 25 miles to the top of Mt. Hamilton, I spotted a lemonade stand, where several children and a couple of adults were gathered. I was in the process of deciding whether it was worth stopping for a taste, when a small boy about 4 years old screamed at me, "Lem-nade! Fif-fy cents!"

His sales technique convinced me—I stopped. The boy and an older sister who was 9 or 10 approached me. "I'll take some," I told them. By now the 4-year-old had walked up so close to me that I almost fell over him. He waved an empty cup and yelled at me again. I was baffled by his blabber and asked him to repeat himself. I was able to make out "Pink or yellow?" and I inquired which he thought was best. "Pink," he answered without hesitation. I told him that I'd take his recommendation. His sister, who had not said a word, immediately went to pour my glass. In the meantime, I gave the 4-year-old a dollar and said, "I'll have two."

The 4-year-old galloped off with my money. His sister returned with the lemonade. I took the cup and began to drink. The sister continued to stand in front of me and, finally realizing that I did not understand her behavior, very politely extended her hand. "Oh," I said as I pointed to the 4-year-old, "I already paid him."

The girl smiled and skipped back toward the table loaded with pitchers, cups, and money box. The *cha-ching* of money filling the till had clearly excited her, but she composed herself and returned to stand in her spot behind the table.

As I sipped, I noticed that other children were present. Two boys, who by garb and demeanor appeared to be late-stage middle schoolers, were sprawled on the grass by the sidewalk, conversing in hushed tones. Two girls, heads taller than the boys but apparently preteens as well, stood a few feet behind the stand. The girls were standing with their heads together, chatting and giggling. They at least had selected a position that implied they intended to help with the lemonade enterprise, even though they were currently ignoring it. In fact, only three people seemed to be actively engaged in the lemonade project: the 4-year-old salesman, his more reserved sister, and an adult woman, who I assumed was their mother.

Standing on the grass beyond the commotion was a brightly smiling man. He was clearly enjoying the whole event and struck up a conversation with me. As I suspected, this was Dad. The 4-year-old was already back at the street, hollering at potential customers. "He's our top salesman," Dad told me. "What's the reason for the lemonade stand?" I asked. "What will you use the money for?" The friendly and gregarious father started to answer me, but he managed to stop himself and, instead, he fielded the question to the diligent 9-year-old. "Megan, would you like to explain what we're doing?" His daughter, still standing very politely behind the sales table, told me about the people that the money would benefit: the money would provide tools and supplies so that the recipients would be able to grow their own food. I commended their efforts and pedaled homeward.

My experience at the lemonade stand was an interactive reminder of the kinds of behavior and contrasts among individuals and age groups that evoke questions about human development. What processes transform excited 4-year-olds and diligent 9-year-olds into self-absorbed preteens? Why were the boys able to blow off their responsibilities without feeling guilty, whereas the girls were compelled to at least appear to be helping? Are the temperament differences in siblings due to age, genetics, or the influence of their same-sex role models? If adults are capable of interpreting the jabber of a toddler, why does that child's diction ever improve? Can parents effectively foster altruism and enterprise in their offspring? When do young children begin to grasp the concept of number correspondence (I never received my second cup of lemonade)? Do children who live in impoverished communities pass through the same social and developmental milestones as those who live in healthier communities? For that matter, why does a woman who is approaching 50 get on a bicycle and ride 25 miles uphill?

Introduction to Developmental Psychology

The aim of this book is to seek answers for these and many other fascinating questions about developing persons by reviewing the theories, methods, discoveries, and many practical accomplishments of the modern developmental sciences. This introductory chapter lays the groundwork for the remainder of the book by addressing important issues about the nature of human development and how knowledge about development is gained. What does it mean to say that people "develop" over time? How is your experience of development different from that of developing persons in past eras or in other cultures? When were scientific studies of human development first conducted and why are they necessary? And what strategies, or research methods, do scientists use to study the development of children and adolescents? Let's begin by considering the nature of development.

What Is Development?

development
systematic continuities and changes in the individual over the course of life.

developmental continuities
ways in which we remain stable over time or continue to reflect our past.

developmental psychology
branch of psychology devoted to identifying and explaining the continuities and changes that individuals display over time.

developmentalist
any scholar, regardless of discipline, who seeks to understand the developmental process (e.g., psychologists, biologists, sociologists, anthropologists, educators).

maturation
developmental changes in the body or behavior that result from the aging process rather than from learning, injury, illness, or some other life experience.

Development refers to systematic continuities and changes in the individual that occur between conception (when the father's sperm penetrates the mother's ovum, creating a new organism) and death. By describing *changes* as "systematic" we imply that they are orderly, patterned, and relatively enduring, so that temporary mood swings and other transitory changes in our appearances, thoughts, and behaviors are therefore excluded. We are also interested in **"continuities"** in development, or ways in which we remain the same or continue to reflect our past.

If development represents the continuities and changes an individual experiences from "womb to tomb," the developmental sciences refer to the study of these phenomena and are a multidisciplinary enterprise. Although **developmental psychology** is the largest of these disciplines, many biologists, sociologists, anthropologists, educators, physicians, and even historians share an interest in developmental continuity and change and have contributed in important ways to our understanding of both human and animal development. Because the science of development is multidisciplinary, we use the term **developmentalist** to refer to any scholar—regardless of discipline—who seeks to understand the developmental process.

What Causes Us to Develop?

To grasp the meaning of development, we must understand two important processes that underlie developmental change: maturation and learning. **Maturation** refers to the biological unfolding of the individual according to species-typical biological inheritance and an individual person's biological inheritance. Just as seeds become mature plants, assuming that they receive adequate moisture and nourishment, human beings grow within the womb. The human maturational (or species typical) biological program calls for us to become capable of walking and uttering our first meaningful words at about 1 year of age, to reach sexual maturity between age 11 and 15, and then to age and die on roughly similar schedules. Maturation is partly responsible for psychological changes such as our increasing ability to concentrate, solve problems, and understand another person's thoughts or feelings. So one reason that we humans are so similar in many important respects is that our common species heredity guides all of us through many of the same developmental changes at about the same points in our lives.

learning
a relatively permanent change in behavior (or behavioral potential) that results from one's experiences or practice.

The second critical developmental process is **learning**—the process through which our *experiences* produce relatively permanent changes in our feelings, thoughts, and behaviors. Let's consider a very simple example. Although a certain degree of physical maturation is necessary before a grade school child can become reasonably proficient at dribbling a basketball, careful instruction and many, many hours of practice are essential if this child is ever to approximate the ball-handling skills of a professional basketball player. Many of our abilities and habits do not simply unfold as part of maturation; we often learn to feel, think, and behave in new ways from our observations of and interactions with parents, teachers, and other important people in our lives, as well as from events that we experience. This means that we change in response to our *environments*—particularly in response to the actions and reactions of the people around us. Of course, most developmental changes are the product of *both* maturation and learning. And as we will see throughout this book, some of the more lively debates about human development are arguments about which of these processes contributes most to particular developmental changes.

What Goals Do Developmentalists Pursue?

normative development
developmental changes that characterize most or all members of a species; typical patterns of development.

ideographic development
individual variations in the rate, extent, or direction of development.

Three major goals of the developmental sciences are to describe, to explain, and to optimize development (Baltes, Reese, & Lipsitt, 1980). In pursuing the goal of *description,* human developmentalists carefully observe the behavior of people of different ages, seeking to specify how people change over time. Although there are typical pathways of development that virtually all people follow, no two persons are exactly alike. Even when raised in the same home, children often display very different interests, values, abilities, and behaviors. Thus, to adequately describe development, it is necessary to focus both on typical patterns of change (or **normative development**) and on individual variations in patterns of change (or **ideographic development**). So, developmentalists seek to understand the important ways that developing humans resemble each other and how they are likely to differ as they proceed through life.

Adequate description provides us with the "facts" about development, but it is only the starting point. Developmentalists next seek to explain the changes they have observed. In pursuing this goal of *explanation,* developmentalists hope to determine *why* people develop as they typically do and *why* some people develop differently than others. Explanation centers both on normative changes *within* individuals and variations in development *between* individuals. As we will see throughout the text, it is often easier to describe development than to conclusively explain how it occurs.

Finally, developmentalists hope to *optimize* development by applying what they have learned in attempts to help people develop in positive directions. This is a practical side to the study of human development that has led to such breakthroughs as ways to:

- Promote strong affectional ties between fussy, unresponsive infants and their frustrated parents.

Developmental psychology has provided research to identify methods that could be used to assist learning-disabled children with their schoolwork.

- Assist children with learning difficulties to succeed at school.
- Help socially unskilled children and adolescents to prevent the emotional difficulties that could result from having no close friends and being rejected by peers.

Many believe that such *optimization* goals will increasingly influence research agendas in the 21st century (Fabes et al., 2000; Lerner, Fisher, & Weinberg, 2000), as developmentalists show greater interest in solving real problems and communicating the practical implications of their findings to the public and policymakers (McCall & Groark, 2000). Yet, this heavier focus on *applied* issues in no way implies that traditional descriptive and explanatory goals are any less important, because optimization goals often cannot be achieved until researchers have adequately described normal and abnormal pathways of development and their causes (Schwebel, Plumert, & Pick, 2000).

Some Basic Observations about the Character of Development

Now that we have defined development and talked very briefly about the goals that developmentalists pursue, let's consider some of the conclusions they have drawn about the character of development.

A continual and cumulative process. Although no one can specify precisely what adulthood holds in store from even the most meticulous examination of a person's childhood, developmentalists have learned that the first 12 years are an extremely important part of the life span that sets the stage for adolescence and adulthood. Who we are as adolescents and adults also depends on the experiences we have later in life. Obviously, you are not the same person you were at age 10 or at age 15. You have probably grown somewhat, acquired new academic skills, and developed very different interests and aspirations from those you had as a fifth-grader or a high school sophomore. And the path of such developmental change stretches ever onward, through middle age and beyond, culminating in the final change that occurs when we die. In sum, human development is best described as a *continual* and *cumulative* process. The one constant is change, and the changes that occur at each major phase of life can have important implications for the future.

© Elizabeth Crews

Developmentalists label the first year of life *infancy.*

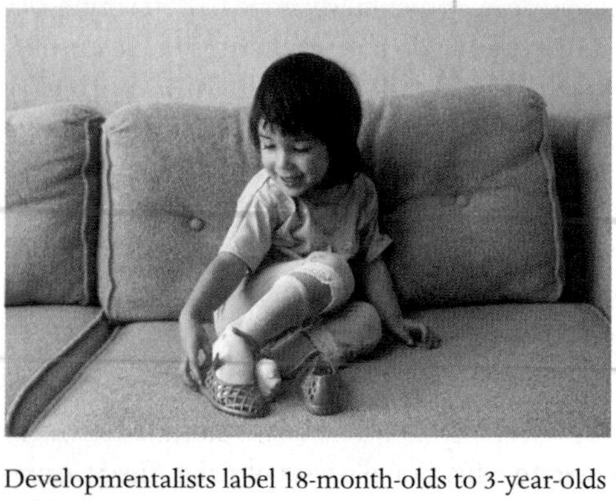

© Elizabeth Crews

Developmentalists label 18-month-olds to 3-year-olds *toddlers.*

Table 1.1 presents a chronological overview of the life span as developmentalists see it. Our focus in this text is on development during the first five periods of life—prenatal development, infancy and toddlerhood, preschool, middle childhood, and adolescence. By examining how children develop from the moment they are conceived until they reach young adulthood, we will learn about ourselves and the determinants of our behavior. Our survey will also provide some insight as to why no two individuals are ever exactly alike. Our survey won't provide answers to every important question you may have about developing children and adolescents. The study of human development is still a relatively young discipline with many unresolved issues. But as we proceed, it should become quite clear that developmentalists have provided an enormous amount of very practical information about young people that can help us to become better educators, child/adolescent practitioners, and parents.

A holistic process. It was once fashionable to divide developmentalists into three camps: (1) those who studied *physical growth* and development, including bodily changes and the sequencing of motor skills, (2) those who studied *cognitive* aspects of development, including perception, language, learning, and thinking, and (3) those who concentrated on *psychosocial* aspects of development, including emotions, personality, and the growth of interpersonal relationships. Today we know that this classification is misleading, for researchers who work in any of these areas have

TABLE 1.1 A Chronological Overview of Human Development

Period of life	Approximate age range
1. Prenatal period	Conception to birth
2. Infancy	First year of life
3. Toddlerhood	18-month-olds to 3-year-olds
4. Preschool period	3 to 5 years of age
5. Middle childhood	5 to 12 or so years of age (until the onset of puberty)
6. Adolescence	12 or so to 20 years of age (many developmentalists define the end of adolescence as the point at which the individual begins to work and is reasonably independent of parental sanctions)
7. Young adulthood	20 to 40 years of age
8. Middle age	40 to 65 years of age
9. Old age	65 years of age or older

NOTE: The age ranges listed here are approximate and may not apply to any particular individual. For example, a few 10-year-olds have experienced puberty and are properly classified as adolescents. Some teenagers are fully self-supporting, with children of their own, and are best classified as young adults.

found that changes in one aspect of development have important implications for other aspects. Let's consider an example.

What determines a person's popularity with peers? If you were to say that social skills are important, you would be right. Social skills such as warmth, friendliness, and willingness to cooperate are characteristics that popular children typically display. Yet there is much more to popularity than meets the eye. We now have some indication that the age at which a child reaches puberty, an important milestone in physical development, has an effect on social life. For example, boys who reach puberty early enjoy better relations with their peers than do boys who reach puberty later (Livson & Peskin, 1980). Children who do well in school also tend to be more popular with their peers than children who perform somewhat less well in school.

holistic perspective
a unified view of the developmental process that emphasizes the important interrelationships among the physical, mental, social, and emotional aspects of human development.

plasticity
capacity for change; a developmental state that has the potential to be shaped by experience.

We see, then, that popularity depends not only on the growth of social skills but also on various aspects of both cognitive and physical development. As this example illustrates, development is not piecemeal but **holistic**—humans are physical, cognitive, and social beings, and each of these components of self depends, in part, on changes taking place in other areas of development. This holistic perspective is one of the dominant themes of human development today, around which this book is organized.

© Elizabeth Crews

Developmentalists label 3- to 5-year-olds *preschoolers*.

Plasticity. **Plasticity** refers to a capacity for change in response to positive or negative life experiences. Although we have described development as a continual and cumulative process and noted that past events often have implications for the future, developmentalists know that the course of development can change abruptly if important aspects of one's life change. For example, somber babies living in barren, understaffed orphanages often become quite cheerful and affectionate when placed in socially stimulating adoptive homes (Rutter, 1981). Highly aggressive children who are intensely disliked by peers often improve their social status after learning and practicing the social skills that popular children display (Mize & Ladd, 1990; Shure, 1989). It is indeed fortunate that human development is so plastic, for children who have horrible starts can often be helped to overcome their deficiencies.

Historical/cultural context. No single portrait of development is accurate for all cultures, social classes, or racial and ethnic groups. Each culture, subculture, and social class transmits a particular pattern of beliefs, values, customs, and skills to its younger generations, and the content of this cultural socialization has a strong influence on the attributes and competencies that individuals display. Development is also influenced by societal changes: historical events such as wars, technological breakthroughs such as the development of the Internet, and social causes such as the gay and lesbian rights movement. Each generation develops in its own way, and each generation changes the world for succeeding generations. So we should not automatically assume that developmental patterns observed in North American or European children (the most heavily studied populations) are optimal, or even that they characterize persons developing in other eras or cultural settings (Laboratory of Comparative Human Cognition, 1983). Only by adopting a historical/cultural perspective can we fully appreciate the richness and diversity of human development. Let's look at the historical context of the science of human development in more detail.

© Elizabeth Crews

Developmentalists label the period from about 5 years old to the onset of puberty *middle childhood*.

Human Development in Historical Perspective

Contemporary Western societies can be described as "child-centered": Parents focus much of their lives on their children, spend a great deal of money to care for and educate their children, and excuse children from shouldering the full responsibilities of adulthood until attaining the legal age of 14 to 21 (depending on the society), when they have presumably gained the wisdom and skills to adapt to adult life. Childhood and adolescence were not always regarded as the very special and sensitive periods that we regard them as today. To understand how developmentalists think about and approach the study of children, it is necessary to see how the concept of childhood has changed over time. You may be surprised just how recent our modern viewpoint really is. Of course, it was only after people came to view childhood as a very special period that they began to study children and the developmental process.

Childhood in Premodern Times

In the early days of recorded history, children had few if any rights, and their lives were not always valued by their elders. Archeological research, for example, has shown that the ancient Carthaginians often killed children as religious sacrifices and embedded them in the walls of buildings to "strengthen" these structures (Bjorklund & Bjorklund, 1992). Until the 4th century A.D., Roman parents were legally entitled to kill their deformed, illegitimate, or otherwise unwanted infants. After this active infanticide was outlawed, unwanted babies were often left to die in the wilderness, or were sold as servants or as objects for sexual exploitation upon reaching middle childhood (deMause, 1974). Even "wanted" children were often treated rather harshly by today's standards. For example, boys in the city-state of Sparta were exposed to a strict regimen designed to train them for the grim task of serving a military state. As infants, they were given cold baths to "toughen" them. At age 7, when children in modern society are entering second grade, Spartan boys were taken from their homes and housed in public barracks, where they

Developmentalists label the period from the onset of puberty to about 20 years old *adolescence.*

were often beaten or underfed to instill the discipline they would need to become able warriors (deMause, 1974; Despert, 1965).

Not all early societies treated their children as harshly as the citizens of Carthage, Rome, and Sparta. Yet, for several centuries A.D., children were viewed as family "possessions" who had no rights (Hart, 1991) and whom parents were free to exploit as they saw fit. It wasn't until the 12th century A.D. in Europe that legislation equated infanticide with murder (deMause, 1974)!

Children fared a little better during the medieval era. Medieval children were not coddled or indulged to the extent that today's children are. They were often dressed in miniature versions of adult clothing and were depicted in artwork working alongside adults in the shop or the field or drinking and carousing with adults at parties. And except for exempting very young children from criminal culpability, medieval law generally made no distinctions between childhood and adult offenses (Borstelmann, 1983; Kean, 1937). But childhood was generally recognized as a distinct phase of life and children were thought to have certain needs above and beyond those of adults (see Borstelmann, 1983; Cunningham, 1996; Kroll, 1977).

Toward Modern-Day Views on Childhood

During the 17th and 18th centuries, attitudes toward children and child rearing began to change. Religious leaders of that era stressed that children were innocent and helpless souls who should be shielded from the wild and reckless behavior of adults. One method of accomplishing this objective was to send young people to school. Although the primary purpose of schooling was to provide a proper moral and religious education, it was now recognized that teaching important subsidiary skills such as reading and writing would transform the innocents into "servants and workers" who would provide society "with a good labor force" (Aries, 1962, p. 10). Although children were still considered family possessions, parents were now discouraged from abusing their sons and daughters and were urged to treat them with more warmth and affection (Aries, 1962; Despert, 1965).

Formal recognition of adolescence as a distinct phase of life came later, during the early years of the 20th century (Hall, 1904). The spread of industry in Western societies is probably the event most responsible for the "invention" of adolescence. As immigrants poured into industrialized nations and took jobs that had formerly been filled by children and teenagers, young people became economic liabilities rather than assets (Remley, 1988). The increasingly complex technology of industrial operations placed a premium on obtaining an educated labor force. So laws were passed in the late 19th century to restrict child labor and make schooling compulsory (Kett, 1979). Suddenly teens were spending much of their time surrounded by age-mates and separated from adults. As they hung out with friends and developed their own peer cultures, teenagers came to be viewed as a distinct class of individuals who had clearly emerged from the innocence of childhood but who were not yet ready to assume adult responsibilities (Hall, 1904).

After World War II, the adolescent experience broadened as increasing numbers of high school graduates postponed marriages and careers to pursue college (and postgraduate) educations. Part of the reason for these changes is the increased life span (due, in part, to medical advances) in our current culture compared to that of earlier eras. Because of this, there is the opportunity to take time for exploration in adolescence. Today, it is not at all unusual for young people to delay their entry into the adult world until their mid to late 20s (Hartung & Sweeney, 1991; Vobejda, 1991). And we might add that society condones this "extended adolescence" by requiring workers to obtain increasingly specialized training to pursue their chosen careers (Elder, Liker, & Cross, 1984).

Early philosophical perspectives on childhood. Why did attitudes toward children change so drastically in the 17th and 18th centuries? It is likely that the thinking of influential social philosophers contributed meaningfully to the "new look" at children and child care. Lively speculation about human nature led these philosophers to carefully consider each of the following issues:

- Are children inherently good or bad?
- Are children driven by inborn motives and instincts; or, rather, are they products of their environments?
- Are children actively involved in shaping their characters; or are they passive creatures molded by parents, teachers, and other agents of society?

Debates about these philosophical questions produced quite different perspectives on children and child rearing. For example, Thomas Hobbes's (1651/1904) doctrine of **original sin** held that children are inherently selfish egoists who must be restrained by society, whereas Jean Jacques Rousseau's (1762/1955) doctrine of **innate purity** maintained that children are born with an intuitive sense of right and wrong that society often corrupts. These two viewpoints clearly differ in their implications for child rearing. Proponents of original sin argued that parents must actively control their egoistic children; the innate purists argued that parents should give their children more freedom to follow their inherently positive inclinations.

original sin
the idea that children are inherently negative creatures who must be taught to rechannel their selfish interests into socially acceptable outlets.

innate purity
the idea that infants are born with an intuitive sense of right and wrong that is often misdirected by the demands and restrictions of society.

tabula rasa
the idea that the mind of an infant is a "blank slate" and that all knowledge, abilities, behaviors, and motives are acquired through experience.

Another influential view on children and child rearing was suggested by John Locke (1690/1913), who believed that the mind of an infant is a **tabula rasa,** or "blank slate," and that children have no inborn tendencies. In other words, children are neither inherently good nor inherently bad, and how they turn out depends entirely on their worldly experiences. Locke argued in favor of disciplined child rearing to ensure that children would develop good habits and acquire few bad ones.

These philosophers also differed on the question of children's participation in their own development. Hobbes maintained that children must learn to rechannel their naturally selfish interests into socially acceptable outlets; in this sense, they are passive subjects to be molded by parents. Locke, too, believed that the child's role is passive, because the mind of an infant is a blank slate on which experience writes its lessons. But a strikingly different view was proposed by Rousseau, who believed that children are actively involved in the shaping of their own intellects and personalities. In Rousseau's words, the child is not a "passive recipient of the tutor's instruction" but a "busy, testing, motivated explorer. The active searching child, setting his own problems, stands in marked contrast to the receptive one . . . on whom society fixes its stamp" (quoted in Kessen, 1965, p. 75).

Clearly these philosophers had some interesting ideas about children and child rearing. But how could anyone decide whether their views were correct? Unfortunately, the philosophers collected no objective data to back their pronouncements, and the few observations they did make were limited and unsystematic. Can you anticipate the next step in the evolution of the developmental sciences?

Children as subjects of study: the baby biographies. The first glimmering of a systematic study of children can be traced to the late 19th century. This was a period in which investigators from a variety of academic backgrounds began to observe the development of their own children and to publish these data in works known as **baby biographies.**

baby biography
a detailed record of an infant's growth and development over a period of time.

Perhaps the most influential of the baby biographers was Charles Darwin, who made daily records of the early development of his son (Darwin, 1877; and see Charlesworth, 1992). Darwin's curiosity about child development stemmed from his earlier theory of evolution. Quite simply, he believed that young, untrained infants share many characteristics with their nonhuman ancestors, and he advanced the (now discredited) idea that the development of the individual child retraces the entire evolutionary

Julia Margaret Cameron/The Bridgeman Art Library/Getty Images

Charles Darwin

history of the species, thereby illustrating the "descent of man." So Darwin and many of his contemporaries viewed the baby biography as a means of answering questions about our evolutionary past.

Baby biographies left much to be desired as works of science. Different baby biographers emphasized very different aspects of their children's behavior, so that different baby biographies were difficult to compare. In addition, parents are not entirely objective about their own children, and baby biographers may also have let their assumptions about the nature of development bias their observations so that they "found" what they were looking for. Finally, each baby biography was based on a single child—and often the child of a distinguished individual, at that. Conclusions based on a single case may not hold true for other children.

Despite these shortcomings, baby biographies were a step in the right direction. The fact that eminent scientists such as Charles Darwin were now writing about developing children implied that human development was a topic worthy of scientific scrutiny.

Origins of a Science of Development

Corbis-Bettman

American psychologist G. Stanley Hall (1846–1924) is recognized as one of the founders of developmental psychology.

G. Stanley Hall conducted the first large-scale scientific investigations of children, and because of this he is considered by most to be the founder of developmental psychology as a research discipline (White, 1992). Well aware of the shortcomings of baby biographies, Hall set out in the late 19th century to collect more objective data on larger samples. Specifically, he was interested in children's thinking, and he developed a now familiar research tool—the *questionnaire*—to explore "the contents of children's minds" (Hall, 1891). By asking children questions about a range of topics, Hall discovered that children's understanding of the world grows rapidly during childhood and that the "logic" of young children is not very logical at all. Hall later wrote an influential book titled *Adolescence* (1904) that was the first work to call attention to adolescence as a unique phase of the life span.

At about the time Hall was using questionnaires to study children's minds, a young European neurologist was trying a different method of probing the mind and revealing its contents. The neurologist's approach was very fruitful, providing information that led him to propose a theory that revolutionized thinking about children and childhood. The neurologist was Sigmund Freud. His ideas came to be known as *psychoanalytic theory.*

Hulton Archive/Getty Images

Sigmund Freud

In many areas of science, new theories are often revisions or modifications of old theories. But in Freud's day, there were few "old" theories of human development to modify. Freud was truly a pioneer, formulating his psychoanalytic theory from the thousands of notes and observations he made while treating patients for various kinds of emotional disturbances.

Freud's highly creative and unorthodox theorizing soon attracted a lot of attention. Shortly after the publication of Freud's earliest theoretical monographs, the *International Journal of Psychoanalysis* was founded, and other researchers began to report their tests of Freud's thinking. By the mid-1930s much of Freud's work had been translated into other languages, and the impact of psychoanalytic theory was felt around the world. Over the years, Freud's theory continued to generate new research and prompt other researchers to revise and extend his thinking. The field of developmental psychology was thriving by the time Freud died in 1939.

Freud's work—and other scientists' reactions to it—aptly illustrates the role that theories play in the science of human development. Although the word *theory* is an imposing term, theories are something that everybody has. If we were to ask you why males and females appear very different as adults when they seem so very similar as infants, you would undoubtedly have some opinions on the issue. Your answer would state or at least reflect your own underlying theory of the development of sex differences. So a **theory** is a set of concepts and propositions that describe and explain some aspect of experience. In the field of psychology, theories help us describe and explain various patterns of behavior.

theory
a set of concepts and propositions designed to organize, describe, and explain an existing set of observations.

hypothesis
a theoretical prediction about some aspect of experience.

Good theories have another important feature: the ability to predict future events. These theoretical predictions, or **hypotheses,** are then tested by collecting data. The data we obtain when testing hypotheses provides information about the theory's ability to explain new observations. It may also lead to new theoretical insights that extend our knowledge even further.

Today there are many theories that have contributed to our understanding of child and adolescent development, and in Chapter 2 we will examine several of the more influential of these viewpoints. Although it is quite natural for people reading about various theories to favor one, the scientist uses a rather stringent yardstick to evaluate theories: He or she will formulate hypotheses and conduct research to determine whether the theory can adequately predict and explain new observations. Thus, there is no room for subjective bias when evaluating a theory. Theories in the developmental sciences are only as good as their ability to predict and explain important aspects of development.

In the next section of the chapter, we will focus on the research methods that developmentalists use to test their theories and gain a better understanding of child and adolescent development.

CONCEPT CHECK 1.1 Introduction to Developmental Psychology

Check your understanding of the science and history of developmental psychology by answering the following questions. Answers appear in the Appendix.

Multiple Choice: Select the best answer for each question.

_____ 1. According to developmentalists, the *primary* cause of developmental change is
a. maturation
b. learning
c. experience
d. the product of both maturation and learning
e. the product of both learning and experience

_____ 2. Among the following, who would *not* be considered a "developmentalist"?
a. a sociologist
b. an anthropologist
c. a historian
d. *all* of the above might be considered developmentalists
e. *none* of the above would be considered developmentalists

_____ 3. The goals of the developmental sciences discussed in the text include
a. the description of development
b. the explanation of development
c. the optimization of development
d. all of the above

_____ 4. Enrique is a developmental psychologist. He studies children's adjustment following their parents' divorce and remarriage. He finds that sullen children who become withdrawn and isolated after their parents divorce can be helped to become happier and more social through play therapy. Which aspect of development change does Enrique's research most reflect?
a. Development is a continual and cumulative process.
b. Development is marked by plasticity.
c. Development is a holistic process.
d. Development depends upon the historical and cultural context in which it occurs.

Fill in the Blank: Fill in the blank with the appropriate word or phrase.

5. In the developmental sciences, typical patterns of change are called _______, whereas individual variations in patterns of change are called _______.

Matching: Match the theorist in the first column with the correct theory in the second column, and the theorist's view of children's participation in their own development in the third column.

The Theorist	The Theory	View of Children
6. Hobbes	blank slate	passive
7. Rousseau	original sin	passive
8. Locke	innate purity	active

Short Answer: Briefly answer the following question.

9. Explain the scientific significance of "baby biographies." Why were these publications scientifically flawed?

Essay: Provide a more detailed answer to the following question.

10. Trace the progression of developmental science from the early philosophical debates to the publication of scientifically collected data and theory on development.

Research Strategies: Basic Methods and Designs

When detectives are assigned cases to solve, they first gather facts, formulate hunches, and then sift through clues or collect additional information until one of their hunches proves correct. Unraveling the mysteries of development is in many ways a similar endeavor. Investigators must carefully observe their subjects, analyze the information they collect, and use these data to draw conclusions about the ways people develop.

Other times theories direct the collection of data that can lead to new discoveries and new ideas. For example, aspects of the developmental theories of Jean Piaget guided Esther Thelen and her research team (2002) as they investigated one newborn reflex. Long ago, Piaget (1952) conjectured that as children develop, new behavioral patterns are built upon earlier behavioral patterns. For many years, newborns have been observed to possess a stepping reflex. Immediately post delivery, when a newborn is held upright and its feet touch a flat surface, the newborn "steps." Weeks later, the infant no longer steps when held upright. The usual explanation for the disappearance of the stepping reflex is that it is a consequence of normal neurological development. In light of Piaget's thinking about how human behaviors are built upon previously existing behaviors, Thelen and her colleagues were dissatisfied with the notion that the stepping reflex simply disappears. According to Piaget's theory, the reflex should continue until it becomes subsumed by later behaviors such as crawling or walking. Thelen's team began to observe the reflex as it occurred among newborns and as it receded with age. They observed that lighter-weight babies, those that did not experience rapid weight gains after birth, retained the reflex longer than babies who quickly gained weight. As a result of their observations, the researchers were able to find the reflex that had "disappeared." To test for the reflex, rather than simply holding older babies upright, they submerged the legs of these heavier babies in water. As the chubby infants' feet touched the bottom of the pool, they stepped; the reflex had *not* disappeared. Thelen and her colleagues concluded that the stepping reflex was still intact, but because the babies' muscle strength did not increase as rapidly as their weight, their weak muscles could not lift their chubby legs. In this way, Piaget's theory inspired observation that yielded information about the abilities of newborns. Had Thelen and her team not been familiar with Piaget's theory, they might not have gone looking for the stepping reflex at all.

Research Methods in Child and Adolescent Development

Our focus in this section is on the methods researchers use to gather information about developing children and adolescents. Our first task is to understand why developmentalists consider it absolutely essential to collect all these facts. We will then discuss the advantages and disadvantages of five basic fact-finding strategies: self-report methodologies, systematic observation, case studies, ethnography, and psychophysiological methods. Finally, we will consider the ways developmentalists might design their research to detect and explain age-related changes in children's feelings, thoughts, abilities, and behaviors.

The Scientific Method

Modern developmental psychology is appropriately labeled a scientific enterprise because those who study development have adopted the **scientific method** that guides their attempts at understanding. There is nothing mysterious about the scientific method. It refers to the use of objective and replicable methods to gather data for the purpose of testing a theory or hypothesis. It dictates that, above all, investigators must be *objective* and must allow their data to decide the merits of their thinking.

scientific method
the use of objective and replicable methods to gather data for the purpose of testing a theory or hypothesis. It dictates that, above all, investigators must be *objective* and must allow their data to decide the merits of their thinking.

In earlier eras, when social philosophers such as Hobbes, Locke, and Rousseau were presenting their views on children and child rearing, their largely unsubstantiated claims were often accepted as fact. People assumed that great minds always had great insights. Very few individuals questioned the word of these well-known scholars because the scientific method was not yet a widely accepted criterion for evaluating knowledge.

The intent here is not to criticize the early social philosophers. In fact, today's developmentalists (and children) are deeply indebted to these thinkers for helping to modify the ways in which society regarded and treated children. However, great minds may on occasion produce miserable ideas that can do a great deal of harm if those ideas are uncritically accepted and influence the way people are treated. The scientific method, then, is a valuable safeguard that helps to protect the scientific community and society at large against flawed reasoning. Protection is provided by the practice of evaluating the merits of various theoretical pronouncements against the objective record, rather than simply relying on the academic, political, or social credibility of the theorist. Of course, this also means that the theorist whose ideas are being evaluated must be equally objective and willing to discard pet notions when there is evidence against them.

Gathering Data: Basic Fact-Finding Strategies

No matter what aspect of development we hope to study—be it the perceptual capabilities of newborn infants, the growth of friendships among grade-school children, or the reasons some adolescents begin to use drugs—we must find ways to *measure* what interests us. Today researchers are fortunate in having many tried-and-true procedures they might use to measure behavior and test their hypotheses about human development. But regardless of the technique one employs, scientifically useful measures must always display two important qualities: **reliability** and **validity.**

reliability
the extent to which a measuring instrument yields consistent results, both over time and across observers.

validity
the extent to which a measuring instrument accurately reflects what the researchers intended to measure.

A measure is *reliable* if it yields consistent information over time and across observers. Suppose you go into a classroom and record the number of times each child behaves aggressively toward others, but your research assistant, using the same scheme to observe the same children, does not agree with your measurements. Or you measure each child's aggressiveness one week but come up with very different aggressiveness scores while applying the same measure to the same children a week later. Clearly, your observational measure of aggression is *unreliable* because it yields highly inconsistent information. To be reliable and thus useful for scientific purposes, your measure would have to produce comparable estimates of children's aggression from independent observers (*interrater reliability*), and yield similar scores for individual children from one testing to another shortly thereafter (*temporal stability*).

A measure is *valid* if it measures what it is supposed to measure. An instrument must be reliable before it can possibly be valid. Yet reliability, by itself, does not guarantee validity (Miller, 1997). For example, a highly reliable observational scheme intended as a measure of children's aggression may provide grossly overinflated estimates of aggressive behavior if the investigator simply classifies all acts of physical force as examples of aggression. What the researcher has failed to recognize is that much high-intensity behavior may simply represent enjoyable forms of rough-and-tumble play without harmful or aggressive intent. Researchers must demonstrate they are measuring the attribute they say they are measuring before we can have much faith in the data they collect or the conclusions they reach.

Keeping in mind the importance of establishing the reliability and validity of measures, let us consider some of the different ways in which aspects of human development might be measured.

Self-report methodologies. Three common procedures developmentalists use to gather information and test hypotheses are interviews, questionnaires (including psychological tests), and the clinical method. Although these approaches are similar in that each asks participants to answer questions posed by the investigator, they differ in the extent to which the investigator treats individual participants alike.

Interviews and Questionnaires. Researchers who opt for interview or questionnaire techniques will ask the child (or the child's parents) a series of questions pertaining to such aspects of development as the child's conduct, feelings, beliefs, or characteristic methods of thinking. Collecting data via a questionnaire (and most psychological tests)

structured interview or structured questionnaire
a technique in which all participants are asked the same questions in precisely the same order so that the responses of different participants can be compared.

simply involves putting questions on paper and asking participants to respond to them in writing, whereas interviews require participants to respond orally to the investigator's queries. If the procedure is a **structured interview** or **structured questionnaire,** all who participate in the study are asked the same questions in the same order. The purpose of this standardized or structured format is to treat each person alike so the responses of different participants can be compared.

One interesting use of the interview technique is a project in which kindergarten, second-grade, and fourth-grade children responded to 24 questions designed to assess their knowledge of social stereotypes about males and females (Williams, Bennett, & Best, 1975). Each question came in response to a different short story in which the central character was described by either stereotypically masculine adjectives (for example, *aggressive, forceful, tough*) or stereotypically feminine adjectives (for example, *emotional, excitable*). The child's task was to indicate whether the character in each story was male or female. Williams and associates found that even kindergartners could usually tell whether the stories referred to boys or girls. In other words, these 5-year-olds were quite knowledgeable about gender stereotypes, although children's thinking became much more stereotyped between kindergarten and the second grade. One implication of these results is that stereotyping of the sexes must begin very early if kindergartners are already thinking along stereotyped lines. (We'll learn more about the development of children's gender and their ideas about gender in Chapter 13.)

Andrew Fuligni and Sara Pedersen (2002) used self-report methods to assess the familial obligations felt among culturally diverse young adults in the United States. They developed questionnaires to measure (1) the young adults' sense of family duty, which included obligation to support and assist their families, plus the degree of respect they had for their families, (2) how this sense of family duty influenced their educational choices, occupational choices, and emotional well-being, and (3) the extent to which they provided assistance to their families, and their plans for future support of their families. (The questionnaire is illustrated in Table 1.2.)

Despite the fact that, in the United States, the transition to young adulthood is viewed as a time for adolescents to become increasingly independent and to pursue personal goals, results from Fuligni and Pederson's study indicated that a sense of family duty permeates the lives of many young adults. In fact, they found that sense of family obligation increased for all participants as they left high school and became engaged in the first years of their adult lives.

By using the questionnaire method, Fuligni and Pedersen were able to collect information from a very large sample of adolescents (745 participants), and they were able to use the structured questionnaire to assess the participants' attitudes across time by having them complete the same questionnaire once when the participants were high school seniors, and again 1 to 3 years later. Thus, the questionnaire method was a very appropriate tool for such an investigation.

Nevertheless, interviews and questionnaires have some very real shortcomings. Neither approach can be used with very young children who cannot read or comprehend speech very well. Investigators must also hope that the answers they receive are honest and accurate, and are not merely attempts by respondents to present themselves in a favorable or socially desirable way. Many adolescents, for example, may be unwilling to admit they regularly masturbate, or smoke marijuana, or enjoy the risks of shoplifting. Clearly, inaccurate or untruthful responses lead to erroneous conclusions. Investigators must also be careful to ensure that participants of all ages interpret questions in the same way; otherwise, the age trends observed in the study may reflect differences in children's ability to comprehend and communicate rather than real underlying changes in their feelings, thoughts, or behaviors. Finally, researchers who interview both developing children and their parents (or teachers) may have trouble determining which set of reports is more accurate if the children's descriptions of their own behaviors differ from those of the other informants (Hussong, Zucker, Wong, Fitzgerald, & Puttler, 2005).

Despite these potential shortcomings, structured interviews and questionnaires can be excellent methods of obtaining large amounts of useful information in a short period

TABLE 1.2 Items Comprising Measures of Attitudes Regarding Family Obligations

Current Assistance

Answer Scale: (1) almost never to (5) almost always

1. Spend time with your grandparents, cousins, aunts, and uncles
2. Spend time at home with your family
3. Run errands that the family needs done
4. Help your brothers or sisters with their homework
5. Spend holidays with your family
6. Help out around the house
7. Spend time with your family on weekends
8. Help take care of your brothers and sisters
9. Eat meals with your family
10. Help take care of your grandparents
11. Do things together with your brothers and sisters

Respect for Family

Answer Scale: (1) not important at all to (5) very important

1. Treat your parents with great respect
2. Follow your parents' advice about choosing friends
3. Do well for the sake of your family
4. Follow your parents' advice about choosing a job or major in college
5. Treat your grandparents with great respect
6. Respect your older brothers and sisters
7. Make sacrifices for your family

Future Support

Answer Scale: (1) not important at all to (5) very important

1. Help your parents financially in the future
2. Live at home with your parents until you are married
3. Help take care of your brothers and sisters in the future
4. Spend time with your parents even after you no longer live with them
5. Live or go to college near your parents
6. Have your parents live with you when you get older

Adapted from Fuligni, A. J. & Pedersen, S. (2005). Family Obligation and the Transition to Young Adulthood. *Developmental Psychology, 38*, 856-868. Copyright © 2005 by the American Psychological Association. Adapted with permission.

of time. Both approaches are particularly useful when the investigator emphasizes to participants that their responses will be confidential and/or challenges them to report exactly what they know about an issue, thereby maximizing the likelihood of a truthful or accurate answer. In the gender stereotyping study, for example, the young participants probably considered each question a personal challenge or a puzzle to be solved and were thus motivated to answer accurately and to display exactly what they knew about males and females. Under the circumstances, then, the structured interview was an excellent method of assessing children's perceptions of the sexes.

clinical method
a type of interview in which a participant's response to each successive question (or problem) determines what the investigator will ask next.

The Clinical Method. The **clinical method** is very similar to the interview technique. The investigator is usually interested in testing a hypothesis by presenting the research participant with a task or stimulus of some sort and then inviting a response. After the participant responds, the investigator typically asks a second question or introduces a new task to clarify the participant's original answer. Although participants are often asked the same questions initially, each participant's answer determines what he or she is asked next. Thus, the clinical method is a flexible approach that considers each participant to be unique.

Jean Piaget, a famous Swiss psychologist, relied extensively on the clinical method to study children's moral reasoning and intellectual development. The data from Piaget's research are largely protocol records of his interactions with individual children. Here is a

Investigator using the clinical method. All participants are asked the same questions at first, but each participant's answers to the initial questions determine what the researcher will ask next.

small sample from Piaget's work (1932/1965, p. 140) on the development of moral reasoning, which shows that this young child thinks about lying in a very different way than adults do:

> Do you know what a lie is?—*It's when you say what isn't true.*—Is 2 + 2 = 5 a lie?—*Yes, it's a lie.*—Why?—*Because it isn't right.*—Did the boy who said 2 + 2 = 5 know it wasn't right or did he make a mistake?—*He made a mistake.*—Then if he made a mistake, did he tell a lie or not?—*Yes, he told a lie.*

Like structured interviews, clinical methods are often useful for gathering large amounts of information in relatively brief periods. This strategy's flexibility is also an advantage: By asking follow-up questions that are tailored to the participant's original answers it is often possible to obtain a rich understanding of the meaning of those answers. However, the flexibility of the clinical method is also a potential shortcoming. It may be difficult, if not impossible, to directly compare the answers of participants who are asked different questions. Furthermore, tailoring one's questions to the participant's responses raises the possibility that the examiner's preexisting theoretical biases may affect the particular follow-up questions asked and the interpretations provided. Because conclusions drawn from the clinical method depend, in part, on the investigator's *subjective* interpretations, it is always desirable to verify these insights using other research techniques.

naturalistic observation
a method in which the scientist tests hypotheses by observing people as they engage in everyday activities in their natural habitats (for example, at home, at school, or on the playground).

Observational methodologies. Often researchers prefer to observe people's behavior directly rather than asking them questions about it. One method that many developmentalists favor is **naturalistic observation**—observing people in their common, everyday (that is, natural) surroundings (Pellegrini, 1996). To observe children, this usually means going into homes, schools, or public parks and playgrounds and carefully recording what they do. Rarely will the investigator try to record every event that occurs; they are usually testing a specific hypothesis about one type of behavior, such as cooperation or aggression, and will focus their attention and data collection exclusively on acts of this kind. One strength of naturalistic observation is the ease with which it can be applied to infants and toddlers, who often cannot be studied through methods that demand verbal skills. But perhaps the greatest advantage of naturalistic observation is that it illustrates how people actually behave in everyday life (Willems & Alexander, 1982).

However, naturalistic observation also has its limitations. First, some behaviors occur so infrequently (for example, heroic rescues) or are so socially undesirable (for example, overt sex play or thievery) that they are unlikely to be witnessed by an unknown observer in the natural environment. Second, many events are usually happening at the same time in a natural setting, and any (or some combination) of them may affect people's behavior. This makes it difficult to pinpoint the causes of participants' actions or of any developmental trends in behavior. Finally, the mere presence of an observer can sometimes make people behave differently than they otherwise would. Children may "show off" when they have an audience, whereas parents may be on their best behavior, showing a strong reluctance, for example, to spank a misbehaving child as they normally might. For these reasons, researchers often attempt to minimize **observer influence** by (1) videotaping their participants from a concealed location or (2) spending time in the setting before collecting their "real" data so that the individuals they are observing will grow accustomed to their presence and behave more naturally.

observer influence
tendency of participants to react to an observer's presence by behaving in unusual ways.

Several years ago, Mary Haskett and Janet Kistner (1991) conducted an excellent piece of naturalistic observation to compare the social behaviors of nonabused preschoolers with those of day-care classmates identified by child protection agencies as having been physically abused by their parents. The investigators first defined examples of the behaviors they wished to record—both *desirable* behaviors such as appropriate social initiations and positive play, and *undesirable* behaviors such as aggression and negative verbalizations. They then monitored 14 abused and 14 nonabused preschool children as they mingled with peers in a play area of a day-care facility. Observations were made according to a **time-sampling** procedure: each child was observed during three 10-minute play sessions on three different days. To minimize their influence on the play activities, observers stood outside the play area while making their observations.

The results were disturbing. As shown in Figure 1.1, abused children initiated fewer social interactions than their nonabused classmates and were somewhat socially withdrawn. And when they did interact with playmates, the abused youngsters displayed many more aggressive acts and other negative behaviors than did their nonabused companions. Indeed, nonabused children often blatantly ignored the positive social initiations of an abused child, as if they did not want to get involved with him or her.

In sum, Haskett and Kistner's observational study shows that abused children are unattractive playmates who are likely to be disliked and even rejected by peers. But as is almost always the case in naturalistic observational research, it is difficult to pinpoint the exact cause of these findings. Did the negative behaviors of abused children cause their peers to reject them? Or did the peer rejection cause the abused children to display negative behaviors? Either possibility can account for Haskett and Kistner's results.

© Corbis

Children's tendency to perform for observers is one of the problems that researchers must overcome when using the method of naturalistic observation.

How might observational researchers study unusual or undesirable behaviors that they are unlikely to observe in the natural environment? One way is to conduct **structured observations** in the laboratory. In a structured observational study, each participant is exposed to a setting that might cue the behavior in question, and is then surreptitiously observed (via a hidden camera or through a one-way mirror) to see if he or she performs the behavior. For example, Leon Kuczynski (1983) got children to promise to help him with a boring task and then left them alone to work in a room where attractive toys were present. This procedure enabled Kuczynski to determine whether children would break a promise to work when they thought there was no one present to observe their transgression. Kuczynski found that some of the children did break the promise to work, whereas others continued with the work even when they thought no one was watching.

Aside from being a feasible way of studying behaviors that occur infrequently or are not openly displayed in the natural environment, structured observations also ensure that every participant in the sample is exposed to the *same* eliciting stimuli and has an *equal opportunity* to perform the target behavior—circumstances that are not always true in the natural environment. Of course, the major disadvantage of structured observation is that participants may not always respond in a contrived laboratory setting as they would in everyday life.

time-sampling
a procedure in which the investigator records the frequencies with which individuals display particular behaviors during the brief time intervals each is observed.

structured observation
an observational method in which the investigator cues the behavior of interest and observes participants' responses in a laboratory.

In an interesting example of structured observation, Tronick et al. (2005) studied the interaction between 4-month-olds and their mothers, with a specific interest in how the mother–infant interactions of babies prenatally exposed to cocaine compared to those of nonexposed infants. To find out, they brought 695 mother–infant pairs into a laboratory setting, 236 of whom had been exposed to cocaine prenatally. Cameras were positioned so that both the infant's face and the mother's face were videotaped for three 2-minute periods. During the first 2 minutes mother and child were allowed to interact normally. During the second period the mother was instructed to present a "still face" to the infant; that is, she was told not to laugh, smile, talk to, or touch the infant. During the third

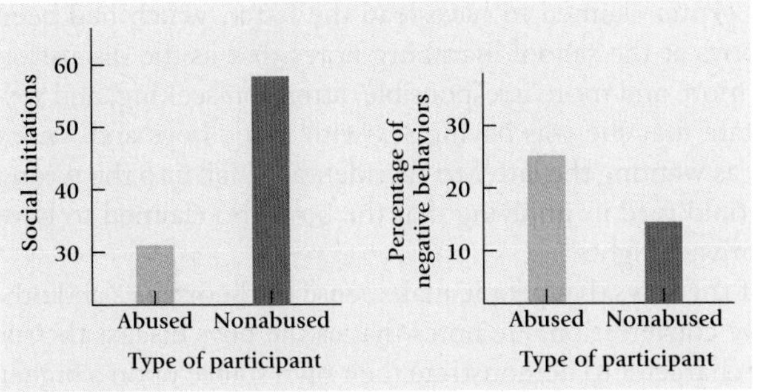

Figure 1.1 Social initiations and negative behaviors of abused and nonabused preschool children. Compared with their nonabused companions, abused youngsters initiate far fewer social interactions with peers and behave more negatively toward them.

2-minute period, the mother was to resume normal interaction with her child. This face-to-face still-face procedure allowed the researchers to observe the interactions of interest in a little over 6 minutes, rather than traveling to 695 different homes and waiting for hours and hours for the behaviors to occur.

As Tronick and colleagues suspected, the interaction patterns of the cocaine-exposed mother–infant pairs were different from those of the nonexposed pairs. For the most part, the cocaine-exposed infants and their mothers did not appear to be engaged in the kind of social interaction that facilitates both social and cognitive development in later months. Previous research suggests that the quality of caregiver–infant interactions is extremely important to the healthy social and cognitive development of very young children (Ainsworth, 1979, 1989). Positive, synchronized interactions provide the infant with the foundation for forming other positive, supportive relationships later on in life. Such relationships also enable the child to investigate objects and the rest of the world without excessive fear (Bowlby, 1973, 1988).

Unfortunately, compared to nonexposed infants, the cocaine-exposed 4-month-olds were hypervigilant: they spent more time monitoring their mothers' reactions and behaviors and less time exploring the toys in the lab. In addition, the interactions of the cocaine-exposed pairs were less synchronized: often the child would be emotionally neutral while the mother was emotionally negative. In the highest exposure group, mother and infant spent more time negatively engaged and less time positively engaged than all other pairs. Overall, the cocaine-exposed infants hiccupped and spit up more than their nonexposed peers, and those with highest exposure were more passive and distant than both nonexposed infants and those exposed to lower levels of cocaine. However, despite these differences, when the mothers presented the still face, the cocaine-exposed 4-month-olds behaved in the same way as the nonexposed infants: they expected Mother to be engaged with them, so the still face was surprising, frustrating, and even stressful. Tronick and colleagues point out that the cocaine-exposed infants' behaviors during the still-face episode indicated that the infants did have the ability to interact and connect with their caregivers. The infants' behaviors also suggested that their mothers were providing some degree of social interaction, and that intervention strategies might improve the developmental outcomes of the cocaine-exposed babies.

case study
a research method in which the investigator gathers extensive information about the life of an individual and then tests developmental hypotheses by analyzing the events of the person's life history.

Case studies. Any or all of the methods we have discussed—structured interviews, questionnaires, clinical methods, and behavioral observations—can be used to compile a detailed portrait of a single individual's development through the **case study** method. In preparing an individualized record, or "case," the investigator typically seeks many kinds of information about the participant, such as his or her family background, socioeconomic status, health records, academic or work history, and performance on psychological tests. Much of the information included in any case history comes from interviews with and observations of the individual, although the questions asked and observations made are typically not standardized and may vary considerably from case to case. The baby biographies of the 19th and early 20th centuries are examples of case studies.

Case studies may also be used to describe groups. For example, Michael Bamburg (2004) conducted a project investigating identity development in 10-, 12- and 15-year-old boys. During the project, information was collected from journal entries, oral accounts, open-ended one-on-one interviews, and group discussions. From the information collected, Bamburg chose an excerpt from a single segment of conversation to illustrate how adolescent males construct their identities within the moment-to-moment course of a conversation. During the conversation, five ninth-grade boys discussed a rumor they had heard during the previous school year which related the story of a sexually active female classmate who had supposedly revealed in a letter that she was pregnant. One of the ninth-graders in the discussion group claimed to have read the letter, which had been passed around among several boys at the school. Bamburg notes that as the discussion unfolds, the girl is portrayed as more and more irresponsible, attention-seeking, and sexually promiscuous. The boys state that she was having sex with many boys and "more than just sex." They portray her as wanting the letter to "accidentally" fall into the wrong hands so that many students would read it, implying that the boy who claimed to have read the letter had violated no privacy rights.

Bamburg argues that one of the ways that people make sense of themselves and others is through socially interactive conversation. He notes that as the boys discuss the rumor about the girl, they use her character to demonstrate their own stance upon a higher moral ground. Bamburg found that the group's engagement in "slut-bashing" allows the boys to construe their identities as morally superior to and more adult than the girl's, while also illustrating how the boys subtly endorse a stereotypic double standard for girls in comparison to boys. Thus, their conversation reveals more about themselves as they would like to be seen by the adult moderator of the discussion than it does about the girl's character. Analysis of the discussion also provides insight into how, as a group, adolescent boys develop and maintain attitudes that may adversely affect both themselves and adolescent girls. Because we all engage in the "local management" of our identities and self-presentation, this *group case study* reveals information that is different from what we might glean in an individual case study.

Although many developmentalists have used case studies to great advantage, there are major drawbacks to this approach. For example, it is often difficult to directly compare subjects who have been asked different questions, taken different tests, and been observed under different circumstances. Case studies may also lack *generalizability;* that is, conclusions drawn from the experiences of the small number of individuals studied may simply not apply to most people. The ninth-graders in Bamburg's discussion group, for example, were all from a large city in the eastern United States, and theories posited as a result of analyzing their discussion may not apply to boys in Finland or Southeast Asia. For these reasons, any conclusions drawn from case studies should always be verified through the use of other research techniques.

ethnography
method in which the researcher seeks to understand the unique values, traditions, and social processes of a culture or subculture by living with its members and making extensive observations and notes.

Ethnography. **Ethnography**—a form of participant observation often used in the field of anthropology—is becoming increasingly popular among researchers who hope to understand the effects of culture on developing children and adolescents. To collect their data, ethnographers often live within the cultural or subcultural community they are studying for periods of months, or even years. The data they collect is typically diverse and extensive, consisting largely of naturalistic observations, notes made from conversations with members of the culture, and interpretations of these events. These data are eventually used to compile a detailed portrait of the cultural community and draw conclusions about how the community's unique values and traditions influence aspects of the development of its children and adolescents.

Vanderle: Almeida/AFP/Getty Images

Ethnographic researchers attempt to understand cultural influences by living within the community and participating in all aspects of community life.

Detailed ethnographic portraits of a culture or subculture that arise from close and enduring contact with members of the community can lead to a richer understanding of that community's traditions and values than is possible through a small number of visits, in which outsiders make limited observations and conduct a few interviews (LeVine et al., 1994). Extensive cultural or subcultural descriptions are particularly useful to investigators hoping to understand cultural conflicts and other developmental challenges faced by minority children and adolescents in diverse multicultural societies (Segal, 1991; see also Patel, Power, & Bhavnagri, 1996). But despite these clear strengths, ethnography is a highly *subjective* method because researchers' own cultural values and theoretical biases can cause them to misinterpret what they have experienced. In addition, ethnographic conclusions pertain only to the culture or subculture studied and cannot be assumed to generalize to other contexts or social groups.

A recent example of ethnographic research was conducted by Posada et al. (2004). Because the various questionnaires and behavioral coding schemes typically used to assess caregiver–infant interactions were developed in studies using Caucasian, middle-class participants from industrialized countries, Posada and colleagues chose ethnographic methods to assess mother–infant interactions in middle- to lower-middle-class families in Bogotá, Colombia. They then compared the results derived from observations made in the Colombian households to results derived using previously developed assessments.

In a traditionally ethnographic manner, observers made eight to nine 2-hour, unstructured visits to 27 Colombian homes. During the visits, mothers were told to carry on with their daily routines, behaving as they normally would. The observers interacted with the families naturally. After each visit, they transcribed their observations. Repeat visits were conducted by the same observer.

From the observers' transcripts, 10 domains of maternal caregiving were identified. Using an inductive approach, two of the researchers and an ethnographic expert reviewed the transcripts. On first pass, they identified major caregiving themes. Then they reviewed the transcripts in more detail, focusing on specifying the major domains and identifying subdomains. In this way they were able to develop a set of culture-sensitive scales that could be used alongside previously developed measures in order to assess the universality of infant-sensitive maternal care.

The 10 scales of maternal sensitivity derived from the observations included domains such as promptness of response, enjoyment of interaction, interactive smoothness, and quality of physical contact. Results from the ethnographically derived Colombian scales were highly consistent with results from measures previously developed for Caucasian, middle-class, and upper-middle-class families, lending credence to the notion that sensitive caregiving behaviors are similar across cultures and socioeconomic circumstances, at least within the first few years of an infant's life.

Psychophysiological methods. In recent years, developmentalists have turned to **psychophysiological methods**—techniques that measure the relationship between physiological responses and behavior—to explore the biological underpinnings of children's perceptual, cognitive, and emotional responses. Psychophysiological methods are particularly useful for interpreting the mental and emotional experiences of infants and toddlers who are unable to report such events (Bornstein, 1992).

psychophysiological methods
methods that measure the relationships between physiological processes and aspects of children's physical, cognitive, social, or emotional behavior/development.

Heart rate is an involuntary physiological response that is highly sensitive to one's psychological experiences. Compared to their normal resting, or *baseline* levels, infants who are carefully attending to an interesting stimulus may show a decrease in heart rate; those who are uninterested in it may show no heart rate change, and others who are afraid of or angered by the stimulus may show a heart rate increase (Campos, Bertenthal, & Kermoian, 1992; Fox & Fitzgerald, 1990).

Measures of brain function are also very useful for assessing psychological state. For example, electroencephalogram (EEG) recordings of brain wave activity can be obtained by attaching electrodes to the scalp. Because different patterns of EEG activity characterize different arousal states, such as sleep, drowsiness, and alertness, investigators can track these patterns and determine how sleep cycles and other states of arousal change with age. Novel stimuli or events also produce short-term changes in EEG activity. So an investigator who hopes to test the limits of infant sensory capabilities can present novel sights and sounds and look for changes in brain waves (called *event-related potentials,* or *ERPs*) to determine whether these stimuli have been detected, or even discriminated, because two stimuli sensed as "different" will produce different patterns of brain activity (Bornstein, 1992).

Though very useful, psychophysiological responses are far from perfect indicators of psychological states. Even though an infant's heart rate or brain wave activity may indicate that he or she is attending to a stimulus, it is often difficult to determine exactly which aspect of that stimulus (shape, color, etc.) has captured attention.

TABLE 1.3 Strengths and Limitations of Seven Common Research Methods

Method	Strengths	Limitations
Self-reports		
Interviews and questionnaires	Relatively quick way to gather much information; standardized format allows the investigator to make direct comparisons between data provided by different participants.	Data collected may be inaccurate or less than completely honest, or may reflect variations in respondents' verbal skills and ability to understand questions.
Clinical methods	Flexible methodology that treats subjects as unique individuals; freedom to probe can be an aid in ensuring that the participant understands the meaning of the questions asked.	Conclusions drawn may be unreliable in that participants are not all treated alike; flexible probes depend, in part, on the investigator's subjective interpretations of the participant's responses; can be used only with highly verbal participants.
Systematic observations		
Naturalistic observation	Allows study of behavior as it actually occurs in the natural environment.	Observed behaviors may be influenced by observer's presence; unusual or undesirable behaviors are unlikely to be observed during the periods when observations are made.
Structured observation	Offers a standardized environment that provides every child an opportunity to perform target behavior. Excellent way to observe infrequent or socially undesirable acts.	Contrived observations may not always capture the ways children behave in the natural environment.
Case Studies	Very broad method that considers many sources of data when drawing inferences and conclusions about individual participants.	Kind of data collected often differs from case to case and may be inaccurate or less than honest; conclusions drawn from individual cases are subjective and may not apply to other people.
Ethnography	Provides a richer description of cultural beliefs, values, and traditions than is possible in brief observational or interview studies.	Conclusions may be biased by the investigator's values and theoretical viewpoints; results cannot be generalized beyond the groups and settings that were studied.
Psychophysiological methods	Useful for assessing biological underpinnings of development and identifying the perceptions, thoughts, and emotions of infants and toddlers who cannot report them verbally.	Cannot indicate with certainty what participants sense or feel; many factors other than the one being studied can produce a similar physiological response.

Furthermore, changes in physiological responses often reflect mood swings, fatigue, hunger, or even negative reactions to the physiological recording equipment, rather than a change in the infant's attention to a stimulus or emotional reactions to it. For these reasons, physiological responses are more likely to be valid indications of psychological experiences when participants (particularly very young ones) are initially calm, alert, and contented.

Table 1.3 provides a brief review of the data-gathering methods we have examined thus far. In the sections that follow, we will consider how investigators might design their research to test hypotheses and detect developmental continuities and changes.

Detecting Relationships: Correlational, Experimental, and Cross-Cultural Designs

Once researchers have decided what they want to study, they must then devise a research plan, or design, that permits them to identify relationships among events and behaviors and to specify the causes of these relationships. Here we consider the three general research designs that investigators might employ: correlational, experimental, and cross-cultural designs.

correlational design
a type of research design that indicates the strength of associations among variables; though correlated variables are systematically related, these relationships are not necessarily causal.

The Correlational Design

In a **correlational design,** the investigator gathers information to determine whether two or more variables of interest are meaningfully related. If the researcher is testing a specific hypothesis (rather than conducting preliminary descriptive or exploratory research), he or she will be checking to see whether these variables are related as the hypothesis specifies they should be. No attempts are made to structure or to manipulate the participants' environment in any way. Instead, correlational researchers take people as they find them—already "manipulated" by natural life experiences—and try to determine whether variations in people's life experiences are associated with differences in their behaviors or patterns of development.

To illustrate the correlational approach to hypothesis testing, let's work with a simple theory specifying that youngsters learn a lot from watching television and are apt to imitate the actions of the characters they observe. One hypothesis we might derive from this theory is that the more frequently children observe TV characters who display violent and aggressive acts, the more inclined they will be to behave aggressively toward their own playmates. After selecting a sample of children to study, our next step in testing our hypothesis is to measure the two variables that we think are related. To assess children's exposure to violent themes on television, we might use the interview or naturalistic observational methods to determine what each child watches, and then count the number of aggressive acts that occur in this programming. To measure the frequency of the children's own aggressive behavior toward peers, we could observe our sample on a playground and record how often each child behaves in a hostile, aggressive manner toward playmates. Having now gathered the data, it is time to evaluate our hypothesis.

correlation coefficient
A numerical index, ranging from −1.00 to +1.00, of the strength and direction of the relationship between two variables.

The presence (or absence) of a relationship between variables can be determined by examining the data with a statistical procedure that yields a **correlation coefficient** (symbolized by an r). This statistic provides a numerical estimate of the strength and the direction of the relationship between two variables. It can range in value from +1.00 to −1.00. The absolute value of r (disregarding its sign) tells us the *strength* of the relationship. Thus, correlation coefficients of −.70 and +.70 are of equal strength, and both are stronger than a moderate correlation of .30. An r of .00 indicates that the two variables are not systematically related. The sign of the correlation coefficient indicates the *direction* of the relationship. If the sign is positive, this means that as one variable increases, the other variable also increases. For example, height and weight are positively correlated: as children grow taller, they tend to get heavier (Tanner, 1990). Negative correlations indicate inverse relationships: as one variable increases, the other decreases. Among grade school students, for example, aggression and popularity are negatively correlated: Children who behave more aggressively tend to be less popular with their peers (Crick, 1996).

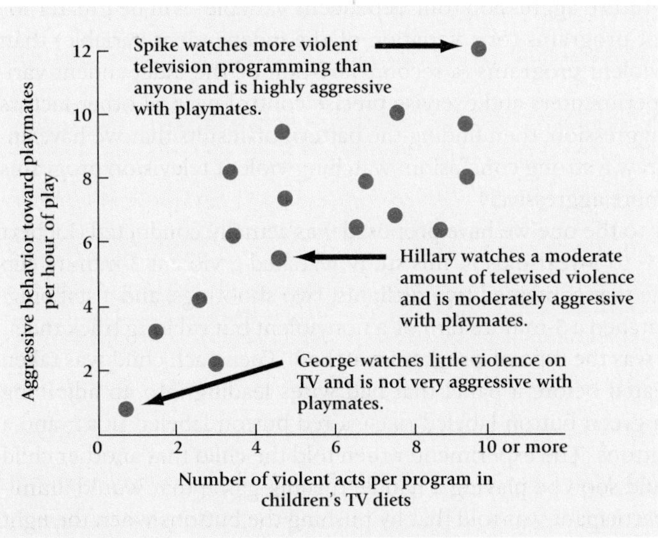

Figure 1.2 Plot of a hypothetical positive correlation between the amount of violence that children see on television and the number of aggressive responses they display. Each dot represents a specific child who views a particular level of televised violence (shown on the horizontal axis) and commits a particular number of aggressive acts (shown on the vertical axis). Although the correlation is less than perfect, we see that the more acts of violence a child watches on TV, the more inclined he or she is to behave aggressively toward peers.

Now let's return to our hypothesized positive relationship between televised violence and children's aggressive behavior. A number of investigators have conducted correlational studies similar to the one we have designed, and the results (reviewed in Liebert & Sprafkin, 1988) suggest a moderate positive correlation (between +.30 and +.50) between the two variables of interest: Children who watch a lot of violent television programming are more likely to behave aggressively toward playmates than are other children who watch little violent programming (see Figure 1.2 for a visual display).

Do these correlational studies establish that exposure to violent TV programming *causes* children to behave more aggressively? No, they do not! Although we have detected a relationship between exposure to televised violence and children's aggressive behavior, the causal direction of the relationship is not at all indicated by this design. An equally plausible alternative explanation is that relatively aggressive children are more inclined to prefer violent programming. Another possibility is that the association between TV viewing and aggressive behavior is actually caused by a third variable we have not measured. For example, perhaps parents who fight a lot at home (an unmeasured variable) cause their children to become more aggressive *and* to favor violent TV programming. If this were true, the latter two variables may be correlated, even though their relationship to each other is not one of cause and effect.

In sum, the correlational design is a versatile approach that can detect systematic relationships between any two or more variables that we might be interested in and are capable of measuring. However, its major limitation is that it cannot indicate that one thing causes another. How, then, might a researcher establish the underlying causes of various behaviors or other aspects of human development? One solution is to conduct experiments.

The Experimental Design

experimental design
a research design in which the investigator introduces some change in the participant's environment and then measures the effect of that change on the participant's behavior.

independent variable
the aspect of the environment that an experimenter modifies or manipulates in order to measure its impact on behavior.

dependent variable
the aspect of behavior that is measured in an experiment and assumed to be under the control of the independent variable.

In contrast to correlational studies, **experimental designs** permit a precise assessment of the cause-and-effect relationship that may exist between two variables. Let's return to the issue of whether viewing violent television programming *causes* children to become more aggressively inclined. In conducting a laboratory experiment to test this (or any) hypothesis, we would bring participants to the lab, expose them to different treatments, and record their responses to these treatments as data.

The different treatments to which we expose our participants represent the **independent variable** of our experiment. To test the hypothesis we have proposed, our independent variable (or treatments) would be the type of television program that our participants observe. Half the children might view a program in which characters behave in a violent or aggressive manner toward others, whereas the other half would watch a program that contains no violence.

Children's reactions to the television shows would become the data, or **dependent variable,** in our experiment. Because our hypothesis centers on children's aggression, we would want to measure (as our dependent variable) how aggressively children behave after watching each type of television show. A dependent variable is called "dependent" because its value presumably "depends" on the independent variable. In the present case, we are hypothesizing that future aggression (our dependent variable) will be greater for children who watch violent programs (one variation of the independent variable) than for those who watch nonviolent programs (a second variation of the independent variable). If we are careful experimenters and exercise precise control over *all* other factors that may affect children's aggression, then finding the pattern of results that we have anticipated will allow us to draw a strong conclusion: watching violent television programs *causes* children to behave more aggressively.

An experiment similar to the one we have proposed was actually conducted (Liebert & Baron, 1972). Half the 5- to 9-year-olds in this study watched a violent 3-minute clip from the *Untouchables*—one that contained two fistfights, two shootings, and a stabbing. The remaining children watched a 3-minute film of a nonviolent but exciting track meet. So the *independent variable* was the type of program watched. Then each child was taken into another room and seated before a panel that had wires leading into an adjoining room. On the panel was a green button labeled HELP, a red button labeled HURT, and a white light between the buttons. The experimenter then told the child that another child in the adjoining room would soon be playing a handle-turning game that would illuminate the white light. The participant was told that by pushing the buttons when the light was lit, he or she could either *help* the other child by making the handle easy to turn or *hurt* the child by making the handle become very hot. When it was clear that the participant understood the instructions, the experimenter left the room, and the light came on 20 times over the next several minutes. So each participant had 20 opportunities to help or hurt another child. The total amount of time each participant spent pushing the HURT button served as a measure of his or her aggression—the *dependent variable* in this study.

The results were clear: Despite the availability of an alternative, helping response, both boys and girls were much more likely to press the HURT button if they had watched the violent television program. So it appears that a mere 3-minute exposure to televised violence can *cause* children to behave more aggressively toward a peer, even though the aggressive acts they witnessed on television bore no resemblance to those they committed themselves.

When students discuss this experiment in class, someone invariably challenges this interpretation of the results. For example, one student recently proposed an alternative explanation that "maybe the kids who watched the violent film were naturally more aggressive than those who saw the track meet." In other words, he was suggesting that a **confounding variable**—children's preexisting levels of aggression—had determined their willingness to hurt a peer and that the independent variable (type of television program) had had no effect at all! Could he have been correct? How do we know that the children in the two experimental conditions really didn't differ in some important way that may have affected their willingness to hurt a peer?

confounding variable
some factor other than the independent variable that, if not controlled by the experimenter, could explain any differences across treatment conditions in participants' performance on the dependent variable.

experimental control
steps taken by an experimenter to ensure that all extraneous factors that could influence the dependent variable are roughly equivalent in each experimental condition; these precautions must be taken before an experimenter can be reasonably certain that observed changes in the dependent variable were caused by the manipulation of the independent variable.

random assignment
a control technique in which participants are assigned to experimental conditions through an unbiased procedure so that the members of the groups are not systematically different from one another.

This question brings us to the crucial issue of **experimental control.** In order to conclude that the independent variable is causally related to the dependent variable, the experimenter must ensure that all other confounding variables that could affect the dependent variable are *controlled*—that is, equivalent in each experimental condition. One way to equalize these extraneous factors is to do what Liebert and Baron (1972) did: randomly assign children to their experimental treatments. The concept of *randomization,* or **random assignment,** means that each research participant has an equal probability of being exposed to each experimental treatment. Assignment of individual participants to a particular treatment is accomplished by an unbiased procedure such as the flip of a coin. If the assignment is truly random, there is only a very slim chance that participants in the two (or more) experimental treatments will differ on any characteristic that might affect their performance on the dependent variable. All these confounding variables will have been randomly distributed within each treatment and equalized across the different treatments. Because Liebert and Baron randomly assigned children to experimental treatments, they could be reasonably certain that children who watched the violent TV program were not naturally more aggressive than those who watched the nonviolent TV program. So it was reasonable for them to conclude that the former group of children were more aggressive *because* they had watched a TV program in which violence and aggression were central.

The greatest strength of the experimental method is its ability to establish unambiguously that one thing causes another. Yet, critics of laboratory experimentation have argued that the tightly controlled laboratory environment is often contrived and artificial and that children are likely to behave differently in these surroundings than they would in a natural setting. Urie Bronfenbrenner (1977) charged that a heavy reliance on laboratory experiments made developmental psychology "the science of the strange behavior of children in strange situations with strange adults" (p. 19). Similarly, Robert McCall (1977) noted that experiments tell us what *can* cause a developmental change but do not necessarily pinpoint the factors that *actually do* cause such changes in natural settings. Consequently, it is quite possible that conclusions drawn from laboratory experiments do not always apply to the real world. One step that scientists can take to counter this criticism and assess the **ecological validity** of their laboratory findings is to conduct a *field experiment.*

ecological validity
state of affairs in which the findings of one's research are an accurate representation of processes that occur in the natural environment.

The field experiment. How can we be more certain that a conclusion drawn from a laboratory experiment also applies in the real world? One way is to seek converging evidence for that conclusion by conducting a similar experiment in a natural setting—that is, a **field experiment.** This approach combines all the advantages of naturalistic observation with the more rigorous control that experimentation allows. In addition, participants are typically not apprehensive about participating in a "strange" experiment because all the activities they undertake are everyday activities. They may not even be aware that they are participating in an experiment.

field experiment
an experiment that takes place in a naturalistic setting such as home, school, or a playground.

Let's consider a field experiment (Leyens et al., 1975) that sought to test the hypothesis that heavy exposure to media violence can cause viewers to become more aggressive. The participants were Belgian delinquents who lived together in cottages at a minimum-security institution for adolescent boys. Before the experiment began, the experimenters observed each boy in their research sample to measure his characteristic level of aggression. These initial assessments served as a *baseline* against which future increases in aggression could be measured. The baseline observations suggested that the institution's four cottages could be divided into two subgroups consisting of two cottages populated by relatively aggressive boys and two cottages populated by less aggressive peers. Then the experiment began. For a period of one week, violent movies (such as *Bonnie and Clyde* and *The Dirty Dozen*) were shown each evening to one of the two cottages in each subgroup, and neutral films (such as *Daddy's Fiancée* and *La Belle Américaine*) were shown to the other cottages. Instances of physical and verbal aggression among residents of each cottage were recorded twice daily (at lunchtime and in the evenings after the movie) during the movie week and once daily (at lunchtime) during a posttreatment week.

The most striking result of this field experiment was the significant increase in physical aggression that occurred in the evenings among residents of both cottages assigned to the violent-film condition. Because the violent movies contained a large number of physically aggressive incidents, it appears that they evoked similar responses from the boys who watched them. But as shown in Figure 1.3, violent movies prompted larger increases in aggression among boys who were already relatively high in aggression. Exposure to the violent movies caused the highly aggressive boys to become more verbally aggressive as well—an effect that these boys continued to display through the movie week *and* the posttreatment week.

The results of the Belgian field experiment are consistent with Liebert and Baron's (1972) laboratory study in suggesting that exposure to media violence does instigate aggressive behavior. Yet it also qualifies the laboratory findings by implying that the instigating effects of media violence in the natural environment are likely to be stronger and more enduring for the more aggressive members of the audience.

The natural (or quasi-) experiment. There are many issues to which an experimental design either cannot be applied or should not be used for ethical reasons. Suppose, for example, that we wish to study the effects of social deprivation in infancy on children's intellectual development. Clearly we cannot ask one group of parents to lock their infants in an attic for 2 years so that we can collect the data we need. It is unethical to subject children to any experimental treatment that would adversely affect their physical or psychological well-being.

natural (or quasi) experiment a study in which the investigator measures the impact of some naturally occurring event that is assumed to affect people's lives.

However, we might be able to accomplish our research objectives through a **natural (or quasi-) experiment** in which we observe the consequences of a natural event that participants have experienced. If we were able to locate a group of children who had been raised in impoverished institutions with very limited contact with caregivers over the first 2 years, we could compare their intellectual development with that of children raised at home with their families. This comparison would provide valuable information about the likely effect of early social deprivation on children's intellectual development. The "independent variable" in a natural experiment is the "event" that participants experience (in our example, the social deprivation experienced by institutionalized infants). The "dependent variable" is whatever outcome measure one chooses to study (in our example, intellectual development).

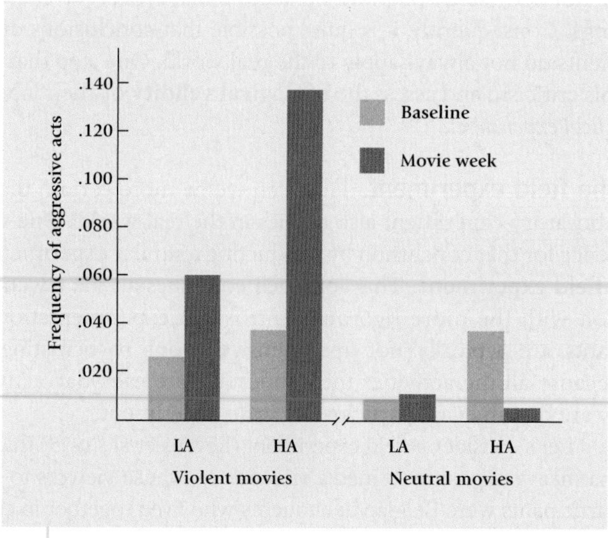

Figure 1.3 Mean physical aggression scores in the evening for highly aggressive (HA) and less aggressive (LA) boys under baseline conditions and after watching violent movies or neutral movies. *Adapted from "Effects of Movie Violence on Aggression in a Field Setting as a Function of Group Dominance and Cohesion," by J. P. Leynes, R. D. Parke, L. Camino, & L. Berkowitz, 1975,* Journal of Perception and Social Psychology, *1, 346–360. Copyright © 1975 by the American Psychological Association. Adapted by permission.*

Let's note, however, that researchers conducting natural experiments do not control the independent variable, nor do they randomly assign participants to experimental treatments. Instead, they merely observe and record the apparent outcomes of a natural happening or event. And in the absence of tight experimental control, it is often hard to determine precisely what factor is responsible for any group differences that are found. Suppose, for example, that our socially deprived institution children showed a poorer pattern of intellectual outcomes than children raised at home. Is the *social deprivation* that institutionalized children experienced the factor that causes this difference? Or is it that institutionalized children differed in other ways from family-reared children (for example, were more sickly as infants, were more poorly nourished, or simply had less intellectual potential) that might explain their poorer outcomes? Without randomly assigning participants to treatments and controlling other factors that may vary across treatments (for example, nutrition received), we simply cannot be certain that social deprivation is the factor responsible for the poor intellectual outcomes that institutionalized children display.

Despite its inability to make precise statements about cause and effect, the natural experiment is useful nonetheless. It can tell us whether a natural event could *possibly* have influenced those who experienced it and, thus, can provide some meaningful clues about cause and effect.

Table 1.4 summarizes the strengths and limitations of each of the general research designs we have discussed. Before moving on to consider specifically developmental research designs, let's consider one more research strategy used by scientists to verify the generalizability of their theories and hypotheses: the cross-cultural design.

Cross-Cultural Designs

Scientists are often hesitant to publish a new finding or conclusion until they have studied enough people to determine that their "discovery" is reliable. However, their conclusions are frequently based on participants living at one point in time within one particular culture or subculture, and it is difficult to know whether these conclusions apply to future generations or even to children currently growing up in other societies or subcultures (Lerner, 1991). Today, the generalizability of findings across samples and settings has become an important issue, for many theorists have implied that there are "universals" in human development—events and outcomes that all children share as they progress from infancy to adulthood.

TABLE 1.4 Strengths and Limitations of General Research Designs

Design	Procedure	Strengths	Limitations
Correlational	Gathers information about two or more variables without researcher intervention.	Estimates the strength and direction of relationships among variables in the natural environment.	Does not permit determination of cause-and-effect relationships among variables.
Laboratory experiment	Manipulates some aspect of participants' environment (independent variable) and measures its impact on participants' behavior (dependent variable).	Permits determination of cause-and-effect relationships among variables.	Data obtained in artificial laboratory environment may lack generalizability to the real world.
Field experiment	Manipulates independent variable and measures its impact on the dependent variable in a natural setting.	Permits determination of cause-and-effect relationships and generalization of findings to the real world.	Experimental treatments may be less potent and harder to control when presented in the natural environment.
Natural (quasi-) experiment	Gathers information about the behavior of people who experience a real-world (natural) manipulation of their environment.	Permits a study of the impact of natural events that would be difficult or impossible to simulate in an experiment; provides strong clues about cause-and-effect relationships.	Lack of precise control over natural events or the participants exposed to them prevents the investigator from establishing definitive cause-and-effect relationships.

cross-cultural comparison
a study that compares the behavior and/or development of people from different cultural or subcultural backgrounds.

Cross-cultural studies are those in which participants from different cultural or subcultural backgrounds are observed, tested, and compared on one or more aspects of development. Studies of this kind serve many purposes. For example, they allow the investigator to determine whether conclusions drawn about the development of children from one social context (such as middle-class, white youngsters in the United States) also characterize children growing up in other societies or those from different ethnic or socioeconomic backgrounds within the same society (for example, American children of Hispanic ancestry or those from economically disadvantaged homes). So the **cross-cultural comparison** guards against the overgeneralization of research findings and is the only way to determine whether there are truly "universals" in human development.

Souza et al. (2004) used a cross-cultural comparison to examine two groups of children and adolescents who had been diagnosed with attention deficit hyperactivity disorder (ADHD). The groups were from two industrialized cities in Brazil: Pôrto Alegre in the south and Rio de Janeiro in the southeast. Because children and adolescents diagnosed with ADHD in the United States are typically depressed, defiant, or anxious, the researchers conducting the study wondered whether ethnic and cultural factors might be associated with differences in the kinds of emotional troubles and disorders that accompany ADHD. The results revealed that the patterns of disorders associated with ADHD did not differ between the two geographic regions. Oppositional defiant disorder was the most common co-diagnosis for both regions, and depressive and anxiety disorders occurred among children from the two groups at about the same rates. Results from the Brazilian study were congruent with results from similar studies in the United States and other countries. Therefore, it appears that, among children and adolescents from diverse cultures in developing and industrialized nations, the pattern of emotional disorders accompanying ADHD is quite stable.

Other investigators who favor the cross-cultural approach are looking for *differences* rather than similarities. They recognize that human beings develop in societies that have very different ideas about issues such as the proper times and procedures for disciplining children, the activities that are most appropriate for boys and for girls, the time at which childhood ends and adulthood begins, the treatment of the aged, and countless other aspects of life (Fry, 1996). They have also learned that people from various cultures differ in the ways they perceive the world, express their emotions, think, and solve problems. So apart from its focus on universals in development, the cross-cultural approach also illustrates that human development is heavily influenced by the cultural context in which it occurs.

For example, earlier we discussed the invention of adolescence in Western societies. Cross-cultural comparisons have shown us that many of the world's cultures have no concept of adolescence as a distinct phase of life. The St. Lawrence Eskimos, for example, simply distinguish boys from men (or girls from women), following the tradition of many preliterate societies that passage to adulthood occurs at puberty (Keith, 1985). And yet, other cultures' depictions of the life span are much more intricate than our own. The Arasha of East Africa, for example, have at least six meaningful age strata for males: youths, junior warriors, senior warriors, junior elders, senior elders, and retired elders.

The fact that age does not have the same meaning in all eras or cultures reflects a basic truth that we have already touched on and will emphasize repeatedly throughout this book: The course of human development in one historical or cultural context is apt to differ, and to differ substantially, from that observed in other eras and cultural settings (Fry, 1996). Aside from our biological link to the human race, we are largely products of the times and places in which we live. (See Box 1.1 for a dramatic illustration of cultural diversity in gender roles.)

It is important to note that cross-cultural comparisons do not always examine similarities and differences among people of different nationalities, but that this method is also used to compare cultural differences within a specific nation. For example, many studies examine differences among subcultures within the United States because the experiences that these subcultures have can be quite different.

For example, the Fuligni and Pedersen study that was mentioned earlier as an example of a questionnaire methodology was in fact a cross-cultural comparison to assess the familial obligations felt among culturally diverse young adults in the United States.

FOCUS ON RESEARCH

A Cross-Cultural Comparison of Gender Roles

One of the greatest values of cross-cultural comparisons is that they can tell us whether a developmental phenomenon is or is not universal. Consider the roles that males and females play in our society. In our culture, playing the masculine role has traditionally required traits such as independence, assertiveness, and dominance. Females are expected to be more nurturant and sensitive to other people. Are these masculine and feminine roles universal? Could biological differences between the sexes lead inevitably to sex differences in behavior?

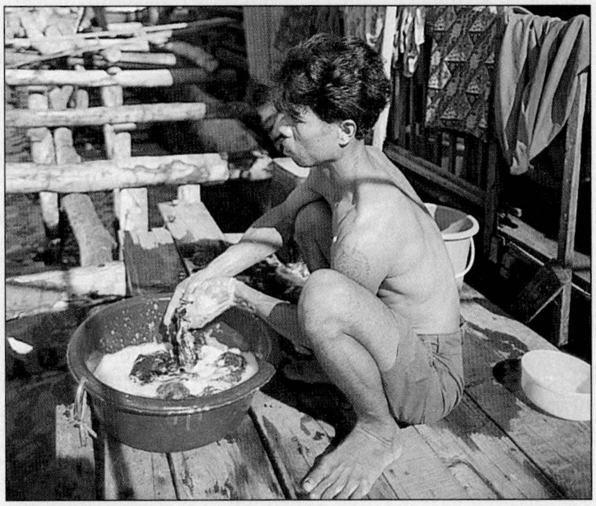
Jeffrey Aaronson/Network Aspen

The roles assumed by men and women may vary dramatically from culture to culture.

Many years ago, anthropologist Margaret Mead (1935) compared the gender roles adopted by people in three tribal societies on the island of New Guinea, and her observations are certainly thought provoking. In the Arapesh tribe, both men and women were taught to play what we would regard as a feminine role: They were cooperative, nonaggressive, and sensitive to the needs of others. Both men and women of the Mundugumor tribe were brought up to be aggressive and emotionally unresponsive to other people—a masculine pattern of behavior by Western standards. Finally, the Tchambuli displayed a pattern of gender-role development that was the direct opposite of the Western pattern: Males were passive, emotionally dependent, and socially sensitive, whereas females were dominant, independent, and assertive.

Mead's cross-cultural comparison suggests that cultural learning may have far more to do with the characteristic behavior patterns of men and women than biological differences do. So we very much need cross-cultural comparisons such as Mead's. Without them, we might easily make the mistake of assuming that whatever holds true in our society holds true everywhere; with their help, we can begin to understand the contributions of biology and environment to human development.

Cross-culturally, the researchers were interested in how the ethnic subgroups espoused by the young adults differed in their attitudes toward offering familial assistance as they moved into early adulthood. They contrasted Filipino, East Asian, Latin American, and European American subcultures. The researchers also looked at how generational status was related to sense of family duty. They compared young adults who were born outside the United States (first generation citizens) with young adults who were born inside the United States but had at least one parent who was born outside the United States (second generation citizens), and with young adults whose parents were both born inside the United States.

Fuligni and Pedersen found that although a sense of family obligation increased for all participants as they left high school and became engaged in the first years of their adult lives, the increase was strongest among young adults from Latino and European backgrounds. They also found that young adults from Latin American and Filipino backgrounds reported a stronger sense of family duty than those from other backgrounds. So too, did young adults from families that had immigrated more recently. First generation young adults were more likely to believe that continuing to support the family in the future was more important than did third generation young adults. Fuligni and Pedersen (2002) suggest that first generation young adults may feel a responsibility for parents who have been in the United States a relatively short time and who may need more assistance with language and cultural issues.

Studies examining subcultures within nations such as Fuligni and Pedersen's are increasingly adding to our understanding of how environmental and societal factors can influence development. But to truly understand how developmental change occurs, we need to use research methods designed to illuminate those changes. This is the topic of our next section.

CONCEPT CHECK 1.2 Understanding Research Methods and Designs

Check your understanding of basic research methods used in developmental psychology and research designs by answering the following questions. Answers appear in the Appendix.

Multiple Choice: Select the best answer for each question.

_____ 1. Suppose Dr. Smith is a developmental psychologist who is interested in whether intelligence changes as children develop. She creates a test of intelligence and administers it to a group of children. Her results lead her to conclude that her test actually measured years of schooling, not intelligence. What scientific ideal did her study violate?
  a. Her measure was not reliable.
  b. Her measure was not valid.
  c. Her experiment did not follow the scientific method.
  d. Her treatment groups were not randomly assigned.

_____ 2. The belief that investigators should be objective and use scientific data to test their theories is known as the
  a. scientific attitude
  b. scientific objective
  c. scientific method
  d. scientific value

_____ 3. If you were to check to make sure that two observers obtained the same results when observing the same event, you would be measuring
  a. validity
  b. interrater reliability
  c. temporal stability
  d. temporal validity

_____ 4. Which of the following methods would be *least* practical to use when studying infants?
  a. naturalistic observation
  b. structured observation
  c. psychophysiological methods
  d. the clinical method

Matching: Select the research method that is best suited for investigating each of the following research questions. Select from the following research methods:

a. structured interview
b. ethnography
c. naturalistic observation
d. structured observation
e. psychophysiological methods

5. _______ Will young elementary school children break a solemn promise to watch a sick puppy when no one is around to detect their transgression?
6. _______ Do 6-year-olds know any negative stereotypes about minority group members?
7. _______ Can 6-month-old infants discriminate the colors red, green, blue, and yellow?
8. _______ Are the aggressive actions that boy playmates display toward each other different from those that occur in girls' play groups?
9. _______ How does life change for boys from the Sambia tribe once they have experienced tribal rites of puberty?

Short-Answer: Test your knowledge of correlation and causation by briefly answering the following question:

10. Dr. Chang finds that the better children feel about themselves (that is, the higher their self-esteem as reported in an interview), the higher their grades are in school. What can we conclude about the relationship between self-esteem and school grades from this study?

Research Strategies and Studying Development

In the previous sections we considered data collection methods and research designs that could be used in many areas of psychological research. The designs we considered were helpful for identifying relationships between variables (the correlational design), for detecting causal relationships between variables (the various experimental designs), and for evaluating the generalizability of our theories (the cross-cultural comparisons). In the next sections we will consider additional research designs that can be combined with the ones we've already considered to give us information about *developmental* continuities and changes. These are designs that allow us to make inferences about how people change over time.

Research Designs for Studying Development

Developmentalists are not merely interested in examining people's progress at one particular phase of life; instead, they hope to determine how people's feelings, thoughts, abilities, and behaviors *develop* or *change* over time. Four basic approaches allow us to chart these developmental trends: the cross-sectional design, the longitudinal design, the sequential design, and the microgenetic design.

The Cross-Sectional Design

cross-sectional design
a research design in which subjects from different age groups are studied at the same point in time.

cohort
a group of people of the same age who are exposed to similar cultural environments and historical events as they are growing up.

In a **cross-sectional design** people who *differ in age* are studied at *the same point in time.* In cross-sectional research, participants at each age level are *different* people. That is, they come from different cohorts, where a **cohort** is defined as a group of people of the same age who are exposed to similar cultural environments and historical events as they are growing up. By comparing participants in the different age groups, investigators can often identify age-related changes in whatever aspect of development they happen to be studying.

An experiment by Brian Coates and Willard Hartup (1969) is an excellent example of a cross-sectional experimental design. Coates and Hartup were interested in determining why preschool children are less proficient than first- or second-graders at learning new responses displayed by an adult model. Their hypothesis was that younger children do not spontaneously *describe* what they are observing, whereas older children produce verbal descriptions of the modeled sequence. When asked to perform the actions they have witnessed, the preschoolers are at a distinct disadvantage because they have no verbal "learning aids" that would help them to recall the model's behavior.

To test these hypotheses, Coates and Hartup designed an interesting cross-sectional experiment. Children from two age groups—4- to 5-year-olds and 7- to 8-year-olds—watched a short film in which an adult model displayed 20 novel responses, such as throwing a beanbag between his legs, lassoing an inflatable toy with a hula hoop, and so on. Some of the children from each age group were instructed to describe the model's actions, and they did so as they watched the film (induced-verbalization condition). Other children were not required to describe the model's actions as they observed them (passive-observation condition). When the show ended, each child was taken to a room that contained the same toys seen in the film and was asked to demonstrate what the model had done with these toys.

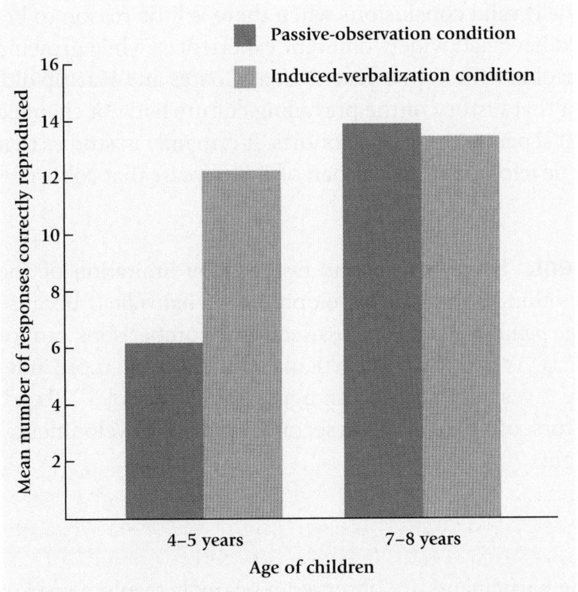

Figure 1.4 Children's ability to reproduce the behavior of a social model as a function of age and verbalization instructions. *Adapted from "Age and Verbalization in Observational Learning," by B. Coates & W. W. Hartup, 1969,* Developmental Psychology, 1, *556–562. Adapted by permission of the author.*

Figure 1.4 illustrates the three interesting findings that emerged from this experiment. First, the 4- to 5-year-olds who were *not* told to describe what they had seen (that is, the passive observers) reproduced *fewer* of the model's responses than the 4- to 5-year-olds who described the model's behavior (the induced verbalizers) or the 7- to 8-year-olds in either experimental condition. This finding suggests that 4- to 5-year-old children may not produce the verbal descriptions that would help them to learn unless they are explicitly instructed to do so. Second, the performance of younger and older children in the induced-verbalization condition was comparable. So younger children can learn just as much as older children by observing a social model *if the younger children are told to describe what they are observing.* Finally, 7- to 8-year-olds in the passive-observation condition reproduced about the same number of behaviors as 7- to 8-year-olds in the induced-verbalization condition. This finding suggests that instructions to describe the model's actions had little effect on 7- to 8-year-olds, who will apparently describe what they have seen, even when not told to. Taken together, the results imply that 4- to 5-year-olds may often learn less from social models because they, unlike older children, do not spontaneously produce the verbal descriptions that would help them to remember what they have observed.

An important advantage of the cross-sectional design is that the investigator can collect data from children of different ages over a short time. For example, Coates and Hartup did not have to wait 3 years for their 4- to 5-year-olds to become 7- to 8-year-olds in order to test their developmental hypotheses. They merely sampled from two age groups and tested both samples simultaneously. Yet there are two important limitations of cross-sectional research.

Cohort effects. Recall as we noted above that in cross-sectional research, participants at each age level are *different* people. That is, they come from different cohorts, where a cohort was defined as a group of people of the same age who are exposed to similar cultural environments and historical events as they are growing up. The fact that cross-sectional comparisons always involve different cohorts presents us with a thorny interpretive problem, for any age differences that are found in the study may not always be due to age or development but, rather, may reflect other cultural or historical factors that distinguish members of different cohorts. Stated another way, cross-sectional comparisons *confound age and cohort effects.*

An example should clarify the issue. For years, cross-sectional research had consistently indicated that young adults score slightly higher on intelligence tests than middle-aged adults, who, in turn, score much higher than the elderly. But does intelligence decline with age, as these findings would seem to indicate? Not necessarily! Later research (Schaie, 1990) revealed that individuals' intelligence test scores remain relatively stable over the years and that the earlier studies were really measuring something quite different: age differences in education. The older adults in the cross-sectional studies had had less schooling and, therefore, scored lower on intelligence tests than the middle-aged and young adult samples. Their test scores had not declined but, rather, had always been lower than those of the younger adults with whom they were compared. So the earlier cross-sectional research had discovered a **cohort effect,** not a true developmental change.

cohort effect
age-related difference among cohorts that is attributable to cultural/historical differences in cohorts' growing-up experiences rather than to true developmental change.

Despite this important limitation, the cross-sectional comparison is still the design developmentalists use most often. Why? Because it has the advantage of being quick and easy; we can go out this year, sample individuals of different ages, and be done with it. Moreover, this design is likely to yield valid conclusions when there is little reason to believe that the cohorts being studied have had widely different experiences while growing up. So if we compared 4- to 5-year-olds with 7- to 8-year-olds, as Coates and Hartup did, we might feel reasonably confident that history or the prevailing culture had not changed in any major way in the 3 years that separate these two cohorts. It is mainly in studies that attempt to make inferences about development over a span of many years that cohort effects present a serious problem.

Data on individual development. There is a second noteworthy limitation of the cross-sectional design: it tells us nothing about the development of *individuals* because each person is observed *at only one point in time.* So cross-sectional comparisons cannot provide answers to questions such as "When will this particular child become more independent?" or "Will this aggressive 2-year-old become an aggressive 5-year-old?" To address issues like these, investigators often turn to a second kind of developmental comparison, the longitudinal design.

The Longitudinal Design

longitudinal design
a research design in which one group of subjects is studied repeatedly over a period of months or years.

In a **longitudinal design,** the same participants are observed repeatedly over a period of time. The time period may be relatively brief—6 months to a year—or it may be very long, spanning a lifetime. Researchers may be studying one particular aspect of development, such as intelligence, or many. By repeatedly testing the same participants, investigators can assess the *stability* (continuity) of various attributes for each person in the sample. They can also identify normative developmental trends and processes by looking for commonalities, such as the point(s) at which most children undergo various changes and the experiences, if any, that children seem to share prior to reaching these milestones. Finally, the tracking of several participants over time will help investigators to understand *individual differences* in development, particularly if they are able to establish that different kinds of earlier experiences lead to different outcomes.

Several very noteworthy longitudinal projects have followed children for decades and have assessed many aspects of development (see, for example, Kagan & Moss, 1962; Newman et al., 1997). However, most longitudinal studies are much more modest in direction and scope. For example, Carolee Howes and Catherine Matheson (1992) conducted a study in which the pretend play activities of a group of 1- to 2-year-olds were repeatedly observed at 6-month intervals over 3 years. Using a classification scheme that assessed the cognitive complexity of play, Howes and Matheson sought to determine (1) whether play did reliably become more complex with age, (2) whether children reliably differed in the complexity of their play, and (3) whether the complexity of a child's play reliably forecasted his or her social competencies with peers. Not surprisingly, all children displayed increases in the complexity of their play over the 3-year period, although there were reliable individual differences in play complexity at each observation point. In addition, there was a clear relationship between the complexity of a child's play and social competence with peers: Children who engaged in more complex forms of play at any given age were the ones who were rated as most outgoing and least aggressive at the next observation period 6 months later. So this longitudinal study shows that complexity of pretend play not only increases with age but is also a reliable predictor of children's future social competencies with peers.

Although we have portrayed the longitudinal design in a very favorable manner, this approach has several potential drawbacks as well. For example, longitudinal projects can be very *costly* and *time-consuming*. These points are especially important in that the focus of theory and research in the developmental sciences is constantly changing, and longitudinal questions that seem exciting at the beginning of a 10- or 20-year project may seem rather trivial by the time the project ends. **Practice effects** can also threaten the validity of longitudinal studies: Participants who are repeatedly interviewed or tested may become test-wise or increasingly familiar with the content of the test itself, showing performance improvements that are unrelated to normal patterns of development. Longitudinal researchers may also have a problem with **selective attrition;** children may move away or become bored with participating, or they may have parents who, for one reason or another, will not allow them to continue in the study. The end result is a smaller and potentially **nonrepresentative sample** that not only provides less information about the developmental issues in question but also may limit the conclusions of the study to those children who do not move away and who remain cooperative over the long run.

practice effect
changes in participants' natural responses as a result of repeated testing.

selective attrition
nonrandom loss of participants during a study which results in a nonrepresentative sample.

nonrepresentative sample
a subgroup that differs in important ways from the larger group (or population) to which it belongs.

cross-generational problem
the fact that long-term changes in the environment may limit conclusions of a longitudinal project to that generation of children who were growing up while the study was in progress.

There is another shortcoming of long-term longitudinal studies that students often see right away—the **cross-generational problem.** Children in a longitudinal project are typically drawn from one cohort and are likely to have very different kinds of experiences than children from other eras. Consider, for example, how the times have changed since the 1930s and 1940s, when children in some of the early long-term longitudinal studies were growing up. Today, in this age of dual-career families, more children are attending day-care centers and nursery schools than ever before. Modern families are smaller than the past, meaning that children now have fewer brothers and sisters. Families also move more frequently than they did in the 1930s and 1940s, so that many children from the modern era are exposed to a wider variety of people and places than was typical in the past. And no matter where they may be living, today's children grow up in front of televisions, video games, and computers, influences that were not available during the 1930s and 1940s. So children of earlier eras lived in a very different world, and we cannot be certain that those children developed in precisely the same way as today's children. In sum, cross-generational changes in the environment may limit the conclusions of a longitudinal project to those participants who were growing up while the study was in progress.

Lambert/Hulton Archive/Getty Images

Andrew Olney/Getty Images

Leisure activities of the 1930s (top) and today (bottom). As these photos illustrate, the kinds of experiences that children growing up in the 1930s had were very different from those of today's youth. Many believe that cross-generational changes in the environment may limit the results of a longitudinal study to the youngsters who were growing up while the research was in progress.

We have seen that the cross-sectional and the longitudinal designs each have distinct advantages and disadvantages. Might it be possible to combine the best features of both approaches? A third kind of developmental comparison—the sequential design—tries to do just that.

The Sequential Design

Sequential designs combine the best features of cross-sectional and longitudinal studies by selecting participants of different ages and following each of these cohorts over time. To illustrate, imagine that we wished to study the development of children's logical reasoning abilities between the ages of 6 and 12. We might begin in 2006 by testing the logical reasoning of a sample of 6-year-olds (the 2000 birth cohort) and a sample of 8-year-olds (the 1998 birth cohort). We could then retest the reasoning abilities of both groups in 2008 and 2010. Notice that the design calls for us to follow the 2000 cohort from ages 6 through 10 and the 1998 cohort from ages 8 through 12. A graphic representation of this research plan appears in Figure 1.5.

There are three major strengths of this sequential design. First, it allows us to determine whether cohort effects are influencing our results by comparing the logical reasoning of same-aged children who were born in different years. As shown in the figure, cohort effects are assessed by comparing the logical reasoning of the two samples when each is aged 8 and 10. If the samples do not differ, we can assume that cohort effects are not operating. Figure 1.5 also illustrates a second major advantage of our sequential design: it allows us to make both longitudinal and cross-sectional comparisons in the same study. If the age trends in logical reasoning are similar in both the longitudinal and the cross-sectional comparisons, we can be quite confident that they represent true developmental changes in logical reasoning abilities. Finally, sequential designs are often more efficient than standard longitudinal designs. In our example, we could trace the development of logical reasoning over a 6-year age range, even though our study would take only 4 years to conduct. A standard longitudinal comparison that initially sampled 6-year-old participants would take 6 years to provide similar information. Clearly, this combination of the cross-sectional and longitudinal designs is a rather versatile alternative to either of these approaches.

The Microgenetic Design

Cross-sectional, longitudinal, and sequential designs provide only a broad outline of developmental changes without necessarily specifying why or how these changes take place. **Microgenetic designs,** currently favored by many researchers who study children's cognitive development, are used in an attempt to illuminate the processes that are thought to promote developmental changes. The logic is straightforward: children who are thought to be ready for an important developmental change are exposed repeatedly to experiences that are thought to produce the change and their behavior is monitored *as it is changing.*

Cognitive theorists have used this approach to specify how children come to rely on new and more efficient strategies for solving problems. By studying participants intensively over a period of hours, days, or weeks and carefully analyzing their problem-solving behavior, it is often possible to specify how their thinking and strategizing is

sequential design
a research design in which subjects from different age groups are studied repeatedly over a period of months or years.

microgenetic design
a research design in which participants are studied intensively over a short period of time as developmental changes occur; attempts to specify how or why those changes occur.

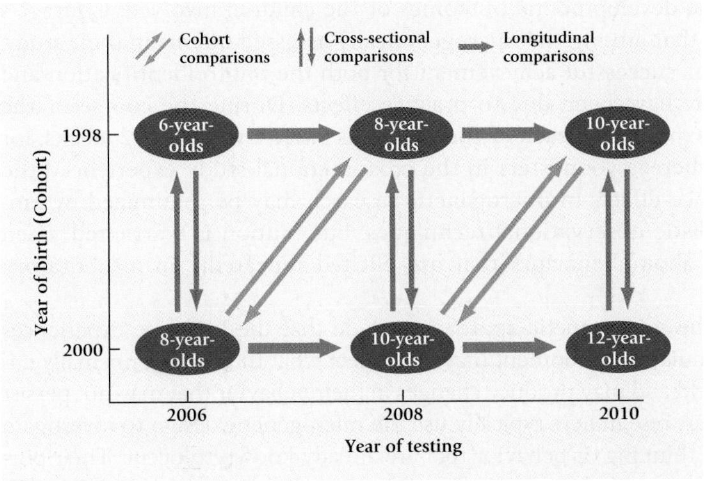

Figure 1.5 Example of a sequential design. Two samples of children, one born in 1998 and one born in 2000, are observed longitudinally between the ages of 6 and 12. The design permits the investigator to assess cohort effects by comparing children of the same age who were born in different years. In the absence of cohort effects, the longitudinal and cross-sectional comparisons in this design also permit the researcher to make strong statements about the strength and direction of any developmental changes.

changing to advance their cognitive competencies (Siegler & Svetina, 2002), arithmetic skills (Siegler & Jenkins, 1989), memory (Coyle & Bjorklund, 1997), and language skills (Gershkoff-Stowe & Smith, 1997). Although the microgenetic approach is a new method, it holds great promise for illuminating the kinds of experiences that can promote changes in such areas of social and personality development as self-concept and self-esteem, social cognition (that is, understanding others' behaviors and forming impressions of others), reasoning about moral issues, and thinking about gender-role stereotypes, to name a few.

A clever example of a study that used the microgenetic approach was conducted by Courage, Edeson, and Howe (2004). Actually, they combined microgenetic and cross-sectional approaches in their study of the development of visual self-recognition in infants. In the microgenetic component of the study, each of 10 toddlers was assessed biweekly between the ages of 15 and 23 months. In the cross-sectional component, 10 toddlers were assessed in each of 9 age groups, the youngest consisting of 15-month-olds, the next 16-month-olds, and so on through 23 months. All children in the study were assessed using three visual tasks. In the first task, each child's parent surreptitiously marked the infant's nose with blue paint. Thirty seconds later a mirror was placed in front of the child. Upon seeing themselves in the mirror, children who touched hand to nose, or commented about appearance change, were designated "recognizers." Children who stared at the image, or looked shy or embarrassed, were designated as "ambiguous," and children who did not respond with either recognizer or ambiguous behaviors were designated "nonrecognizers." A second task required the children to identify a photograph of self that was presented with two other Polaroid pictures of children of the same age and sex. During the third task, the experimenters suspended a toy behind each infant's head so that the infant could see the toy in a mirror. Infants were considered successful when they turned to locate the toy in real space.

The microgenetic data revealed that prior to mastery of the visual recognition task, children experienced a period during which they successfully identified themselves at some times and failed to identify themselves at others. As well, this ambiguous period was short for some children, being observed during only a single session, and much longer, lasting four sessions, for other children. The cross-sectional data told another story. Month-to-month changes in self-recognition represented by the successive age groups appeared to be more abrupt. A sharp increase in self-recognition ability that occurred between 16 months and 17 months in the cross-sectional data was not apparent in the microgenetic data. However, the mean age of mirror self-recognition fell within the 16-month to 17-month range for the 10 infants who participated in the microgenetic component of the study, suggesting some convergence of results between the two approaches. The average age of success for the photo identification and toy location tasks was younger in the microgenetic component than in the cross-sectional component.

Although microgenetic techniques present a unique opportunity to witness and record the actual process of change as it occurs during development, there are disadvantages to the microgenetic approach. First, it is difficult, time-consuming, and costly to track large numbers of children in such a detailed manner. Recall that Courage and colleagues recorded the progress of only 10 toddlers in the microgenetic component of their study, whereas they included 90 toddlers in the cross-sectional component. Also, the frequency of observations required by the microgenetic method may affect the developmental outcomes of the children involved. Courage's research group notes that among the microgenetically assessed infants in their study, the lower mean age of successful achievement for both the photo identification and toy location tasks may have been due to practice effects. During the course of the study, these toddlers experienced each of the two tasks twice a week for 32 weeks, for a total of 64 trials, whereas youngsters in the cross-sectional study experienced the task only once. Practice effects in microgenetic research may be minimized by employing more naturalistic observational techniques, but caution is warranted when drawing conclusions about behaviors that are elicited repeatedly in a laboratory setting.

So criticisms of the microgenetic approach include that the intensive experiences children receive to stimulate development may not reflect what they would normally encounter in the real world and may produce changes in their behavior that may not persist over the long run. Thus, researchers typically use the microgenetic design to investigate age-related changes in thinking or behavior that are already known to occur. Their purpose is to specify more precisely *how* or *why* these changes might occur by studying children as the changes take place.

To help you review and compare the four major developmental designs, Table 1.5 provides a brief description of each, along with its major strengths and weaknesses.

Isn't it remarkable how many methods and designs that developmentalists have at their disposal? This diversity of available procedures is a definite strength because findings gained through one procedure can then be checked and perhaps confirmed through other procedures. Indeed, providing such *converging evidence* serves a most important function by demonstrating that the conclusion a researcher draws is truly a "discovery" and not merely an artifact of the method or the design used to collect the original data. So there is no "best method" for studying children and adolescents; each of the approaches we have considered has contributed substantially to our understanding of human development.

TABLE 1.5 Strengths and Limitations of Four Developmental Designs

Design	Procedure	Strengths	Limitations
Cross-sectional	Observes people of different ages (or cohorts) at one point in time.	Demonstrates age differences, hints at developmental trends; relatively inexpensive; takes little time to conduct.	Age trends may reflect extraneous differences between cohorts rather than true developmental change; provides no data on the development of individuals because each participant is observed at only one point in time.
Longitudinal	Observes people of one cohort repeatedly over time.	Provides data on the development of individuals; can reveal links between early experiences and later outcomes; indicates how individuals are alike and how they are different in the ways they change over time.	Relatively time-consuming and expensive; selective attrition may yield nonrepresentative sample that limits the generalizability of one's conclusions; cross-generational changes may limit one's conclusions to the cohort that was studied.
Sequential	Combines the cross-sectional and the longitudinal approaches by observing different cohorts repeatedly over time.	Discriminates true developmental trends from cohort effects; indicates whether developmental changes experienced by one cohort are similar to those experienced by other cohorts; often less costly and time-consuming than the longitudinal approach.	More costly and time-consuming than cross-sectional research; despite being the strongest design, may still leave questions about whether a developmental change is generalizable beyond the cohorts studied.
Microgenetic	Children are observed extensively over a limited time period when a developmental change is thought to occur.	Extensive observation of changes as they occur can reveal how and why changes occur.	Extensive experience given to stimulate change may be somewhat atypical and produce change that may not persist over long periods.

Ethical Considerations in Developmental Research

When designing and conducting research with humans, researchers may face thorny issues centering on *research ethics*—the standards of conduct that investigators are ethically bound to honor in order to protect their research participants from physical or psychological harm. Some ethical issues are easily resolved: One simply does *not* conduct experiments that will cause physical or psychological damage, such as physical abuse, starvation, isolation for long periods, and the like. However, most ethical issues are far more subtle. Here are some of the dilemmas that developmentalists may have to resolve during their careers as researchers:

- Can children or adolescents be exposed to temptations that virtually guarantee that they will cheat or break other rules?
- Am I ever justified in deceiving participants, either by misinforming them about the purpose of my study or by telling them something untrue about themselves (for example, "You did poorly on this test," when they actually did very well)?
- Can I observe my participants in the natural setting without informing them that they are the subjects of a scientific investigation?
- Is it acceptable to tell children that their classmates think that an obviously incorrect answer is "correct" to see whether participants will conform to the judgments of their peers?
- Am I justified in using verbal disapproval as part of my research procedure?

Before reading further, you may wish to think about these issues and formulate your own opinions. Then read Table 1.6 and reconsider each of your viewpoints.

TABLE 1.6 Major Rights of Children and Responsibilities of Investigators Involved in Psychological Research

Ethical considerations are especially complex when children participate in psychological research. Children are more vulnerable than adolescents and adults to physical and psychological harm. Moreover, young children may not always fully understand what they are committing themselves to when they agree to participate in a study. In order to protect children who participate in psychological research and to clarify the responsibilities of researchers who work with children, the American Psychological Association (1992) and the Society for Research in Child Development (1993) have endorsed special ethical guidelines, the more important of which are as follows:

Protection from Harm[a]

The investigator may use no research operation that may harm the child either physically or psychologically. Psychological harm is difficult to define; nevertheless, its definition remains the responsibility of the investigator. When an investigator is in doubt about the possible harmful effects of the research operations, he or she must seek consultation from others. When harm seems possible, he or she is obligated to find other means of obtaining the information or abandon the research.

Informed Consent

The informed consent of parents as well as others who act in the child's behalf—teachers, superintendents of institutions—should be obtained, preferably in writing. Informed consent requires that the parent or other responsible adult be told all features of the research that may affect his or her willingness to allow the child to participate. Moreover, federal guidelines in the United States specify that all children 7 years of age and older have the right to have explained to them, in understandable language, all aspects of the research that could affect their willingness to participate. Of course, children of any age always have the right to choose not to participate or to discontinue participation in research at any time. This provision is a tricky one, however: Even if they are told that they can stop participating in a study at any time, young children may not really grasp how to do so or may not really believe that they can stop without incurring a penalty of some kind. However, children are much more likely to understand their rights of assent and to exercise them if the researcher carefully explains that he or she would not be upset if the child chose not to participate or to stop participating (Abramovitch et al., 1995).

Confidentiality

Researchers must keep in confidence all information obtained from research participants. Children have the right to concealment of their identity on all data collected and reported, either in writing or informally. The one exception is most states have laws that prohibit an investigator from withholding the names of suspected victims of child abuse or neglect (Liss, 1994).

Deception/Debriefing/Knowledge of Results

Although children have the right to know the purposes of a study in advance, a particular project may necessitate concealment of information, or deception. Whenever concealment or deception is thought to be essential to the conduct of research, the investigator must satisfy a committee of peers that this judgment is correct. If deception or concealment is used, participants must later be debriefed—that is, told, in language they can understand, the true purpose of the study and why it was necessary to deceive them. Children also have the right to be informed, in language they can understand, of the results of the research in which they have participated.

[a] Ross Thompson (1990) has published an excellent essay on this topic that I would recommend to anyone who conducts (or plans to conduct) research with children.

Have any of your opinions changed? As you can see, the tabled guidelines are very general; they do not explicitly permit or prohibit specific operations or practices such as those described in the preceding dilemmas. In fact, any of the listed dilemmas can be resolved in ways that permit an investigator to use the procedures in question and still remain well within current ethical guidelines. For example, it is generally considered permissible to observe young children in natural settings (for example, at school or in a park) without informing them that they are being studied if the investigator has previously obtained the **informed consent** (see Table 1.5) of the adults responsible for the children's care and safety in these settings. Ethical guidelines are just that: guidelines. The ultimate responsibility for treating children fairly and protecting them from harm is the investigator's.

informed consent
the right of research participants to receive an explanation, in language they can understand, of all aspects of research that may affect their willingness to participate.

benefits-to-risks ratio
a comparison of the possible benefits of a study for advancing knowledge and optimizing life conditions versus its costs to participants in terms of inconvenience and possible harm.

How, then, do investigators decide whether to use a procedure that some may consider questionable on ethical grounds? They generally weigh the advantages and disadvantages of the research by carefully calculating its possible *benefits* (to humanity or to the participants) and comparing them with the potential *risks* that participants may face (Greig & Taylor, 2004). If the **benefits-to-risk ratio** is favorable, and if there are no other less risky procedures that could be used to produce these same benefits, the investigator will generally proceed. However, there are safeguards against overzealous researchers who underestimate the riskiness of their procedures. In the United States and Canada, for example, universities, research foundations, and government agencies that fund research with children have set up "human-subjects review committees" to provide second (and sometimes third) opinions on the ethical ramifications of all proposed research. The function of these review committees is to reconsider the potential risks and benefits of the proposed research and, more important, to help ensure that all possible steps are taken to protect the welfare of those who may choose to participate in the project.

confidentiality
the right of participants to concealment of their identity with respect to the data that they provide.

protection from harm
the right of research participants to be protected from physical or psychological harm.

Clashes between the ethical provisions of **confidentiality** and **protection from harm** can pose serious ethical dilemmas for researchers who learn that the well-being of one or more participants (or their associates) may be seriously at risk for such life-threatening events as suicidal tendencies or untreated sexually transmitted diseases. These are risks that many investigators may feel ethically bound to report or to help the participant to self-report to the appropriate medical, social, or psychological services. Indeed, adolescents view reporting of these very serious risks (or, alternatively, helping the participant to self-report) in a very favorable way; and they may perceive inaction on the investigator's part as an indication that the problem is considered unimportant, that no services are available to assist them, or that knowledgeable adults cannot be depended upon to help youngsters in need. (See Fisher et al., 1996, for an excellent discussion of the confidentially dilemmas researchers may face and adolescents' views about appropriate courses of action for researchers to take.)

Of course, final approval of all one's safeguards and reporting procedures by a review committee does not absolve investigators of the need to reevaluate the benefits and costs of their projects, even while the research is in progress (Thompson, 1990). Suppose, for example, that a researcher studying children's aggression in a playground setting came to the conclusion that his subjects had (1) discovered his own fascination with aggressive behavior and (2) begun to beat on one another in order to attract his attention. At that point, the risks to participants would have escalated

Frank Pedrick/The Image Works

Ethical considerations may force an investigator to abandon procedures that cause harm or pose unforeseen risks to research participants.

far beyond the researcher's initial estimates, and he would be ethically bound (in our opinion) to stop the research immediately.

In the final analysis, guidelines and review committees do not guarantee that research participants will be treated responsibly; only investigators can do that by constantly reevaluating the consequences of their operations and by modifying or abandoning any procedure that may compromise the welfare or the dignity of those who have volunteered to participate.

CONCEPT CHECK 1.3 Understanding Developmental Research Designs

Check your understanding of developmental research designs by answering the following questions. Answers appear in the Appendix.

Multiple Choice: Select the best answer for each question.

_____ 1. Which of the following is a disadvantage of the *longitudinal research design?*
   a. It does not evaluate individual differences in development.
   b. It is subject to the cross-generational problem.
   c. It violates the scientific method.
   d. It may cause developmental delays and trauma to the participants.

_____ 2. Which of the following is a disadvantage of the *cross-sectional research design?*
   a. It does not evaluate individual differences in development.
   b. It is subject to the cross-gender problem.
   c. It violates the scientific method.
   d. It may cause developmental changes that would not occur naturally and which may not be long lasting.

_____ 3. Which of the following is a disadvantage of the *microgenetic research design?*
   a. It does not evaluate individual differences in development.
   b. It confounds cohort and age effects.
   c. It violates the scientific method.
   d. It may cause developmental changes that would not occur naturally and which may not be long lasting.

Fill in the Blank: Complete the following sentences with the appropriate word or phrase.

4. One primary problem with longitudinal designs is that participants may drop out of the study before it is concluded. This is called _____.
5. A group of children who are the same age and develop in the same cultural and historical times is called a _____.
6. Making sure that any research conducted with children causes no harm and passes the benefits-to-risk ratio test is ultimately the responsibility of _____.

Matching: Match the following developmental research designs to the appropriate research questions. Choose from the following designs:

a. cross-sectional design
b. longitudinal design
c. sequential design
d. microgenetic design

7. _____ A developmentalist hopes to determine whether all children go through the same stages of intellectual development between infancy and adolescence.
8. _____ A developmentalist wants to quickly assess whether 4-, 6-, and 8-year-old children differ in their willingness to donate part of their allowance to children less fortunate then themselves.
9. _____ A developmentalist wants to determine how and why third-grade children acquire memory strategies.

Short-Answer: Briefly answer the following question.

10. Suppose you are a developmental psychologist and you are interested in learning about how elementary school children (first- through fifth-graders) change in their altruistic behavior (that is, their willingness to help others who are in need).
   a. Design a cross-sectional study to answer the research question.
   b. Design a longitudinal study to answer the research question.

APPLYING RESEARCH TO YOUR LIFE

Becoming a Wise Consumer of Developmental Research

At this point, you may be wondering, "Why do I need to know so much about the methods that developmentalists use to conduct research?" This is a reasonable question given that the vast majority of students who take this course will pursue other careers and will never conduct a scientific study of developing children or adolescents.

Our answer is straightforward: Although survey courses such as this one are designed to provide a solid overview of theory and research in the discipline to which they pertain, they should also strive to help you evaluate the relevant information you may encounter in the years ahead. And you will encounter such information. Even if you don't read academic journals in your role as a teacher, school administrator, nurse, probation officer, social worker, or other professional who works with developing persons, then certainly you will be exposed to such information through the popular media—television, newspapers, magazines, and the like. How can you know whether that seemingly dramatic and important new finding you've just read or heard about should be taken seriously?

This is an important issue, for new information about human development is often chronicled in the popular media several months or even years before the data on which the media reports are based finally make their appearance in professional journals. What's more, less than 30 percent of the findings developmentalists submit are judged worthy of publication by reputable journals in our discipline. So many media reports of "dramatic" new findings are based on research that other scientists do not regard as very dramatic, or even worth publishing.

Even if a media report is based on a published article, coverage of the research and its conclusions is often misleading. For example, one TV news story reported on a published article, saying that there was clear evidence that "alcoholism is inherited." As we will see in Chapter 3, this is a far more dramatic conclusion than the authors actually drew. Another metropolitan newspaper report summarized a recent article from the prestigious journal *Developmental Psychology* with the headline "Day care harmful for children." What was never made clear in the newspaper article was the researcher's (Howes, 1990) conclusion that *very-low-quality* day care may be harmful to the social and intellectual development of *some* preschool children but that most youngsters receiving good day care suffer no adverse effects.

We don't mean to imply that you can never trust what you read; rather, we'd caution you to be skeptical and to evaluate media (and journal) reports, using the methodological information presented in this chapter. You might start by asking: How were the data gathered, and how was the study designed? Were appropriate conclusions drawn given the limitations of the method of data collection and the design (correlational vs. experimental; cross-sectional vs. longitudinal) that the investigators used? Was there random assignment to treatment groups? Have the results of the study been reviewed by other experts in the field and published in a reputable academic journal? And please don't assume that published articles are beyond criticism. Many theses and dissertations in the developmental sciences are based on problems and shortcomings that students have identified in previously published research. So take the time to read and evaluate published reports that seem especially relevant to your profession or to your role as a parent. Not only will you have a better understanding of the research and its conclusions, but any lingering questions and doubts you may have can often be addressed through a letter, an e-mail message, or a phone call to the author of the article.

So we encourage you to become a knowledgeable consumer in order to get the most out of what the field of human development has to offer. Our discussion of research methodology was undertaken with these objectives in mind, and a solid understanding of these methodological lessons should help you to properly evaluate the research you will encounter, not only throughout this text but from many other sources in the years to come.

SUMMARY

What Is Development?

- **Development** refers to the systematic continuities and changes that people display over the course of their lives that reflect the influence of biological **maturation** and **learning.**
- **Developmentalists** come from many disciplines and all study the process of development.
- **Developmental psychology** is the largest of these disciplines.
- **Normative developments** are typical developments characterizing all members of a species; **ideographic developments** describe those that vary across individuals.
- Developmentalists' goals are to describe, to explain, and to optimize development.
- Human development is a continual and cumulative process that is **holistic,** highly **plastic,** and heavily influenced by the historical and cultural contexts in which it occurs.

Human Development in Historical Perspective

- In medieval times, children were afforded few of the rights and protections of today's youth.
- The 17th- and 18th-century philosophies of **original sin, innate purity,** and **tabula rasa** contributed to a more humane view of children.
- In the 19th century scientists began to record the development of their infant sons and daughters in **baby biographies.**
- The scientific study of development did not emerge until the early 1900s when G. Stanley Hall began to collect data and formulate **theories** about human development.
- Soon, other researchers were deriving **hypotheses** and conducting research to evaluate and extend early theories.

Research Methods in Developmental Psychology

- The **scientific method** is a value system that requires the use of objective data to determine the viability of theories.
- Acceptable research methods possess both **reliability** (produces consistent, replicable results) and **validity** (accurately measures what it is intended to measure).
- The most common methods of data collection in child and adolescent development are:
  - self-reports (questionnaires and interviews)
  - the clinical method (a more flexible interview method)
  - observational methodologies (naturalistic and structured observations)
  - case studies
  - ethnography
  - psychophysiological methods

Detecting Relationships: Correlational, Experimental, and Cross-Cultural Designs

- **Correlational designs** examine relationships as they naturally occur, without any intervention.
- The **correlation coefficient** is used to estimate the strength and magnitude of the association between variables.
- Correlational studies cannot specify whether correlated variables are causally related.
- The **experimental design** identifies cause-and-effect relationships. The experimenter:
  - manipulates one (or more) **independent variables**
  - exercises **experimental control** over all other **confounding variables** (often by **random assignment** of participants to treatments)
  - observes the effect(s) of the manipulation(s) on the **dependent variable**
- Experiments may be performed in the laboratory or in the natural environment (that is, a **field experiment**), thereby increasing the **ecological validity** of the results.
- The impact of events that researchers cannot manipulate or control can be studied in **natural (or quasi-) experiments.** However, lack of control over natural events prevents the quasi-experimenter from drawing definitive conclusions about cause and effect.
- **Cross-cultural studies**
  - Compare participants from different cultures and subcultures on one or more aspects of development
  - Identify universal patterns of development
  - Demonstrate that other aspects of development are heavily influenced by the social context in which they occur

Designs for Studying Development

- The **cross-sectional design**
  - Compares different age groups at a single point in time
  - Is easy to conduct
  - Cannot tell us how *individuals* develop
  - May confuse age trends for trends that may actually be due to **cohort effects** rather than true developmental change
- The **longitudinal design**
  - Detects developmental change by repeatedly examining the same participants as they grow older
  - Identifies developmental continuities and changes and individual differences in development
  - Is subject to such problems as **practice effects** and **selective attrition,** which results in **nonrepresentative samples**

- May be limited to the particular cohort studied because of the **cross-generational** problem
- The **sequential design**
  - Is a combination of the cross-sectional and longitudinal designs
  - Offers researchers the advantages of both approaches
  - Discriminates true developmental trends from troublesome cohort effects
- The **microgenetic design**
  - Studies children intensively over a brief period of time
  - Studies children when developmental changes normally occur
  - Attempts to specify how and why developmental changes occur

Ethical Considerations in Developmental Research

- Research conducted with children and adolescents raises some challenging ethical issues.
- The benefits to be gained from the research should always exceed the risks to participants.
- But no matter how positive this **benefits-to-risks ratio,** participants have the rights to:
  - expect **protection from harm**
  - give **informed consent** to participate (or to stop participating)
  - have their data treated with **confidentiality**
  - receive explanations for any deception that may have been necessary to collect their data

KEY TERMS

development 2
developmental continuities 2
developmental psychology 2
developmentalist 2
maturation 2
learning 3
normative development 3
ideographic development 3
holistic perspective 5
plasticity 5
original sin 8
innate purity 8
tabula rasa 8
baby biography 8
theory 9
hypothesis 10
scientific method 11
reliability 12
validity 12
structured interview or structured questionnaire 13
clinical method 14
naturalistic observation 15
observer influence 15
time-sampling 16
structured observation 16
case study 17
ethnography 18
psychophysiological methods 19
correlational design 20
correlation coefficient 21
experimental design 22
independent variable 22
dependent variable 22
confounding variable 23
experimental control 23
random assignment 23
ecological validity 23
field experiment 23
natural (or quasi-) experiment 24
cross-cultural comparison 26
cross-sectional design 29
cohort 29
cohort effect 30
longitudinal design 30
practice effect 31
selective attrition 31
nonrepresentative sample 31
cross-generational problem 31
sequential design 32
microgenetic design 32
informed consent 36
benefits-to-risk ratio 36
confidentiality 36
protection from harm 36

MEDIA RESOURCES

The Human Development Book Companion Website

See the companion website http://www.thomsonedu.com/psychology/shaffer for flashcards, practice quiz questions, Internet links, updates, critical thinking exercises, discussion forums, games, and more

Thomson NOW! http://www.thomsonedu.com

Go to this site for the link to ThomsonNOW, your one-stop shop. Take a pre-test for this chapter, and ThomsonNOW will generate a personalized study plan based on your test results. The study plan will identify the topics you need to review and direct you to online resources to help you master those topics. You can then take a post-test to help you determine the concepts you have mastered and what you will still need to work on.

Lori Adamski Peek/Getty Images

CHAPTER

2 Theories of Human Development

Erin Richman, a graduate student, had an idea for her graduate thesis. She came to me and expressed her opinion that participating in sports contributes strongly to young women's self-esteem. When I asked her why she thought this, she jokingly replied, "It worked for me!" I laughed and said, "You'll need more of a conceptual framework than that to guide your proposed research," and sent her off to think about the issue. Several days later, having read what limited research was available, she returned with a theory: She proposed that sports participation for teenage girls promotes positive body images, perceptions of physical competence, and more flexible outlooks on what it means to be a woman, all of which should contribute positively to a young woman's sense of self-worth. Erin now had specified a relationship that she believed to be true and also a theory to explain why that relationship was true. Within weeks, she had refined her theory to the point of formulating a research design and selecting measures to assess all the important variables. The research that she then conducted provided ample support for her theory and resulted not only in a graduate thesis, but also in a published scientific article (her findings will be discussed in Chapter 12).

The Nature of Scientific Theories

theory
a set of concepts and propositions designed to organize, describe, and explain an existing set of observations.

parsimony
a criterion for evaluating the scientific merit of theories; a parsimonious theory is one that uses relatively few explanatory principles to explain a broad set of observations.

falsifiability
a criterion for evaluating the scientific merit of theories. A theory is falsifiable when it is capable of generating predictions that could be disconfirmed.

heuristic value
a criterion for evaluating the scientific merit of theories. A heuristic theory is one that continues to stimulate new research and new discoveries.

A scientific **theory** is nothing more than a set of concepts and propositions that a scientist believes to be true about a specific area of investigation. Some theories in the developmental sciences are broad in scope, seeking to explain the development of global domains, such as personality or cognition. Others are limited to a specific issue, such as the impact of sports participation on women's self-esteem. But the basis of all scientific theories is that they help us to organize our thinking about the aspects of experience that interest us. In the developmental sciences, theories provide us with a "lens" through which we can interpret our specific observations about developing individuals.

What are the characteristics of a good theory? Ideally, it should be concise, or **parsimonious,** and yet be able to explain a broad range of phenomena. A theory with few principles that accounts for a large number of empirical observations is far more useful than a theory that requires many more principles and assumptions to explain the same number of observations. Good theories are **falsifiable**—that is, capable of making explicit predictions about future events so that the theory can be supported or disconfirmed. And good theories are not limited to what is already known. Instead, they are **heuristic**—meaning that they build on existing knowledge by continuing to generate testable hypotheses that, if confirmed by future research, will lead to a much richer understanding of the phenomena of interest (see Figure 2.1). When a theory is parsimonious, falsifiable, and heuristic, even its disconfirmation may reveal information that can be used in generating new, more accurate theories. Later in this chapter we will review Piaget's theory of cognitive development. It meets all the qualifications of a good theory, and yet portions of the theory have been disconfirmed by research. Nevertheless, the basic model that Piaget proposed continues to generate new research and new theories, as we saw in Chapter 1 when discussing Thelen's research on infant motor development. Furthermore, whether completely accurate or not, good theories also continue to

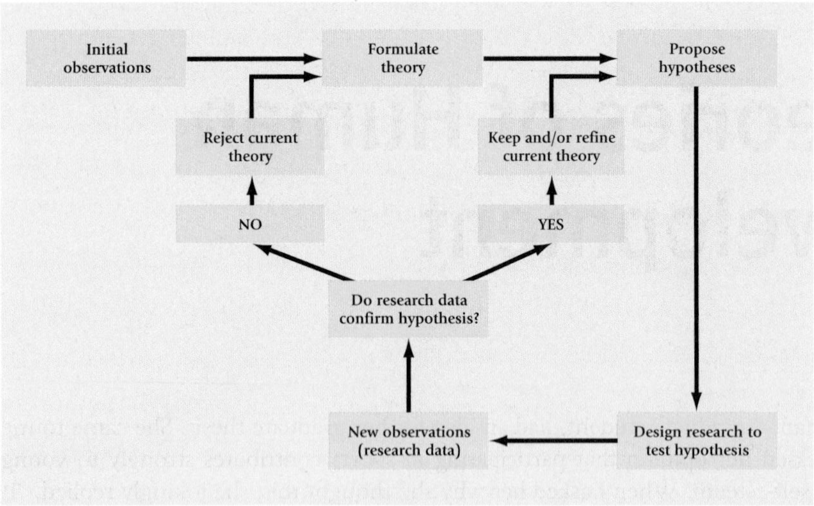

Figure 2.1 The role of theory in scientific investigation.

generate new knowledge, much of which may have practical implications that truly benefit humanity. For example, Piaget's theory has been extremely influential in the field of education, guiding teachers in the development of effective strategies for learning. In this sense, there is nothing quite so practical as a *good* theory.

In the developmental sciences there have been many theories proposed about different aspects of human development. In the process of generating, testing, and confirming or disconfirming these theories, a very basic set of themes has emerged that nearly every theory addresses. Before beginning our review of some of the specific theories in human development, it may be helpful to consider these themes that underlie most developmental science. We will return to these themes throughout the book as a way of organizing and orienting the specific developmental theories and facts we uncover.

Themes in the Study of Human Development

Is developmental outcome (that is, who we are as adults) more a function of our biology or of the environments we encounter as we grow? How much do children contribute to their own development versus being clay that is molded by parenting practices and other external forces? What does development look like, from a wide angle? Is it a slow, continuous process or a series of relatively quick changes that occur abruptly and propel the child from developmental level to developmental level? And how much do different aspects of development influence each other? That is, does children's thinking influence their social and biological development, or are these aspects of development isolated and unrelated to each other? These are some of the questions with which developmental scientists have grappled throughout the history of the science, and which developmental theories continue to address. Let's take a look at each of these major themes in the study of human development to see what the basic issues are.

The Nature/Nurture Theme

Is human development primarily the result of nature (biological forces) or nurture (environmental forces)? Perhaps no theoretical controversy has been any more heated than this **nature/nurture issue.** Here are two opposing viewpoints:

nature/nurture issue
the debate among developmental theorists about the relative importance of biological predispositions (nature) and environmental influences (nurture) as determinants of human development.

> Heredity and not environment is the chief maker of man. . . . Nearly all of the misery and nearly all of the happiness in the world are due not to environment. . . . The differences among men are due to differences in germ cells with which they were born (Wiggam, 1923, p. 42).
>
> Give me a dozen healthy infants, well formed, and my own specified world to bring them up in and I'll guarantee to take any one at random and train him to become any type of specialist I might select—doctor, lawyer, artist, merchant, chief, and yes, even beggar-man and thief, regardless of his talents, penchants, tendencies, abilities, vocations, and race of his ancestors. There is no such thing as an inheritance of capacity, talent, temperament, mental constitution, and behavioral characteristics. (Watson, 1925, p. 82)

Of course, there is a middle ground that is endorsed by many contemporary researchers who believe that the relative contributions of nature and nurture depend on the aspect of development in question. However, they stress that all complex human attributes such as intelligence, temperament, and personality are the end products of a long and involved interplay between biological predispositions and environmental forces (Bornstein & Lamb, 2005; Garcia Coll, Bearer, & Lerner, 2003; Gottlieb, 2003; Lerner, 2002). Their advice to us, then, is to think less about nature *versus* nurture and more about how these two sets of influences combine or *interact* to produce developmental change.

The Active/Passive Theme

activity/passivity issue
a debate among developmental theorists about whether children are active contributors to their own development or, rather, passive recipients of environmental influence.

Another topic of theoretical debate is the **active/passive** theme. Are children curious, active creatures who largely determine how agents of society treat them? Or are they passive souls on whom society fixes its stamp? Consider the implications of these opposing viewpoints. If we could show that children are extremely malleable—literally at the mercy of those who raise them—then perhaps individuals who turned out to be less than productive would be justified in suing their overseers for poor parenting. Indeed, one troubled young man in the United States used this logic to bring a malfeasance suit against his parents. Perhaps you can anticipate the defense that the parents' lawyer offered. Counsel argued that the parents had tried many strategies in an attempt to raise their child right but that he responded favorably to none of them. The implication is that this young man played an *active* role in determining how his parents treated him and is largely responsible for creating the climate in which he was raised.

The active/passive theme goes beyond considering the child's conscious choices and behaviors. That is, developmentalists consider a child active in development whenever any aspect of the child has an effect on the environment the child is experiencing. So a temperamentally difficult infant who challenges the patience of his loving but frustrated parents is actively influencing his development, even though he is not consciously *choosing* to be temperamentally difficult. Similarly, a young preteen girl who has gone through the biological changes of puberty earlier than most of her classmates and friends did not choose this event. Nevertheless, the fact that she appears so much more mature than her peers is likely to have dramatic effects on the ways others treat her and the environment she experiences in general.

Which of these perspectives do you consider the more reasonable? Think about it, for very soon you will have an opportunity to state your views on this and other topics of theoretical debate.

The Continuity/Discontinuity Theme

Think for a moment about developmental change. Do you think that the changes we experience occur very gradually? Or would you say that these changes are rather abrupt?

continuity/discontinuity issue
a debate among theorists about whether developmental changes are quantitative and continuous, or qualitative and discontinuous (i.e., stagelike).

quantitative change
incremental change in degree without sudden transformations; for example, some view the small yearly increases in height and weight that 2- to 11-year-olds display as quantitative developmental changes.

On one side of this **continuity/discontinuity issue** are continuity theorists who view human development as an additive process that occurs gradually and continuously, without sudden changes. They might represent the course of developmental change with a smooth growth curve like the one in Figure 2.2 (left). On the other hand, discontinuity theorists describe the road to maturity as a series of abrupt changes, each of which elevates the child to a new and presumably more advanced level of functioning. These levels, or "stages," are represented by the steps of the discontinuous growth curve in Figure 2.2 (right).

A second aspect of the continuity/discontinuity issue centers on whether developmental changes are quantitative or qualitative in nature. **Quantitative changes** are changes in degree or amount. For example, children grow taller and run a little faster with each passing year; and they acquire more and more knowledge about the world around

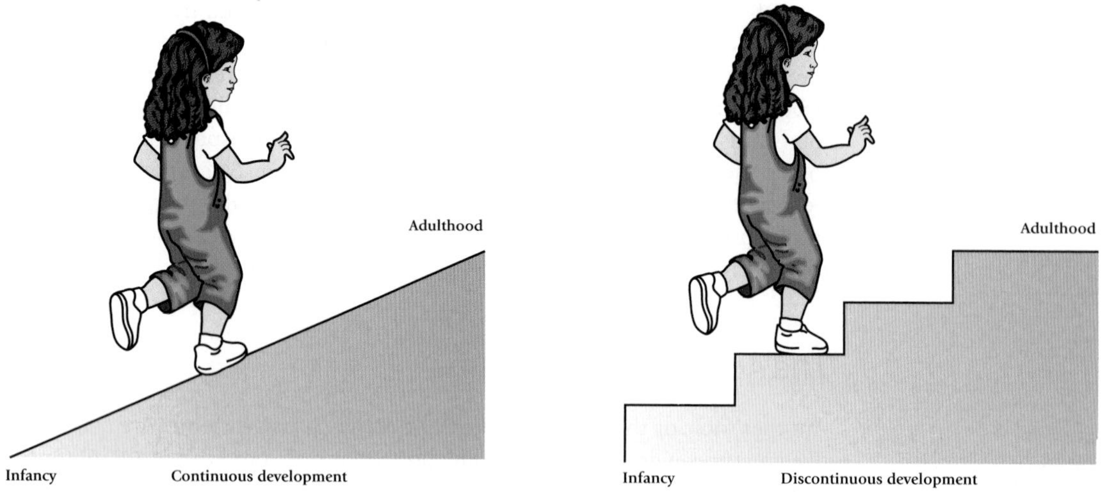

Figure 2.2 The course of development as described by continuity and discontinuity (stage) theorists.

qualitative change
changes in kind that make individuals fundamentally different than they were before; the transformation of a prelinguistic infant into a language user is viewed by many as a qualitative change in communication skills.

developmental stage
a distinct phase within a larger sequence of development; a period characterized by a particular set of abilities, motives, behaviors, or emotions that occur together and form a coherent pattern.

them. **Qualitative changes** are changes in form or kind—changes that make the individual fundamentally different in some way than he or she was earlier. The transformation of a tadpole into a frog is a qualitative change. Similarly, an infant who lacks language may be qualitatively different from a preschooler who speaks well, and an adolescent who is sexually mature may be fundamentally different from a classmate who has yet to reach puberty. Continuity theorists generally think that developmental changes are basically quantitative in nature, whereas discontinuity theorists tend to portray development as a sequence of qualitative changes. Discontinuity theorists are the ones who claim that we progress through **developmental stages,** each of which is a distinct phase of life characterized by a particular set of abilities, emotions, motives, or behaviors that form a coherent pattern.

Societies may take different positions on the continuity/discontinuity issue. Some Pacific and Eastern cultures, for example, have words for infant qualities that are never used to describe adults, and adult terms such as *intelligent* or *angry* are never used to characterize infants (Kagan, 1991). People in these cultures view personality development as discontinuous, and infants are regarded as so fundamentally different from adults that they cannot be judged on the same personality dimensions. North Americans and Northern Europeans are more inclined to assume that personality development is a continuous process and to search for the seeds of adult personality in babies' temperaments.

The Holistic Nature of Development Theme

The final major theme that has intrigued developmental scientists is the extent to which development is a holistic process versus a segmented, separate process. The question is whether different aspects of human development, such as cognition, personality, social development, biological development, and so forth, are interrelated and influence each other as the child matures. Early views of development tended to take a more segmented approach, with scientists limiting themselves to one area of development and attempting to study that development in isolation from influences from the other areas. Today most developmental scientists adopt a more holistic perspective, believing that all areas of development are interdependent and that one cannot truly understand development change in one area without at least a passing knowledge of what is happening developmentally in other areas of the child's life. It can be a challenge to take such a holistic perspective because it makes it necessary to consider many more variables when attacking a

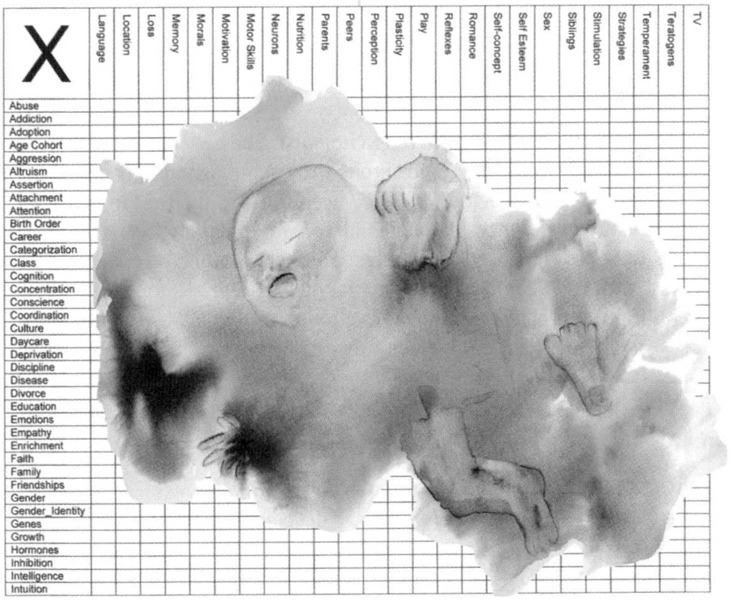

Figure 2.3 Psychologists attempt to tease apart the biological (red), cognitive (yellow), social (blue), and contextual (white) factors that influence human development. However, development is holistic and at a very early age the variables that we choose to study have already begun to interact. A single domain or variable never influences development independently of other factors. The chosen variable's effect is modified and modulated by the influences of other domains and their variables, just as they are modified and modulated by it. Like the colors in this illustration, influences from the four domains interact to produce confluent effects that are not easily traced to a single, or even a handful, of individual factors. *Used by permission of Julia Cline.*

developmental problem. Nevertheless, we try to at least acknowledge the holistic nature of development and look for ways in which various aspects of developmental change interrelate as we study children's development (see Figure 2.3).

These, then, are the major developmental controversies that theories resolve in different ways. You may wish to clarify your own stand on these issues by completing the brief questionnaire in Concept Check 2.1. At the end of the chapter, Table 2.4 indicates how the major developmental theories address these same questions so that you can compare their assumptions about human development with your own.

In this chapter, we will examine the basic premises of six broad theoretical traditions that have each had a major impact on the science of human development: the *psychoanalytic* viewpoint, the *learning* viewpoint, the *cognitive-developmental* viewpoint, the *information-processing* viewpoint, the *evolutionary* viewpoint, and the *ecological systems* viewpoint. Although these theories are central to our discipline and could be characterized as the conceptual basis of developmental psychology, there are many other recent viewpoints that have emerged as extensions of or complements to "the grand theories," and we will consider the strengths and weaknesses of these alternative approaches throughout the text.

CONCEPT CHECK 2.1 Theories and Themes in Human Development

In this concept check you will identify your own views on the four basic themes in studying human development. You will also be able to check your understanding of the role of theories and themes in the developmental sciences. Answers appear in the Appendix.

Survey: Where do you stand on major developmental themes? Answer each of the following multiple-choice questions by selecting the answer that most reflects your *own* views about development. Use the key in the Appendix to match your views to different theoretical perspectives on the themes. Flip forward in the text to Table 2.4 and enter your views on the bottom line of the table.

_____ 1. Biological influences (heredity, maturation) and environmental influences (culture, parenting styles, schools and peers) both contribute to development. Overall, however:
   a. Biological factors contribute more than environmental factors.
   b. Biological and environmental factors are equally important.
   c. Environmental factors contribute more than biological factors.

_____ 2. Children and adolescents are:
   a. active beings who play a major role in determining their own developmental outcomes
   b. passive beings whose developmental outcomes largely reflect the influences of other people and circumstances beyond their control

_____ 3. Development proceeds:
   a. through distinct stages so that the individual changes abruptly into a quite different kind of person than he or she was at an earlier stage
   b. continuously, in small increments without abrupt changes

_____ 4. Various aspects of child development, such as cognitive, social, and biological development
   a. are basically distinct and interact little with each other in the course of the child's development
   b. are interrelated, with each area of development having effects upon the other areas of development so that we cannot seriously consider one aspect without also addressing the other areas of development

CONTINUED

Matching: Check your understanding of key qualities of scientific theories by matching the term to its definition.

5. ________ heuristic
6. ________ parsimonious
7. ________ falsifiable

a. capable of making explicit predictions about future events so that the theory can be supported or disconfirmed.
b. builds on existing knowledge by continuing to generate testable hypotheses that may lead to a deeper understanding of the phenomena of interest
c. uses a small number of principles to explain a large range of phenomena

Identification: Use your understanding of the basic themes in studying human development to identify the following researcher's views.

Dr. Damone is a child psychologist. She believes that all children in the world go through the same distinct phases of intellectual development. However, she also believes in individual differences among children. She thinks that very smart parents will have the smartest children, even if the children are raised by undereducated nannies. She thinks the children's intelligence will show through as long as they have many puzzles to solve and other challenges to master on their own. Dr. Damone believes in:

8. a. nature — b. nurture
9. a. the active child — b. the passive child
10. a. continuous development — b. discontinuous development

The Psychoanalytic Viewpoint

Sigmund Freud (1856–1939) is a theorist who has had a great impact on Western thought. He challenged prevailing notions about human nature by proposing that we are driven by motives and conflicts of which we are largely unaware and that our personalities are shaped by our early life experiences. In this section, we will first consider Freud's **psychosexual theory** of human development and then compare Freud's theory with that of his best-known follower, Erik Erikson.

psychosexual theory
Freud's theory that states that maturation of the sex instinct underlies stages of personality development, and that the manner in which parents manage children's instinctual impulses determines the traits that children display.

Freud's Psychosexual Theory

Freud was a practicing neurologist who formulated his theory of human development from his analyses of his emotionally disturbed patients' life histories. Seeking to relieve their nervous symptoms and anxieties, he relied heavily on such methods as hypnosis, free association (a quick spilling out of one's thoughts), and dream analysis, because they gave some indication of **unconscious motives** that patients had **repressed** (that is, forced out of their conscious awareness). By analyzing these motives and the events that caused their repression, Freud concluded that human development is a conflictual process: As biological creatures, we have basic sexual and aggressive **instincts** that *must* be served; yet society dictates that many of these drives must be restrained. According to Freud, the ways in which parents manage these sexual and aggressive urges in the first few years of their child's life play a major role in shaping their children's personalities.

unconscious motives
Freud's term for feelings, experiences, and conflicts that influence a person's thinking and behavior, but lie outside the person's awareness.

repression
a type of motivated forgetting in which anxiety-provoking thoughts and conflicts are forced out of conscious awareness.

instinct
an inborn biological force that motivates a particular response or class of responses.

Three Components of Personality

Freud's psychosexual theory proposes that three components of personality—the id, ego, and superego—develop and gradually become integrated in a series of five developmental psychosexual stages. Only the **id** is present at birth. Its sole function is to satisfy inborn biological instincts, and it will try to do so immediately. Young infants often do seem to be "all id." When hungry or wet, they fuss and cry until their needs are met.

The **ego** is the conscious, rational component of the personality that reflects the child's emerging abilities to perceive, learn, remember, and reason. Its function is to find realistic means of gratifying instincts, such as when a hungry toddler, remembering how she gets

id
psychoanalytic term for the inborn component of the personality that is driven by the instincts.

ego
psychoanalytic term for the rational component of the personality.

food, seeks out mom and says "cookie." As their egos mature, children become better at controlling their irrational ids and finding appropriate ways to gratify their needs.

However, realistic solutions to needs are not always acceptable, as a hungry 3-year-old who is caught stealing cookies between meals may soon discover. The final component of personality, or **superego,** is the seat of the conscience. It develops between the ages of 3 and 6 as children *internalize* (take on as their own) the moral values of their parents (Freud, 1933). Once the superego emerges, children do not need an adult to tell them that they have been good or bad. They are now aware of their own transgressions and will feel guilty or ashamed of their unethical conduct. So the superego is truly an internal censor. It insists that the ego find socially acceptable outlets for the id's undesirable impulses.

superego
psychoanalytic term for the component of the personality that consists of one's internalized moral standards.

These three components of personality inevitably conflict (Freud, 1940/1964). In the mature, healthy personality, a dynamic balance operates: the id communicates basic needs, the ego restrains the impulsive id long enough to find realistic methods of satisfying these needs, and the superego decides whether the ego's problem-solving strategies are morally acceptable. The ego is "in the middle"; it must strike a balance between the opposing demands of the id and the superego while accommodating the realities of the external world.

Stages of Psychosexual Development

Freud thought that sex was the most important instinct because he discovered that his patients' mental disturbances often revolved around childhood sexual conflicts they had repressed. Freud's (1940/1964) view of sex was very broad, encompassing such activities as thumb-sucking and urinating that we would not consider erotic. Freud believed that as the sex instinct matured, its focus shifted from one part of the body to another, and that each shift brought on a new stage of psychosexual development. Table 2.1 briefly describes each of Freud's five stages of psychosexual development.

Freud believed that parents permitting too much or too little gratification of sexual needs would cause the child to become obsessed with whatever activity was encouraged or discouraged. The child might then **fixate** on that activity (that is, display arrested development) and retain some aspect of it throughout life. For example, an infant who was strongly punished for and thus conflicted about sucking her thumb might express this oral fixation in adulthood through such activities as smoking or oral sex. The

fixation
arrested development at a particular psychosexual stage which can prevent movement to higher stages.

TABLE 2.1 Freud's Stages of Psychosexual Development

Psychosexual stage	Age	Description
Oral	Birth to 1 year	The sex instinct centers on the mouth because infants derive pleasure from such oral activities as sucking, chewing, and biting. Feeding activities are particularly important. For example, an infant weaned too early or abruptly may later crave close contact and become overdependent on a spouse.
Anal	1 to 3 years	Voluntary urination and defecation become the primary methods of gratifying the sex instinct. Toilet-training produces major conflicts between children and parents. The emotional climate that parents create can have lasting effects. For example, children who are punished for toileting "accidents" may become inhibited, messy, or wasteful.
Phallic	3 to 6 years	Pleasure is now derived from genital stimulation. Children develop an incestuous desire for the opposite-sex parent (called the *Oedipus complex* for boys and Electra complex for girls). Anxiety stemming from this conflict causes children to internalize the sex-role characteristics and moral standards of their same-sex parental rival.
Latency	6 to 11 years	Traumas of the phallic stage cause sexual conflicts to be repressed and sexual urges to be rechanneled into school work and vigorous play. The ego and superego continue to develop as the child gains more problem-solving abilities at school and internalizes societal values.
Genital	age 12 onward	Puberty triggers a reawakening of sexual urges. Adolescents must now learn how to express these urges in socially acceptable ways. If development has been healthy, the mature sex instinct is satisfied by marriage and raising children.

important implication for developmental psychology was Freud's claim that early childhood experiences and conflicts heavily influence our adult interests, activities, and personalities.

Contributions and Criticisms of Freud's Theory

How plausible do you think Freud's ideas are? Do you think that we are driven by sexual and aggressive instincts? Or might the sexual conflicts that Freud thought so important have been reflections of the sexually repressive Victorian era in which he and his patients lived?

Few developmentalists today are strong proponents of Freud's theory. There is not much evidence that the early oral, anal, and genital conflicts that Freud stressed predict adult personality (Bem, 1989; Crews, 1996). One reason for this may be that Freud's theory was based on the recollections of a small number of emotionally disturbed adults whose experiences may not apply to most people.

Yet, we should not reject all of Freud's ideas because some of them are a bit outlandish. Perhaps Freud's greatest contribution was his concept of *unconscious motivation.* When psychology emerged in the mid-19th century, investigators focused on isolated aspects of *conscious* experience, such as sensory processes and perceptual illusions. It was Freud who first proclaimed that the vast majority of psychic experience lay below the level of conscious awareness. Freud also deserves great credit for focusing attention on the influence of early experience on later development. Debates continue about exactly how critical early experiences are, but most developmentalists today agree that some early experiences do have lasting effects. Finally, Freud instigated the study of the emotional side of human development—the loves, fears, anxieties, and other emotions that play important roles in our lives. For these reasons, Freud was a great pioneer who dared to navigate murky, uncharted waters that his predecessors had not even thought to explore. In the process, he changed our views of human development.

Erikson's Theory of Psychosocial Development

As Freud became widely read, he attracted many followers. However, Freud's pupils did not always agree with him, and eventually they began to modify some of his ideas and became important theorists in their own right. Among the best known of these scholars was Erik Erikson.

Comparing Erikson with Freud

Although Erikson (1963, 1982) accepted many of Freud's ideas, he differed from Freud in two important respects. First, Erikson (1963) stressed that children are *active,* curious explorers who seek to adapt to their environments, rather than passive slaves to biological urges who are molded by their parents. Erikson has been labeled an "ego" psychologist because he believed that at each stage of life, people must cope with social *realities* (in ego function) in order to adapt successfully and display a normal pattern of development. So in Erikson's theory, the ego is far more than a simple mediator of the opposing demands of the id and superego.

A second critical difference between Erikson and Freud is that Erikson places much less emphasis on sexual urges and far more emphasis on cultural influences than Freud did. Erikson's thinking was shaped by his own varied experiences. He was born in Denmark, raised in Germany, and spent much of his adolescence wandering throughout Europe. After receiving his professional training, Erikson came to the United States, where he studied college students, combat soldiers, civil rights workers in the South, and Native Americans. Having observed many similarities and differences in development across

UPI/Corbis-Bettman

Erik Erikson (1902–1994) emphasized the sociocultural determinants of personality in his theory of psychosocial development.

TABLE 2.2 Erikson's and Freud's Stages of Development

Approximate age	Erikson's stage or "psychosocial" crisis	Erikson's viewpoint: significant events and social influences	Corresponding Freudian stage
Birth to 1 year	Basic trust versus mistrust	Infants must learn to trust others to care for their basic needs. If caregivers are rejecting or inconsistent, the infant may view the world as a dangerous place filled with untrustworthy or unreliable people. The primary caregiver is the key social agent.	Oral
1 to 3 years	Autonomy versus shame and doubt	Children must learn to be "autonomous"—to feed and dress themselves, to look after their own hygiene, and so on. Failure to achieve this independence may force the child to doubt his or her own abilities and feel shameful. Parents are the key social agents.	Anal
3 to 6 years	Initiative versus guilt	Children attempt to act grown up and will try to accept responsibilities that are beyond their capacity to handle. They sometimes undertake goals or activities that conflict with those of parents and other family members, and these conflicts may make them feel guilty. Successful resolution of this crisis requires a balance: The child must retain a sense of initiative and yet learn not to impinge on the rights, privileges, or goals of others. The family is the key social agent.	Phallic
6 to 12 years	Industry versus inferiority	Children must master important social and academic skills. This is a period when the child compares him- or herself with peers. If sufficiently industrious, children acquire the social and academic skills to feel self-assured. Failure to acquire these important attributes leads to feelings of inferiority. Significant social agents are teachers and peers.	Latency
12 to 20 years	Identity versus role confusion	This is the crossroad between childhood and maturity. The adolescent grapples with the question "Who am I?" Adolescents must establish basic social and occupational identities, or they will remain confused about the roles they should play as adults. The key social agent is the society of peers.	Early genital (adolescence)
20 to 40 years (young adulthood)	Intimacy versus isolation	The primary task at this stage is to form strong friendships and to achieve a sense of love and companionship (or a shared identity) with another person. Feelings of loneliness or isolation are likely to result from an inability to form friendships or an intimate relationship. Key social agents are lovers, spouses, and close friends (of both sexes).	Genital
40 to 65 years (middle adulthood)	Generativity versus stagnation	At this stage adults face the tasks of becoming productive in their work and raising their families or otherwise looking after the needs of young people. These standards of "generativity" are defined by one's culture. Those who are unable or unwilling to assume these responsibilities become stagnant and self-centered. Significant social agents are the spouse, children, and cultural norms.	Genital
Old age	Ego integrity versus despair	The older adult looks back at life, viewing it as either a meaningful, productive, and happy experience or a major disappointment full of unfulfilled promises and unrealized goals. One's life experiences, particularly social experiences, determine the outcome of this final life crisis.	Genital

these diverse social groups, Erikson emphasized *social* and *cultural* aspects of development in his own **psychosocial theory.**

psychosocial theory
Erikson's revision of Freud's theory that emphasizes sociocultural (rather than sexual) determinants of development and posits a series of eight psychosocial conflicts that people must resolve successfully to display healthy psychological adjustment.

Eight Life Crises (or Psychosocial Stages)

Erikson believed that people face eight major crises, which he labeled psychosocial stages, during the course of their lives. Each crisis emerges at a distinct time dictated by biological maturation and the social demands that developing people experience at particular points in life. Each crisis must be resolved successfully to prepare for a satisfactory resolution of the next life crisis. Table 2.2 briefly describes the psychosocial stages and lists the Freudian psychosexual stage to which it corresponds. Notice that Erikson's developmental stages do not end at adolescence or young adulthood as Freud's do. Erikson believed that the problems of adolescents and young adults are very different from those faced by parents who are raising children or by the elderly who may be grappling with retirement, a sense of uselessness, and the end of their lives. Most contemporary developmentalists agree (Sheldon & Kasser, 2001).

Contributions and Criticisms of Erikson's Theory

Many people prefer Erikson's theory to Freud's because they do not believe that people are dominated by sexual instincts. A theory like Erikson's, which stresses our rational, adaptive nature, is much easier to accept. Also, Erikson's theory emphasizes social conflicts and personal dilemmas that people may remember, are currently experiencing, can easily anticipate, or observe in people they know.

Erikson does address many of the central issues of life in his eight psychosocial stages. We will discuss his ideas on such topics as the emotional development of infants in Chapter 11, the growth of the self-concept in childhood and the identity crisis facing adolescents in Chapter 12, and the influence of friends and playmates on social development in Chapter 16 (see also Sigelman & Rider, 2003, for a discussion of Erikson's contributions to the field of adult development).

On the other hand, Erikson's theory can be criticized for being vague about the *causes* of development. What kinds of experiences must people have in order to successfully resolve various psychosocial conflicts? How does the outcome of one psychosocial stage influence personality at a later stage? Erikson is not very explicit about these important issues. So his theory is really a *descriptive* overview of human social and emotional development that does not adequately *explain* how or why this development takes place.

Psychoanalytic Theory Today

Freud and Erikson are only two of many psychoanalysts who had a meaningful influence on the study of human development (Tyson & Tyson, 1990). For example, Karen Horney (1967) challenged Freud's ideas about sex differences in development and is now widely credited as a founder of the discipline we know today as the psychology of women. Alfred Adler (1929/1964), a contemporary of Freud's, was among the first to suggest that *siblings* (and sibling rivalries) are important contributors to social and personality development, a proposition we will explore in detail in Chapter 15. And Harry Stack Sullivan (1953) wrote extensively about how close, same-sex friendships during middle childhood set the stage for intimate love relationships later in life (see Chapter 16 for a discussion of this and other contributions that friends may make to social and personality development). Although their theories differ in focus, all these psychoanalytic theorists place more emphasis on *social* influences on development and much less emphasis on the role of sexual instincts than Freud.

Despite these important contributions, many contemporary developmentalists have largely rejected the psychoanalytic perspective because its propositions are very difficult to either falsify or confirm. Suppose, for example, that we wanted to test a basic Freudian hypothesis that the "healthy" personality is one in which the id, ego, and superego are roughly equal in strength. How could we do it? There are objective tests that we could use to select "mentally healthy" persons, but we have no instrument that measures the relative strengths of the id, ego, and superego. The point is that many psychoanalytic hypotheses are untestable by any method other than the interview or a clinical approach, and unfortunately, these techniques are time-consuming, expensive, and among the least objective of all methods used to study human development.

Another reason that so many developmentalists abandoned the psychoanalytic perspective is that other theories seem more compelling. One perspective favored by many is the learning approach, to which we now turn.

John B. Watson (1878–1958) was the father of behaviorism and the first social-learning theorist.

The Learning Viewpoint

Earlier, we discussed John B. Watson, a developmentalist who claimed that he could take a dozen healthy infants and mold them to be whatever he chose—doctor, lawyer, beggar, and so on—regardless of their backgrounds or ancestry. What a bold statement! It implies that nurture is everything and that nature, or hereditary endowment, counts for nothing. Watson was a strong proponent of the importance of learning in

behaviorism
a school of thinking in psychology that holds that conclusions about human development should be based on controlled observations of overt behavior rather than speculation about unconscious motives or other unobservable phenomena; the philosophical underpinning for the early theories of learning.

habits
well-learned associations between stimuli and responses that represent the stable aspects of one's personality.

human development and the father of a school of thought known as **behaviorism** (Horowitz, 1992).

Watson's Behaviorism

A basic premise of Watson's (1913) behaviorism is that conclusions about development should be based on observations of overt behavior rather than on speculations about unconscious motives or cognitive processes that are unobservable. Watson believed that well-*learned* associations between external stimuli and observable responses (called **habits**) are the building blocks of development. Like John Locke, Watson viewed the infant as a *tabula rasa* to be written on by experience. Children have no inborn tendencies; how they turn out depends entirely on their rearing environments and the ways in which their parents and other significant people in their lives treat them. According to this perspective, children do not progress through a series of distinct stages dictated by biological maturation, as Freud (and others) have argued. Instead, development is viewed as a continuous process of behavioral change that is shaped by a person's unique environment and may differ dramatically from person to person.

To prove just how malleable children are, Watson set out to demonstrate that infants' fears and other emotional reactions are acquired rather than inborn. In one demonstration, for example, Watson and Rosalie Raynor (1920) presented a gentle white rat to a 9-month-old boy named Albert. Albert's initial reactions were positive; he crawled toward the rat and played with it as he had previously with a dog and a rabbit. Then, two months later, Watson attempted to instill a fear response. Every time Albert reached for the white rat, Watson would slip behind him and bang a steel rod with a hammer. Little Albert eventually associated the white rat with the loud noise and came to fear the furry playmate. This illustrated that fears are easily learned. (Of course, with our ethical concerns for the welfare of children, we would never conduct an experiment like this one today!)

Watson's belief that children are shaped by their environments carried a stern message for parents: They were largely responsible for what their children would become. Watson (1928) cautioned parents that they should begin to train their children at birth and cut back on the coddling if they hoped to instill good habits. Treat them, he said

> . . . as though they were young adults . . . Let your behavior always be objective and kindly firm. Never hug and kiss them, never let them sit on your lap. . . . Shake hands with them in the morning. Give them a pat on the head if they have made an extraordinarily good job of a difficult task. . . . In a week's time, you will find how easy it is to be perfectly objective . . . [yet] kindly. You will be utterly ashamed at the mawkish, sentimental way you have been handling [your child] (pp. 81–82).

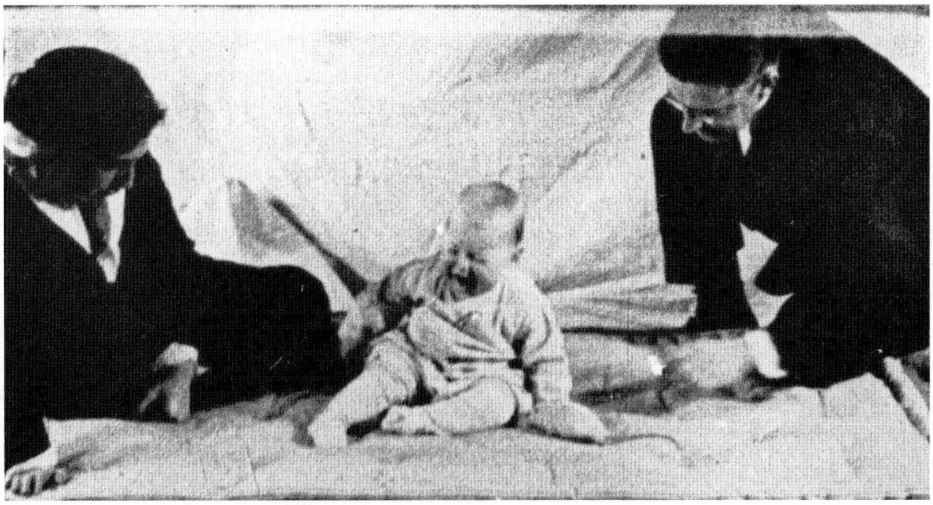

This is a frame from a 1920 film. It shows distressed Little Albert, the rat, Rosalie Rayner (on the left) and John Watson (on the right). *Owens, K. B. (2002).* Child and adolescent development: An integrated approach. *Belmont, CA: Wadsworth/Thomson.*

Since Watson's day, several theories have been proposed to explain how we learn from our social experiences and form the habits Watson proposed. Perhaps the one theorist who did more than anyone to advance the behaviorist approach was B. F. Skinner.

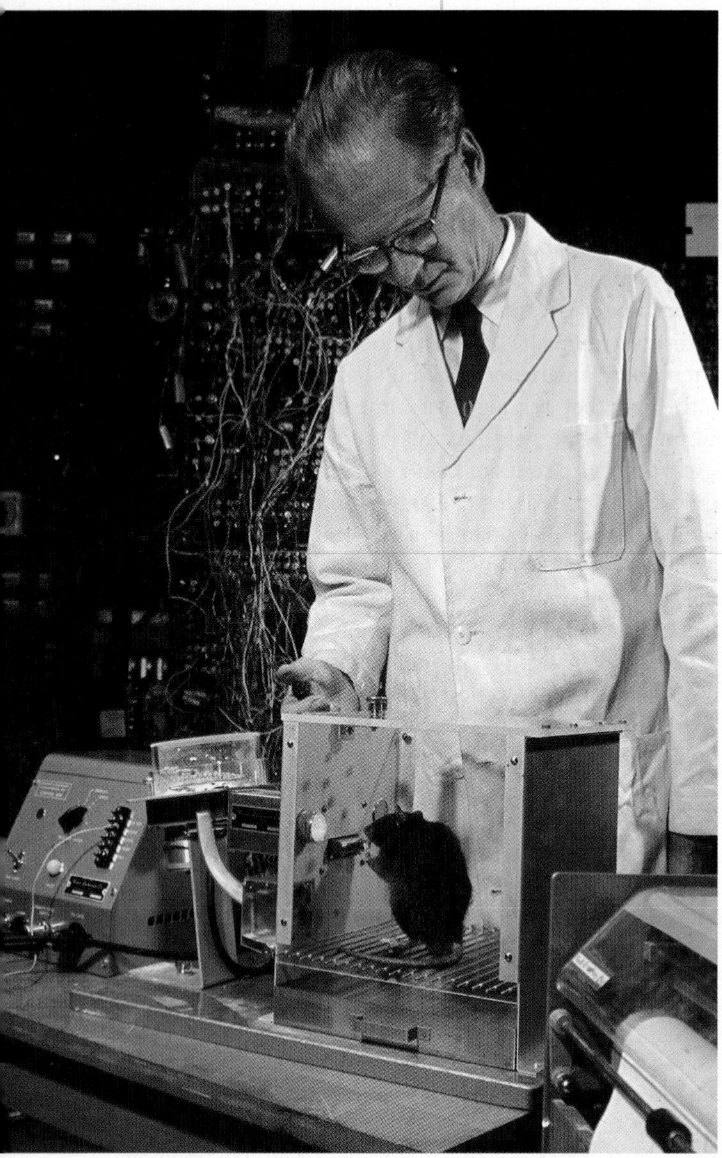

Nina Leen/Time & Life Pictures/Getty Images

B. F. Skinner (1904–1990) proposed a learning theory that emphasized the role of external stimuli in controlling human behavior.

Skinner's Operant Learning Theory

Through his research with animals, Skinner (1953) proposed a form of learning he believed is the basis for most habits. Skinner argued that both animals and humans repeat acts that lead to favorable outcomes and suppress those that lead to unfavorable outcomes. So a rat that presses a bar and receives a tasty food pellet is apt to perform that response again. In the language of Skinner's theory, the bar-pressing response is called an **operant,** and the food pellet that strengthens this response (by making it more probable in the future) is called a **reinforcer.** Applied to children, a young girl may form a habit of showing compassion toward distressed playmates if her parents consistently reinforce her kindly behavior with praise. A teenage boy may become more studious if his efforts are rewarded by higher grades. **Punishers** are consequences that suppress a response and decrease the likelihood that it will recur. If the rat that had been reinforced for bar pressing were given a painful shock each time it pressed the bar, the "bar pressing" habit would begin to disappear. Applied to children, a teenage girl who is grounded every time she stays out beyond her curfew is apt to begin coming home on time.

Skinner's theory was that habits develop as a result of unique **operant learning** experiences. One boy's aggressive behavior may increase over time because his playmates "give in" to (reinforce) his forceful tactics. Another boy may become relatively nonaggressive because his playmates actively suppress (punish) aggressiveness by fighting back. The two boys may develop in entirely different directions based on their different histories of reinforcement and punishment. According to Skinner, there is no "aggressive stage" in child development nor an "aggressive instinct" in people. Instead, he claimed that the majority of habits that children acquire—the very responses that make up their unique "personalities"—are freely emitted operants that have been shaped by their consequences. This *operant learning theory* claims that development depends on *external* stimuli (reinforcers and punishers) rather than internal forces such as instincts, drives, or biological maturation.

Today's developmentalists agree that human behavior can take many forms and that habits can emerge and disappear over a lifetime, depending on whether they have positive or negative consequences (Gewirtz & Pelaez-Nogueras, 1992; Stricker et al., 2001). Yet many believe that Skinner placed too much emphasis on operant behaviors shaped by external stimuli (reinforcers and punishers) while ignoring important *cognitive* contributors to learning. One such critic is Albert Bandura, who proposed a cognitive social-learning theory of development that is widely respected today.

operant
the initially voluntary act that becomes more or less probable of occurring depending on the consequence that it produces.

reinforcer
any consequence of an act that increases the probability that the act will recur.

punisher
any consequence of an act that suppresses that act and/or decreases the probability that it will recur.

operant learning
a form of learning in which voluntary acts (or operants) become either more or less probable, depending on the consequences they produce.

Bandura's Cognitive Social-Learning Theory

Can human social learning be explained by research with animals? Bandura (1977, 1986, 1992, 2001) doesn't think so. He agrees with Skinner that operant conditioning is an important type of learning, particularly for animals. However, Bandura argues that people are *cognitive* beings—active information processors—who, unlike animals, think about the relationships between their behavior and its consequences. They are often more affected by what they *believe* will happen than by what they actually experience. Consider your own situation as a student. Your education is costly and time-consuming and imposes many stressful demands. Yet, you tolerate the costs and toil because you *anticipate* greater rewards after you graduate. Your behavior is not shaped by immediate consequences; if it were, few students would ever make it through the trials and turmoil of college. Instead, you persist as a student because you have *thought about* the long-term benefits of obtaining an education and have decided that the benefits outweigh the short-term costs you must endure.

observational learning
learning that results from observing the behavior of others.

Bandura emphasizes **observational learning** as a central developmental process. Observational learning is simply learning that results from observing the behavior of other people (called *models*). A 2-year-old may learn how to approach and pet the family dog by simply watching his older sister do it. An 8-year-old may learn a very negative attitude toward a minority group after hearing her parents talk about this group in a disparaging way. Observational learning could not occur unless cognitive processes were at work. We must *attend* carefully to a model's behavior, actively digest, or *encode,* what we observe, and then *store* this information in memory (as an image or a verbal label) in order to imitate what we have observed. And, as we will see in Box 2.1, children do not need to be reinforced to learn this way.

Observational learning permits young children to quickly acquire thousands of new responses in a variety of settings where their "models" are pursuing their own interests and are not trying to teach them anything. In fact, many of the behaviors that children observe, remember, and may imitate are actions that models display but would like to discourage—practices such as swearing, smoking, or eating between meals. So Bandura claims children are continually learning both desirable and undesirable behaviors by observation and that, because of this, child development proceeds very rapidly along many different paths.

environmental determinism
the notion that children are passive creatures who are molded by their environments.

Social Learning as Reciprocal Determinism

Early versions of learning theory were largely tributes to Watson's doctrine of **environmental determinism:** Young, unknowing children were viewed as passive recipients of environmental influence—they would become whatever parents, teachers, and other agents of society groomed them to be. Bandura (1986, 1989) disagrees, stressing that children and adolescents are active, thinking beings who contribute in many ways to their

Courtesy of Albert Bandura

Albert Bandura (b. 1925) has emphasized the cognitive aspects of learning in his social-learning theory.

© United Feature Syndicate, Inc.

Children learn through modeling the behaviors of others they observe, even the family cat!

FOCUS ON RESEARCH An Example of Observational Learning

In 1965 Bandura made what then was considered a radical statement: Children can learn by merely observing the behavior of a social model *even without first performing the responses themselves or receiving any reinforcement for performing them.* Clearly, this "no-trial" learning is inconsistent with Skinner's theory, which claims that one must perform a response and then be reinforced in order to have learned that response.

Bandura (1965) then conducted a now-classic experiment to prove his point. Nursery-school children each watched a short film in which an adult model directed an unusual sequence of aggressive responses toward an inflatable Bobo doll, hitting the doll with a mallet while shouting "sockeroo," throwing rubber balls while shouting "bang, bang," and so on. There were three experimental conditions:

Children in the *model-rewarded* condition saw a second adult give the aggressive model candy and soda for a "championship performance."

Children in the *model-punished* condition saw a second adult scold and spank the model for beating up Bobo.

Children in the *no-consequence* condition simply saw the model behave aggressively.

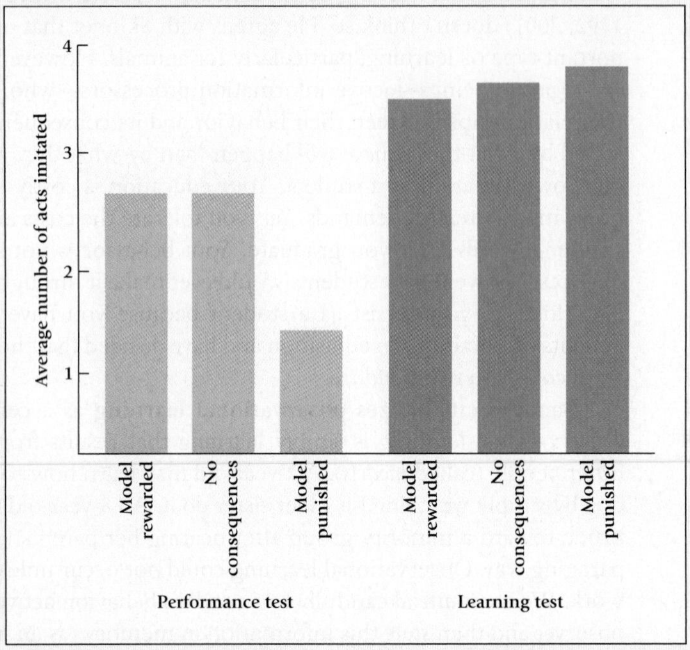

Average number of aggressive responses imitated during the performance test and the learning test for children who had seen a model rewarded, punished, or receive no consequences for his action. Adapted from "Influence of Models' Reinforcement Contingence on the Acquisition of Imitative Responses," by A. Bandura, 1965, Journal of Personality and Social Psychology, 1, 589–595. Copyright © 1995, 1965 by the American Psychological Association. Adapted with permission.

When the film ended, each child was left alone in a playroom that contained a Bobo doll and the props that the model had used to beat up Bobo. Hidden observers then recorded all instances in which the child imitated one or more of the model's aggressive acts. These observations revealed how willing children were to *perform* the responses they had witnessed. The results of this "performance" test appear on the left-hand side of the figure. Notice that children in the model-rewarded and no-consequences conditions imitated more of the model's aggressive acts than those who had seen the model punished for aggressive behavior. Clearly, this looks very much like the kind of no-trial observational learning that Bandura had proposed.

CONTINUED

own development. Observational learning, for example, requires the child to *actively* attend to, encode, and retain the behaviors displayed by social models. And children are often free to choose the models to whom they will attend; so they have some say about *what* they will learn from others.

reciprocal determinism
the notion that the flow of influence between children and their environments is a two-way street; the environment may affect the child, but the child's behavior also influences the environment.

Bandura (1986) proposed the concept of **reciprocal determinism** to describe his view that human development reflects an interaction among an active person (P), the person's behavior (B), and the environment (E) (see Figure 2.4). Unlike Watson and Skinner, who maintained that the environment (E) shaped a child's personality and her behavior, Bandura and others (most notably Richard Bell, 1979) propose that links among persons, behaviors, and environments are *bidirectional.* Thus, a child can influence his environment by virtue of his own conduct.

Consider an example.

Suppose that a 4-year-old (P) discovers that he can get the best toys by assaulting his playmates (B). In this case, possession of the desired toy is a favorable outcome (E) that reinforces the child's aggressive behavior (B). But note that the reinforcer here is produced by the child himself through his aggressive actions. Not only has his

But an important question remained. Had children in the first two conditions actually learned more from observing the model than those who had seen the model punished? To find out, Bandura devised a test to see just how much they had learned. Each child was now offered trinkets and fruit juice for reproducing all the model's behaviors that he or she could recall. As we see in the right-hand side of the figure, this "learning test" revealed that children in each of the three conditions had learned about the same amount by observing the model. Apparently, children in the model-punished condition had imitated fewer of the model's responses on the initial performance test because they felt that they too might be punished for striking Bobo. But when offered a reward, they showed that they had learned much more than their initial performances had implied.

In sum, it is important to distinguish what children *learn* by observation from their willingness to *perform* these responses. Clearly, reinforcement is not necessary for observational learning—that is, for the formation of images or verbal descriptions that would enable the observer to imitate the model's acts. However, the reinforcing or punishing consequences that the model received may well affect the observer's tendency to *perform* what he or she already has learned by observation.

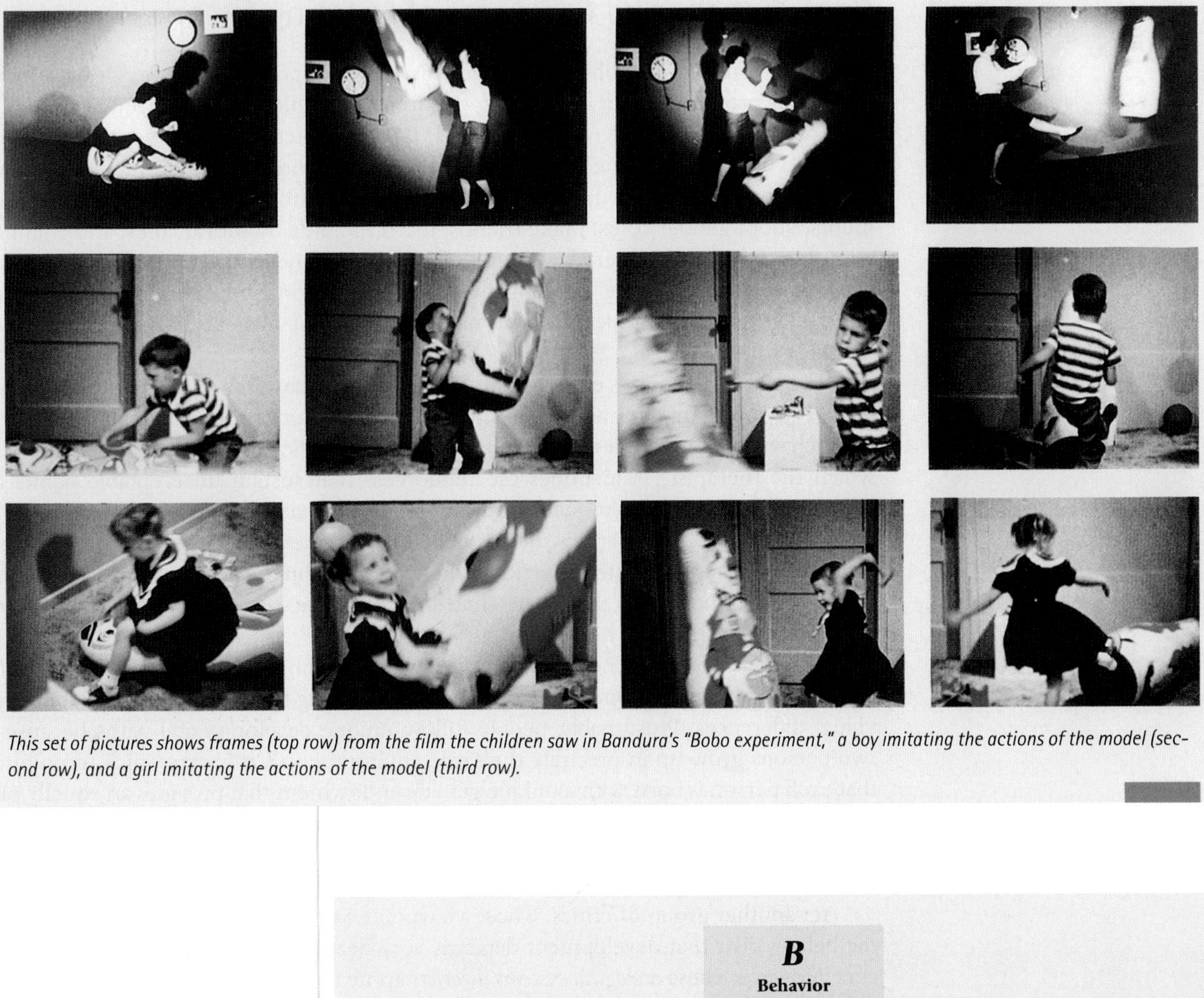

Courtesy of Albert Bandura

This set of pictures shows frames (top row) from the film the children saw in Bandura's "Bobo experiment," a boy imitating the actions of the model (second row), and a girl imitating the actions of the model (third row).

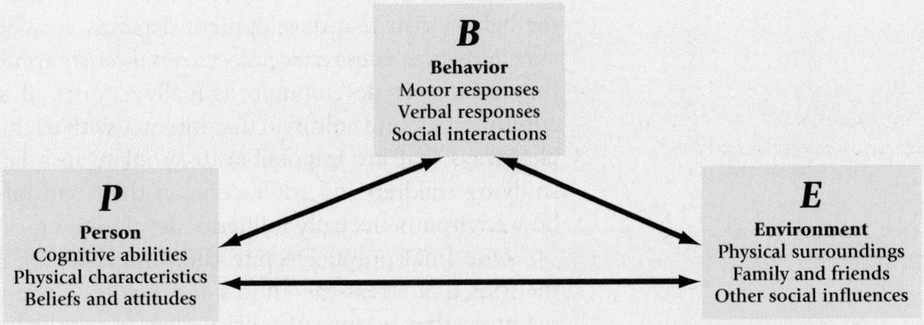

Figure 2.4 Bandura's model of reciprocal determinism. *Adapted from "The Self System in Reciprocal Determinism," by Albert Bandua, 1978,* American Psychologist, *33, 335. Copyright © 1978 by the American Psychological Association. Adapted by permission.*

(P) bullying behavior (B) been reinforced (by obtaining the toy), but *the nature of the play environment (E) has changed.* Playmates who were victimized may be more inclined to "give in" to the bully, which, in turn, can make him more likely to pick on these same children in the future (Anderson & Bushman, 2002; Putallaz & Bierman, 2004; Putallaz et al., 2004).

In sum, cognitive learning theorists argue that child development is best described as a continuous *reciprocal interaction* between children and their environments. The environment that a child experiences surely affects her, but her behavior affects the environment as well. The implication is that children are actively involved in shaping the very environments that will influence their growth and development.

Contributions and Criticisms of Learning Theories

Perhaps the major contribution of the learning viewpoint is the wealth of information it has provided about developing children and adolescents. Learning theories are very precise and testable (Horowitz, 1992). By conducting tightly controlled experiments to determine how children react to various environmental influences, learning theorists have begun to understand how and why children form emotional attachments, adopt gender roles, make friends, learn to abide by moral rules, and change in countless other ways over the course of childhood and adolescence. As we will see throughout the text, the learning perspective has contributed substantially to our knowledge of many aspects of human development (see also Gewirtz & Pelaez-Nogueras, 1992; Grusec, 1992).

The learning theory's emphasis on the immediate causes of overt behaviors has also produced important clinical insights and practical applications. For example, many problem behaviors can now be quickly eliminated by behavioral modification techniques in which the therapist (1) identifies the reinforcers that sustain unacceptable habits and eliminates them while (2) modeling or reinforcing alternative behaviors that are more desirable. Thus, distressing antics such as bullying or name-calling can often be eliminated in a matter of weeks with behavior modification techniques, whereas psychoanalysts might require months to probe the child's unconscious, searching for the unconscious drive that underlies these hostilities.

Despite its strengths, however, many view the learning approach as an oversimplified account of human development. Consider what learning theorists have to say about individual differences. Presumably, people follow unique developmental paths because no two persons grow up in precisely the same environment. Critics are quick to point out that each person is born with a unique genetic endowment that provides an equally plausible explanation for his or her individuality. So learning theorists may have oversimplified the issue of individual differences in development by downplaying the contribution of important biological influences.

Yet another group of critics, whose viewpoint we will soon examine, can agree with the behaviorists that development depends very heavily on the contexts in which it occurs. However, these *ecological systems theorists* argue that the environment that so powerfully influences development is really a series of social systems (for example, families, communities, and cultures) that interact with each other and with the individual in complex ways that are impossible to simulate in a laboratory. Their point is that only by studying children and adolescents in their natural settings are we likely to understand how environments truly influence development.

One final point: Despite the popularity of recent cognitively oriented learning theories that stress the child's active role in the developmental process, some critics maintain that learning theorists devote too little attention to *cognitive* influences on development. Proponents of this *cognitive-developmental* viewpoint believe that a child's mental abilities change in ways that behaviorists completely ignore. Further, they argue that a child's impressions of and reactions to the environment depend largely on his or her level of **cognitive development.** Let's now turn to this viewpoint and see what it has to offer.

cognitive development
age-related changes that occur in mental activities such as attending, perceiving, learning, thinking, and remembering.

CONCEPT CHECK 2.2 Psychoanalytic and Learning Viewpoints

Check your understanding of the psychoanalytic viewpoint (including Freud's and Erikson's theories) and the learning viewpoint (including Watson's, Skinner's, and Bandura's theories) in child development. Answers appear in the Appendix.

Multiple Choice: Select the best alternative for each question.

_____ 1. Freud's psychosexual theory of development emphasized all of the following *except*
  a. conscious drives and motivations
  b. repression of unconscious feelings or events
  c. the coordination of the id, ego, and superego
  d. sexual and aggressive instincts

_____ 2. Whose theory focuses on psychosocial stages or life crises that individuals must resolve during their lives to achieve healthy development?
  a. Freud's
  b. Erikson's
  c. Watson's
  d. Bandura's

_____ 3. Watson and Raynor conditioned 9-month-old Albert to be afraid of a white rat (which he had initially played with and enjoyed). These findings led Watson to develop advice for parents, suggesting that they
  a. bang a steel rod with a hammer behind their children whenever the child did something that they wished to discourage
  b. show careful attention and physical acts of affection for their children so that they would not develop irrational fears
  c. begin to train their children at birth and do not coddle their children in order to instill good habits in the children

Matching: Considering Skinner's Operant Learning Theory, match the following terms with their definitions.

4. _______ reinforcer
5. _______ operant
6. _______ punisher

a. the freely emitted response that produces a result to influence learning
b. a consequence that *suppresses* a response and *decreases* the likelihood that it will recur
c. a consequence that *strengthens* a response and *increases* the likelihood that it will recur

True or False: Indicate whether each of the following statements is true or false.

7. (T)(F) Dr. Macalister is interested in studying adolescent's identity development. She believes that adolescents struggle with breaking away from their parents and with forming their own ideas about who they are. Dr. Macalister's theory and research is most closely associated with Erikson's psychosocial theory of development.

8. (T)(F) Dr. Rosen studies children's observational learning. He believes that children can learn a great deal by simply observing the behaviors of people around them. He also believes that children influence the actual environments they experience. Dr. Rosen's research and theory is most closely associated with Bandura's cognitive social learning theory.

Short Answer: Briefly answer the following question.

9. The id, ego, and superego have been compared to the three branches of a democratic government. Which component of the Freudian personality seems to serve an executive function? A judicial function? A legislative function?

Essay: Provide a more detailed answer to the following question.

10. Three "Learning Perspectives" were discussed in this chapter: Watson's, Skinner's, and Bandura's. Compare the similarities among these theories in terms of their principles and assumptions. Contrast how the theories differ from each other in the principles and assumptions.

The Cognitive-Developmental Viewpoint

No theorist has contributed more to our understanding of children's thinking than Jean Piaget (1896–1980), a Swiss scholar who began to study intellectual development during the 1920s. Piaget was truly a remarkable individual. At age 10, he published his first scientific article about the behavior of a rare albino sparrow. His early interest in the ways that animals adapt to their environments eventually led him to pursue a doctoral degree

Yves de Braine/Black Star

In his cognitive-developmental theory, Swiss scholar Jean Piaget (1896–1980) focused on the growth of children's knowledge and reasoning skills.

in zoology, which he completed in 1918. Piaget's secondary interest was *epistemology* (the branch of philosophy concerned with the origins of knowledge), and he hoped to be able to integrate his two interests. Thinking that psychology was the answer, Piaget journeyed to Paris, where he accepted a position at the Alfred Binet laboratories, working on the first standardized intelligence test. His experiences in this position had a profound influence on his career.

In testing mental ability, an estimate is made of the person's intelligence based on the number and kinds of questions that he or she answers correctly. However, Piaget soon found that he was more interested in children's *incorrect* answers than their correct ones. He first noticed that children of about the same age produced the same kinds of wrong answers. But why? As he questioned children about their misconceptions, using the clinical method he had learned while working in a psychiatric clinic, he began to realize that young children are not simply less intelligent than older children; rather their thought processes are completely different. Piaget then set up his own laboratory and spent 60 years charting the course of intellectual growth and attempting to determine how children progress from one type (or stage) of thinking to another.

Piaget's View of Intelligence and Intellectual Growth

Influenced by his background in biology, Piaget (1950) defined *intelligence* as a basic life process that helps an organism to *adapt* to its environment. By adapting, Piaget means that the organism is able to cope with the demands of its immediate situation. For example, the hungry infant who grasps a bottle and brings it to her mouth is behaving adaptively, as is the adolescent who successfully interprets a road map while traveling. As children mature, they acquire ever more complex "cognitive structures" that aid them in adapting to their environments.

scheme
an organized pattern of thought or action that a child constructs to make sense of some aspect of his or her experience; Piaget sometimes uses the term cognitive structures as a synonym for schemes.

A cognitive structure—or what Piaget called a **scheme**—is an organized pattern of thought or action that is used to cope with or explain some aspect of experience. For example, many 3-year-olds insist that the sun is alive because it comes up in the morning and goes down at night. According to Piaget, these children are operating on the basis of a simple cognitive scheme that "things that move are alive." The earliest *schemes,* formed in infancy, are motor habits such as rocking, grasping, and lifting, which prove to be adaptive indeed. For example, a curious infant who combines the responses of extending an arm (reaching) and grasping with the hand is suddenly capable of satisfying her curiosity by exploring almost any interesting object that is no more than an arm's length away. Simple as these behavioral schemes may be, they permit infants to operate toys, to turn dials, to open cabinets, and to otherwise master their environments. Later in childhood, cognitive schemes take the form of "actions of the head" (for example, mental addition or subtraction) that allow children to manipulate information and think logically about the issues and problems they encounter in everyday life. At any age, children rely on their current cognitive schemes to understand the world around them. And because cognitive schemes take different forms at different ages, younger and older children may often interpret and respond to the same objects and events in very different ways.

How do children grow intellectually? Piaget claimed that infants have no inborn knowledge or ideas about reality, as some philosophers have claimed. Nor are children simply given information or taught how to think by adults. Instead, they *actively construct* new understandings of the world based on their own experiences. Children watch what goes on around them; they experiment with objects they encounter; they make connections or associations between events; and they are puzzled when their current understandings (or schemes) fail to explain what they have experienced.

Piaget believed that children are naturally curious explorers who are constantly trying to make sense of their surroundings.

To illustrate, let's return for a moment to the 3-year-old who believes that the sun is alive (Opfer & Gelman, 2001). Surely this idea is not something the child learned from an adult; it was apparently constructed by the child on the basis of her own worldly experiences. After all, many things that move *are* alive. So long as the child clings to this understanding, she may regard any new moving object as alive; that is, new experiences will be interpreted in terms of her current cognitive schemes, a process Piaget called **assimilation.** Eventually, however, this child will encounter moving objects that almost certainly couldn't be alive, such as a paper airplane that was nothing more than a sheet of newsprint before dad folded it, or a wind-up toy that invariably stops moving until she winds it again. Now here are contradictions (or what Piaget termed **disequilibriums**) between the child's understanding and the facts. It becomes clear to the child that her "objects-that-move-are-alive" scheme needs to be revised. She is prompted by these disconfirming experiences to **accommodate**—that is, to alter her existing schemes so that they provide a better explanation of the distinction between animate and inanimate objects (perhaps by concluding that only things that move under their own power are alive).

Piaget believed that we are continually relying on the complementary processes of assimilation and accommodation to adapt to our environments. Initially, we attempt to understand new experiences or solve problems using our current cognitive schemes (assimilation). But we often find that our existing schemes are inadequate for these tasks, which then prompts us to revise them (through accommodation) so that they provide a better "fit" with reality (Piaget, 1952). Additionally, we also may create new schemes to adapt to the disequilibriums experienced in our environments.

Biological maturation also plays an important role: As the brain and nervous system mature, children become capable of increasingly complex cognitive schemes that help them to construct better understandings of what they have experienced (Piaget, 1970). Eventually, curious, active children, who are always forming new schemes and reorganizing their knowledge, progress far enough to think about old issues in entirely new ways; that is, they pass from one stage of cognitive development to the next higher stage.

Four Stages of Cognitive Development

Piaget proposed four major stages of cognitive development: the *sensorimotor* stage (birth to age 2), the *preoperational* stage (ages 2 to 7), the *concrete-operational* stage (ages 7 to 11 or 12), and the *formal-operational* stage (ages 11–12 and beyond). These stages form what Piaget called an **invariant developmental sequence**—that is, all children progress through the stages in exactly the order in which they are listed. They cannot skip stages because each successive stage builds on the previous stage and represents a more complex way of thinking.

Table 2.3 summarizes the key features of Piaget's four cognitive stages. Each of these periods of intellectual growth will be discussed in much greater detail when we return to the topic of cognitive development in Chapter 7.

assimilation
Piaget's term for the process by which children interpret new experiences by incorporating them into their existing schemes.

disequilibriums
imbalances or contradictions between one's thought processes and environmental events. On the other hand, equilibrium refers to a balanced, harmonious relationship between one's cognitive structures and the environment.

accommodation
Piaget's term for the process by which children modify their existing schemes in order to incorporate or adapt to new experiences.

invariant developmental sequence
a series of developments that occur in one particular order because each development in the sequence is a prerequisite for the next.

Contributions and Criticisms of Piaget's Viewpoint

Like Freud and Watson, Piaget was an innovative renegade. He was unpopular with psychometricians because he claimed that their intelligence tests only measure what children know and tell us nothing about the most important aspect of intelligence—how children think. In addition, Piaget dared to study an unobservable concept, cognition, that had fallen from favor among psychologists from the behaviorist tradition (Beilin, 1992).

By the 1960s, times changed. Piaget's early theorizing and research legitimized the study of children's thinking, and his early work linking moral development to cognitive development (see Chapter 14) contributed immensely to a whole new area of

TABLE 2.3 Piaget's Stages of Cognitive Development

Approximate age	Stage	Primary schemes or methods of representing experience	Major developments
Birth to 2 years	Sensorimotor	Infants use sensory and motor capabilities to explore and gain a basic understanding of the environment. At birth they have only innate reflexes with which to engage the world. By the end of the sensorimotor period, they are capable of complex sensorimotor coordinations.	Infants acquire a primitive sense of "self" and "others," learn that objects continue to exist when they are out of sight (object permanence), and begin to internalize behavioral schemes to produce images or mental schemes.
2 to 7 years	Preoperational	Children use symbolism (images and language) to represent and understand various aspects of the environment. They respond to objects and events according to the way things appear to be. Thought is egocentric, meaning that children think everyone sees the world in much the same way that they do.	Children become imaginative in their play activities. They gradually begin to recognize that other people may not always perceive the world as they do.
7 to 11 years	Concrete operations	Children acquire and use cognitive operations (mental activities that are components of logical thought).	Children are no longer fooled by appearances. By relying on cognitive operations, they understand the basic properties of and relations among objects and events in the everyday world. They are becoming much more proficient at inferring motives by observing others' behavior and the circumstances in which it occurs.
11 years and beyond	Formal operations	Adolescents' cognitive operations are reorganized in a way that permits them to operate on operations (think about thinking). Thought is now systematic and abstract.	Logical thinking is no longer limited to the concrete or the observable. Adolescents enjoy pondering hypothetical issues and, as a result, may become rather idealistic. They are capable of systematic, deductive reasoning that permits them to consider many possible solutions to a problem and to pick the correct answer.

developmental research—*social cognition*. Social-cognitive theorists such as Lawrence Kohlberg and Robert Selman argued that the same mind that gradually constructs increasingly sophisticated understandings of the physical world also comes, with age, to form more complex ideas about sex differences, moral values, emotions, the meaning and obligations of friendship, and countless other aspects of social life. The development of social cognition is a primary focus of Chapter 12, and the links between one's social-cognitive abilities and various aspects of social and personality development are discussed throughout the text.

Piaget's theory has also had a strong impact on education. For example, popular *discovery-based* educational programs are based on the premise that young children do not think like adults and that they learn best by having "hands-on" educational experiences with their environment. So a preschool teacher in a Piagetian classroom might introduce the difficult concept of number by presenting her pupils with different numbers of objects to stack, color, or arrange. The idea is that new concepts like number are best taught by methods in which curious, active children can apply their existing schemes and make the critical "discoveries" for themselves.

Although Piaget's pioneering efforts left a deep and lasting imprint on our thinking about development (see Beilin, 1992), many of his ideas have been challenged (Miller, 2002). It now appears that Piaget regularly underestimated the intellectual capabilities of infants, preschoolers, and grade-school children, all of whom show much greater problem-solving skills when presented with simplified tasks that are more familiar and thereby allow them to display their competencies (Bjorklund, 2005). Other investigators found that performance on Piagetian problems can be improved dramatically through training programs, which challenges Piaget's assumption that individualized discovery learning is the best way to promote intellectual growth.

Sociocultural Influences: Lev Vygotsky's Viewpoint

sociocultural theory
Vygotsky's perspective on development, in which children acquire their culture's values, beliefs, and problem-solving strategies through collaborative dialogues with more knowledgeable members of society.

One of the first important challenges to Piaget's theory came from Russian developmentalist Lev Vygotsky (1934/1962). Vygotsky's **sociocultural theory** focused on how *culture*—the beliefs, values, traditions, and skills of a social group—is transmitted from generation to generation. Rather than depicting children as independent explorers who make critical discoveries on their own, Vygotsky viewed cognitive growth as a *socially mediated activity*—one in which children gradually acquire new ways of thinking and behaving through cooperative dialogues with more knowledgeable members of society (see also Gauvain, 2001; Rogoff, 2002, 2003). Vygotsky also rejected the notion that all children progress through the same stages of cognitive growth. He argued that the new skills children master through their interactions with more competent people are often specific to their culture rather than universal cognitive structures. So from Vygotsky's perspective (which we will explore in depth in Chapter 7), Piaget largely ignored important social and cultural influences on human development.

Is Cognitive Development Stagelike?

Piaget's notion that cognitive growth proceeds through an invariant sequence of stages has come under increasing attack in recent years (Bjorklund, 2005). Several influential developmentalists continue to believe that cognitive growth *is* stagelike but that Piaget's description of these stages is simply too broad (Case & Okamoto, 1996). However, *information-processing* theorists take a dramatically different point of view. Let's now examine the most important assumptions of this interesting and influential perspective.

The Information-Processing Viewpoint

information-processing theory
a perspective that views the human mind as a continuously developing, symbol-manipulating system, similar to a computer, into which information flows, is operated on, and is converted to output (answers, inferences, and solutions to problems).

By 1990, many developmentalists, disenchanted by the narrow, anti-mentalistic bias of behaviorism and the problems they saw in Piaget's theory, turned to such fields as cognitive psychology and computer science, seeking new insights about children's thinking (Bjorklund, 2005; Shultz, 2003; Siegler & Alibali, 2005). Digital computers, which rely on mathematically specified programs to operate on information and generate solutions to problems, provided the framework for a new **information-processing perspective** on cognitive development. According to the information-processing theory, the human mind is like a computer into which information flows, is operated on, and is converted to output—that is, answers, inferences, or solutions to problems (Klahr, 1992; Siegler, 1996). Continuing to use the computer analogy, information-processing theorists view cognitive development as the age-related changes that occur in the mind's *hardware* (that is, the brain and the peripheral nervous system) and *software* (mental processes such as attention, perception, memory, and problem-solving strategies).

Like Piaget, information-processing theorists acknowledge that biological maturation is an important contributor to cognitive growth. But unlike Piaget, who was vague about the connections between biological and cognitive development, informational-processing theorists contend that maturation of the brain and nervous system enables children and adolescents to process information faster (Kail, 1992). As a result, developing children become better at sustaining attention, at recognizing and storing task-relevant information, and at executing mental programs that allow them to operate on what they have stored to answer questions and solve problems. Yet, information-processing theorists are also keenly aware that the strategies that children develop for attending to and processing information are greatly influenced by their *experiences*—that is, by the kinds of problems presented to them, by the kinds of instruction they receive at home and at school, and even by the skills that their culture or subculture specifies as important.

In what is perhaps their biggest break with Piaget, information-processing theorists propose that cognitive development is a *continuous* process that is not stagelike. Presumably, the strategies we use to gather, store, retrieve, and operate on information evolve gradually over the course of childhood and adolescence. So cognitive development from an information-processing perspective involves small *quantitative* rather than large qualitative changes.

Contributions and Criticisms of the Information-Processing Viewpoint

The information-processing perspective on cognitive development has changed the ways developmentalists (and educators) view children's thinking. As we will see in Chapter 8, information-processing theorists have provided a host of new insights on the growth of many cognitive abilities that Piaget did not emphasize, and their research has also filled in many of the gaps in Piaget's earlier theory. Furthermore, the rigorous and intensive research methods favored by information-processing researchers have enabled them to identify how children and adolescents approach various problems and why they may make logical errors. Educators have seen the practical utility of this research: if teachers understand exactly *why* children are having difficulties with their reading, math, or science lessons, it becomes easier to suggest alternative strategies to improve student performances (Siegler & Munakata, 1993).

Despite its many strengths, the information-processing theory is subject to criticism. Some question the utility of a theory based on the thinking that children display in artificial laboratory studies, arguing that it may not accurately reflect their thinking in everyday life. Others contend that the computer model on which information-processing theory is based seriously underestimates the richness and diversity of human cognition. After all, people (but not computers) can dream, create, and reflect on their own and other's states of consciousness, and the information-processing theory does not adequately explain these cognitive activities. Although there is some merit to both criticisms, information-processing researchers are addressing them by studying children's memories for everyday events and activities, as well as the reasoning they display in conversations with parents and peers, and the strategies they use in processing social information to form impressions of themselves and other people in their natural environments (see, for example, Hayden, Haine, & Fivush, 1997; Heyman & Gelman, 1999; Kupersmidt & Dodge, 2004).

You may have noticed that both Piaget and the information-processing theorists contend that intellectual development is heavily influenced by the forces of nature (biological maturation) *and* nurture (the environments that children and adolescents experience, which provide the input on which they operate to construct knowledge and develop problem-solving strategies). We will examine two additional theoretical perspectives, both of which concur that nature *and* nurture make important contributions to human development. However, one of these theories, *ethology,* emphasizes the biological side of development, whereas the other, *ecological systems theory,* stresses the crucial role that *contexts* play in influencing developmental outcomes. Let's first consider the ethological viewpoint.

The Ethological (or Evolutionary) Viewpoint

Behaviorist John Watson may have taken such an extreme environmental stand as he did partly because other prominent theorists of his era, most notably Arnold Gesell (1880–1961), took an equally extreme but opposing position that human development is largely a matter of biological maturation. Gesell (1933) believed that children, like plants, simply "bloomed," following a pattern and timetable laid out in their genes; how parents raised their young was thought to be of little importance.

ethology
the study of the bioevolutionary basis of behavior and development.

Although today's developmentalists have largely rejected Gesell's radical claims, the notion that biological influences play a significant role in human development is alive and well in **ethology**—the scientific study of the evolutionary basis of behavior and the contributions of evolved responses to the human species' survival and development (Bjorklund & Pelligrini, 2002; Gaulin & McBurney, 2001; Geary & Bjorklund, 2000). The origins of this discipline can be traced to Charles Darwin; however, modern ethology arose from the work of Konrad Lorenz and Niko Tinbergen, two European zoologists whose animal research highlighted some important links between evolutionary processes and adaptive behaviors (Dewsbury, 1992). Let's now examine the central assumptions of classical ethology and their implications for human development.

Assumptions of Classical Ethology

The most basic assumption ethologists make is that members of all animal species are born with a number of "biologically programmed" behaviors that are (1) products of evolution and (2) adaptive in that they contribute to survival. Many species of birds, for example, seem to come biologically prepared to engage in such instinctual behaviors as following their mothers (a response called *imprinting* that helps to protect the young from predators and to ensure that they find food), building nests, and singing songs. (Konrad Lorenz is credited with discovering the imprinting process through his experiments with geese in which he actually caused them to imprint on *him* instead of their mothers!) These biologically programmed characteristics are thought to have evolved as a result of the Darwinian process of **natural selection;** that is, over the course of evolution, birds with genes promoting these adaptive behaviors were more likely to survive and to pass their genes on to offspring than were birds lacking these adaptive characteristics. Over many, many generations, the genes underlying the most adaptive behaviors became widespread in the species, characterizing nearly all individuals.

natural selection
an evolutionary process, proposed by Charles Darwin, stating that individuals with characteristics that promote adaptation to the environment will surive, reproduce, and pass these adaptive characteristics to offspring; those lacking these adaptive characteristics will eventually die out.

So ethologists focus on inborn or instinctual responses that (1) all members of a species share and (2) may steer individuals along similar developmental paths. Where might one search for these adaptive behaviors and study their developmental implications? Ethologists have always preferred to study their subjects in their natural environment because they believe that the inborn behaviors that shape human (or animal) development are most easily identified and understood if observed in the settings where they evolved and have proven to be adaptive (Hinde, 1989).

Nina Leen/Time Life Pictures/Getty Images

Konrad Lorenz studied imprinting in geese. As you can see in this photo, a flock of geese imprinted on him instead of their mother. They followed him everywhere and considered him their mother.

Ethology and Human Development

Instinctual responses that seem to promote survival are relatively easy to spot in animals. But do humans really display such behaviors? And if they do, how might these preprogrammed responses influence their development?

Human ethologists such as John Bowlby (1969, 1973) believe that children display a wide variety of preprogrammed behaviors. They also claim that each of these responses promotes a particular kind of experience that will help the individual to survive and develop normally. For example, the cry of a human infant is thought to be a biologically programmed "distress signal" that attracts the attention of caregivers. Not only are infants said to be biologically programmed to convey their distress with loud, lusty cries, but ethologists also believe that caregivers are biologically predisposed to respond to such signals. So the adaptive significance of an infant's crying ensures that (1) the infant's basic needs (for example, hunger, thirst, safety) are met and (2) the infant will have sufficient contact with other human beings to form primary emotional attachments (Bowlby, 1973).

Although ethologists are critical of learning theorists for largely ignoring the biological bases of human development, they are well aware that development requires learning. For example, the infant's cries may be an innate signal that promotes the human contact from which emotional attachments emerge. However, these emotional attachments do not happen automatically. The infant must first *learn* to discriminate familiar faces from those of strangers before becoming emotionally attached to a caregiver. Presumably, the adaptive significance of this discriminatory learning goes back to a period in evolutionary history when humans traveled in nomadic tribes and braved the elements. In those days, it was crucial that an infant become attached to caregivers and wary of strangers, for failure to stay close to caregivers and to cry in response to a strange face might make the infant easy prey for a predatory animal.

Now consider the opposite side of the argument. Some caregivers who suffer from various life stresses of their own (for example, prolonged illnesses, depression, an unhappy marriage) may be routinely inattentive or neglectful, so that an infant's cries rarely promote any contact with them. Such an infant will probably not form secure emotional attachments to her caregivers and may become rather shy and emotionally unresponsive to other people for years to come (Ainsworth, 1979, 1989). What this infant has learned from her early experiences is that her caregivers are undependable and are not to be trusted. Consequently, she may become ambivalent or wary around her caregivers and may later assume that other regular companions, such as teachers and peers, are equally untrustworthy people who should be avoided whenever possible.

How important are an individual's early experiences? Like Freud, ethologists believe early experiences are *very* important. In fact, they have argued that there may be "critical periods" for the development of many attributes. A *critical period* is a limited time span during which developing organisms are biologically prepared to display adaptive patterns of development, provided they receive the appropriate input (Bailey & Symons, 2001; Bruer, 2001). Outside this period, the same environmental events or influences are thought to have no lasting effects. Although this concept of critical period does seem to explain certain aspects of animal development, such as imprinting in young birds, many human ethologists think that the term *sensitive period* is a more accurate description of human development. A **sensitive period** refers to a time that is optimal for the emergence of particular competencies or behaviors and in which the individual is particularly sensitive to environmental influences. The time frames of sensitive periods are less rigid or well-defined than those of critical periods. It is possible for development to occur outside of a sensitive period but is much more difficult to foster (Bjorklund & Pelligrini, 2002).

sensitive period
period of time that is optimal for the development of particular capacities, or behaviors, and in which the individual is particularly sensitive to environmental influences that would foster these attributes.

Some ethologists believe that the first 3 years of life are a sensitive period for the development of social and emotional responsiveness in people (Bowlby, 1973). The argument is that we are most susceptible to forming close emotional ties during the first 3 years, and should we have little or no opportunity to do so during this period, we would find it much more difficult to make close friends or to enter into intimate emotional relationships with others later in life. This is a provocative claim about the emotional lives of people, which we will examine carefully when we discuss early social and emotional development in Chapter 11.

In sum, ethologists acknowledge that we are heavily influenced by our experiences (Gottlieb, 1996); yet they emphasize that people are inherently biological creatures whose inborn characteristics affect the kinds of learning experiences they are likely to have.

Contributions and Criticisms of the Ethological Viewpoint

If this text had been written 40 years ago, it would not have included a section on ethological theory. Although ethology became popular in the 1960s, the early ethologists studied animal behavior. Only within the past 25 years have ethologists made a serious attempt to specify evolutionary contributors to human development, and many of their hypotheses may still be considered speculative (Lerner & von Eye, 1992). Nevertheless, human ethologists have made important contributions to our discipline by reminding us that every child is a biological creature who comes equipped with a number of adaptive, genetically programmed characteristics—attributes that influence other people's reactions to the child and, thus, the course that development will take. In addition, ethologists have made a major methodological contribution by showing us the value of (1) studying human development in normal, everyday settings and (2) comparing human development with that of other species.

One intriguing ethological notion that we will discuss in detail in Chapter 11 is that infants are inherently sociable creatures who are quite capable of promoting and sustaining social interactions from the day they are born. This viewpoint contrasts sharply with that of behaviorists, who portray the newborn as a *tabula rasa,* and with Piaget's "asocial" infant who enters the world equipped only with a few basic reflexes. Ethologists also believe that humans have evolved in ways that predispose us to develop and display prosocial motives such as **altruism** that contribute to the common good, permitting us to live and work together in harmony. Box 2.2 describes some observations suggesting that there may be a biological basis for certain aspects of altruism.

altruism
a selfless concern for the welfare of others that is expressed through prosocial acts such as sharing, cooperating, and helping.

On the other hand, evolutionary approaches are like psychoanalytic theory in being very hard to test. How does one prove that various motives, mannerisms, and behaviors are inborn, adaptive, or products of evolutionary history? Such claims are often difficult to confirm. Ethological theory has also been criticized as a retrospective explanation of development. One can easily apply evolutionary concepts to explain what has already happened, but can the theory *predict* what is likely to happen in the future? Many developmentalists believe that it cannot.

Finally, proponents of other viewpoints (most notably, learning theory) have argued that even if there is a biological basis for certain human motives or behaviors, these predispositions will soon become so modified by learning that it may not be helpful to spend much time wondering about their prior evolutionary significance. Even strong, genetically influenced attributes can be modified by experience. Consider, for example, that young mallard ducklings clearly prefer mallards' vocal calls to those of other birds—a behavior that ethologists claim is innate and adaptive as a product of mallard evolution. Yet Gilbert Gottlieb (1991) found that duckling embryos that were exposed to chicken calls before hatching preferred the call of a chicken to that of a mallard mother! In this case, the ducklings' *prenatal experiences* overrode a genetic predisposition. People have a much greater capacity for learning than ducklings do, leading many critics to argue that cultural learning experiences quickly overshadow innate evolutionary mechanisms in shaping human conduct and character.

Despite these criticisms, the evolutionary perspective remains a valuable addition to the developmental sciences. Not only has it provided a healthy balance to the heavy environmental emphasis of learning theories by identifying important biological contributions to human development, but it has also reinforced a crucial premise of the final theory we will review, the ecological systems theory: There is much to be learned about the process of development by studying children and adolescents in their everyday environments.

The Ecological Systems Viewpoint

American psychologist Urie Bronfenbrenner offers an exciting new perspective on child and adolescent development that addresses many of the shortcomings of earlier "environmentalist" approaches. Behaviorists John Watson and B. F. Skinner had defined

FOCUS ON RESEARCH

Is Altruism Part of Human Nature?

Darwin's notion of survival of the fittest seems to argue against altruism as an inborn motive. Many have interpreted Darwin's idea to mean that powerful, self-serving individuals who place their own needs ahead of others' are the ones who are most likely to survive. If this were so, evolution would favor the development of selfishness and egoism—not altruism—as basic components of human nature.

©LWA-Dann Tardif/Corbis

Infants who heard another infant crying soon began to cry themselves.

Martin Hoffman (1981) has challenged this point of view, listing several reasons why the concept of survival of the fittest actually implies altruism. His arguments hinge on the assumption that human beings are more likely to receive protection from natural enemies, satisfy all their basic needs, and successfully reproduce if they live together in cooperative social units. If this assumption is correct, cooperative, altruistic individuals would be the ones who are most likely to survive long enough to pass along their "altruistic genes" to their offspring; individualists who go it alone would probably succumb to famine, predators, or some other natural disaster that they could not cope with by themselves. So, over thousands of generations, natural selection would favor the development of innate social motives such as altruism. Presumably, the tremendous survival value of being "social" makes altruism, cooperation, and other social motives much more plausible as components of human nature than competition, selfishness, and the like.

It is obviously absurd to argue that infants routinely help other people. However, Hoffman believes that even newborn babies are capable of recognizing and experiencing the emotion of others. This ability, known as **empathy**, is thought to be an important contributor to altruism, for a person must recognize that others are distressed in some way before he or she is likely to help. So Hoffman is suggesting that at least one aspect of altruism—empathy—is present at birth.

Hoffman's claim is based on an experiment (Sagi & Hoffman, 1976) in which infants less than 36 hours old listened to (1) another infant's cries, (2) an equally loud computer simulation of a crying infant, or (3) no sounds at all (silence). The infants who heard a real infant crying soon began to cry themselves, to display physical signs of agitation such as kicking, and to grimace. Infants exposed to the simulated cry or to silence cried much less and seemed not to be very discomforted. (A second study by Martin & Clark, 1982, has confirmed these observations.)

Hoffman argues that there is something quite distinctive about the human cry. His contention is that infants listen to and experience the distress of another crying infant and become distressed themselves. Of course, this finding does not conclusively demonstrate that humans are altruistic by nature. But it does imply that the capacity for empathy, at least in a rudimentary form, may be present at birth and thus may serve as a biological basis for the eventual development of altruistic behavior.

"environment" as any and all external focuses that shape the individual's development. Although modern learning theorists such as Bandura (1986, 1989) have backed away from this view by acknowledging that environments both influence and *are influenced by* developing individuals, they continued to provide only vague descriptions of the environmental contexts in which development takes place.

What Bronfenbrenner's **ecological systems theory** (1989, 1993, 2005; Brofenbrenner & Morris, 2006) provides is a detailed analysis of environmental influences. This approach also concurs that a person's biologically influenced characteristics interact with environmental forces to shape development, so it is probably more accurate to describe this perspective as a *bioecological* theory (Bronfenbrenner, 1995).

empathy
the ability to experience the same emotions that someone else is experiencing, or in more advanced forms, the ability to understand another person's emotional state or psychological experience.

ecological systems theory
Bronfenbrenner's model emphasizing that the developing person is embedded in a series of environmental systems that interact with one another and with the person to influence development.

Bronfenbrenner's Contexts for Development

Bronfenbrenner (1979) begins by assuming that *natural* environments are the major source of influence on developing persons—and one that is often overlooked by researchers who choose to study development in the highly artificial context of the laboratory. He defines environment (or the natural ecology) as "a set of nested structures, each inside the next, like a set of Russian dolls" (p. 22). In other words, the developing person is said to be at the center of and embedded in several environmental systems, ranging from immediate settings such as the family to more remote contexts such as the broader culture (see Figure 2.5). Each of these systems is thought to interact with the others and with the individual to influence development in important ways (see also Cole, 2005). Let's take a closer look.

The Microsystem

microsystem
the immediate settings (including role relationships and activities) that the person actually encounters; the innermost of Bronfenbrenner's environmental layers or contexts.

Bronfenbrenner's innermost environmental layer, or **microsystem,** refers to the activities and interactions that occur in the person's immediate surroundings. For most young infants, the microsystem may be limited to the family. Yet, this system eventually becomes much more complex as children are exposed to day care, preschool classes, youth groups, and neighborhood playmates. Children are influenced by the people in their microsystems. In addition, their own biologically and socially influenced characteristics—their habits, temperaments, physical characteristics, and capabilities—influence the behavior of companions (that is, their microsystem) as well. For example, a temperamentally difficult infant can alienate her parents or even create friction between them that may be sufficient to damage their marital relationship (Belsky, Rosenberger, & Crnic, 1995). And interactions between any two individuals in microsystems are likely to be influenced by third parties. Fathers, for example, clearly influence mother-infant interactions: happily married mothers who have close supportive relationships with their husbands tend to interact much more patiently and sensitively with their infants than mothers who experience marital tension, little support from their spouses, or feel that they are raising their children on their own (Cox et al., 1989, 1992). So microsystems are truly dynamic contexts for development in which each person influences and is influenced by all other persons in the system.

The Mesosystem

mesosystem
the interconnections among an individual's immediate settings or microsystems; the second of Bronfenbrenner's environmental layers or contexts.

The second of Bronfenbrenner's environmental layers, or **mesosystem,** refers to the connections or interrelationships among such microsystems as homes, schools, and peer groups. Bronfenbrenner argues that development is likely to be optimized by strong, supportive links between microsystems. For example, youngsters who have established secure and harmonious relationships with parents are especially inclined to be accepted by peers and to enjoy close, supportive friendships during childhood and adolescence (Clark & Ladd, 2000; Hodges, Finnegan, & Perry, 1999). A child's ability to learn at school depends on the quality of instruction that his teachers provide and also on the extent to which parents value scholastic activities and consult or cooperate with teachers (Gottfried, Fleming, & Gottfried, 1998; Luster & McAdoo, 1996). Nonsupportive links between microsystems can spell trouble. For example, when peer groups devalue academics, they often undermine an adolescent's scholastic performance, despite the best efforts of parents and teachers to encourage academic achievement (Steinberg, Dornbusch, & Brown, 1992).

In his ecological systems theory, Urie Bronfenbrenner (b. 1917) describes how multiple levels of the surrounding environment influence child and adolescent development.

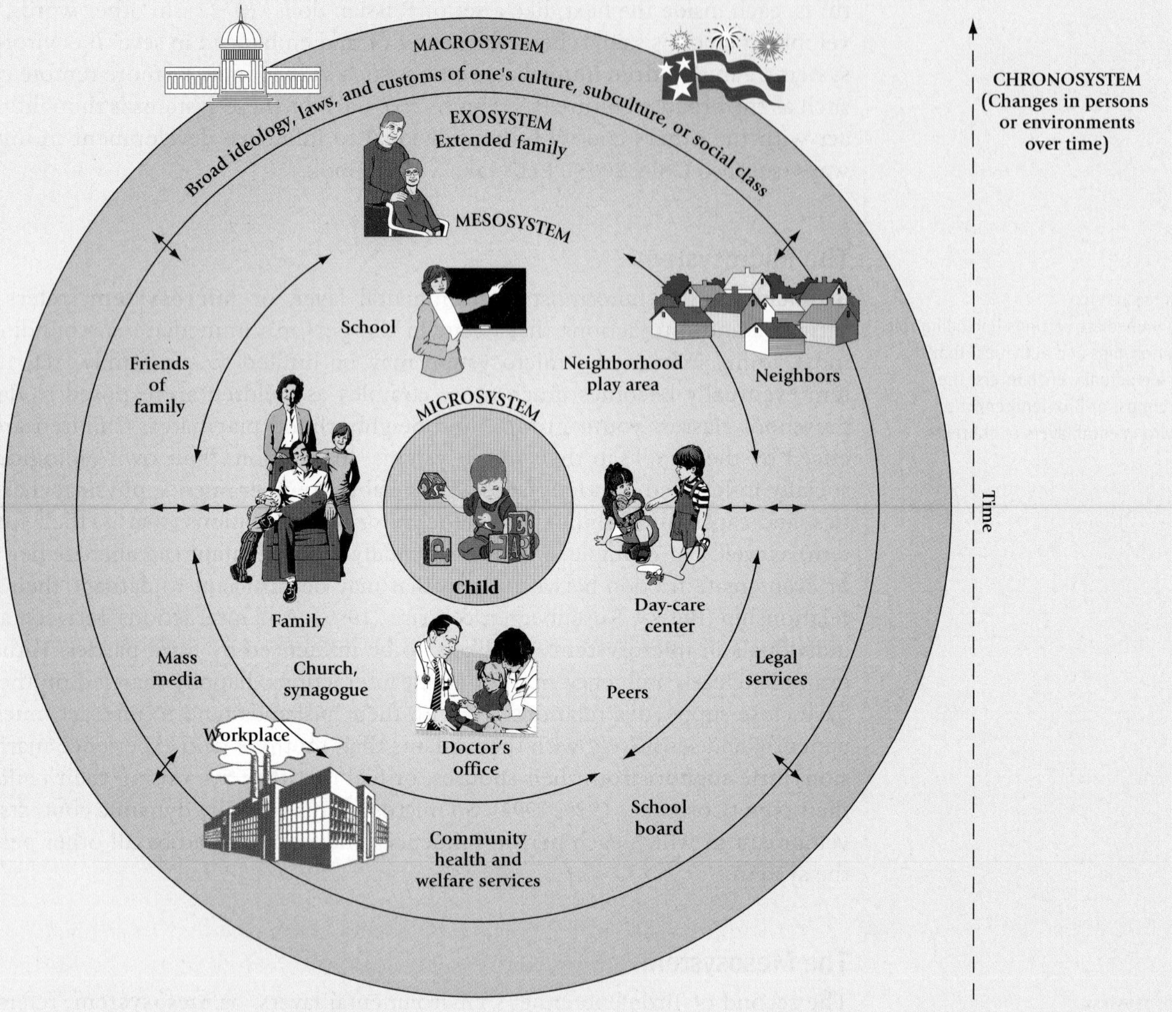

Figure 2.5 Bronfenbrenner's ecological model of the environment as a series of nested structures. The microsystem refers to relations between the child and the immediate environment, the mesosystem to connections among the child's immediate settings, the exosystem to social settings that affect but do not contain the child, and the macrosystem to the overarching ideology of the culture. *Based on Bronfenbrenner, 1979.*

exosystem
social systems that children and adolescents do not directly experience but that may nonetheless influence their development; the third of Bronfenbrenner's environmental layers or contexts.

The Exosystem

Bronfenbrenner's third environmental layer, or **exosystem,** consists of contexts that children and adolescents are not a part of but that may nevertheless influence their development. For example, parents' work environments are an exosystem influence. Children's emotional relationships at home may be influenced considerably by whether or not their parents enjoy their work (Greenberger, O'Neal, & Nagel, 1994). Similarly, children's experiences in school may also be affected by their exosystem—by a social integration plan adopted by the school board, or by a factory closing in their community that results in a decline in the school's revenue.

macrosystem
the larger cultural or subcultural context in which development occurs; Bronfenbrenner's outermost environmental layer or context.

The Macrosystem

Bronfenbrenner also stresses that development occurs in a **macrosystem**—that is, a cultural, subcultural, or social class context in which microsystems, mesosystems, and exosystems are imbedded. The macrosystem is really a broad, overarching ideology that dictates (among other things) how children should be treated, what they should be taught, and the goals for which they should strive. These values differ across cultures (and subcultures and social classes) and can greatly influence the kinds of experiences children have in their homes, neighborhoods, schools, and all other contexts that affect them, directly or indirectly. To cite one example, the incidence of child abuse in families (a microsystem experience) is much lower in those cultures (or macrosystems) that discourage physical punishment of children and advocate nonviolent ways of resolving interpersonal conflict (Belsky, 1993; Gilbert, 1997).

chronosystem
in ecological systems theory, changes in the individual or the environment that occur over time and influence the direction development takes.

Finally, Bronfenbrenner's model includes a temporal dimension, or **chronosystem,** which emphasizes that changes *in the child* or in any of the ecological contexts of development can affect the direction that development is likely to take. Cognitive and biological changes that occur at puberty, for example, contribute to increased conflict between young adolescents and their parents (Paikoff & Brooks-Gunn, 1991; Steinberg, 1988). And the effects of environmental changes also depend upon the age of the child. For example, even though a divorce hits hard at youngsters of all ages, adolescents are less likely than younger children to experience the guilty sense that *they* were the cause of the breakup (Hetherington & Clingempeel, 1992).

Contributions and Criticisms of Ecological Systems Theory

The ecological perspective provides a much richer description of environment (and environmental influences) than anything offered by learning theorists. Each of us functions in particular microsystems that are linked by a mesosystem and embedded in the larger contexts of an exosystem and a macrosystem. It makes little sense to an ecological theorist to study environmental influences in laboratory contexts. Instead, they argue that only by observing transactions between developing children and their ever-changing *natural* settings will we understand how individuals influence and are influenced by their environments.

Bronfenbrenner's detailed analysis of environmental influences has suggested many ways in which the development of children and adolescents might be optimized. To illustrate, imagine a working mother who is having a tough time establishing a pleasant relationship with her temperamentally difficult infant. At the level of the microsystem, a successful intervention might be to assist the father to become a more sensitive companion who assumes some of the drudgery of child care and encourages the mother to be more responsive to and patient with their baby (Howes & Markman, 1989). At the level of the exosystem, mothers (and fathers) can often be helped to improve their relationships with their children if their community has parenting classes or groups where parents can express their concerns, enlist others' emotional support, and learn from each other how to elicit more favorable reactions from their children (Lyons-Ruth et al., 1990). And at the level of the macrosystem, a social policy guaranteeing parents the right to take paid or unpaid leave from their jobs to attend to family matters may be an especially important intervention indeed, allowing distressed parents more time to resolve difficulties that arise with their children (Clarke et al., 1997).

Yet, despite its strengths, the ecological systems theory falls far short of being a complete account of human development. It is characterized as a bioecological model, but it really has very little to say about specific biological contributors to development. The emphasis on complex transactions between developing persons and their ever-changing environments is both a strength and a weakness of ecological systems theory (Dixon & Lerner, 1992). Where are the normative patterns of development? Must we formulate different theories for persons from different environments—one for Thai women born in the 1940s, and another for Hispanic Americans born in the 1970s? If unique individuals influence and are influenced by their unique environments, is each life span unique? In sum, ecological systems theory may focus too heavily on ideographic aspects of change to ever provide a coherent normative portrait of human development; for this reason, it qualifies as an important complement to rather than a replacement for other developmental theories.

CONCEPT CHECK 2.3 Cognitive Developmental, Ethological, and Ecological Systems Viewpoints

Check your understanding of the cognitive-developmental viewpoints (Piaget's theory, information-processing perspectives), the ethological or evolutionary viewpoint, and the ecological systems viewpoint by answering the following questions. Answers appear in the Appendix.

Matching: Match the theoretical viewpoint to its description by selecting the theory's title. Choose from the following options:

a. Piaget's cognitive-developmental theory
b. information-processing theory
c. ethology
d. ecological systems theory
e. Vygotsky's sociocultural theory

_____ 1. Theory claiming that children are "prepared" to display adaptive patterns of development, provided that they receive appropriate kinds of environmental inputs at the most appropriate times.

_____ 2. Theory claiming that children actively construct knowledge and which has stimulated discovery-based educational programs.

_____ 3. Theory claiming that the natural environment that influences a developing child is a complex interlocking set of contexts that influence and are influenced by the child.

_____ 4. Theory claiming that the developing human mind is a system that operates on stimulus input to convert it to output—inferences, solutions, etc.

_____ 5. Theory claiming that cognitive growth is socially mediated and that there are no universal cognitive stages.

Fill in the Blank: Complete the following sentences by filling in the blanks with the appropriate word or phrase.

6. Piaget proposed that children use the processes of _____ and _____ to resolve disequilibriums and help them adapt to their environments.

7. The evolutionary perspective argues that certain adaptive characteristics in humans are most likely to develop during _____, provided that the environment fosters this development.

Short Answer: Provide a brief answer to the following questions.

8. List and provide an example of each of Bronfenbrenner's ecological systems theory's interacting contexts or systems.

9. Dr. Helpful has been asked to create a lesson plan for the local elementary school. She bases her lesson plan on the theoretical viewpoint that she adheres to in her research. Her view is that children learn best when they are given challenges to solve through their own trial-and-error and that children should be encouraged to discover solutions to problems rather than just being told the answers in lecture format. Which theoretical position does Dr. Helpful adhere to? What type of lesson plan is she most likely to create?

Essay: Provide a more detailed answer to the following question.

10. After a divorce, children fare much better if their divorced parents can agree on how their children should be raised and support each other's parenting efforts. Which developmental theory seems best suited to explaining this finding and how might it do so?

Special Study Session: Table 2.4 contains a grid describing the philosophical underpinnings of each theory you've learned about in this chapter. To maximize your learning of this material, consider covering up the rows of the table one at a time and reciting the information from the cells. Alternatively, you could photocopy the Table, cut it into individual cells and see if you can reconstruct the Table from memory.

Theories and World Views

Now that we have completed our survey of the major theories of human development, how might we compare them? One way is to group the theories into even grander categories, for each is grounded in a broader set of philosophical assumptions, or *world view.* By examining the fundamental assumptions that underlie different theories, we can perhaps better appreciate just how deeply some of their disagreements run.

Early developmental theories adopted either of two broad world views (Overton, 1984). The **mechanistic model** compares people to machines by viewing them as (1) a collection of parts (behaviors) that can be decomposed, much as machines can be taken apart piece by piece; (2) passive, changing mostly in response to outside influences (much as machines depend on external energy sources to operate); and (3) changing gradually

mechanistic model
view of children as passive entities whose developmental paths are primarily determined by external (environmental) influences.

or continuously as their parts (specific behavior patterns) are added or subtracted. The **organismic model** compares people to other living organisms by viewing them as (1) whole beings who cannot be understood as a simple collection of parts; (2) active in the developmental process, changing under the guidance of internal forces (such as instincts or maturation); and (3) evolving through distinct (discontinuous) stages as they mature.

organismic model
view of children as active entities whose developmental paths are primarily determined by forces from within themselves.

Which theorists have adopted which model? Clearly, learning theorists such as Watson and Skinner favor the mechanistic world view, for they see human beings as passively shaped by environmental events and they analyze human behavior response by response. Bandura's social learning theory is primarily mechanistic, yet it reflects the important organismic assumption that human beings are active creatures who both influence and are influenced by their environments. Psychoanalytic theorists such as Freud and Erikson and cognitive-developmentalists from the Piagetian tradition all base theories primarily on the organismic model: Given some nourishment from their surroundings, people will progress through discontinuous steps or stages, directed largely by forces lying within themselves, much as seeds evolve into blooming plants. Finally, ethologists also portray humans as active, holistic beings with biological predispositions that channel or guide development. However, they are less inclined than other organismic theorists to view the course of development as discontinuous, or stagelike.

contextual model
view of children as active entities whose developmental paths represent a continuous, dynamic interplay between internal forces (nature) and external influences (nurture).

Another broad world view, the **contextual model,** has recently emerged as the perspective that many developmentalists favor (Bornstein & Lamb, 2005; Lerner, 1996). The contextual model views development as the product of a dynamic interplay between person and environment. People are assumed to be active in the developmental process (as in the organismic model) *and* the environment is active as well (as in the mechanistic model). Development may have both universal aspects *and* aspects peculiar to certain cultures, times, or individuals. The potential exists for both qualitative and quantitative change, and development may proceed along many different paths depending on the intricate interplay between internal forces (nature) and external influences (environment).

Although none of the theories we've reviewed provides a pure example of the contextual world view, three come reasonably close: Information-processing theorists describe children and adolescents as active processors of environmental input whose capabilities are heavily influenced by maturation *and* by the kinds of social and cultural experiences they encounter. Although they view development as basically continuous rather than stagelike, many information-processing theorists concede that changes that occur within particular intellectual domains may be uneven, and that qualitative leaps in one's intellectual performances are possible. Vygotsky's sociocultural theory, that we touched on briefly, makes similar assumptions.

Bronfenbrenner's ecological systems theory also adopts a contextual world view. Bronfenbrenner does make the mechanistic assumption that humans are heavily influenced by many environmental contexts, ranging from home settings to the wider society in which they live. Yet, he is clearly aware that children and adolescents are active biological beings who change as they mature, and whose behaviors and biologically influenced attributes influence the very environments that are influencing their development. So development is viewed as the product of a truly dynamic interplay between an active person and an ever-changing active environment, and it is on this basis that the ecological systems approach qualifies as a contextual theory.

Table 2.4 summarizes the philosophical assumptions and "world views" underlying each of the broad theoretical perspectives we have reviewed. As you compare the viewpoints you expressed in Concept Check 2.1 with those of the theorists, see if you can clearly determine your own world views on human nature and the character of human development.

In case you are wondering, we don't expect you to choose one of these theories as a favorite and reject the others. Indeed, because different theories emphasize different aspects of development, one may be more relevant to a particular issue or to a particular age group than another. Today, many developmentalists are theoretical **eclectics:** Individuals who rely on many theories, recognizing that none of the grand theories can explain all aspects of development and that each makes some contribution to our

eclectics
those who borrow from many theories in their attempts to predict and explain human development.

TABLE 2.4 A Summary of the Philosophies Underlying Seven Major Developmental Perspectives

Theory	Active vs. Passive Child	Continuous vs. Discontinuous Development	Nature vs. Nurture	Holistic vs. Modular Development	World view
	Child influences her own development Or *Development is primarily a function of environmental influence*	*Development is primarily a matter of growth and refinement* Or *Development proceeds through a series of qualitatively distinct stages*	*Genetics & biology are the primary determinants of development* Or *Experience is the primary determinant of development*	*Biological, cognitive, and social development all interact* Or *Each aspect of development is considered separately*	*Mechanistic: children passive, development driven by environment* Or *Organismic: children active, development driven by child* Or *Contexual: children active, development a dynamic interplay of nature & nurture*
Psychoanalytic perspective	Active	Discontinuous	Both	Modular	Organismic
Learning perspective	Passive	Continuous	Nurture	Modular	Mechanistic
Piaget's cognitive developmental theory	Active	Discontinuous	Both	Holistic	Organismic
Ethological perspective	Active	Both	Nature	Holistic	Organismic
Information-processing perspective	Active	Continuous	Both	Modular	Contexual
Vygotsky's sociocultural theory	Active	Continuous	Both	Holistic	Contexual
Ecological systems perspective	Both	Both	Nurture	Holistic	Contexual
My Viewpoint (from Concept Check 2-1)					

understanding. For the remainder of this book, we will borrow from many theories to integrate their contributions into a unified, holistic portrait of the developing person. Yet, we will also continue to explore theoretical controversies, which often produce some of the most exciting breakthroughs in the field. So please join us now in examining not just the specific facts about human development, but also the broader theoretical insights that have helped to generate these facts and give them a larger meaning.

SUMMARY

The Nature of Scientific Theories

- A **theory** is a set of concepts and propositions that describe and explain observations. Good theories are:
  - **parsimonious** (concise and yet applicable to a wide range of phenomena)
  - **falsifiable**
  - **heuristic** (they build on existing knowledge by continuing to generate testable hypotheses, leading to new discoveries and important practical applications)

Themes in the Study of Human Development

- Theories of human development differ with respect to their stands on four basic themes:
  - Is development primarily determined by **nature** or **nurture?**
  - Are humans **actively** or **passively** involved in their development?
  - Is development a quantitative and **continuous** process, or a qualitative and **discontinuous** process?
  - Are various areas of development interrelated (and holistic), or basically separate and distinct?

The Psychoanalytic Viewpoint

- The psychoanalytic perspective:
  - Originated with Sigmund Freud's **psychosexual theory,** with basic tenets:
    - People are driven by inborn sexual and aggressive instincts that must be controlled.
    - People's behavior was said to reflect **unconscious motives** that people **repress.**
- Freud proposed five stages of psychosexual development:
  - oral, anal, phallic, latency, and genital
  - During development, three components of personality, the **id, ego,** and **superego,** become integrated.

- Eric Erikson's **psychosocial theory** extended Freud's theory by
  - Concentrating less on the sex instinct
  - Concentrating more on sociocultural determinants of development
  - Arguing that people progress through a series of eight psychosocial conflicts
    - The conflicts begin with "trust versus mistrust" in infancy and conclude with "integrity versus despair" in old age.
    - Each conflict must be resolved in favor of the positive trait (trust, for example) for healthy development.

The Learning Viewpoint

- The learning viewpoint, or **behaviorism,** originated with John B. Watson:
  - Viewed infants as ***tabula rasae*** who develop **habits** from learning experiences
  - Viewed development as a continuous process
  - Viewed the environment as responsible for the direction of individuals' development
- B. F. Skinner proposed **operant learning** theory:
  - Claimed that development reflects the **operant** conditioning of children who are **passively** shaped by the **reinforcers** and **punishments** that accompany their behaviors
- Albert Bandura proposed cognitive social-learning theory:
  - Viewed children as *active* information processors
  - Viewed **observational learning** as the source of children's learning
  - Rejected Watson's **environmental determinism**
  - Proposed **reciprocal** determinism in which children have a hand in creating the environments that influence their development

Cognitive-Developmental Viewpoints

- Jean Piaget pioneered the cognitive-developmental viewpoint:
  - This theory views children as active explorers who construct cognitive **schemes.**
  - The processes of **assimilation** and **accommodation** enable children to resolve **disequilibriums** and adapt to their environments.
  - Piaget described **cognitive development** as an **invariant sequence** of four stages:
    - sensorimotor
    - preoperational
    - concrete-operational
    - formal-operational
  - The child's stage of development determines how she will interpret various events and what she learns from her experiences.
- Lev Vygotsky proposed the **sociocultural theory:**
  - Views cognitive growth as a socially mediated activity
  - Views cognitive growth as heavily influenced by culture
- **Information-processing perspectives** were adapted to explain cognitive development.
  - View the mind as a complex symbol-manipulating system
    - Information flows into the system, is operated on, and is converted to output (answers, inferences, and solutions).
  - View cognitive development as continuous
    - Children and adolescents gradually become better at:
      - attending to information
      - remembering and retrieving information
      - formulating strategies to solve problems

The Ethological (Or Evolutionary) Viewpoint

- The ethological or evolutionary viewpoint:
  - Views humans as born with adaptive attributes that have evolved through **natural selection**
  - Says that adaptive attributes channel development to promote survival
  - Views humans as influenced by their experiences
  - Argues that certain adaptive characteristics are most likely to develop during **sensitive periods,** provided that the environment fosters this development
  - Emphasizes that humans' biologically influenced attributes affect the kind of learning experiences they are likely to have

The Ecological Systems Viewpoint

- Urie Bronfenbrenner proposed the **ecological systems theory:**
  - Views development as the product of transactions between an ever-changing person and an ever-changing environment
  - Bronfenbrenner proposes that the natural environment actually consists of interacting contexts or systems:
    - **microsystem**
    - **mesosystem**
    - **exosystem**
    - **macrosystem**
    - **chronosystem**
  - This detailed analysis of person-environment interactions has stimulated many new interventions to optimize development.

Theories and World Views

- Theories can be grouped according to world views that underlie them.
  - Today developmentalists prefer the **contextual world** view:
    - Accounts for the complexity and diversity of human development
- Older theories fell into other world views:
  - The **mechanistic world view:**
    - Sees humans as machines and the sum of their parts
    - Is preferred by learning theorists
  - The **organismic world view:**
    - Sees humans as entities that are more complex than the sum of their parts
    - Is preferred by stage theorists
- Most contemporary developmentalists are theoretically **eclectic:**
  - They recognize that no single theory offers a totally adequate account of human development.
  - They believe that each theory contributes importantly to our understanding of development.

KEY TERMS

theory 43
parsimonious 43
falsifiable 43
heuristic 43
nature/nurture issue 44
active/passive theme 45
continuity/discontinuity issue 45
quantitative changes 45
qualitative changes 46
developmental stages 46
psychosexual theory 48
unconscious motives 48
repressed 48
instincts 48
id 48
ego 48
superego 49
fixate 49
psychosocial theory 51
behaviorism 53
habits 53
operant 54
reinforcer 54
punisher 54
operant learning 54
observational learning 55
environmental determinism 55
reciprocal determinism 56
cognitive development 58
scheme 60
assimilation 61
disequilibriums 61
accommodate 61
invariant developmental sequence 61
sociocultural theory 63
information-processing perspective 63
ethology 64
natural selection 65
sensitive period 66
altruism 67
empathy 68
ecological systems theory 68
microsystem 69
mesosystem 69
exosystem 70
macrosystem 70
chronosystem 71
mechanistic model 72
organismic model 73
contextual model 73
eclectics 73

MEDIA RESOURCES

The Human Development Book Companion Website

See the companion website http://www.thomsonedu.com/psychology/shaffer for flashcards, practice quiz questions, Internet links, updates, critical thinking exercises, discussion forums, games, and more.

ThomsonNOW! http://www.thomsonedu.com
Go to this site for the link to ThomsonNOW, your one-stop shop. Take a pre-test for this chapter, and ThomsonNOW will generate a personalized study plan based on your test results. The study plan will identify the topics you need to review and direct you to online resources to help you master those topics. You can then take a post-test to help you determine the concepts you have mastered and what you will still need to work on.

Child and Adolescent Development CD-ROM

For more information about the concepts covered in this chapter, go to Module II: Cognition, Language, and Learning

- Cognitive Development

James Porto/Getty Images

CHAPTER

3 Hereditary Influences on Development

Can you remember when you were first introduced to the concept of heredity? Consider the experience of one first-grader at a parent–teacher conference. The teacher asked the boy whether he knew in which country his ancestors had lived before coming to the United States. He proudly proclaimed "The Old West" because he was "half cowboy and half black." The adults had a good laugh and then tried to convince the boy that he couldn't be of African American ancestry because his parents were not, that he could only become what mom and dad already were. Evidently, the limitations of heredity did not go over too well. The boy quickly frowned as he asked, "You mean I can't be a fireman?"

genotype
the genetic endowment that an individual inherits.

phenotype
the ways in which a person's genotype is expressed in observable or measurable characteristics.

This chapter approaches human development from a hereditary perspective, seeking to determine how one's **genotype** (the genes that one inherits) is expressed as a **phenotype** (one's observable or measurable characteristics). We will first explore how hereditary information is transmitted from parents to their children and how the mechanics of heredity make us unique individuals. We will then review the evidence for hereditary contributions to such important psychological attributes as intelligence, personality, mental health, and patterns of behavior. This evidence implies that many of our most noteworthy phenotypic characteristics are influenced by the genes passed to us by our parents. And yet, the biggest lesson from this chapter is that genes, by themselves, determine less than you might imagine. As we will see, most complex human characteristics are the result of a long and involved interplay between the forces of nature (heredity) and nurture (environment) (Anastasi, 1958; Brown, 1999; Plomin et al., 2001).

Principles of Hereditary Transmission

conception
the moment of fertilization, when a sperm penetrates an ovum, forming a zygote.

To understand the workings of heredity, we must start at **conception,** the moment when an ovum released by a woman's ovary and on its way to the uterus via the fallopian tube is fertilized by a man's sperm. Once we establish what is inherited at conception, we can examine the mechanisms by which genes influence the characteristics we display.

The Genetic Material

zygote
a single cell formed at conception from the union of a sperm and an ovum.

chromosome
a threadlike structure made up of genes; in humans there are 46 chromosomes in the nucleus of each body cell.

The very first development that occurs after conception is protective: When a sperm cell penetrates the lining of the ovum, a biochemical reaction repels other sperm, thus preventing them from repeating the fertilization process. Within a few hours, the sperm cell begins to disintegrate, releasing its genetic material. The ovum also releases its genetic material, and a new cell nucleus forms around the hereditary information provided by the father's sperm and the mother's ovum. This new cell, called a **zygote,** is only 1/20th the size of the head of a pin. Yet this tiny cell contains the biochemical material for the zygote's development from a single cell into a recognizable human being.

What hereditary material is present in a human zygote? The new cell nucleus contains 46 elongated, threadlike bodies called **chromosomes,** each of which consists of

genes
hereditary blueprints for development that are transmitted unchanged from generation to generation.

deoxyribonucleic acid (DNA)
long, double-stranded molecules that make up chromosomes.

mitosis
the process in which a cell duplicates its chromosomes and then divides into two genetically identical daughter cells.

thousands of chemical segments, or **genes**—the basic units of heredity that work to build a single protein (Brown, 1999). With one exception that we will soon discuss, chromosomes come in matching pairs. Each member of a pair corresponds to the other in size, shape, and the hereditary functions it serves. One member of each chromosome pair comes from the mother's ovum and the other from the father's sperm cell. Thus, each parent contributes 23 chromosomes to each of their children.

The genes on each chromosome also function as pairs, the two members of each gene pair being located at the same sites on their corresponding chromosomes. Genes are actually stretches of **deoxyribonucleic acid,** or **DNA,** a complex, "double helix" molecule that resembles a twisted ladder and provides the chemical basis for development. A unique feature of DNA is that it can duplicate itself. The rungs of this ladder-like molecule split in the middle, opening somewhat like a zipper. Then each remaining half of the molecule guides the replication of its missing parts. This special ability of DNA to replicate itself is what makes it possible for a one-celled zygote to develop into a marvelously complex human being.

Growth of the Zygote and Production of Body Cells

As the zygote moves through the fallopian tube toward its prenatal home in the uterus, it begins to replicate itself through the process of **mitosis.** At first, the zygote divides into two cells, but the two soon become four, four become eight, eight become sixteen, and so on. Just before each division, the cell duplicates its 46 chromosomes, and these duplicate sets move in opposite directions. The division of the cell then proceeds, resulting in two new cells, each of which has the identical 23 pairs of chromosomes (46 in all) and thus the same genetic material as the original cell. This remarkable process is illustrated in Figure 3.1.

By the time a child is born, he or she consists of billions of cells, created through mitosis, that make up muscles, bones, organs, and other bodily structures. Mitosis continues throughout life, generating new cells that enable growth and replacing old ones that are damaged. With each division, the chromosomes are duplicated, so that every new cell contains an exact copy of the 46 chromosomes we inherited at conception.

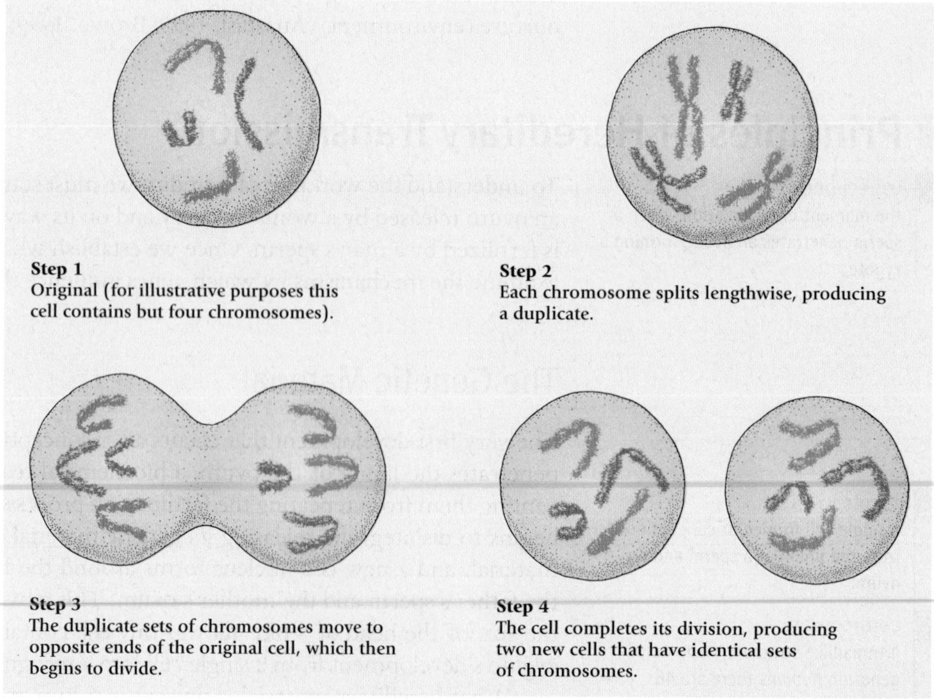

Step 1
Original (for illustrative purposes this cell contains but four chromosomes).
Step 2
Each chromosome splits lengthwise, producing a duplicate.
Step 3
The duplicate sets of chromosomes move to opposite ends of the original cell, which then begins to divide.
Step 4
The cell completes its division, producing two new cells that have identical sets of chromosomes.

Figure 3.1 Mitosis: the way that cells replicate themselves.

The Germ (or Sex) Cells

In addition to body cells, human beings have *germ* cells that serve one special hereditary function—to produce *gametes* (sperm in males and ova in females). This is a different type of cell reproduction than the process of mitosis. The process shares some of the characteristics of mitosis, but it differs in ways that make the resulting cells able to join with gametes to create a unique cell that will become a unique individual. Only the germ cells reproduce in this way. Let's explore this process in more detail.

Production of Gametes through Meiosis

meiosis
the process in which a germ cell divides, producing gametes (sperm or ova) that each contain half of the parent cell's original complement of chromosomes; in humans, the products of meiosis contain 23 chromosomes.

crossing-over
a process in which genetic material is exchanged between pairs of chromosomes during meiosis.

Male germ cells in the testes and female germ cells in the ovaries produce sperm and ova through a process called **meiosis** that is illustrated in Figure 3.2. The germ cell first duplicates its 46 chromosomes. Then an event called **crossing-over** often takes place: Adjacent duplicated chromosomes cross and break at one or more points along their length, exchanging segments of genetic material. This transfer of genes during crossing-over creates new and unique hereditary combinations. (For a more detailed look at crossing-over, see the Box on p. 82.) Next, pairs of duplicated chromosomes (some of which have been altered by crossing-over) segregate into two new cells that each contains 46 chromosomes. Finally, the new cells divide so that each of the resulting gametes contains 23 single, or *unpaired,* chromosomes. At conception, then, a sperm with 23 chromosomes unites with an ovum with 23 chromosomes, producing a zygote with a full set of 46 chromosomes.

Brothers and sisters who have the same mother and father have inherited 23 chromosomes from each of these parents. Why is it, then, that offspring of the same parents sometimes barely resemble each other? The reason is that meiosis makes us genetically unique.

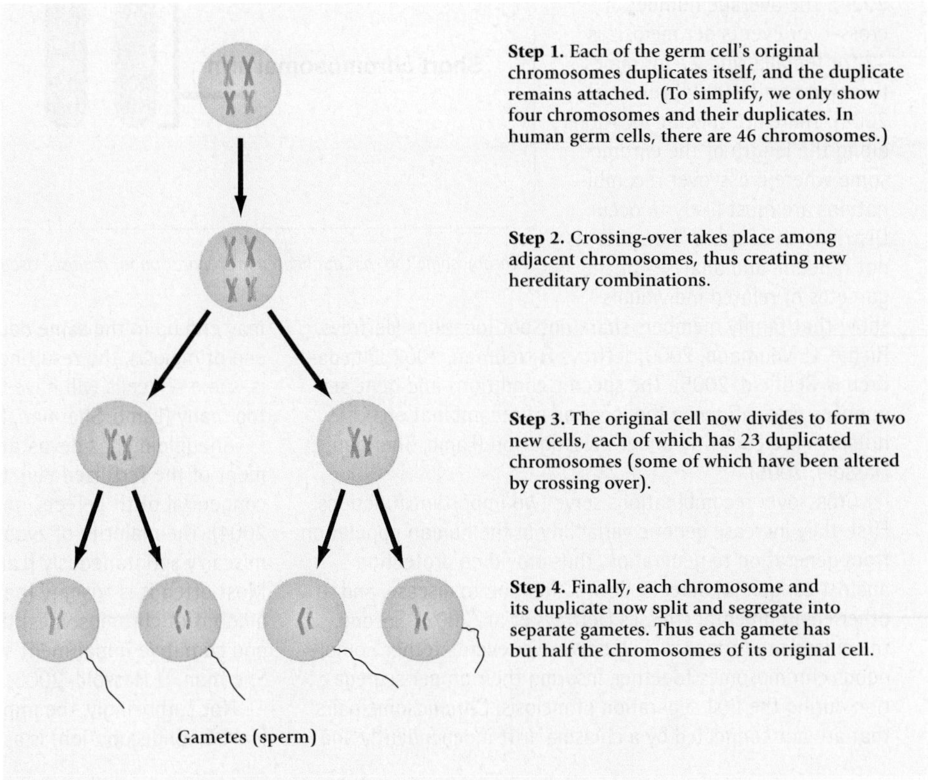

Step 1. Each of the germ cell's original chromosomes duplicates itself, and the duplicate remains attached. (To simplify, we only show four chromosomes and their duplicates. In human germ cells, there are 46 chromosomes.)
Step 2. Crossing-over takes place among adjacent chromosomes, thus creating new hereditary combinations.
Step 3. The original cell now divides to form two new cells, each of which has 23 duplicated chromosomes (some of which have been altered by crossing over).
Step 4. Finally, each chromosome and its duplicate now split and segregate into separate gametes. Thus each gamete has but half the chromosomes of its original cell.
Gametes (sperm)

Figure 3.2 Diagram of the meiosis of a male germ cell.

FOCUS ON RESEARCH: Crossing-Over and Chromosome Segregation During Meiosis

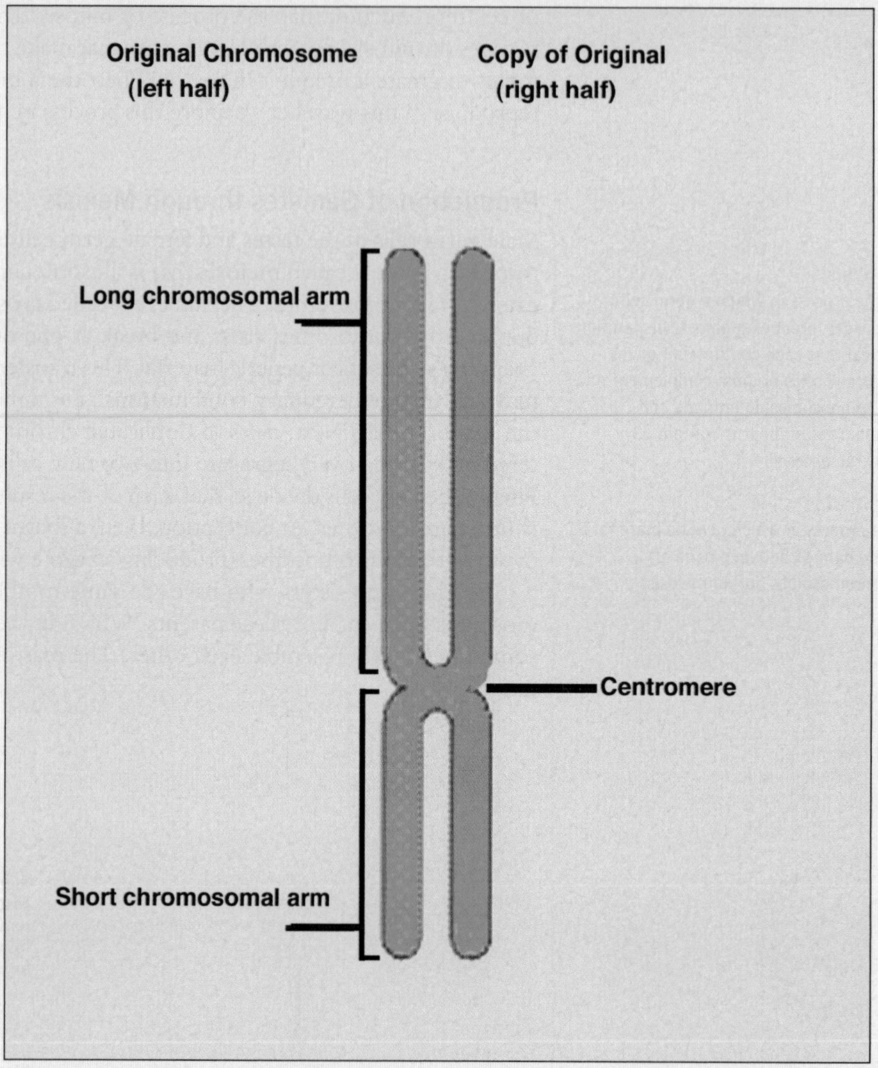

A chromosome that has duplicated in preparation for meiosis. Used by permission of Julia Cline.

During meiosis, chromosomes duplicate. The original strand and its duplicate are held together by a structure called the centromere. Each chromosome has both a short and long arm extending from the centromere, giving them the X-shaped configuration that you may recognize in the figure at the right. After duplication, homologous chromosomes come together in pairs; that is, grand-maternal and grand-paternal chromosomes that contain similar genes line up beside one another (right). At this point during meiosis the arms of grand-maternal and grand-paternal chromosomes swap genetic material, causing cross-over recombinations to occur (Lamb et al., 2005; Lynn et al., 2004). The cross-over site is called a chiasma, which is simply a Greek word for a cross-shaped mark.

Cross-over events occur quite frequently during meiosis (Broman et al., 1998; Jeffreys, Richie, & Neumann, 2000; Lynn et al., 2004). The average number of cross-over events per meiosis is 42 for females and 27 for males (Broman et al., 1998; Lynn et al., 2004). There are specific locations along the length of the chromosome where cross-over recombinations are most likely to occur. Distribution of these "hotspots" is not random, and analyses of the gametes of related individuals show that family members share hotspot locations (Jeffreys, Richie, & Neumann, 2000; Jeffreys & Neuman, 2002; Pineda-Krch & Redfield, 2005). The specific conditions and gene sequences that influence the location of recombination hotspots are currently under investigation (Lamb, Sherman, & Hassold, 2005).

Cross-over recombinations serve two important functions. First, they increase genetic variability in the human population from generation to generation, thus providing protection against congenital defects, decimation due to disease, and other environmental stresses (Jeffreys et al., 2002). Second, the chiasmata formed during cross-over events tether homologous chromosomes together, insuring their proper segregation during the first separation of meiosis. Chromosome pairs that are not connected by a chiasma drift independently and may end up in the same daughter cell. Consequently, at the end of meiosis, the resulting gametes will be aneuploid: that is, some sex cells will have too few chromosomes and some too many (Lamb, Sherman, & Hassold, 2005; Lynn et al., 2004).

Aneuploidy has devastating consequences for the development of the fertilized egg. It can cause spontaneous abortion, congenital birth defects, and mental retardation (Lynn et al., 2004). The majority of zygotes having too few chromosomes miscarry spontaneously (Lamb, Sherman, & Hassold, 2005). Most often it is trisomy (having more than the necessary amount of chromosomes) that leads to congenital defects and cognitive impairment such as Down syndrome (Lamb, Sherman, & Hassold, 2005; Lynn et al., 2004).

Not surprisingly, the improper separation of chromosomes (called nondisjunction) is associated with low frequencies of

CONTINUED

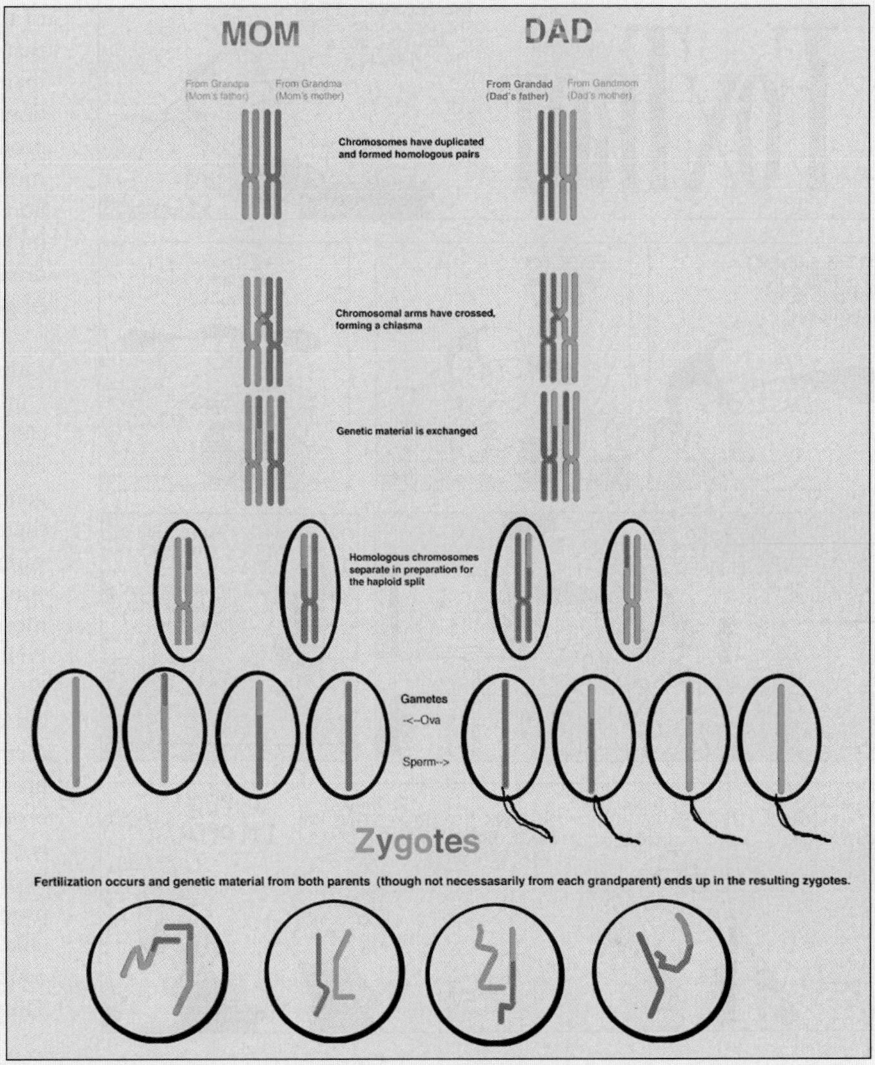

Recombination via cross-over between homologous grandparent genes during meiosis and four of the 16 possible zygote combinations. Used by permission of Julia Cline.

cross-over (Lamb, Sherman, & Hassold, 2005; Lamb et al., 2005; Lynn et al., 2004). Decreasing cross-over frequencies are, in turn, associated with increasing maternal age (Lamb et al., 2005). The rate of trisomic pregnancies in women 25 years old and younger is about 2 percent, whereas the rate for women over the age of 40 is nearly 35 percent (Lamb, Sherman, & Hassold, 2005). For some chromosomes, nondisjunction may also occur when chiasma form too close or too far away from the centromere (Lamb, Sherman, & Hassold, 2005). Lamb and colleagues (2005) investigated the location of nondisjunctions associated with pregnancies that were trisomic at chromosome 21, the trisomy associated with Down syndrome. Their results revealed that women under the age of 29 produced trisomic offspring with nondisjunction occurring only very near to or very far from the centromere, whereas nondisjunctions among women 29 and older were distributed along the length of the chromosomal arm (Lamb et al., 2005). The gametes of the younger women were vulnerable to improper separation at sites that are universally vulnerable due to their location on chromosome 21. The older women were susceptible at those sites as well as many others. Lamb and colleagues (2005, p. 96) characterize the results of the study as they pertain to older women: "As a woman ages, her meiotic machinery accumulates the effects of years of environmental and age-related insults, becoming less efficient and more error-prone."

Other cross-over mistakes include the misalignment of paternal and maternal chromosomes (causing nonhomologous material to be exchanged) as well as exchanges between the arm of a chromosome and that of its duplicate (Lynn et al., 2005). Fortunately, cellular mechanisms have evolved that promote crossover between homologues and depress cross-over between chromosomes and their duplicates (Lynn et al., 2004). Direct observations of meiosis in progress as well as indirect analyses of genotype data in families continue to reveal the mechanisms and mishaps that induce variety into the combinations of genes transferred from generation to generation (Lynn et al., 2004).

Hereditary Uniqueness

independent assortment
the principle stating that each pair of chromosomes segregates independently of all other chromosome pairs during meiosis.

When a pair of chromosomes segregates during meiosis, it is a matter of chance which of the two chromosomes will end up in a particular new cell. And because each chromosome pair segregates independently of all other pairs according to the principle of **independent assortment,** there are many different combinations of chromosomes that could result from the meiosis of a single germ cell. Because human germ cells contain 23 chromosome pairs,

each of which is segregating independently of the others, the laws of probability tell us that each parent can produce 2^{23}—more than 8 million—different genetic combinations in their sperm or ova. If a father can produce 8 million combinations of 23 chromosomes and a mother can produce 8 million, any couple could theoretically have 64 *trillion* babies without producing two children who inherited precisely the same set of genes!

In fact, the odds of exact genetic replication in two siblings are even smaller than 1 in 64 trillion. Why? Because the *crossing-over* process, which occurs during the earlier phases of meiosis, actually alters the genetic composition of chromosomes and thereby increases the number of possible variations in an individual's gametes far beyond the 8 million that could occur if chromosomes segregated cleanly, without exchanging genetic information.

Of course, brothers and sisters resemble one another to some extent because their genes are drawn from a gene pool provided by the same two parents. Each brother or sister inherits half of each parent's genes, although two siblings never inherit the same half, owing to the random process by which parental chromosomes (and genes) segregate into the sperm and ovum that combine to produce each child. Thus, each individual is genetically unique.

Multiple Births

monozygotic (identical) twins twins who develop from a single zygote that later divides to form two genetically identical individuals.

dizygotic (fraternal) twins twins that result when a mother releases two ova at roughly the same time and each is fertilized by a different sperm, producing two zygotes that are genetically different.

There is one circumstance under which two people will share a genotype. Occasionally, a zygote will split into separate but identical cells, which then become two individuals. These are called **monozygotic** (or **identical**) **twins** because they have developed from a *single* zygote and have *identical* genes. Identical twins occur in about 1 of every 250 births around the world (Plomin, 1990). Because they are genetically identical, monozygotic twins should show very similar developmental progress if genes have much effect on human development.

More common, occurring in approximately 1 of every 125 births, are **dizygotic** (or **fraternal**) **twins**—pairs that result when a mother releases *two* ova at the same time and each is fertilized by a *different* sperm (Brockington, 1996). Even though fraternal twins are born together, they have no more genes in common than any other pair of siblings. As illustrated in Figure 3.3, fraternal twins often differ considerably in appearance and may not even be the same sex.

Male or Female?

A hereditary basis for sex differences becomes quite clear if we examine the chromosomes of normal men and women. These chromosomal portraits, or *karyotypes,* reveal

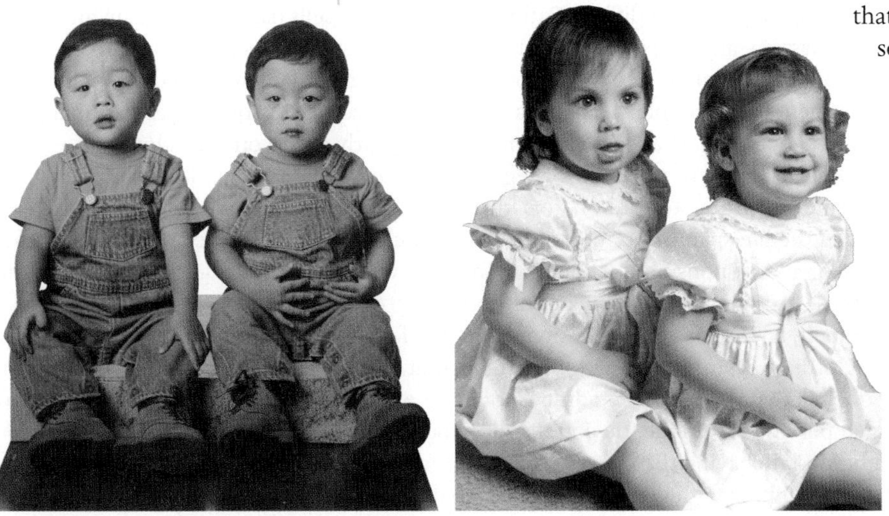

Barbara Penoyar/Getty Images

Katherine Kipp

Figure 3.3 Identical, or monozygotic, twins (left) develop from a single zygote. Because they have inherited identical sets of genes, they look alike, are the same sex, and share all other inherited characteristics. Fraternal, or dizygotic, twins (right) develop from separate zygotes and have no more genes in common than siblings born at different times. Consequently, they may not look alike (as we see in this photo) and may not even be the same sex.

that 22 of the 23 pairs of human chromosomes (called *autosomes*) are similar in males and females. Sex is determined by the 23rd pair (called the *sex chromosomes*). In males, the 23rd pair consists of one elongated body known as an **X chromosome** and a short, stubby companion called a **Y chromosome.** In females, both these sex chromosomes are X chromosomes (see Figure 3.4).

Throughout history, mothers have often been belittled, tortured, divorced, and even beheaded for failing to bear their husbands a male heir! This is both a social and a biological injustice in that *fathers* determine the sex of their children. When the sex chromosomes of a genetic (XY) male segregate into gametes during meiosis, half of the sperm produced will contain an X chromosome and half will contain a Y chromosome. On the other hand, the ova produced by a genetic (XX) female all carry an X chromosome. So a child's sex is determined by whether an X-bearing or a Y-bearing *sperm* fertilizes the ovum.

So far, so good: We have a genetically unique boy or girl who has inherited thousands of genes on his or her 46 chromosomes (Lemonick, 2001). Now an important question: How do genes influence development and a person's phenotypic characteristics?

What Do Genes Do?

How do genes promote development? At the most basic, biochemical level, they call for the production of amino acids, which form enzymes and other proteins that are necessary for the formation and functioning of new cells (Mehlman & Botkin, 1998). Genes, for example, regulate the production of a pigment called melanin in the iris of the eye. People with brown eyes have genes that call for much of this pigment, whereas people with lighter (blue or green) eyes have genes that call for less pigmentation.

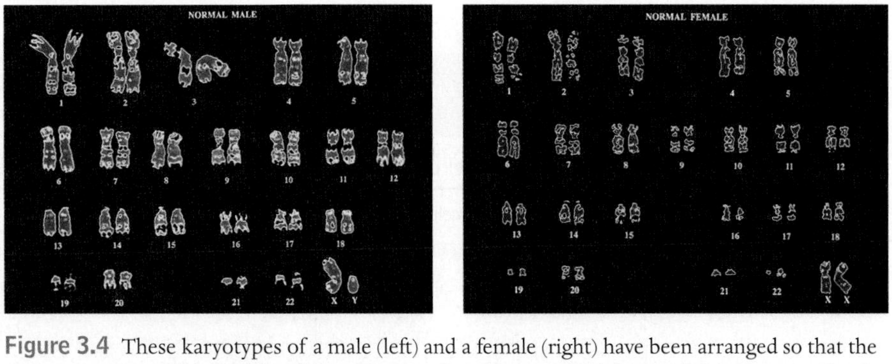

Biphoto Associates/Science Source/Photo Researchers Inc.

Figure 3.4 These karyotypes of a male (left) and a female (right) have been arranged so that the chromosomes could be displayed in pairs. Note that the twenty-third pair of chromosomes for the male consists of one elongated X chromosome and a Y chromosome that is noticeably smaller, whereas the twenty-third pair for the female consists of two X chromosomes.

X chromosome
the longer of the two sex chromosomes; normal females have two X chromosomes, whereas normal males have but one.

Y chromosome
the shorter of the two sex chromosomes; normal males have one Y chromosome, whereas females have none.

Genes also guide cell differentiation, making some cells parts of the brain and central nervous system, and others parts of the circulatory system, bones, skin, and so on. Genes influence and are influenced by the biochemical environment surrounding them during development. For example, a particular cell might become part of an eyeball or part of an elbow depending on what cells surround it during early embryonic development.

Some genes are responsible for regulating the pace and timing of development. That is, specific genes are "turned on" or "turned off" by other regulatory genes at different points in the life span (Plomin et al., 2001). Regulatory genes, for example, might "turn on" the genes responsible for the growth spurt we experience as adolescents, and then shut these growth genes down in adulthood.

Finally, an important point: Environmental factors clearly influence how genes function (Gottlieb, 1996). Consider, for example, that a child who inherits genes for tall stature may or may not be tall as an adult. Should he experience very poor nutrition for a prolonged period early in life, he could end up being only average or even below average in height, despite having the genetic potential for exceptional stature. So environmental influences combine with genetic influences to determine how a genotype is translated into a particular phenotype—the way one looks, feels, thinks, and behaves.

Environment affects the actions of genes at several different levels. For example, the nucleus contains the chromosomes and genes. The environment within this nucleus may affect the expression of genetic material. The internal environment that surrounds the cell may affect the gene's expression. Finally, the external environment affects the expression of the genetic material, as we illustrated previously with the nutrition and stature example.

In addition, some of the effects of the external environment are experienced by all humans, and some are experienced by only some people. The former are called "experience-expectant interactions," and the latter are called "experience-dependent interactions" (Greenough, Black, & Wallace, 2002; Johnson, 2005; Pennington, 2001). These various levels of gene-environment interactions are summarized in Table 3.1. The most important point to take away from this discussion is the realization that genes do *not* simply "code" for human characteristics, but that they interact with the environment at many levels to produce proteins that eventually influence human characteristics.

Another way to approach the riddle of how genes influence development is to consider the major patterns of genetic inheritance: the ways in which parents' genes are expressed in their children's phenotypes.

How Are Genes Expressed?

There are four main patterns of genetic expression: simple dominant-recessive inheritance, codominance, sex-linked inheritance, and polygenic (or multiple gene) inheritance.

TABLE 3.1 Different Levels of Gene-Environment Interaction That Influence Genetic Expression

Level of Environment	Type of Gene-Environment Interaction
Intracellular (surrounding the nucleous)	Molecular
Extracellular (surrounding the cell)	Cellular
External environment (outside the body)	Organism-environment
	Experience-expectant
	Experience-dependent

Source: Adapted from Johnson, 2005.

Single-Gene Inheritance Patterns

Genes influence human characteristics in different ways. Sometimes human characteristics are determined by the actions of a single gene. Sometimes the characteristics are determined by the actions of many genes working together: this is known as polygenic inheritance. Understanding single-gene inheritance patterns can help us build an understanding of the actions of genes and their interactions with the environment. From there we can then turn to understanding the mechanisms at work when many genes interact to influence characteristics. Thus, our first task is to examine patterns of single-gene inheritance.

alleles
alternative forms of a gene that can appear at a particular site on a chromosome.

simple dominant-recessive inheritance
a pattern of inheritance in which one allele dominates another so that only its phenotype is expressed.

dominant allele
a relatively powerful gene that is expressed phenotypically and masks the effect of a less powerful gene.

recessive allele
a less powerful gene that is not expressed phenotypically when paired with a dominant allele.

homozygous
having inherited two alleles for an attribute that are identical in their effects.

heterozygous
having inherited two alleles for an attribute that have different effects.

carrier
a heterozygous individual who displays no sign of a recessive allele in his or her own phenotype but can pass this gene to offspring.

Simple Dominant-Recessive Inheritance. Many human characteristics are influenced by only one pair of genes (called **alleles**): one from the mother, one from the father. Although he knew nothing of genes, a 19th-century monk named Gregor Mendel contributed greatly to our knowledge of single gene-pair inheritance by cross-breeding different strains of peas and observing the outcomes. His major discovery was a predictable pattern to the way in which two alternative characteristics (for example, smooth seeds vs. wrinkled seeds, green pods vs. yellow pods) appeared in the offspring of cross-breedings. He called some characteristics (for example, smooth seeds) "dominant" because they appeared more often in later generations than their opposite traits, which he called "recessive" traits. Among peas and among humans, an offspring's phenotype often is not simply a "blend" of the characteristics of mother and father. Instead, one of the parental genes often dominates the other, and the child resembles the parent who contributed the dominant gene. To illustrate the principles of **simple dominant-recessive inheritance,** consider the fact that about three-fourths of us have the ability to see distant objects clearly (that is, normal vision), whereas the remaining one-fourth of us cannot and are myopic (nearsighted). The gene associated with normal vision is a **dominant allele.** A weaker gene calling for nearsightedness is a **recessive allele.** So a person who inherits one allele for normal vision and one allele for myopia would display a phenotype of normal vision because the normal-vision gene overpowers (that is, dominates) the nearsightedness gene.

Because a normal-vision allele dominates a nearsightedness allele, we represent the normal-vision gene with a capital *N* and the nearsightedness gene with a lower-case *n*. Perhaps you can see that there are three possible genotypes for this visual characteristic: (1) two normal-vision alleles (NN), (2) two nearsightedness alleles (nn), and (3) one of each (Nn). People whose genotype for an attribute consists of two alleles of the same kind are said to be **homozygous** for that attribute. Thus, an *NN* individual is homozygous for normal-vision and will pass only genes for normal vision to his or her children. An *nn* individual is homozygous nearsighted (the only way one can actually be nearsighted is to inherit two of these recessive alleles) and will pass nearsightedness genes to his or her children. Finally, an *Nn* individual is said to be **heterozygous** for this visual trait because he or she has inherited alternative forms of the allele. This person will have normal vision, because the N allele is dominant. And what kind of allele will the heterozygous person pass along to children? Either a normal-vision gene or a nearsightedness gene! Even though a heterozygous person has normal vision, exactly half the gametes produced by this individual will carry a gene for normal vision, and half will carry a gene for nearsightedness.

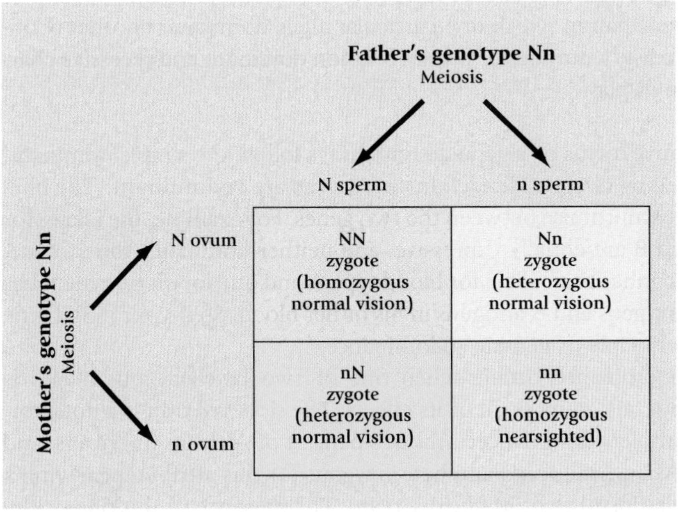

Figure 3.5 Possible genotypes (and phenotypes) resulting from a mating of two heterozygotes for normal vision.

Can two individuals with normal vision ever produce a nearsighted child? The answer is yes—if each parent is heterozygous for normal vision and is a **carrier** of the recessive allele for nearsightedness. In Figure 3.5, the genotype of a *carrier father* appears at the head of

APPLYING RESEARCH TO YOUR LIFE

Examples of Dominant and Recessive Traits in Human Heredity

Our discussion of dominant and recessive genes has centered on two particular alleles, a gene for normal vision and a gene for nearsightedness. Listed here are a number of other dominant and recessive characteristics in human heredity (Connor, 1995; McKusick, 1995).

A quick glance through the list reveals that most of the undesirable or maladaptive attributes are recessive. For this we can be thankful. Otherwise genetically linked diseases and defects might become widespread and eventually destroy the species.

One important genetic disease produced by a *dominant* gene is **Huntington's disease**, a condition that causes a gradual deterioration of the nervous system, leading to a progressive decline in physical and mental abilities and ultimately to death. Although some victims of Huntington's disease die in young adulthood, the disease normally appears much later, usually after 40. Fortunately, the dominant allele that is responsible for this lethal condition is very rare.

Dominant Traits	Recessive Traits
Dark hair	Blond hair
Full head of hair	Pattern baldness
Curly hair	Straight hair
Facial dimples	No dimples
Farsightedness	Normal vision
Normal vision	Color blindness*
Extra digits	Five digits
Pigmented skin	Albinism
Type A blood	Type O blood
Type B blood	Type O blood
Normal blood clotting	Hemophilia*
Huntington's disease*	Normal physiology
Normal blood cells	Sickle-cell anemia*
Normal physiology	Cystic fibrosis*
Normal physiology	Phenylketonuria*
Normal physiology	Tay-Sachs disease*

*These conditions are discussed elsewhere in the chapter.

Huntington's disease
a genetic disease, caused by a dominant allele, that typically appears later in life and causes the nervous system to degenerate.

codominance
condition in which two heterozygous but equally powerful alleles produce a phenotype in which both genes are fully and equally expressed.

the columns, and that of a *carrier mother* appears at the left of the rows. What kind of vision will their children have? The various possibilities appear in the four quadrants of the chart. If a sperm bearing a normal-vision (N) allele unites with an ovum carrying a normal-vision (N) allele, the result is an NN, or a child that is homozygous for normal-vision. If a sperm bearing an N gene fertilizes an ovum carrying an n gene, or if an n sperm fertilizes an N ovum, the result is a heterozygous child with normal vision. Finally, if both sperm and ovum carry an n gene, the child will be nearsighted. Because each of these four combinations is equally likely in any given mating, the odds are 1 in 4 that a child of two Nn parents will be nearsighted. This graphic representation of parents' alleles and their possible combinations to form unique inheritable traits is called a *Punnett Square.*

The normal vision/nearsightedness trait is one of thousands of human attributes determined by a single gene pair in which one particular allele dominates another (Connor, 1995). The Box above lists a number of other common dominant and recessive characteristics that people can display.

Science Source/Photo Researchers Inc.

Figure 3.6 Normal (round) and "sickled" (elongated) red blood cells from a person with sickle cell anemia.

Codominance. Alternative forms of a gene do not always follow the simple dominant-recessive pattern described by Gregor Mendel. Instead, some are **codominant:** The phenotype they produce is a compromise between the two genes. For example, the alleles for human blood types A and B are equally expressive, and neither dominates the other. A heterozygous person who inherits an allele for blood type A and one for blood type B has equal proportions of A-antigens and B-antigens in his or her blood. So if your blood type is AB, you illustrate this principle of genetic codominance.

Another type of codominance occurs when one of two heterozygous alleles is stronger than the other but fails to mask all of its effects. The *sickle cell* trait is a noteworthy example of this "incomplete dominance." About 8 percent of African Americans (and relatively few whites or Asian Americans) are heterozygous for this attribute, carrying a recessive "sickle cell" allele (Institute of Medicine, 1999). The presence of this one sickle-cell gene causes some of the person's red blood cells to assume an unusual crescent, or sickle, shape (see Figure 3.6). Sickled cells can be a problem because they tend to cluster together, distributing less oxygen throughout the circulatory system. Yet overt symptoms of circulatory distress, such as painful swelling of the joints and fatigue, are rarely experienced by these sickle-cell "carriers," unless they experience oxygen deprivation as they might after physical exertion at high altitudes or while under anesthesia (Strachan & Read, 1996).

The consequences are much more severe for those individuals who inherit *two* recessive sickle-cell genes. They will develop a severe blood disorder, called **sickle-cell anemia,** that causes massive sickling of red blood cells and inefficient distribution of oxygen at all times. Many who suffer from this painful disease die from heart or kidney failure or respiratory diseases during childhood (Institute of Medicine, 1999).

sickle-cell anemia
a genetic blood disease that causes red blood cells to assume an unusual sickled shape and to become inefficient at distributing oxygen.

sex-linked characteristic
an attribute determined by a recessive gene that appears on the X chromosome; more likely to characterize males.

polygenic trait
a characteristic that is influenced by the action of many genes rather than a single pair.

Sex-Linked Inheritance. Some traits are called **sex-linked characteristics** because they are determined by genes located on the sex chromosomes. In fact, the vast majority of these sex-linked attributes are produced by recessive genes that are found only on X chromosomes. Who do you suppose is more likely to inherit these recessive X-linked traits, males or females?

The answer is males, a point we can easily illustrate with a common sex-linked characteristic, red/green color blindness. Many people cannot distinguish red from green, an inability caused by a recessive gene that appears only on X chromosomes. Now recall that a normal (XY) male has but one X chromosome—the one he inherited from his mother. If this X chromosome carries a recessive gene for color blindness, the male will be color-blind. Why? Because there is no corresponding gene on his Y chromosome that might counteract the effect of this "color blind" allele. A genetic female who inherits but one gene for color blindness will not be color-blind, for the color-normal gene on her second X chromosome will dominate the color-blindness gene, enabling her to distinguish red from green (see Figure 3.7). So, a female cannot be color-blind unless *both* of her X chromosomes contain a recessive gene for color blindness.

Immediately, we have reason to suspect that more males than females will be color-blind. Indeed, roughly 8 white males in 100 cannot distinguish red from green, whereas only 1 in 144 white females are red/green color-blind (Burns & Bottino, 1989).

There are more than 100 sex-linked characteristics other than color blindness, and many of them are disabling (Plomin et al., 2001). These include hemophilia (a disease in which the blood does not clot), two kinds of muscular dystrophy, degeneration of the optic nerve, and certain forms of deafness and night blindness. Because these disorders are determined by recessive genes on X chromosomes, males are much more likely than females to suffer their harmful effects.

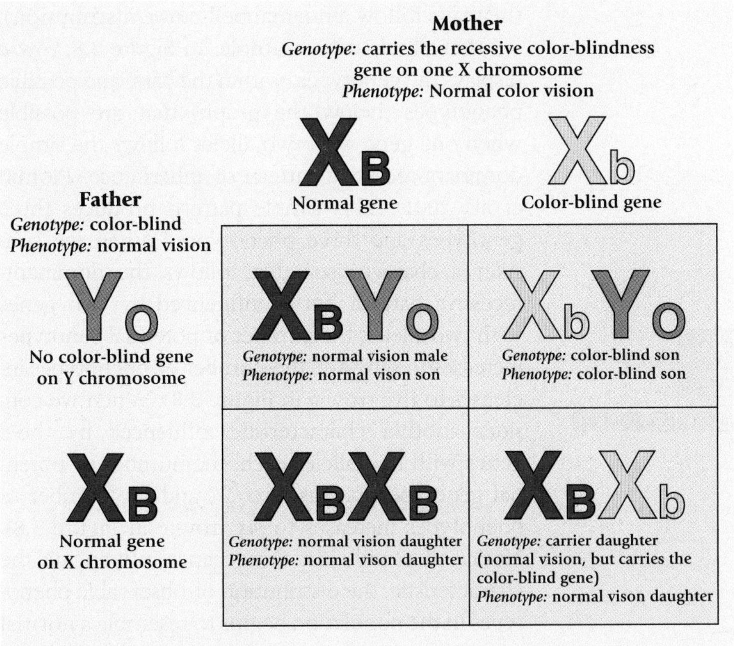

Figure 3.7 Sex-linked inheritance of red/green color blindness. In the example here, the mother can distinguish reds from greens but is a carrier because one of her X chromosomes contains a color-blind allele. Notice that her sons have a 50 percent chance of inheriting the color-blind allele and being color-blind, whereas none of her daughters would display the trait. A girl can be color-blind only if her father is color-blind and her mother is at least a carrier of the color-blindness gene.

Polygenic Inheritance

To this point, we have considered only those traits that are influenced by a single pair of alleles. However, most important human characteristics are influenced by many pairs of alleles and are called **polygenic traits.** Examples of polygenic traits include height, weight, intelligence, skin color, temperamental attributes, susceptibility to cancer, and a host of others (Plomin et al., 2001). As the number of genes that contribute to a particular characteristic increases, the number of possible genotypes and phenotypes quickly increases. As a result, the observ-

CONCEPT CHECK 3.1 Understanding Principles of Hereditary Transmission

Check your understanding of the principles of hereditary transmission by answering the following questions. Answers appear in the Appendix.

Multiple Choice: Select the best answer for each question.

_____ 1. The genes a person inherits are called his _______; the observable characteristics a person inherits are called his _______.
a. gene; chromosome
b. chromosome; gene
c. phenotype; genotype
d. genotype; phenotype

_____ 2. DNA is to gene as
a. gene is to chromosome
b. meiosis is to mitosis
c. crossing-over is to independent assortment
d. germ cell is to gamete

_____ 3. Which of the following is *not* a process that contributes to each gamete receiving a unique set of chromosomes?
a. meiosis
b. mitosis
c. crossing-over
d. independent assortment

_____ 4. Each human cell contains 22 pairs of _______ and 1 pair of _______.
a. genes; alleles
b. alleles; genes
c. autosomes; sex chromosomes
d. sex chromosomes; autosomes

_____ 5. *Dizygotic* twins result from
a. the fertilization of two different ova by two different sperm

CONTINUED

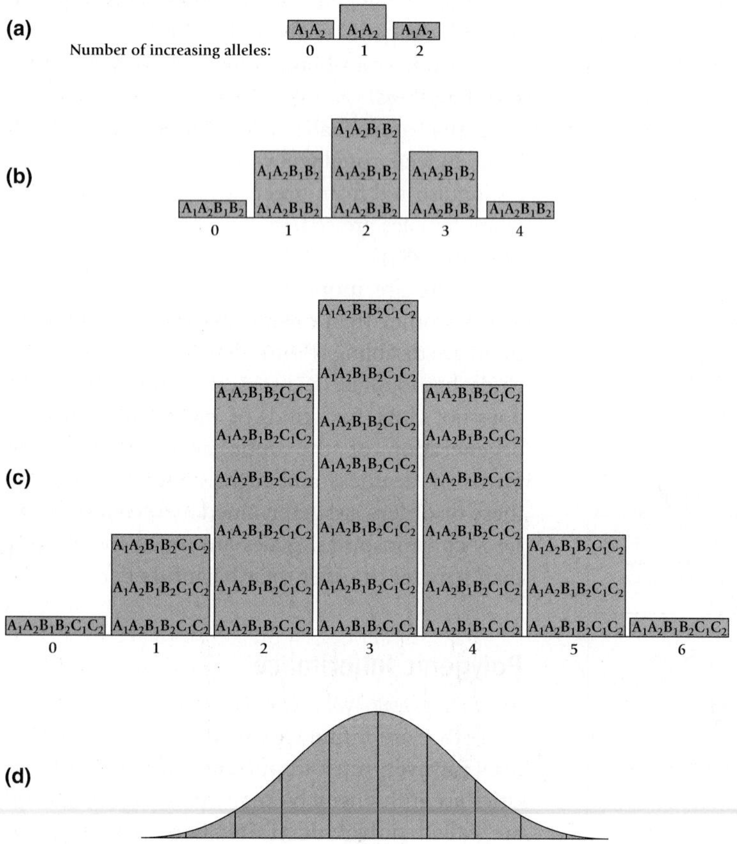

Figure 3.8 Single-gene and multiple-gene distributions for traits with additive gene effects: (a) A single gene with two alleles yields three genotypes and three phenotypes. (b) Two genes, each with two alleles, yield nine genotypes and five phenotypes. (c) Three genes, each with two alleles, yield twenty-seven genotypes and seven phenotypes. (d) Normal bell-shaped curve of continuous variation. *From R. Plomin, J.C. DeFries, G.E. McClearn, and P. McGuffink,* Behavioral Genetics, *4th ed. Copyright © 1980, 1990, 1997, 2001 by Worth Publishers/W. H. Freeman and Company. Reprinted by permission.*

able traits for polygenic traits are not either/or possibilities (such as the eye color and red/green color-blindness examples we discussed previously). Instead, the observable traits follow a pattern of continuous variation with few people having the traits at the extremes, and most people having the traits in the middle of the distribution (that is, the traits follow a normal bell-curve distribution).

Let's look at an example. In Figure 3.8, row *a* displays the genotypes (within the bars) and possible phenotypes (below the graph) that are possible when one gene with two alleles follows the simple dominant-recessive pattern of inheritance (Plomin et al., 2001). This simple pattern produces three genotypes and three phenotypes. When we consider a characteristic that follows the dominant-recessive pattern but is influenced by two genes with two alleles, the number of potential genotypes increases to nine and the number of phenotypes increases to five (row *b* in Figure 3.8). When we consider another characteristic influenced by three genes with two alleles each, the number of potential genotypes increases to 27, and the number of phenotypes increases to six (row *c* in Figure 3.8). Notice that with just three genes influencing the characteristic, the distribution of observable phenotypes in the population begins to resemble a normal curve (row *d* in Figure 3.8)!

This illustrates the complexity we face when dealing with polygenic characteristics. In addition to this complexity, we could also imagine increased complexity when we consider that some of the many genes would follow other patterns of inheritance, such as codominance, incomplete dominance, or sex-linked inheritance. Clearly, polygenic

b. the fertilization of a single ova by two different sperm
c. the division of the zygote into two different individuals
d. the division of the gamete into two germ cells

Short Answer: Briefly answer the following questions.

6. List four levels of environment that interact with genetic action to influence traits and characteristics.
7. Most people can curl their tongues—a simple dominant-recessive trait that is determined by a dominant gene. Your father can curl his tongue, but neither your mother nor your sister can. Prepare a Punnett Square demonstrating the possible genotypes and phenotypes of you and your siblings.
8. Consider a situation in which both parents *cannot* curl their tongues. Prepare a Punnett Square of the possible genotypes and phenotypes of their children. From this chart, compute the probability that one of their children can curl his or her tongue.
9. A color-blind mother and a color-blind father have a son and a daughter. Prepare a Punnett Square of genotypes and phenotypes of these children and use it to answer the following questions: What is the probability that the boy will be color-blind? The girl will be color-blind?

Essay: Provide a more detailed answer to the following question.

10. Describe four patterns of genetic inheritance of behavioral characteristics. Which pattern would be most important to psychologists? Why?

characteristics are much more complex than simple single-gene characteristics. And most of the characteristics that psychologists are interested in exploring (intelligence, personality, mental health) are influenced by many, many genes. So we must be careful not to expect a simple formula for understanding inheritance of these behavioral characteristics.

To date, nobody knows exactly how many pairs of alleles influence physical stature (height), intelligence, or other polygenic traits. All we can say is that unknown numbers of genes, interacting with environmental influences, create a wide range of individual differences in most important human attributes.

Hereditary Disorders

congenital defect
a problem that is present (though not necessarily apparent) at birth; such defects may stem from genetic and prenatal influences or from complications of the birth process.

Although the vast majority of newborn infants are healthy at birth, approximately 5 of every 100 have a congenital problem of some kind (Schulman & Black, 1993). **Congenital defects** are those that are present at birth, although many of these conditions are not detectable when the child is born. For example, the gene that produces Huntington's disease is present from the moment of conception. But as we learned in the Box on p. 82, the gradual deterioration of the nervous system associated with this condition is not apparent at birth and will not ordinarily appear until much later—usually after age 40.

In Chapter 4, we will consider a variety of congenital defects that are likely to result from abnormalities in the birth process or from harmful conditions in prenatal development. Here we will look only at those problems that are caused by abnormal genes and chromosomes, that is, inherited congenital disorders. Figure 3.9 provides a graphic representation of the different sources of congenital disorders that may help you organize your thinking about the differences between chromosomal and genetic abnormalities, and congenital disorders caused by environmental effects.

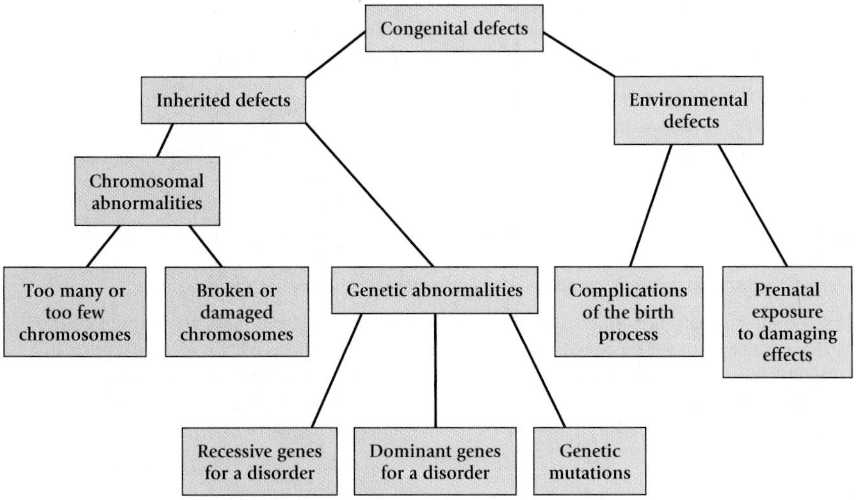

Figure 3.9 Sources of congenital defects.

Chromosomal Abnormalities

When a germ cell divides during meiosis, the distribution of its 46 chromosomes into sperm or ova is sometimes uneven. In other words, one of the resulting gametes may have too many chromosomes, while the other has too few. If these abnormal germ cells are conceived, the vast majority of these chromosomal abnormalities are lethal, and will fail to develop or will be spontaneously aborted. However, some chromosomal abnormalities are not lethal. Approximately 1 child in 250 is born with either one chromosome too many or one too few (Plomin et al., 2001).

Abnormalities of the Sex Chromosomes

Many chromosomal abnormalities involve the 23rd pair—the sex chromosomes. Occasionally males are born with an extra X or Y chromosome, producing the genotype XXY or XYY, and females may survive if they inherit a single X chromosome (XO) or even three (XXX), four (XXXX), or five (XXXXX) X chromosomes. Each of these conditions has somewhat different developmental implications, as we will see in examining four of the more common sex chromosome abnormalities in Table 3.2.

TABLE 3.2 Four Common Sex Chromosome Abnormalities

Name/genotype(s)	Incidence	Developmental implications
Female abnormalities		
Turner's syndrome; XO	1 in 2,500 female births	*Appearance:* Phenotypically female but small in stature with stubby fingers and toes, a webbed neck, a broad chest, and small, underdeveloped breasts. Normal sexual development lacking at puberty although Turner females can assume a more "womanly" appearance by taking the female hormone estrogen. *Fertility:* Sterile. *Intellectual characteristics:* Normal verbal intelligence but frequently score below average on tests of spatial abilities such as puzzle assembly or the mental rotation of figures.
Poly-X or "superfemale" syndrome; XXX, XXXX, or XXXXX	1 in 1,000 female births	*Appearance:* Phenotypically female and normal in appearance. *Fertility:* Fertile; produce children with the usual number of sex chromosomes. *Intellectual characteristics:* Score somewhat below average in intelligence, with greatest deficits on tests of verbal reasoning. Developmental delays and intellectual deficits become more pronounced with an increase in the number of extra X chromosomes inherited.
Male abnormalities		
Klinefelter's syndrome; XXY or XXXY	1 in 750 male births	*Appearance:* Phenotypically male with the emergence of some female secondary sex characteristics (enlargement of the hips and breasts) at puberty. Significantly taller than normal (XY) males. In the past Klinefelter males from Eastern-bloc countries may have competed as females in athletic events, leading to the current practice of administering sex tests to all female Olympic athletes. *Fertility:* Have underdeveloped testes and are sterile. *Intellectual characteristics:* About 20 to 30% of Klinefelter males are deficient in verbal intelligence, and their deficiencies become more pronounced with an increase in the number of extra X chromosomes inherited.
Supermale syndrome; XYY, XYYY, or XYYYY	1 in 1,000 male births	*Appearance:* Phenotypic males who are significantly taller than normal (XY) males, have large teeth, and often develop severe acne during adolescence. *Fertility:* Typically fertile although many of these men have abnormally low sperm counts. *Intellectual characteristics:* Although once thought to be subnormal intellectually and prone to violence and aggression, both these assumptions have been proved wrong by research. IQs of supermales span the full range of those observed in normal (XY) males. Moreover, careful studies of large numbers of XYYs indicate that they are no more violent or aggressive than normal males and are sometimes shy and retiring.

Sources: Robinson et al., 1992; Plomin et al., 1997; Shafer & Kuller, 1996.

Abnormalities of the Autosome

autosomes
the 22 pairs of human chromosomes that are identical in males and females.

Several hereditary abnormalities are attributable to the **autosomes**—that is, the 22 pairs of chromosomes that are similar in males and females. The most common type of autosomal abnormality occurs when an abnormal sperm or ovum carrying an extra autosome combines with a normal gamete to form a zygote that has 47 chromosomes (2 sex chromosomes and 45 autosomes). In these cases the extra chromosome appears along with one of the 22 pairs of autosomes to yield three chromosomes of that type, or a *trisomy.*

Down syndrome
a chromosomal abnormality (also known as trisomy-21) caused by the presence of an extra 21st chromosome; people with this syndrome have a distinctive physical appearance and are moderately to severely retarded.

By far the most frequent of all autosomal abnormalities (occurring once in every 800 births) is **Down syndrome,** or trisomy-21, a condition in which the child inherits all or part of an extra 21st chromosome. Children with Down syndrome are mentally retarded, with IQs that average 55 (the average IQ among normal children is 100). Typically this means they are mildly or moderately mentally retarded. They may also have congenital eye, ear, and heart defects and are usually characterized by a number of distinctive physical features, including a sloping forehead, protruding tongue, short stubby limbs, slightly flattened nose, and almond-shaped eyes (see Figure 3.10). Although intellectually impaired, these youngsters reach many of the same developmental milestones as normal children, but at a slower pace (Carr, 1995; Evans & Gray, 2000). Most of these youngsters learn to care for their basic needs, and some learn to read and write (Carr, 1995; Gibson & Harris, 1988). Developmental progress appears to be best when parents and other family members strive to include Down syndrome children in most family activities, are patient and work hard to properly stimulate them, and provide them with lots of emotional support (Atkinson et al., 1995; Hauser-Cram et al., 1999).

Genetic Abnormalities

mutation
a change in the chemical structure or arrangement of one or more genes that has the effect of producing a new phenotype.

Parents who are themselves healthy are often amazed to learn that their child could have a hereditary defect. Their surprise is certainly understandable, for most genetic problems are recessive traits that few if any close relatives may have had. In addition, these problems simply will not appear unless both parents carry the harmful allele *and* the child inherits this particular gene from each parent. The exceptions to this rule are sex-linked defects that a *male* child will display if the recessive alleles for these traits appear on his X chromosome that he inherited from his mother.

Earlier in the chapter, we discussed two recessive hereditary defects, one that is sex-linked (color blindness) and one that is not (sickle-cell anemia). Table 3.3 describes a number of additional debilitating or fatal diseases that are attributable to a single pair of recessive alleles. Each of these defects can be detected prior to birth, as we will discuss later on in the chapter.

Figure 3.10 Children with Down syndrome can lead happy lives if they receive affection and encouragement from their companions.

Some genetic abnormalities are caused by *dominant alleles.* In this case, the child will develop the disorder by inheriting the dominant allele from either parent. The parent contributing the allele for the disorder will also display the defect (because he or she carries the dominant allele). One example of a dominant genetic disorder is Huntington's disease (review Box 3.1).

Genetic abnormalities may also result from **mutations**—that is, changes in the chemical structure of one or more genes that produce a new phenotype. Many mutations occur spontaneously and are harmful or even fatal. Mutations can also be induced by environmental hazards such as toxic industrial waste, radiation, agricultural chemicals that enter the food supply, and possibly even some of the additives and preservatives in processed foods (Burns & Bottino, 1989).

TABLE 3.3 Brief Descriptions of Major Recessive Hereditary Diseases

Disease	Description	Incidence	Treatment	Prenatal detection
Cystic fibrosis (CF)	Child lacks enzyme that prevents mucus from obstructing the lungs and digestive tract. Many who have CF die in childhood or adolescence, although advances in treatment have enabled some to live well into adulthood.	1 in 2,500 Caucasian births; 1 in 15,000 African American births	Bronchial drainage; dietary control; gene replacement therapy	Yes
Diabetes	Individual lacks a hormone that would enable him or her to metabolize sugar properly. Produces symptoms such as excessive thirst and urination. Can be fatal if untreated.	1 in 2,500 births	Dietary control; insulin therapy	Yes
Duchenne-type muscular dystrophy	Sex-linked disorder that attacks the muscles and eventually produces such symptoms as slurred speech and loss of motor capabilities.	1 in 3,500 male births; rare in females	None. Death from weakening of heart muscle or respiratory infection often occurs between ages 7 and 14	Yes
Hemophilia	A sex-linked condition sometimes called "bleeder's disease." Child lacks a substance that causes the blood to clot. Could bleed to death if scraped or cut.	1 in 3,000 male births; rare in females	Blood transfusions; precautions to prevent cuts and scrapes	Yes
Phenylketonuria (PKU)	Child lacks an enzyme to digest foods (including milk) containing the amino acid phenylalanine. Disease attacks nervous system, producing hyperactivity and severe mental retardation.	1 in 10,000 Caucasian births; rare in children of African or Asian ancestry	Dietary control	Yes
Sickle-cell anemia	Abnormal sickling of red blood cells causes inefficient distribution of oxygen, pain, swelling, organ damage, and susceptibility to respiratory diseases.	1 in 600 African American births; even higher incidence in Africa and Southeast Asia	Blood transfusions; painkillers; drug to treat respiratory infections; bone marrow transplantation (if suitable donor is found)	Yes
Tay-Sachs disease	Causes degeneration of the central nervous system starting in the first year. Victims usually die by age 4.	1 in 3,600 births to Jews of European descent and French Canadians	None	Yes

Sources: Kuller, Cheschier, & Cefalo, 1996; Strachan & Read, 1996.

Might mutations ever be beneficial? Evolutionary theorists think so. Presumably, any mutation that is induced by stressors present in the natural environment may provide an "adaptive" advantage to those who inherit the mutant genes, thus enabling these individuals to survive. The sickle-cell gene, for example, is a mutation that originated in Africa, Southeast Asia, and other tropical areas where malaria is widespread. Heterozygous children who inherit a single sickle-cell allele are well adapted to these environments because the mutant gene makes them more resistant to malarial infection and thus more likely to survive (Plomin et al., 1997). Of course, the mutant sickle-cell gene is not advantageous in environments where malaria is not a problem.

Predicting, Detecting, and Treating Hereditary Disorders

In years gone by, many couples whose relatives were affected by hereditary disorders were reluctant to have children, fearing that they too would bear an abnormal child. Today there are options for predicting whether a couple is at risk for a hereditary disorder, options for prenatal detection of hereditary disorders, and options for medical treatment of hereditary disorders (both prenatally and after birth). These options help take away the mystery and fear of the unknown, and allow couples to make reasoned decisions about having children. In the sections that follow, we will discuss each of these options, following a developmental progression of sorts as we consider prediction before conception, detection after conception but before birth, and treatment after conception and before and after birth.

Predicting Hereditary Disorders

genetic counseling
a service designed to inform prospective parents about genetic diseases and to help them determine the likelihood that they would transmit such disorders to their children.

Genetic counseling is a service that helps prospective parents to assess the likelihood that their children will be free of hereditary defects. (It is important to remember that "genetic counseling" refers to the prediction of both chromosomal abnormalities and genetic abnormalities.) Genetic counselors are trained in genetics, the interpretation of family histories, and counseling procedures. They may be geneticists, medical researchers, or practitioners, such as pediatricians. Although any couple who hopes to have children might wish to talk with a genetic counselor about the hereditary risks their children may face, genetic counseling is particularly helpful for couples who either have relatives with hereditary disorders or have already borne a child with a hereditary disorder.

Genetic counselors normally begin by obtaining a complete family history, or *pedigree,* from each prospective parent to identify relatives affected by hereditary disorders. These pedigrees are used to estimate the likelihood that the couple would bear a child with a chromosomal or genetic disorder; in fact, pedigrees are the only basis for determining whether children are likely to be affected by certain disorders (one type of diabetes and some forms of muscular dystrophy, for example). Yet, a pedigree analysis *cannot* guarantee that a child will be healthy, even when no genetic disorders are found among blood relatives. Fortunately, DNA analyses from parents' blood tests can now determine whether *parents* carry genes for many serious hereditary disorders, including all those listed in Table 3.3, as well as Huntington's disease and the **fragile-X syndrome** (Strachan & Read, 1996).

fragile-X syndrome
abnormality of the X chromosome caused by a defective gene and associated with mild to severe mental retardation, particularly when the defective gene is passed from mother to child.

Once all the information and test results are in, the genetic counselor helps the couple consider the options available to them. For example, one couple went through genetic counseling and learned that they were both carriers for Tay-Sachs disease, a condition that normally kills an affected child within the first 3 years of life (see Table 3.3). The genetic counselor explained to this couple that there was one chance in four that *any* child they conceived would inherit a recessive allele from each of them and have Tay-Sachs disease. However, there was also one chance in four that the child would inherit the dominant gene from each parent, and there were two chances in four that the child would be just like its parents—phenotypically normal but a carrier of the recessive Tay-Sachs allele. After receiving this information, the young woman expressed strong reservations about having children, feeling that the odds were just too high to risk having a baby with a fatal disease.

At this point, the counselor informed the couple that before they made a firm decision against having children, they ought to be aware of procedures that can detect many genetic abnormalities, including Tay-Sachs disease, early in a pregnancy. These screening procedures cannot reverse any defects that are found, but they allow expectant parents to decide whether to terminate a pregnancy rather than give birth to a child with a fatal disease. This leads us from a consideration of predicting hereditary disorders to a consideration of detecting hereditary disorders that might exist.

Detecting Hereditary Disorders

amniocentesis
a method of extracting amniotic fluid from a pregnant woman so that fetal body cells within the fluid can be tested for chromosomal abnormalities and other genetic defects.

Because the overall rate of chromosomal abnormalities dramatically increases after age 35, older pregnant women often undergo a prenatal screening know as **amniocentesis.** A large, hollow needle is inserted into the woman's abdomen to withdraw a sample of the amniotic fluid that surrounds the fetus (see Figure 3.11). Fetal cells in this fluid can then be tested to determine the sex of the fetus and the presence of chromosomal abnormalities such as Down syndrome. In addition, more than 100 genetic disorders—including Tay-Sachs disease, cystic fibrosis, one type of diabetes, Duchenne muscular dystrophy,

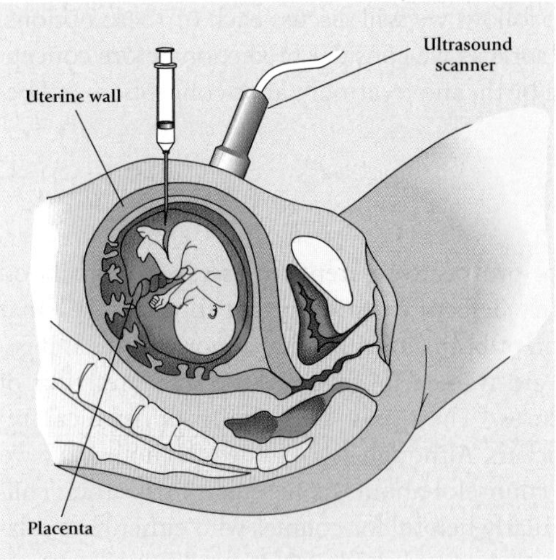

Figure 3.11 In amniocentesis, a needle is inserted through the abdominal wall into the uterus. Fluid is withdrawn and fetal cells are cultured, a process that takes about 3 weeks. *Adapted from* Before We Are Born, *4th Ed., by K. L. Moore & T. V. N. Persaud, 1993, p. 89. Philadelphia: Saunders. Adapted with permission of the author and publisher.*

sickle-cell anemia, and hemophilia—can now be diagnosed by analyzing fetal cells in amniotic fluid (Whittle & Connor, 1995). Although amniocentesis is considered a very safe procedure, it triggers a miscarriage in a very small percentage of cases. In fact, the risk of miscarriage (currently about 1 chance in 150) is thought to be greater than the risk of a birth defect if the mother is under age 35 (Cabaniss, 1996).

A major disadvantage of amniocentesis is that it is not easily performed before the 11th to 14th week of pregnancy, when amniotic fluid becomes sufficiently plentiful to withdraw for analysis (Kuller, 1996). Because the results of the tests will not come back for another 2 weeks, parents have little time to consider a second-trimester abortion if the fetus has a serious defect and abortion is their choice.

An alternative procedure is **chorionic villus sampling (CVS),** which collects tissue for the same tests as amniocentesis and can be performed during the 8th or 9th week of pregnancy (Kuller, 1996). As shown in Figure 3.12, there are two approaches to CVS. Either a catheter is inserted through the mother's vagina and cervix, or a needle through her abdomen, into a membrane called the *chorion* that surrounds the fetus. Fetal cells are then extracted and tested for hereditary abnormalities, with the results typically available within 24 hours. So CVS often allows parents to know whether their fetus bears a suspected abnormality very early on, leaving them more time to carefully consider the pros and cons of continuing the pregnancy in the event that the fetus is abnormal. But despite its advantages, CVS is currently recommended only to parents at very high risk of conceiving an abnormal child, for it entails a greater chance of miscarriage (about 1 chance in 50) than does amniocentesis, and its use has, in rare instances, been linked to limb deformities in the fetus (Kuller, 1996).

chorionic villus sampling (CVS)
an alternative to amniocentesis in which fetal cells are extracted from the chorion for prenatal tests. CVS can be performed earlier in pregnancy than is possible with amniocentesis.

ultrasound
method of detecting gross physical abnormalities by scanning the womb with sound waves, thereby producing a visual outline of the fetus.

Fortunately, a much safer early screening technique may be widely available in the near future (Springen, 2001). The procedure involves DNA analysis of fetal cells that begin to enter the mother's bloodstream early in pregnancy and which, when isolated from the mother's cells, can be tested to determine whether the fetus carries any chromosomal or genetic abnormalities. DNA screening will almost surely become more common once scientists are better able to locate and test fetal cells in the mother's bloodstream with absolutely no risk to the fetus.

A very common and very safe prenatal diagnostic technique is **ultrasound** (sonar), a method of scanning the womb with sound waves that is most useful after the 14th week of pregnancy (Cheschier, 1996). Ultrasound provides the attending physician with an outline of the fetus in much the same way that sonar reveals outlines of the fish beneath a fishing boat. It is particularly helpful for detecting multiple pregnancies and gross physical defects as well as the age and sex of the fetus. It is also used to guide practitioners as they perform amniocentesis and CVS (see Figures 3.11 and 3.12). Ultrasound is even a pleasant experience for many parents who seem to enjoy "meeting" their baby. In fact, it is common practice today for expectant parents to be given a photograph (even a 3-D photograph, as depicted in Figure 3.13) or videotape of the ultrasound procedure.

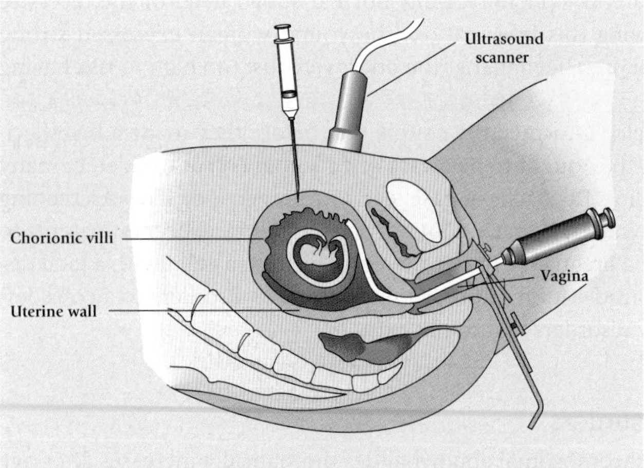

Figure 3.12 Chorionic villus sampling can be performed much earlier in pregnancy, and results are available within 24 hours. Two approaches to obtaining a sample of chorionic villi are shown here: inserting a thin tube through the vagina into the uterus or a needle through the abdominal wall. In either of these methods, ultrasound is used for guidance. *Adapted from* Before We Are Born, *4th Ed., by K. L. Moore & T. V. N. Persaud, 1993, p. 89. Philadelphia: Saunders. Adapted with permission of the author and publisher.*

Treating Hereditary Disorders

Prenatal detection of a hereditary disorder leaves many couples in a quandary, particularly if their religious background or personal beliefs are opposed to abortion. If the disease in question is invariably fatal, like Tay-Sachs, the couple must decide either to violate their moral principles and terminate the pregnancy or to have a baby who will appear normal and healthy but will rapidly decline and die young.

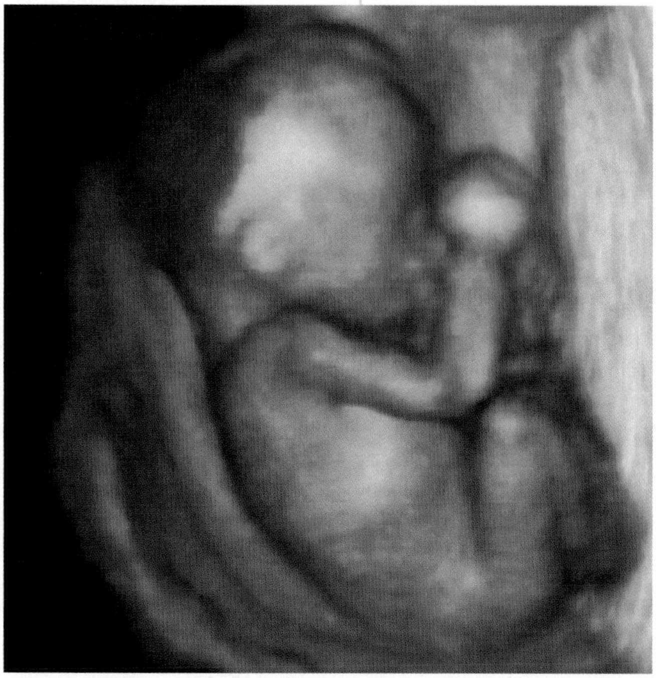

Dr. Najeeb Layyous/Photo Researchers, Inc.

Figure 3.13 Three-dimensional ultrasound images of the developing fetus are the expectant parents' first introduction to their child.

Might this quandary someday become a thing of the past? Very possibly. Less than 50 years ago, medical science could do little for children with another degenerative disease of the nervous system—**phenylketonuria,** or **PKU.** Like Tay-Sachs disease, PKU is a metabolic disorder. Affected children lack a critical enzyme that would allow them to metabolize phenylalanine, a component of many foods, including milk. As phenylalanine accumulates in the body, it is converted to a harmful substance, phenylpyruvic acid, that attacks the nervous system. Prior to the medical advances we enjoy today, the majority of children who inherited this disorder soon became hyperactive and severely retarded.

The major breakthroughs came in the mid-1950s when scientists developed a diet low in phenylalanine, and in 1961, when they developed a simple blood test that could determine if a child had PKU within a few days after birth. Newborn infants are now routinely screened for PKU (and other metabolic disorders), and affected children are immediately placed on a low-phenylalanine diet for PKU (or other dietary restrictions depending on any metabolic disorders which are found). The outcome of this therapeutic intervention is a happy one: children who remain on the diet throughout middle childhood suffer few if any of the harmful consequences of this formerly incurable disease. Outcomes are best when individuals with PKU remain on the special diet *for life.* This is particularly true of PKU women who hope to have children of their own; if they abandon the diet and their phenylalanine levels are high, they face great risk of either miscarrying or of bearing a mentally deficient child (Verp, 1993).

Today, the potentially devastating effects of many other hereditary abnormalities can be minimized or controlled. For example, new medical and surgical techniques, performed on fetuses in the uterus, have made it possible to treat some hereditary disorders by delivering drugs or hormones to the developing fetus (Hunter & Yankowitz, 1996), performing bone marrow transplants (Hajdu & Golbus, 1993), or surgically repairing some genetically transmitted defects of the heart, neural tube, urinary tract, and respiratory system (Yankowitz, 1996). In addition, children born with either Turner's syndrome or Klinefelter's syndrome can be placed on hormone therapy to make them more normal in appearance. Diabetes can be controlled by a low-sugar diet and by periodic doses of insulin, which help the patient to metabolize sugar. And youngsters who have such blood disorders as hemophilia or sickle-cell anemia may now receive periodic transfusions to provide them with the clotting agents or the normal red blood cells they lack.

Advances in the treatment of cystic fibrosis (CF) illustrate the remarkable rate at which researchers are gaining the knowledge to combat hereditary diseases. Not so long ago, about all that could be done for CF patients was to administer antibiotics to lessen the discomfort of their chronic lung obstructions and infections. But in 1989, researchers located the CF gene, and only one year later, two research teams succeeded at neutralizing the damaging effects of this gene in the laboratory (Denning et al., 1991). Soon thereafter came the development and testing of a gene replacement therapy that involves inserting normal genes, carried by genetically engineered cold viruses, into the noses and lungs of patients with cystic fibrosis in the hope that these imported genes can override the effects of the CF genes. A similar genetic therapy has been attempted for adenosine deaminese deficiency, an inherited disorder of the immune system. Although both approaches have had some limited success, they produce their benefits by lessening the patients' symptoms rather than by curing the disorders and must be repeated frequently to remain effective (Mehlman & Botkin, 1998).

Finally, advances in *genetic engineering* are raising the possibility of **germline gene therapy**—a process by which harmful genes are altered or replaced with healthy ones in the early embryonic stage, thereby permanently correcting a genetic defect. This approach

phenylketonuria (PKU)
a genetic disease in which the child is unable to metabolize phenylalanine; if left untreated, it soon causes hyperactivity and mental retardation.

germline gene therapy
a procedure, not yet perfected or approved for use with humans, in which harmful genes would be repaired or replaced with healthy ones, thereby permanently correctly a genetic defect.

APPLYING RESEARCH TO YOUR LIFE

Ethical Issues Surrounding Treatments for Hereditary Disorders

Although many children and adolescents with hereditary disorders have clearly benefited from new treatments only recently introduced, scientists and society at large are now grappling with thorny ethical issues that have arisen from the rapid progress being made (Dunn, 2002; Weinberg, 2002). Here is a small sampling of these concerns.

Issues Surrounding Fetal Surgery

Most fetal surgical procedures are still experimental and often induce miscarriages and other harmful consequences. Consider that the risk of fetal death in urinary tract surgery is about 5 to 10 percent from the surgery itself, with another 20 to 30 percent suffering serious complications from the operation; and urinary tract surgery is safer than most other surgical procedures preformed on fetuses (Yankowitz, 1996). Is it really in a fetus's best interests to undergo an operation that may end its life or produce birth defects? Should parents be held legally responsible if they choose to continue a pregnancy while refusing a fetal surgical procedure that might prevent their child from suffering from a serious handicap? Think about these questions, for they are some of the very issues that medical and legal practitioners are now debating.

Issues Surrounding Gene Replacement Therapy

All current gene replacement therapies for humans involve insertion of normal genes into patients' somatic (body) tissues to relieve the *symptoms* of genetic disorders. Are there major ethical problems here? Most observers think not (Strachan & Read, 1996). Clearly, investigators and practitioners are ethically bound to ensure the safety of their patients, especially because the techniques of somatic gene therapies are experimental and can have side effects. Yet, by limiting treatment to the patient's body cells, any consequences of the procedure are confined to the patient, who is usually suffering from a debilitating and even life-threatening disease for which no other effective therapy is available (Mehlman & Botkin, 1998). Thus, the benefits of somatic gene therapy are likely to greatly outweigh its costs. Many view this kind of treatment as analogous to (and at least as acceptable as) other medical procedures such as organ transplants. Some would even consider it *unethical* were parents to withhold somatic gene therapy from a seriously ill child who might benefit from the procedure.

Issues Surrounding Germline Gene Therapy

The hottest debates about new genetic technologies center around the prospect of *germline gene therapy,* in which attempts would be made to repair or replace abnormal genes at the early embryonic stage and thereby "cure" genetic defects. This technology, which could be widely available by 2040 (Nesmith & McKenna, 2000), would bring us to the edge of a slippery slope where human beings will be capable of altering genotypes. This prospect seems perfectly acceptable to many observers, provided it is limited to correcting diagnosed genetic defects (Begley, 2000). However, others point out that permanent modification of a patient's genotype has consequences not only for the patient, but also for all individuals who inherit the modified gene in the future. Germline gene therapy would therefore deny the rights of these descendants to have any choice about whether their genetic makeup should have been modified in the first place, a state of affairs that some view as ethically unacceptable (see Strachan & Read, 1996).

Other critics have argued that approval of germline gene therapy for use with humans will inevitably place us on the path toward *positive eugenics*—that is, toward genetic enhancement programs that could involve artificial selection for genes thought to confer advantageous traits. This possibility is frightening to many. Who would decide which traits are advantageous and should be selected? Some have argued that parents who have produced many embryos via in vitro fertilization will begin to play God, using DNA screening and/or germline gene therapy to create what they judge to be the most perfect baby they can produce (Begley, 2000, 2001). Even if the motives of those who would alter genotypes were beyond reproach, would they really be any better at engineering a hardy human race than nature already has through the process of natural selection? Of course, the biggest concern that many people have about germline genetic engineering is its potential for political and social abuse. In the words of two molecular geneticists (Strachan & Read, 1996, p. 586):

> "The horrifying nature of *negative eugenics* programs (most recently in Nazi Germany and in many states in the USA where compulsory sterilization of [feeble-minded] individuals was practiced well into the present century) serves as a reminder . . . of the potential Pandora's box of ills that could be released if ever human germline gene therapy were to be attempted."

has been used successfully to correct certain genetic disorders in animals (Strachan & Read, 1996), but the kinds of ethical issues raised in Box 3.3 may keep it from being used with humans for some time to come.

In sum, many abnormal children can lead normal lives if their hereditary disorders are detected and treated before serious harm has been done. And inspired by recent successes in

CONCEPT CHECK 3.2 Understanding Chromosomal and Genetic Abnormalities

Check your understanding of how and why chromosomal and genetic abnormalities form, and the causes and effects of the most common hereditary disorders by answering the following questions. Answers appear in the Appendix.

Multiple Choice: Select the best answer for each question.

_____ 1. All of the following can result in congenital disorders *except* which?
   a. abnormal genes
   b. abnormal chromosomes
   c. abnormal contact between mother and child during postnatal development
   d. abnormalities in prenatal development

_____ 2. "Genetic counseling" refers to the prediction of:
   a. chromosomal abnormalities
   b. genetic abnormalities
   c. both a and b
   d. neither a nor b

_____ 3. The complete family history a genetic counselor will use to determine the likelihood that a child will inherit a congenital disorder is called the:
   a. pedigree
   b. DNA analysis
   c. DNA map
   d. background check

_____ 4. Which test to detect congenital disorders during prenatal development can be performed earliest in the pregnancy (at 8 to 9 weeks), allowing the parents more time to consider terminating the pregnancy?
   a. amniocentesis
   b. ultrasound
   c. chorionic villus sampling

True or False: Identify whether the following statements are true or false.

5. (T)(F) Amniocentesis can only detect the sex of the fetus, *not* whether or not it has any genetic disorders.
6. (T)(F) Predicting, detecting, and treating genetic disorders are the three ways a couple can deal with the possibility that their child will inherit a disorder.

Short Answer: Briefly answer the following questions.

7. Describe the cause and effects of the most common autosomal abnormality, Down syndrome.
8. Describe the three methods of dealing with hereditary disorders.

Essay: Provide more detailed answers to the following questions.

9. Imagine that you and your partner have discovered that there is a 75 percent chance that your child will inherit Tay-Sachs disease. Write an essay describing your preferred plan of action: Do you terminate your (or your partner's) pregnancy, continue the pregnancy without medication and hope for the best, or continue the pregnancy and treat the fetus using medically groundbreaking, yet experimental methods? Why?
10. Imagine that you or your partner is pregnant with your first child. A genetic counselor has determined that your child has a 50 percent chance of inheriting cystic fibrosis. Which method, or methods, if any, do you use to detect the disorder: amniocentesis, chorionic villus sampling, or ultrasound? Why?

fetal medicine, genetic mapping, and gene replacement therapy, geneticists and medical practitioners are hopeful that many untreatable hereditary disorders will become treatable, or even curable, in the near future (Mehlman & Botkin, 1998; Nesmith & McKenna, 2000).

Hereditary Influences on Behavior

We have seen that genes play a major role in determining our appearance and many of our physical characteristics. But to what extent does heredity affect such characteristics as intelligence, personality, or mental health?

In recent years, investigators from the fields of genetics, zoology, population biology, and psychology have asked the question, "Are there certain abilities, traits, and patterns of behavior that depend very heavily on the particular combination of genes that an individual inherits, and if so, are these attributes likely to be modified by one's experiences?" Those who focus on these issues in their research are known as *behavioral geneticists*.

Behavioral Genetics

behavioral genetics
the scientific study of how genotype interacts with environment to determine behavioral attributes such as intelligence, personality, and mental health.

Before we take a closer look at the field of **behavioral genetics,** it is necessary to dispel a common myth. Although behavioral geneticists view development as the process through which one's *genotype* (the set of genes one inherits) is expressed in one's *phenotype* (observable characteristics and behaviors), they are not strict hereditarians. They recognize, for example, that even physical characteristics such as height depend to some extent on environmental variables, such as the adequacy of one's diet (Plomin, 1990). They acknowledge that the long-term effects of one's genotype on behavioral characteristics such as intelligence, personality, and mental health also depend on one's environment. In other words, the behavioral geneticist is well aware that even attributes that have a strong hereditary component are often modified in important ways by environmental influences (Brown, 1999).

Behavioral geneticists differ from ethologists and other scientists, who are also interested in the biological bases of development. Ethologists study inherited attributes that characterize *all* members of a species, make them *alike,* and contribute to *common* developmental outcomes. Behavioral geneticists focus on the biological bases for *variation* among members of a species. They are concerned with determining how the unique combination of genes that each of us inherits might make us *different* from one another. Let's now consider the methods they use to approach this task.

Methods of Studying Hereditary Influences

heritability
the amount of variability in a trait that is attributable to hereditary factors.

There are two major strategies that behavioral geneticists use to assess hereditary contributions to behavior: *selective breeding* and *family studies.* Each of these approaches attempts to specify the **heritability** of various attributes—that is, the amount of variation in a trait or a class of behavior, within a specific population, that is attributable to hereditary factors.

selective breeding experiment
a method of studying genetic influences by determining whether traits can be bred in animals through selective mating.

Selective Breeding. Deliberately manipulating the genetic makeup of animals to study hereditary influences on behavior is much like what Gregor Mendel did to discover the workings of heredity in plants. A classic example of such a **selective breeding experiment** is R. C. Tryon's (1940) attempt to show that maze-learning ability is a heritable attribute in rats. Tryon first tested a large number of rats for the ability to run a complex maze. Rats that made few errors were labeled "maze-bright;" those that made many errors were termed "maze-dull." Then, across several generations, Tryon mated bright rats with other bright rats and dull rats with dull rats. He also matched the environments to which the rats were exposed to rule out environmental differences and their contribution to differences in maze-learning performance. As we see in Figure 3.14, differences in the maze-learning performances of the maze-bright and maze-dull groups became progressively greater across generations. This indicated that maze-learning ability in rats is influenced by their genetic makeup. Other investigators have used this selective breeding technique to show that genes contribute to behavioral characteristics such as activity level, emotionality, aggressiveness, and sex drive in rats, mice, and chickens (Plomin et al., 2001).

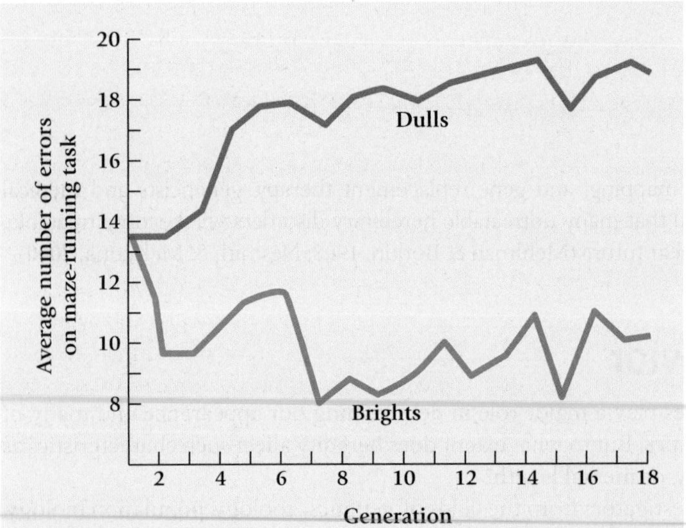

Figure 3.14 Maze-running performance by inbred maze-bright and maze-dull rats over 18 generations. *From* Behavioral Genetics: A Primer, *3rd ed., by R. Plomin, J. C. DeFries, & G. E. McClearn, 1997. Copyright © W. H. Freeman and Company.*

Family Studies. Because people don't take kindly to the idea of being selectively bred by experimenters, human behavioral genetics relies on an alternative methodology known as the family study. In a typical family study, persons who live together are compared to see how similar they are on one or more attributes. If the attributes in question are heritable, then the similarity between any two pairs of individuals who live in the same environment should increase as a function of their **kinship**—the extent to which they have the same genes.

kinship
the extent to which two individuals have genes in common.

twin design
study in which sets of twins that differ in zygosity (kinship) are compared to determine the heritability of an attribute.

adoption design
study in which adoptees are compared with their biological relatives and their adoptive relatives to estimate the heritability of an attribute, or attributes.

Two kinds of family (or kinship) studies are common today. The first is the **twin design,** which asks the question, "Are pairs of identical twins reared together more similar to each other on various attributes than pairs of fraternal twins reared together?" (Segal, 1997). If genes affect the attribute(s) in question, then identical twins should be more similar, for they have 100 percent of their genes in common (kinship = 1.00) whereas fraternal twins share only 50 percent (kinship = .50).

The second common family study is the **adoption design,** which focuses on adoptees who are genetically unrelated to other members of their adoptive families. A researcher searching for hereditary influences would ask, "Are adopted children similar to their biological parents, whose *genes* they share (kinship = .50), or are they similar to their adoptive parents, whose *environment* they share?" If adoptees resemble their biological parents in intelligence or personality, even though these parents did not raise them, then genes must be influential in determining these attributes.

Family studies can also help us to estimate the extent to which various abilities and behaviors are influenced by the environment. To illustrate, consider a case in which two genetically unrelated adopted children are raised in the same home. Their degree of kinship with each other and with their adoptive parents is .00. Consequently, there is no reason to suspect that these children will resemble each other or their adoptive parents unless their common environment plays some part in determining their standing on the attribute in question. Another way the effects of environment can be inferred is to compare identical twins raised in the same environment with identical twins raised in different environments. The kinship of all pairs of identical twins, reared together or apart, is 1.00. So if identical twins reared together are more alike on an attribute than identical twins reared apart, we can infer that the environment plays a role in determining that attribute.

concordance rate
the percentage of cases in which a particular attribute is present for one member of a twin pair if it is present for the other.

Estimating the Contribution of Genes and Environment. Behavioral geneticists rely on some simple and some not so simple mathematical calculations to (a) determine whether or not a trait is genetically influenced and (b) estimate the degree to which heredity *and* environment account for individual differences in that trait. When studying traits that a person either does or does not display (for example, a drug habit or clinical depression), researchers calculate and compare **concordance rates**—the percentages of pairs of people (for example, identical twins, fraternal twins, parents and their adoptive children) in which *both* members of the pair display the trait if one member has it. Suppose that you are interested in determining whether homosexuality in men is genetically influenced. You might locate gay men who have twins, either identical or fraternal, and then track down their twin siblings to determine whether they too are gay. As shown in Figure 3.15, the concordance rate for identical twins in one such study was much higher (29 of the 56 co-twins of gay men were also gay) than the concordance rate for fraternal twins (12 of the 54 co-twins were also gay). This suggests that genotype does contribute to a man's sexual orientation. But because identical twins are not perfectly concordant for sexual orientation (that is, every gay twin does not have a co-twin who is also gay), we can also conclude that their *experiences* (that is, environmental influences) must also have influenced their sexual orientations. After all, 48 percent of the identical twin pairs had *different* sexual orientations, despite their identical genes. (Concordance rates for a number of other behavioral dimensions that have been investigated in twin studies are displayed in Figure 3.16.)

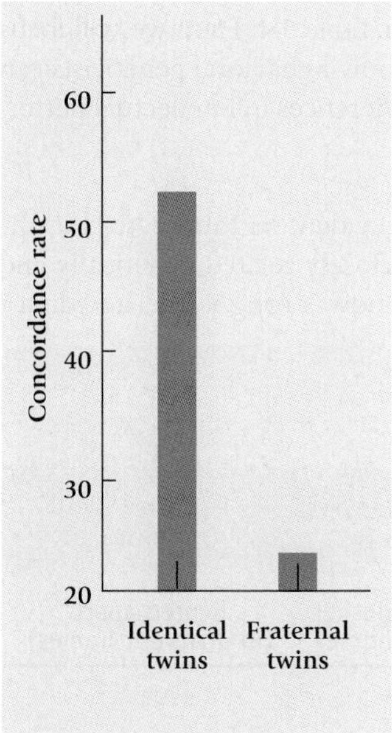

Figure 3.15 Concordance rates for homosexuality in 110 male twin pairs. From the higher concordance for identical twin pairs, we can infer that genes influence one's sexual orientation. *Based on "A Genetic Study of the Male Sexual Orientation," by J. M. Bailey & R. C. Pillard, 1991,* Archives of General Psychiatry, *48, 1089–1096. Copyright 1991 by the Archives of General Psychiatry. Adapted by permission.*

For continuous traits that can assume many values (for example, height, intelligence), behavioral geneticists estimate hereditary contributions by calculating *correlation coefficients* rather than concordance rates. In a study of IQ scores, for example, a correlation coefficient would indicate whether the IQ scores of twins are systematically related to the IQ scores of their co-twins. Larger correlations indicate closer resemblances in IQ,

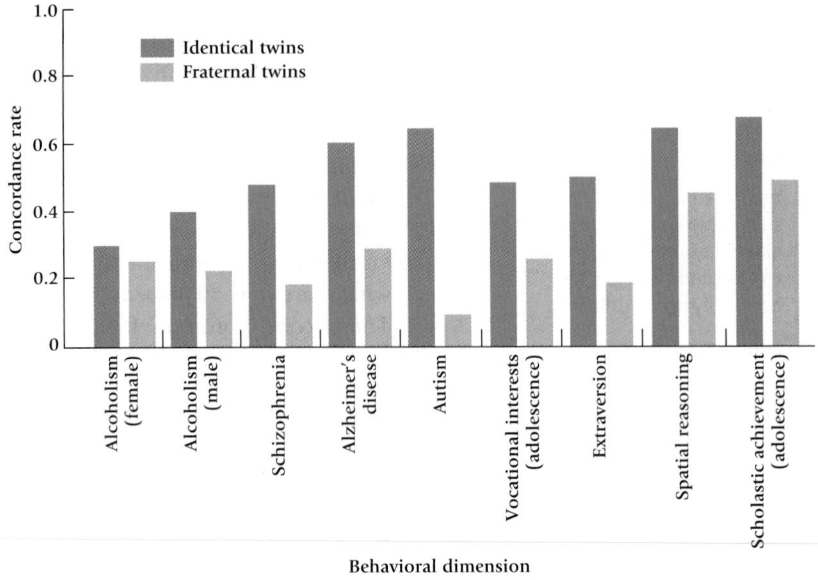

Figure 3.16 Concordance rates for identical and fraternal twins for several behavioral dimensions.
From R. Plomin, M.J. Owen, and P. McGuffin, "The genetic basis of complex human behaviors," Science, 264, *1733–1739. Copyright © 1994 by the American Association for the Advancement of Science. Reprinted by permission.*

thus implying that if one twin is quick to learn, the other is quick too, and if one twin is slow to learn, the other is probably slow as well.

As we noted earlier, behavioral genetics studies always tell us about *both* genetic and environmental influences on development. This point is easily illustrated by considering a review of family studies of intellectual performance (IQ) based on 113,942 pairs of children, adolescents, or adults, the results of which appear in Table 3.4. Here we will focus on the twin correlations (identical and fraternal) to show how behavioral geneticists can estimate the contributions of three factors to individual differences in intellectual performance (IQ).

Gene Influences. Genetic influences on IQ are clearly evident in Table 3.4. The correlations become higher when pairs of people are more closely related genetically and are highest when the pairs are identical twins. But just how strong is the hereditary influence?

TABLE 3.4 Average Correlation Coefficients for Intelligence-Test Scores from Family Studies Involving Persons at Four Levels of Kinship

Genetic relationship (kinship)	Reared together (in same home)	Reared apart (in different homes)
Unrelated siblings (kinship = .00)	+.34	−.01[a]
Adoptive parent/adoptive offspring (kinship = .00)	+.19	–
Half-siblings (kinship = .25)	+.31	–
Biological parent/child (kinship = .50)	+.42	+.22
Siblings (kinship = .50)	+.47	+.24
Twins		
Fraternal (kinship = .50)	+.60	+.52
Identical (kinship = 1.00)	+.86	+.72

[a]This is the correlation obtained from random pairings of unrelated people living apart.
Source: Based on "Family Studies of Intelligence: A Review," by T. J. Bouchard, Jr., and M. McGue, 1981, Science, 212, pp. 1055–1059.

heritability coefficient
a numerical estimate, ranging from .00 to +1.00, of the amount of variation in an attribute that is due to hereditary factors.

Behavioral geneticists use statistical techniques to estimate the amount of variation in a trait that is attributable to hereditary factors. This index, called a **heritability coefficient,** is calculated as follows from twin data:

$$H = (r \text{ identical twins} - r \text{ fraternal twins}) \times 2$$

In words, the equation reads: Heritability of an attribute equals the correlation between identical twins minus the correlation between fraternal twins, all multiplied by a factor of 2 (Plomin, 1990).

Now we can estimate the contribution that genes make to individual differences in intellectual performance. If we focus on sets of twins raised together from Table 3.4, our estimate becomes:

$$H = (.86 - .60) \times 2 = .52$$

The resulting heritability estimate for IQ is .52, which, on a scale ranging from 0 (not at all heritable) to 1.00 (totally heritable) is moderate at best. We might conclude that, within the populations from which our twins reared together came, IQ is influenced to a moderate extent by hereditary factors. However, it appears that much of the variability among people on this trait is attributable to nonhereditary factors—that is, to environmental influences and to errors we may have made in measuring the trait (no measure is perfect).

Interestingly, the data in Table 3.4 also allows us to estimate the contributions of *two* sources of environmental influence:

nonshared environmental influence (NSE)
an environmental influence that people living together do not share which should make these individuals different from one another.

Nonshared Environmental Influences. **Nonshared environmental influences** (**NSE**) are experiences that are unique to the individual—experiences that are *not* shared by other members of the family and, thus, make family members *different* from each other (Rowe & Plomin, 1981; Rowe, 1994). Where is evidence of nonshared environmental influence in Table 3.4? Notice that identical twins raised together are not perfectly similar in IQ, even though they share 100 percent of their genes and the same family environment: A correlation of +.86, though substantial, is less than a perfect correlation of +1.00. Because identical twins share the same genes and family environment, any *differences* between twins raised together must necessarily be due to differences in their *experiences.* Perhaps they were treated differently by friends, or perhaps one twin favors puzzles and other intellectual games more than the other twin does. Because the only factor that can make identical twins raised together any *different* from each other are experiences they do *not* share, we can estimate the influence of nonshared environmental influences by the following formula (Rowe & Plomin, 1981):

$$\text{NSE} = 1.00 - r \text{ (identical twins reared together)}$$

So, the contribution of nonshared environmental influences to individual differences in IQ performance (that is, 1.00 − .86 = .14) is small, but detectable nevertheless. As we will see, nonshared environmental influences make a bigger contribution to other attributes, most notably personality traits.

shared environmental influence (SE)
an environmental influence that people living together share which should make these individuals similar to one another.

Shared Environmental Influences. **Shared environmental influences** (**SE**) are experiences that individuals living in the same home environment share and that conspire to make them *similar* to each other. As you can see in Table 3.4, both identical and fraternal twins (and, indeed, biological siblings and pairs of unrelated individuals) show a greater intellectual resemblance if they live together than if they live apart. One reason that growing up in the same home may increase children's degree of intellectual similarity is that parents model similar interests for *all* their children and tend to rely on similar strategies to foster their intellectual growth (Hoffman, 1991; Lewin et al., 1993).

How do we estimate the contribution of shared environmental influences (SE) to a trait? One rough estimate can be made as follows:

$$SE = 1.00 - (H + NSE)$$

Translated, the equation reads: Shared environmental influences on a trait equal 1 (the total variation for that trait) minus the variation attributable to genes (*H*) *and* the variability attributable to nonshared environmental influences (NSE). Previously, we found that the heritability (*H*) of IQ in our twins-reared-together sample was .52, and the contribution of nonshared environment (NSE) was a .14. So, the contribution of shared environmental influences to individual differences in IQ (that is SE = 1 − [.52 + .14] = .34) is moderate and meaningful.

Myths about Heritability Estimates. Although heritability coefficients are useful for estimating whether genes make any meaningful contribution to various human attributes, these statistics are poorly understood and often misinterpreted. One of the biggest misconceptions that people hold is the notion that heritability coefficients can tell us whether we have inherited a trait. *This idea is simply incorrect.* When we talk about the heritability of an attribute, we are referring to the extent to which *differences* among individuals with that attribute are related to differences in the genes that they have inherited (Plomin et al., 2001). To illustrate that *heritable* means something other than *inherited,* consider that everyone inherits two eyes. Agreed? Yet the heritability of eyes is .00 simply because everyone has two and there are no individual differences in "eyeness" (except for those attributable to environmental events such as accidents).

In interpreting heritability coefficients, it is important to recognize that these estimates apply only to populations and *never to individuals.* So if you studied the heights of many pairs of 5-year-old twins and estimated the heritability of height to be .70, you could infer that a major reason that 5-year-olds differ in height is that they have different genes. But because heritability estimates say nothing about individuals, it is clearly inappropriate to conclude from an *H* of .70 that 70 percent of Juan Miguel's height is inherited and the remaining 30 percent reflects the contribution of environment.

Let's also note that heritability estimates refer only to the particular trait in question as displayed by members of a *particular population* under *particular environmental circumstances.* Indeed, heritability coefficients may differ substantially for different research populations raised in different environments (Rowe, 1999). Suppose, for example, that we located a large number of identical and fraternal twin infants, each of whom was raised in an impoverished orphanage in which his or her crib was lined with sheets that prevented much visual or social contact with other infants or with adult caregivers. Previous research suggests that, if we measured how sociable these infants are, we would find that they vary somewhat in sociability, but virtually all of them are much less sociable than babies raised at home—a finding that we could reasonably attribute to their socially deprived early environment. But because all these twins experienced the same deprived environment, the only reason that they might show any differences in sociability is the result of differences in their genetic predispositions. The heritability coefficient for sociability would actually approach 1.0 in this position—a far cry from the *H* coefficients of .25 to .40 found in studies of other infants raised at home with parents (Plomin et al., 2001).

Finally, people have assumed that clearly heritable traits cannot be modified by environmental influences. This, too, is a false assumption! The depressed sociability of institutionalized infants can be improved substantially by placing them in socially responsive adoptive homes. Similarly, children who score low on the heritable attribute of IQ can dramatically improve their intellectual and academic performances when exposed to intellectually stimulating home and school environments. To assume that *heritable* means *unchangeable* (as some critics of compensatory education have done) is to commit a potentially grievous error based on a common misconception about the meaning of heritability coefficients.

In sum, the term *heritable* is not a synonym for *inherited,* and heritability estimates, which may vary widely across populations and environments, can tell us nothing about the development of individuals. And though heritability estimates are useful for helping us to determine whether there is any hereditary basis for the *differences* people display on any attribute we might care to study, they say nothing about children's capacity for change and should not be used to make public policy decisions that could constrain children's development or adversely affect their welfare.

Hereditary Influences on Intellectual Performance

As we have seen from data presented in Table 3.4, IQ is a moderately heritable attribute; genes account for about half the total variation in people's IQ scores. But because the correlations presented in Table 3.4 are based on studies of children *and* adults, they do not tell us whether the contributions of genes and environment to individual differences in intellectual performance might change over time. Might genes be more important early in life, whereas differences in our home and school experiences increasingly account for the variations we show in intellectual performance as we get older? Sensible as this idea may sound, it seems to be wrong. As children mature, genes actually appear to contribute *more* (rather than less) to individual differences in their IQs (Plomin et al., 1997).

Consider a longitudinal study of the intellectual development of twins reported by Ronald Wilson (1978, 1983). Wilson found that identical twins were no more similar than same-sex fraternal twins on tests of infant mental development during the first year of life. By age 18 months, however, genetic influences were already detectable. Not only did identical twins show a greater resemblance in test performance than fraternal twins did, but *changes* in test scores from one testing to the next also became more similar for identical twins than for fraternal twins. If one identical twin had a big spurt in mental development between 18 and 24 months of age, the other twin was likely to show a similar spurt at the same time. So it seemed as if genes were now influencing both the *course* and the *extent* of infants' mental development.

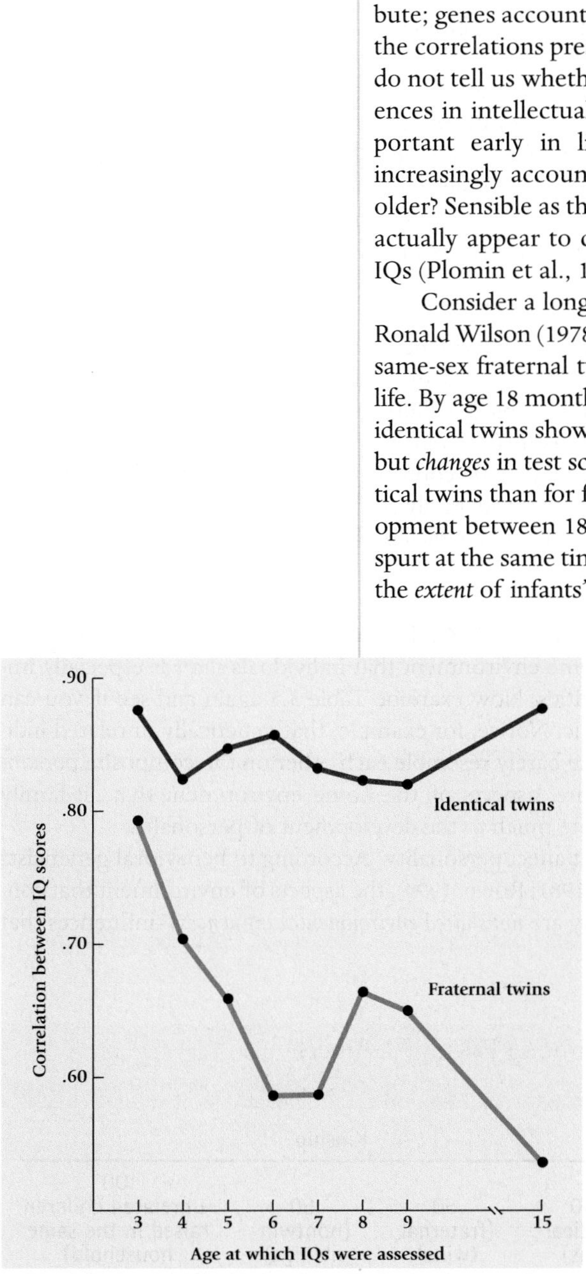

Figure 3.17 Changes in the correlation between the IQ scores of identical and fraternal twins over childhood. *From "The Louisville Twin Study: Developmental Synchronies in Behavior," by R. S. Wilson, 1983,* Child Development, *54, pp. 298–316. Copyright © 1983 by The Society for Research in Child Development, Inc. Reprinted by permission.*

Figure 3.17 shows what happened as these twins continued to develop. Identical twins remained highly similar in their intellectual performance (average $r = +.85$) from age 3 through age 15. Fraternal twins, on the other hand, were most similar intellectually at age 3 ($r = +.79$) and gradually became less similar over time. By age 15, they showed no greater intellectual resemblance ($r = +.54$) than pairs of nontwin siblings. Notice, then, that if we calculated heritability coefficients at each age shown in the figure, the heritability of IQ for these twin samples would actually increase from infancy to adolescence.

Adoption studies paint a similar picture. The IQs of adopted children are correlated with the intellectual performances of *both* their biological parents (suggesting a genetic influence) and their adoptive parents (indicating effects of shared family environment). By adolescence, the resemblance to biological parents is still apparent, but adoptees no longer resemble their adoptive parents intellectually (Scarr & Weinberg, 1978). What seems to be happening, both in the twin and the adoption studies, is that the influence of shared environment on intellectual performance declines with age, whereas the influence of both genes and nonshared environmental influences become increasingly stronger. There is a very influential theory that accounts for these changing patterns of influence on IQ scores and on personality traits as well. But before we examine this theory, let's briefly review the evidence that suggests that our personalities are influenced by the genes we have inherited.

introversion/extroversion
the opposite poles of a personality dimension: introverts are shy, anxious around others, and tend to withdraw from social situations; extroverts are highly sociable and enjoy being with others.

empathic concern
a measure of the extent to which an individual recognizes the needs of others and is concerned about their welfare.

Hereditary Contributions to Personality

Although psychologists have typically assumed that the relatively stable habits and traits that make up our personalities are shaped by our environments, family studies and other longitudinal projects reveal that many core dimensions of personality are genetically influenced. For example, **introversion/extroversion**—the extent to which a person is shy, retiring, and uncomfortable around others versus outgoing and socially oriented—shows about the same moderate level of heritability as IQ does (Plomin et al., 1997). Another important attribute that is genetically influenced is **empathic concern:** a person high in empathy recognizes the needs of others and is concerned about their welfare. In Box 2.2, we saw that newborn infants react to the distress of another infant by becoming distressed themselves—a finding that implies to some investigators that the capacity for empathy may be innate. But are there any biological bases for *individual differences* in empathic concern?

Indeed there are. As early as 14 to 20 months of age, identical twin infants are already more similar in their levels of concern for distressed companions than same-sex fraternal twin infants are (Zahn-Waxler, Robinson, & Emde, 1992). And by middle age, identical twins who have lived apart for many years since leaving home still resemble each other on measures of empathic concern ($r = +.41$), whereas same-sex fraternal twins do not ($r = +.05$), thus suggesting that this attribute is a reasonably heritable trait (Matthews et al., 1981).

How much genetic influence? To what extent are our personalities influenced by the genes we have inherited? We get some idea by looking at personality resemblances among family members, as shown in Table 3.5. Note that identical twins are more similar to each other on this composite measure of personality than fraternal twins are. Were we to use the twin data to estimate the genetic contribution to personality, we might conclude that many personality traits are moderately heritable (i.e., $H = +.40$). Of course, one implication of a moderate heritability coefficient is that personality is also heavily influenced by environmental factors.

Which Aspects of Environment Influence Personality? Developmentalists have traditionally assumed that the home environment that individuals *share* is especially important in shaping their personalities. Now examine Table 3.5 again and see if you can find some problems with this logic. Notice, for example, that genetically unrelated individuals who live in the same home barely resemble each other on the composite personality measure ($r = .07$). Therefore, aspects of the home environment that all family members *share* must not contribute much to the development of personality.

How, then, does environment affect personality? According to behavioral geneticists David Rowe and Robert Plomin (1981; Rowe, 1994), the aspects of environment that contribute most heavily to personality are *nonshared environmental influences*—influences that

TABLE 3.5 Personality Resemblances among Family Members at Three Levels of Kinship

	Kinship			
	1.00 (identical twins)	.50 (fraternal twins)	.50 (nontwin siblings)	.00 (unrelated children raised in the same household)
Personality attributes (average correlations across several personality traits)	.50	.30	.20	.07

Sources: Loehlin, 1985; Loehlin & Nichols, 1976.

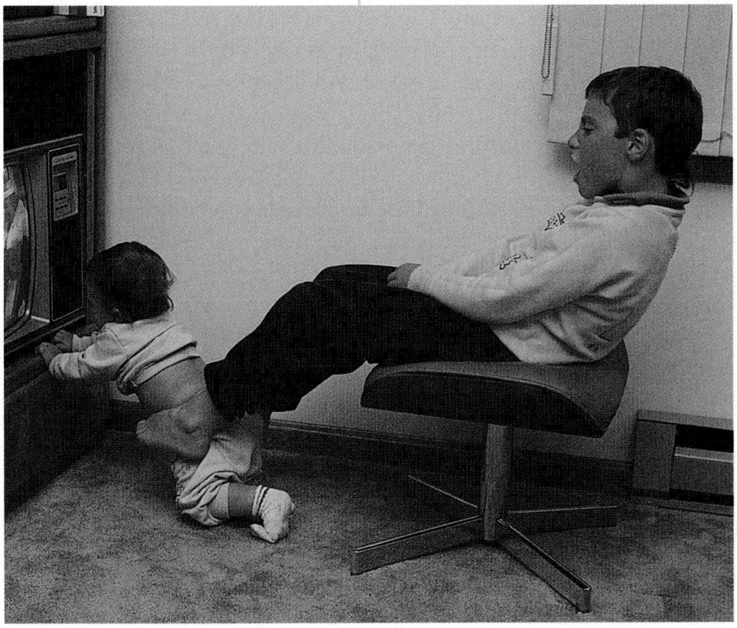

Sibling interactions produce many nonshared experiences that contribute to sibling personality differences.

make individuals *different* from each other. And there are many sources of "nonshared" experience in a typical home. Parents, for example, often treat sons differently than daughters, or first-born children differently than younger ones. To the extent that siblings are not treated alike by parents, they will experience different environments, which will increase the likelihood that their personalities will differ in important ways. Interactions among siblings provide another source of nonshared environmental influence. For example, an older sibling who habitually dominates a younger one may become generally assertive and dominant as a result of these home experiences. But for the younger child, this home environment is a dominating environment that may foster the development of such personality traits as passivity, tolerance, and cooperation.

Measuring the Effects of Nonshared Environments. How could we ever measure the impact of something as broad as nonshared environments? One strategy used by Denise Daniels and her associates (Daniels, 1986; Daniels & Plomin, 1985) is simply to ask pairs of adolescent siblings whether they have been treated differently by parents and teachers or have experienced other important differences in their lives (for example, differences in their popularity with peers). Daniels finds that siblings do report such differences, and, more important, the greater the *differences* in parental treatment and other experiences that siblings report, the more dissimilar siblings are in their personalities. Although correlational studies of this sort do not conclusively establish that differences in experiences *cause* differences in personality, they do suggest that some of the most important environmental influences on development may be nonshared experiences unique to each member of the family (Dunn & Plomin, 1990).

Do Siblings Have Different Experiences Because They Have Different Genes? Stated another way, isn't it possible that a child's genetically influenced attributes might affect how other people respond to her, so that a physically attractive youngster, for example, is apt to be treated very differently by parents and peers than a less attractive sibling would be? Although genes do contribute to some extent to the different experiences that siblings have (Pike et al., 1996; Plomin et al., 1994), there is ample reason to believe that our highly individualized, unique environments are not entirely due to our having inherited different genes. How do we know this?

The most important clue comes from studies of identical twins. Because identical twins are perfectly matched from a genetic standpoint, any *differences* between them must necessarily reflect the contribution of environmental influences that they do *not* share. Identical twins do report differences in their environments that have implications for their personalities and social adjustment. For example, one recent study found that a twin who receives warmer treatment from a parent (an NSE) or who establishes closer relationships with teachers (an NSE) is typically less emotionally distressed than his or her identical co-twin (Crosnoe & Elder, 2002). And the greater the discrepancies in the ways that identical twins are treated by their parents, the less similar the twins are in their personalities and social behaviors (Asbury et al., 2003). Clearly, these nonshared environmental influences cannot be attributed to the twins' different genes, because identical twins have identical genotypes! This is why the formula for estimating the contribution of nonshared environmental influences (that is $1 - r$ [identical twins raised together]) makes sense, for the estimate it provides is based on environmental influences that are *not* in any way influenced by genes.

With these facts in mind, let's return to Table 3.5. Here we see that the average correlation for identical twins across many personality traits is only +.50, which implies that identical twins are similar in some respects and different in others. Applying the formula for estimating NSE (1 − .50 = **.50**) tells us that nonshared environmental influences are very important contributors to personality—at least as important as genes are.

In sum, the family environment does contribute importantly to personality, but not simply because it has a standard effect on all family members that makes them alike. True, there are some important areas of socialization for which parents do treat all their children alike and foster similarities among them. For example, parents often model and encourage the same moral, religious, social, and political interests and values in all their children. For these and many other psychological characteristics, *shared environmental influences* are often as important or even more important than genes in creating likenesses between brothers and sisters (Bussell et al., 1999; Hoffman, 1991, 1994). But when it comes to the shaping of many other basic personality traits, it is the *nonshared* experiences people have—in concert with genetic influences—that contribute most to their phenotypes (Plomin et al., 2001; Reiss et al., 2000).

Hereditary Contributions to Behavior Disorders and Mental Illness

Is there a hereditary basis for mental illness? Might some people be genetically predisposed to commit deviant or antisocial acts? Although these ideas seemed absurd 30 years ago, it now appears that the answer to both questions is a qualified yes.

schizophrenia
a serious form of mental illness characterized by disturbances in logical thinking, emotional expression, and interpersonal behavior.

Consider the evidence for **schizophrenia**—a serious mental illness, characterized by severe disturbances in logical thinking, emotional expression, and social behavior, which typically emerges in late adolescence or early adulthood. A survey of several twin studies of schizophrenia suggests an average concordance rate of .48 for identical twins but only .17 for fraternal twins (Gottesman, 1991). In addition, children who have a biological parent who is schizophrenic are at increased risk of becoming schizophrenic themselves, even if they are adopted by another family early in life (Loehlin, 1992). These are strong indications that schizophrenia is genetically influenced.

bipolar disorder
a psychological disorder characterized by extreme fluctuations in mood.

neurotic disorder
an irrational pattern of thinking or behavior that a person may use to contend with stress or to avoid anxiety.

In recent years, it has also become quite clear that heredity contributes to abnormal behaviors and conditions such as alcoholism, criminality, depression, hyperactivity, **bipolar disorder,** and a number of **neurotic disorders** (Plomin et al., 2001; Rowe, 1994.). Now, it is possible that you may have close relatives who were diagnosed as alcoholic, neurotic, bipolar, or schizophrenic. Rest assured that this does *not* mean that you or your children will develop these problems. Only 9 percent of children who have one schizophrenic parent ever develop any symptoms that might be labeled "schizophrenic" (Plomin et al., 2001). Even if you are an identical twin whose co-twin has a serious psychiatric disorder, the odds are only between 1 in 2 (for schizophrenia) and 1 in 20 (for most other disorders) that you would ever experience anything that even approaches the problem that affects your twin.

Because identical twins are usually *discordant* (that is, not alike) with respect to mental illnesses and behavior disorders, environment must be a very important contributor to these conditions. In other words, people do not inherit behavioral disorders; instead they inherit *predispositions* to develop certain illnesses or deviant patterns of behavior. And even when a child's family history suggests that such a genetic predisposition may exist, it usually takes a number of very stressful experiences (for example, rejecting parents, a failure or series of failures at school, or a family breakup due to divorce) to trigger a mental illness (Plomin & Rende, 1991; Rutter, 1979). Clearly, these findings provide some basis for optimism, for it may be possible someday to prevent the onset of most genetically influenced disorders should we (1) learn more about the environmental triggers that precipitate these disturbances while (2) striving to develop interventions or therapeutic techniques that will help high-risk individuals to maintain their emotional stability in the face of environmental stress (Plomin & Rutter, 1998).

Theories of Heredity and Environment Interactions in Development

Only 50 years ago, developmentalists were embroiled in the nature/nurture controversy: Was heredity or environment the primary determinant of human potential? (See, for example, Anastasi, 1958.) Although this chapter has focused on biological influences, it should now be clear that *both* heredity and environment contribute importantly to development and that the often extreme positions taken by hereditarians and environmentalists in the past are greatly oversimplified. Today, behavioral geneticists no longer think in terms of nature *versus* nurture; instead, they try to determine how these two important influences might combine or interact to promote developmental change.

The Canalization Principle

Although both heredity and environment contribute to most human traits, our genes influence some attributes more than others. Many years ago, Conrad Waddington (1966) used the term **canalization** to refer to cases where genes limit or restrict development to a small number of outcomes. One example of a highly canalized human attribute is babbling in infancy. All infants, even deaf ones, babble in pretty much the same way over the first 8 to 10 months of life. The environment has little if any effect on this highly canalized attribute, which simply unfolds according to a maturational program. Less canalized attributes such as intelligence, temperament, and personality can be deflected away from their genetic pathways in any of several directions by a variety of life experiences.

canalization
genetic restriction of phenotype to a small number of developmental outcomes; a highly canalized attribute is one for which genes channel development along predetermined pathways, so that the environment has little effect on the phenotype that emerges.

We now know that potent environmental influences can also limit, or canalize, development. In Chapter 2, for example, we discussed Gilbert Gottlieb's (1991a) intriguing finding that duckling embryos exposed to chicken calls before hatching come to prefer the calls of chickens to those of their own mothers. In this case, the ducklings' prenatal experiences (environment) overrode the presumably canalized genetic predisposition to favor the vocalization of their own species. Environments may also canalize human development. For example, early environments in which nutrition and social stimulation are inadequate can permanently stunt children's growth and impair their intellectual development.

In sum, the canalization principle is a simple idea—and yet, a very useful one that illustrates that (1) there are multiple pathways along which an individual might develop, (2) nature and nurture combine to determine these pathways, and (3) either genes or environment may limit the extent to which the other factor can influence development. Irving Gottesman makes the same points about gene influences in a slightly different way in his own theory of genotype/environment interactions (discussed in the following section).

The Range-of-Reaction Principle

According to Gottesman (1963), genes typically do not rigidly canalize behavior. Instead, an individual genotype establishes a range of possible responses to different kinds of life experiences: the so-called **range of reaction.** In other words, Gottesman claims that a genotype sets boundaries on the range of possible phenotypes that one might display to different environments. An important corollary is that, because people differ genetically, no two individuals should respond in precisely the same way to any particular environment.

range-of-reaction principle
the idea that genotype sets limits on the range of possible phenotypes that a person might display in response to different environments.

The concept of reaction range, as applied to intellectual performance, is illustrated in Figure 3.18. Here we see the effects of varying degrees of environmental enrichment on the IQs of three children: Juan, who has high genetic potential for intellectual development, Tony, whose genetic endowment for intelligence is average, and Freddie, whose potential for intellectual growth is far below average. Notice that under similar environmental conditions, Juan always outperforms the other two children. Juan also has the widest reaction range, in that his IQ might vary from well below average in a restricted

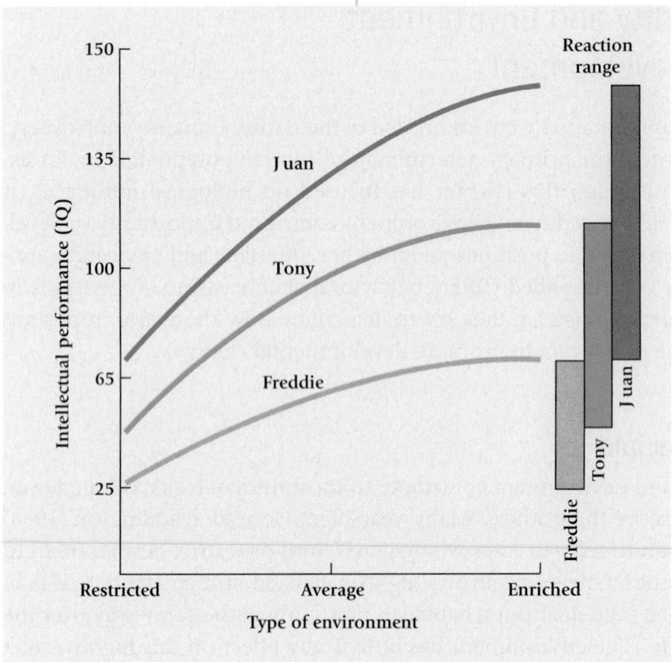

Figure 3.18 Hypothetical reaction ranges for the intellectual performances of three children in restricted, average, and intellectually enriching environments. *Adapted from "Heritability of Personality: A Demonstration," by I. Gottesman, 1963,* Psychological Monographs, *11 (Whole No. 572). Copyright © 1963 by the American Psychological Association.*

environment to far above average in an enriched environment. As is expected, Freddie has a very limited reaction range; his potential for intellectual development is low, and, as a result, he shows smaller variation in IQ across environments than do the other two children.

In sum, the range-of-reaction principle is a clear statement about the interplay between heredity and environment. Presumably, one's genotype sets a range of possible outcomes for any particular attribute, and the environment largely influences where, within that range, he or she will fall.

Genotype/Environment Correlations

Up until now, we have talked as if heredity and environment were independent sources of influence that somehow combined to determine our observable characteristics, or phenotypes. This view is probably much too simple. Many behavioral geneticists now believe that our genes may actually influence the kinds of environments that we are likely to experience (Plomin, DeFries, & Loehlin, 1977; Scarr & McCartney, 1983). How? In at least three ways.

Passive Genotype/Environment Correlations. According to Scarr and McCartney (1983), the kind of home environment that parents provide for their children is influenced, in part, by the parents' own genotypes. And because parents also provide their children with genes, it so happens that the rearing environments to which children are exposed are correlated with (and are likely to suit) their own genotypes.

Koki Iino/Getty Images

Passive genotype-environment correlations occur when the parent provides an environment that is related to the genotype of the child, which the parent also provided.

passive genotype/environment correlations
the notion that the rearing environments that biological parents provide are influenced by the parents' own genes, and hence are correlated with the child's own genotype.

The following example illustrates a developmental implication of these **passive genotype/environment correlations.** Parents who are genetically predisposed to be athletic may create a very "athletic" home environment by encouraging their children to play vigorously and to take an interest in sporting activities. Besides being exposed to an athletic environment, the children may have inherited their parents' athletic genes, which might make them particularly responsive to that environment. So children of athletic parents may come to enjoy athletic pursuits for *both* hereditary and environmental reasons, and the influences of heredity and environment are tightly intertwined.

Evocative Genotype/Environment Correlations. Earlier, we noted that the environmental influences that contribute most heavily to many aspects of personality are nonshared experiences that make individuals *different* from one another. Might the differences in environments that children experience be partly due to the fact that they have inherited different genes and may elicit different reactions from their companions?

evocative genotype/environment correlations
the notion that our heritable attributes affect others' behavior toward us and thus influence the social environment in which development takes place.

Scarr and McCartney (1983) think so. Their notion of **evocative genotype/environment correlations** assumes that a child's genetically influenced attributes will affect the behavior of others toward him or her. For example, smiley, active babies receive more attention and positive social stimulation than moody and passive ones (Deater-Deckard & O'Connor, 2000). Teachers may respond more favorably to physically attractive students than to their less attractive classmates. Clearly, these reactions of other people to the child (and the child's genetically influenced attributes) are environmental influences that play an important role in shaping that child's personality. So once again, we see an intermingling of hereditary and environmental influences: Heredity affects the character of the social environment in which the personality develops.

Active Genotype/Environment Correlations. Finally, Scarr and McCartney (1983) propose that the environments that children prefer and seek out will be those that are most compatible with their genetic predispositions. For example, a child genetically predisposed to be extroverted is likely to invite friends to the house, to be an avid party-goer, and to generally prefer activities that are socially stimulating. Similarly, a child who is genetically predisposed to be shy and introverted may actively avoid large social gatherings and choose instead to pursue activities (such as playing video games) that can be enjoyed alone. So one implication of these **active genotype/environment correlations** is that people with different genotypes will select different "environmental niches" for themselves—niches that may then have a powerful effect on their future social, emotional, and intellectual development.

active genotype/environment correlations
the notion that our genotypes affect the types of environments that we prefer and seek out.

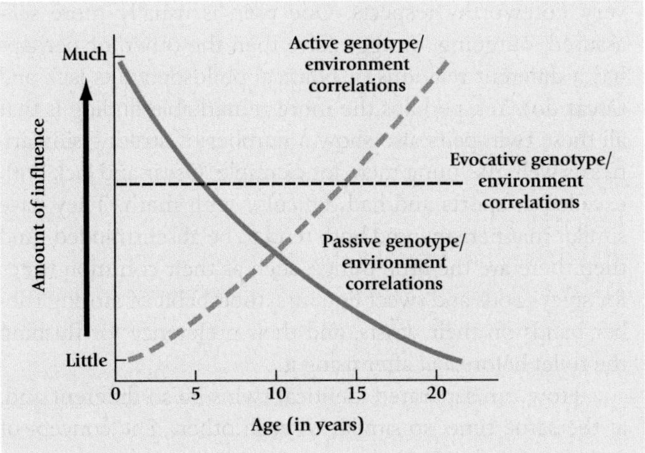

Figure 3.19 Relative influence of passive, evocative, and active (niche-picking) genotype/environment correlations as a function of age.

How Do Genotype/Environment Correlations Influence Development? According to Scarr and McCartney (1983), the relative importance of active, passive, and evocative gene influences changes over the course of childhood. During the first few years, infants and toddlers are not free to roam the neighborhood, choosing friends and building environmental niches; most of their time is spent at home in an environment that parents structure for them, making passive genotype/environment correlations particularly important early in life. But once children reach school age and venture away from home on a daily basis, they suddenly become much freer to select their own interests, activities, friends, and hangouts. Therefore, active, niche-building correlations should exert greater influence on development as the child matures (see Figure 3.19). Finally, evocative genotype/environment correlations are always important; that is, a person's genetically influenced attributes and patterns of behavior may influence the ways other people react to him or her throughout life.

If Scarr and McCartney's theory has any merit, then virtually all siblings other than identical twins should become less similar over time as they emerge from the relatively similar rearing environments that parents impose during their early years and begin to actively select different environmental niches for themselves. Indeed, there is ample support for this idea. Pairs of genetically unrelated adoptees who live in the same home do show some definite similarities in conduct and in intellectual performance during early and middle childhood (Scarr & Weinberg, 1978). Because these adoptees share no genes with each other or with their adoptive parents, their resemblances must be due to their common rearing environments. Yet, by late adolescence, genetically unrelated siblings barely resemble each other in intelligence, personality, or any other aspect of behavior, presumably because they have selected very different environmental niches, which, in turn, have steered them along different developmental paths (Scarr, 1992; Scarr & McCartney, 1983). Even fraternal twins, who have 50 percent of their genes in common, are much less alike as adolescents or adults than they were as children (McCartney, Harris, & Bernieri, 1990; and recall the declining resemblance in fraternal twins' IQs over time as shown in Figure 3.17). Apparently the genes that fraternal twins do *not* share cause these individuals to select different environmental niches, which, in turn, contribute to their declining resemblance over time.

On the other hand, pairs of identical twins bear a close behavioral resemblance throughout childhood and adolescence. Why? For two reasons: (1) Not only do identical twins evoke similar reactions from other people, but (2) their identical genotypes predispose them to prefer and select very similar environments (that is, friends, interests, and activities), which will then exert comparable influences on these twin pairs and virtually guarantee that they will continue to resemble one another. Even identical twins raised apart should be similar in some respects because their identical genes cause them to seek out and to prefer similar activities and experiences. Let's take a closer look.

Separated Identical Twins. Thomas Bouchard and his associates (Bouchard et al., 1990; Neimark, 2000) have studied nearly 100 pairs of separated identical twins—people with identical genes who were raised in different home environments. One such pair was Oscar Stohr and Jack Yufe. Oscar was raised as a Catholic by his mother in Nazi-dominated Europe. He became involved in the Hitler Youth Movement during World War II and is now employed as a factory supervisor in Germany. Jack, a store owner, was raised as a Jew and came to loathe Nazis while growing up in a Caribbean country halfway around the world. Today, Jack is a political liberal, whereas Oscar is very, very conservative.

Like every pair of separated identical twins that Bouchard has studied, Oscar and Jack are different in some very noteworthy respects. One twin is usually more self-assured, outgoing, or aggressive than the other, or perhaps has a different religious or political philosophy (as Jack and Oscar do). Yet, perhaps the more remarkable finding is that all these twin pairs also show a number of striking similarities as well. As young men, for example, Oscar and Jack both excelled at sports and had difficulty with math. They have similar mannerisms, and both tend to be absentminded. And then there are the little things, such as their common tastes for spicy foods and sweet liqueurs, their habit of storing rubber bands on their wrists, and their preference for flushing the toilet before *and* after using it.

Robert Burroughs

Jack Yufe (left) and Oscar Stohr (right).

How can separated identical twins be so different and, at the same time, so similar to each other? The concept of *active gene influences* helps to explain the uncanny resemblances. When we learn that twins grew up in different environments, we tend to think of these settings as more dissimilar than they really are. In fact, identical twins raised apart are members of the same historical period who are likely to be exposed to many of the same kinds of objects, activities, educational experiences, and historical events as they are growing up. So, if identical twins are genetically predisposed to select comparable aspects of the environment for special attention, and if their "different" environments provide them with reasonably similar sets of experiences from which to build their environmental niches, then these individuals should resemble each other in many of their habits, mannerisms, abilities, and interests.

Why, then, do separated identical twins often differ? According to Scarr and McCartney (1983), twins could be expected to differ on any attribute for which their rearing environments are so dissimilar as to prevent them from ever establishing comparable niches. Oscar Stohr and Jack Yufe are a prime example. They are alike in many ways because their separate rearing environments permitted them access to many of the same kinds of experiences (for example, sports, math classes, spicy foods, rubber bands), thereby enabling these genetically identical individuals to develop several similar habits, mannerisms, and interests. However, it was almost inevitable that they would differ in their political ideologies because their sociopolitical environments (Nazi-dominated Europe vs. the laid-back Caribbean) were so dissimilar as to prevent them from ever building the kinds of "niches" that would have made them staunch political allies.

Contributions and Criticisms of the Behavioral Genetics Approach

Behavioral genetics is a relatively new discipline that is having a strong influence on the way scientists look at human development (Dick & Rose, 2002). We now know, for example, that many attributes previously thought to be shaped by environment are influenced, in part, by genes. As Scarr and McCartney put it, we are products of "cooperative efforts of the nature/nurture team, directed by the genetic quarterback" (1983, p. 433). In effect, genes may exert many of their influences on human development by affecting the experiences we have, which in turn influence our behavior. And one very important implication of their viewpoint is that many of the "environmental" influences on development that have previously been identified may reflect, in part, the workings of heredity (Plomin et al., 2001; see also Turkheimer, 2000).

Of course, not all developmentalists would agree that genetic endowment is the "quarterback" of the "nature/nurture team" (Gottlieb, 1996; Wachs, 1992). Students often object to Scarr and McCartney's theory because they sometimes read it to mean that genes *determine* environments. But this is not what the theory implies. What Scarr and McCartney are saying is this:

1. People with different genotypes are likely to evoke different responses from others and to select different environmental niches for themselves.
2. Yet, the responses they evoke and the niches they select depend to no small extent on the particular individuals, settings, and circumstances they encounter. Although a child may be genetically predisposed to be outgoing and extroverted, for example, it would be difficult to act on this predisposition if she lived in the wilds of Alaska with a reclusive father. In fact, this youngster could well become rather shy and reserved when raised in such an asocial environment.

In sum, genotypes and environments *interact* to produce developmental change and variations in developmental outcomes. True, genes exert some influence on those aspects of the environment that we are likely to experience. But the particular environments available to us limit the possible phenotypes that are likely to emerge from a particular genotype (Gottlieb, 1991b; 1996). Perhaps Donald Hebb (1980) was not too far off when he said that behavior is determined 100 percent by heredity and 100 percent by the environment, for it seems that these two sets of influences are complexly intertwined.

Interesting as these new ideas may be, critics argue that the behavioral genetics approach is merely a descriptive overview of how development might proceed rather than a well-articulated explanation of development. One reason for this sentiment is that we know so little about how genes exert their effects. Genes are coded to manufacture amino acids, not to produce such attributes as intelligence or sociability. Though we now suspect that genes affect behavior indirectly by influencing the experiences we evoke from others or create for ourselves, we are still a long way from understanding how or why genes might impel us to prefer particular kinds of stimulation or to find certain activities especially satisfying (Plomin & Rutter, 1998). In addition, behavioral geneticists apply the term "environment" in a very global way, making few if any attempts to measure environmental influences directly or to specify *how* environments act on individuals to influence their behavior. Perhaps you can see the problem: the critics contend that one has not explained development by merely postulating that unspecified environmental forces influenced in unknown ways by our genes will somehow shape our abilities, conduct, and character (Bronfenbrenner & Ceci, 1994; Gottlieb, 1996).

How exactly do environments influence people's abilities, conduct, and character? What environmental influences, at what ages, are particularly important? These are questions that we will be seeking to answer throughout this text. We begin in our next chapter by examining how environmental events that occur even before a child is born combine with nature's scheme to influence the course of prenatal development and the characteristics of newborn infants.

CONCEPT CHECK 3.3 Understanding Hereditary Influences on Behavior

Check your understanding of how more complex behavioral characteristics like personality and intelligence are influenced by genotype, phenotype, and experience by answering the following questions. Answers appear in the Appendix.

Multiple Choice: Select the best answer for each question.

_____ 1. In an example of "selective breeding," the scientist Tyron:
   a. bred pea plants and observed their combinations of characteristics
   b. bred rats and tested their maze-running abilities
   c. observed differences in the genetics of identical twins versus fraternal twins
   d. tested how adoption and living with nonbiological parents affect a child's phenotype

_____ 2. The "heritability coefficient" involves comparing _____ to _____.
   a. identical twins in the same environment; identical twins in different environments
   b. fraternal twins in the same environment; fraternal twins in different environments
   c. identical twins; fraternal twins
   d. fraternal twins; nontwin siblings

_____ 3. Heredity contributes to all of the following conditions *except* which?
   a. schizophrenia
   b. bipolar disorder
   c. anorexia nervosa
   d. alcoholism

_____ 4. The limited number of ways a person will respond to the environment is determined by his or her genotype. The possible responses a person could make is called his or her:
   a. possible outcome scenario
   b. range of reaction
   c. nonshared environmental influences
   d. shared environmental influences

True or False: Identify whether the following statements are true or false.

5. (T)(F) Genes are more important earlier in life, whereas experience alone determines intellectual performance after adolescence.
6. (T)(F) Genes influence both the course and the extent of infants' mental development.
7. (T)(F) Both nonshared environmental influences and genetic influences contribute to phenotypes.

Short Answer: Briefly answer the following questions.

8. Briefly describe Tyron's selective breeding experiment and his findings. How did his findings influence other scientists' views of genetics?
9. Describe the two types of family studies used to observe the effect of genotypes on phenotypes and explain which process you would rather use when conducting research of your own. Why would you use this process?

Essay: Provide a more detailed answer to the following question.

10. Describe the principle of active gene influences. What kind of situations are identical twins reared in separate environments likely to share?

Applying Developmental Themes to Hereditary Influences on Development

Throughout this book we will be examining how research and theory on particular topics that we've investigated relate to the four central developmental themes: the active child, nature and nurture interactions, qualitative and quantitative changes in development, and the holistic nature of child development. In this chapter we see that these themes arise even before birth, because hereditary influences on development play into each of these issues.

Scarr and McCartney's genotype/environment correlations theory raises interesting possibilities for the active nature of child development. Recall that the active child refers to how the child's characteristics influence his or her development, and that this influence need not reflect conscious choices or behaviors. According to the genotype/environment correlation theory, the child is active in his or her development through passive genotype/environment correlations, because these depend upon the genotype of the child. The child is also active in evocative genotype/environment correlations, because these also depend upon the responses elicited by the child's genotype. Finally, the child is active in the choices of environment he or she pursues in the active genotype/environment correlations. Clearly, this theory (and the data that support it) is strong evidence for the child's active role in development.

Our discussion of the hereditary influences on development throughout the chapter emphasized the interaction of nature and nurture in driving development. We discussed behavioral genetic methods for attempting to measure the relative contribution of heredity, shared environmental effects, and nonshared environmental effects on various behavioral characteristics. We saw that although we could partition effects using concordance rates, kinship correlations, and heritability estimates, we nonetheless were always left acknowledging that nature and nurture interact in development in complex and immeasurable ways.

We also covered a few examples of qualitative and quantitative developmental changes in this chapter. The process of meiosis, by which a germ cell divides and becomes gametes, is an example of a qualitative change. The process of mitosis, by which the body cells divide, is an example of a quantitative change in development.

A more theoretical example of qualitative changes in development draws on the genotype/environment correlation theory again. Recall that the relative influence of the different types of genotype/environment correlations changes across development, with passive effects being stronger influences early in development, and active effects being stronger influences later in development.

Our final theme concerns the holistic nature of child development. Perhaps this theme is the most basic idea from our investigation of hereditary influences on development. We saw in this chapter that heredity and environment influence all aspects of child development: physical, social, cognitive, and behavioral. Clearly heredity is an important building block for understanding the child as an integrated labyrinth of influences and outcomes in all aspects of psychological functioning.

SUMMARY

Principles of Hereditary Transmission

- Development begins at **conception,** when a sperm cell from the father penetrates an ovum from the mother, forming a **zygote.**
- A normal human zygote contains 46 **chromosomes** (23 from each parent), each of which consists of several thousand strands of **deoxyribonucleic acid** (or **DNA**) known as **genes.** Genes are the biological basis for the development of the zygote into a person.
- Development of the zygote occurs through **mitosis**—new body cells are created as the 23 paired chromosomes in each cell duplicate themselves and separate into 2 identical new cells.
- Specialized germ cells divide by **meiosis** to produce gametes (sperm or ova) that each contain 23 unpaired chromosomes. **Crossing-over** and the **independent assortment** of chromosomes ensure that each gamete receives a unique set of genes from each parent.
- **Monozygotic** (or **identical**) **twins** result when a single zygote divides to create two cells that develop independently into two individuals.
- **Dizygotic** (or **fraternal**) twins result when two different ova are each fertilized by a different sperm cell, then develop independently into two individuals.
- Gametes contain 22 **autosomes** and 1 sex chromosome. Females' sex chromosomes are both X chromosomes, males' sex chromosomes are an X and a Y chromosome.
- Ova contain an **X chromosome.** Sperm contain either an X or a Y chromosome. Therefore, fathers determine the sex of their children (depending on whether the sperm that fertilizes the ova contains an X or a Y chromosome).
- Genes produce enzymes and other proteins that are necessary for the creation and functioning of new cells, and regulate the timing of development. Internal and external environments influence how genes function.
- There are many ways in which one's **genotype** may affect **phenotype**—the way one looks, feels, thinks, or behaves.
    - Some characteristics are determined by a single pair of **alleles,** one of which is inherited from each parent.
        - In simple **dominant/recessive** traits, the individual displays the phenotype of the **dominant allele.**
        - If a gene pair is **codominant,** the individual displays a phenotype in between those produced by the dominant and the **recessive alleles.**
        - **Sex-linked characteristics** are those caused by recessive genes on the X chromosome when there is no corresponding gene on the Y chromosome to mask its effects; they are more common in males.
    - Most complex human attributes, such as intelligence and personality traits, are **polygenic,** or influenced by many genes rather than a single pair.

Hereditary Disorders

- Occasionally, children inherit **congenital defects** (for example, **Huntington's disease**) that are caused by abnormal genes and chromosomes.
    - Chromosomal abnormalities occur when the individual inherits too many or too few chromosomes.
    - A major **autosomal** disorder is **Down syndrome,** in which the child inherits an extra 21st chromosome.
    - Many genetic disorders can be passed to children by parents who are not affected but are **carriers** of a recessive allele for the disorder.
    - Genetic abnormalities may also result from **mutations**—changes in the structure of one or more genes that can occur spontaneously or result from environmental hazards such as radiation or toxic chemicals.

Genetic Counseling, Prenatal Detection, and Treatment of Hereditary Disorders

- **Genetic counseling** informs prospective parents about the odds of giving birth to a child with a hereditary disorder. Family histories and medical tests are used to determine if the parents are at risk.
- **Amniocentesis, chorionic villus sampling,** and **ultrasound** are used for prenatal detection of many genetic and chromosomal abnormalities.
- Medical interventions such as special diets, fetal surgery, drugs and hormones, and gene replacement therapy can reduce the harmful effects of many heredity disorders (for example, **phenylketonuria,** or **PKU**).

Hereditary Influences on Behavior

- **Behavioral genetics** is the study of how genes and environment contribute to individual variations in development.
- Although animals can be studied in **selective breeding** experiments, human behavioral geneticists must conduct family studies (often **twin designs** or **adoption designs**), estimating the **heritability** of various attributes from similarities and differences among family members who differ in **kinship.**
- Hereditary contributions to various attributes are estimated using **concordance rates** and **heritability coefficients.**
- Behavioral geneticists can also determine the amount of variability in a trait that is attributable to **nonshared environmental influences** and **shared environmental influences.**
- Family studies reveal that heritability influences intellectual performance, **introversion-extroversion** and **empathic concern,** and predispositions to display such disorders as **schizophrenia, bipolar disorder, neurotic disorders,** alcoholism, and criminality.

Theories of Hereditary and Environment Interactions in Development

- The **canalization** principle implies that genes limit development to certain outcomes that are difficult for the environment to alter.
- The **range-of-reaction** principle states that heredity sets a range of developmental potentials and the environment influences where in that range the individual will fall.
- A more recent theory proposes three avenues by which genes influence the environments we are likely to experience: through **passive genotype/environment correlations, evocative genotype/environment correlations,** and **active genotype/environment correlations.**
- The relative influence of the different genotype/environment correlations changes across development, with passive effects predominating in early life, evocative effects operating throughout life, and active effects not playing a role until later childhood and adolescence.

Contributions and Criticisms of the Behavioral Genetics Approach

- Behavioral genetics has had a strong influence on our outlook on human development by showing that many attributes previously thought to be environmentally determined are influenced, in part, by genes.
- It has also helped to defuse the nature versus nurture debate by illustrating that these two sources of influence are complexly intertwined.
- Behavioral genetics has been criticized as an incomplete theory of development that describes, but fails to explain, how either genes or environment influence our abilities, conduct, and character.

KEY TERMS

genotype 79
phenotype 79
conception 79
zygote 79
chromosomes 79
genes 80
deoxyribonucleic acid (DNA) 80
mitosis 80
meiosis 81
crossing-over 81
independent assortment 83
monozygotic (identical) twins 84
dizygotic (fraternal) twins 84
X chromosome 85
Y chromosome 85
alleles 87
simple dominant-recessive inheritance 87
dominant allele 87
recessive allele 87
homozygous 87
heterozygous 87
carrier 87
Huntington's disease 88
codominance 88
sickle-cell anemia 89
sex-linked characteristics 89
polygenic traits 89
congenital defects 91
autosomes 93
Down syndrome 93
mutations 93
genetic counseling 95
fragile-X syndrome 95
amniocentesis 95
chorionic villus sampling (CVS) 96
ultrasound 96
phenylketonuria (PKU) 97
germline gene therapy 97
behavioral genetics 100
heritability 100
selective breeding experiment 100
kinship 101
twin design 101
adoption design 101
concordance rates 101
heritability coefficient 103
nonshared environmental influences (NSE) 103
shared environmental influences (SE) 103
introversion/extroversion 106
empathic concern 106
schizophrenia 108
bipolar disorder 108
neurotic disorders 108
canalization 109
range of reaction 109
passive genotype/environment correlations 111
evocative genotype/environment correlations 111
active genotype/environment correlations 111

MEDIA RESOURCES

The Human Development Book Companion Website

See the companion website http://www.thomsonedu.com/psychology/shaffer for flashcards, practice quiz questions, Internet links, updates, critical thinking exercises, discussion forums, games, and more

ThomsonNOW! http://www.thomsonedu.com
Go to this site for the link to ThomsonNOW, your one-stop shop. Take a pre-test for this chapter, and ThomsonNOW will generate a personalized study plan based on your test results. The study plan will identify the topics you need to review and direct you to online resources to help you master those topics. You can then take a post-test to help you determine the concepts you have mastered and what you will still need to work on.

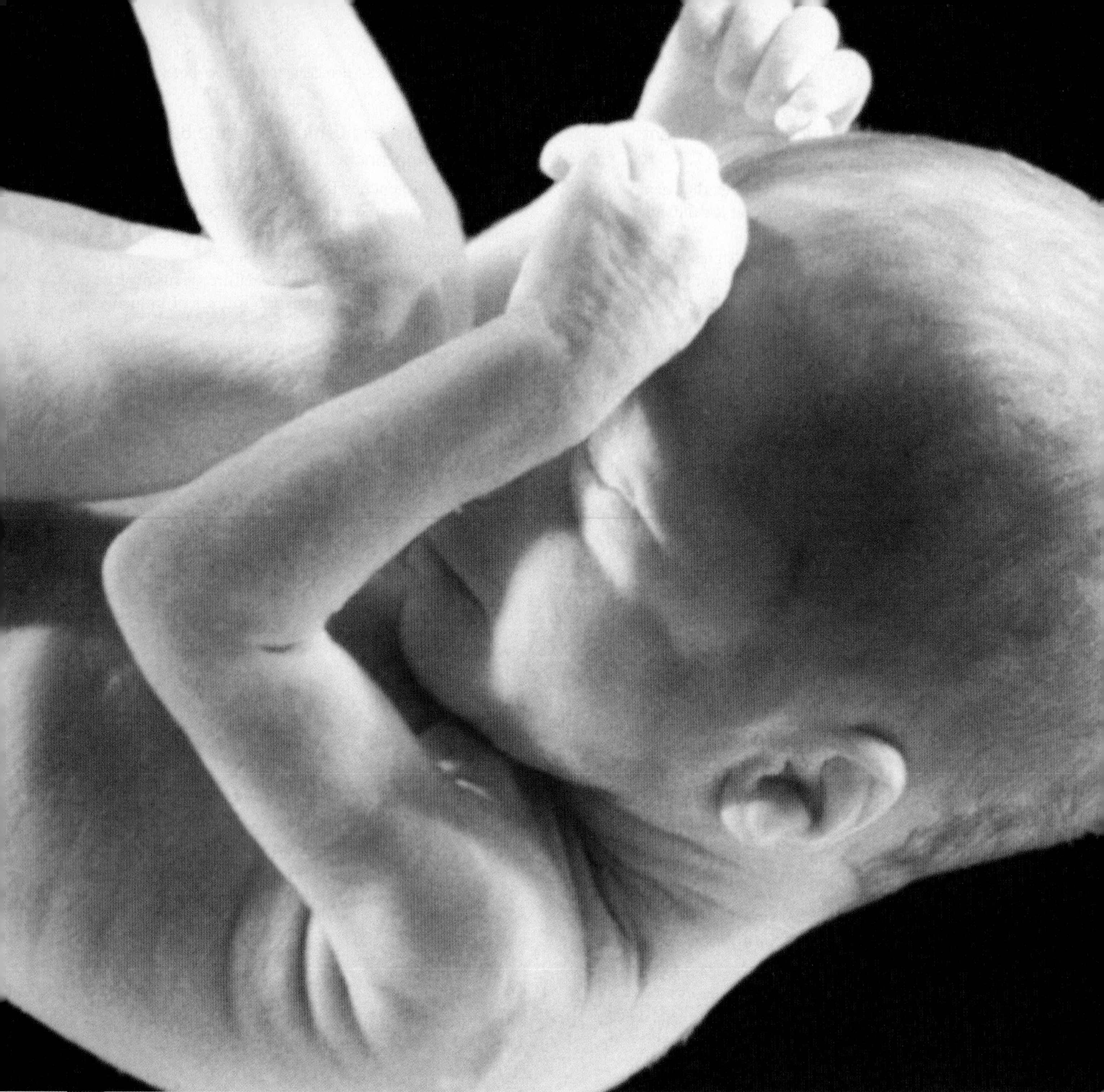

© Ralph Hutchings/Visuals Unlimited

CHAPTER

4 Prenatal Development and Birth

If you mention pregnancy in a room full of women, each one who has borne a child will have a story to tell. There will be laughter about food cravings, body shape, and balance issues. There will be tales of babies who arrive early and attend their own showers, as well as recollections of induced labors that jettisoned infants who were reluctant to leave the womb. There will be complaints about advice from the medical world that was later discovered to be prenatally hazardous. Young, healthy women who had never smoked or ingested alcohol, who carefully consumed a nutrient-rich variety of fruits, vegetables and other foods, who made sure they were well rested, and who enjoyed the support of spouse, friends, and family may talk about miscarriage, premature births, or other life-threatening complications that accompanied their pregnancies. Older mothers, or those who inadvertently or intentionally drank alcohol, smoked cigarettes or marijuana, and who paid little heed to their diets, will boast about plump, Gerber-baby newborns that are now at the top of their high school classes. While these women express relief that their offspring seem to have dodged the bullets that they themselves launched, others speak of how they deal with consequences they might have avoided. A few of the women in the room may sit quietly and reflect upon what it was like to be pregnant as a teenager, a single parent, or a widow. As an observer, you will note that nearly every woman in the room was, or has become, keenly aware that a mother's behavioral choices during pregnancy may affect the outcome of her child.

prenatal development
development that occurs between the moment of conception and the beginning of the birth process.

In this chapter we will discuss normal **prenatal development** as well as the things that can go wrong. You will see that the timetable inside the womb differs drastically from what we observe externally as the three familiar trimesters that demark the experience of the pregnant woman. Inside the womb, there are three stages as well, but these stages pass quickly as the organism becomes a zygote, then an embryo, and finally a fetus. The transition from embryo to fetus occurs at 8 weeks, a full month before the pregnant woman enters the second trimester of her pregnancy and, often, before she is aware that she is pregnant. At this point, all of the embryo's major organs are formed. The rest of the prenatal period is a time of growth, developing function, and the refinement of organs and structures that already exist. This means that a woman may pass through the most critical periods of pregnancy before she even knows she is pregnant. Even though she may be aware that behaviors such as ceasing to consume alcohol or monitoring the nutritional value of her diet are beneficial, her window of opportunity for minimizing risk may pass before she realizes that she has reason to make behavioral changes.

In this chapter, we present information about both maternal and paternal behaviors that may impact the course of prenatal development. Some of these behaviors are associated with negative impacts, such as low birth weight, cognitive deficits, or birth defects. Others are associated with healthy newborn outcomes and positive outcomes for the maturing child. Just because a risk or benefit is associated with a certain behavior does not mean that engaging in the behavior will ensure that outcome. For example, both increasing maternal age and alcohol consumption during pregnancy are associated with severe cognitive deficits in newborns, but, as noted above, many women who wait to conceive or who drink alcohol while pregnant, bear perfectly healthy, bright newborns. In addition, although good nutrition, adequate amounts of sleep, and support from the baby's father are associated with positive newborn outcomes, young women with healthy lifestyles who receive both emotional and behavioral support from a spouse or partner may still bear newborns with birth defects or low IQs. The behavioral information in this chapter provides a means for prospective parents to minimize the risks that threaten healthy prenatal development, but perhaps the most important message of the chapter is that all sexually active men and women should be aware of the possibility of a pregnancy, the critical period of the early weeks of pregnancy, and the wisdom of adjusting their lifestyles to provide a healthy prenatal environment, just in case.

From Conception to Birth

In Chapter 3 we learned that development begins in the fallopian tube when a sperm penetrates the wall of an ovum, forming a zygote. From the moment of conception, it will take approximately 266 days for this tiny, one-celled zygote to become a fetus of some 200 billion cells that is ready to be born.

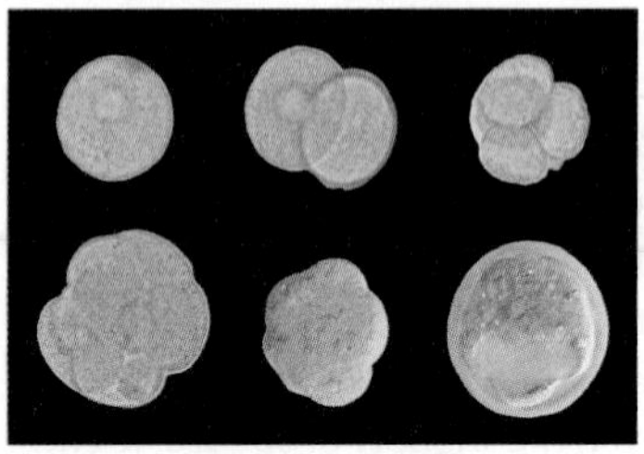

Within hours, the fertilized ovum (zygote) divides, beginning a continuous process of cell differentiation.

Prenatal development is often divided into three major phases. The first phase, called the **period of the zygote,** lasts from conception through implantation, when the developing zygote becomes firmly attached to the wall of the uterus. The period of the zygote normally lasts about 10 to 14 days (Leese, 1994). The second phase of prenatal development, the **period of the embryo,** lasts from the beginning of the third week through the end of the eighth. This is the time when virtually all the major organs are formed and the heart begins to beat (Corsini, 1994). The third phase, the **period of the fetus,** lasts from the ninth week of pregnancy until the baby is born. During this phase, all the major organ systems begin to function, and the developing organism grows rapidly (Malas et al., 2004).

The Period of the Zygote

As the fertilized ovum, or zygote, moves down the fallopian tube toward the uterus, it divides by mitosis into two cells. These two cells and all the resulting cells continue to divide, forming a ball-like structure, or **blastocyst,** that will contain 60 to 80 cells within 4 days of conception (see Figure 4.1). Cell differentiation has already begun. The inner layer of the blastocyst will become the **embryo,** whereas the outer layer of cells will develop into tissues that protect and nourish the embryo.

period of the zygote
first phase of prenatal development, lasting from conception until the developing organism becomes firmly attached to the wall of the uterus.

period of the embryo
second phase of prenatal development, lasting from the third through the eighth prenatal week, during which the major organs and anatomical structures take shape.

period of the fetus
third phase of prenatal development, lasting from the ninth prenatal week until birth; during this period, all major organ systems begin to function and the fetus grows rapidly.

blastocyst
name given to the ball of cells formed when the fertilized egg first begins to divide.

embryo
name given to the prenatal organism from the third through the eighth week after conception.

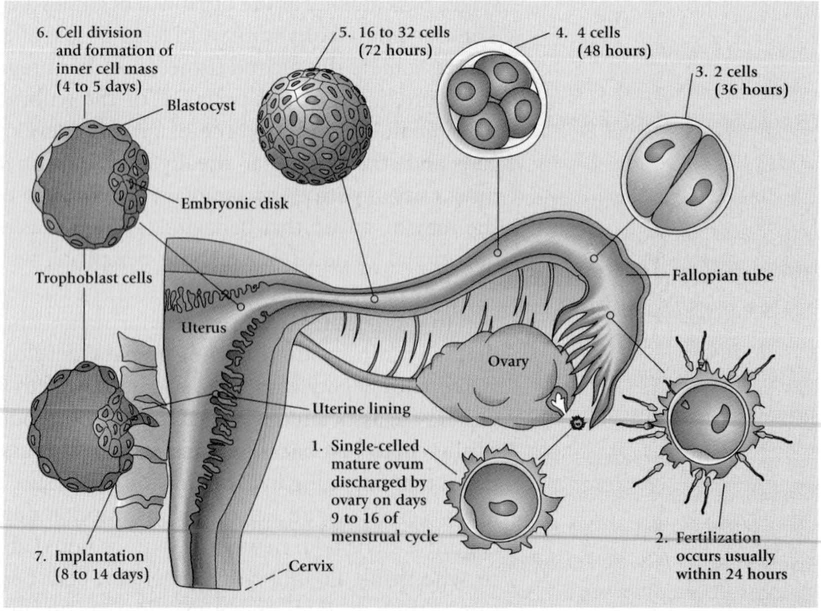

Figure 4.1 The period of the zygote.

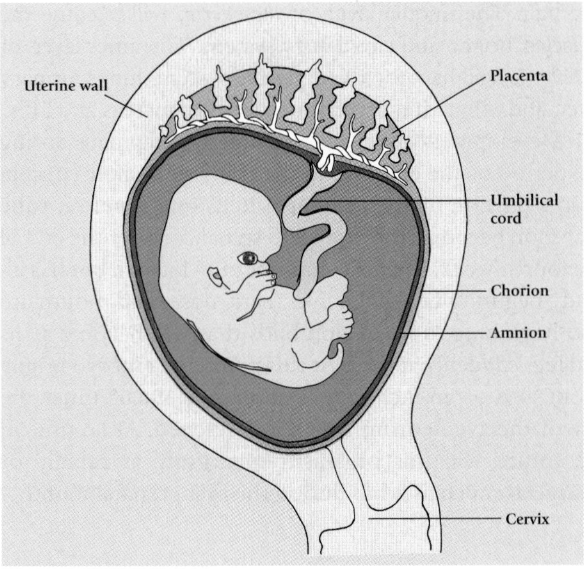

Figure 4.2 The embryo and its prenatal environment.

Implantation

As the blastocyst approaches the uterus 6 to 10 days after conception, small, burrlike tendrils emerge from its outer surface. Upon reaching the uterine wall, these tendrils burrow inward, tapping the mother's blood supply. This is **implantation.** Implantation is quite a development in itself. There is a specific "window of implantation" during which the blastocyst must communicate (biologically) with the uterine wall, position itself, attach and invade. This implantation choreography takes about 48 hours and occurs 7 to 10 days after ovulation, with the entire process completing about 10 to 14 days after ovulation (Hoozemans et al., 2004). Once the blastocyst is implanted it looks like a small translucent blister on the wall of the uterus (see Figure 4.1).

Only about half of all fertilized ova are firmly implanted, and perhaps as many as half of all such implants are either genetically abnormal and fail to develop, or burrow into a site incapable of sustaining them and are miscarried (Moore & Persaud, 1993; Simpson, 1993). So nearly three zygotes out of four fail to survive the initial phase of prenatal development.

Development of Support Systems

Once implanted, the blastocyst's outer layer rapidly forms four major support structures that protect and nourish the developing organism (Sadler, 1996). One membrane, the **amnion,** is a watertight sac that fills with fluid from the mother's tissues. The purposes of this sac and its *amniotic fluid* are to cushion the developing organism against blows, regulate its temperature, and provide a weightless environment that will make it easier for the embryo to move. Floating in this watery environment is a balloon-shaped *yolk sac* that produces blood cells until the embryo is capable of producing its own. This yolk sac is attached to a third membrane, the **chorion,** which surrounds the amnion and eventually becomes the lining of the **placenta**—a multipurpose organ that we will discuss in detail (see Figure 4.2). A fourth membrane, the *allantois,* forms the embryo's **umbilical cord.**

Purpose of the Placenta

Once developed, the placenta is fed by blood vessels from the mother and the embryo, although its hairlike villi act as a barrier that prevents these two bloodstreams from mixing. This placental barrier is semipermeable, meaning that it allows some substances to pass through, but not others. Gases such as oxygen and carbon dioxide, salts, and various nutrients such as sugars, proteins, and fats are small enough to cross the placental barrier. However, blood cells are too large (Gude et al., 2004).

Maternal blood flowing into the placenta delivers oxygen and nutrients into the embryo's bloodstream by means of the umbilical cord, which connects the embryo to the placenta. The umbilical cord also transports carbon dioxide and metabolic wastes from the embryo. These waste products then cross the placental barrier, enter the mother's bloodstream, and are eventually expelled from the mother's body along with her own metabolic wastes. Thus, the placenta plays a crucial role in prenatal development because this organ is the site of all metabolic transactions that sustain the embryo.

implantation
the burrowing of the blastocyst into the lining of the uterus.

amnion
a watertight membrane that surrounds the developing embryo, serving to regulate its temperature and to cushion it against injuries.

chorion
a membrane that becomes attached to the uterine tissues to gather nourishment for the embryo.

placenta
an organ, formed from the lining of the uterus and the chorion, that provides for respiration and nourishment of the unborn child and the elimination of its metabolic wastes.

umbilical cord
a soft tube containing blood vessels that connects the embryo to the placenta.

The Period of the Embryo

The period of the embryo lasts from implantation (roughly the third week) through the eighth week of pregnancy. By the third week, the embryonic disk is rapidly differentiating into three cell layers. The outer layer, or *ectoderm,* will become the nervous system, skin,

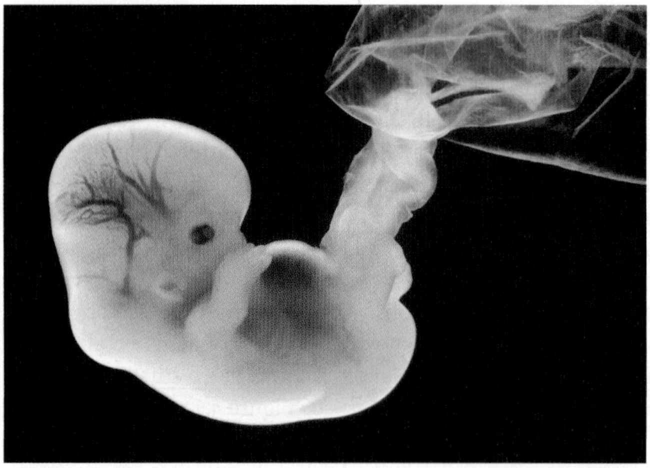

Figure 4.3 A human embryo at 40 days.

and hair. The middle layer, or *mesoderm,* will become the muscles, bones, and circulatory system. The inner layer, or *endoderm,* will become the digestive system, lungs, urinary tract, and other vital organs such as the pancreas and liver.

Development proceeds at a breathtaking pace during the period of the embryo. In the third week after conception, a portion of the ectoderm folds into a **neural tube** that soon becomes the brain and spinal cord. By the end of the fourth week, the heart has not only formed but has already begun to beat. The eyes, ears, nose, and mouth are also beginning to form, and buds that will become arms and legs suddenly appear. At this point, the embryo is only about ¼th of an inch long, but already 10,000 times the size of the zygote from which it developed. At no time in the future will this organism ever grow as rapidly or change as much as it has during the first prenatal month.

neural tube
the primitive spinal cord that develops from the ectoderm and becomes the central nervous system.

The Second Month

During the second month, the embryo becomes much more human in appearance as it grows about 1/30th of an inch per day. A primitive tail appears (see Figure 4.3), but it is soon enclosed by protective tissue and becomes the tip of the backbone, the coccyx. By the middle of the fifth week, the eyes have corneas and lenses. By the seventh week, the ears are well formed, and the embryo has a rudimentary skeleton. Limbs are now developing from the body outward; that is, the upper arms appear first, followed by the forearms, hands, and then fingers. The legs follow a similar pattern a few days later. The brain develops rapidly during the second month, and it directs the organism's first muscular contractions by the end of the embryonic period.

During the seventh and eighth prenatal weeks, the embryo's sexual development begins with the appearance of a genital ridge called the *indifferent gonad.* If the embryo is a male, a gene on its Y chromosome triggers a biochemical reaction that instructs the indifferent gonad to produce testes. If the embryo is a female, the indifferent gonad receives no such instructions and will produce ovaries. The embryo's circulatory system now functions on its own, for the liver and spleen have assumed the task of producing blood cells.

By the end of the second month, the embryo is slightly more than an inch long and weighs less than 1/4th of an ounce. Yet it is already a marvelously complex being. At this point, all the major structures of the human are formed and the organism is beginning to be recognizable as a human (Apgar & Beck, 1974).

The Period of the Fetus

fetus
name given to the prenatal organism from the ninth week of pregnancy until birth.

The last seven months of pregnancy, or period of the **fetus,** is a period of rapid growth (see Figure 4.4) and refinement of all organ systems. This is the time during which all major organ systems begin to function and the fetus begins to move, sense, and behave (although not intentionally). This is also a time when individuality emerges as different fetuses develop unique characteristics, such as different patterns of movement and different facial expressions.

The Third Month

During the third prenatal month, organ systems that were formed earlier continue their rapid growth and become interconnected. For example, coordination between the nervous and muscular systems allow the fetus to perform many interesting maneuvers in its watery environment—kicking its legs, making fists, twisting its body—although these activities are far too subtle to be felt by the pregnant woman. The digestive and excretory

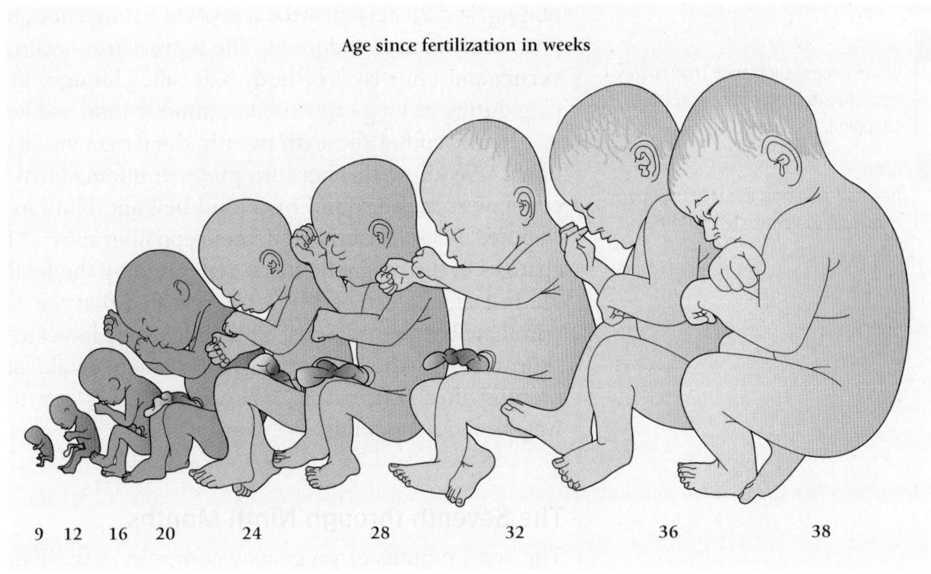

Figure 4.4 Rate of body growth during the fetal period. Increase in size is especially dramatic from the 9th to the 20th week. *Adapted from Before We Are Born, 4th Ed., by K. L. Moore & T. V. N. Persaud, 1993, p. 89. Philadelphia: Saunders. Adapted with permission of the author and publisher.*

systems are also working together, allowing the fetus to swallow, digest nutrients, and urinate (El-Haddad et al., 2004; Ross & Nijland, 1998). Sexual differentiation is progressing rapidly. The male testes secrete *testosterone*—the male sex hormone responsible for the development of a penis and scrotum. In the absence of testosterone, female genitalia form. By the end of the third month, the sex of a fetus can be detected by ultrasound and its reproductive system already contains immature ova or sperm cells. All these detailed developments are present after 12 weeks even though the fetus is a mere 3 inches long and still weighs less than an ounce.

The Fourth through Sixth Months

Development continues at a rapid pace during the 13th through 24th weeks of pregnancy. At age 16 weeks, the fetus is 8 to 10 inches long and weighs about 6 ounces. From 15 or 16 weeks through about 24 or 25 weeks, simple movements of the tongue, lips, pharynx, and larynx increase in complexity and coordination, so that the fetus begins to suck, swallow, munch, hiccup, breathe, cough, and snort, thus, preparing itself for extrauterine life (Miller, Sonies, & Macedonia, 2003). In fact, infants born prematurely may have difficulty breathing and suckling because they exit the womb at an early stage in the development of these skills—simply put, they haven't had enough time to practice (Miller, Sonies, & Macedonia, 2003). During this period the fetus also begins kicking that may be strong enough to be felt by the pregnant woman. The fetal heartbeat can easily be heard with a stethoscope, and as the amount of bone and cartilage increases as the skeleton hardens (Salle et al., 2002) the skeleton can be detected by ultrasound. By the end of the 16th week, the fetus has assumed a distinctly human appearance, although it stands virtually no chance of surviving outside the womb.

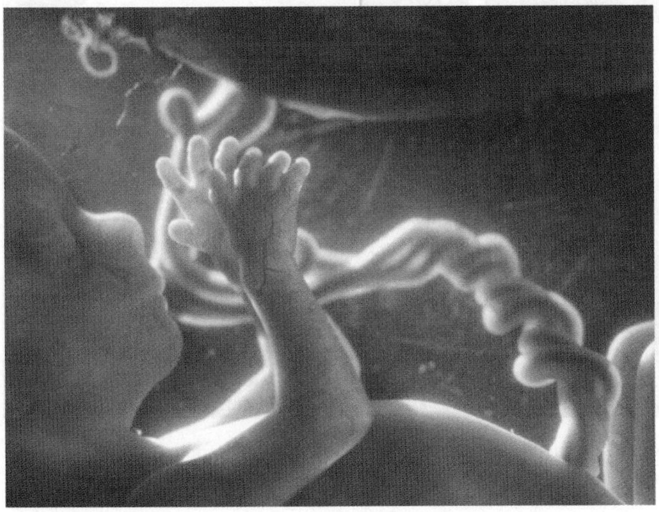

Nestle/Petit Format/Photo Researchers, Inc.

At 12 weeks after conception, the fetus is about 3 inches long and weighs almost 1 ounce. All major organ systems have formed and several are already functioning.

During the fifth and sixth months, the nails harden, the skin thickens, and eyebrows, eyelashes, and scalp hair suddenly appear. At 20 weeks, the sweat glands are func-

vernix
white cheesy substance that covers the fetus to protect the skin from chapping.

lanugo
fine hair covering the fetus's body which helps vernix stick to the skin.

tioning, and the fetal heartbeat is often strong enough to be heard by placing an ear on the pregnant woman's abdomen. The fetus is now covered by a white cheesy substance called **vernix** and a fine layer of body hair called **lanugo.** Vernix protects fetal skin against chapping during its long exposure to amniotic fluid and lanugo helps vernix stick to the skin.

By the end of the sixth month, the fetus's visual and auditory senses are clearly functional. We know this because preterm infants born only 25 weeks after conception become alert at the sound of a loud bell and blink in response to a bright light (Allen & Capute, 1986). Also, magnetoencephalography (MEG) has been used to document changes in the magnetic fields generated by the fetal brain in response to auditory stimuli. In fact, the use of MEG has revealed that the human fetus has some ability to discriminate between sounds. This ability may indicate the presence of a rudimentary, fetal short-term memory system (Huotilainen et al., 2005). These abilities are present 6 months after conception, when the fetus is approximately 14 to 15 inches long and weighs about 2 pounds.

The Seventh through Ninth Months

age of viability
a point between the 22nd and 28th prenatal weeks when survival outside the uterus is possible.

The last 3 months of pregnancy comprise a "finishing phase" during which all organ systems mature rapidly, preparing the fetus for birth. Indeed, somewhere between 22 and 28 weeks after conception (usually in the seventh month), fetuses reach the **age of viability**—the point at which survival outside the uterus is possible (Moore & Persund, 1993). Research using fetal monitoring techniques reveals that 28- to 32-week-old fetuses suddenly begin to show better organized and more predictable cycles of heart rate activity, gross motor activity, and sleepiness/waking activity, findings that indicate that their developing nervous systems are now sufficiently well organized to allow them to survive should their birth be premature (DiPietro et al., 1996; Groome et al., 1997). Nevertheless, many fetuses born this young will still require oxygen assistance because the tiny *pulmonary alveoli* (air sacs) in their lungs are too immature to inflate and exchange oxygen for carbon dioxide on their own (Moore & Persaud, 1993).

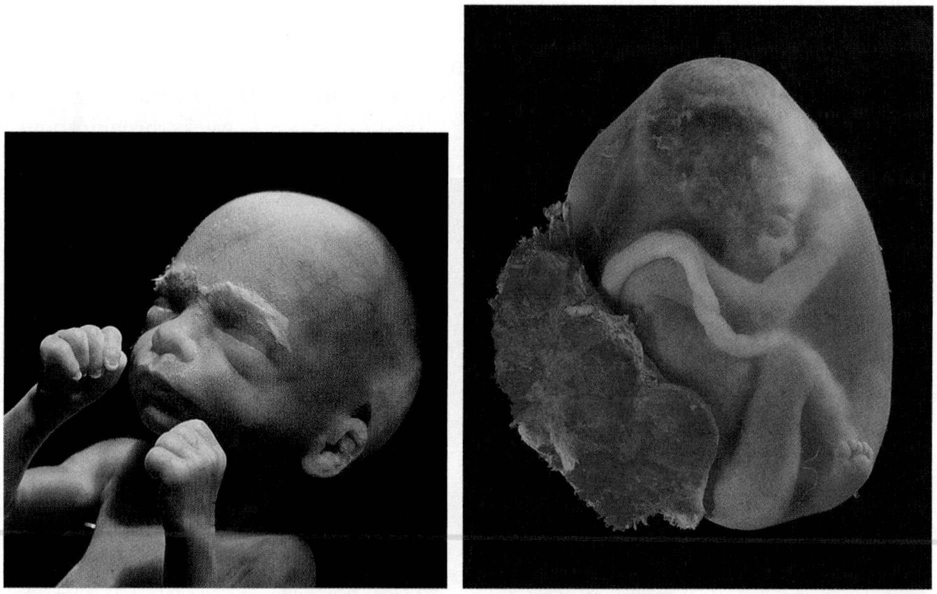
Lennart Nilsson/Albert Bonniers Forlag AB, A CHILD IS BORN

Left: This 24-week-old fetus has reached the age of viability and stands a slim chance of surviving outside the womb. From this point on, odds of survival in the event of a premature birth will increase with each day that passes.

Right: This 36-week-old fetus, covered with the cheese-like vernix that protects the skin against chapping, completely fills the uterus and is ready to be born within the next 2 weeks.

By the end of the seventh month, the fetus weighs nearly 4 pounds and is about 16 to 17 inches long. One month later, it has grown to 18 inches and put on another 1 to 2 pounds. Much of this weight comes from a padding of fat deposited just beneath the skin that later helps to insulate the newborn infant from changes in temperature. By the middle of the ninth month, fetal activity slows and sleep increases (DiPietro et al., 1996; Sahni et al., 1995). The fetus is now so large that the most comfortable position within a restricted, pear-shaped uterus is likely to be a head-down posture at the base of the uterus, with the limbs curled up in the so-called fetal position. At irregular intervals over the last month of pregnancy, the pregnant woman's uterus contracts and then relaxes—a process that tones the uterine muscles, dilates the cervix, and helps to position the head of the fetus into the gap between the pelvic bones through which it will soon be pushed. As the uterine contractions become stronger, more frequent, and regular, the prenatal period draws to a close. The pregnant woman is now in the first stage of labor, and within a matter of hours she will give birth.

A brief overview of prenatal development is presented in Table 4.1. Note that the stages of development through which the developing organism passes *do not* correspond to the trimester stages used to describe the pregnant woman's experience. In fact, the developing organism passes through all three stages of prenatal development in the pregnant woman's first trimester. Furthermore, because the organism becomes a fetus at about 8 weeks after conception, it is not at all uncommon for a woman not to realize she is pregnant before the periods of the zygote and embryo have passed.

TABLE 4.1 A Brief Overview of Prenatal Development

Trimester	Period	Weeks	Size	Major developments
First	Zygote	1		One-celled zygote divides and becomes a blastocyst.
	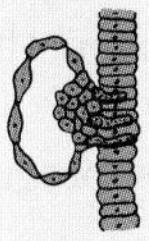	2		Blastocyst implants into uterine wall; structures that nourish and protect the organism—amnion, chorion, yolk sac, placenta, umbilical cord—begin to form.
	Embryo	3–4	1/4 in.	Brain, spinal cord, and heart form, as do the rudimentary structures that will become the eyes, ears, nose, mouth, and limbs.
		5–8	1 in. 1/4 oz	External body structures (eyes, ears, limbs) and internal organs form. Embryo produces its own blood and can now move.
	Fetus 	9–12	3 in. 1 oz	Rapid growth and interconnections of all organ systems permit such new competencies as body and limb movements, swallowing, digestion of nutrients, urination. External genitalia form.
Second	Fetus 	13–24	14–15 in. 2 lb	Fetus grows rapidly. Fetal movements are felt by the mother, and fetal heartbeat can be heard. Fetus is covered by vernix to prevent chapping; it also reacts to bright lights and loud sounds.
Third	Fetus 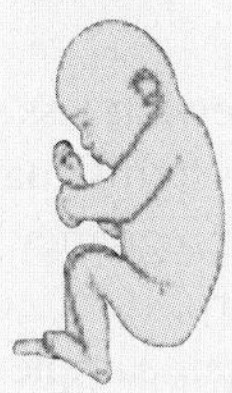	25–38	19–21 in. 7–8 lb	Growth continues and all organ systems mature in preparation for birth. Fetus reaches the age of viability and becomes more regular and predictable in its sleep cycles and motor activity. Layer of fat develops under the skin. Activity becomes less frequent and sleep more frequent during last 2 weeks before birth.

Potential Problems in Prenatal Development

Although the vast majority of newborn infants have followed the "normal" pattern of prenatal development just described, some encounter environmental obstacles that may channel their development along an abnormal path. In the following sections, we will consider a number of environmental factors that can harm developing embryos and fetuses. We will also consider interventions used to prevent abnormal outcomes.

Teratogens

teratogens
external agents such as viruses, drugs, chemicals, and radiation that can harm a developing embryo or fetus.

The term **teratogen** refers to any disease, drug, or other environmental agent that can harm a developing embryo or fetus by causing physical deformities, severely retarded growth, blindness, brain damage, and even death. The list of known and suspected teratogens has grown frighteningly long over the years, making many of today's parents quite concerned about the hazards their developing embryos and fetuses could face (Friedman & Polifka, 1996; Verp, 1993). Before considering the effects of some of the major teratogens, let's emphasize that about 95 percent of newborn babies are perfectly normal and that many of those born with defects have mild, temporary, or reversible problems (Gosden, Nicolaides, & Whitling, 1994; Heinonen, Slone, & Shapiro, 1977). Let's also lay out a few principles about the effects of teratogens that will aid us in interpreting the research that follows:

- The effects of a teratogen on a body part or organ system are worst during the period when that structure is forming and growing most rapidly.
- Not all embryos or fetuses are equally affected by a teratogen; susceptibility to harm is influenced by the embryo's or fetus's and the pregnant woman's genetic makeup and the quality of the prenatal environment.
- The same defect can be caused by different teratogens.
- A variety of defects can result from a single teratogen.
- The longer the exposure to or higher the "dose" of a teratogen, the more likely it is that serious harm will be done.
- Embryos and fetuses can be affected by *fathers'* as well as by pregnant women's exposure to some teratogens.
- The long-term effects of a teratogen often depend on the quality of the *postnatal* environment.
- Some teratogens cause "sleeper effects" that may not be apparent until later in the child's life.

sensitive period
a period during which an organism is quite susceptible to certain environmental influences; outside this period, the same environmental influences must be much stronger to produce comparable effects.

Let's look more closely at the first principle from the list because it is very important. Each major organ system or body part has a **sensitive period** when it is most susceptible to teratogenic agents, namely, the time when that particular part of the body is forming. Recall that most organs and body parts are rapidly forming during the period of the embryo (weeks 3 through 8 of prenatal development). As we see in Figure 4.5, this is precisely the time—before a woman may even know that she is pregnant—that most organ systems are most vulnerable to damage. The most crucial period for gross physical defects of the head and central nervous system is the third through the fifth prenatal weeks. The heart is particularly vulnerable from the middle of the third through the middle of the sixth prenatal week; the most vulnerable period for many other organs and body parts is the second prenatal month. Is it any wonder, then, that the period of the embryo is often called the critical phase of pregnancy?

Once an organ or body part is fully formed, it becomes somewhat less susceptible to damage. However, as Figure 4.5 also illustrates, some organ systems (particularly the eyes, genitals, and nervous system) can be damaged throughout pregnancy. Several years ago, Olli Heinonen and his associates (Heinonen, Slone, & Shapiro, 1977) concluded that many of the birth defects found among the 50,282 children in their sample were *anytime malformations*—problems that could have been caused by teratogens at any point during

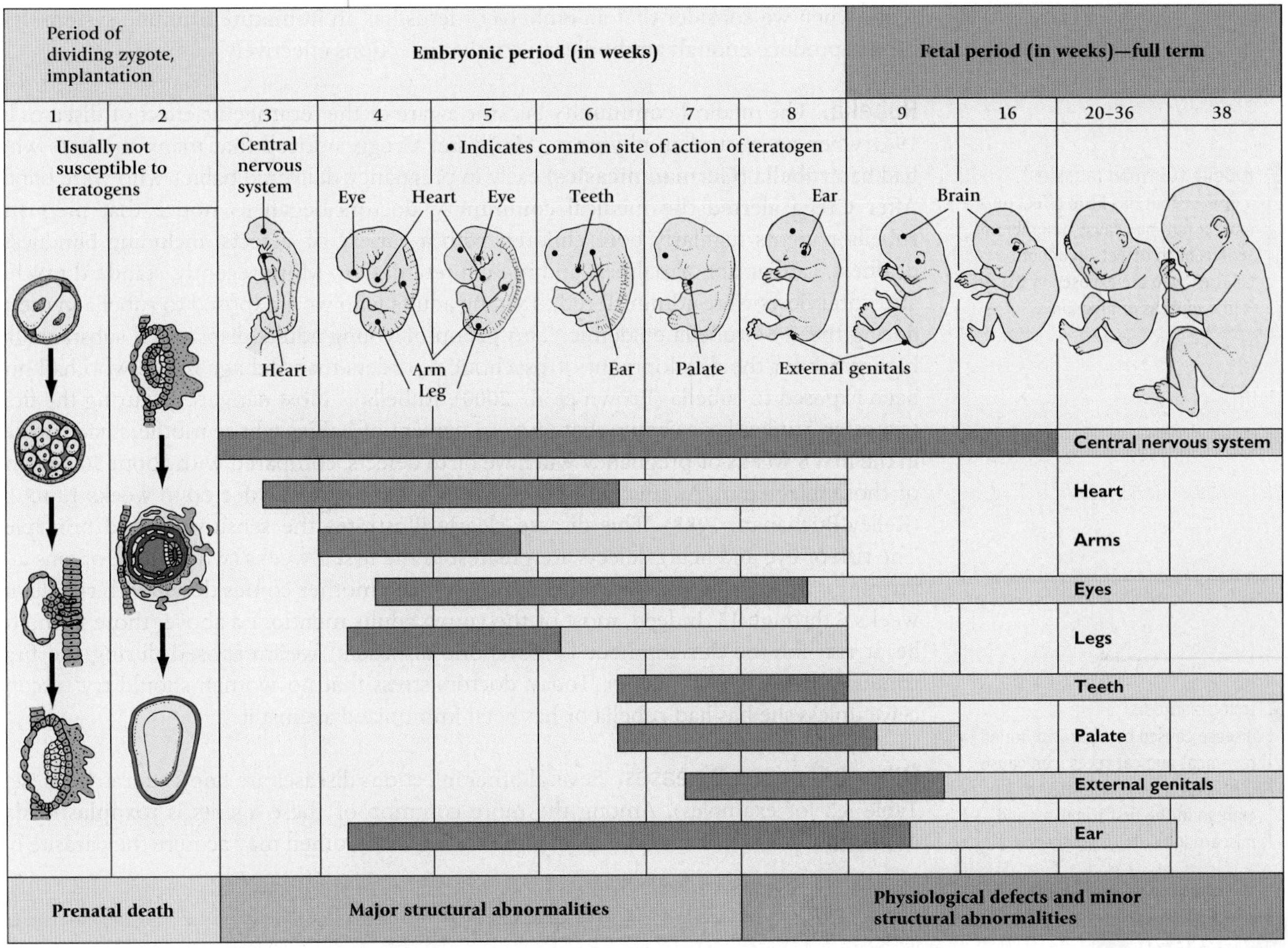

Figure 4.5 The critical periods of prenatal development. Each organ or structure has a critical period when it is most sensitive to damage from teratogens. Dark band indicates the most sensitive periods. Light band indicates times that each organ or structure is somewhat less sensitive to teratogens, although damage may still occur. *Adapted from* Before We Are Born, *4th Ed., by K. L. Moore & T. V. N. Persaud, 1993, p. 89. Philadelphia: Saunders. Adapted with permission of the author and publisher.*

the 9-month prenatal period. So it seems that the entire prenatal period could be considered a sensitive period for human development.

Teratogens can have subtle effects on babies' behavior that are not obvious at birth but nevertheless influence their psychological development. For example, we will see that babies whose mothers consumed as little as an ounce of alcohol a day while pregnant usually display no obvious physical deformities; however, they are often slower to process information and may score lower on IQ tests later in childhood than children whose mothers did not drink (Jacobson & Jacobson, 1996). These results may reflect subtle effects of alcohol on the development of the fetal brain. But there is another possibility. Postnatally, caregivers may have been less inclined to stimulate a sluggish baby who was slow to respond to their bids for attention. And, over time, those depressed levels of stimulation (rather than any effect of alcohol on the brain) may have stunted the child's intellectual development.

With these principles in mind, let's now consider some of the diseases, drugs, chemicals, and other environmental hazards that can adversely affect prenatal development or have other harmful consequences.

Diseases Suffered by the Pregnant Woman

Some disease agents are capable of crossing the placental barrier and doing much more damage to a developing embryo or fetus than to the pregnant woman herself. This makes sense when we consider that an embryo or fetus has an immature immune system that cannot produce enough antibodies to combat infections effectively.

rubella (German measles)
a disease that has little effect on a mother but may cause a number of serious birth defects in unborn children who are exposed in the first 3 to 4 months of pregnancy.

Rubella. The medical community became aware of the teratogenic effect of diseases in 1941 when an Australian physician, McAllister Gregg, noticed that many mothers who had had **rubella (German measles)** early in pregnancy delivered babies who were blind. After Gregg alerted the medical community, doctors began to notice that pregnant rubella patients regularly bore children with a variety of defects, including blindness, deafness, cardiac abnormalities, and mental retardation. More recently, standard psychiatric interviews were administered to young adults who were exposed to rubella in utero during the 1964 rubella epidemic. This group of young adults displayed a substantially higher risk for the development of psychotic disorders than did age-mates who had not been exposed to rubella (Brown et al., 2000). Rubella is most dangerous during the first trimester. Studies have shown that 60 to 85 percent of babies whose mothers had rubella in the first 8 weeks of pregnancy will have birth defects, compared with about 50 percent of those infected in the third month and 16 percent of those infected in weeks 13 to 20 (Kelley-Buchanan, 1988). This disease clearly illustrates the sensitive period principle. The risk of eye and heart defects are greatest in the first 8 weeks (when these organs are forming), whereas deafness is more common if the mother comes down with rubella in weeks 6 through 13. Indeed, most of the young adults mentioned above (those found to be at risk for the development of psychotic disorders) were exposed during the first trimester (Brown et al., 2000). Today, doctors stress that no woman should try to conceive unless she has had rubella or has been immunized against it.

toxoplasmosis
disease caused by a parasite found in raw meat and cat feces; can cause birth defects if transmitted to an embryo in the first trimester and miscarriage later in pregnancy.

Other Infectious Diseases. Several other infectious diseases are known teratogens (see Table 4.2 for examples). Among the more common of these agents is **toxoplasmosis,** caused by a parasite found in many animals. Pregnant women may acquire the parasite by

TABLE 4.2 Common Diseases That May Affect an Embryo, Fetus, or Newborn

	Effects			
Disease	Miscarriage	Physical malformations	Mental impairment	Low birth weight/ premature delivery
Sexually transmitted diseases (STDs)				
Acquired immunodeficiency syndrome (AIDS)	?	?	?	+
Herpes simplex (genital herpes)	+	+	+	+
Syphilis	+	+	+	+
Other maternal diseases/conditions				
Chickenpox	0	+	+	+
Cholera	+	0	?	+
Cytomegalovirus	+	+	+	+
Diabetes	+	+	+	0
Influenza	+	+	?	?
Malaria	+	0	0	+
Mumps	+	0	0	0
Rubella	+	+	+	+
Toxemia	+	0	+	?
Toxoplasmosis	+	+	+	+
Tuberculosis	+	+	+	+
Urinary tract infection (bacterial)	+	0	0	+

Note: + = established finding; 0 = no clear evidence; ? = possible effect.
Sources: Carrington, 1995; Cates, 1995; Faden & Kass, 1996; Kelley-Buchanan, 1988.

eating undercooked meat or by handling the feces of a family cat that has eaten an infected animal. Although toxoplasmosis produces only mild coldlike symptoms in adults, it can cause severe eye and brain damage if transmitted to the prenatal organism during the first trimester, and can induce a miscarriage if it strikes later in pregnancy (Carrington, 1995). Pregnant women can protect themselves against infection by cooking all meat until it is well-done, thoroughly washing any cooking implements that came in contact with raw meat, and avoiding the garden, a pet's litter box, or other locations where cat feces may be present.

Sexually Transmitted Diseases. Finally, no infections are more common and few are more hazardous than sexually transmitted diseases. According to one estimate, as many as 32 million adolescents and adults in the United States either have or have had a sexually transmitted disease (STD) that is capable of producing serious birth defects or otherwise compromising their children's developmental outcomes (Cates, 1995). Three of these diseases—*syphilis, genital herpes,* and *acquired immunodeficiency syndrome (AIDS)*—are especially hazardous.

syphilis
a common sexually transmitted disease that may cross the placental barrier in the middle and later stages of pregnancy, causing miscarriage or serious birth defects.

Syphilis is most harmful in the middle and later stages of pregnancy because syphilitic spirochetes (the microscopic organisms that transmit the disease) cannot cross the placental barrier until the 18th prenatal week. This is fortunate, for the disease is usually diagnosed with a blood test and treated with antibiotics long before it could harm a fetus. However, the pregnant woman who receives no treatment runs the risk of miscarrying or of giving birth to a child who has serious eye, ear, bone, heart, or brain damage (Carrington, 1995; Kelley-Buchanan, 1988).

genital herpes
a sexually transmitted disease that can infect infants at birth, causing blindness, brain damage, or even death.

The virus causing **genital herpes** (herpes simplex) can also cross the placental barrier, although most infections occur at birth as the newborn comes in contact with lesions on the mother's genitals (Gosden, Nicolaides, & Whitting, 1994; Roe, 2004). Unfortunately, there is no cure for genital herpes, so pregnant women cannot be treated, and the consequences of a herpes infection can be severe: this incurable disease kills about one-third of all infected newborns and causes such disabilities as blindness, brain damage, and other serious neurological disorders in another 25 to 30 percent (Ismail, 1993). For these reasons, pregnant women with active herpes infections are now routinely advised to undergo a **cesarean delivery** (a surgical birth in which the baby is delivered through an incision in the mother's abdomen) to avoid infecting their babies.

cesarean section
surgical delivery of a baby through an incision made in the mother's abdomen and uterus.

acquired immune deficiency syndrome (AIDS)
a viral disease that can be transmitted from a mother to her fetus or neonate and that results in a weakening of the body's immune system and, ultimately, death.

The STD of greatest concern today is **acquired immunodeficiency syndrome (AIDS),** a relatively new and incurable disease caused by the human immunodeficiency virus (HIV), which attacks the immune system and makes victims susceptible to a host of other opportunistic infections that will eventually kill them. Transfer of bodily fluids is necessary to spread HIV; consequently, people are normally infected during sexual intercourse or by sharing needles while injecting illegal drugs. Worldwide, more than 4 million women of childbearing age carry HIV and could transmit it to their offspring (Faden & Kass, 1996). Infected mothers may pass the virus (1) prenatally, through the placenta; (2) while giving birth, when there may be an exchange of blood between mother and child as the umbilical cord separates from the placenta; or (3) after birth, if the virus is passed through the mother's milk during breast-feeding (Institute of Medicine, 1999). Despite all these possibilities, it appears that fewer than 25 percent of babies born to HIV-infected mothers are infected themselves. Prenatal transmission of HIV is reduced by nearly 70 percent among mothers taking the antiviral drug ZDV (formerly known as AZT), without any indication that this drug (or HIV) causes birth defects (Institute of Medicine, 1999; but see also Jourdain et al., 2004).

What are the prospects for babies born infected with HIV? Early reports were extremely depressing, claiming that the virus would devastate immature immune systems during the first year, causing most HIV-infected infants to develop full-blown AIDS and die by age 3 (Jones et al., 1992). However, several recent studies (reviewed in Hutton, 1996) find that more than half of all HIV-infected infants are living beyond age 6, with a fair percentage surviving well into adolescence. The antiviral drug ZDV, which interferes with HIV's ability to infect new cells, is now used to treat HIV-infected children, many of whom improve or remain stable for years if treatment is started early (Hutton, 1996).

However, virtually all HIV-infected youngsters will eventually die from complications of their infection, whereas a much larger group of children who escaped HIV infection from their mothers will have to deal with the grief of losing their mothers to AIDS (Hutton, 1996).

Mother-to-child transmission of HIV in the United States is most common among inner-city, poverty-stricken women who take drugs intravenously or have sexual partners who do (Eldred & Chaisson, 1996). Many experts believe that interventions aimed at modifying unsafe sexual practices and unsafe drug use may be about the only effective means to combat the HIV epidemic, for it may be many years before a cure for AIDS is found (Institute of Medicine, 1999).

Drugs

People have long suspected that drugs taken by pregnant women could harm the prenatal organism. Even Aristotle thought as much when he noted that many drunken mothers have feeble-minded babies (Abel, 1981). Today, we know that these suspicions were often correct and that even mild drugs that have few if any lasting effects on a pregnant woman may prove extremely hazardous to a developing embryo or fetus. Unfortunately, the medical community learned this lesson the hard way.

The Thalidomide Tragedy. In 1960 a West German drug company began to market a mild tranquilizer, sold over the counter, that was said to alleviate the periodic nausea and vomiting (commonly known as "morning sickness," although pregnant women may experience it at any time of day) that many women experience during the first trimester of pregnancy. Presumably, the drug was perfectly safe; in tests on pregnant rats, it had no ill effects on mother or offspring. The drug was **thalidomide.**

thalidomide
a mild tranquilizer that, taken early in pregnancy, can produce a variety of malformations of the limbs, eyes, ears, and heart.

What came to pass quickly illustrated that drugs that are harmless in tests with laboratory animals may turn out to be violent teratogens for human beings. Thousands of women who had used thalidomide during the first two months of pregnancy were suddenly giving birth to babies with horrible birth defects. Thalidomide babies often had badly deformed eyes, ears, noses, and hearts, and many displayed *phocomelia*—a structural abnormality in which all or parts of limbs are missing and the feet or hands may be attached directly to the torso.

Alistair Berg/FSP/Gamma Liaison

This boy has no arms or hands—two of the birth defects that may be produced by thalidomide.

The kinds of birth defects produced by thalidomide depended on when the drug was taken. Babies of mothers who had taken the drug on or around the 21st day after conception were likely to be born without ears. Those whose mothers had used thalidomide on the 25th through the 27th day of pregnancy often had grossly deformed arms or no arms. If a mother had taken the drug between the 28th and 36th day, her child might have deformed legs or no legs. But if she had waited until the 40th day before using thalidomide, her baby was usually not affected (Apgar & Beck, 1974). However, most mothers who took thalidomide delivered babies with no apparent birth defects—a finding that illustrates the dramatic differences that individuals display in response to teratogens.

Other Common Drugs. Despite the lessons learned from the thalidomide tragedy, about 60 percent of pregnant women take at least one prescription or over-the-counter drug. Unfortunately, some of the most commonly used drugs are suspect. Heavy use of aspirin, for example, has been linked to fetal growth retardation, poor motor control, and even infant death (Barr et al., 1990; Kelley-Buchanan, 1988), and the use of ibuprofen in the third trimester increases the risk of a prolonged delivery and pulmonary hypertension in newborns (Chomitz, Chung, & Lieberman, 2000). Some studies have linked heavy use of caffeine (that is, more than four soft drinks or cups of coffee per day) to such complications as miscarriage and low birth weight (Larroque, Kaminski, & Lelong, 1993; Larsen, 2004; Leviton, 1993). However, the harmful outcomes attributed to caffeine may well have been caused by other drugs these mothers had used (Friedman & Polifka, 1996)—most notably alcohol and nicotine, which we will discuss.

Several other prescription drugs pose a slight risk to developing embryos and fetuses. For example, antidepressants containing lithium can produce heart defects when taken in the first trimester (Friedman & Polifka, 1996). Medications containing sex hormones (or their active biochemical ingredients) can also affect a developing embryo or fetus. For example, oral contraceptives contain female sex hormones and, if a woman takes the pill without knowing that she is pregnant, her child faces a slightly increased risk of heart defects and other minor malformations (Gosden, Nicolaides, & Whitting, 1994; Heinonen, Slone, & Shapiro, 1977).

diethylstilbestrol (DES)
a synthetic hormone, formerly prescribed to prevent miscarriage, that can produce cervical cancer in female offspring and genital-tract abnormalities in males.

One synthetic sex hormone that can have serious long-term effects is **diethylstilbestrol (DES)**—the active ingredient of a drug that was widely prescribed for the prevention of miscarriages between the mid-1940s and 1965. The drug seemed safe enough; newborns whose mothers had used DES appeared to be normal in every way. But in 1971 physicians clearly established that 17- to 21-year-old females whose mothers had used DES were at risk for developing abnormalities of the reproductive organs, including a rare form of cervical cancer. Clearly, the risk of cancer is not very great; fewer than 1 in 1,000 DES daughters have developed the disease thus far (Friedman & Polifka, 1996). However, there are other complications. For example, DES daughters who themselves become pregnant are more likely than nonexposed women to miscarry or to deliver prematurely. What about DES sons? Although there is no conclusive evidence that prenatal exposure to DES causes cancer in sons, a small number of men who were exposed to DES before birth developed minor genital trait abnormalities but remain fertile (Wilcox et al., 1995).

Clearly, the vast majority of pregnant women who take aspirin and caffeine, oral contraceptives, or DES deliver perfectly normal babies. And under proper medical supervision, use of medications to treat a mother's ailments is usually safe for mother and fetus (McMahon & Katz, 1996). Nevertheless, new drugs are often approved and used without adequate testing for their possible teratogenic effects; the fact that some drugs that do adults no harm can produce congenital defects has convinced many pregnant women to restrict or eliminate their intake of all drugs during pregnancy.

fetal alcohol syndrome (FAS)
a group of serious congenital problems commonly observed in the offspring of mothers who abuse alcohol during pregnancy.

fetal alcohol effects (FAE)
a group of mild congenital problems that are sometimes observed in children of mothers who drink sparingly to moderately during pregnancy.

Alcohol. Alcohol affects development of the fetus directly and indirectly by compromising the function of the placenta (Vuorela et al., 2002). Knowing this, should a no-drug policy be extended to alcohol? Most contemporary researchers think so. In 1973 Kenneth Jones and his colleagues (1973) described a **fetal alcohol syndrome** (FAS) that affects many children of alcoholic mothers. The most noticeable characteristics of fetal alcohol syndrome are defects such as microcephaly (small head) and malformations of the heart, limbs, joints, and face (Abel, 1998). FAS babies are likely to display excessive irritability, hyperactivity, seizures, and tremors. They are also smaller and lighter than normal, and their physical growth lags behind that of normal age-mates. Finally, the majority of the 3 in 1,000 babies born with FAS score well below average in intelligence throughout childhood and adolescence, and more than 90 percent of them display major adjustment problems as adolescents and young adults (Asher, 2002; Disney, 2002; Stratton, Howe, & Battaglia, 1996).

How much can a pregnant woman drink without harming her baby? Perhaps a lot less than you might imagine. In keeping with the dosage principle of teratology, the symptoms of FAS are most severe when the "dose" of alcohol is highest—that is, when the pregnant woman is clearly an alcoholic. Yet, even moderate "social drinking" (1 to 3 ounces a day) can lead to a set of less serious problems, called **fetal alcohol effects (FAE),** in some babies. These effects include retarded physical growth and minor physical abnormalities as well as such problems as poor motor skills, difficulty paying attention, subnormal intellectual performance, and verbal learning deficits (Cornelius et al., 2002; Day et al., 2002; Jacobson et al, 1993; Streissguth et al., 1993; Willford et al., 2004). Magnetic resonance imaging (MRI) has also revealed structural anomalies in the brains of children with both FAS

George Steinmetz

This girl's widely spaced eyes, flattened nose, and underdeveloped upper lip are three of the common physical symptoms of fetal alcohol syndrome.

and FAE (Autti-Rämö et al., 2002). The risks of FAE are greatest should pregnant women binge occasionally, having five or more drinks per drinking occasion (Abel, 1998; Jacobson & Jacobson, 1999). In fact, a pregnant woman who consumes five or more drinks per week is placing herself at risk for first-trimester miscarriage (Kesmodel et al., 2002). Yet, even a pregnant woman who drinks less than an ounce of alcohol a day is more likely than a nondrinker to have an infant whose mental development is slightly below average (Jacobson & Jacobson, 1996). In a longitudinal study that followed infants from the neonatal period through 6 years of age, infants prenatally exposed to alcohol displayed higher levels of negative effects than their unexposed counterparts. Even more troubling, infants who were exposed to alcohol in utero and who displayed higher levels of negative effects were more likely to report depressive symptoms at age 6. This scenario was more pronounced in girls (O'Connor, 2001). There is no well-defined sensitive period for fetal alcohol effects; drinking late in pregnancy can be just as risky as drinking soon after conception (Jacobson et al., 1993). Finally, drinking can affect the male reproductive system, leading to reduced sperm motility, lower sperm count, and abnormally formed sperm. Some research even indicates that newborns whose fathers use alcohol are likely to have lower birth weights than newborns whose fathers do not use alcohol (Frank et al., 2002). In 1981, the U.S. Surgeon General concluded that *no amount* of alcohol consumption is entirely safe and has since advised pregnant women not to drink at all.

Cigarette Smoking. Fifty years ago, neither doctors nor pregnant women had any reason to suspect that cigarette smoking might affect an embryo or fetus. Now we know otherwise. A positive association between smoking during the first trimester and **cleft lip,** with or without **cleft palate,** was reported by Little and colleagues (2004). Also, abnormal lung function and hypertension in newborns of women who smoked during pregnancy have been found (Bastra, Hadders-Algra, & Neeleman, 2003). Reviews of the literature have concluded that smoking clearly increases the risk of miscarriage or death shortly after birth in otherwise normal infants and is a leading contributor to fetal growth retardation and low-birth-weight deliveries (Blake et al., 2000; Chomitz, Cheung, & Lieberman, 2000; Cnattingius, 2004; Haug et al., 2000). Smoking during pregnancy is also associated with higher incidences of ectopic pregnancies (when the zygote implants on the wall of the fallopian tube instead of the uterus), as well as sudden infant death syndrome (which we will discuss in detail in Chapter 5) (Cnattingius, 2004; Sondergaard et al., 2002).

cleft lip
a congenital disorder in which the upper lip has a vertical (or pair of vertical) openings or grooves.

cleft palate
a congenital disorder in which the roof of the mouth does not close properly during embryonic development, resulting in an opening or groove in the roof of the mouth.

Furthermore, Schuetze and Zeskind (2001) report that smoking during pregnancy may also affect the regulation of autonomic activity in neonates. In their research, during both quiet and active sleep, the hearts of neonates exposed to nicotine in utero beat more rapidly than those of neonates whose mothers did not smoke during pregnancy. Schuetze and Zeskind also report that the heart rates of nicotine-exposed neonates are less variable than those of nonexposed infants and that both tremors and changes of behavioral state are more frequent among nicotine-exposed newborns (see Chapter 5 for a description of infant behavioral states).

During pregnancy, smoking introduces nicotine and carbon monoxide into both the pregnant woman's and fetus's bloodstreams, which impairs the functioning of the placenta, especially the exchange of oxygen and nutrients to the fetus. Nicotine diffuses rapidly through the placenta. Fetal concentrations of nicotine may be as much as 15 percent higher than those of the smoking women (Bastra, Hadders-Algra, & Neeleman, 2003). And all these events are clearly related in that the more cigarettes pregnant women smoke per day, the greater their risk of miscarriage or of delivering a low-birth-weight baby who may struggle to survive. Newborn infants of fathers who smoke are also likely to be smaller than normal. Why? One reason may be that pregnant women who live with smokers become "passive smokers," who inhale nicotine and carbon monoxide that can hamper fetal growth (Friedman & Polifka, 1996).

The long-term effects of exposure to tobacco products are less clear. Some research has found that children whose mothers smoked during pregnancy or whose parents continue to smoke after they are born tend to be smaller on average, more susceptible to respiratory infections, and show slightly poorer cognitive performance early in childhood than do children of nonsmokers (Diaz, 1997; Chavkin, 1995). Mattson and colleagues (2002) cite specific studies that suggest that nicotine has some powerful interactive effects when combined with certain prescribed and illicit drugs. Because nicotine is a stimulant, they point out, it may actually increase the teratogenic effects of other drugs by increasing their transport across the placenta. Cnattingius (2004) and Linnet et al. (2003) report an association between maternal smoking during pregnancy and conduct disorders, including ADHD-related disorders. Bastra, Hadders-Algra, and Neeleman (2003) found associations between maternal smoking and externalizing behaviors and attention deficit, as well as poorer performance in spelling and math. In this study, children (1,186 of them between 5½ and 11 years) whose mothers also smoked postnatally were the poorest performers on school-related tasks. Thus, evidence is overwhelming that smoking during pregnancy can harm fetuses (not to mention, of course, the harmful long-term effects that this habit can have on parents). For these reasons, physicians today routinely advise pregnant women and their partners to stop smoking, if not forever, at least during the pregnancy.

Illicit Drugs. In the United States, use of recreational drugs such as marijuana, cocaine, and heroin has become so widespread that as many as 700,000 infants are born each year having been exposed to one or more of these substances in the womb (Chavkin, 1995). A variety of cognitive and behavioral defects are associated with illicit drug use. For example, examination of the brain tissue of human fetuses reveals that marijuana use during pregnancy is associated with changes in the functioning of the basal nucleus of the amygdala, an area of the brain that is involved in the regulation of emotional behavior. These changes are more prevalent in male fetuses and may indicate that in utero exposure to marijuana causes impairment of emotional regulation, especially for boys (Wang et al., 2004). Pregnant women who report using the drug two or more times per week often deliver babies who display tremors, sleep disturbances, and a lack of interest in their surroundings over the first week or two of life (Brockington, 1996; Fried, 1993, 2002). These behavioral disturbances appear to place infants at risk for adverse outcomes later in childhood. When compared to children not exposed to marijuana in utero, 10-year-olds whose mothers smoked one or more marijuana joints per day during the first trimester of pregnancy exhibited poorer performance on achievement tests for reading and spelling. Teacher evaluations of the classroom performance of the marijuana-exposed children were also lower than those of their nonexposed peers. Second-trimester marijuana use was associated with deficits in reading comprehension as well as underachievement. In addition, the marijuana-exposed 10-year-olds presented more symptoms of anxiety and depression (Goldschmidt et al., 2004).

Although heroin, methadone, and other addicting narcotic agents do not appear to produce gross physical abnormalities, women who use these drugs are more likely than nonusers to miscarry, deliver prematurely, or have babies who die soon after birth (Brockington, 1996). The first month of life is often difficult for the 60 to 80 percent of babies who are born addicted to the narcotic their mother has taken. When deprived of the drug after birth, addicted infants experience withdrawal symptoms such as vomiting, dehydration, convulsions, extreme irritability, weak sucking, and high-pitched crying (Brockington, 1996; D'Apolito & Hepworth, 2001). In addition, during the first month of life these drug-exposed neonates have trouble coordinating breathing and swallowing (Gewolb et al., 2004). Symptoms such as restlessness, tremors, and sleep disturbances may persist for as long as 3 to 4 months. However, longer-term studies reveal that some infants prenatally exposed to opioid drugs show normal developmental progress by age 2, and that indifferent parenting, along with other social and environmental risk factors, may be the most likely contributors to the poor progress of these children, rather than their prenatal exposure to drugs (Brockington, 1996; Hans & Jeremy, 2001). In one such study, children prenatally exposed to multiple drug abuse were placed in homes with foster parents who were recruited specifically to care for neonates at risk. Over the first three years of life these children showed developmental improvements, indicating that specialized caregiving may help compensate for early drug-related deficits. It is important to note, however, that even under these optimal caregiving conditions, boys who had been prenatally exposed to drugs earned significantly lower scores on assessments of infant development than did unexposed children or girls who were also exposed to drugs in utero.

These results suggest that boys may be especially vulnerable to the effects of maternal prenatal drug abuse (Vibeke & Slinning, 2001).

Today, much concern centers on the risks associated with cocaine use, particularly the use of "crack" cocaine, a cheap form of the drug that delivers high doses through the lungs. Cocaine is known to constrict the blood vessels of both mother and fetus, thereby elevating fetal blood pressure and hampering the flow of nutrients and oxygen across the placenta (Chavkin, 1995; MacGregor & Chasnoff, 1993). As a result, babies of cocaine-using mothers, particularly mothers who use crack cocaine, are often miscarried or born prematurely. And, like the babies of heroin or methadone users, they often display tremors, sleep disturbances, a sluggish inattention to the environment, and a tendency to become extremely irritable when aroused (Askin & Diehl-Jones, 2001; Brockington, 1996; Eidin, 2001; Lester et al., 1991; Singer et al., 2002a).

In addition, prenatal cocaine exposure has been linked to a variety of postpartum developmental deficits, including lower IQ scores (Singer et al., 2002a, b; Singer et al., 2004), impaired visual-spatial abilities (Arendt et al., 2004a, b), and problems with skills that are critical to language development—auditory attention and comprehension, as well as verbal expression (Delaney-Black et al., 2000; Lewis et al., 2004; Singer et al., 2001). Because cocaine-using mothers are often malnourished and prone to use other teratogens such as alcohol (Eidin, 2001; Friedman & Polifka, 1996), it is difficult to determine the extent to which prenatal cocaine exposure contributes to these deficits, even when researchers use investigative methodologies that account for such additional factors (Arendt et al., 2004a, b). However, several studies indicate that aspects of both the prenatal and postnatal environment may influence the severity of cocaine-related developmental deficits (Arendt et al., 2004a, b). For example, maternal distress has been shown to contribute to poor fetal growth over and above contributions made by prenatal exposure to cocaine (Singer et al., 2002b). Also, when compared to prenatal cocaine exposure, maternal vocabulary and quality of the home environment (Lewis et al., 2004; Singer et al., 2004) have emerged as stronger predictors of developmental outcomes related to IQ and language development. Even visual-spatial deficits associated with cocaine exposure appear to occur more frequently in less-than-optimal home environments (Arendt et al., 2004a, b).

Some investigators suspect that the unpleasant demeanor that many cocaine babies display interferes with the emotional bonding that normally occurs between infants and their caregivers (Eidin, 2001). One study found that a majority of cocaine-exposed infants failed to establish secure emotional ties to their primary caregivers in the first year (Rodning, Beckwith, & Howard, 1991). Other studies find that babies exposed to higher levels of cocaine derive less joy from learning than nonexposed infants do (Alessandri et al., 1993), and by age 18 months are displaying clear decrements in their intellectual development as well (Alessandri, Bendersky, & Lewis, 1998). These poor outcomes may stem from the infants' prior exposure to cocaine and their resulting negative emotional demeanor, their exposure to other teratogens (for example, alcohol and tobacco) commonly used by substance-abusing parents, or the less than adequate stimulation and care these babies may receive from drug-using parents. Further research is necessary to clarify this issue and properly assess the long-term impact of cocaine (and other narcotic agents) on *all* aspects of development (Keyser-Marcus, 2004).

Table 4.3 catalogs a number of other drugs and their known or suspected effects on unborn children. What should we make of these findings? Assuming that our first priority is the welfare of unborn children, then perhaps Virginia Apgar summarized it best: "A woman who is pregnant, or who thinks she could possibly be pregnant should not take any drugs whatsoever unless absolutely essential—and then only when [approved] by a physician who is aware of the pregnancy" (Apgar & Beck, 1974, p. 445).

Environmental Hazards

Another class of teratogens is environmental hazards. These include chemicals in the environment that the pregnant woman cannot control and may not even be aware of. There are also environmental hazards that the pregnant woman can regulate. Let's examine these teratogens and their effects.

TABLE 4.3 Partial List of Drugs and Treatments Used by the Mother That Affect (or Are Thought to Affect) the Fetus or the Newborn

Maternal drug use	Effect on fetus/newborn
Alcohol	Small head, facial abnormalities, heart defects, low birth weight, and mental retardation (see text).
Amphetamines Dextroamphetamine Methamphetamine	Premature delivery, stillbirth, irritability, and poor feeding among newborns.
Antibiotics Streptomycin Terramycin Tetracycline	Heavy use of streptomycin by mothers can produce hearing loss in fetuses. Terramycin and tetracycline may be associated with premature delivery, restricted skeletal growth, cataracts, and staining of the baby's teeth.
Aspirin Ibuprofen	See text. (In clinical doses, acetaminophen is a very safe alternative to aspirin and ibuprofen.)
Barbiturates	All barbiturates taken by the mother cross the placental barrier. In clinical doses, they cause the fetus or newborn to be lethargic. In large doses, they may cause anoxia (oxygen starvation) and restrict fetal growth. One barbiturate, primidone, is associated with malformations of the heart, face, and limbs.
Hallucinogens LSD	Lysergic acid diethylamide (LSD) slightly increases the likelihood of limb deformities.
Marijuana	Heavy marijuana use during pregnancy is linked to behavioral abnormalities in newborns (see text).
Lithium	Heart defects, lethargic behavior in newborns.
Narcotics Cocaine Heroin Methadone	Maternal addiction increases the risk of premature delivery. Moreover, the fetus is often addicted to the narcotic agent, which results in a number of complications. Heavy cocaine use can seriously elevate fetal blood pressure and even induce strokes (see text).
Sex hormones Androgens Progestogens Estrogens DES (diethylstilbestrol)	Sex hormones contained in birth control pills and drugs to prevent miscarriages taken by pregnant women can have a number of harmful effects on babies, including minor heart malformations, cervical cancer (in female offspring), and other anomalies (see text).
Tranquilizers (other than thalidomide) Chlorpromazine Reserpine Valium	May produce respiratory distress in newborns. Valium may also produce poor muscle tone and lethargy.
Tobacco	Parental cigarette smoking is known to restrict fetal growth and to increase the risk of spontaneous abortion, stillbirth, and infant mortality (see text).
Vitamins	Excessive amounts of vitamin A taken by pregnant women can cause cleft palate, heart malformations, and other serious birth defects. The popular antiacne drug Accutane, derived from vitamin A, is one of the most powerful teratogens, causing malformations of the eyes, limbs, heart, and central nervous system.

Sources: Chavkin, 1995; Chomitz, Cheung, & Lieberman, 2000; Friedman & Polifka, 1996.

Radiation. Soon after the atomic blasts of 1945 in Japan, scientists became painfully aware of the teratogenic effects of radiation. Not one pregnant woman who was within one-half mile of these explosions gave birth to a live child. In addition, 75 percent of the pregnant women who were within a mile and a quarter of the blasts had seriously handicapped children who soon died, and the infants who did survive were often mentally retarded (Apgar & Beck, 1974; Vorhees & Mollnow, 1987).

We don't know exactly how much radiation it takes to harm an embryo or fetus. Even if an exposed child appears normal at birth, the possibility of developing complications later in life cannot be dismissed. For these reasons, pregnant women are routinely advised to avoid X-rays, particularly of the pelvis and abdomen, unless they are crucial for their own survival.

Chemicals and Pollutants. Pregnant women routinely come in contact with potentially toxic substances in their everyday environments, including organic dyes and coloring agents, food additives, artificial sweeteners, pesticides, and cosmetic products, some of which are known to have teratogenic effects in animals (Verp, 1993). Unfortunately, the risks associated with a large number of these common chemical additives and treatments remain to be determined.

There are also pollutants in the air we breathe and the water we drink. For example, pregnant women may be exposed to concentrations of lead, zinc, or mercury discharged into the air or water by industrial operations or present in house paint and water pipes. These "heavy metals" are known to impair the physical health and mental abilities of adults and children and to have teratogenic effects (producing physical deformities and mental retardation) on developing embryos and fetuses. Polluting chemicals called *PCBs* (polychlorinated biphenyls), now outlawed but once widely used in plastics and carbon paper, represent another hazard. Joseph Jacobson and his colleagues (1984, 1985) found that even low-level exposure to PCBs, resulting from mothers' eating of contaminated fish from Lake Michigan, was enough to make newborns smaller on average and less responsive and neurologically mature than babies whose mothers did not eat polluted fish. At age 4, these children still performed poorly on tests of short-term memory and verbal reasoning ability, with the extent of their deficits corresponding to the "dose" of PCB that they received before birth (Jacobson, Jacobson, & Humphrey, 1990; Jacobson et al., 1992). In other studies, prenatal PCB exposure has been associated with difficulty in maintaining attention and slower reaction times (Grandjean et al., 2001), and with problems with spatial reasoning skills (Guo et al., 1995). Furthermore, these effects may be compounded by lactational exposure to PCB post birth (Vreugdenhil et al., 2004). In one study, 9-year-olds were asked to complete a complex task that required planning and integration skills, as well as sustained attention and the use of spatial working memory. During conception, pregnancy, and the nursing period, the mothers of the children tested lived in a highly industrial section of Rotterdam, where they were exposed to varying levels of PCB, thus exposing their children prenatally, and augmenting the exposure if the mothers chose to breast-feed their newborns. Children who were exposed to higher levels of PCB performed more poorly on the complex task than did children who were exposed to lower levels of PCB. In addition, 9-year-olds who were breast-fed performed more poorly than children who were formula-fed. In fact, the children who were least proficient at the task were those who had been exposed to high levels of PCB in utero and whose mothers had breast-fed them for longer periods of time (see Figure 4.6) (Vreugdenhil et al., 2004).

Even a father's exposure to environmental toxins can affect a couple's children. Studies of men in a variety of occupations reveal that prolonged exposure to radiation, anesthetic gases, and other toxic chemicals can damage a father's chromosomes, increasing

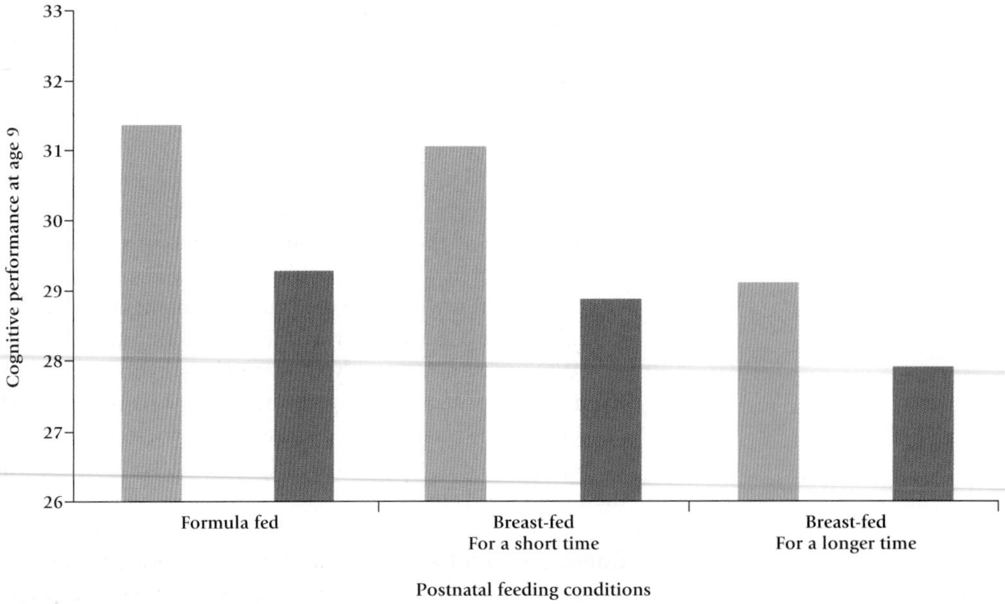

Figure 4.6 Average cognitive test performance at age 9, based on child's level of exposure to PCB prenatally and through breast-feeding. Light bars are children who were exposed to low levels of PCB; dark bars are children who were exposed to high levels of PCB. *From Vreugenhil et al., "Effects of Perinatal Exposure to PCBs on Neuropsychological Functions in the Rotterdam Cohort at 9 Years of Age,"* Neuropsychology, *18, 185–193. Reprinted by permission of Elsevier.*

the likelihood of his child's being miscarried or displaying genetic defects (Gunderson & Sackett, 1982; Merewood, 2000; Strigini et al., 1990). And even when expectant mothers do *not* drink alcohol or use drugs, they are much more likely to deliver a low-birth-weight baby or one with other defects if the father is a heavy drinker or drug user (Frank et al., 2002; Merewood, 2000). Why? Possibly because certain substances (for example, cocaine and maybe even alcohol, PCBs, and other toxins) can apparently bind directly to live sperm or cause mutations in them, thereby altering prenatal development from the moment of conception (Merewood, 2000; Yazigi, Odem, & Polakoski, 1991). Taken together, these findings imply that (1) environmental toxins can affect the reproductive system of either parent so that (2) both mothers *and* fathers should limit their exposure to known teratogens.

Characteristics of the Pregnant Woman

In addition to teratogens, a pregnant woman's nutrition, her emotional well-being, and even her age can affect the outcome of her pregnancy. These are characteristics that can affect the prenatal environment and in that way affect the organism's development. And, as discussed in Box 4.1, the prenatal environment may have long-term as well as immediate effects on the developing organism.

The Pregnant Woman's Diet

Sixty years ago, doctors routinely advised pregnant women to gain no more than 2 pounds a month while pregnant and believed that a total gain of 15 to 18 pounds was quite sufficient to ensure healthy prenatal development. Today pregnant women are more often advised to eat a healthy, high-protein, high-calorie diet on which they gain 2 to 5 pounds during the first 3 months of pregnancy and about a pound a week thereafter, for a total increase of 25 to 35 pounds (Chomitz, Cheung, & Lieberman, 2000). Why has the advice changed? Because we now know that inadequate prenatal nutrition can be harmful.

Severe malnutrition, as often occurs during periods of famine, stunts prenatal growth and produces small, underweight babies (Susser & Stein, 1994). The precise effects of malnutrition depend on when it occurs. During the first trimester, malnutrition can disrupt the formation of the spinal cord and induce miscarriages. During the third trimester, malnutrition is more likely to result in low-birth-weight babies with small heads who may fail to survive the first year of life (Susser & Stein, 1994; and see Figure 4.7). Indeed, autopsies of stillborn infants whose mothers were malnourished during the third trimester reveal fewer brain cells and lower brain weights than is typical among babies born to well-nourished mothers (Goldenberg, 1995; Winick, 1976).

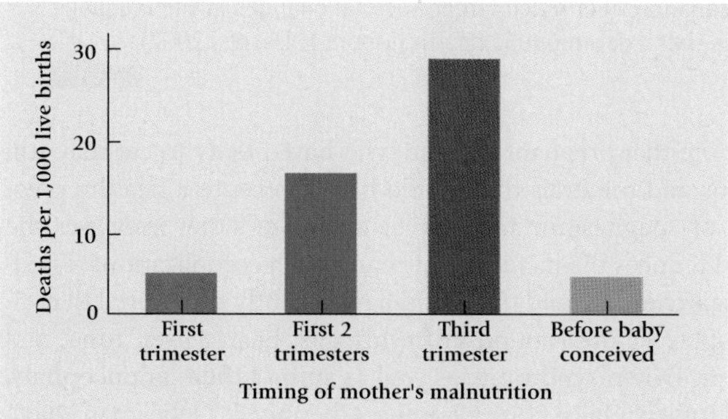

Figure 4.7 Incidence of infant mortality in the first 12 months for babies born to Dutch mothers who had experienced famine during World War II. *Adapted from Stein & Susser, 1976.*

Not surprisingly then, babies born to malnourished mothers sometimes show cognitive deficits later in childhood, and one contributor to these deficits is the babies' own behavior. Malnourished babies whose diets remain inadequate after birth are often apathetic and quick to become irritated when aroused—qualities that can disrupt the parent-infant relationship, and lead parents to fail to provide the kinds of playful stimulation and emotional support that would foster their social and intellectual development (Grantham-McGregor et al., 1995). Fortunately, dietary supplements, especially when combined with stimulating day care and programs that help parents to become more sensitive, responsive caregivers, can significantly reduce or even eliminate the potentially damaging long-term effects of prenatal malnutrition (Grantham-McGregor et al., 1994; Super, Herrera, & Mora, 1990; Zeskind & Ramey, 1981).

FOCUS ON RESEARCH Fetal Programming Theory

It is generally accepted that the plasticity of a newborn brain is adaptive because it allows the infant to develop in ways that are compatible with the environment into which it is born. In a similar manner, brain plasticity from infancy through childhood also allows for environmentally adaptive growth. Gradually, as the child interacts with the surrounding environment, some neural pathways are reinforced and others are not. The brain begins to take on a more definite organization that is less malleable, but also well suited for the child's environment.

Fetal programming theory takes that perspective a step backward along the developmental path by focusing on the uterus as an environment that may influence the development of the prenatal brain and other regulatory systems (Barker, 1994; Holmang, 2001; Moore & Davies, 2002; Sallout & Walker, 2003). The brain (as well as other organs and systems) is "programmed" in a manner that is adaptive for the uterine environment. Because this programming persists post birth, it may influence the child's developmental outcomes. If the programming that was adaptive in the uterine environment is not so in the postnatal environment, negative, long-term developmental consequences may result. Therefore, anything that alters the uterine environment has the potential to limit or influence developmental processes and outcomes in a lasting manner (Plageman, 2004; Wilcoxin & Redei, 2004).

For example, recent evidence suggests that slight metabolic changes in the fetuses of diabetic mothers (a fetal reaction to uterine hyperinsulinism) may create a predisposition to the development of insulin resistance and non-insulin-dependent diabetes later in life. This programmed predisposition influences the development of insulin resistance and diabetes over and above any predisposition that may be inherited from the diabetic mothers (Phillips, 2004; Plageman, 2004). Also, fetal programming effects related to prenatal maternal anxiety have been implicated in the incidence of mixed-handedness among $3^1/_2$-year-olds (Glover et al., 2004).

Fetal programming theory differs from but does not contradict the concept of sensitive or critical periods in development. In fact, some associations between the operation of fetal programming factors and adult chronic disease are more pronounced during particular gestational phases. That is, certain fetal programming phenomena occur during sensitive periods (Holmang, 2001). For instance, in the handedness study mentioned above, a higher incidence of mixed-handedness was associated with prenatal maternal anxiety at 18 weeks but not at 32 weeks (Glover et al., 2004). Fetal programming theory differs from the concept of the sensitive period in that programming theory focuses on subtle changes in metabolism, autonomic and endocrine functions, and the central nervous system rather than more obvious teratogenic effects, such as those associated with prenatal exposure to thalidomide. The changes are considered responses to the uterine environment and, though slight, they are permanent, making the emerging infant more susceptible to chronic diseases in adulthood.

Although researchers pursuing evidence for fetal programming most often focus on aspects of the uterine environment that produce adverse effects, fetal programming operates in healthy uterine environments as well and presumably makes a positive contribution to the adaptive development of the fetus in the same way that it makes negative ones: by creating subtle permanent changes. In this way, fetal programming is congruent with the concept of the sensitive period—for sensitivity to input at critical points in development may also be a positive adaptive process, necessary for the proper maturation of the fetus or child. For example, early on, there is a critical period during which infant eyes and ears must have things to see and hear in order to develop properly. Fetal programming is simply a metaphor that presents a slightly different perspective from which to consider developmental processes, and therefore, may call attention to changes and outcomes that have previously gone unnoticed.

Finally, the most prolific area of research involving fetal effects has centered on nutrition and other uterine influences resulting in low birth weight (Holmang, 2002; Moore & Davies, 2002; Sallout & Walker, 2003). Low birth weight is an important predictor of cardiovascular disease, stroke, type 2 diabetes, insulin resistance and deficiency, hypertension, and obesity (Holmang, 2001; Sallout & Walker, 2003). Because low birth weight is more common among groups with lower socioeconomic status (SES), it would be logical to predict that the prevalence of cardiovascular disease, type 2 diabetes, and other diseases associated with low birth weight would be greater among groups of low SES. In fact, this is true. By providing a framework for ferreting out very small metabolic changes in utero, fetal programming theory may provide a means to effect much larger, societal changes in the inequalities that exist in public health (Moore & Davies, 2002).

folic acid
B-complex vitamin that helps to prevent defects of the central nervous system.

spina bifida
a bulging of the spinal cord through a gap in the spinal column.

anencephaly
a birth defect in which the brain and neural tube fail to develop (or develop incompletely) and the skull does not close.

Finally, it is important to note that pregnant women who have plenty to eat may still fail to obtain all of the vitamins and minerals that would help to ensure a healthy pregnancy. Adding small amounts of magnesium and zinc to a mother's diet improves the functioning of the placenta and reduces the incidence of many birth complications (Friedman & Polifka, 1996). Also, researchers around the world have recently discovered that diets rich in **folic acid,** a B-complex vitamin found in fresh fruits, beans, liver, tuna, and green vegetables, help to prevent Down syndrome, as well as **spina bifida, anencephaly,** and other defects of the neural tube (Cefalo, 1996; Chomitz, Cheung, & Lieberman, 2000; Mills, 2001; Reynolds, 2002). Most women consume less than half the recommended daily allowance of folic acid, and intensive campaigns are now under way to persuade all women of childbearing age to take vitamin-mineral supplements that provide them with at least 0.4 mg (but not more than 1.0 mg) of folic acid a day (Cefalo, 1996). Folic acid enrichment is particularly important from the time of conception through the first 8 weeks of pregnancy, when the neural tube is forming (Friedman & Polifka, 1996). However, these supplementation campaigns are controversial. Many fear that some women encouraged to take vitamin-mineral supplements may assume that "more is better" and end up ingesting too much vitamin A, which in very high doses can *produce* birth defects (review Table 4.3). Yet, under proper medical supervision, vitamin-mineral supplements are considered quite safe (Friedman & Polifka, 1996).

The Pregnant Woman's Emotional Well-Being

Although most women are happy about conceiving a child, many pregnancies are unplanned. Does it matter how a woman feels about being pregnant or about her life while she is pregnant?

Indeed it may, at least in some cases. When a pregnant woman becomes emotionally aroused, her glands secrete powerful activating hormones such as adrenaline. These hormones may then cross the placental barrier, enter the fetus's bloodstream, and increase the fetus's motor activity. Stress may, in other conditions, decrease fetal motor activity. DiPietro, Costigan, and Gurewitsch (2003) monitored fetal heart rate and motor activity while pregnant women completed a difficult cognitive task that can increase temporary stress while attempting the activity. Increased variability in fetal heart rate and decreased motor activity were associated with increased maternal stress during the task. Maternal stress measures included skin conductance and heart rate, self-ratings, and observer ratings. In the fetus, the changes in heart rate variability and motor activity occurred very quickly. DiPietro and her colleagues suggest that the rapid changes they observed may indicate a sensory reaction on the part of the fetus. That is, the fetus may detect (hear) differences in sounds made by the maternal heart and vascular systems, as well as changes in the mother's voice. Therefore, stress-induced changes in the fetus may be caused by the sensory experience the fetus has, in addition to maternal heart rate and changes in the hormones as they cross the placenta when the pregnant woman is under stress.

Temporarily stressful episodes such as a fall, a frightening experience, or an argument have few if any harmful consequences for a mother or her fetus (Brockington, 1996). However, prolonged and severe emotional stress is associated with stunted prenatal growth, premature delivery, low birth weight, and other birth complications (Lobel, 1994; Paarlberg et al., 1995; Weerth, Hees, & Buitelaar, 2003). Others have found that babies of highly stressed mothers tend to be highly active, irritable, and irregular in their feeding, sleeping, and bowel habits (Sameroff & Chandler, 1975; Vaughn et al., 1987). Experiments with rhesus monkeys suggest a causal relationship between maternal stress and low birth weight and irregular infant demeanor (Schneider et al., 1999).

In a small study of 17 mothers and their full-term, healthy infants, maternal levels of salivary cortisol, a hormone important to regulation of the human stress response, were sampled at 37 and 38 weeks prior to delivery. Post delivery, mother-infant pairs were videotaped at home during bath time. As illustrated in Figure 4.8, the infants of mothers with higher prenatal cortisol levels fussed and cried more during baths than did those of mothers with lower cortisol levels. The high-cortisol infants also exhibited more negative facial expressions. In addition, mothers in the high-cortisol group reported that their infants were temperamentally difficult, displaying higher levels of emotionality and activity than low-cortisol infants. For the most part, differences in negative reactions to bathing disappeared for the two groups as they approached 18 to 20 weeks post birth. The authors suggested that this disappearance might be attributed to the infants' maturing perceptions and capabilities. In general, newborns may experience being splashed with water as aversive. However, a 5-month-old, even a temperamentally difficult one, may experience splashing Mother as quite fun. The authors further suggest that other activities may reveal lingering temperamental differences in the two groups of children (Weerth, Hees, & Buitelaar, 2003).

Van der Bergh and Marcoen (2004) report several long-term consequences of maternal stress that appear to be associated with a sensitive period during gestation. These include an

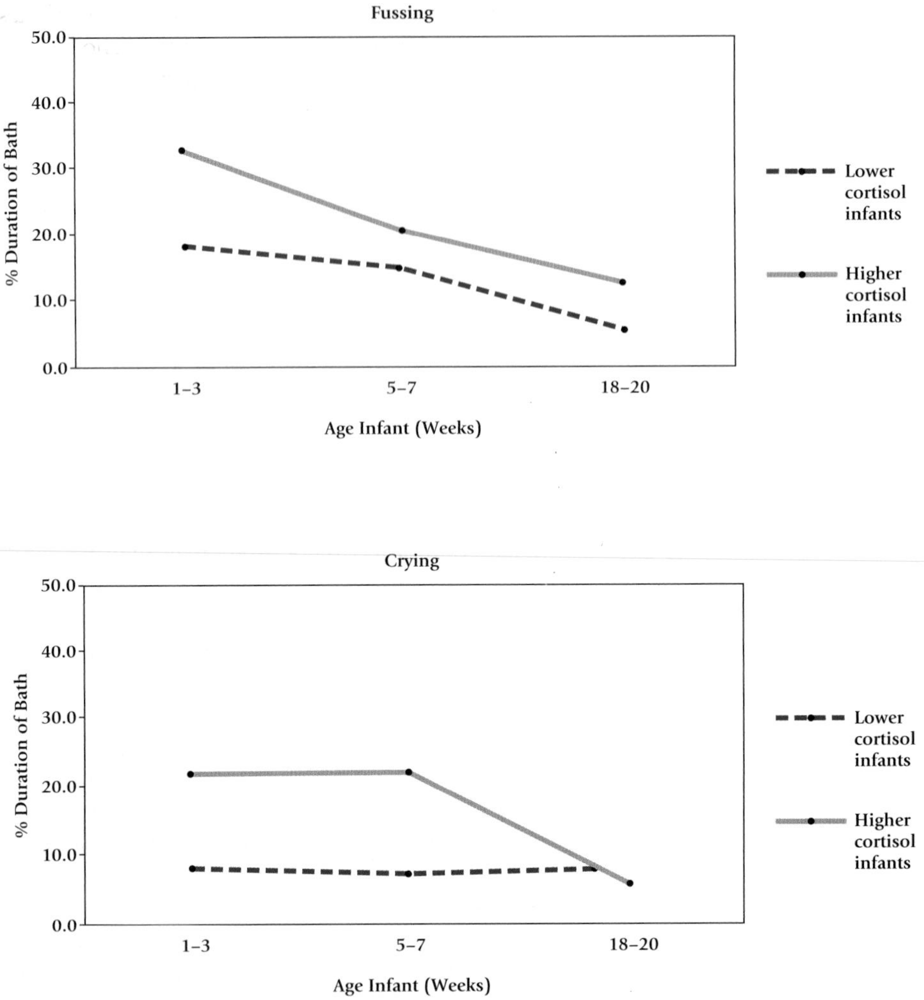

Figure 4.8 Percent of bath time that infants spent fussing and crying. The figure compares infants whose mothers experienced high levels of cortisol (a hormone related to stress) to infants whose mothers experienced low levels of cortisol during pregnancy. *From Weerth et al., "Prenatal maternal cortisol levels and infant behavior during the first 5 months,"* Early Human Development, *74, 193–151. Reprinted by permission of Elsevier.*

increased risk for childhood development of ADHD symptoms, externalizing problems (such as temper tantrums and aggressive behaviors toward other children), and anxiety. Van der Bergh and Marcoen's research suggests that children are especially susceptible when the prenatal stress experience occurs between weeks 12 and 22 of the gestational period.

How might emotional stress stunt fetal growth and contribute to birth complications and newborn behavioral irregularities? A link between prolonged stress and growth retardation or low birth weight may reflect the influence of stress hormones, which divert blood flow to the large muscles and impede the flow of oxygen and nutrients to the fetus. Stress may also weaken the pregnant woman's immune system, making her (and her fetus) more susceptible to infectious diseases (Cohen & Williamson, 1991; DiPietro, 2004). Finally, emotionally stressed mothers may be inclined to eat poorly, smoke, or use alcohol and drugs, all of which are known to promote fetal growth retardation and low birth weight (DiPietro, 2004; Paarlberg et al., 1995). Of course, a mother whose source of stress continues after her baby is born may not make the most sensitive caregiver, which, coupled with a baby who is already irritable and unresponsive, can perpetuate the infant's difficult behavioral profile (Brockington, 1996; Vaughn et al., 1987).

Interestingly, not all highly stressed mothers experience the complications we have discussed. Why? Because it seems that the presence of objective stressors in a woman's life is far less important than her ability to *manage* such stress (McCubbin et al., 1996). Stress-related complications are much more likely when pregnant women (1) are ambivalent or negative about their marriages or their pregnancies, and (2) have no friends or other bases of social support to turn to for comfort (Brockington, 1996). Counseling aimed at managing and reducing stress may help these women immensely. In one study, babies of stressed pregnant women who received such counseling weighed significantly more at birth than babies of stressed pregnant women who received no help (Rothberg & Lits, 1991).

Finally, in a recent literature review, Janet DiPietro (2004) reports that both negative and positive developmental outcomes have been associated with prenatal maternal stress. She and her colleagues have noted that, as pregnant women report greater numbers of daily hassles, the synchrony of fetal heart rate and movement (an important indicator of developing neurological integration) is diminished. However, DiPietro and her colleagues (2003) also report a strong association between higher maternal anxiety midway through pregnancy and higher scores on motor and mental development assessments at two years. DiPietrio points out that, as reported above, stress hormones may cross the placental barrier and that, since one group of such hormones, the glucocorticoids, are also involved in the maturation progress of fetal organs, maternal stress may actually promote prenatal development rather than diminish it. DiPietrio suggests that moderate amounts of maternal stress, as opposed to low or high maternal stress levels, may be necessary for healthy development in utero.

The Pregnant Woman's Age

neonate
a newborn infant from birth to approximately 1 month of age

The safest time to bear a child appears to be from about age 16 to age 35 (Dollberg et al., 1996). There is a clear relationship between a woman's age and the risk of death for her fetus or **neonate** (newborn). Risk of infant mortality increases substantially for mothers 15 years old and younger (Phipps, Sowers, & Demonner, 2002). Compared with mothers in their 20s, mothers younger than 16 experience more birth complications and are more likely to deliver prematurely and have low-birth-weight babies (Koniak-Griffin & Turner-Pluta, 2001).

Why are younger mothers and their offspring at risk? The major reason is simply that pregnant teenagers are often from economically impoverished family backgrounds characterized by poor nutrition, high levels of stress, and little access to supervised prenatal care (Abma & Mott, 1991). Teenage mothers and their babies are usually *not* at risk when they receive good prenatal care and competent medical supervision during the birth process (Baker & Mednick, 1984; Seitz & Apfel, 1994a).

What risks do women face should they delay childbearing until after age 35? There is an increased incidence of miscarriage, due in part to the older woman's greater likelihood of conceiving children with chromosomal abnormalities. The risks of other complications during pregnancy and delivery are also greater for older women, even when they receive adequate prenatal care (Dollberg et al., 1996). Even so, it is important to emphasize that the vast majority of older women—particularly those who are healthy and well-nourished—have normal pregnancies and healthy babies (Brockington, 1996).

Prevention of Birth Defects

Reading a chapter such as this one can be frightening to anyone who hopes to have a child. It is easy to come away with the impression that "life before birth" is a veritable minefield: So many hereditary accidents are possible, and even a genetically normal embryo or fetus may encounter a large number of potential hazards while developing in the womb.

But clearly there is another side to this story. Recall that the majority of genetically abnormal embryos do not develop to term. And it is important to emphasize that the prenatal environment is not so hazardous when we note that more than 95 percent of newborn babies are perfectly normal and that many of the remaining 5 percent have minor congenital problems that are only temporary or easily correctable (Gosden, Nicolaides, & Whitting, 1994). Although there *is* reason for concern, parents can significantly reduce the odds that their babies will be abnormal if they follow the recommendations in Table 4.4. Apgar and Beck (1974, p. 452) remind us that "Each pregnancy is different. Each unborn child has a unique genetic make-up. The prenatal environment a mother provides is never quite the same for another baby. Thus, we believe no amount of effort is too great to increase the chances that a baby will be born normal, healthy, and without a handicapping birth defect."

TABLE 4.4 Reducing the Likelihood of Congenital Disorders

Virginia Apgar and Joan Beck (1974) suggest these ways that prospective parents can significantly reduce the likelihood of bearing a child with a congenital disorder.

- ✓ If you think a close relative has a disorder that might be hereditary, you should take advantage of genetic counseling.
- ✓ The ideal age for a woman to have children is between 16 and 35.
- ✓ Every pregnant woman needs good prenatal care supervised by a practitioner who keeps current on medical research in the field of teratology and who will help her deliver her baby in a reputable, modern hospital.
- ✓ No woman should become pregnant unless she is sure that she has either had rubella or been immunized against it.
- ✓ From the beginning of pregnancy, a woman should be tested for STDs and do everything possible to avoid exposure to contagious diseases.
- ✓ Pregnant women should avoid eating undercooked red meat or having contact with any cat (or cat feces) that may carry toxoplasmosis infection.
- ✓ A pregnant woman should not take any drugs unless absolutely essential—and then only when approved by a physician who is aware of the pregnancy.
- ✓ Unless it is absolutely essential for her own well-being, a pregnant woman should avoid radiation treatments and X-ray examinations.
- ✓ Cigarettes should not be smoked during pregnancy.
- ✓ A nourishing diet, rich in proteins and adequate in vitamins, minerals, and total calories, is essential during pregnancy.

CONCEPT CHECK 4.1 Prenatal Development

Check your understanding of prenatal development and some of the problems that can occur in prenatal development by answering the following questions. Answers appear in the Appendix.

Multiple Choice: Select the best answer for each of the following multiple-choice questions.

_____ 1. Which of the following events marks the transition between when we label the developing organism a "zygote" to when we begin to label it an "embryo"?
a. conception
b. ovulation
c. implantation
d. cell division

_____ 2. The organ that is responsible for the transmission of nutrients and wastes between the developing organism and the pregnant woman is called the
a. amnion
b. placenta
c. chorion
d. embryonic disk

_____ 3. The most critical period in prenatal development for potential damage to the developing organism from teratogens is the period of the
a. embryo
b. zygote
c. fetus
d. blastocyst

Matching: Check your understanding of the effects of teratogens by matching the teratogen to the effect it may have on the developing organism.

4. rubella
5. toxoplasmosis
6. thalidomide

a. eye and brain damage; late-pregnancy miscarriage
b. missing or malformed arms and legs
c. blindness, deafness, mental retardation

Fill in the Blank: Check your understanding of the material by filling in the blanks in the following sentences with the correct word or phrase.

7. When a pregnant woman drinks alcohol during her pregnancy, she risks having a child born with _____ if the prenatal damage was not severe, or _____ if the prenatal damage from alcohol was very severe.
8. Two methods of obtaining cells from the developing organism for the purpose of karotyping and examining the cells for genetic or chromosomal abnormalities are _____ and _____.
9. Sexual differentiation begins when a gene on the _____ chromosome instructs the _____ to produce testes, if the developing organism is a male.
10. Erica was born in 1960 and she appeared at birth to be a normal, healthy girl. Her life proceeded normally until she turned 20. Then she discovered that she had a rare form of reproductive organ cancer and that she would be unlikely to be able to have children herself. Her doctor wondered whether her mother had taken _____ during her pregnancy with Erica. He suspected that the drug could have been a teratogen that caused Erica's reproductive abnormalities.

Birth and the Perinatal Environment

perinatal environment
perinatal refers to the time around birth, both before and after birth; perinatal environment refers to the environment surrounding birth.

The **perinatal environment** is the environment surrounding birth; it includes influences such as medications given to the mother during delivery, delivery practices, and the social environment shortly after the baby is born. As we will see, this perinatal environment is an important one that can affect a baby's well-being and the course of her future development.

The Birth Process

first stage of labor
the period of the birth process lasting from the first regular uterine contractions until the cervix is fully dilated.

second stage of labor
the period of the birth process during which the fetus moves through the birth canal and emerges from the mother's body (also called the delivery).

third stage of labor
expulsion of the placenta (afterbirth).

Childbirth is a three-stage process (see Figure 4.9). The **first stage of labor** begins as the mother experiences uterine contractions spaced at 10- to 15-minute intervals, and it ends when her cervix has fully dilated so that the fetus's head can pass through. This phase lasts an average of 8 to 14 hours for firstborn children and 3 to 8 for later-borns. As labor proceeds, the uterus contracts more frequently and intensely. When the head of the fetus is positioned at the cervical opening, the second phase of labor is about to begin.

The **second stage of labor,** or *delivery,* begins as the fetus's head passes through the cervix into the vagina and ends when the baby emerges from the mother's body. This is the time when the mother may be told to bear down (push) with each contraction to assist her child through the birth canal. A quick delivery may take a half-hour, whereas a long one may last more than an hour and a half.

The **third stage of labor,** or *afterbirth,* takes only 5 to 10 minutes as the uterus once again contracts and expels the placenta from the mother's body.

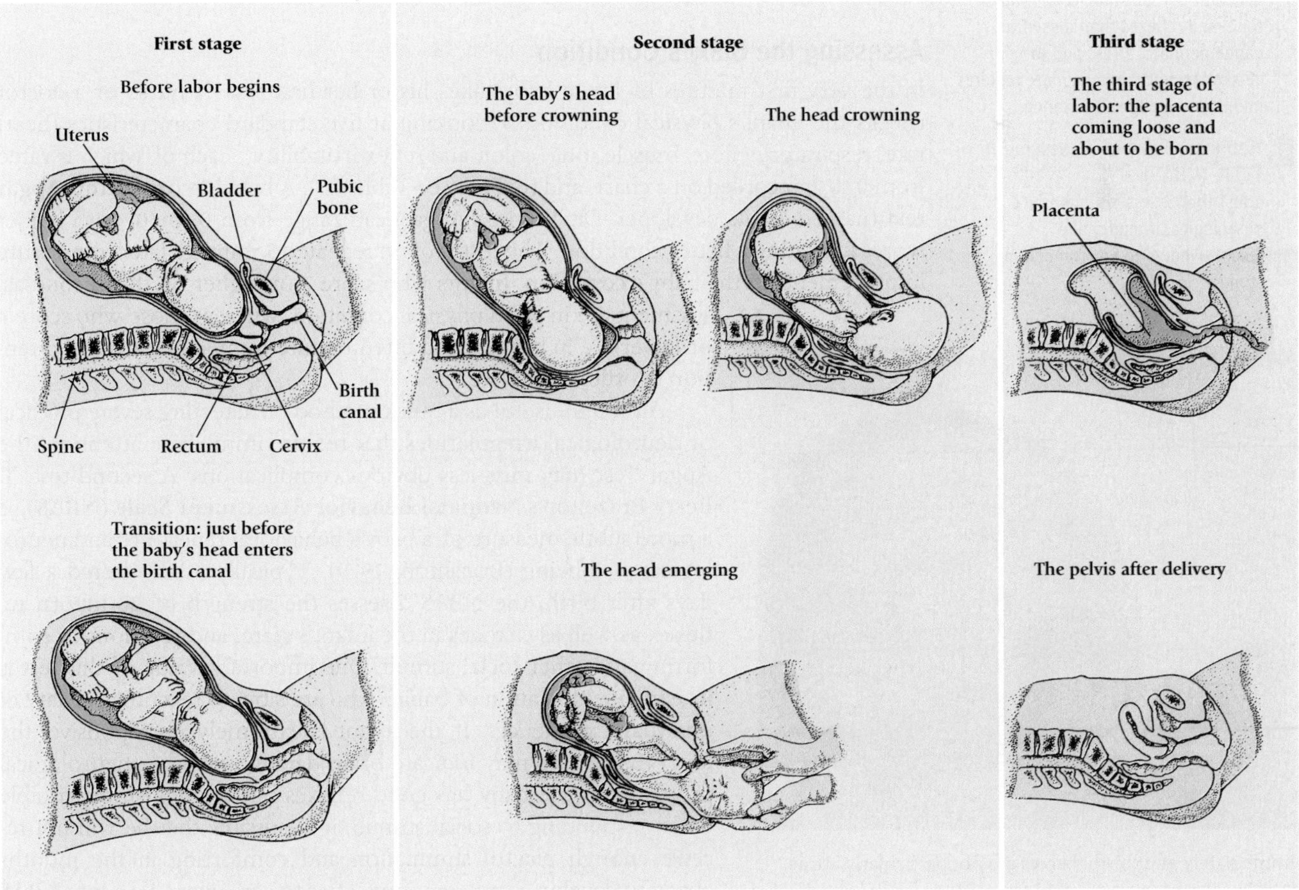

Figure 4.9 The three stages of childbirth.

The Baby's Experience

It was once thought that birth was an extremely hazardous and torturous ordeal for a contented fetus who is suddenly expelled from a soft, warm uterus into a cold, bright world where, for the first time, it may experience chills, pain, hunger, and the startling rush of air into its lungs. Yet, few people today would describe birth and birthing practices as the "torture of the innocents" as French obstetrician Frederick LeBoyer (1975) has. Fetuses *are* stressed by birth, but their own production of activating stress hormones is adaptive, helping them to withstand oxygen deprivation by increasing their heart rate and the flow of oxygenated blood to the brain (Nelson, 1995). Birth stress also helps to ensure that babies are born wide awake and ready to breathe. Aiden MacFarlane (1977) has carefully observed many newborn babies, noting that most of them quiet down and begin to adapt to their new surroundings within minutes of that first loud cry. So birth is a stressful ordeal, but hardly a torturous one.

The Baby's Appearance

To a casual observer, many newborns may not look especially attractive. Often born bluish in color from oxygen deprivation during the birth process, babies' passage through the narrow cervix and birth canal may also leave them with flattened noses, misshapen foreheads, and an assortment of bumps and bruises. As the baby is weighed and measured, parents are likely to see a wrinkled, red-skinned little creature, about 20 inches long and weighing about 7½ pounds, who is covered with a sticky substance. But even though newborns may hardly resemble the smiley bouncing infants who appear in baby food commercials, most parents think that their baby is beautiful nevertheless, and are usually eager to become acquainted with this new member of the family.

Apgar test
a quick assessment of the newborn's heart rate, respiration, color, muscle tone, and reflexes that is used to gauge perinatal stress and to determine whether a neonate requires immediate medical assistance.

Neonatal Behavior Assessment Scale (NBAS)
a test that assesses a neonate's neurological integrity and responsiveness to environmental stimuli.

Assessing the Baby's Condition

In the very first minutes of life, a baby takes his or her first test. A nurse or a doctor checks the infant's physical condition by looking at five standard characteristics (heart rate, respiratory effort, muscle tone, color, and reflex irritability), each of which is rated from 0 to 2, recorded on a chart, and totaled (see Table 4.5). A baby's score on this **Apgar test** (named for its developer, Dr. Virginia Apgar) can range from 0 to 10, with higher scores indicating a better condition. The test is often repeated 5 minutes later to measure improvements in the baby's condition. Infants who score 7 or higher on this second assessment are in good physical condition, whereas those who score 4 or lower are in distress and often require immediate medical attention in order to survive.

Although useful as a quick method of detecting severe physical or neurological irregularities that require immediate attention, the Apgar Test may miss less obvious complications. A second test, T. Berry Brazelton's **Neonatal Behavior Assessment Scale (NBAS),** is a more subtle measure of a baby's behavioral repertoire and neurological well-being (Brazelton, 1979). Typically administered a few days after birth, the NBAS assesses the strength of 20 inborn reflexes, as well as changes in the infant's state, and reactions to comforting and other social stimuli. One important value of this test is its early identification of babies who are slow to react to a variety of everyday experiences. If the infant is extremely unresponsive, the low NBAS score may indicate brain damage or other neurological problems. If the baby has good reflexes but is sluggish or irritable when responding to social stimuli, it is possible that he will not receive enough playful stimulation and comforting in the months ahead to develop secure emotional ties to caregivers. So a low NBAS score provides a warning that problems could arise.

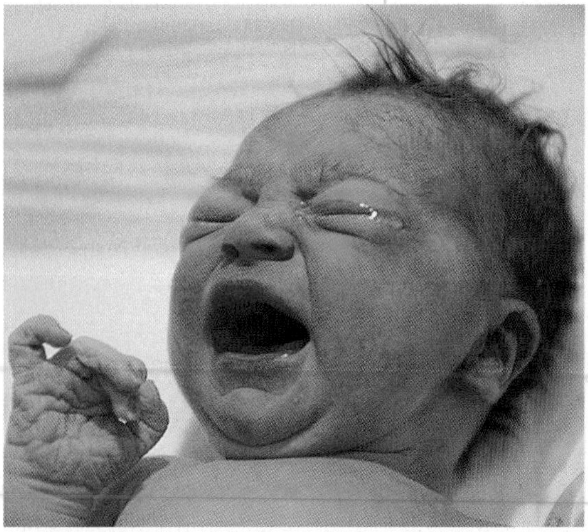

David Sams/Stock Boston

Immediately after birth, babies are not particularly attractive, but their appearance improves dramatically over the first few weeks of life.

TABLE 4.5 The Apgar Test

Characteristic	Score 0	Score 1	Score 2
Heart rate	Absent	Slow (fewer than 100 beats per minute)	Over 100 beats per minute
Respiratory effort	Absent	Slow or irregular	Good; baby is crying
Muscle tone	Flaccid, limp	Weak, some flexion	Strong, active motion
Color	Blue or pale	Body pink, extremities blue	Completely pink
Reflex irritability	No response	Frown, grimace, or weak cry	Vigorous cries, coughs, sneezes

Note: Letters in Apgar are an acronym for the test's five criteria:
A = Appearance, P = Pulse, G = Grimace, A = Activity level, R = Respiratory effort.

Fortunately, the NBAS can be an excellent teaching tool to help parents get off to a good start with their babies. Several studies show that mothers and fathers who take part as the NBAS is administered often learn much about their baby's behavioral capabilities, as well as how they might successfully quiet their fussy infant or elicit such pleasing responses as smiles and attentive gazes. When observed 1 month later, NBAS-trained parents are generally more responsive toward and involved with their infants than are parents in control groups who received no training (see Britt & Myers, 1994). Others have had similar success with filmed NBAS sessions (which illustrate newborns' social and perceptual capabilities) coupled with discussions, undertaken with the baby present, that stress the importance of affectionate handling and sensitively adapting one's caregiving to the baby's unique characteristics (Wendland-Carro, Piccinini, & Millar, 1999). So NBAS training and other similar interventions appear to be highly effective at starting parents and babies on the right foot. What's more, parents enjoy these simple, inexpensive programs, which seem especially well-suited for (1) young, inexperienced caregivers who know little about babies or (2) families with a baby who scores low on the NBAS and may otherwise frustrate parents with his irritable or unresponsive demeanor (Wendland-Carro, Piccinini, & Millar, 1999).

Labor and Delivery Medications

In the United States, as many as 95 percent of mothers receive some kind of medication (and often several) while giving birth. These drugs may include analgesics and anesthetics to reduce pain, sedatives to relax the mother, and stimulants to induce or intensify uterine contractions. Obviously, these agents are administered in the hope of making the birth process easier for the mother, and their use is often essential to save a baby's life in a complicated delivery. However, a strong dose of birth medications can have some undesirable consequences.

Mothers who receive large amounts of anesthesia, for example, are often less sensitive to uterine contractions and do not push effectively during the delivery. As a result, their babies may have to be pulled from the birth canal with *obstetrical forceps* (a device that resembles a pair of salad tongs) or a *vacuum extractor* (a plastic suction cup attached to the baby's head). Unfortunately, in a small number of cases, application of these devices to a baby's soft skull can cause cranial bleeding and brain damage (Brockington, 1996).

Labor and delivery medications also cross the placenta and, in heavy doses, can make babies lethargic and inattentive. Infants of heavily medicated mothers smile infrequently, become irritable when aroused, and are difficult to feed or cuddle in the first weeks of life (Brackbill, McManas, & Woodward, 1985). Some researchers fear that parents could fail to become very involved with or attached to such a sluggish, irritable, and inattentive baby (Murray et al., 1981).

APPLYING RESEARCH TO YOUR LIFE

Cultural and Historical Variations in Birthing Practices

Although nearly 99 percent of all babies in the United States are born in a hospital to a mother in bed, the majority of infants in many other cultures are still born at home, often with the mother in a vertical or squatting position, surrounded by family members and assisted by other women (Philpott, 1995). Cultures clearly differ in the rituals surrounding birth (Steinberg, 1996). Among the Pokot people of Kenya, cultural rituals help to ensure strong social support of the birth mother (O'Dempsey, 1988). The whole community celebrates the coming birth, and the father-to-be must stop hunting and be available to support his wife. A midwife, assisted by female relatives, delivers the baby. The placenta is then ceremoniously buried in the goat enclosure, and the baby is given a tribal potion for its health. Mothers are secluded for a month to recover and are given 3 months, free of other chores, to devote themselves to their babies (Jeffery & Jeffery, 1993).

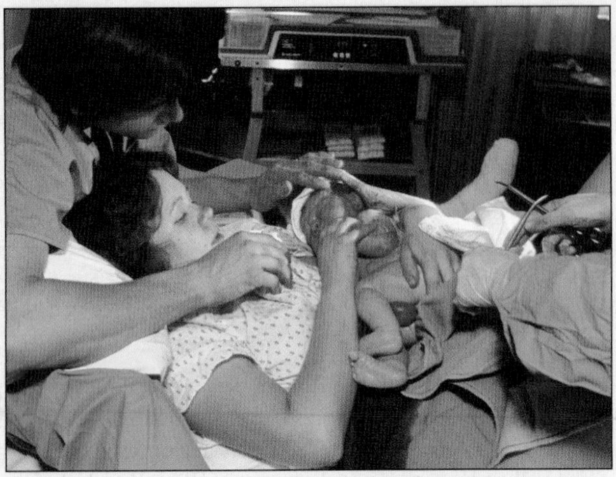
Tom Tucker/Science Source/Photo Researchers Inc.

More women today are choosing to give birth at home or in alternative birth centers to share the joy of childbirth with family members.

Childbirth is viewed as disgusting and shameful in Uttar Predesh in northern India. Babies are delivered by poorly paid attendants, who discourage a mother's cries of pain and offer little social support. The mother is isolated for days after a birth, and her "dirty" baby's head is shaved to avoid "polluting" others.

Interestingly, hospital birthing in the United States is a relatively recent practice; before 1900, only 5 to 10 percent of U.S. babies were born in a hospital to a heavily medicated mother who was flat on her back with her legs in stirrups. Today, many parents favor a return to the practice of viewing birth as a natural family event rather than a medical crisis to be managed with high technology (Brockington, 1996). Two approaches to childbirth that reflect these concerns are the natural childbirth philosophy and the home birthing movement.

Natural or Prepared Childbirth

The **natural,** or **prepared, childbirth** movement is a philosophy based on the idea that childbirth is a normal and natural part of life rather than a painful ordeal that women should fear. The natural childbirth movement arose in the mid-20th century from the work of Grantly Dick-Read, in England, and Fernand Lamaze in France. These two obstetricians claimed

CONTINUED

So are mothers best advised to avoid all labor and delivery medications? Probably not. Some women are at risk of birth complications because they are small or are delivering large fetuses, and drugs given in appropriate doses can ease their discomfort without disrupting the delivery. In addition, doctors today are more likely than those of the past to use less toxic drugs in smaller doses at the safest times, so that taking medications is not as risky as it once was (Simpson & Creehan, 1996).

The Social Environment Surrounding Birth

Only 30 years ago, most hospitals barred fathers from delivery rooms and whisked babies away from their mothers to nurseries within minutes of a delivery. However, the times have changed—so much so that a birth today is much more likely to be a dramatic experience for both parents.

natural, or prepared, childbirth a delivery in which physical and psychological preparations for the birth are stressed and medical assistance is minimized.

The Mother's Experience

The first few minutes after birth can be a special time for a mother to thoroughly enjoy her baby, provided she is given the opportunity. Marshall Klaus and John Kennell (1976) that most women could give birth quite comfortably, without medication, if they had been taught to associate childbirth with pleasant feelings and to ready themselves for the process by learning exercises, breathing methods, and relaxation techniques that make childbirth easier (Dick-Read, 1933/1972; Lamaze, 1958).

Parents who decide on a prepared childbirth usually attend classes for 6 to 8 weeks before the delivery. They learn what to expect during labor and may even visit a delivery room and become familiar with the procedures used there as part of their preparation. They are also given a prescribed set of exercises and relaxation techniques to master. Typically, the father (or another companion) acts as a coach to assist the mother in toning her muscles and perfecting her breathing for labor. The birthing partner is also encouraged to physically and emotionally support the mother during the delivery.

Research reveals that there are many benefits to natural childbirth, not least of which is the important social support mothers receive from their spouses and other close companions. When mothers attend childbirth classes regularly and have a companion present in the delivery room to assist and encourage them, they experience less pain during delivery, use less medication, and have more positive attitudes toward themselves, their babies, and the whole birth experience (Brockington, 1996; Wilcock, Kobayashi, & Murray, 1997). As a result, many physicians today routinely recommend natural childbirth to their patients.

Home Births

Since the 1970s, a small but growing number of families have largely rejected the medical model of childbirth, choosing instead to deliver their babies at home with the aid of a certified nurse-midwife trained in nonsurgical obstetrics. They believe that home deliveries will reduce the mother's fear and offer maximum social support by encouraging friends and family to be there, rather than a host of unfamiliar nurses, aides, and physicians. They are also hoping to reduce their reliance on childbirth medications and other unnecessary and potentially harmful medical interventions. Indeed, it appears that the relaxed atmosphere and the social support available at a home delivery do have a calming effect on many mothers. Women who deliver at home have shorter labors and use less medication than those who deliver in hospitals (Beard & Chapple, 1995; Brackbill, McManus, & Woodward, 1985).

Are home births as safe as hospital deliveries? Childbirth statistics from many industrialized countries suggest that they are, as long as the mother is healthy, the pregnancy has gone smoothly, and the birth is attended by a well-trained midwife (Ackermann-Liebrich et al., 1996). Yet unexpected, life-threatening complications can occur in any delivery, and such complications are quite common in some developing nations, occurring in more than 15 percent of home deliveries there (Caldwell, 1996).

Fortunately, there are other options for couples who seek safety and the advantages of giving birth in a comfortable homelike environment. Many hospitals have created **alternative birth centers,** which provide a homelike atmosphere but still make medical technology available. Still other birthing centers operate independently of hospitals and place the task of delivery in the hands of certified nurse-midwives (Beard & Chapple, 1995). In either case, spouses, friends, and often even the couple's children can be present during labor, and healthy infants can remain in the same room with their mothers (rooming-in) rather than spending their first days in the hospital nursery. So far, the evidence suggests that giving birth in well-run alternative birth centers is no more risky to healthy mothers and their babies than hospital deliveries are (Fullerton & Severino, 1992; Harvey et al., 1996). However, mothers at risk for birth complications are always best advised to deliver in a hospital, where life-saving technologies are immediately available should they be needed.

believe that the first 6 to 12 hours after birth are a sensitive period for **emotional bonding** when a mother is especially ready to respond to and develop a strong sense of affection for her baby (Kennell, & Klaus, 1976). In a study testing this hypothesis, Klaus and Kennell (1976) had half of a group of new mothers follow the then-traditional hospital routine: They saw their babies briefly after delivery, visited with them 6 to 12 hours later, and had half-hour feeding sessions every 4 hours thereafter for the remainder of a 3-day hospital stay. The other mothers were in an "extended contact" group and were permitted 5 "extra" hours a day to cuddle their babies, including an hour of skin-to-skin contact that took place within 3 hours of birth.

In a follow-up 1 month later, mothers who had been allowed early extended contact with their babies appeared to be more involved with them and held them closer during feeding sessions than did mothers who had followed the traditional hospital routine. One year later, the extended-contact mothers were still the more highly involved group of caregivers, and their 1-year-olds outperformed those in the traditional-routine group on tests of physical and mental development. Apparently, extended early contact in the hospital fostered mothers' affection for their newborns, which, in turn, may have motivated those mothers to continue to interact in highly stimulating ways with their babies. In response to this and other similar studies, many hospitals have altered their routines to allow the kinds of early contact that can promote emotional bonding.

alternative birth center
a hospital birthing room or other independent facility that provides a homelike atmosphere for childbirth but still makes medical technology available.

emotional bonding
term used to describe the strong affectionate ties that parents may feel toward their infant; some theorists believe that the strongest bonding occurs shortly after birth, during a sensitive period.

Does this mean that mothers who have no early contact with their newborns miss out on forming the strongest possible emotional ties to them? No, it does not! Later research has shown that early contact effects are nowhere near as significant or long-lasting as Klaus and Kennell presumed (Eyer, 1992; Goldberg, 1983). Other research reveals that most adoptive parents, who rarely have any early contact with their infants, nevertheless develop emotional bonds with their adoptees that are just as strong, on average, as those seen in nonadoptive homes (Levy-Shiff, Goldschmidt, & Har-Even, 1991; Singer et al., 1985). So even though early contact can be a very pleasant experience that can help a mother begin to form an emotional bond with her child, she need not fear that problems will arise should something prevent her from having this experience.

postpartum depression
strong feelings of sadness, resentment, and despair that may appear shortly after childbirth and can linger for months.

engrossment
paternal analogue of maternal emotional bonding; term used to describe fathers' fascination with their neonates, including their desire to touch, hold, caress, and talk to the newborn baby.

Postpartum Depression. Unfortunately, there is a "down side" to the birth experience for some mothers. These mothers may find themselves depressed, tearful, irritable, and even resentful of their babies shortly after birth. Milder forms of this condition, called the *maternity blues,* may characterize as many as 40 to 60 percent of all new mothers (Kessel, 1995), whereas slightly more than 10 percent of new mothers experience a more serious depressive reaction, called **postpartum depression.** Many of these severely depressed women do not want their infants and perceive them to be difficult babies. These mothers also interact less positively with their infants and in some cases seem downright hostile toward them (Campbell et al., 1992). Whereas the maternity blues usually pass within a week or two, postpartum depression may last for months.

Hormonal changes following childbirth, along with new stresses associated with the responsibilities of parenthood, probably account for milder, short-lived symptoms of maternal depression post birth (Hendrick & Altshuler, 1999; Wile & Arechiga, 1999). A maternal history of depressive episodes, binge drinking and cigarette use during pregnancy, plus life stresses over and above that associated with parenthood are often associated with manifestations of more severe postpartum depression (Brockington, 1996; Homish, 2004; Whiffen, 1992). The availability of social support may influence postpartum outcomes. Lack of social support—particularly a poor relationship with the father—dramatically increases the odds of a negative postpartum experience (Field et al., 1988; Gotlib et al., 1991). Reciprocally, new mothers with positive perceptions about the availability of social support report more positive perceptions of their newborns (Priel & Besser, 2002). The attachment bond that develops between an infant and a mother who remains chronically depressed, withdrawn, and unresponsive is likely to be insecure. Infants in this situation may develop depressive symptoms and behavior problems of their own (Campbell, Cohn, & Myers, 1995; Murray, Fiori-Cowley, & Hooper, 1996). Consequently, mothers experiencing more than a mild case of the maternity blues should seek professional help.

Jeff Persons/Photo Researchers Inc.

This father displays a fascination with his newborn that is known as engrossment.

The Father's Experience

Fathers, like mothers, experience the birth process as a significant life event that involves a mix of positive and negative emotions. New fathers interviewed in one study admitted that their fears mounted during labor, but said that they tried hard to appear calm nonetheless. Although they described childbirth as a most agonizing and stressful ordeal, their negative emotions usually gave way to relief, pride, and joy when the baby finally arrived (Chandler & Field, 1997).

Like new mothers, new fathers often display a sense of **engrossment** with the baby—an intense fascination with and a strong desire to touch, hold, and caress this newest member of the family (Greenberg & Morris, 1974; Peterson, Mehl, & Liederman, 1979). One young father put it this way: "When I came up to see (my) wife . . . I go look at the kid and then I pick her up and put her down . . . I keep going back to the kid. It's like a magnet. That's what I can't get over, the fact that I feel like that" (Greenberg & Morris, 1974, p. 524). Some studies find that fathers who have handled and helped care for their babies in the hospital later spend more time with them at home than other fathers who have not had these early contacts with their newborns (Greenberg & Morris, 1974). Other studies have failed to find these long-term effects on father-infant interactions, but suggest that early contact with a newborn can make fathers feel closer to their partners and more a part of the family (Palkovitz, 1985). So a father who is present at birth not only plays an important supportive role for the mother, but is just as likely as the mother to enjoy close contact with their newborn.

Potential Problems at Birth

Childbirth does not always proceed as smoothly as indicated in our earlier account of the "normal" delivery. Three birth complications that can adversely influence a baby's development are anoxia (oxygen deprivation), a premature delivery, and low birth weight.

Anoxia

anoxia
a lack of sufficient oxygen to the brain; may result in neurological damage or death.

breech birth
a delivery in which the fetus emerges feet first or buttocks first rather than head first.

Nearly 1 percent of babies are born showing signs of **anoxia,** or oxygen deprivation. In many cases, the child's supply of oxygen is interrupted because the umbilical cord has become tangled or squeezed during childbirth, as can easily happen when infants are lying in the **breech position** and are born feet or buttocks first. In fact, breech babies are often delivered by cesarean section to protect against anoxia (Lin, 1993a). Other cases of anoxia occur when the placenta separates prematurely, interrupting the supply of food and oxygen to the fetus. Anoxia can also happen after birth if sedatives given to the mother cross the placental barrier and interfere with the baby's breathing or if mucus ingested during childbirth becomes lodged in the baby's throat. Although newborns can tolerate oxygen deprivation far longer than older children and adults, permanent brain damage can result if breathing is delayed for more than 3 to 4 minutes (Nelson, 1995).

RH factor
a blood protein that, when present in a fetus but not the mother, can cause the mother to produce antibodies. These antibodies may then attack the red blood cells of subsequent fetuses who have the protein in their blood.

Another potential cause of anoxia is a genetic incompatibility between an RH-positive fetus, who has a protein called **RH factor** in its blood, and an RH-negative mother, who lacks this substance. During labor and delivery when the placenta is deteriorating, RH-negative mothers are often exposed to the blood of their RH-positive fetuses, and they begin to produce RH antibodies. If these antibodies enter a fetus's bloodstream, they can attack red blood cells, depleting oxygen and possibly producing brain damage and other birth defects. Firstborns are usually not affected because an RH-negative mother has no RH antibodies until she gives birth to an RH-positive child. Fortunately, problems stemming from an RH incompatibility can now be prevented by administering *rhogam* after the delivery, a vaccine that prevents the RH-negative mother from forming the RH antibodies that could harm her next RH-positive baby.

Children who experience mild anoxia are often irritable at birth and may score below average on tests of motor and mental development throughout the first 3 years (Sameroff & Chandler, 1975). However, these differences between mildly anoxic and normal children get smaller and smaller and are usually not detectible by age 7 (Corah et al., 1965). Prolonged oxygen deprivation, however, can cause neurological damage and permanent disabilities. For example, motor skill proficiency was negatively associated with the amount of perinatal oxygen deprivation experienced by 4- to 6-year-olds. That is, the greater the deprivation, the less proficient the child (Stevens, 2000). Other research has found that prenatal anoxia is associated with an increased vulnerability to adult heart disease (Zhang, 2005).

Complications of Low Birth Weight

More than 90 percent of babies in the United States are born between the 37th and 42nd weeks of pregnancy and are considered "timely." The average full-term, or "timely," infant is 19 to 21 inches long and weighs about 3,500 grams (7½ pounds).

preterm babies
infants born more than three weeks before their normal due dates.

The remaining 7 percent of babies weigh less than 2,500 grams (5½ pounds) at birth (Chomitz, Cheung, & Lieberman, 2000). There are two kinds of low-birth-weight babies. Most are born more than 3 weeks before their due dates and are called **preterm babies**.

small-for-date babies infants whose birth weight is far below normal, even when born close to their normal due dates.

Although small in size, the body weights of these babies are often appropriate for the amount of time they spent in the womb. Other low-birth-weight babies, called **small for date,** have experienced slow growth as fetuses and are seriously underweight, even when born close to their normal due dates. Although both kinds of low-birth-weight babies are vulnerable and may have to struggle to survive, small-for-date infants are at greater risk of serious complications. For example, they are more likely to die during the first year or to show signs of brain damage. They are also more likely than preterm infants to remain small in stature throughout childhood, to experience learning difficulties and behavior problems at school, and to perform poorly on IQ tests (Goldenberg, 1995; Taylor et al., 2000).

What are the causes of low birth weight? We have already seen that mothers who smoke and drink heavily, use drugs, or are malnourished are likely to deliver undersized babies. Indeed, low-income women are particularly at risk, largely because they experience higher levels of stress than other mothers do, and their diets and the prenatal care they receive are often inadequate (Chomitz, Cheung, & Lieberman, 2000; Fowles & Gabrielson, 2005; Mehl-Madrona, 2004). Yet another frequent contributor to undersized babies is multiple births (see Figure 4.10). Multiple fetuses generally gain much less weight than a singleton after the 29th week of pregnancy. And in addition to being small for date, triplets and quadruplets rarely develop to term in the uterus; in fact, they are often born 5 to 8 weeks early (Papiernik, 1995).

Interestingly, over and above biological influences, psychosocial factors have been associated with both gestational duration and birth weight (Mehl-Madrona, 2004; Schmid, 2000). In one study, changes in psychosocial factors emerged as predictors of birth weight. For example, mothers who demonstrated increases in the use of coping skills between the first and second trimester bore infants with greater birth weights than mothers who did not augment their coping behaviors. Also, increases in the amount of social support available to mothers during the second and third trimesters were associated with longer gestational periods (Schmid, 2000). Even the support and presence of unwed adolescent fathers may increase the chances that an unwed adolescent mother will bear a child of normal birth weight. Padilla and Reichman (2001) report that newborns of unwed adolescent parents had significantly higher birth weights when the teenaged father contributed monetarily to the mother's income or when the two parents lived together. Taken together, these findings may provide information relevant to planning prenatal interventions aimed at preventing both premature birth and low birth weight.

Short-Term Consequences of Low Birth Weight

The most trying task for a low-birth-weight baby is simply surviving the first few days of life. Although more of these infants are surviving each year, between 40 and 50 percent of

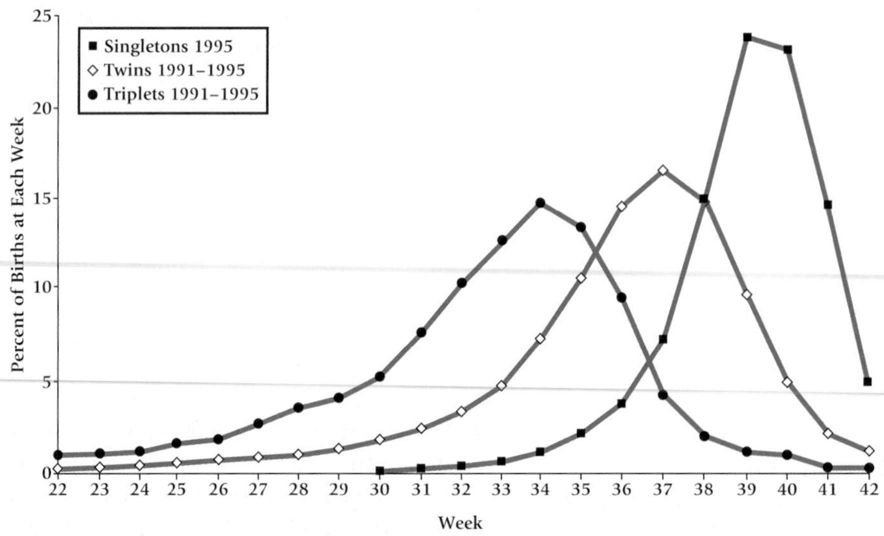

Figure 4.10 Gestational age at birth for singletons, twins, and triplets. *From Amiel-Tison et al., "Fetal adaptation to stress: Part I: acceleration of fetal maturation and earlier birth triggered by placental insufficiency in humans,"* Early Human Development, *78, 15–27. Reprinted by permission of Elsevier.*

those who weigh less than 1,000 grams (2.2 pounds) die at birth or shortly thereafter, even in the best hospitals. Small-for-date babies are often malformed, undernourished, or genetically abnormal—factors that will hinder them as they struggle to survive. Moreover, preterm infants are likely to experience a number of additional problems as a consequence of their general immaturity. For example, infant auditory skills, specifically the ability to discriminate between differing sounds and maternal voice recognition, were assessed for two groups of infants. One group consisted of full-term infants that were 1 to 3 days old. The other group consisted of preterm infants who were 1 to 3 days older than their original due date. In other words, the groups compared were of equivalent age from date of conception. Compared to the full-term infants, the preterm infants exhibited atypical patterns of neural activity during the auditory discrimination and sound recognition tasks. As well, the preterm infants did not recognize their own mothers' voices, whereas the full-term infants did (Therien et al., 2004).

When compared to full-term infants, preterm infants exhibit slower processing speeds throughout the first year of life (Rose, Feldman, & Jankowski, 2002). Together this evidence suggests that brain development and neural pattern formation in preterm infants differs from that of full-term infants. In fact, magnetic resonance imaging (MRI) techniques have revealed differences in brain structure that persist into young adulthood. In particular, the way that gray and white matter is distributed in the brain differs for very-low-birth-weight individuals when compared to their normal-birth-weight agemates (Allin et al., 2004). The consequences of these differences in the brain development of preterm infants are as yet unclear.

Preterm and low-birth-weight babies' most serious difficulty is breathing. A preterm infant often has very little *surfactin,* a substance that normally coats the lungs during the last 3 to 4 weeks of pregnancy to prevent them from collapsing. A deficiency of surfactin may result in **respiratory distress syndrome (RDS),** a serious respiratory ailment in which the affected child will breathe very irregularly and may stop breathing altogether. But the treatments for problems that preterm and low-birth-weight babies experience are not straightforward. Their problems are severe, as well as difficult to treat. For example, dexamethasone is a steroid used postnatally to treat RDS. Postnatal treatment with dexamethasone is a major risk factor for delayed psychomotor development at 18 and 24 months (Stoelhorst et al., 2003).

respiratory distress syndrome
a serious condition in which a preterm infant breathes very irregularly and is at risk of dying (also called hyaline membrane disease).

On the other hand, even though many preterm infants experience respiratory distress and other problems related to immaturity, Claudine Amiel-Tison and her colleagues (2004) report that despite a general reduction in overall growth, the maturation of the brain, lungs, heart, and other organs is accelerated in fetuses that are at high risk for preterm delivery. She and her colleagues cite evidence suggesting that prioritizing early organ maturation in lieu of increase in overall size is an adaptive response to stressors (such as sharing the womb with a sibling, malnutrition, or even maternal distress) that prepares the fetuses for their impending preterm birth.

Preterm infants often spend their first few weeks of life in heated *isolettes* that maintain their body temperature and protect them from infection. Isolettes are aptly named because they do isolate: the infant is fed, cleaned, and changed through a hole in the device that is much too small to allow visiting parents to cuddle and love their baby in the usual way. Furthermore, preterm infants can try the patience of caregivers. Compared with full-term infants, they are slow to initiate social interactions and often respond to a parent's bids for attention by looking away, fussing, or actively resisting such overtures (Eckerman et al., 1999; Lester, Hoffman, & Brazelton, 1985). Mothers of preterm infants often remark that their babies are "hard to read," causing the mothers to become rather frustrated as their persistent attempts to carry on a social dialogue are apparently rebuffed by an aloof, fussy, squirming little companion (Lester, Hoffman, & Brazelton, 1985). Indeed preterm infants are at risk of forming less secure emotional ties to their caregivers than other babies do (Mangelsdorf et al., 1996; Wille, 1991); and although the vast majority of them are never mistreated, they are more likely than full-term infants to become targets of child abuse (Brockington, 1996).

Finally, evidence suggests that long-term effects of preterm or low-birth-weight status is related to the severity of the abnormality (Burns et al., 2004). In a longitudinal study follow-

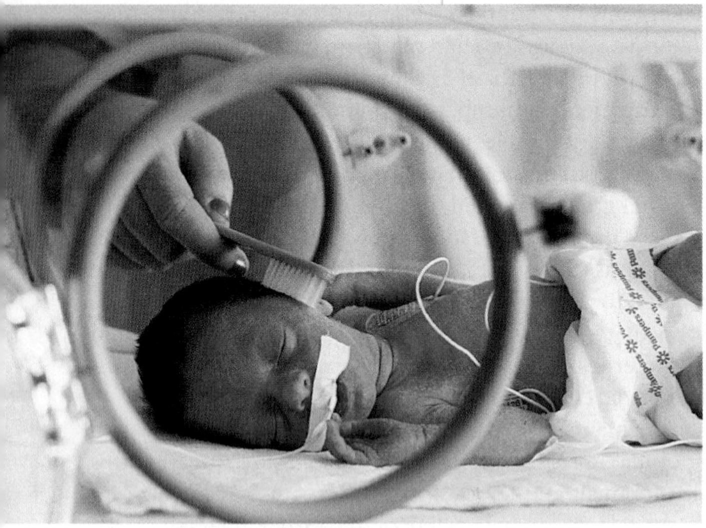

Isolettes do isolate. The holes in the apparatus allow parents and hospital staff to care for, talk to, and touch the baby, but close, tender cuddling is nearly impossible.

ing small-for-date infants from birth to 18 months, Harding and McCowan (2003) report that infants with less severe growth restriction and longer gestational periods "have a good chance of catch-up growth by six months." That is, at sixth months, newborns that were less severely premature and underweight were comparable in weight and stature to their full-term peers. More severely premature and underweight newborns, especially those who were shorter at birth and boys, took longer to catch up with full-term peers.

Interventions for Preterm Infants

Twenty years ago, hospitals permitted parents little if any contact with preterm infants for fear of harming these fragile little creatures. Today, parents are encouraged to visit their child often in the hospital and to become actively involved during their visits by touching, caressing, and talking to their baby. The objective of these early-acquaintance programs is to allow parents to get to know their child and to foster the development of positive emotional ties. But there may be important additional benefits, for babies in intensive care often become less irritable and more responsive and show quicker neurological and mental development if they are periodically rocked, stroked, massaged, or soothed by the sound of a mother's voice (Barnard & Bee, 1983; Feldman & Eidelman, 2003; Ferber et al., 2005; Field, 1995; Scafidi et al., 1986, 1990).

Preterm and other low-birth-weight babies can also benefit from programs that teach their parents how to provide them with sensitive and responsive care at home (Veddovi et al., 2004). In one study, a pediatric nurse visited periodically with mothers and taught them how to read and respond appropriately to the atypical behaviors their preterm infants displayed. Although the intervention lasted only 3 months, the low-birth-weight infants whose mothers participated had caught up intellectually with normal-birth-weight peers by the age of 4 (Achenbach et al., 1990). When combined with stimulating day-care programs, parental interventions not only foster the cognitive growth of low-birth-weight children, but can reduce the likelihood of their displaying behavioral disturbances as well (Brooks-Gunn et al., 1993; Hill, Brooks-Gunn, & Waldfogel, 2003; Spiker, Ferguson, & Brooks-Gunn, 1993). These interventions are most effective when they continue into the grade-school years (Bradley et al., 1994; McCarton et al., 1997).

Of course, not all low-birth-weight infants (or their parents) have opportunities to participate in successful interventions. What happens to them?

Long-Term Consequences of Low Birth Weight

Over the years, many researchers have reported that preterm and other low-birth-weight infants were likely to experience more learning difficulties later in childhood, to score lower on IQ tests, and to suffer more emotional problems than normal-birth-weight infants (Caputo & Mandell, 1970; Saigal et al., 2000; Weindrich et al., 2003). Preterm female infants may be more likely to develop eating disorders, especially if they are also small for date (Cnattingius et al., 1999). Low-birth-weight girls also progress through puberty more quickly and attain a final height that is smaller than normal-weight girls (Ibanez et al., 2000 DONE). Low birth weight has been associated with type 2 diabetes, hypertension, and coronary artery disease in adults (Sallout & Walker, 2003).

Today we know that the long-term prognosis for low-birth-weight children depends largely on the environment in which they are raised (Reichman, 2005). Outcomes are likely to be especially good when mothers are knowledgeable about the factors that promote healthy development. These mothers are likely to be highly involved with their children and

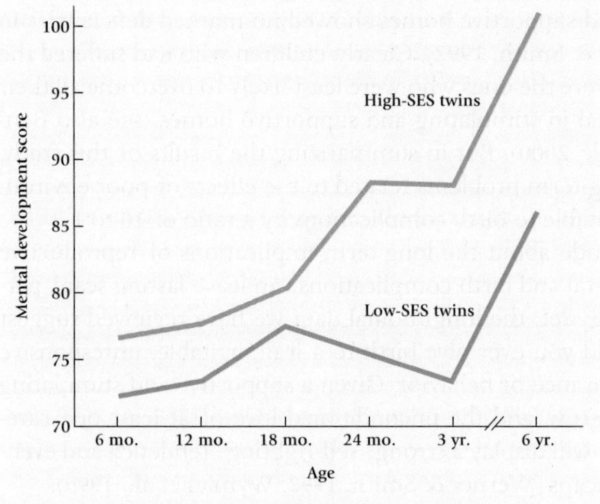

Figure 4.11 Age trends in intellectual development for low-birth-weight twins from middle-class (high-SES) and lower socioeconomic (low-SES) backgrounds. *Adapted from "Risk and Resilience in Early Mental Development," by R. S. Wilson, 1985,* Developmental Psychology, 21, *795–805. Copyright © 1985 by the American Psychological Association.*

to create a stimulating home environment that fosters cognitive and emotional growth (Benasich & Brooks-Gunn, 1996; Caughy, 1996). By contrast, low-birth-weight children from less stable or economically disadvantaged families are likely to remain smaller in stature than full-term children, experience more emotional problems, and show some long-term deficits in intellectual performance and academic achievement (Kopp & Kahler, 1989; Rose & Feldman, 1996; Taylor et al., 2000).

Consider what Ronald Wilson (1985) found in his study of developing twins. Although twins are generally small for date and are often preterm, Wilson focused closely on twins who were especially small at birth (weighing under 1,750 grams, or less than 3¾ pounds). In Figure 4.11, we see that these preterm, low-birth-weight babies were indeed below average in mental performance throughout the first 3 years of life (a score of 100 on the test reflects average intellectual performance). Yet, the figure also shows that low-birth-weight twins from middle-class (high SES) homes eventually made up their intellectual deficits, scoring average (or slightly above) on the tests by age 6, whereas their counterparts from low-income (low SES) backgrounds remained substantially below average in their intellectual performance. So the long-term prognosis for preterm and small-for-date children seems to depend very critically on the *postnatal environment* in which they are raised.

Reproductive Risk and Capacity for Recovery

We have now discussed many examples of what can go wrong during the prenatal and perinatal periods, as well as some steps that expectant parents can take to try to prevent such outcomes. Once they occur, some of these damaging effects are irreversible: a baby blinded by rubella, for example, will never regain its sight, and a child who is mentally retarded from fetal alcohol syndrome or severe anoxia will always be mentally retarded. And yet, there are many adults walking around today who turned out perfectly normal even though their mothers smoked, drank, or contracted harmful diseases while pregnant or received heavy doses of medication while in labor and childbirth. Why is this? As we have already emphasized, not all embryos, fetuses, and newborns that are exposed to teratogens and other early hazards are affected by them. But what about those who are affected? Is it possible that many of these infants will eventually overcome their early handicaps later in life?

Indeed it is, and we now have some excellent longitudinal studies to tell us so. In 1955, Emmy Werner and Ruth Smith began to follow the development of all 670 babies born that year on the Hawaiian island of Kauai. At birth, 16 percent of these infants showed moderate to severe complications, another 31 percent showed mild complications, and 53 percent appeared normal and healthy. When the babies were reexamined at age 2, there was a clear relationship between severity of birth complications and developmental progress: the more severe their birth complications, the more likely children were to be lagging in their social and intellectual development. However, effects of the postnatal environment were already apparent. In homes rated high in emotional support and educational stimulation, children who had suffered severe birth complications scored slightly below average on tests of social and intellectual development. But in homes low in emotional support and educational stimulation, the intellectual performance of children who had experienced equally severe complications was *far* below average (Werner & Smith, 1992).

Werner and Smith then followed up on the children at ages 10 and 18, and again as young adults. What they found was striking. By age 10, early complications no longer predicted children's intellectual performance very well, but certain characteristics of the children's home environments did. Children from unstimulating and unresponsive home environments continued to perform very poorly on intelligence tests, whereas their counterparts from stimulating and supportive homes showed no marked deficiencies in intellectual performance (Werner & Smith, 1992). Clearly, children who had suffered the most severe early complications were the ones who were least likely to overcome all their initial handicaps, even when raised in stimulating and supportive homes (see also Bendersky & Lewis, 1994; Saigal et al., 2000). But in summarizing the results of this study, Werner and Smith noted that long-term problems related to the effects of poor environments outnumbered those attributable to birth complications by a ratio of 10 to 1.

What, then, are we to conclude about the long-term implications of reproductive risk? First, we do know that prenatal and birth complications can leave lasting scars, particularly if these insults are severe. Yet, the longitudinal data we have reviewed suggest ample reason for optimism should you ever give birth to a frail, irritable, unresponsive baby that is abnormal in its appearance or behavior. Given a supportive and stimulating home environment in which to grow, and the unconditional love of at least one caregiver, a majority of these children will display a strong "self-righting" tendency and eventually overcome their initial handicaps (Werner & Smith, 1992; Wyman et al., 1999).

CONCEPT CHECK 4.2 Birth and the Perinatal Environment

Check your understanding of the process of birth and the perinatal environment from the perspective of the baby, mother, and father by answering the following questions. Answers appear in the Appendix.

Multiple Choice: Select the best alternative for each question.

_____ 1. A severe form of depression suffered by about 10 percent of new mothers leaves these women feeling like they don't want their babies, perceiving their babies to be "difficult," and not interacting with their babies. These feelings can last for months. This form of depression is known as
- a. maternity depression
- b. maternity blues
- c. postpartum depression
- d. post-birth depression

_____ 2. Oxygen deprivation at birth is called
- a. breech delivery
- b. anoxia
- c. oxygen depletion
- d. umbilical cord abnormality

_____ 3. A disorder in which a deficiency in surfactin causes irregular breathing or stopping breathing is called
- a. persistent fetal respiration
- b. persistent respiratory distress
- c. respiratory distress syndrome
- d. respiratory surfactin disorder

Fill in the Blank: Check your understanding of birth and the perinatal environment by completing the following statements with the correct word or phrase.

4. The delivery of a baby occurs during the _______ stage of labor.

5. Juanita seemed fine at birth and scored well on the Apgar test. However, a few days after her birth she was given the _______ test that assessed her reflexes, changes in her state, her reactions to comforting, and her reactions to social stimuli. She scored very low on this test and the doctors suspected that she might have _______.

6. When a mother is unable to push effectively during delivery, a baby is sometimes pulled from the birth canal using _______ or _______.

Matching: Check your understanding of the perinatal environment by matching the experience a parent feels upon delivery to the psychological term for this effect.

7. engrossment
8. emotional bonding

a. a mother's initial emotional response to her newborn, with close contact with the newborn soon after birth
b. a father's initial emotional response to his newborn, with close contact with the newborn soon after birth

Essay: Provide a more detailed answer to the following questions to demonstrate your understanding of birth and the potential complications that can occur at birth.

9. Discuss the short-term and long-term consequences of low birth weight on babies' long-term development.
10. Discuss how postnatal interventions can overcome early postnatal distress, such as preterm or low-birth-weight deliveries.

Applying Developmental Themes to Prenatal Development and Birth

We can now turn to an examination of how our four developmental themes are revealed in prenatal development and birth. Recall that our four recurring developmental themes include: the active child, nature and nurture interactions in development, qualitative and quantitative changes in development, and the holistic nature of child development. Before reading on, can you think of any examples from the chapter that relate to these themes?

Let's begin with the active child theme. Before reading this chapter you may have guessed that prenatal development is a relatively passive experience for the developing organism. But we have learned that the fetus's behavior before birth does play an important role in development. The fetus needs to move and to practice using its mouth, lungs, and digestive system, all in preparation for the great environmental change that occurs at birth. These are active child effects even though they are not conscious choices to be active.

Another example concerns one of the principles of teratogenic effects on the developing organism. It states that the extent of damage caused by any particular teratogen will depend on the developing organism's genotype. Some will be severely damaged, others may escape effects of the teratogen, all based (in part) on individual differences in genotype across developing organisms. So this is another example of the active child effect, which precedes consciousness and choice.

Looking next at nature and nurture interactions, it would be difficult to pinpoint any aspect of prenatal development or birth that did not involve the reciprocal interaction of nature and nurture on development. Returning to the teratogen example, the principles of teratogenic effects, taken together, represent an integration of biological influences and environmental influences. One does not operate without the other. Even the birth process represents an interaction of nature and nurture. There is a strong biological determinism about the birth process, proceeding through each stage in order and with little potential for interruption or interference from the environment during a normal birth. But the environment surrounding the birth clearly influences the health of the baby and the mother, and the feelings of bonding and engrossment that the parents feel for their new baby.

We encountered three different qualitative stage progressions in this chapter. The developing organism proceeds through three qualitatively distinct stages in prenatal development: the zygote, the embryo, and the fetus. The pregnant woman goes through three qualitatively distinct stages during pregnancy: The first, second, and third trimester. (And remember that the stages of the developing organism do not correspond chronologically to the pregnant woman's stages.) Finally, we saw that the birth process can be divided into three qualitatively distinct stages: labor, birth, and afterbirth. As usual, however, we can also see quantitative change in prenatal development. For example, the period of the fetus consists mainly of quantitative changes as the organism grows in size and refines the structures and functions that first develop in the period of the embryo.

Finally, we can consider the holistic nature of child development when we recall that prenatal development affects a child's future physical development as well as cognitive and emotional development, especially in cases in which teratogenic effects interfere with these aspects of development. We saw many examples of problems in prenatal development causing later mental retardation, and some cases of emotional disturbances. When examining the birth process we saw that emotional and social support for the woman giving birth was just as important as the physical assistance she needs with this process. And after birth, parents who are trained to respond to and engage their infants in social interaction are more likely to have infants who are able to overcome early physical complications.

In sum, we saw evidence for each of the enduring developmental themes in our examination of prenatal development and birth. Perhaps now it is easier to see that the developing organism is active in its own development, that it moves through a series of both qualitative and quantitative changes as it develops, that both nature and nurture play important roles in the prenatal period, and that we must always consider the child holistically.

SUMMARY

From Conception to Birth

- **Prenatal development** is divided into three phases:
  - The **period of the zygote** lasts about 2 weeks, from conception until the zygote (or blastocyst) is firmly **implanted** in the wall of the uterus.
    - The inner layer of the blastocyst will become the **embryo.**
    - The outer layer forms the **amnion, chorion, placenta,** and **umbilical cord**—support structures that help to sustain the developing prenatal organism.
  - The **period of the embryo** lasts from the beginning of the third through the eighth week of pregnancy.
    - This is the period when all major organs are formed and some have begun to function.
  - The **period of the fetus** lasts from the ninth prenatal week until birth.
    - All organ systems become integrated in preparation for birth.
    - Fetuses move and begin to use organ systems during this period in preparation for the use of those systems after birth.

Potential Problems in Prenatal Development

- **Teratogens** are external agents such as diseases, drugs, and chemicals that can harm the developing organism.
  - Teratogenic effects are worst when a body structure is forming (usually during the period of the embryo) and when the "dose" of the teratogen is high.
  - Teratogenic effects differ for different genotypes. One teratogen can cause many birth defects, and different teratogens can cause the same birth defect.
  - Teratogenic effects can be altered by the postnatal environment (through rehabilitation efforts). Some teratogenic effects (like DES) are not apparent at birth but become apparent later in a child's life.
- Maternal characteristics also influence prenatal development.
  - Pregnant women who are malnourished (particularly during the third trimester) may deliver a preterm baby who may fail to survive.
  - Supplements of **folic acid** help to prevent **spina bifida** and other birth defects.
  - Malnourished babies are often irritable and unresponsive, interfering with positive developmental outcomes.
  - Pregnant women under severe emotional stress risk pregnancy complications.
  - Complications are also more likely among women over 35 and teenage pregnant women who lack adequate prenatal care.

Birth and the Perinatal Environment

- Childbirth is a three-step process:
  - It begins with contractions that dilate the cervix (**first stage of labor**).
  - Followed by the baby's delivery (**second stage of labor**).
  - And finally the afterbirth is expelled (**third stage of labor**).
- The **Apgar test** is used to assess the newborn's condition immediately after birth.
- The **Neonatal Behavioral Assessment Scale (NBAS),** administered a few days later, is a more extensive measure of the baby's health and well-being.
- Labor and delivery medication given to mothers to ease pain can, in large doses, interfere with the baby's development.
- Many mothers feel exhilarated shortly after birth if they have close contact with their babies and begin the process of **emotional bonding** with them.
- Fathers are often **engrossed** with their newborns.
- The support of fathers during pregnancy and childbirth can make the birth experience easier for mothers.

Potential Problems at Birth

- **Anoxia** is a potentially serious birth complication that can cause brain damage and other defects. Mild anoxia usually has no long-term effects.
- Women who abuse alcohol and drugs, who smoke, or who receive poor prenatal care risk delivering preterm or low-birth-weight babies.
  - **Small-for-date** babies usually have more severe and longer lasting problems than do **preterm** infants.
  - Interventions to stimulate these infants and to teach their parents how to respond appropriately to their sluggish or irritable demeanor can help to normalize their developmental progress.
- The problems stemming from both prenatal and birth complications are often overcome in time, provided that the child is not permanently brain damaged and has a stable and supportive postnatal environment in which to grow.

KEY TERMS

prenatal development 119
period of the zygote 120
period of the embryo 120
period of the fetus 120
blastocyst 120
embryo 120
implantation 121
amnion 121
chorion 121
placenta 121
umbilical cord 121
neural tube 122
fetus 122
vernix 124
lanugo 124
age of viability 124
teratogens 126
sensitive period 126
rubella (German measles) 128
toxoplasmosis 128
syphilis 129
genital herpes 129
cesarean delivery 129
acquired immune deficiency syndrome (AIDS) 129
thalidomide 130
diethylstilbestrol (DES) 131
fetal alcohol syndrome (FAS) 131
fetal alcohol effects (FAE) 131
cleft lip 132
cleft palate 132
folic acid 138
spina bifida 138
anencephaly 138
neonate 141
perinatal environment 143
first stage of labor 143
second stage of labor 143
third stage of labor 143
Apgar test 144
Neonatal Behavior Assessment Scale (NBAS) 144
natural childbirth 146
alternative birth center 147
emotional bonding 147
postpartum depression 148
engrossment 148
anoxia 149
breech birth 149
RH factor 149
preterm babies 149
small-for-date babies 150
respiratory distress syndrome (RDS) 151

MEDIA RESOURCES

The Human Development Book Companion Website

See the companion website http://www.thomsonedu.com/psychology/shaffer for flashcards, practice quiz questions, Internet links, updates, critical thinking exercises, discussion forums, games, and more.

http://www.thomsonedu.com
Go to this site for the link to ThomsonNOW, your one-stop shop. Take a pre-test for this chapter, and ThomsonNOW will generate a personalized study plan based on your test results. The study plan will identify the topics you need to review and direct you to online resources to help you master those topics. You can then take a post-test to help you determine the concepts you have mastered and what you will still need to work on.

Child and Adolescent Development CD-ROM

For more information about the concepts covered in this chapter, go to

Module I: Physical Development

- Prenatal Physical Development
- Module I Media

CHAPTER 5

Infancy

Imagine that you are a neonate, only 5 to 10 minutes old, who has just been sponged, swaddled, and handed to your mother. As your eyes meet hers, she smiles and says "Hi there, sweetie" in a high-pitched voice as she moves her head closer and gently strokes your cheek. What would you make of all this sensory input? How would you interpret these experiences?

sensation
detection of stimuli by the sensory receptors and transmission of this information to the brain.

perception
the process by which we categorize and interpret sensory input.

Developmentalists are careful to distinguish between sensation and perception. **Sensation** is the process by which sensory receptor neurons detect information and transmit it to the brain. Clearly, neonates "sense" the environment. They gaze at interesting sights, react to sounds, tastes, and odors, and are likely to cry up a storm when poked by a needle for a blood test. But do they "make sense" of these sensations? **Perception** is the interpretation of sensory input: recognizing what you see, understanding what is said to you, or knowing that the odor you've detected is fresh-baked bread. Are newborns capable of drawing any such inferences? Do they perceive the world, or merely sense it?

We might also wonder whether very young infants can associate their sensations with particular outcomes. When, for example, might a baby first associate her mother's breast with milk and come to view Mom as a valuable commodity who eliminates hunger and other kinds of distress? Are infants capable of modifying their behavior in order to persuade Mom to attend to them? These are questions of *learning*—the process by which our behaviors change as a result of experience.

In this chapter we will examine the life of the newborn and infant. We will begin by considering the newborn's capabilities at birth and then consider how the infant's senses, perceptions, and learning mature through the period of infancy. A common theme we will encounter is that the infant is much more capable than we might imagine. This is especially true as we begin, considering the capabilities of the newborn from the moment of birth.

The Newborn's Readiness for Life

In the past, newborns were often characterized as fragile and helpless little organisms who were simply not prepared for life outside the womb. This view may once have been highly adaptive, helping to ease parents' grief in earlier eras when medical procedures were rather primitive and a fair percentage of newborns died. Even today, in cultures where many newborns die because of poor health and medical care, parents often do not name their newborns until they are 3 months old and have passed the critical age for newborn death (Brazelton, 1979).

Actually, newborns are much better prepared for life than many doctors, parents, and developmentalists had initially assumed. All of a newborn's senses are in good working order and she sees and hears well enough to detect what is happening around her and respond adaptively to many of these sensations. Very young infants are also quite capable of learning and can even remember some of the particularly vivid experiences they have had. Two other indications that neonates are quite well adapted for life are their repertoire of inborn reflexes and their predictable patterns, or cycles, of daily activity.

Newborn Reflexes

One of the neonate's greatest strengths is a full set of useful reflexes. A reflex is an involuntary and automatic response to a stimulus, as when the eye automatically blinks in response to a puff of air. Table 5.1 describes some reflexes that healthy newborns display. Some of these graceful and complex patterns of behavior are called survival reflexes because they have clear adaptive value (Berne, 2003). Examples include the *breathing reflex*, the *eye-blink reflex* (which protects the eyes against bright lights or foreign particles), and the *sucking* and *swallowing reflexes*, by which the infant takes in food. Also implicated in feeding is the *rooting reflex*—an infant who is touched on the cheek will turn in that direction and search for something to suck.

Not only do survival reflexes offer some protection against aversive stimulation and enable an infant to satisfy very basic needs, but they (and some of the primitive reflexes we discuss next) may also have a very positive impact on caregivers. Mothers, for

TABLE 5.1 Major Reflexes Present in Full-Term Neonates

Name	Response	Development and course	Significance
Survival reflexes			
Breathing reflex	Repetitive inhalation and expiration.	Permanent	Provides oxygen and expels carbon dioxide.
Eye-blink reflex	Closing or blinking the eyes.	Permanent	Protects the eyes from bright light or foreign objects.
Pupillary reflex	Constriction of pupils to bright light; dilation to dark or dimly lit surroundings.	Permanent	Protects against bright lights; adapts the visual system to low illumination.
Rooting reflex	Turning the head in the direction of a tactile (touch) stimulus to the cheek.	Disappears over the first few weeks of life and is replaced by voluntary head turning.	Orients baby to the breast or bottle.
Sucking reflex	Sucking on objects placed (or taken) into the mouth.	Permanent	Allows baby to take in nutrients.
Swallowing reflex	Swallowing	Permanent	Allows baby to take in nutrients.
Primitive reflexes			
Babinski reflex	Fanning and then curling the toes when the bottom of the foot is stroked.	Usually disappears within the first 8 months–1 year of life.	Its presence at birth and disappearance in the first year are an indication of normal neurological development.
Palmar grasping reflex	Curling of the fingers around objects (such as a finger) that touch the baby's palm.	Disappears in first 3–4 months and is then replaced by a voluntary grasp.	Its presence at birth and later disappearance are an indication of normal neurological development.
Moro reflex	A loud noise or sudden change in the position of the baby's head will cause the baby to throw his or her arms outward, arch the back, and then bring the arms toward each other as if to hold onto something.	The arm movements and arching of the back disappear over the first 4–6 months; however, the child continues to react to unexpected noises or a loss of bodily support by showing a startle reflex (which does not disappear).	Its presence at birth and later disappearance are indications of normal neurological development.
Swimming reflex	An infant immersed in water will display active movements of the arms and legs and involuntarily hold his or her breath (thus giving the body buoyancy); this swimming reflex will keep an infant afloat for some time, allowing easy rescue.	Disappears in the first 4–6 months.	Its presence at birth and later disappearance are an indication of normal neurological development.
Stepping reflex	Infants held upright so that their feet touch a flat surface will step as if to walk.	Disappears in the first 8 weeks unless the infant has regular opportunities to practice this response.	Its presence at birth and later disappearance are an indication of normal neurological development.

Note: Preterm infants may show little or no evidence of primitive reflexes at birth, and their survival reflexes are likely to be weak. However, the missing primitive reflexes typically appear soon after birth and disappear a little later than they do among full-term infants.

example, may feel quite gratified and competent as caregivers when their hungry babies immediately stop fussing and suck easily at the nipple. And few parents can resist the feeling that their baby enjoys being close when he grasps their fingers tightly as his palm is touched. So if these survival reflexes help to endear infants to older companions, who can protect them and attend to their needs, then they have tremendous "survival" value indeed (Bowlby, 1969, 1988).

Other so-called primitive reflexes in the table are not nearly as useful; in fact, many are believed to be remnants of our evolutionary history that have outlived their original purpose. The *Babinski reflex* is a good example. Why would it be adaptive for infants to fan their toes when the bottoms of their feet are stroked? We don't know. Other primitive reflexes may still have some adaptive value, at least in some cultures (Bowlby, 1969; Fentress & McLeod, 1986). The *swimming reflex,* for example, may help keep afloat an infant who is accidentally immersed in a pond or a river. The *grasping reflex* may help infants who are carried in slings or on their mothers' hips to hang on. Finally, other responses such as the *stepping reflex* may be forerunners of useful voluntary behaviors such as crawling and walking that develop later in infancy (Thelen, 1984).

Primitive reflexes normally disappear during the first few months of life. Why? Because they are controlled by the lower "subcortical" areas of the brain and are lost once the higher centers of the cerebral cortex mature and begin to guide voluntary behaviors. But even if many primitive reflexes are not very useful to infants, they are important diagnostic indicators to developmentalists (Stirniman & Stirniman, 1940). If these reflexes are not present at birth—or if they last too long in infancy—we have reason to suspect that something is wrong with a baby's nervous system.

In sum, a full complement of infant reflexes tells us that newborns are quite prepared to respond adaptively to a variety of life's challenges. And the timely appearance and disappearance of certain reflexes is one important sign that a baby's nervous system is developing normally.

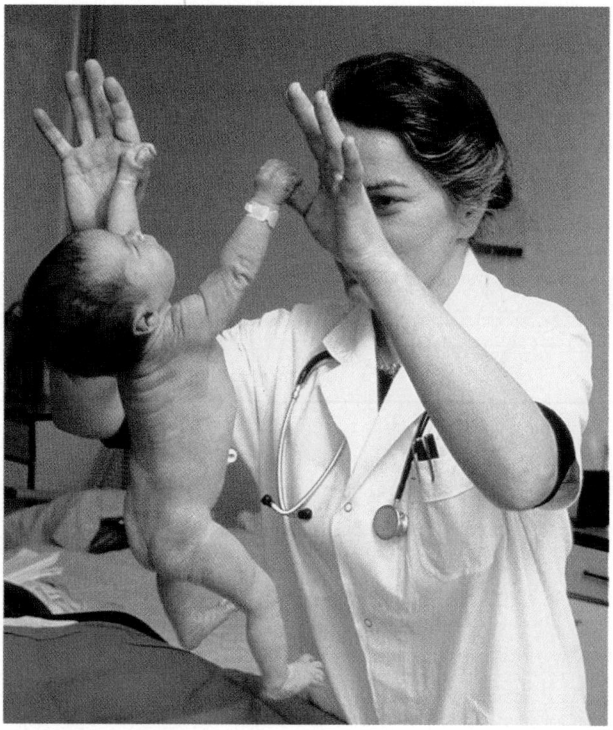

Cunha/Petit Format/Photo Researchers Inc.

Newborns' grasping reflexes are quite stong, often allowing them to support their own weight.

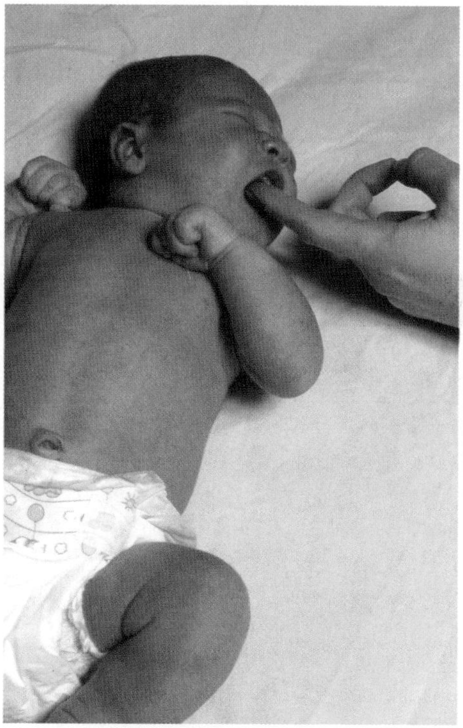

© Spencer Grant/PhotoEdit

This infant illustrates the rhythmical sucking, or *sucking reflex,* that neonates display when objects are placed into their mouths.

Infant States

Newborns also display organized patterns of daily activity that are predictable and foster healthy developmental outcomes. In a typical day (or night), a neonate moves in and out of six infant states, or levels of arousal, that are described in Table 5.2. During the first month, a baby may move rapidly from one state to another, as mothers observe when their wide-awake babies suddenly nod off to sleep in the middle of a feeding. Neonates spend about 70 percent of their time (16 to 18 hours a day) sleeping and only 2 to 3 hours in the alert, inactive (attentive) state, when they are most receptive to external stimulation (Berg & Berg, 1987; Thoman, 1990). Sleep cycles are typically brief, lasting from 45 minutes to 2 hours. These frequent naps are separated by periods of drowsiness, alert or inalert activity, and crying, any of which occur (as red-eyed, sleep deprived, parents well know) at all hours of the day and night.

The fact that neonates pass through a predictable pattern of states during a typical day indicates that their internal regulatory mechanisms are well organized. Research on infant states also makes it clear that newborns show a great deal of individuality (Thoman & Whitney, 1989). For example, one newborn in one study was alert for only about 15 minutes a day, on average, whereas another was alert for more than 8 hours daily (Brown, 1964). Similarly, one infant cried about 17 percent of the time while awake, but another spent 39 percent of its awake time crying. These differences have some obvious implications for parents, who may find it far more pleasant to be with a bright-eyed baby who rarely cries than with one who is often fussy and inattentive (Colombo & Horowitz, 1987).

Developmental Changes in Infant States

Two of the states in Table 5.2—sleep and crying—show regular patterns of change over the first year and provide important information about the developmental progress a baby is making.

Changes in Sleep

As infants develop, they spend less time sleeping and more time awake, alert, and attending to their surroundings. By age 2 to 6 weeks, babies are sleeping only 14 to 16

TABLE 5.2 Infant States of Arousal

State	Description	Daily duration in newborn (hours)
Regular sleep	Baby is still, with eyes closed and unmoving. Breathing is slow and regular.	8–9
Irregular sleep	Baby's eyes are closed but can be observed to move under the closed eyelids (a phenomenon known as rapid eye movements, or REMs). Baby may jerk or grimace in response to stimulation. Breathing may be irregular.	8–9
Drowsiness	Baby is falling asleep or waking up. Eyes open and close and have a glazed appearance when open. Breathing is regular but more rapid than in regular sleep.	½–3
Alert inactivity	Baby's eyes are wide open and bright, exploring some aspect of the environment. Breathing is even, and the body is relatively inactive.	2–3
Alert activity	Baby's eyes are open and breathing is irregular. May become fussy and display various bursts of diffuse motor activity.	1–3
Crying	Intense crying that may be difficult to stop and is accompanied by high levels of motor activity.	1–3

Source: Wolff, 1966.

hours a day; and somewhere between 3 and 7 months of age, many infants reach a milestone that parents truly appreciate—they begin to sleep through the night and require but two or three shorter naps during the day (Berg & Berg, 1987; St. James-Roberts & Plewis, 1996).

From at least 2 weeks before they are born throughout the first month or two of life, babies spend at least half their sleeping hours in REM sleep, a state of active irregular sleep characterized by rapid eye movements (REMs) under their closed eyelids and brain-wave activity more typical of wakefulness than of regular (non-REM) sleep (Groome et al., 1997; Ingersoll & Thoman, 1999). However, REM sleep declines steadily after birth and accounts for only 25 to 30 percent of total sleep for a 6-month-old.

Why do fetuses and newborns spend so much time in REM sleep and why does it decline so dramatically over the first few months? The most widely accepted theory is that this active REM sleep early in life provides fetuses and very young infants, who sleep so much, with enough internal stimulation to allow their nervous systems to develop properly (Boismier, 1977). Consistent with this autostimulation theory is the finding that babies who are given lots of interesting visual stimuli to explore while awake will spend less time in REM sleep than infants who do not have these experiences (Boismier, 1977). Perhaps the reason REM sleep declines sharply over the first 6 months is that the infant's brain is rapidly maturing, she is becoming more alert, and there is simply less need for the stimulation provided by REM activity.

Few babies have problems establishing regular sleep cycles unless their nervous system is abnormal in some way. Yet one of the major causes of infant mortality is a very perplexing sleep-related disorder called crib death, or **sudden infant death syndrome (SIDS),** that we will examine more carefully in the Box on p. 164.

sudden infant death syndrome (SIDS)
the unexplained death of a sleeping infant who suddenly stops breathing (also called *crib death*)

The Functions and Course of Crying

A baby's earliest cries are unlearned and involuntary responses to discomfort—distress signals by which the infant makes caregivers aware of his needs. Most of a newborn's early cries are provoked by such physical discomforts as hunger, pain, or a wet diaper, although chills, loud noises, and even sudden changes in illumination (as when the light over a crib goes off) are often enough to make a baby cry.

An infant's cry is a complex vocal signal that may vary from a soft whimper to piercing shrieks and wails. Experience clearly plays a role in helping adults to determine why an infant may be crying, for parents are better than nonparents at this kind of problem solving, and mothers (who have more contact with infants) are better than are fathers (Holden, 1988). Philip Zeskind and his associates (1985) found that adults perceive the intense cries of hungry babies as just as arousing and urgent as equally intense "pain" cries. So crying probably conveys only one very general message—"Hey, I'm distressed"—and the effectiveness of this signal at eliciting attention depends more on the *amount* of distress it implies than on the *kind* of distress that the baby is experiencing (Green, Gustafson & McGhie, 1998; Zeskind et al., 1992).

Developmental Changes in Crying. Babies around the world cry most often during their first 3 months of life (St. James-Roberts & Plewis, 1996). In fact, the declines we see early in life in both crying and REM sleep suggest that both these changes are meaningfully related to the maturation of a baby's brain and central nervous system (Halpern, MacLean, & Baumeister, 1995). And what role do parents play? Will those who are especially responsive to their infant's cries produce a spoiled baby who enslaves them with incessant demands for attention?

Probably not. Mary Ainsworth and her associates (1972) found that babies of mothers who responded quickly to their cries came to cry very little. Sensitive, responsive parenting may result in a less fussy baby because a sensitive and attentive caregiver is more likely to prevent a baby from becoming highly distressed in the first place (Lewis & Ramsay, 1999). (Methods of soothing fussy and crying babies are discussed in

APPLYING RESEARCH TO YOUR LIFE

Sudden Infant Death Syndrome

Each year in the United States as many as 5,000 to 6,000 seemingly healthy infants suddenly stop breathing and die in their sleep. These deaths are unexpected, unexplained, and classified as examples of **sudden infant death syndrome (SIDS).** In industrialized societies, SIDS is the leading cause of infant mortality in the first year of life, accounting for more than one-third of all such deaths (American Academy of Pediatrics, 2000; Tuladhar et al., 2003).

Although the exact cause of SIDS is not known, we do know that boys and preterm or other low-birth-weight babies who had poor Apgar scores and experienced respiratory distress as newborns are most susceptible (American Academy of Pediatrics, 2000; Frick, 1999) and that the central nervous systems of infants with SIDS suffer from chronic hypoxia—that is, the brains of infants with SIDS do not receive the proper amount of oxygen. Mothers of SIDS victims are also more likely to smoke, to have used illicit drugs, and to have received poor prenatal care (Dwyer et al., 1991; Frick, 1999). Both prenatal exposure to alcohol and parental postnatal use of alcohol have been associated with a higher incidence of SIDS (Friend, Goodwin, & Lipsitt, 2004; Lipsitt, 2003).

SIDS is most likely to occur during the winter months among infants who are 2 to 4 months of age and who have a respiratory infection such as a cold. SIDS victims are also more likely to be sleeping on their stomachs than on their backs, and they are often wrapped tightly in clothing and/or covered in blankets at the time of their death. These findings have led some researchers to propose that factors that contribute to overheating the infant—more clothing or blankets and higher room temperatures—may seriously increase the risk of SIDS. Yet, risks associated with overheating are particularly evident when infants also sleep on their stomachs (American Academy of Pediatrics, 2000; Kahn et al., 2003). Research conducted on healthy infants demonstrates that sleeping on the stomach may involve more work for infant cardiovascular systems than sleeping on the back. When infants sleep on their stomachs, their heart rates are higher than when they sleep on their backs. Also, when infants are aroused from a prone (face down) sleeping position, it takes longer for heart rates to increase than when infants are aroused from a supine (face up) sleeping position. This research suggests that poor autonomic heart rate control may be a factor contributing to the onset of SIDS (Tuladhar et al., 2003).

Many (but not all) SIDS victims have abnormalities in the *arculate nucleus,* a portion of the brain that seems to be involved early in infancy in controlling breathing and waking during sleep (Kinney et al., 1995; Panigrahy et al., 1997). Normally, when a very young infant senses inadequate oxygen intake while sleeping, the brain will trigger waking, crying, and changes in heart rate to compensate for insufficient oxygen. However, abnormalities of the arculate nucleus, which may stem from prenatal exposure to a toxic substance (such as illicit drugs or tobacco products), may prevent a very young infant from becoming aroused when oxygen intake is inadequate (Franco et al., 1998; Frick, 1999). So when babies with abnormalities in the lower brain centers are sleeping prone, are heavily bundled, or have a respiratory infection that may restrict breathing, they may not struggle sufficiently to breathe and thus may succumb to SIDS (Iyasu et al., 2002; Ozawa et al., 2003; Sawaguchi et al., 2003a–d, g–n). Nevertheless, it is important to note that (1) not all SIDS victims have identifiable brain abnormalities, and (2) researchers, as yet, have no foolproof screening tests to predict which babies are at highest risk of SIDS.

It is important to note that investigation into the etiology of SIDS is methodologically limited. One of the major sources of information about the state and composition of arousal centers and neuron structure are the histological studies of the brains of SIDS victims. A proper control group for comparison should consist of infants who died at similar age and were not victims of SIDS or other hypoxic events. Many infants who die during the first year of life and are not victims of SIDS are victims of choking, suffocation, and other oxygen-deprivation events (Sawaguchi, 2003j). The advent of noninvasive methods of observation, such as MRIs and optical topography, may yet provide a way around this problem.

Fortunately, there are some effective strategies for reducing the incidence of SIDS. In 1994, the American Academy of Pediatrics instituted the *Back to Sleep* campaign, instructing hospitals, child-care facilities, and parents not to place young infants on their stomachs to sleep. Since the issuance of this simple instruction, the percentage of American babies who sleep on their stomachs has decreased from more than 70 percent to approximately 20 percent and, more important, the number of SIDS babies has declined by 40 percent (American Academy of Pediatrics, 2000). The American Academy of Pediatrics Task Force on SIDS has recently made the following recommendations, hoping to further decrease the incidence of SIDS (Kahn et al., 2003):

Don't place infants down to sleep on waterbeds, sofas, soft mattresses, or other soft surfaces.

Soft materials that may obstruct the infant's breathing (for example, unnecessary pillows, stuffed toys, or comforters) should be kept away from the infant's sleeping environment.

Infants should be lightly clothed for sleep and the bedroom temperature kept comfortable for a lightly clothed adult so as to avoid infant overheating.

Create a smoke-free zone around the baby. Mothers should not smoke during pregnancy and no one should smoke in the infant's presence.

If possible, consider breast-feeding. There is some evidence that SIDS is less common in breast-fed infants.

Unfortunately, SIDS can still occur, even when parents follow all these guidelines. And SIDS has a devastating impact on most affected families: Parents often feel bitter or extremely guilty over their loss, and siblings may also grieve deeply over the death of a baby brother or sister and begin to display problem behaviors (Brockington, 1996). These families need social support and, fortunately, parent support groups can often help them to cope with their loss and allay their concerns about losing another child to SIDS, should they decide to conceive again. Current information on SIDS and SIDS support groups can be obtained from the National SIDS Alliance, 1314 Bedford Avenue, Suite 210, Baltimore, MD 21208; phone: 1-800-221-7437; online: http://sidsalliance.org.

APPLYING RESEARCH TO YOUR LIFE

Methods of Soothing a Fussy Baby

Although babies can be delightful companions when alert and attentive, they may irritate the most patient of caregivers when they fuss, cry, or are difficult to pacify. Many people think that a crying baby is either hungry, wet, or in pain, and if the infant has not eaten in some time, feeding may be a very effective method of pacification. Presentation of a mild sucrose solution is particularly effective at calming distressed newborns (Blass, 1997), although even a nipplelike pacifier is often sufficient to quiet a fussy baby (Campos, 1989). Of course, the soothing effect of a pacifier may be short-lived if the baby really is hungry.

Jean-Gerard Sidaner/Photo Researchers Inc.

In many cultures, babies are kept quite contented through swaddling and having ample close contact with their mothers, who stand ready to nurse at the baby's first whimper.

Other Soothing Techniques

When feeding or diaper changing doesn't work, rocking, stroking, singing lullabies, and other forms of continuous, rhythmic stimulation will often quiet restless babies (Campos, 1989; Rock & Trainor, 1999). Swaddling (wrapping the infant snugly in a blanket) is also comforting because the wraps provide continuous tactile sensation all over the baby's body. Perhaps the infant's nervous system is programmed to respond to soft, rhythmic stimulation, because studies have repeatedly shown that rocking, swaddling, and continuous rhythmic sounds have the effect of decreasing a baby's muscular activity and lowering heart and respiratory rates (Campos, 1989).

One particularly effective method of soothing crying infants is simply to pick them up. Whereas soft, rhythmic stimulation may put babies to sleep, lifting is likely to have the opposite effect (Korner, 1972), causing them to become visually alert, particularly if their caregivers place them against their shoulder—an excellent vantage point for visual scanning. Anneliese Korner (1972) believes that parents who often soothe their infants by picking them up may be doing them a favor, because the visual exploration from this technique helps babies to learn more about their environment.

Individual and Cultural Differences in Soothability

Just as infants differ in their sleeping patterns and daily rhythms, they also differ in their irritability and their ability to be soothed (Korner, 1996). Even in the first few days of life, some infants are easily distressed and difficult to soothe, whereas others are rarely perturbed and will calm easily should they become overstimulated. There are also cultural differences in infant soothability: Caucasian babies tend to be much more restless and more difficult to calm than Chinese American, Native American, or Japanese infants (Freedman, 1979; Nugent, Lester, & Brazelton, 1989). These differential reactions to stress and soothing are present at birth and may be genetically influenced. Yet it is also clear that child-rearing practices can affect a baby's demeanor. Many Asian, South American, and Native American mothers, for example, are often successful at improving the dispositions of even their most irritable babies by swaddling them, carrying them around (in slings or pouches) as they do their chores, and nursing at the baby's first whimper (Nugent, Lester, & Brazelton, 1989; Tronick, Thomas, & Daltabuit, 1994).

A baby who is not easily soothed can make a parent feel anxious, frustrated, or downright incompetent—reactions that may contribute to a poor parent-child relationship. For this reason, parents of difficult infants need to cast aside their preconceptions about the typical or "perfect" baby and learn how to adjust to the characteristics of their own child. Indeed, the Neonatal Behavioral Assessment Scale (NBAS) training described in Chapter 4 was designed with just this objective in mind by (1) showing parents that even an irritable or unresponsive baby can react positively to them and (2) teaching the parents how to elicit these favorable responses.

the Box). Pediatricians and nurses are trained to listen carefully to the vocalizations of a newborn infant because congenital problems are sometimes detectable by the way an infant cries. Preterm babies, for example, and those who are malnourished, brain-damaged, or born addicted to narcotics, often emit shrill, nonrhythmic cries that are perceived as much more "sickly" and aversive than those of healthy full-term infants (Frodi, 1985; Zeskind, 1980). In fact, Barry Lester (1984) reports that it is even possible to discriminate preterm infants who will develop normally from those who are likely to experience later deficiencies in cognitive development by analyzing their crying in the first few days and weeks of life. So the infant cry is not only an important communicative prompt for parents but is a meaningful diagnostic tool as well.

CONCEPT CHECK 5.1 Infant Development

Check your understanding of the newborn's readiness for life by answering the following questions. Answers appear in the Appendix.

Multiple Choice: Select the best answer for each of the following multiple-choice questions.

_____ 1. Markus notices that his newborn son spends many hours sleeping. While his son sleeps, his eyes appear to be moving rapidly under his closed eyelids. Markus also finds that when he spends time giving his new son lots of different things to look at and explore visually, this eye movement during sleep is less pronounced. Developmental psychologists would say that Markus's experiences support the _______ theory.
   a. irregular sleep
   b. REM sleep
   c. autostimulation
   d. visual stimulation

_____ 2. Which of the following is *not* a viable recommendation to help lower the chances of sudden infant death syndrome?
   a. Keep soft materials that could obstruct the infant's breathing away from the infant's sleeping environment.
   b. Have the baby tested for the SIDS virus by a pediatrician.
   c. Create a smoke-free zone around the baby.
   d. Consider breast-feeding the baby, if possible.

_____ 3. Which of the following statements is *false* concerning infants' crying?
   a. Crying is an infant state by which an infant communicates his or her distress.
   b. Shrill and nonrhythmic crying may be an indication of brain damage.
   c. Crying diminishes rapidly over the first 2 weeks of life as the baby's brain matures.
   d. Crying diminishes over the first 6 months of life, partially because parents become better at preventing infants from becoming distressed.

Matching: Check your understanding of infant states by matching the name of the infant state to the description of that state.

a. regular sleep
b. irregular sleep
c. drowsiness
d. alert inactivity
e. alert activity
f. crying

4. Baby's eyes are open and breathing is irregular; may become fussy and display various bursts of diffuse motor activity.
5. Intense crying that may be difficult to stop and is accompanied by high levels of motor activity.
6. Baby is still, with eyes closed and unmoving; breathing is slow and regular.

Fill in the Blank: Check your understanding of the material by filling in the blanks in the following sentences with the correct word or phrase.

7. _______ is the detection of sensory stimulation.
8. The interpretation of what is sensed is called _______.
9. _______ reflexes disappear in the first year of life, signifying that development is proceeding normally.
10. _______ reflexes help newborns adapt to their surroundings and satisfy basic needs.

Research Methods Used to Study the Infant's Sensory and Perceptual Experiences

As recently as the early 1900s, many medical texts claimed that human infants were functionally blind, deaf, and impervious to pain for several days after birth. Babies were believed to be unprepared to extract any "meaning" from the world around them. Today we know otherwise. Why the change in views? It is not that babies have become any more capable or any smarter. Instead, researchers have gotten smarter and have developed some ingenious research methods for understanding what nonverbal infants can sense and perceive (Bertenthal & Longo, 2002). Let's briefly discuss four of these techniques.

preference method
a method used to gain information about infants' perceptual abilities by presenting two (or more) stimuli and observing which stimulus the infant prefers.

The Preference Method

The **preference method** is a simple procedure in which at least two stimuli are presented simultaneously to see whether infants will attend more to one of them than the other(s)

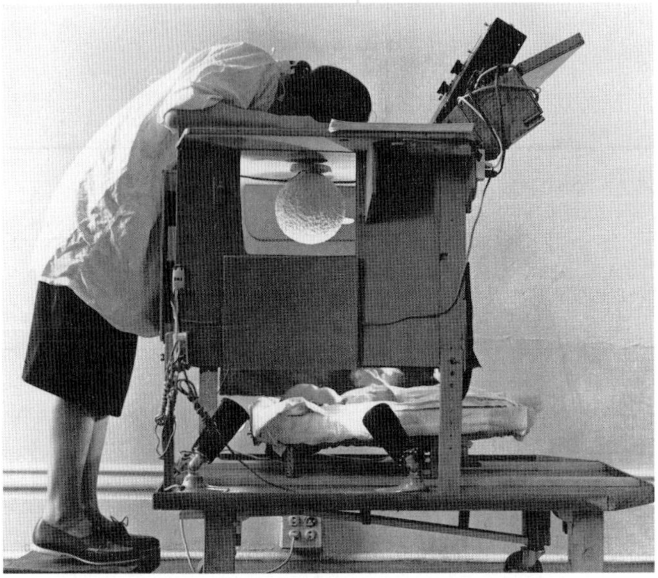

David Linton

Figure 5.1 The looking chamber that Fantz used to study infants' visual preferences.

(Houston-Price & Nakai, 2004). This approach became popular during the early 1960s after Robert Fantz used it to determine whether very young infants could discriminate visual patterns (for example, faces, concentric circles, newsprint, and unpatterned disks). Babies were placed on their backs in a *looking chamber* (see Figure 5.1) and shown two or more stimuli. An observer located above the looking chamber then recorded the amount of time the infant gazed at each of the visual patterns. If the infant looked longer at one target than the other, it was assumed that she preferred that pattern.

Fantz's early results were clear. Newborns could easily discriminate (or tell the difference between) visual forms, and they preferred to look at patterned stimuli such as faces or concentric circles rather than at unpatterned disks. Apparently the ability to detect and discriminate patterns is innate (Fantz, 1963).

The preference method has one major shortcoming. If an infant shows no preferences among the target stimuli, it is not clear whether she failed to discriminate them or simply found them equally interesting. Fortunately, each of the following methods can resolve this ambiguity.

The Habituation Method

habituation
a decrease in one's response to a stimulus that has become familiar through repetition.

dishabituation
increase in responsiveness that occurs when stimulation changes.

Perhaps the most popular strategy for measuring infant sensory and perceptual capabilities is the habituation method. **Habituation** is the process in which a repeated stimulus becomes so familiar that responses initially associated with it (for example, head or eye movements, changes in respiration or heart rate) no longer occur. Thus, habituation is a simple form of learning. As the infant stops responding to the familiar stimulus, he is telling us that he recognizes it as something that he has experienced before (Bertenthal & Longo, 2002). For this reason, the habituation method is also referred to as a "familiarization-novelty" procedure (Brookes et al., 2001; Houston-Price & Nakai, 2004).

To test an infant's ability to discriminate two stimuli that differ in some way, the investigator first presents one of the stimuli until the infant stops attending or otherwise responding to it (habituates). Then the second stimulus is presented. If the infant discriminates this second stimulus from the first, he will **dishabituate**—that is attend closely to it while showing a change in respiration or heart rate. If the infant fails to react, it is assumed that the differences between the two stimuli were too subtle for him to detect. Because babies habituate and dishabituate to so many different kinds of stimulation—sights, sounds, odors, tastes, and touches—the habituation method is very useful for assessing their sensory and perceptual capabilities.

However, distinguishing between habituation and preference effects can be tricky (Houston-Price & Nakai, 2004). Infants display preference when they are familiar with—but not too familiar with—a stimulus. When presented with two stimuli, initially infants show no preference—they don't look at one toy, person, and picture any more frequently than they look at the other. When one stimulus does capture their attention, they begin to look at it more often and, for a short time, when presented with this partially familiar stimulus and an unfamiliar stimulus, they will spend more time looking at the partially familiar stimulus. When they become thoroughly familiar with the original stimulus, they become ready to move on, so to speak, and will spend less time looking at the familiar stimulus than its unfamiliar partner (see Figure 5.2 for an example of this sequence of attentional events). In order to properly categorize infant looking behaviors, researchers must pay careful attention to the familiarization timeline of each infant being tested (Houston-Price & Nakai, 2004).

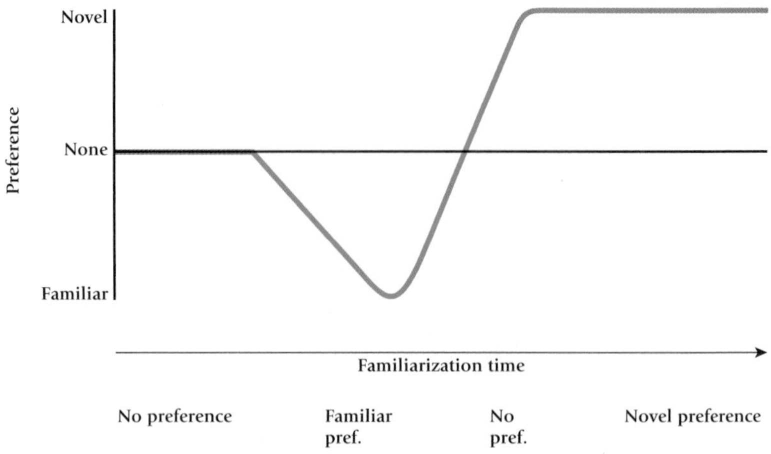

Figure 5.2 A model of the effect of familiarization time on an infant's preference for a novel vs. familiar stimulus. *From Michael A. Hunter and Elinor W. Ames,* A multifactor model of infant preferences for novel and familiar stimuli, *Fig. 2, 1988. Reprinted by permission of Greenwood Publishing Group, Inc., Westport, CT.*

evoked potential
a change in patterning of the brain waves which indicates that an individual detects (senses) a stimulus.

high-amplitude sucking method
a method of assessing infants' perceptual capabilities that capitalizes on the ability of infants to make interesting events last by varying the rate at which they suck on a special pacifier.

The Method of Evoked Potentials

Yet another way of determining what infants can sense or perceive is to present them with a stimulus and record their brain waves. Electrodes are placed on the infant's scalp above those brain centers that process the kind of sensory information that the investigator is presenting (see Figure 5.3). This means, for example, that responses to visual stimuli are recorded from the back of the head, at a site above the occipital lobe. If the infant senses the particular stimulus presented, she will show a change in the patterning of her brain waves, or evoked potential. Stimuli that are not detected will produce no changes in the brain's electrical activity. The **evoked potentials** can even tell us whether infants can discriminate various sights or sounds, because two stimuli that are sensed as "different" produce different patterns of electrical activity.

The High-Amplitude Sucking Method

Finally, most infants can exert enough control over their sucking behavior to use it to show us what they can sense and to give us some idea of their likes and dislikes. The **high-amplitude sucking method** provides infants with a special pacifier containing electrical circuitry that enables them to exert some control over the sensory environment (see Figure 5.4). After the researcher establishes an infant's baseline sucking rate, the procedure begins. Whenever the infant sucks faster or harder than she did during the baseline observations (high-amplitude sucking), she trips the electrical circuit in the pacifier, thereby activating a slide projector or tape recorder that introduces some kind of sensory stimulation. Should the infant detect this stimulation and find it interesting, she can make it last by displaying bursts of high-amplitude sucking. But once the infant's interest wanes and her sucking returns to the baseline level, the stimulation stops. If the investigator then introduces a second stimulus that elicits an increase in high-amplitude sucking, he could conclude that the infant has discriminated the second stimulus from the first.

This procedure can even be modified to let the infant show us which of two stimuli she prefers. If we wanted to determine whether babies prefer rap music to lullabies, we could adjust the circuitry in the pacifier so that high-amplitude sucking activates one kind of music and low-amplitude (or no) sucking activates the other. By then noting what the baby does, we could draw some inferences about which of these musical compositions she prefers. Clearly, this high-amplitude sucking method is a clever and versatile technique!

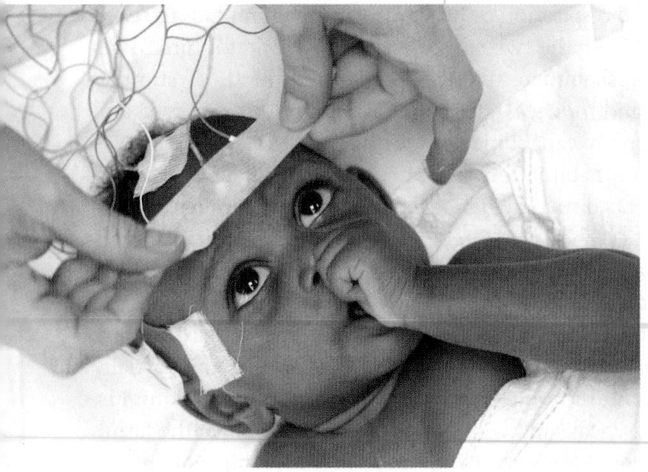

Figure 5.3 An EEG cap is used to place electrodes around the baby's head to record electrode activity at appropriate places on the baby's brain.

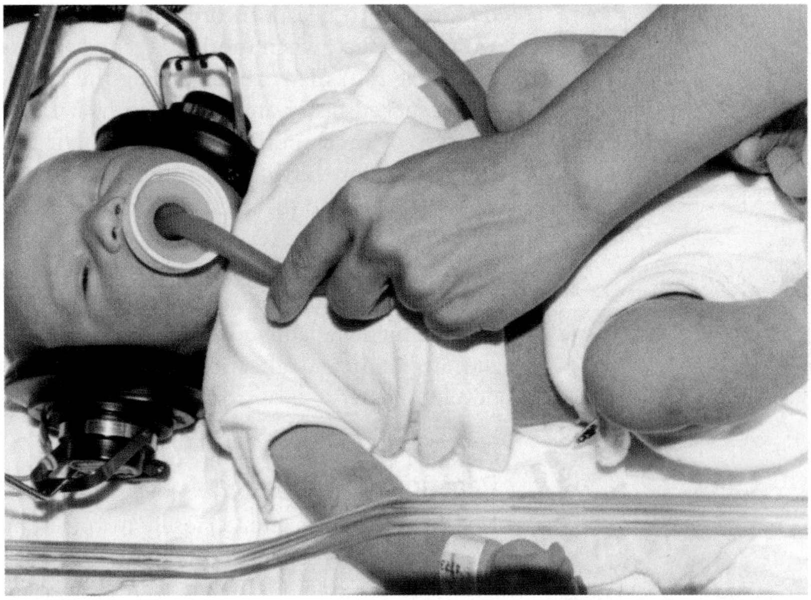

Courtesy of Anthony DeCasper

Figure 5.4 The high-amplitude sucking apparatus.

Infant Sensory Capabilities

Let's now see what these creative research methods have revealed about babies' sensory and perceptual capabilities. How well do newborns sense their environments? Better, perhaps, than you might imagine. We'll begin our exploration of infants' sensory world by examining their auditory capabilities.

Hearing

Soft sounds that adults hear must be made noticeably louder before a neonate can detect them (Aslin, Pisoni, & Jusczyk, 1983). In the first few hours of life, infants may hear about as well as an adult with a head cold. Their insensitivity to softer sounds could be due, in part, to fluids that have seeped into the inner ear during the birth process. Despite this minor limitation, neonates are capable of discriminating sounds that differ in loudness, duration, direction, and frequency (Bower, 1982). They hear rather well indeed. And they impart meaning to sounds fairly early. For example, at 4 to 6 months, infants react to a rapidly approaching auditory stimulus in the same way that they react to approaching visual stimuli: they blink in anticipation of a collision (Freiberg, Tually, Crassini, 2001).

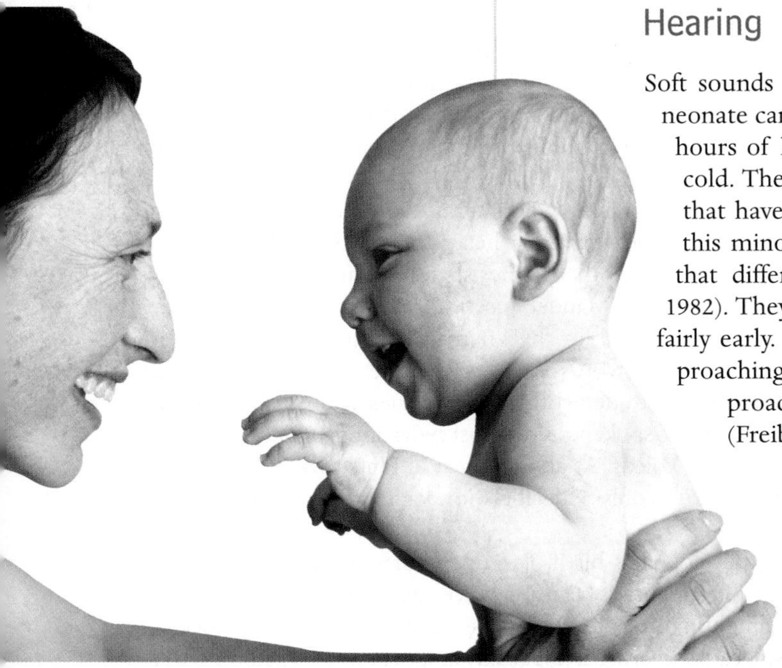

© Bill Aron/PhotoEdit

Very young infants are particularly responsive to the sound of human voices.

Reactions to Voices

Young infants are particularly attentive to voices, especially high-pitched feminine voices (Ecklund-Flores & Turkewitz, 1996). But can they recognize their mother's voices? Research by Anthony DeCasper and his associates (DeCasper & Fifer, 1980; DeCasper & Spence, 1986, 1991) reveals that newborns suck faster

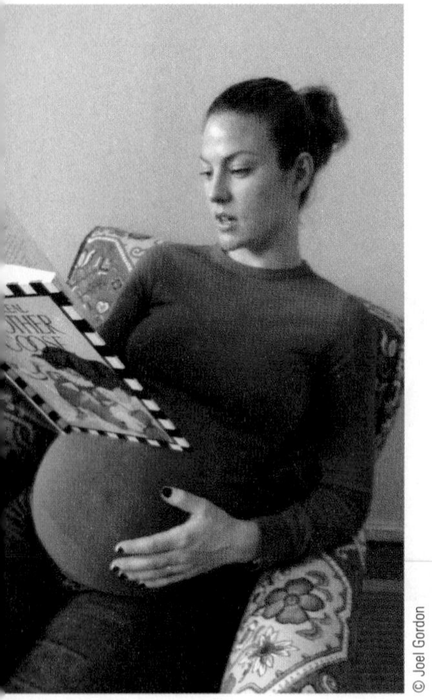
© Joel Gordon

on a nipple to hear a recording of their mother's voice than a recording of another woman. In fact, when mothers recited a passage (for example, portions of Dr. Seuss's *Cat in the Hat*) many times during the last 6 weeks of their pregnancies, their newborns sucked faster and harder to hear those particular passages than to hear other samples of their mother's speech. Might these preferences reflect the experiences a baby had before birth, as he listened to his mother's muffled voice through the uterine wall? Probably so, because DeCasper and Spence (1994) found that fetuses in their third trimester experienced changes in their heart rate between familiar and novel passages read by their mothers, a clear indication that the fetuses were learning sound patterns before birth. This special responsiveness to Mother's voice after birth may even be highly adaptive if it encourages a mother to talk to her infant and to provide the attention and affection that foster healthy social, emotional, and intellectual development.

Reactions to Language

Not only do babies attend closely to voices, but they are also able to discriminate basic speech sounds—called **phonemes**—very early in life. Peter Eimas (1975b, 1985) pioneered research in this area by demonstrating that infants 2 to 3 months old could distinguish consonant sounds that are very similar (for example, *ba* and *pa*). In fact, infants less than 1 week old can tell the difference between the vowels *a* and *i* (Clarkson & Berg, 1983), and can even segment words into discrete syllables (Bijeljac-Babic, Bertoncini, and Mehler, 1993). Just as babies divide the spectrum of light into basic color categories, they seem to divide speech sounds into categories corresponding to the basic sound units of language (Miller & Eimas, 1996). In fact, 3- to 6-month-old infants are actually better than adults are at perceiving certain phonemes that are *not* a part of the language their companions speak (Best & McRoberts, 2003; Jusczyk, 1995; Werker & Desjardins, 1995). This capability was demonstrated using a reinforcement paradigm. For example, infants were placed in an infant seat with a display of mechanical toys beside them. They listened to a recording of voices saying "A" or "I" (or phonemes from different languages than the one spoken in their homes). For half of the infants, the mechanical toys would be activated after one syllable was uttered, and for the other half of the infants, the mechanical toys would be activated after the other syllable was uttered. Infants learned the reinforcement contingencies, and would turn their heads in anticipation of the mechanical toys being activated when they heard the correct syllable or phoneme. This demonstrated their abilities to distinguish the language sounds (and to learn the reinforcement contingencies of the experiment), even for sounds that weren't a part of their companions' language. These are impressive accomplishments indeed!

phonemes
smallest meaningful sound units that make up a spoken language.

Finally, babies soon learn to recognize words that they hear often. By age 4½ months, for example, they will reliably turn their heads to hear their own name but not to hear other names, even when these other names share the same stress pattern as their own (Abbey vs. Johnny, for example) (Mandel, Jusczyk, & Pisoni, 1995). Babies this young probably do not know that the word for their name refers to *them,* but they are able to recognize such frequently heard words very early in life. At 5 months, if the speaker is loud enough, infants are able to detect their own names against a background of babbling voices. The volume of the spoken name must be around 10 decibels higher than the volume of the background voices. At about 1 year, infants turn in response to their own names when the names are only 5 decibels louder than background voices (Newman, 2005).

Clearly, hearing is highly developed at birth. Even newborns are remarkably well-prepared for such significant achievements as (1) using voices to identify and discriminate their companions and (2) segmenting speech into smaller units—the building blocks of language. This is significant because hearing is especially important to development, as the research on hearing loss in the Box on p. 171 suggests.

FOCUS ON RESEARCH Causes and Consequences of Hearing Loss

How important is hearing to human development? We gain some insight on this issue from the progress made by otherwise healthy youngsters whose hearing is impaired by a common childhood infection.

Otitis media, a bacterial infection of the middle ear, is the most frequently diagnosed disease among infants and preschool children. Almost all children are infected at least once, with up to one-third of them experiencing recurring infections despite receiving adequate medical care (Halter et al, 2004; Vernon-Feagans, Manlove, & Volling, 1996). Antibiotics can eliminate the bacteria that causes this disease (Pichichero & Casey, 2005) but will do nothing to reduce the buildup of fluid in the middle ear, which often persists without any symptoms of pain or discomfort. Unfortunately, this fluid may produce mild to moderate hearing loss that can last for months after an infection has been detected and treated (Halter et al., 2004; Vernon-Feagans, Manlove, & Volling, 1996). Temporary insertion of ventilating tubes may be prescribed to ensure drainage of fluid buildup (Halter et al., 2004).

Due to the widespread use of antibacterial treatment, drug-resistant strains of otitis media have developed (Rosenfeld, 2004). Fortunately, for less severe infections, "watchful waiting" presents an alternative to the automatic prescription of antibiotics. Children with nonsevere otitis media may be treated with symptom-relieving medicines and their parents educated about signs of the development of a more severe infection. As parents watch and wait, the immune systems of many children will eliminate the infection without assistance from antibiotic medication (McCormick et al., 2005; Wald, 2005).

Otitis media strikes hardest between 6 months and 3 years of age. As a result, developmentalists have feared that youngsters with recurring infections may have difficulties understanding others' speech, which could hamper their language development as well as other cognitive and social skills that normally emerge early in childhood. And there is reason for concern. Children who have had recurring ear infections early in life do show delays in language development and poorer academic performance early in elementary school than peers whose bouts with the disease were less prolonged (Friel-Patti & Finitzo, 1990; Teele, Klein, & Chase et al., 1990). They also exhibit impaired auditory attention skills (Asbjornsen et al., 2005). Compared to those who have no history of chronic OM, very young children with histories of chronic OM perform more poorly on tasks that involve syllable and phoneme awareness (Nittrouer & Burton, 2005). Older children with histories of chronic OM have more difficulty when asked to recall a series of words, as well as more difficulty comprehending syntactically complex sentences (Nittrouer & Burton, 2005). Another study found that 3-year-olds with chronic OM may be at risk of developing poor social skills, for they spend more time playing alone and they have fewer positive contacts with day-care classmates than other children do (Vernon-Feagans, Manlove, & Volling, 1996). Although longitudinal research is needed to determine whether the problems associated with chronic OM will persist later in childhood and adolescence, current research implies that young children with mild to moderate hearing loss are likely to be developmentally disadvantaged, and that otitis media, a major contributor to early hearing loss, needs to be detected early and treated aggressively (Jung et al., 2005).

Taste and Smell

Infants are born with some very definite taste preferences. For example, they apparently prefer sweets, because both full-term and premature babies suck faster and longer for sweet liquids than for bitter, sour, salty, or neutral (water) solutions (Crook, 1978; Smith & Blass, 1996). Different tastes also elicit different facial expressions from newborns. Sweets reduce crying and produce smiles and smacking of the lips, whereas sour substances cause infants to wrinkle their noses and purse their lips. Bitter solutions often elicit expressions of disgust—a down turning of the corners of the mouth, tongue protrusions, and even spitting (Blass & Ciaramitaro, 1994; Ganchrow, Steiner, & Daher, 1983). These facial expressions become more pronounced as solutions become sweeter, more sour, or more bitter, suggesting that newborns can discriminate different concentrations of a particular taste.

Newborns are also capable of detecting a variety of odors, and they react vigorously by turning away and displaying expressions of disgust in response to unpleasant smells such as vinegar, ammonia, or rotten eggs (Rieser, Yonas, & Wilkner, 1976; Steiner, 1979). In the first 4 days after birth, babies already prefer the odor of milk to that of amniotic fluid (in which they have been living for 9 months) (Marlier, Scholl, & Soussignan, 1998). And a 1- to 2-week-old breast-fed infant can already recognize his mother (and discriminate her from other women) by the smell of her breasts and underarms (Cernoch & Porter, 1985; Porter et al., 1992). Like it or not, each of us has a

otitis media
common bacterial infection of the middle ear that produces mild to moderate hearing loss.

unique "olfactory signature"—a characteristic odor that babies can use as an early means of identifying their closest companions.

To demonstrate this discrimination of mother by smell, Macfarlane (1977) asked nursing mothers to wear breast pads in their bras between nursings (such pads absorb milk and odors from the breast that may be emitted between nursings). Next, 2-day-old or 6-day-old nursing infants were observed lying down with a breast pad from their own mother on one side of their heads, and the breast pad of another nursing mother on the other side of their heads. Macfarlane found that the 2-day-old infants showed no difference in which breast pad they turned too. In contrast, the 6-day-old infants consistently turned to the side facing their mother's breast pad. This demonstrated that the infants had learned their mother's unique smell in their first week of life, and had also developed a preference for her smell over the smells of other nursing women.

Touch, Temperature, and Pain

Receptors in the skin are sensitive to touch, temperature, and pain. Earlier in the chapter we learned that newborn infants reliably display a variety of reflexes if they are touched in the appropriate areas. Even while sleeping, neonates habituate to stroking at one locale but respond again if the tactile stimulation shifts to a new spot—from the ear to the chin, for example (Kisilevsky & Muir, 1984).

Sensitivity to touch clearly enhances infants' responsiveness to their environments. In Chapter 4, we learned that premature infants show better developmental progress when they are periodically stroked and massaged in their isolettes. The therapeutic effect of touch is due, in part, to the fact that gentle stroking and massaging arouses inattentive infants and calms agitated ones, often causing them to smile at and become more involved with their companions (Field et al., 1986; Stack & Muir, 1992). Later in the first year, babies begin to use their sense of touch to explore objects—first with their lips and mouths, and later with their hands. So touch is a primary means by which infants acquire knowledge about their environment, which contributes so crucially to their early cognitive development (Piaget, 1960).

Newborns are also quite sensitive to warmth, cold, and to changes in temperature. They refuse to suck if the milk in their bottles is too hot, and they maintain their body heat by becoming more active should the temperature of a room suddenly drop (Pratt, 1954).

Do babies experience much pain? Apparently so, for even 1-day-old infants cry loudly when pricked by a needle for a blood test. In fact, very young infants show greater distress upon receiving an inoculation than 5- to 11-month-olds do (Axia, Bonichini, & Benini, 1999).

Male babies are highly stressed by circumcision, an operation that is usually done without anesthesia because giving these pain-killing drugs to infants in itself is very risky (Hill, 1997). While the surgery is in progress, infants emit high-pitched wails that are similar to the cries of premature babies or those who are brain damaged (Porter, Porges, & Marshall, 1988). Moreover, plasma cortisol, a physiological indicator of stress, is significantly higher just after a circumcision than just before the surgery (Gunnar et al., 1985). Findings such as these challenge the medical wisdom of treating infants as if they are insensitive to pain. Fortunately, researchers have found that babies treated with a mild topical anesthetic before circumcision and given a sugary solution to suck afterward are less stressed by the operation and are able to sleep more peacefully (Hill, 1997).

Vision

Vision may be the least mature of the newborn's sensory capabilities. Changes in brightness elicit a subcortical *pupillary reflex,* which indicates that the neonate is sensitive to light (Pratt, 1954). Babies can also detect movement in the visual field and track a visual stimulus with their eyes, as long as the target moves slowly (Banks & Salapatek, 1983).

The newborn's limited powers of accommodation and pour visual acuity make the mother's face look fuzzy (photo A) rather than clear (photo B), even when viewed from close up. (Try it yourself, by moving the photos to within 6–8 inches of your face.)

Steve McAlister/Getty Images

A: Newborn's view *B: Adult's view*

Newborn infants are more likely to track faces (or facelike stimuli) than other patterns (Johnson et al., 1991). Demonstrating this preference, Johnson and his colleaguesprepared three head-shaped cut-outs with different drawings on them: one was a human face, one a scrambled version of face parts, and one was blank. They moved these cutouts in the visual field of infants just minutes old to 5 weeks old. They found that the infants were more likely to follow (both with their eyes and with their heads) the movement of the cut-out with the human face than either of the other two stimuli. This demonstrated that infants just minutes old could track a visual stimulus with their eyes and heads, and that they showed a preference for the human face. Why do babies display this preference? One possibility is that it represents an adaptive remnant of our evolutionary history—a reflex, controlled by subcortical areas of the brain, that serves to orient babies to their caregivers and promote social interactions (Johnson et al., 1991).

Neonates see the world in color, although they have trouble discriminating blues, greens, and yellows from whites (Adams & Courage, 1998). However, rapid development of the visual brain centers and sensory pathways allows their color vision to improve quickly. By 2 to 3 months of age, babies can discriminate all the basic colors (Brown, 1990; Matlin & Foley, 1997), and by age 4 months they are grouping colors of slightly different shades into the same basic categories—the reds, greens, blues, and yellows—that adults do (Bornstein, Kessen, & Weiskopf, 1976).

visual acuity
a person's ability to see small objects and fine detail.

visual contrast
the amount of light/dark transition in a visual stimulus.

Despite these impressive capabilities, very young infants do not resolve fine detail very well (Kellman & Banks, 1998). Studies of **visual acuity** suggest that a neonate's distance vision is about 20/600, which means that she sees at 20 feet what an adult with excellent vision sees at 600 feet. What's more, objects at any distance look rather blurry to a very young infant, who has trouble *accommodating*—that is, changing the shape of the lens of the eye to bring visual stimuli into focus. Given these limitations, it is perhaps not surprising that many patterns and forms are difficult for a very young infant to detect; she simply requires sharper **visual contrasts** to "see" them than adults do (Kellman & Banks, 1998). However, acuity improves very rapidly over the first few months. By age 6 months, babies' visual acuity is about 20/100, and by age 12 months they see about as well as adults do (Kellman & Banks, 1998).

In sum, the young infant's visual system is not operating at peak efficiency, but it certainly is working. Even newborns can sense movement, colors, changes in brightness, and a variety of visual patterns—as long as these patterned stimuli are not too finely detailed and have a sufficient amount of light/dark contrast. Visual functions evident in

TABLE 5.3 The Newborn's Sensory Capabilities

Sense	Newborn capabilities
Vision	Least-well-developed sense; accommodation and visual acuity limited; is sensitive to brightness; can discriminate some colors; tracks moving targets.
Hearing	Turns in direction of sounds; less sensitive to soft sounds than an adult would be but can discriminate sounds that differ in such dimensions as loudness, direction, and frequency. Particularly responsive to speech; recognizes mother's voice.
Taste	Prefers sweet solutions; can discriminate sweet, salty, sour, and bitter tastes.
Smell	Detects a variety of odors; turns away from unpleasant ones. If breast-fed, can identify mother by the odor of her breast and underarm area.
Touch	Responsive to touch, temperature change, and pain.

newborns are largely experience-independent. As infants explore the world with their eyes, experience-dependent mechanisms—such as synaptic reinforcement—begin to contribute to the development of visual acuity. Thus, both experience-independent and experience-dependent mechanisms promote the development of the infant visual systems (Johnson, 2001).

In sum, each of the major senses is functioning at birth (see Table 5.3 for a review) so that even neonates are well prepared to sense their environments. But do they interpret this input? Can they perceive?

Visual Perception in Infancy

Although newborn infants see well enough to detect and even discriminate some patterns, we might wonder what they "see" when looking at these stimuli. If we show them a □ do they see a square, or must they learn to construct a square from an assortment of lines and angles? When do they interpret faces as meaningful social stimuli or begin to distinguish the faces of close companions from those of strangers? Can neonates perceive depth? Do they think receding objects shrink, or do they know that these objects remain the same size and only look smaller when moved away? These are precisely the kinds of questions that have motivated curious investigators to develop research methods to determine what infants see.

Perception of Patterns and Forms

Recall Robert Fantz's observations of infants in his looking chamber: babies only 2 days old could easily discriminate visual patterns. In fact, of all the targets that Fantz presented, the most preferred stimulus was a face! Does this imply that newborns already interpret faces as a meaningful pattern?

Early Pattern Perception (0 to 2 Months)

Apparently not. When Fantz (1961) presented young infants with a face, a stimulus consisting of scrambled facial features, and a simpler stimulus that contained the same amount of light and dark shading as the facelike and scrambled face drawings, the infants were just as interested in the scrambled face as the normal one (see Figure 5.5).

Later research revealed that very young infants prefer to look at high contrast patterns with many sharp boundaries between light and dark areas, and at moderately complex patterns that have curvilinear features (Kellman & Banks, 1998). So faces and scrambled faces may have been equally interesting to Fantz's young subjects because these targets had the same amount of contrast, curvature, and complexity.

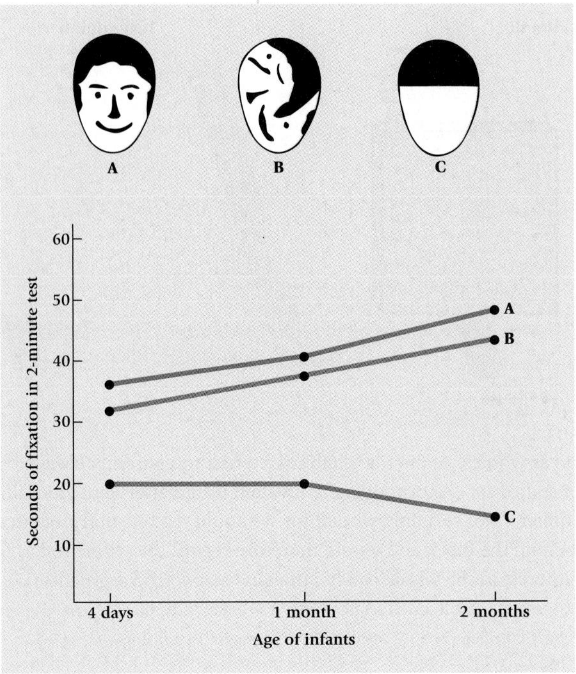

Figure 5.5 Fantz's test of young infants' pattern preferences. Infants preferred to look at complex stimuli rather than at a simpler black-and-white oval. However, the infants did not prefer the facelike figure to the scrambled face. *Adapted from "The Origin of Form Perception," by R. L. Fantz, May 1961,* Scientific American, *204, p. 72 (top). Copyright © 1961 by Scientific American, Inc. Adapted by permission of the artist, Alex Semenoick.*

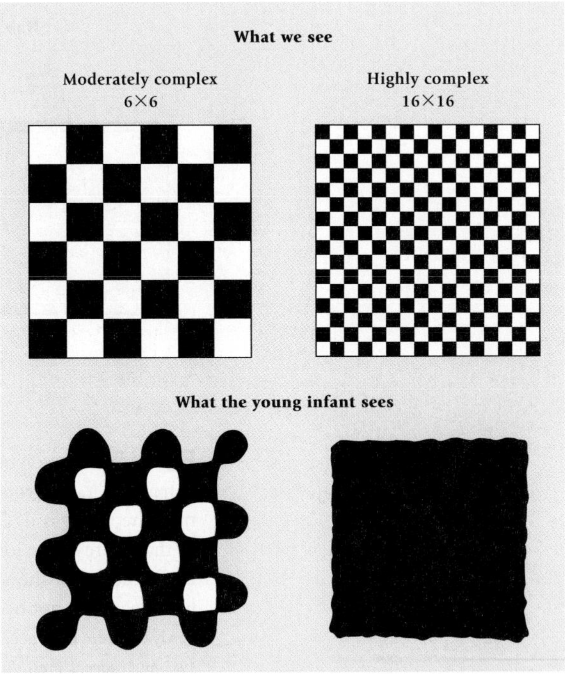

Figure 5.6 What patterns look like to the young eye. By the time these two checkerboards are processed by eyes with poor vision, only the checkerboard on the left may have any pattern left to it. Poor vision in early infancy helps to explain a preference for moderately complex rather than highly complex stimuli. *Adapted from "Infant Visual Perception," by M. S. Banks, in collaboration with P. Salapatek, 1983, in* Handbook of Child Psychology, Vol. 2: Infancy and Developmental Psychology, *by M. M. Haith & J. J. Campos (Eds.). Copyright © 1983 by John Wiley & Sons, Inc. Adapted by permission of John Wiley & Sons, Inc.*

By analyzing the characteristics of stimuli that very young infants will or will not look at, we can estimate what they see. Figure 5.6, for example, indicates that babies less than 2 months old see only a dark blob when looking at a highly complex checkerboard, probably because their immature eyes don't accommodate well enough to resolve the fine detail. However, the infant sees a definite pattern when gazing at the moderately complex checkerboard (Banks & Salapatek, 1983). Martin Banks and his associates have summarized the looking preferences of very young infants quite succinctly: babies prefer to look at whatever they see well (Banks & Ginsburg, 1985), and the things they see best are moderately complex, high-contrast targets, particularly those that capture their attention by moving.

Later Form Perception (2 Months to 1 Year)

Between 2 and 12 months of age, the infant's visual system is rapidly maturing. She now sees better and is capable of making increasingly complex visual discriminations. She is also organizing what she sees to perceive visual forms.

To demonstrate this new ability to perceive forms, Philip Kellman and Elizabeth Spelke (1983; Kellman, Spelke, & Short, 1986) presented infants with a display consisting of a rod partially hidden by a block in front of it (see Figure 5.7, displays A and B). Would they perceive the rod as a whole object, even though part of it was not visible, or would they act as though they had seen two short and separate rods?

To find out, 4-month-olds were first presented with either display A (a stationary hidden rod) or display B (a moving hidden rod) and allowed to look at it until they habituated

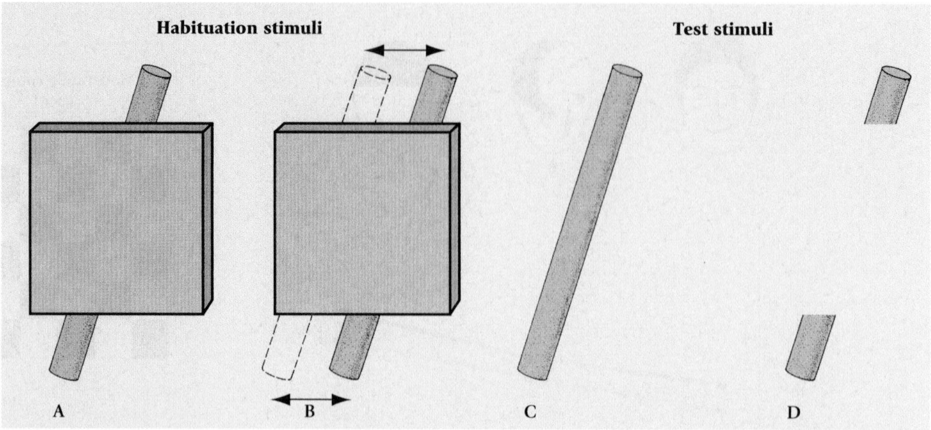

Figure 5.7 Perceiving objects as wholes. An infant is habituated to a rod partially hidden by the block in front of it. The rod is either stationary (A) or moving (B). When tested afterward, does the infant treat the whole rod (C) as "familiar"? We certainly would, for we could readily interpret cues that tell us that there is one long rod behind the block and would therefore regard the whole rod as familiar. But if the infant shows more interest in the whole rod (C) than in the two rod segments (D), he or she has apparently not been able to use available cues to perceive a whole rod. *Adapted from "Perception of Partly Occluded Objects in Infancy," by P. J. Kellman & E. S. Spelke, 1983,* Cognitive Psychology, *15, 483–524. Copyright © 1983 by Academic Press, Inc. Adapted by permission.*

and were no longer interested. Then infants were shown displays C (a whole rod) and D (two rod segments), and their looking preferences were recorded. Infants who had habituated to the *stationary* hidden rod (display A) showed no clear preference for display C or display D in the later test. They were apparently not able to use available cues, such as the two identical rod tips oriented along the same line, to perceive a whole rod when part of the rod was hidden. Infants did apparently perceive the *moving* rod (display B) as "whole," for after habituating to this stimulus, they much preferred to look at the two short rods (display D) than at a whole rod (display C, which they now treated as familiar). It seems that these latter infants inferred the rod's wholeness from its synchronized movement—the fact that its parts moved in the same direction at the same time. So infants rely heavily on motion cues to identify distinct forms (Johnson et al., 2002; Johnson & Mason, 2002).

Interestingly, this impressive ability to use object movement to perceive form is apparently not present at birth (Slater et al., 1990), but has developed by 2 months of age (Johnson & Aslin, 1995). By age 3 to 4 months, infants can even perceive form in some stationary scenes that capture their attention. Look carefully at Figure 5.8. Do you see a square in this display? So do 3- to 4-month-olds (Ghim, 1990)—a remarkable achievement indeed, for the boundary of this "square" is a *subjective contour* that must be constructed mentally rather than simply detected by the visual system.

Figure 5.8 By 3 months of age, infants are perceiving subjective contours such as the "square" shown here. *Adapted from "Development of Visual Organization: The Perception of Subjective Contours," by B. I. Berthnthal, J. J. Campos, & M. M. Haith, 1980,* Child Development, 51, *1077–1080. Copyright © 1980 by The Society for Research in Child Development, Inc. Adapted by permission.*

Further strides in form perception occur later in the first year as infants come to detect more and more about structural configurations from the barest of cues (Craton, 1996). At about 8 months, infants no longer need kinetic cues to perceive a partially obscured rod as whole (Johnson & Richard, 2000; Kavšek, 2004). Twelve-month-old infants are even better at constructing form from limited information. After seeing a single point of light move so as to trace a complex shape such as a !, 12-month-olds (but not 8- or 10-month-olds) prefer to look at actual objects with *different* shapes. This preference for novelty on the part of the 12-month-olds indicates that they have perceived the form traced earlier by the light and now find it less interesting than other novel forms (Rose, 1988; Skouteris, McKenzie, & Day, 1992).

Explaining Form Perception

Newborns are biologically prepared to seek visual stimulation and make visual discriminations. These early visual experiences are important, for they keep the visual neurons firing and contribute to the maturation of the visual centers of the brain (Nelson, 1995). By about 2 to 3 months of age, maturation has progressed to the point of allowing an infant to see more detail, scan more systematically, and begin to construct visual forms, including one for faces in general, as well as more specific configurations that represent the faces of familiar companions. All the while, infants are continuing their visual explorations and gaining knowledge that will permit them to make even finer distinctions among visual stimuli, and to draw some general inferences about the significance of such forms as an elongated toy that rattles when shaken or a gleeful look on a father's face.

Notice, then, that the growth of form perception results from a continuous interplay, or interaction, among the baby's inborn equipment (a working, but immature, visual sense), biological maturation, and visual experiences (or learning). Let's see if this same interactive model holds for spatial perception as well.

Perception of Three-Dimensional Space

Because we adults easily perceive depth and the third dimension, it is tempting to conclude that newborns can too. But when are infants capable of perceiving depth and making reasonably accurate inferences about size and spatial relations? We'll briefly consider research designed to answer these questions.

Size Constancy

Very young infants have shown some intriguing abilities to interpret movement across the third dimension. For example, a 1-month-old reacts defensively by blinking his eyes as a looming object approaches his face (Nanez & Yonas, 1994). Three- to five-month-olds react differently to looming objects than to looming openings. Along with pressing the head backward and throwing the arms outward, infants' heightened blinking response has been interpreted as anticipation of an impending collision (Schmuckler & Li, 1998). As an object moves closer to an observer (i.e., as it looms), it consumes more of the visual field and, consequently, the observer sees less and less of what is behind the object. However, as an aperture, i.e., an opening, approaches, more and more of what is behind the opening becomes visible, while room for seeing what is in front or beside the opening, decreases. Their increased rate of blinking has been interpreted as acknowledgement of an impending collision, while lower frequencies of blinking have been interpreted as acknowledgement of an impending pass through the aperture (Schmuckler & Li, 1998). But do very young infants display **size constancy,** recognizing that an object remains the same size when its image on the retina becomes larger as it moves closer or smaller as it moves further away?

size constancy
the tendency to perceive an object as the same size from different distances despite changes in the size of its retinal image.

Until recently, researchers claimed that size constancy could not emerge until 3 to 5 months of age, after infants had developed good binocular vision (stereopsis) that would help them to make accurate spatial inferences. But even newborns know something about an object's real size, although this ability is not yet fully developed.

Apparently, binocular vision does contribute to its development, for 4-month-olds, who show greater evidence of size constancy, are those whose binocular capabilities are most mature (Aslin, 1987). Movement cues also contribute: inferences about real size among $4\frac{1}{2}$-month-olds are more likely to be accurate if the infants have watched an object approach and recede (Day & McKenzie, 1981). Size constancy steadily improves throughout the first year; however, this ability is not fully mature until 10 to 11 years of age (Day, 1987).

Use of Pictorial Cues

Albert Yonas and his associates have studied infants' reactions to monocular depth cues—the tricks artists and photographers use to portray depth and distance on a two-dimensional surface. In the earliest of these studies (Yonas, Cleaves, & Pettersen, 1978),

Figure 5.9 This bank of windows is actually a large photograph taken at a 45-degree angle, and the two edges of this stimulus are in fact equidistant from an infant seated directly in front of it. If infants are influenced by pictorial cues to depth, they should perceive the right edge of the photo to be nearer to them and indicate as much by reaching out to touch this edge rather than the more "distant" edge to their left. *Adapted with permission from "Development of Sensitivity to Pictorial Depth," by A. Yonas, W. Cleaves, and L. Pettersen, 1978,* Science, *200, 77–79. Copyright © 1978 by the American Association for the Advancement of Science.*

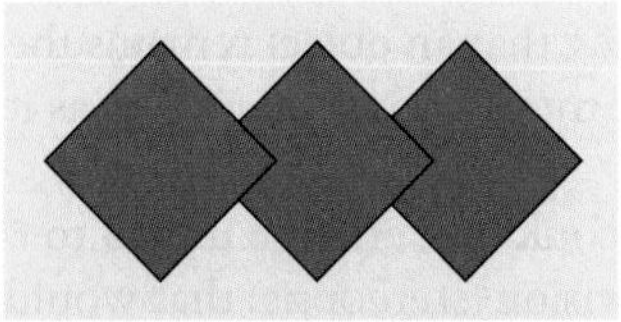

Figure 5.10 If infants are sensitive to the pictorial cue of interposition, they should reliably reach for the "closet" area of a visual display (left side in this example.) Seven-month-olds show this reaching preference, whereas 5-month-olds do not. *From "Infants' Perceptions of Pictorially Specified Interposition," by C. E. Granrud and A. Yonas, 1984,* Journal of Experiemental Child Psychology, *377, 500–511. Copyright © 1984 by Academic Press. Reprinted by permission.*

infants were exposed to a photograph of a bank of windows taken at a 45-degree angle. As we see in Figure 5.9, the windows on the right appear (to us at least) to be much closer than those on the left. So if infants perceive pictorial depth cues, they might be fooled into thinking that the windows on the right are closer and should reach to the right. But if they are insensitive to pictorial cues, they should reach out with one hand about as often as they do with the other.

What Yonas found is that 7-month-olds reliably reached toward the windows that appeared nearest, whereas 5-month-olds displayed no such reaching preferences. In later research, Yonas found that 7-month-olds are also sensitive to pictorial cues such as interposition (see Figure 5.10), relative size, and other two-dimensional pictorial cues, whereas 5-month-olds are not (Yonas, Arterberry, & Granrud, 1987; Arterberry, Yonas, & Bensen, 1989).

In sum, infants become sensitive to different spatial cues at different ages. From a limited capacity for size constancy at birth, babies extract spatial information from kinetic cues (that is, from looming and other moving objects) between 1 and 3 months of age, binocular cues at 3 to 5 months (Schor, 1985), and monocular (pictorial cues) by age 6 to 7 months. Do these impressive accomplishments imply that a 6- to 7-month-old infant perceives depth and knows enough to avoid crawling off the edge of a sofa or a staircase? Let's see what researchers have learned from their attempts to answer these questions.

Development of Depth Perception

Eleanor Gibson and Richard Walk (1960) developed an apparatus they called the **visual cliff** to determine whether infants can perceive depth. The visual cliff (see Figure 5.11) consists of an elevated glass platform divided into two sections by a center board. On the "shallow" side, a checkerboard pattern is placed directly under the glass. On the "deep" side, the pattern is placed several feet below the glass, creating the illusion of a sharp drop-off, or a "visual cliff." The investigator tests an infant for depth perception by placing him on the center board and then asking the child's mother to try to coax the infant to cross both the "shallow" and the "deep" sides. Testing infants 6½ months of age and older, Gibson and Walk (1960) found that 90 percent of them would cross the shallow side but fewer than 10 percent would cross the deep side. Apparently, most infants of crawling age clearly perceive depth and are afraid of drop-offs.

© Mark Richards/PhotoEdit

Figure 5.11 An infant at the edge of the visual cliff.

visual cliff
an elevated platform that creates an illusion of depth, used to test the depth perception of infants.

Might children who are too young to crawl also perceive depth? To find out, Joseph Campos and his associates (1970) recorded changes in infants' heart rates when they were lowered face down over the "shallow" and "deep" sides of the apparatus. Babies as young as 2 months of age showed a decrease in heart rate when over the deep side but no change in heart rate on the shallow side. Why a decrease in heart rate? When we are afraid, our hearts beat faster, not slower. A decrease in heart rate is a sign of interest. So 2-month-old infants detect a difference between the deep and shallow sides, but they have not learned to fear drop-offs.

Motor Development and Depth Perception. One reason that many 6- to 7-month-olds come to fear drop-offs is that they are more sensitive to kinetic, binocular, and monocular depth cues than younger infants are. Yet, this fear also depends very heavily on the experiences infants have creeping and crawling about and perhaps falling now and then. Joseph Campos and his associates (1992) found that infants who have crawled for a couple of weeks are much more afraid of drop-offs than infants of the same age who are not yet crawling. In fact, precrawlers quickly develop a healthy fear of heights when given special walkers that allow them to move about on their own. So motor development provides experiences that change infants' interpretation of the *meaning* of depth. And as we shall see in Chapter 6, infants who have begun to move about on their own are better than those who haven't at solving other spatial tasks, such as finding hidden objects.

Why does self-produced movement make such a difference? Probably because young creepers and crawlers have discovered that the visual environment changes when they move, so that they are more inclined to use a spatial landmark to help them define where they (and hidden objects) are in relation to the larger spatial layout. Self-produced movement also makes an infant more sensitive to *optical flow*—the sensation that other objects move when she does—which may promote the development of new neural pathways in the sensory and motor areas of the brain that underlie improvements in both motor skills and spatial perception (Bertenthal & Campos 1987; Higgins, Campos, & Kermoian, 1996; Schmuckler & Tsang-Tong, 2000).

Perhaps you have already inferred by now that the *interactive* model that best explains the growth of form perception applies equally well to the development of spatial abilities. Maturation of the visual sense enables infants to see better and to detect a greater variety of depth cues, while also contributing to the growth of motor skills. Yet experience is equally important: the first year is a time when curious infants are constantly making new and exciting discoveries about depth and distance relations as they become ever more skilled at reaching for and manipulating objects and at moving about to explore stairs, sloped surfaces, and other "visual cliffs" in their natural environments (Bertenthal, 1993; Bushnell & Boudreau, 1993).

Now let's consider how infants come to integrate information from more than one sense to make perceptual inferences.

Intermodal Perception

Suppose you are playing a game in which you are blindfolded and are trying to identify objects by touch. A friend places a small, spherical object in your hand. As you finger it, you determine that it is about 1½ inches in diameter, that it weighs a couple of ounces, and that it is very hard and covered with many small "dimples." You then say "aha" and conclude that the object is a ________.

A colleague who conducts this exercise in class reports that most students easily identify the object as a golf ball—even if they have never touched a golf ball in their lives. This is an example of **intermodal perception**—the ability to recognize by one sensory modality (in this case, touch) an object that is familiar through another (vision). As adults, we can make many inferences of this kind. When do babies first display these abilities?

intermodal perception
the ability to use one sensory modality to identify a stimulus or pattern of stimuli that is already familiar through another modality.

The senses are integrated at birth, and babies expect to touch and feel objects that they can see and reach. However, vision and touch are soon differentiated, so that this year-old infant might even enjoy making an object disappear at her slightest touch.

Are the Senses Integrated at Birth?

It would obviously be useful for an infant who is attempting to understand the world to be able to integrate information gained by viewing, fingering, sniffing, or otherwise exploring objects. Do the senses function in an integrative way early in life?

Suppose that you captured a baby's attention by floating a soap bubble in front of her face. Would she reach for it? If she did, how do you think she would react when the bubble pops at her slightest touch?

Thomas Bower and his associates (1970) exposed neonates to a situation similar to the soap-bubble scenario. The subjects were 8- to 31-day-old infants who could see an object well within reaching distance while they were wearing special goggles. Actually, this *virtual object* was an illusion created by a shadow caster. If the infant reached for it, his or her hand would feel nothing at all. Bower and his associates found that the infants did reach for the virtual object and that they often became frustrated to tears when they failed to touch it. These results suggest that vision and touch are integrated: infants expect to feel objects that they can see and reach, and an incongruity between vision and the tactile sense is discomforting.

Other research on auditory-visual incongruities (Aronson & Rosenbloom, 1971) reveals that 1- to 2-month-olds often become distressed when they *see* their talking mothers behind a soundproof screen but *hear* their mothers' voices through a speaker off to the side. Their discomfort implies that vision and hearing are integrated: a baby who sees his mother expects to hear her voice coming from the general direction of her mouth.

Even a newborn's ability to recognize his or her mother's face may depend on early intermodal integration. Shortly after birth, newborns have shown a preference for their mother's face over the faces of strangers—they look toward their mothers' faces more often and for longer periods of time than they look at strangers' faces. This preference has been demonstrated when olfactory cues have been controlled, that is, the experimenters prevented the newborns from sniffing the moms out (Sai, 1990; Bushnell & Sai, 1989). However, when newborns are prevented from hearing their mothers' voices, they show no preference for gazing at their mothers' faces in comparison to strangers' faces. Apparently, newborns must both see and hear Mom before they become able to recognize her (Sai, 2005). Infants are able to learn the face-voice associations of strangers as early as 3½ months (Brookes et al., 2001).

In sum, the senses are apparently integrated early in life. Nevertheless, infants' negative emotional responses to confusing sensory stimulation says very little about their ability to use one sense to recognize objects and experiences that are already familiar through another sense.

Development of Intermodal Perception

Although intermodal perception has never been observed in newborns, it seems that babies only 1 month old have the ability to recognize by sight at least some of the objects they have previously sucked. In one study, Eleanor Gibson and Arlene Walker (1984) allowed 1-month-old infants to suck either a rigid cylinder or a spongy, pliable one. Then the two objects were displayed visually to illustrate that the spongy cylinder would bend and the rigid one would not. The results were clear: infants who had sucked on a spongy object preferred to look at the rigid cylinder, whereas those who had sucked on a rigid cylinder now gazed more at the pliable one. Apparently these infants could "visualize" the object they had sucked and now considered it less interesting than the other stimulus, which was new to them.

Because 30-day-old infants have had lots of experience sucking on both spongy objects (nipples) and rigid ones (their own thumbs), we cannot necessarily conclude that intermodal perception is innate. And before we get too carried away with the remarkable proficiencies of 1-month-olds, let's note that (1) oral-to-visual perception is the only cross-modal skill that has ever been observed in infants this young, and (2) this ability is weak, at best, in very young infants and improves dramatically over the first year (Maurer, Stager, & Mondloch, 1999; Rose, Gottfried, & Bridger, 1981). Even the seemingly related ability to match tactile sensations (from grasping) with visual ones does not appear until 4 to 6 months of age (Rose, Gottfried, & Bridger, 1981; Streri & Spelke, 1988), largely because infants younger than this cannot grasp objects well (Bushnell & Boudreau, 1993).

Intermodal matching between vision and hearing emerges at about 4 months of age—precisely the time that infants begin to *voluntarily* turn their heads in the direction of sounds (Bahrick, Netto, & Hernandez-Reif, 1998). By age 4 months, infants can even match visual and auditory cues for distance. So if they are listening to a sound track in which engine noise is becoming softer, they prefer to watch a film of a train moving away rather than one showing a train approaching (Pickens, 1994; Walker-Andrews & Lennon, 1985). Clearly, 4-month-olds know what sights go with many sounds, and this auditory / visual matching continues to improve over the next several months.

As the separate sensory systems mature, intermodal perception continues to assist infants in learning about and exploring their worlds. When habituated to a serial presentation of objects that emit a series of idiosyncratic noises, both 4- and 8-month-olds are able to differentiate between the habituated presentation and a presentation of the same object-sound pairings in a different serial order. However, when the object-sound pairings are separated and the presentation order of only one modality, either sound or sight, is manipulated independently, 4-month-olds no longer detect the difference between the habituated presentation and the presentations in which the sounds or objects are presented out of order. In contrast, 8-month-old infants are able to detect the single modality differences in presentation. For the younger infants, the object-sound pairings elicits an intermodal perceptual response that draws attention to the serial relationship, thus laying the foundation for the more advanced order-detection skills demonstrated by the 8-month-olds (Leckowicz, 2004).

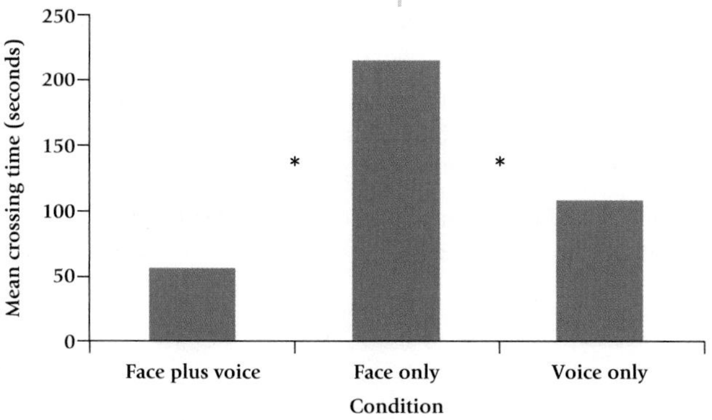

Figure 5.12 Mean times for infants to cross the visual cliff as a function of condition. *From A. Vaish and T. Strian, "Is visual reference necessary? Contributions of facial versus vocal cues in 12-month-olds,"* Developmental Science, 7, *261–269. Reprinted by permission of Blackwell Publishing.*

In some situations, infants as old as 1 year may demonstrate a stronger response to stimuli perceived by more than one sense. During a visual cliff procedure, 12-month-olds crossed the cliff more quickly when they received both visual and auditory cues from their mothers. They crossed somewhat less quickly when receiving auditory cues alone, and crossing times were slowest when infants received visual cues only (see Figure 5.12). Also, the infants looked to their mothers more when they received both auditory and visual cues. There was no significant difference between the amount and number of times that infants looked toward Mom in the voice only and face only conditions. With respect to the overall influence of voice, think about a parent running up behind an infant who is about to do something dangerous or naughty. Infants often receive voice-only cues, and even when facing a child in a precarious position, a parent's voice can reach the child before the parent can (Vaish & Strian, 2004).

Explaining Intermodal Perception

The intersensory redundancy hypothesis suggests that the amodal detection of a stimulus aids in the development and differentiation of individual senses (Bahrick & Lickliter, 2000). That is, the multiple sensory modalities of a stimulus object draw an infant's attention, and as the infant attends to and interacts with that object, the infant gathers comparative input that refines individual sensory modalities. Consequently, the infant's perceptual system advances from an amodal state, in which various sensory inputs are received as a whole, to an intermodal state, in which the infant can separate sound from sight, sight from smell, etc. For example, because both visual and auditory senses are activated, an infants' attention may be captured very quickly by the kneading and purring of a kitten. As the infant watches and listens, both auditory and visual input interact with the infants' developing senses—vision and hearing—so that the infant learns to hear and see with more acuity. If the kitten were silent, the opportunity for the infant to differentiate between auditory and visual input would not be available. Therefore, according to the intersensory

CONCEPT CHECK 5.2 Infant Sensation and Perception

Check your understanding of the research methods used to study infants' sensation and perception, as well as the infant's sensory and perceptual experiences, by answering the following questions. Answers appear in the Appendix.

Multiple Choice: Select the best alternative for each question.

_____ 1. Visual perception develops rapidly in the first year. At what age do we describe infants as "stimulus seekers" who prefer to look at moderately complex, high-contrast stimuli (especially those that move)?
a. 0 to 2 months
b. 2 to 6 months
c. 6 to 9 months
d. 9 to 12 months

_____ 2. Researchers devised a clever method for investigating infants' depth perception. With this method, researchers learned when infants can perceive, but do not fear, changes in depth. The method also revealed when infants begin to fear changes in depth. This research method was
a. the habituation method
b. the visual cliff
c. the high-amplitude sucking method
d. the preference method

_____ 3. The ability to recognize by one sensory modality an object or experience that is already familiar through another sensory modality is termed
a. sensory integration
b. sensory learning
c. intermodal perception
d. visual integration

Fill in the Blank: Check your understanding of newborn's sensory capabilities by selecting the correct word or phrase to complete the following sentences.

4. Newborns' visual acuity is (poor/good/very good) compared to adults' visual acuity.
5. Newborns can hear and discriminate sounds (very poorly/very well).
6. Newborns are (insensitive/quite sensitive) to touch, temperature, and pain.

Matching: Check your understanding of the research methods used to study sensation and perception by matching the name of the research method to the description of that method.

a. the preference method
b. the habituation method
c. the method of evoked potentials
d. the high-amplitude sucking method

7. Two pictures are presented to the infant and the length of time the infant looks at each picture is measured and compared.
8. A pacifier is connected to a speaker system and the infant controls whether she listens to her mother's voice or a stranger's voice by sucking or not sucking on the pacifier.

Essays: Provide a more detailed answer to the following questions to demonstrate your understanding of perceptual development in infancy.

9. Describe how a loss of sensory ability as the infant develops is an indication that cultural experiences influence perceptual development.
10. Discuss the causes and consequences of hearing loss in infancy.

redundancy hypothesis, attending to multimodal stimuli actually promotes perceptual differentiation (Bahrick & Lickliter, 2000; Bahrick, Lickliter, Flom, 2004). In this sense, the intermodal sensory perception of a newborn may be viewed as quite different from the intermodal sensory perception of a 6-month-old infant. At birth, sensory perception is amodal—or undifferentiated—and as infants experience multimodal sensory stimuli, they develop true intermodal perception. That is, as infants learn to see, hear, smell, taste and feel, they are able to distinguish and then reintegrate sensory modalities that are becoming more and more differentiated (Bahrick, 2000).

Cultural Influences on Infant Perception

How is perception influenced by one's culture and cultural traditions? Although people in different cultures rarely differ in such basic perceptual capabilities as the ability to discriminate forms, patterns, and degrees of brightness or loudness (Berry et al., 1992), culture can have some subtle but important effects on perception.

For example, each of us begins life biologically prepared to acquire any language that humans speak. But as we are exposed to a particular language, we become especially sensitive to the sound patterns that are important to that language (that is, to its distinctive features) and less sensitive to auditory distinctions our language deems irrelevant. So all infants easily discriminate the consonants *r* and *l* (Eimas, 1975a). So can you if your native language is English, French, Spanish, or German. However, Chinese and Japanese make no distinction between *r* and *l*, and adult native speakers of these languages cannot make this auditory discrimination as well as infants can (Miyawaki et al., 1975).

Music is another cultural tool that influences our auditory perception. Michael Lynch and his associates (1990) had 6-month-old infants and American adults listen to melodies in either the Western major/minor scale or the Javanese pelog scale, which sounds a bit strange to Western adults. Inserted within the melodies was an occasional "mistuned" note that violated the musical scale. Remarkably, 6-month-old infants often detected these mistuned notes, regardless of whether they violated a Western or a Javanese melody. Apparently babies are born with the potential to perceive "musicality" and to discriminate "good" music from "bad" music in a variety of musical scales. American adults were much less sensitive to bad notes in the unfamiliar Javanese musical system than to mistuned notes in their native Western scale, suggesting that their years of experience with the Western musical system had shaped their perceptions of music.

These findings illustrate two general principles of development that are very important. First, the growth of perceptual abilities, like so many other aspects of development, is not simply a matter of adding new skills; it is also a matter of losing unnecessary ones. Second, our culture largely determines which sensory inputs are "distinctive" and how they should be interpreted. We learn not to hear certain phonemes if they are not distinctive to the language we speak. So the way we perceive the world depends not only on the detection of the objective aspects in our sensory inputs (**perceptual learning**) but also on *cultural* learning experiences that provide a framework for interpreting these inputs.

perceptual learning
changes in one's ability to extract information from sensory stimulation that occur as a result of experience.

Let's now take a closer look at learning and see if we can determine why many developmentalists include it (along with maturation and perception) among the most fundamental developmental processes.

Basic Learning Processes in Infancy

learning
a relatively permanent change in behavior (or behavioral potential) that results from one's experiences or practice.

Learning is one of those deceptively simple terms that are actually quite complex. Most psychologists think of learning as a change in behavior (or behavior potential) that meets the following three requirements (Domjan, 1993):

The individual now thinks, perceives, or reacts to the environment in a *new way.*

This change is clearly the result of a person's *experiences*—that is, attributable to repetition, study, practice, or the observations the person has made, rather than to hereditary or maturational processes or to physiological damage resulting from injury.

Figure 5.13 Support habituation and test events; containment test events.

The change is *relatively permanent*. Facts, thoughts, and behaviors that are acquired and immediately forgotten have not really been learned, and temporary changes due to fatigue, illness, or drugs do not qualify as learned responses.

Let's now consider four fundamental ways in which infants learn: habituation, classical conditioning, operant conditioning, and observational learning.

Habituation: Early Evidence of Information-Processing and Memory

Earlier, we touched on one very simple and often overlooked form of learning called *habituation*—the process by which we stop attending or responding to a stimulus repeated over and over. Habituation can be thought of as learning to become disinterested in stimuli that are recognized as familiar and nothing to get excited about. It can occur even before a baby is born: 27- to 36-week-old fetuses initially become quite active when a vibrator is placed on the mother's abdomen, but soon stop moving (that is, habituate), as if they process these vibrations as a familiar sensation that is no longer worthy of attention (Madison, Madison, & Adubato, 1986).

How do we know that an infant is not merely fatigued when he stops responding to a familiar stimulus? We know because when a baby has habituated to one stimulus, he often *dishabituates*—that is, attends to or even reacts vigorously to a slightly different stimulus. Dishabituation, then, indicates that the baby's sensory receptors are not simply fatigued and that he can discriminate the familiar from the unfamiliar.

Developmental Trends

Habituation improves dramatically throughout the first year. Infants less than 4 months old may require long exposures to a stimulus before they habituate; 5- to 12-month-olds may recognize the same stimulus as familiar after a few seconds of sustained attention and are likely to retain this knowledge for days or even weeks (Fagan, 1984; Richards, 1997). Sometime between 10 and 14 months, infants not only habituate to objects, but to objects in relation to one another. After viewing toys that sit atop upside-down containers, infants habituate to this support configuration and choose to take a longer look at a containment configuration—in which the same toys are seated inside the same, now right-side-up, containers (Casasola, 2005). This trend toward rapid habituation and habituation to relationships between objects is undoubtedly related to the maturation of the sensory areas of the cerebral cortex. As the brain and the senses continue to mature, infants process information faster and detect more about a stimulus and its relationship to its surroundings during any given exposure (Richards, 1997; Rovee-Collier, 1997).

Individual Differences

Infants reliably differ in the rate at which they habituate. Some are highly efficient information processors: they quickly recognize repetitive sensory inputs and are very slow to forget what they have experienced. Others are less efficient: they require longer exposures to brand a stimulus as "familiar" and may soon forget what they have learned. Might these early individual differences in learning and memory have any implications for later development?

Apparently so. Infants who habituate rapidly during the first 6 to 8 months of life are quicker to understand and use language during the second year (Tamis-LeMonda & Bornstein, 1989) and reliably outscore their slower habituating age-mates on standardized intelligence tests later in childhood (McCall & Carrigher, 1993; Rose & Feldman, 1995). Why? Probably because rate of habituation measures the speed at which information is processed, as well as attention, memory, and preferences for novelty—all of which underlie the complex mental activities and problem-solving skills normally measured on IQ tests (Rose & Feldman, 1995, 1996).

Classical Conditioning

A second way that infants learn is through classical conditioning. In classical conditioning, a neutral stimulus (the **conditioned stimulus,** or **CS**) that initially has no effect on the infant eventually elicits a response (the **conditioned response,** or **CR**) of some sort by virtue of its association with a second stimulus (the **unconditioned stimulus,** or **UCS**) that always elicits the response.

Though it is extremely difficult and was once thought impossible, even newborns can be classically conditioned. Lewis Lipsitt and Herbert Kaye (1964), for example, paired a neutral tone (the CS) with the presentation of a nipple (a UCS that elicits sucking) to infants 2 to 3 days old. After several of these conditioning trials, the infants began to make sucking motions at the sound of the tone, before the nipple was presented. Clearly, their sucking qualifies as a classically conditioned response because it is now elicited by a stimulus (the tone) that does not normally elicit sucking behavior.

classical conditioning
a type of learning in which an initially neutral stimulus is repeatedly paired with a meaningful nonneutral stimulus so that the neutral stimulus comes to elicit the response originally made only to the nonneutral stimulus.

conditioned stimulus (CS)
an initially neutral stimulus that comes to elicit a particular response after being paired with a UCS that always elicits the response.

conditioned response (CR)
a learned response to a stimulus that was not originally capable of producing the response.

unconditioned stimulus (UCS)
a stimulus that elicits a particular response without any prior learning.

Yet there are important limitations on classical conditioning in the first few weeks of life. Conditioning is likely to be successful only for biologically programmed reflexes, such as sucking, that have survival value. Furthermore, neonates process information very slowly and require more time than an older participant to associate the conditioned and unconditioned stimuli in classical conditioning experiments (Little, Lipsitt, & Rovee-Collier, 1984). But despite these early limitations in information processing, classical conditioning is almost certainly one of the ways in which very young infants recognize that certain events occur together in the natural environment and learn other important lessons, such as that bottles or breasts give milk, or that other people (notably caregivers) signify warmth and comfort.

Operant Conditioning

operant conditioning
a form of learning in which freely emitted acts (or operants) become either more or less probable depending on the consequences they produce.

In classical conditioning, learned responses are *elicited* by a conditioned stimulus. **Operant conditioning** is quite different: the learner first *emits* a response of some sort (that is, *operates* on the environment) and then associates this action with the pleasant or unpleasant consequences it produces. B. F. Skinner (1953) made this form of conditioning famous. He argued that most human behaviors are those we emit voluntarily (that is, *operants*) and that become more or less probable, depending on their consequences. This basic principle makes a good deal of sense: we do tend to repeat behaviors that have favorable consequences and to limit those that produce unfavorable outcomes (see Figure 5.14).

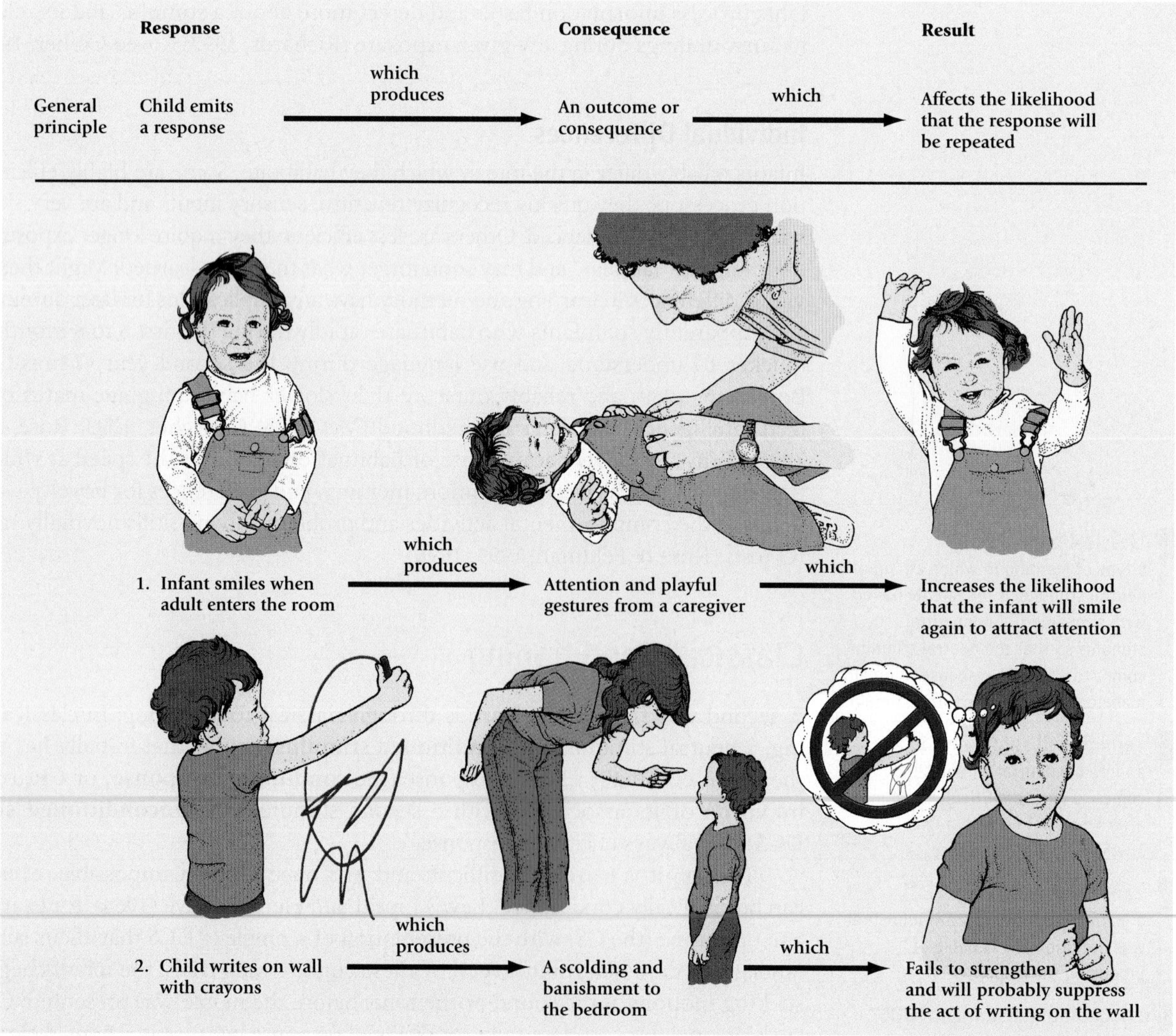

Figure 5.14 Basic principles of operant conditioning.

Operant Conditioning in Infancy

Even babies born prematurely are susceptible to operant conditioning (Thoman & Ingersoll, 1993). However, successful conditioning in very young infants is generally limited to the few biologically significant behaviors (for example, sucking, head-turning) that they can control (Rovee-Collier, 1997). Newborns are also very inefficient information processors who learn very slowly. So if you hoped to teach 2-day-old infants to turn their heads to the right and offered them a nippleful of milk every time they did, you would find that they took about 200 trials, on average, to acquire this simple habit (Papousek, 1967). Older infants learn much faster: a 3-month-old requires only about 40 trials to display a conditioned head-turning response, and 5-month-olds acquire this habit in fewer than 30 trials. Apparently, older infants are quicker to associate their behavior (in this case, head turning) with its consequences (a tasty treat)—an advance in information-processing that seems to explain infants' increasing susceptibility to operant conditioning over the first few months of life.

Can Infants Remember What They Have Learned? Earlier, we noted that very young infants seem to have very short memories. Minutes after they have habituated to a stimulus, they may begin to respond once again to that stimulus, as if they no longer recognize it as familiar. Yet, the simple act of recognizing a stimulus as "familiar" may not be terribly meaningful to a neonate, or even a 2-month-old. Might young infants be better at remembering behaviors they have performed and that have proved to be reinforcing?

Yes indeed, and a program of research by Carolyn Rovee-Collier (1995, 1997; Hayne & Rovee-Collier, 1995) makes this point quite clearly. Rovee-Collier's procedure was to place an attractive mobile over the cribs of 2- to 3-month-old infants and to run a ribbon from the mobile to the infants' ankles (see Figure 5.15). Within a matter of minutes, these young participants discovered that they could make the mobile move by kicking their legs, and they took great pleasure in doing so. But would they remember how to make the mobile move a week later? To succeed at this memory task, the infant not only had to *recognize* the mobile, but also had to *recall* that it moves and that kicking was the way to get it to move.

The standard procedure for testing an infant's memory was to place the child back in the crib to see whether kicking occurred when he or she saw the mobile. Rovee-Collier and her associates found that 2-month-old infants remembered how to make the mobile move for up to 3 days after the original learning, whereas 3-month-olds recalled this kicking response for more than a week. Clearly, a very young infant's memory is much more impressive than habituation studies would have us believe.

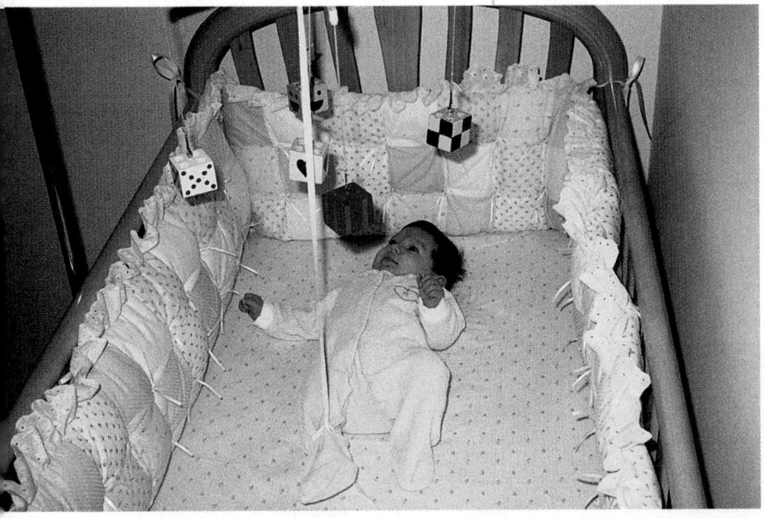

Figure 5.15 When ribbons are attached to their ankles, 2- to 3-month-old infants soon learn to make a mobile move by kicking their legs. But do they remember how to make the mobile move when tested days or weeks after the original learning? These are the questions that Rovee-Collier has explored in her fascinating research on infant memory.

Why do infants eventually forget how to make the mobile move? It is not that their previous learning has been lost, for even 2 to 4 weeks after the original training, infants who were "reminded" of their previous learning by merely seeing the mobile move, looked briefly at it and then kicked up a storm as soon as the ribbon was attached to their ankles (Rovee-Collier, 1997). Infants who received no reminder did not try to make the mobile move when given an opportunity. So even 2- to 3-month-old infants can *retain* meaningful information for weeks, if not longer. However, they find it hard to *retrieve* what they have learned from memory unless they are given explicit reminders. Interestingly, these early memories are highly *context-dependent:* if young infants are not tested under the same conditions in which the original learning occurred (that is, with the same or a highly similar mobile), they show little retention of previously learned responses (Hayne & Rovee-Collier, 1995; Howe & Courage, 1993). So a baby's earliest memories can be extremely fragile.

The Social Significance of Early Operant Learning. Because even newborns are capable of associating their behaviors with their outcomes, they should soon learn that they can elicit favorable responses from other people. For example, a baby may come to display such sociable gestures as smiling or babbling because he discovers that those responses often attract attention and affection from caregivers. At the same time, caregivers are learning how to elicit favorable reactions from their baby, so that their social interactions gradually become smoother and more satisfying for both the infant and her companions. It is fortunate, then, that babies can learn, for in so doing, they are likely to become ever more responsive to other people, who, in turn, become more responsive to them. As we will see in Chapter 11, these positive reciprocal interactions provide a foundation for the strong emotional attachments that often develop between babies and their closest companions.

Newborn Imitation or Observational Learning

observational learning
learning that results from observing the behavior of others.

The last form of basic learning we will consider is **observational learning,** which results from observing the behavior of other people. Almost anything can be learned by watching (or listening to) others. For example, a child may learn how to speak a language and tackle math problems, as well as how to swear, snack between meals, and smoke by imitating his parents. As we saw in Chapter 2, observational learning takes center stage in Albert Bandura's (1977, 1989) social learning theory. Recall that new responses acquired by observation need not be reinforced or even performed before they are learned. Instead this *cognitive* form of learning occurs as the observer attends carefully to the model and constructs *symbolic representations* (for example, images or verbal summaries) of the model's behavior. These mental symbols are then stored in memory and retrieved later to guide the observer's performance of what he or she has observed.

encoding
the process by which external stimulation is converted to a mental representation.

Of course, successful observational learning not only requires the capacity to imitate others, but also the ability to **encode** a model's behavior and rely on mental symbols to reproduce what one has witnessed. When do these abilities first emerge?

Newborn Imitation

Researchers once believed that infants were unable to imitate the actions of another person until the latter half of the first year (Piaget, 1951). But beginning in the late-1970s, a number of studies began to report that babies less than 7 days old were apparently able to imitate a number of adult facial gestures, including sticking out their tongues, opening and closing their mouths, protruding their lower lips (as if they were sad), and even displays of happiness (Field et al., 1982; Meltzoff & Moore, 1977) (see Figure 5.16).

Interestingly, these early imitative displays become much harder to elicit over the first 3 to 4 months of life (Abravanel & Sigafoos, 1984). Some have interpreted this to mean that the neonate's limited capacity for mimicry may be a largely involuntary *reflexive* scheme that disappears with age (as many other reflexes do), only to be replaced later by voluntary imitative responses (Kaitz et al., 1988; Vinter, 1986). Others have argued that

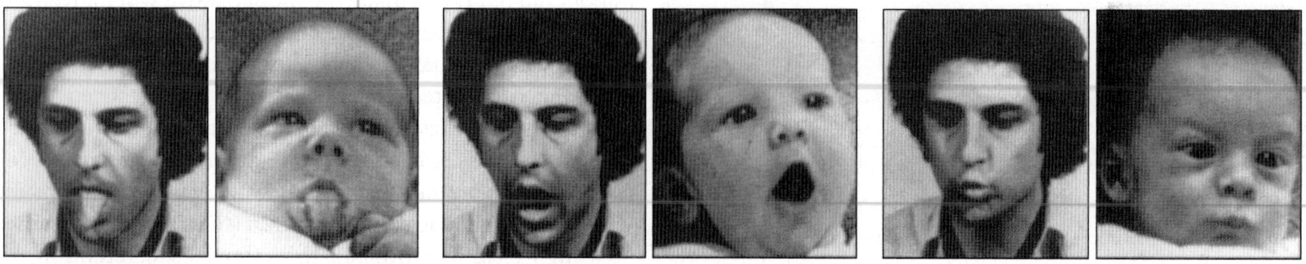

Courtesy of A.N. Meltzoff & A.K. Moore, University of Washington

Figure 5.16 Sample photographs from videotaped recording of 2- and 3-week-old infants imitating tongue protrusion, mouth opening, and lip protrusion.

the two most reliable displays—tongue protrusions and mouth openings—are not imitative responses at all, but simply reflect the baby's early attempts to explore with their mouths those sights they find particularly interesting (Jones, 1996). However, Andrew Meltzoff (1990) contends that these early expressive displays are *voluntary, imitative* responses because babies will often match an adult's facial expression after a short delay, even though the model is no longer posing that expression. Meltzoff's view is that neonatal imitation is simply another example of *intermodal* matching—one in which babies match facial movements they can "see" in the model's face to those they can "feel" in their own faces (Meltzoff & Moore, 1992). However, critics contend that if neonatal imitation represented an infant's *voluntary* intermodal matching, it should get stronger with age rather than disappearing (Bjorklund, 2005). So the underlying cause of these early matching facial displays remains a topic of debate. But regardless of whether we choose to call it imitation, reflexive behavior, or exploration, a newborn's responsiveness to facial gestures may serve a useful function in that it is likely to warm the hearts of caregivers and help ensure that they and their baby get off to a good start.

Advances in Imitation and Observational Learning

An infant's capacity to imitate *novel* responses that are not a part of her behavioral repertoire becomes much more obvious and more reliable between 8 and 12 months of age (Piaget, 1951). At first, the model must be present and must continue to perform the new response before the child is able to imitate. But by age 9 months, some infants can imitate very simple acts (such as closing a wooden flap) up to 24 hours after they first observe them (Meltzoff, 1988c). This **deferred imitation**—the ability to reproduce the actions of a model at some point in the future—develops rapidly during the second year. By age 14 months, nearly half the infants in one study imitated the simple actions of a televised model after a 24-hour delay (Meltzoff, 1988a). And this study probably underestimates their imitative capabilities, for 12- to 15-month-olds are much more inclined to recall and later imitate the actions of *live* rather than televised models (Barr & Hayne, 1999). Indeed, nearly all the 14-month-olds in one experiment were able to imitate at least three (of six) novel behaviors displayed by a live model after a delay of 1 week (Meltzoff, 1988b). In their second year, children are also able to adopt more efficient procedures than those they observe. One week after watching a chilly model push a button to turn on a light, 14-month-olds imitated the model by pushing the button to turn on the light, but they pushed the button using their hands. The model, who was clasping a blanket around herself, had pushed the button with her head (Gergely et al., 2002). And 2-year-olds are able to reproduce the behavior of absent models, even when the materials available to them differ somewhat from those that the model used (Herbert & Hayne, 2000).

deferred imitation
the ability to reproduce a modeled activity that has been witnessed at some point in the past.

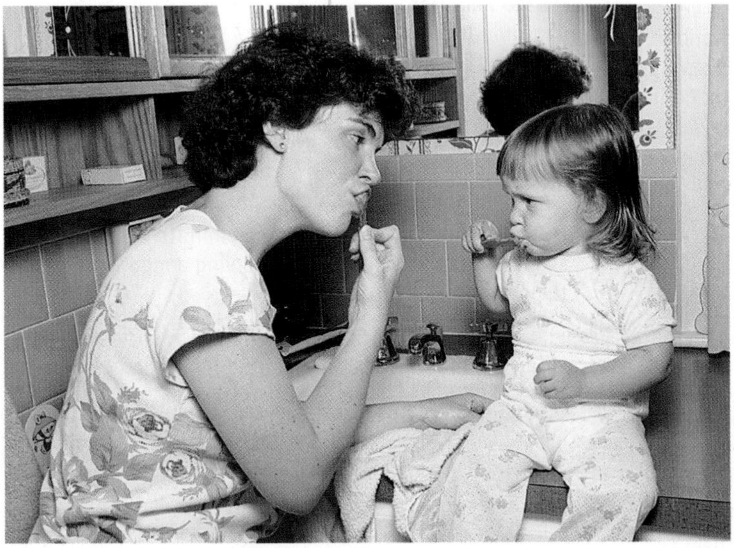
Peter Chapman

By age 2, toddlers are already acquiring important personal and social skills by imitating the adaptive acts of social models.

Thompson and Russell (2004) have demonstrated that infants in their second year can reproduce the dynamic actions of an event when no model is present. They created a "ghost condition" during which infants observed a toy on a rug move toward them. The toy was moved via remote control and the movement of the rug was counterintuitive. That is, rather than the pulling, pushing was the action necessary to move the rug/toy combination. The 14- to 26-month-old infants in this ghost condition successfully pushed the rug to gain access to the toy. Performance in the "ghost condition" was significantly better than when a human model pushed the rug to gain access to the toy. Thompson and Russell propose that observational learning can occur without a model. They call this particular mode of observational learning "emulation" (as opposed to "imitation," which involves a model).

In sum, many of the behavioral changes that occur in infants as they develop are the result of learning. They learn not to dwell too long on stimuli that they are already familiar with (habituation). They may come to like, dislike, or fear almost anything if their encounters with these objects and events have occurred under pleasant or unpleasant circumstances (classical conditioning). They form habits, some good and some bad, by associating various actions with their reinforcing and punishing consequences (operant conditioning). And they acquire new habits and behaviors by observing the behaviors of social models (observational learning). Clearly, then, learning is an important developmental process that leads infants to both become like other people and to develop their own idiosyncrasies.

CONCEPT CHECK 5.3 Basic Learning Processes in Infancy

Check your understanding of the infant learning processes by answering the following questions. Answers appear in the Appendix.

True or False: Demonstrate your understanding of learning processes by indicating whether each of the following statements is true or false.

1. (T)(F) Fetuses have been found to learn through habituation procedures.
2. (T)(F) Learning can be a change in behavior that is a result of hereditary or maturational processes, or to physiological damage resulting from injury.
3. (T)(F) Individual differences in infant habituation patterns are correlated with standardized intelligence test scores later in childhood.

Multiple Choice: Select the best answer for each of the following multiple-choice questions.

_____ 4. Researchers paired a tone with the presentation of a nipple to infants 2 to 3 days old. After several of these trials, the infants began sucking motions at the sound of the tone, before the nipple was presented. In this classical conditioning learning demonstration, the *tone* would be considered the
a. unconditioned stimulus
b. unconditioned response
c. conditioned stimulus
d. conditioned response

_____ 5. Rachel and Ross discover that when they sing rap music to their infant daughter, Emma, she smiles and laughs. They try other methods to get her to laugh, but she consistently laughs only when they sing rap music to her. Consequently, they eventually sing rap music to her over and over to enjoy her laughter. In this situation, Rachel and Ross have learned to sing to Emma because of her laughter. What type of learning is this?
a. operant conditioning
b. classical conditioning
c. observational learning
d. imitation

_____ 6. Researchers examined infant learning by teaching infants to kick their legs when a mobile hanging over their cribs was attached to their legs by a ribbon. This form of learning is
a. habituation
b. classical conditioning
c. operant conditioning
d. observational learning

Matching: Check your understanding of observational learning by matching each description of learning with the term used to describe it.

a. newborn imitation
b. deferred imitation
c. infant imitation

7. Between 8 and 12 months, infants can imitate novel behaviors that a model presents and continues to perform while the infant imitates.
8. As early as 7 days after birth, the infant can imitate facial expressions such as tongue protrusions.
9. By 9 months of age, the infant can imitate novel responses up to 24 hours after observing a model perform the response.

Essay: Demonstrate your understanding of infant learning by answering the following question in the form of an essay.

10. Discuss the benefits of early learning in infancy for forming social relationships and attachments between the infant and her caregivers.

Applying Developmental Themes to Infant Development, Perception, and Learning

Now that we have considered the newborn's readiness for life, the growth of basic perceptual abilities, and the means by which infants learn from their experiences, we might reflect for a moment on the issue of how our developmental themes are applied in these areas of infant development.

Our first theme is that of the active child, or how the child participates in his or her own development. We have seen evidence of this in the findings that perceptual development is the growth of *interpretive* skills: a complex process that depends on the maturation of the brain and the sensory receptors, the kinds of sensory experiences the child has available to analyze and interpret, his emerging motor skills, and even the social/cultural context in which he is raised. So in both conscious and unconscious ways, children are active in their perceptual development. Infants are also highly active in their development though the various learning processes they experience. Finally, infants can be thought of as actively contributing to their own development through some of the losses they have in healthy development, such as the loss of primitive reflexes over the first year of life, and the loss of the ability to perceive some sensory distinctions (such as sounds that are not used in their native language) over the first year of life.

Our second theme, the interaction of nature and nurture in development, borrows the example of the interpretive skills of perception mentioned above. Sensory and perceptual development clearly require both nature and nurture to proceed. The infant's brain and sensory receptors mature over the first year and this maturation limits and guides the development of what the infant is able to sense and perceive. But the infant's abilities are also guided by the sensory experiences she has and how her experiences and motor developments shape her perceptions of what she senses.

By definition, the various forms of learning the infant experiences early in life (habituation, classical conditioning, operant conditioning, and observational learning) all require experience (or nurture) to develop. And yet we also saw many examples of how infants' developing cognitive abilities—to retain and retrieve from memory the things they observed and learned—provided examples of how their biological development (or nature) set limits on their developing learning abilities.

Learning also provided examples of qualitative and quantitative changes in development across infancy. Some of the changes in the ability to learn through observation and conditioning improved quantitatively; the infant gradually became better able to retain, recall, and use what he had learned over longer delays. Some of the changes in learning, such as newborn imitation, changed qualitatively: infants were able to express this ability very early in life, but then passed through a developmental stage at a few months of age when they were not able to imitate, and finally reached another stage of development when imitation seemed to take a different form and they again could imitate facial expressions. Another basic example of qualitative change in infancy is the change from expressing newborn reflexes to the loss of these reflexes across the first year of life.

Finally, although we have focused heavily on perceptual growth in this chapter, we should remember that development is a holistic enterprise and that a child's maturing perceptual abilities influence all aspects of development. Take intellectual development, for example. As we will see in Chapter 7, Jean Piaget argued that all the intellectual advances of the first 2 years spring from the infant's sensory and motor activities. How else, he asked, could infants ever come to understand the properties of objects without being able to see, hear, or smell them, to fondle them, or to hold them in their mouths? How could infants ever use language without first perceiving meaningful regularities in the speech they hear? So Piaget (and many others) claim that perception is central to everything—there is nothing we do (consciously, at least) that is not influenced by our interpretation of the world around us.

SUMMARY

- **Sensation:** the detection of sensory stimulation
- **Perception:** the interpretation of what is sensed

The Newborn's Readiness for Life

- **Survival reflexes** help newborns adapt to their surroundings and satisfy basic needs.
- **Primitive reflexes** are not as useful; their disappearance in the first year is a sign that development is proceeding normally.
- Newborns' sleep-waking cycle becomes better organized over the first year:
  - Babies move into and out of six **infant states** in a typical day and spend up to 70 percent of their time sleeping
  - **REM sleep** is characterized by twitches, jerks, and rapid eye movements.
    - **Autostimulation theorists** believe the function of the REM state is to provide infants with necessary stimulation that helps develop the central nervous system.
  - **Sudden infant death syndrome** is a leading cause of infant mortality.
- Crying is the state by which infants communicate distress.
  - A baby may be brain damaged if his cries are shrill and nonrhythmic.
  - Crying diminishes over the first 6 months as the brain matures and caregivers become better at preventing infants' distress.

Research Methods Used to Study the Infant's Sensory and Perceptual Capabilities

- Methods of determining what infants might be sensing or perceiving include:
  - the **preference method**
  - the **habituation method**
  - the **method of evoked potentials**
  - the **high-amplitude sucking method**

Infant Sensory Capabilities

- Hearing:
  - Young infants can hear very well: even newborns can discriminate sounds that differ in loudness, direction, duration and frequency.
  - They already prefer their mother's voice to that of another woman, and are quite sensitive to **phonemic** contrasts in the speech they hear.
  - Even mild hearing losses, such as those associated with **otitis media,** may have adverse developmental effects.
- Taste, smell, and touch:
  - Babies are also born with definite taste preferences, favoring sweets over sour, bitter, or salty substances.
  - They avoid unpleasant smells and soon come to recognize their mothers by odor alone if they are breast-fed.
  - Newborns are also quite sensitive to touch, temperature, and pain
- Vision:
  - Newborns can see patterns and colors and can detect changes in brightness.
  - Their **visual acuity** is poor by adult standards but improves rapidly over the first 6 months.

Visual Perception in Infancy

- Visual perception develops rapidly in the first year:
  - 0 to 2 months: Babies are "stimulus seekers" who prefer to look at moderately complex, high-contrast targets, particularly those that move.
  - 2 to 6 months: Infants begin to explore visual targets more systematically, become increasingly sensitive to movement, and begin to perceive visual forms and recognize familiar faces.
  - 9 to 12 months: Infants can construct forms from the barest of cues.
- Newborns display some **size constancy** but lack stereopsis and are insensitive to pictorial cues to depth; consequently, their spatial perception is immature.
- By the end of the first month, they become more sensitive to kinetic cues and respond to looming objects.
- Infants develop sensitivities to binocular cues (by 3 to 5 months) and pictorial cues (at 6 to 7 months).
  - Experiences through motor developments leads to a fear of heights (as on the **visual cliff**) and to making more accurate judgments about size constancy and other spatial relations.

Intermodal Perception

- Signs that senses are integrated at birth:
  - looking in the direction of sound-producing sources
  - reaching for objects they can see
  - expecting to see the source of sounds or to feel objects for which they are reaching
- **Intermodal perception:**
  - Intermodal perception is the ability to recognize by one sensory modality an object or experience that is already familiar through another modality.
  - Possible once the infant can process through two different senses.

Cultural Influences on Infant Perception

- Influences may involve losing the ability to detect sensory input that has little sociocultural significance.

Basic Learning Processes in Infancy

- **Learning:**
  - a relatively permanent change in behavior
  - results from experience (repetition, practice, study, or observations) rather than from heredity, maturation, or physiological change resulting from injury
- **Habituation:**
  - a process in which infants come to recognize and thus cease responding to stimuli that are presented repeatedly
  - the simplest form of learning
  - may be possible even before birth
  - improves dramatically over the first few months of life
- **Classical conditioning:**
  - A neutral **conditioned stimulus (CS)** is repeatedly paired with an **unconditioned stimulus (UCS)** and, eventually, the CS alone comes to elicit a response called a **conditioned response (CR).**
  - Newborns can be classically conditioned if the responses have survival value, but are less susceptible to this kind of learning than older infants.
- **Operant conditioning:**
  - The subject first emits a response and then associates this action with a particular outcome.
- **Observational learning:**
  - This occurs as the observer attends to a model and constructs symbolic representations of its behavior.
  - These symbolic codes are stored in memory and may be retrieved at a later date to guide the child's attempts to imitate the behavior he or she has witnessed.
  - Infants become better at imitating social models and may even display **deferred imitation** by the end of the first year.
  - Improvement enables children to rapidly acquire many new habits by attending to social models.

KEY TERMS

sensation 159
perception 159
sudden infant death syndrome (SIDS) 163
preference method 166
habituation 167
dishabituation 167
evoked potential 168
high-amplitude sucking method 168
phonemes 170
otitis media 171
visual acuity 173
visual contrast 173
size constancy 177
visual cliff 178
intermodal perception 179
perceptual learning 183
learning 183
classical conditioning 185
conditioned stimulus (CS) 185
conditioned response (CR) 185
unconditioned stimulus (UCS) 185
operant conditioning 186
observational learning 188
encoding 188
deferred imitation 189

MEDIA RESOURCES

The Human Development Book Companion Website

See the companion website http://www.thomsonedu.com/psychology/shaffer for flashcards, practice quiz questions, Internet links, updates, critical thinking exercises, discussion forums, and more

Thomson NOW! http://www.thomsonedu.com
Go to this site for the link to ThomsonNOW, your one-stop shop. Take a pre-test for this chapter, and ThomsonNOW will generate a personalized study plan based on your test results. The study plan will identify the topics you need to review and direct you to online resources to help you master those topics. You can then take a post-test to help you determine the concepts you have mastered and what you will still need to work on.

Child and Adolescent Development CD-ROM

For more information about the concepts covered in this chapter, go to

Module I: Physical Development

- Physical Development During Infancy
- Module I Media

Module II: Cognition, Language, and Learning

- Learning

Anne Ackermann/Getty Images

CHAPTER

6 Physical Development: The Brain, Body, Motor Skills, and Sexual Development

"My, my, she is already walking! What a smart little girl!"

"Look at you go. Oops, fall down, go boom!"

"Get your rest, little guy, it will help you grow big and strong."

"He's growing like a weed—and his arms are too long!"

"Only 11 and she's got her period! What's the world coming to!"

"All that girl thinks about is boys!"

Have you ever heard adults make these kinds of statements about developing children and adolescents? Few aspects of development are more interesting to the casual observer than the rapid transformation of a seemingly dependent and immobile little baby into a running, jumping bundle of energy who grows and changes at what may seem to be an astounding pace, and who may one day surpass the physical stature of his or her parents. Those physical changes that many find so fascinating are the subject of this chapter.

We will begin by focusing on the changes that occur in the body, the brain, and motor skills throughout childhood. Then we will consider the impact of puberty—both the dramatic physical changes that adolescents experience and their social and psychological impacts. Finally, we will close by discussing the factors that influence physical growth and development throughout the first 20 years of life.

Having experienced most (if not all) of the changes covered in this chapter, you may assume that you know quite a bit about physical development. Yet students often discover that there is much they *don't* know. To check your own knowledge, take a minute to decide whether the following statements are true or false:

1. Babies who walk early are inclined to be especially bright.
2. The average 2-year-old is already about half of his/her adult height.
3. Half the nerve cells (neurons) in the average baby's brain die (and are not replaced) over the first few years of life.
4. Most children walk when they are ready, and no amount of encouragement will enable a 6-month-old to walk alone.
5. Hormones have little effect on human growth and development until puberty.
6. Emotional trauma can seriously impair the growth of young children, even those who are adequately nourished, free from illness, and not physically abused.

Answers to pretest: 1. F; 2. T; 3. T; 4. T; 5. F; 6. T

Jot down your responses and we will see how you did on this "pretest" as we discuss these issues throughout the chapter. (If you would like immediate feedback, the correct answers appear at the bottom of the page).

An Overview of Maturation and Growth

Adults are often amazed at how quickly children grow. Even tiny babies don't remain tiny for long. In the first few months of life, they gain nearly an ounce each day and an inch each month. Yet the dramatic increases in height and weight that we see are accompanied by a number of important *internal* developments in the muscles, bones, and central nervous system that will largely determine the physical feats that children are capable of performing at different ages. In this section of the chapter, we will briefly chart the course of physical development from birth through adolescence and see that there is a clear relationship between the external aspects of growth that are so noticeable and the internal changes that are much harder to detect.

Changes in Height and Weight

Babies grow very rapidly during the first 2 years, often doubling their birth weight by 4 to 6 months of age and tripling it (to about 21 to 22 pounds) by the end of the first year. Growth is very uneven in infancy. One study found that babies may remain the same length for days or weeks at a time before showing spurts of more than a centimeter in a single day (Lampl, Veldhuis, & Johnson, 1992). By age 2, toddlers are already half their eventual adult height and have quadrupled their birth weight to 27 to 30 pounds. If children continued to grow at this rapid pace until age 18, they would stand at about 12 feet, 3 inches and weigh several tons!

From age 2 until puberty, children gain about 2 to 3 inches in height and 6 to 7 pounds in weight each year. During middle childhood (ages 6 to 11), children may seem to grow very little; over an entire year, gains of 2 inches and 6 pounds are hard to detect on a child who stands 4 to 4½ feet tall and weighs 60 to 80 pounds (Eichorn, 1979). But as shown in Figure 6.1, physical growth and development are once again obvious at puberty, when adolescents enter a 2- to 3-year growth spurt, during which they may post an annual gain of 10 to 15 pounds and 2 to 4 inches in height. After this large growth spurt, there are typically small increases in height until full adult stature is attained in the mid to late teens (Tanner, 1990).

cephalocaudal development
a sequence of physical maturation and growth that proceeds from the head (cephalic region) to the tail (or caudal region).

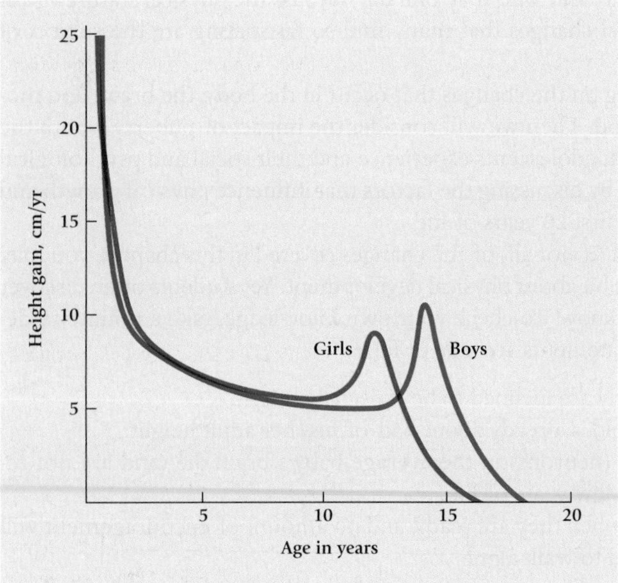

Figure 6.1 Gain in height per year by males and females from birth through adolescence. At about age 10½, girls begin their growth spurt. Boys follow some 2½ years later and grow faster than girls once their growth begins. *Based on a figure in* Archives of the Diseases in Childhood, 41, *by J.M. Tanner, R.H. Whithouse, and A. Takaishi, 1966, pp. 454–471.*

Changes in Body Proportions

To a casual observer, newborns may appear to be "all head"—and for good reason. The newborn's head is already 70 percent of its eventual adult size and represents one-quarter of total body length, the same fraction as the legs.

As a child grows, body shape rapidly changes (see Figure 6.2). Development proceeds in a **cephalocaudal** (head downward) direction. The trunk grows fastest during the first year. At 1 year of age, a child's head now accounts for only 20 percent of total body length. From the child's first birthday until the adolescent growth spurt, the legs grow rapidly, accounting

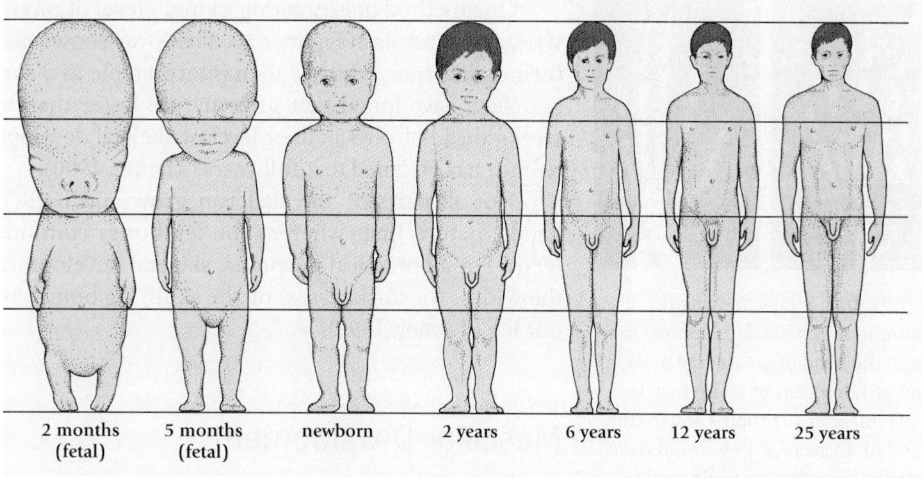

Figure 6.2 Proportions of the human body from the fetal period through adulthood. The head represents 50 percent of body length at 2 months after conception but only 12 to 13 percent of adult stature. In contrast, the legs constitute about 12 to 13 percent of the total length of a 2-month-old fetus, but 50 percent of the height of a 25-year-old adult.

for more than 60 percent of the increase in height (Eichorn, 1979). During adolescence the trunk once again becomes the fastest-growing segment of the body, although the legs are also growing rapidly at this time. When we reach our eventual adult stature, our legs will account for 50 percent of total height and our heads only 12 percent.

proximodistal development
a sequence of physical maturation and growth that proceeds from the center of the body (the proximal region) to the extremities (distal regions).

While children grow upward, they are also growing outward in a **proximodistal** (center outward) direction (Kohler & Rigby, 2003). During prenatal development, for example, the chest and internal organs form first, followed by the arms and legs, then the hands and feet. Throughout infancy and childhood, the arms and legs continue to grow faster than the hands and feet. However, this center-outward growth pattern reverses just before puberty, when the hands and feet begin to grow rapidly and become the first body parts to reach adult proportions, followed by the arms and legs and, finally, the trunk. One reason teenagers often appear so clumsy or awkward is that their hands and feet (and later their arms and legs) may suddenly seem much too large for the rest of their bodies (Tanner, 1990).

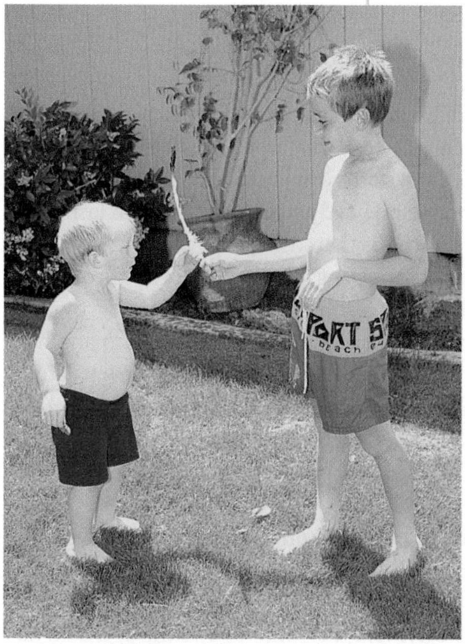

Body proportions change rapidly over the first few years as chubby toddlers become long-legged children.

Skeletal Development

The skeletal structures that form during the prenatal period are initially soft cartilage that will gradually ossify (harden) into bony material. At birth, most of the infant's bones are soft, pliable, and difficult to break. One reason that newborns cannot sit up or balance themselves when pulled to a standing position is that their bones are too small and too flexible.

The neonate's skull consists of several soft bones that can be compressed to allow the child to pass through the cervix and the birth canal, making childbirth easier for the mother and the baby. These skull bones are separated by six soft spots, or *fontanelles,* that are gradually filled in by minerals to form a single skull by age 2, with pliable points at the seams where skull bones join. These seams, or *sutures,* allow the skull to expand as the brain grows larger.

Other parts of the body—namely the ankles and feet and the wrists and hands—develop more (rather than fewer) bones as the child matures. In Figure 6.3, we see that the wrist and hand bones of a 1-year-old are both fewer and less interconnected than the corresponding skeletal equipment of an adolescent.

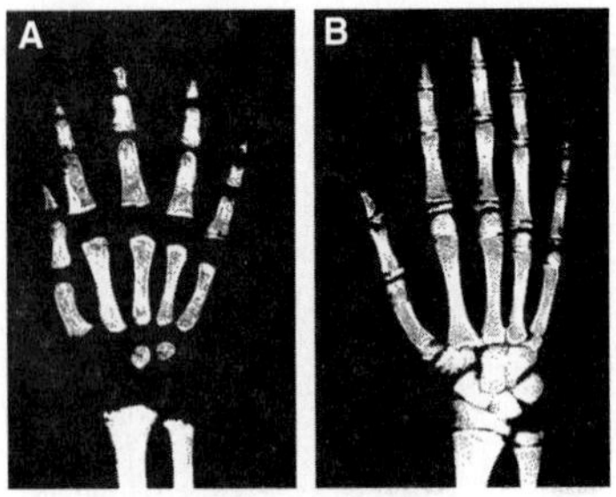

Figure 6.3 X-rays showing the amount of skeletal development seen in (a) the hand of an average male infant at 12 months or an average female infant at 10 months and (b) the hand of an average 13-year-old male or an average 10½-year-old female.

One method of estimating a child's level of physical maturation is to X-ray his or her wrist and hand (as in Figure 6.3). The X-ray shows the number of bones and the extent of their ossification, which is then interpretable as a **skeletal age.** Using this technique, researchers have found that girls mature faster than boys. At birth, girls are only 4 to 6 weeks ahead of boys in their level of skeletal development; but by age 12, the gender difference has widened to 2 full years (Tanner, 1990).

Not all parts of the skeleton grow and harden at the same rate. The skull and hands mature first, whereas the leg bones continue to develop until the mid to late teens. For all practical purposes, skeletal development is complete by age 18, although the widths (or thicknesses) of the skull, leg bones, and hands increase slightly throughout life (Tanner, 1990).

skeletal age
a measure of physical maturation based on the child's level of skeletal development.

Muscular Development

Newborns are born with all the muscle fibers they will ever have (Tanner, 1990). At birth, muscle tissue is 35 percent water, and it accounts for no more than 18 to 24 percent of a baby's body weight (Marshall, 1977). However, muscle fibers soon begin to grow as the cellular fluid in muscle tissue is bolstered by the addition of protein and salts.

Muscular development proceeds in cephalocaudal and proximodistal directions, with muscles in the head and neck maturing before those in the trunk and limbs. Like many other aspects of physical development, the maturation of muscle tissue occurs very gradually over childhood and then accelerates during early adolescence. One consequence of this muscular growth spurt is that members of both sexes become noticeably stronger, although increases in both muscle mass and physical strength (as measured in tests of large-muscle activity) are more dramatic for boys than for girls (Malina, 1990). By the mid-20s, skeletal muscle accounts for 40 percent of the body weight of an average male, compared with 24 percent for the average female.

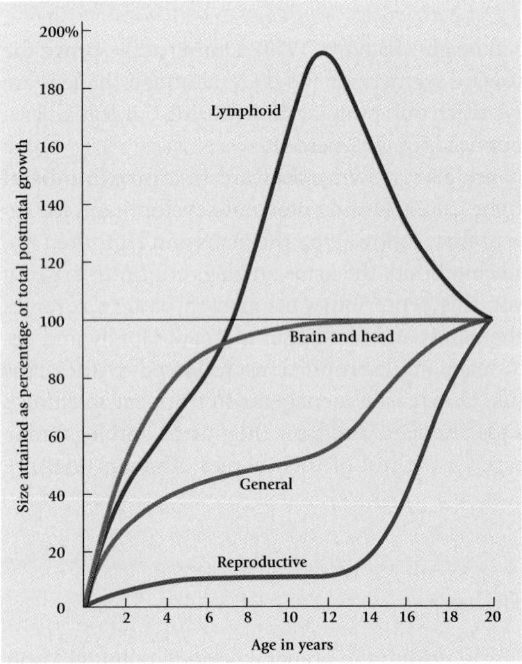

Figure 6.4 Growth curves for different body systems. Each curve plots the size of a group of organs or body parts as a percentage of their size at age 20 (which is the 100 percent level on the vertical scale). The "general" curve describes changes in the body's size as well as the growth of respiratory and digestive organs and musculature. The brain and head grow more rapidly than the body in general, and the reproductive organs are the slowest to reach adult size. (The lymph nodes and other parts of the lymphoid system, which function as part of the immune system, also grow rapidly and actually exceed adult size during late childhood and adolescence.) *From* Growth at Adolescence, *2nd ed., by J. M. Tanner, 1962. Oxford, England: Blackwell. Copyright © 1962 by Blackwell Scientific Publications, Inc. Reprinted by permission of Blackwell Science, Ltd.*

Variations in Physical Development

To this point, we have been discussing sequences of physical growth that all humans display. However, physical development is a very uneven process in which different bodily systems display unique growth patterns. As we see in Figure 6.4, the brain and head actually grow much faster and are quicker to reach adult proportions than the rest of the body, whereas the genitals and other reproductive organs grow very slowly throughout childhood and develop rapidly in adolescence. Notice also that growth of the lymph tissues—which make up part of the immune system and help children to fight off infections—actually overshoots adult levels late in childhood, before declining rapidly in adolescence.

Individual Variations

Not only is the development of body systems an uneven or asynchronous process, but there are sizable individual variations in the rates at which children grow (Kohler & Rigby, 2003). Look carefully at the photo on p. 199. These two boys are the same age, although one has already reached puberty and looks much older. As we will see later in the chapter, two grade-school friends might begin the pubertal transition from child to adult as much as 5 years apart!

© Novastock/PhotoEdit

There are large individual variations in the timing of the adolescent growth spurt as we see in comparing the stature of these two boys of the same age.

Cultural Variations

Finally, there are meaningful cultural and subcultural variations in physical growth and development. As a rule, people from Asia, South America, and Africa tend to be smaller than North Americans, Northern Europeans, and Australians. In addition, there are cultural differences in the *rate* of physical growth. Asian-American and African-American children, for example, tend to mature faster than European-American and European children (Berkey et al., 1994; Herman-Giddens et al., 1997).

What accounts for these variations in growth? Current thinking is that asynchronies in the maturation of different body systems are built in to our species heredity—that is, the common maturational program that all humans share (Tanner, 1990). And later in the chapter, we will see that heredity, in concert with such environmental factors as the food people eat, the diseases they may encounter, and even the emotional climate in which they live, can produce significant variations in the rates at which they grow and the statures they attain (Kohler & Rigby, 2003).

Development of the Brain

The brain grows at an astounding rate early in life, increasing from 25 percent of its eventual adult weight at birth to 75 percent of adult weight by age 2. Indeed, the last 3 prenatal months and the first 2 years after birth have been termed the period of the **brain growth spurt** because more than half of one's adult brain weight is added at this time (Glaser, 2000). Between the seventh prenatal month and a child's first birthday, the brain increases in weight by about 1.7 grams a day, or more than a milligram per minute.

brain growth spurt
the period between the seventh prenatal month and 2 years of age when more than half of the child's eventual brain weight is added.

However, an increase in brain weight is a general index that tells us very little about how or when various parts of the brain mature and affect other aspects of development. Let's take a closer look at the internal organization and development of the brain.

Neural Development and Plasticity

The human brain and nervous system consists of more than a trillion highly specialized cells that work together to transmit electrical and chemical signals across many trillions of **synapses,** or connective spaces between the cells (see Figure 6.5). **Neurons** are the basic unit of the brain and nervous system—the cells that receive and transmit neural impulses. Neurons are produced in the neural tube of the developing embryo. From there, they migrate along pathways laid down by a network of *guiding cells* to form the major parts of the brain. The vast majority of the neurons a person will ever have—some 100 to 200 billion of them—have already formed by the end of the second trimester of pregnancy, before the brain growth spurt has even begun (Kolb & Fantie, 1989; Rakic, 1991). Until recently, it was thought that no new neurons were produced after a baby was born. However, scientists have established that formation of new neurons in the hippocampus (an area of the brain important to learning and memory) occurs throughout life (Kemperman & Gage, 1999).

synapse
the connective space (juncture) between one nerve cell (neuron) and another.

neurons
nerve cells that receive and transmit neural impulses.

What, then, accounts for the brain growth spurt? One major contributor is the development of a second type of nerve cell, called **glia,** which nourish the neurons and eventually encase them in insulating sheaths of a waxy substance called *myelin.* Glia are far more numerous than neurons are, and they continue to form throughout life (Tanner, 1990).

glia
nerve cells that nourish neurons and encase them in insulating sheaths of myelin.

Neural Development: Cell Differentiation and Synaptogenesis

Influenced by the sites to which they migrate, neurons assume specialized functions—as cells of the visual or auditory areas of the brain, for example. If a neuron that would normally migrate to the visual area of the brain is instead transplanted to the area that

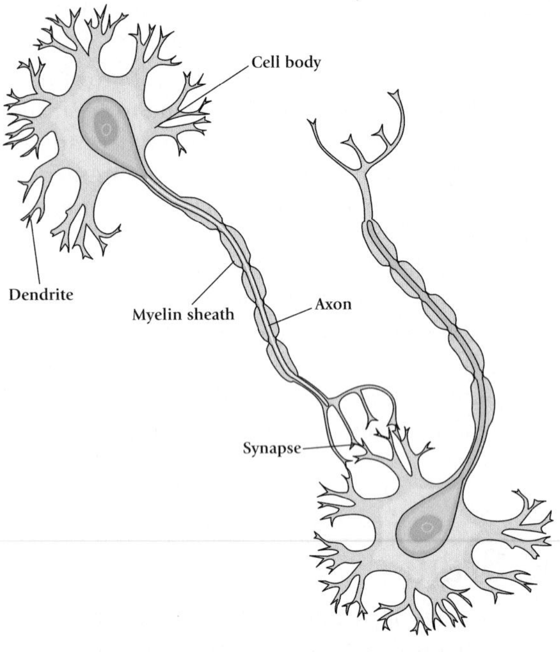

Figure 6.5 Two neurons forming a synapse. A synapse between neurons links the axon of one to the dendrites of the other. When the first neuron is activated, it releases neurotransmitters that stimulate (or inhibit) electrical activity in the second neuron. *From "Is there a neural basis for cognitive transitions in school-age children?" by J. Janowsky and R. Carper in A. J. Samaroff & M. M. Haith (Eds.),* The 5–7 Year Shift: Age of Reason & Response, *pp. 33–56. Copyright © 1996 by the University of Chicago Press. Used with permission.*

controls hearing, it will change to become an auditory neuron instead of a visual neuron (Johnson, 1998, 2005). So individual neurons have the potential to serve any neural function, and the function each serves depends on where it ends up.

Meanwhile, the process of **synaptogenesis**—the formation of synaptic connections among neurons—is proceeding rapidly during the brain growth spurt. This brings us to an intriguing fact about the developing nervous system: the average infant has far more neurons and neural connections than adults do (Elkind, 2001). The reason is that neurons that successfully interconnect with other neurons crowd out those that don't, so that about half the neurons produced early in life also die early in life (Elkind, 2001; Janowsky & Finlay, 1986). Meanwhile, surviving neurons form hundreds of synapses, many of which will disappear if the neuron is not properly stimulated (Huttenlocher, 1994). If we likened the developing brain to a house under construction, we might imagine a builder who merrily constructs many more rooms and hallways than he needs, and then later goes back and knocks about half of them out!

What is happening here reflects the remarkable **plasticity** of the young infant's brain—the fact that its cells are highly responsive to the effects of experience (Stiles, 2000). As William Greenough and his colleagues (1987) explain, the brain has evolved so that it produces an excess of neurons and synapses in preparation for receiving any and all kinds of sensory and motor stimulation that a human being could conceivably experience. Of course, no human being has this broad a range of experiences, so much of one's neural circuitry remains unused. Presumably, then, neurons and synapses that are most often stimulated continue to function. Other surviving neurons that are stimulated less often lose their synapses (a process called *synaptic pruning*) and stand in reserve to compensate for brain injuries or to support new skills (Elkind, 2001; Huttenlocher, 1994). Note the implication then: the development of the brain early in life is not due entirely to the unfolding of a maturational program. It is the result of both a biological program and early experience (Greenough, Black, & Wallace, 1987; Johnson, 1998, 2005).

Neural Plasticity: The Role of Experience

How do we know that early experience plays such a dramatic role in the development of the brain and central nervous system? The first clue came from research by Austin Riesen and his colleagues (Riesen, 1947; Riesen et al., 1951). Riesen's subjects were infant chimpanzees that were reared in the dark for periods ranging up to 16 months. His results were striking. Dark-reared chimps experienced atrophy of the retina and the neurons that make up the optic nerve. This atrophy was reversible if the animal's visual deprivation did not exceed 7 months, but was irreversible and often led to total blindness if the deprivation lasted longer than a year. So neurons that are not properly stimulated will degenerate (Elkind, 2001; Rapoport et al., 2001).

Might we then foster the neural development of an immature, maleable brain by exposing participants to enriched environments that provide a wide variety of stimulation? Absolutely. Animals raised with lots of companions and many toys to play with have brains that are heavier and display more extensive networks of neural connections than those of littermates raised under standard laboratory conditions (Greenough & Black, 1992; Rosenzweig, 1984). What's more, the brains of animals raised in stimulating environments lose some of their complexity if the animals are moved to less stimulating quarters (Thompson, 1993).

In one human study, head circumference, a rough indicator of brain size, was assessed in 221 children at a gestational age of 18 weeks, again at birth, and finally at 9 years of age. The head circumferences of children from high socioeconomic status (SES)

synaptogenesis
formation of connections (synapses) among neurons.

plasticity
capacity for change; a developmental state that has the potential to be shaped by experience.

homes, and those whose mothers had earned college degrees, were significantly larger than the head circumferences of children from low SES homes and whose mothers had no degrees (Gale et al., 2004). So, even though genes may provide rough guidelines as to how the brain should be configured, early experience largely determines the brain's specific architecture (Rapoport et al., 2001).

Brain Differentiation and Growth

Not all parts of the brain develop at the same rate. At birth, the most highly developed areas are the lower (subcortical) brain centers, which control states of consciousness, inborn reflexes, and vital biological functions such as digestion, respiration, and elimination. Surrounding these structures are the *cerebrum* and *cerebral cortex,* the areas most directly implicated in voluntary bodily movements, perception, and higher intellectual activities such as learning, thinking, and language. The first areas of the cerebrum to mature are the *primary motor areas* (which control simple motor activities such as waving the arms), and the *primary sensory areas* (which control sensory processes such as vision, hearing, smelling, and tasting). Thus, one reason human neonates are reflexive, "sensory-motor" beings is that only the sensory and motor areas of the cortex are functioning well at birth. By 6 months of age, the primary motor areas of the cerebral cortex have developed to the point that they now direct most of the infant's movements. Inborn responses such as the palmar grasp and the Babinski reflex should have disappeared by now, thus indicating that the higher cortical centers are assuming proper control over the more primitive subcortical areas of the brain.

Myelinization

As brain cells proliferate and grow, some of the glia begin to produce a waxy substance called *myelin,* which forms a sheath around individual neurons. This myelin sheath acts like an insulator to speed up the transmission of neural impulses, allowing the brain to communicate more efficiently with different parts of the body.

myelinization
the process by which neurons are enclosed in waxy myelin sheaths that will facilitate the transmission of neural impulses.

Myelinization follows a definite chronological sequence that is consistent with the maturation of the rest of the nervous system. At birth or shortly thereafter, the pathways between the sense organs and the brain are reasonably well myelinated. As a result, the neonate's sensory equipment is in good working order. As neural pathways between the brain and the skeletal muscles myelinate (in a cephalocaudal and proximodistal pattern), the child becomes capable of increasingly complex motor activities such as lifting its head and chest, reaching with its arms and hands, rolling over, sitting, standing, and eventually walking and running. Although myelinization proceeds very rapidly over the first few years of life (Herschkowitz, 2000), some areas of the brain are not completely myelinated until the mid to late teens or early adulthood (Fischer & Rose, 1995; Kennedy et al., 2002; Rapoport et al., 2001; Sowell et al., 1999). For example, the *reticular formation* and the *frontal cortex*—parts of the brain that allow us to concentrate on a subject for lengthy periods—are not fully myelinated at puberty (Tanner, 1990). This may be one reason that the attention spans of infants, toddlers, and school-age children are much shorter than those of adolescents and adults.

In addition, as myelinization enhances the efficiency between the more primitive, emotive subcortical areas of the brain and the more regulatory prefrontal cortical areas of the brain, an infant or child's ability to process and respond to socially important emotional input—such as the expressions of fear or disapproval on a parent's face—may improve. As well, a child's ability to monitor his or her own emotional reactions increases (Herba & Phillips, 2004). For example, in a rush to grab the next present, a 3- or 4-year-old may quickly discard a disappointing birthday gift, such as clothing, whereas a 6-year-old may pause and give a polite "thank you" to Grandma, thus managing to mask disappointment and delay the gratification of exploring the next, more desirable gift. A teenager may display an even more complex inhibition pattern—smiling politely when a gift of unfashionable clothing is received from Grandma, and scowling and protesting when a similar fashion *faux pas* is passed along from Mom (who should know better).

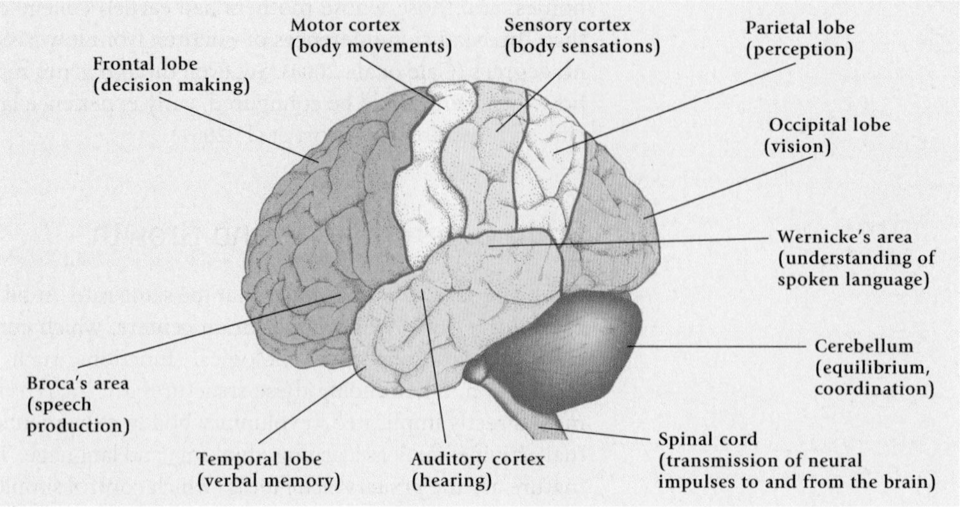

Figure 6.6 Lateral view of the left cerebral cortex and some of the functions that it controls. Although the cerebellum and spinal cord ar not part of the cerebral cortex, they serve important functions of their own.

Cerebral Lateralization

cerebrum
the highest brain center; includes both hemispheres of the brain and the fibers that connect them.

corpus callosum
the bundle of neural fibers that connects the two hemispheres of the brain and transmits information from one hemisphere to the other.

cerebral cortex
the outer layer of the brain's cerebrum that is involved in voluntary body movements, perception, and higher intellectual functions such as learning, thinking, and speaking.

cerebral lateralization
the specialization of brain functions in the left and the right cerebral hemispheres.

The highest brain center, the **cerebrum,** consists of two halves (or *hemispheres*) connected by a band of fibers called the **corpus callosum.** Each of the hemispheres is covered by a **cerebral cortex**—an outer layer of gray matter that controls sensory and motor processes, perception, and intellectual functioning. Although identical in appearance, the left and right cerebral hemispheres serve different functions and control different areas of the body. The left cerebral hemisphere controls the right side of the body, and, as illustrated in Figure 6.6, it contains centers for speech, hearing, verbal memory, decision making, language processing, and expression of positive emotions. The right cerebral hemisphere, on the other hand, controls the left side of the body and contains centers for processing visual-spatial information, nonlinguistic sounds such as music, tactile (touch) sensations, and expressing negative emotions (Fox et al., 1995). Thus, the brain is a *lateralized* organ. **Cerebral lateralization** also involves a preference for using one hand or one side of the body more than the other. About 90 percent of adults rely on their right hands (or left hemispheres) to write, eat, and perform other motor functions, whereas these same activities are under the control of the right hemisphere among most people who are left-handed. However, the fact that the brain is a lateralized organ does not mean that each hemisphere is totally independent of the other; the corpus callosum, which connects the hemispheres, plays an important role in integrating their respective functions.

When do the two cerebral hemispheres begin to become lateralized? Brain lateralization may originate during the prenatal period and be well under way at birth (Kinsbourne, 1989). For example, about two-thirds of all fetuses end up positioned in the womb with their right ears facing outward, and it is thought that this gives them a right ear advantage and illustrates the left hemisphere's specialization in language processing (Previc, 1991). From the first day of life, speech sounds stimulate more electrical activity in the left side of the cerebral cortex than in the right (Molfese, 1977). In addition, most newborns turn to the right rather than to the left when they lie on their backs, and these same babies later tend to reach for objects with their right hands (Kinsbourne, 1989). So it seems that the two cerebral hemispheres may be biologically programmed to assume different functions and have already begun to differentiate by the time a baby is born (Kinsbourne, 1989; Witelson, 1987).

However, the brain is not completely specialized at birth; throughout childhood we come to rely more and more on one particular hemisphere or the other to serve particular functions. Consider, for example, that even though left- or right-handedness is apparent early and is reasonably well established by age 2, lateral preferences become stronger with age. In one experiment, preschoolers and adolescents were asked to pick up a crayon, kick a ball, look into a small, opaque bottle, and place an ear to a box to hear a sound. Only 32 percent of the preschoolers, but more than half of the adolescents, showed a consistent lateral preference by relying exclusively on one side of the body to perform all four tasks (Coren, Porac, & Duncan, 1981).

Because the immature brain is not completely specialized, young children often show a remarkable ability to bounce back from traumatic brain injuries as neural circuits that might otherwise have been lost assume the functions of those that have died (Kolb & Fantie, 1989; Rakic, 1991). Although adolescents and adults who suffer brain damage often regain a substantial portion of the functions they have lost, especially with proper therapy, their recoveries are rarely as rapid or as complete as those of younger children (Kolb & Fantie, 1989). So the remarkable recuperative power of the human brain (that is, its plasticity) is greatest early in life, before cerebral lateralization is complete.

Development of the Brain During Adolescence

Through the ages, adults have noticed that when children reach the teenage years, they suddenly begin to ask hypothetical "what if" questions and to ponder weighty abstractions such as truth and justice. Are these changes in thinking tied to late developments in the brain?

Many researchers now believe that they are (Case, 1992; Somsen et al., 1997). For example, myelinization of the higher brain centers, which continues well into adolescence, may not only increase adolescents' attention spans, but also explains why they process information much faster than grade-school children (Kail, 1991; Rapoport et al., 2001). Furthermore, we now know that the brain retains at least some of its plasticity well beyond puberty (Nelson & Bloom, 1997), and that reorganizations of the neural circuitry of the *prefrontal cortex,* which is involved in such higher-level cognitive activities as strategic planning, continues until at least age 20 (Spreen, Risser, & Edgell, 1995; Stuss, 1992). Additionally, brain volume increases through early- to mid-adolescence and then decreases during late adolescence, suggesting that some pubertal reorganizations may involve synaptic pruning (Rapoport et al., 2001; Kennedy et al., 2002). So, even though changes in the brain during adolescence are less dramatic than those earlier in life, it is likely that some of the cognitive advances that teenagers display become possible only after their brains undergo a process of reorganization and specialization (Barry et al., 2002, 2005).

CONCEPT CHECK 6.1 Overview of Physical Development and Brain Development

Check your understanding of general trends in maturation and growth and the development of the brain by answering the following questions. Answers appear in the Appendix.

Multiple Choice: Select the best alternative for each question.

_____ 1. The fact that a newborn's head is 70 percent of its adult size and a full half of its body length is best explained by which concept of development?
   a. the skeletal age trend
   b. the cephalocaudal trend
   c. the proximodistal trend
   d. the fontenelle trend

_____ 2. Which of the following body parts actually *overshoots* adult levels in childhood and then declines to adult levels later in adolescence?
   a. the head and brain
   b. the muscular system
   c. the lymphoid system
   d. the skeletal system

_____ 3. The basic unit of the brain and nervous system are the cells that receive and transmit neural impulses. These cells are called
   a. glia cells
   b. neurons
   c. myelin
   d. synapses

CONTINUED

_____ 4. Scientists believe that the human brain has evolved so that the infant brain can be highly responsive to the effects of experience. The brain is thought to produce an excess of neurons and synapses so that it can be responsive to many different kinds of sensory and motor stimulation. This responsiveness also results in synaptic and neural degeneration when the neurons that are not stimulated do not continue to function. This aspect of brain development is termed
   a. plasticity
   b. myelinization
   c. cerebral cortexification
   d. cerebral lateralization

_____ 5. Gretchen is having a baby. She learned that brain lateralization may occur during the prenatal period and be well under way at birth. This understanding led her to fully expect the positioning of her fetus when it was examined with ultrasound. Like two-thirds of all fetuses, her fetus was positioned in her womb
   a. with its left ear facing outward
   b. with its right ear facing outward
   c. with its ears facing upward
   d. with its ears facing downward

True or False: Indicate whether each of the following statements is true or false.

6. (T)(F) At birth, an infant's bones are very stiff and brittle and easy to break.
7. (T)(F) Individual neurons have the potential to serve any neural function, depending on where their migration delivers them.
8. (T)(F) Very few neurons produced early in life die; instead, they are adapted for different functions in the nervous system.
9. (T)(F) Although the brain is lateralized at birth, lateral preferences continue to become stronger across age through adolescence.

Short Answer: Briefly answer the following question.

10. Explain the ways in which the development of the brain and nervous system help us to understand why babies are reflexive, "sensory-motor" beings at birth.

Motor Development

One of the more dramatic developments of the first year of life is the remarkable progress that infants make in controlling their movements and perfecting motor skills. Writers are fond of describing newborns as "helpless babes"—a characterization that largely stems from the neonate's inability to move about on her own. Clearly, human infants are disadvantaged when compared with the young of other species, who can follow their mothers to food (and then feed themselves) very soon after birth.

However, babies do not remain immobile for long. By the end of the first month, the brain and neck muscles have matured enough to permit most infants to reach the first milestone in locomotor development: lifting their chins while lying flat on their stomachs. Soon thereafter, children lift their chests as well, reach for objects, roll over, and sit up if someone supports them. Investigators who have charted motor development over the first 2 years find that motor skills evolve in a definite sequence, which appears in Table 6.1. Although the ages at which these skills first appear vary considerably from child to child, infants who are quick to proceed through this motor sequence are not necessarily any brighter or otherwise advantaged, compared with those whose rates of motor development are average or slightly below average. Thus, even though the age norms in Table 6.1 are a useful standard for gauging an infant's progress as he or she begins to sit, stand, and take those first tentative steps, a child's rate of motor development really tells us very little about future developmental outcomes.

Basic Trends in Locomotor Development

The two fundamental "laws" that describe muscular development and myelinization also hold true for motor development during the first few years. Motor development proceeds in a *cephalocaudal* (head-downward) direction, with activities involving the head, neck,

TABLE 6.1 Age Norms (in Months) for Important Motor Developments (Based on European American, Latino, and African American Children in the United States)

Skill	Month when 50% of infants have mastered the skill	Month when 90% of infants have mastered the skill
Lifts head 90° while lying on stomach	2.2	3.2
Rolls over	2.8	4.7
Sits propped up	2.9	4.2
Sits without support	5.5	7.8
Stands holding on	5.8	10.0
Crawls	7.0	9.0
Walks holding on	9.2	12.7
Plays pat-a-cake	9.3	15.0
Stands alone momentarily	9.8	13.0
Stands well alone	11.5	13.9
Walks well	12.1	14.3
Builds tower of two cubes	13.8	19.0
Walks up steps	17.0	22.0
Kicks ball forward	20.0	24.0

Sources: Bayley, 1993; Frankenberg & Dodds, 1967.

and upper extremities preceding those involving the legs and lower extremities. At the same time, development is *proximodistal* (center-outward), with activities involving the trunk and shoulders appearing before those involving the hands and fingers. The kicking movements displayed by infants during the first few months present a problem for the cephalocaudal perspective and are usually dismissed as unintentional movements generated by the central nervous system (Lamb & Yang, 2000). However, Galloway and Thelen (2004) present evidence that contradicts the "cephalocaudal rule." First they point to evidence demonstrating that infants alter the pattern of their leg movements when rewarded. For example, when rewarded, infants change from alternating leg kicks to simultaneous kicks (Thelen, 1994), as well as from flexed leg movements to extended leg movements (Angulo-Kinzler, 2001; Angulo-Kinzler, Ulrich, & Thelen, 2002). They note that even Piaget (1952) noticed that his son repeated leg kicks that shook a toy. Finally, Galloway and Thelen (2004) presented six infants with toys at both foot and hand level. The infants first made contact with the toy at around 12 weeks and did so by lifting a leg to touch the toy. First contact with hands was made at around 16 weeks, much later than the intentional foot contact. Extended contact with their feet also preceded extended contact with their hands. Galloway and Thelen suggest that the structure of the hip joint may contribute to infants' early ability to control their legs because the hip joint is more stable and constrained than the shoulder joint. Therefore the amount of motion to be controlled is much smaller for the hip joint than for the shoulder joint. Control of the shoulder joint may call for much more experience, practice, and activity to master. Therefore, infants are able to coordinate hip movement earlier than shoulder movement, contradicting the cephalocaudal rule-of-thumb.

How do we explain the sequencing and timing of early motor development? Let's briefly consider three possibilities: the *maturational viewpoint,* the *experiential* (or practice) *hypothesis,* and a newer *dynamical systems theory* that views motor development (and the whole of development) as a product of a complex transaction among the child's physical capabilities, goals, and the experiences she has had (Kenrick, 2001; Thelen, 1995).

The Maturational Viewpoint

The maturational viewpoint (Shirley, 1933) describes motor development as the unfolding of a genetically programmed sequence of events in which the nerves and muscles mature in a *downward* and *outward* direction. As a result, children gradually gain more control over the lower and peripheral parts of their bodies, displaying motor skills in the sequence shown in Table 6.1.

One clue that maturation plays a prominent role in motor development comes from cross-cultural research. Despite their very different early experiences, infants from around the world progress through roughly the same sequence of motor milestones. In addition, early studies in which one identical twin was allowed to practice motor skills (such as climbing stairs or stacking blocks) while the co-twin was denied these experiences suggested that practice had little effect on motor development: when finally allowed to perform, the unpracticed twin soon matched the skills of the co-twin who had had many opportunities to practice (Gesell & Thompson, 1929; McGraw, 1935). Taken together, these findings seemed to imply that maturation underlies motor development and that practice merely allows a child to perfect those skills that maturation has made possible.

The Experiential (or Practice) Hypothesis

Although no one denies that maturation contributes to motor development, proponents of the experiential viewpoint believe that opportunities to practice motor skills are also important. Consider what Wayne Dennis (1960) found when he studied two groups of institutionalized orphans in Iran who had spent most of their first 2 years lying flat on their backs in their cribs. These infants were never placed in a sitting position, were rarely played with, and were even fed in their cribs with their bottles propped on pillows. Was their motor development affected by these depriving early experiences? Indeed it was! None of the 1- to 2-year-olds could walk and less than half of them could even sit unaided. In fact, only 15 percent of the 3- to 4-year-olds could walk well alone! So Dennis concluded that maturation is *necessary but not sufficient* for the development of motor skills. In other words, infants who are physically capable of sitting, crawling, or walking will not be very proficient at these activities unless they have opportunities to practice them.

Not only does a lack of practice inhibit motor development but cross-cultural research illustrates that a variety of enriching experiences can even accelerate the process. Cross-cultural studies tell us that the ages at which infants attain major motor milestones are heavily influenced by parenting practices. The Kipsigis of Kenya, for example, work to promote motor skills. By their eighth week, infants are already practicing their "walking" as parents grasp them by the armpits and propel them forward. Also, throughout their first few months, infants are seated in shallow holes, dug so that the sides support their backs and maintain an upright posture. Given these experiences, it is perhaps not surprising that Kipsigi infants sit unassisted about 5 weeks earlier and walk unaided about a month earlier than Western infants do.

Similarly, Brian Hopkins (1991) has compared the motor development of white infants in England with that of black infants whose families emigrated to England from Jamaica. As in several other comparisons of black and white infants, the black infants displayed such important motor skills as sitting, crawling, and walking at earlier ages. Do these findings reflect genetic differences between blacks and whites? Probably not, because black babies were likely to acquire motor skills early *only* if their mothers had followed traditional Jamaican routines for handling infants and nurturing motor development. These routines include massaging infants, stretching their limbs, and holding them by the arms while gently shaking them up and down. Jamaican mothers expect early motor development, work to promote it, and get it.

Dovetailing nicely with the cross-cultural work are experiments conducted by Philip Zelazo and his associates (1972, 1993) with North American infants. Zelazo found that 2- to 8-week-old babies who were regularly held in an upright posture and encouraged to practice their stepping reflex showed a strengthening of this response (which usually disappears early in life). They also walked at an earlier age than did infants in a control group who did not receive this training.

Why might having one's limbs stretched or being held (or sat) in an upright posture hasten motor development? Esther Thelen's (1986; Thelen & Fisher, 1982) view is that babies who are often placed in an upright position develop strength in the neck, trunk, and legs (an acceleration of muscular growth), which, in turn, promotes the early development of such motor skills as standing and walking. So it seems that both maturation and experience are important contributors to motor development. Maturation does place some limits on the age at which the child will first be capable of sitting, standing, and walking. Yet experiences such as upright posturing and various forms of practice may influence the age at which important maturational capabilities are achieved and translated into action.

Motor Skills as Dynamic, Goal-Directed Systems

dynamical systems theory
a theory that views motor skills as active reorganizations of previously mastered capabilities that are undertaken to find more effective ways of exploring the environment or satisfying other objectives.

Although they would certainly agree that both maturation and experience contribute to motor development, proponents of an exciting new perspective—**dynamical systems theory**—differ from earlier theorists. They do not view motor skills as genetically programmed responses that simply "unfold" as dictated by maturation and opportunities to practice. Instead, they view each new skill as a *construction* that emerges as infants *actively* reorganize existing motor capabilities into new and more complex action systems. At first, these new motor configurations are likely to be tentative, inefficient, and uncoordinated. New walkers, for example, spend a fair amount of time on their backsides and are not called "toddlers" for nothing. But over a period of time, these new motor patterns are modified and refined until all components mesh and become smooth, coordinated actions such as bouncing, crawling, walking, running, and jumping (Thelen, 1995; Whitall & Getchell, 1995).

But why would infants work so hard to acquire new motor skills? Unlike earlier theories that did not address this issue, the dynamical systems theory offers a straightforward answer: Infants hope to acquire and perfect new motor skills that will help them to get to interesting objects they hope to explore or to accomplish other goals they may have in mind (Thelen, 1995). Consider what Eugene Goldfield (1989) learned in studying infants' emerging ability to crawl. Goldfield found that 7- to 8-month-old infants began to crawl on their hands and knees only after they (1) regularly turned and raised their heads toward interesting sights and sounds in the environment, (2) had developed a distinct hand/arm preference when reaching for such stimuli, and (3) had begun to thrust (kick) with the leg opposite to the outstretched arm. Apparently, visual orientation motivates the infant to approach interesting stimuli she can't reach, reaching steers the body in the right direction, and kicking with the opposite leg propels the body forward. So, far from being a preprogrammed skill that simply unfolds according to a maturational plan, crawling (and virtually all other motor skills) actually represents an active and intricate *reorganization* of *several existing capabilities* that is undertaken by a curious, active infant who has a particular *goal* in mind.

H. Bruhat/Rapho/The Liaison Agency

According to dynamical systems theory, new motor skills emerge as curious infants reorganize their existing capabilities in order to achieve important objectives.

Why, then, do all infants proceed through the same general sequence of locomotor milestones? Partly because of their human maturational programming, which sets the stage for various accomplishments, and partly because each successive motor skill must necessarily build on specific component activities that have developed earlier. How does experience fit in? According to the dynamical systems theory, a real world of interesting objects and events provides infants with many reasons to want to reach out or to sit up, crawl, walk, and run—that is, with *purposes* and *motives* that might be served by actively reorganizing their existing skills into new and more complex action systems (Adolph, Vereijken, & Denny, 1998). Of course, no two infants have exactly the same set of experiences (or goals), which may help to explain why each infant coordinates the component activities of an emerging motor skill in a slightly different way (Thelen et al., 1993).

In sum, the development of motor skills is far more interesting and complex than earlier theories had assumed. Though maturation plays a very important role, the basic motor skills of the first 2 years do not simply unfold as part of nature's grand plan. Rather, they emerge largely because goal-driven infants are constantly recombining actions they can perform into new and more complex action systems that will help them to achieve their objectives.

Fine Motor Development

Two other aspects of motor development play especially important roles in helping infants to explore and adapt to their surroundings: *voluntary reaching* and *manipulatory* (or hand) *skills.*

Development of Voluntary Reaching

An infant's ability to reach out and manipulate objects changes dramatically over the first year. Recall that newborns come equipped with a grasping reflex. They are also inclined to reach for things, although these primitive thrusts (or *prereaches*) are really little more than uncoordinated swipes at objects in the visual field. Prereaching is truly a hit-or-miss proposition (Bower, 1982). By 2 months of age, infants' reaching and grasping skills may even seem to deteriorate: the reflexive palmar grasp disappears and prereaching occurs much less often (Bower, 1982). However, these apparent regressions set the stage for the appearance of *voluntary* reaching. Babies 3 months of age and older display this new competency as they extend their arms and make in-flight corrections, gradually improving in accuracy until they can reliably grasp their objectives (Hofsten, 1984; Thelen et al., 1993). However, infants clearly differ in how they reach for objects. Some infants will flap their arms at first and must learn to dampen their enthusiasm, whereas others start off reaching tentatively and will soon learn that they must supply more power to grasp their objectives (Thelen et al., 1993). So, here again, we see that reaching is a motor skill that does not simply "unfold"; instead, babies reach in different ways and take their own unique pathways to refining this important skill.

It was once thought that early reaching required visual guidance of the hand and arm for infants to locate their target. However, research indicates that infants only 3 months old are just as successful at reaching for and grasping objects they can only hear (in the dark) as they are at grabbing those they can see (Clifton et al., 1993). By age 5 months, infants are becoming proficient at reaching for and touching (1) stationary illuminated objects that suddenly darken to become invisible as they begin their reaches (McCarty & Ashmead, 1999), as well as (2) glowing objects that move in the dark (Robin, Berthier, & Clifton, 1996)—even though these young reachers cannot see what their hands are doing. So, far from being totally controlled by vision, early reaches are also dependent on **proprioceptive information** from the muscles, tendons, and joints that help infants to guide their arms and hands to any interesting objects within arm's length.

proprioceptive information
sensory information from the muscles, tendons, and joints that help one to locate the position of one's body (or body parts) in space.

Development of Manipulatory Skills

Once an infant is able to sit well and to reach inward, across her body, at about 4 to 5 months, she begins to grasp interesting objects with *both* hands and her exploratory activities forever change. Rather than merely batting or palming objects, she is now apt to transfer them from hand to hand or to hold them with one hand and finger them with the other (Rochat, 1989; Rochat & Goubet, 1995). Indeed, this fingering activity may be the primary method by which 4- to 6-month-olds gain information about objects, for their unimanual (one-handed) grasping skills are poorly developed: the reflexive palmar grasp has already disappeared by this age, and the **ulnar grasp** that replaces it is itself a rather clumsy, clawlike grip that permits little tactile exploration of objects by touch.

ulnar grasp
an early manipulatory skill in which an infant grasps objects by pressing the fingers against the palm.

During the latter half of the first year, fingering skills improve and infants become much more proficient at tailoring all their exploratory activities to the properties of the objects they are investigating (Palmer, 1989). Now, wheeled toys are likely to be scooted rather than

The pincer grasp is a crucial motor milestone that underlies the development of many coordinated manual activities.

Bruce Plotkin/The Image Works

banged, spongy objects are squeezed rather than scooted, and so on. The next major step in the growth of hand skills occurs near the end of the first year as infants use their thumbs and forefingers to lift and explore objects (Halverson, 1931). This **pincer grasp** transforms the child from a little fumbler into a skillful manipulator who may soon begin to capture crawling bugs and to turn knobs and dials, thereby discovering that he can use his newly acquired hand skills to produce any number of interesting results.

Throughout the second year, infants become much more proficient with their hands. At 16 months of age, they can scribble with a crayon, and by the end of the second year, they can copy a simple horizontal or vertical line and even build towers of five or more blocks. What is happening is quite consistent with the dynamical systems theory: infants are gaining control over simple movements and then integrating these skills into increasingly complex, coordinated systems (Fentress & McLeod, 1986). Building a tower, for example, requires the child to first gain control over the thumb and the forefinger and then use the pincer grip as part of a larger action sequence that involves reaching for a block, snatching it, laying it squarely on top of another block, and then delicately releasing it. Despite their ability to combine simple motor activities into increasingly complex sequences, even 2- to 3-year-olds are not very good at catching and throwing a ball, cutting food with utensils, or drawing within the lines of their coloring books. These skills will emerge later in childhood as the muscles mature and children become more proficient at using visual information to help them coordinate their actions.

Psychological Implications of Early Motor Development

pincer grasp
a grasp in which the thumb is used in opposition to the fingers, enabling an infant to become more dexterous at lifting and fondling objects.

Life changes dramatically for both parents and infants once a baby is able to reach out and grasp interesting objects, especially after he can crawl or walk to explore these treasures. Suddenly, parents find they have to child-proof their homes, limit access to certain areas, or else run the risk of experiencing a seemingly endless string of disasters including torn books, overturned vases, unraveled rolls of toilet paper, and irritated pets whose tails the little explorer has pulled. Placing limits on explorations often precipitates conflicts and a "testing of the wills" between infants and their parents (Biringen et al., 1995). Nevertheless, parents are often thrilled by their infant's emerging motor skills, which not only provide clear evidence that development is proceeding normally, but also permit such pleasurable forms of social interaction as pat-a-cake, chase, and hide-and-seek.

Aside from the entertainment value it provides, an infant's increasing control over bodily movements has other important cognitive and social consequences. Mobile infants may feel much more bold, for example, about meeting people and seeking challenges if they know that they can retreat to their caregivers for comfort should they feel insecure (Ainsworth, 1979). Achieving various motor milestones may also foster perceptual development. For example, crawlers (as well as noncrawlers who are made mobile with the aid of special walkers) are better able to search for and

John Eastcott/The Image Works

Life becomes more challenging for parents as infants perfect their motor skills.

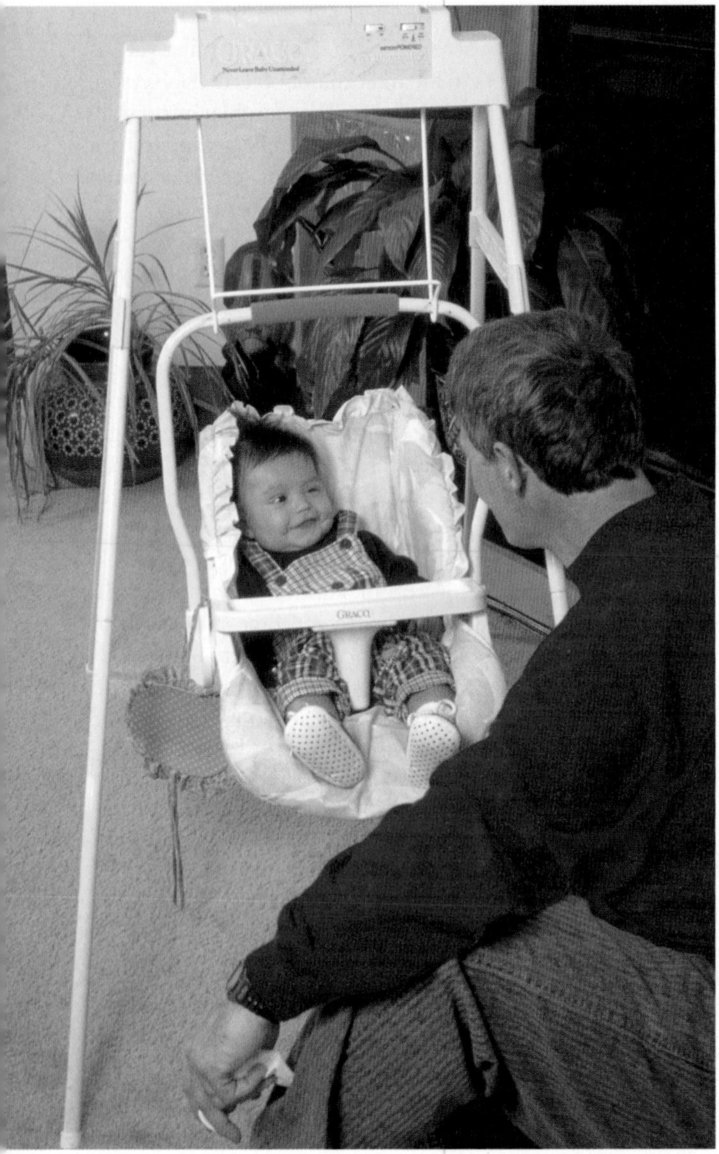
© Michelle D. Bridwell/PhotoEdit

find hidden objects than infants of the same age who are not mobile (Kermoian & Campos, 1988). The self-produced movement of crawling and walking also makes infants more aware of *optic flow,* the perceived movement of objects in the visual field as well as the perceived movements of the foreground and background in which the objects are imbedded. Such perceptions are influenced by the relative movements of the observer or the objects being observed. For example, an infant who is seated in a mechanical swing may watch the family dog grow larger and then smaller in a rhythmic manner, as does the sofa in front of which the dog is seated (the background) and the rug on which both the dog and the mechanical swing rest (the foreground). In fact, as the section of rug that the dog is seated on grows larger, the edges of the rug disappear. The outer ends of the sofa may disappear as well. Both the edges of the rug and the ends of the sofa reappear as the dog shrinks. However, if the swing winds down and the infant is stationary, the synchronized optic flow of dog, sofa, and rug ceases. Now that the swing has stopped its anxiety-producing movement, the dog may wish to investigate the infant. As the dog approaches the stationary infant and swing, the dog grows bigger while the sofa (background) and the rug (foreground) remain the same. The pattern of optic flow generated by the dog moving toward the infant is quite different from the pattern generated by the motion of the infant seated in the activated mechanical swing. The infant will experience yet a third pattern of optical flow if, while Mom and Dad are preoccupied, big brother releases her from the swing and allows her to approach the dog unsupervised. The rug and the sofa will grow larger, expanding outward and escaping the infant's visual field, as the dog expands to fill the field completely—unless the dog's previous experience with big brother's infancy was traumatic. Then the crawling infant will perceive the dog as constant in size, as the background and foreground change (i.e., the dog maintains a safe distance, as it leads the infant all over the house).

As infants mature and begin to add crawling and walking to their array of motor skills, their adeptness in using optic flow to distinguish between self-locomotion and other-locomotion improves. They also learn to use optic flow to detect smaller and smaller changes in locomotion trajectories and velocities, thereby improving at avoiding collisions and correcting balance miscalculations (Gilmore & Rettke, 2003; Gilmore, Baker, & Grobman, 2004). Optic flow displays must simulate at least a 22-degree change in heading before most noncrawlers recognize the change (Gilmore, Baker, & Grobman, 2004). By 4 months of age, some infants can distinguish 16-degree changes in headings (Gilmore and Rettke, 2003). In comparison, adults distinguish 1-degree changes, and under some circumstances, less than 1 degree (Royden, Crowell, & Banks, 1994; Warren, Morris, & Kalish, 1998).

So, optic flow and an infant's gradual understanding of it helps the child to orient herself in space, improves her posture, and causes her to crawl or walk more efficiently (Higgins, Campos, & Kermoian, 1996). Also, crawling and walking both contribute to an understanding of distance relationships and a healthy fear of heights (Adolph, Eppler, & Gibson, 1993; Campos, Bertenthal, & Kermoian, 1992). Experienced crawlers and experienced walkers are better able to use landmarks to find their way than infants who have just begun to crawl or to walk—that is, locomotion influences spatial memory (Clearfield, 2004). So, once again, we see that human development is a holistic enterprise: changes in motor skills have clear implications for other aspects of development.

Top-heavy toddlers often lose their balance when they try to move very quickly.

Beyond Infancy: Motor Development in Childhood and Adolescence

The term *toddler* aptly describes most 1- to 2-year-olds, who often fall down or trip over stationary objects when they try to get somewhere in a hurry. But as children mature, their locomotor skills increase by leaps and bounds. By age 3, children can walk or run in a straight line and leap off the floor with both feet, although they can only clear very small (8- to 10-inch) objects in a single bound and cannot easily turn or stop quickly while running. Four-year-olds can skip, hop on one foot, catch a large ball with both hands, and run much farther and faster than they could one year earlier (Corbin, 1973). By age 5, children are becoming rather graceful: like adults, they pump their arms when they run and their balance has improved to the point that some of them can learn to ride a bicycle. Despite (or perhaps because of) the rapid progress they are making, young children often overestimate the physical feats they can perform, and the bolder or less inhibited ones are likely to be somewhat accident prone, ending up with bruises, burns, cuts, scrapes, and an assortment of other injuries (Schwebel & Plumert, 1999).

With each passing year, school-age children can run a little faster, jump a little higher, and throw a ball a little further (Herkowitz, 1978; Keough & Sugden, 1985). The reasons that children are improving at these large-muscle activities is that they are growing larger and stronger, and are also fine-tuning their motor skills. As shown in Figure 6.7, young children throw only with the arm, whereas adolescents are usually able to coordinate shoulder, arm, and leg movements to put the force of their bodies behind their throws. So, older children and adolescents can throw farther than younger children can, not solely because they are bigger and stronger, but because they also use more refined and efficient techniques of movement (Gallahue, 1989).

At the same time, eye-hand coordination and control of the small muscles are improving rapidly so that children can make more sophisticated use of their hands. Three-year-olds find it difficult to button their shirts, tie their shoes, or copy simple designs. By

Figure 6.7 As these initial tosses and mature throws illustrate, large-muscle activities become more refined with age. *From Science and Medicine of Exercise and Sport, 2nd ed., by Warren K. Johnson and Elsworth R. Buskirk, 1974. Copyright © 1974 by Warren K. Johnson and Ellsworth R. Buskirk. Reprinted by permission of Pearson Education, Inc.*

age 5, children can accomplish all of these feats and can even cut a straight line with scissors or copy letters and numbers with a crayon. By age 8 or 9, they can use household tools such as screwdrivers and have become skilled performers at games such as jacks and Nintendo that require hand-eye coordination. Finally, older children display quicker reaction times than younger children (Williams et al., 1999), which helps to explain why they usually beat younger playmates at "action" games such as dodge ball or ping-pong.

Boys and girls are nearly equal in physical abilities until puberty, when boys continue to improve on tests of large-muscle activities, whereas girls' skills level off or decline (Thomas & French, 1985). These sex differences are, in part, attributable to biology: adolescent boys have more muscle and less fat than adolescent girls and might be expected to outperform them on tests of physical strength (Tanner, 1990). Yet biological developments do not account for all the difference in large-muscle performance between boys and girls (Smoll & Schutz, 1990), nor do they adequately explain the declining performance of many girls, who continue to grow taller and heavier between ages 12 and 17. Jacqueline Herkowitz (1978) believes that the apparent physical decline of adolescent girls is a product of gender-role socialization: with their widening hips and developing breasts, girls are often encouraged to become less tomboyish and more interested in traditionally feminine (and less athletic) activities.

There is clearly an element of truth to this notion in that female athletes show no apparent decline in large-muscle performance over time. Furthermore, as gender roles have changed in the past few decades, female athletes have been steadily improving their performances, and the male/female gap in physical performance has narrowed dramatically (Dyer, 1977; Whipp & Ward, 1992). So it seems that adolescent girls would almost certainly continue to improve on tests of large-muscle activity should they choose to remain physically active. And as we see in Box 6.1, they may experience important psychological benefits as well by remaining physically active throughout the teenage years.

Puberty: The Physical Transition from Child to Adult

adolescent growth spurt
the rapid increase in physical growth that marks the beginning of adolescence.

puberty
the point at which a person reaches sexual maturity and is physically capable of fathering or conceiving a child.

The onset of adolescence is heralded by two significant changes in physical development. First, children change dramatically in size and shape as they enter the **adolescent growth spurt** (Pinyerd & Zipf, 2005). Second, they also reach **puberty** (from the Latin word *pubertas,* meaning "to grow hairy"), the point in life when an individual reaches sexual maturity (Mustanski et al., 2004) and becomes capable of producing a child (Pinyerd & Zipf, 2005).

The Adolescent Growth Spurt

The term *growth spurt* describes the rapid acceleration in height and weight that marks the beginning of adolescence (a growth rate which is faster than any growth rate since the children were infants) (Pinyerd & Zipf, 2005). Girls typically enter the growth spurt by age 10½, reach a peak growth rate by age 12 (about 1.3 years before menarche), and return to a slower rate of growth by age 13 to 13½ (Pinyerd and Zipf, 2005; Tanner, 1988). Most girls gain only about 2.5 cm in height after menarche (Grumbach & Styne, 2003). Boys lag behind girls by 2 to 3 years: they typically begin their growth spurt by age 13, peak at age 14 (mid-puberty), and return to a more gradual rate of growth by age 16. Because girls mature much earlier than boys, it is not at all uncommon for females to be the tallest two or three students in a middle school classroom. By the end of the growth spurt boys have increased 28 to 31 cm in height and girls 27.5 to 29 cm (Abbassi, 1998).

In addition to growing taller and heavier, the body assumes an adultlike appearance during the adolescent growth spurt. Perhaps the most noticeable changes are the appearance of breasts and a widening of the hips for girls, and a broadening of the shoulders for boys. Facial features also assume adult proportions as the forehead protrudes, the nose and jaw become more prominent, and the lips enlarge.

FOCUS ON RESEARCH

Sports Participation and Self-Esteem among Adolescent Females

© Smiley N. Pool/Dallas Morning News/Corbis

Recently, developmentalists have begun to consider the benefits of **physically active play**, speculating that it serves as a mechanism for building muscle strength and endurance and possibly for reducing levels of fat in children's growing bodies (Pellegrini & Smith, 1998). Physically active play typically peaks in early to middle childhood and declines thereafter. This reduction in vigorous physical activity is much more apparent for girls than for boys, which undoubtedly helps to explain the decline in large-muscle strength often see among girls during the adolescent years.

Interestingly, over the past 30 years, our society has become much more supportive of one kind of physical activity for girls—participation in competitive and noncompetitive sports. Title IX, a federal law banning discrimination on the basis of gender in federally funded institutions, passed in 1972 and has resulted in dramatic increases in funding for female athletic programs at the college level. High school programs for female athletes have expanded greatly over the same period, and even private corporations such as Nike have entered the playing field with an ad campaign featuring young girls pleading "If you let me play sports . . . ," and then citing various health and social benefits that can result from sports participation. One of the benefits to which the ads alluded was an enhanced sense of self-worth (or self-esteem) among female athletes.

Is there any basis for the latter claim? To find out, Erin Richman and David Shaffer (2000) constructed an elaborate questionnaire to measure both the depth and breadth of female freshman college students' participation in formal and informal sporting activities during their high school years. These researchers also asked their participants to complete instruments designed to assess their current (1) levels of self-esteem, (2) feelings of physical competence, (3) body images, and (4) possession of such desirable "masculine" attributes as assertiveness and a healthy sense of competition.

The results provided some support for the claims made in the Nike ad campaign. First, there was a clear relation between girls' participation in sports during high school and their later self-esteem: girls who had earlier participated to a greater extent in sports enjoyed higher levels of general self-worth as college students. Further analysis revealed that the apparently beneficial effect of earlier sporting activities on girls' college self-esteem reflected the findings that (1) sports participation was associated with increases in perceived physical competencies, development of a more favorable body image, and acquisition of desirable masculine attributes (such as assertiveness), and (2) all these developments, in turn, were positively correlated with (and apparently fostered) participants' college self-esteem.

In sum, it appears that girls' participation in sporting activities during the adolescent years may well contribute to an enhanced sense of self-worth—but this was true only to the extent that sporting activities fostered physical competencies, more favorable body images, and such desirable personal attributes as assertiveness (see also Ackerman, 2002; Lehman& Koerner, 2005; Malcom, 2003; Shakib, 2003). These findings imply that gym classes and formal team sports might be more beneficial to a larger number of girls if educators and coaches were to emphasize and devise ways to measure and to illustrate the physical gains and psychological benefits of formal and informal sporting activities, while concentrating less on the outcomes of competitive sports and/or the physical deficiencies of the less athletically competent girls under their tutelage.

Sexual Maturation

Maturation of the reproductive system occurs at roughly the same time as the adolescent growth spurt and follows a predictable sequence for girls and boys.

Sexual Development in Girls

For most girls, sexual maturation begins at about age 9 to 11 as fatty tissue accumulates around their nipples, forming small "breast buds" (Herman-Giddens et al., 1997; Pinyerd & Zipf 2005). Full breast development, which takes about 3 to 4 years, finishes around age 14 (Pinyerd & Zipf, 2005). Usually pubic hair begins to appear a little later, although

physically active play
moderate to vigorous play activities such as running, jumping, climbing, play fighting, or game playing that raise a child's metabolic rate far above resting levels.

as many as one-third of all girls develop some pubic hair before their breasts begin to develop (Tanner, 1990).

As a girl enters her growth spurt, the breasts grow rapidly and the sex organs begin to mature. Internally, the vagina becomes larger, and the walls of the uterus develop a powerful set of muscles that may one day be used to accommodate a fetus during pregnancy and to push it through the cervix and vagina during the birth process. Externally, the mons pubis (the soft tissue covering the pubic bone), the labia (the fleshy lips surrounding the vaginal opening), and the clitoris all increase in size and become more sensitive to touch (Tanner, 1990).

menarche
the first occurrence of menstruation.

At about age 12, the average girl in Western societies reaches **menarche**—the time of her first menstruation (Pinyerd & Zipf, 2005). Though it is generally assumed that a girl becomes fertile at menarche, young girls often menstruate without ovulating and *may* remain unable to reproduce for 12 to 18 months after menarche (Tanner, 1978; Pinyerd & Zipf, 2005). Anovulatory menstrual cycles (menstruation without ovulation) are often associated with irregular and painful periods. After 1 to 2 years, cycles become ovulatory, more regular, and less painful (Pinyerd & Zipf, 2005). In the year following menarche, female sexual development concludes as the breasts complete their development and axillary (underarm) hair appears (Pinyerd & Zipf, 2005). Hair also appears on the arms, legs and, to a lesser degree, on the face (Pinyerd & Zipf, 2005).

Sexual Development in Boys

For boys, sexual maturation begins at about 11 to 12 (9.5 to 13.5) with an enlargement of the testes (Pinyerd & Zipf, 2005). The growth of the testes is often accompanied or soon followed by the appearance of unpigmented pubic hair (Pinyerd & Zipf, 2005). As the testes grow, the scrotum also grows; it thins and darkens, and descends to its pendulous adult position (Pinyerd & Zipf, 2005). Meanwhile, the penis lengthens and widens. At about age 13 to 14½, sperm production begins (Pinyerd & Zipf, 2005). By the time the penis is fully developed at age 14½ to 15, most boys will have reached puberty and are now capable of fathering a child (Tanner, 1990).

Somewhat later, boys begin to sprout facial hair, first at the corners of the upper lip, then on the sides of the face, and finally on the chin and jawline (Mustanski et al., 2004; Pinyerd & Zipf, 2005). Body hair also grows on the arms and legs, although signs of a hairy chest may not appear until the late teens or early 20s, if at all. Another hallmark of male sexual maturity is a lowering of the voice as the larynx grows and the vocal cords lengthen. In fact, many men may laugh (years later) about hearing their voices "cracking" up and down between a squeaky soprano and a deep baritone, sometimes within a single sentence.

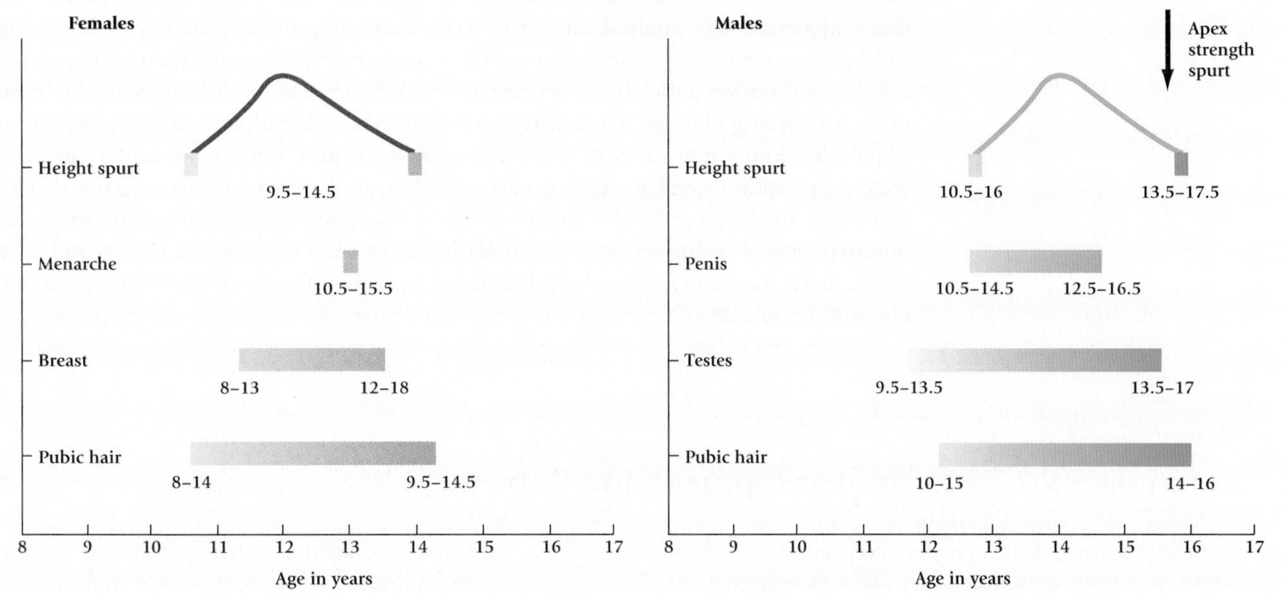

Figure 6.8 Milestones in the sexual maturation of girls (a) and boys (b). The numbers represent the variation among individuals in the ages at which each aspect of sexual maturation begins or ends. For example, we see that the growth of the penis may begin as early as age 10½ or as late as 14½. *From* Fetus into Man: Physical Growth from Conception to Maturity, *2nd ed., by J. M. Tanner, 1978. Cambridge, Mass.: Harvard University Press. Copyright © 1978, 1990 by J. M. Tanner.*

Bob Daemmrich/Stock Boston

In early adolescence, girls are maturing more rapidly than boys.

secular trend
a trend in industrialized societies toward earlier maturation and greater body size now than in the past.

Individual Differences in Physical and Sexual Maturation

So far, we have been describing developmental norms, or the average ages when adolescent changes take place. But as Figure 6.8 indicates, there are many individual differences in the timing of physical and sexual maturation. An early-maturing girl who develops breast buds at age 8, starts her growth spurt at age 9½, and reaches menarche at age 10½ may nearly complete her growth and pubertal development before the late developing girls in her class have even begun. Individual differences among boys are at least as great: some boys reach sexual maturity by age 12½ and are as tall as they will ever be by age 13, whereas others begin growing later and do not reach puberty until their late teens. This perfectly normal biological variation may be observed in any middle school classroom, where one will find a wide assortment of bodies, ranging from those that are very childlike to those that are quite adultlike.

Secular Trends—Are We Maturing Earlier?

About 25 years ago, women in one family were surprised when a sixth-grader began to menstruate shortly after her 12th birthday. The inevitable comparisons soon began, as the girl learned that neither of her great-grandmothers had reached this milestone until age 15, and that her grandmother had been nearly 14 and her mother 13. At this point, the girl casually replied, "Big deal! Lots of girls in my class have got their periods."

As it turns out, this young woman was simply "telling it like it is." In 1900, when her great-grandmother was born, the average age of first menstruation was 14 to 15. By 1950, most girls were reaching menarche between 13½ and 14, and recent norms have dropped even further, to age 12½ (Tanner, 1990). Today, the definition of "early" puberty remains puberty begun before 8 years of age for girls and 9 years of age for boys (Saenger, 2003). This **secular trend** toward earlier maturation started more than 100 years ago in the industrialized nations of the world, where it has now leveled off, and it has begun happening in the more prosperous nonindustrialized countries as well (Coleman & Coleman, 2002). In addition, people in industrialized nations have been growing taller and heavier over the past century. What explains these secular trends? Better nutrition and advances in medical care seem to be most responsible (Tanner, 1990). Today's children are more likely than their parents or grandparents to reach their genetic potentials for maturation and growth because they are better fed and less likely to experience growth-retarding illnesses. Even within our own relatively affluent society, poorly nourished adolescents mature later than well-nourished ones. Girls who are tall and overweight as children tend to mature early (Graber et al., 1994), whereas many dancers, gymnasts, and other girls who engage regularly in strenuous physical activity may begin menstruating very late or stop menstruating after they have begun (Hopwood et al., 1990). Here, then, are strong clues that nature and nurture interact to influence the timing of pubertal events.

CONCEPT CHECK 6.2 Motor Development and Puberty

Check your understanding of motor development and developmental changes associated with puberty by answering the following questions. Answers appear in the Appendix.

True or False: Indicate whether each of the following statements is true or false.

1. (T)(F) Infants who proceed through stages of motor development more quickly than the average are likely to be more intelligent later in childhood than infants who are average or behind average.
2. (T)(F) Infants who are mobile (can crawl or walk easily) are less fearful about meeting strangers because they know they can easily escape to their caregivers if they should begin to feel insecure in the new situation.
3. (T)(F) Generally, girls reach sexual maturity earlier than boys.
4. (T)(F) Girls become capable of having children as soon as they have their first menstruation.
5. (T)(F) The *secular trend* refers to the fact that children today are reaching sexual maturity at later ages than their grandparents and great-grandparents.

Multiple Choice: Select the best alternative for each question.

_____ 6. Zach has a young son, about 6 months old. Zach believes that helping his son practice motor skills will help his son achieve motor skills alone earlier than if he did not help his son practice. Consequently, when Zach plays with his son he helps his son practice sitting and walking and encourages his son's efforts. Zach's viewpoints about motor development are most closely aligned with which scientific view of motor development?
a. the maturational viewpoint
b. the experiential viewpoint
c. the developmental sequence viewpoint
d. the dynamical systems viewpoint

_____ 7. In a study of orphaned children who were confined to their cribs during their first 2 years of life, Dennis found that
a. Maturation determined the age at which young toddlers could sit, crawl, and walk, regardless of their experiences.
b. Experience determined the age at which young toddlers could sit, crawl, and walk, regardless of their maturational age.
c. Maturation was necessary but not sufficient for the development of such motor skills as sitting, walking, and crawling.
d. Experience was the determining factor, regardless of age, of when young toddlers could sit, crawl, or walk.

_____ 8. The ability to grasp an object using the thumb and forefinger is called the
a. pincer grasp
b. ulnar grasp
c. proprioceptive grasp
d. forefinger grasp

_____ 9. Boys and girls are nearly equal in physical abilities until puberty, when
a. Girls continue to improve on tests of large-muscle activities, whereas boys' skills level off or decline.
b. Boys continue to improve on tests of large-muscle activities, whereas girls' skills level off or decline.
c. Boys and girls continue to improve on tests of large-muscle activities.
d. Boys' and girls' skills level off or decline.

_____ 10. Which of the following is *not* one of the changes associated with the adolescent growth spurt?
a. Girls and boys grow taller and heavier.
b. Girls and boys assume adult facial features as their foreheads protrude, and their noses and jaws become more prominent.
c. Girls and boys experience a widening of their hips.
d. Girls develop breasts and boys experience a broadening of their shoulders.

The Psychological Impacts of Puberty

What do adolescents think about the dramatic physical changes they are experiencing? In Western cultures, girls typically become quite concerned about their appearance and worry about how other people will respond to them (Cauffman & Steinberg, 1996; Greif & Ulman, 1982). In general, teenage girls hope to be perceived as attractive, and changes that are congruent with the "feminine ideal" of slimness are often welcomed. However, they are often concerned that they are growing too tall or too large (Swarr & Richards, 1996; Wichstrom, 1999), and their body images become increasingly negative from early to late adolescence (Rosenblum & Lewis, 1999). Even well-proportioned teenage girls may try to compensate for perceived physical faults by slouching, not wearing high-heeled shoes, or trying diets (Rosen, Tracey, & Howell, 1990). Girls whose bodies develop at a pace that is different from average (much faster or much slower) are particularly prone to internalizing a negative body image (Pinyerd & Zipf, 2005).

Girls' reactions to menarche are mixed (Greif & Ulman, 1982). They are often excited but somewhat confused as well, especially if they mature very early or have not been told what to expect (Brooks-Gunn, 1988). Few girls today are traumatized by menarche, but at the same time, few are overjoyed about becoming a woman (Koff & Rierden, 1995; Moore, 1995).

Boys' body images are more positive than girls' (Rosenblum & Lewis, 1999), and they are much more likely than girls to welcome their weight gains (Richards et al., 1990). Teenage boys also hope to be tall, hairy, and handsome, and they may become preoccupied with the aspects of body image that center on physical and athletic prowess (Simmons & Blyth, 1987). Whereas menarche is a memorable event for girls, boys are often only dimly aware of the physical changes they are experiencing (Zani, 1991). They rarely tell anyone about their first ejaculation, often were not prepared for it, and like girls, express mixed reactions to becoming sexually mature (Gaddis & Brooks-Gunn, 1985; Stein & Reiser, 1994).

Adolescent Body Image and Unhealthy Weight Control Strategies

So, during adolescence the bodies of girls and boys begin to mature into those of men and women. For teenagers, feelings about this process and its end product become an important part of identity development. A teenager who has positive feelings about his or her body, particularly about the appearance of that body, is more likely to have high self-esteem and to have positive peer relationships (Stice & Whitenton, 2002). A teenager who is dissatisfied with his or her body and who focuses on its shortcomings in comparison to unrealistic cultural and social ideals of attractiveness is likely to experience depression and to engage in unhealthy weight control behaviors (Fichter, 2005; Sim & Zeman, 2004; Stice, 2002; Stice & Bearman, 2001). Body image dissatisfaction, the discrepancy between a teen's assessment of his or her physical appearance and that teen's internal picture of the ideal body, has emerged as a strong predictor of teenage depression, and one of the most important predictors of eating disorders, exercise dependence, and steroid use among teens (Stice & Whitenton, 2002). It is important to note that the two "measurements" from which body image dissatisfaction is determined are subjective—both body image, what a teenager thinks he or she looks like, and ideal body image, a teenager's conceptualization of the perfect body, are derived largely from what a teenager believes about appearance and its importance in his or her life (Canpolat et al., 2005).

Among adolescents, the prevalence and nature of body image dissatisfaction differs for the two sexes, as do the weight control strategies teens use in their attempts to modify their non-ideal bodies (McCabe & Ricciardelli, 2004a, b). Boys who express dissatisfaction with their bodies tend to fall into two groups: those who wish to lose weight and those who wish to become larger and more muscular (Kostanski et al., 2004). That is, boys' dissatisfaction increases as weight increases only among those who weigh more

© Tony Freeman/PhotoEdit

than average. Among boys who weigh less than average, body image dissatisfaction increases as weight decreases. Boys of average weight express little body image dissatisfaction (Presnell, Bearman, & Stice, 2004; Toro et al., 2004).

In comparison, adolescent girls are more unified in their goals: as a whole, they feel compelled to be thin. For girls, as weight increases, body image dissatisfaction also increases (Presnell et al., 2004). Unlike adolescent boys, very few adolescent girls express satisfaction with their bodies (Beato-Fernández et al., 2004; Gusella, Clark, & Van Roosmalen, 2004). As Marion Kostanski and her colleagues (2004) have said, "Body dissatisfaction among adolescent and adult groups has been found to be so predominant for women that it is considered to be a normative component of their living within modern Western society."

In general, the weight control strategies selected by teens correspond to the kinds of body image dissatisfaction that they experience. Girls diet to become thin and to reduce weight. For the most part, boys choose strategies that they believe will increase muscle mass (McCabe & Ricciardelli, 2004a; McCreary & Sasse, 2000; Toro et al., 2005): they exercise and participate in sports (Toro et al., 2005) and they take dietary supplements and may use steroids (McCabe & Ricciardelli, 2004b). Heavier boys are also likely to diet in order to lose fat—but not necessarily to lose weight, as girls do (McCabe & Ricciardelli, 2004a).

In addition to the adverse emotional consequences associated with body image dissatisfaction, engaging in extreme methods of weight control may compromise the healthy development of an adolescent's body. The adolescent growth period is critical to the achievement of normal adult stature and reproductive capability (Seidenfeld, Sosin, & Rickert, 2004). The most obvious of the physical consequences of unhealthy weight control are those concerned with nutrition and growth. Adolescent girls who continually diet are especially at risk (Neumark-Sztainer et al., 2004a, b). They consume significantly fewer fruits, vegetables, and grains than girls who do not diet. Their intakes of calcium, iron, vitamins, and zinc are also lower. On the other hand, boys who diet tend to consume higher quantities of fruit than boys who do not diet (Neumark-Sztainer et al., 2004a, b).

For those adolescents who progress beyond simple dieting to the development of eating disorders, the consequences of unhealthy weight control involve much more than simple nutrition (Neumark-Sztainer et al., 2005). Eating disorders that befall adolescents include anorexia nervosa, bulimia nervosa, and less extreme, but serious manifestations of the symptoms comprising anorexia and bulimia (APA, 2000). Teenagers with **anorexia nervosa** are obsessively concerned about weight gain, refuse to maintain normal body weights, and are quite persistent in their denial of the peril of maintaining such extremely low body weights (APA, 2000; Fichter, 2005; Seidenfeld, Sosin, & Rickert, 2004). Adolescents with **bulimia nervosa** engage in binge eating: they consume large amounts of food in short periods of time. They follow binges with behaviors designed to prevent weight gain, such as self-induced vomiting, overzealous exercise, or laxative ingestion (APA, 2000; Seidenfeld, Sosin, & Rickert, 2004). Adolescents engaging in anorexic behavior often

anorexia nervosa
a life-threatening eating disorder characterized by self-starvation and a compulsive fear of getting fat.

bulimia
a life-threatening eating disorder characterized by recurrent eating binges followed by such purging activities as heavy use of laxatives or vomiting.

appear thin, even emaciated, while adolescents engaging in bulimic behaviors will most likely be somewhat overweight. Consequently, within the general population of adolescents, bulimia is much harder to diagnose than anorexia (Seidenfeld, Sosin, & Rickert, 2004).

Both anorexia and bulimia occur more frequently among girls and women than among boys and men. However, the prevalence of eating disorders among males may be underestimated due to the perception that eating disorders are a feminine malady. In most cases, eating-disordered behavior is secretive, and adolescent boys, who view such behaviors as characteristic of girls, may be even more motivated to hide their symptoms (Ray, 2004).

Eating disorders usually first occur between the ages 12 and 26, with a peak occurring between ages 14 and 18 (APA, 2000; Gerlinghoff & Backmund, 2004). However, preadolescents and children 3 to 10 years old have been known to exhibit symptoms, suggesting that the foundation for fully developed anorexia and bulimia may be laid at a very young age (Goëb et al., 2005). Unfortunately for some individuals, the morbid fear of obesity and unhealthy weight control behaviors associated with eating disorders are persistant and may continue into adulthood (Gerlinghoff & Backmund, 2004), but the majority of adolescents diagnosed with eating disorders do not retain symptoms this long. As adults, however, they are at risk for other psychiatric disorders, especially those involving depression and anxiety (Halvorsen & Heyerdahl, 2004; Herpertz-Dahlmann et al., 2001).

Physical consequences associated with the development of bulimia include damage to the esophageal tube and tooth enamel erosion due to induced vomiting, as well as the development of obesity (Nilsson & Hägglöf, 2005). Although obesity in childhood is only a moderate predictor of obesity in adulthood, obesity during adolescence more strongly predicts adult obesity (Gordon-Larson et al., 2004). Therefore, bulimia in adolescence may place individuals at risk for many obesity-related health issues later in life such as diabetes, heart attack, and stroke (Colton et al., 2004).

Fortunately, death rates associated with anorexia have fallen (Nilsson & Hägglöf, 2005). However, physical consequences of the starvation associated with anorexia are numerous. Both thyroid and cardiac function may be compromised and structural damage to the heart may occur (Olivares et al., 2005; Reijonen et al., 2003). Anorexics may experience constipation and emaciation (Reijonen et al., 2003). Bone density scans of girls who starve themselves reveal levels of calcium that are far below normal (Gordon, 2003; Stoffman et al., 2005). During adolescence, at least half of an individual's adult bone mass is laid down, with peak adult bone mass occurring during young adulthood. Anorexic behaviors prevent the intake of sufficient calcium and minerals to complete this process. Girls with extremely low body weights also experience amenorrhea—the cessation of menstrual periods (Seidenfeld, Sosin, & Rickert, 2004). Because estrogen and other reproductive hormones regulate the rate of material turnover in the bones, amenorrhea also adversely affects bone density. Thus, whereas both anorexic boys and girls may fail to lay down calcium, anorexic girls also experience bone loss due to the hormonal effects of amenorrhea (Gordon, 2003).

With the restoration of adequate consumption of nutrients and the resulting weight gain, cardiac and thyroid function return to normal, as long as there has been no permanent damage to the heart muscles (Cooke & Sawyer, 2004; Olivares et al., 2005), and the female reproductive system also resumes its normal cycle (Nilsson & Hägglöf, 2005; Swenne, 2004). However, in order for the menstrual cycles to return, weight gain goals must be set on an individual basis. Target weights based on population norms for age and height are often too low for many girls (Swenne, 2004). With increased intake of nutrients, the bones once again begin to lay down calcium, but even so, individuals diagnosed with anorexia have an increased incidence of fractures and are at risk for the early development of osteoperosis (Gordon, 2003; Gordon et al., 2002).

A host of factors related to the family appear to influence eating and weight control behaviors for all teens. A chaotic or tumultuous home environment may place adolescents at risk for developing eating disorders, as does recent experience with a family-related loss, such as the death of a family member or divorce (Ray, 2004; Shannon, 2004). Both high levels of conflict and low levels of emotional expressiveness among family members are associated with adolescent bulimia and, on any day within such families, an adolescent's bulimic episodes appear to be catalyzed by family hassles and conflict that the teenager experienced earlier that day (Okon et al., 2003). Teens with a family history of eating disorders and those coming from families in which appearance and body image are emphasized are also likely to use unhealthy weight control strategies and to develop full-blown eating disorders (Ray, 2004; Shannon, 2004). Another family factor that seems to be related strongly to teen body image dissatisfaction and weight behavior problems is the feeling of being unloved by one or both parents (Beato-Fernández et al., 2004).

Intrapersonal factors that influence body image dissatisfaction and the development of unhealthy weight control strategies among teens are both emotional and behavioral. Emotional factors include a tendency on the part of the adolescent to internalize stress, intense emotions, and feelings (Fichter, 2005; Thompson & Stice, 2001). Bulimic girls seem to have a particularly difficult time with the outward expression of emotion. In one study, girls with bulimia were more reluctant to express feelings than girls who were depressed or had a history of psychological problems but did not have eating disorders. The bulimic girls also took longer to retrieve emotional information and had trouble identifying their own moods (Sim & Zeman, 2004). Dysthymia, the type of depression associated with bulimia, ranks low on the emotional scale among depressions. *Dysthymia* is described as a persistent and consistent low-energy depression, without the mood swings and deeply felt sadnesses and despondencies that characterize other kinds of depression (Perez, Joiner, & Lewinsohn, 2004).

Behavioral factors that appear to have the most influence on eating and weight control strategies among teens are participation in certain sports and dieting. Participation in sports that have a weight requirement (such as wrestling or rowing) or sports in which thinness is an advantage (such as distance running or cycling) has been associated with disordered eating and excessive exercise, as well as the use of steroids and food supplements (Hausenblas & Carron, 1999; McCabe & Ricciardelli, 2004b; Patel et al., 2003). Dieting places teens at risk for both the development of serious eating disorders and obesity (Neumark-Sztainer et al., 2005; Stice, 2001). Perfectionistic behavior has also been associated with eating disorders in teens (Fichter, 2005).

Treatments for adolescents with high body-image dissatisfaction and those who employ unhealthy weight control strategies include a variety of approaches, but the most effective involve the family of the adolescent. For instance, many studies point to the fact that outcome improves when an adolescent is treated on an outpatient basis with high familial involvement (Fleminger, 2005; Krautter & Lock, 2004; Nilsson & Hägglöf, 2005; Stanford & McCabe, 2005). Parent education and family support groups are also beneficial (Cook-Darzens et al., 2005; Holtkamp et al., 2005). In fact, a study of teenagers who were able to recover from eating disorders without professional treatment revealed that the earlier a teen's parents intervened, the shorter duration of the disorder and the more complete the teen's recovery (Woods, 2004). Thus, it has become apparent that the parents and family of teenagers can be instrumental in the prevention and treatment of eating disorders, even though no single, specific pattern of family dysfunction has been associated with their development (Beato-Fernández et at., 2004). Programs and therapists that focus on the strengths of individual families and that tailor treatment to support these strengths may be more effective than more generalized approaches to family involvement (Beato-Fernández et al., 2004; Cook-Darzens et al., 2005; Eisler, 2005; Woods, 2004).

In addition, studies related to individual treatment issues have produced interesting results. When adolescent girls sent for bone density scans found themselves to be the single young person in a waiting room filled with elderly women, they experienced an acute awareness of the physical damage caused by their anorexic behaviors (Stoffman et al., 2005). This suggests that novel ways of altering the perspectives of anorexic adolescents may assist them in forming more realistic views of the consequences of their actions. In another study, having noted that boys are raised to focus upon the instrumental capabilities of their bodies (what they can do) and girls the ornamental aspects (how they look), researchers had adolescent girls who had been diagnosed with eating disorders complete an assessment that included standard questions about appearance, along with questions about the instrumental aspects of body image (Gusella, Clark, & Van Roosmalen, 2004). The girls were surprised to find themselves considering how their bodies worked *for* them. The girls also discovered that many of their anorexic symptoms, such as bloating and headaches, reinforced negative associations about their body function. The authors suggest that finding ways to incorporate "body competence and healthy functioning into the general definition of body image or body concept is beneficial for girls" (Gusella, Clark, & Van Roosmalen, 2004).

Other research points to the preventive measures that may be directed toward all adolescents. For example family meals are associated with higher self-esteem among teenagers, and high self-esteem is possibly the single most potent protective factor against body image dissatisfaction (Beato-Fernández et al., 2004; Eisenberg et al., 2005; Neumark-Sztainer et al., 2004b). Therefore, frequent, structured family meals, during which the atmosphere is positive, may prevent the development of unhealthy weight control behaviors among teens. In fact, adolescent girls who participated in three to four family meals per week were one-third less likely to exhibit unhealthy weight control behaviors than girls who participated in family meals less frequently (Eisenberg et al., 2004).

Still other research suggests that creating environments at both the familial and school level that emphasize health and fitness rather than appearance is also likely to increase body image satisfaction (Kelly et al., 2005; Stice & Bearman, 2001; Stice & Whitenton, 2002). Body image is an important aspect of adolescent identity development that influences a teen's emotional as well as physical health. Expanding the concept of body image beyond the male and female appearance ideals promoted by the popular cultures of industrialized nations and promoting high self-esteem may inoculate teens against body image dissatisfaction, preventing the development of self-destructive weight control strategies that often lead to diagnoses of serious eating disorders.

Social Impacts of Pubertal Changes

Adolescents who are maturing physically and sexually not only come to feel differently about themselves, but come to be viewed and treated differently by other people. In many nonindustrialized societies, rituals called **rites of passage** inform the whole community that a child has become an adult (Schlegel & Barry, 1991). Among the Kaguru of eastern Africa, for example, pubertal boys are led into the bush, stripped, and shaved of all hair, which symbolizes losing their status as children (Beidelman, 1971). They then undergo the painful experience of circumcision without anesthesia, learn about tribal sexual practices, and are taught ritual songs and riddles that instruct them in the ways of manhood. Finally, they are "anointed" with red earth to mark their new status and led back to the village for celebrations and feasts. The Kaguru girl is initiated when she experiences her first menstruation. Her genital area is cut as a mark of her new status, and she is instructed in the ways of womanhood, usually by her grandmother, before being welcomed back into society as an adult.

rites of passage
rituals that signify the passage from one period of life to another (for example, puberty rites).

Although our society has no universal rites of passage to mark one's transition from childhood to adolescence or from adolescence to adulthood, pubertal changes may nonetheless have social consequences. Lawrence Steinberg (1981, 1988) reports that around age 11 to 13, when pubertal changes are peaking, European American adolescents become more independent and feel less close to their parents, with whom they often argue (see also Paikoff & Brooks-Gunn, 1991). These standoffs are more likely to involve squabbles about unmade beds, late hours, and loud music than arguments about core values, but they can be unpleasant nonetheless. Hormonal changes in early adolescence may contribute to these conflicts as well as to moodiness, bouts of depression, and restlessness (Buchanan, Eccles, & Becker, 1992; Udry, 1990). However, none of these experiences is inevitable. In fact, Mexican American boys and their parents appear to become *closer* rather than more distant as puberty arrives, suggesting that cultural beliefs about the family or about the significance of becoming more adultlike can influence parent-child relations during adolescence (Molina & Chassin, 1996).

Even when parent-child relations are disrupted early in adolescence, they typically become warmer again later in adolescence, once the pubertal transition is over (Greenberger & Chen, 1996; Smetana & Gaines, 1999). Parents can help their children successfully adjust to puberty by maintaining close relationships, being patient, and helping adolescents to accept themselves and all the physical and social changes they are experiencing (Swarr & Richards, 1996). Clearly, the early teenage years are a period when biological changes interact with changes in the social environment to influence how adolescence is experienced (Magnusson, 1995; Paikoff & Brooks-Gunn, 1991).

Does Timing of Puberty Matter?

Think back for a moment to your own adolescence when you first realized that you were rapidly becoming a man or a woman. Did this happen to you earlier than to your friends, or later? Do you think that the timing of these events could have influenced your personality or social life?

Timing of puberty does have some meaningful implications, although its impact differs somewhat for boys and girls.

Possible Impacts on Boys

Longitudinal research conducted at the University of California suggests that boys who mature early enjoy a number of social advantages over boys who mature late. One study followed the development of 16 early-maturing and 16 late-maturing male adolescents over a 6-year period and found late maturers to be more eager, anxious, and attention-seeking (and also rated by teachers as less masculine and less physically attractive) than early maturers (Jones & Bayley, 1950). Early maturers tended to be poised and confident in social settings and were more likely to win athletic honors and election to student offices. Although this study was based on only 32 boys in California, other researchers have found that late-maturing males do tend to feel somewhat socially inadequate and inferior (Duke et al., 1982; Livson & Peskin, 1980). Late-maturing boys also have lower educational aspirations than early maturers do, and they even score lower on school achievement tests early in adolescence (Dubas, Graber, & Petersen, 1991).

Why is the early-maturing boy advantaged? One reason may be that his greater size and strength often make him a more capable athlete, which in turn is apt to bring social recognition from adults and peers (Simmons & Blyth, 1987). The early maturer's adultlike appearance may also prompt others to overestimate his competencies and to grant him privileges and responsibilities normally reserved for older individuals. Indeed, parents hold higher educational and achievement aspirations for early-maturing than for late-maturing sons (Duke et al., 1982), and they have fewer conflicts with early maturers about issues such as acceptable curfews and the boy's choice of friends (Savin-Williams & Small, 1986). Perhaps you can see how this generally positive, harmonious atmosphere might promote the poise or self-confidence that enables early maturers to become popular and to assume positions of leadership within the peer group.

© Barbara Stitzer/PhotoEdit

Early-maturing males tend to be poised and confident in social settings and popular with their peers.

Do these differences between early and late maturers persist into adulthood? In general, they fade over time. By twelfth-grade, for example, differences in academic performance between early and late maturers have already disappeared (Dubas, Graber, & Petersen, 1991). However, Jones (1965) found that early-maturing boys from the University of California study were still somewhat more sociable, confident, and responsible in their 30s than their peers who had matured later. So some of the advantages of early maturation may carry over into adulthood.

Possible Impacts on Girls

For girls, maturing early may be somewhat of a *disadvantage.* Although early breast development is associated with a favorable body image and increased self-confidence (Brooks-Gunn & Warren, 1988), several studies find that early-maturing girls are somewhat less outgoing and less popular than their prepubertal classmates (Aro & Taipale, 1987; Clausen, 1975; Faust, 1960) and are likely to report more symptoms of anxiety and depression as well (Ge, Conger, & Elder, 1996, 2001; Stice, Presnell & Bearman, 2001; Wichstrom, 1999). Intuitively, these findings make sense. A girl who matures very early may look very different from female classmates, who may tease her. She will look older and is often noticeably heavier than the boys in the class, who will not mature for 2 to 3 years and are not yet all that enthused about an early maturer's more womanly attributes (Caspi et al., 1993; Halpern et al., 1999). As a result, early-maturing girls often seek (or are sought out by) older companions, particularly boys, who often steer them away from academic pursuits and into less desirable activities (such as smoking, drinking, drug use, and sex) that they are not yet prepared to handle (Caspi et al., 1993; Dick et al., 2000; Wiesner & Ittel, 2002; Stice, Presnell, & Bearman, 2001). Indeed, risks of psychological distress among early-maturing girls are much higher when they attend coed schools and have lots of boys as friends (Caspi et al., 1993; Ge, Conger, & Elder, 1996).

Some of the curses of early maturity can be long-lasting. One Swedish study, for example, found that early-maturing girls continued to perform more poorly at school and were more likely to drop out than their late-maturing or on-time classmates (Stattin & Magnusson, 1990). Yet, most early-maturing girls fare better over time. Not only are they often admired later in middle school once the female peer group discovers that early-maturing girls tend to be popular with boys (Faust, 1960), but as young adults, women who matured early are no less well-adjusted than their late-maturing peers (Stattin & Magnusson, 1990).

Overall, then, both the advantages of maturing early and the disadvantages of maturing late are greater for boys than for girls. But even though late-maturing boys and early-maturing girls are more likely to be distressed, the psychological differences between early and late maturers become smaller and more mixed in nature by adulthood. Finally, let's note that the differences between early and late maturers are not large, and that many factors other than timing of puberty influence whether or not this period of life goes smoothly.

Adolescent Sexuality

The biological upheaval of puberty brings about major hormonal changes, one of which is increased production of androgens in both boys and girls, which dramatically increases one's sex drive (Graber & Bastiani, 2001; Smith, Guthrie, & Oakley, 2005; Spencer et al., 2002; Udry, 1990; Weisfeld & Woodard, 2004). Although grade-school children often play kiss-and-chase games that prepare them for heterosexual relationships later in life (Thorne, 1993), the new urges they feel make adolescents increasingly aware of their own **sexuality**—an aspect of development that greatly influences their self-concepts. One major hurdle adolescents face is figuring out how to properly manage and express their sexual feelings, an issue that is heavily influenced by the social and cultural contexts in which they live (Weisfeld & Woodard, 2004).

sexuality
aspect of self referring to one's erotic thoughts, actions, and orientation.

Cultural Influences on Sexuality

Societies clearly differ in the education they provide children about sexual matters and in their attempts prepare them for their roles as mature sexual beings (Ford & Beach, 1951; Nieto, 2004; Schalet, 2000). On the island of Ponape, for example, 4- and 5-year-olds receive a thorough "sex education" from adults and are encouraged to experiment with one another. Among the Chewa of Africa, parents believe that practice makes perfect; so, with the blessings of their parents, older boys and girls build huts and play at being husbands and wives in trial marriages. *Restrictive cultures* view sexuality as a taboo subject and vigorously suppress its expression. In New Guinea, for example, Kwoma children are punished for sex play and are not allowed to touch themselves. In fact, a Kwoma boy caught with an erection is likely to have his penis beaten with a stick!

Where do the United States and other Western societies fall on this continuum of sexual permissiveness/restrictiveness? Most can be classified as relatively restrictive. If you are like many Western children and adolescents, the "facts of life" may have come as a shock to you, having been related not by your parents, but by an older sibling or peer. In fact, you may have had trouble imagining your parents ever having done what it takes to conceive you (Walters, 1997). American parents generally discourage overt sex play and often find ways to elude the sexually explicit questions their children may ask (Thorne, 1993). Mainly, adults leave the task of preparing for sexual relations up to the children themselves, and many children and adolescents end up learning from their peers how they should relate to members of the other sex (Whitaker & Miller, 1999).

Sexual Attitudes and Behavior

How, then, do Western adolescents, who receive so little guidance from adults, ever learn to manage sexual urges and to incorporate their sexuality into their self-concepts? These tasks have never been easy and, as we see in Box 6.2, can be especially trying for teenagers who find themselves attracted to members of their own sex. Judging from letters to advice columns, adults seem to think that modern adolescents, driven by raging hormones, are almost obsessed with sex and feel quite free to express their sexuality. How accurate is this portrayal?

Sexual Attitudes. Adolescents have become increasingly liberal in their thinking about sex throughout the 20th century, with recent attitudes reverting only slightly to a more conservative viewpoint due to fears of contracting AIDS (Carroll, 1988; McKenna, 1997). Yet, it is clear that today's youth have changed some of their attitudes about sex while retaining many of the same views held by their parents and grandparents.

What has changed? For one thing, adolescents now firmly believe that premarital sex *with affection* is acceptable, although, like teens of earlier eras, they think that casual or exploitative sex is wrong, even if they have had such experiences (Astin et al., 1994). Still, only a minority of sexually active adolescents in one survey (25 percent of the males and 48 percent of the females) cited affection for their partner as the reason they first had intercourse (Laumann et al., 1994).

A second major change in teenage attitudes about sex is the decline of the **double standard**—the idea that many sexual practices viewed as appropriate for males (for example, premarital sex, promiscuity) are less appropriate for females. The double standard hasn't completely disappeared, for college students of the 1990s still believed that a woman who has many sexual partners is more immoral than an equally promiscuous man (Robinson et al., 1991). But Western societies are rapidly moving toward a single standard of sexual behavior for both males and females. Nevertheless, adolescent girls and boys tend to differ in their attitudes about sex and sexuality: boys are generally more permissive and accepting of premarital sex than girls (Lesch & Kruger, 2005; Smith et al., 2005). Boys are more likely to see experience with sexual intercourse as a positive part of self than girls are (Rucibwa et al., 2003; Tolman, Striepe, & Harmon, 2003; Welles, 2005).

double standard
the view that sexual behavior that is appropriate for members of one gender is less appropriate for the other.

FOCUS ON RESEARCH The Origins of Sexual Orientation

Much of the task of establishing one's sexual identity is becoming aware of one's *sexual orientation*—one's preference for sexual partners of the same or opposite sex. Sexual orientation exists on a continuum and not all cultures categorize sexual preferences as ours does (Paul, 1993), but we commonly describe people as having primarily heterosexual, homosexual, or bisexual orientations. Most adolescents establish a heterosexual orientation without much soul-searching. For the 3 to 6 percent of youths who are attracted to members of their own sex, the process of accepting that they have a homosexual orientation and establishing a positive identity in the face of negative societal attitudes can be long and torturous (Hershberger & D'Augelli, 1995; Lasser & Tharinger, 2003; Patterson, 1995b; Savin-Williams, 2001). It is not that homosexual youths are especially critical of themselves, for their levels of general self-esteem are quite comparable to those of heterosexual peers (Savin-Williams, 1995, 2001). Despite this fact, they may be anxious or even depressed, often because they fear rejection from family members or physical and verbal abuse from peers were their orientation to become known (Dubé & Savin-Williams, 1999; Hershberger & D'Augelli, 1995). Consequently, many gay or lesbian youth do not gather the courage to "come out" until their mid-20s, if they come out at all (Garnets & Kimmel, 1991; Miller, 1995; Savin-Williams, 2001).

How do adolescents become homosexual or heterosexual? In addressing this issue, John Money (1988) emphasizes that sexual orientation is not a choice we make but, rather, something that happens to us. In other words, we do not prefer to be gay or straight; we simply turn out that way. Yet not everyone agrees with this viewpoint: Diana Baumrind (1995) has noted that many bisexual individuals may actively choose to adopt a heterosexual identity, even though they have been sexually attracted to members of both sexes. Similarly, Celia Kitzinger and Sue Wilkinson (1995) find that many women with more than 10 years of heterosexual experience, and who had always viewed themselves as heterosexuals, make a transition to lesbianism later in adulthood (see also Diamond, 2000). Similarly, it now appears that some men become gay later in life after having thought of themselves as (and having lived as) heterosexuals (Savin-Williams, 1995). Clearly these findings imply that at least some homosexual individuals were not predestined to be homosexual and had at least some say in the matter.

How, then, might homosexual individuals become homosexual? Part of the answer lies in the genetic code, it seems. Michael Bailey and his colleagues (Bailey & Pillard, 1991; Bailey et al., 1993, 2000) find that identical twins are more alike in sexual orientation than fraternal twins are. But as we see in the table, only about half of identical twin pairs share the same sexual orientation. This means that environment contributes at least as much as genes to the development of sexual orientation.

What environmental factors might help to determine whether a person with a genetic predisposition toward homosexuality comes to be attracted to same-sex companions? We really don't know yet. The old psychoanalytic view that male homosexuality stems from having a domineering mother and a weak father has received little support (LeVay, 1996). Nor is there any compelling evidence for the long-standing "seduction hypothesis"—the idea that homosexuals have been lured into the lifestyle by an older same-sex companion. Even the once popular notion that fathers' rejection of their sons makes them effeminate and pushes them toward homosexuality has failed to gain much support (Bell et al., 1981; Green, 1987). And growing up with a gay or lesbian parent also seems to have little impact on later sexual orientation (Bailey et al., 1995; Golombok & Tasker, 1996). A more promising hypothesis is that hormonal influences during the prenatal period may be important. For example, women exposed before birth to diethylstilbestoral (DES) or to heightened levels of androgen are more likely than other women to express a bisexual or lesbian orientation—a finding which suggests that high doses of sex hormones prenatally may dispose at least some females to homosexuality (Dittman et al., 1992; Meyer-Bahlberg et al., 1995). However, the fact is that no one yet knows exactly which factors in the prenatal or postnatal environment contribute, along with genes, to a homosexual orientation (Berenbaum & Snyder, 1995; Paul, 1993).

TABLE 6.2 Concordance Rates for Homosexuality Among Male and Female Identical and Fraternal Twin Pairs

	Identical Twins	Fraternal Twins
If one male twin is gay/bisexual, then both are.	52%	22%
If one female twin is gay/bisexual, then both are.	48%	16%

Source: Male figures are from Bailey & Pillard, 1991; female figures are form Bailey et al., 1993.

Suggested Further Reading

Rahman & Wilson (2003). Born gay? The psychobiology of human sexual orientation. *Personality and Individual Differences, 34,* 1337–1382.

Mustanski (2002). A critical review of recent biological research on human sexual orientation. *Annual Review of Sex Research, 13,* 89–141.

Mustanski & Bailey (2003). A therapist's guide to the genetics of human sexual orientation. *Sexual & Relationship Therapy, 18,* 429–436.

Friedman, Silvestre, Gold, Markovic, Savin-Williams, Huggins, & Sell (2004). Adolescents define sexual orientation and suggest ways to measure it. *Journal of Adolescence, 27,* 303–317.

Galupo & St. John (2001). Benefits of cross-sexual orientation friendships among adolescent females. *Journal of Adolescence, 24,* 83–93.

Finally, sexual attitudes today are highly variable and seem to reflect an increased confusion about sexual norms (Lesch & Kruger, 2005; Tolman, Striepe, & Harmon 2003; Welles, 2005). As Philip Dreyer (1982) notes, the "sex with affection" idea is very ambiguous: Must one truly be in love, or is mere liking enough to justify sexual intercourse? It is now up to the individual(s) to decide. Yet these decisions are tough because adolescents receive mixed messages from many sources. On the one hand, they are often told by parents, clergy, and advice columnists to value virginity and to avoid such consequences as pregnancy and sexually transmitted diseases. On the other hand, adolescents are strongly encouraged to be popular and attractive, and the more than 12,000 glamorous sexual innuendos and behaviors that they see annually on television (many of which depict promiscuity in a favorable way and occur between *unmarried* couples) may convince them that sexual activity is one means to these ends (Associated Press, 1999). Apparently, the behavior of older siblings adds to the confusion, for younger brothers and sisters of a sexually active sibling tend to be sexually active themselves, often at an earlier age than the older siblings were (East, 1996; Rodgers & Rowe, 1988). One young adolescent, lamenting the strong social pressures she faced to become sexually active, offered this amusing definition of a virgin: "An awfully ugly third grader" (Gullotta, Adams, & Alexander, 1986, p. 109). In years gone by, the norms of appropriate behavior were much simpler: sex was fine if you were married (or perhaps engaged), but it should otherwise be avoided. This is not to say that your parents or grandparents always resisted the temptations they faced, but they probably had a lot less difficulty than today's adolescents in deciding whether what they were doing was acceptable or unacceptable.

Sexual Behavior. Not only have sexual attitudes changed over the years, but so have patterns of sexual behavior. Generally, today's adolescents are involved in more intimate forms of sexual activity (masturbation, petting, and intercourse) at earlier ages than adolescents of earlier eras (Bingham & Crockett, 1996; Forrest & Singh, 1990). Figure 6.9 shows the percentages of high school students from different historical periods who reported ever having experienced premarital intercourse. Notice that the long-term increase in sexual activity at the high school level may have peaked, for recent data indicate that about half of high school girls (down from 55 percent in 1990) and 55 percent of high school boys (down from 60 percent in 1990) have ever had intercourse (McKenna, 1997). (By comparison, some 70 to 80 percent of college students have had sexual intercourse). Notice also from Figure 6.9 that the sexual behavior of girls has changed more than that of boys so that differences in boys' and girls' adolescent sexual activity have all but disappeared. Finally, it is clearly a myth to assume that today's youth are having sex as early and as often as circumstances permit. Only about 30 percent of U.S. adolescents have had sex by age 15, and their experiences are usually limited to one partner (Hendrick, 1994). Girls are more likely than boys to insist that sex and love—physical and emotional intimacy—go together (Welles, 2005), and they are more likely than boys to have been in a steady relationship with their first sexual partner (Darling, Davidson, & Passarello, 1992). This attitudinal gap between the sexes can sometimes create misunderstandings and hurt feelings, and it may partially explain why girls are less likely than boys to describe their first sexual experience as satisfying (Darling, Davidson, & Passarello, 1992; de Gaston, Jensen, & Weed, 1995).

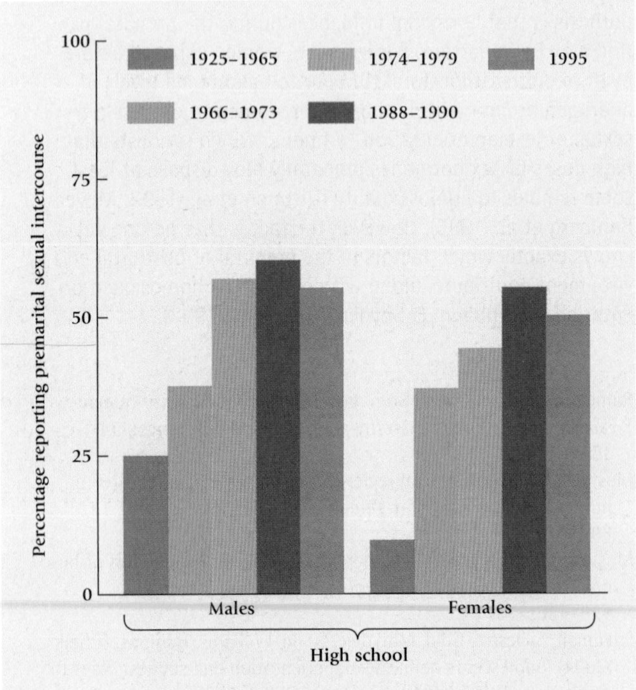

Figure 6.9 Historical changes in the percentages of high school students reporting premarital sexual intercourse. *Data for first three time periods adapted from Dreyer, 1982; data for more recent periods from Baier, Rosenzweig, & Whipple, 1991; Centers for Disease Control, 1992; Reinisch et al., 1992; McKenna, 1997.*

In sum, both the sexual attitudes and the sexual behaviors of adolescents have changed dramatically in this century—so much so that some kind of sexual involvement is now part of the average adolescent's experience (McKenna, 1997). This is true of all major ethnic groups and social classes, and differences in sexual activity among social groups are shrinking dramatically (Forrest & Singh, 1990; Hendrick, 1994).

Personal and Social Consequences of Adolescent Sexual Activity

Who is most inclined to become sexually active early in adolescence, and how risky is this activity? Research has identified a number of factors that contribute to early sexual involvement. Teenagers who have intercourse very early tend to be early maturers from low-income families, who are having difficulties at school, whose friends are sexually active, and who are already involved in such activities as alcohol or substance abuse (Bingham & Crockett, 1996; Fagot et al., 1998; Scaramella et al., 1998). Indeed, the finding that African American, Native American, and Hispanic American adolescents are more likely than adolescents of other ethnicities to be sexually involved at earlier ages probably reflects the fact that more teenagers from those social groups are living in poverty and having difficulties at school and have friends or older siblings who are sexually active (Coley & Chase-Lansdale, 1998; East, 1996; Feldman & Middleman, 2002).

Sadly, large numbers of sexually active adolescents fail to use contraception, largely because they are (1) uninformed about reproductive issues, (2) too cognitively immature to take seriously the possibility that their behavior could have serious long-term consequences, and (3) concerned that other people (including their partners) will think negatively of them if they appear prepared and thus "ready" to have sex (Coley & Chase-Lansdale, 1998). Of course, unsafe sex places them at risk of experiencing two serious consequences: sexually transmitted diseases and teenage pregnancy. Even teenaged girls who receive negative pregnancy test results, thus having escaped one pregnancy, continue to be at high risk for future pregnancy and sexually transmitted disease (Debitko, et al, 2005).

Sexually Transmitted Disease

In the United States, approximately one in five sexually active adolescents contracts a sexually transmitted disease (STD) such as syphilis, gonorrhea, chlamydia, genital herpes, or AIDS—that, left untreated, can cause problems ranging from sterility to death in the infected individual and, as we noted in Chapter 4, can lead to birth defects and other complications for his or her children (Cates, 1995). Clearly, risk of STD is highest for teenagers who fail to use condoms regularly and for those who have sex with multiple partners.

As the number of cases of AIDS has grown, so too have efforts to educate children and adolescents about how to prevent this deadly disease. The incidence of AIDS in the United States is growing fastest among 13- to 19-year-olds, particularly African American and Hispanic adolescents from urban backgrounds (Institute of Medicine, 1999). Most states now require some form of AIDS education in public schools, and there is evidence that these programs can increase grade-school children's knowledge about this disease and its prevention (Gill & Beazley, 1993; Osborne, Kistner, & Helgamo, 1993), particularly when they are tailored to the cultural traditions, beliefs, and values of the children most likely to become sexually active (see Sigelman et al., 1996).

Teenage Pregnancy and Childbearing

Adolescents who are sexually active face another important consequence: each year in the United States, more than 1 million unmarried teenage girls become pregnant. And although as many as 50 percent of these pregnancies end in miscarriages or abortions, an estimated 2 million U.S. babies are born to adolescent mothers every 4 years (Miller et al., 1996). The incidence of teenage pregnancy is about twice as high in the United States as in Canada and most European nations, ranging from a high of 16 pregnancies per 100 teenage girls in California to 6 pregnancies per 100 girls in North Dakota (Allan

Guttmacher Foundation, as cited by McKenna, 1997). Out-of-wedlock births are more common among such economically disadvantaged groups as African Americans, Hispanics, and Native Americans, and about two-thirds of these adolescent mothers choose to keep their babies rather than place them in adoptive homes. In South Africa 33 percent of all women giving birth are under 18 years old (Lesch & Kruger, 2005). Economic poverty is associated with higher rates of teen pregnancy, abortion, and childbearing (McCulloch, 2001). Also, poverty at the community level is associated with higher rates of teen pregnancy (South & Baumer, 2000; Benson, 2004).

In Switzerland, a survey conducted to assess health intervention needs of adolescents revealed that although HIV/AIDS was the most prevalent parental concern, most important to teens themselves were the issues of pregnancy and contraception (Michaud, 2003).

Consequences for Adolescent Mothers. Unfortunately for the adolescent who gives birth, the consequences are likely to include an interrupted education, loss of contact with her social network, and if she is one of the 50 percent who drop out of school, a future of low paying (or no) jobs that perpetuate her economic disadvantage (Coley & Chase-Lansdale, 1998; Fergusson & Woodward, 2000). In addition, many adolescent girls, particularly younger ones, are not psychologically prepared to become parents, a fact that can greatly affect their babies' developmental outcomes.

Research has shown that pregnant teens often come from highly dysfunctional families (Corcoran, 2001). Younger sisters of teen mothers can be important as caregivers for the baby, but younger sisters of teen mothers are also likely to experience early sexual intercourse and to use drugs (East and Jacobson, 2001). Pregnant teens are more likely to be involved in incidences of violence than nonpregnant teens (Martin et al., 1999), and violence toward pregnant teenagers is a risk factor for preterm delivery (Covington, Justason, & Wright, 2001). However, pregnant teenagers have higher self-esteem and greater life satisfaction when they have the social support of their own parents. Therefore, social workers may deal with some of the negative effects of pregnancy for teenagers by supporting family communication (Benson, 2004).

Consequences for Babies of Adolescent Mothers. As we noted in Chapter 4, teenage mothers, particularly those from economically disadvantaged backgrounds, are more likely than older mothers to be poorly nourished, to use alcohol and drugs while pregnant, and to fail to obtain adequate prenatal care. Consequently, many adolescent mothers experience more prenatal and birth complications than older mothers and are more likely to deliver premature or small-for-date babies (Chomitz, Cheung, & Lieberman, 2000).

Not only are their babies at risk for getting off to a rocky start, but so are many adolescent mothers, who are intellectually ill-prepared for the responsibilities of motherhood and who rarely receive adequate financial or social support from a teenage father (Fagot et al., 1998). Compared with older mothers, adolescent mothers know less about child development, view their infants as more difficult, experience greater parenting stress, and respond to their babies with less sensitivity and affection (Miller et al., 1996). It is not completely clear at this point whether the poor parenting practices that characterize many adolescent mothers occur because these mothers are so young or because the adolescent mothers studied come from extremely disadvantaged backgrounds in which parenting (regardless of the parent's age) is generally less sensitive and stimulating (Coley & Chase-Lansdale, 1998). But regardless of how we choose to interpret it, this pattern of parenting can have long-term consequences, because children born to teenagers often show sizable intellectual deficits and emotional disturbances during the preschool years, and poor academic achievement, poor peer relations, and delinquent behaviors later in childhood (Hardy et al., 1998; Miller et al., 1996; Spieker et al., 1999). A teenage mother's life situation and her child's developmental progress may improve later on, especially if she returns to school and avoids having more children; nevertheless, she (and her children) are likely to remain economically disadvantaged compared to peers who postpone parenthood until their 20s (Hardy et al., 1998).

Some kind of sexual involvement is now part of the average adolescent's experience.

Dealing with the Problem of Teenage Sexuality

How might we delay the onset of sexual behavior and reduce the incidence of teenage pregnancies and STDs? Many developmentalists now believe that the crucial first steps to accomplishing these aims should begin at home. Parents consistently underestimate the sexual activity of their teens (particularly younger teens) and are reluctant to communicate just how strongly opposed they are to teenage sexual activity (Jaccard, Dittus, & Gordon, 1998). Yet, it is becoming quite clear that early and frank discussions about sexual matters between parents and their teens (or even preteens) can be a helpful preventative strategy. Research from the U.S. Centers for Disease Control and Prevention (Miller et al., 1998; Whitaker & Miller, 1999) reveals that parent-child communications about sexual risk and condom use, undertaken *before* teens initiate sex, appear to (1) delay the onset of adolescent sexual relations and (2) promote regular condom use once teens do become sexually active—outcomes that clearly lessen the likelihood that adolescents will conceive a child or contract STDs (see also Lesch & Kruger, 2005; Meschke, Bartholomae, & Zentall, 2002; Welles, 2005).

Promising interventions from outside the family are also beginning to emerge. One noteworthy approach is the privately funded *Teen Outreach* program now underway at nearly 50 locales around the United States. Adolescents in *Teen Outreach* perform volunteer service activities (for example, peer tutoring, hospital work) and take part in regular classroom discussions centering on such topics as their volunteer work, future career options, and current and future relationship decisions. A recent evaluation of *Teen Outreach* at 25 sites nationwide revealed that the incidence of pregnancy among female participants was less than half that of girls from similar social and family backgrounds who had not participated in the program (Allen et al., 1997). Apparently, productively engaged adolescents who have reason to be optimistic about their futures and their abilities to manage personal relationships are much less likely to become pregnant.

Finally, formal sex education that goes beyond the biological facts of reproduction can indeed be an effective intervention. Programs that are most successful at delaying sexual activity and at increasing contraceptive use among older sexually active adolescents generally rely on a two-pronged approach of (1) teaching preteens and young adolescents that abstinence can shield them from potentially costly medical and emotional risks associated with sexual activity, and (2) providing older teens with ample information about contraceptives and about strategies they can use to resist pressures to have sex (Frost & Forrest, 1995; Lowy, 2000). And, in light of evidence from Western Europe that free distribution of condoms does *not* encourage sexually inactive teenagers to become sexually active, many educators are calling for similar contraceptive programs in the United States (Lowy, 2000). Those who favor earlier and more extensive sex education and free access to contraception believe that there is little chance of preventing the harmful consequences of teenage sexuality unless more adolescents either postpone sex or practice safer sex.

Causes and Correlates of Physical Development

Although we have now charted the course of physical development from birth through adolescence, we've touched only briefly on the factors that influence growth. What *really* causes children to grow in the first place? And why do their bodies change so dramatically at adolescence, when growth accelerates? As we will see in the pages that follow, physical development results from a complex and continuous interplay between the forces of nature and nurture.

Biological Mechanisms

Clearly, biological factors play a major role in the growth process. Although children do not all grow at the same rate, we have seen that the *sequencing* of both physical maturation and motor development is reasonably consistent from child to child. Apparently, these regular maturational sequences that all humans share are species-specific attributes—products of our common genetic heritage.

Effects of Individual Genotypes

Aside from our common genetic ties to the human race, we have each inherited a unique combination of genes that influence our physical growth and development. For example, family studies clearly indicate that height is a heritable attribute: identical twins are much more similar in height than fraternal twins, whether the measurements are taken during the first year of life, at 4 years of age, or in early adulthood (Tanner, 1990). Rate of maturation is also genetically influenced: female identical twins reach menarche within 2 to 3 months of each other, whereas fraternal twin sisters are typically about 10 to 12 months apart (Kaprio et al., 1995). In fact, genetics has a strong influence upon the onset and progression of puberty for both boys and girls (Mustanski et al., 2004). Similar genetic influences hold for milestones in skeletal growth and even for the appearance of teeth in infants.

How does genotype influence growth? We are not completely certain, although it appears that our genes regulate the production of hormones, which have major effects on physical growth and development.

Hormonal Influences: The Endocrinology of Growth

Hormones begin to influence development long before a child is born. As we learned in Chapter 4, a male fetus assumes a malelike appearance because (1) a gene on his Y chromosome triggers the development of testes, which (2) secrete a male hormone (testosterone) that is necessary for the development of a male reproductive system. By the fourth prenatal month, the thyroid gland has formed and begins to produce **thyroxine,** a hormone that is essential if the brain and nervous system are to develop properly. Babies born with a thyroid deficiency soon become mentally handicapped if this condition goes undiagnosed and untreated (Tanner, 1990). Those who develop a thyroid deficiency later in childhood will not suffer brain damage because their brain growth spurt is over. However, they will begin to grow very slowly, a finding that indicates that a certain level of thyroxine is necessary for normal growth and development.

thyroxine
a hormone produced by the thyroid gland; essential for normal growth of the brain and the body.

The most critical of the *endocrine* (hormone-secreting) glands is the **pituitary,** a "master gland" located at the base of the brain that triggers the release of hormones from all other endocrine glands. In addition to regulating the endocrine system, the pituitary produces a **growth hormone (GH)** that stimulates the rapid growth and development of body cells. Growth hormone is released in small amounts several times a day. When parents tell their children that lots of sleep will help them to grow big and strong, they are right: GH is normally secreted into the bloodstream about 60 to 90 minutes after a child falls asleep (Tanner, 1990). And GH is essential for normal growth and development as well. Children who lack this hormone do grow, and they are usually well proportioned as adults, but they will stand only about 130 cm (or a little over 4 feet) tall (Tanner, 1990).

pituitary
a "master gland" located at the base of the brain that regulates the endocrine glands and produces growth hormone.

growth hormone (GH)
the pituitary hormone that stimulates the rapid growth and development of body cells; primarily responsible for the adolescent growth spurt.

During infancy and childhood, physical growth seems to be regulated by thyroxine and the pituitary growth hormone. What, then, triggers the adolescent growth spurt and other pubertal changes?

Research (reviewed in Tanner, 1990) has clarified the endocrinology of adolescence far beyond what we knew only 20 to 25 years ago. Long before any noticeable physical changes occur, pituitary secretions stimulate a girl's ovaries to produce more **estrogen** and a boy's testes to produce more **testosterone.** Once these sex hormones reach a critical level, the hypothalamus (a part of the brain) instructs the pituitary to secrete more growth hormone (GH). This increase in GH seems to be wholly responsible for the adolescent growth spurt in girls and is primarily responsible for boys' growth spurt. As for sexual maturation, the female hormone estrogen triggers the growth of a girl's breasts, uterus, vagina, pubic and underarm hair, and the widening of her hips. In boys, testosterone is responsible for growth of the penis and prostate, voice changes, and the development of facial and body hair. And although GH may be the primary contributor to the

estrogen
female sex hormone, produced by the ovaries, that is responsible for female sexual maturation.

testosterone
male sex hormone, produced by the testes, that is responsible for male sexual maturation.

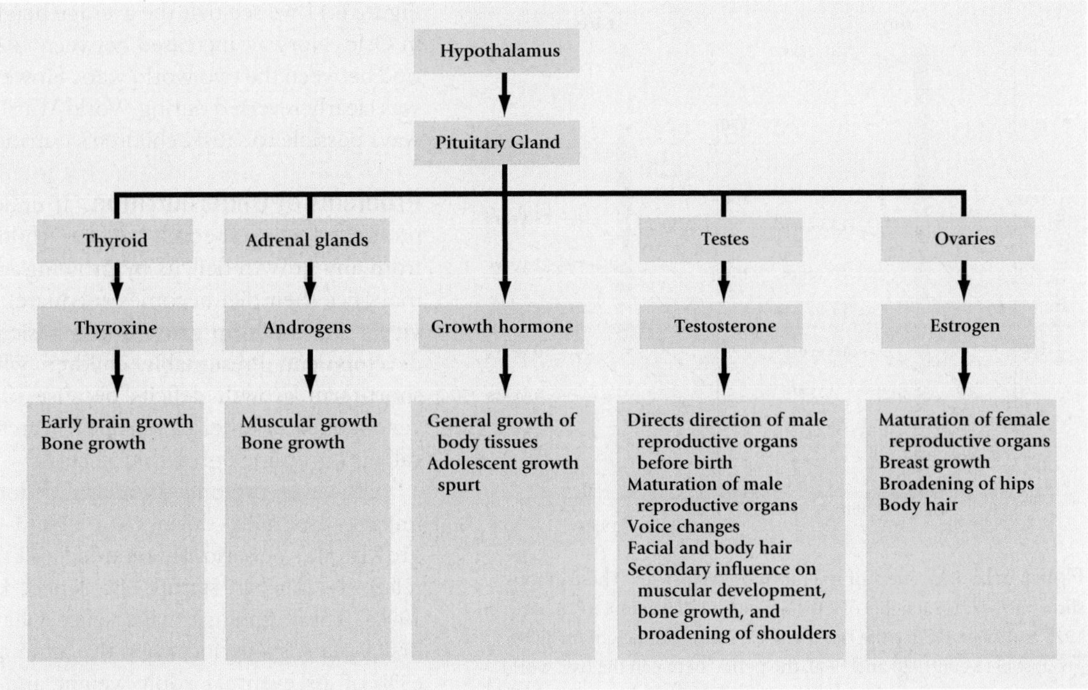

Figure 6.10 Hormonal influences on physical development.

male growth spurt, testosterone exerts its own independent effects on the growth of a boy's muscles, the broadening of his shoulders, and the extension of his backbone. So it seems that adolescent boys experience larger growth spurts than adolescent girls simply because testosterone promotes muscular and bone growth in ways that estrogen does not. Finally, androgen secreted by *adrenal glands* plays a secondary role in promoting the maturation of muscles and bones in both sexes (Tanner, 1990).

What causes the pituitary to activate the endocrine glands and precipitate the dramatic physical changes of adolescence? No one can say for sure. We know that skeletal maturity, which seems to be genetically controlled, is an excellent predictor of when menarche will occur (Tanner, 1990). Yet, any simple "genetic clock" theory that focuses on a singular precipitating factor is probably oversimplified because the timing of breast growth, testicular development, and many other pubertal events are not closely synchronized with skeletal age (or with each other). So, we have learned a great deal about *how* hormones affect human growth and development (see Figure 6.10 for a brief review). However, the events responsible for the timing and regulation of these hormonal influences remain unclear.

Environmental Influences

Three kinds of environmental influence can have a major effect on physical growth and development: nutrition, illnesses, and the quality of care that children receive.

Nutrition

Diet is perhaps the most important environmental influence on human growth and development. As you might expect, children who are inadequately nourished grow very slowly, if at all. The dramatic effect of malnutrition on physical development can be seen by comparing the heights of children before and during wartime periods when food is scarce. In

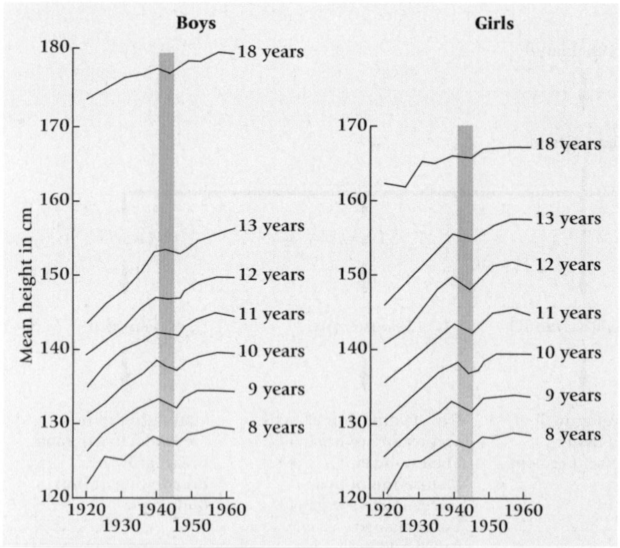

Figure 6.11 The effect of malnutrition on growth. These graphs show the average heights of Oslo schoolchildren ages 8 to 18 between 1920 and 1960. Notice the trend toward increasing height (in all age groups) between 1920 and 1940, the period between the two world wars. This secular trend was dramatically reversed during World War II (the shaded section of the graphs), when nutrition was often inadequate. *Reprinted by permission of the publisher from* Fetus into Man: Physical Growth from Conception to Maturity, *2nd ed., by J. M. Tanner, 1978. Cambridge, Mass.: Harvard University Press. Copyright © 1978, 1990 by J. M. Tanner.*

Figure 6.11 we see that the average heights of schoolchildren in Oslo, Norway, increased between 1920 and 1940—the period between the two world wars. However, this secular trend was clearly reversed during World War II, when it was not always possible to satisfy children's nutritional needs.

Problems of Undernutrition. If undernutrition is neither prolonged nor especially severe, children usually recover from any growth deficits by growing much faster than normal once their diet becomes adequate. James Tanner (1990) views this **catch-up growth** as a basic principle of physical development. Presumably, children who have experienced short-term growth deficits because of malnutrition grow very rapidly in order to regain (or catch up to) their genetically programmed growth trajectory.

However, prolonged undernutrition has a more serious impact, especially during the first 5 years of life: brain growth may be seriously retarded and the child may remain relatively small in stature (Barrett & Frank, 1987; Tanner, 1990). These findings make sense when we recall that the first 5 years is a period when the brain normally gains about 65% of its eventual adult weight and the body grows to nearly two-thirds of its adult height.

In many of the developing countries of Africa, Asia, and Latin America, as many as 85 percent of all children under age 5 experience some form of undernutrition (Barrett & Frank, 1987). When children are severely undernourished, they are likely to suffer from either of two nutritional diseases—*marasmus* or *kwashiorkor*—each of which has a slightly different cause.

Marasmus affects babies who get insufficient protein and too few calories, as can easily occur if a mother is malnourished and does not have the resources to provide her child with a nutritious commercial substitute for mother's milk. A victim of marasmus becomes very frail and wrinkled in appearance as growth stops and the body tissues begin to waste away. Even if these children survive, they remain small in stature and often suffer impaired social and intellectual development (Barrett & Frank, 1987).

Kwashiorkor affects children who get enough calories but little if any protein. As the disease progresses, the child's hair thins, the face, legs, and abdomen swell with water, and severe skin lesions may develop. In many poor countries of the world, one of the few high-quality sources of protein readily available to children is mother's milk. So breast-fed infants do not ordinarily suffer from marasmus unless their mothers are severely malnourished; however, they may develop kwashiorkor when they are weaned from the breast and denied their primary source of protein.

In Western industrialized countries, the preschool children who do experience protein/calorie deficiencies are rarely so malnourished as to develop marasmus or kwashiorkor. However, **vitamin and mineral deficiencies** affect large numbers of children in the United States, particularly African American and Hispanic children from lower socioeconomic backgrounds (Pollitt, 1994). Especially common among infants and toddlers are iron and zinc deficiencies that occur because rapid growth early in life requires more of these minerals than a young child's diet normally provides. Thus, children whose diets are deficient in zinc grow very slowly (Pollitt et al., 1996).

Prolonged iron deficiency causes **iron deficiency anemia,** a condition which not only makes children inattentive and listless, thereby restricting their opportunities for social interaction, but also retards their growth rates and is associated with poor performances on tests of motor skills and intellectual development. Unfortunately, these behavioral and intellectual deficiencies are hard to completely overcome, even after the anemia is corrected by supplementing the child's diet (Lozoff, et al., 1998; Pollitt, et al.,

catch-up growth
a period of accelerated growth in which children who have experienced growth deficits grow very rapidly to "catch up to" the growth trajectory that they are genetically programmed to follow.

marasmus
a growth-retarding disease affecting infants who receive insufficient protein and too few calories.

kwashiorkor
a growth-retarding disease affecting children who receive enough calories but little if any protein.

vitamin/mineral deficiency
a form of malnutrition in which the diet provides sufficient protein and calories but is lacking in one or more substances that promote normal growth.

iron deficiency anemia
a listlessness caused by too little iron in the diet that makes children inattentive and may retard physical and intellectual development.

1996). So, iron deficiencies are a major health problem in the United States and around the world. Even mild cases later in childhood are associated with poor performances on school achievement tests (Watkins & Pollitt, 1999), and children who experience prolonged vitamin/mineral deficiencies are also less resistant to a variety of illnesses that can affect intellectual performance and retard physical growth.

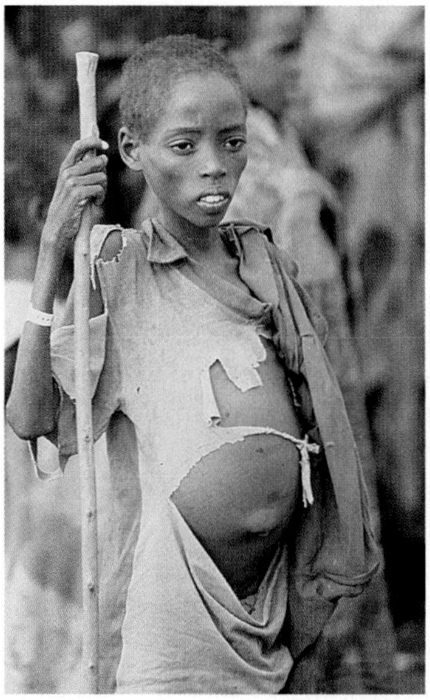

Jean Michel Turpin/Liaison/Getty Images

This child's swollen stomach and otherwise emaciated appearance are symptoms of kwashiorkor. Without adequate protein in the diet, children with kwashiorkor are more susceptible to many diseases and may die from illnesses that well-nourished children can easily overcome.

Intervention Strategies. Recall from Chapter 4 that malnutrition can cause young children to be lethargic, inattentive, irritable, and intolerant of stressful situations—a behavioral profile that places them at risk of alienating their caregivers and thereby receiving little social or intellectual stimulation. In other words, many of the long-term effects of undernutrition may stem, in part, from the unstimulating environments in which malnourished children live and have inadvertently helped to create (Barrett & Frank, 1987; Valenzuela, 1990, 1997).

Nutritional supplements for malnourished children can make them much more receptive to social or intellectual stimulation (Pollitt et al., 1996). Yet, the results of several intervention studies indicate that dietary supplements alone are not enough! Malnourished children are least likely to display long-term deficits in physical growth and social/intellectual development when their diets are supplemented *and* they receive ample social and intellectual stimulation, either through high-quality day-care (Zeskind & Ramey, 1981) or through a home visitation program that teaches caregivers about the importance of such stimulation and shows them how to provide it (Ciliska et al., 2001; Grantham-McGregor et al., 1994; Super, Herrera, & Mora, 1990).

Problems of Overnutrition. Dietary excess (eating too much) is yet another form of poor nutrition that is increasing in Western societies and can have several long-term consequences (Galuska et al., 1996). The most immediate effect of overnutrition is that children may become **obese** and face added risk of diabetes, high blood pressure, and heart, liver, or kidney disease. Obese children may also find it difficult to make friends with agemates, who are apt to tease them about their size and shape. Indeed, obese youngsters are often among the least popular students in grade school classrooms (Sigelman, Miller, & Whitworth, 1986; Staffieri, 1967).

obese
a medical term describing individuals who are at least 20 percent above the ideal weight for their height, age, and sex.

Is a plump baby likely to become an obese adolescent or adult? Not necessarily, for there is only a slight correlation between chubbiness in infancy and obesity later in life (Roche, 1981). However, obese grade-school children and adolescents are much more likely than their thinner peers to be obese in later adolescence and adulthood (Cowley, 2001). Heredity definitely contributes to these trends, for identical twins—even those raised apart—have very similar body weights, whereas the body weights of same-sex fraternal twins may differ dramatically (Stunkard et al., 1990). Yet, a genetic predisposition does not guarantee obesity. Highest levels of obesity are found among children who eat a high-fat diet and who do not get sufficient exercise to burn the calories they've consumed (Cowley, 2001; Fischer & Birch, 1995).

Bad eating habits that can lead to obesity are often established early in life (Birch, 1990). Some parents overfeed infants because they almost always infer that a fussy baby must be hungry. Other parents use food to reinforce desirable behaviors (for example, "clean your room and you can have some ice cream"), or they bribe their children to eat foods they do not want (for example, "no dessert until you eat your peas") (Olvera-Ezzell, Power, & Cousins, 1990; Smith, 1997). Unfortunately, children may attach a special significance to eating that extends far beyond its role in reducing hunger if they are encouraged to view food as a reward. Moreover, use of high-fat desserts or snacks as a reward may convince young children that the healthier foods they are being "bribed" to eat must really be yucky stuff after all (Birch, Marlin, & Rotter, 1984).

In addition to their poor eating habits, obese children are less active than normal weight peers. Of course, their inactivity may both contribute to obesity (obese children burn fewer calories) and be a consequence of their overweight condition. One strong clue that activity restriction contributes to obesity is that the amount of time children spend in the sedentary activity of watching television is one of the best predictors of fu-

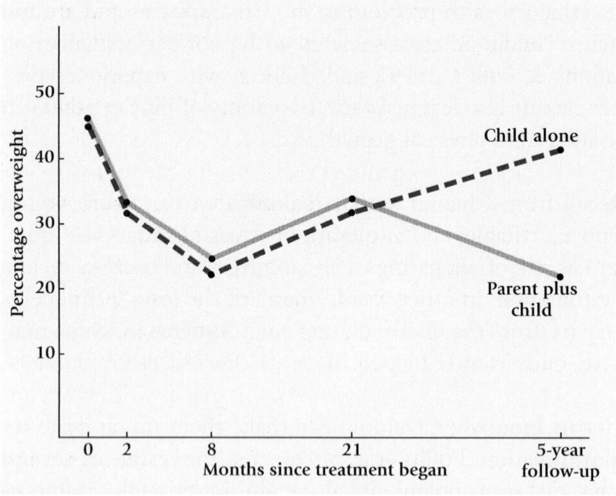

Figure 6.12 Average percentage of excess body weight for obese children who participated in a weight-loss program with and without a parent. *Adapted from "Long-Term Effects of Family-Based Treatment of Childhood Obesity," by L. H. Epstein, R. R. Wing, R. Koeske, & A. Valoski, 1987,* Journal of Consulting and Clinical Psychology, *55, 91–95. Adapted by permission of the author.*

ture obesity (Cowley, 2001). Television may also promote poor eating habits: not only do children tend to snack while passively watching TV, but the foods they see advertised are mostly high-calorie products containing lots of fat and sugar and few beneficial nutrients (Tinsley, 1992).

Crash diets for obese children are often counterproductive. Severe dietary restrictions can interfere with the development of the brain, muscles, and bones early in life, and older children on restrictive diets may feel mistreated, rejected, and inclined to partake in binge eating should the opportunity arise (Kolata, 1986). To date, the most effective treatments for childhood obesity have been behavioral approaches that involve obese youngsters *and* their parents. In one particularly effective program (Epstein et al., 1987, 1990), parents and their obese children were taught to revise their eating and exercise habits, to carefully monitor their own behavior to ensure compliance with the regimen, and to encourage other family members to exercise more and eat healthier foods. In addition, children in this program entered into contracts with their parents whereby they could earn rewards for losing weight. As shown in Figure 6.12, obese children who received this intensive family therapy not only lost weight, but had kept it off when observed during a follow-up 5 years later. Obese youngsters who had participated in the same program without their parents were unable to maintain the weight loss they had initially achieved. Here, then, is a strong indication that childhood obesity is a *family* problem that is most likely to be overcome when family members work together to change a home environment that has permitted children to become obese.

Illnesses

Among children who are adequately nourished, common childhood illnesses such as measles, chicken pox, or even pneumonia have little if any effect on physical growth and development. Major illnesses that keep a child in bed for weeks may temporarily retard growth, but after recovering, the child will ordinarily show a growth spurt (catch-up growth) that makes up for the progress lost while he or she was sick (Tanner, 1990).

Yet, diseases are likely to permanently stunt the growth of children who are moderately to severely undernourished. A poor diet weakens the immune system so that childhood diseases strike an undernourished child sooner and harder (Pollitt et al., 1996). Not only does malnutrition increase one's susceptibility to disease, but diseases contribute to malnutrition by suppressing a child's appetite and limiting the body's ability to absorb and utilize nutrients (Pollitt, 1994). In developing countries where gastrointestinal infections and upper respiratory illnesses are common, young school-age children who have been relatively disease-free are already 1 to 2 inches taller and 3 to 5 pounds heavier on average than their more "sickly" peers (Martorell, 1980; Roland, Cole, & Whitehead, 1977), and are outperforming them on a variety of cognitive tests as well (Pollitt, 1994).

Emotional Stress and Lack of Affection

Finally, otherwise healthy children who experience too much stress and too little affection are likely to lag far behind their age-mates in physical growth and motor development. This *failure-to-thrive* syndrome may characterize as many as 6 percent of preschool children in the United States and up to 5 percent of all patients admitted to pediatric hospitals (Lozoff, 1989).

nonorganic failure to thrive
an infant growth disorder, caused by lack of attention and affection, that causes growth to slow dramatically or stop.

Nonorganic failure to thrive is a growth disorder that appears early, usually by 18 months of age. Babies who display it stop growing and appear to be wasting away, in much the same way that malnourished infants with marasmus do. These infants do not have an obvious illness, and no other biological cause for their condition is apparent.

Affected babies often have trouble feeding and, in many cases, their growth retardation is undoubtedly attributable to poor nutrition (Brockington, 1996; Lozoff, 1989). Of course, a major question is, why would an otherwise healthy baby have trouble feeding?

One clue comes from these babies' behaviors around caregivers. They are generally apathetic and withdrawn, will often watch their caregivers closely, but are unlikely to smile or cuddle when they are picked up. Why? Because their caregivers are typically cool and aloof, impatient with them, and sometimes even physically abusive (Brockington, 1996). So even though caregivers offer enough food for those babies to thrive, their impatience and hostility causes babies to withdraw and to become aloof themselves to the point of feeding poorly and displaying few, if any, positive social responses.

deprivation dwarfism
a childhood growth disorder that is triggered by emotional deprivation and characterized by decreased production of GH, slow growth, and small stature.

Deprivation dwarfism is a second growth-related disorder that stems from emotional deprivation and a lack of affection. It appears later, usually between 2 and 15 years of age, and is characterized by small stature and dramatically reduced rates of growth, even though children who display this disorder do not look especially malnourished and usually receive adequate nutrition and physical care. What seems to be lacking in their lives is a positive involvement with another person, namely with their primary caregivers, who themselves are likely to be depressed by an unhappy marriage, economic hardships, or some other personal problem (Brockington, 1996; Roithmaier et al., 1988). It appears that deprivation dwarfs grow very slowly because their emotional deprivation depresses the endocrine system and inhibits the production of growth hormone. Indeed, when these youngsters are removed from their homes and begin to receive attention and affection, secretion of GH quickly resumes, and they display catch-up growth, even when they eat the same diet on which they formerly failed to thrive (Brockington, 1996; Gardner, 1972).

The prognoses for children affected by nonorganic failure to thrive and deprivation dwarfism is very good if the caregiving problems responsible for these disorders are corrected by individual or family therapy, or if the affected child is placed with caring foster parents (Brockington, 1996). However, if nonorganic failure to thrive is not identified and corrected in the first 2 years, or if the emotional neglect that underlies deprivation dwarfism persists for several years, affected children may remain smaller than normal and display long-term emotional problems and intellectual deficiencies as well (Drotar, 1992; Lozoff, 1989).

In sum, failure to thrive provides yet another indication that children require love and responsive caregiving if they are to develop normally. Fortunately, there is hope for preventing these deprivation-related disorders if parents whose children are at risk can be identified early, which they often can be. Even before giving birth, women whose children may fail to thrive are more likely than other mothers to feel unloved by their parents, to reject their own mothers as a model, and to say their own childhoods were unhappy. Within days of giving birth, these mothers are already having more problems feeding and soothing their babies than other mothers are (Lozoff, 1989). Clearly, these families need help and would almost certainly benefit from early interventions that teach parents how to be more sensitive and responsive caregivers.

CONCEPT CHECK 6.3 Psychological Impacts of Puberty and Causes of Growth and Development

Check your understanding of the psychological impacts of puberty as well as the causes and correlates of growth and development by answering the following questions. Answers appear in the Appendix.

True or False: Indicate whether each of the following statements is true or false.

1. (T)(F) "Rites of passage" are rituals observed in many nonindustrialized countries that are used to mark the child's puberty and transition from child to adolescent.
2. (T)(F) One cross-cultural similarity in child-rearing is that the vast majority of societies are relatively restrictive in their views of adolescent sexuality, view sex as a taboo subject, and vigorously suppress its expression.

CONTINUED

Matching: Match the following nutritional deficits with their definitions.

3. kwashiorkor
4. iron deficiency anemia
5. overnutrition
6. marasmus

a. a wasting away of body tissues caused by insufficient protein and calories
b. a disease marked by a swollen abdomen and severe skin lesions caused by insufficient protein
c. a disease that is associated with diabetes, high blood pressure, and heart or kidney disease
d. a disease that makes children listless and inattentive, retards their growth, and causes them to score poorly on tests of intelligence

Multiple Choice: Select the best alternative for each question.

_____ 7. Research has found that the timing of puberty can have effects on adolescents' self-esteem and personality. Which of the following most accurately describes the effects of timing of puberty on girls and boys?
a. Early maturing boys and early maturing girls both show advantages to their self-esteem associated with maturing early.
b. Later maturing boys and later maturing girls both show disadvantages to their self-esteem associated with maturing later.
c. Early maturing boys show disadvantages and early maturing girls show advantages to their self-esteem associated with maturing earlier.
d. Early maturing boys show advantages and early maturing girls show disadvantages to their self-esteem associated with maturing earlier.

_____ 8. The "double standard" view of sexuality (that is, the idea that sexual practices are appropriate for males but not for females) has
a. Remained the same in the past few decades.
b. Increased in the past few decades.
c. Decreased in the past few decades.
d. Reversed in the past few decades.

_____ 9. In the United States, large numbers of sexually active adolescents fail to use contraception, largely because of all of the following reasons *except*
a. They are uninformed about reproductive issues.
b. They are too cognitively immature to take seriously the possibility that their behavior could have serious long-term consequences.
c. They are largely unable to obtain contraceptive devices because of the restrictiveness of the culture.
d. They are concerned that others will think negatively of them if they appear prepared to have sex.

Short Answer: Briefly answer the following question.

10. Describe the *Teen Outreach* program for adolescents and explain how it helps to prevent early sexual activity and lower incidence of STDs and pregnancy among participating teens.

Applying Developmental Themes to Physical Development

Before we close our discussion of physical development, let's take a brief look at how our developmental themes are reflected in the various aspects of physical development, including the development of the brain and body, the development of motor skills, and puberty and sexual development. Recall that our developmental themes include the active child, the interplay of nature and nurture in development, qualitative and quantitative developmental changes, and the holistic nature of development.

Our first theme is that of the active child, or how the child participates in his or her own development both, intentionally and through unconscious implications of his or her nature. One dramatic piece of evidence that the child is active in development is the fact that the child's early experiences direct the synaptic pruning that occurs in the first few years of life. Children who are reared in stimulating environments may develop dramatically different brain organizations than those who are reared in impoverished environments. We saw an example of this in the orphans who were left lying on their backs in cribs for the first 2 years of life and, as a result, were severely handicapped in their motor development when finally freed from this restriction. Further support for this active role in development came from Riesen's work with dark-reared chimpanzees, which revealed that atrophy of the neurons that make up the optic nerve led to blindness if the young chimps were unable to see for longer than 7 months, suggesting that the active use of these neurons was necessary for normal visual development. Turning to the development of motor skills, dynamical systems theory clearly sees the child as active in the development of motor skills early in life, as the infants use goals and objectives to actively reorganize existing motor capabilities into new and more complex action systems. And finally, we saw evidence that the adolescent's activity can even affect the timing of puberty. Adolescent females who are engaging in extremely strenuous physical activity and those who are afflicted with anorexia may begin menstruating very late or stop after they have begun.

The interactions of nature and nurture in their effects on physical development expand the influence of the active child to include the environment in which the child is reared. For example, both heredity and environmental factors such as the food people eat, the diseases they may contract, and even the emotional climate of their lives can produce significant variations in the rates at which they grow and the statures they eventually attain. We saw that the early development of the brain is the result of both a biological program and early experiences. The effects on the timing of puberty also illustrate the interactions of nature and nurture on physical development. Both genetic influences (as demonstrated by twin and family studies) and environmental influences (such as the cessation of pubertal development seen in girls who are involved in extremely strenuous physical activity) interact to influence the timing of pubertal events.

Physical development across childhood and adolescence is marked by both qualitative and quantitative changes. We saw that babies may remain the same length for days or weeks at a time before showing spurts of more than a centimeter in a single day, a dramatic qualitative change. Quantitative changes mark the period of physical development during middle childhood (ages 6 to 11) when children may seem to grow very little. This is because their rate of growth is slow and steady throughout these years. Another qualitative change concerns the body's physical proportions. Across childhood, body shape changes from infancy to childhood, and then dramatically during the adolescent growth spurt and puberty, when the child takes on adult proportions. Qualitative physical changes also influence cognitive abilities (which is also an example of the holistic nature of development). We saw that researchers believe that the cognitive advances of adolescence experience occur only after a qualitative change in brain development including reorganizations and specializations. And of course the adolescent growth spurt and the physical changes of puberty are a clear example of a qualitative change in physical development.

Finally, looking at the holistic nature of development, we saw many examples of the effects physical development can have on social, intellectual, and psychological aspects of development in this chapter. Indeed, these effects are the reason a chapter on physical development is included in a developmental psychology textbook! Some examples include the fact that individual differences in the rates at which children grow have strong consequences for their social and personality development. One area where such differences are seen is in the changes in the structures of the brain during adolescence, including myelinization of the higher brain centers and reorganizations of the neural circuitry of the prefrontal cortex that are responsible for the dramatic changes in the types of thought that occupy adolescents as compared to younger children. Looking at motor skill development, we saw that the dynamical systems theory sees early motor development as a holistic enterprise, involving the infants' cognitive goals and objectives, leading to the reorganization of simple motor skills into more complex motor systems. We saw that experienced crawlers and walkers are better able to use landmarks to guide their adventures than are infants who have just begun to crawl or walk. This suggests that locomotion influences spatial memory, another example of how various aspects of development work together in a holistic manner. Turning to the physical changes of adolescence, we saw that physically active girls and teenagers experience important psychological benefits such as increased self-esteem. Furthermore, the many social and psychological implications of maturing early or late, for both girls and boys (but in opposite directions), is more evidence of how physical development is linked to other aspects of development in a holistic manner. The cultural influences on an adolescent's developing sexuality links social influences to physical development. And finally, the dramatic social, cultural, and intellectual implications of early sexual behavior and teenage pregnancy (implications for both the teenage mothers and their babies) is yet another example of physical development interacting with other aspects of development in a holistic manner.

SUMMARY

An Overview of Maturation and Growth

- The body is constantly changing between infancy and adulthood.
  - Height and weight increase rapidly during the first 2 years.
  - Growth becomes more gradual across middle childhood.
  - In early adolescence there is rapid growth spurt when height and weight again increase rapidly.
- The shape of the body and body proportions also change because various body parts grow at different rates.
  - Physical development follows a **cephalocaudal** (head downward) and a **proximodistal** (center-outward) direction: structures in the upper and central regions of the body mature before those in the lower and peripheral regions.
- Skeletal and muscular development parallel the changes occurring in height and weight.
  - Bones become longer and thicker and gradually harden, completing their growth and development by the late teens.
  - **Skeletal age** is a measure of physical maturation.
  - Muscles increase in density and size, particularly during the growth spurt of early adolescence.
- Physical growth is quite uneven, or asynchronous:
  - The brain, the reproductive system, and the lymph tissues mature at different rates.
  - There are sizable individual and cultural variations in physical growth and development.

Development of the Brain

- A **brain growth spurt** occurs during the last 3 months of the prenatal period and the first 2 years of life.
  - **Neurons** form **synapses** with other neurons.
  - **Glia** form to nourish the neurons and encase them in myelin—a waxy material that speeds the transmission of neural impulses.
- Many more neurons and synapses are formed than are needed:
  - Those that are used often will survive.
  - Neurons that are stimulated less often either die or lose their synapses and stand in reserve to compensate for brain injuries.
  - Up until puberty, the brain shows a great deal of **plasticity;** this allows it to change in response to experience and to recover from many injuries.
- The highest brain center, or **cerebrum,** consists of two hemispheres connected by the **corpus callosum.**
  - Each hemisphere is covered by a **cerebral cortex.**
  - The brain may be **lateralized** at birth so that the two hemispheres assume different functions.
  - Children come to rely increasingly on one particular hemisphere or the other to perform each function.
- **Myelinization** and reorganization of the neural circuitry of the cerebral cortex continue throughout adolescence.

Motor Development

- Like the physical structures of the body, motor development proceeds in a cephalocaudal and proximodistal direction.
  - Motor skills evolve in a definite sequence:
    - Infants gain control over their heads, necks, and upper arms before they become proficient with their legs, feet, and hands.
  - Motor skills that infants display do not unfold according to a maturational timetable: experience is important as well:
    - Institutionalized children who have few opportunities to practice motor skills have retarded motor development.
    - Cross-cultural research shows that motor development can be accelerated.
  - According to **dynamical systems theory,** each new motor skill represents an active and intricate reorganization of several existing capabilities that infants undertake to achieve important objectives.
- Fine motor skills improve dramatically in the first year.
  - Prereaching is replaced by voluntary reaching.
  - The claw-like **ulnar grasp** is replaced by the **pincer grasp.**
  - Reaching and grasping skills transform infants into skillful manipulators who soon reorganize their existing capabilities to copy lines and build towers of blocks.
- Emerging motor skills often thrill parents and allow new forms of play.

- Emerging motor skills support other aspects of perceptual, cognitive, and social development.
- With each passing year, children's motor skills improve.
  - Boys become notably stronger than girls early in adolescence because of their greater muscular development and the fact that girls are less inclined to remain physically active.

Puberty: The Physical Transition from Child to Adult

- At about age 10½ for females and age 13 for males, the **adolescent growth spurt** begins.
  - Adolescents grow taller and heavier.
  - Adolescents' bodies and faces assume a more adult-like appearance.
- Sexual maturation:
  - begins about the same time as the adolescent growth spurt
  - follows a predictable sequence
- For girls, **puberty** includes:
  - the onset of breast and pubic-hair development
  - a widening of the hips, enlarging of the uterus and vagina
  - **menarche** (first menstruation)
  - and completion of breast and pubic-hair growth
- For boys, puberty includes:
  - development of the testes and scrotum
  - the emergence of pubic hair
  - the growth of the penis and the ability to ejaculate
  - the appearance of facial hair
  - and a lowering of the voice
- There are great individual differences in the timing of sexual maturation.
- The **secular trend** refers to the fact that people in industrialized societies are reaching sexual maturity earlier than in the past.
  - People are also growing taller and heavier than people in the past.
  - The secular trend is due to improved nutrition and health care.

The Psychological Impacts of Puberty

- Girls' reactions to their changing bodies:
  - They hope to be attractive.
  - They worry about their weight.
  - Their reactions to menarche are mixed.
- Boys' reactions to their changing bodies:
  - They have better body images than girls.
  - They are somewhat more positive about their first ejaculation than girls are about menarche.
- Some girls, and fewer boys, develop such poor body images that they become afflicted with eating disorders.
  - **Anorexia** and **bulimia** are two serious eating disorders in which the afflicted starve themselves or binge eat and purge in efforts to attain unrealistic and unhealthy body images.
  - Cultural, personal, emotional, and environmental influences all contribute to the development of these disorders.
- Societies differ in their reactions to puberty.
  - Many nonindustrialized societies:
    - take pubertal changes as a sign that a child has become an adult
    - mark this transition with formal **rites of passage**
  - In other societies:
    - Parent-child conflicts often heighten at puberty and usually decline later in adolescence.
- Timing of puberty can have personal and social consequences.
  - Early-maturing boys and on-time and late-maturing girls:
    - have better body images
    - feel more self-confident
    - display better social adjustment than late-maturing boys and early-maturing girls
  - These effects do not hold for all individuals and tend to fade over time.
- The hormonal changes of puberty bring about an increase in sex drive and the responsibility of managing one's **sexuality.**
  - This transition may be particularly difficult for teenagers who are sexually attracted to same-sex peers.
  - Sexual attitudes have become increasingly liberal over the years.
    - A majority of adolescents now think that sex with affection is acceptable.
    - Teens seem to be rejecting the **double standard** for sexual behavior.
    - Teenage sexual activity has increased, more for girls than for boys.
  - Large numbers of sexually active teenagers fail to use contraception regularly.
    - This increases the risk of contracting sexually transmitted diseases (STDs) or becoming pregnant.
- Adolescent pregnancy and childbearing represent a major social problem in the United States.
  - Teenage mothers:
    - are often poor and ill-prepared psychologically to be parents
    - often drop out of school and perpetuate their economic disadvantage
  - Poor teenage parenting contributes to the emotional problems and cognitive deficiencies that children of teenage parents often display.
  - Discussions about sexual matters at home, improved sex education and contraceptive services, and programs such as *Teen Outreach* can help to reduce sexual risk and the rate teenage pregnancy.

Causes and Correlates of Physical Development

- Physical development results from a complex interplay between biological and environmental forces.
  - Individual genotypes set limits for stature, shape, and tempo of growth.
  - Growth is heavily influenced by hormones released by the endocrine glands as regulated by the **pituitary.**
  - **Growth hormone** (GH) and **thyroxine** regulate growth throughout childhood.
  - At adolescence, other endocrine glands secrete hormones.
    - **Estrogen** from the ovaries triggers sexual development in girls.
    - **Testosterone** from the testes instigates sexual development in boys.
- Adequate nutrition, in the form of total calories, protein, and vitamins and minerals, is necessary for children to reach their growth potentials.
  - **Marasmus, kwashiorkor,** and **iron deficiency anemia** are three growth-retarding diseases that stem from undernutrition.
  - In industrialized countries, **obesity** is a nutritional problem, with many physical and psychological consequences.
- Chronic infectious diseases can combine with poor nutrition to stunt physical and intellectual growth.
  - **Nonorganic failure to thrive** and **deprivation dwarfism** illustrate that affection and sensitive, responsive caregiving are important to ensure normal growth.

KEY TERMS

cephalocaudal development 196
proximodistal development 197
skeletal age 198
brain growth spurt 199
synapse 199
neurons 199
glia 199
synaptogenesis 200
plasticity 200
myelinization 201
cerebrum 202
corpus callosum 202
cerebral cortex 202
cerebral lateralization 202
dynamical systems theory 207
proprioceptive information 208
ulnar grasp 208
pincer grasp 209
adolescent growth spurt 212
puberty 212
physically active play 213
menarche 214
secular trend 215
anorexia nervosa 218
bulimia 218
rites of passage 221
sexuality 223
double standard 224
thyroxine 230
pituitary 230
growth hormone (GH) 230
estrogen 230
testosterone 230
catch-up growth 232
marasmus 232
kwashiorkor 232
vitamin/mineral deficiency 232
iron deficiency anemia 232
obese 233
nonorganic failure to thrive 234
deprivation dwarfism 235

MEDIA RESOURCES

The Human Development Book Companion Website

See the companion website http://www.thomsonedu.com/psychology/shaffer for flashcards, practice quiz questions, Internet links, updates, critical thinking exercises, discussion forums, games, and more

Thomson NOW! http://www.thomsonedu.com
Go to this site for the link to ThomsonNOW, your one-stop shop. Take a pre-test for this chapter, and ThomsonNOW will generate a personalized study plan based on your test results. The study plan will identify the topics you need to review and direct you to online resources to help you master those topics. You can then take a post-test to help you determine the concepts you have mastered and what you will still need to work on.

Child and Adolescent Development CD-ROM

For more information about the concepts covered in this chapter, go to

Module I: Physical Development

- Physical Development During Infancy
- Physical Development in Childhood and Adolescence
- Module I Media

Veer/Michael Malyszko/Getty Images

CHAPTER 7

Cognitive Development: Piaget's Theory and Vygotsky's Sociocultural Viewpoint

TEACHER (to a class of 9-year-olds): For artwork today, I'd like each of you to draw me a picture of a person who has three eyes.

BILLY: How? Nobody has three eyes!

If you were asked to account for the reaction of this 9-year-old, you might be tempted to conclude that he either lacks imagination or is being sarcastic. Actually, Billy's feelings about the art assignment are rather typical (see the Box on page 269), because 9-year-olds think differently than adults do, and they often find it difficult to reflect on hypothetical propositions that have no basis in reality.

cognition
the activity of knowing and the processes through which knowledge is acquired.

cognitive development
changes that occur in mental activities such as attending, perceiving, learning, thinking, and remembering.

Our next three chapters examine the growth of **cognition**—a term psychologists use to refer to the activity of knowing and the mental processes by which human beings acquire and use knowledge to solve problems. The cognitive processes that help us to understand and to adapt to the environment include such activities as attending, perceiving, learning, thinking, and remembering—in short, the unobservable events and undertakings that characterize the human mind (Bjorklund, 2005).

The study of **cognitive development**—the changes that occur in children's mental abilities over the course of their lives—is one of the more diverse and exciting topics in all of developmental sciences. In this chapter we begin our exploration of the developing mind, focusing first on the many important contributions of Swiss psychologist Jean Piaget, who charted what he (and others) believed to be a *universal* pattern of intellectual growth that unfolds during infancy, childhood, and adolescence. We then examine Lev Vygotsky's *sociocultural* viewpoint—a theory that claims that cognitive growth is heavily influenced by one's culture and may be nowhere near as universal as Piaget and his followers assumed (Wertsch & Tulviste, 1992).

Chapter 8 introduces a third influential perspective on the developing mind: *information processing,* a viewpoint that arose, in part, from questions left unanswered by Piaget's earlier work. Our attention then shifts in Chapter 9 to the *psychometric,* or intelligence testing, approach, where we discuss the many factors that contribute to individual differences in children's intellectual performance.

Piaget's Theory of Cognitive Development

You were introduced to Piaget in Chapter 2. By far the most influential theorist in the history of child development, Piaget combined his earlier interests in zoology and

genetic epistemology
the experimental study of the development of knowledge, developed by Piaget.

epistemology (the branch of philosophy concerned with the origins of knowledge) to develop a new science that he termed **genetic epistemology,** which he defined as the experimental study of the origin of knowledge. (Piaget used the term *genetic* in an older sense, meaning essentially developmental.)

Piaget began his studies by carefully observing his own three children as infants: how they explored new toys, solved simple problems that he arranged for them, and generally came to understand themselves and their world. Later, Piaget studied larger samples of children through what became known as the *clinical method,* a flexible question-and-answer technique he used to discover how children of different ages solve various problems and thought about everyday issues. From these naturalistic observations of topics ranging from the rules of games to the laws of physics, Piaget formulated his grand theory of intellectual growth.

What Is Intelligence?

intelligence
in Piaget's theory, a basic life function that enables an organism to adapt to its environment.

cognitive equilibrium
Piaget's term for the state of affairs in which there is a balanced, or harmonious, relationship between one's thought processes and the environment.

constructivist
one who gains knowledge by acting or otherwise operating on objects and events to discover their properties.

Piaget's background in zoology is quite apparent from his definition of **intelligence** as *a basic life function* that helps the organism adapt to its environment. We observe such adaptation as we watch a toddler figure how to turn on the TV, a school-age child decide how to divide candies among friends, or an adolescent struggle at solving a geometry problem. Piaget proposed that intelligence is "a form of *equilibrium* toward which all cognitive structures tend" (1950, p. 6). His point was simply that all intellectual activity is undertaken with one goal in mind: to produce a balanced, or harmonious, relationship between one's thought processes and the environment. Such a balanced state of affairs is called **cognitive equilibrium,** and the process of achieving it is called *equilibration.* Piaget stressed that children are active and curious explorers who are constantly challenged by many novel stimuli and events that are not immediately understood. He believed that these imbalances (or *cognitive disequilibria*) between the children's modes of thinking and environmental events prompt them to make mental adjustments that enable them to cope with puzzling new experiences and thereby restore cognitive equilibrium. So we see that Piaget's view of intelligence is an "interactionist" model that implies that mismatches between one's internal mental schemes (existing knowledge) and the external environment stimulate cognitive activity and intellectual growth.

There is a very important assumption that underlies Piaget's view of intelligence: If children are to know something, they must *construct* that knowledge themselves. Indeed, Piaget described the child as a **constructivist**—an individual who acts on novel objects and events and thereby gains some understanding of their essential features. Children's constructions of reality (that is, interpretations of objects and events) depend on the knowledge they have available to them: The more immature the child's cognitive system, the more limited his or her interpretation of an event. For example, 4-year-old Robin told his mom after school one day, "*Mommy, today at recess, a big cold wind came and almost blew me down! I think it knew that I was hot and it came to cool me down!*" This child is making an important assumption that dominates his attempt at understanding—namely that inanimate things, in this case wind, have intentions. He does not make the distinction between animate and inanimate objects, at least not the type of distinction that adults make. As a result, he constructs a very different interpretation of "reality" than his mother does.

Elizabeth Crews/The Image Works

Infants develop a broad range of behavioral schemes that they can use to explore and "understand" new objects and to solve simple problems.

How We Gain Knowledge: Cognitive Schemes and Cognitive Processes

scheme
an organized pattern of thought or action that one constructs to interpret some aspect of one's experience (also called cognitive structure).

According to Piaget, cognition develops through the refinement and transformation of mental structures, or **schemes** (Piaget & Inhelder, 1969). Schemes are unobservable mental systems that underlie intelligence. A scheme is a pattern of thought or action and is most simply viewed as some enduring knowledge base by which children interpret their world. Schemes, in effect, are representations of reality. Children know their world through their schemes. Schemes are the means by which children interpret and organize experience. For Piaget, cognitive development is the development of schemes, or structures. Children enter the world with some reflexes by which they interpret their surroundings, and what underlies these reflexes are schemes.

How do children construct and modify their intellectual schemes? Piaget believed that all schemes, all forms of understanding, are created through the workings of two inborn intellectual processes: *organization* and *adaptation*.

organization
an inborn tendency to combine and integrate available schemes into coherent systems or bodies of knowledge.

Organization is the process by which children combine existing schemes into new and more complex intellectual schemes. For example, an infant who has "gazing," "reaching," and "grasping" reflexes soon organizes these initially unrelated schemes into a more complex structure—*visually directed reaching*—that enables him to reach out and discover the characteristics of many interesting objects in the environment. Although cognitive schemes may assume radically different forms at different phases of development, the process of organization is unchanging. Piaget believed that children are constantly organizing whatever schemes they have into more complex and adaptive structures.

adaptation
an inborn tendency to adjust to the demands of the environment.

assimilation
the process of interpreting new experiences by incorporating them into existing schemes.

The goal of organization is to promote **adaptation,** the process of adjusting to the demands of the environment. According to Piaget, adaptation occurs through two complementary activities: *assimilation* and *accommodation*.

Assimilation is the process by which children try to interpret new experiences in terms of their existing models of the world, the schemes they already possess. The young child who sees a horse for the first time may try to assimilate it into one of her existing schemes for four-legged animals and thus may think of this creature as a "doggie." In other words, the child is trying to adapt to this novel stimulus by construing it as something familiar.

accommodation
the process of modifying existing schemes in order to incorporate or adapt to new experiences.

Yet truly novel objects, events, and experiences may be difficult to interpret in terms of one's existing schemes. For example, our young child may soon notice that this big animal she is labeling a doggie has funny-looking feet and a most peculiar bark, and she may seek a better understanding of the observations she has made. **Accommodation,** the complement of assimilation, is the process of modifying existing structures in order to account for new experiences. So the child who recognizes that a horse is not a dog may invent a name for this new creature or perhaps say "What dat?" and adopt the label that her companions use. In so doing, she has modified (accommodated) her scheme for four-legged animals to include a new category of experience—horses.

Piaget believed that assimilation and accommodation work together to promote cognitive growth. They do not always occur equally as in the preceding example; but assimilations of experiences that do not quite "jibe" with existing schemes eventually introduce cognitive conflict and prompt accommodations to those experiences. And the end result is adaptation, a state of equilibrium, or balance, between one's cognitive structures and the environment.

Table 7.1 provides one example of how cognitive growth might proceed from Piaget's point of view—a perspective that stresses that cognitive development is an *active* process in which children are regularly seeking and *assimilating* new experiences, *accommodating* their cognitive structures to these experiences, and *organizing* what they know into new and more complex schemes. So two inborn activities—organization and adaptation—make it possible for children to construct progressively greater understandings of the world in which they live.

TABLE 7.1 A Small Sample of Cognitive Growth from Piaget's Perspective

	Piagetian concept	Definition	Example
Start	Equilibrium	Harmony between one's schemes and one's experience.	Toddler who has never seen anything fly but birds thinks that all flying objects are "birdies."
	Assimilation	Tries to adapt to new experience by interpreting it in terms of existing schemes.	Seeing an airplane in the sky prompts child to call the flying object a birdie.
	Accommodation	Modifies existing schemes to better account for puzzling new experience.	Toddler experiences conflict or disequilibrium upon noticing that the new birdie has no feathers and doesn't flap its wings. Concludes it is not a bird and invents a new name for it (or asks, "What dat?"). Successful accommodation restores equilibrium—for the moment, at least.
Finish	Organization	Rearranges existing schemes into new and more complex structures.	Forms hierarchical scheme consisting of a superordinate class (flying objects) and two subordinate classes (birdies and airplanes).

Note: As an exercise, you may wish to apply Piaget's concepts to chart the further elaborations of the child's schemes upon encountering a butterfly and a Frisbee.

CONCEPT CHECK 7.1 Understanding Piagetian Assumptions and Concepts

Check your understanding of the basic assumptions and concepts of Piaget's theory by answering the following questions. Answers appear in the appendix.

Multiple Choice: Select the best alternative for each question.

_____ 1. According to Piaget, *accommodation* refers to
- a. the modification or distortion of new information in order to incorporate it into current schemes
- b. the fact that every structure has its genesis in previous structures
- c. the tendency to integrate structures into higher order systems of structures
- d. the changing of a current scheme in order to incorporate new information

_____ 2. According to Piaget, *cognitive equilibration* refers to the
- a. tendency to integrate structures into higher order systems or structures
- b. individual seeking to stabilize his or her cognitive structures
- c. tendency to modify structures in order to incorporate new information into existing structures
- d. fact that every structure has its genesis (that is, its origins) in earlier structures

_____ 3. Professor Johanson believes that children's thinking follows an invariant developmental sequence. It is likely that Professor Johanson generally
- a. agrees with Piaget and is a stage theorist
- b. agrees with Piaget and is *not* a stage theorist
- c. disagrees with Piaget and believes that children's thinking is uneven at different times in development
- d. disagrees with Piaget and believes that children's thinking strongly reflects sociocultural influence

Matching: Match the following concepts with their definitions.

a. schemes
b. constructivist
c. cognitive equilibration
d. intelligence
e. organization
f. assimilation

4. _______ In Piaget's theory, a basic life function that enables an organism to adapt to its environment.
5. _______ Piaget's term for the state of affairs in which there is a balanced, or harmonious, relationship between one's thought processes and the environment.
6. _______ The process of interpreting new experiences by incorporating them into existing schemes.
7. _______ One who gains knowledge by acting or otherwise operating on objects and events to discover their properties.
8. _______ An organized pattern of thought or action that one constructs to interpret some aspect of one's experience.
9. _______ An inborn tendency to combine and integrate available schemes into coherent systems or bodies of knowledge.

Essays: Provide a detailed answer to the following questions.

10. Discuss Piaget's concept of adaptation. How do assimilation and accommodation "work" together to result in adaptation?
11. How did Piaget define *intelligence?* How is this different from the way most people define the term?

Piaget's Stages of Cognitive Development

invariant developmental sequence
a series of developments that occur in one particular order because each development in the sequence is a prerequisite for those appearing later.

Piaget identified four major periods, or stages, of cognitive development: the *sensorimotor stage* (birth to 2 years), the *preoperational stage* (2 to 7 years), the *stage of concrete operations* (7 to 11 years), and the *stage of formal operations* (11 years and beyond). These stages of intellectual growth represent qualitatively different levels of functioning and form what Piaget calls an **invariant developmental sequence;** that is, all children progress through the stages in the same order. Piaget argued that stages can never be skipped because each successive stage builds on the accomplishments of previous stages.

Although Piaget believed that the sequencing of intellectual stages is fixed, or invariant, he recognized that there are tremendous individual differences in the ages at which children enter or emerge from any particular stage. In fact, his view was that cultural factors and other environmental influences may either accelerate or retard a child's rate of intellectual growth, and he considered the age norms that accompany his stages (and substages) as only rough approximations at best.

The Sensorimotor Stage (Birth to 2 Years)

sensorimotor period
Piaget's first intellectual stage, from birth to 2 years, when infants are relying on behavioral schemes as a means of exploring and understanding the environment.

During the **sensorimotor stage,** infants coordinate their *sensory* inputs and *motor* capabilities, forming behavioral schemes that permit them to "act on" and to get to "know" their environment. How much can they really understand by relying on overt actions to generate knowledge? More than you might imagine. During the first 2 years, infants develop from reflexive creatures with very limited knowledge into planful problem solvers who have already learned a great deal about themselves, their close companions, and the objects and events in their everyday world. So drastic is the infant's cognitive growth that Piaget divided the sensorimotor period into six substages (see Table 7.2) that describe the

TABLE 7.2 Summary of the Piaget's Account of Sensorimotor Development

Substage	Methods of solving problems or producing interesting outcomes	Imitation	Object concept
1. Reflex activity (0–1 month)	Exercising and accommodation of inborn reflexes.	Some reflexive imitation of motor responses.[1]	Tracks moving object but ignores its disappearance.
2. Primary circular reactions (1–4 months)	Repeating interesting acts that are centered on one's own body.	Repetition of own behavior that is mimicked by a companion.	Looks intently at the spot where an object disappeared.[2]
3. Secondary circular reactions (4–8 months)	Repeating interesting acts that are directed toward external objects.	Same as in Substage 2.	Searches for partly concealed object.
4. Coordination of secondary schemes (8–12 months)	Combining actions to solve simple problems (first evidence of intentionality).	Gradual imitation of novel responses; deferred imitation of very simple motor acts after a brief delay.	Clear signs of emerging object concept; searches for and finds concealed object that has *not* been visibly displaced.
5. Tertiary circular reactions (12–18 months)	Experimenting to find new ways to solve problems or reproduce interesting outcomes.	Systematic imitation of novel responses; deferred imitation of simple motor acts after a long delay.	Searches for and finds object that has been *visibly* displaced.
6. Invention of new means through mental combinations (18–24 months)	First evidence of insight as the child solves problems at an internal, symbolic level.	Deferred imitation of complex behavioral sequences.	Object concept is complete; searches for and finds objects that have been hidden through *invisible* displacements.

[1]Imitation of simple motor acts (such as tongue protrusions, head movements, and the opening and closing of one's lips or hands) is apparently an inborn, reflexlike ability that bears little relation to the voluntary imitation that appears later in the first year.

[2]Many researchers now believe that object permanence may be present very early and that Piaget's reliance on search procedures badly underestimated what young infants know about objects (see Box on p. 252).

Blowing bubbles is an accommodation of the sucking reflex and one of the infant's earliest primary circular reactions.

child's gradual transition from a *reflexive* to a *reflective* being. Our review will focus on three important aspects of sensorimotor development: *problem-solving skills* (or means/ends activities), *imitation,* and the growth of the *object concept.*

Development of Problem-Solving Abilities

Reflex Activity (Birth to 1 Month). Piaget characterized the first month of life as a stage of **reflex activity**—a period when an infant's actions are pretty much confined to exercising innate reflexes, assimilating new objects into these reflexive schemes (for example, sucking on blankets and toys as well as on nipples), and accommodating their reflexes to these novel objects. Granted, this is not high intellect, but these primitive adaptations represent the beginning of cognitive growth.

Primary Circular Reactions (1 to 4 Months). The first nonreflexive schemes emerge at 1 to 4 months of age as infants discover by chance that various responses that they can emit and control (for example, sucking their thumbs, making cooing sounds) are satisfying and, thus, worth repeating. These simple repetitive acts, called **primary circular reactions,** are always centered on the infant's own body. They are called "primary" because they are the first motor habits to appear and "circular" because they are repetitive.

Secondary Circular Reactions (4 to 8 Months). Between 4 and 8 months of age, infants are discovering (again by chance) that they can make interesting things happen to objects beyond their own bodies, such as making a rubber duck quack by squeezing it. These new schemes, called **secondary circular reactions,** are also repeated for the pleasure they bring. According to Piaget, 4- to 8-month-olds' sudden interest in external objects indicates that they have begun to differentiate themselves from objects they can control in the surrounding environment.

Is an infant who delights in such repetitive actions as swatting a brightly colored mobile or making a toy duck quack engaging in *planful* or *intentional* behavior? Piaget said no: The secondary circular reaction is not a fully intentional response, because the interesting result it produces was discovered by chance and was not a purposeful goal the first time the action was performed.

Coordination of Secondary Reactions (8 to 12 Months). Truly planful responding first appears between 8 and 12 months of age, during the substage of the **coordination of secondary circular reactions,** as infants begin to coordinate two or more actions to achieve simple objectives. For example, if you were to place an attractive toy under a cushion, a 9-month-old might lift the cushion with one hand while using the other to grab the toy. In this case, the act of lifting the cushion is not a pleasurable response in itself, nor is it emitted by chance. Rather, it is part of a larger *intentional* scheme in which two initially unrelated responses—lifting and grasping—are coordinated as a means to an end. Piaget believed that these simple coordinations of secondary schemes represent the earliest form of *goal-directed behavior,* and thus true problem solving.

Tertiary Circular Reactions (12 to 18 Months). Between 12 and 18 months of age, infants begin to actively experiment with objects and try to invent new methods of solving problems or reproducing interesting results. For example, an infant who had originally squeezed a rubber duck to make it quack may now decide to drop it, step on it, and crush it with a pillow to see whether these actions will have the same or different effects on the toy. Or she may learn from her explorations that flinging is more efficient than

reflex activity
first substage of Piaget's sensorimotor stage; infants' actions are confined to exercising innate reflexes, assimilating new objects into these reflexive schemes, and accommodating their reflexes to these novel objects.

primary circular reactions
second substage of Piaget's sensorimotor stage; a pleasurable response, centered on the infant's own body, that is discovered by chance and performed over and over.

secondary circular reactions
third substage of Piaget's sensorimotor stage; a pleasurable response, centered on an external object, that is discovered by chance and performed over and over.

coordination of secondary circular reactions
fourth substage of Piaget's sensorimotor stage; infants begin to coordinate two or more actions to achieve simple objectives. This is the first sign of goal-directed behavior.

spitting as a means of getting food to stick to the wall. Although parents may be less than thrilled by such exciting new cognitive advances, these trial-and-error exploratory schemes, called **tertiary circular reactions,** reflect an infant's active curiosity—her strong motivation to learn about the way things work.

tertiary circular reactions
fifth substage of Piaget's sensorimotor stage; an exploratory scheme in which the infant devises a new method of acting on objects to reproduce interesting results.

Symbolic Problem Solving (18 to 24 Months). The crowning achievement of the sensorimotor stage occurs as infants begin to internalize their behavioral schemes to construct mental symbols, or images, that they can then use to guide future conduct. Now the infant can experiment *mentally* and may show a kind of "insight" in how to solve a problem. Piaget's son Laurent nicely illustrates this symbolic problem solving, or **inner experimentation:**

inner experimentation
in the sixth substage of Piaget's sensorimotor stage, the ability to solve simple problems on a mental, or symbolic, level without having to rely on trial-and-error experimentation.

> Laurent is seated before a table and I place a bread crust in front of him, out of reach. Also, to the right . . . I place a stick, about 25 cm. long. At first, Laurent tries to grasp the bread . . . and then he gives up. . . . Laurent again looks at the bread, and without moving, looks very briefly at the stick, then suddenly grasps it and directs it toward the bread . . . [he then] draws the bread to him (Piaget, 1952, p. 335).

Clearly, this is not trial-and-error experimentation. Instead, Laurent's problem solving occurred at an internal, symbolic level as he visualized the stick being used as an extension of his arm to obtain a distant object.

Development of Imitation

Piaget recognized the adaptive significance of imitation, and he was very interested in its development. His own observations led him to believe that infants are incapable of imitating *novel* responses displayed by a model until 8 to 12 months of age (the same age at which they show some evidence of intentionality in their behavior). However, the imitative schemes of infants this young are rather imprecise. Were you to bend and straighten your finger, the infant might mimic you by opening and closing her entire hand (Piaget, 1951). Indeed, precise imitations of even the simplest responses may take days (or even weeks) of practice (Kaye & Marcus, 1981), and literally hundreds of demonstrations may be required before an 8- to 12-month-old will catch on and begin to enjoy sensorimotor games such as peekaboo or pat-a-cake.

Voluntary imitation becomes much more precise at age 12 to 18 months, as we see in the following example:

> At [1 year and 16 days of age, Jacqueline] discovered her forehead. When I touched the middle of mine, she first rubbed her eye, then felt above it and touched her hair, after which she brought her hand down a little and finally put her finger on her forehead (Piaget, 1951, p. 56).

According to Piaget, **deferred imitation**—the ability to reproduce the behavior of an *absent* model—first appears at 18 to 24 months of age. Consider the following observation of the antics of Jacqueline, Piaget's 16-month-old daughter:

deferred imitation
the ability to reproduce a modeled activity that has been witnessed at some point in the past.

> Jacqueline had a visit from a little boy (18 months of age) who, in the course of the afternoon got into a terrible temper. He screamed as he tried to get out of a playpen and pushed it backward, stamping his feet. Jacqueline stood watching him in amazement, never having witnessed such a scene before. The next day, she herself screamed in her playpen and tried to move, stamping her foot . . . several times in succession (Piaget, 1951, p. 63).

Piaget believed that older infants are capable of deferred imitation because they can now construct mental symbols, or images, of a model's behavior that are stored in memory and retrieved later to guide the child's re-creation of the modeled sequence.

Other investigators disagree with Piaget, arguing that deferred imitation, and thus symbolic representation, begins much earlier. (Deferred imitation was discussed in Chapter 5.) For example, research has shown that 6-month-olds are able to imitate very simple acts (for example, button-pressing to activate a noise-making toy) after 24 hours (Collie & Hayne, 1999), and toddlers have been shown to imitate particularly memorable events up to 12 months after first witnessing them (Bauer et al., 2000; Meltzoff, 1995). So a capacity for deferred imitation—imitation requiring the infant to construct, store, and then retrieve mental symbols—is present much earlier than Piaget had thought; this finding questions Piaget's account of the nonsymbolic sensorimotor child.

Development of Object Permanence

object permanence
the realization that objects continue to exist when they are no longer visible or detectable through the other senses.

One of the more notable achievements of the sensorimotor period is the development of **object permanence,** the idea that objects continue to exist when they are no longer visible or detectable through the other senses. If you removed your watch and covered it with a coffee mug, you would still know that the watch continues to exist. But because very young infants rely so heavily on their senses and their motor skills to "understand" an object, they seem to operate as if objects exist only if they can be immediately sensed or acted upon. Indeed, Piaget (1954) and others have found that 1- to 4-month-olds will not search for attractive objects that are hidden from view. If a watch that interests them is covered by a mug, they soon lose interest, almost as if they believe that the watch no longer exists or has been transformed into a mug. At age 4 to 8 months, infants will retrieve toys that are partially concealed or placed beneath a semitransparent cover; but their continuing failure to search for objects that are *completely* concealed suggested to Piaget that, from the infant's perspective, disappearing objects no longer exist.

Clearer signs of an emerging object concept appear by 8 to 12 months of age. However, object permanence is far from complete, as we see in Piaget's demonstration with his 10-month-old daughter:

> Jacqueline is seated on a mattress without anything to . . . distract her . . . I take her [toy] parrot from her hands and hide it twice . . . under the mattress, on her left [point A]. Both times Jacqueline looks for the object immediately and grabs it. Then I take it from her hands and move it very slowly *before her eyes* to the corresponding place on her right, under the mattress [point B]. Jacqueline watches this movement . . . but at the moment when the parrot disappears [at point B] she turns to her left and looks where it was before [at point A] (Piaget, 1954, p. 51; italics added).

A-not-B error
tendency of 8- to 12-month-olds to search for a hidden object where they previously found it even after they have seen it moved to a new location.

Jacqueline's response is typical of 8- to-12-month-olds, who will search for a hidden object *where they found it previously* rather than where they saw it last (Markovitch & Zelazo, 1999). Piaget's account of this **A-not-B error** was straightforward: Jacqueline acted as if her *behavior* determines where the object will be found; consequently, she does not treat the object as if it exists independent of her own activity.

Between 12 and 18 months of age, the object concept improves. Toddlers now track the visible movements of objects and search for them *where they were last seen*. However, object permanence is not complete, because the child cannot make the mental inferences necessary to understand *invisible displacements.* So if you conceal a toy in your hand, place your hand behind a barrier and deposit the toy there, remove your hand, and then ask the child to find the toy, 12- to 18-month-olds will search *where the toy was last seen*—in your hand—rather than looking behind the barrier.

By 18 to 24 months of age, toddlers are capable of *mentally representing* such invisible displacements and using these mental inferences to guide their search for objects that have disappeared. At this point, they fully understand that objects have a "permanence" about them and take great pride at locating their objectives in sophisticated games of hide and seek.

Jean-Claude Le Jeune/Stock Boston

Playing peekaboo is an exciting activity for infants who are acquiring object permanence.

Challenges to Piaget's Account of Sensorimotor Development: Neo-Nativism and Theory Theories

Piaget was an amazing observer of infants, and at the level of describing infant problem-solving that most people (including parents) actually see, Piaget's account of infant development is generally accurate (see Table 7.2 for a summary), although somewhat incomplete (Bjorklund, 2005). Yet Piaget generally underestimated infants' cognitive capabilities, and many researchers today believe that new theories are needed to completely capture the richness of infant intelligence.

neo-nativism
the idea that much cognitive knowledge, such as object concept, is innate, requiring little in the way of specific experiences to be expressed, and that there are biological constraints, in that the mind/brain is designed to process certain types of information in certain ways.

Neo-nativism. The most articulate criticism of Piaget's infancy theory comes from **neo-nativists**—theorists who believe that infants are born with substantial innate knowledge about the physical world, which requires much less time and experience to be demonstrated than Piaget proposed (Gelman & Williams, 1998; Spelke & Newport, 1998). This can be seen in the description of the work of Baillargeon (1987) on object permanence described in the Box on p. 252. As the research presented in this box indicates, infants know something about the permanency of objects very early on; such knowledge does not have to be "constructed" as Piaget proposed, but is part of an infant's genetic heritage. This does not mean that there is no development or that no experience is necessary for the mature expression of an ability, but rather that babies are prepared by evolution to make sense of certain aspects of their physical world that are universally experienced (such as the permanency of objects).

Similarly, others argue that not only do infants know more about physical properties of objects than we once expected, but, from the very earliest months of life, infants are symbolic beings, a perspective very different from the one argued by Piaget (Meltzoff, 1990). Research on deferred imitation (and neonatal imitation discussed in Chapter 5) is consistent with this position, and caused Andrew Meltzoff (1990, p. 20) to argue that "in a very real sense, there may be no such things as a purely 'sensorimotor period' in the normal human infant."

The early display of symbolic ability is illustrated in innovative research by Karen Wynn (1992), who used techniques similar to those of Baillargeon (1987) presented in Box 7.1 to assess simple arithmetic abilities in infants. In Wynn's experiment, 5-month-old infants were shown a sequence of events that involved the addition or subtraction of elements. Two of these sequences are shown in Figure 7.1. One sequence (the "possible outcome") led to the conclusion that 1 + 1 = 2; the other sequence (the "impossible

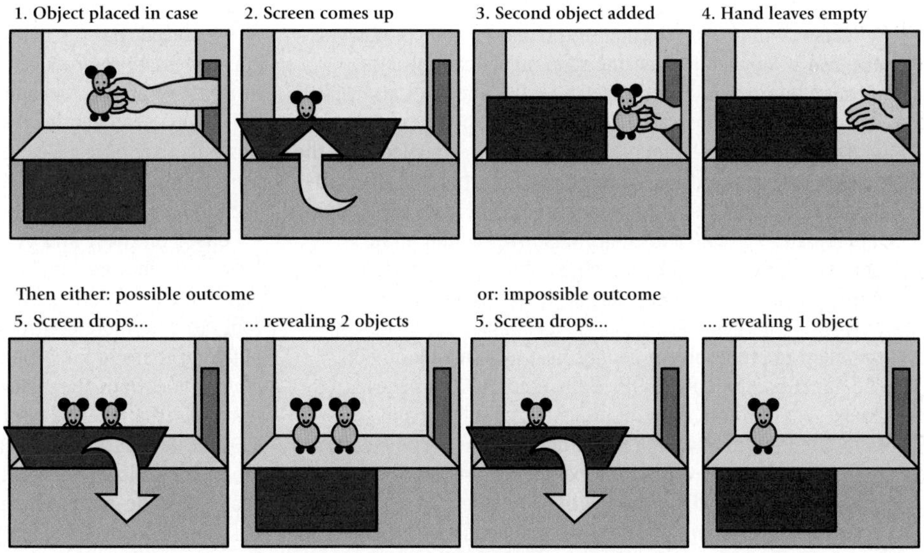

Figure 7.1 Sequence of events for the 1 + 1 = 2 (possible) outcome and the 1 + 1 = 1 (impossible) outcome from the experiment by Wynn (1992). *From "Addition and Subtraction by Human Infants," by K. Wynn, 1992,* Nature, *358, 749–750. Reprinted by permission.*

FOCUS ON RESEARCH Why Infants Know More about Objects than Piaget Assumed

Do very young infants really believe that vanishing objects cease to exist? Renee Baillargeon (1987) doubts it, and her research illustrates a theme that has been echoed by many contemporary researchers: young infants know more about objects than Piaget thought they did; in fact, they may never be totally ignorant about the permanence of objects.

The trick in demonstrating what very young infants know is to conduct tests appropriate to their developmental level. Unfortunately, 3- to 4-month-old infants have limited motor skills, so that their inability to search for things (Piaget's tests) really says very little about their knowledge of objects.

Baillargeon (1987; Baillargeon & De Voss, 1991) used the habituation/dishabituation paradigm to assess what $3^1/_2$- to $4^1/_2$-month-old infants may know about objects and their properties. Baillargeon (1987) first habituated each infant to a screen that moved 180 degrees, from being flat with its leading edge facing the infant, rising continuously through an arc until it rested in the box with its leading edge being farthest away from the infant (see panel *a* of figure). Once habituated to this event, infants were shown a colorful wooden block with a clown face painted on it, placed to the rear of the flat screen. (Actually, the block was an illusion created by a mirror.) Then, as illustrated in the figure, the screen was rotated to produce either a *possible* event (the screen would stop as if stopped by the box, panel *b*) or an *impossible* event (the screen rotated 180 degrees, passing through the box, panel *c*). Baillargeon reasoned that if babies thought the box still existed, even when hidden by the screen, they should stare longer at the screen and be more surprised when it appeared to pass through the solid box (impossible event) than when it bumped the box and stopped its forward motion (possible event). That is exactly what most of the $4^1/_2$-month-olds and many of the $3^1/_2$-month-olds did, taking great interest in the impossible event.

Infants' performance in the "impossible event" condition reflects not only a knowledge of the permanence of objects, but also a knowledge that one solid object cannot pass through another. Elizabeth Spelke (1991; Spelke et al., 1992) has similarly demonstrated in a series of experiments that infants as young as $2^1/_2$ months of age have a knowledge of the solidity and continuity of objects (the fact that a moving object continues on its path), and more recent research by Baillargeon and her colleagues has illustrated young infants' understanding of support (an object must be supported or it falls), collisions (an object that is hit by another object moves) (Baillargeon, Kotovsky, & Needham, 1995), and containment (a larger object cannot fit into a smaller object) (Aguiar & Baillargeon, 1998). Baillargeon (2004) believes, like Spelke, that infants' general principles of solidity and continuity are innate. However, Baillargeon claims, infants early representations of events they experience are impoverished and become more elaborated with experience.

It was once thought that memory deficits also explained the *A-not-B error* that 8- to 12-month-olds display. But we now know that infants this old have reasonably good memories and are actually quite surprised if a hidden object turns out *not* to be where they have last seen it (at point B) (Baillargeon & Graber, 1988). So 8- to 12-month-olds who commit A-not-B errors will often remember that an object has been hidden at new location B; what they may lack is the ability to *inhibit* the tendency to search where they have previously found the object. Indeed, Adele Diamond (1985) claims that some infants who search inappropriately for hidden objects at point A hardly look there at all, as if they realize this is not the right place to search but simply cannot stop themselves. Diamond (1985) tested 25 infants in the A-not-B task, beginning at about $7^1/_2$ months and continuing until 12 months of age. She reported that the delay between hiding and searching that was necessary to produce an A-not-B error increased with age at a rate of about 2 seconds per month. That is, $7^1/_2$-month-old infants searched for the hidden object at the erroneous A position after only a 2-second delay. By 12 months of age, infants made the error only if 10 seconds had passed between the hiding of the object and the beginning of the search.

Based on these and other data Diamond (1991, 1995) believes that maturational changes in the frontal lobes of the cerebral cortex during the second 6 months of life permit infants to gain more control over their motor responses, thus allowing them to inhibit an impulse to search for hidden objects at locations they know are incorrect. And she may be right. Martha Bell and Nathan Fox (1992) found that 7- to 12-month-olds who *avoid* making A-not-B errors show far more frontal lobe electrical activity while performing the task than their age-mates who search less appropriately.

Though we've considered only a portion of the evidence, it is clear that Piaget's reliance on active search procedures caused him (1) to badly underestimate what very young infants know about objects and (2) to misinterpret why infants display the A-not-B error.

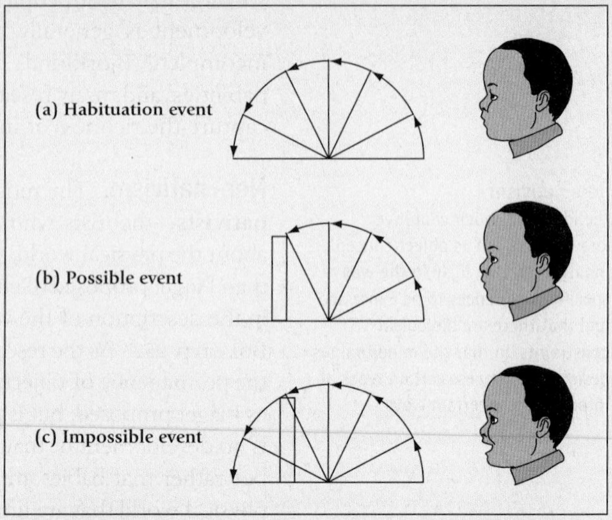

Fig. Box 7.1-1 Representations of the habituation stimulus and the possible and impossible events shown to young infants in Baillargeon's (1987) experiment. Babies took great interest in the "impossible" event, thus suggesting that they knew that the block continues to exist and that the screen shouldn't have passed through it. *Based on Baillargeon, 1987.*

outcome") led to the conclusion that 1 + 1 = 1. Infants sat in front of a stage and watched as one object was placed in it (step 1 in Figure 7.1). A screen was then raised, hiding the object (step 2 in Figure 7.1). The infant then watched as a second object was placed behind the screen (steps 3 and 4 in Figure 7.1). The screen was then lowered, revealing either two objects (the "possible outcome") or one object (the "impossible outcome"). If infants have some primitive concept of addition, they should be surprised and thus spend more time looking at the "impossible outcome." This was exactly what occurred, both for the addition problem shown in Figure 7.1 and for a simple subtraction problem (2 − 1 = 1). These findings have been replicated by others (Simon, Hespos, & Rochat, 1995; Uller et al., 1999).

How can these results best be interpreted? Infants seem not to be making only a perceptual discrimination between two displays (that is, telling the difference between a display with one item in it and another with two). Rather, when they watch as one item is added to another behind a screen, they expect to see two items when the screen is dropped. This requires a certain level of object permanence and memory, but also some rudimentary ideas about addition. They must infer that the second object was added to the first, without actually seeing that this was done (recall that the screen blocked their vision). These findings are provocative and suggest substantially greater quantitative (symbolic) knowledge in young infants than proposed by Piaget. However, others question Wynn's interpretation, and suggest that babies are not responding on the basis of *number* but, rather, to the total amount of *substance* present (Mix, Huttenlocker, & Levine, 2002). In other words, infants are not doing primitive (and unconscious) addition and subtraction, but are reacting to changes in the amount of "stuff" that is present in the various arrays. For example, rather than reflecting infants' abstract understanding of integers (that is, there should be "1" or "2" objects behind the screen), their behavior may be based on representations of the actual objects (for example, ♥ versus ♥♥ suggesting that decisions are based more on perceptual than conceptual relations (Uller et al., 1999; see Mandler, 2000). And regardless of which interpretation one prefers, it does not justify the conclusion that babies are born knowing basic arithmetic or that infants and toddlers should be able to learn complicated mathematics given proper instructions.

Theory Theories. There are other theorists who acknowledge that infants indeed come into the world with more knowledge than Piaget proposed, but who believe that, beyond the very early stages of sensorimotor development, Piaget's constructivist account is generally close to the truth. These are the *theory theorists,* who combine aspects of neo-nativism with Piagetian constructivism (Gopnik & Meltzoff, 1997; Karmiloff-Smith, 1992). The basic idea behind **theory theories** is that infants are prepared from birth to make sense of certain classes of information (about objects and language, for example), much as neo-nativists propose; but such innate knowledge is incomplete and requires substantial experience for infants to construct reality, much as Piaget proposed. Infants do this by constructing "theories" about how the world works and testing and modifying their theories, much as scientists do, until the models in their brains resemble the way the world is structured. Developmental change following theory theory is similar to that described by Piaget. According to Alison Gopnik and Andrew Meltzoff (1997, p. 63), "We will typically see a pattern in which the child holds to a particular set of predictions and interpretations for some time; the child has a particular theory. Then we may expect a period of disorganization, in which the theory is in crisis. And finally, we should see a new, equally coherent and stable theory emerge." This is reminiscent of Piaget's concept of equilibration, discussed earlier in this chapter.

> **theory theories**
> theories of cognitive development that combine neo-nativism and constructivism, proposing that cognitive development progresses by children generating, testing, and changing theories about the physical and social world.

One question that is fair to ask of the theory-theory approach is that, if development is the process of testing and changing theories, why do children all over the globe end up with basically the same adult theories of the world? Experience plays an important role in this formulation, and experiences will surely vary considerably between children growing up in information-age societies and those growing up in traditional hunter-gatherer societies. And of course adults in these cultures do differ considerably in their thinking, but their understanding of the physical and social world are remarkably the same. How can a theory theory explain such similarity of cognitive functioning? Consistent with the ideas of evolutionary developmental psychologists (Bjorklund & Pellegrini, 2002; Hernández Blasi & Bjorklund, 2003), Gopnik and Meltzoff propose that children around the world are born with the same initial theories and that powerful mechanisms revise current theories when children are faced with conflicting evidence. That is, all infants

CONCEPT CHECK 7.2 Understanding Infant Intelligence

Check your understanding of Piaget's view of infant intelligence and what more recent research has found about infant intelligence by answering the following questions. Answers appear in the appendix.

Multiple Choice: Select the best alternative for each question.

_____ 1. The first major period in Piaget's stage theory is the *sensorimotor stage,* which lasts from birth to approximately 2 years of age. According to Piaget, children at this stage
- a. are not able to comprehend the world yet, and must rely on others to do their thinking for them
- b. are able to think logically and comprehend their environment
- c. are of little interest to experimental psychologists because they are unable to verbalize fluently
- d. are able to comprehend the world around them through their actions on it

_____ 2. According to Piaget, *imitation* is the purest example of
- a. accommodation
- b. assimilation
- c. the coordination of both assimilation and accommodation
- d. abstract representation

_____ 3. Six-month-old Pedro is playing with his stuffed toy rabbit in his crib. He sets the rabbit down, and as he moves to reach his bottle, his blanket covers this toy. Pedro then turns to reach for his rabbit, but seeing only a bump in his blanket, he cries. According to Piaget, Pedro's actions in this situation reflect a lack of
- a. object permanence
- b. deferred imitation
- c. primary circular reactions
- d. assimilation

_____ 4. Piaget's concept of *object permanence* refers to the
- a. knowledge that objects have an existence in space and time independent of one's perceptions of and action on them
- b. knowledge that an inanimate object (i.e., a ball) will remain in a given location when put there, although an animate object (i.e., a rabbit) may not
- c. tendency for semantic knowledge of objects to remain permanently in long-term memory
- d. ability to memorize the spatial location of permanent objects in the environment

Matching: Match the following concepts with their definitions.

- a. invariant developmental sequence
- b. coordination of secondary circular reactions
- c. A-not-B error
- d. neo-nativism
- e. theory theories
- f. primary circular reactions

5. _____ The tendency of 8- to 12-month-olds to search for a hidden object where they previously found it even after they have seen it moved to a new location.
6. _____ Second substage of Piaget's sensorimotor stage; a pleasurable response, centered on the infant's own body, that is discovered by chance and performed over and over.
7. _____ A series of developments that occur in one particular order because each development in the sequence is a prerequisite for those appearing later.
8. _____ Theories of cognitive development that combine neo-nativism and constructivism, proposing that cognitive development progresses by children generating, testing, and changing theories about the physical and social world.
9. _____ The fourth substage of Piaget's sensorimotor stage; infants begin to coordinate two or more actions to achieve simple objectives. This is the first sign of goal-directed behavior.
10. _____ The idea that much cognitive knowledge, such as object concept, is innate, requiring little in the way of specific experiences to be expressed, and that there are biological constraints, in that the mind/brain is designed to process certain types of information in certain ways.

Essays: Provide a detailed answer to the following questions.

11. Discuss the development of imitation through the sensorimotor period.
12. Discuss the development of object permanence through the sensorimotor period. What evidence is there to suggest that Piaget underestimated infants' knowledge of objects?

start with the same ideas about how the world works and modify these theories as they grow. They also try to solve basically the same problems about how the physical and social world works, and they get similar information at about the same time in their lives. We will have more to say about a particular type of theory theory later in this chapter, namely children's development of *theory of mind.*

Summing Up

Piaget's theory of infant cognitive development has been one of the most influential ever proposed. It uncovered previously unknown phenomena (for example, object permanence) and generated nearly a century of research. However, it has become obvious in recent decades that new theories are necessary to account for the greater cognitive abilities that infants have been shown to possess. Yet, as new research accumulates, it also has become clear that we do not want to throw out Piaget with the baby's bath water. Many of Piaget's ideas, particularly *constructivism,* have been shown to have staying power and have become incorporated in contemporary theories of infant development.

The Preoperational Stage (2 to 7 Years) and the Emergence of Symbolic Thought

preoperational period
Piaget's second stage of cognitive development, lasting from about age 2 to age 7, when children are thinking at a symbolic level but are not yet using cognitive operations.

symbolic function
the ability to use symbols (for example, images and words) to represent objects and experiences.

representational insight
the knowledge that an entity can stand for (represent) something other than itself.

The **preoperational period** is marked by the appearance of the **symbolic function**—the ability to make one thing—a word or an object—stand for, or represent, something else. Judy DeLoache (1987, 2000) refers to the knowledge that an entity can stand for something other than itself as **representational insight.** This transition from the curious hands-on-everything toddler to the contemplative, symbolic preschool child is remarkable indeed. Consider, for example, that because 2- to 3-year-olds can use words and images to represent their experiences, they are now quite capable of reconstructing the past and thinking about or even comparing objects that are no longer present. And just how much does the ability to construct mental symbols transform a child's thinking? David Bjorklund (2005) answers by noting that the average, symbolic 3-year-old probably has more in common intellectually with a 21-year-old adult than with a 12-month-old infant. Although a 3-year-old's thinking will change in many ways over the next several years, it is similar to an adult's in that both preschool children and adults think by manipulating mental symbols such as images and language, with most "thinking" being done covertly, "in the head."

Language is perhaps the most obvious form of symbolism that young children display. Although most infants utter their first meaningful word by the end of the first year, it is not until about 18 months of age—the point at which they show other signs of symbolism such as inner experimentation—that they combine two (or more) words to form simple sentences. Does the use of language promote cognitive development? Piaget said no, arguing instead that language merely reflects what the child *already knows* and contributes little to new knowledge. In other words, he believed that cognitive development promotes language development, not vice versa. (We will have more to say about Piaget's ideas about the relationship between language and thought later in this chapter.)

A second major hallmark of the early preoperational period is the blossoming of *pretend* (or *symbolic*) play. Toddlers often pretend to be people they are not (mommies, superheroes), and they may play these roles with props such as a shoe box or a stick that symbolize other objects such as a baby's crib or a gun. Although some parents are concerned when their preschool children immerse themselves in a world of make-believe and begin to invent imaginary playmates, Piaget felt that these are basically healthy activities. According to Marc Bornstein and his colleagues (1996), "In symbolic play, young children advance upon their cognitions about people, objects, and actions and in this way construct increasingly sophisticated representations of the world" (p. 2923). In Box 7.2, we focus briefly on children's play and see how these "pretend" activities may contribute in a positive way to the child's social, emotional, and intellectual development.

APPLYING RESEARCH TO YOUR LIFE

Play Is Serious Business

Play is an intrinsically satisfying activity—something young children do for the sheer fun of it (Rubin, Fein, & Vandenberg, 1983). In contrast to earlier views that childhood play activities were a frivolous waste of time, Piaget (1951) was fascinated by the young child's play. He believed that play provided a glimpse of the child's emerging cognitive schemes in action while allowing young players to practice and strengthen whatever competencies they possess.

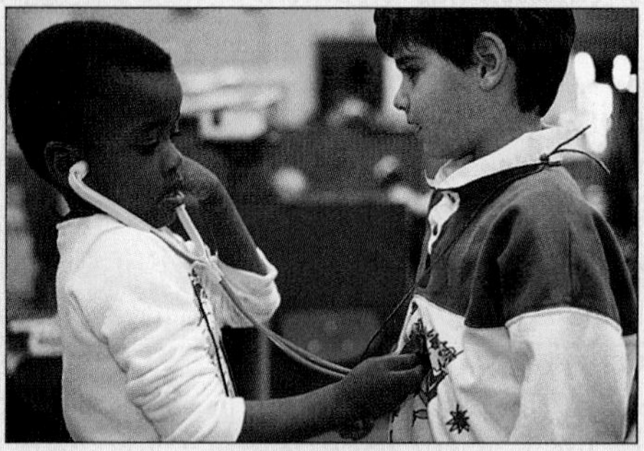
© Jeff Greenberg/PhotoEdit

The reciprocal roles children enact during pretend play promote the growth of social skills and interpersonal understanding.

Sensorimotor play begins very early and develops in much the same way in all cultures (Pellegrini & Smith, 1998). Infants progress from playing with their own bodies (for example, sucking their thumbs), to manipulating external objects such as rattles and stuffed animals, to fully *functional play*—using objects to serve the functions they normally serve—which appears by the end of the first year. So a 12-month-old is now more inclined to push the bottoms on a toy phone rather than merely sucking on or banging the toy.

Perhaps the most exciting breakthrough in play activities is the emergence of *symbolic* (or *pretend*) *play* at 11 to 13 months of age. The earliest "pretend" episodes are simple ones in which infants pretend to engage in familiar activities such as eating, drinking, or sleeping. But by 18 to 24 months of age, toddlers have progressed to a point where they will pretend to perform multiple acts in a meaningful sequence; they can also coordinate their actions with those of a play partner, making social games of imitating each other and sometimes even cooperating to achieve a goal (Brownell & Carriger, 1990; Howes & Matheson, 1992). Parents can foster this development by providing toddlers with a secure base of affection and by playing along with their child's little dramas (O'Reilly & Bornstein, 1993; Slade, 1987).

Symbolic play truly blossoms during Piaget's preoperational period. By age 2, toddlers can use one object (a block) to symbolize another (a car) and are now using language in inventive ways to create rich fantasy worlds for themselves. They clearly understand pretense: if you hand them a towel and suggest that they wipe up the imaginary tea you just spilled, they will do it (Harris, Kavanaugh, & Meredith, 1994). Think about this: Because there is no tea in sight, the child's willingness to clean it up suggests that he can construct a mental representation of someone else's pretend event and then act according to this representation. Pretend play becomes increasingly social and increasingly complex between ages 2 and 5. More importantly, children combine their capacity for increasingly social play and their capacity for understanding pretense to cooperate with each other at *planning* their pretend activities: They name and assign roles that each player will enact, propose play scripts, and may even stop playing to modify the script if necessary (Howes & Matheson, 1992). Indeed, play episodes are among the most complex social interactions that preschoolers have (Pellegrini & Bjorklund, 2004).

What good is play? Intellectually, play provides a context for using language to communicate and using the mind to fantasize, plan strategies, and solve problems. Children often show more advanced intellectual skills during pretend play than they do when performing other activities, suggesting that play fosters cognitive development (Lillard, 1993). Indeed, preschool children who engage in a great deal of pretend play (or who are trained to do so) perform better on tests of Piagetian cognitive development, language skills, and creativity than children who "pretend" less often (Fisher, 1992; Johnsen, 1991).

Preschool pretend activities may also promote social development. To be successful at social pretend play, children must adopt different roles, coordinate their activities, and resolve any disputes that may arise. Children may also learn about and prepare for adult roles by "playing house" or "school" and stepping into the shoes of their mothers, fathers, or nursery school teachers (Pellegrini & Bjorklund, 2004). Perhaps due to the social skills they acquire (for example, an ability to cooperate) and the role-taking experiences they have, preschool children who participate in a lot of *social* pretend play tend to be more socially mature and more popular with peers than age-mates who often play without partners (Howes & Matheson, 1992).

Finally, play may foster healthy emotional development by allowing children to express feelings that bother them or to resolve emotional conflicts (Fein, 1986). If Latoya, for example, has been scolded at lunch for failing to eat her peas, she may gain control of the situation at play as she scolds her doll for picky eating or persuades the doll to "eat healthy" and consume the peas. Indeed, playful resolutions of such emotional conflicts may even be an important contributor to children's understanding of authority and the rationales that underlie all those rules they must follow (Piaget & Inhelder, 1969).

Let it never be said that play is useless. Although children play because it is fun, not because it sharpens their skills, players indirectly contribute to their own social, emotional, and intellectual development, enjoying themselves all the while. In this sense, play truly is the child's work—and is serious business indeed!

New Views on Symbolism

Piaget's emphasis on the symbolic nature of preoperational children's thought has captured the attention of developmentalists. Judy DeLoache and her colleagues, for example, have explored preschool children's abilities to use scale models and pictures as symbols (DeLoache, 1987, 2000; Uttal, Schreiber, & DeLoache, 1995). In DeLoache's studies, children are asked to find a toy hidden in a room. Prior to searching for the toys children are shown a scale model of the room, with the experimenter hiding a miniature toy (Snoopy) behind a chair in the model. The miniature toy and the model chair correspond to a large Snoopy and real chair in the adjoining "real" room. Children are then asked to find the toy in the real room (Retrieval 1). After searching for the toy in the real room, they return to the model and are asked to find where the miniature toy was hidden (Retrieval 2). If children cannot find the large toy in the real room (Retrieval 1) but *can* find the miniature toy in the scale model (Retrieval 2), their failure to find the large toy cannot be due to forgetting where the miniature toy was hidden. A better interpretation would be that the children have no representational insight and cannot use the model in a symbolic fashion to guide their search.

DeLoache reported that the 3-year-olds performed well in *both* retrieval tasks, indicating that they remembered where the miniature toy was hidden and used the information from the scale model to find the large toy in the real room. The 2½-year-olds showed good memory for where the miniature toy had been hidden, but performed very poorly when trying to find the large toy in the real room. Apparently, 2½-year-olds failed to recognize that the scale model was a symbolic representation of the large room.

It is not that 2½-year-olds have no representational insight. If given a *photo* that shows Snoopy's hiding place in the real room, 2½-year-olds (but not 2-year-olds) can find him when given the opportunity. Why do they do better with a two-dimensional photo than with an actual three-dimensional scale model? DeLoache believes that scale models are harder to use as symbols because 2½-year-olds lack **dual representation**—the ability to think about an object in two different ways at the same time. Dual representation is not required with photos because the primary purpose of a photo is to represent something else. But a scale model is an interesting object in its own right, and 2½-year-olds may not recognize that it is also a representation of the larger room. If DeLoache is right, then anything that induces young children to pay less attention to the scale model as an object should persuade them to use it as a symbol and thereby improve their search for the hidden toy. Indeed, DeLoache (2000) reports that 2½-year olds who are not allowed to play with the scale model but only to look through its windows do focus less on the interesting qualities of the scale model itself, treating it more like a symbol that helps them to find the hidden toy in the real room.

dual representation (dual encoding)
the ability to represent an object simultaneously as an object itself and as a representation of something else.

Although representational insight and dual-representational abilities improve appreciably between 2½ and 3 years of age, they remain rather tentative and are easily disrupted. Consider, for example, that when 3-year-olds must wait 5 minutes after seeing a toy hidden in the scale model to make their initial search, they were typically unsuccessful at finding the toy in the larger room. It is not that they forget where the toy was hidden in the scale model. Instead they don't seem to remember over a 5-minute delay that the scale model is a symbolic representation of the real room (Uttal et al., 1995). So dual representation—the ability to keep in mind the relationship between a symbol and its referent—is rather fragile in 3-year-olds but improves substantially over the preschool years.

Deficits in Preoperational Reasoning

But despite important new strengths that the use of symbols provided, Piaget's descriptions of preoperational intelligence focused mainly on the limitations, or deficiencies, in children's thinking. Indeed, he called this period "preoperational" because he believed that preschool children have not yet acquired the operational schemes that enable them to think logically. He claimed, for example, that young children often display **animism**—a willingness to attribute life and lifelike qualities (for example, motives and intentions) to inanimate objects. The 4-year-old who believed that the wind blew on him to cool him off

animism
attributing life and lifelike qualities to inanimate objects.

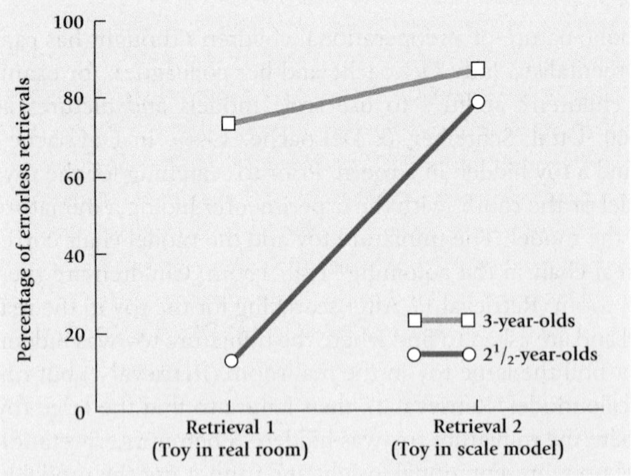

Figure 7.2 The number of errorless retrievals (correctly locating the hidden toy) for 2½- (younger) and 3-year-olds (older) on a model task. Retrieval 1 involved locating the real toy in the real room; Retrieval 2 involved locating the miniature toy in the model. *From "Rapid Change in the Symbolic Functioning of Very Young Children," by J. S. DeLoache, 1987. Science, 238, 1556–1557. Copyright © 1987 by the American Association for the Advancement of Science.*

provides a clear example of the animistic logic that children are likely to display during the early preschool years.

According to Piaget, the most striking deficiency in children's preoperational reasoning—a deficiency that contributes immensely to the other intellectual shortcomings they display—is their **egocentrism,** a tendency to view the world from one's own perspective and to have difficulty recognizing another person's point of view. Piaget demonstrated this by first familiarizing children with an asymmetrical mountain scene (see Figure 7.2) and then asking them what an observer on the opposite side of the table would see as he gazed at the scene. Often, 3- and 4-year-olds said the other person would see exactly what they saw, thus failing to consider the other's different perspective. Other examples of this self-centered thinking appear in the statements young children make. Take the telephone conversation of 4-year-old Kelly with her uncle Dave:

DAVE: So you're going to a party today. Great. What are you wearing?
KELLY: This.

Kelly probably pointed to her new dress while talking into the phone, seemingly unaware that her uncle couldn't know what she was talking about. Consequently, her speech is not adapted to the needs of her listener, reflecting instead her egocentric point of view.

egocentrism
the tendency to view the world from one's own perspective while failing to recognize that others may have different points of view.

appearance/reality distinction
ability to keep the true properties or characteristics of an object in mind despite the deceptive appearance the object has assumed; notably lacking among young children during the preconceptual period.

Finally, Piaget claimed that the young children's egocentric focus on the way things appear to be makes it nearly impossible for them to distinguish appearances from reality. Consider Rheta DeVries's (1969) classic study of the **appearance/reality distinction.** Children 3 to 6 years of age were introduced to a cat named Maynard. After the children had petted Maynard, DeVries hid Maynard's head and shoulders behind a screen while she strapped a realistic mask of a dog's face onto Maynard's head (see Figure 7.3). The children were then asked questions about Maynard's identity such as "What kind of animal is it now?" and "Does it bark or meow?" Even though Maynard's back half and tail remained in full view during the transformation, nearly all the 3-year-olds focused on Maynard's new appearance and concluded that he really was a dog. By contrast, most 6-year-olds could distinguish appearances from reality, correctly noting that Maynard the cat now merely looked like a dog.

Why do 3-year-olds fail to distinguish between the misleading visual appearance of an object and its actual identity? Their problem, according to John Flavell and his associates (1986), is that they are not yet proficient at *dual encoding*—at representing an object in more than one way at a time. Just as young children have difficulty representing a scale model as both an *object* and a *symbol* (DeLoache, 2000), they struggle to construct simultaneous mental representations of an object that looks like something other than what it really is.

To illustrate, Flavell and his colleagues (1983, 1989) found that 3-year-olds who were shown a toy sponge that looked like a rock were apt to say that not only does it look like a rock, but it "really and truly is a rock." Their representation of the object's identity was based on its single most salient feature—its deceptive appearance. Yet, when 3-year-old children are persuaded to play a trick on someone (for example, "Let's trick Sally and make her think that this sponge really is a rock, and not just a sponge that looks like one"), many 3-year-olds are capable of this kind of pretense, forming dual representations of this object as a sponge (reality) that only looks like a rock (appearance) (Rice et al., 1997). Clearly, symbolic play activities, in which children pretend that objects (such as a large cardboard box) are something other than what they really are (for example, a fort) are an important contributor to dual representation and to children's gradually emerging abilities to distinguish misleading appearances from reality (Golomb & Galasso, 1995). But, as we'll see in the next section, these abilities develop gradually over the preschool period.

Figure 7.3 Piaget's three-mountain problem. Young preoperational children are egocentric. They cannot easily assume another person's perspective and often say that another child viewing the mountain from a different vantage point sees exactly what they see from their own location.

Children become less egocentric and more proficient at classifying objects on the basis of shared perceptual attributes such as size, shape, and color over the preschool years. But their thinking still shows a number of limitations. Piaget described the preschool child's thinking as intuitive because their understanding of objects and events is still largely based, or **"centered,"** on their single most salient perceptual feature—the way things appear to be—rather than on logical or rational thought processes.

The most frequently cited examples of children's intuitive reasoning come from Piaget's famous conservation studies (Flavell, 1963). One of these experiments begins with the child adjusting the amounts of liquid in two identical containers until each is said to have "the same amount to drink." Next the child sees the experimenter pour the liquid from one of these tall, thin containers into a short, broad container. He is then asked whether the remaining tall, thin container and the shorter, broader container have the same amount of liquid (see Figure 7.4 for an illustration of the procedure). Children younger than 6 or 7 will usually say that the tall, thin receptacle contains *more* liquid than the short, broad one. The child's thinking about liquids is apparently *centered* on one perceptual feature—the relative heights of the columns (tall column = more liquid). In Piaget's terminology, preoperational children are incapable of **conservation:** They do not yet realize that certain properties of objects (such as volume, mass, or number) remain unchanged when the objects' appearances are altered in some superficial way.

centration (centered thinking)
in Piaget's theory, the tendency of preoperational children to attend to one aspect of a situation to the exclusion of others; contrast with *decentration.*

conservation
the recognition that the properties of an object or substance do not change when its appearance is altered in some superficial way.

decentration
in Piaget's theory, the ability of concrete operational children to consider multiple aspects of a stimulus or situation; contrast with *centration.*

reversibility
the ability to reverse, or negate an action by mentally performing the opposite action (negation).

Why do preschool children fail to conserve? The answer, according to Piaget, is that these children lack two cognitive operations that would help them to overcome their perceptually-based intuitive reasoning. The first of these operations is **decentration**—the ability to concentrate on more than one aspect of a problem at the same time. Children are unable to attend *simultaneously* to both height and width when trying to solve the conservation of liquid problem. They center their attention either on the difference in height or width and make their decisions on differences in that single dimension. Consequently, they fail to recognize that increases in the width of a column of liquid compensate for decreases in its height to preserve (or conserve) its absolute amount. Preschoolers also lack **reversibility**—the ability to mentally undo or negate an action (see Figure 7.5). So an intuitive 5-year-old faced with the conservation-of-liquids problem is unable to mentally reverse what he has seen to conclude that the liquid in the short, broad beaker is still the same water and would attain its former height if it were poured back into its original container.

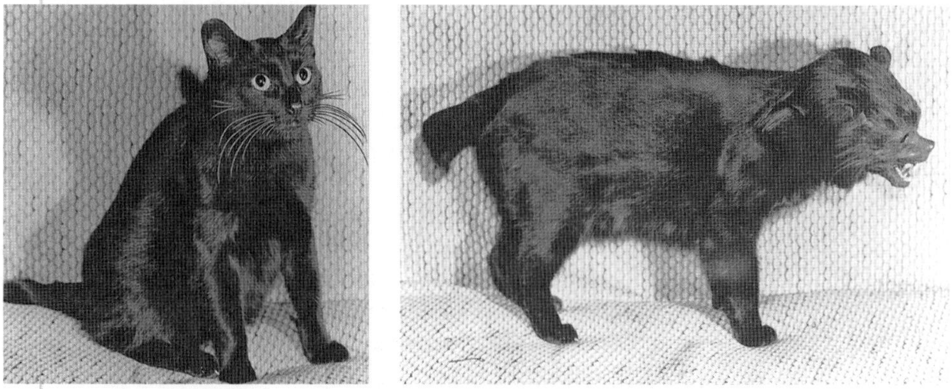

Figure 7.4 Maynard the cat, without and with a dog mask. Three-year-olds who met Maynard before his change in appearance nonetheless believed that he had become a dog.

Courtesy of Rheta de Vries

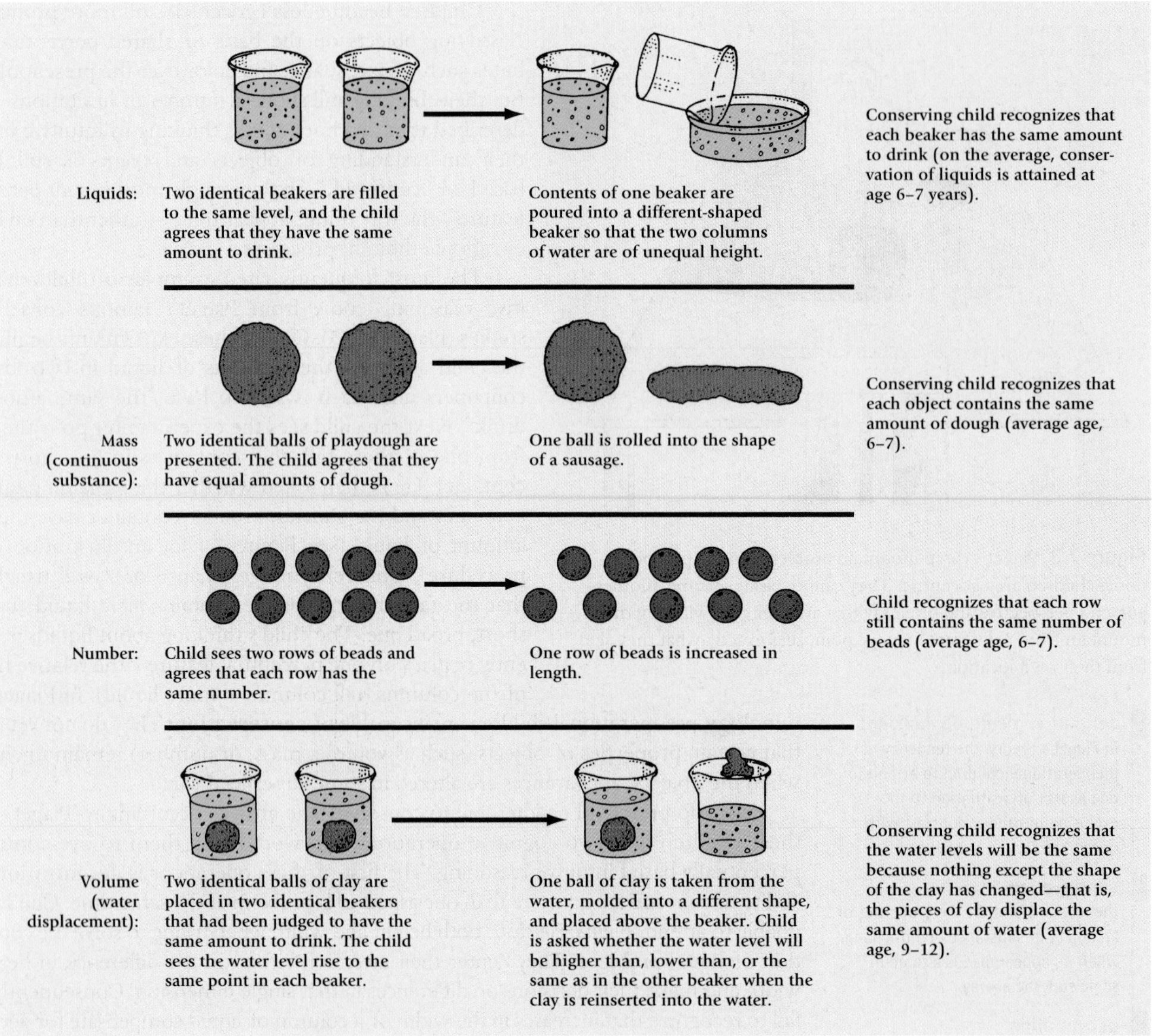

Figure 7.5 Some tests of a child's ability to conserve.

Did Piaget Underestimate the Preoperational Child?

Are preschool children really as intuitive, illogical, and egocentric as Piaget assumed? Can a child who has no understanding of cognitive operations be taught to conserve? Let's see what later research can tell us.

New Evidence on Egocentrism. Numerous experiments indicate that Piaget underestimated the ability of preschool children to recognize and appreciate another person's point of view. For example, Piaget and Inhelder's three-mountain task has been criticized as being unusually difficult, and more recent research has shown that children look much less egocentric when provided with less complicated visual displays (Gzesh & Surber, 1985; Newcombe & Huttenlocher, 1992). John Flavell and his associates (1981), for example, showed 3-year-olds a card with a dog on one side and a cat on the other. The card was then held vertically between the child (who could see the dog) and the experimenter (who could see the cat), and the child was asked which animal the experimenter could see. The 3-year-olds performed flawlessly, indicating that they could assume the experimenter's perspective and infer that he must see the cat rather than the animal they were looking at.

FOCUS ON RESEARCH Cognitive Development and Children's Humor

Developmental differences in the appreciation of humor have been hypothesized to be a function of children's level of cognitive development—specifically, their ability to deal with symbols—and have been interpreted in terms of Piaget's theory. Most developmental researchers have proposed that humor is reflected in the child's ability to perceive *incongruity*, noticing (or creating) a discrepancy between what is usual or expected and what is experienced (McGhee, 1979; Shultz & Robillard, 1980). Of course, incongruity can be defined only by what a child already knows, both world knowledge and general cognitive capabilities. Thus, a child's ability to make and understand jokes will depend on his or her level of cognitive development.

According to Paul McGhee (1976, 1979), incongruity is most likely to be perceived as humorous when the discrepancy is of some intermediate magnitude. The funniest jokes, for both adults and children, are those that take a little mental effort to figure out. Too easy, and they are boring; too difficult, and they are not worth the effort.

McGhee (1976) tested this theory by assessing children's appreciation of jokes as a function of their level of cognitive development. In one experiment, McGhee tested children in grades 1, 2, and 5 and college students. Within the first and second grades, half of the children were classified as conservers on conservation-of-weight tasks, and half were classified as nonconservers. All the fifth-grade and college students were conservers. The participants were read jokes requiring a knowledge of conservation for their appreciation. (For example: "Mr. Jones went into a restaurant and ordered a whole pizza for dinner. When the waiter asked if he wanted it cut into six or eight pieces, Mr. Jones said: 'Oh, you'd better make it six. I could never eat eight!'") After reading each joke, the experimenter asked each person to rate the joke on a five-point scale for how funny it was.

McGhee evaluated the children's appreciation of the jokes as a function of their level of cognitive development (that is, conservers or nonconservers) and grade level. The children who found the jokes funniest were the first- and second-grade conservers. Nonconservers generally did not find the humor in the jokes, nor did the older children and adults, though for different reasons. For the nonconservers, there was nothing to laugh about. The response given by Mr. Jones in the example joke is one they might have given themselves. In contrast, the joke was trivial for the fifth-graders, taking little in the way of mental effort. Only for the young conservers was the joke funny. These children had only recently mastered conservation, making the challenge of interpreting the joke greatest for them.

Most critical for humor, according to McGhee, is the ability to represent objects and events symbolically. McGhee proposed that humor requires comparing some event with a similar event in memory, and he believes that children do not develop this ability sufficiently well until sometime between their first and second birthdays. He sees humor as a type of intellectual play that requires symbols.

McGhee proposed four stages of humor development, beginning when the capacity for fantasy and make-believe develops, sometime late in the second year with the transition from sensorimotor to preoperational thought. In stage 1, typifying children between 18 and 24 months, children substitute one object for another in a playful game of pretending. For example, Piaget (1951) observed his daughter Jacqueline at 15 months clutching a cloth that vaguely resembled her pillow. She held it in her hand, sucked her thumb, and lay down, closing her eyes. But while she was pretending to sleep, she was laughing hard. To this toddler, pretending the cloth was her pillow was funny.

Children's first verbal jokes occur in stage 2. The simplest of these jokes involves calling something by its wrong name. A 2-year-old finds great mirth in calling the family dog a cow, in labeling a hamburger macaroni and cheese, or in pointing to her eye and calling it a nose. Such humor might not seem all that sophisticated, but it requires greater abstraction than the object-dependent humor of stage 1. Children no longer need a physical prop to make a joke. The word is enough.

Soon, however, children's humor becomes more complex, usually beginning around age 3. Now, it is not enough merely to call a dog a cat. Because of 3-year-olds' increasing knowledge of things in their environment, distortions must be more drastic for something to be funny. So, for example, a cow that says "oink oink" and has a curlicue tail is funny, whether that cow is seen in a picture or is just imagined.

What is humorous to a stage 3 child is often a function of how absurd something looks. Consistent with Piaget's description of preoperational children, preschoolers' attention is often drawn to perceptual or literal stimulus features. This over-reliance on appearance affects children's humor. A picture of an elephant sitting in a tree is funny to a 3-year-old, as is a picture of a fish swimming inside a car filled with water. These pictures are funny to 3-year-olds not because they defy logic but just because they are unusual. The incongruity is visual, not logical.

Beginning around 6 or 7 years of age with the advent of concrete operations, children's humor makes a more drastic change and starts to resemble the humor of adults. According to McGhee, the ability to understand double meanings of words and sentences is the hallmark of stage 4 and much of adult humor. A sentence with a serious (and obvious) meaning taken one way can be funny if viewed differently. A favorite of 6-year-old Heidi involved a woman mailing three socks to her son away in the army. Why did she mail three socks? Because he had written saying he had "grown another foot." Appreciation of the joke requires an understanding of the double meaning of "grown another foot." Most 7-year-olds have the ability to represent two meanings of a single word or phrase simultaneously, and from this time on, humor takes a distinctly adult form, although most adults are still likely to groan at jokes that have an 8-year-old rolling on the floor with laughter. (Such as this joke that 8-year-old Jeffrey thought was hilarious and apparently had made up

CONTINUED

himself: "Why did the brave chicken cross the road? 'Cause he wanted to prove that he wasn't chicken. Get it?")

Research has clearly demonstrated that children's understanding and appreciation of humor varies as a function of their level of cognitive development. Other factors, of course, affect humor. Some topics (aggression, sex) are more likely to be a source of humor than others, and humor plays an important role in greasing the gears of social interaction. Yet, the core of humor is cognitive. Simple visual jokes can be comprehended by 3-year-olds. But as the basis of jokes becomes more abstract and less dependent on visual cues, it becomes increasingly difficult for children to identify and resolve the conflict. Children's abilities to represent events, both real and unreal, and to view multiple meanings of a single situation determine what they find funny.

Flavell's study investigated young children's *perceptual* perspective-taking—that is, the ability to make correct inferences about what another person can see or hear. Can preoperational children engage in *conceptual* perspective-taking by making correct inferences about what another person may be thinking or feeling when these mental states differ from their own? The answer is a qualified yes. In one study (Hala & Chandler, 1996), 3-year-olds were asked to play a trick on a person (Lisa) by moving some biscuits from their distinctive biscuit jar to a hiding place, so that Lisa would be fooled. When later asked where Lisa will look for the biscuits and where she will think the biscuits are, children who helped plan the deception performed quite well, saying that Lisa would look in the biscuit jar. In contrast, children who merely observed the experimenter planning the deception did not perform so well. Rather, they were more likely to answer this *false-belief task* erroneously, stating that Lisa would look for the biscuits in the new hiding place. In other words, when they planned to deceive someone, 3-year-olds were later able to take the perspective of that person. When they were not actively involved in the deceit, however, they performed egocentrically, stating that the unsuspecting person would look for the biscuits where they knew them to be (see also Carlson, Moses, & Hix, 1998). Such tasks have been proposed to assess children's *theory of mind,* a topic we will discuss in greater detail shortly.

Clearly, preoperational children are not nearly as egocentric as Piaget thought. Nevertheless, Piaget was right in claiming that young children often rely on their own perspectives and thus fail to make accurate judgments about other people's motives, desires, and intentions; and they do often assume that if they know something, others will too (Ruffman & Olson, 1989; Ruffman et al., 1993). Today, researchers believe that children gradually become less egocentric and better able to appreciate others' points of view as they learn more and more—particularly about other people and causes of their behavior. In other words, perspective-taking abilities are not totally absent at one stage and suddenly present at another; they develop slowly and become more refined from early in life into adulthood (Bjorklund, 2005).

Another Look at Children's Reasoning. Piaget was quite correct in stating that preschool children are likely to provide animistic answers to many questions and to make logical errors when thinking about cause-and-effect relationships. Yet Susan Gelman and Gail Gottfried (1996) find that 3-year-olds do *not* routinely attribute life or lifelike qualities to inanimate objects, even such inanimates as a robot that can be made to move. In addition, most 4-year-olds recognize that plants and animals grow and will heal after an injury, whereas inanimate objects (for example, a table with a broken leg) will not (Backschneider, Shatz, & Gelman, 1993). Although preschool children do occasionally display animistic responses, these judgments stem not so much from a general belief that moving inanimates have lifelike qualities (Piaget's position) as from the (typically accurate) presumption that *unfamiliar* objects that appear to move *on their own* are alive (Dolgin & Behrend, 1984).

Can Preoperational Children Conserve?

According to Piaget (1970b), children younger than 6 or 7 cannot solve conservation problems because they have not yet acquired the operation of reversibility—the cognitive operation that enables them to discover the constancy of attributes such as mass and volume. Piaget also argued that one cannot teach conservation to children younger than 6 or 7, for these preoperational youngsters are much too intellectually immature to understand and use logical operations such as reversibility.

However, many researchers have demonstrated that nonconservers as young as 4 years of age, and even children with mental retardation, can be *trained* to conserve by a variety of techniques (Gelman, 1969; Hendler & Weisberg, 1992). One approach that has proved particularly effective is **identity training**—teaching children to recognize that the object or substance transformed in a conservation task is still the same object or substance, regardless of its new appearance. For example, a child being trained to recognize identities on a conservation of liquids task might be told: "It may look like less water when we pour it from a tall, thin glass into this shorter one, but it is the same water, and there has to be the same amount to drink." Dorothy Field (1981) showed that 4-year-olds who received this training not only conserved on the training task but could also use their new knowledge about identities to solve a number of conservation problems on which they had not been trained. Field also reported that nearly 75 percent of the 4-year-olds who had received some kind of identity training were able to solve at least three (out of five) conservation problems that were presented to them 2½ to 5 months after their training had ended. So contrary to Piaget's viewpoint, many preoperational children can learn to conserve, and their initial understanding of this law of nature seems to depend more on their ability to recognize identities than on their use of reversibility and decentration.

identity training
an attempt to promote conservation by teaching nonconservers to recognize that a transformed object or substance is the same object or substance, regardless of its new appearance.

The Development of Theory of Mind (TOM)

In discussing challenges to Piaget's theory of sensorimotor development, we introduced *theory theories,* which postulate, essentially, that infants possess some ideas of how the world is structured (theories) and modify these theories as a function of experience until their understanding of the world more resembles that of adults. The most investigated theory is not associated with infant intelligence, however, but develops during Piaget's preoperational period: **theory of mind** (TOM). In general, the phrase "theory of mind" is used to refer to children's developing concepts of mental activity—an understanding of how the human mind works and a knowledge that humans are cognitive beings whose mental states are not always shared with or accessible to others. Henry Wellman (1990) has proposed that adults' TOM is based on **belief-desire reasoning** (see Figure 7.6). We understand that our behavior, and the behavior of others, is based on what we know, or believe, and what we want, or desire. Such an understanding of intentional behavior is the basis of nearly all social interaction among people beyond preschool age, and it develops.

theory of mind
a person's concepts of mental activity; used to refer to how children conceptualize mental activity and how they attribute intention to and predict the behavior of others; see also belief-desire reasoning.

belief-desire reasoning
the process whereby we explain and predict what people do based on what we understand their desires and beliefs to be.

Very young children may view desire as the most important determinant of behavior because their own actions are so often triggered by desires and they may assume that other people's conduct reflects similar motives. For example, when 14-month-olds have

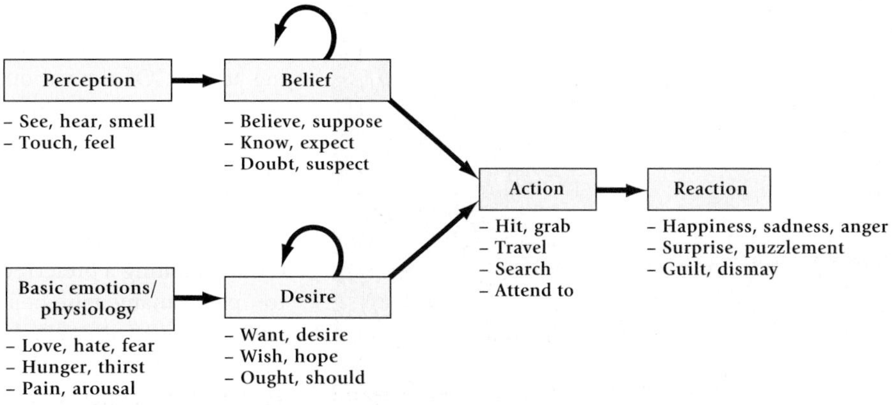

Figure 7.6 A simplified scheme depicting belief-desire reasoning. *Reprinted by permission. From* The Child's Theory of Mind *by H.M. Wellman. Copyright © 1990 MIT Press. Reprinted by permission.*

the options of giving a woman a food treat of either crackers or broccoli, they give her the crackers, even though they had just seen her express disgust to the crackers. Eighteen-month-olds, however, will offer the woman the vegetables, apparently realizing that the woman's desires are different from their own (Repacholi & Gopnik, 1997).

false-belief task
a type of task used in theory-of-mind studies, in which the child must infer that another person does not possess knowledge that he or she possesses (that is, that other person holds a belief that is false).

The most frequently used tool to assess children's theory of mind is the **false-belief task.** Consider the following scenario.

> Jorge puts some chocolate in a blue cupboard and goes out to play.
> In his absence, his mother moves the chocolate to the green cupboard.
> When Jorge returns, he wants his chocolate. Where does he look for it?

Three-year-olds say "in the green cupboard." They know where the chocolate is, and because beliefs represent reality, they assume that Jorge will be driven by his *desire* for chocolate to look in the right place. From a Piagetian perspective, children are making an egocentric response, believing that because they know where the chocolate is hidden, Jorge will know its location as well. In contrast, 4- to 5-year-olds display a belief-desire theory of mind: They understand that beliefs are merely mental representations of reality that may be inaccurate and that someone else may not share; thus, they know that Jorge will look for his chocolate in the blue cupboard where he *believes* it is (beliefs determine behavior, even if they are false) rather than in the green cupboard where they know it is (Wellman & Woolley, 1990).

© Myrleen Ferguson Cate/PhotoEdit

Sibling interactions involving deception or trickery contribute to the development of a theory of mind.

It's not that younger children don't have the capacity to recognize a false belief or its implications. For example, if 3-year-olds collaborate with an adult in formulating a deceptive strategy in a hide-the-object game, their performance improves substantially on other false-belief tasks (Sodian et al., 1991). Nevertheless, between 3 and 4 years of age is when children normally achieve a much richer understanding of mental life and more clearly understand how beliefs and desires motivate their own behavior and also the behavior of other people (Wellman, Cross, & Watson, 2001; Wellman & Liu, 2004).

How do children manage to construct a theory of mind so early in life? One perspective is that human infants may be just as biologically prepared and as motivated to acquire information about mental states as they are to share meaning through language (Meltzoff, 1995). As the Box on p. 265 illustrates, there are even those who believe that theory of mind is a product of evolution and that the human brain has specialized modules that allow children to construct an understanding of mental activities.

Why do 3-year-olds fail at the false-belief task? Some researchers have proposed that they lack a set of cognitive skills, collectively referred to as *executive function,* necessary to perform false-belief tasks properly. Executive functions refer to cognitive abilities involved in planning, executing, and inhibiting actions. Of the various components of executive function related to theory of mind, inhibition mechanisms have received the most attention (Carlson, Loses, & Claxton, 2004; Flynn, O'Malley, & Wood, 2004). *Cognitive inhibition* refers to the ability to inhibit certain thoughts and behaviors at specified times, and its development will be discussed in greater detail in Chapter 8. Inhibiting a preferred, or dominant, response is necessary to "pass" many false-belief tasks. For example, Joan Peskin (1992) showed preschool children a series of stickers, some more attractive than others. She then introduced "Mean Monkey," a hand puppet controlled by the experimenter, who played a game with the children. Mean Monkey would ask the children which of the stickers they really wanted and which stickers they

FOCUS ON RESEARCH

Is Theory of Mind Biologically Programmed?

Some theorists claim that the capacities underlying self-consciousness and complex theories of mind are products of human evolution and are the basis for our social intelligence and the development of cultures (Baron-Cohen, 1995, 2005; Mitchell, 1997). Presumably, our ancestors would have found it highly adaptive to understand beliefs, desires, and other mental states, for this ability to read minds allows for the evolution of cooperative divisions of labor that help to ensure survival, as well as more accurate assessments of the motives of rival groups that might threaten survival.

Simon Baron-Cohen (1995) has proposed that humans possess information-processing mechanisms that are specialized for theory of mind. One such mechanism is the *shared-attention mechanism* (SAM), which is said to develop between 9 and 18 months of age and allows two or more individuals to understand that they are attending to the same thing. Another such mechanism is the *theory of mind module* (TOMM), which develops between 18 and 48 months of age and permits children to eventually discriminate such mental states as beliefs, desires, and intentions.

Indeed, there is some evidence that development of a belief-desire theory of mind may reflect processing skills that are *domain specific*—that is, apart from normal intelligence. For example, about 85 percent of both 4-year-olds with normal intelligence and retarded children with Down syndrome pass false-belief problems. Yet shared attention and understanding of false beliefs are lacking in children with *autism*, even though these autistic children may perform quite well on other intellectual tasks. Autism is a severe psychiatric disorder; affected children seem to be in a world of their own and they have difficulties with most forms of social interaction. Baron-Cohen (1995) claims that autistic individuals lack TOMM and display severe deficits in reading minds, or *mindblindness.* Imagine how confusing and frightening it would be to interact with other humans if you lacked the capacity to understand their desires or recognize that they may try to deceive you. Temple Grandin, a woman with autism who is intelligent enough to be a professor of animal sciences, described having to compensate for her lack of mind-reading skills by actively creating a memory bank of how people behave and what emotions they are likely to express in particular situations (Sacks, 1993). Although she can grasp simple emotions like happiness, she never could quite understand what *Romeo and Juliet* was all about.

In other research Baron-Cohen and his colleagues (1999) observed deficits in theory of mind in three highly successful autistic (Asperger syndrome) adults, despite above-average performance on IQ and other cognitive tests. Neurological research has shown that people with autism show deficits in the same brain region (left frontal lobe) that normal adults use in processing theory-of-mind tasks (Sabbagh & Taylor, 2000). And researchers have found substantial genetic influence on theory-of-mind tasks among 199 3-year-old same-sex twins that was independent of a general measure of verbal ability, consistent with the idea that theory of mind is not simply a function of general intellectual functioning (Hughes & Cutting, 1999).

Baron-Cohen's nativist theory is understandably controversial. What is clear at this point is that not everyone believes that autistic children's mind-reading problems are attributable to their lack of a specialized theory of mind module (TOMM). They might also stem from deficits that autistic children show in shared attention (Leekam, Lopez, & Moore, 2000), or from more general problems they display at tying together related pieces of information to reach appropriate conclusions (Jarrold et al., 2000).

did not want; he then selected the children's favorite sticker, leaving them with the least desirable ones. By 4 years of age, children understood the dynamics of the interchange and quickly learned to tell Mean Monkey the opposite of their true desires. Younger children rarely caught on and played most of the game telling Mean Monkey the truth and not getting the stickers they wanted. In other research, 3-year-old children were shown a series of windows, some of which had treats in them (Russell et al., 1991). Children had to select the *nontreat* window to get the treat, something that they had a difficult time doing, and repeatedly failed to get a treat, seemingly being unable to inhibit their "pick-the-treat" response.

Other, more social factors also seem to influence TOM development. Pretend play, for example, is an activity that prompts children to think about mental states. As toddlers and preschool children conspire to make one object represent another or to enact pretend roles such as cops and robbers, they become increasingly aware of the creative potential of the human mind—an awareness that beliefs are merely mental constructions that can influence ongoing behavior, even if they misrepresent reality (as they often do during pretend play) (Hughes & Dunn, 1999; Taylor & Carlson, 1997). Young children also have ample opportunity to learn how the mind works from family conversations centering on the discussion of motives, intentions, and other mental states (Sabbagh & Callanan, 1998), as well as on the resolution of conflicts among siblings and reasoning about moral issues (Dunn, 1994). Indeed, researchers have found that preschoolers with siblings, especially those with older siblings, do better on false-belief tasks and are quicker to acquire a belief-desire theory of mind than children without siblings are (see Ruffman et al., 1998, for a review). Having siblings may provide more opportunities for pretend play as well as more interactions involving deception or trickery—experiences that illustrate that beliefs need not reflect reality to influence one's own or another's behavior. However, preschoolers who perform especially well on false-belief tasks also interact with a larger number of adults, which implies that children are apprentices to a variety of tutors as they acquire a theory of mind (Lewis et al., 1996).

Summing Up

Taken together, the evidence we have reviewed suggests that preschool children are not nearly as illogical or egocentric as Piaget assumed. Today, many researchers believe that Piaget underestimated the abilities of preschool children because his problems were too complex to allow them to demonstrate what they actually knew. If we were to ask you "What do quarks do?," you probably couldn't tell us unless you are a physics major. Surely, this is an unfair test of your "causal logic," just as Piaget's tests were when he questioned preschool children about phenomena that were equally unfamiliar to them (for example, "What causes the wind?"). Even when they were thinking about familiar concepts, Piaget required children to verbally justify their answers—to state rationales that these young, relatively inarticulate preschoolers were often incapable of providing (to Piaget's satisfaction, at least). Yet later research consistently indicates that Piaget's participants may have had a reasonably good understanding of many ideas that they couldn't articulate (for example, distinctions between animates and inanimates) and would have easily displayed such knowledge if asked different questions or given nonverbal tests of the same concepts (Bullock, 1985; Waxman & Hatch, 1992).

Clearly, Piaget was right in arguing that preschool children are more intuitive, egocentric, and illogical than older grade-school children. Yet, it is now equally clear that: (1) preschoolers are capable of reasoning logically about simple problems or concepts that are familiar to them, and (2) a number of factors other than lack of cognitive operations may account for their poor performances on Piaget's cognitive tests.

The Concrete-Operational Stage (7 to 11 Years)

concrete-operational period
Piaget's third stage of cognitive development, lasting from about age 7 to age 11, when children are acquiring cognitive operations and thinking more logically about real objects and experiences.

During Piaget's **concrete-operational period,** children rapidly acquire cognitive operations and apply these important new skills when thinking about objects and events that they have experienced. A cognitive operation is an internal mental activity that enables children to modify and reorganize their images and symbols to reach a logical conclusion. With these powerful new operations in their cognitive arsenal, grade-school children progress far beyond the static and centered thinking of the preoperational stage. For every limitation of the preoperational child, we can see a corresponding strength in the concrete operator (see Table 7.3). Below we provide a couple of examples of operational thought: *conservation* and *relational logic.*

Conservation

Concrete-operational children can easily solve several of Piaget's conservation problems. Faced with the conservation of liquids puzzle, for example, a 7-year-old concrete operator can *decenter* by focusing simultaneously on both the height and width of the two containers. She also displays *reversibility*—the ability to mentally undo the pouring process and imagine the liquid in its original container. Armed with these cognitive operations, she now knows that the two different containers each have the same amount of liquid; she uses logic, not misleading appearances, to reach her conclusion.

Relational Logic An important hallmark of concrete-operational thinking is a better understanding of quantitative relations and relational logic. Do you remember an occasion when your gym teacher said, "Line up by height from tallest to shortest"?

TABLE 7.3 A Comparison of Preoperational and Concrete-operational Thought

Concept	Preoperational thought	Concrete-operational thought
Egocentrism	Children typically assume that others share their point of view.	Children may respond egocentrically at times but are now much more aware of others' divergent perspectives.
Animism	Children are likely to assume that unfamiliar objects that move on their own have lifelike qualities.	Children are more aware of the biological bases for life and do not attribute lifelike qualities to inanimates.
Causality	Limited awareness of causality. Children occasionally display transductive reasoning, assuming that one of two correlated events must have caused the other.	Children have a much better appreciation of causal principles (although this knowledge of causality continues to develop into adolescence and beyond).
Perception-bound thought/ centration	Children make judgments based on perceptual appearances and focus on a single aspect of a situation when seeking answers to a problem.	Children can ignore misleading appearances and focus on more than one aspect of a situation when seeking answers to a problem (decentration).
Irreversibility/ reversibility	Children cannot mentally undo an action they have witnessed. They cannot think back to the way an object or situation was before the object or situation changed.	Children can mentally negate changes they have witnessed to make before/after comparisons and consider how changes have altered the situation.
Performance on Piagetian tests of logical reasoning	Their egocentrism and their perception-bound, centered reasoning means that children often fail conservation tasks, have difficulty grouping objects into hierarchies of classes and subclasses, and display little ability to order objects *mentally* along such quantitative dimensions as height or length.	Their declining egocentrism and acquisition of reversible cognitive operations permit concrete-operational children to conserve, correctly classify objects on several dimensions, and mentally order objects on quantitative dimensions. Conclusions are now based on logic (the way things *must* necessarily be) rather than on the way they appear to be.

mental seriation
a cognitive operation that allows one to mentally order a set of stimuli along a quantifiable dimension such as height or weight.

transitivity
the ability to recognize relations among elements in a serial order (for example, if A > B and B > C, then A > C).

horizontal décalage
Piaget's term for a child's uneven cognitive performance; an inability to solve certain problems even though one can solve similar problems requiring the same mental operations.

Carrying out such an order is really quite easy for concrete operators, who now are capable of **mental seriation**—the ability to mentally arrange items along a quantifiable dimension such as height or weight. By contrast, preoperational youngsters perform poorly on many seriation tasks (see Figure 7.7) and would struggle to comply with the gym teacher's request.

Concrete-operational thinkers also have mastered the related concept of **transitivity,** which describes the necessary relations among elements in a series. If, for example, Juan is taller than Pedro, and Mark is taller than Sam, who is taller, Juan or Sam? It follows logically that Juan must be taller than Sam, and the concrete operator grasps the transitivity of these size relationships. Lacking the concept of transitivity, the preoperational child relies on perceptions to answer the question and might insist that Juan and Sam stand next to each other so that she can determine who is taller. Preoperational children probably have a better understanding of such transitive relations than Piaget gave them credit for (Trabasso, 1975), but they still have difficulty grasping the logical necessity of transitivity (Chapman & Lindenberger, 1988; Markovits & Dumas, 1999).

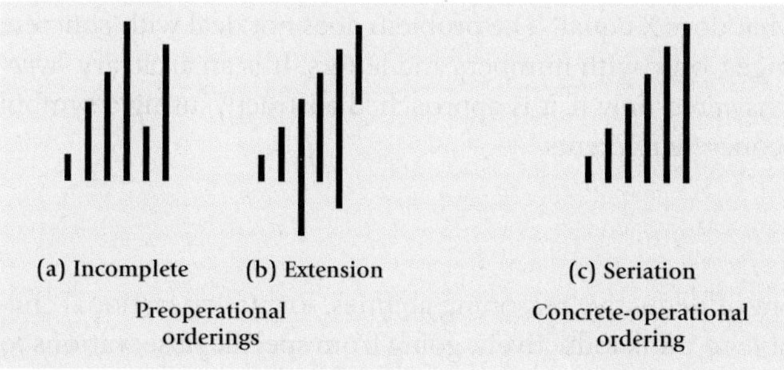

Figure 7.7 Children's performance on a simple seriation task. If asked to arrange a series of sticks from shortest to longest, preoperational children often line up one end of the sticks from shortest to longest, preoperational children often line up one end of the sticks and create an incomplete ordering (a) or order them so the top of each successive stick extends higher than the preceding stick (b). Concrete operators, by contrast, can use the inverse cognitive operations greater than (>) and less than (<) to quickly make successive comparisons and create a correct serial ordering (c).

The Sequencing of Concrete Operations. While examining Figure 7.5, you may have noticed that some forms of conservation (for example, mass) are understood much sooner than others (volume). Piaget was aware of this and other developmental inconsistencies, and he coined the term **horizontal décalage** to describe them.

Why does the child display different levels of understanding of conservation tasks that seem to require the same mental operations? According to Piaget, horizontal décalage occurs because problems that appear quite similar may actually differ in complexity. For example, conservation of volume (see Figure 7.5) is not attained until ages 9 to 12 because it is a complex task that requires the child to simultaneously consider the operations involved in the conservation of both liquids *and* mass and then to determine whether there are any meaningful relationships between these two phenomena.

Although we have talked as if concrete operations were a set of skills that appeared rather abruptly over a brief period, this was not Piaget's view. Piaget always maintained that operational abilities develop gradually and sequentially as the simpler skills that appear first are consolidated, combined, and reorganized into increasingly complex mental structures.

After reviewing some of the intellectual accomplishments of the concrete-operational period, we can see why many societies begin formal education at 6 to 7 years of age. According to Piaget, this is precisely the time when children are decentering from perceptual illusions and acquiring the cognitive operations that enable them to comprehend arithmetic, think about language and its properties, classify animals, people, objects, and events, and understand the relations between uppercase and lowercase letters, letters and the printed word, and words and sentences.

The Formal-Operational Stage (11 to 12 Years and Beyond)

According to Piaget, the impressive thinking of concrete-operational children is limited because they can apply their operational schemes only to objects, situations, or events that are real or imaginable. The transitive inferences of concrete operators, for example, are likely to be accurate only for real objects that are (or have been) physically present. Seven- to eleven-year-olds cannot yet apply this relational logic to abstract signifiers such as the Xs, Ys, and Zs that we use in algebra. By contrast, formal operations, first seen between the ages of 11 and 13 years of age, are mental actions performed on *ideas* and *propositions.* No longer is thinking tied to the factual or observable, for formal operators can reason quite logically about hypothetical processes and events that may have no basis in reality.

Hypothetico-Deductive Reasoning

formal operations
Piaget's fourth and final stage of cognitive development, from age 11 or 12 and beyond, when the individual begins to think more rationally and systematically about abstract concepts and hypothetical events.

hypothetico-deductive reasoning
in Piaget's theory, a formal operational ability to think hypothetically.

The benchmark of **formal operations** is what Piaget referred to as **hypothetico-deductive reasoning** (Inhelder & Piaget, 1958). *Deductive reasoning,* which entails reasoning from the general to the specific, much as Sherlock Holmes would do in examining the clues to a crime to catch the villain, is not, in itself, a formal operational ability. Concrete-operational children can arrive at a correct conclusion if they are provided with the proper concrete "facts" as evidence. Formal-operational children, on the other hand, are not restricted to thinking about previously acquired facts, but can generate hypotheses; what is possible is more important to them than what is real. In the Box on p. 269 we can see the differences between concrete-operational and formal-operational thinking as children consider a hypothetical proposition presented in the form of an art assignment.

Hypothetical thinking is also critical for most forms of mathematics beyond simple arithmetic. If $2X + 5 = 15$, what does X equal? The problem does not deal with concrete entities such as apples or oranges, only with numbers and letters. It is an arbitrary, *hypothetical* problem that can be answered only if it is approached abstractly, using a symbol system that does not require concrete referents.

Thinking Like a Scientist

inductive reasoning
the type of thinking that scientists display, where hypotheses are generated and then systematically tested in experiments.

In addition to the development of deductive reasoning abilities, formal-operational children are hypothesized to be able to think inductively, going from specific observations to broad generalizations. **Inductive reasoning** is the type of thinking that scientists display, where hypotheses are generated and then systematically tested in experiments.

Inhelder and Piaget (1958) used a series of tasks to assess scientific reasoning, one of which was the *pendulum problem.* Given strings of different lengths, objects of different weights to attach to one end of the strings, and a hook on which to hang the other end, the child's task is to discover which factor or factors influence how fast the string pendulum oscillates (that is, swings back and forth during a set time period). Is it the length of the string that matters? The heaviness of the weight? The force with which the weight is

FOCUS ON RESEARCH Children's Responses to a Hypothetical Proposition

Piaget (1970a) argued that the thinking of concrete operators is reality bound. Presumably, most 9-year-olds would have a difficult time thinking about objects that don't exist or events that could never happen. By contrast, children entering the stage of formal operations are said to be quite capable of considering hypothetical propositions and carrying them to a logical conclusion. Indeed, Piaget suspected that many formal operators would even enjoy this type of cognitive challenge.

Some years ago, a group of concrete operators (9-year-old fourth-graders) and a group of children who were at or rapidly approaching formal operations (11- to 12-year-old sixth graders) completed the following assignment:

Suppose that you were given a third eye and that you could choose to place this eye anywhere on your body. Draw me a picture to show where you would place your extra eye, and then tell me why you would put it there.

All the 9-year-olds placed the third eye on the forehead between their two natural eyes. It seems as if these children called on their concrete experiences to complete their assignment: Eyes are found somewhere around the middle of the face in all people. One 9-year-old boy remarked that the third eye should go between the other two because "that's where a cyclops has his eye." The rationales for this eye placement were rather unimaginative. Consider the following examples:

JIM (age 9½): I would like an eye beside my two other eyes so that if one eye went out, I could still see with two.

VICKIE (age 9): I want an extra eye so I can see you three times.

TANYA (age 9½): I want a third eye so I could see better.

In contrast, the older, formal-operational children gave a wide variety of responses that were not at all dependent on what they have seen previously. Furthermore, these children thought out the advantages of this hypothetical situation and provided rather imaginative rationales for placing the extra eye in unique locations. Here are some sample responses:

KEN (age 11½): (draws the extra eye on top of a tuft of hair) I could revolve the eye to look in all directions.

JOHN (age 11½): (draws his extra eye in the palm of his left hand) I could see around corners and see what kind of cookie I'll get out of the cookie jar.

TONY (age 11): (draws a close-up of a third eye in his mouth) I want a third eye in my mouth because I want to see what I am eating.

When asked their opinions of the three-eye assignment, many of the younger children considered it rather silly and uninteresting. One 9-year-old remarked, "This is stupid. Nobody has three eyes." However, the 11- to 12-year-olds enjoyed the task and continued to pester their teacher for "fun" art assignments "like the eye problem" for the remainder of the school year (Shaffer, 1973).

So the results of this demonstration are generally consistent with Piaget's theory. Older children who are at or rapidly approaching the stage of formal operations are more likely than younger, concrete operators to generate logical and creative responses to a hypothetical proposition and to enjoy this type of reasoning.

A systematic approach to problem solving is one of the characteristics of formal-operational thinking.

pushed? The height from which the weight is released? Or might two or more of these variables be important?

The key to solving this problem is to first identify the four factors that might control the pendulum's oscillation and then to systematically test each of these hypotheses, varying one factor at a time while holding the others constant. Each successive hypothesis is tested in an if–then fashion: "If the weight on the string matters, then I should see a difference in oscillation when I compare a string with a heavy weight to a same-length string with a light weight, while holding other factors constant." Formal operators, who rely on this systematic approach to hypothesis generation and testing, eventually discover that the "weight hypothesis" is wrong and that the pendulum's oscillation depends on only one factor: the length of the string.

By contrast, 9- to 10-year-old concrete operators are not able to generate and systematically test the full range of possibilities that would permit them to draw the appropriate conclusion. They often begin with a reasonable hypothesis ("Maybe string length matters"), but they can't isolate the effects of each variable. For example, they may test the string-length hypothesis without holding weight constant; should they find that a short string with a heavy weight oscillates faster than a longer one with a lighter weight, they are likely to erroneously conclude that both string length and weight control the pendulum's oscillation. Although subsequent research has not always supported Piaget's observations about scientific reasoning, it is generally agreed that it is a late-developing ability that is not easily demonstrated in many adults (Kuhn, Amsel, & O'Loughlin, 1988; Moshman, 1998). Older concrete operators can be trained to think more like formal operators when seeking solutions to problems (Adey & Shayer, 1992), but they are unable to generate these rational and methodical problem-solving strategies on their own. Even elementary school children can be trained to use scientific reasoning with explicit instructions, but transfer of such trained strategies is limited to older preadolescent children only (Chen & Klahr, 1999).

In sum, formal-operational thinking is rational, systematic, and abstract. The formal operator can now think planfully about thought and can operate on ideas and hypothetical concepts, including those that contradict reality.

Personal and Social Implications of Formal Thought

Formal-operational thinking is a powerful tool that may change adolescents in many ways—some good, and some not so good. First the good news. As we will see in Chapter 12, formal operations may pave the way for thinking about what is possible in one's life, forming a stable identity, and achieving a much richer understanding of other people's psychological perspectives and the causes of their behavior. Formal-operational thinkers are also better equipped to make difficult personal decisions that involve weighing alternative courses of action and their probable consequences for themselves and other people (see Chapter 14, for example, on the development of moral reasoning). So advances in cognitive growth help to lay the groundwork for changes in many other aspects of development.

Now the bad news: Formal operations may also be related to some of the more painful aspects of the adolescent experience. Unlike younger children who tend to accept the world as it is and to heed the dictates of authority figures, formal operators, who can imagine hypothetical alternatives to present realities, may begin to question everything from their parents' authority to impose strict curfews to the government's need for spending billions of dollars on weapons and the exploration of outer space when so many people are hungry and homeless. Indeed, the more logical inconsistencies and other flaws that adolescents detect in the real world, the more confused they become and the more inclined they are to become frustrated with or even to display rebellious anger toward the agents (for example, parents, the government) thought to be responsible for these imperfect states of affairs. Piaget (1970a) viewed this idealistic fascination with the way things "ought to be" as a perfectly normal outgrowth of the adolescent's newly acquired abstract reasoning abilities, and he thus proclaimed formal operations the primary cause of the "generation gap."

Does Everyone Reach Formal Operations?

Piaget (1970b) believed that the transition from concrete-operational to formal-operational reasoning takes place very gradually. For example, 11- to 13-year-olds who are entering formal operations are able to consider simple hypothetical propositions such as the three-eye problem mentioned in the Box on p. 269. However, they are not yet proficient at generating and testing hypotheses, and it may be another 3 to 4 years before they are capable of the planful, systematic reasoning that is necessary to deduce what determines how fast a pendulum will swing. Piaget never identified a stage of reasoning beyond formal operations, and he believed that most people show at least some signs of this highest level of intellect by ages 15 to 18.

Other investigators find that adolescents are much slower to acquire formal operations than Piaget had thought. In fact, Edith Neimark's (1979) review of the literature

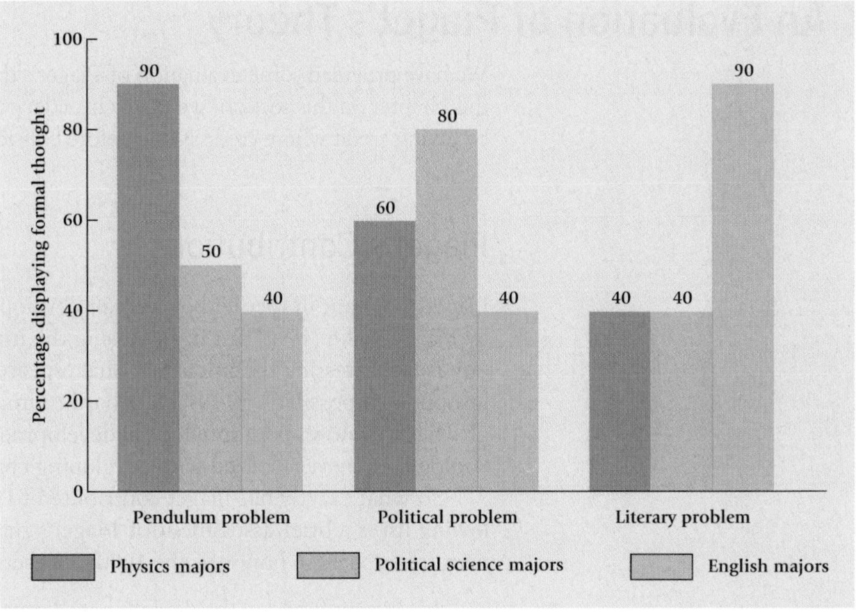

Figure 7.8 Expertise and formal operations. College students show the greatest command of formal-operational thought in the subject area most related to their major. *Adapted from "Individual Differences in College Students' Performance on Formal Operations Tasks," by R. De Lisi & J. Staudt, 1980,* Journal of Applied Developmental Psychology, 1, *163–174. Reprinted with permission from Excerpta Medica, Inc.*

suggests that a sizable percentage of American adults do not often reason at the formal level, and apparently there are some cultures—particularly those where formal schooling is rare or nonexistent—in which no one solves Piaget's formal-operational problems. Why do some people fail to attain formal operations? Cross-cultural research provides one clue: They may not have had sufficient exposure to the kinds of schooling that stress logic, mathematics, and science—experiences that Piaget believed help the child to reason at the formal level (Cole, 1990; Dasen, 1977).

In the later stages of his career, Piaget (1972) suggested another possibility: Perhaps nearly all adults are capable of reasoning at the formal level, but do so only on problems that hold their interest or are of vital importance to them. Indeed, Steven Tulkin and Melvin Konner (1973) found that preliterate Bushman hunters who fail Piaget's test problems often do reason at the formal level on at least one task: tracking prey. Clearly, this is an activity of great importance to them that requires the systematic testing of inferences and hypotheses. A similar phenomenon has been observed among high school and college students. Not only do 12th-graders reason more abstractly about relevant everyday issues with which they are already familiar (Ward & Overton, 1990), but as we see in Figure 7.8, physics, English, and social science majors are all more likely to perform at the formal level on problems that fall within their own academic domains (De Lisi & Staudt, 1980).

It seems likely, then, that each person has an optimal, or "highest," level of cognitive performance that will show itself in familiar or well-trained content domains (Fischer, 1980; Fischer & Bidell, 1998). However, performance is likely to be inconsistent across domains unless the person has had a chance to build knowledge and to practice reasoning in all these content areas (Marini & Case, 1994). So we must be careful not to underestimate the cognitive capabilities of adolescents and adults who fail Piaget's formal-operational tests, for their less-than-optimal performances on these physical-science problems may simply reflect either a lack of interest or a lack of experience with the subject matter rather than an inability to reason at the formal level.

One interesting (and perhaps counterintuitive for some) finding is that formal operational abilities seem to be accelerated in contemporary adolescents relative to those of earlier generations (Flieller, 1999). Tests of formal operational abilities given to groups of French adolescents between 1967 and 1996 reveal higher scores for the latter cohorts. This suggests that today's adolescents are cognitively more advanced than adolescents at the same age 25 and 30 years ago. This is similar to the effect of increasing IQ scores found over the past 60 years (Flynn, 1987), the so-called Flynn effect, which will be discussed in Chapter 9.

An Evaluation of Piaget's Theory

We have provided some evaluation of Piaget's theory of cognitive development throughout this chapter. In this section, we take a broader view of this monumental theory. Let us start by giving credit where credit is due before considering the challenges to Piaget's viewpoint.

Piaget's Contributions

Piaget is a giant in the field of human development. As one anonymous scholar quoted by Harry Beilin (1992) put it, "assessing the impact of Piaget on developmental psychology is like assessing the impact of Shakespeare on English literature or Aristotle on philosophy—impossible" (p. 191). It is hard to imagine that we would know even a fraction of what we know about intellectual development had Piaget pursued his early interests in zoology and never worked with developing children.

So what exactly has Piaget contributed to the field of human development? The following list is a brief assessment of Piaget's major contributions made by several prominent researchers in honor of the 100th anniversary of Piaget's birth (see Brainerd, 1996):

1. Piaget founded the discipline we know today as cognitive development. His interest in children's thinking insured that this field would be "developmental" and not merely apply to children the ideas and methods from the study of adult thinking.
2. Piaget convinced us that children are curious, active explorers who play an important role in their own development. Although Piaget's assumptions that children actively construct their own knowledge may seem obvious today, this viewpoint was innovative and counter to the thinking of his time.
3. Piaget's theory was one of the first to try to *explain,* and not just *describe,* the process of development. Largely prompted by his theory, many theorists today have taken seriously the need to explain transitions in children's thinking (Fischer & Bidell, 1998; Nelson, 1996; Pascual-Leone, 2000; Siegler, 1996).
4. Piaget's description of broad sequences of intellectual development provides a reasonably accurate overview of how children of different ages think. He may have been wrong about some of the specifics, but, as Robert Siegler (1991, p. 18) notes, "His descriptions feel right. . . . The general trends . . . appeal to our intuitions and our memories of childhood."
5. Piaget's ideas have had a major influence on thinking about social and emotional development as well as many practical implications for educators.
6. Finally, Piaget asked important questions and drew literally thousands of researchers to the study of cognitive development. And as often happens when heuristic theories such as Piaget's are repeatedly scrutinized, some of this research led to new insights while pointing to problems with his original ideas.

Challenges to Piaget

Over the past 35 years, critics have pointed to several apparent shortcomings of Piaget's theory. We briefly consider four of these criticisms.

Piaget Failed to Distinguish Competence from Performance

We have commented repeatedly throughout this chapter that Piaget underestimated the cognitive capabilities of infants, toddlers, and preschool children. One reason for this consistent underestimation of children's abilities is that Piaget was concerned with identifying the underlying *competencies,* or cognitive structures, that presumably determined how children perform on various cognitive tasks. He tended to assume that a child who failed one of his problems simply lacked the underlying concepts, or thought structures, he was testing.

We now know that this assumption is not valid because many factors other than a lack of critical competencies might undermine one's performance on a cognitive test. We've seen, for example, that 4- and 5-year-olds who seem to know the differences between animates and inanimates failed Piaget's tests largely because Piaget required them to explain principles they understood (critical competency) but could not articulate. His tendency to equate task performances with competencies (and to ignore motivation, task familiarity, and all other factors that influence performance) is a major reason that his age norms for various cognitive milestones were often so far off target.

Does Cognitive Development Really Occur in Stages?

Piaget maintained that his stages of intellectual development are *holistic structures,* that is, coherent modes of thinking that are applied across a broad range of tasks. To say that a child is concrete-operational, for example, implies that he relies on cognitive operations and thinks logically about the vast majority of intellectual problems that he encounters.

Recently this holistic-structures assumption has been challenged by researchers who question whether cognitive development is at all stagelike (Bjorklund, 2005; Siegler, 2000). From their perspective, a "stage" of cognitive development implies that abrupt changes in intellectual functioning occur as the child acquires several new competencies over a relatively brief period. Yet we've seen that cognitive growth doesn't happen that way. Major transitions in intellect occur quite gradually, and there is often very little consistency in the child's performance on tasks that presumably measure the abilities that define a given stage. For example, it may be years before a 7-year-old who can seriate or conserve number will be able to conserve volume (see Figure 7.5). Furthermore, it now appears that different concrete-operational and formal-operational problems are mastered in different orders by different children, a finding that suggests that there is a lot less consistency and coherence to cognitive growth than Piaget assumed (Case, 1992; Larivée, Narmandeau, & Parent, 2000).

So is cognitive development truly stagelike? The issue is still hotly debated and far from being resolved. Some theorists insist that cognitive development is coherent and does progress through a series of stages, though not necessarily through the same stages that Piaget proposed (Case & Okamoto, 1996). Yet many other theorists believe that intellectual development is a complex, multifaceted process in which children gradually acquire skills in many different content areas such as deductive reasoning, mathematics, visual–spatial reasoning, verbal skills, and moral reasoning to name a few (Bjorklund, 2005; Fischer & Bidell, 1998). Although development within each of these domains may occur in small, orderly steps, there is no assumption of consistency across domains. Thus, a 10-year-old who enjoys solving word puzzles and playing verbal games might outperform most age-mates on tests of verbal reasoning but function at a much lower level in less familiar domains, such as hypothesis testing or mathematical reasoning.

In sum, many aspects of cognitive development are orderly and coherent (and some would say stagelike) *within particular intellectual domains.* Yet, there is very little evidence for strong consistencies in development across domains or for broad, holistic cognitive stages of the kind Piaget described.

Does Piaget "Explain" Cognitive Development?

Even those researchers who claim that cognitive growth is stagelike are bothered by Piaget's account of how children move from one stage of intellect to the next. Recall Piaget's interactionist viewpoint: Presumably children are (1) constantly assimilating new experiences in ways that their level of maturation allows, (2) accommodating their thinking to these experiences, and (3) reorganizing their structures into increasingly complex mental schemes that enable them to reestablish cognitive equilibrium with novel aspects of the environment. As children continue to mature, assimilate more complex information, and alter and reorganize their schemes, they eventually come to view familiar objects and events in new ways and move from one stage of intellect to the next.

This rather vague explanation of cognitive growth raises more questions than it answers. What maturational changes are necessary before children can progress from sensorimotor to preoperational intellect or from concrete operations to formal operations? What kinds of experiences must a child have before he will construct mental symbols, use cognitive operations, or operate on ideas and think about hypotheticals? Piaget was simply not very clear about these or any other mechanisms that might enable a child to move to a higher stage of intellect. As a result, a growing number of researchers now look on his theory as an elaborate description of cognitive development that has limited explanatory power (Gelman & Baillargeon, 1983; Kuhn, 1992).

Piaget Devoted Too Little Attention to Social and Cultural Influences

Children live in varied social and cultural contexts that affect the way their world is structured. Although Piaget admitted that cultural factors may influence the rate of cognitive growth, developmentalists now know that culture influences *how* children think as well (Gauvain, 2001; Rogoff, 1998, 2003). Piaget also paid too little attention to the ways that children's minds develop through their *social interactions* with more competent individuals. It would be an overstatement to say that Piaget ignored social influences on cognitive development. As we will see in Chapters 12 and 14, Piaget felt that conflict among peers was a major contributor to cognitive disequilibrium and intellectual growth, particularly the growth of perspective-taking skills and moral reasoning. Nevertheless, Piaget's descriptions emphasized the *self-directed* character of cognitive growth, almost as if children were isolated scientists, exploring the world and making critical discoveries largely on their own. Today, we know that children develop many of their most basic (and not so basic) competencies by collaborating with parents, teachers, older siblings, and peers. Indeed, the belief that social interaction contributes importantly to cognitive growth is a cornerstone of the *sociocultural perspective* on cognitive development offered by one of Piaget's contemporaries, Lev Vygotsky.

sociocultural theory
Vygotsky's perspective on cognitive development, in which children acquire their culture's values, beliefs, and problem-solving strategies through collaborative dialogues with more knowledgeable members of society.

Vygotsky's Sociocultural Perspective

In order to view Piaget's work from a new vantage point, let's consider a perspective on cognitive development that has been arousing a great deal of interest lately—the **sociocultural theory** of Lev Vygotsky (1934/1962; 1930–1935/1978; and see Gauvain, 2001; Rogoff, 1990, 1998, 2003; Wertsch & Tulviste, 1992). This Russian developmentalist was an active scholar in the 1920s and 1930s when Piaget was formulating his theory. Unfortunately, Vygotsky died at the age of 38 before his work was complete. Nevertheless, he left us with much food for thought by insisting that (1) cognitive growth occurs in a sociocultural context that influences the form it takes, and (2) many of a child's most noteworthy cognitive skills evolve from social interactions with parents, teachers, and other more competent associates.

The sociocultural theory of Lev Vygotsky (1896–1934) views cognitive development as a socially mediated process that may vary from culture to culture.

The Role of Culture in Intellectual Development

The crux of the sociocultural perspective as advocated by Vygotsky was that children's intellectual development is closely tied to their culture. Children do *not* develop the same type of mind all over the world, but learn to use their species-typical brain and mental abilities to solve problems and interpret their surroundings consistent with the demands and values of their culture. For Vygotsky, human cognition, even when carried out in isolation, is inherently *sociocultural*, affected by the beliefs, values, and tools of intellectual adaptation passed to individuals by their culture. And because these values and intellectual tools may vary substantially from culture to culture, Vygotsky believed that neither the course nor the content of intellectual growth was as universal as Piaget assumed.

CONCEPT CHECK 7.3 Understanding Operations

Check your understanding of older children's cognitive development by answering the following questions. Answers appear in the appendix.

Multiple Choice: Select the best alternative for each question.

_____ 1. Glen's mother has dark hair and is short; Glen thinks that all mothers have dark hair and are short. This is an example of
a. conservation
b. disequilibrium
c. egocentrism
d. accommodation

_____ 2. The *preoperational* child is characterized by
a. introspective and abstract thinking
b. logical, concrete, and nonabstract thinking
c. symbolic, intuitive, and egocentric thinking
d. logical, abstract, and egocentric thinking

_____ 3. A 5-year-old child suggests that John, who is 6 feet tall, must be older than his Aunt Mary, who is only 5 feet tall. This approach of interpreting age based solely on the height of an individual can be attributed to this child's
a. seeing events as specific *states* and ignoring *transformations*
b. egocentricity
c. inability to deal with a superordinate and subordinate concept simultaneously
d. perceptual centration

_____ 4. Children's developing concepts of mental activity, including some coherent framework for organizing facts and making predictions, is referred to as
a. dual encoding
b. reflective abstraction
c. theory of mind
d. representational insight

Matching: Match the following concepts with their definitions.

a. representational insight
b. animism
c. conservation
d. theory of mind
e. horizontal décalage
f. hypothetico-deductive reasoning

5. _______ A person's concepts of mental activity; used to refer to how children conceptualize mental activity and how they attribute intention to and predict the behavior of others.
6. _______ The knowledge that an entity can stand for (represent) something other than itself.
7. _______ The recognition that the properties of an object or substance do not change when its appearance is altered in some superficial way.
8. _______ In Piaget's theory, a formal operational ability to think hypothetically.
9. _______ Attributing life and lifelike qualities to inanimate objects.
10. _______ Piaget's term for a child's uneven cognitive performance; an inability to solve certain problems even though one can solve similar problems requiring the same mental processes.

Essays: Provide a detailed answer to the following questions.

11. What are some of the cognitive abilities that differentiate preoperational from concrete operational children?
12. How are false-belief tasks used to assess belief-desire reasoning in children?

ontogenetic development
development of the individual over his or her lifetime.

microgenetic development
changes that occur over relatively brief periods of time, in seconds, minutes, or days, as opposed to larger-scale changes, as conventionally studied in ontogenetic development.

phylogenetic development
development over evolutionary time.

Vygotsky proposed that we should evaluate development from the perspective of four interrelated levels in interaction with children's environments—*microgenetic, ontogenetic, phylogenetic,* and *sociohistorical.* **Ontogenetic development** refers to development of the individual over his or her lifetime, and is the topic of this book and the level of analysis for nearly all developmental psychologists. **Microgenetic development** refers to changes that occur over relatively brief periods of time, such as the changes that one may see in a child solving addition problems every week for 11 consecutive weeks (Siegler & Jenkins, 1989), or even the changes in the use of memory strategies that children use over five different trials in the course of a 20-minute session (Coyle & Bjorklund, 1997). This is obviously a finer-grained analysis than that afforded by the traditional ontogenetic level. **Phylogenetic development** refers to changes over evolutionary time, measured in thousands and even millions of years. Here, Vygotsky anticipated the current evolutionary psychology perspective, believing that an understanding of the species' history can provide insight into child development (Bjorklund & Pellegrini, 2002; Ellis & Bjorklund,

sociohistorical development changes that have occurred in one's culture and the values, norms, and technologies such a history has generated.

2005). Finally, **sociohistorical development** refers to the changes that have occurred in one's culture and the values, norms, and technologies such a history has generated. It is this sociohistorical perspective that modern-day researchers have emphasized most about Vygotsky's ideas.

Tools of Intellectual Adaptation

tools of intellectual adaptation Vygotsky's term for methods of thinking and problem-solving strategies that children internalize from their interactions with more competent members of society.

Vygotsky proposed that infants are born with a few *elementary mental functions*—attention, sensation, perception, and memory—that are eventually transformed by the culture into new and more sophisticated *higher mental functions.* Take memory, for example. Young children's early memorial capabilities are limited by biological constraints to the images and impressions they can produce. However, each culture provides its children with **tools of intellectual adaptation** that permit them to use their basic mental functions more adaptively. For example, children in information-age societies might enhance their memory by taking notes, whereas their age-mates in preliterate societies might represent each object they must remember by tying a knot in a string. Such socially transmitted memory strategies and other cultural tools teach children how to use their minds—in short, *how* to think. And because each culture also transmits specific beliefs and values, it teaches children *what* to think as well.

One subtle difference in cultural tools of intellectual adaptation that can make a noticeable difference on children's cognitive task performance is found in how a language names its numbers. For example, in all languages, the first ten digits must be learned by rote. However, after that, some languages take advantage of the base-ten number system and name numbers accordingly. English does this beginning at 20 (twenty-one, twenty-two, and so on). However, the teen numbers in English are not so easily represented. Rather, 11 and 12 also must be memorized. Not until 13 does a base-ten system begin (three + ten = "thirteen"), and even then, several of the number names do not correspond to the formula digit + ten. "Fourteen," "sixteen," "seventeen," "eighteen," and "nineteen" do, but the number names for "thirteen" and "fifteen" are not as straightforward (that is, they are not expressed as "threeteen" and "fiveteen"). Moreover, for the teen numbers, the digit unit is stated first ("*four*teen," "*six*teen"), whereas the decade unit is stated first for the numbers 20 through 99 ("*twenty*-one," "*thirty*-two"). Thus, the number system becomes regular in English beginning with the 20s.

Other languages, such as Chinese, have a more systematic number-naming system. In Chinese, as in English, the first ten digits must be memorized. However, from this point, the Chinese number-naming system follows a base-ten logic, with the name for 11 translating as "ten one," the name for 12 translating as "ten two," and so on. Table 7.4 shows the names for the numbers 1 to 20 in both English and Chinese. Kevin Miller and his colleagues (1995) reasoned that differences in the number-naming systems between English and Chinese might be associated with early mathematical competence, specifically counting. They tested 3- through 5-year-old children in Champaign-Urbana, Illinois, and Beijing, China. They asked each child to count as high as possible. There were no cultural differences for the 3-year-olds, but the Chinese children began to show an advantage by age 4, and this advantage was even larger at age 5. Further analyses indicated that cultural differences were limited to the teens decade. Although almost all children could count to 10 (94 percent of the American children and 92 percent of the Chinese children), only 48 percent of the American children could count to 20, compared with 74 percent of the Chinese children. Once children could count to 20, there were no cultural differences for counting to 100. These findings indicate how differences in the number-naming system of a language can contribute to early differences in a cognitive skill. This early difference in a tool of intellectual adaptation might contribute to later differences in mathematical abilities found between Chinese and American children (Stevenson & Lee, 1990).

TABLE 7.4 Chinese and English number words from 1 to 20. The more systematic Chinese numbering system follows a base-ten logic (i.e., 11 translating as "ten one" ["shi yee"]) requiring less rote memorization, which may explain why Chinese-speaking children learn to count to 20 earlier than English-speaking children.

Number	Chinese word	English word
1	yee	one
2	uhr	two
3	sahn	three
4	suh	four
5	woo	five
6	lyo	six
7	chee	seven
8	bah	eight
9	jyo	nine
10	shi	ten
11	shi yee	eleven
12	shi uhr	twelve
13	shi shan	thirteen
14	shi suh	fourteen
15	shi woo	fifteen
16	shi lyo	sixteen
17	shi chee	seventeen
18	shi bah	eighteen
19	shi jyo	nineteen
20	ershi	twenty

The Social Origins of Early Cognitive Competencies and the Zone of Proximal Development

Vygotsky agreed with Piaget that young children are curious explorers who are actively involved in learning and discovering new principles. However, unlike Piaget, Vygotsky believed that many of the truly important "discoveries" that children make occur within the context of cooperative, or collaborative, *dialogues* between a skillful tutor, who models the activity and transmits verbal instructions, and a novice pupil, who first seeks to understand the tutor's instruction and eventually internalizes this information, using it to regulate his or her own performance.

To illustrate collaborative (or guided) learning as Vygotsky viewed it, let's imagine that Tanya, a 4-year-old, has just received her first jigsaw puzzle. She attempts to work the puzzle but gets nowhere until her father sits down beside her and gives her some tips. He suggests that it would be a good idea to put together the corners first, points to the pink area at the edge of one corner piece and says, "Let's look for another pink piece." When Tanya seems frustrated, he places two interlocking pieces near each other so that she will notice them, and when Tanya succeeds, he offers words of encouragement. As Tanya gradually gets the hang of it, he steps back and lets her work more and more independently.

The Zone of Proximal Development

How do collaborative dialogues foster cognitive growth? First, Vygotsky would say that Tanya and her father are operating in what he called the **zone of proximal development**—the difference between what a learner can accomplish independently and what he or she can accomplish with the guidance and encouragement of a more skilled partner. It is in this zone that sensitive instruction should be aimed and in which new cognitive growth can be expected to occur. Tanya obviously becomes a more competent puzzle-solver with her father's help than without it. More importantly, she will internalize the problem-solving techniques that she uses in collaboration with him and ultimately use them on her own, rising to a new level of independent mastery.

zone of proximal development
Vygotsky's term for the range of tasks that are too complex to be mastered alone but can be accomplished with guidance and encouragement from a more skillful partner.

One feature of social collaboration that fosters cognitive growth is **scaffolding,** the tendency of more expert participants to carefully tailor the support they provide to the novice learner's current situation so that he can profit from that support and increase his understanding of a problem (Wood, Bruner, & Ross, 1976). Scaffolding occurs not just in formal educational settings, but any time a more expert person adjusts his input to guide a child to a level near the limits of his or her capabilities. The behavior of Tanya's father in the preceding example reflects not only working in the zone of proximal development but also scaffolding.

scaffolding
process by which an expert, when instructing a novice, responds contingently to the novice's behavior in a learning situation, so that the novice gradually increases his or her understanding of a problem.

All the responsibility for determining the extent of adult involvement is not on the adult. Both adults and children jointly determine the degree to which children can function independently. For example, children who are less able to solve problems on their own will elicit more support from adults than will more capable children. More skilled children need less adult support, or scaffolding, to solve a problem (Plumert & Nichols-Whitehead, 1996).

We have been careful not to use the word "competence" in describing children's problem-solving abilities. In Vygotsky's sociocultural perspective, learning and development are the result of interacting in specific culturally defined tasks that have specific rules. Unlike other theories of cognitive development (for example, Piaget's), "competence" is not an absolute level beyond which a child cannot exceed, but rather is task specific (Fischer & Bidell, 1998). A child can show an elevated level of ability on one highly practiced task but be much less adept on a very similar, perhaps even objectively less-demanding, task. A child's level of intellectual functioning is always evaluated by performance on specific tasks or in specific culturally determined situations.

guided participation
adult-child interactions in which children's cognitions and modes of thinking are shaped as they participate with or observe adults engaged in culturally relevant activities.

Bob Daemmrich/Stock Boston

According to Vygotsky, new skills are easier to acquire if children receive guidance and encouragement from a more competent associate.

Apprenticeship in Thinking and Guided Participation

In many cultures, children do not learn by going to school with other children, nor do their parents formally teach such lessons as weaving and hunting. Instead, they learn through **guided participation**—by actively *participating* in culturally relevant activities alongside more skilled partners who provide necessary aid and encouragement (Gauvain, 2001; Rogoff, 1998). Guided participation is an informal "apprenticeship in thinking" in which children's cognitions are shaped as they partake, alongside adults or other more skillful associates, in everyday culturally relevant experiences. Barbara Rogoff believes that cognitive growth is shaped as much or more by these informal adult–child transactions as it is by more formal teaching or educational experiences.

The idea of an apprenticeship, or guided participation, may seem reasonable in cultures where children are integrated early into the daily activities of adult life, such as the agrarian Mayans of Guatemala and Mexico, or the !Kung of Africa whose hunting-and-gathering lifestyle has remained virtually unchanged for thousands of years. But this idea is not as easily grasped for a culture such as our own, because many aspects of cognitive development in Western culture have shifted from parents to professional educators, whose job it is to teach important cultural knowledge and skills to children. Nevertheless, learning certainly occurs at home in modern societies, particularly during the preschool years. And in many ways, these home-learning experiences prepare children for the schooling that will follow. For example, formal education in the United States and Europe involves children responding to adults' questions when the adults already know the answers. It also involves learning and discussing things that have no immediate relevance—knowledge for knowledge's sake. Such **context-independent learning,** foreign to so many cultures, is fostered from infancy and early childhood in our own culture (Rogoff, 1990). Consider the following interchange between 19-month-old Brittany and her mother:

context-independent learning learning that has no immediate relevance to the present context, as is done in modern schools; acquiring knowledge for knowledge's sake.

MOTHER: Brittany, what's at the park?
BRITTANY: Babyswing.
MOTHER: That's right, the babyswing. And what else?
BRITTANY: (shrugs)
MOTHER: A slide?
BRITTANY: (smiling, nods yes)
MOTHER: And what else is at the park?
BRITTANY: (shrugs)
MOTHER: A see . . .
BRITTANY: Seesaw!
MOTHER: That's right, a seesaw.

This type of conversation is typical for an American mother and her child, and it is a good example of Vygotsky's zone of proximal development. Brittany, in this case, was not only learning to recall specific objects with her mother's help, but was also learning the importance of remembering information *out of context* (mother and daughter were in their living room at the time, miles from the park). Brittany was learning that she could be called upon to state facts to her mother that her mother already knew. She was also learning that she could depend on her mother to help provide answers when she was unable to generate them herself. Figure 7.9 provides a list of some of the functions that such "shared remembering" between parent and child can have on memory development.

Working in the Zone of Proximal Development in Different Cultures

Although the process of guided participation may be universal, how it is carried out varies from culture to culture. Rogoff and her colleagues (1993) classified cultures into two general types: (1) cultures such as ours, where, beginning in the preschool years, children are often segregated from adults and receive much culturally important information in school; and (2) cultures where children are in close contact most of the day with adults, observing and interacting with them while they perform culturally important activities. Rogoff then observed 14 families with toddlers in each of four communities, two where culturally important information is transmitted mainly "out of context," through formal schooling (Salt Lake City, in the United States, and Keçiören, a middle-class community in Turkey), and two where culturally important information is transmitted mainly in context (the Guatemalan Mayan town of San Pedro and Dhol-Ki-Patti, a tribal village in India).

Figure 7.9 Some functions of shared remembering in children's memory development *Source: Gauvain, M. (2001).* The Social Context of Cognitive Development. *New York: Guilford, p. 111.*

- ☑ Children learn about memory process, for example, strategies
- ☑ Children learn ways of remembering and communicating memories with others, for example, narrative structure
- ☑ Children learn about themselves, which contributes to the development of the self-concept
- ☑ Children learn about their own social and cultural history
- ☑ Children learn values important to the family and the community, that is, what is worth remembering
- ☑ Promotes social solidarity

Toddlers and their caregivers were observed while performing routine activities (e.g., feeding, dressing), playing social games (e.g., peekaboo), and playing with novel objects (e.g., an embroidery hoop, a jumping jack—a marionette that kicks its legs). The following excerpts are two examples of guided participation, one from the middle-class community in Salt Lake City, and the other from the tribal Indian village of Dhol-Ki-Patti.

> SALT LAKE CITY: *A 21-month-old boy and his mother, exploring a glass jar that contains a peewee doll.*
>
> Sandy's mother held the jar up and chirped excitedly, "What is it? What's inside?" and then pointed to the peewee doll inside. "Is that a little person?" When Sandy pulled down on the jar, she suggested, "Can you take the lid off?"
>
> Sandy inspected the round knob on top and said, "Da ball."
>
> "Da ball, yeah," his mother confirmed. "Pull the lid," she encouraged, and demonstrated pulling on the knob. "Can you pull?" Sandy put his hand on hers, and they pulled the lid off together triumphantly. "What's inside?" asked his mother, and took the peewee out. "Who is that?"
>
> Sandy reached for the lid, and mother provided running commentary. "OK you put the lid back on." And when Sandy exclaimed "Oh!" his mother repeated "Oh!" after him. When Sandy lost interest, his mother asked with mock disappointment, "Oh, you don't want to play anymore?" and suggested, "We could make him play peekaboo."
>
> When Sandy took the peewee out, she asked, "Where did she go?" and sang, "There, she's all gone," as she covered the peewee with her hands, "Aaall gone." (Rogoff et al., 1993, p. 81)

> DHOL-KI-PATTI, INDIA: *An 18-month-old girl and her mother, playing with a jumping jack.*
>
> Roopa was not holding the top and bottom strings taut enough to cause the jumping jack to jump, so her mother took Roopa's hand in her own, grasped the bottom string with both hands, and pulled on the string twice, saying, "Pull here, pull here," as she demonstrated. She then released her hold of Roopa's hand to enable Roopa to do it on her own.
>
> But the jumping jack fell to the ground because Roopa was not holding it tight. The mother, quick to help, lifted the jumping jack as Roopa reached for it. Twice again, she pulled on the bottom string with her left hand, repeating, "Pull it here." Then she released her hold, letting Roopa take the object. She held her hands close to (but not touching) Roopa's, ready to help if necessary. (Rogoff et al., 1993, p. 114)

Although toddlers and caregivers in all communities interacted in ways permitting all participants to develop an understanding of the task at hand, there were important differences between the middle-class and more traditional communities. As illustrated in these examples, parents in Salt Lake City (and the Turkish town) placed a far greater emphasis on verbal than nonverbal instruction, with the adults providing a good deal of structure to foster children's involvement in learning, including praise and other techniques to motivate their charges. By contrast, parents in the Mayan and Indian villages used more explicit *nonverbal* communication and only occasionally instructed their children in a particular task. In these communities, children are around adults most of the day, and they can observe competent adult behavior and interact with adults while they perform the important tasks of their society. Rogoff and her colleagues concluded that children's observation skills are more important and better developed in traditional than in middle-class communities, with children in the traditional communities being better at learning by emulating adult behavior.

Rogoff's findings make it clear that there is not one single path to becoming an effective member of society and that different forms of guided participation are likely to be used depending on the requirements culture places upon adults and children. One form is not necessarily better than another. It depends on how a competent adult in a society is expected to behave and on what skills a competent child is expected to acquire.

"Playing" in the Zone of Proximal Development

Another important behavior that is often guided by older, more expert associates is children's pretend, or symbolic play. Investigators have found that young children are more likely to engage in symbolic play when they are playing with someone else rather than alone, and that mothers in particular bring out high levels of symbolic play in their children (Bornstein et al., 1996; Youngblade & Dunn, 1995). Close examination of play episodes between mothers and their 21-month-old toddlers reveal that many mothers adjust their level of play to that of their child. What's more, mothers who know the most about the development of play provide the most challenging play interactions by adjusting their own playful behavior to a level just beyond the child's own. Consistent with Vygotsky's idea of a zone of proximal development and Rogoff's idea of guided participation, young children who interact with a more skilled partner who structures the situation appropriately, advance in their skills faster than those who lack that support (Damast, Tamis-LeMonda, & Bornstein, 1996).

Similar mother-child play patterns are found across cultures, attesting to the universality of play development, but there are also differences between cultures. For example, Chinese children are more likely to engage in pretend play with their caregivers than with other children, whereas the reverse is true for Irish American children (Haight et al., 1999). In other research, Argentine mothers were more likely than American mothers to involve their 20-month-old children in symbolic play, whereas the opposite pattern was found for exploratory play (Bornstein et al., 1999).

Why might it be important to facilitate symbolic play, and what might the consequences to cognitive development be of different play styles in different cultures? Children learn about "people, objects, and actions" through symbolic play, and research indicates that such play might be related to other aspects of cognitive development. Researchers have found a relationship between the amount of cooperative social play preschoolers engage in (often with a sibling or parent) and later understanding of other peoples' feelings and beliefs (Astington & Jenkins, 1995; Youngblade & Dunn, 1995). Indeed, an understanding that other people have thoughts, feelings, and beliefs other than one's own reflects a *theory of mind,* discussed earlier in this chapter. Developing an advanced theory of mind is necessary if children are to succeed in any society, and it appears that the guided participation afforded by parents, siblings, and other more expert partners during symbolic play contributes to this development.

It is easy to think of cognitive development as something that "just happens" exactly the same way for children worldwide. After all, evolution has provided all humans with a uniquely human nervous system. Yet intelligence is also rooted in the environment, particularly in the culture. Understanding how cultural beliefs and technological tools influence cognitive development through child-rearing practices helps us better comprehend the process of development and our role as guides in fostering that process.

Implications for Education

Vygotsky's theory has some rather obvious implications for education. Like Piaget, Vygotsky stressed active rather than passive learning and took great care to assess what the learner already knew, thereby estimating what he was capable of learning. The major difference in approaches concerns the role of the instructor. Whereas students in Piaget's classroom would spend more time in independent, discovery-based activities, teachers in Vygotsky's classroom would favor guided participations in which they structure the learning activity, provide helpful hints or instructions that are carefully tailored to the child's current abilities, and then monitor the learner's progress, gradually turning over more of the mental activity to their pupils. Teachers may also arrange cooperative learning exercises in which students are encouraged to assist each other; the idea here is that the less competent members of the team are likely to benefit from the instruction they receive from their more skillful peers, who also benefit by playing the role of teacher (Palinscar, Brown, & Campione, 1993).

Is there any evidence that Vygotsky's collaborative-learning approach might be a particularly effective educational strategy? Consider what Lisa Freund (1990) found when she had 3- to 5-year-olds help a puppet decide which furnishings (for example, sofas, beds, bathtubs, and stoves) should be placed in each of six rooms of a dollhouse that the puppet was moving into. First, children were tested to determine what they already knew about proper furniture placement. Then each child worked at a similar task, either alone (as might be the case in Piaget's discovery-based classroom) or with his or her mother (Vygotsky's guided learning). Then to assess what they had learned, children performed a final, rather complex, furniture-sorting task. The results were clear: Children who had sorted furniture with help from their mothers showed dramatic improvements in sorting ability, whereas those who had practiced on their own showed little improvement at all, even though they had received some corrective feedback from the experimenter.

Similar advances in problem-solving skills have been reported when children collaborate with peers, as opposed to working alone (Azmitia, 1992; Johnson & Johnson, 1987), and the youngsters who gain the most from these collaborations are those who were initially much less competent than their partners (Tudge, 1992). David Johnson and Roger Johnson (1987) conducted an analysis of 378 studies that compared achievement of people working alone versus cooperatively and found that cooperative learning resulted in superior performance in more than half of the studies; in contrast, working alone resulted in improved performance in fewer than 10 percent of the studies.

There appear to be at least three reasons why cooperative learning is effective (Johnson & Johnson, 1989). First, children are often more motivated when working problems together. Second, cooperative learning requires children to explain their ideas to one another and to resolve conflicts. These activities help young collaborators to examine their own ideas more closely and to become better at articulating them so that they can be understood. Finally, children are more likely to use high-quality cognitive strategies while working together—strategies that often lead to ideas and solutions that no one in the group would likely have generated alone.

As with other aspects of sociocultural theory, the effectiveness of collaborative learning varies by culture. American children, accustomed to competitive "do your own work" classrooms, sometimes find it difficult to adjust to the shared decision making found in cooperative learning (see Rogoff, 1998), although they get better at cooperative decision making with practice (Socha & Socha, 1994). As the structure of schools changes to support peer collaboration, with teachers' roles being that of active participants in the children's learning experiences and not simply directors of it, the benefits of cooperative learning are sure to increase (Rogoff, 1998).

The Role of Language in Cognitive Development

From Vygotsky's viewpoint, language plays two critical roles in cognitive development by (1) serving as the primary vehicle through which adults pass culturally valued modes of thinking and problem solving to their children, and (2) eventually becoming one of the more powerful "tools" of intellectual adaptation in its own right. As it turns out, Vygotsky's perspective on language and thought contrasts sharply with those of Piaget.

Piaget's Theory of Language and Thought

As Piaget (1926) recorded the chatterings of preschool children, he noticed that they often talked to themselves as they went about their daily activities, almost as if they were play-by-play announcers ("Put the big piece in the corner. Not that one, the pink one").

Indeed, two preschool children playing close to each other sometimes carried on their own separate monologues rather than truly conversing, something Piaget referred to as *collective monologues*. Piaget called these self-directed utterances **egocentric speech**—talk not addressed to anyone in particular and not adapted in any meaningful way so that a companion might understand it.

egocentric speech
Piaget's term for the subset of a young child's utterances that are nonsocial—that is, neither directed to others nor expressed in ways that listeners might understand.

What part might such speech play in a child's cognitive development? Very little, according to Piaget, who saw egocentric speech as merely reflecting the child's ongoing mental activity. However, he did observe that speech becomes progressively more social and less egocentric toward the end of the preoperational stage, which he attributed to children's increasing ability to assume the perspective of others and thus adapt their speech so that listeners might understand. So here was another example of how cognitive development (a decline in egocentrism) was said to promote language development (a shift from egocentric to communicative speech), rather than the other way around.

Vygotsky's Theory of Language and Thought

Vygotsky agreed with Piaget that the child's earliest thinking is prelinguistic and that early language often reflects what the child already knows. However, he argued that thought and language eventually merge and that many of the nonsocial utterances that Piaget called "egocentric" actually illustrate the transition from prelinguistic to verbal reasoning.

Vygotsky noticed that preschool children's self-directed monologues occur more often in some contexts than in others, specifically as they attempt to solve problems or achieve important goals, and that this nonsocial speech increased substantially whenever these young problem solvers encountered obstacles in pursuing their objectives. He concluded that nonsocial speech is not egocentric but communicative; it is a "speech for self," or **private speech,** that helps young children to plan strategies and regulate their behavior so that they are more likely to accomplish their goals. Viewed through this theoretical lens, language may thus play a critical role in cognitive development by making children more organized and efficient problem solvers. Vygotsky also observed that private speech becomes more abbreviated with age, progressing from the whole phrases that 4-year-olds produce, to single words, to simple lip movements that are more common among 7- to 9-year-olds (see photo). His view was that private speech never completely disappears; it serves as a **cognitive self-guidance system** and then goes "underground," becoming silent, or *inner speech*—the covert verbal thought that we use to organize and regulate our everyday activities.

private speech
Vygotsky's term for the subset of a child's verbal utterances that serve a self-communicative function and guide the child's thinking.

cognitive self-guidance system
in Vygotsky's theory, the use of private speech to guide problem-solving behavior.

Which Viewpoint Should We Endorse?

Contemporary research sides squarely with Vygotsky's theory over that of Piaget (see Berk, 1992). It seems that the *social speech* that occurs during guided learning episodes (for example, the conversation between Tanya and her father as they worked jointly on a puzzle) gives rise to much of the *private speech* (Tanya's talking aloud as she tries to work the puzzle on her own) that preschool children display. Also consistent with Vygotsky's claims, children rely more heavily on private speech when facing difficult rather than easy tasks and deciding how to proceed after making errors (Berk, 1992), and their performance often improves after using self-instruction (Berk & Spuhl, 1995). Furthermore, it is the brighter preschool children who rely most heavily on private speech, a finding that links this "self-talk" to cognitive *competence* rather than the cognitive immaturity (egocentrism) that Piaget claimed it represents (Berk, 1992). Finally, private speech does eventually go underground, progressing from words and phrases to whispers and mutterings, to inner speech (Bivens & Berk, 1990), al-

According to Vygotsky, private speech is an important tool used by preschool and young grade-school children to plan and regulate their problem-solving activities.

though it persists on problem-solving tasks into adolescence, even though such speech is not associated with improved task performance (Winsler, 2003).

So private speech does appear to be an important tool in intellectual adaptation—a means by which children plan and regulate their mental activities to solve problems and make new discoveries.

Vygotsky in Perspective: Summary and Evaluation

Vygotsky's sociocultural theory offers a new lens through which to view cognitive development by stressing the importance of specific social processes that Piaget (and others) largely overlooked. According to Vygotsky, children's minds develop as they (1) take part in cooperative dialogues with skilled partners on tasks that are within their zones of proximal development, and (2) incorporate what skillful tutors say to them into what they say to themselves. As social speech is translated into private speech and then inner speech, the culture's preferred methods of thinking and problem solving—or tools of intellectual adaptation—work their way from the language of competent tutors into the child's own thinking.

Unlike Piaget, who stressed *universal* sequences of cognitive growth, Vygotsky's theory leads us to expect wide variations in cognitive development across cultures that reflect differences in children's cultural experiences. So children in Western cultures acquire context-independent memory and reasoning skills that prepare them for highly structured Western classrooms, whereas children of Australian aborigines and African Bushmen hunters acquire elaborate spatial reasoning skills that prepare them to successfully track the prey on which their lives depend. Neither set of cognitive capacities is necessarily more "advanced" than the other; instead, they represent alternative forms of reasoning, or "tools of adaptation," that have evolved because they enable people to adapt successfully to cultural values and traditions (Rogoff, 1998; Vygotsky, 1978).

As we see in Table 7.5, Vygotsky's theory challenges many of Piaget's most basic assumptions and has attracted a lot of attention lately among Western developmentalists, whose own research efforts tend to support his ideas. Yet many of Vygotsky's writings are only now being translated from Russian to other languages (Wertsch & Tulviste, 1992), and his theory has not received the intense scrutiny that Piaget's has. Nevertheless, at least some of his ideas have already been challenged. Barbara Rogoff (1990, 1998), for example, argues that guided participations that rely heavily on the kinds of verbal instruction that Vygotsky emphasized may be less adaptive in some cultures or less useful for some forms of learning than for others. A young child learning to stalk prey in Australia's

TABLE 7.5 Comparing Vygotsky's and Piaget's Theories of Cognitive Development

Vygotsky's sociocultural theory	Piaget's cognitive-developmental theory
1. Cognitive development varies across cultures.	Cognitive development is mostly universal across cultures.
2. Cognitive growth stems from social interactions (from guided learning within the zone of proximal development as children and their partners "co-construct" knowledge).	Cognitive development stems largely from independent explorations in which children construct knowledge on their own.
3. Social processes become individual-psychological processes (for example, social speech becomes private speech and, eventually, inner speech).	Individual (egocentric) processes become social processes (for example, egocentric speech is adapted in ways to allow more effective communication).
4. Adults are especially important as change agents (by transmitting their culture's tools of intellectual adaptation that children internalize).	Peers are especially important as change agents (because peer contacts promote social perspective taking, a topic we will explore in detail in Chapter 12).

outback or to plant, care for, and harvest rice in Southeast Asia may profit more from observation and practice than from verbal instruction and encouragement. Other investigators are finding that collaborative problem solving among peers does not always benefit the collaborators and may actually undermine task performance if the more competent collaborator is not very confident about what he knows or if he fails to adapt his instruction to a partner's level of understanding (Levin & Druyan, 1993; Tudge, 1992). But despite whatever criticism his theory may generate in the years ahead, Vygotsky has provided a valuable service by reminding us that cognitive growth, like all other aspects of development, is best understood when studied in the cultural and social contexts in which it occurs.

The reader may get the impression that, compared to Piaget, Vygotsky got off pretty easy in the "criticism" department. As we mentioned earlier, this is due in part to the fact that Vygotsky's theory and the sociocultural approach in general is relatively new to Western psychologists and has thus received less scrutiny that Piaget's theory. But there is another reason that Vygotsky's approach has received less criticism than Piaget's. Unlike Piaget, whose theory generated many testable hypotheses that could be disproved, Vygotsky's approach may not truly deserve the label "theory," but be better thought of as a general perspective used to guide research and interpret children's intellectual development. A sociocultural perspective tells us that context matters—that the environments in which children grow up will influence how they think and what they think about. This is considered a general truism today, much as Piaget's view of the child as an intellectually active being is viewed as "a known fact." And although researchers from a sociocultural perspectives can and do formulate specific testable hypotheses, disconfirmation of these hypotheses rarely implies disconfirmation of the underlying theory. Cultural context matters, but how it matters is to be discovered. In other words, Vygotsky's sociocultural perspective does not provide as many specific hypotheses to test as did Piaget's theory, making its refutation difficult, if not impossible.

We do not mean to minimize the contribution of Vygotsky and his followers. We believe that such a perspective is inherently correct—that children's intellects are influenced by the culture in which they develop. However, this perspective does not eliminate a need to look at developmental universals (such as Piaget proposed) or the role of biology on development. Vygotsky himself was clearly aware of this, listing sociohistorical development as only one of four levels of analysis that must be used to evaluate behavior (the others being microgenetic, ontogenetic, and phylogenetic development). Cognitive development (as development in general) results from the continuous and bidirectional interaction between a child and his or her environment over time at all levels of organization, beginning at conception and the genetic level and progressing through the cultural level. Vygotsky's approach provides a valuable perspective to this view of development, but, as Piaget's theory, by itself it is not the whole answer.

CONCEPT CHECK 7.4 Understanding Vygotsky's Sociocultural Theory

Check your understanding of Vygotsky's concepts and theory by answering the following questions. Answers appear in the appendix.

Multiple Choice: Select the best alternative for each question.

_____ 1. Vygotsky discussed four perspectives of development that should be considered in any theory of intellectual development. Which one of the following is *not* one of the perspectives proposed by Vygotsky?

a. microgenetic development
b. phylogenetic development
c. sociocultural development
d. prenatal development

CONTINUED

_____ 2. Miller and his colleagues observed that Chinese children learned to count to 20 before American children. They attribute this difference to differences in
a. the number words used in Chinese and English
b. the amount of instruction in counting that Chinese and American children receive
c. the amount of scaffolding that Chinese and American children receive
d. genetic dispositions, with Chinese children being genetically disposed to better arithmetic abilities than most American children

_____ 3. Five-year-old Erin sits on the floor with her mother as they play a board game. Erin rolls a two and a three on the dice. She picks up her game piece, a small toy dog, moving it along the board as she says, "I move my doggie one, two . . . then I move my doggie one, two, three." Erin's behavior reflects
a. Piaget's perspective, that private speech reflects the child's egocentricity of thought and represents the child's unsuccessful attempt at social speech.
b. Piaget's perspective, that private speech is a necessary precursor to social speech in that it serves as preparation (practice) for successful social communication.
c. Vygotsky's perspective, that private speech serves as a cognitive self-guidance system for young children.
d. Both Piaget's and Vygotsky's perspectives, that private speech is presymbolic and serves only to initiate or inhibit overt motor actions and has no influence on cognition.

Matching: Match the following concepts with their definitions.

a. tools of intellectual adaptation
b. zone of proximal development
c. scaffolding
d. ontogenetic development
e. microgenetic development
f. guided participation

4. _______ Vygotsky's term for the range of tasks that are too complex to be mastered alone but can be accomplished with guidance and encouragement from a more skillful partner.
5. _______ Development of the individual over his or her lifetime.
6. _______ Adult-child interactions in which children's cognitions and modes of thinking are shaped as they participate with or observe adults engaged in culturally relevant activities.
7. _______ Changes that occur over relatively brief periods of time, in seconds, minutes, or days, as opposed to larger-scale changes, as conventionally studied in ontogenetic development.
8. _______ Process by which an expert, when instructing a novice, responds contingently to the novice's behavior in a learning situation, so that the novice gradually increases his or her understanding of a problem.
9. _______ Vygotsky's term for methods of thinking and problem-solving strategies that children internalize from their interactions with more competent members of society.

Essays: Provide a detailed answer to the following questions.

10. Discuss the concepts of the zone of proximal development and apprenticeship in thinking as they relate to cognitive development.
11. How can Vygotsky's sociocultural theory be applied to education?

Applying Developmental Themes to Piaget's and Vygotsky's Theories

Now that we've learned about the cognitive developmental theories of Piaget and Vygotsky, let's consider how these theories address our four developmental themes: the active child, nature and nurture interactions, quantitative and qualitative developmental changes, and the holistic nature of development. Consider first the theme of the active child. This theme is particularly important in Piaget's theory. In fact, it was Piaget who brought to developmental psychologists' attention the fact that infants and children are active, hands-on, creatures—in many ways the sculptors of their own development. Unlike the views that were fashionable in psychology in the early decades of the 20th century, Piaget did not see the child as molded by environmental pressures and their parents, nor as the inevitable product of the unfolding of a genetic plan. Rather, Piaget viewed the child as playing a primary role in development. It is because of Piaget that we can no longer give serious consideration to either the environmentalist view of children shaped by external forces or the maturationalist view of children as products of their heredity. Vygotsky also advocated the idea of an active child, although his emphasis on the role that significant others in a child's world play in cognitive development contrasts sharply with Piaget's views.

Piaget's and Vygotsky's theories also emphasize the interaction of nature and nurture in development. Piaget's "active child" follows a species-typical course of cognitive development, influenced by the common biological inheritance shared by all human beings. But this course is also influenced by the child's surroundings. The experiences children have as they explore their environment and their social and educational worlds especially affect the rate of their development.

Vygotsky placed greater weight on the role that adults and other cultural agents have on children's thinking, believing that nurture has a greater role in cognitive development than that proposed by Piaget. But in addition to emphasizing the sociocultural influences on children's development, Vygotsky also made it clear that one must consider the evolutionary past in explaining contemporary behavior and development. This focus on the ancient origins of behavior illustrates Vygotsky's recognition that one cannot account for children's cognitive development by sociocultural factors alone; one must also take "human nature" into consideration.

With respect to the issue of qualitative versus quantitative changes, Piaget's theory heavily emphasizes qualitative changes. For Piaget, children's thinking is different in type or kind at each major stage in development, with smaller changes within a stage also occurring in a step-by-step fashion (recall Piaget's description of sensorimotor development). In fact, this is one area for which Piaget has been criticized. Although Piaget's account of children's thinking is valuable, it tends to overstate how stagelike cognitive development truly is. Contemporary developmentalists generally believe that cognitive development consists of both qualitative and quantitative changes. Piaget's description of qualitative changes is generally accurate, but it is also limited because he basically ignored more quantitative types of changes. Vygotsky's theory was less concerned with the qualitative or quantitative nature of developmental changes and focused more on the source of the change (mainly from the social environment). Nevertheless, it's fair to say that Vygotsky was more apt to see changes as less stagelike than Piaget.

In this chapter devoted to cognitive development, it's not surprising that there has been less emphasis on the holistic nature of development. However, both Piaget's and Vygotsky's theories were intended to apply to more than children's thinking. Piaget believed that children's cognitive development influenced their social and emotional development. We'll see in later chapters that Piaget's theory has been applied to issues far removed from intelligence, including gender identification and moral development. And Vygotsky's emphasis on the sociocultural influences on children's thinking makes it clear that cognitive development cannot be viewed in isolation. The social environment, starting with the family, extending to peers and eventually to the entire culture, is the context in which cognition develops.

SUMMARY

- This and the following two chapters are devoted to an examination of **cognition,** the mental processes by which humans acquire and use knowledge, and to **cognitive development.**

Piaget's Theory of Cognitive Development

- Piaget's theory of **genetic epistemology** (cognitive development) defines **intelligence** as a basic life function that helps the child to adapt to the environment.
- Piaget described children as active explorers who construct **schemes** to establish **cognitive equilibrium** between one's thinking and one's experiences.
- Schemes are **constructed** and modified through the processes of **organization** and **adaptation.**
- Adaptation consists of two complementary activities: **assimilation** (attempts to fit new experiences to existing schemes) and **accommodation** (modifying existing schemes in response to new experiences).

■ Cognitive growth results as assimilations stimulate accommodations, which induce the reorganization of schemes, which permit further assimilations, and so on.

Piaget's Stages of Cognitive Development

■ Piaget claimed that intellectual growth proceeds through an **invariant sequence** of stages that can be summarized as follows:

■ **Sensorimotor period** (age 0–2). From basic **reflex activity,** infants over the first 2 years come to know and understand objects and events by acting on them. Subsequent substages involve the construction of schemes via **primary** and **secondary circular reactions,** the **coordination of secondary circular reactions** (which are the first signs of goal-directed behavior), and **tertiary reactions.** These behavioral schemes are eventually internalized to form mental symbols that support such achievements as **inner experimentation.**

- Although Piaget's general sequences of sensorimotor development have been confirmed, recent evidence indicates that Piaget's explanation of **A-not-B errors** was incorrect and that infants achieve such milestones as **deferred imitation** and **object permanence** earlier than Piaget had thought.
- Alternative approaches, such as **neo-nativism** and **theory theories,** assume, counter to Piaget, that infants possess innate knowledge that directs their early development.

■ **Preoperational period** (roughly 2 to 7 years). Symbolic reasoning increases dramatically as children in the **preoperational period** rely on the **symbolic function** and display **representational insight.** Symbolism gradually becomes more sophisticated as children acquire a capacity for **dual representation** (or **dual encoding**).

- Piaget described the thinking of 2- to 7-year-olds as **animistic** and **egocentric,** characterized by **centration.**
- Although preoperational children often fail to make **appearance/reality distinctions,** recent research indicates that they are much more logical and less egocentric when thinking about familiar issues or about simplified versions of Piaget's tests.
- Procedures such as **identity training** enable preoperational children to solve **conservation** tasks, indicating that preschool children possess an early capacity for logical reasoning that Piaget overlooked.
- During the preoperational period, children acquire a **belief-desire reasoning,** a reflection of **theory of mind** (TOM), in which children come to understand that their behavior and the behavior of others is based on what they know or believe, and what the want or desire. TOM is usually assessed using **false-belief tasks.**
- Children's ability to perform theory-of-mind tasks is influenced by the development of executive functions, such as inhibition, and by social factors, such as interacting with siblings.

■ **Concrete operations** (age 7 to 11 years). During concrete operations, children acquire such cognitive operations as **decentration** and **reversibility** that enable them to think logically and systematically about tangible objects, events, and experiences.

- Becoming operational in their thinking permits children to conserve, **mentally seriate,** and display **transitivity.** However, concrete operators can only apply their logic to real or tangible aspects of experience and cannot reason abstractly.
- Piaget noted that children's cognitive accomplishments were often uneven, with children being unable to solve certain problems even though they could solve similar problems requiring the same mental operations, a phenomenon he referred to as **horizontal décalage**.

■ **Formal operations** (age 11 or 12 and beyond). Formal-operational reasoning is rational, abstract, and involves both **hypothetico-deductive** and **inductive reasoning.**

- Attainment of formal operations may sometimes contribute to confusion and idealism. Formal operations may elude those adolescents and adults who have not been exposed to educational experiences that foster this reasoning. And even at this highest level, performance is uneven: Adults are most likely to display formal operations in areas of special interest or expertise.

An Evaluation of Piaget's Theory

■ Piaget founded the field of cognitive development, discovered many important principles about developing children, and influenced thousands of researchers in psychology and related fields.

■ Although Piaget seems to have adequately described general sequences of intellectual development, his tendency to infer underlying competencies from intellectual performances often led him to underestimate children's cognitive capabilities.

■ Some investigators have challenged Piaget's assumption that development occurs in stages, whereas others have criticized his theory for failing to specify how children progress from one "stage" of intellect to the next, and for underestimating social and cultural influences on intellectual development.

Vygotsky's Sociocultural Perspective

■ Vygotsky's **sociocultural theory** emphasizes social and cultural influences on intellectual growth.

■ He proposed that we should evaluate development from the perspective of four interrelated levels in interaction with children's environments—**microgenetic, ontogenetic, phylogenetic,** and **sociohistorical.**

■ Each culture transmits beliefs, values, and preferred methods of thinking or problem solving—its **tools of intellectual adaptation**—to each successive generation.

Thus, culture teaches children what to think and how to go about it.

- Children acquire cultural beliefs, values, and problem-solving strategies in the context of collaborative dialogues with more skillful partners as they gradually internalize their tutor's instructions to master tasks within their **zone of proximal development.**
- Learning occurs best when more skillful associates properly **scaffold** their intervention.
- Much of what children acquire from more skillful associates occurs through **guided participation**—a process that may be highly **context-independent** (in Western cultures) or may occur in the context of day-to-day activities (as is most common in traditional cultures).
- Unlike Piaget, who argued that children's self-talk, or **egocentric speech,** plays little if any role in constructing new knowledge, Vygotsky claimed that a child's **private speech** becomes a **cognitive self-guidance system** that regulates problem-solving activities and is eventually internalized to become covert, verbal thought. Recent research favors Vygotsky's position over Piaget's, suggesting that language plays a most important role in children's intellectual development.
- Vygotsky provided a valuable service by reminding us that cognitive growth is best understood when studied in the social and cultural contexts in which it occurs. Although this theory has fared well to date, it has yet to receive the intense scrutiny that Piaget's theory has.

KEY TERMS

cognition 243
cognitive development 243
genetic epistemology 244
intelligence 244
cognitive equilibrium 244
constructivist 244
scheme 245
organization 245
adaptation 245
assimilation 245
accommodation 245
invariant developmental sequence 247
sensorimotor period 247
reflex activity 248
primary circular reactions 248
secondary circular reactions 248
coordination of secondary circular reactions 248
tertiary circular reactions 249
inner experimentation 249
deferred imitation 249
object permanence 250
A-not-B error 250
neo-nativism 251
theory theories 252
preoperational period 255
symbolic function 255
representational insight 255
dual representation 257
animism 257
egocentrism 258
appearance/reality distinction 258
dual encoding 258
centration (centered thinking) 259
conservation 259
decentration 259
reversibility 259
identity training 263
theory of mind 263
belief-desire reasoning 263
false-belief task 264
concrete-operational period 266
mental seriation 267
transitivity 267
horizontal décalage 267
formal operations 268
hypothetico-deductive reasoning 268
inductive reasoning 268
sociocultural theory 274
ontogenetic development 275
microgenetic development 275
phylogenetic development 275
sociohistorical development 276
tools of intellectual adaptation 276
zone of proximal development 278
scaffolding 278
guided participation 278
context-independent learning 279
egocentric speech 283
private speech 283
cognitive self-guidance system 283

MEDIA RESOURCES

The Human Development Book Companion Website

See the companion website http://www.thomsonedu.com/psychology/shaffer for flashcards, practice quiz questions, Internet links, updates, critical thinking exercises, discussion forums, games, and more

ThomsonNOW! http://www.thomsonedu.com

Go to this site for the link to ThomsonNOW, your one-stop shop. Take a pre-test for this chapter, and ThomsonNOW will generate a personalized study plan based on your test results. The study plan will identify the topics you need to review and direct you to online resources to help you master those topics. You can then take a post-test to help you determine the concepts you have mastered and what you will still need to work on.

Child and Adolescent Development CD-ROM

For more information about the concepts covered in this chapter, go to

Module II: Cognition, Language, and Learning

- Cognitive Development
- Module II Media

Photo Alto Photography/Veer.com

CHAPTER

8 Cognitive Development: Information-Processing Perspectives

Piaget's and Vygotsky's theories have had a profound influence on our understanding of cognitive development. Piaget saw children as active agents in their own development, always constructing knowledge and changing their cognitive structures to better understand the world. Vygotsky saw children as active participants in collaborative dialogues with others, acquiring the tools of thought appropriate for their culture. Yet the shortcomings of these approaches led many scholars to believe that a fresh outlook on human cognition was necessary.

Then came the digital computer—a wondrous new invention that intrigued many scientists with its capacity for rapidly and systematically converting input (or information) into output (answers and solutions). Might the operations of a computer be similar in certain limited respects to the workings of the human mind? Proponents of a third influential viewpoint on cognitive development—the *information-processing perspective*—thought so (Klahr & MacWhinney, 1998).

How is the human mind similar to a computer? One way is that both the mind and a computer have a limited capacity for processing information, associated with their hardware and software. Computer *hardware* is the machine itself—its keyboard (or input system), storage capacity, and logic units. The mind's hardware is the nervous system, including the brain, the sensory receptors, and their neural connections. The computer's *software* consists of the programs used to store and manipulate information—word-processing programs, statistics programs, and the like. The mind, too, has its software—rules, strategies, and other "mental programs" that specify how information is registered, interpreted, stored, retrieved, and analyzed. As children's brains and nervous systems mature (hardware improvements) and as they adopt new strategies for attending to information, interpreting it, remembering what they have experienced, and monitoring their mental activities (software improvements), they are able to perform increasingly complex cognitive feats with greater speed and accuracy.

Roy Botterell/Stone

Information Flow and the Multistore Model

There is no single information-processing theory of cognition or cognitive development. Yet central to all information-processing perspectives is the idea that people use a variety of cognitive operations, or strategies, to process information through a limited-capacity system. Nearly 40 years ago, Richard Atkinson and Richard Shiffrin (1968) developed a **multistore model** of the information-processing system, and this model continues to be a useful guide for understanding how people think. A slightly updated version of their important and influential model appears in Figure 8.1.

multistore model information-processing model that depicts information as flowing through three processing units (or stores): the sensory store, the short-term store (STS), and the long-term store (LTS).

sensory store (or sensory register) first information-processing store, in which stimuli are noticed and are briefly available for further processing.

short-term store (STS) second information-processing store, in which stimuli are retained for several seconds and operated on (also called working memory).

long-term store (LTS) third information-processing store, in which information that has been examined and interpreted is permanently stored for future use.

As we see in the figure, the first of these components is the **sensory store** (or **sensory register**). This is the system's log-in unit; it simply holds raw sensory input as a kind of afterimage (or echo) of what you have sensed. There are separate sensory registers for each sense modality (for example, vision, hearing), and presumably they can hold large quantities of information, but only for very brief periods of time (milliseconds in the case of vision). The contents of sensory stores are thus extremely volatile and soon disappear without further processing.

Should you attend to this information, however, it passes into the **short-term store (STS),** a processing unit that can store a limited amount of information (perhaps five to nine pieces) for several seconds. Thus the capacity of the short-term store is sufficient to allow you to retain a telephone number for perhaps as long as it takes you to dial it. But unless this information is rehearsed or otherwise operated on, it too is soon lost. The short-term store has also been referred to as the *primary memory,* or *working memory,* because all conscious intellectual activity is thought to take place here. So short-term, or working, memory has two functions: (1) to store information temporarily so that (2) we can do something with it.

Finally, new information that is operated on while in the short-term store passes into the **long-term store (LTS)**—a vast and relatively permanent storehouse of information that includes your knowledge of the world, your impressions of past experiences and events, and the strategies that you use to process information and solve problems.

This brief description may give the impression that the person plays a relatively passive role in information processing. This is not the case. People must decide what

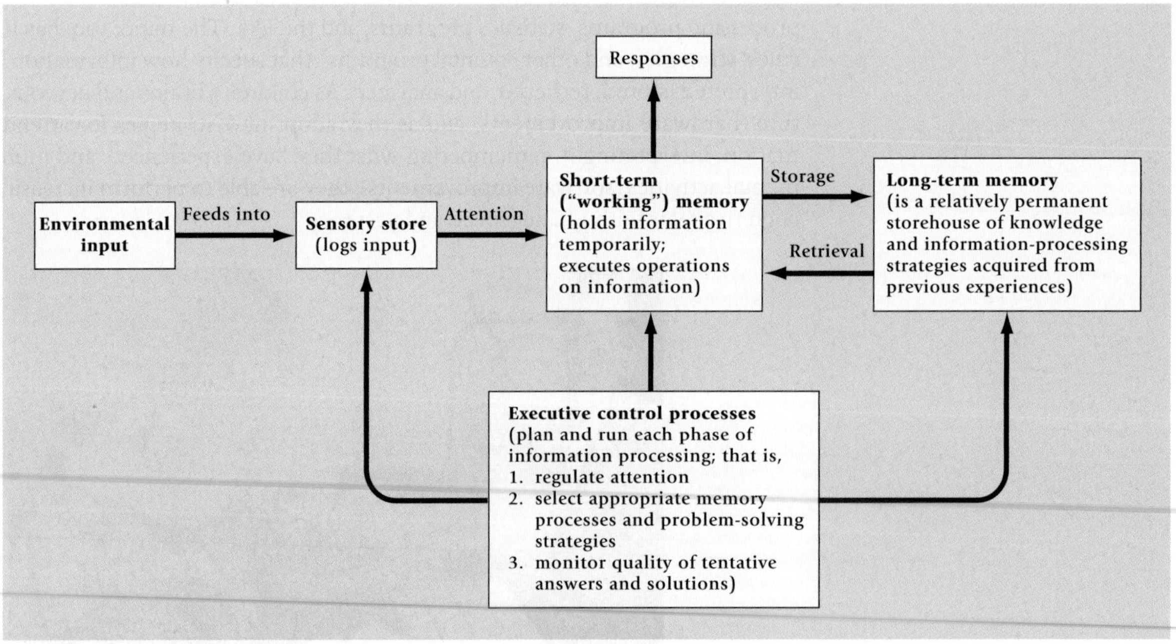

Figure 8.1 A schematic model of the human information processing system. *Adapted from "Human Memory: A Proposed System and Its Control Processes," by R. C. Atkinson and R. M. Shiffrin, 1968, in K. W. Spence and J. T. Spence (eds.),* The Psychology of Learning and Motivation: Advances in Research and Theory. *Copyright © 1968 by Academic Press, Inc. Adapted by permission.*

information to attend to and which, if any, strategies to execute in order to move information through the system. So information does not simply flow on its own through the various stores, or processing units, of the system; instead, we actively channel the input. This is why most information-processing models include **control processes,** or **executive functions**—the processes involved in planning and monitoring what you attend to and what you do with this input. We sometimes refer to such executive functions as **metacognition**—knowledge of one's cognitive abilities and processes related to thinking.

executive control processes
the processes involved in regulating attention and in determining what to do with information just gathered or retrieved from long-term memory.

metacognition
one's knowledge about cognition and about the regulation of cognitive activities.

Our executive functions are thought to be largely under voluntary control and are, in fact, what most clearly distinguish human information processors from computers. Unlike computers, we humans must initiate, organize, and monitor our own cognitive activities. We decide what to attend to; we select our own strategies for retaining and retrieving this input; we call up our own programs for solving problems; and last but not least, we are often free to choose the very problems that we attempt to solve. Clearly, we humans are rather versatile information processors, although modern science is still a bit in the dark in knowing precisely how complex thinking is achieved. But what we do know (or think we know) is that the process is one in which higher-level cognition emerges as a result of *self-organization* in dynamic systems (Lewis, 2000; Thelen & Smith, 1998). That is, lower-level units (sensations, features of a stimulus) interact and, as a result, organize into higher-order units (a perception, a concept), a phenomenon not too dissimilar from Piaget's idea of how assimilation and accommodation operate to yield more advanced stages of cognitive development. Admittedly, we have a lot to learn about the procedures underlying the emergence of executive functions; however, by examining their development and looking at how individual differences in executive functioning relate to performance on cognitive tasks, much can be learned about children's thinking and possibly ways to enhance it through educational intervention.

In this chapter we examine developmental differences in several important aspects of children's thinking that have been examined from an information-processing perspective, including attention, memory, reasoning, and arithmetic. Before examining children's thinking in each of these specific domains, we first look at aspects of children's information processing that influence all types of thinking. Two of these are examples of hardware: the capacity of the short-term store and speed of processing. Two others can be considered as forms of software: children's use of strategies and children's understanding of what it means to think, which is closely related to metacognition, or executive functioning. A fifth factor that is related to the other four and that influences nearly all forms of children's thinking is **knowledge base,** what children know about the things they are thinking about.

knowledge base
one's existing information about a topic or content area.

CONCEPT CHECK 8.1 Understanding the Information-Processing Model

Check your understanding of the Information-Processing model of cognitive development by answering the following questions. Answers appear in the Appendix.

Matching: Match the following concepts with their definitions:

a. metacognition
b. sensory register
c. short-term store (STS)
d. executive control processes
e. long-term store (LTS)
f. multistore model

1. ______ The second information-processing store, in which stimuli are retained for several seconds and operated on (also called working memory).
2. ______ The information-processing model that depicts information as flowing through three processing units (or stores).
3. ______ The first information processing store, in which stimuli are noticed and are briefly available for further processing.
4. ______ One's knowledge about cognition and about the regulation of cognitive activities.
5. ______ The third information-processing store, in which information that has been examined and interpreted is permanently stored for future use.
6. ______ The processes involved in regulating attention and in determining what to do with information just gathered or retrieved from long-term memory.

Developmental Differences in "Hardware": Information-Processing Capacity

"Capacity" within an information-processing system can be expressed in a variety of ways. It is sometimes used to refer to the total amount of "space" available to store information, sometimes to how long information can be retained in a storage unit, and sometimes to how quickly information can be processed. In the following sections we examine the capacity of the short-term store (STS), specifically age changes in how much information can be held in the STS, and in developmental differences in the speed which information can be processed.

Development of the Short-Term Store

memory span
a general measure of the amount of information that can be held in the short-term store.

Traditionally, the capacity of the short-term store (STS) has been assessed by tests of **memory span.** Memory span refers to the number of *rapidly presented* and *unrelated* items (for example, digits) that a person can recall in exact order. Age differences in memory span are highly reliable (Figure 8.2). In fact, they are so reliable that memory span is used as one indication of general intelligence on the two most widely used intelligence tests for children. Short-term memory has even been assessed in infants using looking-time procedures like those described in Chapter 5. Not surprisingly, results show that the amount of visual information infants can keep in mind at a time increases over the first year of life (Pelphrey et al., 2004; Ross-Sheehy, Oakes, & Luck, 2003).

span of apprehension
the number of items that people can keep in mind at any one time, or the amount of information that people can attend to at a single time without operating mentally to store this information.

Yet, memory span may not be the purest test of the capacity of the STS because children (especially older children) may be using strategies or taking advantage of their greater knowledge base for the materials they are asked to remember, each of which may increase their span. Clearer evidence for developmental differences in the actual *capacity* of the STS comes from a study by Nelson Cowan and his colleagues (1999). Cowan assessed age differences in **span of apprehension,** a term used to refer to the number of items that people can keep in mind at any one time, or can attend to at once without operating mentally on this information. Does span of apprehension represent an absolute capacity of the short-term store, and does it increase with age? In the study by Cowan and colleagues (1999), first- and fourth-grade children and adults played a computer game. Over earphones they also heard series of digits that they were to ignore. Occasionally and unexpectedly, however, they were signaled to recall, in exact order, the most recently presented set of digits they had heard. Participants were not explicitly attending to the digits, making it unlikely that they were using any encoding strategies to remember them; performance on this task thus seems to be a fair test of span of apprehension—the capacity of the STS. Average span of apprehension was about 3.5 digits for adults, about 3 digits for fourth-grade children, and about 2.5 digits for first-grade children. Cowan and his colleagues interpreted these significant age differences as reflecting a true developmental difference in the capacity of the STS—a difference that serves as the foundation for age differences on memory span tasks.

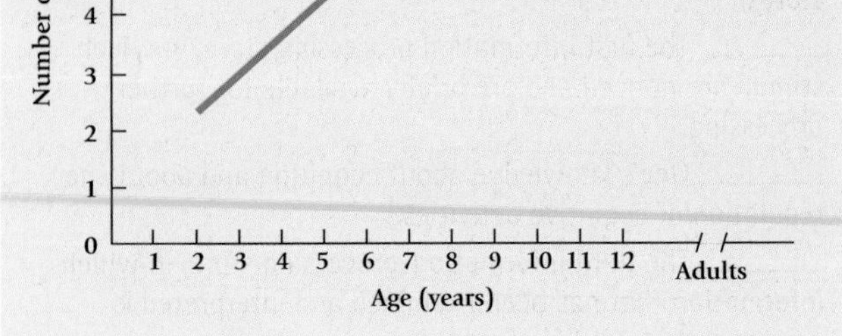

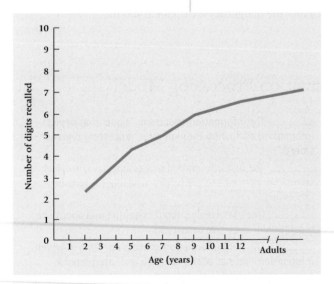

Figure 8.2 Children's memory span for digits (digit span) shows regular increases with age. *Adapted from "Memory Span: Sources of Individual and Developmental Differences," by F. N. Dempster, 1981,* Psychological Bulletin, *89, 63–100. Copyright © 1981 by the American Psychological Association. Adapted with permission from the publisher and author.*

Although span of apprehension tasks seem to eliminate age differences in strategies, what about knowledge? As it turns out, what children know about the randomly presented items they are asked to remember affects their memory span. In a classic study by Michelene Chi (1978), a group of graduate students was given two simple memory tests. The first was a digit-span task. On a second test they were shown chess

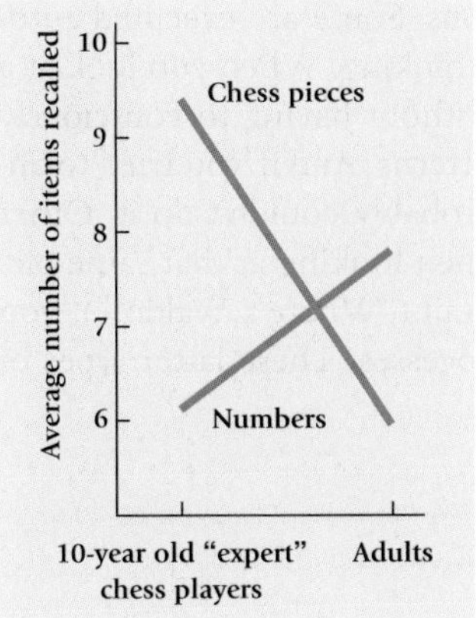

Figure 8.3 Knowledge base affects memory. Children who are chess "experts" recall more about locations of chess pieces than "novice" adults do. However, adults recall more about numbers than children do, a finding Chi attributes to adults' greater familiarity with (or knowledge of) numbers. *From "Knowledge Structures and Memory Development," by M. H. T. Chi, 1978, in R. S. Siegler (Ed.),* Children's Thinking: What Develops? *Copyright © 1978 by Lawrence Erlbaum Associates, Inc. Reprinted by permission.*

pieces on a chess board (about one chess piece per second) and then given the pieces and asked to place them at their previous positions on the board. Their performance on these tasks was compared with that of a group of 10-year-olds. However, these were not typical 10-year-olds; they were all chess experts—winners of local tournaments or members of chess clubs. If younger children simply have smaller short-term stores than adults, the graduate students should outperform the 10-year-olds on both memory tests. But this is not what Chi found. As we see in Figure 8.3, the child experts clearly outperformed the adults when memory for chess pieces was tested. However, their remarkable performance was limited to what they knew well, because they performed much worse than adults did when their memory for digits was tested (see also Schneider et al., 1993).

These findings indicate that having a detailed knowledge base for a particular domain (in this case, chess) facilitates memory performance for information from that domain but not necessarily for information from other areas. How does being an expert in a subject such as chess result in improved memory span? Although a number of possibilities have been suggested, the factor that seems to play the most crucial role is ease of item identification—how quickly the child identifies items to be remembered. Children who are experts in a domain can rapidly process information in that domain and thus have an advantage when it comes to memory span. Their speed of item identification is an indication of their *domain-specific* processing efficiency. Yet, in domains in which they are not experts, older children tend to process most types of information faster than younger children, and faster processing contributes to larger memory spans (Chuah & Maybery, 1999; Luna et al., 2004).

Changes in Processing Speed

It's not just identifying items on memory-span tasks that show age-related improvements in speed of processing. Robert Kail (1997) found that general developmental changes in processing speed are similar across a variety of different problems, ranging from simple tasks in which participants must determine whether the objects in two pictures have the same name (for example, are they both pictures of bananas?) to complex mental arithmetic (see also Miller & Vernon, 1997). Kail concedes that our past experiences (such as being a chess expert) can influence speed of processing within a particular domain, but he believes that biological maturation is primarily responsible for broad age-related differences in speed of information processing.

What maturational developments might underlie age-related changes in processing speed? Increased myelination of neurons in the associative (thinking) areas of the brain and the elimination of unnecessary (or excess) neural synapses that could interfere with efficient information processing are two possible candidates. As we noted in Chapter 6, myelin is a fatty substance that surrounds nerves and facilitates transmission of nerve impulses. Whereas myelination of most sensory and motor areas of the brain is accomplished within the first several years of life, myelination of the associative area is not complete until adolescence or young adulthood. Many theorists have proposed that age differences in myelination are directly responsible for age differences in speed of information processing and, ultimately, for age differences in the efficient use of limited mental capacity (Bjorklund & Harnishfeger, 1990; Kail & Salthouse, 1994).

Developmental Differences in "Software": Strategies and What Children Know about "Thinking"

Age differences in information-processing hardware—how much children can hold in mind at one time and how quickly they can process information—will clearly influence how effectively they can "think." Yet central to the information-processing perspective is that people possess a variety of cognitive operations that they apply to information and that both the quantity and quality of these operations change with age.

Cognitive processes vary along a number of dimensions. Some are executed automatically, so that you may not even be aware that you are thinking. When you look at a drawing, for example, you effortlessly "see" the images without having to consciously concentrate on converting the light waves into coherent patterns. And if you tried to analyze how you performed such a complicated feat, you probably couldn't do it. Other cognitive processes are more conscious and effortful. If, when looking at that same picture, for example, you were searching for a particular detail ("Where's Waldo?"), you would need to use more focused and planful cognitive processes. These latter types of processes, called *strategies,* change substantially with age.

The Development of Strategies

strategies
goal-directed and deliberately implemented mental operations used to facilitate task performance.

Strategies, a particular subset of executive functions, are usually defined as deliberately implemented, goal-directed operations used to aid task performance (Harnishfeger & Bjorklund, 1990; Schneider & Pressley, 1997). Much of our conscious thinking is guided by strategies, and even young children may discover or invent strategies when they encounter problems in everyday life. Yet many strategies that children living in information-age societies find so useful are explicitly taught in school (Moely, Santulli, & Obach, 1995). These include strategies involved in mathematics, reading, memory, and scientific problem solving.

Age differences in strategy use account for a substantial portion of the age-related differences that we see in children's cognitive performance. Generally speaking, younger children use fewer strategies and use them far less effectively than older children do. Yet the development of cognitive strategies is much more complex than this statement would imply, because even young children can use some strategies effectively, and the more sophisticated strategies that older children select do not always help them as much as you might expect. For example, in research in which children remembered the names of their current classmates, the recall of youngsters who remembered the names by seating arrangement, for instance, was no better than that of children who remembered the names in a seemingly random order (Bjorklund & Bjorklund, 1985). In this case, it seems that having a detailed knowledge of one's classmates made the use of a strategy superfluous. It's also worth noting that, although recall in this study was high, most children were typically far from perfect, whether they used a strategy or not.

Production and Utilization Deficiencies

© Laura Dwight/Corbis

Young children devise simple strategies for solving the problems they face.

Developmentalists once believed that preschool children were *astrategic;* that is, they didn't use any strategies when approaching most problems. Later research seriously questioned this interpretation. Consider that even 18- to 36-month-olds use simple strategies to locate objects in hide-and-seek games. If instructed to remember where a stuffed animal (Big Bird) has been hidden so that they can later wake him up from his nap, these young children strategically remind themselves where the animal is by repeatedly looking at or pointing to its hiding place (DeLoache, 1986). In another example, Michael Cohen (1996) asked 3- and 4-year-olds to play store, a game in which they had to fill customers' vegetable orders by relying on such strategies as adding, subtracting, or making no changes in the number of objects (for example, tomatoes) in an existing display. These young children used a variety of possible strategies and became more efficient (that is, made fewer moves to fill an order) with practice. Clearly, preschool children can be strategic in their thinking and problem solving, although the strategies they devise tend to be simple and to increase in efficiency with age.

Do younger children lack the cognitive capacity to execute and benefit from the more effective strategies older children use? One way to find out is to teach them new strategies to see if their cognitive performance improves. Dozens of training studies of this kind have been conducted, and their findings are reasonably consistent: Children who do not use a strategy on their own can be trained to do so and often benefit from its use (Bjorklund & Douglas, 1997; Harnishfeger & Bjorklund, 1990). So rather than being astrategic or lacking cognitive capacity, younger children often display what has been termed **production deficiencies;** they merely fail to *produce* effective strategies, even though they are often quite capable of putting those strategies to good use. So, for example, young children who do not rehearse lists of words or sentences in preparation for a memory test will do so when given specific instructions, and, as a result, their memory performance typically improves. However, improvement is often short-lived, is usually greater for older than for younger children, and young children trained to use a strategy rarely perform as well as older children who use the same strategy spontaneously (see Schneider & Bjorklund, 1998, 2003).

production deficiency
a failure to spontaneously generate and use known strategies that could improve learning and memory.

But acquiring a new and more sophisticated strategy does not always lead to significant improvements in task performance. Instead, children who spontaneously generate and use such strategies often display what Patricia Miller (2000; Miller & Seier, 1994) calls a **utilization deficiency.** Even when children are trained to use a new strategy at school or in the laboratory, they often display utilization deficiencies by failing to benefit immediately from its use (Bjorklund et al., 1997).

utilization deficiency
a failure to benefit from effective strategies that one has spontaneously produced; thought to occur in the early phases of strategy acquisition when executing the strategy requires much mental effort.

Consider a specific example of children who were successfully trained to use a strategy but showed little or no subsequent benefit from it (Bjorklund et al., 1994). In this study fourth-grade children were given sets of categorically related words (for instance, different examples of *fruits, furniture, tools,* and *mammals*) that they could sort into groups prior to a memory test. Both the extent to which children grouped the words by category prior to the recall test (sorting) and the extent to which they remembered words from the same category together (clustering) have been shown to be effective memory strategies. After an initial free-recall phase ("Study the words any way you'd like and remember them in any order you'd like"), children were given specific instructions in the use of an organization strategy (sort the words by category and remember words from the same category together—Phase 2). After training, they were given a new list of words to remember to see if they would generalize the strategy they had learned (Phase 3). A second generalization trial was given a week later (Phase 4). Children showed improvements in recall, sorting, and clustering as a result of training (Phase 2), and maintained their high levels of strategy use (sorting and clustering) in Phases 3 and 4. But levels of recall fell to their earlier levels on these latter phases, reflecting a utilization deficiency.

Why do children display utilization deficiencies if the new and more sophisticated strategies that they are acquiring are generally better ways to approach the problems they face? One possibility is that executing a novel strategy may require so much mental effort that children have few cognitive resources left to gather and store information relevant to the problems they face (Bjorklund et al., 1997; Miller & Seier, 1994). Second, new strategies are often intrinsically interesting to children. Much as Piaget proposed that children use a scheme just for the sheer joy of exercising it, children may use a strategy for the novelty of trying something different (Siegler, 1996). Third, younger children in particular may know less about how to monitor their cognitive activities and may not even be aware that they are failing to benefit from using a new strategy. However, this poor metacognition may actually be beneficial in the long run if it prompts children to practice the effortful new strategy until it can be executed much quicker and becomes a truly effective aid for problem solving (Bjorklund et al., 1997).

Clearly, the fact that children display both production deficiencies and utilization deficiencies implies that the growth of strategic thinking is a slow and uneven process. In fact, Robert Siegler's recent studies of children's problem-solving strategies show just how uneven the process can be.

Multiple-Strategy and Variable-Strategy Use

Children's strategies do not develop in a stagelike fashion, with earlier strategies being replaced by more complicated and effective strategies. Rather, children of all ages have a variety of strategies available to them and select among those strategies when trying to solve a problem.

Consider what Robert Siegler and his colleagues (1996, 2000) found when researching young children's arithmetic strategies. In learning to add, young children frequently use a *sum* strategy that involves counting both numbers out loud (for example, for 5 + 3 = ?, saying, "1, 2, 3, 4, 5 [pause], 6, 7, 8."). A more sophisticated strategy is to begin with the larger number (in this case, 5) and count up from there (e.g., saying, "5 [pause], 6, 7, 8."). This is called the *min* strategy. A more sophisticated strategy still, known as *fact retrieval,* is "just knowing" the answer, and retrieving it directly from long-term memory without having to count at all (for example, simply answering "8" to the question How much is 5 + 3?). When looking at cross-sectional data, one gets the impression that children progress from using the sum strategy to using the min strategy to using fact retrieval. Yet closer examination reveals that individual children use a variety of these strategies at any given time, and the frequency that each strategy is used varies with age, with older children using more sophisticated strategies more often. Multiple-strategy and variable-strategy use has been found in other cognitive domains, including serial recall (remembering a list of digits in exact order) (McGilly & Siegler, 1990); simple same-different tasks (Blöte et al., 1999); spelling (Rittle-Johnson & Siegler, 1999); free recall (Coyle & Bjorklund, 1997); tic-tac-toe (Crowley & Siegler, 1993); and scientific reasoning (Schauble, 1990), among others.

adaptive strategy choice model Siegler's model to describe how strategies change over time; the view that multiple strategies exist within a child's cognitive repertoire at any one time, with these strategies competing with one another for use.

Siegler and his colleagues (1996, 2000) formulated the **adaptive strategy choice model** to describe children's multiple strategy use and how strategies change over time. Basically, Siegler believes that children of any age have a variety of strategies that compete for use on problems for which they are relevant. Sometimes one strategy will "win" the mental competition (the min strategy, for example) and sometimes another strategy will win (fact retrieval, for example). With age, experience, and improved information-processing abilities, more sophisticated strategies are apt to win, so that min, on average, replaces sum as a preferred strategy, and later on, fact retrieval replaces min. But for new problems or problems with which children are less familiar, the older *fallback strategies* often come up as the winners. So from Siegler's perspective, strategy development is not the simple matter of abandoning older, less sophisticated strategies for newer, more powerful ones. Rather, multiple strategies reside side by side in a child's mind, and old strategies never die; they simply lie in wait for a chance to be used when a newer, more preferred strategy doesn't quite fit or fails to produce the correct answer. So, Siegler does not see strategies developing in a steplike fashion, but rather as a series of overlapping waves, as illustrated in Figure 8.4.

As the work of Siegler and others makes clear, the issue facing cognitive developmentalists today is not whether young children can be strategic—they are, from an early

Figure 8.4 Siegler's adaptive strategy choice model of development. Change in strategy use is seen as a series of overlapping waves, with different strategies being used more frequently at different ages. *Adapted from* Emerging Minds: The Process of Change in Children's Thinking, *by R. S. Seilger. New York: Oxford University Press, 1996.*

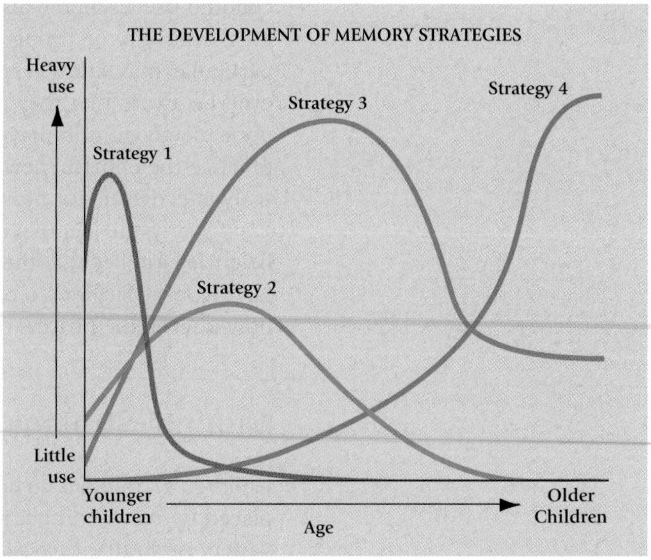

age. Rather, developmentalists must now determine what combination of strategies children use within different cognitive domains. They must explain why the simpler strategies that younger children prefer gradually give way to the more sophisticated and effective strategies used by older children, adolescents, and adults, and how variations in strategy use might be related to cognitive performance and development (Coyle, 2001).

As is likely obvious, cognitive strategies can be of great use in the classroom. (This goes for college students as well as children in elementary school.) Some researchers have looked at the specific strategy instruction children receive over the course of a normal school day (Moely, Santulli, & Obach, 1995) and others have developed research-based techniques to teach strategies to school children (Pressley & Woloshyn, 1995). For example, Michael Pressley and Vera Woloshyn (1995) provide examples of the following strategies that can be used by children for the task of reading comprehension: summarization (abstracting the gist of a text), mental imagery (constructing mental images), self-generation of questions (teaching children to generate their own questions and answers), question-answering strategies (questions provided by the teacher or textbook author), story grammar (using the narrative structure of a text to generate questions), and activating prior knowledge (making use of what the reader already knows to aid comprehension of new material), among others. Although this example is specific to reading instruction, and methods of instruction will vary with individual children, it provides an idea of how teachers can help children learn important academic knowledge and skills via strategy training. Pressley and Woloshyn (1995) provide a general model for how to teach strategies, which is summarized in Table 8.1.

What Children Know about Thinking

Four-year-old Joshua had pushed his father's patience too far. "Joshua," said his father, "I want you to go over to that corner and just *think* about all this for a while." Instead of following his father's orders, Joshua stood where he was, not defiantly, but with a confused look and quivering lips, as if he were trying to say something but was afraid to. "What's the matter now?" his father asked, his irritation still showing. "But, Daddy," Joshua said,

TABLE 8.1 General model of how to teach strategies

Teach a few strategies at a time, intensively and extensively, as part of the ongoing curriculum; in the beginning, teach only one at a time, until students are familiar with the "idea" of strategy use.
Model and explain each new strategy.
Model again and re-explain strategies in ways that are sensitive to aspects of strategy use that are not well understood. (The students are constructing their understanding of the strategy, refining the understanding a little bit at a time.)
Explain to students where and when to use strategies, although students will also discover some such metacognitive information as they use strategies.
Provide plenty of practice, using strategies for as many appropriate tasks as possible. Such practice increases proficient execution of the strategy, knowledge of how to adapt it, and knowledge of when to use it.
Encourage students to monitor how they are doing when they are using strategies.
Encourage continued use of and generalization of strategies, for example, by reminding students throughout the school day about when they could apply strategies they are learning about.
Increase students' motivation to use strategies by heightening student awareness that they are acquiring valuable skills that are at the heart of competent functioning with learning tasks.
Emphasize reflective processing rather than speedy processing; do all possible to eliminate high anxiety in students; encourage students to shield themselves from distraction so they can attend to the academic task.

Source: Pressley, M., & Woloshyn, V. (1995). *Cognitive strategy instruction that really improves children's academic performance* (second edition). Cambridge, MA: Brookline Books.

implicit cognition
thought that occurs without awareness that one is thinking.

explicit cognition
thinking and thought processes of which we are consciously aware.

"I don't know *how* to think." Obviously, 4-year-old Joshua did know how to think. He just didn't know that he did.

You don't necessarily have to know what you're doing to do a good job of it, at least when it comes to thinking. Much of our day-to-day cognition is **implicit,** or unconscious. For example, despite the fact that we are all highly proficient speakers of our mother tongue, very few of us can consciously enumerate all the linguistic rules that underlie our language. Of course, much of the richness of cognition—both children's and adults'—comes from the type of thought that is conscious, or **explicit.** Aspects of explicit cognition become especially important when we consider executive functions. To a large extent, in order to regulate our thinking, it helps to understand what thinking is. It seems obvious that Joshua lacked knowledge about what it means to think, and we should not be surprised if his cognition were limited by his lack of understanding.

Preschool children often confuse various forms of thinking. For example, they seem not to be aware of the difference between remembering, knowing, and guessing (Johnson & Wellman, 1980; Schwanenflugel et al., 1998). Young children also think they have greater control of their thoughts than they really do. For example, John Flavell, Frances Green, and Eleanor Flavell (1998) asked 5-, 9-, and 13-year-old children and adults a series of questions related to mental uncontrollability. Will a child who hears a strange noise automatically wonder what that noise is, even if he or she doesn't want to? Is it possible to go for 3 days without thinking about anything? Adults and older children understood that the mind "has a mind of its own" better than younger children did. That is, they understood that the mind will sometimes think about things even if the person has no interest in thinking about it (the source of an unexpected noise, for example), and that one cannot avoid thinking for an extended period of time.

Researchers have shown that children's awareness of their own thoughts and the distinction between consciousness and unconsciousness develop gradually during childhood. For example, many 5-year-old and some 7- and 8-year-old children believe that people continue to wish, pretend, think, and hear things while still sound asleep and not dreaming (Cormier et al., 2004; Flavell et al., 1999) or even after death (Bering & Bjorklund, 2004; Bering, Hernández-Blasi, & Bjorklund, in press). In other research, 5- and 8-year-old children and adults were asked to "think of nothing" for about half a minute. Most adults and 8-year-olds said that, try as they might, thinking of nothing was not possible. By contrast, most 5-year-olds claimed that they were able to keep *all* thoughts from their minds and were unaware of the stream of consciousness that seemingly runs through every waking person's mind (Flavell et al., 2000). This and other research (see Flavell, 1999) indicates that children have a lot to learn about thinking.

Knowledge of one's thought processes, termed *metacognition,* is important for many aspects of higher-order thinking and problem solving. Although we do perform some complicated cognitive tasks unconsciously (or implicitly), many learning and memory tasks are best accomplished when we are consciously aware of the mental processes involved. The benefits of good metacognition for several cognitive challenges will become clear later in this chapter. But first, we take a brief look at the other side of the coin, cognition without awareness, and see that young children are often as good as adults at certain implicit cognitive tasks.

Implicit Cognition, or Thought Without Awareness

We previously defined *implicit cognition* as thought without awareness. Annette Karmiloff-Smith (1992) developed a theory that postulates that most of infants' and young children's knowledge is implicit. For example, young infants' knowledge of physical objects or young children's (and adults') knowledge of language would be represented implicitly. This knowledge, impressive as it may be, is similar to the knowledge a spider

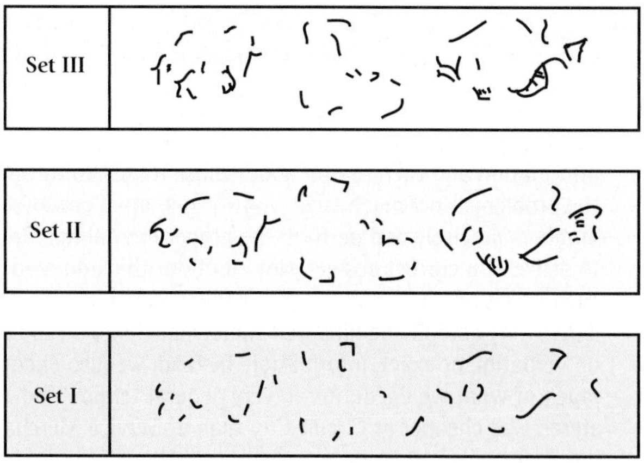

Figure 8.5 Incomplete drawings similar to these are used in studies of implicit memory. *From Gollin, E. S., Factors affecting the visual recognition of incomplete objects: A comparative investigation of children and adults.* Perceptual and Motor Skills, *15, 583–590, 1962. © Southern Universities Press 1962.*

has about making a web, a blue jay has about building a nest, or a newborn goat has about avoiding falling off cliffs.

Related to this is the idea that *implicit learning* (acquiring new knowledge without explicit awareness) is an early-developing ability. For example, research has shown that 6- and 10-year-old children learn serial sequences of responses (that is, learning which of several responses follows one another) as well as adults do, despite having no explicit (verbalizable) knowledge of what they have learned (Meulemans, Van der Linden, & Perruchet, 1998; Vinter & Perruchet, 2000). Implicit memory (memory without awareness) has also been proposed to be an early-developing ability that shows little improvement across childhood. For example, one procedure used to assess implicit memory in children involves the use of fragmented pictures such as those shown in Figure 8.5. A fragmented (incomplete) picture is presented, and children are asked to identify it. This is very difficult to do initially, but as more of the picture is completed it becomes increasingly easier to identify the object. In experiments using this task, children are shown the series of degraded pictures and later given another task involving those degraded pictures. Do children perform this second task better (faster or more accurately) for pictures they had previously seen than for those they hadn't seen, despite the fact that they do not remember seeing any of the pictures before? The answer is generally yes, and more important, there are few age differences in magnitude of this "implicit memory" effect (Drummey & Newcombe, 1995; Hayes & Hennessy, 1996).

Although there has been relatively little developmental research on implicit learning and memory, what research there is presents a consistent picture. Substantial age differences are found on tests of *explicit* learning and memorization and on children's understanding of what it means to think; but few age differences are found on tests of *implicit* learning or memory (Hayes & Hennessy, 1996; Vinter & Perruchet, 2000). Both implicit and explicit cognition can be thought of in terms of information-processing mechanisms; yet the very different developmental patterns they display indicate that cognitive development is multifaceted and does not follow a single course for all types of thinking.

Alternative perspectives to traditional information-processing models have been proposed and help explain age differences in children's thinking. Two such approaches, fuzzy-trace theory and developmental differences in inhibition, are discussed briefly in the Boxes on pages 302 and 303, respectively.

We have described the basic premises of information-processing theory and have discussed the development of processing hardware and software in a very general way. Now we will trace the development of four crucial information-processing attributes—attention, memory, reasoning, and arithmetic skills—and will comment on the practical and theoretical importance of these developments.

fuzzy-trace theory
theory proposed by Brainerd and Reyna that postulates that people encode experiences on a continuum from literal, verbatim traces to fuzzy, gistlike traces.

gist
a fuzzy representation of information that preserves the central content but few precise details.

inhibition
the ability to prevent ourselves from executing some cognitive or behavioral response.

FOCUS ON RESEARCH Fuzzy-Trace Theory: An Alternative Viewpoint

Most traditional accounts of human information processing assume that we solve problems by encoding discrete pieces of information and then reason about those items. So to solve the problem "How much is 27 + 46?," one must encode both numbers precisely and perform the proper mental operations to arrive at a correct answer. Not all of our thinking requires such precision. In fact, most of our thinking about everyday issues may actually be hindered somewhat by trying to rely on verbatim, or exact, information. Instead, we also encode much of what we encounter in very general terms ("The stereo was cheaper at Circuit City than at Service Merchandise") and solve problems using this less-than-exact information ("I'll buy the stereo at Circuit City").

Charles Brainerd's and Valerie Reyna's (2001, 2004) **fuzzy-trace theory** takes this fact of mental life into account, proposing that there are important developmental differences in how children represent information to solve problems. At the core of fuzzy-trace theory is the idea that memory representations (or memory traces) exist on a continuum from literal *verbatim* representations to vague, *fuzzy* representations, called **gist**, that preserve the essential content without all of the precise details. The theory also assumes that gistlike representations, or fuzzy traces, are not merely degraded forms of our verbatim representations. Indeed, we encode both verbatim and fuzzy, gistlike representations of the information we encounter and use whichever representation is easier or more appropriate for the problem we are trying to solve.

Fuzzy and verbatim traces differ in important ways. Compared with verbatim traces, fuzzy traces are more easily accessed and generally require less effort to use. Also, verbatim traces are more susceptible to interference and forgetting than fuzzy traces are. For example, when comparing the price of two shirts at two stores, the exact prices of the shirts may be quickly forgotten. More resistant to forgetting, however, will be the information that the shirt at The Gap was cheaper than the comparable shirt at Old Navy. If your problem is to decide which shirt is the better buy, you can rely on the gistlike knowledge of the relative price of the two shirts. If, however, you are trying to decide if you have enough money to purchase either of the shirts, you will need the verbatim information.

Although people generally find it easier and actually prefer to reason using fuzzy traces rather than verbatim representations of information, this varies with age. Before age 6 or 7, children seem to be biased toward encoding and remembering verbatim traces whereas older children, like adults, are more inclined to encode and remember fuzzy, gistlike traces (Brainerd & Gordon, 1994; Marx & Henderson, 1996). Charles Brainerd and L. L. Gordon (1994), for example, gave preschool and second-grade children simple numerical problems to solve, based on the following background information: "Farmer Brown owns many animals. He owns 3 dogs, 5 sheep, 7 chickens, 9 horses, and 11 cows." They were then asked a series of questions, some requiring verbatim knowledge for their correct answer, such as: "How many cows does Farmer Brown own: 11 or 9?" And others requiring only gist information, such as: "Which of Farmer Brown's animals are the most: cows or horses?"

They found that preschoolers performed better on the verbatim questions than on gist-based ones, whereas second-graders performed better on gist-based questions than on verbatim items (see accompanying figure). The second-graders performed just as well as preschoolers on the verbatim questions. The only age difference was that preschoolers were not as good as second-graders at solving gist-based problems.

Fuzzy-trace theory has been useful for describing developmental changes in the ways that children encode information and use it to solve problems. Relying on gist information is easier than trying to retrieve verbatim details and is just as effective (or more so) for solving a large number of problems that children face. Some tasks, such as mental arithmetic, do require verbatim representations. But a major reason that young children may think more slowly and less efficiently than older children do is that they often get bogged down processing unnecessary verbatim details that consume much of their limited cognitive resources and interfere with effective problem solving.

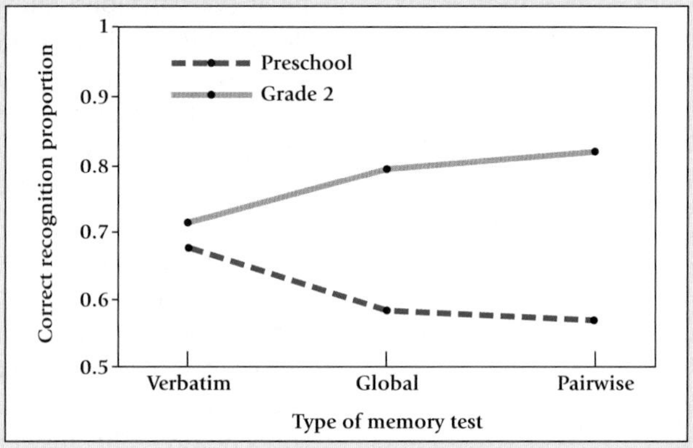

Fuzzy-trace theory. Proportion of correct recognition responses for verbatim, global, and pairwise problems for preschool and grade-2 children. From C. J. Brainerd and L. L. Gordon, "Development of verbatim and gist memory for numbers," *Developmental Psychology, 30,* 163–177. Copyright © 1994 by the American Psychological Association. Reprinted by permission.

A gistlike representation, or fuzzy trace, preserves the central content of a scene or an event without all the precise details. This boy may remember that he saw a dog chasing a cat without recalling the color of the animals or the fact that the cat wore a red collar.

FOCUS ON RESEARCH

Can Age Changes in Inhibition Account for Changes in Cognitive Development?

Researchers have proposed that age changes in children's abilities to *inhibit* preferred or well-established responses may play an important role in cognitive development (Diamond & Taylor, 1996; Harnishfeger, 1995). Whereas traditional information-processing theories have emphasized the *activation* of operations and knowledge, these alternative accounts propose that *inhibiting* an operation or preventing some piece of knowledge from getting into consciousness may be equally important for cognitive development (see also Dempster, 1993).

Deficits in **inhibition** are thought to influence cognition both in infancy and childhood. Recall from Chapter 7 that infants solving Piaget's A-not-B problem will often reach for a hidden object at location A, even after seeing it hidden at location B. They cannot inhibit their tendency to search where they had previously found the object (at point A) despite seemingly "knowing" better.

Age-related changes in inhibitory processes have also been noted for a number of other cognitive challenges that older children face. For example, children's ability to selectively forget unimportant information is affected by their ability to keep the to-be-forgotten information out of mind. Older grade-school children are simply better able to execute these inhibitory processes than younger children are (Lehman et al., 1997; Wilson & Kipp, 1998). In general, young children have a difficult time executing anything other than their preferred or predominant response. Children's ability to regulate their conduct (which involves inhibiting unacceptable responses as well as performing more desirable acts) also improves with age (Jones, Rothbart, & Posner, 2003; Kochanska et al., 1996).

What factors contribute to the development of inhibitory control? Neurological maturation seems to. In Chapter 7 we learned that infants' ability to inhibit inappropriate responses in A-not-B search problems is related to maturation of the frontal lobes of the cerebral cortex. Furthermore, both preschool children and adults with lesions of the frontal lobes show the same difficulties performing tasks in which verbal instructions require them to inhibit a dominant response. So if told to tap a pencil one more time (or one less time) than an experimenter does, both young children and brain-damaged adults have trouble inhibiting their preferred tendency to imitate the number of taps the experimenter displays (Diamond & Taylor, 1996). Taken together, these findings imply that maturation of the frontal lobes plays a major role in permitting us to inhibit various thoughts and behaviors.

Katherine Kipp Harnishfeger and David Bjorklund (Bjorklund & Harnishfeger, 1990; Harnishfeger, 1995; Harnishfeger & Bjorklund, 1994) proposed a model of "inefficient inhibition" to account for the influence of inhibitory mechanisms on cognitive development. The central idea in their model is that age differences in the ability to keep task-inappropriate information out of working memory influences task performance. Young children may not only have difficulty ignoring task-irrelevant input from the environment, but they also have a difficult time suppressing task-irrelevant *thoughts.* This greater amount of task-irrelevant information in working memory results in "cognitive clutter," which effectively reduces functional working-memory space and prevents the successful execution of other cognitive strategies (Lorsbach, Katz, & Cupak, 1998).

Recognizing that inhibitory processes play an important role in cognitive development seems to be an important step forward in helping us arrive at a better understanding of children's thinking. Yet the inhibitory perspective should be seen as supplementing information-processing views of development and not replacing them. Age changes in inhibition may *permit* certain other abilities to be expressed, but they do not *cause* them to develop in the first place. Stated another way, improvements in inhibitory control may promote cognitive growth by reducing cognitive clutter, thereby allowing more advanced information-processing abilities to emerge.

CONCEPT CHECK 8.2

Understanding Developmental Differences in Information Processing

Check your understanding of developmental differences in information processing by answering the following questions. Answers appear in the Appendix.

Multiple Choice: Select the best alternative for each question.

_____ 1. Patricia Miller and her colleagues have suggested a transitional period of strategy development, in which children use a strategy although it does not facilitate their task performance. This phenomenon is referred to as a

a. mediation deficiency
b. utilization deficiency
c. production deficiency
d. limited capacity

CONTINUED

______ 2. Concerning development, fuzzy-trace theory makes specific predictions about how gist and verbatim processing changes with age. What does the theory predict?
a. Young children do not extract gist traces, but process only verbatim traces. Older children and adults extract both types of traces.
b. Young children do not extract verbatim traces, but process only gist traces. Older children and adults extract both types of traces.
c. Compared to older children, young children prefer to operate on the verbatim end of the trace continuum; older children and adults prefer to operate on the gist end of the trace continuum.
d. Compared to older children, young children prefer to operate on the gist end of the trace continuum; older children and adults prefer to operate on the verbatim end of the trace continuum.

______ 3. Brett played a dice game with his mother. Sometimes he counted all the pips on each dice to compute his move; sometimes he just looked at the two dice and "knew" how many spaces he could move; and sometimes he said the number of one die ("6") and counted up the number on the second die ("7, 8, 9") to compute his move. Josh's strategic behavior best reflects which of the following theories?
a. Siegler's adaptive strategy choice model
b. Brainerd & Reyna's fuzzy-trace theory
c. Miller's utilization deficiency theory
d. Flavell's metacognition theory

Matching: Match the following concepts with their definitions.

a. memory span
b. implicit cognition
c. explicit cognition
d. span of apprehension
e. a fuzzy representation of information that preserves the central content but few precise details
f. a failure to spontaneously generate and use known strategies that could improve learning and memory

4. ________ A general measure of the amount of information that can be held in the short-term store.
5. ________ A fuzzy representation of information that preserves the central content but few precise details.
6. ________ Thinking and thought processes of which we are consciously aware.
7. ________ A failure to spontaneously generate and use known strategies that could improve learning and memory.
8. ________ The number of items that people can keep in mind at any one time, or the amount of information that people can attend to at a single time without operating mentally to store this information.
9. ________ Thought that occurs without awareness that one is thinking.

Essays: Provide a detailed answer to the following questions.

10. Discuss how age differences in inhibition/resistance to interference may contribute to cognitive development.
11. Discuss the development of strategies. What factors affect the likelihood that children of different ages will use strategies and that they will be effective?

The Development of Attention

Clearly, a person must first detect and attend to information before it can be encoded, retained, or used to solve problems. Although even young infants attend to a variety of sensory inputs, objects and events often capture their attention: A 1-month-old baby does not choose to attend to a face; instead, faces attract his attention. Similarly, preschoolers who seem totally immersed in one activity can quickly lose interest and just as quickly get caught up in another activity. But as children grow older, they become better able to sustain their attention, more selective in what they attend to, and know more about attention.

Changes in Sustained Attention

attention span
capacity for sustaining attention to a particular stimulus or activity.

Visit a nursery school and you will see that teachers are likely to switch classroom activities every 15 to 20 minutes. Why? Because young children have very short **attention spans;** they cannot sustain attention, or concentrate, on any single activity for very long. Even when doing things they like, such as playing with toys or watching TV, 2- and 3-year-olds often look away, move about, and direct their attention elsewhere, spending far less time on the activity at hand than older children do (Ruff & Capozzoli, 2003; Ruff, Capozzoli, & Weisberg, 1998). Part of younger children's problem in trying to concentrate is that their attention is easily captured by distractions and they are often unable to inhibit the intrusion of task-irrelevant thoughts (see the Box on p. 303).

The capacity for sustained attention gradually improves throughout childhood and early adolescence, and these improvements may be due, in part, to maturational changes in the central nervous system. For example, the *reticular formation,* an area of the brain responsible for the regulation of attention, is not fully myelinated until puberty. Perhaps this neurological development helps explain why adolescents and young adults are suddenly able to spend hours on end cramming for upcoming exams or typing furiously to make morning deadlines on term papers.

Selective Attention: Ignoring Information That Is Clearly Irrelevant

selective attention
capacity to focus on task-relevant aspects of experience while ignoring irrelevant or distracting information.

Would young children perform as well as older children if they were told in advance which information is most relevant to the tasks they face and did not have to be so planful? Probably not, because younger children display little ability to display **selective attention**—to concentrate only on task-relevant stimuli and to not be distracted by other noise in the environment. Consider what Patricia Miller and Michael Weiss (1981) found when they told 7-, 10-, and 13-year-olds to remember the locations of a number of animals, each of which was hidden behind a different cloth flap. When each flap was lifted to reveal an animal, the children could also see a household object positioned either above or below the animal. Here, then, is a learning task that requires the child to attend selectively to certain information (the animals) while ignoring other potentially distracting input (the household objects). When the children were tested to see whether they had learned where each animal was located, the 13-year-olds outperformed the 10-year-olds, who, in turn, performed slightly better than the 7-year-olds. Miller and Weiss then tested to see whether children had attended to the incidental (irrelevant) information by asking them to recall which household object had been paired with each animal. They found exactly the opposite pattern on this incidental-learning test: 13-year-olds recalled *less* about the household objects than either 7- or 10-year-olds. In fact, both of the younger groups recalled as much about the irrelevant objects as about the locations of the animals. Taken together, these findings indicate that older children are much better than younger ones at concentrating on relevant information and filtering out extraneous input that may interfere with task performance.

attention-deficit hyperactivity disorder (ADHD)
an attentional disorder involving distractibility, hyperactivity, and impulsive behavior that often leads to academic difficulties, poor self-esteem, and social or emotional problems.

Despite these normal trends, many grade-school children find it nearly impossible to sustain their attention for long periods of time or to develop planful attentional strategies. In the Box on p. 306 we take a closer look at this **attention-deficit hyperactivity disorder (ADHD)** and its implications for children's academic, social, and emotional development.

Meta-Attention: What Do Children Know about Attention?

Do young children know more about attentional processes than their behavior might indicate? Indeed they do. Even though 4-year-olds generally cannot overcome distractions when performing selective-attention tasks, they are apparently aware that distractions can be a problem because they realize that two stories will be harder to understand if the storytellers speak simultaneously rather than taking turns (Pillow, 1988). Yet when 4-year-olds are told that a woman is examining a set of decorative pins to select one as a gift, they are largely unaware that she would be thinking primarily about the pins and

APPLYING RESEARCH TO YOUR LIFE

Attention-Deficit Hyperactivity Disorder

> They can't sit still; they don't pay attention to the teacher; they mess around and get into trouble; they try to get others into trouble; they are rude; they get mad when they don't get their way (Henker & Whalen, 1989, p. 216).

These and other similar descriptions are widely endorsed by classmates of those 3 to 5 percent of grade-school children (mostly boys) diagnosed as having *attention-deficit hyperactivity disorder (ADHD).* ADHD youngsters display three major symptoms: (1) they are highly *impulsive,* often acting before thinking and blurting out whatever is on their minds; (2) they are *inattentive,* frequently failing to listen and displaying an inability to concentrate or to finish tasks; and (3) they are *hyperactive,* constantly fidgeting, squirming, or moving about (American Psychiatric Association, 1994). As you might expect, these youngsters perform miserably on tests of sustained and selective attention. They also do poorly in school and will often alienate both teachers and classmates by their failure to comply with requests and their disruptive and aggressive behavior (see Barkley, 1997).

It was once believed that hyperactive children simply outgrew their problems after reaching puberty. Although they do generally become less fidgety and overactive during the teenage years, many people diagnosed in childhood as having ADHD will continue to display serious adjustment problems later in life. For example, attention-disordered adolescents are likely to struggle both socially and academically, and they frequently drop out of high school or impulsively commit reckless, delinquent acts without thinking about the consequences (Wender, 1995). The picture is somewhat more positive by early adulthood, as the majority of all ADHD individuals seem to be functioning well in their jobs (Wender, 1995). But for many with ADHD, young adulthood is characterized by above-average rates of job changes (or dismissals), marital disruptions, traffic accidents, legal infractions, and other personality problems or emotional disorders (see Barkley, 1997).

According to Russell Barkley (1997), the primary cause of ADHD is problems in behavioral inhibition. Barkley defined behavioral inhibition as the ability to inhibit a prepotent response, to resist interference, and to stop an ongoing response, much as it was described in Box 8.2. Behavioral inhibition affects working memory, self-regulation of emotion, internalization of speech, which is critical in directing problem solving and reflecting upon one's behavior, and in what Barkley calls reconstitution, which involves the "creation of novel, complex goal-directed behaviors" (p. 72). Given the importance of these abilities for cognition and successful day-to-day functioning, children with deficits in behavioral inhibition would be especially disadvantaged.

What causes ADHD? Unfortunately, we do not yet have a clear answer. Some people may be genetically predisposed to develop the disorder in that concordance rates in ADHD are higher for pairs of identical twins than for fraternal twins or

CONTINUED

would not have other things on her mind (Flavell, Green, & Flavell, 1995). It is as if these preschoolers simply do not realize what is involved in selective attention, even though they know something about distractions.

In other research Miller and Weiss (1982) asked 5-, 7-, and 9-year-olds to answer a series of questions about factors known to affect performance on incidental-learning tasks (that is, a task such as the animals and objects test described earlier). Although knowledge about attentional processes generally increased with age, even the 5-year-olds realized that they should at least *look* first at task-relevant stimuli and then *label* these objects as an aid to remembering them. The 7- and 10-year-olds further understood that they must *attend selectively* to task-relevant stimuli and *ignore* irrelevant information in order to do well on these problems. But before thinking that young preschoolers know nothing about attention, consider the findings of Michael Tomasello and Katharina Haberl (2003). Twelve- and eighteen-month-old infants interacted with an adult who expressed great interest in one of three toys (a novel toy, one she hadn't seen previously), saying, for example, "Wow! Cool." The adult then asked the children "Can you give it to me?" Infants at both ages were able to comply, indicating that they realized that looking at an object, that is, attending to it, and getting excited about it indicated a preference for that object. This knowledge of attention (in this case, attention in other people) may not be on par with understanding that a person is likely thinking about something she is looking at, but it does reveal that the roots of understanding attention are found in infancy.

ordinary siblings (Levy et al., 1997). Environment also matters. The incidence of ADHD is higher among children who were exposed *prenatally* to alcohol, drugs, and the disease rubella (Millberger et al., 1996), and a harsh, highly controlling style of parenting may also contribute to, or at least aggravate, the problem in some cases (Sroufe, 1997). However, earlier theories linking the syndrome to food additives, excessive dietary intake of sugar, lead poisoning, and brain damage have received little support (Henker & Whalen, 1989).

Interestingly, some critics claim that ADHD is overdiagnosed in the United States and may represent more of an adaptational problem than a disorder (Jensen et al., 1997; Panksepp, 1998). From this perspective, many children diagnosed as having ADHD are simply highly active and playful youngsters whose impulsiveness and heightened motor activity may once have been advantages (as is true today for people in hunter-gatherer societies), but simply does not mesh with the focused attention that is required for success in modern schools. Nevertheless, even adaptational problems require some intervention if these children are to adapt.

What can be done to help children labeled as having ADHD? One treatment that seems to help about 70 percent of these children is to administer stimulant drugs such as Ritalin or Concerta (Lore, 2000). Although it may seem odd to give overactive children drugs that increase their heart rates and respiratory levels, stimulants work because they subtly alter brain chemistry in ways that make ADHD children better able to focus their attention and less distractible and disruptive (Barkley, 1997). Important side benefits of this increased attentional focusing are that both academic performance and peer relations often improve (Pelham et al., 1993). However, critics of this approach argue that stimulants do little more than suppress ADHD symptoms while possibly producing such serious side effects as curbing appetites, disrupting sleep cycles, and reducing children's desire to play and to acquire any number of important skills that are not taught at school (Panksepp, 1998).

Gains in scholastic performance have also been achieved through cognitive-behavioral programs that teach ADHD children how to set academic goals that require sustained attention while allowing these youngsters to reinforce their successes with tokens that can be exchanged for prizes. Indeed, many ADHD children seem to benefit most from a *combination* of drug and behavior therapies (Cantwell, 1996). And recently, researchers have found that if parents can remain warm and supportive but firm in their demands, their hyperactive sons display fewer problem behaviors and are much better accepted by peers (Hinshaw et al., 1997). So, family therapies aimed at teaching often-exasperated adults to become more patient and to effectively manage the antics of a child with ADHD are likely to enhance the effectiveness of existing drug and behavioral interventions (Hinshaw et al., 1997).

A final note: Although therapeutic interventions do improve the self-esteem, social behaviors, and academic performance of ADHD children, many of these treated individuals are no better adjusted as adults than hyperactive peers who received no therapy (Hart et al., 1995). Undoubtedly the long-term prognosis will improve as we learn more about this condition. At present, we can say that the many problems associated with ADHD clearly illustrate just how important the regulation of attention is—not only to cognitive development and academic performance, but to one's social and emotional development as well.

Memory: Retaining and Retrieving Information

Central to the study of cognition and its development is memory. Whether an infant searches for his bottle that slipped under his blanket, a 7-year old recalls the names of his classmates so her mother can address Valentine Day cards, or a 17-year-old prepares for an essay exam on the American Revolution, all involve memory—the processes by which we store and retrieve information.

In this section we first look at memory development over infancy. We then trace the development of two general kinds of memory over childhood: *event memory* and *strategic memory*. **Event memory** refers to memories such as what you ate for breakfast this morning, Britney Spears's opening number at last year's concert, or the joy your mother displayed when your baby brother was born. Memory for events, including **autobiographical memories** of things that happened to you, is what most people think of as "natural" memory, and it rarely requires use of any strategies. We examine the growth of event memory and look at recent research examining children's memory for events when serving as eyewitnesses. In contrast, **strategic memory** refers to the processes involved when we consciously try to retain or retrieve such information as a telephone number, the route to a theater across town, or the text of the Gettysburg Address for a U.S. history class. Information-processing researchers have investigated a variety of memory strategies, or **mnemonics,** that might promote academic performance, and we examine the development of several such strategies and some of the factors that influence their development.

event memory
long-term memory for events.

autobiographical memory
memory for important experiences or events that have happened to us.

strategic memory
processes involved as one consciously attempts to retain or retrieve information.

mnemonics (memory strategies)
effortful techniques used to improve memory, including rehearsal, organization, and elaboration.

Memory Development in Infancy

There's no doubt that babies remember things, but how do you prove it? And how do you figure out how long they remember something or what, exactly, it is they're remembering? Those questions went unanswered for most of the last century, but clever techniques were developed to test infant memory, and now it is one of the hottest topics in cognitive development.

So how do you test infant memory? We saw in Chapter 7 that techniques based on children's looking time can be used as an indication of memory. For example, children will *habituate,* or decrease their looking time, when a stimulus, such as a picture, is presented repeatedly. But they will increase their looking time, or *dishabituate,* when a new picture is shown. When infants dishabituate it implies that they recognize that the new stimulus that is before their eyes is different from the original stimulus, which is not before them but only in their memories. Using variants of these techniques, Joseph Fagan (1973, 1974) was able to show that 5- to 6-month-old babies form visual memories after only brief exposures to pictures (5 to 10 seconds), and that these memories can last as long as 2 weeks. (See Rose, Feldman, and Jankowski, [2004] for a review of contemporary research looking at infant visual recognition memory.) In other research discussed in Chapter 5, newborns preferred to listen to stories their mothers had read to them the 6 weeks before their birth than other stories, a clear indication of prenatal auditory memories (DeCasper & Spence, 1984; Spence, 1996).

Research using operant-conditioning techniques has also been used to demonstrate memory in young infants. As you may recall from Chapter 5, Carolyn Rovee-Collier and her colleagues have shown that infants will "remember" a context where they were previously reinforced (kicking their leg when placed in a crib to see a mobile move) by displaying the same when placed in the same or similar crib (even though the mobile does not move) some significant time later (Rovee-Collier, 1999). This *conjugate-reinforcement procedure* has shown that young babies are very sensitive to context. Change even a small part of the context, such as the liner of the crib, and young infants don't seem to recognize it and will not kick their legs. But this procedure, and a similar one (the train task) used with older infants, also reveals that infants' memories for their actions increase with age. The mobile task described in Chapter 5 can be used for infants between about 2 and 6 months. The train task uses the same logic as the mobile task and can be used with infants between about 6 and 18 months of age. In the train task, infants sit in front of a miniature train set. They can learn to move the train by pressing a lever in front of them, and memory is tested by bringing the babies back after some delay and measuring the rate at which they press the lever when it is not connected to the train. The maximum number of weeks that infants between 2 and 18 months of age demonstrated retention under standard conditions on the mobile and train tasks is shown in Figure 8.6 (Rovee-Collier, 1999). As can be seen, the duration of infants' memories showed gradual but steady increases with age, reflecting a continuously developing memory system.

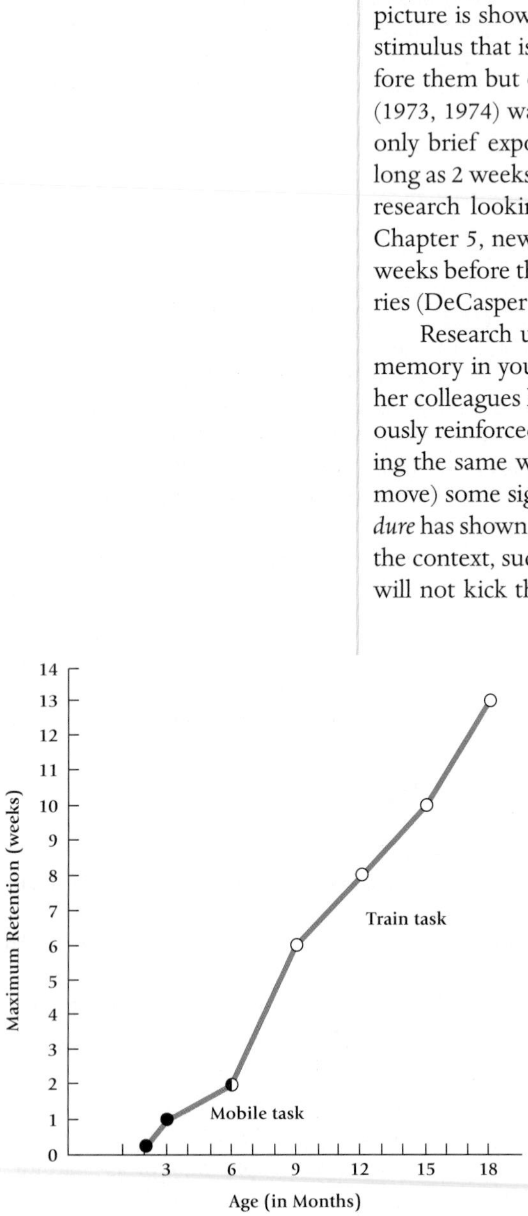

Figure 8.6 Maximum duration of retention from 2 to 18 months of age. Filled circles show retention on the mobile task, and open circles show retention on the train task; 6-month-olds were trained and tested on both tasks. *From C. Rovee-Collier, "The development of infant memory,"* Current Directions in Psychological Science, 8, *80–85, 1999. Reprinted by permission of Blackwell Publishing.*

The procedure that has become the workhorse of infant memory research involves *deferred imitation.* We discussed deferred imitation in the previous chapter. There we noted that children's ability to observe a model perform some task and then reproduce that behavior after some significant delay, reflects a form of symbolic representation. But it also reflects memory. The basic procedure involves a model demonstrating some novel behavior to an infant, such as pressing one's head against the top of a box to make the box light up. Sometime later (perhaps minutes, perhaps months) the infants are given the object. If they display the novel behavior at a greater rate than a control group of infants, who had not seen the novel behavior displayed, the inference is that they remembered the action and chose to display it when given the chance. The results of recent research are quite striking, showing that infants as young as 6 months can remember simple actions over the course of a day (Collie & Hayne, 1999), whereas some infants as young as 13 months old can remember novel actions for up to a year (see Bauer, 2004; Meltzoff, 1995)! These results suggest that preverbal infants and toddlers do represent events in their long-term memories, and, under the right conditions, can access those memories months later.

Age differences in how long babies can remember actions using the deferred imitation procedures have also been found. For example, in a series of studies, Patricia Bauer and her colleagues (Bauer, 2004; Bauer et al., 2000) showed 9- to 20-month-old infants a series of three-step sequences. (For example, the model placed a bar across two posts, hung a plate from the bar, and then struck the plate with a mallet.) One to twelve months later the babies were tested again. About half of the youngest babies demonstrated deferred imitation of simpler two-sequence actions following a 1-month delay, although these infants required at least three exposures to the events before showing imitation. Levels of performance were considerably higher for 13-month-olds and further increased for the 16- and 20-month-old infants (Bauer et al., 2000). Figure 8.7 presents the percentage of infants at 13 months, 16 months, and 20 months of age who showed imitation after 1-month, 3-month, 6-month, 9-month, and 12-month delays. As can be seen in the figure, nearly 80 percent of the 13-month-olds demonstrated deferred imitation after 1 month, but fewer than half did after a 6-month delay. In contrast, nearly 70 percent of the 20-month-olds were still imitating the novel behavior they had seen after a 12-month delay. These findings are similar to those reported by Rovee-Collier using a very different task and illustrate that infants are able to form long-term memories early in life and that the ability to retain these memories increases gradually during the first 2 years.

The age-related pattern of deferred imitation is consistent with what we know about brain development during this time (Bauer, 2004; C. Nelson, 1997). Long-term memory requires the integration of brain activity from multiple sites, including the hippocampus, which develops early, and the prefrontal cortex and structures within the temporal lobe, which develop more slowly. The early developing hippocampus presumably underlies the deferred imitation of simple actions seen by 6-month-olds (Collie & Hayne, 1999), but other brain areas must mature before infants can retain more complicated information for longer periods. Not until the second year of life do these systems (hippocampus, prefrontal lobe, temporal lobe) begin to coalesce, with development continuing well into the third year. The relatively gradual development of these brain structures correlates with the relatively gradual improvement in long-term retention of infants during this same period (Bauer et al., 2000).

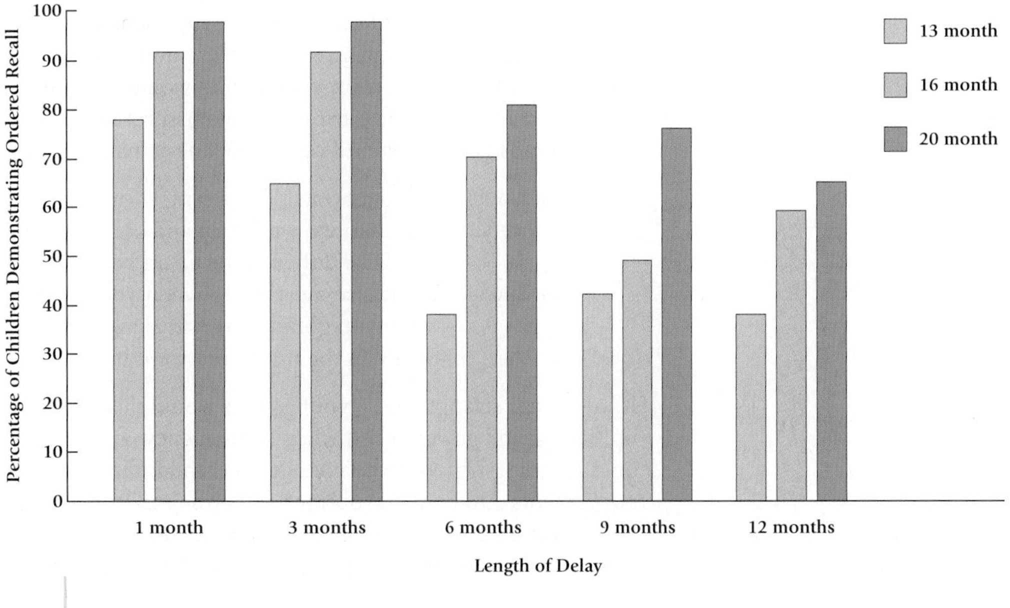

Figure 8.7 Percentage of 13-, 16-, and 20-month-old infants displaying deferred imitation of three-step sequences as a function of length of delay. *From Bauer et al., "Parameters of remembering and forgetting in the transition from infancy to early childhood,"* Monographs of the Society for Research in Child Development, 65 *(Serial No. 263). Reprinted by permission of Blackwell Publishing.*

The Development of Event and Autobiographical Memory

Although infant memory is quite impressive, and far more sophisticated at an early age than we once thought, when most people think about memory they think about remembering episodes, or events, particularly those that happen to them. *Event memory* in general, and our memory for particularly important personal experiences, or *autobiographical memory,* are almost always expressed through language, and as we'll see, event and autobiographical memories are closely tied to language skills and to our ability to represent our experiences in storylike narratives (Nelson, 1996).

Origins of Event Memory

Many researchers propose that deferred imitation, discussed in the preceding section, represents the first evidence of event memory, albeit a nonverbal form. If infants and toddlers can recall events that happened months ago, why do we display **infantile amnesia**—an inability to remember much that happened to us during the first few years? Though the answers remain elusive, some speculations about this fascinating memory lapse are presented in the Box on p. 311.

infantile amnesia
a lack of memory for the early years of one's life.

Development of Scripted Memory

What events do toddlers and preschool children remember best? They tend to recall well recurring events that typically happen in familiar contexts. Katherine Nelson and her colleagues (1996) find that young children organize familiar routines into **scripts,** schemes for certain experiences that preserve the ordering and causal relations among the events that unfold. For example, a 4-year-old describing her fast-food restaurant script might say, "You drive there, go in, get in line, get hamburgers and fries, eat, and go home." Even 2-year-olds can organize information in a scriptlike fashion (Fivush, Kuebli, & Clubb, 1992). And although scripted knowledge may become more elaborate with age, preschool children continue to learn and remember what usually happens at snack time at school, at birthday parties, at fast-food restaurants, at bedtime at home, and in a variety of other familiar settings (Nelson, 1996).

script
a general representation of the typical sequencing of events (i.e., what occurs and when) in some familiar context.

Forming scripts thus appears to be a way that young children organize and interpret their experiences and make predictions about what they can expect on similar occasions in the future. However, young children's organization of events into scripts has its costs because it results in their tending not to remember much in the way of novel, atypical (or nonscript) information. In one study (Fivush & Hamond, 1990), 2½-year-olds were questioned about such recent noteworthy events as a trip to the beach, a camping trip, or a ride on an airplane. Rather than recalling the novel aspects of these special events, children were more likely to focus on what adults would consider to be routine information. So when describing a camping trip, one child first recalled sleeping outside, which is unusual, but then mostly remembered very mundane activities (Fivush & Hamond, 1990, p. 231):

INTERVIEWER: You slept outside in a tent? Wow, that sounds like a lot of fun.
CHILD: And then we waked up and eat dinner. First we eat dinner, then go to bed, and then wake up and eat breakfast.
INTERVIEWER: What else did you do when you went camping? What did you do when you got up, after breakfast?
CHILD: Umm, in the night, and went to sleep.

It may seem strange that a young child would talk about such routine events as waking up, eating, and going to bed when so many new and exciting things must have happened on a camping trip. But the younger the child, the more he or she may need to embed novel events into familiar routines. According to Robyn Fivush and Nina Hamond (1991), everything is new to 2-year-olds, who are most concerned with making some sense of the events they experience.

APPLYING RESEARCH TO YOUR LIFE

What Happened to Our Early Childhood Memories?

David and Barbara Bjorklund (1992, p. 206) recount the following story:

> We received a letter from a woman . . . who was worried because her 10-year-old son could remember very little from his preschool days. She said that she and her husband had always tried to be good parents but thought that her son's inability to remember things from early childhood was an indication that either they hadn't done a very good job after all, or they had done a truly terrible job and her son was repressing this painful period of his life. We assured her that her son's inability to remember events much before his fourth birthday is quite normal, and is certainly not an indication that those events were unimportant.

Though infants are quite capable of remembering, most adults recall almost nothing that happened to them before age 3; and if they do have memories, many of them turn out to be pure fiction. JoNell Usher and Ulric Neisser (1993) studied this lack of memory for the early years, or *infantile amnesia,* by questioning college students about experiences they had had early in life—experiences such as the birth of a younger sibling, a stay in the hospital, a family move, or the death of a family member. To assess recall, a series of questions was asked about each event the participant had experienced (for example, Who told you your mother was going to the hospital to give birth? What were you doing when she left? Where were you when you first saw the new baby?). As we see in the accompanying figure, the percentage of questions college students could answer increased substantially the older the person was when he or she had experienced the event. Usher and Neisser concluded that the earliest age of *any* meaningful recall was about age 2 for the birth of a sibling or a hospitalization and age 3 for the death of a family member or a family move. Even 9- and 10-year-olds who are shown photographs of their day-care classmates from 6 or 7 years earlier have difficulty discriminating these youngsters, who were once very familiar to them, from other young day-care children they had never seen before (Newcombe & Fox, 1994). So if infants can remember their experiences, why can't grade-school children and adults remember much about what their lives were like as infants and toddlers?

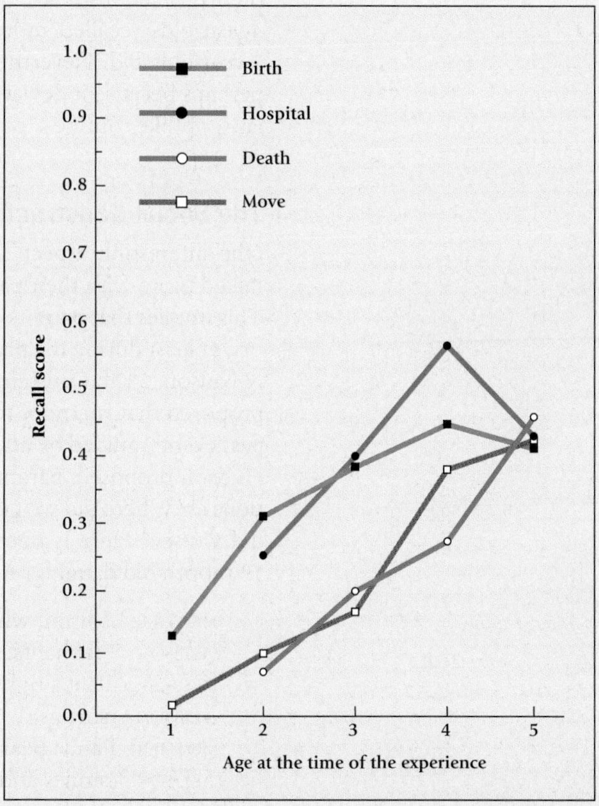

College students' recall of early life events increases as a function of their age at the time of the event. From J. A. Usher and U. Neisser, "Childhood amnesia and the beginnings of memory of four early life events," *Journal of Experimental Psychology: General, 122,* 155–165. Copyright © 1993 by the American Psychological Association. Reprinted by permission.

Sigmund Freud thought infantile amnesia simply reflected our tendency to repress the emotional conflicts of early childhood. Contemporary researchers have rejected Freud's view in favor of more cognitive explanations. For example, infants do not use language and adults do, so it is possible that early memories are stored in some nonverbal code that we cannot retrieve once we become language users (Sheingold & Tenney, 1982). Even slightly older children, who can talk, may not represent their experiences in the same way as older children and adults do. It is not until about 4 years that most children *easily* encode and remember their experiences in terms of narratives—stories about their lives—and this usually with much help from adults. It is only after being guided by adults that children learn to code memories and realize that language can be used to share memories with others (Fivush & Nelson, 2004; Nelson, 1996). Mark Howe (2003) suggests yet another interesting possibility: Maybe what is lacking in infancy is not cognitive or language ability, but a sense of "self" around which personal experiences can be organized. Once an infant gains a firm sense of self (discussed in Chapter 12) at about 18 to 24 months, events may become more memorable when encoded as "things that happened to *me.*" Interestingly, research indicates that each of these theories may have some truth to them. For example, in one study toddlers were shown a series of actions and were tested 6 to 12 months later for both their verbal and nonverbal memory for these actions (Simcock & Hayne, 2002). Children who were more verbally sophisticated at the time of initial testing tended to verbally recall some aspects of the event (see also Bauer, Wenner, & Kroupina, 2002), but children were seemingly not able to translate earlier preverbal experiences into language. According to Simcock and Hayne, "children's verbal reports were frozen in time, reflecting their verbal skill at the time of encoding, rather than at the time of test" (2002, p. 229). In other research, both the development of a sense of self and adult assistance in constructing personal narratives helped young preschool children to remember past events that happened to them (Harley & Reese, 1999). So our lack of both linguistic proficiency and a concept of "selfhood" for the first 18 to 24 months help explain why our early life experiences remain a blank for most of us.

As children grow older, they eventually remember more specific and atypical information over extended periods, especially if the event sequence they experienced is highly unusual and particularly noteworthy. For example, Hamond and Fivush (1991) interviewed 3- and 4-year-olds 6 or 18 months after they had gone to Disney World. All children recalled a great deal of information about their trip, even after 18 months. The 4-year-olds recalled more details and required fewer prompts to describe them than 3-year-olds did. Nevertheless, recall for this single, special experience was quite good, perhaps because it deviated so far from, and could not easily be assimilated into, a familiar scriptlike routine.

The Social Construction of Autobiographical Memories

One interesting aspect of Hamond and Fivush's (1991) study was that children who talked more with their parents about the Disney World trip recalled more about the trip. This implies that parents play an important role in the growth of autobiographical memory, at least during the preschool years, a point recently made by several theorists (Fivush & Nelson, 2004; Ornstein, Haden, & Hedrick, 2004). Judith Hudson (1990), for example, proposed that memory for events begins as a joint activity in which children talk about past events, guided by adults who expand on their skimpy recollections. In most families, Hudson proposed, parents begin talking about the past by asking such contextual questions as: Where did we go this morning? What did we see? Who went with us? What else did we see? Here is one example of a conversation in which a mother prompted her 19-month-old daughter to recall details of their morning trip to a zoo:

MOTHER: Allison, what did we see at the zoo?
ALLISON: Elephants.
MOTHER: That's right! We saw elephants. And what else?
ALLISON: (shrugs)
MOTHER: Panda bear? Did we see a panda bear?
ALLISON: (smiles and nods)
MOTHER: Can you say panda bear?
ALLISON: Panda bear.
MOTHER: Good! Elephants and panda bears. What else?
ALLISON: Elephunts.
MOTHER: That's right, elephants. And also a gorilla.
ALLISON: Go-rilla!

Elizabeth Crews/The Image Works

By encouraging children to reconstruct past events in which they have participated, parents foster the development of autobiographical memory.

From these interchanges, children learn that the important facts to remember about events are the whos, whens, and wheres of their experiences. Furthermore, when parents request this information in ways that reconstruct the temporal order and causal sequences among events and ask children to evaluate these happenings (what was your favorite part?), they are helping youngsters to organize their experiences into storylike narratives and to recall them as events that have personal significance—as "things that happened to me" (Boland, Haden, & Ornstein, 2003; Farrant & Reese, 2000). Clearly, these joint reconstructions of past experiences should remind us of Vygotsky's ideas about the social construction of knowledge and Rogoff's ideas about guided participation. Indeed, 2- to 3½-year-olds whose parents have often collaborated with them by asking questions about past events recall more autobiographical experiences 1 to 2 years later than do age-mates whose parents have rarely questioned them about the past (Harley & Reese, 1999; Reese, Haden, & Fivush, 1993).

Interestingly, parents' co-constructions of past events become increasingly detailed as their children develop more competent language and narrative skills (Haden, Hayne, & Fivush, 1997). So over the preschool years, autobiographical memory appears and blossoms as children, guided by their parents, learn to construct increasingly detailed personal narratives in which they place their experiences in the larger context of their own lives.

Children as Eyewitnesses

One topic related to event memory that has attracted a lot of attention over the past decade concerns the reliability of children as eyewitnesses. Not surprisingly, much of the interest came about because of children's increasing participation in the legal system, either as victims of or as witnesses to purported crimes (Ceci & Bruck, 1998). Issues of interest both to psychologists and to the legal profession include the following:

- How much do children of different ages remember of events they witness?
- How accurate are their memories?
- How susceptible are children to suggestion?

Age Differences in Eyewitness Memory

Eyewitness memory is really no different from event memory, except that some misdeed or traumatic experience is usually embedded in the witnessed event. Research in which children observe and are later asked to recall such events yields the typical developmental differences in event memory, with older children remembering far more than younger children (Ornstein, Gordon, & Larus, 1992; Poole & Lindsay, 1995). But even though preschool (and young grade-school) children recall few precise details, what they do remember is generally accurate and central to the witnessed event (Bjorklund, Brown, & Bjorklund, 2001; Poole & White, 1995). For example, in a video involving a boy and a girl in which the boy stole a bike, young children typically recalled the bike theft but were much less likely than older children or adults to describe the participants, characteristics of the bicycle, or details of the setting (Cassel & Bjorklund, 1995). When children are prompted with more specific cues (for example, "Tell me what the girl looked like."), they recall more information. However, in addition to remembering more *correct* facts, they also tend to relate some *incorrect* "facts" as well, reducing the overall accuracy of their recall (Goodman et al., 1994). And unfortunately, these *false memories* often persist and may be as, or more, resistant to forgetting as true memories are (Brainerd & Reyna, 2004).

How Suggestible Are Child Witnesses?

The fact that children sometimes report and retain false memories implies that their recall of witnessed or experienced events may be highly susceptible to suggestion. Research has shown that people of all ages report more inaccurate information if asked leading questions that suggest inaccurate facts or events (for example, "He touched your penis, didn't he?"). And most of the available evidence implies that children younger than 9 or 10 are far more susceptible to such memory distortions than older children, adolescents, and adults are (Ceci & Bruck, 1998; Lindberg, Keiffer, & Thomas, 2000).

Don't misunderstand: False memories can be induced in people of all ages (Lindberg, Keiffer, & Thomas, 2000; Loftus & Pickrell, 1995). Nevertheless, it is much easier to create them in preschool and young grade-school children, even when the memories address events that allegedly happened to them and the children initially deny the experiences. Stephen Ceci and his associates (1994), for example, asked preschool children and 6-year-olds if they could ever remember having experienced events such as catching a finger in a mousetrap. Although almost no one admitted to recalling these *fictional* events in the initial interviews, after repeated questioning, more than 50 percent of the younger preschool children and about 40 percent of the 5- and 6-year-olds said that these events had happened to them and often provided vivid accounts of their experiences! Furthermore, many children continued to believe that these events actually happened even after being told by the interviewers and their parents that the events were just made up and had never taken place.

Plausibility is an important factor here. Even though getting one's finger caught in a mousetrap might be an event that few children have ever actually experienced, it is one that could happen in many households. Kathy Pezdek and Danielle Hodge (1999) demonstrated that about one third of 5- to 7-year-old children "remembered" being lost in a mall (which they had not been) whereas only 1 of 19 children "remembered" being given an enema. Although most of these children knew what an enema was, the event was implausible. If such an embarrassing and invasive event had happened to them, they certainly would have remembered. Pezdek and Hodge also found that children reported more details for true memories than for false ones. So even though there is no "Pinocchio test" for determining whether a memory is true or not, on average, children's recollections of events that actually did happen to them tend to be clearer and more detailed than their recollections of planted, or false, memories (Pezdek & Taylor, 2000).

In sum, it is often possible to convince young children to confirm an interviewer's allegations by falsely recalling information or experiences that never happened, particularly when the suggestions and accusations are strong, persistent, and plausible. Why are younger children so suggestible? Such social factors as a young child's desire to please adults or to comply with their requests almost certainly contributes to their heightened suggestibility. So, too, does a young child's preference for encoding and reporting exact details (which are more prone to forgetting) rather than gist information, which is easier to remember over the long run (Brainerd & Reyna, 2004). Therefore, when an interviewer suggests a fact that children haven't encoded or can't recall (for example, "The man who touched your sister had a scar on his face, didn't he?"), younger children, who are especially motivated to recall details, may answer yes and remain convinced that this is what they really saw.

Implications for Legal Testimony

Although most states rarely ask children age 5 or under to testify in court, 6- to 10-year-olds are often called as witnesses. What steps might legal practitioners take to help ensure that testimony provided by child witnesses is accurate and not tainted by false memories?

Judging from the research on children's eyewitness memory, the most important step might be to place sensible limitations on the ways children are interviewed so as to lessen the likelihood of suggestibility. This can be accomplished by asking questions in nonleading ways, by limiting the number of times children are interviewed, and by cautioning children that it is better to say "I don't remember" than it is to guess or to go along with what an interviewer is implying (Poole & Lamb, 1998). Remaining friendly and patient with a child, rather than stern and adversarial, also seems to lessen the probability that children will report inaccurate details or construct false memories. Children who are victims of abuse who are interviewed following these general guidelines tend to report more accurate and less inaccurate information than when these procedures are not followed (Pipe et al., 2004). Table 8.2 presents the recommended sequences of phases for interviewing potential child-abuse victims, from the National Institute of Child Health and Human Development (NICHD) guidelines (adapted from Poole & Lamb, 1998).

Other procedures have been used to spare children the traumas of having to face an abusive parent in court or to answer pointed questions about uncomfortable issues, such as sexual abuse, that they may not understand and can easily misreport. For example, young children are sometimes asked to act out with dolls what they have experienced, or to answer questions about sensitive issues posed by a puppet with whom they feel more comfortable. However, these methods are controversial because they may not improve the accuracy of children's testimony (Greenhoot et al., 1999) and can even induce some young witnesses to imply the occurrence of inappropriate physical and sexual contact that never happened (Bruck et al., 1995). Other children are spared the discomfort of facing family members in the emotionally charged atmosphere of the courtroom by testifying on videotape, which is later entered as evidence during the trial. Although this procedure can lessen children's emotional concerns (that is anxiety, fear of punishment)

TABLE 8.2 Sequence of phases for interviewing children, as recommended by the NICHD guidelines

Introduction of parties and their roles
The "truth and lie ceremony" (warning the child of the necessity to tell the truth)
Rapport building
Description of a recent salient event
First narrative account of the allegation
Narrative accounts of the last incident (if the child reports multiple incidents)
Cue question (for example, "You said something about a barn. Tell me about that.")
Paired direct-open questions about the last incident
Narrative account of first incident
Cue questions
Paired direct-open questions about the first incident
Narrative accounts of another incident that the child remembers
Cue questions
Paired direct-open questions about this incident
If necessary, leading questions about forensically important details not mentioned by the child
Invitation for any other information the child wants to mention
Return to neutral topic

Source: Adapted from Poole & Lamb, 1998, pp. 98–99.

rehearsal
a strategy for remembering that involves repeating the items one is trying to retain.

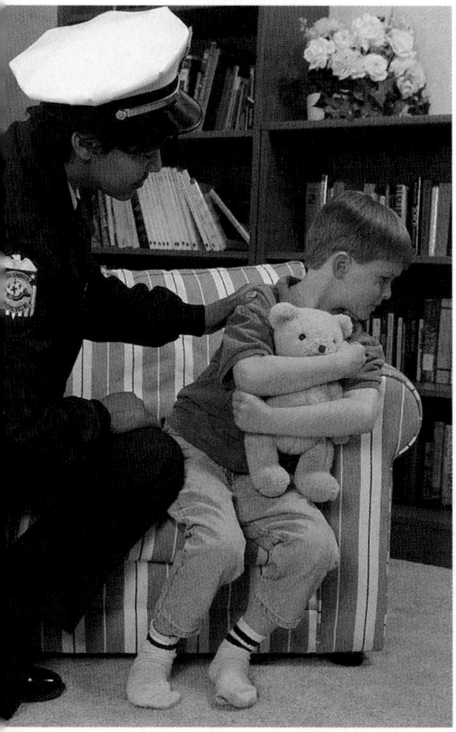
Mark C. Burnett/Photo Researchers, Inc.

Child witnesses are susceptible to reporting false memories. To guard against this possibility, adults must be patient and supportive and must avoid asking leading questions when possible.

and increase reporting accuracy, it is important that the interrogators be impartial and question children in nonleading ways that are unlikely to promote false memories (Bruck, Ceci, & Hembrooke, 1998).

The Development of Memory Strategies

We discussed earlier in this chapter how deliberately implemented *strategies* play an important role in information-processing accounts of children's cognitive development. Although strategies have been examined for a broad range of topics and contents, they have been the focus of extensive research in the area of memory development. Researchers have studied a variety of memory strategies, and, not surprisingly, they find that the number of such strategies and their effectiveness increase with age (Bjorklund & Douglas, 1997). However, as is the case with cognitive strategies in general (Siegler, 1996), children at any age use a variety of different strategies, although the sophistication of the "average" strategy that children use increases with age (Coyle & Bjorklund, 1997). In the following sections, we discuss research on the development of several memory strategies, or *mnemonics,* and look at the role that metamemory and knowledge have on memory strategies and memory development.

Rehearsal

One very simple yet effective strategy that people use to retain new information is **rehearsal**—repeating something until we think we will remember it. When instructed to try to remember a group of toys they have been shown, 3- to 4-year-olds look very carefully at the objects and often label them (once); but they rarely rehearse (Baker-Ward, Ornstein, & Holden, 1984; Oyen & Bebko, 1996). In contrast, 7- to 10-year-olds rehearse more efficiently than younger children do, and the more they rehearse, the more they remember (Flavell, Beach, & Chinsky, 1966). Older children also rehearse *differently* than

Playing strategy games with a more competent opponent often contributes more to the development of effective memory skills than learning the skills yourself.

younger children. If asked to recall a list of words presented one at a time, 5- to 8-year-olds usually rehearse each word in just that way—one at a time. Twelve-year-olds, by comparison, are more likely to use *active,* or *cumulative rehearsal,* repeating several earlier items as they rehearse each successive word. For example, when attempting to remember a list of words, children may say the most recent word on the list ("table") and then repeat it several times with earlier words on the list (for example, "table, lion, yard, table, yard, lion"). As a result, they remember more words than children who rehearse just one item at a time (Guttentag, Ornstein, & Siemans, 1987; Ornstein, Naus, & Liberty, 1975). As with most strategies, young children can be trained to use sophisticated cumulative rehearsal, and as a result, improve their performance (Cox et al., 1989), although the levels of recall are rarely as high as those shown by older children.

Why don't young children rehearse more efficiently? Possibly because their attempts to execute the more complex strategy require so much of their limited working-memory capacity that they are unable to retrieve enough information to form useful clusters. A study by Peter Ornstein and his associates (1985) supports this interpretation. The researchers tried to teach 7-year-olds to use the "clustering" rehearsal strategy and found that the children did so only if the stimulus cards (with the words written on them) remained visible. So when these younger children were able to form item clusters without having to expend mental effort retrieving the items, they could execute the complex rehearsal strategy. By contrast, 12-year-olds relied on the "clustering" strategy regardless of whether earlier items were visually displayed. Apparently, this efficient rehearsal technique has become so automatized for most 12-year-olds that they implement it almost effortlessly, thus leaving themselves ample space in working memory for retrieving items to rehearse.

Organization

Although rehearsal can be a very effective strategy, in one sense, it's a rather unimaginative one. If someone merely repeats the names of to-be-remembered items, he or she may not notice certain meaningful relations among the items that might make them easier to remember. A better strategy in many cases may be **organization.** Consider the following example:

organization
a strategy for remembering that involves grouping or classifying stimuli into meaningful (or manageable) clusters that are easier to retain.

List 1: boat, match, nail, coat, grass, nose, pencil, dog, cup, flower
List 2: knife, shirt, car, fork, boat, pants, sock, truck, spoon, plate

Although these 10-item lists should be equally difficult to recall if one simply rehearses them, the second list is actually much easier for most people. The reason is that its items can be grouped into three semantically distinct categories (eating utensils, clothes, and vehicles) that can serve as cues for storage and retrieval. Until about age 9 to 10, children are not usually any better at recalling items that can be *semantically organized* (such as List 2) than those that are difficult to categorize (such as List 1) (Hasselhorn, 1992). This finding suggests that young children make few attempts to organize information for later recall.

Young children can be easily trained to use an organizational strategy, however, when given explicit instructions to group, or sort, related items together during study (for example, "Put the pictures that are the same type of thing, or are in the same category together") and to recall items by category (for example, "When you remember the pictures, remember the ones from the same category together") (Black & Rollins, 1982; Lange & Pierce, 1992). Thus, they show a *production deficiency,* as we discussed earlier, indicating that young children are capable of organizing information for recall, but they generally fail to do so spontaneously. And, as with rehearsal, training children to use an organizational strategy rarely eliminates age differences, and, under most conditions, they fail to generalize the strategy to new situations or new sets of materials (Cox & Waters, 1986).

Retrieval Processes

retrieval
class of strategies aimed at getting information out of the long-term store.

free recall
a recollection that is not prompted by specific cues or prompts.

cued recall
a recollection that is prompted by a cue associated with the setting in which the recalled event originally occurred.

Getting information into your long-term store won't do much good unless you can get that information *out,* or **retrieve** it. Young children are notoriously bad at retrieving information on their own. This is where the distinction between **free recall** and **cued recall** becomes important. In free recall, children are given a general prompt for information, such as, "Tell me what happened at school today." When these kinds of general prompts are provided, young children have a difficult time retrieving much information (Kobasigawa, 1974; Schneider & Bjorklund, 1998). However, if more focused cued-recall questions are asked, prompting younger children to retrieve more specific information, they often remember things rather well. One 5-year-old boy who had spent the afternoon with his grandparents seeing his first play, *Little Shop of Horrors,* was asked by his mother, "Well, how was your afternoon?" The child replied, "OK." The mother persisted with a second general prompt: "Well, did you have a good time?" The child said, "Yeah." However, when cued by his grandmother to "tell about Audrey II, the plant," he provided extensive details, telling how the plant ate some of the main characters, talked, and sang, and how it took three people underneath it to make it move. The child had a wealth of information, but it could only be retrieved when specific cues were provided.

Young children can be instructed in the use of rehearsal, organization, and retrieval strategies, and their memory performance typically increases (Bjorklund & Douglas, 1997). However, when given the opportunity to use their newly learned strategy on a new set of materials, children frequently revert back to their nonstrategic ways. Why do they fail to make good use of a strategy they have just used successfully? One gets the feeling that younger children simply know less about memory aids and the circumstances under which it is appropriate to use them. They also know less in general than older children do, and their limited knowledge may hinder their attempts to categorize or elaborate on materials they are trying to remember. Let's see what researchers have learned in attempting to evaluate these hypotheses.

Metamemory and Memory Performance

metamemory
one's knowledge about memory and memory processes.

Earlier, we used the term *metacognition* to refer to knowledge of the workings of one's mind, including one's mental strong and weak points. One important aspect of metacognition is **metamemory**—one's knowledge of memory and memory processes. Children display metamemory if they recognize, for example, that there are limits to what they can remember; that some things are easier to remember than others; or that certain strategies are more effective than others at helping them to remember (Schneider & Bjorklund, 1998, 2003).

How do we know what children know about their memories? One straightforward way is simply to ask them. Interview studies of this kind reveal that even 3- and 4-year-olds have some idea that the mind has a limited capacity and that some materials will be easier to learn and retain than others (O'Sullivan, 1997). For example, preschoolers realize that remembering many items is more difficult than remembering a few (Yussen & Bird, 1979) and that the longer they study materials the more they are likely to retain (Kreutzer, Leonard, & Flavell, 1975). Yet they usually overestimate how much they will remember and know very little about forgetting, even saying that it is just as easy to remember something (like a phone number) over a long period of time as over a short period (Kreutzer, Leonard, & Flavell, 1975). It is almost as if preschool children view information they have retained as a "mental copy" of reality that is filed away in one of the mind's drawers and will be available for use whenever they need it.

Knowledge about memory increases substantially between ages 4 and 12 as children come to regard the mind as an active, constructive agent that stores only interpretations

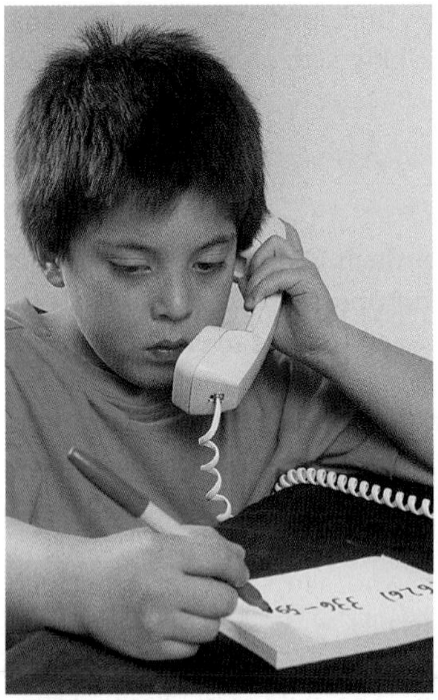

Metamemory improves dramatically in middle childhood. This 8-year-old is now aware that writing down a phone number is an effective strategy to ensure that he retains this information.

(rather than copies) of reality. Many 5-year-olds, for example, now know that items such as phone numbers are quickly forgotten unless they write them down, thus displaying an awareness that external cues can help them to remember (Kreutzer, Leonard, & Flavell, 1975). Yet knowledge about memory strategies develops very gradually. Children younger than 7 are often unaware that strategies such as rehearsal and organization may be useful to them (Justice et al., 1997); and even if they realize that related items are easier to remember than unrelated items, they often cannot say why this is so (O'Sullivan, 1996). And although 7- and 9-year-olds now realize that rehearsing and categorizing are more effective strategies than merely looking at items or labeling them once, not until age 11 or older do children recognize that organization is more effective than rehearsal (Justice et al., 1997).

Does a person's metamemory influence how well he or she will perform on memory tasks? The evidence is mixed. Some studies report only low to moderate positive correlations between memory and metamemory, implying that good metamemory is not always necessary for good recall (see Cavanaugh & Perlmutter, 1982). Nevertheless, studies that have trained children to use memory strategies are often more successful when training includes a metamemory component such as making children aware that being strategic has improved their memory performance (Ghatala et al., 1986).

So children's understanding of how or why memory strategies work seems to be the best metacognitive predictor of their use of these techniques. Indeed, the finding that measures of metamemory and memory are often more highly correlated among children 10 years and older (DeMarie & Ferron, 2003; Schneider & Pressley, 1997) undoubtedly reflects the fact that older children have had more time to discover why various memory strategies make remembering easier.

Knowledge Base and Memory Development

As we noted earlier, children who are experts in a particular domain, such as chess, have longer memory spans when tested on information from their area of expertise (Chi, 1978). Consider an implication of this finding. Because older children generally know more about the world than younger ones do, they are relative experts on most topics. Thus age differences in recall memory could be due as much to increases in children's knowledge base as to increases in their use of strategies (Bjorklund, 1987; Schneider & Bjorklund, 2003).

Consider what David and Barbara Bjorklund (1985) found when testing grade-school children's memory for one area in which children have some considerable expertise: the identities of their classmates. Some students were given a specific strategy for performing this task (recall names row by row) whereas others were left to their own devices. Nearly all the children using the efficient row-by-row strategy listed the names they recalled in perfect row-by-row order, yet they left out (forgot) just as many classmates as did children using other schemes, even those who professed to use no strategy at all. In other words, use of the row-by-row strategy did not gain these children anything in the way of greater memory performance, presumably because they were all experts when it came to their current classmates, making the row-by-row strategy unnecessary.

This is not to say that strategy use is unimportant to knowledgeable individuals. In their own areas of expertise, whether the topic is math, chess, dinosaurs, or soccer, children seem to develop highly specialized strategies for processing information that make learning and remembering new information about that topic much easier (Bjorklund, 1987; Hasselhorn, 1995). Think about the difference between reading about a topic that you already know well and reading about an unfamiliar topic. In the first case you can process the information quickly by linking it to existing knowledge. That is, you already have a scheme for organizing or elaborating new information. However, learning and retaining information about an unfamiliar topic is much more effortful because you have no existing conceptual pegs to hang it on.

Just how important is one's knowledge base to memory performance? In one study conducted in Germany, third-, fifth-, and seventh-grade soccer experts' and nonexperts' ability to recall information about a soccer-related story was assessed (Schneider, Korkel, & Weinert, 1989). Schneider and his colleagues reported that children's recall of the story was influenced more by their knowledge about soccer than by their general intellectual

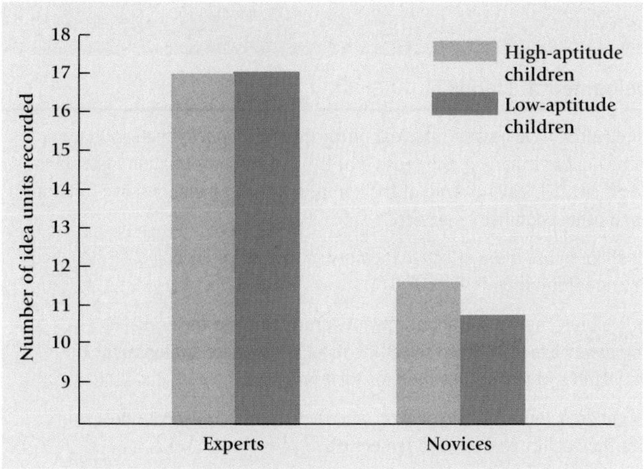

Figure 8.8 Number of idea units remembered about a soccer story for high-aptitude and low-aptitude soccer experts and soccer novices. In this case, being an expert eliminated any effect of academic aptitude (IQ) on performance. *Adapted from data presented in Schneider, Körkel, & Weinert, 1989.*

aptitude! As we see in Figure 8.8, experts recalled more than novices, even when the experts were of low general aptitude and the novices were high in general mental ability. Although low-ability experts do not always outperform high-ability novices on all tasks, experts generally recall far more new information about their area of expertise than do novices of the same intellectual level (Schneider, Bjorklund, & Maier-Brückner, 1996).

In sum, knowledge is power, and the more one knows about a topic, the more one can learn and remember. Detailed general knowledge may result in improved memory performance because the better established the information is in one's mind, the more easily it can be activated, or brought to consciousness (Bjorklund, 1987; Kee, 1994). Because older children usually know more than younger children do about most subjects, they expend less mental effort to activate what they know, leaving them with more mental capacity to encode, classify, and execute other cognitive operations on the new material they encounter.

Culture and Memory Strategies

Cultures clearly differ in the extent to which they support and encourage particular memory strategies (Kurtz, 1990; Mistry, 1997). Rehearsal and organization, for example, are especially helpful to children from industrialized societies, whose school activities involve a great deal of rote memorization and list learning. Yet these same strategies may not be so useful to unschooled children from nonindustrialized societies, whose most important memory tasks might involve recalling the location of objects (water, game animals) in a natural setting or remembering instructions passed along in the context of proverbs or stories. In list-learning experiments Western children rely heavily on strategies acquired at school and clearly outperform their unschooled peers from nonindustrialized societies (Cole & Scribner, 1977; Rogoff & Waddell, 1982). Yet their superior performance does not extend to other kinds of memory tasks. Unschooled Australian aboriginal children, for example, are better than their Anglo Australian peers at remembering the location of objects in natural settings (Kearins, 1981), and African adolescents display better recall for orally transmitted stories than American adolescents (Dube, 1982). In fact, Western children actually remember less if they try to rehearse or to organize information in these latter kinds of memory tasks (Rogoff, 1990).

These findings make perfectly good sense when viewed through the lens of Vygotsky's sociocultural theory. Cognitive development always occurs within a particular cultural context, which not only defines the kinds of problems that children must solve but also dictates the strategies (or tools of intellectual adaptation) that enable them to master these challenges.

Summing Up

How might we briefly summarize the ground we have covered? One way is to review Table 8.3, which describes four general conclusions about the development of strategic memory that have each gained widespread support.

Let's also note that these four aspects of development interact with each other rather than developing independently. For example, automation of some processes, such as "just knowing" how much 5 plus 6 equals, may leave the child with enough working memory capacity to use effective memory strategies that were just too mentally demanding earlier in childhood (Case, 1992; Kee, 1994). Or a child's expanding knowledge base may permit faster information processing and suggest ways that information can be categorized and elaborated (Bjorklund, 1987). So there is no one best explanation for the growth of memory skills. All the developments that we have discussed contribute in important ways to the dramatic improvements that occur in children's strategic memory.

TABLE 8.3 Four Major Contributors to the Development of Learning and Memory

Contributor	Developmental trends
1. *Working memory capacity*	Older children have greater information-processing *capacity* than younger children do, particularly in the sense that they process information faster (and more efficiently), leaving more of their limited working memory space for storage and other cognitive processes.
2. *Memory strategies*	Older children use more effective *memory strategies* for encoding, storing, and retrieving information.
3. *Metamemory*	Older children know more about memory processes, and their greater *metamemory* allows them to select the most appropriate strategies for the task at hand and to carefully monitor their progress.
4. *Knowledge base*	Older children know more in general, and their greater *knowledge base* improves their ability to learn and remember.

CONCEPT CHECK 8.3 Understanding Memory Development

Check your understanding of memory development by answering the following questions. Answers appear in the Appendix.

Multiple Choice: Select the best alternative for each question.

_____ 1. Research on event memory has identified parents as a contributor to children's memory development. Which of the following is *not* one of the ways parents contribute to their children's developing ability to recall events?
a. Parents teach their children specific memory strategies, such as organization and rehearsal.
b. Parents ask many questions, directing their children to form narratives.
c. Parents show children the directions conversations should go and how to construct narratives.
d. Parents provide cues to help their children remember.

_____ 2. Recalling items from the same category together in a free-recall task has been referred to as
a. rehearsal
b. elaboration
c. clustering (organization)
d. selective combination

_____ 3. Monica was telling her friend that she can remember *nothing* before the age of 4. Monica's inability to recall events from early in her life reflects
a. script-based narratives
b. infantile amnesia
c. poor metamemory
d. inefficient mnemonics

Matching: Match the following concepts with their definitions.

a. autobiographical memory
b. metamemory
c. script
d. organization
e. retrieval
f. mnemonics

4. _______ A strategy for remembering that involves grouping or classifying stimuli into meaningful (or manageable) clusters that are easier to retain.
5. _______ A general representation of the typical sequencing of events (i.e., what occurs and when) in some familiar context.
6. _______ Effortful techniques used to improve memory, including rehearsal, organization, and elaboration.
7. _______ Memory for important experiences or events that have happened to us.
8. _______ One's knowledge about memory and memory processes.
9. _______ Class of strategies aimed at getting information out of the long-term store.

Essays: Provide a detailed answer to the following questions.

10. Discuss the development of memory in infancy. What are the ways in which memory can be tested in preverbal infants? How long do those memories last?

11. What are the best techniques for interviewing children who may have been victims or witnesses of a crime? How reliable are children as eyewitnesses?

Analogical Reasoning

reasoning
a particular type of problem solving that involves making inferences.

analogical reasoning
reasoning that involves using something one knows already to help reason about something not known yet.

Reasoning is a special type of problem solving, one that usually requires that one make an *inference.* That is, to reason, one must go beyond the information given. It is not enough just to figure out the rules associated with some game. In reasoning one must take the evidence presented and arrive at a *new conclusion* based on that evidence. The result is often new knowledge (DeLoache, Miller, & Pierroutsakos, 1998).

Perhaps the type of reasoning that people are most familiar with is **analogical reasoning.** Analogical reasoning involves using something you already know to help you understand something you don't know yet. Classic analogical reasoning problems are stated "A is to B as C is to ______." For example, *dog* (A) is to *puppy* (B) as *cat* (C) is to ?. The answer here, of course, is *kitten.* By knowing the relation between the first two elements in the problem (a *puppy* is a baby *dog*), one can use that knowledge to complete the analogy for the new item (*cat*). Analogies are thus based on *similarity relations.* One must understand the similarity between dogs and cats and puppies and kittens if one is to solve the analogy.

Analogical reasoning is a tremendously important ability that can help a person to quickly acquire new knowledge as long as he or she understands the base relation and can apply it appropriately to new contexts. You can probably remember examples from your own education in which analogies were used to help you learn or solve problems. I can remember achieving a better understanding of the configurations of molecular components in chemistry by comparing them with interplanetary bodies (a sun, planets, and comets). Can young children reason by analogy? If so, can they use these skills to infer rules that they can use to solve novel problems?

Analogical reasoning is often assessed on intelligence tests, and gifted children show a sizable advantage over their normal peers in reasoning by analogy (Muir-Broaddus, 1995). This suggests to some researchers that analogical reasoning is a complex skill that is not well developed before adolescence (Inhelder & Piaget, 1958). Others, however, have proposed that analogical thinking serves as the basis for many other reasoning and problem-solving skills and might be present at birth (Goswami, 1996, 2003)!

How can there be such divergence of opinion about when analogical reasoning emerges? Part of the problem lies in the nature of the problems children are asked to solve. In cases when successful problem solving is not seen until late childhood or adolescence, the problems often involve objects or concepts with which children are unfamiliar. Perhaps more than any other factor, knowledge about the objects and relations among objects is critical in determining whether a child will solve or fail to solve a problem. Other factors also contribute to a child's success on analogical-reasoning problems, including memory for the premises and metacognitive knowledge (DeLoache, Miller, & Pierroutsakos, 1998; Goswami, 2003). In the following sections we review age trends in children's ability to solve analogical-reasoning problems and look at some of the factors that contribute to these cognitive developments.

Analogical Reasoning in Young Children

relational primacy hypothesis
the hypothesis that analogical reasoning is available in infancy.

Counter to Piaget's account of analogical reasoning, Usha Goswami (1996) proposed the **relational primacy hypothesis,** suggesting that analogical reasoning is available early in infancy. In one of the few experiments to assess analogical reasoning in infancy, Zhe Chen, Rebecca Sanchez, and Tammy Campbell (1997) tested 1-year-old infants (Experiment 1). The basic task involved placing a desirable toy out of reach of the infants, with a barrier between the babies and the toy. Two strings, one attached to the toy and one not, were also out of the infants' reach, but each string was on a cloth that *was* within reach. To get the toy, the infants had to pull the cloth toward them and then pull the string attached to the toy. There were three similar tasks, although the toy, the barrier, and the

Figure 8.9 The configuration of the three problems 1-year-olds solved to test their reasoning by analogy. *From Z. Chen, R. P. Sanchez, & T. Campbell (1997), Beyond to within their grasp: The rudiment of analogical problem solving in 10- and 13-month-olds.* Developmental Psychology, *33, 790–801. Copyright © 1997 by the American Psychological Association. Reprinted with permission.*

color of the cloth varied across the three tasks. These are illustrated in Figure 8.9. If infants did not solve the problem after 100 seconds, their parents modeled the correct solution for them. The primary research question was: After solving an initial problem, either with or without parental modeling, would the infants see the similarity with the later problems and be more apt to solve them? That is, would infants use analogical reasoning?

Few infants solved the first problem spontaneously (most required modeling by a parent). However, the percentage of infants solving the problems increased from 29 percent for the first problem, to 43 percent for the second, to 67 percent for the third.

So it seems that 1-year-olds are able to use analogical reasoning to solve simple problems. However, these perceptual analogies are very different from the classic problems used in research: Often the similarity between objects is *relational* rather than *perceptual*. Consider a study by Usha Goswami and Ann Brown (1990), who showed 4-, 5-, and 9-year-old children sets of pictures of the "A as to B as C is to ______" type. Children were given four alternatives and had to choose which of the four best completed the analogy. An example of a problem used in this study is shown in Figure 8.10. In this problem children must discover the relation between bird and nest (a bird lives in a nest) and make the analogous inference for *dog* (that is, dog house). Children of all ages performed far better than expected by chance (59 percent, 66 percent, and 94 percent correct for the 4-, 5-, and 9-year-olds, respectively, with chance = 25 percent). Note that children are not solving the problem based on *perceptual similarity.* The bird and dog look nothing alike, nor do the nest and the dog house. To solve this problem, they must do so on the basis of *relational similarity*—the relation between the A and B terms (bird and nest) is used to find the best match for the C term (dog). This is clearly a more advanced form of analogical reasoning than that demonstrated by the 1-year-old infants in the study by Chen and his colleagues (1997).

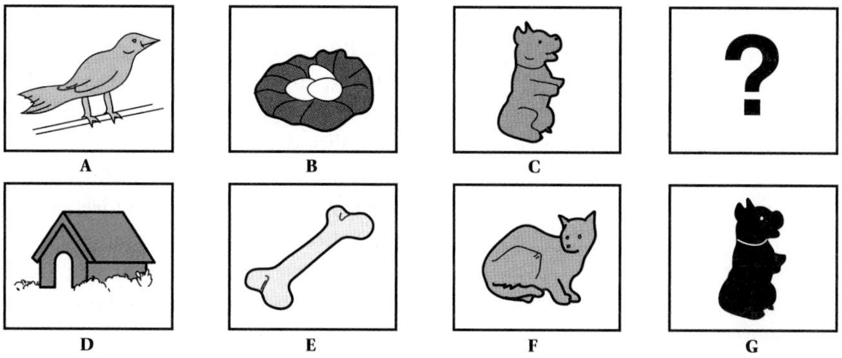

Figure 8.10 Example of problem used in Goswami & Brown. Children must select from set of pictures in bottom row (pictures D through G) the one that best completes the visual analogy on the top row (the correct answer is D). *From U. Goswami & A. L. Brown (1990). Higher-order structure and relational reasoning: Contrasting analogical and thematic relations.* Cognition, *36, 207–226. Reprinted by permission of Elsevier Science Ltd.*

The Role of Knowledge in Children's Analogical Reasoning

One factor that affects whether children will use relational similarity to solve an analogical-reasoning problem is their knowledge, or familiarity, with the underlying relations used to make the analogy. Remember, the function of analogical reasoning is to use something you *know* to help you understand something you *don't* know. From this perspective, analogical reasoning can only make sense if a child is familiar with the base relation. You might get a better understanding of the human nervous system, for example, if you see it as analogous to electrical circuits. But if you know nothing about electrical circuits, it won't help you understand the nervous system at all, no matter how well developed your analogical reasoning abilities are.

The role of familiarity is illustrated in a study by Goswami (1995) that used a familiar children's story, *Goldilocks and the Three Bears* ("The Daddy Bear has all the big things, the Mummy Bear has all the medium-sized things, and the Baby Bear has all the tiny things") to help children make *transitive mappings.* A transitive relation involves relations among at least three objects. If object A is longer than object B, and object B is longer than object C, then object A must be longer than object C (that is, $A > B > C$). Can young children use the transitive relation on one dimension (for example, Daddy Bear, Mummy Bear, and Baby Bear) as an analogy for mapping transitive relations on another dimension, such as size or loudness, for instance?

In Goswami's (1995) study, 3- and 4-year-old children were asked to use the relation in the Goldilocks story (Daddy Bear > Mummy Bear > Baby Bear) to classify objects that differed in quantity (a lot versus a medium amount versus a little pizza, candy, or lemonade), or to rank order (three levels) certain phenomena on the basis of loudness (of footsteps), pitch (of voices), temperature (of porridge), saltiness (of porridge), width (of beds), or height (of mirrors). Four-year-olds generally performed well on all these tasks, using the Three Bears analogy to map onto other dimensions. Three-year-olds did less well although they performed above chance levels on most tasks.

Goswami's findings are really quite remarkable. Piaget claimed that children cannot make transitive inferences until age 6 to 7, when they enter his concrete-operational stage of cognitive development. Yet Goswami's 3- and 4-year-olds were quite capable of transitivity by analogy, *as long as the basis for the analogy* (in this case, the Three Bears story) *was familiar to them.*

The Role of Metacognition in Children's Analogical Reasoning

To what extent is *explicit* awareness of the relations between entities on analogical reasoning tasks important in solving problems? Can children think analogically but be unable to articulate what they are doing? Might such knowledge be *implicit,* and unavailable to consciousness? It certainly appears that the knowledge that the infants in the study by Chen and his colleagues (1997) had must have been implicit. These preverbal children's metacognitive understanding of the problem and their solutions to them was likely nonexistent. How important is explicit, metacognitive knowledge for analogical reasoning during childhood?

Apparently, metacognitive knowledge is very important. Successful training of analogical reasoning in preschool children is best accomplished when children receive explicit instruction about the rationale that underlies the analogy (Brown & Kane, 1988). Consider a program of research by Ann Brown and her associates (Brown & Kane, 1988; Brown, Kane, & Long, 1989) who assessed preschool children's **learning to learn** by analogy.

learning to learn
improvements in performance on novel problems as a result of acquiring a new rule or strategy from the earlier solution of similar problems.

In Brown and Kane's studies, preschool children were given a series of problems in which they had to move some gumballs in one bowl on a table to another out-of-reach bowl, without leaving their chairs. They had various objects available to them that they could use to solve the problem, including scissors, an aluminum cane, tape, string, and a sheet of paper. Before solving the problem, children heard a story about a genie who had a similar problem of moving some jewels from one bottle within his reach to another bottle out of his reach. If children in the experimental condition did not "solve" the problem, they were told that the genie could roll his carpet into a tube that could be used to transport the jewels. They were then given a similar problem (the Easter Bunny needing to transport eggs by using a rolled-up blanket), and then a third (a farmer transporting cherries using a rolled-up rug). Children who received this series of problems, and who were made aware of the solution to the first problem when they failed, showed a large learning-to-learn effect. For the "rolling" solution, 46 percent of the children used analogical reasoning to solve the second problem, and 98 percent of the children did so for the third task. In contrast, control children who received the three sets of rolling problems but who did not get the hints performed far worse: only 20 percent solved the first novel problem and 30 percent solved the second. So it seems that metacognitive awareness really does improve analogical problem solving. After solving the first two rolling problems, one 4-year-old commented at the beginning of the third problem: "And all you need to do is get this thing rolled up? I betcha!" Brown and Kane (1988) commented that the "aware" children had developed a mind-set to look for analogies, expecting to extract some general rule to solve problems and to be able to use knowledge they acquired in new contexts.

In sum, analogical reasoning, which seems to be present in a simple implicit form *in infancy,* gradually develops and becomes more explicit throughout childhood. This is an important finding that has clear educational implications: Even preschool children can use analogies to acquire new information and become better problem solvers as long as they (1) understand the base relation from which inferences might be drawn, and (2) are (or are made) aware of the value of reasoning by analogy.

Development of Arithmetic Skills

Another kind of reasoning that is heavily emphasized and almost essential to children growing up in today's information-age societies is quantitative, or arithmetic, reasoning. When are human beings first capable of processing quantitative information?

Remarkable as it may seem, this may be a very early-developing ability (Geary, 1995). Very young infants can easily discriminate visual displays containing four or fewer objects, and by 5 months they can learn that a particular numerical cue (for example, two objects rather than one or three) presented to their left means that an interesting stimulus will soon appear to their right (Canfield & Smith, 1996). We also saw in Chapter 7 how 5-month-olds display a rudimentary understanding of simple addition and subtraction (Wynn, 1992). By 16 to 18 months toddlers have even acquired a sense of ordinal relationships, recognizing, for example, that three objects are more than two (Strauss & Curtis, 1981). These early understandings, coupled with the acquisition and use of such quantitative labels as *big, lots, small,* and *little,* reveal that toddlers are quite well prepared for such feats as learning to count and to think about quantities.

Counting and Arithmetic Strategies

Elizabeth Crews

Counting on one's fingers is an early strategy that children use to solve arithmetic problems, one that is used less frequently as they develop more mathematical knowledge.

Counting normally begins shortly after children begin to talk. However, early counting strategies are very imprecise, often consisting of no more than uttering a few number words (for example, "one, three, four, six") while pointing to objects that a companion has counted (Fuson, 1988). By age 3 to 4 most children can count accurately, establishing a one-to-one correspondence between number words and the items they represent (Gallistel & Gelman, 1992). And by age 4½ to 5, most children have acquired the principle of **cardinality**—the knowledge that the last word in a counting sequence (e.g., "1, 2, 3, 4, 5") represents the number of items in a set (Bermejo, 1996). These developments in counting are especially important because they pave the way for the emergence of simple arithmetic strategies.

cardinality
principle specifying that the last number in a counting sequence specifies the number of items in a set.

Children's earliest arithmetic strategies are based on counting, at first out loud, and often using fingers or other props. The *sum* strategy we discussed earlier is perhaps the simplest method of adding numbers. Given the problem, "What is 2 + 3?," the child begins by counting out the first number ("1, 2") and then counts out the second, starting from the cardinal value of the first (". . . 3, 4, 5"). Although the sum strategy is quite accurate, it takes a lot of time to execute and is not very effective for problems where larger numbers (for example, 22 + 8) are involved.

More sophisticated addition strategies take shortcuts in counting. For example, a 6-year-old using the *min* strategy performs the minimum number of counts. Asked for the sum of 8 + 3, this child would start with the cardinal value of the larger number and count up from there (that is, "8 . . . 9, 10, 11"). Although preschoolers may use rules other than the sum and min strategies to add (and subtract) numbers, their approaches almost always involve counting by ones the concrete objects to be added or subtracted (Carpenter & Moser, 1982).

Development of Mental Arithmetic

At some point during the early grade-school years, children's solutions to simple arithmetic problems become covert. They no longer count objects on their fingers, but perform arithmetic operations mentally. The earliest mental arithmetic strategies may still involve counting, but the counting is now done "in their heads." However, the many experiences children have adding and subtracting numbers, coupled with knowledge about number systems that is often taught at school, soon permit grade-school children to use other, more efficient arithmetic strategies. For example, knowledge of the base-10 number system underlies *decomposition* strategies, in which children transform an original problem into two simpler problems. Given 13 + 3= ?, for example, a child might think "13 is 10 + 3; 3 + 3 = 6; 10 + 6 = 16 so the answer is 16." Initially, use of a decomposition strategy may be slower than the min strategy, particularly for simple problems where not many counts are involved. But as children become practiced at decomposing numbers into base-10 components, they solve problems faster by decomposition, particularly if they are working with larger numbers (for example, 26 + 17) for which counting strategies are laborious (Siegler, 1996). Finally, children come to solve many simple arithmetic problems by *fact retrieval*. They simply know the correct answer (that is, 8 + 6 is 14) and retrieve it from long-term memory.

Once children begin to perform arithmetic computations in their heads, it's more difficult for a researcher to know exactly what they are doing. However, it is possible to infer their arithmetic strategies from the time it takes them to arrive at a correct answer. If children are using the min strategy, for example, their reaction times for addition problems should increase as the size of the smaller of the two numbers (that is, the number of counts it requires) increases. If children are using fact retrieval, by contrast, they should answer very quickly, regardless of the numbers involved.

The arithmetic strategies children use increase in sophistication with age, but they do not follow a stagelike pattern. As we discussed earlier in this chapter when introducing Robert Siegler's (1996) *adaptive strategy choice model,* children have multiple strategies available to them that compete with one another for use. Thus, although preschool children rarely use fact retrieval, they do occasionally, particularly for simple problems such as those involving doubles ($2 + 2 = ?$) (Bjorklund & Rosenblum, 2001). Likewise, older children and adults typically use more sophisticated strategies such as fact retrieval to solve most problems, but will fall back to use counting strategies such as min on occasion (Bisanz & LeFevre, 1990).

Math Disabilities

Math is difficult for many children, with some displaying specific math disabilities. Math disabilities can be identified as early as kindergarten. Children with math disabilities tend to have several types of difficulties (Geary, 1993). First, they have poor *procedural skills* (Geary, Brown, & Samaranayake, 1991). For instance, young children display a poor knowledge of the rules of counting and they use a more immature mix of arithmetic strategies than normal children do. Second, math-disabled children show deficits in memory retrieval; they retrieve fewer facts from long-term memory (that is, they use fact retrieval less often), and when they do, they are often wrong (Jordan, Hanich, & Kaplan, 2003). Although these children often show substantial improvement in their procedural knowledge with time and practice, their problems with fact retrieval tend not to improve to the level of their age-mates as they get older (see Geary, 1993).

A factor likely related to math-disabled children's retrieval deficits is working-memory capacity. Researchers have repeatedly found that math-disabled children have smaller working-memory spans than nondisabled children (Geary et al., 2004; Passolunghi & Siegl, 2004). For example, David Geary and his colleagues (1991) reported that the working memory spans for math-disabled children (4.2 words) were about one word less than for nondisabled children (5.3 words). This deficit might be the result of faster decay of information (that is, the memory representations might disappear more quickly in working memory for math-disabled children), of slower counting speed, or of a slower domain-general speed-of-processing capacity (Bull & Johnston, 1997). Because these children make computation errors, they arrive at many incorrect answers, and these answers can become part of their long-term memory representations of arithmetic facts. Unfortunately, they are wrong.

Cultural Influences on Mathematics Performance

One of the major claims that Vygotsky made in his sociocultural theory was that cognitive development always occurs in a cultural context that influences the way one thinks and solves problems. Can this important principle possibly hold for a rule-bound domain such as arithmetic?

Arithmetic Competencies of Unschooled Children

Although children in most cultures learn to count and acquire some very simple arithmetic strategies during the preschool years, the computational procedures on which higher mathematics are based are typically taught at school. Does this imply that children who receive minimal or no schooling are hopelessly incompetent in math?

One might answer "yes" if math competencies are measured by the paper-and-pencil tests so often used in Western societies. However, these tests often badly underestimate the skills of unschooled children.

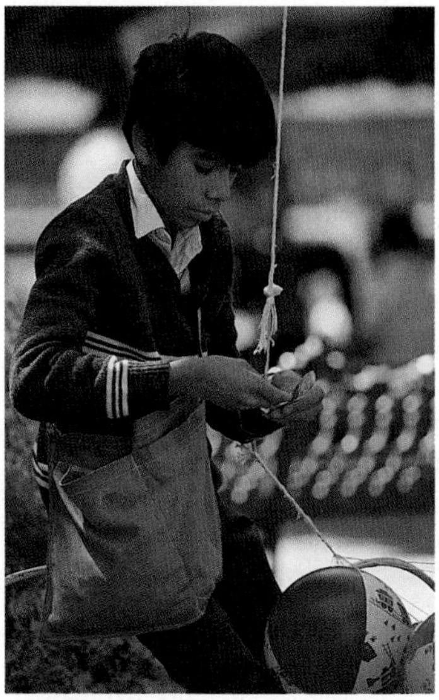
David Wells/The Image Works

Although unschooled street vendors may often fail at paper-and-pencil math problems, they display sophisticated arithmetic skills when making change during sales transactions.

T. N. Carraher and associates (1985), for example, examined the mathematical competencies of unschooled 9- and 15-year-old street vendors in Brazil. They found that problems embedded in real-life contexts (for example, "If a large coconut costs 76 cruzeiros, and a small one costs 50, how much do the two cost together?") were solved correctly 98 percent of the time. By contrast, the same problems presented in a standard, out-of-context way (that is, "How much is 76 + 50?") were answered correctly only 37 percent of the time. Street vendors can quickly and accurately add and subtract currency values in their heads, just as they must when conducting street transactions where mistakes can have economic consequences. In contrast, the same numerical problems presented in out-of-context paper-and-pencil formats have little practical application, and unschooled participants are apparently less motivated to expend the effort necessary to solve them. Other unschooled participants, such as bricklayers and lottery bookies, also develop flexible arithmetic competencies that they use with great skill in their own work (Schliemann, 1992).

Cultural Variations in Arithmetic Among Schooled Children

Much has been written, both in the popular and the scholarly presses, about the fact that East Asian youngsters from China, Taiwan, and Japan typically outperform American children in certain academic subjects, most notably mathematics. The reality is, American schoolchildren perform significantly more poorly in mathematics than children from East Asian cultures beginning in the first grade, with the magnitude of the cultural difference increasing with age (Baker, 1992; Stevenson & Lee, 1990).

In attempting to explain these findings, researchers quickly ruled out the possibility that East Asian students are inherently smarter than Americans; first-graders in the U.S., Taiwan, and Japan perform equally well on standardized intelligence tests (Stevenson et al., 1985). Yet East Asian first-graders already rely on a more sophisticated mix of basic arithmetic strategies than American first-graders do, including the relatively sophisticated (for first-graders) decomposition and fact retrieval strategies (Geary, Fan, & Bow-Thomas, 1992). And other research reveals that the math-strategy advantage that East Asian children display is already apparent during the *preschool* period (Geary et al., 1993).

A critic might say, so what? We are talking about the most basic of arithmetic strategies that American children clearly master by the end of elementary school. Yet David Geary and his colleagues have shown that the sophistication of early arithmetic strategies and speed of fact retrieval predicts later performance in more complex forms of mathematics (Geary & Burlingham-Dubre, 1989; Geary & Widaman, 1992). So if early mastery of basic skills promotes more complex mathematical competencies, it may not be surprising that East Asian students display a consistent mathematical advantage over their American peers at all levels of schooling.

Now the obvious question becomes: Why are young East Asians so advantaged in acquiring basic mathematical skills? Let's briefly consider some linguistic and instructional supports for acquiring mathematical concepts that are available to East Asian children but not to their American counterparts.

Linguistic supports. Basic differences in how the Chinese (and Japanese and Korean) versus the English language represents numbers seem to contribute to some of the early differences in arithmetic proficiency. Recall from Chapter 7 that the number words in Chinese for 11, 12, and 13 are translated as "ten-one," "ten-two," and "ten-three," which helps children learn to count sooner than American children, who must use the more idiosyncratic number words of "eleven," "twelve," and "thirteen" (Miller et al., 1995). The Chinese number-naming system also helps children to understand that the 1 in 13 has a place value of 10 (rather than 1). By contrast, English words for two-digit numbers in the teens are irregular and do not convey the idea of tens and ones. In one study, Korean second- and third-graders had an excellent understanding of the meaning of digits in multidigit numbers, knowing that the 1 in 186 stood for "hundreds" and the eight stands for "eight-tens." Consequently, they performed very well on three-digit addition and subtraction problems (for example, What is 142 + 318?), even though they had not yet received any formal instruction on adding or subtracting numbers this large (Fuson & Kwon, 1992).

Other research has suggested that language may also play a role in understanding more complicated arithmetic, specifically fractions. Irene Miura and her colleagues (1999) studied 6- and 7-year-old Croatian, Korean, and U.S. children's understanding of fractions and reported significantly greater understanding for the East Asian than for the Western children. They then looked at the way fractions are expressed in the Korean versus the English and Croatian languages. In Western languages the fraction ⅓ is expressed as "one third." In Korean, one third is spoken as *sam bun ui il,* which is literally translated as "of three parts, one." Miura and her colleagues argue that the intuitively clear way fractions are expressed in Korean helps children better understand the concept of the whole divided into parts and is primarily responsible for the early superiority of Korean children's understanding of fractions.

The finding that children's early arithmetic abilities differ as a function of their culture's language is consistent with Vygotsky's ideas about the importance of a culture's *tools of intellectual adaptation* for influencing thought. Cultures affect thinking not only in obvious ways, such as the provision of formal versus informal education, but also in less obvious ways, such as how the language describes and organizes important concepts.

Instructional supports. Several East Asian instructional practices support the rapid learning of math facts and computational procedures involved in multidigit addition and subtraction. East Asian students practice computational procedures more than American students do (Stevenson & Lee, 1990), and practice of this sort fosters the retrieval of math facts from memory (Geary et al., 1992). And the type of instruction provided seems to matter. For example, Asian teachers instructing students how to carry a sum from one column of a multidigit number to the next will say to "bring up" the sum instead of "carrying" it. The term bring up (rather than carry) may help children learning multidigit addition to remember that each digit to the left in a multidigit number is a base-10 increment of the cardinal value of that digit (that is, the 5 in 350 represents "50," rather than "5," and the 3 represents "300"). Furthermore, Asian math texts also help children to avoid confusing place values by having different color codes for the hundreds, tens, and ones columns of multidigit numbers (Fuson, 1992).

How much do these linguistic and instructional supports contribute to the superior math performance of East Asian students? They almost certainly matter, but they are hardly the sole contributors. Consider that Asian students have always had the linguistic advantages over their American counterparts; yet Americans who received their elementary school educations during the 1930s were quicker to acquire basic mathematical competencies than today's American students are, showing a proficiency for mathematics that rivals today's East Asian students (Geary et al., 1996). So differences in mathematical competencies between East Asian and American students seem to be a relatively recent phenomenon that undoubtedly reflects broader cultural differences in educational philosophies and supports for education and the differences in linguistic and instructional supports for mathematics learning that we have discussed here. Indeed,

Linguistic supports, instructional supports, and lots of practice help explain the high proficiency that East Asian students often display in mathematics.

CONCEPT CHECK 8.4 Understanding Children's Arithmetic Development

Check your understanding of the development of children's arithmetic abilities by answering the following questions. Answers appear in the Appendix.

Multiple Choice: Select the best alternative for each question.

_____ 1. According to the *min* model, children's reaction times to solve addition problems vary as a function of

a. retrieval of arithmetic facts
b. spreading activation
c. the second, smaller addend
d. knowledge base

_____ 2. Siegler and his colleagues have conducted a series of experiments to investigate the nature of arithmetic-strategy development. They concluded that

a. children move from the sum to the min to fact-retrieval strategies in a regular, stagelike progression
b. children's developmental progression through stages of arithmetic strategy usage follows steps in biological maturation
c. children's developmental progression in strategy usage does not follow a stagelike progression; rather, children of every age use a variety of arithmetic strategies
d. arithmetic strategy development is primarily a matter of replacing less sophisticated strategies with more efficient and mature strategies

Essays: Provide a detailed answer to the following questions.

3. Discuss the type of information-processing problems experienced by children with math disabilities.
4. Cross-cultural differences have been observed in children's mathematical abilities. Discuss differences both between children in schooled and nonschooled societies, and between children in different schooled societies. How might the language that children speak influence their mathematical performance?

we will see just how true this speculation is in Chapter 16, where we will examine the many roles that schooling plays in the social, emotional, and intellectual lives of developing children and adolescents.

Evaluating the Information-Processing Perspective

Today, the information-processing perspective has become the dominant approach to the study of children's intellectual development, and justifiably so. Simply stated, information-processing researchers have provided a reasonably detailed description of how such cognitive processes as attention, memory, and metacognition—processes that Piaget did not emphasize—change with age and influence children's thinking. Furthermore, the detailed examination of certain domain-specific academic skills that information-processing theorists have undertaken has led to important instructional changes that enhance scholastic performances.

Despite these obvious strengths, the information-processing approach has several drawbacks that render it incomplete as an explanation of cognitive development. Some of the stronger challenges have come from the developing field of cognitive neuroscience, which is concerned with identifying evolutionary and neurological contributors to intellectual growth. Research on the neural correlates of inhibition that we reviewed in the Box on p. 303 and the brain correlates of infant memory development (Bauer, 2004) are small steps in this direction. Other researchers are looking seriously at the relations between brain and cognitive development in infancy and childhood and developing new theories that integrate these different levels of organization (Byrnes & Fox, 1998; Johnson, 2000). In fact, James Byrnes and Nathan Fox (1998) propose that research in developmental cognitive neuroscience has placed us on the threshold of a new revolution, equivalent to the cognitive revolution of 50 years ago that replaced behavioral perspectives of how children learn and think.

Still other critics point out that information-processing theorists have paid little attention to important social and cultural influences on cognition that Vygotsky and others emphasized. And those who favor the elegant coherence of Piaget's stage model question what they see as the "fragmented" approach of information-processing theorists, who focus on specific cognitive processes and view development as the gradual acquisition of skills in many different domains. These critics contend that information-processing researchers have succeeded in breaking cognition into pieces, but haven't been able to put it back together into a broad, comprehensive theory of intellectual development. Although this criticism has some merit, information-processing theorists would reply by noting that it was the many problems with Piaget's broad-brush account of cognitive development that helped stimulate their work in the first place.

Even some of the central assumptions on which information-processing theory rests have been assailed in some quarters. For example, critics have argued that the classic mind–computer analogy badly underestimates the richness of human cognitive activity. After all, people can dream, speculate, create, and reflect on their own (and other people's) cognitive activities and mental states whereas computers most certainly cannot (Kuhn, 1992). Furthermore, the classic assumption that all cognitive activities take place in a single, limited-capacity working memory store has been challenged. Charles Brainerd and Johannas Kingma (1985), for example, proposed that working memory should be viewed as a series of independent stores, each with its own resources and each performing such specific operations as information encoding, information retrieval, and execution of strategies. Of course, we have already discussed another alternative to traditional information-processing models—fuzzy-trace theory—which claims that we process information at more than one level rather than merely making verbatim mental copies of what we experience.

In sum, the information-processing approach is itself a developing theory (or set of theories) that has greatly advanced our understanding of children's intellectual growth while experiencing some very real growing pains of its own. We like to think of this model as a necessary complement to, rather than a replacement for, Piaget's earlier framework. And our guess is that this new look at cognitive development will continue to evolve, aided by advances in cognitive neuroscience and other complementary perspectives (see Fischer & Bidell, 1998), eventually filling in many of the gaps that remain in its own framework and that of Piaget, and thereby contributing to a comprehensive theory of intellectual growth that retains the best features of several approaches.

Applying Developmental Themes to Information-Processing Perspectives

Let's turn now to a brief consideration of how an information-processing perspective relates to our four themes: the active child, nature and nurture interactions, quantitative and qualitative developmental changes, and the holistic nature of development.

The concept of an active child is not as obvious in an information-processing perspective as it was in Piaget's theory. Information-processing researchers often focus on limitations in the system that restrict how much information a child will encode, store, or retrieve. Children seem to play little active role in the capacity of their short-term store or the rate at which they process information. On the other hand, information-processing theorists have also focused on children's use of strategies—deliberately implemented, conscious, and goal-directed cognitive operations used to improve task performance. How children learn to exert intentional control over their own learning and thinking is a central issue in cognitive development, and information-processing research on strategies and metacognition clearly reflects children as active participants in their own learning, not the passive recipients of information that travels through their information-processing systems. Thus, we can see the information-processing perspective as embracing an active child model after all.

Our second theme concerns the interaction of nature and nurture in development. To what extent is children's cognition the result of biological processes that mature relatively independently of specific experience or, conversely, the product of input from the outside world? It may seem, for example, that talking about the hardware and software of information-processing systems implies a good deal of biological determinism: here is the system the child is born with and characteristics of this system will expand with age (short-term memory will increase, processing speed will be faster). From this view, experience plays only a minor role. (We know, of course, that even advocates of this viewpoint would believe that experience is necessary for the inherited system to develop properly.) But this interpretation of the development of information-processing systems is incomplete. Information-processing theorists also emphasize that experience plays a critical role in thinking and cognitive development. For example, many researchers have stressed the role of knowledge base as a principal *cause* of cognitive development. The more children know about any topic, the faster they can process that information, the more they can retain, and the more easily they can learn new information related to that topic. In sum, information-processing researchers may not make the nature-nurture relationships explicit in much of their writing, but they are modern theorists and recognize, at least implicitly, the complex relationship between nature and nurture which affects children's thinking across development.

We commented in the previous chapter that Piaget was the classic stage theorist, postulating *qualitative* changes in children's thinking over time. Information-processing theorists generally take the opposite position: most aspects of cognitive development vary *quantitatively* and continuously over time. With increasing age, children process information faster, they hold more items in their short-term stores, and possess more knowledge about the things they think about. These are all things that vary quantitatively. According to information-processing perspectives, any abrupt changes in how children think are caused by underlying quantitative and continuously changing operations, such as working memory or speed of processing. This doesn't mean that there is no room for a few qualitatively-based changes in cognition that can be explained in information-processing terms; but these are few in number. We expect that most researchers who would describe themselves as proponents of the information-process perspective believe that the most important changes in children's thinking are quantitative, not qualitative, in nature.

Finally, what do information-processing theorists have to say about the holistic nature of development? As with Piaget and Vygotsky's theories, information-processing theorists believe that the operations they are studying are used by children not only in researchers' laboratories, but also in the real world. Children with limited memory spans cannot be expected to keep track of complicated story plots involving many different characters, to remember the long list of chores their parents dictate to them, or to memorize the presidents of the United States. In fact, information-processing approaches probably have more to say about reasons why children succeed and fail in school (and ways to remediate poor academic performance) than any other perspective (see the Box on p. 332). And information-processing perspectives are not limited to cognition in the classroom, but also apply to social relations. Although the strategies children use to solve arithmetic problems are likely very different in nature to those they use to make friends, social behavior and its development can also be viewed through the lens of information processing theories (Dodge, 1986), as we will discover in detail in Chapter 12.

APPLYING RESEARCH TO YOUR LIFE

Some Educational Implications of Information-Processing Research

Piaget stressed that teachers should view children as naturally inquisitive beings who learn best by *constructing* and *discovering* knowledge from *moderately novel* aspects of experience—that is, from information that challenges their current understanding and forces them to reevaluate what they already know. Information-processing theorists can certainly agree with Piaget on this point. However, their own guidelines for effective instruction are much more explicit than Piaget's and come closer to the views of Lev Vygotsky (1978), implying that teachers (and parents or other more competent associates) should take a more *active, directive* role than Piaget had envisioned. The following six implications for instruction flow directly from the research we have reviewed on the development of strategic memory, attention, and problem solving.

1. *Analyze the requirements of problems that you present to your students.* Know what information must be encoded and what mental operations must be performed to arrive at a correct answer or to otherwise grasp the lesson to be learned. Without such knowledge, it may be difficult to tell why students are making errors or to help them overcome their mistakes.
2. *Reduce short-term memory demands to a bare minimum.* Problems that require young grade-school children to encode more than three or four bits of information are likely to overload their short-term storage capacity and prevent them from thinking logically about this input. The simplest possible version of a new problem or concept is what teachers should strive to present. If a problem involves several steps, students might be encouraged to break it down into parts (or subroutines). Once children grasp a concept and their information processing becomes more "automated," they will have the short-term storage capacity to succeed at more complex versions of these same problems (Case, 1992).
3. *Encourage children to "have fun" using their memories.* Strategic games such as 20 questions or concentration are not only enjoyable to grade-school children, but also help them to appreciate the advantages of being able to retain and to retrieve information for a meaningful purpose.
4. *Provide opportunities to learn effective memory strategies.* A teacher can do this by grouping materials into distinct categories as she talks about them or by giving children easily categorizable sets of items to sort and classify. Question-and-answer games of the form "Tell me why leopards, lions, and house cats are alike" or "How do dragonflies and hummingbirds differ from helicopters and missiles?" are challenging to young children and make them aware of conceptual similarities and differences on which organizational strategies depend.
5. *Provide opportunities for analogical reasoning.* Creative use of analogical puzzles and games encourages children to use what they know to reason and master novel challenges (Goswami, 1995). Proficiency at analogical reasoning may be particularly useful for helping children and adolescents to grasp unfamiliar or unobservable concepts. Inducing students to think about concrete models that they can see or easily imagine (for example, the arc of a spark across a spark plug, or the operation of a digital computer) should help those who are practiced at reasoning by analogy to grasp more abstract or less tangible phenomena (such as transmission of neural impulses across a synapse, or the workings of the human mind).
6. *Structure lessons so that children are likely to acquire metacognitive knowledge and to understand why they should plan, monitor, and control their cognitive activities.* Simply teaching appropriate information-processing strategies does not guarantee that students will use them. If these skills are to transfer to settings other than the training task, it is important that children understand *why* these strategies will help them to achieve their objectives and *when* it is appropriate to use them. The instructor can help by offering suggestions to the child ("You might find it easier to remember the months of the year if you group them according to seasons. Summer includes . . ."), or asking questions that remind children of strategies already taught ("Why is it important to summarize what you've read? Why do you need to double-check your answer?"). All these approaches have proved quite successful at furthering children's metacognitive skills and persuading them to apply this knowledge to the intellectual challenges they face.

SUMMARY

Information Flow and the Multistore Model

- Information-processing theorists use the analogy of he mind as a computer, with information flowing through a *limited-capacity system* composed of mental hardware and software.
- The **multistore model** depicts the human information-processing system as consisting of a **sensory register** to detect, or "log in," input; a **short-term store (STS),** where information is stored temporarily until we can operate on it; and a permanent or **long-term store (LTS).**
- Also included in most information processing models is a concept of **executive control processes,** or **metacognition,** which includes processes by which we plan, monitor, and control all phases of information processing.

Developmental Differences in Information-Processing Capacity

- Age differences in information-processing hardware have been examined by assessing **memory span** and **span of apprehension** to evaluate capacity of the STS. Although substantial age differences in the STS have been found, many developmental differences in memory can be attributed to increases in **knowledge base** and how quickly children can process information.
- Research on developmental changes in information-processing software have focused mainly on **strategies**—goal-directed operations used to aid task performance.
- Frequent findings include **production deficiencies,** in which children fail to produce a strategy spontaneously but can do so when instructed, and **utilization deficiencies,** in which children experience little or no benefit when they use a new strategy.
- Children of all ages have been found to use multiple and variable strategies in solving problems, a phenomenon that is explained by Robert Siegler's **adaptive strategy choice model.**
- Children's understanding of what it means to think increases over the preschool and early school years. Few or no developmental differences are observed for **implicit cognition,** cognition that is performed without conscious awareness, in contrast to **explicit cognition,** or cognition with awareness.

Alternative Viewpoints

- A recent alternative to the multistore model of information processing is **fuzzy-trace theory,** which claims that we process information at both a **gist** and a *verbatim* level and accounts nicely for some age differences in memory and problem solving. Other alternative approaches emphasize the role of inhibition in children's intellectual development.

The Development of Attention

- With age the **attention spans** of children and adolescents increase dramatically, owing, in part, to increasing myelination of the central nervous system.
- Attention also becomes more planful and more **selective** with age, as children and adolescents steadily improve in their ability to concentrate on task-relevant stimuli and to not be distracted by other noise in the environment.
- **Attention-deficit hyperactivity disorder** (**ADHD**) describes children who find it difficult to sustain their attention for long or to develop planful attentional strategies.

Memory: Retaining and Retrieving Information

- Infant memory has been tested by a variety of measures, most recently the *conjugate-reinforcement procedure* and *deferred imitation.* Deferred imitation may be an indication of *explicit,* or *declarative,* memory, has been found in infants as young as 6 months, and the duration of these memories increases with the age of the infants.
- Although infants can remember events that happened earlier in time, most of us display infantile amnesia—an inability to recall much about the first few years of life.
- Early **event memory,** specifically, **autobiographical memory,** is based on **scripts,** or schematic organizations of recurring real-world events organized in terms of their causal and temporal sequences. Even very young children organize their experiences in terms of scripts, which become more detailed with age.
- Autobiographical memory improves dramatically during the preschool years. Parents play an important role in the growth of autobiographical memories by discussing past events, providing clues about what information is important to remember, and helping children to recall their experiences in rich personal narratives.
- One aspect of autobiographical memory that has received much attention is age differences in eyewitness memory and suggestibility. As in general event memory, the accuracy of children's eyewitness memory increases with age. Young children are generally more susceptible to suggestion than older children and are more likely to form *false memories.* Steps to increase the accuracy of children's eyewitness testimony in legal proceedings include limiting the number of times child witnesses are interrogated, asking questions in nonleading ways, and cautioning the child against guessing or providing answers merely to please the interrogator.
- The effective use of memory strategies, or **mnemonics,** increases with age. Frequently used memory strategies include **rehearsal, organization,** and **retrieval.**
- Memory strategies are usually assessed on either **free-recall** or **cued-recall** tasks, the latter of which provide

specific cues, or prompts, to aid retrieval. The particular memory strategies that one acquires are heavily influenced by culture and the kinds of information that children are expected to remember.

■ Metamemory (or knowledge of the workings of memory) increases with age and contributes to developmental and individual differences in strategic memory.

■ Another reason for the dramatic improvements in strategic memory between infancy and adolescence is that older persons know more than younger ones do, and this larger knowledge base improves one's ability to access information and to devise memory strategies for use in learning and remembering.

Analogical Reasoning

■ **Reasoning** is a special type of problem solving that requires that one make an inference.

■ **Analogical reasoning** involves applying what one knows about one set of elements to infer relations about different elements.

■ The **relational primacy hypothesis** proposes that analogical reasoning is available early in infancy.

■ Many factors affect children's analogical reasoning; two important ones are *metacognition,* or a conscious awareness of the basis on which one is solving a problem, and *knowledge* of the relations on which the analogy is based.

Development of Arithmetic Skills

■ Even infants are capable of processing and using quantitative information, and toddlers have already acquired a rudimentary understanding of ordinal relationships.

■ Counting begins once children begin to talk, and preschoolers gradually construct such basic mathematical understandings as the principle of **cardinality.** Early arithmetic strategies usually involve counting out loud; but eventually, children perform simple arithmetic operations in their heads, using increasingly sophisticated arithmetic strategies.

■ Yet children of any age actually use a variety of strategies to solve math problems, as described by Siegler's *adaptive strategy choice model.*

■ Children with math disabilities show deficits in procedural skills and retrieval of facts from long-term memory, and have shorter short-term memory than nondisabled children.

■ There are sizable cultural variations in mathematics performance and the use of arithmetic strategies. Unschooled children develop arithmetic strategies that they apply quite skillfully to the practical problems they encounter.

■ Among those who are taught arithmetic strategies at school, East Asian children consistently outperform their American age-mates, owing, in part, to the structure of their languages and to instructional practices that aid them in retrieving math facts and acquiring computational skills and other mathematical knowledge.

Evaluating the Information-Processing Perspective

■ Despite its many strengths, the information-processing perspective has been criticized for largely ignoring neurological and sociocultural influences on cognitive growth, for failing to provide a broad, integrative theory of children's intelligence, and for underestimating the richness and diversity of human cognitive activities.

KEY TERMS

MEDIA RESOURCES

The Human Development Book Companion Website

See the companion website http://www.thomsonedu.com/psychology/shaffer for flashcards, practice quiz questions, Internet links, updates, critical thinking exercises, discussion forums, games, and more

ThomsonNOW! http://www.thomsonedu.com
Go to this site for the link to ThomsonNOW, your one-stop shop. Take a pre-test for this chapter, and ThomsonNOW will generate a personalized study plan based on your test results. The study plan will identify the topics you need to review and direct you to online resources to help you master those topics. You can then take a post-test to help you determine the concepts you have mastered and what you will still need to work on.

Child and Adolescent Development CD-ROM

For more information about the concepts covered in this chapter, go to

Module II: Cognition, Language, and Learning

- Cognitive Development
- Module II Media

© Joel Gordon

CHAPTER

9 Intelligence: Measuring Mental Performance

When he was 3 years old, the 19th-century philosopher John Stuart Mill began to study Greek under his father's direction. At age 6½ he wrote a history of Rome. He tackled Latin at age 8 when he also began his study of geometry and algebra. Mill's IQ score has been estimated at 190, on a scale on which 100 is average, 140 is gifted, and only 0.01 percent of the population score above 160 (Cox, 1926).

At age 27, Susan lives in an institution for the mentally retarded. She has been labeled profoundly retarded, has an IQ of 37, and usually responds to people with smiles. She cannot read, write, feed, or even dress herself. Yet, remarkably, she can flawlessly recite just about any poem after having heard it only once.

As these examples indicate, the range of human cognitive potential is immense. So far, our explorations of cognitive development have focused mainly on what human minds have in common. Piaget, after all, was interested in identifying *universal* stages in the way thinking is organized or structured. Similarly, information-processing theorists have been primarily concerned with understanding the basic cognitive processes on which *all* people rely to learn, remember, and solve problems.

In this chapter, we continue our exploration of how the human mind changes over the course of childhood and adolescence, but with a greater emphasis on individual differences in cognitive performance. We will begin by introducing yet another perspective on intellectual development—the psychometric approach—which has led to the creation and widespread use of intelligence tests. Unlike the Piagetian and information-processing approaches, which focus on cognitive *processes,* psychometricians are more *product-oriented.* They seek to determine how many and what kinds of questions children can answer correctly at different ages and whether or not this index of intellectual performance can predict such developmental outcomes as scholastic achievement, occupational attainments, and even health and life satisfaction.

There may be some surprises ahead as we consider what a person's score on an intelligence test implies about his or her ability to learn, perform in academic settings, or succeed at a job. Perhaps the biggest surprise for many people is learning that intelligence test scores, which can change dramatically over the course of one's life, are assessments of intellectual *performance* rather than innate potential or intellectual *capacity.* True, heredity does affect intellectual performance, but so do a variety of environmental factors that we will examine, including one's cultural and socioeconomic background, one's home environment, the schooling one receives, and even social and emotional factors in the testing situation itself. We will then evaluate the merits of preschool educational programs such as "Project Head Start," which was designed to promote the scholastic performances of children who perform poorly on intelligence tests. Finally, we will explore the growth of highly valued creative talents that are not adequately represented on our current intelligence tests.

What Is Intelligence?

If you were to ask five people to summarize in a single sentence what intelligence means to them, and then to list attributes that characterize highly intelligent people, you would probably find some similarities in their answers. Chances are their summary sentences will state that intelligence is how "smart" someone is compared to other people, or perhaps that it represents one's capacity for learning or problem-solving. However, you would probably also find that your five interviewees would show some meaningful differences in the attributes they view as characterizing highly intelligent individuals. Simply stated, intelligence does not mean the same thing to all people (Neisser et al., 1996).

And so it goes with behavioral scientists. Although few topics have generated as much research as intelligence and intelligence testing, even today there is no clear consensus about what intelligence is. Clearest agreement comes in "one-sentence" characterizations. Piaget (1970), for example, defined intelligence as "adaptive thinking or action." In a recent survey, 24 experts provided somewhat different one-sentence definitions of what intelligence meant to them, but virtually all these definitions centered in some way on the ability to think abstractly or to solve problems effectively (Sternberg, 1997).

So why is there still no singular definition of intelligence? Because different theorists have very different ideas about which attributes (and how many of them) are core aspects of this construct they call intelligence. Let's now consider some of the more influential viewpoints on the nature of intelligence, beginning with the psychometric perspective.

Psychometric Views of Intelligence

psychometric approach
a theoretical perspective that portrays intelligence as a trait (or set of traits) on which individuals differ; psychometric theorists are responsible for the development of standardized intelligence tests.

The research tradition that spawned the development of intelligence tests is the **psychometric approach** (Thorndike, 1997). According to psychometric theorists, intelligence is an intellectual trait or a set of traits that differ among people and so characterizes some people to a greater extent than others. The theorists' goal, then, is to identify precisely what those traits might be and to *measure* them so that intellectual differences among individuals can be described. But from the start, psychometricians could not agree on the *structure* of intelligence. Was it a single ability that influenced how people performed on all cognitive tests. Or, alternatively, was intelligence best described as many distinct abilities?

Alfred Binet (1857–1911), the father of intelligence testing.

Alfred Binet's Singular Component Approach

Alfred Binet and Theodore Simon produced the forerunner of our modern intelligence tests. In 1904, Binet and Simon were commissioned by the French government to construct a test that would identify "dull" children who might profit from remedial instruction (Boake, 2002; White, 2000). They then devised a large set of tasks measuring skills presumed to be necessary for classroom learning: attention, perception, memory, numerical reasoning, verbal comprehension, and so on. Items that clearly distinguished normal children from those described by teachers as dull or slow were kept in the final test.

In 1908 the Binet-Simon test was revised and all test items were age-graded (Boake, 2002; White, 2000). For example, problems that were passed by most 6-year-olds but few 5-year-olds were assumed to reflect the mental performance of a typical 6-year-old; those passed by most 12-year-olds but few 11-year-olds were said to measure the intellectual skills of an average 12-year-old, and so on. This age-grading of test items for ages 3 to 13 allowed a more precise assessment of a child's level of intellectual functioning. A child who passed all items at the 5-year-old level but none at the 6-year-old level was said to have a **mental age (MA)** of 5 years. A child who passed all items at the 10-year-old level and half of those at the 11-year-old level would have an MA of 10½ years.

mental age (MA)
a measure of intellectual development that reflects the level of age-graded problems a child is able to solve.

Thus, Binet and Simon had created a test that enabled them to identify slow learners and to estimate all children's levels of intellectual development. This information was useful for school administrators, who began to use children's mental ages as a guideline for planning curricula for both normal and retarded students (Boake, 2002; White, 2000).

The Multicomponent View of Intelligence

Other psychometric theorists were quick to challenge the notion that a single score, such as mental age, adequately represented human intellectual performance. Their point was that intelligence tests (even Binet's earliest versions) require people to perform a variety of tasks such as defining words or concepts, extracting meaning from written passages, answering general information questions, reproducing geometric designs with blocks, and solving arithmetic puzzles (see Figure 9.1 for some sample items). Couldn't these different subtests be measuring a number of distinct mental abilities rather than a single, overarching ability?

factor analysis
a statistical procedure for identifying clusters of tests or test items (called factors) that are highly correlated with one another and unrelated to other test items.

One way of determining whether intelligence is a single attribute or many different attributes is to ask people to perform a large number of mental tasks and then analyze their performances using a statistical procedure called **factor analysis.** This technique identifies clusters of tasks, called *factors,* that are highly correlated with one another and unrelated to other tasks on the test. Each factor (if more than one are found) presumably

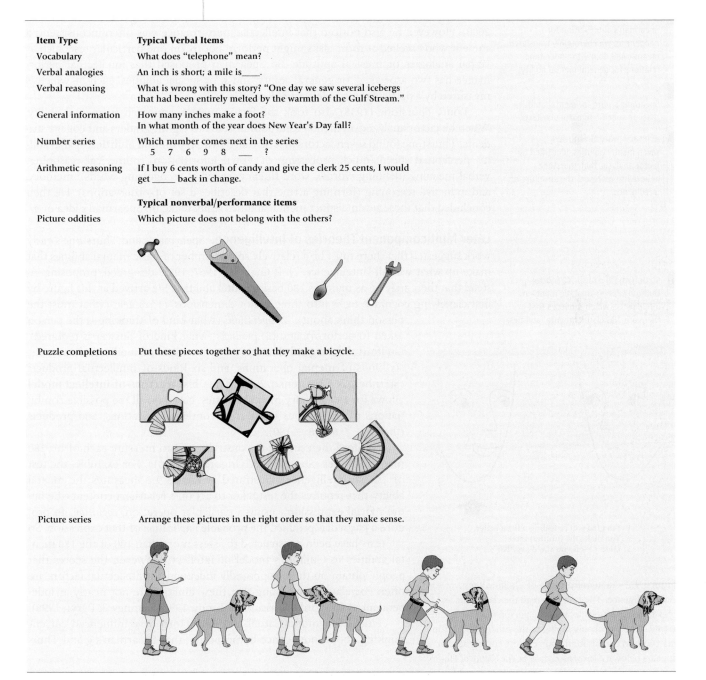

Item Type	Typical Verbal Items
Vocabulary	What does "telephone" mean?
Verbal analogies	An inch is short; a mile is____.
Verbal reasoning	What is wrong with this story? "One day we saw several icebergs that had been entirely melted by the warmth of the Gulf Stream."
General information	How many inches make a foot? In what month of the year does New Year's Day fall?
Number series	Which number comes next in the series 5 7 6 9 8 ___ ?
Arithmetic reasoning	If I buy 6 cents worth of candy and give the clerk 25 cents, I would get ____ back in change.
	Typical nonverbal/performance items
Picture oddities	Which picture does not belong with the others?

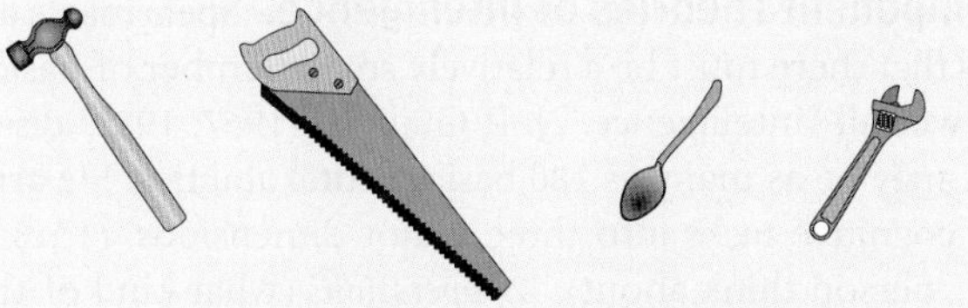

Puzzle completions	Put these pieces together so that they make a bicycle.

Picture series	Arrange these pictures in the right order so that they make sense.

Figure 9.1 Items similar but not identical to those appearing on intelligence tests for children.

represents a distinct mental ability. Suppose, for example, we found that people performed very similarly on four items that require verbal skills and on three items that require mathematical skills, but that their verbal skill score was not correlated with their score on the math items. Under these circumstances, we might conclude that verbal ability and mathematical ability are distinct intellectual factors. But if subjects' verbal and math scores were highly correlated with each other and with scores for all other kinds of mental problems on the test, we might conclude that intelligence is a single attribute rather than a number of separate mental abilities.

Early Multicomponent Theories of Intelligence. Charles Spearman (1927) was among the first to use factor analysis to try to determine whether intelligence was one or many abilities (Bower, 2003). He found that a child's scores across a variety of cognitive tests were moderately correlated and thus inferred that there must be a *general mental factor,* which he called ***g***, that affects one's performance on most cognitive tasks (Bower, 2000). However, he also noticed that intellectual performance was often inconsistent: a student who excelled at most tasks might perform poorly on one particular test, such as verbal analogies or musical aptitude. So Spearman proposed that intellectual performance has two aspects: *g*, or general ability, and ***s***, or special abilities, each of which is measured by a particular test (Hefford & Keef, 2004).

g
Spearman's abbreviation for *neogenesis,* which, roughly translated, means one's ability to understand relations (or general mental ability).

s
Spearman's term for mental abilities that are specific to particular tests.

primary mental abilities
seven mental abilities, identified by factor analysis, that Thurstone believed to represent the structure of intelligence.

Louis Thurstone (1938) also took the factor analysis approach to mental ability. When he factor-analyzed 50 mental tests administered to eighth-graders and college students, Thurstone found seven factors that he called **primary mental abilities:** spatial ability, perceptual speed (quick processing of visual information), numerical reasoning, verbal meaning (defining words), word fluency (speed at recognizing words), memory, and inductive reasoning (forming a rule that describes a set of observations). He then concluded that these seven distinct mental abilities really make up Spearman's idea of *g*.

Later Multicomponent Theories of Intelligence. Spearman's and Thurstone's early work suggested that there must be a relatively small number of basic mental abilities that make up what we call "intelligence." J. P. Guilford (1967, 1988) disagreed, proposing instead that there may be as many as 180 basic mental abilities. He arrived at this figure by first classifying cognitive tasks into three major dimensions: (1) *content* (what must the person think about), (2) *operations* (what kind of thinking is the person asked to perform), and (3) *products* (what kind of answer is required). Guilford then argued that there are five kinds of intellectual contents, six kinds of mental operations, and six kinds of intellectual products (Sternberg & Grigorenko, 2001). Thus, his **structure-of-intellect model** allows for 180 primary mental abilities, based on all the possible combinations of the various intellectual contents, operations, and products (that is, $5 \times 6 \times 6 = 180$).

structure-of-intellect model
Guilford's factor-analytic model of intelligence, which proposes that there are 180 distinct mental abilities.

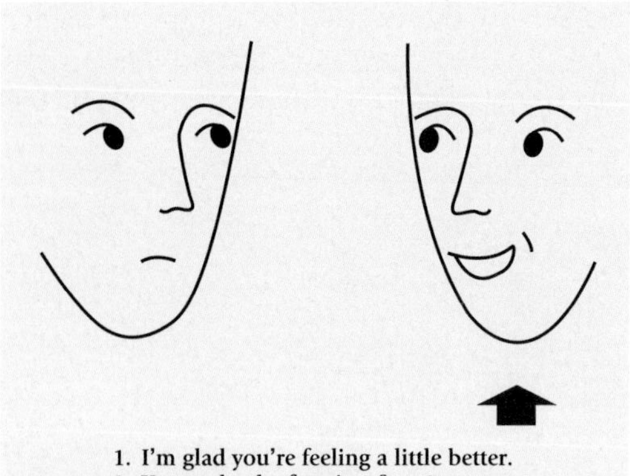
1. I'm glad you're feeling a little better.
2. You make the funniest faces!
3. Didn't I tell you she'd say "No"?

Figure 9.2 An item from one of Guilford's tests of social intelligence. The task is to read the characters' expressions and to decide what the person marked by the arrow is most probably saying to the other person. You may wish to try this item yourself (the correct answer appears below). *Adapted from a table in* The Nature of Human Intelligence, *by J. P. Guilford, 1967. Copyright © 1967 by McGraw-Hill, Inc. Adapted by permission.*

Guilford then set out to construct tests to measure each of his 180 mental abilities (Sternberg & Grigorenko, 2001). For example, the test of "social intelligence" illustrated in Figure 9.2 measures the mental ability that requires the test taker to act on a *behavioral* content (the figure's facial expression), using a particular operation, *cognition,* to produce a particular product, the probable *implication* of that expression. So far, tests have been constructed to assess more than 100 of the 180 mental abilities in Guilford's model of intellect. However, the scores that people obtain on these supposedly independent intellectual factors are often correlated, suggesting that these abilities are not nearly as independent as Guilford has assumed (Brody, 1992; Romney & Pyryt, 1999).

Finally, Raymond Cattell and John Horn have influenced current thinking about intelligence by proposing that Spearman's *g* and Thur-

Answer to Figure 9.2: Statement 3

stone's primary mental abilities can be reduced to two major dimensions of intellect: *fluid intelligence* and *crystallized intelligence* (Cattell, 1963; Horn & Noll, 1997). **Fluid intelligence** refers to one's ability to solve novel and abstract problems of the sort that are not taught and are relatively free of cultural influences (Jay, 2005; Gray, Chabris, & Braver, 2003). Examples of the kinds of problems that tap fluid intelligence are the verbal analogies and number series tests from Figure 9.1, as well as tests of one's ability to recognize relationships among otherwise meaningless geometric figures (see Figure 9.8 on page 362 for an example). **Crystallized intelligence** is the ability to solve problems that depend on knowledge acquired as a result of schooling and other life experiences (Jay, 2005). Tests of general information ("At what temperature does water boil?"), word comprehension ("What is the meaning of *duplicate?*"), and numerical abilities are all measures of crystallized intelligence.

fluid intelligence
the ability to perceive relationships and solve relational problems of the type that are not taught and are relatively free of cultural influences.

crystallized intelligence
the ability to understand relations or solve problems that depend on knowledge acquired from schooling and other cultural influences.

A Recent Hierarchical Model. So what have we learned from factor-analytic studies of intelligence? Perhaps that Spearman, Thurstone, and Cattell and Horn were all partially correct. Indeed, many psychometricians today favor **hierarchical models of intelligence**—models in which intelligence is viewed as consisting of (1) a general ability factor at the top of the hierarchy, which influences one's performance on many cognitive tests, and (2) a number of specialized ability factors (something similar to Thurstone's primary mental abilities) that influence how well one performs in particular intellectual domains (for example, on tests of numerical reasoning or tests of spatial skills). The most elaborate of these hierarchical models, based on analyses of hundreds of studies of mental abilities conducted over the past 50 years, is John Carroll's **three-stratum theory of intelligence** (Esters & Ittenbach, 1999). As shown in Figure 9.3, Carroll (1993) represents intelligence as a pyramid, with *g* at the top and eight broad intellectual abilities at the second level. This model implies that each of us may have particular intellectual strengths or weaknesses depending on the patterns of "second stratum" intellectual abilities we display. It also explains how a person of below average general ability (*g*) might actually excel in a narrow third-stratum domain (for example, reciting poems heard only once, like Susan in our chapter opener) if she displays an unusually high second-stratum ability (general memory) that fosters good performance in that domain (Johnson & Bouchard, 2005).

hierarchical model of intelligence
model of the structure of intelligence in which a broad, general ability factor is at the top of the hierarchy, with a number of specialized ability factors nested underneath.

three-stratum theory of intelligence
Carroll's hierarchical model of intelligence with *g* at the top of the hierarchy, eight broad abilities at the second level, or stratum, and narrower domains of each second-stratum ability at the third stratum.

So hierarchical models depict intelligence as *both* an overarching general mental ability *and* a number of more specific abilities that each pertain to a particular intellectual domain. Are we now closer to a consensus on the definition of intelligence? Unfortunately no, because a growing number of researchers believe that no single psychometric theory of intelligence fully captures what it means to be intelligent (Neisser et al., 1996). Let's now examine two alternative viewpoints that should help us to appreciate some of the limitations of today's intelligence tests.

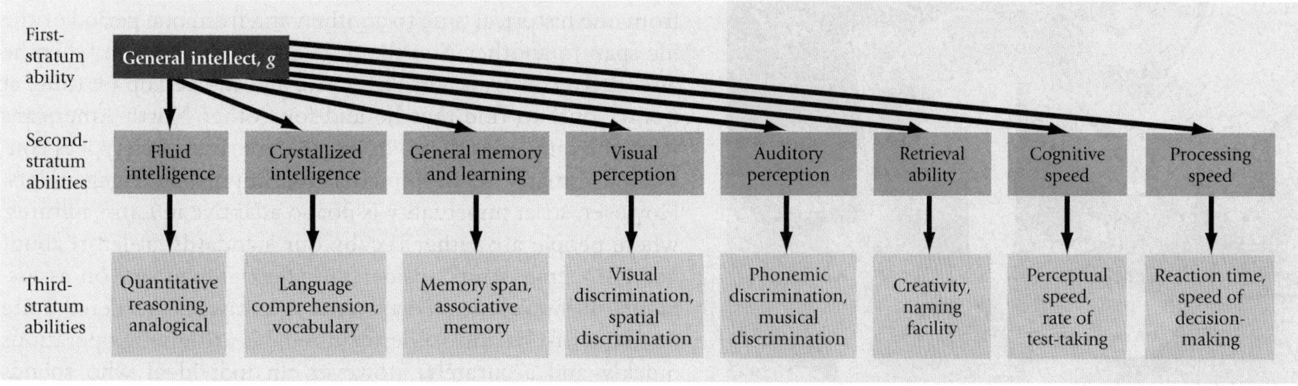

Figure 9.3 John Carroll's three-stratum hierarchical model of intelligence. Second-stratum abilities are arranged from left to right in terms of their decreasing correlation with *g*. So fluid intelligence and the reasoning it supports (for example, quantitative reasoning) are more closely associated with general mental ability *g* than are auditory perception, cognitive speed, and the third-stratum skills that these abilities support. *From* Human Cognitive Abilities: A Survey of Factor-Analytic Studies, *by J. B. Carroll, 1993. Copyright 1993 by Cambridge University Press. Reprinted by permission.*

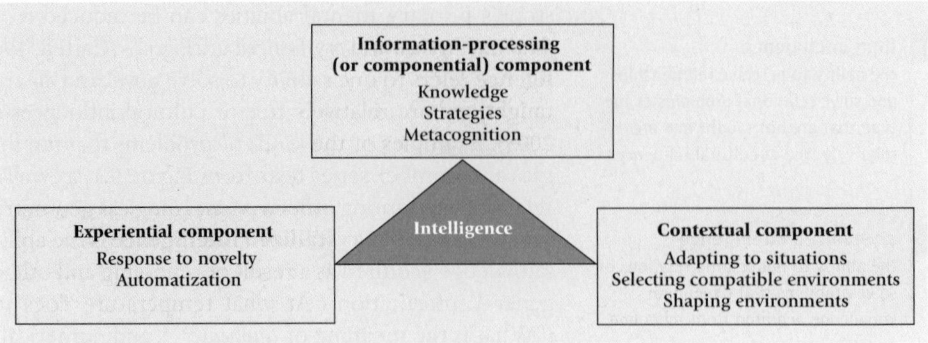

Figure 9.4 Sternberg's triarchic theory of intelligence.

A Modern Information-Processing Viewpoint

One recurring criticism of psychometric models of intelligence is that they are very narrow, focusing primarily on intellectual content, or what the child knows, rather than on the processes by which this knowledge is acquired, retained, and used to solve problems. Furthermore, traditional intelligence tests do not measure other attributes that people commonly think of as indications of intelligence, such as common sense, social and interpersonal skills, and the talents that underlie creative accomplishments in music, drama, and athletics (Gardner, 1983).

triarchic theory
a recent information-processing theory of intelligence that emphasizes three aspects of intelligent behavior not normally tapped by IQ tests: the *context* of the action; the person's *experience* with the task (or situation); and the *information-processing strategies* the person applies to the task (or situation).

Recently, Robert Sternberg (1985, 1991) proposed a **triarchic theory of intelligence** that emphasizes three aspects, or components, of intelligent behavior: *context, experience,* and *information-processing skills* (see Figure 9.4) (Sternberg, 2003; Tigner & Tigner, 2000). As we will see in reviewing this model, Sternberg's view of intelligence is much, much broader than that of psychometric theorists (Bower, 2000).

The Contextual Component

First, Sternberg argues that what qualifies as "intelligent" behavior will depend in large part on the context in which it is displayed. According to Sternberg, intelligent people are those who can successfully adapt to their environment or can shape that environment to suit them better. These people display practical intelligence, or "street smarts." Psychologists, Sternberg believes, must begin to understand intelligence as adaptive *real world* behavior, not as behavior in taking tests (Sternberg, 1997, 2003).

Cameraman/The Image Works

The sophisticated ability that this child displays is considered intelligent in his culture, but is not measured by traditional IQ tests.

From a contextual perspective, what is meant by intelligent behavior may vary from one culture or subculture to another, from one historical time to another, and from one period of the life span to another. Sternberg describes an occasion when he attended a conference in Venezuela and showed up on time, at 8 A.M., only to find that he and four other North Americans were the only ones there. In North American society it is considered "smart" to be punctual for important engagements. However, strict punctuality is not so adaptive in Latin cultures, where people are rather lax (by our standards, at least) about being on time. And consider the effects of history on assessments of intelligence. Forty years ago, it was considered quite intelligent to be able to perform mental arithmetic operations quickly and accurately. However, an individual who spends countless hours perfecting those same skills today might be considered somewhat less than intelligent given that computers and calculators can perform these computations much faster.

The Experiential Component

According to Sternberg, a person's experience with a task helps to determine whether that person's performance qualifies as intelligent behavior. He believes that relatively novel tasks require active and conscious information processing and are the best measures of a person's reasoning abilities, as long as these tasks are not *so* foreign that the person is unable to apply what he may know (for example, if geometry problems were presented to 5-year-olds). So, responses to *novel* challenges are an indication of the person's ability to generate good ideas or fresh insights (Sternberg, 2003).

In daily life, however, people also perform more or less intelligently on familiar tasks (such as balancing a checkbook, or quickly extracting the most important information from a newspaper). This second kind of experiential intelligence reflects *automatization,* or increasing efficiency of information processing with practice. According to Sternberg, it is a sign of intelligence when we develop automatized routines for performing everyday tasks accurately and efficiently so that we don't have to waste much time or conscious thought when accomplishing them.

The experiential component of Sternberg's theory has a most important implication for intelligence testers: it is crucial to know how familiar specific test items are to examinees in order to test their intelligence fairly. For example, if the items on an intelligence test are generally familiar to members of one cultural group but novel to members of another (for example, questions about restaurants or banks, which one cultural group may have experience with whereas the second group may not), the second group will perform much worse than the first, thereby reflecting a **cultural bias** in the testing procedure. A valid comparison of the intellectual performances of people from diverse cultural backgrounds requires the test items to be equally familiar (or unfamiliar) to all test takers.

cultural bias
the situation that arises when one cultural or subcultural group is more familiar with test items than another group and therefore has an unfair advantage.

The Componential (or Information-Processing) Component

Sternberg's major criticism of psychometric theorists is that they estimate a test taker's intelligence from the quality (or correctness) of her answers, while completely ignoring how she produces intelligent responses. Sternberg is an information-processing theorist who believes that we must focus on the *componential aspects* of intelligent behavior—that is, the cognitive processes by which we size up the requirements of problems, formulate strategies to solve them, and then monitor our cognitive activities until we've accomplished our goals. He, along with other information-processing theorists, argue that some people process information faster and more efficiently than others and that our cognitive tests could be improved considerably by measuring these differences and treating them as important aspects of intelligence (Burns & Nettelbeck, 2003; Sternberg, 2003; Tigner & Tigner, 2000).

In sum, Sternberg's triarchic theory provides us with a very rich view of the nature of intelligence. It suggests that if you want to know how intelligent Charles, Chico, and Chenghuan are, you had better consider (1) the *context* in which they are performing (that is, the culture and historical period in which they live, and their ages), (2) their *experience* with the tasks and whether their behavior qualifies as responses to novelty or automatized processes, and (3) the *information-processing skills* that reflect how each person is approaching these tasks. Unfortunately, the most widely used intelligence tests are not based on such a broad and sophisticated view of intellectual processes.

Gardner's Theory of Multiple Intelligences

theory of multiple intelligences
Gardner's theory that humans display as many as nine distinct kinds of intelligence, each linked to a particular area of the brain, and several of which are not measured by IQ tests.

Howard Gardner (1983, 1999) is another theorist who criticizes the psychometricians for trying to describe a person's intelligence with a single score. In his book *Frames of Mind,* Gardner (1983) outlined his **theory of multiple intelligences,** proposing that humans display at least seven distinctive kinds of intelligence (Hefford & Keef, 2004). Since that

TABLE 9.1 Gardner's Mulitple Intelligence

Type of intelligence	Intellectual processes	Cerebral Systems	Vocational end-states
Linguistic	Sensitivity to the meaning and sounds of words, to the structure of language, and to the many ways language can be used.	Left hemisphere, temporal and frontal lobes	Poet, novelist, journalist
Spatial	Ability to perceive visual-spatial relationships accurately, to transform these perceptions, and to re-create aspects of one's visual experience in the absence of the pertinent stimuli.	Right hemisphere, parietal Posterior Occipital lobe	Engineer, sculptor, cartographer 
Logical-mathematical	Ability to operate on and to perceive relationships in abstract symbol systems and to think logically and systematically in evaluating one's ideas.	Left parietal lobes and adjacent temporal and occipital association areas Left hemisphere for verbal naming Right hemisphere for spatial organization Frontal system for planning and goal setting	Mathematician, scientist 
Musical	Sensitivity to pitch, melody; ability to combine tones and musical phrases into larger rhythms; understanding of the emotional aspects of music.	Right anterior temporal Frontal lobes	Musician, composer
Body-kinesthetic	Ability to use the body skillfully to express oneself or achieve goals; ability to handle objects skillfully.	Cerebral motor strip Thalamus Basal ganglia Cerebellum	Dancer, athlete 
Interpersonal	Ability to detect and respond appropriately to the mood, temperaments, motives, and intentions of others.	Frontal lobes as integrating station between internal and external states\people	Therapist, public relations specialist, salesperson
Intrapersonal	Sensitivity to one's own inner states; recognition of personal strengths and weaknesses and ability to use information about the self to behave adaptively.	Frontal lobes as integrating station between internal and external states\people	Contributes to success in almost any walk of life
Naturalist	Sensitively to the factors influencing, and influenced by, organisms (fauna and flora) in the natural environment	Left parietal lobe (discriminating living from nonliving things)	Biologist, naturalist 
Spiritual/existential (speculative at this point)	Sensitivity to issues related to the meaning of life, death, and other aspects of the human condition.	Hypothesized as specific regons in the right temporal lobe	Philosopher, theologian

Adapted from *Frames of Mind: The Theory of Multiple Intelligence*, by Howard Gardner, Perseus Books Group, 1983; and Branton Shearer, "Multiple Intelligences Theory after 20 Years," *Teachers College Record, 106*, 2–16, 2004.

time, Gardner has added an eighth intelligence to the list and has speculated about a ninth form of intelligence (see Table 9.1).

Gardner (1999) does not claim that these nine abilities represent the universe of intelligences. But he makes the case that each ability is distinct, is linked to a specific area of the brain, and follows a different developmental course (Shearer, 2004). As support for these ideas, Gardner points out that injury to a particular area of the brain usually influences only one ability (linguistic or spatial, for example), leaving others unaffected.

As further evidence for the independence of these abilities, Gardner notes that some individuals are truly exceptional in one ability but poor in others. This is dramatically clear in cases of the *savant syndrome*—mentally retarded people with an extraordinary talent. Leslie Lemke is once such individual: he is blind, has cerebral palsy, and is mentally retarded, and he could not talk until he was an adult. Yet he can hear a musical piece once and play it flawlessly on the piano or imitate songs in German or Italian perfectly, even though his own conversational speech is still primitive. And despite their abysmal performance on intelligence tests, other mentally retarded individuals with savant skills can draw well enough to gain admittance to art school or calculate almost instantaneously what day of the week January 16, 1909,* was (O'Connor & Hermelin, 1991). Finally, Gardner notes that different intelligences develop at different times. Many of the great composers and athletes, for example, begin to display their immense talents in childhood, whereas logical-mathematical intelligence often shows up much later in life.

Gardner's ideas have had an impact, particularly on investigators who study the development of creativity and special talents—a topic we will explore later in this chapter. Nevertheless, critics have argued that even though such talents as musical or athletic prowess are important human characteristics, they are not the same kinds of *mentalistic* activities as those most people view as the core of intelligence (Bjorklund, 2005; Shearer, 2004). And although children gifted in the visual arts or athletics are often notably better in these areas than in Gardner's other intelligences (see Winner, 2000), current intelligence tests do tap Gardner's logical, spatial, and mathematical intelligences, which are moderately correlated rather than highly distinct (Jensen, 1998). Perhaps it is too early, then, to totally reject the concept of *g*, or general mental ability. Yet Gardner is almost certainly correct in arguing that we surely misrepresent and underestimate the talents of many individuals by trying to characterize their "intelligence" with a single test score (Shearer, 2004).

How Is Intelligence Measured?

When psychometricians began to construct intelligence tests nearly 100 years ago, their concern was not with defining the nature of intelligence but with the more practical goals of determining which schoolchildren were likely to be slow learners. Recall that Binet and Simon produced a test that accomplished this goal and characterized each child's intellectual development with a single score, or *mental age*. Among the more popular of our contemporary intelligence tests for children is a direct descendant of Binet and Simon's early test.

The Stanford-Binet Intelligence Scale

In 1916, Lewis Terman of Stanford University translated and published a revised version of the Binet scale for use with American children. This test came to be known as the **Stanford-Binet Intelligence Scale** (Boake, 2002; White, 2000).

Stanford-Binet Intelligence Scale
modern descendent of the first successful intelligence test that measures general intelligence and four factors: verbal reasoning, quantitative reasoning, spatial reasoning, and short-term memory.

intelligence quotient (IQ)
a numerical measure of a person's performance on an intelligence test relative to the performance of other examinees.

Like Binet's scale, the original version of the Stanford-Binet consisted of age-graded tasks designed to measure the average intellectual performance of children aged 3 through 13. But unlike Binet, who classified children according to mental age, Terman used a ratio measure of intelligence, developed by Stern (1912), that came to be known as an **intelligence quotient,** or **IQ** (Boake, 2002). The child's IQ, which was said to be a measure of his brightness or rate of intellectual development, was calculated by dividing his mental age by his chronological age and then multiplying by 100:

$$IQ = \frac{MA}{CA} \times 100$$

Notice that an IQ of 100 indicates average intelligence; it means that a child's mental age *is exactly equal to* her chronological age. An IQ greater than 100 indicates that the child's per-

*It was a Saturday.

formance is comparable to that of people older than she is, whereas an IQ less than 100 means that her intellectual performance matches that of children younger than herself.

A revised version of the Stanford-Binet is still in use (Thorndike, Hagen, & Sattler, 1986). Its **test norms** are now based on representative samples of people (6-year-olds through adults) from many social-class and ethnic backgrounds. The revised test continues to measure abilities thought to be important to academic success, namely verbal reasoning, quantitive reasoning, visual-spatial reasoning, and short-term memory. However, the concept of mental age is no longer used to calculate IQ on the Stanford-Binet or any other modern intelligence test. Instead, individuals receive **deviation IQ scores** that reflect how well or poorly they do *compared with others of the same age.* An IQ of 100 is still average, and the higher (or lower) the IQ score an individual attains, the better (or worse) her performance is compared to age-mates.

test norms
standards of normal performance on psychometric instruments that are based on the average scores and the range of scores obtained by a large, representative sample of test takers.

deviation IQ score
an intelligence test score that reflects how well or poorly a person performs compared with others of the same age.

The Wechsler Scales

David Wechsler has constructed two intelligence tests for children, both of which are widely used. **The Wechsler Intelligence Scale for Children-IV (WISC-IV)** is appropriate for children aged 6 to 16, whereas the *Wechsler Preschool and Primary Scale of Intelligence-III (WPPSI-III)* is designed for children between ages 3 and 8 (Baron, 2005; Lichtenberger, 2005; Wechsler, 1989, 1991).

Wechsler Intelligence Scale for Children (WISC-IV)
widely used individual intelligence test that includes a measure of general intelligence and both verbal and performance intelligence.

One reason Wechsler constructed his own intelligence tests is that he believed that earlier versions of the Stanford-Binet were overloaded with items that require verbal skills (Boake, 2002). He felt that this heavy bias toward verbal intelligence discriminated against children who have certain language handicaps—for example, those for whom English is a second language or those who have reading difficulties or are hard of hearing. To overcome this problem, Wechsler's scales contain verbal subtests similar to those on the Stanford-Binet as well as *nonverbal,* or "performance" subtests. Items on the performance subtests are designed to measure such predominantly nonverbal skills as the ability to assemble puzzles, solve mazes, reproduce geometric designs with colored blocks, and rearrange sets of pictures so that they tell a meaningful story. Test-takers receive three scores: a *verbal IQ, a performance IQ,* and a *full-scale IQ* based on a combination of the verbal and performance measures (Saklofske et al., 2005).

The Wechsler scales soon became popular. Not only did the new performance subscales allow children from all backgrounds to display their intellectual strengths, but the tests were also sensitive to inconsistencies in mental skills that may be early signs of neurological problems or learning disorders. For example, children who display reading disorders often do much worse on the verbal component of the WISC.

Distribution of IQ Scores

If a girl or boy scores 130 on the Stanford-Binet or the WISC, we know that his or her IQ is above average. But how bright is he or she? To tell, we would have to know something about the way IQs are distributed in the population at large.

One interesting feature of all modern IQ tests is that people's scores are **normally distributed** around an IQ of 100 (see Figure 9.5). This patterning of scores is hardly an accident. By definition, the average score made by examinees from each age group is set at 100, and this is the most common score that people make (Neisser et al., 1996). Note that approximately half the population scores below 100 and half above. Moreover, roughly equal numbers of examinees obtain IQs of 85 and 115 (15 points from the average) or 70 and 130 (30 points from average). To determine the meaning of an IQ of 130, we can look at Table 9.2, which shows what percentage of the population the person outperforms by scoring at that level. Here we see that an IQ of 130 equals or exceeds the IQs of 97 percent of the population; it is a very high IQ indeed. Similarly, fewer than 3 percent of all test takers obtain IQs below 70, a cutoff that is commonly used today to define mental retardation.

normal distribution
a symmetrical, bell-shaped curve that describes the variability of certain characteristics within a population; most people fall at or near the average score, with relatively few at the extremes of the distribution.

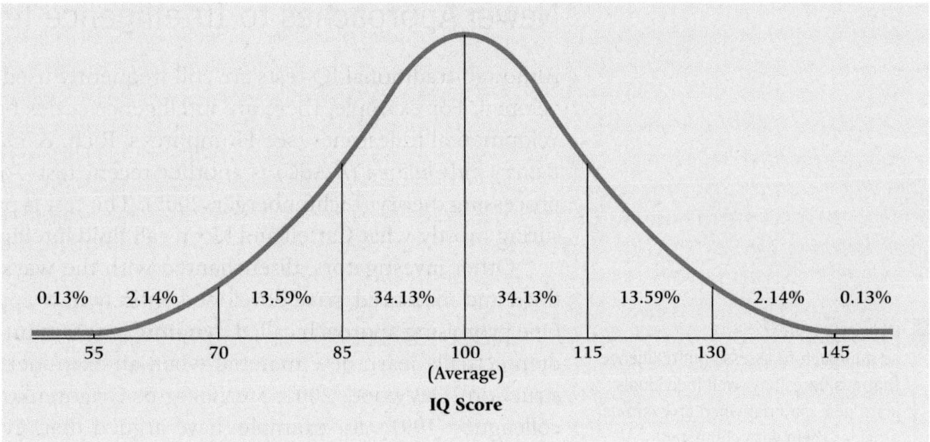

Figure 9.5 The approximate distribution of IQ scores people make on contemporary intelligence tests. These tests are constructed so that the average score made by examinees in each age group is equivalent to an IQ of 100. Note that more than two-thirds of all examinees score within 15 points of this average (that is, IQs of 85–115) and that 95 percent of the population scores with 30 of average (IQs of 70–130). *From David Bjorklund,* Children's Thinking: Cognitive Development and Individual Differences, *4th ed., p. 437, Belmont, CA: Thomson, 2005.*

Group Tests of Mental Performance

Because the Stanford-Binet and the Wechsler scales must be administered individually by a professionally trained examiner and can take more than an hour to assess each person's IQ, psychometricians soon saw the need for more cost effective, paper-and-pencil measures that could be group-administered to quickly assess the intellectual performance of large numbers of army recruits, job applicants, or students in a city's public schools. Indeed, you have almost certainly taken a *group test* of scholastic aptitude at some point in your life. Among the more widely used of these tests are the Lorge-Thorndike Test, which is designed for grade school and high school students, the Scholastic Aptitude Test (SAT) and the American College Test (ACT) taken by many college applicants, and the Graduate Record Examination (GRE) often required of applicants to graduate school. These instruments are sometimes called "achievement" tests because they call for specific information that the examinee has learned at school (that is, crystallized intelligence) and are designed to predict future academic achievement.

TABLE 9.2 The Meaning of Different IQ Scores

An IQ of	Equals or exceeds (% of the population)
160	99.99
140	99.3
135	98
130	97
125	94
120	89
115	82
110	73
105	62
100	50
95	38
90	27
85	18
80	11
75	6
70	3
65	2
62	1

Newer Approaches to Intelligence Testing

Although traditional IQ tests are still frequently used, new tests are constantly being developed. For example, there are intelligence scales based on Piagetian concepts and developmental milestones (see Humphreys, Rich, & Davey, 1985). *The Kaufman Assessment Battery for Children (K-ABC)* is another recent test—one based on modern information-processing theory (Lichtenberger, 2005). The test is primarily nonverbal in content, measuring mostly what Cattell and Horn call fluid intelligence (Kaufman & Kaufman, 1983).

dynamic assessment
an approach to assessing intelligence that evaluates how well individuals learn new material when an examiner provides them with competent instruction.

Other investigators, disenchanted with the ways in which intelligence has been defined and measured, have developed entirely new approaches to intellectual assessment. One promising approach called **dynamic assessment** attempts to evaluate how well children actually learn new material when an examiner provides them with competent instruction (Haywood, 2001; Sternberg & Grigorenko, 2001). Reuven Feuerstein and his colleagues (1997), for example, have argued that, even though intelligence is often defined as a potential to learn from experience, IQ tests typically assess what has already been learned, not what *can* be learned (Bower, 2003; White, 2000). The traditional psychometric approach may be biased against children from culturally diverse or economically disadvantaged backgrounds who have lacked opportunities to learn what the tests measure (White, 2000). Feuerstein's *Learning Potential Assessment Device* asks children to learn new things with the guidance of an adult who provides increasingly helpful hints—precisely the kind of collaborative learning that Vygotsky emphasized in his sociocultural theory. This test interprets intelligence as the ability to learn quickly with minimal guidance. Robert Sternberg (1985, 1991) used a similar approach in a test he has constructed based on his triarchic theory of intelligence. To better understand the information processes involved in verbal comprehension, for example, Sternberg does not ask people to define words they learned in the past, as IQ tests so often do. Instead, he places an unfamiliar word in a set of sentences and asks people to learn, from its context, what the new word means, just as they must do in real life.

In sum, modern perspectives on intelligence are now beginning to be reflected in the content of intelligence tests (Sternberg, 1997). However, these new tests and testing procedures have a very short history, and it remains to be seen whether they will eventually replace more traditional assessments of mental performance, such as the WISC and the Stanford-Binet.

Assessing Infant Intelligence

None of the standard intelligence tests can be used with children much younger than 2½ because the test items require verbal skills and attention spans that infants do not have. However, attempts have been made to measure infant "intelligence" by assessing the rate at which babies achieve important developmental milestones. Perhaps the best known and most widely used of the infant tests is the *Bayley Scales of Infant Development* (Bayley, 1969, 1993). This instrument, designed for infants aged 2 to 30 months, has three parts: (1) the *motor* scale (which assesses such motor capabilities as grasping a cube, throwing a ball, or drinking from a cup); (2) the *mental* scale (which includes adaptive behaviors such as categorizing objects, searching for a hidden toy, and following directions); and (3) the *Infant Behavioral Record* (a rating of the child's behavior on dimensions such as goal directedness, fearfulness, and social responsivity) (see Table 9.3). On the basis of the first two scores, the infant is given a **DQ,** or **developmental quotient,** rather than an IQ. The DQ summarizes how well or poorly the infant performs in comparison to a large group of infants the same age (Lichtenberger, 2005).

developmental quotient (DQ)
a numerical measure of an infant's performance on a developmental schedule relative to the performance of other infants of the same age.

Do DQs Predict Later IQs?

Infant scales are very useful for charting babies' developmental progress and for diagnosing neurological disorders and other signs of mental retardation, even when these

TABLE 9.3 Description of Subscales of the Bayley Scale of Infant Development

Bayley Scale of Infant Development Subscale	Description
Mental	Assesses the child's current level of cognitive, language, and personal/social development and includes items that measure memory, problem solving, early number concepts, generalization, classification, vocalizations, language, and social skills.
Motor	Measures the child's level of gross and fine motor development via items associated with crawling, sitting, standing, walking, etc., for gross motor movement and items related to the use of writing, grasping, and imitation of hand movements for fine motor movement.
Behavior rating	This scale is completed by the examiner regarding the child's behaviors during the test administration and assesses the child's attention/arousal (for children under 6 months of age), orientation/engagement toward the tasks and the examiner, emotional regulation, and quality of motor movement.

Adapted from "The Stability of Mental Test Performance Between Two and Eighteen Years," by M. P. Honzik, J. W. MacFarlane, & L. Allen, 1948, *Journal of Experimental Education, 17,* 309–324.

conditions are fairly mild and difficult to detect in a standard neurological exam (Columbo, 1993; Honzik, 1983). However, these tests generally fail to predict a child's later IQ or scholastic achievements (Honzik, 1983; Rose et al., 1989). In fact, a DQ measured early in infancy may not even predict the child's DQ later in infancy.

Why do infant tests do such a poor job at predicting children's later IQs? Perhaps the main reason is that infant tests and IQ tests tap very different kinds of abilities. Infant scales are designed to measure sensory, motor, language, and social skills, whereas standardized IQ tests such as the WISC and the Stanford-Binet emphasize more abstract abilities such as verbal reasoning, concept formation, and problem solving. So to expect an infant test to predict the later results of an IQ test is like expecting a yardstick to tell us how much someone weighs. There may be some correspondence between the two measures (a yardstick indicates height, which is correlated with weight; DQ indicates developmental progress, which is related to IQ), but the relationship is not very great.

New Evidence for Continuity in Intellectual Performance

Is it foolish, then, to think that we might ever accurately forecast a child's later IQ from his or her behavior during infancy? Maybe not. As we learned in Chapter 5, information-processing theorists have discovered that certain measures of infant attention and memory are much better at predicting IQ during the preschool and grade-school years than are the Bayley scales or other measures of infant development. Three attributes appear especially promising: how quickly infants look when presented with a visual target (*visual reaction time*), the rate at which they *habituate* to repetitive stimuli, and the extent to which they prefer novel stimuli to familiar ones (*preference for novelty*). Measures of these information-processing skills obtained during the first 4 to 8 months of life have an average correlation of .45 with IQ in childhood, with visual reaction time corresponding more closely to later measures of performance IQ, and the other measures predicting better for verbal IQ (Dougherty & Haith, 1997; McCall & Carriger, 1993).

So there is some continuity between infant intelligence and childhood intelligence after all. Perhaps we can now characterize the "smart" infant as one who prefers and seeks out novel experiences and who soaks up new information quickly—in short, a speedy and efficient information processor.

TABLE 9.4 Correlations of IQs Measured during the Preschool Years and Middle Childhood, with IQs Measured at Ages 10 and 18

Age of child	Correlation with IQ at age 10	Correlation with IQ at age 18
4	.66	.42
6	.76	.61
8	.88	.70
10	–	.76
12	.87	.76

Source: Adapted from Honzik, MacFarlane, & Allen, 1948.

Stability of IQ in Childhood and Adolescence

It was once assumed that a person's IQ reflected his or her genetically determined intellectual capacity and would remain quite stable over time. In other words, a child with an IQ of 120 at age 5 was expected to obtain a similar IQ at age 10, 15, or 20.

How much support is there for this idea? As we have seen, infant DQs do not predict later IQ test scores very well at all. But starting at about age 4, there is a meaningful relationship between early and later IQs (Sameroff et al., 1993), and the relationship grows even stronger during middle childhood. Table 9.4 summarizes the results of a longitudinal study of more than 250 children conducted at the University of California (Honzik, Macfarlane, & Allen, 1948). In examining these data, we see that the shorter the interval between two testings, the higher the correlations between children's IQ scores. But even after a number of years have passed, IQ seems to be a reasonably stable attribute. After all, the scores that children obtain at age 8 are still clearly related to those they obtain 10 years later at age 18.

There is something that these correlations are not telling us, however. Each of them is based on a large group of children, and they do not necessarily mean that the IQs of *individual children* remain stable over time. Robert McCall and his associates (1973) looked at the IQ scores of 140 children who had taken intelligence tests at regular intervals between ages 2½ and 17. Their findings were remarkable: more than half of these individuals displayed large fluctuations in IQ over time, and the average range of variation in the IQ scores of the test-takers whose scores fluctuated was more than 20 points.

So it seems that IQ is more stable for some children than for others. Clearly, these findings challenge the notion that IQ is a reflection of one's absolute potential for learning or intellectual capacity; if it were, the intellectual profiles of virtually all children would be highly stable, showing only minor variations due to errors of measurement.

Alan S. Weiner/The Liaison Agency/Getty Images

Impoverished environments dampen intellectual growth, leading to a progressive decline in children's IQ scores.

What, then, does an IQ represent, if not one's intellectual competence or ability? Today, many experts believe that an IQ score is merely an estimate of the person's intellectual performance at one particular point in time—an estimate that may or may not be a good indication of the person's intellectual capacity.

Interestingly, children whose IQs change the most usually do not fluctuate randomly: their scores tend to either increase or decrease over time. Who are the gainers and who are the losers? Gainers typically come from homes in which parents are interested in their children's intellectual accomplishments, urge them to achieve, and are neither too strict nor too lax in their child-rearing practices (Honzik, Macfarlane, & Allen, 1948; McCall, Applebaum, & Hogarty, 1973). On the other hand, meaningful declines in IQ often occur among children who live in poverty, especially when that poverty is prolonged rather than tempo-

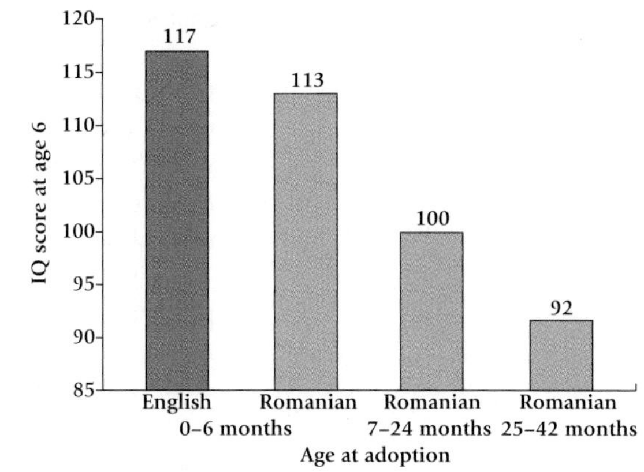

Figure 9.6 Mental performance at age 6 years for early-adopted English children and Romanian orphans adopted at different ages. Notice that the longer the Romanian children had lived in the barren institutional environment, the lower their cognitive performances at age 6—a finding that supports the cumulative-deficit hypothesis. *Adapted from T. G. O'Connor, M. Rutter, C. Beckett, L. Keaveney, J. M. Kreppner, & the English and Romanian Adoptees Study Team (2000). The effects of global severe privation on cognitive competence: Extension and longitudinal follow-up.* Child Development, 71, *376–390. Reprinted by permission.*

cumulative-deficit hypothesis the notion that impoverished environments inhibit intellectual growth and that these inhibiting effects accumulate over time.

rary (Duncan & Brooks-Gunn, 1997). Otto Klineberg (1963) proposed a **"cumulative-deficit" hypothesis** to explain this: presumably, impoverished environments dampen intellectual growth, and these inhibiting effects accumulate over time. Consequently, the longer children remain in a barren intellectual environment, the worse they perform on IQ tests.

Support for the cumulative-deficit effect comes from a study of the intellectual performance of Romanian children adopted into middle-class English homes after spending varying amounts of time in understaffed, poverty-stricken Romanian institutions (O'Connor et al., 2000). As we see in Figure 9.6, the 6-year-old mental performance scores of Romanian children adopted in the first 6 months of life were comparable to those of English children adopted within their first 6 months. Romanian children adopted later showed lingering cognitive deficits at age 6, with children who had spent more time in the poverty-stricken orphanages posting the lowest scores (or larger deficits).

What Do Intelligence Tests Predict?

We have seen that IQ tests measure intellectual performance rather than capacity and that a person's IQ may vary considerably over time. Given these qualifications, it seems reasonable to ask whether IQ scores can tell anything very meaningful about the people who were tested. For example, does IQ predict future academic accomplishments? Is it in any way related to a person's health, occupational status, or general life satisfaction? Let's first consider the relationship between IQ and academic achievement.

IQ as a Predictor of Scholastic Achievement

Because the original purpose of IQ testing was to estimate how well children would perform at school, it should come as no surprise that modern intelligence tests predict academic achievement quite well (Ackerman et al., 2001; White, 2000). The average correlation between children's IQ scores and their current and future grades at school is about .50 (Neisser et al., 1996). In addition, scholastic aptitude tests such as the ACT or SAT are also reliable predictors of the grades that high school students will make in college.

Not only do students with high IQs tend to do better in school, but they stay there longer (Brody, 1997); that is, they are less likely to drop out of high school and more likely than other high school graduates to attempt and complete college.

Some have argued that IQ tests predict scholastic performance because both measures depend on the abstract reasoning abilities that make up Spearman's *g*, or general mental ability (Jensen, 1998). However, critics of this viewpoint argue that both IQ tests and measures of scholastic achievement reflect knowledge and reasoning skills that are culturally valued (White, 2000). One line of evidence consistent with this viewpoint is that schooling, which largely reflects cultural values, actually improves IQ test performance (Ceci & Williams, 1997). How? By transmitting factual knowledge pertinent to test questions, promoting memory strategies and categorization skills that are measured on IQ tests, and encouraging attitudes and behaviors (such as trying hard and working under pressure) that foster successful test-taking skills (Ceci, 1991; Huttenlocker, Levine, & Vevea, 1998). Viewed from this perspective, then, IQ tests could almost be considered tests of academic achievement (White, 2000).

Finally, let's keep in mind that the moderate correlations between IQ and scholastic performance are based on group trends and that the IQ score of any individual student may not accurately reflect her current or future academic accomplishments (Ackerman et al., 2001). Clearly, academic performance also depends very heavily on such factors as a student's work habits, interests, and motivation to succeed (Neisser et al., 1996). So even though IQ (and aptitude) tests predict academic achievement better than any other type of test, judgments about a student's prospects for future success should never be based on a test score alone. Indeed, studies have consistently shown that the best single predictor of a student's future grades is not an IQ or aptitude score but, rather, the grades the student has previously earned (Minton & Schneider, 1980).

IQ as a Predictor of Vocational Outcomes

Do people with higher IQs get better jobs? Are they more successful in their chosen occupations than co-workers who test lower in intelligence?

There is a clear relationship between IQ and occupational status: professional and other white-collar business persons consistently score higher in IQ than blue collar or manual workers (White, 2000), although the IQ gap across occupations is smaller for recent cohorts than was true earlier in the 20th century, perhaps due to improvements over time in educational opportunities for the less wealthy (Weakliem, McQuillan, & Schauer, 1995). Generally, the average IQ for an occupation increases as the prestige of the occupation increases. And one contributor to this relationship is the link between IQ and education (Brody, 1997). Yet IQs vary considerably in every occupational group, and many people in low-status jobs have high IQs.

Does IQ predict job performance? Are bright lawyers, electricians, or farmhands more successful or productive than their less intelligent colleagues? The answer here is also yes. The correlations between mental test scores and such indications of job performance as ratings from supervisors average about +.50—about as high as IQ correlates with academic achievement (Hunter & Hunter, 1984; Neisser et al., 1996). However, an astute manager or personnel officer would never rely exclusively on an IQ score to decide who to hire or to promote. One reason for looking beyond IQ is that people differ in **tacit (or practical) intelligence**—the ability to size up everyday problems and take steps to solve them, which is not closely related to IQ, but which predicts job performance rather well (Sternberg et al., 1995). In addition, other variables such as prior job performance, interpersonal skills, and motivation to succeed may be as important or even more important than IQ as predictors of future job performance (Neisser et al., 1996).

tacit (or practical) intelligence ability to size up everyday problems and solve them; only modestly related to IQ.

IQ as a Predictor of Health, Adjustment, and Life Satisfaction

Are bright people any healthier, happier, or better adjusted than those of average or below-average intelligence? Let's see what researchers have learned by considering the life outcomes of people at opposite ends of the IQ continuum: the intellectually gifted and the mentally retarded.

In 1922, Lewis Terman began a most interesting longitudinal study of more than 1,500 California children who had IQs of 140 or higher—a study that continues today. The purpose of the project was to collect as much information as possible about the abil-

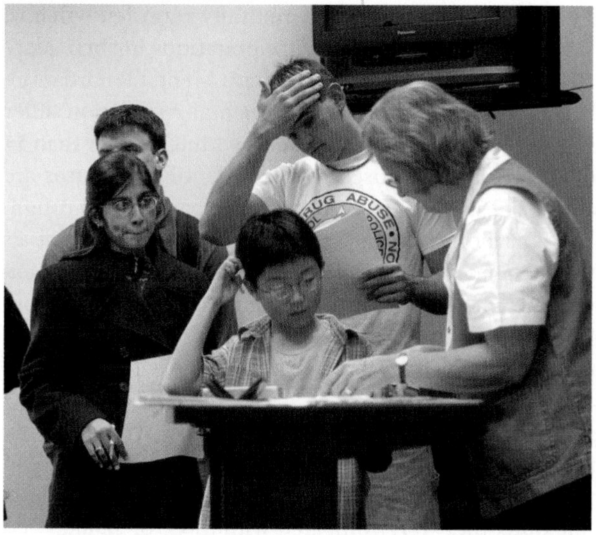

Nancy Stone/Chicago Tribune

Some gifted children as young as 11 or 12 thrive as college students, particularly if they have the support and encouragement of their parents.

ities and personal characteristics of these "gifted" children and to follow up on them every few years for the rest of their lives to see what they were accomplishing.

It soon became clear that these children were exceptional in many respects other than intelligence. For example, they had learned to walk and talk much sooner than most toddlers, and their general health, as determined from physicians' reports, was much better than average. The gifted children were rated by teachers as better adjusted emotionally and more morally mature than their less intelligent peers. And although they were no more popular, on average, than their classmates, the gifted children were quicker to take charge and assume positions of leadership. Taken together, these findings demolish the stereotype of child prodigies as frail, sickly youngsters who are socially inadequate and emotionally immature.

Yet it is inappropriate to conclude that intellectually gifted children are immune to adjustment problems. Other studies find that very high-IQ children are about twice as likely as nongifted peers to feel socially isolated, depressed, and to even try to hide their abilities in the hope of becoming more popular (Winner, 2000). Intellectually gifted youngsters who display these adjustment problems may profit from skipping grades or otherwise having their education accelerated so that they are challenged academically and exposed to peers who think as complexly as they do. Yet, a decision to accelerate the education of gifted children should always be made on an individual basis, for some accelerated children do become anxious and depressed at being so far behind their older classmates both socially and emotionally (Winner, 1997).

What becomes of gifted children as adults? Most of Terman's gifted sample remained remarkable in many respects. Fewer than 5 percent were rated as seriously maladjusted, and the incidence of problems such as ill health, alcoholism, and delinquent behavior was but a fraction of that normally observed in the general population (Terman, 1954), although they were no less likely to divorce (Holahan & Sears, 1995). The occupational attainments of the gifted men were impressive. By middle age, 88 percent were working in professional or semiprofessional jobs. As a group they had taken out more than 200 patents and written some 2,000 scientific reports, 100 books, 375 plays or short stories, and more than 300 essays, sketches, magazine articles, and critiques. Due to the influence of gender-role expectations during the period covered by Terman's study, most of the gifted women sacrificed career aspirations to raise families (Schuster, 1990; Tomlinson-Keasey & Little, 1990). However, more recent cohorts of gifted women are pursuing careers more vigorously and seem to have a greater sense of well-being than gifted women in Terman's study did (Schuster, 1990; Subotnik, Karp, & Morgan, 1989).

In short, most of Terman's participants were well-adjusted people living happy, healthy, and highly productive lives. Nevertheless, approximately 15 percent of the sample were not particularly happy or successful as middle-aged adults (Shurkin, 1992; Terman, 1954). In their analysis of factors that predicted the paths these adults' lives took over a 40-year period, Carolyn Tomlinson-Keasey and Todd Little (1990) found that the most well-adjusted and successful participants had highly educated parents who offered them lots of love and intellectual stimulation. The least successful of the group were likely to have experienced disruption of family ties due to their parents' divorce and less social support and encouragement (see also Friedman et al., 1995). So a high IQ, by itself, does not guarantee health, happiness, or success. Even among a select sample of children with superior IQs, the quality of the home environment contributes substantially to future outcomes and accomplishments.

What about the other end of the IQ continuum? Do mentally retarded individuals have much hope of succeeding in life or achieving happiness? Although our stereotypes about mental retardation might persuade us to say no, research suggests a different conclusion.

mental retardation
significant sub-average intellectual functioning associated with impairments in adaptive behavior in everyday life.

About 3 percent of school-age children are classified as **mentally retarded**—that is, as significantly below average in intellectual functioning, with limitations in such adaptive behaviors as self-care and social skills (American Association on Mental Retardation, 1992; Roeleveld, Zielhuis, & Gabreels, 1997). Individuals with mental retardation differ greatly in their levels of functioning. Severely retarded individuals with IQs lower than 55 are often affected by *organic retardation*—deficits caused by such identifiable causes are Down syndrome, diseases, or injuries. These individuals may require basic care throughout life, often in institutions. More common, however, are mildly retarded individuals (IQs 55 to 70) who usually display *cultural-familial retardation*—deficits reflecting a combination of low genetic potential and an unstimulating rearing environment (Simonoff, Bolton, & Rutter, 1996). Mildly retarded individuals can learn both academic and practical lessons at school, and they can often work and live independently or with occasional help as adults.

What kinds of life outcomes do mildly retarded individuals display? We gain some clues from a follow-up study of men and women (average IQ < 67) who had been placed in special education classes for the mentally retarded during the 1920s and 1930s (Ross et al., 1985). Nearly 40 years later, their life outcomes were compared with those of siblings and nonrelated peers, and with the highly favorable attainments of Terman's gifted sample.

Generally, the mentally retarded adults had less favorable life outcomes in middle age than the nonretarded groups (see also Schalock et al., 1992). As we see in the Table 9.5, about 80 percent of the retarded men were employed, but they usually held semiskilled or unskilled jobs that required little education or intellectual ability. Retarded women usually married and became homemakers. Compared with nonretarded peers, retarded men and women fared worse on other counts as well. For example, they had lower incomes, less adequate housing, poorer social skills, and a greater dependency on others.

Yet the authors of this study still found grounds for optimism. After all, the vast majority of these mildly retarded individuals had worked and married, and they were generally satisfied with their accomplishments. In fact, only one in five reported having *any* need for public assistance in the 10 years before they were interviewed. Clearly, they were faring much better than common stereotypes about the mentally retarded would lead us to believe.

So this study, like others before it, reveals that many individuals labeled mildly retarded by schools, and who do indeed have some difficulty mastering academic lessons, often "vanish" into the adult population after they leave school. Apparently, they adapt to the demands of adult life, displaying a fair amount of the practical intelligence or "street smarts" that Sternberg (1997) talks about, and that is not measured by standardized IQ tests. As the authors put it, "It does not take as many IQ points as most people believe to be productive . . . and self-fulfilled" (Ross et al., 1985, p. 149).

TABLE 9.5 Midlife Occupations of Mentally Retarded, Nonretarded, and Gifted Males

Occupational classification	Mentally retarded subjects (n = 54), %	Nonretarded siblings (n = 31), %	Nonretarded peers (n = 33), %	Terman's gifted sample (n = 757), %
Professional, managerial	1.9	29.1	36.4	86.3
Retail business, skilled trade, agricultural	29.6	32.3	39.4	12.5
Semiskilled, minor or business, clerical	50.0	25.8	15.2	1.2
Slightly skilled, unskilled	18.5	13.0	9.4	0.0

Source: Adapted from *Lives of Mentally Retarded: A Forty-Year Follow-up*, by R. T. Ross, M. J. Begab, E. H. Dondis, J. S. Giampiccolo, Jr., & C. E. Meyers. Copyright © 1985 by Stanford University Press. Adapted with permission.

CONCEPT CHECK 9.1 Understanding Theories of Intelligence and Intelligence Testing

Check your understanding of different perspectives on the meaning of intelligence, different approaches to intelligence testing, and what intelligence tests predict by answering the following questions. Answers appear in the Appendix.

Matching: Match the following descriptions of theories of intelligence to the correct name for the theory below.

a. the triarchic theory
b. the psychometric approach
c. the theory of multiple intelligences

1. ______ The theoretical perspective that portrays intelligence as a trait (or set of traits) on which individuals differ.
2. ______ Gardner's theory that humans display as many as nine distinct kinds of intelligence, each linked to a particular area of the brain.
3. ______ Sternberg's theory that intelligence should be considered contextually, experientially, and in terms of information-processing components.

Multiple Choice: Select the best answer for each question.

______ 4. The currently used deviation IQ is determined by:
a. comparing the child's mental age to chronological age

$$IQ = \frac{MA}{CA} \times 100$$

b. comparing the child's performance to other children of his or her own age
c. comparing how much the child's performance deviates from adult performance
d. subtracting missed items from 100 and dividing by the child's chronological age

______ 5. Joanna has been labeled mildly mentally retarded with an IQ of 65, and displays cultural-familial retardation. We can most likely assume that Joanna:
a. has deficits caused by Down syndrome, disease, or injury
b. will require basic institutional care throughout her life
c. has deficits reflecting a combination of low genetic potential and an unstimulating rearing environment
d. cannot attend to her basic self-care and social skills

______ 6. Infant development scales such as the Bayley Scales of Infant Development have been found to be:
a. poor predictors of later IQ, probably because IQ performance is such an unstable attribute
b. good predictors of later IQ, probably because IQ is such a stable attribute
c. good predictors of later IQ, probably because intelligence is so highly canalized
d. poor predictors of later IQ, probably because infant tests and later IQ tests tap different abilities

______ 7. Dr. Smahtee is a clinical psychologist who administers intelligence tests to children as one aspect of his professional work. His view of intelligence is consistent with the psychometric perspective of Cattell and Horn. On one test he asks children to name as many of the United States' capitals as they can remember. With this test, Dr. Smahtee assumes he is testing the children's:
a. *g*, or general intelligence
b. fluid intelligence
c. crystallized intelligence
d. motor intelligence

Short Answer: Provide brief answers to the following questions.

8. Wechsler developed his own intelligence tests because he was dissatisfied with the Stanford-Binet. What did he feel was the major problem with the Stanford-Binet? What is one advantage to having separate verbal and performance scales?
9. Assume that Desean, Jesse, and Chris have completed a standardized IQ test. Desean's IQ score is 135, Jesse's IQ score is 100, and Chris's IQ score is 80. Explain the meaning of each of their scores.

Essay: Provide a more detailed answer to the following question.

10. List the nine kinds of intelligence Gardner proposed in his theory of multiple intelligences, and identify vocations in which each type of intelligence would be a valuable asset.

Factors That Influence IQ Scores

Why do people differ so dramatically in the scores that they make on IQ tests? In addressing this issue, we will briefly review the evidence for hereditary and environmental influences and then take a closer look at several important social and cultural correlates of intellectual performance.

The Evidence for Heredity

In Chapter 3, we reviewed two major lines of evidence indicating that heredity affects intellectual performance and that about half the variation in IQ scores within a particular population of test takers is due to genetic differences among these individuals.

Twin Studies

The intellectual resemblance between pairs of individuals living in the same home increases as a function of their kinship (that is, genetic similarity). For example, the IQ correlation for identical twins, who inherit identical genes, is substantially higher than the IQ correlations for fraternal twins and nontwin siblings, who have only half of their genes in common (Bower, 2003).

Adoption Studies

Adopted children's IQs are more highly correlated with the IQs of their biological parents than with those of their adoptive parents. This finding can be interpreted as evidence for a genetic influence on IQ, for adoptees share genes with their biological parents but not with their adoptive caregivers.

We also learned in Chapter 3 that a person's genotype may influence the type of environment that he or she is likely to experience. Indeed, Scarr and McCartney (1983) have proposed that people seek out environments that are compatible with their genetic predispositions, so that identical twins (who share identical genes) select and experience more similar environments than fraternal twins or nontwin siblings do. This is a major reason that identical twins resemble each other intellectually throughout life, whereas the intellectual resemblances between fraternal twins or nontwin siblings become progressively smaller over time (McCartney, Harris, & Bernieri, 1990).

Do these observations imply that a person's genotype determines his environment and exerts the primary influence on his intellectual development? No, they do not! A child who has a genetic predisposition to seek out intellectual challenges could hardly be expected to develop a high IQ if she is raised in a barren environment that offers few such challenges for her to meet. Alternatively, a child who does not gravitate toward intellectual activities might nevertheless obtain an average or above-average IQ if raised in a stimulating environment that continually provides her with cognitive challenges that she must master. Let's now take a closer look at how environment might influence intellectual performance.

The Evidence for Environment

The evidence for environmental effects on intelligence comes from a variety of sources. For example, we learned in Chapter 3 that there is a small to moderate intellectual resemblance between pairs of *genetically unrelated* children who live in the same household—a resemblance that can only be attributable to their common rearing environment because they share no genes. Earlier in this chapter we noted that children who remain in impoverished rearing environments show a progressive decline (or cumulative-deficit) in IQ, thus implying that economic disadvantage inhibits intellectual growth.

Might we then promote intellectual development and improve children's IQs by enriching the environments in which they live? Indeed we can, and at least two lines of evidence tell us so.

The Flynn Effect

Flynn effect
systematic increase in IQ scores observed over the 20th century.

People have been getting smarter throughout the 20th century. Average IQs in all countries studied have increased about 3 points per decade since 1940, a phenomenon called the **Flynn effect** after its discoverer, James Flynn (1987, 1996; Howard, 2005; Teasdale & Owen, 2005). An increase this large that occurs this quickly cannot be due to evolution and must therefore have environmental causes. So what might be responsible for improving IQ scores?

Worldwide improvements in education could increase IQs in three ways: helping people to become more test-wise, more knowledgeable in general, and more likely to rely on sophisticated problem-solving strategies (Flieller, 1999; Flynn, 1996). Yet, improved education is probably not the sole contributor because the Flynn effect is much clearer on measures of fluid intelligence, even though one might expect crystallized intelligence to benefit most from educational enrichment. Twentieth-century improvements in nutrition and health care are two other potent environmental factors that many believe to have contributed to improved intellectual performance by helping to optimize the development of growing brains and nervous systems (Flynn, 1996; Neisser, 1998).

Adoption Studies

Other investigators have charted the intellectual growth of adopted children who left disadvantaged family backgrounds and were placed with highly educated adoptive parents (Scarr & Weinberg, 1983; Skodak & Skeels, 1949). By the time these adoptees were 4 to 7 years old, they were scoring well above average on standardized IQ tests (about 110 in Scarr and Weinberg's study and 112 in Skodak and Skeels's). Interestingly, the IQ scores of these adoptees were still correlated with the IQs of their *biological* mothers, thus reflecting the influence of heredity on intellectual performance. And yet, the *actual* IQs these adoptees attained were considerably higher (by 10 to 20 points) than one would expect on the basis of the IQ and educational levels of their biological parents. Furthermore, the adoptees' levels of academic achievement remained slightly above the national norm well into adolescence (Weinberg, Scarr, & Waldman, 1992; Waldman, Weinberg, & Scarr, 1994). So the *phenotype* that one displays on a genetically influenced attribute like intelligence is clearly influenced by one's environment. Because the adopting parents in these studies were themselves highly educated and above average in intelligence, it seems reasonable to assume that they were providing enriched, intellectually stimulating home environments that fostered the cognitive development of their adopted children.

Social and Cultural Correlates of Intellectual Performance

So environment is truly a powerful force that may either promote or inhibit intellectual growth. Yet our use of the term "environment" here is very global, and the evidence that we have reviewed does not really tell us which of the life experiences children have are most likely to affect their intellectual development. In this section, we will look more closely at environmental influences and see that a child's performance on IQ tests depends to some extent on parental attitudes and child-rearing practices, the socioeconomic status of the family, and even the sociocultural group to which the family belongs.

Home Environment and IQ

Earlier, we implied that the quality or character of the home environment may play an important role in determining children's intellectual performance and eventual life

TABLE 9.6 Ten Environmental Risk Factors Associated with Low IQ and Mean IQs at Age 4 of Children Who Did or Did Not Experience Each Risk Factor

Risk factor	Mean IQ at age 4: Child experienced risk factor	Mean IQ at age 4: Child did not experience risk factor
Child is member of minority group	90	110
Head of household is unemployed or low-skilled worker	90	108
Mother did not complete high school	92	109
Family has four or more children	94	105
Father is absent from family	95	106
Family experienced many stressful life events	97	105
Parents have rigid child-rearing values	92	107
Mother is highly anxious/distressed	97	107
Mother has poor mental health/diagnosed disorder	99	107
Mother shows little positive affect toward child	88	107

Source: Data and descriptions compiled from "Stability of intelligence from Preschool to Adolescence: The Influence of Social and Family Risk Factors," by A.J. Sameroff, R. Seifer, A. Bladwin, and C. Baldwin, 1993, *Child Development, 64,* 80–97.

outcomes. Several years ago, Arnold Sameroff and his colleagues (1993) listed 10 environmental factors that place children at risk of displaying low IQ scores, 9 of which were characteristics of children's homes and families (or family members). These researchers measured each of the IQ risk factors shown in Table 9.6 at age 4, and again when the children in their sample were 13 years old. Each of these "risk factors" was related to IQ at age 4, and most of them also predicted IQ at age 13. In addition, the greater the number of these risk factors affecting a child, the lower his or her IQ; which particular risk factors a child experienced were less important than how many he or she experienced. This same pattern of outcomes has now been replicated (through age 4) in a contemporary sample of low-income African families (Burchinal, Roberts, Hooper, and Zeisel, 2000). It is clearly not conducive to intellectual development to grow up in a economically disadvantaged home with highly stressed or poorly educated parents who provide low levels of intellectual stimulation.

Assessing the Character of the Home Environment

HOME inventory
a measure of the amount and type of intellectual stimulation provided by a child's home environment.

Exactly how do parents influence a child's intellectual development? In an attempt to find out, Bettye Caldwell and Robert Bradley have developed a widely used instrument, called the **HOME inventory** (*H*ome *O*bservation for *M*easurement of the *E*nvironment), that allows an interviewer/observer to visit an infant, a preschooler, or a school-age child at home and determine how intellectually stimulating (or impoverished) that home environment is (Caldwell & Bradley, 1984). The infant version of the HOME inventory, for example, consists of 45 statements, each of which is scored *yes* (the statement is true of this family) or *no* (the statement is not true of this family). To gather the information necessary to complete the inventory, the researcher (1) asks the child's parent (usually the mother) to describe her daily routine and child-rearing practices, (2) carefully observes the parent as she interacts with her child, and (3) notes the kinds of play materials that the parent makes available to the child. The 45 bits of information collected are then grouped into the six subscales in Table 9.7. The home then receives a score on each subscale. The higher the scores across all six subscales, the more intellectually stimulating the home environment.

TABLE 9.7 Subscales and Sample Items for the HOME Inventory (Infant Version)

Subscale 1: Emotional and verbal responsivity of parent (11 items)	
Sample items:	Parent responds verbally to child's vocalizations or verbalizations
	Parent's speech is distinct, clear, and audible
	Parent caresses or kisses child at least once
Subscale 2: Avoidance of restriction and punishment (8 items)	
Sample items:	Parent neither slaps nor spanks child during visit
	Parent does not scold or criticize child during visit
	Parent does not interfere with or restrict child more than three times during visit
Subscale 3: Organization of physical and temporal environment (6 items)	
Sample items:	Child gets out of house at least four times a week
	Child's play environment is safe
Subscale 4: Provision of appropriate play materials (9 items)	
Sample items:	Child has a push or pull toy
	Parent provides learning facilitators appropriate to age: mobile, table and chairs, highchair, playpen, and so on
	Parent provides toys for child to play with during visit
Subscale 5: Parental involvement with child (6 items)	
Sample items:	Parent talks to child while doing household work
	Parent structures child's play periods
Subscale 6: Opportunities for variety in daily stimulation (5 items)	
Sample items:	Father provides some care daily
	Child has three or more books of his or her own

Source: Adapted from the *Manual for the HOME Observation for Measurement of the Environment*, by B. M. Caldwell & R. H. Bradley, 1984, University of Arkansas. Copyright © 1984. Adapted by permission.

Does the HOME Predict IQ?

Research conducted in the United States consistently indicates that the scores that families obtain on the HOME Inventory do predict the intellectual performances of toddlers, preschoolers, and elementary-school-aged children, regardless of their social class or ethnic backgrounds (Gottfried, Fleming, & Gottfried, 1998; Jackson et al., 2000; Luster & Dubow, 1992; Espy, Molfese, & DiLalla, 2001). Furthermore, gains in IQ from age 1 to age 3 are likely to occur among children from stimulating homes. On the other hand, children from families with low HOME scores often experience 10 to 20 point declines in IQ over the same period—much as the cumulative deficit hypothesis would predict (Bradley et al., 1989).

Which Aspects of the Home Environment Matter Most? Although all of the HOME subscales are moderately correlated with children's IQ scores, some are better predictors of intellectual performance than others. During infancy, HOME subscales measuring *parental involvement* with the child, provision of *age-appropriate play materials,* and opportunities for *variety in daily stimulation* are the best predictors of children's later IQs and scholastic achievement (Bradley, Caldwell, & Rock, 1988; Gottfried et al., 1994). And preschool measures of *parental warmth* and *stimulation of language and academic behaviors* are also closely associated with children's future intellectual performances (Bradley & Caldwell, 1982; Bradley, Caldwell, & Rock, 1988).

What these findings imply, then, is that an intellectually stimulating home is one in which parents are warm, verbally engaging, and eager to be involved with their child (Fagot & Gauvain, 1997; Hart & Risley, 1995; MacPhee, Ramey, & Yeates, 1984). These parents describe new objects, concepts, and experiences clearly and accurately, and they

Bob Daemmrich/The Image Works

Orderly home environments in which family members are warm, responsive, and eager to be involved with one another are precisely the kind of setting that promotes children's intellectual development.

provide the child with a variety of challenges that are appropriate for her age or developmental level. They encourage the child to ask questions, solve problems, and think about what she is learning. As the child matures and enters school, they stress the importance of academic achievement and expect her to get good grades (Luster & Dubow, 1992). When you stop and think about it, it is not at all surprising that children from these "enriched" home settings often have high IQs; after all, their parents are obviously concerned about their cognitive development and have spent several years encouraging them to acquire new information and to practice many of the cognitive skills that are measured on intelligence tests.

A Hidden Genetic Effect? It turns out that brighter parents are more likely to provide more intellectually stimulating home environments (Coon et al., 1990). Could the correlation between the quality of home environments and children's IQ scores simply reflect the fact that bright parents transmit genes for high intelligence to their children?

There is some support for this idea in that correlations between HOME scores and IQ scores are higher for biological children, who share genes with their parents, than for adopted children, who are genetically unrelated to other members of their family (Braungart, Fulker, & Plomin, 1992). So does the quality of the home environment have any effect on children's intellectual development that does not reflect the influence of genes?

The answer is yes, and there are two lines of evidence that tell us so. First, adopted children's IQ scores rise considerably when they are moved from less stimulating to more stimulating homes (Turkheimer, 1991). Clearly, this change in IQ has to be an environmental effect because adoptees share no genes with their adoptive parents. Equally revealing are the results of a longitudinal study of 112 mothers and their 2- to 4-year-old children conducted by Keith Yeates and his associates (1983). These investigators measured the mothers' IQs, the IQ of each child at ages 2, 3, and 4, and the quality of the families' home environments (as assessed by the HOME). The best predictor of a child's IQ at age 2 was the mother's IQ, just as a genetic hypothesis would suggest. But the picture had changed by the time the children were 4 years old; now the quality of the home environment was a strong predictor of children's IQs, even after the influence of the mothers' IQ was taken into account.

So it appears that the quality of the home environment is truly an important contributor to a child's intellectual development that becomes more apparent later in the preschool period, when IQ becomes a more stable attribute (Sameroff et al., 1993; Yeates et al., 1983). However, let's also note that the relationship between HOME scores and children's IQs does decline somewhat during the elementary school years (Luster & Dubow, 1992), probably because older children are away from home more often and are exposed (or expose themselves) to other people, such as coaches, teachers, and peers, who also influence their intellectual development (Bjorklund, 2005).

Social-Class and Ethnic Differences in IQ

One of the most reliable findings in the intelligence literature is a social class effect: children from lower- and working-class homes average some 10 to 15 points below their middle-class age-mates on standardized IQ tests (Helms, 1997). Infants are apparently the only exception to this rule, as there are no reliable social class differences on infant information-processing measures of habituation and preference for novelty that predict later IQ scores (McCall & Carriger, 1993) or in the developmental quotients (DQs) that infants obtain on infant "intelligence" tests (Golden et al., 1971).

There are also some ethnic variations in intellectual performance. In the United States, children of African American and Native American ancestry score, on average, about 12 to 15 points below their European American classmates on standardized IQ tests. The average IQ scores of Hispanic American children lie in between those of African American and European American classmates, whereas Asian American children score at about the same level or slightly higher on IQ tests than European American children do (Flynn, 1991; Neisser et al., 1996). Different ethnic groups may also display distinctive ability profiles. African American children, for example, often perform better on verbal tests than on other subtests, whereas Hispanic American and Native American children may do particularly well on nonverbal items assessing spatial abilities (Neisser et al., 1996; Suzuki & Valencia, 1997).

Before we try to interpret these social-class and ethnic variations, an important truth is worth stating here—one that is often overlooked when people discover that white and Asian American children outperform their African American or Hispanic classmates on IQ tests. The fact is that we cannot predict anything about the IQ or the future accomplishments of an individual on the basis of his ethnicity or skin color. As we see in Figure 9.7, the IQ distributions for samples of African Americans and white Americans overlap considerably. So even though the average IQ scores of African Americans are somewhat lower than those of whites, the overlapping distributions mean that many African American children obtain higher IQ scores than many white children. In fact, approximately 15 to 25 percent of the African American population scores higher—in many cases, substantially higher—than the majority of the white population.

Why Do Groups Differ in Intellectual Performance?

Over the years, developmentalists have proposed three general hypotheses to account for ethnic and social-class differences in IQ: (1) a *cultural/test bias* hypothesis, that standardized IQ tests and the ways they are administered are geared toward white, middle-class cultural experiences and seriously underestimate the intellectual capabilities of economically disadvantaged children, especially those from minority subcultures; (2) a *genetic* hypothesis that group differences in IQ are hereditary; and (3) an *environmental* hypothesis, that the groups scoring lower in IQ come from intellectually impoverished backgrounds—that is, neighborhoods and home environments that are not very conducive to intellectual growth.

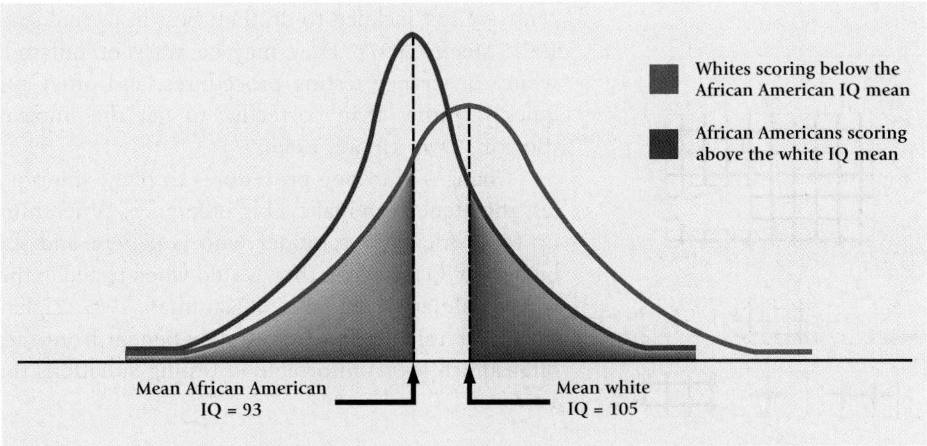

Figure 9.7 Approximate distributions of IQ scores for African American and white children reared by their biological parents. *Based on* Intelligence, *2nd ed., by N. Brody, 1990. San Diego: Academic Press; and "Intelligence: Knowns and Unknowns," by U. Neisser, et al., 1996,* American Psychologist, 51, *77–101.*

The Cultural/Test-Bias Hypothesis

cultural test bias hypothesis
the notion that IQ tests and testing procedures have a built-in, middle-class bias that explains the substandard performance of children from lower-class and minority subcultures.

Those who favor the **cultural/test bias hypothesis** believe that group differences in IQ are an artifact of our tests and testing procedures (Helms, 1992; White, 2000; Resing, 2001; Helms-Lorenz, Van de Vijver, & Poortinga, 2003). To illustrate, they point out that IQ tests currently in use were designed to measure cognitive skills (for example, assembling puzzles) and general information (for example, "What is a 747?") that white, middle-class children are more likely to have acquired. They note that subtests measuring vocabulary and word usage may be harder for African Americans and Latinos, who often speak a different English dialect from that of the white middle class. Even the way language is used varies across ethnic groups. For example, white parents ask a lot of "knowledge-training" questions ("What does a doggie say?"; "Where do Eskimos live?") that require brief answers and are similar to the kinds of questions asked on IQ tests. AfricanAmerican parents are more inclined to ask *real questions* (for example, "Why didn't you come right home after school?") that the parents may not know the answer to—questions that often require elaborate, story-type responses that are quite unlike those called for at school or when taking an IQ test (Heath, 1989). So if IQ tests assess proficiency in the white culture, as many critics contend, minority children are bound to appear deficient (Helms, 1992; Van de Vijver & Tanzer, 2004; Fagan, 2000).

culture fair tests
intelligence tests constructed to minimize any irrelevant cultural biases in test content that could influence test performance.

Does "Test Bias" Explain Group Differences in IQ? Several attempts have been made to construct **"culture fair" IQ tests** that do not place poor people or those from minority subcultures at an immediate disadvantage (Fagan, 2000). For example, the *Raven Progressive Matrices Test* requires the examinee to scan a series of abstract designs, each of which has a missing section. The examinee's task is to complete each design by selecting the appropriate section from a number of alternatives (see Figure 9.8). These problems are assumed to be equally familiar (or unfamiliar) to people from all ethnic groups and social classes, there is no time limit on the test, and the instructions are very simple. Nevertheless, middle-class whites continue to outperform their lower-income and/or African American age-mates on these "culture fair" measures of intelligence (Jensen, 1980). Translating existing tests into the English dialect spoken by urban African American children also does not appear to increase the scores that these children make (Quay, 1971). And finally, IQ tests and various tests of intellectual aptitude (such as the SAT) predict future academic successes just as well as or even better for African Americans and other minorities as for whites (Neisser et al., 1996). Taken together, these findings imply that group differences in IQ scores are not solely attributable to biases in the content of our tests or the dialect in which they are administered. But another possibility remains.

Motivational Factors. Critics have argued that many minority children and adolescents are not inclined to do their best in formal testing situations (Moore, 1986; Ogbu, 1994; Steele, 1997). They may be wary of unfamiliar examiners (most of whom are white) or strange testing procedures, and often appear more interested in answering quickly (rather than correctly) to get the unpleasant testing experience over with (Boykin, 1994; Moore, 1986).

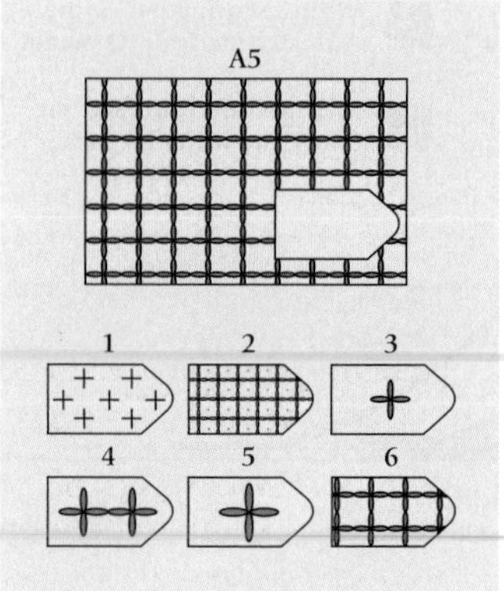

Figure 9.8 An item similar to those appearing in the Raven Progressive Matrices Test.

Changes in testing procedures to make minority examinees more comfortable and less threatened can make a big difference. When minority children are allowed to warm up to a "friendly" examiner who is patient and supportive, they score several points higher on IQ tests than they would when tested in the traditional way by a strange examiner (Kaufman, Kamphaus, & Kaufman, 1985; Zigler et al., 1982). Even minority youngsters from middle-class homes may benefit from these procedural changes, for they are often much less comfortable in testing situations than middle-class whites are (Moore, 1986).

Impacts of Negative Stereotypes. John Ogbu (1994) believes that negative stereotypes about their intellectual abilities may cause some minority youngsters to feel that their life outcomes will be restricted by prejudice and discrimination. Consequently, they may come to reject certain behaviors sanctioned by the majority culture, such as excelling on tests, as less relevant to them or as "acting white."

The Genetic Hypothesis

Controversy surrounding the causes of ethnic differences in IQ scores was fueled by the publication of Richard Herrnstein and Charles Murray's book, *The Bell Curve,* in 1994. These authors argued that ethnic differences in average IQ scores were largely the result of genetic differences between ethnicities (Rowe & Rodgers, 2005).

genetic hypothesis
the notion that group differences in IQ are hereditary.

Level I abilities
Jensen's term for lower-level intellectual abilities (such as attention and short-term memory) that are important for simple association learning.

Level II abilities
Jensen's term for higher-level cognitive skills that are involved in abstract reasoning and problem solving.

Arthur Jensen (1985, 1998) agrees with this **genetic hypothesis.** He claims that there are two broad classes of intellectual abilities that are equally heritable among different ethnic groups. **Level I abilities** include attentional processes, short-term memory, and associative skills—abilities that are important for simple kinds of rote learning. **Level II abilities** allow one to reason abstractly and to manipulate words and symbols to form concepts and solve problems. According to Jensen, Level II abilities are highly correlated with school achievement, whereas Level I abilities are not. Of course, it is predominantly Level II abilities that are measured on IQ tests.

Jensen (1985) finds that Level I tasks are performed equally well by children from all ethnic groups and social classes. However, middle-class and white children outperform lower-income and African American children on the more advanced Level II tasks. Since Level I and Level II tasks are equally heritable *within* each social class and ethnic group, Jensen proposes that the IQ differences *between* groups must be hereditary.

Criticisms of the Genetic Hypothesis. Although Jensen's arguments may sound convincing, the evidence that heredity contributes to within-group differences in intelligence says nothing at all about *between*-group differences in intelligence. Richard Lewontin (1976) makes this point quite clear with an analogy. Suppose that corn seeds with different genetic makeups are randomly drawn from a bag and planted in two fields—one that is barren and one that has fertile soil. Because all the plants within each field were grown in the same soil, their differences in height would have to be due to differences in genetic makeup. But if the plants grown in fertile soil are taller on average than those grown in barren soil (see Figure 9.9), this between-field difference is almost certainly due to environment—the quality of soil in which the plants grew. Similarly, even though genes partially explain individual differences in IQ *within* black groups and white groups, the average difference in IQ *between* the two ethnicities may represent nothing more than differences in the environments they typically experience (Brooks-Gunn et al., 2003; Rowe & Rodgers, 2005).

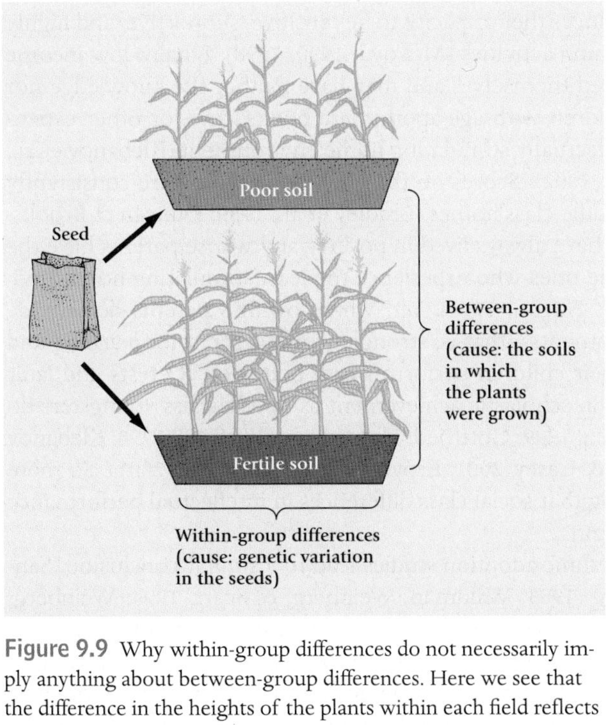

Figure 9.9 Why within-group differences do not necessarily imply anything about between-group differences. Here we see that the difference in the heights of the plants within each field reflects the genetic variation in the seeds that were planted there, whereas the difference in the average heights of the plants across the fields is attributable to an environmental factor: the soils in which they were grown. *Adapted from* Psychology, *Third Edition, by Henry Gleitman. Copyright © 1991, 1986, 1981 by W. W. Norton & Company, Inc. Used by permission of W. W. Norton & Company, Inc.*

Data available on mixed-ethnicity children also fails to support the genetic hypothesis. Eyferth (as cited in Loehlin, Lindzey, & Spuhler, 1975) obtained the IQ scores of German children fathered by African American soldiers, and compared these mixed-ethnicity children to a group of German children fathered by white American servicemen. Clearly, the mixed-ethnicity group should have scored lower than their white agemates if their African American fathers had had fewer IQ-enhancing genes to pass along to them. However, Eyferth found that these two groups of children did not differ in IQ. Similarly, extremely bright African American children have no higher percentage of white ancestors than is typical of the African American population as a whole (Scarr et al., 1977).

Despite this negative evidence, the genetic hypothesis lives on. T. Edward Reed (1997), for example, points to methodological problems with existing studies of mixed-ethnicity children that, in his opinion, call their findings into question. Other investigators claim that differences in head and brain size (with whites having larger heads and brains than African Americans) provide strong evidence that ethnic differences in IQ are largely hereditary (Lynn, 1997; Rushton, 1999). Are these physical differences between blacks and whites truly evidence that genes are responsible for black–white differences in IQ? Ulric Neisser (1997) certainly doesn't think so. He points out that both head and brain size are heavily influenced by such factors as adequacy of prenatal care and nutrition—environmental variables that differ across ethnic groups and can strongly affect children's intellectual performances. So even though IQ is a genetically influenced attribute within all ethnic groups, conclusions drawn in *The Bell Curve* are badly overstated. Simply stated, there is no evidence to conclusively demonstrate that group differences in IQ are genetically determined (Neisser et al., 1996).

The Environmental Hypothesis

environmental hypothesis
the notion that groups differ in IQ because the environments in which they are raised are not equally conducive to intellectual growth.

A third explanation for group differences in IQ is the **environmental hypothesis**—that poor people and members of various minority groups tend to grow up in environments that are much less conducive to intellectual development than those experienced by most whites and other members of the middle class.

Recently, developmentalists have carefully considered how a low-income or poverty-stricken lifestyle is likely to influence a family's children, and several of these findings bear directly on the issue of children's intellectual development (Duncan & Brooks-Gunn, 2000; Garrett, Ng'andu, & Ferron, 1994; McLoyd, 1998; Bradley, Burchinal, & Casey, 2001; Espy, Molfese, & DiLalla, 2001). Consider, for example, that a family's poverty status and lack of adequate income may mean that many children from low-income families are undernourished, which may inhibit brain growth and make them listless and inattentive (Pollitt, 1994). Furthermore, economic hardship creates psychological distress—a strong dissatisfaction with life's conditions that makes lower-income adults edgy and irritable and reduces their capacity to be sensitive, supportive, and highly involved in their children's learning activities (McLoyd, 1990, 1998). Finally, low-income parents are often poorly educated themselves and may have neither the knowledge nor the money to provide their children with age-appropriate books, toys, or other experiences that contribute to an intellectually stimulating home environment (Klebanov et al., 1998; Sellers, Burns, & Guyrke, 2002). Scores on the HOME inventory are consistently lower in low-income than in middle-class homes (Bradley et al., 1989; Duncan & Brooks-Gunn, 2000), and children who have always lived in poverty and whose parents have the fewest financial resources are the ones who experience the least stimulating home environments (Garrett, Ng'andu, & Ferron, 1994). Yet, when low-SES parents do provide more stimulating home environments—that is, strong encouragement for learning and many challenges to master—their children perform much better on IQ tests and later show as much intrinsic interest in scholastic achievement as middle-class youngsters do (DeGarmo, Forgatch, & Martinez, 1999; Gottfried, Fleming, & Gottfried, 1998; Klebanov et al., 1998; Bradley, Burchinal, & Casey, 2001; Espy, Molfese, & DiLalla, 2001). So there are ample reasons for concluding that social-class differences in intellectual performance are largely environmental in origin.

Carefully conducted cross-ethnic adoption studies lead to a similar conclusion. Sandra Scarr and Richard Weinberg (1983; Waldman, Weinberg, & Scarr, 1994; Weinberg, Scarr, & Waldman, 1992) have studied more than 100 African American (or mixed-ethnicity) children who were adopted by white, middle-class families. The adoptive parents were well above average in IQ and highly educated, and many had biological children of their own. Although Scarr and Weinberg found that the childhood IQs of the adoptees were about 6 points lower than the IQs of the white offspring of these same families, this small ethnic difference seems rather insignificant when we look at the absolute performance of the cross-ethnic adoptees. As a group, the African American adoptees obtained an average IQ of 106—6 points above the average for the population as a whole and 15 to 20 points above comparable children who are raised in low-income

African American communities. Ten years later, the average IQs of the cross-ethnic adoptees had declined somewhat (average = 97), although direct comparisons may be misleading because the IQ test used in the follow-up was different from that administered in childhood. Nevertheless, these cross-ethnic adolescent adoptees remained well above the average IQ obtained by low-income African American youth, and they scored slightly higher than the national norm in academic achievement. Scarr and Weinberg (1983) concluded that:

> The high IQ scores for the black and interracial [adoptees] . . . mean that (a) genetic differences do not account for a major portion of the IQ performance difference between racial groups, and (b) African American and interracial children *reared in the [middle class] culture of the tests and the schools* perform as well as other . . . children in similar families (p. 261, italics added).

It is important to note that Scarr and her associates are not suggesting that white parents are better parents or that disadvantaged children would be better off if they were routinely placed in middle-class homes. In fact, they caution that debates about who might make better parents only distract us from the more important message of the cross-ethnic adoption study, namely that much of the intellectual and academic discrepancies that have been attributed to ethnicity may largely reflect ethnic differences in socioeconomic status. Indeed, there is ample evidence for this preposition. Consider that nearly two-thirds of poverty-stricken people in the United States are white, and IQ scores of children from this disadvantaged subgroup closely resemble those of children from disadvantaged ethnic minority groups (U.S. Bureau of the Census, 1999). What's more, Charlotte Patterson and her associates (1990) found that variation in socioeconomic status is a better predictor of the academic competencies of African American and white schoolchildren than ethnicity is (see also Greenberg et al., 1999). Finally, the research described in Box 9.1 proceeds one step further by suggesting that almost all of the differences in IQ test performance between African American and white preschool children reflect differences in the social and economic environments in which these children are raised.

FOCUS ON RESEARCH

Do Socioeconomic Differences Explain Ethnic Differences in IQ?

In 1997 nearly 20 percent of American children—some $13^1/_2$ million in all—were living in families in which total income was not sufficient to meet the families' most basic needs (U.S. Bureau of the Census, 1999). Furthermore, children from minority groups are much more likely to be living under these marginal conditions than white youngsters are, especially African American children, for whom living in poverty early in life is more the rule than the exception (Duncan, Brooks-Gunn, & Klebanov, 1994).

To what extent do socioeconomic differences between African Americans and whites account for ethnic differences in IQ? One way to approach this question is to (1) select a large number of African American and white families, (2) carefully measure several indicators and correlates of each family's socioeconomic status, and (3) determine whether any differences in these socioeconomic variables are associated with (and thus might conceivably explain) ethnic differences in children's intellectual performance.

Jeanne Brooks-Gunn and her associates (1996) conducted such a study as part of a larger longitudinal investigation of low-birth-weight children. All of the children in this sample, who were now healthy 5-year-olds, had recently taken a standardized IQ test. In addition, such social class indicators and correlates as family income, average neighborhood income, mother's educational level, mother's verbal ability, number of parents living at home, and quality of the home environment (as assessed by the HOME inventory) were available for the family of each child. Like other investigators, Brooks-Gunn and her colleagues found that African American children obtained lower IQs, on average, than white children did. Furthermore, the African American families scored lower on each of the above indicators and correlates of socioeconomic status. So how close was the association between ethnic differences in IQ and differences in socioeconomic status?

To find out, Brooks-Gunn and her associates (1996) submitted their data to a sophisticated correlational analysis that allowed them to estimate how much of the ethnic difference in intellectual performance is accounted for by each indicator/correlate of socioeconomic status. This is accomplished statistically by holding each socioeconomic variable constant for all children and then estimating what the IQ difference

CONTINUED

between African Americans and whites would be had they been raised under the same conditions—that is, with the same financial circumstances, home environments, and so on.

The results of this analysis appear in the accompanying table. Because African American children and white children differed in ways other than socioeconomic status that are known to influence intellectual performance (for example, in birth weight), it was necessary to first estimate the contribution of these background variables to ethnic differences in intellectual performance. As we see in the table, ethnic differences in IQ are hardly affected, dropping from 18.1 points actually observed to an estimated 17.8 points after controlling for background differences between the groups. However, after adjusting for the lower average incomes of African American families, estimated ethnic differences in IQ drop 52 percent, to 8.5 points. Further adjustments to compensate for the lower levels of maternal education, maternal verbal ability, and the greater number of single-parent households among the African American sample reduced the IQ differences only minimally, from 8.5 to 7.8 points. But when the data were further analyzed to compensate for the less stimulating home environments in which African American children lived, there remained an IQ difference of only 3.4 points that was not accounted for by ethnic differences in socioeconomic status and home environments.

Of course, these findings are correlational data that we must interpret cautiously. Nevertheless, they strongly suggest that much of the IQ difference between African Americans and whites is really a social class effect and that African American children would perform comparably with whites if raised under similar socioeconomic circumstances. Indeed, we have reviewed other evidence that supports this conclusion, namely Scarr and Weinberg's cross-ethnic adoption study. When raised in similar middle-class environments, African American and white children differ only minimally in intellectual performance and score at or above the national average on tests of academic achievement.

Estimated Differences in Intellectual Performance of African American and White Preschool Children after Adjusting for Ethnic Differences in Background Variables, Socioeconomic Status, and Other Family Characteristics

Analysis performed	Ethnic difference in IQ (points)
Unadjusted (actual IQ scores)	18.1
After adjusting for race differences in:	
Background variables	17.8
Family/neighborhood income	8.5
Mother's education, mother's verbal ability, number of parents living at home	7.8
Home environment (HOME scores)	3.4

CONCEPT CHECK 9.2 Understanding Factors That Influence IQ Scores

Check your understanding of factors that influence IQ scores and the social and cultural correlates of intellectual performance by answering the following questions. Answers appear in the Appendix.

Multiple Choice: Select the best answer for each question.

_____ 1. The higher correlation of IQ for identical than fraternal twins is typically interpreted as evidence for the influence of:
a. heredity in intellectual performance
b. environment in intellectual performance
c. both heredity and environment in intellectual performance
d. neither heredity nor environment in intellectual performance

_____ 2. Arthur Jensen identified two broad classes of intellectual abilities. In his classification scheme, abstract reasoning skills would be considered to be:
a. fluid abilities
b. Level I abilities
c. crystallized abilities
d. Level II abilities

_____ 3. The Flynn effect (1996) refers to a long-term trend in which:
a. later generations have become less religious
b. hereditary influences have become stronger
c. IQs have risen in the entire population
d. evolution has expanded the brain's performance

_____ 4. At the annual company party, Joe Plodder got the Employee of the Year award. He said "Ah didn't go to college, but Ah do well because Ah got my smarts from the School of Hard Knocks." In this speech, Joe alluded to his high level of:
a. formal education
b. Flynn effect intelligence
c. crystallized intelligence
d. tacit/practical intelligence

_____ 5. Intellectually stimulating parents are *unlikely* to _______ when interacting with their children.
a. emphasize the importance of academic achievement
b. describe what is happening near or around the child
c. encourage rote memorization
d. encourage the child to ask questions

CONTINUED

True or False: Identify whether the following statements are true or false.

6. (T)(F) One of the three major hypotheses that have been offered to explain ethnic/social class differences in IQ is the disease/general health hypothesis.
7. (T)(F) The motivational factor in IQ testing refers to how hard a child works to excel during the test.

Short Answer: Briefly answer the following questions.

8. Explain what is meant by the Flynn effect and discuss some potential reasons for this effect.
9. List three general hypotheses that have been proposed to account for group differences in intellectual performance and briefly describe the basic premise of each of these hypotheses.

Essay: Provide a more detailed answer to the following question.

10. Identify the six subscales of the HOME inventory and provide an illustrative example of items from each subscale.

Improving Cognitive Performance Through Compensatory Education

compensatory interventions
special educational programs designed to further the cognitive growth and scholastic achievements of disadvantaged children.

Head Start
a large-scale preschool educational program designed to provide children from low-income families with a variety of social and intellectual experiences that might better prepare them for school.

Perhaps the most enduring legacy of President Lyndon B. Johnson's "War on Poverty" in the United States is a variety of preschool education programs that are designed to enrich the learning experiences of economically disadvantaged children. Project Head Start is perhaps the best known of these **compensatory interventions.** The goal of **Head Start** (and similar programs) was to provide disadvantaged children with the kinds of educational experiences that their middle-class peers were presumably getting in their homes and nursery school classrooms. It was hoped that these early interventions would compensate for the disadvantages that these children may have already experienced and place them on roughly equal footing with their middle-class peers by the time they entered the first grade.

The earliest reports suggested that Head Start and comparable programs were a smashing success. Program participants were posting an average gain of about 10 points on IQ tests, whereas the IQs of nonparticipants from similar social backgrounds remained unchanged. However, this initial optimism soon began to wane. When program participants were reexamined after completing a year or two of grade school, the gains they had made on IQ tests had largely disappeared (Gray & Klaus, 1970). In other words, few if any lasting intellectual benefits seemed to be associated with these interventions, thus prompting Arthur Jensen (1969, p. 2) to conclude that "compensatory education has been tried and it apparently has failed."

However, many developmentalists were reluctant to accept this conclusion. They felt that it was shortsighted to place so much emphasis on IQ scores as an index of program effectiveness. After all, the ultimate goal of compensatory education is not so much to boost IQ as to improve children's academic performance. Others have argued that the impact of these early interventions might be cumulative, so that it may be several years before the full benefits of compensatory education are apparent.

Long-Term Follow-Ups

As it turns out, Jensen's critics may have been right on both counts. In 1982 Irving Lazar and Richard Darlington reported on the *long-term* effects of 11 high-quality, university-based early intervention programs initiated during the 1960s. The program participants were disadvantaged preschool children from several areas of the United States. At regular intervals throughout the grade-school years, the investigators examined the participants' scholastic records and administered IQ and achievement tests. The participants and their mothers were also interviewed to determine the children's feelings of self-worth, attitudes about school and scholastic achievement, and vocational aspirations, as well as mothers' aspirations for their children and their feelings about their children's progress at school. Other longitudinal follow-ups of these or similar high-quality interventions have been conducted since 1982 (Barnett, 1995; Berrueta-Clement et al., 1984; Darlington, 1991). Together, these longitudinal studies suggest that program participants score higher in IQ than nonparticipants for 2 to 3 years after the interventions are over, but that their IQ scores eventually decline. Did the program fail then?

No, indeed! Children who participated in the interventions were more likely to meet their school's basic requirements than nonparticipants were. They were less likely to be assigned to special education classes or to be retained in a grade, and they were more likely than nonparticipants to complete high school. Program participants had more positive attitudes about school and (later) about job-related successes than nonparticipants did, and their mothers were more satisfied with their academic performances and held higher occupational aspirations for them as well. There was even some evidence that teenagers who had participated in these high-quality interventions earlier in life were less likely to become pregnant or to be involved in delinquent activities and were more likely to be employed than nonparticipants were (Gormley, 2005; Bainbridge et al., 2005; Barnett & Hudstedt, 2005).

Can we expect to do better than this in the future? Many believe that we can if compensatory education begins earlier in life and lasts longer, and ways are found to help parents become more involved in their children's learning activities (Ramey & Ramey, 1998; Anderson, 2005; Ou, 2005; Anthony et al., 2005; Foster et al., 2005; Shears & Robinson, 2005).

The Importance of Parental Involvement

Comparisons of the impact of early intervention programs suggest that the most effective ones almost always involve parents in one way or another (Raikes, Summers, & Roggman, 2005; Love et al., 2005; Ou, 2005; Downer & Mendez, 2005). For example, Joan Sprigle and Lyn Schaefer (1985) evaluated the long-term benefits of two preschool interventions—Head Start and *Learning to Learn,* a program that educated parents about its goals, provided them with informational updates about their children's progress, and repeatedly emphasized that a partnership between home and school was necessary to ensure the program's success. When the disadvantaged students who had participated in these interventions were later observed in the fourth, fifth, and sixth grades, the outcomes consistently favored the Learning to Learn (LTL) program, in which parents had been heavily involved. Although LTL students did not necessarily outperform those from Head Start on IQ tests, they were making better grades in basic academic subjects (such as reading) and were less likely to have failed a grade in school or to have been placed in costly special education classes for the learning disabled.

two-generation intervention interventions with goals to both stimulate children's intellectual development through preschool day care/education and to assist parents to move out of poverty.

Other investigators favor **two-generation interventions** that not only provide children with high-quality preschool education, but would also provide disadvantaged parents with social support and the educational and vocational training they need to lift themselves out of poverty (Ramey & Ramey, 1998; Duch, 2005). The research described in the Box on p. 369 suggests that this kind of family intervention is likely to improve parents' psychological well-being, which may translate into more effective patterns of parenting and, ultimately, into long-term gains in children's intellectual performances.

The Importance of Intervening Early

Critics of Head Start have argued that it begins too late (often after age 3) and is simply too brief to have any lasting impact. Might interventions that begin in infancy and last for several years produce more enduring gains in the IQs and academic performances of disadvantaged children?

APPLYING RESEARCH TO YOUR LIFE

An Effective Compensatory Intervention for Families

In Chapter 5, we learned that disadvantaged children of teenage mothers are at risk of displaying poor cognitive development and of becoming academic underachievers throughout childhood and adolescence. Victoria Seitz and Nancy Apfel (1994b; Seitz, Rosenbaum, & Apfel, 1985) described a two-generation family intervention that looks very promising as a means of preventing these negative outcomes.

Two-generation family interventions that target disadvantaged children and their parents lead to changes in parenting that benefit all children in the family.

Seitz and Apfel's family intervention was a 30-month program targeting poverty-stricken mothers who had recently delivered healthy firstborn children. It provided pediatric care, developmental evaluations, and monthly home visits by a psychologist, nurse, or social worker, who gave mothers social support, information about child rearing and other family matters, and assistance in obtaining education or vocational training needed to get a job (or a better paying job). The children received stimulating, high-quality day care from a provider who met frequently with mothers to discuss their children's developmental progress and to help them deal constructively with any child-rearing problems they had encountered. Other mothers and their firstborns from the same socioeconomic backgrounds received no intervention and served as a control group.

Ten years later, Seitz and her associates (1985) followed up on the firstborn children of these families to assess their academic progress. They found that children who had received the intervention were doing well. They were much more likely than control children to be attending school regularly and making normal progress, and were much less likely to have been retained in a grade or required costly remedial services such as special education. Clearly, this intervention appeared to benefit the children who had participated.

But there was more—what might be called a *diffusion* effect. Specifically, the younger siblings of the "intervention" and the "control" participants displayed precisely the same differences in scholastic outcomes that the older children did, even though these younger brothers and sisters of children who participated in the intervention had not been born *until after the intervention was over* (Seitz & Apfel, 1994b). Apparently, this family intervention had made the disadvantaged mothers who participated more involved in their children's lives and more confident and effective in their parenting—a change that not only benefited their firstborn child who received stimulating day care, but all of their subsequent children as well. It was an effective intervention indeed!

The Carolina Abecedarian Project (Campbell & Ramey, 1994, 1995) is a particularly ambitious early intervention that was designed to answer these questions. Program participants were selected from families considered to be at risk for producing mildly retarded children. These families were all on welfare, and most were headed by a single parent (the mother) who had scored well below average on a standardized IQ test (obtaining IQs of 70 to 85). The project began when the participating children were only 6 to 12 weeks old, and it continued for the next 5 years. Half of the high-risk children took part in a special day-care program designed to promote their intellectual development. The program was truly a full-time endeavor, running from 7:15 A.M. to 5:15 P.M., five days a week for 50 weeks each year, until the child entered school. The remaining "control" children received exactly the same dietary supplements, social services, and pediatric care given to their age-mates in the experimental group, but they did not attend day care. At regular intervals over the next 15 years, the progress of these two groups of "high risk" children was assessed by administering IQ tests, and periodic tests of academic achievement were also given at school.

The results were striking. Abecedarian program participants began to outperform their counterparts in the control group on IQ tests, starting at age 18 months and

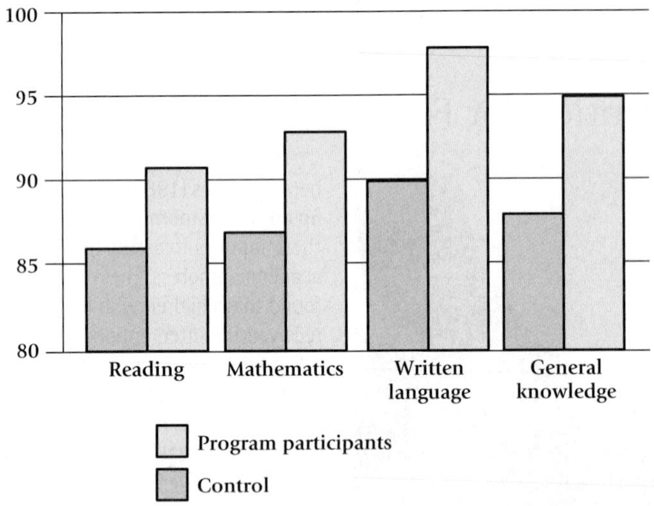

Figure 9.10 Average academic achievement scores at age 12 for Abecedarian preschool program participants and control children. *Adapted with permission from "Effects of Early Intervention on Intellectual and Academic Achievement," by F. A. Campbell & C. T. Ramey,* Child Development, *65, 684–698. Copyright © 1994 by the Society for Research in Child Development.*

maintaining this IQ advantage through age 15. Here, then, is evidence that high-quality preschool interventions that begin very early can have lasting intellectual benefits. They can have lasting educational benefits too, for program participants outperformed the control group in all areas of academic achievement from the third year of school onward (see Figure 9.10).

Finally, the Chicago longitudinal study (Reynolds & Temple, 1998) followed the progress of disadvantaged preschoolers who received high-quality preschool education with heavy parental involvement. Some of these youngsters received additional compensatory education for the first two or three years of school, whereas others did not. By itself, the *preschool* program was successful: participants performed at grade level in academic subjects, whereas program nonparticipants did not. Yet, students who received extended compensatory education did especially well: they scored nearly half a grade level higher in reading and math achievement in the third and the seventh grades and were less likely to require costly special education or to have been retained in a grade than program participants whose involvement ended at school entry. So *extended* compensatory education that helps disadvantaged youngsters to make the transition to a structured classroom environment can be highly effective indeed.

Programs such as the family intervention discussed in the Box on p. 369 and the Abecedarian and Chicago projects are expensive to administer, and there are critics who claim that they would not be worth the high costs of providing them to all disadvantaged families. However, such an attitude may be "penny wise and pound foolish," for Victoria Seitz and her associates (1985) found that extensive two-generation interventions emphasizing quality day-care often pay for themselves by (1) allowing more parents freedom from full-time child care to work, thereby reducing their need for public assistance, and (2) providing the foundation for cognitive growth that enables most disadvantaged children to avoid special education in school—a savings that, by itself, would justify the expense of extensive compensatory interventions (Bainbridge, 2005; Gormley, 2005; Karoly et al., 1998). And when we consider the long-term economic benefits that could accrue later in life, when gainfully employed adult graduates of highly successful interventions pay more taxes than disadvantaged nonparticipants, need less welfare, and are less often maintained at public expense in penal institutions, the net return on each dollar invested in compensatory education could be impressive indeed.

Creativity and Special Talents

giftedness
the possession of unusually high intellectual potential or other special talents.

What do we mean when we say that a child or an adolescent is "gifted"? This term was once limited to people such as those in Terman's longitudinal study with IQs of 140 or higher. However, recent definitions of **giftedness** have been broadened to include not only a high IQ, but also singular talents in particular areas such as music, art, literature, or science (Winner, 2000). Over the years, we have learned that certain abilities not measured by traditional IQ tests help some people to become technical experts in their chosen fields. And at least a few of these experts become truly innovative creators.

What Is Creativity?

Despite their many positive life outcomes, not one of Terman's high-IQ gifted children became truly eminent. Eminent people are not simply experts; they are innovators who are generally described as creative. In fact, creativity may be more important than a high IQ in permitting a Mozart, an Einstein, or a Piaget to break new ground.

What is creativity? Debates about this term have provoked nearly as much controversy as those about the meaning of intelligence (Mumford & Gustafson, 1988). Yet, almost everyone agrees that **creativity** represents an ability to generate novel ideas and innovative solutions—products that are not merely new and unusual but are also appropriate in context and valued by others (Simonton, 2000; Sternberg, 2001; Sternberg & Lubart, 1996). Although long considered a valued attribute, creativity received little attention from the scientific community until the 1960s and 70s, when psychometricians began to try to measure it.

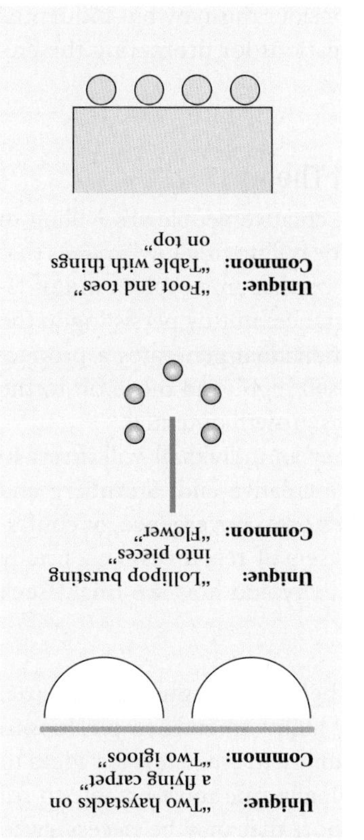

Figure 9.11 Are you creative? Indicate what you see in each of the three drawings. Below each drawing you will find examples of unique and common responses, drawn from a study of creativity in children. *Adapted from* Modes of Thinking in Young Children, *1965 Edition by Michael A. Wallach and Nathan Kogan.*

The Psychometric Perspective

In his structure-of-intellect model, J. P. Guilford (1967, 1988) proposed that creativity represents divergent rather than convergent thinking. **Convergent thinking** requires individuals to generate the one best answer to a problem and is precisely what IQ tests measure. **Divergent thinking** requires one to generate a variety of solutions to problems for which there is no one right answer (Sternberg & Grigorenko, 2001). Divergent thinking can be measured figuratively, as in Figure 9.11, or verbally, as in questions that ask respondents to list all words that can be made from the letters in *BASEBALL,* or a "real-world problem" measure that might ask them to list as many practical uses as possible for common objects such as a clothespin or a cork (Runco, 1992; Torrance, 1988).

Interestingly, divergent thinking is only modestly correlated with IQ (Wallach, 1985; Sternberg & Lubart, 1996; Vincent, Decker, & Mumford, 2002) and seems to be more heavily influenced by children's home environments than by their genes (Plomin, 1990). Specifically, children who score high in divergent thinking have parents who encourage their intellectual curiosity and who grant them a great deal of freedom to select their own interests and to explore them in depth (Getzels & Jackson, 1962; Harrington, Block, & Block, 1987; Runco, 1992). So divergent thinking is a cognitive skill that is distinct from general intelligence and can be nurtured. However, many researchers have become disenchanted with the psychometric approach to creativity once it became obvious that the scores people make on tests of divergent thinking during childhood and adolescence are, at best, only modestly related to their creative accomplishments later in life (Feldhusen & Goh, 1995; Runco, 1992). Clearly, divergent thinking may help to foster creative solutions; but, by itself, it is a woefully incomplete account of what it means to be creative (Amabile, 1983; Simonton, 2000).

The Multicomponent (or Confluence) Perspective

Think for a moment about the characteristics of people whom you consider creative. Chances are that you view them as reasonably intelligent; but it is also likely that they display such characteristics as being highly inquisitive and flexible individuals who love their work, make connections between ideas that others don't, and may be a bit unorthodox and nonconforming, or even rebellious. This "creativity syndrome" may be no accident, for many researchers today generally believe that creativity results from a *convergence* of many personal and situational factors (Gardner, 1993; Simonton, 2000; Sternberg & Lubart, 1996).

If creativity truly reflects all of the attributes above, then it is perhaps understandable why many people with high IQs or who are otherwise gifted are not particularly creative or why so few are truly eminent (Winner, 2000). Yet, Robert Sternberg and Todd Lubart (1996) have argued that most people have the potential to be creative and will be, at least to some degree, if they can marshal the resources that foster creativity and can in-

creativity
the ability to generate novel ideas or works that are useful and valued by others.

convergent thinking
thinking that requires one to come up with a single correct answer to a problem; what IQ tests measure.

divergent thinking
thinking that requires a variety of ideas or solutions to a problem when there is no one correct answer.

vest themselves in the right kinds of goals. Let's briefly consider this new but influential **investment theory of creativity** and its implications for promoting the creative potential of children and adolescents.

K. Cavanagh/Photo Researchers Inc.

Parents of creative children encourage their intellectual curiosity and allow them to explore their interests in depth.

Sternberg and Lubart's Investment Theory

According to Sternberg & Lubart (1996), creative people are willing to "buy low and sell high" in the realm of ideas. "Buying low" means that they invest themselves in ideas or projects that are novel (or out of favor) and may initially encounter resistance. But by persisting in the face of such skepticism, a creative individual generates a product that is highly valued, and can now "sell high" and move on to the next novel or unpopular idea that has growth potential.

What factors determine whether an individual will invest in an original project and bring it to a creative end? Sternberg and Lubart believe that creativity depends on a convergence, or confluence, of six distinct but interrelated sets of resources. Lets briefly consider these components of creativity and how we might seek to promote them.

investment theory of creativity recent theory specifying that the ability to invest in innovative projects and to generate creative solutions depends on a convergence of creative resources, namely background knowledge, intellectual abilities, personality characteristics, motivation, and environmental support/encouragement.

Intellectual Resources. Sternberg and Lubart (1996) believe that three intellectual abilities are particularly important to creativity. One is the ability to *find new problems* to solve or to see old problems in new ways. Another is the ability to *evaluate* one's ideas to determine which are worth pursing and which are not. Finally, one must be able to *sell others* of the value of new ideas in order to gain the support that may be necessary to fully develop them. All three abilities are important. If one cannot evaluate new ideas she has generated or sell others on their value, they are unlikely to ever blossom into creative accomplishments.

Knowledge. A child, an adolescent, or an adult must be familiar with the current state of the art in her chosen area if she is to ever advance or transform it as the groundbreaking artist, musician, or science-fair winner does (Feldhusen, 2002). As Howard Gruber (1982) puts it, "Insight comes to the prepared mind . . ." (p. 22).

Cognitive Style. A *legislative cognitive style*—that is, a preference for thinking in novel and divergent ways of one's own choosing—is important to creativity. It also helps to think in broad, global terms—to be able to distinguish the forest from the trees—which will help in deciding which of one's ideas are truly novel and worth pursuing.

Personality. Previous research indicates that the personality variables most closely associated with high creativity are a willingness to take sensible risks, to persevere in the face of uncertainty or ambiguity, and to have the self-confidence to defy the crowd and pursue ideas that will eventually win recognition.

Motivation. People rarely do creative work in an area unless they have a passion for what they are trying to accomplish and focus on *the work itself* rather than its potential rewards (Amabile, 1983). The groundbreaking Olympic gymnast Olga Korbut put it well: "If gymnastics did not exist, I would have invented it" (Feldman, 1982, p. 35). This does not mean that the prospect of winning Olympic medals had nothing to do with Ms. Korbut's success, for prizes and other incentives indicate what goals are socially valued and encourage people to work on innovative projects. But creativity can truly suffer if children are pushed too hard or focus too heavily on the rewards and lose their intrinsic interest in the work they are pursuing (Simonton, 2000; Winner, 2000).

A Supportive Environment. Several studies of children with special talents in such domains as chess, music, or mathematics reveal that these child "prodigies" are blessed with an environment that nurtured their talents and motivations and praised their accomplishments (Feldman & Goldsmith, 1991; Hennessey & Amabile, 1988; Monass & Engelhard, 1990). Parents of creative youngsters generally encourage intellectual activities and accept their children's idiosyncracies (Albert, 1994; Runco, 1992). They are also quick to recognize unusual talents and often help to foster their growth by soliciting the assistance of expert coaches or tutors. Furthermore, some societies value creativity more than others do and devote many financial and human resources to nurturing creative potential (Simonton, 1994; 2000). Indeed, Olga Korbut's brilliant talent might not have bloomed had gymnastics not been so highly valued in Russian society when she was growing up.

A Test of Investment Theory

If investment theory is sound, then people who have more creative resources at their disposal should generate more creative solutions to problems. Lubart and Sternberg (1995) tested this hypothesis in a study of adolescents and adults. A battery of questionnaires, cognitive tests, and personality measures was first administered to measure five of the six sets of creative resources (environment was not assessed). Participants then worked at innovative problems in writing (create a story about "The Octopus's Sneakers"), art (draw a picture to illustrate "Hope"), advertising (create an ad for brussels sprouts), and science (How might we detect extraterrestrials among us?). Their solutions were then rated for creativity by a panel of judges, who showed high levels of agreement in their ratings.

The results supported investment theory in that all five sets of creativity resources were moderately to highly correlated with the creativity ratings participants received, and participants whose solutions were rated most creative were those who had higher scores across all five kinds of creative resources. Apparently, creativity does reflect the convergence of many factors rather than the possession of a dominant cognitive attribute such as divergent thinking.

Promoting Creativity in the Classroom

How might educators foster creativity in the classroom? Most current programs for gifted students concentrate on enriching and accelerating traditional learning and may do little, beyond providing background knowledge, to promote creativity (Sternberg, 1995; Winner, 1997). Gardner's theory of multiple intelligences has been used as a framework for promoting the growth of intelligences that are not heavily stressed in school. These programs enrich the experiences of all pupils and to foster such abilities as spatial intelligence (through sculpting or painting), kinesthetic-body intelligence (through dance or athletics), and linguistic intelligence (through storytelling). Whether these efforts truly foster creativity is not yet clear, although they have been successful at identifying special talents of children who are not at all exceptional in traditional academic subjects (Ramos-Ford & Gardner, 1997).

The investment theory of creativity suggests several possible means of fostering creative potential. Were teachers to allow students more freedom to design their own art projects or science experiments and to explore any unusual interests in depth, they would more closely approximate the kind of home environment that nurtures curiosity, risk taking, perseverance, intrinsic interest, and a concern with task performance (rather than with such performance outcomes as earning a passing grade). Less emphasis on memorizing facts and obtaining correct answers (convergent thinking) and more emphasis on discussing complex problems that have many possible answers may also help students to develop divergent thinking skills, tolerance for ambiguity, and a global analytic style that fosters creative solutions. Unfortunately, attempts to further the creative potential of children are in their infancy, and it is not yet clear just what procedures work best. However, the research we have reviewed implies that parents and educators might try to be a bit more enthusiastic when youngsters display an unusual passion for an offbeat or otherwise nontraditional interest. By providing such support (and exposure to experts if any are available), we may be helping to nurture the creative potential of our future innovators.

Paul Conklin/Gail Meese Photography

Programs to encourage the development of "intelligences" not usually stressed at school often identify hidden talents and may foster creativity.

CONCEPT CHECK 9.3 Understanding Compensatory Education, Creativity, and Special Talents

Check your understanding of improving cognitive performance through compensatory education and creativity and special talents by answering the following questions. Answers appear in the Appendix.

Multiple Choice: Select the best answer for each question.

_____ 1. The overriding goal of Head Start compensatory preschools has been to:
a. provide employment to teachers
b. prepare low-income children for elementary school
c. boost minority kids' IQ scores with intensive help
d. boost minority kids' IQ scores with effective teaching

_____ 2. Who were the participants in the Carolina Abecedarian Project, a longitudinal intervention program?
a. orphans who suffered neglect in large institutions
b. low-income infants at risk for mental retardation
c. teenagers who had trouble with criminal activity
d. white children of average middle-class families

_____ 3. "Learning to Learn" differs from other preschool interventions because of its special emphasis given to:
a. character-training, emphasizing personal responsibility
b. parental involvement in the program
c. implantation of whites' stem cells into nonwhites
d. well-balanced nutrition, especially at breakfast

_____ 4. Bonzo purchases junk at flea markets and imaginatively refurnishes it into entirely different products, which resell at high prices. Bonzo is ________, according to the Sternberg-Lubart (1996) investment theory.
a. creative
b. financially thrifty
c. a convergent thinker
d. concerned about his own developmental quotient

True or False: Identify whether the following statements are true or false.

5. (T)(F) Creativity may be fostered in schools by encouraging exploration and self-paced learning.
6. (T)(F) The best predictor of academic competency and IQ test performance is family income.
7. (T)(F) The "diffusion effect" reported by Seitz's (1985) two-generation family intervention meant that the gains happened regardless of the program's content.

Short Answer: Briefly answer the following questions.

8. Discuss the research evidence that relates to the long-term impact of early compensatory intervention programs.
9. Explain what creativity is, and contrast divergent and convergent thinking.

Essay: Provide a more detailed answer to the following question.

10. Describe six key components of creativity.

Applying Developmental Themes to Intelligence and Creativity

Our developmental themes are especially relevant to the issues of intelligence and creativity. Developmental psychologists are interested in how the active child influences her own intelligence, the effects of nature and nurture on intelligence, the qualitative and quantitative changes in intelligence across development, and how intelligence relates holistically to the rest of development.

Turning first to the active child effects, in this chapter we saw that the child's phenotype drives his or her activities later in childhood and adolescence, and that his or her experiences impact the intellectual achievements he or she attains. We also saw that the activities a child explores impact the creative achievements he or she attains. Remember that active child effects are not necessarily conscious choices, but also reflect how the child influences his or her development in any way. Consider, then, the results of the compensatory education opportunities we discussed. In a way, those opportunities change the child and result in attitudes and behaviors that change the child's learning outcomes and educational aspirations. This too can be considered an active child effect.

Perhaps the most prominent theme in intelligence is the interaction of nature and nurture in influencing the child's intelligence and cognitive achievements. In this chapter we reviewed clear evidence that genetics and nature effects clearly influence the child's IQ and intelligence. We also reviewed clear evidence that the child's environment has a large impact on later intellectual achievements. Some evidence for nature concerned the genetic effects on IQ scores and the relationships between a child's intelligence and that of his or her biological relatives. The evidence for the influence of the environment concerned the character of the home environment early in life, as well as social and cultural effects on IQ. Clearly, this is one area of development in which both nature and nurture are strong forces directing intellectual attainments.

In contrast, there was little mention of qualitative and quantitative changes in intelligence in this chapter. We did review evidence suggesting that IQ scores change (a great deal for an individual child) across development. But whether those changes are qualitative or quantitative is not an issue to which developmental psychologists have given much attention.

Finally, we saw much evidence of the holistic nature of intelligence in child development. We saw that the child's level of intelligence influences his or her academic future, as well as his or her leadership skills, popularity, emotional development, and general life satisfaction. Clearly, intelligence has a holistic influence on child development and, as such, it should be considered when one attempts to understand the nature of child development as a whole.

SUMMARY

What Is Intelligence?

- The **psychometric approach** defines intelligence as a trait (or set of traits) that allows some people to think and solve problems more effectively than others.
  - Alfred Binet
    - developed the first successful intelligence test
    - defined intelligence as a general mental ability
  - Researchers relying on **factor analysis** argue that intelligence is not a singular trait.
    - Spearman viewed intelligence as a *general mental ability* (or ***g***) and *special abilities* (or ***s***), each of which was specific to a particular test.
    - Thurstone claimed that intelligence consists of seven **primary mental abilities.**
    - Guilford's **structure-of-intellect model** proposes that intelligence consists of 180 mental abilities. Cattel and Horn make a distinction between **fluid intelligence** and **crystallized intelligence.**
    - **Hierarchical models,** such as Carroll's **three-stratum theory of intelligence,** are the most elaborate psychometric classifications of mental abilities to date.
- New viewpoints on intelligence are becoming increasingly influential.
- Robert Sternberg's **triarchic theory** criticizes psychometric theories of intelligence for their failure to consider:
  - the *contexts* in which intelligent acts are displayed
  - the test taker's *experience* with test items
  - the *information-processing strategies* for thinking or solving problems
- Gardner's **theory of multiple intelligences:**
  - contends that human beings display at least nine distinctive kinds of intelligence, several of which are not assessed by traditional intelligence tests

How Is Intelligence Measured?

- Today there are literally hundreds of intelligence tests.
  - The **Stanford-Binet Intelligence Scale** and the **Wechsler Intelligence Scale for Children (WISC-IV)** are widely used.
    - Both scales compare children's performance against **test norms** for age-mates.
    - Both scales assign children **intelligence quotients (IQs),** which are normally distributed around the average score of 100.
- New approaches to intelligence testing include:
  - the **Kaufman Assessment Battery for Children (K-ABC)**

- it is grounded in information-processing theory, and
- it uses **dynamic assessment,** which is compatible with Vygotsky's theory and Sternberg's triarchic theory

- Infant intelligence tests:
  - tap perceptual and motor skills
  - assign **developmental quotient (DQ)** scores
  - are poor predictors of childhood IQs
- Newer measures of infant information-processing capabilities are much better predictors of later intellectual performance.
- IQ is a relatively stable attribute across life for some people.
  - However, many others will show wide variations in their IQ scores over the course of childhood.
  - The fact that IQ can wander upward or downward over time suggests that IQ tests measure intellectual *performance* rather than an inborn capacity for thinking and problem solving.
  - Children whose home environments are stable and stimulating often display IQ stability or increases over time.
  - Children from impoverished backgrounds often display a **cumulative deficit** in IQ.

What Do Intelligence Tests Predict?

- When we consider trends for the population as a whole:
  - IQ scores predict:
    - future academic accomplishments
    - occupational status
    - health and happiness
- But at the individual level:
  - An IQ score is not always a reliable indicator of one's future health, happiness, or success.
  - Besides IQ, one's family background, work habits, education, **tacit (or practical) intelligence,** and motivation to succeed are important contributors to the successes one attains.

Factors That Influence IQ Scores

- Both heredity and environment contribute heavily to intellectual performance.
  - Evidence from twin studies and studies of adopted children indicates that about half the variation among individuals in IQ is attributable to hereditary factors.
  - Regardless of one's genetic predispositions, barren intellectual environments clearly inhibit cognitive growth.
  - Environmental enrichments can clearly promote cognitive growth, as shown by the **Flynn effect.**

Social and Cultural Correlates of Intellectual Performance

- Research with the **HOME Inventory** reveals that:
  - Children who score relatively high in academic achievement and IQ have parents who:
    - create a stimulating home environment
    - become involved in their children's learning activities
    - explain new concepts
    - provide age-appropriate challenges and consistent encouragement
- On average, African American, Native American, Hispanic American, and other children from lower-income backgrounds score lower on IQ tests than middle-class whites and Asian Americans.
  - These differences are still apparent on **culture fair IQ tests.**
  - Some minority students may be less motivated in testing situations.
  - So the **cultural/test bias** does not explain all the group differences in IQ.
- There is no conclusive evidence for the **genetic hypothesis** (or the **Level I–Level II** distinction), which posits that group differences in IQ are hereditary.
- The best explanation for group differences in IQ is the **environmental hypothesis:**
  - Many poor people and minority group members score lower on IQ tests because they grow up in impoverished environments that are much less conducive to intellectual development than those of their middle-class age-mates.

Improving Cognitive Performance Through Compensatory Education

- **Head Start** and other **compensatory interventions** for disadvantaged preschoolers:
  - rarely produce lasting gains in IQ
  - improve children's chances of succeeding in the classroom
  - help to prevent the progressive decline in intellectual performance and academic achievement so often observed among students from disadvantaged backgrounds
- Compensatory education is most effective when it:
  - starts early
  - lasts longer
  - involves children's parents
- Recent *two-generation interventions* and those beginning early in infancy and continuing as children make the transition to school look especially promising.

Creativity and Special Talents

- Definitions of **giftedness** include
  - a high IQ
  - special talents, including **creativity**
- Psychometricians distinguish
  - IQ (which rests on **convergent thinking**)
  - from creativity, or **divergent thinking**
    - Although divergent thinking is only modestly correlated with IQ, it also fails to predict future creativity very well.
- Recent multicomponent (or confluence) perspectives of creativity include:
  - **investment theory of creativity**
    - specifies that a variety of cognitive, personal, motivational, and environmental resources combine to foster creative problem solving
    - looks very promising, both in terms of its existing empirical support and its suggestions for fostering creativity

KEY TERMS

MEDIA RESOURCES

The Human Development Book Companion Website

See the companion website http://www.thomsonedu.com/psychology/shaffer for flashcards, practice quiz questions, Internet links, updates, critical thinking exercises, discussion forums, games, and more

Thomson™ NOW! http://www.thomsonedu.com
Go to this site for the link to ThomsonNOW, your one-stop shop. Take a pre-test for this chapter, and ThomsonNOW will generate a personalized study plan based on your test results. The study plan will identify the topics you need to review and direct you to online resources to help you master those topics. You can then take a post-test to help you determine the concepts you have mastered and what you will still need to work on.

© Corbis

CHAPTER 10

Development of Language and Communication Skills

"Rrrrrruh! Rrrrrruh!" exclaims 11-month-old Delroy as he sits in his walker looking out the window. "What are you saying, little man?" asks his aunt Lateesha. "He's saying Daddy's car is in the driveway; he's home from work!" Delroy's mother replies.

"Oops! It broked. Fix it daggy." (18-month-old Rosalita responding to the arm that has come loose from her doll)

"I can see clearly now . . . ; I see all *icicles* in my way." (2½-year-old Todd singing his rendition of a popular song; the correct lyric is "*obstacles*")

One truly astounding achievement that sets humans apart from the rest of the animal kingdom is our creation and use of **language.** Although animals can **communicate** with one another, their limited number of calls and gestures are merely isolated signals that convey very specific messages (for example, a greeting, a threat, a summons to congregate) in much the same way that single words or stereotyped phrases do in a human language (Tomasello & Camaioni, 1997). On the other hand, human languages are amazingly flexible and productive. From a small number of individually meaningless sounds, children come to generate thousands of meaningful auditory patterns (syllables, words, and even idiosyncratic **vocables** such as Delroy's "Rrrrrruh!") that are eventually combined according to a set of grammatical rules (with a few missteps, such as Rosalita's use of the word "broked") to produce an infinite number of messages. Language is also an

language
a small number of individually meaningless symbols (sounds, letters, gestures) that can be combined according to agreed-on rules to produce an infinite number of messages.

communication
the process by which one organism transmits information to and influences another.

vocables
unique patterns of sound that a prelinguistic infant uses to represent objects, actions, or events.

Animals communicate through a series of calls and gestures that convey a limited number of very specific messages.

inventive tool with which we express our thoughts and interpretations (or in Todd's case, misinterpretations) of what we have seen, heard, or otherwise experienced. In singing the lyrics above, Todd was trying to faithfully reproduce what he had heard. However, most of what children say in any given situation is not merely a repetition of what they have said or heard before; speakers create many novel utterances on the spot, and the topics they talk about may have nothing to do with their current state or the stream of ongoing events. Yet creative as they may be in generating new messages, even 3- and 4-year-olds are generally able to converse quite well with each other, as long as their statements adhere to the rules and social conventions of the language they are speaking.

Although language is one of the most complex and abstract bodies of knowledge we ever acquire, children in all cultures come to understand and use this intricate form of communication very early in life. In fact, some infants are talking before they can walk. How is this possible? Are infants biologically programmed to acquire language? What kinds of linguistic input must they receive in order to become language users? Is there any relation between a child's cooing, gesturing, or babbling and his or her later production of meaningful words? How do infants and toddlers come to attach meaning to words? Do all children pass through the same steps or stages as they acquire their native language? And what practical lessons must children learn to become truly effective communicators? These are but a few of the issues we will consider as we trace the development of children's linguistic skills and try to determine how youngsters become so proficient in using language at such an early age.

Five Components of Language

psycholinguists
those who study the structure and development of children's language.

Perhaps the most basic question that **psycholinguists** have tried to answer is the "what" question: What must children learn in order to master their native language? After many years and literally thousands of studies, researchers have concluded that five kinds of knowledge underlie the growth of linguistic proficiency: *phonology, morphology, semantics, syntax,* and *pragmatics.*

Phonology

phonology
the sound system of a language and the rules for combining these sounds to produce meaningful units of speech.

phonemes
the basic units of sound that are used in a spoken language.

Phonology refers to the basic units of sound, or **phonemes,** that are used in a language and the rules for combining these sounds. Each language uses only a subset of the sounds that humans are capable of generating, and no two languages have precisely the same phonologies—a fact that explains why foreign languages may sound rather strange to us. Clearly, children must learn how to discriminate, produce, and combine the speechlike sounds of their native language in order to make sense of the speech they hear and to be understood when they try to speak (Kelley, Jones, & Fein, 2004).

Morphology

morphology
rules governing the formation of meaningful words from sounds.

Rules of **morphology** specify how words are formed from sounds (Kelley, Jones, & Fein, 2004). In English, these rules include the rule for forming past tenses of verbs by adding *-ed* and the rule for forming plurals by adding *-s,* as well as rules for using other prefixes and suffixes, and rules that specify proper combinations of sounds to form meaningful words. We learn, for example, that *flow* (not *vlow*) is how to describe what the river is doing.

Semantics

semantics
the expressed meaning of words and sentences.

morphemes
smallest meaningful language units.

free morphemes
morphemes that can stand alone as a word (for example, *cat, go, yellow*).

Semantics refers to the *meanings* expressed in words and sentences (Kelley, Jones, & Fein, 2004). The smallest meaningful units of language are **morphemes,** and there are two types. **Free morphemes** can stand alone as words (for example, *dog*), whereas

bound morphemes
morphemes that cannot stand alone but that modify the meaning of free morphemes (for example, the *-ed* attached to English verbs to indicate past tense).

bound morphemes cannot stand alone but change meaning when attached to a free morpheme (for example, adding the bound morpheme *-s* to the word *dog* means that the speaker is talking about more than one pooch). Children must recognize that words and bound grammatical morphemes convey meaning—that they symbolize particular objects, actions, and relations and can be combined to form larger and more complex meanings (sentences)—before they can comprehend others' speech and be understood when they speak.

Syntax

syntax
the structure of a language; the rules specifying how words and grammatical markers are to be combined to produce meaningful sentences.

Language also involves **syntax,** or the rules that specify how words are to be combined to form meaningful phrases and sentences (Kelley, Jones, & Fein, 2004). Consider these three sentences:

1. Garfield Odie bit.
2. Garfield bit Odie.
3. Odie bit Garfield.

Even very young speakers of English recognize that the first sentence violates the rules of English sentence structure, although this word order would be perfectly acceptable in languages with a different syntax, such as French. The second and third sentences are grammatical English sentences that contain the same words but convey very different meanings. They also illustrate how word meanings (semantics) interact with sentence structure (word order) to give the entire sentence a meaning. Children must master rules of syntax before they can become proficient at speaking or understanding a language.

Pragmatics

pragmatics
principles that underlie the effective and appropriate use of language in social contexts.

Children must also master the **pragmatics** of language—knowledge of how language might be used to *communicate effectively* (Diesendruck & Markson, 2001; Kelley, Jones, & Fein, 2004). Imagine a 6-year-old who is trying to explain a new game to her 2-year-old brother. She cannot speak to the toddler as if he were an adult or an age-mate; she will have to adjust her speech to his linguistic capabilities if she hopes to be understood.

sociolinguistic knowledge
culturally specific rules specifying how language should be structured and used in particular social contexts.

Pragmatics also involves **sociolinguistic knowledge**—culturally specified rules that dictate how language should be used in particular social contexts. A 3-year-old may not yet realize that the best way of obtaining a cookie from Grandma is to say "Grandma, may I please have a cookie?" rather than demanding "Gimme a cookie, Grandma!" In order to communicate most effectively, children must become "social editors" and take into account where they are, with whom they are speaking, and what the listener already knows, needs, and wants to hear.

Finally, the task of becoming an effective communicator requires not only a knowledge of the five aspects of language, but an ability to properly interpret and use *nonverbal signals* (facial expressions, intonational cues, gestures, and so on) that often help to clarify the meaning of verbal messages and are important means of communicating in their own right. This brings us to a second basic question: how do young, cognitively immature toddlers and preschool children acquire all this knowledge so quickly?

Theories of Language Development

As psycholinguists began to chart the course of language development, they were amazed that children could learn such a complex symbol system at such a breathtaking pace. After all, some infants are using words (which are arbitrary and abstract signifiers) to refer to objects and activities even before they can walk. And by age 5, children already know and use most of the syntactical structures of their native language, even though they have yet to receive their first formal lesson in grammar. How do they do it?

In addressing the "how" question, we will once again encounter a nativist/empiricist (nature/nurture) controversy. Learning theorists represent the empiricist point of view. From their perspective, language is obviously learned: after all, Japanese children acquire Japanese, French children acquire French, and profoundly deaf children of hearing parents may acquire few formal communication skills unless they receive instruction in sign language. However, other theorists point out that children the world over seem to display similar linguistic achievements at about the same age: they all babble by 4 to 6 months of age, utter their first meaningful word by age 12 to 13 months, begin to combine words by the end of the second year, and know the meanings of many thousands of words and are constructing a staggering array of grammatical sentences by the age of 4 or 5. These **linguistic universals** suggested to nativists that language acquisition is a *biologically programmed* activity that may even involve highly specialized linguistic processing capabilities that operate most efficiently early in childhood (Lidz, Gleitman, & Gleitman 2003; Palmer, 2000; Wilson, 2003).

linguistic universal
an aspect of language development that all children share.

Of course, there is an intermediate point of view—one favored by an increasing number of *interactionists* who believe that language acquisition reflects a complex interplay among a child's biological predispositions, her cognitive development, and the characteristics of her unique linguistic environment. Let's take a closer look at these three different perspectives on language acquisition.

The Learning (or Empiricist) Perspective

Ask most adults how children learn language and they are likely to say that children *imitate* what they hear, are *reinforced* when they use proper grammar, and are *corrected* when they say things wrong. Learning theorists emphasize these same processes—imitation and reinforcement—in their own theories of language learning (Palmer, 2000; Yang, 2004; Zamuner, 2002).

In 1957, B. F. Skinner published a book entitled *Verbal Behavior* in which he argued that children learn to speak appropriately because they are reinforced for grammatically correct speech. He believed that adults begin to shape a child's speech by selectively reinforcing those aspects of babbling that most resemble words, thereby increasing the probability that these sounds will be repeated. Once they have "shaped" sounds into words, adults then withhold further reinforcement (attention or approval) until the child begins combining words, first into primitive sentences and then into longer grammatical utterances. Other social-learning theorists (for example, Bandura, 1971; Whitehurst & Vasta, 1975) add that children acquire much of their linguistic knowledge by carefully listening to and *imitating* the language of older companions. So according to the learning perspective, caregivers "teach" language by modeling and by reinforcing grammatical speech (Nowak, Komarova, & Niyogi, 2002).

Evaluation of the Learning Perspective

Imitation and reinforcement do play some part in early language development. Certainly it is no accident that children end up speaking the same language their parents speak, down to the regional accent. In addition, young children are quicker to acquire and use the proper names for novel toys when reinforced for doing so by receiving the toys to play with (Whitehurst & Valdez-Menchaca, 1988). Finally, children whose parents frequently encourage them to converse by asking questions and making requests are more advanced in their early language development than age-mates whose parents are less conversational (Bohannon & Bonvillian, 1997; Valdez-Menchaca & Whitehurst, 1992).

Despite these observations, learning theorists have had little success accounting for the development of syntax. If parents really "shaped" grammar, as Skinner claimed, then they ought to reliably praise or otherwise reinforce the child's grammatical utterances. Yet, careful analyses of conversations between mothers and young children reveal that a mother's approval or disapproval depends far more on the *truth value* (semantics) of what a child says, *not* on the statement's grammatical correctness (syntax) (Baron, 1992; Brown, Cazden, & Bellugi, 1969). So if a child gazing at a cow says "Him cow" (truthful but grammatically incorrect), mother is likely to approve ("That's right!"); yet, if the child had said "There's a dog!" (grammatically correct, but untruthful), mom would probably correct him ("No silly—that's a *cow!*"). These findings cast doubt on the notion that parents shape syntax by directly reinforcing grammatical speech.

Nor is there much evidence that children acquire grammatical rules by imitating adult speech. Many of a child's earliest sentences are highly creative statements such as "Allgone cookie" or "It broked" that do not appear in adult speech and could not have been learned by imitation. And when young children do try to imitate an adult utterance such as "Look, the kitty is climbing the tree," they condense it to conform to their existing level of grammatical competence, saying something like "Kitty climb tree" (Baron, 1992; Bloom, Hood, & Lightbown, 1974).

How, then, might young children acquire grammatical knowledge if they do not directly imitate adult grammar and are not consistently reinforced for speaking grammatically? A number of psycholinguists have proposed a biological theory of language development—nativism—in an attempt to answer this question.

Noam Chomsky's nativist theory dominated thinking about language development in the 1960s and 1970s.

The Nativist Perspective

According to the nativists, human beings are biologically programmed to acquire language. Linguist Noam Chomsky (1959, 1968) has argued that the structure of even the simplest of languages is incredibly elaborate—far too complex, he believed, to be either taught by parents (as Skinner proposed) or discovered via simple trial-and-error processes by cognitively immature toddlers and preschool children. Instead, Chomsky proposed that we humans (and only humans) come equipped with a **language acquisition device (LAD)**—an inborn linguistic processor that is activated by verbal input. According to Chomsky, the LAD contains a **universal grammar,** or knowledge of rules that are common to all languages. So regardless of the language (or languages) a child has been listening to, the LAD should allow any child to acquire a sufficient vocabulary, combine words into novel, rule-bound utterances, and understand much of what he hears.

Other nativists make similar claims. Dan Slobin (1985), for example, does not assume that children have any innate knowledge of language (as Chomsky did), but instead thinks that they have an inborn **language-making capacity (LMC)**—a set of cognitive and perceptual abilities that are highly specialized for language learning. Presumably these innate mechanisms (an LAD or LMC) enable young children to process linguistic input and to infer the phonological regularities, semantic relations, and rules of syntax that characterize whatever language they are listening to (Palmer, 2000). These inferences about the meaning and structure of linguistic information represent a "theory" of language that children construct for themselves and use to guide their own attempts to

language acquisition device (LAD)
Chomsky's term for the innate knowledge of grammar that humans were said to possess—knowledge that might enable young children to infer the rules governing others' speech and to use these rules to produce language.

universal grammar
in nativist theories of language acquisition, the basic rules of grammar that characterize all languages.

language-making capacity (LMC)
a hypothesized set of specialized linguistic processing skills that enable children to analyze speech and to detect phonological, semantic, and syntactical relationships.

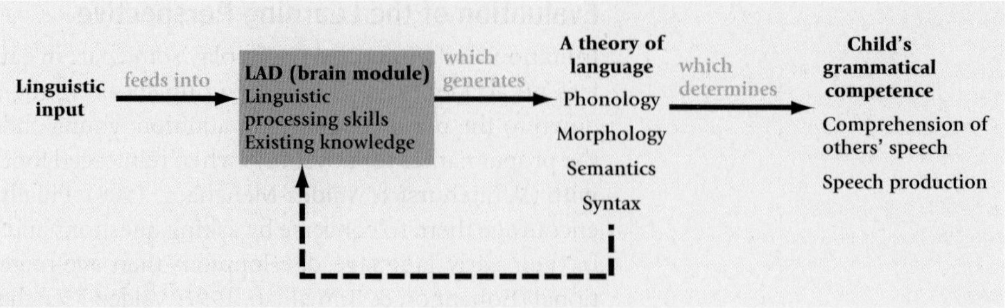

Figure 10.1 A model of language acquisition proposed by nativists.

communicate (see Figure 10.1). Of course, young children are likely to make some erroneous inferences because their linguistic database is very limited; but as they continue to process more and more input, their underlying theories of language will become increasingly elaborate, until they eventually approximate those used by adults. For the nativists, then, language acquisition is quite natural and almost automatic, as long as children have linguistic input to process.

Support for the Nativist Perspective

Are children biologically programmed to acquire language? Several observations seem to suggest that they are. For example, we've noted that children the world over reach certain linguistic milestones at about the same age, despite cultural differences in the structure of their languages. Nativists interpret these *linguistic universals* as clear evidence that language must be guided by some species-specific biological mechanism. Even many retarded children who perform very poorly on a broad range of cognitive tasks nevertheless acquire a near-normal knowledge of syntax and become quite adequate conversationalists (Pinker, 1991).

Also consistent with the nativist viewpoint is the observation that language is species-specific. Although animals can communicate with each other, no species has ever devised anything in the wild that closely resembles an abstract, rule-bound linguistic system. After years of training, apes can learn simple sign languages and other symbolic codes that enable the best of them to communicate with humans at a level comparable to that of a 2- to 2½-year-old child (Savage-Rumbaugh et al., 1993). But only humans spontaneously develop language.

Brain Specialization and Language. As we learned in Chapter 6, the brain is a lateralized organ with major language centers in the left cerebral hemisphere. Damage to one of these language areas typically results in **aphasia**—a loss of one or more language functions, and the symptoms that an aphasic patient displays will depend on the site and the extent of their injury. Injuries to **Broca's area,** near the frontal lobe of the left hemisphere, typically affect speech production rather than comprehension (Martin, 2003; Slobin, 1979). Patients who suffer an injury to **Wernicke's area,** on the temporal lobe of the left hemisphere, may speak fairly well but have difficulty understanding speech (Martin, 2003).

Apparently, the left hemisphere is sensitive to some aspects of language from birth. In the first day of life, speech sounds already elicit more electrical activity from the left side of an infant's brain, whereas music and other nonspeech sounds produce greater activity from the right cerebral hemisphere (Molfese, 1977). Furthermore, we learned in Chapter 5 that infants are quite capable of discriminating important phonetic contrasts in the first few days and weeks of life (Miller & Eimas, 1996). These findings seem to imply that the newborn is "prewired" for speech perception and is prepared to analyze speech-like sounds.

aphasia
a loss of one or more language functions.

Broca's area
structure located in the frontal lobe of the left hemisphere of the cerebral cortex that controls language production.

Wernicke's area
structure located in the temporal lobe of the left hemisphere of the cerebral cortex that is responsible for interpreting speech.

sensitive-period hypothesis (of language acquisition)
the notion that human beings are most proficient at language learning before they reach puberty.

The Sensitive-Period Hypothesis. Many years ago, nativist Erik Lenneberg (1967) proposed that languages should be most easily acquired between birth and puberty, the period when the lateralized human brain is becoming increasingly specialized for linguistic functions. This **sensitive-period hypothesis** for language development was prompted by observations that child aphasics often recover their lost language functions without special therapy, whereas adult aphasics usually require extensive therapeutic interventions to recover even a portion of their lost language skills. Lenneberg's explanation for this intriguing age difference in the ease of language learning was straightforward: presumably, the right hemisphere of a child's relatively unspecialized brain can assume any linguistic functions lost when the left hemisphere is damaged. On the other hand, the brain of a person who is past puberty is already fully specialized for language and other neurological functions. So aphasia may persist in adolescents and adults because the right hemisphere is no longer available to assume linguistic skills lost from a traumatic injury to the left side of the brain.

If language really is most easily acquired before puberty, then children who were largely deprived of a normal linguistic environment should find it difficult to acquire language later in life. Two excellent case studies reflect nicely on this idea. One is the case of Genie, a child who was locked away in a back room as an infant and was not discovered by the authorities until she was nearly 14 years old. While confined, Genie heard very little language; no one was permitted to talk to her, and she was beaten by an abusive father if she made any noise (Curtiss, 1977). Then there is Chelsea, a deaf woman who—because of her deafness and her family's isolation—was 32 years old before she was ever exposed to a formal language system. Extensive efforts were undertaken to teach these women language, and each made remarkable progress, learning the meaning of many words and even producing lengthy sentences that were rich in their semantic content. Yet neither woman has mastered the rules of syntax that virtually all children acquire without formal instruction (Curtiss, 1977, 1988), thus suggesting that learning a first language is easier early in life.

What about learning a second language? Is acquiring a foreign language a tougher task for a postpubertal adolescent whose "sensitive period" for language learning is over? Research by Jacqueline Johnson & Elissa Newport (1989) suggests that it is. Native speakers of Korean or Chinese who had emigrated to the United States at different ages were tested as adults for mastery of English grammar. As we see in Figure 10.2, immigrants who began to learn English between 3 and 7 years of age were as proficient in English as native speakers are. Immigrants who arrived after puberty (particularly after age 15) performed rather poorly.

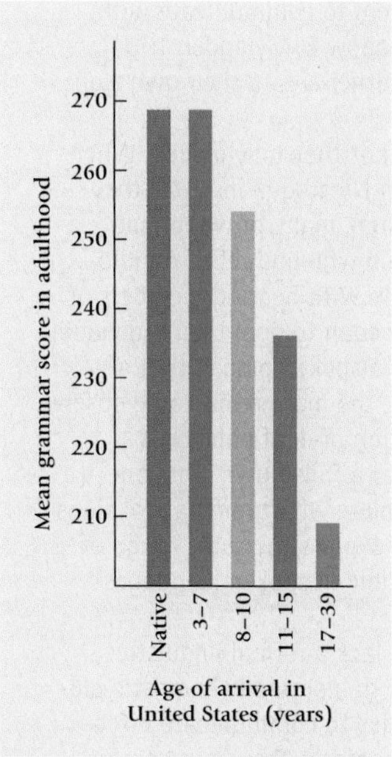

Figure 10.2 As shown here, there is a clear relationship between the age at which immigrants arrived in the United States and their eventual adult performance in English grammar. Those who arrived early in childhood end up performing like native speakers of English, whereas those who arrived as teenagers or adults perform much more poorly. *Adapted from "Critical Period Effects in Second Language Learning: The influence of Maturational State on the Acquisition of English as a Second Language," by J. S. Johnson & E. L. Newport, 1989.* Cognitive Psychology, 21, 60–99. *Copyright © 1989 by Academic Press, Inc. Adapted by permission.*

Finally, there are differences between early and late second language learners in the organization of the brain. Specifically, speaking either of their two languages activates the *same* area of the brain in bilinguals who acquired their second language in early childhood, whereas speaking two languages activates *different* areas of the brain in bilinguals who acquired their second language after puberty (Kim et al., 1997).

Taken together, these findings imply that language learning is easier (and may even occur differently) early in life, almost as if the cognitive system of the young child is especially well suited for this task (Francis, 2005; Stewart, 2004). What's more, nativists interpret the research presented in the Box on p. 386 as a rather dramatic illustration that language acquisition is a natural childhood activity—even if children must "invent" the language they acquire.

Problems with the Nativist Approach

Though most everyone today agrees that language learning is heavily influenced by biological factors, many developmentalists have serious reservations about the nativist approach (Goldberg, 2004; Tomasello, 2003). Some have challenged the findings that nativists cite as support for their theory. For example, the fact that human infants can make important phonemic distinctions in the first days and weeks of life no longer seems to be such compelling support for the existence of a uniquely human LAD. Why? Simply

FOCUS ON RESEARCH On the "Invention" of Language by Children

Suppose that 10 children were raised in isolation by an adult caregiver who attended to their basic needs but never talked or even gestured to them in any way. Would these youngsters devise some method of communicating among themselves? No one can say for sure, for children such as these have never been studied. However, the results of two recent programs of research suggest that these hypothetical children not only would learn to communicate but might even invent their own language.

Transforming Pidgins to True Languages

When adults from different cultures migrate to the same area, they often being to communicate in **pidgin**—a hybrid of their various languages that enables them to convey basic meanings and thus understand each other. In the 1870s for example, large numbers of immigrants from China, Korea, Japan, the Philippines, Portugal, and Puerto Rico migrated to Hawaii to work in the sugar fields. What evolved from this influx was Hawaiian Pidgin English, a communication system with a small vocabulary and a few basic rules for combining words that enabled residents from different linguistic communities to communicate well enough to get by. Yet over the course of generations, this pidgin was transformed into a **creole**—that is, a true language that evolves from a pidgin. Indeed, Hawaiian Creole English was a rich language with a vocabulary that sprang from the pidgin and its foreign language predecessors and had formal syntactical rules. How did this transformation form marginal pidgin to true language occur so rapidly?

Linguist Derek Bickerton (1983, 1984) claims that children of pidgin-speaking parents do not continue to speak pidgin. Instead, they spontaneously invent syntactical rules that creolize the pidgin to make it a true language that future generations may use. How did he decide that children were responsible? One clue was that whenever pidgins arise, they are quickly transformed into creoles, usually within a single generation. But the more important clue was that creole syntax closely resembles the (often grammatically inappropriate) sentences that young children construct when acquiring virtually any language. For example, questions of the form "Where he is going?" and double negatives such as "I haven't got none" are perfectly acceptable in creole languages. Finally, the structure of different creoles is similar the world over—so similar that it cannot be attributed to chance. Bickerton believes that only a nativist model can account for these observations. In his own words: "The most cogent explanation of this similarity . . . is that it derives from . . . a species-specific program for language, genetically coded and expressed . . . in the structures . . . and operation of the human brain" (1984, p. 173).

Unfortunately, no one has yet carefully observed the language development of children whose parents speak pidgins; thus, it is not completely clear that children transform pidgins to creoles by themselves (as Bickerton claims), without adult assistance (Bohannon, MacWhinney, & Snow, 1990; Tomasello, 1995). So let's consider a second set of observations.

Creating a Sign Language

Deaf children often develop sets of gestures that symbolize objects and actions that allow them to communicate with their hearing parents (Goldin-Meadow & Mylander, 1984). Might deaf youngsters raised together create their own sign language?

Recent observations suggest that they may indeed. When the Sandinistas assumed power in Nicaragua in 1979, they established schools for deaf children, many of whom had never met another deaf person and who had relied on idiosyncratic gestures to communicate with hearing members of their families. Soon these pupils began to pool their individual gestures into a system, similar to a spoken pidgin, that allowed them to communicate. Yet, the more remarkable observation is that the second generation of deaf pupils has transformed this "pidgin sign" into a full-blown language—*Nicaraguan Sign Language*—complete with grammatical signs and rules that enable its users to express the same range of ideas and messages that are possible in spoken languages (Brownlee, 1998).

So it seems that children who lack a formal linguistics model—be they deaf or subjected to marginally linguistic pidgins—will create languagelike codes to communicate effectively with their companions. Apparently, they have some linguistic predispositions that serve them well.

pidgins
structurally simple communication systems that arise when people who share no common language come into constant contact.

creoles
languages that develop when pidgins are transformed into grammatically complex "true" languages.

because the young of other species (for example, rhesus monkeys and chinchillas) show similar powers of auditory discrimination (Passingham, 1982).

Others have argued that nativists don't really *explain* language development by attributing it to a built-in language acquisition device. An explanation would require knowing *how* such an inborn processor sifts through linguistic input and infers the rules of language; yet nativists are not at all clear about how an LAD (or LMC) might operate (Moerk, 1989; Palmer, 2000). In some ways, attributing language development to the mysterious workings of an LAD or LMC is like saying that physical growth is biologically programmed—and then stopping there, failing to identify the underlying variables (nutrition, hormones, and so forth) that explain why growth follows the course that it takes (MacNeilage et al., 2000). For these reasons, the nativist approach is woefully incomplete; it is really more of a *description* of language learning than a true explanation.

Finally, there are those who claim that nativists, who focus almost exclusively on biological mechanisms and on the deficiencies of learning theories, have simply overlooked the many ways in which a child's language environment promotes language learning (Brooks, 2004). Let's now turn to a third theoretical viewpoint, which claims that language development reflects an interaction of nature and nurture.

The Interactionist Perspective

interactionist theory
the notion that biological factors and environmental influences interact to determine the course of language development.

Proponents of the **interactionist viewpoint** believe that both learning theorists and nativists are partially correct: language development results from a complex interplay among biological maturation, cognitive development, and an ever-changing linguistic environment that is heavily influenced by the child's attempts to communicate with her companions (Akhtar, 2004; Bohannon & Bonvillian, 1997; McKee & McDaniel, 2004; Tomasello, 1995, 2003; Yang, 2004).

Biological and Cognitive Contributors

Clearly, the remarkable similarities that young children display when learning very different languages imply that biology contributes to language acquisition (MacNeilage et al., 2000). But must we attribute language development to the mysterious workings of an LAD or LMC to explain these linguistic universals?

Apparently not. According to the interactionist viewpoint, young children the world over talk alike and display other linguistic universals because they are all members of the same species who share many common experiences. What is innate is not any specialized linguistic knowledge or processing skills but a sophisticated brain that matures very slowly and predisposes children to develop similar ideas at about the same age—ideas that they are then motivated to express in their own speech (Bates, 1999; Tomasello, 1995). Indeed, there is ample support for links between general cognitive development and language development. For example, words are symbols, and infants typically speak their first meaningful words at about 12 months of age, shortly after they display a capacity for symbolism in pretend play and their *deferred imitation* of adult models (Meltzoff, 1988c). Furthermore, we will see that infants' first words center heavily on objects they have manipulated or on actions they have performed—in short, on aspects of experience they can understand through their sensorimotor schemes (Pan & Gleason, 1997). Finally, words like "gone" and "oh oh" emerge during the second year, about the same time infants are mastering *object permanence* and are beginning to appraise the success or failure of their problem-solving activities (Gopnik & Meltzoff, 1987). So infants and toddlers often seem to talk about whatever cognitive understandings they are acquiring at the moment.

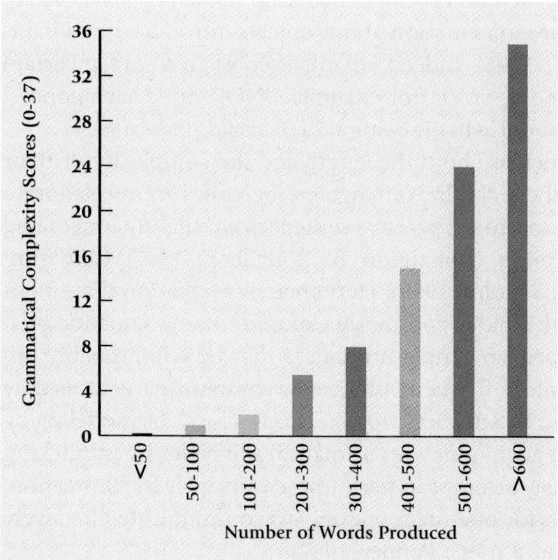

Figure 10.3 Grammatical complexity increases as a function of the size of children's productive vocabulary. *From E. Bates, "On the nature of language," in R. Levi-Montalcini et al. (eds.),* Frontiere della biologia (Frontiers of Biology), The brain of homo sapiens. *Rome: Giovanni Trecanni, 1999. Used by permission of the author.*

Like the nativists, then, interactionists believe that children are biologically prepared to acquire a language. However, the preparation consists *not* of an LAD or LMC but a powerful human brain that slowly matures, allowing children to gain more and more knowledge, which gives them more to talk about (MacNeilage et al., 2000). However, this does not mean that biological maturation and cognitive development totally explain language development. Elizabeth Bates (1999) argues that grammatical speech arises out of social necessity: as children's vocabularies increase beyond 100 to 200 words, they must find ways of organizing all this linguistic knowledge to produce utterances that others will understand. Consistent with Bates's idea, there is a strong relationship between the number of words young children have acquired and the grammatical complexity of their utterances (Robinson & Mervis, 1998) (see Figure 10.3). But how might young children discover subtle points of grammar without the aid of a specialized linguistic processor? Here is where the linguistic environment comes into play.

Environmental Supports for Language Development

Interactionists stress that language is primarily a means of *communicating* that develops in the context of social interactions as children and their companions strive to get their messages across, one way or another (Bohannon & Bonvillian, 1997; Callanan & Sabbagh, 2004; Hoff & Naigles, 2002; MacNeilage et al., 2000; Tomasello, 1995). Over the years, psycholinguists have discovered that parents and older children have distinctive ways of talking to infants and toddlers—that is, communication strategies that seem to foster language learning. Let's see what they have learned.

Lessons from Joint Activities. Long before infants use words, their caregivers show them how to take turns in conversations, even if the only thing these young infants can contribute when their turn comes is a laugh or a babble (Bruner, 1983). As adults continue to converse with young children, they create a supportive learning environment that helps the children grasp the regularities of language (Adamson, Bakeman, & Deckner, 2004; Bruner, 1983; Harris, 1992). For example, parents may go through their children's favorite picture books at bedtime asking "What's this?" or "What does the kitty say?" This gives their children repeated opportunities to learn that conversing involves taking turns, that things have names, and that there are proper ways to pose questions and give answers.

motherese
the short, simple, high-pitched (and often repetitive) sentences that adults use when talking with young children (also called child-directed speech).

Lessons from Child-Directed Speech. Cross-cultural research points to a nearly universal tendency of parents and older siblings to address infants and toddlers with very short, simple sentences that psycholinguists call *child-directed speech,* or **motherese** (Gelman & Shatz, 1977; Kuhl et al., 1997; Thiessen, Hill, & Saffran, 2005). Typically, these utterances are spoken slowly in a high-pitched voice, are often repeated, and emphasize key words (usually words for objects and activities). For example, a mother trying to get her young son to throw a ball might say "*Throw* the *ball,* Andre! Not the rattle. See the *ball?* Yeah, that's the *ball; throw* it!" From the earliest days of life, infants pay more attention to the high-pitched and varied pitch patterns of motherese than to the "flatter" speech that adults use when communicating with each other (Cooper & Aslin, 1990; Pegg, Werker, & McLeod, 1992), and they process more information about objects introduced by infant-directed speech as well (Kaplan et al., 1996). Indeed, infants even seem to grasp certain messages carried in their parents' tone of voice (for example, "NO!" or "That's good!") long before they understand a word about what is being said (Fernald, 1989, 1993).

Interestingly, parents gradually increase both the length and the complexity of their simplified child-directed speech as their children's language becomes more elaborate (Shatz, 1983). And at any given point in time, a parent's sentences are slightly longer and slightly more complex than the child's (Bohannon & Bonvillian, 1997; Cameron-Faulkner, Lieven, & Tomasello, 2003; Sokolov, 1993). Here then, is a situation that might seem ideal for language learning. The child is constantly exposed to new semantic relations and grammatical rules that appear in simple utterances that he will probably understand, particularly if older companions frequently repeat or paraphrase the ideas they are trying to communicate (Bjorklund & Schwartz, 1996). This is a form of modeling by the parent. However, children do not acquire new grammatical principles by mimicking them directly, nor do adults consciously attempt to teach these principles by illustration. Parents speak in child-directed speech for one main reason—to communicate effectively with their children (Fernald & Morikawa, 1993; Penner, 1987).

Lessons from Negative Evidence. Although parents do not reliably attempt to reinforce correct grammar, they do provide the child with *negative evidence;* that is, they respond to ungrammatical speech in ways that subtly communicate that an error has been made and provide information that might be used to correct these errors (Bohannon &

expansions
responding to a child's ungrammatical utterance with a grammatically improved form of that statement.

recasts
responding to a child's ungrammatical utterance with a nonrepetitive statement that is grammatically correct.

Bonvillian, 1997; Saxton, 1997). For example, if a child, says "Doggie go," an adult may respond with an **expansion**—a grammatically correct and enriched version of the child's ungrammatical statement ("Yes, the doggie is going away"). A slightly different form of expansion occurs when adults **recast** the child's sentences into new grammatical forms. For example, a child who says "Doggie eat" might have his sentence recast as "What is the doggie eating?" or "Yes, the doggie is hungry." These recasts are moderately novel utterances that will probably command the child's attention and thereby increase the likelihood that he will notice the new grammatical forms that appear in the adult's speech. Finally, parents are likely to respond to grammatically correct sentences by simply maintaining and extending the conversation (*topic extension*). By carrying on without revising the child's utterance, adults provide a strong clue that the utterance was grammatical (Bohannon & Stanowicz, 1988; Cameron-Faulkner, Lieven, & Tomasello, 2003; Penner, 1987).

Do children profit from negative evidence? Apparently so, for adults who frequently expand, recast, or otherwise extend their children's speech have children who are quicker to acquire grammatical rules and who score relatively high on tests of expressive language ability, compared with children whose parents rely less on these conversational techniques (Bohannon et al., 1996; Valdez-Menchaca & Whitehurst, 1992).

The Importance of Conversation. Would young children learn language just as well by merely listening to others converse? Apparently not. Nativists, who claimed that all children need to acquire language is regular exposure to speech samples, have clearly underestimated the role of *social* interactions in language learning. Mere exposure to speech is simply not enough; children must be actively involved in using language (Locke, 1997). Catherine Snow and her associates, for example, found that a group of Dutch-speaking children, despite the fact that they watched a great deal of German-language television, did not acquire any German words or grammar (Snow et al., 1976). Furthermore, hearing children of profoundly deaf parents often show an approximately normal pattern of language development as long as they spend 5 to 10 hours a week in the company of a hearing/speaking adult who *converses* with them (Schiff-Myers, 1988). True, there are cultures (for example, the Katuli of New Guinea, the natives of American Samoa, and the Trackton people of the Piedmont Carolinas) in which children acquire language without noticeable delays, even though adults rarely restructure their primitive sentences or address them in child-directed speech (Gordon, 1990; Ochs, 1982; Schieffelin, 1986). Yet, even these children regularly participate in social interactions in which language is used, and that is what seems to be most essential in mastering a language (Lieven, 1994).

Summing Up. From an interactionist perspective, then, language development is the product of a complex transaction between nature and nurture. Children are born with a powerful human brain that develops slowly and predisposes them to acquire new understandings, which they are then motivated to share with others (Bates, 1999; Tomasello, 1995). Yet interactionists emphasize—as Vygotsky (1978) did in his model of collaborative learning—that conversations with older companions foster cognitive and language development. As their nervous systems continue to develop, prompted in part by the linguistic input they receive, children grow intellectually and express their new understandings in increasingly complex utterances that prompt close companions to increase the complexity of their replies (Bohannon & Bonvillian, 1997; Sokolov, 1993). As illustrated in Figure 10.4, the pattern of influence is clearly reciprocal: the child's early attempts to communicate influence the speech of older companions, which, in turn, provides information that the child can process to further develop the linguistic centers of the brain, infer linguistic principles, speak more clearly, and influence the speech of companions once again (Tamis-LeMonda, Bornstein, & Baumwell, 2001). Stated another way, the interactionists propose that the language of young children is heavily influenced by a rich, responsive, and ever more complex linguistic environment that they have had a hand in creating (Bloom et al., 1996).

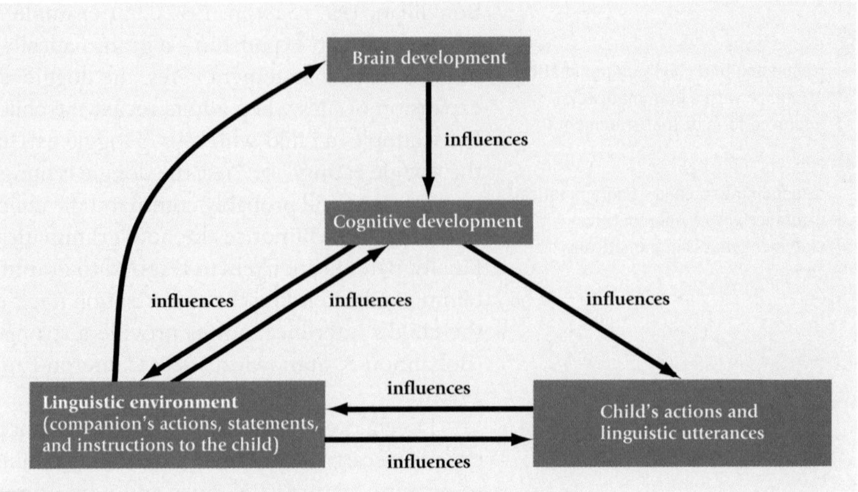

Figure 10.4 An overview of the interactionist perspective on language development.

One final note: Although the interactionist perspective is the approach that many developmentalists favor, the question of how children acquire language is far from resolved. We still know much more about *what* children acquire as they learn a language than about exactly *how* they acquire this knowledge. So let's now chart the course of language development—a process that is well under way long before children utter their first meaningful word.

CONCEPT CHECK 10.1 Understanding Components of Language and Theories of Language Acquisition

Check your understanding of the different components of language and the different theories of language acquisition by answering the following questions. Answers appear in the Appendix.

Matching: Demonstrate your understanding of the five basic components of language by matching the names of these components with their definitions below.

a. morphology
b. phonology
c. pragmatics
d. semantics
e. syntax

1. ________ The sound system of a language and the rules for combining these sounds to produce meaningful units of speech.
2. ________ Rules governing the formation of meaningful words from sounds.
3. ________ The expressed meaning of words and sentences.
4. ________ The structure of a language; the rules specifying how words and grammatical markers are to be combined to produce meaningful sentences.
5. ________ Principles that underlie the effective and appropriate use of language in social contexts.

Multiple Choice: Select the best answer for each question.

____ 6. A learning theorist would most likely claim all of the following events as central to language acquisition *except:*
   a. Children imitate what they hear.
   b. Children are reinforced when they use proper language.
   c. Children are corrected when they use incorrect language.
   d. Children sift language they hear through a biological device in their brains.

____ 7. Damage to part of the brain may result in aphasia, or a loss of one or more language functions. If an aphasic patient can understand what is said *to* him, but cannot *produce* meaningful language, he most likely has had damage to which brain area?
   a. his Broca's area
   b. his Wernicke's area
   c. his language acquisition device
   d. his language-making capacity

____ 8. Interactionist theorists argue that environmental supports help children acquire language. Among these supports are all of the following *except:*
   a. joint social interaction involving language

CONTINUED

b. examples and support of the development of the universal grammar
c. recasts
d. extensions

_____ 9. Brian has always been fascinated by the human brain. He is an undergraduate psychology major and plans to go to graduate school in a cognitive neuroscience program. His lifelong dream is to use brain-imaging techniques with infants and toddlers and be the first person to finally be able to specify where in the brain the language acquisition device is located. If we were to ask Brian what his theoretical views on language acquisition were, he would most likely state:

a. I'm an empiricist!
b. I'm an entomologist!
c. I'm an interactionist!
d. I'm a nativist!

Essay: Provide a detailed answer to the following question.

10. Draw a figure to represent the interactionist view of language acquisition. Explain how this model incorporates nature and nurture influences, and explain the bidirectional aspect of the model.

The Prelinguistic Period: Before Language

prelinguistic phase
the period before children utter their first meaningful words.

For the first 10 to 13 months of life, children are said to be in the **prelinguistic phase** of language development—the period before speaking their first meaningful words. But even though young infants are preverbal, they are quite responsive to language from the day they are born.

Early Reactions to Speech

Newborns seem to be programmed to "tune in" to human speech. When spoken to, neonates often open their eyes, gaze at the speaker, and sometimes even vocalize themselves (Rheingold & Adams, 1980; Rosenthal, 1982). By 3 days of age, an infant already recognizes his or her mother's voice and clearly prefers it to the voice of a female stranger (DeCasper & Fifer, 1980), and newborns suck faster to hear recorded speech than to hear instrumental music or other rhythmic sounds (Butterfield & Siperstein, 1972). So babies can discriminate speech from other sound patterns, and they pay particularly close attention to speech from the very beginning.

Do different samples of speech all sound alike to newborns? Apparently not. Within the first few days after birth, babies begin to discriminate different stress patterns, or rhythms, in two-syllable and three-syllable words (Sansavini, Bertoncini, & Giovanelli, 1997), and they already prefer the sound pattern of the language their mother speaks to that of a foreign language (Moon, Cooper, & Fifer, 1993). One-month-old infants are as capable as adults of discriminating consonant sounds such as *ba* and *da* and *ta,* and by 2 months of age will even recognize that a particular phoneme is still the same sound when spoken at different pitches or intensities by different speakers (Jusczyk, 1995; Marean, Werner, & Kuhl, 1992). In fact, very young infants are actually able to discriminate a wider variety of phonemes than adults can, because adults have lost the ability to make phonemic distinctions that are not important in their native language (Saffran & Thiessen, 2003; Werker & Desjardins, 1995).

It seems, then, that the abilities to discriminate speech from nonspeech and to differentiate a variety of speechlike sounds are either innate or acquired in the first few days and weeks of life. In either case, young infants are remarkably well prepared for the task of decoding the speech they hear.

The Importance of Intonational Cues

Earlier, we noted that adults typically speak to infants in a highly intonated child-directed speech that attracts their attention. Furthermore, adults reliably vary their tone of voice when trying to communicate different "messages" to their preverbal infants (Fernald, 1989; Katz, Cohn, & Moore, 1996). Rising intonations (for example, "look at mom^{my}") are used to recapture the attention of a baby who looks away, whereas falling intonations such as "HEY $_{\text{there!}}$" are often used to comfort or to elicit positive affect (smiles, bright eyes) from a somber baby. These intonational prompts are often successful at affecting a baby's mood or behavior (Fernald, 1989, 1993), and 2- to 6-month-olds frequently produce a vocalization in return that matches the intonation of what they have just heard (Masataka, 1992). This suggests that preverbal infants not only discriminate different intonational patterns but soon recognize that certain tones of voice have a particular meaning. In fact, some researchers believe that a 2- to 6-month-old's successful interpretation of intonational cues may provide some of the earliest evidence that infants understand that speech is a meaningful enterprise (Fernald, 1989, 1993).

During the second half of the first year, infants become increasingly attuned to the "rhythm" of a language, which helps them to segment what they hear, first into phrases, and eventually into words. Phrase boundaries in infant-directed speech are characterized by long pauses that are preceded by very long vowel sounds—acoustic cues that provide ample information about where one phrase ends and another begins (Fisher & Tokura, 1996). By 7 months of age, infants can detect phrase units and clearly prefer to listen to speech that contains natural breaks and pauses to speech in which pauses are inserted at unnatural places, such as the middle of a phrase (Hirsh-Pasek et al., 1987). By age 9 months, infants are becoming sensitive to smaller speech units. They now prefer to listen to speech samples that match the syllabic stress patterns and phonemic combinations of the language their caregivers speak (Jusczyk, Cutler, & Redanz, 1993; Brownlee, 1998; Morgan & Saffran, 1995). So by the last quarter of the first year, infants' increasing familiarity with the phonological aspects of their native language provides important clues about which patterns in an ongoing stream of speech represent individual words (Anthony & Francis, 2005).

Producing Sounds: The Infant's Prelinguistic Vocalizations

coos
vowel-like sounds that young infants repeat over and over during periods of contentment.

babbles
vowel/consonant combinations that infants begin to produce at about 4 to 6 months of age.

The first vocal milestone other than crying occurs by 2 months of age as babies make vowel-like noises called **cooing.** These "ooooohs" and "aaaaahs" are likely to be heard after a feeding when the baby is awake, alert, dry, and otherwise contented. By 4 to 6 months of age, infants have added consonant sounds to their vocal repertoires and are now **babbling**—that is, repeating vowel/consonant combinations such as "mamama" or "papapa" that may sound like words but convey no meaning. Interestingly, deaf infants whose parents are deaf and communicate in sign language will, themselves, babble manually, experimenting with gestures in much the same way that hearing infants experiment with sounds (Petitto & Marentette, 1991).

For the first 6 months, infants the world over (even deaf ones) sound pretty much alike, a finding which suggests that early babbling is heavily influenced by maturation of the brain and the muscles controlling verbal articulation (Hoff-Ginsberg, 1997). The effects of experience soon come into play. Deaf infants, who hear no speech, now begin to fall far behind hearing infants in their ability to produce well-formed, language-like phonemes (Eilers & Oller, 1994; Oller & Eilers, 1988). Hearing infants attend very carefully to others' speech. By the end of the first year, they match the intonation of their babbles to the tonal qualities of the language they hear, and they actually begin to sound as if they are speaking that language (Blake & Boysson-Bardies, 1992; Davis et al., 2000; Davis & MacNeilage, 2000). Apparently, babies are learning the tune before the words (Bates, O'Connell, & Shore, 1987).

As babbling progresses, 10- to 12-month-olds will often reserve certain sounds for particular situations. For example, one infant began to use the *m* sound "*mmmm*" when making requests and the vowel sound "aaaach" when manipulating objects (Blake & Boysson-Bardies, 1992). According to Charles Ferguson (1977), infants who produce these vocables are now aware that certain speech sounds have consistent meanings and are about ready to talk.

What Do Prelinguistic Infants Know about Language and Communication?

Do young infants know more about language than we might think? It now appears that they do and that one of the first things they learn about speech is a practical lesson. During the first 6 months, babies often coo or babble *while* their caregivers are speaking (Rosenthal, 1982). It is almost as if very young infants view talking as a game of noisemaking in which the object is to harmonize with their speaking companions. But by 7 to 8 months of age, infants are typically silent while a companion speaks and wait to respond with a vocalization when their partner stops talking. Apparently they have learned their first rule in the *pragmatics* of language: don't talk while someone else is speaking, for you'll soon have an opportunity to have your say.

Vocal turn-taking may come about because parents typically say something to the baby, wait for the infant to smile, cough, burp, coo, or babble, and address the infant again, thereby inviting another response (Snow & Ferguson, 1977). Of course, infants may also learn about the importance of turn-taking from other contexts in which they assume reversible roles with their companions (Bruner, 1983). Examples of these reciprocal exchanges might include bouts of nose touching, pat-a-cake, and sharing toys. By 4 months of age, infants begin to respond more positively to organized than to disorganized social games (Rochat, Querido, & Striano, 1999). By 9 months of age, they clearly understand the alternation rules of many games. If such activities are interrupted by the adult's failure to take her turn, the infant is likely to vocalize, urge the adult to resume by offering her a toy, or wait for a second or two and take the adult's turn before looking once again at the adult (Ross & Lollis, 1987). So it seems that the ways caregivers structure interactions with an infant may indeed help the child to recognize that many forms of social discourse, including talking, are patterned activities that follow a definite set of rules.

Gestures and Nonverbal Communication

By 8 to 10 months of age, preverbal infants begin to use gestures and other nonverbal responses (for example, facial expressions) to communicate with their companions (Acredolo & Goodwyn, 1990). Two kinds of preverbal gestures are common: *declarative gestures,* in which the infant directs others' attention to an object by pointing at or touching it, and *imperative gestures,* in which the infant tries to convince others to do something by such actions as pointing at candy he wants or tugging at a caregiver's pantleg when he hopes to be picked up. Eventually, some of these gestures become entirely representational and function like words. For example, a 1- to 2-year-old might raise her arms to signify that she wishes to be picked up, hold her arms out to signify an airplane, or even pant heavily to represent the family dog (Acredolo & Goodwyn, 1990; Bates et al., 1989). Once children begin to speak, they often supplement their one- and two-word utterances with a ges-

David M. Grossman/Photo Researchers Inc.

Pointing is an early but very effective means of communication. By the end of the first year, children are calling attention to interesting objects and activities by pointing at them with the index finger.

ture or an intonational cue to ensure that their messages are understood (Butcher & Goldin-Meadow, 2000). And contrary to popular belief, use of gestures to accompany speech actually increases as speech becomes more complex (Iverson & Fagon, 2004; Nicoladis, Mayberry, & Genesee, 1999). In fact, gestures so often accompany vocal communications at all ages (see Goldin-Meadow, 2000) that we might rename the spoken language system as the *speech-gesture system* (Mayberry & Nicoladis, 2000).

Do Preverbal Infants Understand the Meaning of Words?

Although most babies do not utter their first meaningful words until the end of the first year, parents are often convinced that their preverbal infants can understand at least some of what is said to them. However, well-controlled tests of word comprehension suggest that preverbal infants understand the meaning of few, if any, words. In one study, 11- and 13-month-olds were told by their mothers to look at an object that was familiar to them. Mothers were *out of sight* and could not use gestures or other nonverbal cues to direct the infants' attention. The 13-month-olds did understand the meaning of the word that named this object, for they gazed intently at its referent when told to, and they looked very little at other distractor stimuli. Most 11-month-olds did *not* understand the meaning of this word, for they were as likely to gaze at distractor stimuli as at the word's referent (Thomas et al., 1981). So, by age 12 to 13 months infants realize that individual words have meaning. In fact, Sharon Oviatt (1980) found that 12- to 17-month-olds can understand the meaning of many nouns and verbs long before they use them in their own speech. Thus infants seem to know much more about language than they can possibly say. This means that **receptive language** (comprehension) is ahead of **productive language** (expression) from the 12th or 13th month of life and probably even sooner.

receptive language
that which the individual comprehends when listening to others' speech.

productive language
that which the individual is capable of expressing (producing) in his or her own speech.

The Holophrase Period: One Word at a Time

holophrase period
the period when the child's speech consists of one-word utterances, some of which are thought to be holophrases.

holophrase
a single-word utterance that represents an entire sentence's worth of meaning.

In the first stage of meaningful speech, the **holophrase period,** infants utter **holophrases**—single words that often seem to represent an entire sentence's worth of meaning (Brochner & Jones, 2003; Dominey, 2005). At first, the child's productive vocabulary is constrained, in part, by the sounds she can pronounce, so that her very first words may be intelligible only to close companions—for example, "ba" (for "ball") or "awa" (for "I want," as the child points to a cookie) (Hura & Echols, 1996). Sounds that begin with consonants and end with vowels are easiest for infants, whose longer words are often repetitions of the syllables they can pronounce (for example, "mama," "bye-bye").

Phonological development occurs very rapidly. By the middle of the second year, infants' cute and creative pronunciations are already guided by rules or strategies that enable them to produce simplified but more intelligible versions of adult words. For example, they often delete the unstressed syllable of a multisyllable word (saying "poo" for "shampoo"), or replace an ending consonant syllable with a vowel (saying "appo" for "apple") (Ingram, 1986; Lewis, Antone, & Johnson, 1999). The fact that these early pronunciation errors are somewhat similar across languages and are resistant to adults' attempts to correct them suggests that they stem, in part, from biological production constraints, namely, an immature vocal tract. On the other hand, there are tremendous individual differences. All toddlers do not sound alike, even if they have been exposed to the same language (Vihman et al., 1994). Why? Probably because articulating phonemes and combining them into words is a vocal-*motor* skill. Like the dynamic motor systems we discussed in Chapter 6, it reflects the unique paths that individual children follow. They combine the sounds that *they* have been attending closely to and they produce new and more complex patterns. This dynamic system is an attempt to achieve the goal of communicating effectively with their companions (Thelen, 1995; Vihman et al., 1994). As the vocal tract matures during the preschool period, children have more and more opportunities to decipher phonemic combinations that they hear in the speech of older models. They practice these phonemic combinations and their pronunciation errors

TABLE 10.1 Types of Words Used by Children with Productive Vocabularies of 50 Words

Word category	Description and examples	Percentage of utterances
Object words	Words used to refer to classes of objects *(car, doggie, milk)* Words used to refer to unique objects *(Mommy, Rover)*	65
Action words	Words used to describe or accompany actions or to demand attention *(bye-bye, up, go)*	13
Modifiers	Words that refer to properties or quantities of things *(big, hot, mine, allgone)*	9
Personal/social words	Words used to express feelings or to comment about social relationships *(please, thank you, no, ouch)*	8
Function words	Words that have a grammatical function *(what, where, is, to, for)*	4

Source: Adapted from "Structure and Strategy in Learning to Talk," by K. Nelson, 1973, *Monographs of the Society for Research in Child Development, 38,* (Whole No. 149). Copyright © 1973 by The Society for Research in Child Development, Inc. Adapted with permission.

become much less frequent. As a result, most 4- to 5-year-olds already pronounce most words in pretty much the same way that adults do (Ingram, 1986).

Early Semantics: Building a Vocabulary

As infants begin to speak, the growth of their vocabularies proceeds one word at a time (Bloom, 1973). In fact, 3 to 4 months may pass before most children have a vocabulary of 10 words. The pace of word learning quickens dramatically between 18 and 24 months of age, when toddlers may add from 10 to 20 new words a week (Reznick & Goldfield, 1992). This vocabulary spurt is sometimes called the **naming explosion** because, as most parents will attest, toddlers seem to arrive at the wonderful realization that everything has a name and they want to learn all the names they can (Ganger & Brent, 2004; Reznick & Goldfield, 1992). A typical 2-year-old may now produce nearly 200 words (Nelson, 1973) and may comprehend a far greater number (Benedict, 1979).

What do infants talk about? Katherine Nelson (1973) studied 18 infants as they learned their first 50 words and found that nearly two-thirds of these early words referred to *objects* (Bornstein et al., 2004), including familiar people (see Table 10.1). Furthermore, these objects were nearly all either manipulable by the child (for example, balls or shoes) or capable of moving themselves (for example, animals, vehicles); rarely do infants mention objects such as plates or chairs that simply sit there without doing anything. Toddlers' first words also include many references to familiar *actions* as well (Nelson, 1973) (see Table 10.1). In fact, recent research indicates that young infants are especially likely to understand and use words introduced in **multimodal motherese**—that is, exaggerated utterances by an adult that are accompanied by some *action* that calls attention to the referents of these words (Gogate & Bahrick, 2000). So it seems that infants talk mostly about those aspects of experience that they already understand through their own or others' sensorimotor activities.

naming explosion
term used to describe the dramatic increase in the pace at which infants acquire new words in the latter half of the second year; so named because many of the new words acquired are the names of objects.

multimodal motherese
older companion's use of information that is exaggerated and synchronized across two or more senses to call an infant's attention to the referent of a spoken word.

referential style
early linguistic style in which toddlers use language mainly to label objects.

expressive style
early linguistic style in which toddlers use language mainly to call attention to their own and others' feelings and to regulate social interactions.

A large percentage of children's first words are the names of objects that move or can be acted on.

Individual and Cultural Variations in Early Language

Katherine Nelson's (1973) early study revealed an interesting individual difference in the kinds of words infants produced. Most infants displayed what she called a **referential style:** their early vocabularies consisted mainly of words that referred to people or objects. A smaller number of infants displayed an **expressive style:** their vocabularies contained a larger number of personal/social words such as *please, thank you, don't,* and *stop it.* Apparently language serves somewhat different functions for these two groups of children. Referential children seem to think words are for naming objects, whereas expressive

Elizabeth Crews

By emphasizing social routines and concern for others, Japanese mothers encourage their children to adopt an "expressive" language style.

children use words to call attention to their own and others' feelings and to regulate their social interactions (Nelson, 1981).

Another individual difference stems from children's birth order. That is, a child's birth order seems to influence the linguistic environment in ways that could affect her language style. Most firstborns in Western cultures adopt a referential style, perhaps reflecting parents' willingness to label and to ask questions about interesting objects that have captured their attention (Nelson, 1973). Later-borns hear a great deal of speech directed to an older sibling that firstborns haven't heard. So later-borns may spend less time talking with parents about objects and more time listening to simpler speech designed to control their own or their siblings' conduct (Evans, Maxwell, & Hart, 1999; Pine, 1995). As a result, they are more likely than firstborns to conclude that the function of language is to regulate others' behavior, thus prompting them to adopt an expressive language style (Nelson, 1973).

Culture also influences language styles. When talking about a stuffed animal, American mothers treat the interaction as an opportunity to teach the infant about objects ("It's a doggie! Look at its big ears."), thereby encouraging a referential style. Japanese mothers, on the other hand, are more inclined to emphasize social routines and consideration for others ("Give the doggie love!") that seem to promote an expressive style (Fernald & Morikawa, 1993). Indeed, in Asian cultures such as Japan, China, and Korea that stress interpersonal harmony, children are much quicker to acquire verbs and personal/social words than are American children (Gopnik & Choi, 1995; Tardif, Gelman, & Xu, 1999).

Attaching Meaning to Words

fast mapping
process of acquiring a word after hearing it applied to its referent on a small number of occasions.

How do toddlers figure out what words mean? In many cases, they seem to employ a **fast-mapping** process, quickly acquiring (and retaining) a word after hearing it applied to its referent on a small number of occasions (Wilkinson & Mazzitelli, 2003). Apparently, even 13- to 15-month-olds can learn the meaning of new words by fast mapping (Schaefer & Plummert, 1998; Woodward, Markman, & Fitzsimmons, 1994), although the names of objects are more easily acquired at this age than the names of actions or activities (Casasola & Cohen, 2000). Fast mapping clearly improves with age: 18- to 20-month-olds are likely to learn the meaning of novel words that a speaker introduces only if they and the speaker are *jointly attending* to the labeled object or activity (Baldwin et al., 1996). By age 24 months, children are much better at inferring what speakers are talking about and will now fast map a novel word to its referent, even if other objects or events are competing for their attention (Moore, Angelopoulos, & Bennett, 1999).

If 13- to 15-month-olds can fast map word meanings, why do you suppose that children this young produce so few words? One possibility is that fast mapping allows these youngest language users to *comprehend* word meanings, but that they have trouble *retrieving* known words from memory when they try to talk. Consider a recent study in which 14- to 24-month-olds who knew the names of objects hidden in a box and who had seen the objects placed there were asked "What's inside the box?" (Dapretto & Bjork, 2000). Toddlers who had yet to enter that naming explosion generally could not retrieve words *they knew well* to answer correctly, whereas children who had already displayed a vocabulary spurt performed much better. So one important reason why productive vocabulary may be so far behind receptive vocabulary early in life is that 12- to 15-month-olds who are fast mapping the meaning of many new words are often unable to retrieve these words from memory to talk about their referents.

Common Errors in Word Use

Despite their remarkable fast-mapping capabilities, toddlers often attach meanings to words that differ from those of adults (Pan & Gleason, 1997). One kind of error that they frequently make is to use a word to refer to a wider variety of objects or events (Mandler,

overextension
the young child's tendency to use relatively specific words to refer to a broader set of objects, actions, or events than adults do (for example, using the word *car* to refer to all motor vehicles).

underextension
the young child's tendency to use general words to refer to a smaller set of objects, actions, or events than adults do (for example, using *candy* to refer only to mints).

2004; McDonough, 2002; Samuelson, 2002). This phenomenon, called **overextension,** is illustrated by a child's use of the term *doggie* to refer to all furry, four-legged animals. **Underextension,** the opposite of overextension, is the tendency to use a general word to refer to a smaller range of objects—for example, applying the term *cookie* only to chocolate chip cookies (Jerger & Damion, 2005). Why young children overextend or underextend particular words is not always clear, but it is likely that fast mapping contributes to these errors. Suppose, for example, that a mother points to a collie and says "doggie," and then turns toward a fox terrier and says "Look, another doggie." Applying the same name to these perceptually discriminable objects will cause her toddler to mentally abstract their common features, forming a category (Samuelson & Smith, 2000). The child may note that the two things these two animals have in common are four legs and a hairy exterior, thus leading him to "fast map" the word doggie onto these perceptual attributes. And having done so, he may then be inclined to overextend the word doggie to other animals (cats, racoons) that share similar perceptual features (Clark, 1973). Fast mapping could lead to underextensions as well. If the only dog a toddler has ever seen is the family pet, which he has heard his mother refer to as "doggie" a few times, he may initially assume that doggie is the proper name of this particular companion and use the term only when referring to his pet.

Of course, deciphering the meaning of many new words is more difficult than these examples imply because it is often unclear exactly what new words refer to. For example, if mother sees a cat walking alongside a car and exclaims "Oh, there is a kitty!," the child must first decide whether mom is referring to the car or to the animal. If she rules out the car, it is still not obvious whether the word *kitty* refers to four-legged animals, to this particular animal, to the cat's pointed ears, leisurely gait, or even the meowing sound it made. How does the child decide among these many possibilities, all of which may seem plausible to her?

Strategies for Inferring Word Meanings

Determining how young children figure out what new words mean when their referents are *not* immediately obvious (as in the above *"kitty"* example) has proved to be a challenging task that is far from complete. Nameera Akhtar et al. (1996) believe that 2-year-olds are already especially sensitive to *social* and *contextual* cues that would help them to determine what novel aspects of a companion's speech might mean. To illustrate this point, Akhtar et al. had 2-year-olds and two adults play with three *unnamed* objects that were unfamiliar to the children. Then one adult left the room and a fourth unnamed object was added to the mix. Later, when the absent adult returned, she exclaimed, "Look, I see a gazzer! A gazzer!" without pointing or displaying any other clue to indicate which of the four objects she was referring to. Even though "gazzer" could have referred to any of the four unnamed objects, a substantial percentage of these 2-year-olds correctly inferred the speaker's referential intent, picking the *novel* object (which was novel *only for the speaker* and not for them) when asked to show a "gazzer." They realized that the second adult had not previously seen this fourth object and then assumed that she must be talking about whichever object was new to her.

processing constraints
cognitive biases or tendencies that lead infants and toddlers to favor certain interpretations of the meaning of new words over other interpretations.

object scope constraint
the notion that young children will assume that a new word applied to an object refers to the whole object rather than to parts of the object or to object attributes (for example, its color).

mutual exclusivity constraint
notion that young children will assume that each object has but one label and that different words refer to separate and non-overlapping categories.

In addition to using social or contextual cues to infer word meanings, 2-year-olds have a number of other cognitive strategies, or **processing constraints,** that help them narrow down what a new word might possibly mean (de Villiers & de Villiers, 1992; Golinkoff et al., 1996; Hall & Waxman, 1993; Littschwager & Markman, 1994). Several of the more basic constraints that seem to guide children's inferences about word meaning are described in Table 10.2.

Of course, these constraints may often work together to help children learn word meanings. For example, when 2-year-olds hear the words *horn* and *clip* applied to two very different objects, they assign each word correctly to a whole object, rather than to its parts or attributes (**object scope constraint**), and they display **mutual exclusivity** by almost never calling the horn a "clip" (or vice versa) when tested later (Waxman & Senghas, 1992).

TABLE 10.2 Some Processing Strategies, or Constraints, That Guide Young Children's Inferences about the Meaning of New Words

Constraint	Description	Example
Object scope constraint	The assumption that words refer to whole objects rather than to parts of the objects or to object attributes.	The child concludes that the word *kitty* refers to the animal he sees rather than to the animal's ears, tail, meowing vocalizations, or color.
Taxonomic constraint	The assumption that words label categories of *similar* objects that share common perceptual features.	The child concludes that the word *kitty* refers to the animal he has seen *and* to other small, furry, four-legged animals.
Lexical contrast constraint	The assumption that each word has a unique meaning.	The child who already knows the meaning of *doggie* assumes that a label such as *dalmatian*, applied to a dog, refers to that particular kind of dog (subordinate class).
Mutual exclusivity	The assumption that each object has one label and that different words refer to separate, nonoverlapping categories.	The child who already knows the word for *doggie* assumes that the word *kitty* refers to the fleeing animal if he hears someone say "Look at the doggie chasing the kitty."

lexical contrast constraint
notion that young children make inferences about word meanings by contrasting new words with words they already know.

syntactical bootstrapping
notion that young children make inferences about the meaning of words by analyzing the way words are used in sentences and inferring whether they refer to objects (nouns), actions (verbs), or attributes (adjectives).

However, the mutual exclusivity constraint is not very helpful when adults use more than one word to refer to the same object (for example, "Oh, there is a *doggie*—a *cocker spaniel*") (Callanan & Sabbagh, 2004). Under these circumstances, 2-year-olds who already know the word doggie will often apply the **lexical contrast constraint,** concluding that *cocker spaniel* must refer to a particular kind of dog that has the distinctive features (long floppy ears; heavy coat) that this one displays (Taylor & Gelman, 1988, 1989; Waxman & Hatch, 1992). Indeed, this tendency to contrast novel with familiar words may explain how children form hierarchical linguistic categories, eventually recognizing, for example, that a dog is also an animal and a mammal (superordinate categories) as well as a cocker spaniel who has a proper name such as Pokey (subordinate categories) (Mervis, Golinkoff, & Bertrand, 1994).

Syntactical Clues to Word Meaning. Young language learners can also infer word meanings by paying close attention to the way that the word is used in a sentence. For example, a 20- to 24-month-old who hears a new word, *zav,* used as a noun to refer to a toy ("This is a *zav*") is likely to conclude that this new word refers to the toy itself. However, a child who hears *zav* used as an adjective ("This is a *zav* one") is more likely to conclude that *zav* refers to some characteristic of the toy, such as its shape or color (Taylor & Gelmen, 1988; Waxman & Markow, 1998).

Notice, then, children learn word meanings from sentence structure, or *syntactical* clues. Indeed, this **syntactical bootstrapping** may be especially important in helping them to decipher the meaning of new verbs (Gleitman, 1990; Lidz, Gleitman, & Gleitman, 2003; Oller, 2005). Consider the following two sentences:

1. The duck is gorping the bunny. (Gorping refers to a causative action.)
2. The duck and the bunny are gorping. (Gorping is a synchronized action.)

When 2-year-olds hear one or the other of these sentences, they prefer to look at a video that matches what they have heard—for example, looking at a duck *causing* a rabbit to bend over after hearing Sentence 1 (Naigles, 1990). So the verb's syntax—the form that it takes in a sentence—provides important clues as to what it means (Naigles & Hoff-Ginsberg, 1995).

Finally, 2-year-olds can use the meaning of a familiar verb to limit the possible referent of a novel noun. So if they know what "eating" means and hear the sentence "Daddy is eating cabbage," they will map this name onto the leafy substance that dad is consuming rather than wondering whether "cabbage" refers to the ham, cornbread, or any other object on the dining room table (Goodman, McDonough, & Brown, 1998). By age 3, children become so proficient at inferring word meanings from syntactical cues that they trust their understanding of *sentence structure* rather than other processing constraints

when the referent of a new word is unclear or when syntactical cues and other processing constraints would lead to different interpretations (Hall, Quantz, & Persoage, 2000).

Summing Up. Toddlers are remarkably well prepared for the task of figuring out what new words mean. Their strong desire to share meaning with companions makes them especially sensitive to novel aspects of the speech they hear and highly motivated to use contextual cues and other available information to decode new words. By age 2, toddlers can already produce nearly 200 words—a sufficient baseline for lexical contrast. And apparently they already understand enough about sentence structure (syntax) to determine whether many new words are nouns, verbs, or adjectives—another important clue to word meaning. Although it is true that toddlers make some semantic errors, they often seem to know much more about the meaning of words than their errors might indicate. For example, 2-year-olds who say "doggie" when they see a horse can usually discriminate dogs from other animals if they are given a set of animal pictures and asked to find a dog (Naigles & Gelman, 1995). Why, then, might they choose to call a horse a doggie when they can easily tell the animals apart?

One possibility is that toddlers who know relatively few words may use overextension as yet another strategy for learning the names of new objects and activities. A child who sees a horse may call it a doggie, not because he believes it is a dog, but because he has no better word in his vocabulary to describe this animal and he has learned from experience that an incorrect label is likely to elicit reactions such as "No, Marcos, that's a *horse.* Can you say *horsie?* C'mon, say *horsie*" (Ingram, 1989).

When a Word Is More than a Word

Many psycholinguists characterize an infant's one-word utterances as *holophrases* because they often seem less like labels and more like attempts to convey an entire sentence's worth of meaning (Bochner & Jones, 2003; Dominey, 2005). These single-word "sentences" can serve different communicative functions depending on how they are said and the context in which they are said (Greenfield & Smith, 1976). For example, 17-month-old Carmen used the word *ghetti* (spaghetti) three times over a 5-minute period. First, she pointed to the pot on the stove and seemed to be *asking* "Is that spaghetti?" Later, the function of her holophrase was to *name* the spaghetti when shown the contents of the pot, as in "It is spaghetti!" Finally, she left little question that she was *requesting* spaghetti when she tugged at her father's sleeve as he was eating and used a whining tone.

Of course, there are limits to the amount of meaning that can be packed into a single word, but infants in the holphrastic phase of language development do seem to display such basic language functions as naming, questioning, requesting, and demanding—functions

that they will later serve by producing different kinds of sentences. They are also learning an important *pragmatic* lesson: that their one-word messages are often ambiguous and may require an accompanying gesture or intonational cue if they are to be understood (Ingram, 1989).

The Telegraphic Period: From Holophrases to Simple Sentences

telegraphic speech
early sentences that consist of content words and omit the less meaningful parts of speech, such as articles, prepositions, pronouns, and auxiliary verbs.

At about 18 to 24 months of age, children begin to combine words into simple "sentences" such as "Daddy eat," "Kitty go," and "Mommie drink milk" that are remarkably similar in syntax across languages as diverse as English, German, Finnish, and Samoan (see Table 10.3). These early sentences have been called **telegraphic speech** because, like telegrams, they contain only critical content words, such as nouns, verbs, and adjectives, and leave out such frills as articles, prepositions, and auxiliary verbs (Bochner & Jones, 2004).

Why do young children stress nouns and verbs and omit many other parts of speech in their earliest sentences? Certainly not because the omitted words serve no function. Children clearly encode these words in others' speech, for they respond more appropriately to

TABLE 10.3 Similarities in Children's Spontaneous Two-Word Sentences in Four Languages

	Language			
Function of sentence	English	Finnish	German	Samoan
To locate or name	There book	Tuossa Rina (there Rina)	Buch da (book there)	Keith lea (Keith there)
To demand	More milk Give candy	Annu Rina (give Rina)	Mehr milch (more milk)	Mai pepe (give doll)
To negate	No wet Not hungry	Ei susi (not wolf)	Nicht blasen (not blow)	Le'ai (not eat)
To indicate possession	My shoe Mama dress	Täti auto (aunt's car)	Mein ball (my ball) Mamas hut (Mama's hat)	Lole a'u (candy my)
To modify or qualify	Pretty dress Big boat	Rikki auto (broken car)	Armer wauwau (poor dog)	Fa'ali'i pepe (headstrong baby)
To question	Where ball	Missa pallo (where ball)	Wo ball (where ball)	Fea Punafu (where Punafu)

Source: Adapted from *Psycholinguistics*, 2nd ed., by Dan Issac Slobin, 1979, pp. 86–87. Copyright © 1979, 1974, 1971 by Scott, Forseman and Company. Adapted by permission of the author.

fully grammatical sentences (for example, "Get the ball") than to telegraphic (or otherwise ungrammatical) versions of the same idea (such as "Get ball" or "Point to gub ball") (Gerken & McIntosh, 1993; Petretic & Tweney, 1977). Current thinking is that telegraphic children omit words because of their own processing and production constraints. A child who can only generate very short utterances will choose to de-emphasize smaller, less important words in favor of those heavily stressed nouns and verbs that are necessary for effective communication (Gerken, Landau, & Remez, 1990; Valian, Hoeffner & Aubry, 1996).

Interestingly, telegraphic speech is not nearly as universal as earlier researchers had thought. Russian and Turkish children, for example, produce short but reasonably grammatical sentences from the very beginning. Why? Because their languages place more stress on small grammatical markers and have less rigid rules about word order than other languages do (de Villiers & de Villiers, 1992; Slobin, 1985). So it seems whatever is most noticeable about the structure of a language is what children acquire first. And if content words and word-order rules are most heavily stressed (as in English), then young children will include this information and omit the lightly stressed articles, prepositions, and grammatical markers to produce what appear to be "telegraphic" utterances.

A Semantic Analysis of Telegraphic Speech

Psycholinguists have approached early child language as if it were a foreign language and have tried to describe the rules that young children use to form their sentences. Early attempts to specify the structural characteristics, or syntax, of telegraphic speech made it quite clear that many of children's earliest two-word sentences followed at least some grammatical rules. English-speaking children, for example, usually say "Mommy drink" rather than "Drink mommy" or "My ball" rather than "Ball my," thus suggesting that they already realize that some word orders are better than others for conveying meaning (de Villiers & de Villiers, 1992).

However, it soon became obvious that analyses of telegraphic speech based on syntax alone grossly underestimated the young child's linguistic capabilities. Why? Because young children often use the same two-word utterance to convey different meanings (or semantic relations) in different contexts. For example, one of Lois Bloom's (1970) young subjects said "Mommy sock" on two occasions during the same day—once when she picked up her mother's sock and once while her mother was putting a sock on the child's foot. In the first instance, "Mommy sock" seems to imply a possessive relationship—"Mommy's sock." But in the second instance, the child was apparently expressing a different idea, namely "Mommy is putting on my sock." So to properly interpret telegraphic statements, one must determine the child's *meaning* or *semantic intent* by considering not only the words that she generates but also the contexts in which these utterances take place.

The Pragmatics of Early Speech

Because early sentences are incomplete and their meanings often ambiguous, children continue to supplement their words with gestures and intonational cues to ensure that their messages are understood (O'Neill, 1996). Although those who are proficient with the spoken language may consider nonverbal gestures a rather limited and inefficient form of communication, such an attitude is extremely shortsighted. Indeed, many deaf children come to know and use a rather sophisticated language that is based entirely on nonverbal signs and gestures (see the Box on p. 402).

Toddlers are also becoming quite sensitive to many of the social and situational determinants of effective communication. For example, 2-year-olds are rather proficient at vocal turn-taking; they know that speakers "look up" at the listener when they are about to yield the floor, and they now use this same nonverbal cue to signal the end of their own utterances (Rutter & Durkin, 1987). By age 2 to 2½, children know that they must either stand close to a listener or compensate for distance by raising their voices if they

APPLYING RESEARCH TO YOUR LIFE

Learning a Gestural Language

© Richard T. Nowitz/Corbis

Children who are born deaf or who lose their hearing very early in childhood will have a difficult time learning an oral language. Contrary to popular opinion, the deaf do not learn much from lip reading. In fact, many deaf children (especially those of hearing parents) may be delayed in their language development unless they are exposed early to a gestural system such as American Sign Language (ASL) (Mayberry, 1994).

Although ASL is produced by the hands rather than orally, it is a remarkably flexible medium (Bellugi, 1988). Some signs represent entire words; others stand for grammatical morphemes such as the progressive ending *-ing*, the past tense *-ed*, and auxiliaries. Each sign is constructed from a limited set of gestural components in much the same way that the spoken word is constructed from a finite number of distinctive sounds (phonemes). Syntactical rules specify how signs are to be combined to form declarative sentences, to ask questions, and to negate a proposition. And like an oral language, ASL permits the user to sign plays on words (puns), metaphorical statements, and poetry. So people who are proficient in this gestural system can transmit and understand an infinite variety of highly creative messages—they are true language users!

Deaf children who are exposed early to ASL acquire it in much the same way that hearing children acquire an oral language (Bellugi, 1988; Locke, 1997). Indeed, signs are readily visible to the infant and grow from sensorimotor schemes, perhaps explaining why many children produce their first truly referential sign or gesture at about the same time or slightly before hearing children utter their first meaningful words (Folven & Bonvillian, 1991; Goodwyn & Acredolo, 1993). Deaf mothers support sign learning by signing to their infants in "motherese"—that is, signing slowly with exaggerated movements that are repeated often to ensure comprehension (Masataka, 1996, 1998). And the deaf child usually begins by "babbling" in sign, forming rough approximations of signs that parents use—before proceeding to one-word, or "holophrastic," phrases, in which a single sign is used to convey a number of different messages. Furthermore, the linguistic advances of both deaf and hearing children are closely linked to advances in cognitive development; for example, putting signs or words together in sentences happens at about the same age that children put sequences of actions together in their play (Spencer, 1996). Deaf children become quite proficient at fast mapping and using other processing constraints to expand their vocabularies (Lederberg, Prezbindowski, & Spencer, 2000), and when they begin to combine signs, their two-sign sentences are "telegraphic" statements that express the same set of semantic relations that appears in the early speech of hearing children.

Finally, the language areas of the brain develop much the same in deaf children exposed early to sign language as in hearing children exposed to speech. Helen Neville and her colleagues (1997) examined the brain activity of deaf ASL users and hearing individuals as they processed sentences in their respective languages. For the most part, reliance on areas of the left hemisphere of the cerebral cortex to process sentences was just as strong among participants who acquired ASL early in life as among hearing individuals who acquired English early in life. However, early learners of ASL also used their right hemisphere in responding to sentences, perhaps because spatial skills controlled by the right hemisphere come into play in interpreting the gestures of someone who is signing.

What do these striking parallels tell us about theories of language acquisition? They surely imply that language learning depends, to no small extent, on biological processes (Meier, 1991). What isn't clear, however, is whether the linguistic milestones and abilities that deaf and hearing children share reflect (1) the operation of an inborn specialized linguistic knowledge (or LAD) that enables children to acquire any and all languages (nativist position), or (2) the gradual development of a highly plastic (that is, changeable) human brain and achievement of cognitive understandings that children are then motivated to express in languagelike ways to communicate more effectively with their companions (interactionist position).

are to communicate with that person (Johnson et al., 1981; Wellman & Lempers, 1977). And remarkably, 2- to 2½-year-olds are beginning to consider what a partner knows (or doesn't know) when choosing a conversational topic or making a request. They much prefer to talk about events that their partners haven't shared with them or don't already know about (Shatz, 1994), and their requests for assistance in obtaining a toy that is out of reach are much more elaborate and more likely to include a gesture when they know that their partners are unaware of the toy's whereabouts (O'Neill, 1996). In fact, 2½-year-olds can even monitor others' responses to their messages and clarify many utterances that an adult has misunderstood (Levy, 1999). So a child who requested a toy duck and hears an adult say "You asked for the sock" will often repair his failed message with a statement such as "I no want that! Want duck!" (Shwe & Markman, 1997).

CONCEPT CHECK 10.2 Understanding Children's Development of Language Skills

Check your understanding of the prelinguistic period, the holophrase period, and the telegraphic period by answering the following questions. Answers appear in the Appendix.

Fill in the Blank: Fill in the blanks with the correct word or phrase.

1. A young child's tendency to use relatively specific words to refer to a broad set of objects, actions, or events is called a(n) ________.
2. The notion that young children make inferences about the meaning of words by analyzing the way words are used in sentences and inferring whether they refer to objects, actions, or attributes is called ________.
3. The ________ is the single-word utterance that represents an entire sentence's worth of meaning.

Multiple Choice: Select the best answer for each question.

_____ 4. Tamina is preoccupied with pointing at things and asking what they are. She is a toddler who experiences:
   a. the naming explosion
   b. prelinguistic vocables
   c. an overactive language acquisition device (LAD)
   d. metalinguistic awareness

_____ 5. The fact that coos sound the same whether or not the young infant can hear suggests that coos:
   a. convey self-generated meanings for adult listeners
   b. develop with maturation of the brain and vocal organs
   c. are a reflection of the parents' recasts and extensions
   d. arise from the infant's mutual exclusivity constraint

_____ 6. The infant uses *imperative* gestures to get others to:
   a. notice the infant's ideas
   b. expand pidgins into vocables
   c. fulfill the infant's requests
   d. initiate communication via telegraphic speech

_____ 7. Recordo was a father of four children. He liked to keep diaries of their accomplishments in a baby scrapbook. Although his record-keeping did tend to decrease with the birth of each new child, he did manage to record the first words that each child spoke. Recordo was surprised when he compared the baby diaries because his oldest son's first words were very different from the first words of his next three daughters. Recordo's observation illustrates:
   a. the sensitive-period hypothesis
   b. the birth order hypothesis
   c. the sex-difference hypothesis
   d. the critical period hypothesis

Short Answer: Briefly answer the following questions.

8. Define and distinguish between receptive and productive language.
9. Explain what is meant by overextension and underextension and provide examples to illustrate each type of linguistic error.

Essay: Provide a more detailed answer to the following question.

10. List and describe five processing constraints that may guide children's inferences about the meaning of new words.

TABLE 10.4 Samples of One Boy's Speech at Three Ages

	Age	
28 months (telegraphic speech)	**35 months**	**38 months**
Somebody pencil	No—I don't know	I like a racing car
Floor	What dat feeled like?	I broke my racing car
Where birdie go?	Lemme do again	It's broked
Read dat	Don't—don't hold with me	You got some beads
Hit hammer, Mommy	I'm going to drop it—inne dump truck	Who put dust on my hair?
Yep, it fit	Why—cracker can't talk?	Mommy don't let me buy some
Have screw	Those are mines	Why it's not working?

Source: Adapted from *The Acquisition of Language: The Study of Developmental Psycholinguistics,* by D. McNeill, 1970. Harper & Row Publishers. Copyright © 1970 by HarperCollins, Inc.

Finally, young children are also learning certain sociolinguistic prescriptions, such as the need to be polite when making requests, and they are beginning to understand what is polite and what isn't in other people's speech (Baroni & Axia, 1989; Garton & Pratt, 1990). Although we have seen that parents do not intentionally teach grammar to their children, they do instruct them in etiquette (Flavell, Miller, & Miller, 1993). Such common parental prompts as "What do you say?" or "Say the magic word to get a cookie" play an important part in this learning.

In sum, most 2- to 2½-year-olds have learned many pragmatic lessons about language and communication and are usually able to get their meaning across to conversational partners. But even though toddlers can converse with adults and older children, their communication skills pale in comparison with those of a 5-year-old, a 4-year-old, or even many 3-year-olds. Our next task is to determine what it is that preschool children are acquiring that will enable them to become rather sophisticated users of language by the time they enter kindergarten.

Language Learning During the Preschool Period

In the short period from age 2½ to 5, children come to produce sentences that are remarkably complex and adultlike. Table 10.4 gives an inkling of how fast language progresses in the brief span of 7 to 10 months. What are children acquiring that accounts for this language explosion? Surely they are mastering basic morophology and syntax: As we see in Table 10.4, a child of 35 to 38 months is now inserting articles, auxiliary verbs, and grammatical markers (for example, *-ed, -ing*) that were previously omitted, as well as negating propositions and occasionally asking a well-formed question (Hoff-Ginsberg, 1997). And although it is not as obvious from the table, we will see that preschool children are also beginning to understand much more about the pragmatics of language and communication.

Grammatical Development

Development of Grammatical Morphemes

grammatical morphemes
prefixes, suffixes, prepositions, and auxiliary verbs that modify the meaning of words and sentences.

Grammatical morphemes are modifiers that give more precise meaning to the sentences we construct. Use of these meaning modifiers usually appears sometime during the third year as children begin to pluralize nouns by adding *-s,* to signify location with

TABLE 10.5 Order of Acquisition of English Grammatical Morphemes

Morpheme	Example
1. Present progressive: *-ing*	He is sitt*ing* down.
2. Preposition: *in*	The mouse is *in* the box.
3. Preposition: *on*	The book is *on* the table.
4. Plural: *-s*	The dog*s* ran away.
5. Past irregular: for example, *went*	The boy *went* home.
6. Possessive: *-'s*	The girl*'s* dog is big.
7. Uncontractible copula *be:* for example, *are, was*	*Are* they boys or girls? *Was* that a dog?
8. Articles: *the, a*	He has *a* book.
9. Past regular: *-ed*	He jump*ed* the stream.
10. Third person regular: *-s*	She run*s* fast.
11. Third person irregular: for example, *has, does*	*Does* the dog bark?
12. Uncontractible auxiliary *be:* for example, *is, were*	*Is* he running? *Were* they at home?
13. Contractible copula *be:* for example, *-'s, -'re*	That*'s* a spaniel.
14. Contractible auxiliary *be:* for example, *-'s, -'re*	They*'re* running very slowly.

Source: Adapted from *Psychology and Language: An Introduction to Psycholinguistics*, by H. H. Clark & E. V. Clark, p. 345. Copyright © 1977 by Harcourt Brace & Company. Reproduced by permission of the publisher.

This is a wug.
Now there is another one.
There are two of them.
There are two ________

Figure 10.5 A linguistic puzzle used to determine young children's understanding of the rule for forming plurals in English. *From Berko, 1958.*

the prepositional morphemes *in* and *on,* to indicate verb tense with the present progressive *-ing* or the past tense *-ed,* and to describe possessive relations with the inflection *'s.*

Roger Brown (1973) kept records on three children as they acquired 14 grammatical morphemes that frequently appear in English sentences. He found that these three children varied considerably with respect to (1) the age at which they began to use grammatical markers and (2) the amount of time it took them to master all 14 rules. However, all three children in this longitudinal study learned the 14 grammatical morphemes in precisely the order in which they appear in Table 10.5, a finding confirmed in a cross-sectional study of 21 additional children (de Villiers & de Villiers, 1973).

Why do children who have very different vocabularies learn these 14 grammatical markers in one particular order? Brown (1973) soon rejected a frequency-of-mention hypothesis when he found that the grammatical morphemes learned first appear no more often in parents' speech than morphemes acquired later. What he did discover is that the morphemes acquired early are less semantically and syntactically complex than those acquired later. For example, the present progressive *-ing,* which describes an ongoing action, appears before the past regular *-ed,* which describes both action and a sense of "earlier in time." Moreover, *-ed,* which conveys two semantic features, is acquired earlier than the uncontractible forms of the verb *to be* (*is, are, was, were*), all of which are more syntactically complex and specify *three* semantic relations: number (singular or plural), tense (present or past), and action (ongoing process).

Once young children have acquired a new grammatical morpheme, they apply this rule to new as well as to familiar contexts. For example, if the child realizes that the way to pluralize a noun is to add the grammatical inflection *-s,* she has no problem solving the puzzle in Figure 10.5—these two funny-looking creatures are obviously wugs (Berko, 1958).

overregularization
the overgeneralization of grammatical rules to irregular cases where the rules do not apply (for example, saying *mouses* rather than *mice*).

Overregularization. Interestingly, children occasionally overextend new grammatical morphemes to cases in which the adult form is irregular—a phenomenon known as **overregularization** (Clahsen, Hadler, & Weyerts, 2004; Rodriguez-Fornells, Münte, &

Clahsen, 2002). Statements such as "I brushed my *tooths,*" "She *goed,*" or "It *runned* away" are common examples of the kind of overregularization errors that 2½- to 3-year-olds make. Oddly enough, children have often used the *correct* forms of many irregular nouns and verbs (for example, "It *ran* away"; "My *feet* are cold") *before* they learn any grammatical morphemes (Brown, 1973; Mervis & Johnson, 1991). Even after acquiring a new rule, a child's overregularizations are relatively rare, occurring on only about 2½ to 5 percent of those occasions in which irregular verbs are used (Maratsos, 2000; Marcus et al., 1992). So overregularization is not a serious grammatical defect that must be unlearned. Instead, most of their errors seem to occur because children occasionally fail to retrieve the irregular form of a noun or a verb from memory and must then apply their new morpheme (overregularize) to communicate the idea they are trying to express (Marcus et al., 1992).

Mastering Transformational Rules

transformational grammar
rules of syntax that allow one to transform declarative statements into questions, negatives, imperatives, and other kinds of sentences.

In addition to grammatical morphemes, each language has rules for creating variations of the basic declarative sentence. Applying these rules of **transformational grammar,** the declarative statement "I was eating pizza" can easily be modified to produce a *question* ("What was I eating?") or to generate *negative* sentences ("I was *not* eating pizza"), *imperatives* ("Eat the pizza!"), *relative clauses* ("I who hate cheese, was eating pizza"), and *compound sentences* ("I was eating pizza and John was eating spaghetti") (Schoneberger, 2000).

Between the ages of 2 and 2½, most children begin to produce some variations of declarative sentences—many of which depend on their mastery of the auxiliary verb *to be* (de Villiers & de Villiers, 1992). However, children acquire transformational rules in a step-by-step fashion, as we will see by considering the phases that children go through as they learn to ask questions, negate propositions, and generate complex sentences.

Asking Questions. There are two kinds of questions that are common to virtually all languages. *Yes/no questions,* the simpler form that is mastered first, ask whether particular declarative statements are true or false (for example, "Is that a doggie?"). *Wh- questions* call for responses other than a simple yes or no. These queries are called wh- questions because, in English, they almost always begin with a *wh-* word such as *who, what, where, when,* or *why.*

The child's earliest questions often consist of nothing more than a declarative sentence uttered with a rising intonation that transforms it into a yes/no question (for example, "See doggie?"). However, *wh-* words are occasionally placed at the beginning of telegraphic sentences to generate simple *wh-* questions such as "Where doggie?" or "What daddy eat?" During the second phase of question asking, children begin to use the proper auxiliary, or helping, verbs, but their questions are of the form "What daddy is eating?" or "Where doggie is going?" Finally, children learn the transformational rule that calls for moving the auxiliary verb ahead of the subject, and they begin to produce adult-like questions such as "What is daddy eating?"

Lawrence Migdale/Stock Boston

Curious 3- to 5-year-olds display their knowledge of transformational grammar by asking many "who," "what," and "why" questions of their companions.

Producing Negative Sentences. Like questions, children's negative sentences develop in a steplike fashion. Children the world over initially express negations by simply placing a negative word in front of the word or statement they wish to negate, producing such utterances as "No mitten" or "No I go." Notice, however, that these first negatives are ambiguous: "No mitten" can convey *nonexistence* ("There's no mitten"), *rejection* ("I won't wear a mitten"), or *denial* ("That's not a mitten") (Bloom, 1970). This ambiguity is clarified once the child begins to insert the negative word inside the sentence, in front of the word that it modifies (for example, "I not wear mitten" or "That not mitten"). Finally, children learn to combine negative markers with the proper auxiliary verbs to negate sentences in much the same way adults do. Indeed, Peter and Jill de Villiers (1979) describe a delightful experiment in which young children were persuaded to argue with a talking puppet. Whenever the puppet made a declarative statement, such as "He likes bananas," the child's task was to negate the proposition (argue) in any way he or she could. Most

3- to 4-year-olds thoroughly enjoyed this escalating verbal warfare between themselves and the puppet. But more importantly, these young children were already quite capable of using a wide variety of negative auxiliaries, including *wouldn't, wasn't, hasn't,* and *mustn't,* to properly negate almost any sentence the puppet produced.

Producing Complex Sentences. By age 3, most children have begun to produce complex sentences. Relative clauses that modify nouns (for example, "That's the box *that they put it in*"), and conjunctions to join simple sentences ("He was stuck *and* I got him out") are usually the first to appear, followed by embedded sentences (for example, "The man *who fixed the fence* went home") and more intricate forms of questions as well (for example, "John will come, won't he?"; "Where did you say you put my doll?") (de Villiers & de Villiers, 1992). By the end of the preschool period, at age 5 to 6, children are using most of the grammatical rules of their language and speaking much like adults do, even though they have never had a formal lesson in grammar.

Semantic Development

Another reason that preschoolers' language becomes more complex is that 2- to 5-year-olds are beginning to understand and express relational contrasts such as big/little, tall/short, wide/narrow, high/low, in/on, before/after, here/there, and I/you (de Villiers & de Villiers, 1979, 1992). *Big* and *little* are usually the first spatial adjectives to appear, and these terms are soon used to specify a variety of relations. By age 2 to 2½, for example, children can use *big* and *little* to draw proper *normative* conclusions (a 10 cm egg, viewed by itself, is "big" relative to other eggs the child remembers seeing) and *perceptual* inferences (a 10 cm egg placed next to an even larger egg is "little") (Ebeling & Gelman, 1988, 1994). By age 3, children are even capable of using these terms to make appropriate *functional* judgments such as deciding that an oversized article of doll clothing, which is little relative to what the child wears, is nonetheless too "big" to fit the doll in question (Gelman & Ebeling, 1989).

Although preschoolers are becoming increasingly aware of a variety of meaningful relations and are rapidly learning how to properly express them in their own speech, they continue to make some interesting semantic errors. Consider the following sentences:

1. The girl hit the boy.
2. The boy was hit by the girl.

Children younger than 4 or 5 frequently misinterpret *passive* constructions, such as sentence number 2 above. They can easily understand the *active* version of the same idea—that is, sentence 1. But if asked to point to a picture that shows "The boy was hit by the girl," preschoolers usually select a drawing that shows a boy hitting a girl. What they have done is to assume that the first noun is the agent of the verb and that the second is the object; consequently, they interpret the passive construction as if it were an active sentence. Passive sentences based on mental state verbs such as *like* and *know* (for example, "Goofy was liked by Donald") are particularly difficult and are not understood until later in grade school (Sudhalter & Braine, 1985).

It's not that young children lack the cognitive capacity to understand the more syntactically complex passive sentence. Even 3-year-olds can correctly interpret *irreversible* passives like "The candy was eaten by the girl," because it is nonsense to interpret this as an active sentence and assume that the candy was doing the eating (deVilliers & deVilliers, 1979). What's more, 3-year-olds learning new (nonsense) verbs can quickly learn to *produce* passive sentences if they have observed an action, heard a passive sentence to describe that action ("Yes, Big Bird is *meeking* the car"), and are asked questions that focus attention on the object of the action (*Question:* "What happened to the car"; *common answer:* "It got meeked.") (Brooks & Tomasello, 1999). Why, then, do preschoolers often misinterpret passives and rarely produce them? Probably because people speaking to them rarely use passives or ask questions that would encourage their use (Brooks &

Frank Siteman/Stone/Getty Images

Communication skills develop rapidly during the preschool years. Four-year-olds are already quite proficient at adjusting their messages to a listener's level of understanding.

Tomasello, 1999). Indeed, Inuktitut and Zulu children, who hear many passive constructions in speech directed to them, come to understand and to produce passive sentences much earlier than Western children do (Allen & Crego, 1996).

Development of Pragmatics and Communication Skills

During the preschool period, children acquire a number of conversational skills that help them to communicate more effectively and accomplish their objectives. For example, 3-year-olds are already beginning to understand *illocutionary intent*—that the real underlying meaning of an utterance may not always correspond to the literal meaning of the words speakers use. Notice how one 3-year-old used this knowledge to her advantage as she turns a declarative statement into a successful command (Reeder, 1981, p. 135):

> *Sheila:* "Every night I get an ice cream." *Babysitter:* "That's nice, Sheila." *Sheila:* "Even when there's a babysitter, I get an ice cream."
>
> *Babysitter* (to himself): "[B]acked into a corner by a 3-year-old's grasp of language as a social tool!"

Three- to five-year-olds are also learning that they must tailor their messages to their audience if they hope to communicate effectively. Marilyn Shatz and Rochel Gelman (1973) recorded the speech of several 4-year-olds as they introduced a new toy to either a 2-year-old or an adult. An analysis of the tapes revealed that 4-year-old children are already beginning to adjust their speech to their listener's level of understanding. When talking to a 2-year-old, the older children used short sentences and were careful to choose phrases such as "Watch," "Look, Shawtel," and "Look here" that would attract and maintain the toddler's attention. By contrast, 4-year-olds explaining how the toy worked to an adult used complex sentences and were generally more polite.

Referential Communication

An effective communicator is one who not only produces clear, unambiguous messages, but is able to detect any ambiguities in others' speech and ask for clarification. These aspects of language are called **referential communication skills.**

referential communication skills abilities to generate clear verbal messages, to recognize when others' messages are unclear, and to clarify any unclear messages one transmits or receives.

It was once generally assumed that preschool children lacked the abilities to detect uninformative messages and resolve most problems in communication. Indeed, if asked to evaluate the quality of an ambiguous message such as "Look at *that* horse" when a number of horses are in view, preschool children are more likely than their grade-school counterparts to say that this is an *informative* message. Apparently, they often fail to detect linguistic ambiguities because they are focusing on what *they think* the speaker means rather than on the (ambiguous) *literal* meaning of the message (Beal & Belgrad, 1990; Flavell, Miller, & Miller, 1993). Why do preschoolers guess at the meaning of uninformative messages? Possibly because they are often quite successful at inferring the true meaning of ambiguous utterances from other contextual cues, such as their knowledge of a particular speaker's attitudes, preferences, and past behaviors (Ackerman, Szymanski, & Silver, 1990). Four-year-olds are also less likely than seven-year-olds to detect and rephrase their own uninformative messages. In fact, they often assume that their own statements are perfectly informative and that failures to communicate should be blamed on their listeners (Flavell, Miller, & Miller, 1993).

However, most 3- to 5-year-olds display better referential communication skills in the natural environment than on laboratory tasks, particularly when there are contextual cues to help them clarify an otherwise ambiguous message (Ackerman, 1993; Beal & Belgrad, 1990). Even 3-year-olds know that they cannot carry out an unintelligible request made by a yawning adult, and they quickly realize that other impossible requests (such as "Bring me the refrigerator") are problematic as well (Revelle, Wellman, & Karabenick, 1985). These young children also know how they might resolve such breakdowns in communication, for they often say "What?" or "Huh?" to a yawning adult or ask "How? It's too heavy!" when told to retrieve a refrigerator.

In sum, 3- to 5-year-olds are not very good at detecting ambiguities in the *literal* meaning of oral messages. Nevertheless, they are better communicators than many laboratory studies of comprehension monitoring might suggest because they are often successful at inferring what an ambiguous message must mean simply from nonlinguistic contextual information.

Language Learning During Middle Childhood and Adolescence

Although 5-year-olds have learned a great deal about language in a remarkably brief period, many important strides in linguistic competence are made from ages 6 to 14—the grade-school and junior high school years. Not only do schoolchildren use bigger words and produce longer and more complex utterances, they also begin to think about and manipulate language in ways that were previously impossible.

Later Syntactic Development

During middle childhood, children correct many of their previous syntactical errors and begin to use a number of complex grammatical forms that did not appear in their earlier speech. For example, 5- to 8-year-olds are beginning to iron out the kinks in their use of personal pronouns, so that sentences such as "Him and her went" become much less frequent (Dale, 1976). By age 7 to 9, children easily understand and may occasionally even produce such complex *passive* sentences as "Goofy was liked by Donald" (Sudhalter & Braine, 1985) and *conditional sentences* such as "If Goofy had come, Donald would have been delighted" (Boloh & Champaud, 1993).

So middle childhood is a period of syntactical refinement: children are learning subtle exceptions to grammatical rules and coming to grips with the more complex syntactical structures of their native language. However, this process of syntactic elaboration occurs very gradually, often continuing well into adolescence or young adulthood (Clark & Clark, 1977; Eisele & Lust, 1996).

Semantics and Metalinguistic Awareness

Children's knowledge of semantics and semantic relations continues to grow throughout the grade school years, with vocabulary development being particularly impressive. Six-year-olds already understand approximately 10,000 words and continue to expand their *receptive vocabularies* at the rate of about 20 words a day, until they comprehend some 40,000 words by age 10 (Anglin, 1993). Of course grade-school children do not use all these new words in their own speech and may not even have heard many of them before. What they have gained is **morphological knowledge**—knowledge of the meaning of morphemes that make up words—which enables them to analyze the structure of such unfamiliar words as "sourer," "custom-made," or "hopelessness" and quickly figure out what they mean (Anglin, 1993). Finally, adolescents' capacity for formal-operational reasoning permits them to further expand their vocabularies, adding a host of abstract words (for example, "ironic") that they rarely heard (or, if they did, they didn't understand) during the grade-school years (McGhee-Bidlack, 1991).

morphological knowledge
one's knowledge of the meaning of morphemes that make up words.

Grade-school children are also becoming more proficient at *semantic integrations*—that is, at drawing linguistic inferences that enable them to understand more than is actually said. For example, if 6- to 8-year-olds hear "John did not see the rock; the rock was in the path; John fell," they are able to infer that John must have tripped over the rock. Interestingly, however, 6- to 8-year-olds will often assume that the story explicitly described John tripping and are not consciously aware that they have drawn an inference (Beal,

1990). By age 9 to 11, children are better able to make these kinds of linguistic inferences and will recognize them as *inferences* (Beal, 1990; Casteel, 1993), even when the two or more pieces of information that are necessary to draw the "appropriate" conclusion are separated by a number of intervening sentences (Johnson & Smith, 1981; van den Broek, 1989). And once children begin to integrate different kinds of linguistic information, they are able to detect *hidden* meanings that are not immediately obvious from the content of an utterance. For example, if a noisy 6-year-old hears her teacher quip "My, but you're quiet today," the child will probably note the contradiction between the literal meaning of the sentence and its satirical intonation or its context and thereby detect the *sarcasm* in her teacher's remark (Dews et al., 1996).

metalinguistic awareness
a knowledge of language and its properties; an understanding that language can be used for purposes other than communicating.

One reason that school-age children are able to go beyond the information given when making linguistic inferences is that they are rapidly developing **metalinguistic awareness**—an ability to think about language and to comment on its properties (Frost, 2000; Shaoying & Danling, 2005; Whitehurst & Lonigan, 1998). This reflective ability is present to some degree among 4- to 5-year-olds, who are beginning to display much more *phonological awareness* (for example, if you take the *s* sound out of scream, what's left?) and *grammatical awareness* (for example, is "I be sick" the right or wrong way to say it?) than younger children do (de Villiers & de Villiers, 1979). Yet, the metalinguistic competencies that 5-year-olds display are limited compared with those of a 9-year-old, a 7-year-old, or even a 6-year-old (Bialystok, 1986; Ferreria & Morrison, 1994).

An emerging awareness that language is an arbitrary and rule-bound system may have important educational implications (Fielding-Barnsley & Purdie, 2005). Specifically, 4- to 6-year-olds who score relatively high in such phonological skills as detecting phonemes, syllables, and rhymes learn to read much more quickly and remain the most proficient readers throughout the first few grades of school (Lonigan et al., 2000; Roth, Speece, & Cooper, 2002; Whitehurst & Lonigan, 1998). Indeed, this strong relationship between phonological awareness and reading achievement remains even after adjusting for differences in young readers' intelligence, vocabulary, memory skills, and social class. Some theorists believe that some degree of phonological awareness is necessary before a child can learn to read (Wagner et al., 1997), and interventions designed to foster children's phonemic awareness clearly do promote children's reading and speaking skills (Anthony & Francis, 2005; Schneider et al., 1997; Whitehurst & Lonigan, 1998). In fact, one of the strongest arguments in favor of the *phonics method* of reading instruction is that it promotes the very phonological skills that seem so necessary for young children to learn in order to read well.

Research suggests that such home literacy experiences as shared storybook reading with parents do not promote children's phonological skills to any great extent (Whitehurst & Lonigan, 1998). However, shared storybook reading experiences do promote such aspects of emergent literacy as vocabulary growth and letter recognition, which also predict children's success at learning to read (Reese & Cox, 1999; Lonigan et al., 2000).

Joseph Nettis/Stock Boston

By reading to young children, a parent promotes vocabulary growth and letter recognition—two important emergent literacy skills that make learning to read easier.

Further Development of Communication Skills

Earlier, we examined a study (Shatz & Gelman, 1973) in which preschool children adjusted their speech to a listener's level of understanding. Recall that the 4-year-olds in this study were face to face with their 2-year-old or adult companion and thus could see whether or not the listener was responding appropriately to their messages or following their instructions. Could children this young have communicated effectively with their partners if they had been asked to deliver their messages over a telephone?

Probably not. In one early study of children's referential communication skills, 4- to 10-year-olds were asked to describe blocks with unfamiliar graphic designs on them to a peer who was on the other side of an opaque screen so that the peer could identify them (Krauss & Glucksberg, 1977). As shown in Table 10.6, preschool children described these designs in highly idiosyncratic ways that neither communicated much to their listeners nor enabled them to identify which blocks the speaker was talking about. Eight- to ten-year-olds, on the other hand, provided much more informative messages. They realized that their listener could not see what they were referring to, thus requiring them to somehow *differentiate* these objects and make each object's description distinctive if their messages were to be understood.

Four- and five-year-olds perform much better on referential communication tasks that require them to describe the whereabouts of *real* (rather than abstract) objects that are hidden or missing (Plumert, Ewert, & Spear, 1995). But even so, their messages are more ambiguous than those of grade-school children.

Dramatic improvements in referential communication skills during the early grade-school years are due, in part, to the growth of cognitive skills and sociolinguistic understanding. Six- to seven-year-olds have learned from earlier miscommunications about the importance of generating more informative messages. This is also the age at which they are becoming notably less egocentric and acquiring some role-taking skills, two cognitive developments that help them to adapt their speech to the needs of their listeners in such highly demanding situations as talking on the phone (or participating in a referential communication experiment), where it may be difficult to tell whether one's message has been interpreted correctly (Hoff-Ginsberg, 1997). Furthermore, sociolinguistic understanding is required to make the right kinds of speech adjustments, for messages that are clear for one listener may not be for others. For example, a listener who is unfamiliar with the stimuli in a referential communication task (as described earlier and in Table 10.6) may require more differentiating information and more message redundancy than a second person who is already familiar with these objects. Six- to ten-year-olds do provide longer messages to unfamiliar than to familiar listeners, but only the nine- and ten-year-olds among them adjusted the content of their communications to the listeners' needs by providing richer differentiating information to an unfamiliar listener (Sonnenschein, 1986, 1988).

TABLE 10.6 Typical Idiosyncratic Descriptions Offered by Preschool Children When Talking about Unfamiliar Graphic Designs in the Krauss and Glucksberg Communication Game

	Child				
Form	1	2	3	4	5
	Man's legs	Airplane	Drapeholder	Zebra	Flying saucer
	Mother's hat	Ring	Keyhold	Lion	Snake
	Daddy's shirt	Milk jug	Shoe hold	Coffeepot	Dog

Source: Adapted from "Social and Non-Social Speech," by R. M. Krauss & S. Gluckberg, *Scientific American*, February 1977, *236*, p. 104. Copyright © 1977 by Scientific American, Inc. Adapted by permission of the artist, Jerome Kuhl.

© Myrleen Ferguson Cate/PhotoEdit

What we have here is a failure to communicate!

What Role Do Siblings Play in the Growth of Communication Skills?

Most studies of social influences on language development have focused on mother-child pairs (usually mothers and their *firstborn* child). Yet, children with siblings spend a fair amount of time conversing with them or listening as a sibling converses with a parent (Barton & Tomasello, 1991; Brody, 2004). Might conversations involving siblings contribute in a meaningful way to the growth of communication skills?

Yes, indeed, and it appears that interactions among linguistically immature siblings may actually promote effective communication. Consider, for example, that because older siblings are less likely than parents to adjust their speech to a younger sibling's ability to understand (Tomasello, Conti-Ramsden, & Ewert, 1990). The resulting comprehension problems for the younger sibling may make the older sibling more aware of the younger sibling's needs and more inclined to monitor and repair their own ambiguous messages. And because older siblings are also less likely than parents are to correctly *interpret* a younger sibling's uninformative messages, the younger sibling may learn from her failures to communicate and be prompted to speak in ways that are more widely understood (Perez-Granados & Callanan, 1997). So if children truly learn from breakdowns in communication, then chances to converse with relatively immature linguistic partners (such as siblings and peers) would seem to promote the growth of communication skills.

In sum, the rapid pace at which cognitively immature children master the fundamentals of language and communication is truly awe-inspiring. Table 10.7 briefly summarizes the ground we have covered in tracing the evolution of young human beings from preverbal creatures, who are prepared for language learning and motivated to share meaning with their companions, to highly articulate adolescents, who can generate and comprehend an infinite number of messages.

Bilingualism: Challenges and Consequences of Learning Two Languages

Most American children speak only English. However, many children around the world grow up bilingual, acquiring two (or more) languages by the time they reach puberty. In fact, some 6.5 million American schoolchildren speak a language other than English at home (U.S. Bureau of the Census, 1997), and many of them display at least some limitations in their use of the English language.

Does learning two languages rather than one hinder a child's language proficiency or slow her intellectual development? Before 1960, many researchers claimed that it did, pointing to several demonstrations that bilingual children scored significantly lower than their monolingual peers on tests of linguistic knowledge and general intelligence (Hakuta, 1988). However, these early studies were seriously flawed (Francis, 2005; Peña, Bedore, & Rappazzo, 2003). The bilinguals were often first- or second-generation immigrants from lower socioeconomic backgrounds who were not very proficient in English. Furthermore, the tests they took were administered in English (rather than in their language of greatest proficiency), and their performances were compared with samples largely comprised of middle-class, English-speaking monolinguals (Diaz, 1983). No wonder the bilinguals performed so poorly! Unfortunately, these findings were often taken at face value by educators and lawmakers, who have used them as justification for prohibiting the teaching of foreign

TABLE 10.7 Important Milestones in Language Development

Age (years)	Phonology	Semantics	Morphology/syntax	Pragmatics	Metalinguistic awareness
0–1	Receptivity to speech and discrimination of speech sounds Babbling begins to resemble the sounds of native language	Some interpretation of intonational cues in others' speech Preverbal gestures appear Vocables appear Little if any understanding of individual words	Preference for phrase structure and stress patterns of native language	Joint attention with caregiver to objects and events Turn-taking in games and vocalizations Appearance of preverbal gestures	None
1–2	Appearance of strategies to simplify word pronunciations	First words appear Rapid expansion of vocabulary after age 18 months Overextensions and underextensions of word meanings	Holophrases give way to two-word telegraphic speech Sentences express distinct semantic relations Acquisition of some grammatical morphemes	Use of gestures and intonational cues to clarify messages Richer understanding of vocal turn-taking rules First signs of etiquette in children's speech	None
3–5	Pronunciations improve	Vocabulary expands Understanding of spatial relations and use of spatial words in speech	Grammatical morphemes added in regular sequence Awareness of most rules of transformational grammar	Beginning understanding of illocutionary intent Some adjustment of speech to different audiences Some attempts at clarifying obviously ambiguous messages	Some phonemic and grammatical awareness
6–adolescence	Pronunciations become adultlike	Dramatic expansion of vocabulary, including abstract words during adolescence Appearance and refinement of semantic integrations	Acquisition of morphological knowledge Correction of earlier grammatical errors Acquisition of complex syntactical rules	Referential communication improves, especially the ability to detect and repair uninformative messages one sends and receives	Metalinguistic awareness blossoms and becomes more extensive with age

languages until after age 10, so as not to ". . . distract from [students'] ability to assimilate their normal studies in the English language and . . . cause serious emotional disturbances . . ." (Kendler, as cited in Hakuta, 1988, p. 303).

Encouraged in part by the nativist contention that young children should easily acquire any language they hear regularly, psycholinguists in the 1960s began to look more carefully at the process of becoming bilingual. Their findings were clear: Children exposed early (before age 3) to two languages had little difficulty becoming proficient in both. Despite the fact that bilingual toddlers occasionally mixed phonologies and applied the grammar and vocabulary of one language to the second language they were acquiring, by age 3, they were well aware that the two languages were independent systems and that each was associated with particular contexts in which it was to be spoken (Lanza, 1992; Reich, 1986). By age 4, they displayed normal language proficiency in the language of their community and solid to excellent linguistic skills in the second language, depending on how much they had been exposed to it. Even when preschool children acquired a second language *sequentially* (that is, after age 3, when they were already conversant in their native language), it often took no more than a year to achieve near-native abilities in the second language (Reich, 1986).

Ann Clark Beurskens

Contrary to popular belief, learning two (or more) languages rather than one neither hinders a child's language proficiencies nor retards her intellectual growth. Indeed, recent research suggests that there are cognitive advantages to bilingualism.

What about the cognitive consequences of bilingualism? Recent well-controlled studies that have matched bilinguals and monolinguals on important variables such as socioeconomic status consistently find that there are cognitive *advantages* to bilingualism. Not only do fully bilingual children score as high or higher than monolingual peers on tests of IQ, Piagetian conservation problems, and general language proficiency (see, for example, Diaz, 1985; Ginsburg & McCoy, 1982), but they also outperform monolinguals on measures of metalinguistic awareness (Bialystok, 1988), particularly those that call for them to recognize the correspondence between letters, words, and their phonological components (Bialystok, Shenfield, & Codd, 2000), or to detect grammatical errors in speech and written prose (Campbell & Sais, 1995). Bilingual children also outperform monolinguals at *nonlinguistic* tasks that require selective attention to overcome distractions (Bialystok, 1999). Why is the bilingual mind advantaged? Ellen Bialystok and her associates (2000) suggest two reasons. The bilingual advantage at metalinguistic tasks may stem from learning very early that linguistic representations are *arbitrary.* For example, English-French bilinguals learn that the same (canine) animal is symbolized in their two languages by the words "dog" and "chien," which neither look nor sound alike. Second, bilinguals' advantage at ignoring distractions may simply reflect the fact that they are well practiced at monitoring their surroundings and producing the language understood by their immediate companions, while *inhibiting* the distracting second language that is irrelevant to that context.

Despite these positive findings and increased federal support for bilingual education in the United States, public opinion in this country does not support bilingual education. In fact, 18 states have even passed laws making English the official language, thereby providing a strong political argument for instructing non-native English speakers only in English. This may be unfortunate for at least two reasons. First, a total immersion in English-only classrooms can cause some children with *Limited English Proficiency (LEP)* to struggle to grasp their lessons and to flounder academically (see DelCampo & DelCampo, 2000). What's more, minority-language parents are often highly critical of English-only instruction, claiming that it undermines their children's proficiency in their primary language to the extent of disrupting parent-child communications and family relationships (Wong & Filmore, 1991).

Is bilingual education the solution? This question has sparked a firestorm of controversy over the past 20 years, largely because the many approaches to bilingual education that have been attempted differ dramatically in effectiveness (DelCampo & DelCampo, 2000). What now seems clear is that approaches that instruct LEP students 80 to 90 percent of the time in their native language, with only limited exposure to English, are not effective: most LEP youngsters taught this way do not acquire the level of English language literacy skills they will need to succeed in high school and college (DelCampo & DelCampo, 2000). Yet, there appear to be clear benefits of **two-way bilingual education**—preschool or primary-grade programs in which LEP students are taught half the day in English and half in their primary language. Two recent studies of 3½- to 5-year-old Mexican American immigrant children in well-run two-way bilingual preschools in California found that these youngsters not only showed strong gains in English proficiency that will serve them well in the public schools, but also remained just as proficient with Spanish as their ethnic immigrant age-mates who re-

two-way bilingual education programs in which English-speaking (or other majority-language) children and children who have limited proficiency in that language are instructed half of the day in their primary language and the other half in a second language.

mained at home in a predominantly Spanish-language environment (Rodriguez et al., 1995; Winsler et al., 1999).

As debates about the utility of bilingual education rage on in courtrooms, school boards, and families, developmentalists (and the public) should not lose sight of the most important question: how do we provide our millions of LEP children with the best possible education? Although more research is needed, early returns make well-run two-way bilingual education look quite promising. In fact, one pilot program found that even English-speaking students who participate in such programs can benefit by acquiring near-native levels of proficiency in a second language while performing as well (or slightly better) academically as English-speaking age-mates who receive English-only instruction (Sleek, 1994). The costs of providing effective bilingual education to all our students could be formidable, but the cognitive benefits of bilingualism are also formidable (Bialystok, Shenfield, & Codd, 2000). Truly *effective* bilingual education could help to ensure the educational (and future economic) success of our LEP children, promote greater appreciation of ethnic diversity, and address an increasing need for a bilingually competent workforce in our increasingly multicultural world (Hakuta & Garcia, 1989; Sleek, 1994).

CONCEPT CHECK 10.3 Understanding Later Language Development and Bilingualism

Check your understanding of language learning during the preschool period, middle childhood, and adolescence, and the challenges and consequences of bilingualism by answering the following questions. Answers appear in the Appendix.

Multiple Choice: Select the best answer for each question.

_____ 1. During the last phase of question-asking, the child is able to ask an adultlike question such as:
- a. "What is mommy reading?"
- b. "Where mommy?"
- c. "Mommy here?"
- d. "Where mommy go?"

_____ 2. Cross-cultural studies on passives show that children whose language has many passive constructions:
- a. get bored with passives, so actives are preferred
- b. use many passives in their own uttered sentences
- c. have family pets that show humanlike fluencies
- d. become "cognitively choked" on sentences' meanings

_____ 3. Level of _______ is a strong predictor of the child's reading skill in grade school.
- a. holophrase pidginization
- b. overextended underextension
- c. interest in a well-balanced diet
- d. phonological awareness

_____ 4. Conversing with siblings promotes effective communication because:
- a. Telegraphic speech is highly accurate in its content.
- b. Creoles develop more from children than from adults.
- c. Kids in large groups shout at one another.
- d. Noticing siblings' comprehension errors makes the speaker aware of the need to express ideas clearly.

True or False: Identify whether the following statements are true or false.

5. (T)(F) "Overregularization" refers to the young child's tendency to use relatively specific words to refer to a broader set of objects, actions, or events than adults do (for example, using the word *car* to refer to all motor vehicles).
6. (T)(F) "Transformational grammar" refers to rules of syntax that allow one to transform declarative statements into questions, negatives, imperatives, and other kinds of sentences.

Short Answer: Briefly answer the following questions.

8. Describe what morphological knowledge is, and explain how morphological knowledge might allow children to figure out the meanings of novel words.
9. Identify two potential benefits for English-speaking students enrolled in two-way bilingual education programs.

Applying Developmental Themes to Language Acquisition

You may have thought about nature and nurture quite often when reading this chapter. Indeed, our theme of nature and nurture clearly applies to language development, as do our themes of the active child, qualitative and quantitative changes, and the holistic nature of development. Let's review some specific aspects of language development that apply to each of these themes.

Despite the fact that nativists believe in an inborn language acquisition device, which helps the child process and eventually produce speech, the active child theme is central to this chapter. Before their first birthday, infants have already learned that humans take turns when speaking to one another, which usually causes them to wait until a companion is done talking to them before babbling or cooing in reply. Their reply then signals their companion to continue the "conversation" by responding to the infant's vocalization. As development proceeds, toddlers ask many questions, usually about objects' names, purposes, or actions. This active request for information by the toddler leads to the large store of words he will use during the naming explosion. Later, children also use processing constraints to decipher the meanings of words that are not explicitly defined for them. Children alter their speech or mannerisms in order to accommodate the situation, such as being more polite around adults or strangers. Children ask for clarification if they do not understand requests or commands, and are more likely to be aware of a listener's comprehension and slow down or repeat phrases if their listener is lost. Lastly, in middle childhood and early adolescence children pay more attention to the ambiguous words and phrases they hear and try to draw multiple meanings from them. Each of these examples suggests that children are truly active participants in their own language development.

The issue of nature and nurture influences in development was discussed extensively in this chapter, but perhaps the most obvious example of this theme comes from the various theoretical perspectives on language acquisition. Learning theorists tend to be proponents of the nurture perspective, believing that children learn language by conversing with others, being spoken to in child-directed speech, and imitating what they hear. Nativists, on the other hand, are proponents of the nature perspective, believing instead that infants have a special language acquisition device that triggers their speech comprehension, and that infants require nothing more than hearing adults converse in order to acquire a language. The interactionist viewpoint combines these two perspectives by integrating the ideas of a species-specific nervous system that directs the child's language abilities and the assertion that companions' intervention is crucial to an infant's acquisition of language.

Our third theme concerns qualitative and quantitative changes in development. In language development we see distinct qualitative changes across ages as infants' and children's language changes in form or kind. The most obvious examples of these qualitative changes are the stages of prelinguistic, holophrase, and telegraphic language abilities. But there are also many quantitative changes in language development. The acquisition of new words, new grammatical structures, and new syntactical rules across development are excellent examples of quantitative changes. It seems language development may be one of the best examples in developmental psychology of the interplay between qualitative and quantitative changes that occur with age.

Finally, we can see the holistic nature of language development in the way children's interactions with their peers improve as they learn how to communicate. When children learn how to modify their speech in certain circumstances, they better prepare themselves for efficiently conveying their needs and desires, thus making it more likely that they will receive what they have asked for. As children learn how to detect hidden meanings in others' words and how to convey hidden meanings of their own and clarify their own ambiguous phrases, their social interactions with others improve. We also see examples of the holistic nature of language development in the research that suggests that infants and children must have meaningful social interactions involving language in order to acquire language. We saw that culture and birth order are also clear influences on language acquisition. And finally, the interactionist perspective showed us that language acquisition cannot be distinguished from cognitive development.

These are but a few of the many examples that apply our developmental themes to language development. Without a doubt, language acquisition involves the active child, nature and nurture influences, and both qualitative and quantitative developmental changes. And language acquisition is clearly a holistic process intertwined with the child's cognitive and social development and the child's social and cultural life.

SUMMARY

Five Components of Language

- Children must acquire the five aspects of language to communicate effectively:
  - **phonology,** a knowledge of the language's sound system
  - **morphology,** rules specifying how words are formed from sounds
  - **semantics,** an understanding of the meaning of **bound morphemes, free morphemes** (or words), and sentences
  - **syntax,** the rules that specify how words are combined to produce sentences
  - **pragmatics,** the principles governing how language is to be used in different social situations

Theories of Language Development

- Three major theoretical perspectives on language acquisition:
  - **Learning theorists** believe:
    - Children acquire language as they imitate others' speech and are reinforced for grammatically correct utterances, but this is unsupported by research.
    - Adults use **child-directed speech** and reshape their primitive sentences with **expansions** and **recasts.**
    - Children will acquire language as long as they have partners with whom to converse, even without these environmental supports.
  - **Nativists** believe:
    - Human beings are innately endowed with biological linguistic processing capabilities (a **language acquisition device** or **language-making capacity**) that function most efficiently prior to puberty.
    - This means that children require nothing more than being exposed to speech in order to learn to speak the language they hear.
    - Nativists identify **linguistic universals** and observe that language functions are served by **Broca's** and **Wernicke's areas** of the brain.
    - Deaf children of hearing parents and other children exposed to ungrammatical pidgins may create languages of their own.
    - Both first- and second-language learning seem to proceed more smoothly during the "**sensitive period**" prior to puberty.
    - Nativists admit that it is not clear how children sift through verbal input and make the crucial discoveries that further their linguistic competencies.
  - **Interactionist** perspective proponents believe:
    - Children are biologically prepared to acquire language.
    - Instead of a specialized linguistic processor being innate, humans have a nervous system that gradually matures and predisposes them to develop similar ideas at about the same age.
    - Biological maturation affects cognitive development, which, in turn, influences language development.
    - Environment plays a crucial role in language learning, for companions continually introduce new linguistic rules and concepts.

Before Language: The Prelinguistic Period

- Infants are well-prepared for language learning:
  - Development during the **prelinguistic phase** allows them to discriminate speechlike sounds and become sensitive to a wider variety of phonemes than adults are.
  - They are sensitive to intonational cues from birth.
  - By 7 to 10 months of age infants are already segmenting others' speech into phrases and wordlike units.
- Infants begin **cooing** by age 2 months and start to **babble** by age 4 to 6 months.
- They later match the intonation of their babbles to the tonal qualities of the language they hear and may produce their own **vocables** to signify meaning.
- Infants less than 1 year old have already learned that people take turns while vocalizing and that gestures can be used to communicate and share meaning with companions.
- Once infants begin to understand individual words, their **receptive language** is ahead of their **productive language.**

One Word at a Time: The Holophrase Period

- **Holophrase** (or one-word) phase:
  - Infants speak in **holophrases** and spend several months expanding their vocabularies one word at a time.

- Infants talk mostly about moving or manipulable objects that interest them.
- Infants show a vocabulary spurt (**naming explosion**) between 18 and 24 months of age.
- Most children in Western cultures develop a **referential style** of language, whereas a smaller number of Western infants and many infants from social harmony-emphasizing cultures adopt an **expressive style** of language.

- Toddlers use social and contextual cues to **fast map** words onto objects, actions, and attributes.
- Other strategies, or **processing constraints,** such as the **object scope constraint, mutual exclusivity, lexical context,** and **syntactic bootstrapping** help toddlers figure out what new words mean.
- Toddlers still frequently make such semantic errors as **overextensions** and **underextensions.**
- Toddler's one-word utterances are called **holophrases** because they often seem less like labels and more like attempts to communicate an entire sentence's worth of meaning.

From Holophrases to Simple Sentences: The Telegraphic Period

- At 18 to 24 months of age, toddlers begin to produce two- and three-word sentences known as **telegraphic speech** because they omit grammatical markers and smaller, less important words.
- Although telegraphic sentences are not grammatical by adult standards, they are more than random word combinations.
- In their earliest sentences, children follow certain rules of word order when combining words and also express the same categories of meaning (semantic relations).
- Toddlers are also becoming highly sensitive to pragmatic constraints, including the realization that speakers must be more directive and elaborate when a listener doesn't share their knowledge.
- Young children are also learning certain sociolinguistic prescriptions such as the need to be polite when making requests.

Language Learning During the Preschool Period

- During the preschool period (ages 2½ to 5), the child's language becomes much more similar to an adult's.
  - Children begin to add **grammatical morphemes** such as the *-s* for plurality, the *-ed* for past tense, the *-ing* for present progressive, articles, prepositions, and auxiliary verbs to their increasingly long utterances.
  - Though children may **overregularize** grammatical markers, there is a striking uniformity in the order in which these morphemes appear.
  - The preschool period is the time when a child learns rules of **transformational grammar** that will enable him or her to change declarative statements into questions, negations, imperatives, relative clauses, and compound sentences.
  - By the time they enter school, children have mastered most of the syntactical rules of their native language and can produce a wide variety of sophisticated, adult-like messages.
- Also, language becomes increasingly complex during the preschool years because children are beginning to appreciate and use semantic and relational contrasts such as big / little, wide / narrow, more / less, and before / after.
- Preschool children are beginning to understand such pragmatic lessons as the need to tailor their messages to a listener's ability to comprehend if they hope to be understood.
- Children's **referential communication skills** are not well developed, although they have begun to detect at least some of the uninformative messages they receive and to ask for clarification if needed.

Language Learning During Middle Childhood and Adolescence

- Middle childhood and early adolescence is a period of linguistic refinement:
  - Children learn subtle exceptions to grammatical rules and begin to understand even the most complex syntactical structures of their native language.
  - Vocabulary grows rapidly as children acquire **morphological knowledge** and **metalinguistic awareness.**
  - School-age children display much better referential communication skills as they attend more carefully to literal meanings of ambiguous utterances and are more likely to clarify the ambiguous messages they send and receive.
- Cognitive development, the growth of sociolinguistic knowledge, and opportunities to communicate with linguistically immature siblings and peers all contribute to the development of communication skills.

Bilingualism: Challenges and Consequences of Learning Two Languages

- Bilingualism is becoming increasingly common in the United States, and children exposed early and regularly to two languages can easily acquire them both.
- There are cognitive advantages to bilingualism.
- Recent **two-way bilingual education** programs attempt to introduce the millions of limited-English-proficient students in the United States to important English language skills without undermining proficiency in their primary language.

KEY TERMS

language 379
communication 379
vocables 379
psycholinguists 380
phonology 380
phonemes 380
morphology 380
semantics 380
morphemes 380
free morphemes 380
bound morphemes 381
syntax 381
pragmatics 381
sociolinguistic knowledge 381
linguistic universal 382
language acquisition device (LAD) 383
universal grammar 383
language-making capacity (LMC) 383
aphasia 384
Broca's area 384
Wernicke's area 384
sensitive-period hypothesis (of language acquisition) 385
pidgins 386
creoles 386
interactionist theory 387
motherese 388
expansions 389
recasts 389
prelinguistic phase 391
coos 392
babbles 392
receptive language 394
productive language 394
holophrastic period 394
holophrase 394
naming explosion 395
multimodal motherese 395
referential style 395
expressive style 395
fast mapping 396
overextension 397
underextension 397
processing constraints 397
object scope constraint 397
mutual exclusivity constraint 397
lexical contrast constraint 398
syntactical bootstrapping 398
telegraphic speech 400
grammatical morphemes 404
overregularization 405
transformational grammar 406
referential communication skills 408
morphological knowledge 409
metalinguistic awareness 410
two-way bilingual education 414

MEDIA RESOURCES

The Human Development Book Companion Website

See the companion website http://www.thomsonedu.com/psychology/shaffer for flashcards, practice quiz questions, Internet links, updates, critical thinking exercises, discussion forums, games, and more

ThomsonNOW! http://www.thomsonedu.com
Go to this site for the link to ThomsonNOW, your one-stop shop. Take a pre-test for this chapter, and ThomsonNOW will generate a personalized study plan based on your test results. The study plan will identify the topics you need to review and direct you to online resources to help you master those topics. You can then take a post-test to help you determine the concepts you have mastered and what you will still need to work on.

Child and Adolescent Development CD-ROM

For more information about the concepts covered in this chapter, go to
Module II: Cognition, Language, and Learning

- Language
- Module II Media

Hoby Finn/Photo Disc/Getty Images

CHAPTER

11 Emotional Development, Temperament, and Attachment

I (Katherine Kipp) have twin daughters, Rachel and Debby. Debby was sick when she was born and was whisked away that first night to a different hospital that had a better neonatal intensive care unit. Rachel stayed with me in the hospital and came home with me after a few days. I remember falling in love with her. She was amazing. I couldn't take my eyes off her. Everything she did brought joy and intrigue to me. She actually made a pouting-mouth face in those first few days—surely a sign of an extraordinary child, I thought.

I went to visit Debby every day for the week she was in intensive care. It was an hour and a half drive to get there. It was hard to leave Rachel with my Mom and go see Debby because I was so in love with Rachel—it actually physically hurt to be separated from Rachel. After I arrived at Debby's hospital, scrubbed in as if for surgery and donned the sterile robes, I got to visit with her for about an hour each day. At first I could only look at her in the incubator, but eventually I was able to hold her. I was so scared because I didn't "know" her. She was different from Rachel. I didn't feel the same sense of being in love with her. I wondered if I was a bad mother and if I would ever be able to love her as much as I loved Rachel.

But I was able to bring her home after a week, and I fell in love with her too! I developed the same intense feelings for her and the physical need to be with her that I still felt for Rachel. As a first-time mother, I was amazed that I had the capacity to love these two wonderful babies so very much. They were different from the beginning, but my love for each of them was enormous and certainly the most intense feeling I had ever experienced.

I was a student of developmental psychology at the time and knew that I was experiencing what developmentalists call **bonding.** But experiencing the intensity of those feelings certainly put a new spin on my understanding of the terms!

bonding
the strong affectionate ties that parents may feel toward their infant; some theorists believe that the strongest bonding occurs shortly after birth, during a sensitive period.

Do all parents have these intense "falling in love" experiences with their babies? Was it normal to develop those feelings for Rachel before Debby? What made me feel this way about my daughters? Did my daughters have feelings for me (or for anything)? What was that pouty face Rachel made all about? These are some of the questions addressed by research on emotional development and attachment, and we will answer these questions (and more!) in this chapter. We begin by charting age-related changes in children's displays and interpretations of emotions, and by considering some of the roles that emotions play in early social and personality development. We will then look at individual differences in emotional reactivity, or temperament, and will see that the early temperamental attributes that so often explain why young children react differently to everyday events are now considered by many developmentalists to be important building blocks of adult personalities. We will then turn to emotional attachments and explore the processes by which infants and their closest companions establish these intimate affectional ties. Finally, we will review a rapidly expanding base of evidence suggesting that the kind of emotional attachments infants are able to establish can have important implications for their later social, emotional, and intellectual development.

Emotional Development

Do babies have feelings? Do they experience and display specific emotions such as happiness, sadness, fear, and anger the way older children and adults do? Most parents think so. In one study more than half the mothers of 1-month-old infants said that their babies displayed at least five distinct emotional expressions: interest, surprise, joy, anger, and fear (Johnson et al., 1982). One might argue that this is simply a case of proud mothers reading too much into the behavior of their babies, but there is now reliable evidence that even very young infants are emotional creatures.

Displaying Emotions: The Development (and Control) of Emotional Expressions

Carroll Izard and his colleagues have studied infants' emotional expressions by videotaping babies' responses to such events as grasping an ice cube, having a toy taken from them, or seeing their mothers return after a separation (Izard, 1982, 1993). Izard's procedure is to ask raters, who are unaware of the events that an infant has experienced, to tell him what emotion the infant is experiencing from the facial expression the infant displays. These studies reveal that different adult raters observing the same expressions reliably see the same emotion in a baby's face (Figure 11.1). Other investigators find that adults can usually tell which positive emotion a baby is experiencing (e.g., interest versus joy) from facial expressions, but that negative emotions (e.g., fear versus anger) are much more difficult to discriminate on the basis of facial cues alone (Izard et al., 1995; Matias & Cohn, 1993). Nevertheless, most researchers agree that babies communicate a variety of feelings through their facial expressions and that each expression becomes a more recognizable sign of a specific emotion with age (Camras et al., 1992; Izard et al., 1995).

Sequencing of Discrete Emotions

Various emotions appear at different times over the first 2 years of a child's life. At birth babies show interest, distress, disgust, and contentment. Other **basic emotions** that

basic emotions
the set of emotions present at birth or emerging early in the first year that some theorists believe to be biologically programmed.

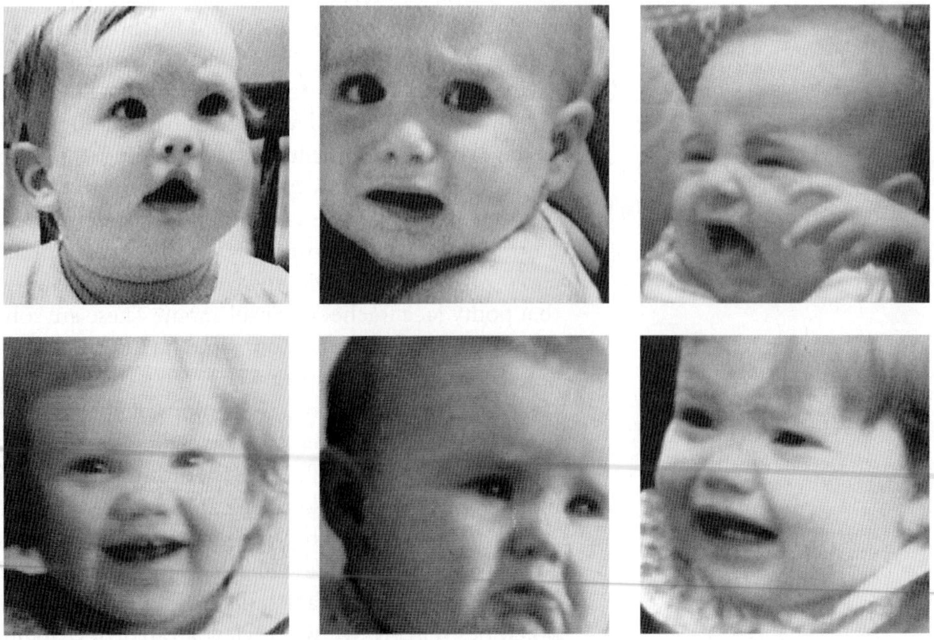

Courtesy of Carroll E. Izard, University of Delaware.

Figure 11.1 Young infants display a variety of emotional expressions.

emerge between 2 and 7 months are anger, sadness, joy, surprise, and fear (Izard et al., 1995). These primary emotions may be biologically programmed because they emerge in all healthy infants at roughly the same ages and are displayed and interpreted similarly in all cultures (Camras et al., 1992; Izard, 1993). Some learning (or cognitive development) may be necessary before babies are able to express emotions that were not present at birth. For example, one of the strongest elicitors of surprise and joy among 2- to 6-month-olds is their discovery that they can exert some control over objects and events, such as learning to kick their feet to make an overhead mobile move or push a button on a toy to make music. Disconfirmation of these *learned* expectancies (as when someone or something prevents them from exerting control, such as when the batteries run out on the mobile or toy) is likely to anger many 2- to 4-month-olds and sadden 4- to 6-month-olds (Lewis, Alessandri, & Sullivan, 1990; Sullivan, Lewis, & Alessandri, 1992).

complex emotions
self-conscious or self-evaluative emotions that emerge in the second year and depend, in part, on cognitive development.

Later in their second year, infants begin to display such **complex emotions** as embarrassment, shame, guilt, envy, and pride. These feelings are sometimes called *self-conscious* emotions because each involves some damage to or enhancement of our sense of self. Michael Lewis and his associates (1989) believe that embarrassment, the simplest self-conscious emotion, will not emerge until the child can recognize herself in a mirror or a photograph (a self-referential milestone we will discuss later in the chapter). *Self-evaluative* emotions such as shame, guilt, and pride may require both self-recognition (that is, the child can recognize herself in a mirror or photograph) and an understanding of rules or standards for evaluating one's conduct.

Most of the available evidence is consistent with Lewis's theory. For example, the only toddlers who become noticeably embarrassed by lavish praise or by requests to show off for strangers are those who display self-recognition (Lewis, Stanger, & Sullivan, 1989). By about age 3, when children are better able to evaluate their performances as good or bad, they begin to show clear signs of pride (smiling, applauding, or shouting "I did it!") when they succeed at a difficult task, such as completing a complicated puzzle with many pieces. They also show signs of shame (a downward gaze with a slumped posture, often accompanied by statements such as "I'm no good at this") should they fail at an easy task, such as failing to piece together a puzzle that has relatively few pieces (Lewis, Alessandri, & Sullivan, 1992; Stipek, Recchia, & McClintic, 1992).

Preschool children may also show evaluative embarrassment, characterized by nervous smiles, self-touching, and gaze aversion, when they fail to complete a task in the allotted time or to otherwise match a standard (Alessandri & Lewis, 1996). Evaluative embarrassment stems from a negative evaluation of one's performance and is much more stressful than the "simple" embarrassment of being the object of others' attention (Lewis & Ramsay, 2002).

The later-developing emotions are truly complex and have different implications for the child's behavior. For example, some investigators make clear distinctions between shame and guilt. Guilt implies that we have in some way failed to live up to our obligations to other people; a child who feels guilty is likely to focus on the interpersonal consequences of his wrongdoing and may try to approach others to make reparations for his harmful acts (Higgins, 1987; Hoffman, 2000). Shame is more self-focused and is not based on a concern for others. Whether it stems from moral transgressions, personal failure, or a social blunder, such as calling someone by the wrong name, shame causes children to focus negatively on themselves and may motivate them to hide or avoid other people (Tangney & Dearing, 2002).

Parents influence a child's experience and expression of self-evaluative emotions. In one study (Alessandri & Lewis, 1996) mothers' reactions were observed as their 4- to 5-year-olds succeeded or failed at a variety of puzzles. They found a clear relationship between the children's signs of pride over their successes, shame over their failures, and the mothers' reactions to these outcomes. When mothers accentuated the negative by being especially critical of failures, children displayed high levels of shame after a failure and little pride after successes. When mothers reacted positively to successes, children displayed more pride in their accomplishments and less shame on those occasions when they did not achieve their objectives.

Consider another interesting parental influence. Clear rule-breaking and other moral transgressions have the potential to make children feel guilty, shameful, or both.

But how parents react to transgressions may determine which emotions children feel, guilty or shameful. Children are more inclined to feel ashamed if parents belittle them ("Claire, you are so bad, stupid, and thoughtless for breaking John's toy."). They are more likely to feel guilty rather than shameful if parents criticize their inappropriate behavior by emphasizing why it was wrong and how it may have harmed others, while encouraging them to do what they can to repair any harm they've done ("Claire, it was wrong to break John's toy. Give him your toy so that he doesn't feel bad.") (Hoffman, 2000; Tangney & Dearing, 2002).

Toddlers and young preschool children are likely to display self-evaluative emotions only when an adult is present to observe their conduct (Harter & Whitesell, 1989; Stipek, Recchia, & McClintic, 1992). This suggests that young children's self-evaluative emotions may stem largely from the reactions they anticipate receiving from adult evaluators. It may be well into the elementary school period before children fully internalize rules or evaluative standards and come to feel especially prideful, shameful, or guilty about their conduct in the absence of external surveillance (Bussey, 1999; Harter & Whitesell, 1989).

Socialization of Emotions and Emotional Self-Regulation

emotional display rules
culturally defined rules specifying which emotions should or should not be expressed under which circumstances.

Each society has a set of **emotional display rules** that specify the circumstances under which various emotions should or should not be expressed (Gross & Ballif, 1991; Harris, 1989). Children in the United States, for example, learn that they are supposed to express happiness or gratitude when they receive a gift from Grandma and, by all means, to suppress any disappointment they may feel should the gift turn out to be underwear. In some ways these emotional codes of conduct are similar to the pragmatic rules of language: children must acquire and use them in order to get along with other people and to maintain their approval.

When does this learning begin? Earlier than you might imagine! Consider that when mothers play with 7-month-old infants, they restrict themselves mainly to displays of joy, interest, and surprise, thus serving as models of only positive emotions for their babies (Malatesta & Haviland, 1982). Mothers also respond selectively to their infants' emotions: over the first several months, they become increasingly attentive to babies' expressions of interest or surprise and less responsive to the infants' negative emotions (Malatesta et al., 1986). Through basic learning processes, babies are trained to display more pleasant faces and fewer unpleasant ones.

However, the emotions that are considered socially acceptable may be quite different in one culture than in another. American parents love to stimulate their babies until they reach peaks of delight. By contrast, caregivers among the Gusii and Aka people of central Africa hardly ever take part in face-to-face play with their babies, seeking instead to keep young infants as calm and contented as possible (Hewlett et al., 1998; LeVine et al., 1994). So American babies learn that intense emotion is okay as long as it is positive, whereas Gusii and Aka babies learn to restrain both positive and negative emotions.

emotional self-regulation
strategies for managing emotions or adjusting emotional arousal to an appropriate level of intensity.

Regulating Emotions. Complying with these emotional lessons, babies must devise strategies for **regulating** and controlling their emotions. This is a difficult task for very young infants, who do manage to reduce at least some of their negative arousal by turning their bodies away from unpleasant stimuli or by sucking vigorously on objects (Mangelsdorf, Shapiro, & Marzolf, 1995). Interestingly, 6-month-old boys find it harder than 6-month-old girls to regulate unpleasant arousal and are more inclined than girls are to fuss and cry in an attempt to elicit regulatory support (soothing) from caregivers (Weinberg et al., 1999).

By the end of the first year infants develop additional strategies for reducing negative arousal such as rocking themselves, chewing on objects, or moving away from people or events that upset them (Kopp, 1989; Mangelsdorf, Shapiro, & Marzolf, 1995). By 18 to 24 months toddlers are more likely to try to control the actions of people ("Up, Daddy!" as a request to be picked up in the presence of a stranger) or objects (e.g., such as the buttons on mechanical toys) that upset them (Mangelsdorf, Shapiro, & Marzolf, 1995). They are also beginning to cope with the frustration of having to wait for snacks or gifts by talking to companions, playing with toys, or otherwise distracting themselves from the source of their disappointments (Grolnick, Bridges, & Connell, 1996). In fact, toddlers this young have even been observed to knit their brows or to compress their lips as they actively attempt to suppress their anger or sadness (Malatesta et al., 1986). Yet toddlers find it almost impossible to regulate fear (Buss & Goldsmith, 1998); instead, they often develop methods of *expressing* fear that successfully attract the attention and comforting of caregivers (Bridges & Grolnick, 1995).

As young preschool children become more talkative and begin to discuss their feelings, parents and other close companions will often help them to deal constructively with negative emotions by distracting them from the most distressing aspects of unpleasant situations (e.g., telling a child who is about to receive a shot to look at a brightly colored poster on the wall) or by otherwise helping them to understand frightening, frustrating, or disappointing experiences (Thompson, 1994, 1998). These supportive interventions are a form of guided instruction of the kind that Vygotsky wrote about—experiences that should help preschoolers to devise effective strategies for regulating their own emotions. Indeed, 2- to 6-year-olds do become better and better at coping with unpleasant emotional arousal. Some methods used by these young children include directing their attention away from frightening events ("I scared of the shark. Close my eyes."), thinking pleasant thoughts to overcome unpleasant ones ("Mommy left me, but when she comes back, we are going to the movies."), and reinterpreting the cause of their distress in a more satisfying way ("He [story character] didn't *really* die . . . it's just pretend.") (Thompson, 1994). Unfortunately, children who are exposed to frequent displays of negative emotion at home, whether it is directed at them or not, often display high levels of negative emotionality that they have difficulty regulating (Caspi et al., 2004; Eisenberg et al., 2001; Maughan & Cicchetti, 2002; Valiente et al., 2004).

Adaptive regulation of emotions may sometimes involve maintaining or intensifying one's feelings rather than suppressing them. For example, children may learn that conveying their anger helps them to stand up to a bully (Thompson, 1994). Parents often call attention to (and thereby seek to maintain) the uneasiness that young children experience after causing another person distress or breaking a rule. Why? Because they hope to persuade youngsters to reinterpret these feelings in ways that cause them to (1) *sympathize* with victims of distress and to act on this concern, or (2) feel *guilty* about their transgressions and become less inclined to repeat them (Dunn, Brown, & Maguire, 1995; Kochanska, 1991). Another form of emotional arousal that parents may seek to maintain or enhance in children is *pride* in their accomplishments, an important contributor to a healthy sense of achievement motivation and to the development of a positive academic self-concept (see Chapter 12 for further discussion of this point). In sum, effective regulation of emotions involves an ability to suppress, maintain, or even intensify emotional arousal to remain productively engaged with the challenges we face or the people we encounter (Cole, Martin, & Dennis, 2004; Campos, Frankel, & Camras, 2004; Thompson, 1994).

Acquiring Emotional Display Rules. An ability to regulate emotions is only the first skill that children must acquire to comply with a culture's emotional display rules. Indeed, these prescriptions often dictate that we not only suppress whatever unacceptable emotions we are experiencing, but also replace them (outwardly, at least) with whatever feeling the display rule calls for in that situation (e.g., acting happy rather than sad on receiving a disappointing gift).

By about age 3 children are beginning to show some limited ability to disguise their true feelings. Michael Lewis and his associates (Lewis, Stanger, and Sullivan, 1989), for example, found that 3-year-olds who had lied about peeking at a forbidden toy showed subtle signs of anguish (detectable on film played in slow motion); however, they were able to mask their feelings well enough to make it impossible for uninformed adult judges to discriminate them from other children who truthfully reported that they hadn't peeked. With each passing year, preschool children become a little better at posing outward expressions

Toddlers and preschool children are not very skilled at masking their true feelings.

that differ from their inner feelings (Peskin, 1992; Ruffman et al., 1993). Yet even 5-year-olds are not especially skilled at disguising their true emotions or at convincing others that their lies are true (Polak & Harris, 1999).

Throughout the grade school years, children become increasingly aware of socially sanctioned display rules, learning more about which emotions to express, and which to suppress, in particular social situations (Eisenberg et al., 2003; Holodynski, 2004; Holodynski & Friedlmeirer, in press; Jones, Abbey, & Cumberland, 1998; Zeman & Shipman, 1997). Perhaps because parents place stronger pressures on girls to act nice in social situations, girls are both more motivated and more skilled at complying with display rules than are boys (Davis, 1995). Furthermore, mothers who emphasize positive emotions in their parent-child interactions tend to have children who are better able to mask disappointment and other negative feelings (Garner & Power, 1996). Yet even simple display rules take some time to fully master. As we see in Figure 11.2, many 7- to 9-year-olds (especially boys) are still unable to act thrilled and to mask all their disappointment on receiving a lousy gift. And even many 12- to 13-year-olds fail to suppress all their anger when taunted by a peer (Underwood et al., 1999) or thwarted by an adult exercising authority (Underwood, Coie, & Herbsman, 1992).

Children's emotional regulation continues to develop throughout adolescence. Recent research by Albert Bandura and his colleagues (2003) suggests that older adolescents' (for example, 14- to 19-year-olds) self-perceptions of their own abilities to control their emotions have a significant impact on many aspects of their social lives. For example, teenagers who believe they are relatively good at managing the expressions of their emotions in public are more prosocial, able to resist peer pressure, and more empathic with their peers.

Compliance with culturally specified rules for displaying emotions occurs earlier and is especially strong among communal peoples such as the Japanese or the Chhetri-Brehmin of Nepal that stress social harmony and place the needs of the social order over those of the individual (Cole & Tamang, 1998; Matsumoto, 1990). Clearly, this socialization of emotions works for the good of society: even in an individualistic culture such as the United States, children's increasing compliance with emotional display rules is largely motivated by a desire to maintain social harmony and to avoid criticism (Saarni, 1990; Zeman & Garber, 1996). Children who have mastered these emotional codes of conduct are viewed as more likable and more competent by their teachers and peers (Jones, Abbey, & Cumberland, 1998).

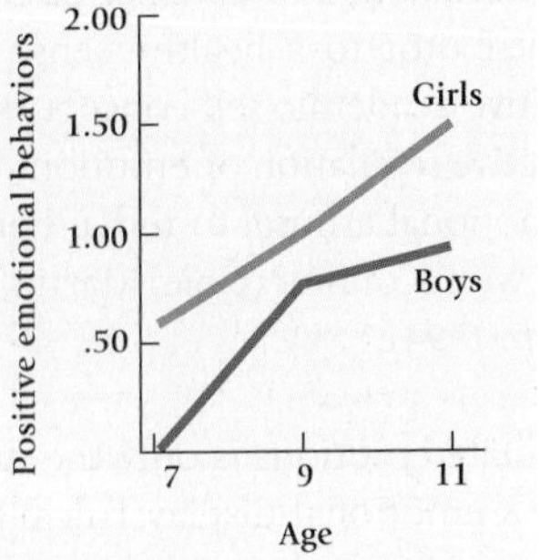

Figure 11.2 With age, children are better able to display positive emotional reactions after receiving a disappointing gift. *Adapted from "An Observational Study of Children's Attempts to Monitor Their Expressive Behavior," by C. Saarni, 1984,* Child Development, *55, 1504–1513. Copyright © 1984 by The Society for Research in Child Development, Inc. Adapted by permission.*

Recognizing and Interpreting Emotions

Currently there is some debate about when babies begin to recognize and interpret the emotional expressions that others display (Kuhana-Kalman & Walker-Andrews, 2001). As we learned in Chapter 5, 3-month-olds can discriminate different emotions posed by adults in photos; however, these demonstrations may simply reflect their powers of visual discrimination and do not necessarily imply that infants this young interpret various expressions as happy, angry, or sad (Nelson, 1987).

Social Referencing

Infants' ability to recognize and interpret particular emotional expressions becomes more obvious between 7 and 10 months (Soken & Pick, 1999)—the point at which they begin to monitor parents' emotional reactions to uncertain situations and to use this information

social referencing
the use of others' emotional expressions to infer the meaning of otherwise ambiguous situations.

to regulate their own behavior (Feinman, 1992). This **social referencing** becomes more common with age (Walden & Baxter, 1989) and soon extends to people other than parents (Repacholi, 1998). By the end of the first year infants typically approach and play with unfamiliar toys if a nearby stranger is smiling, but are apt to avoid these objects if the stranger displays a fearful expression (Klinnert et al., 1986). In one recent study, 12-month-old infants even socially referenced from a televised segment, avoiding and reacting negatively to the presentation of an object that had elicited a fearful reaction from an adult on TV (Mumme & Fernald, 2003). A mother's vocal expressions of emotion seem to convey at least as much information for a 12-month-old infant as her facial expressions do (Mumme, Fernald, & Herrera, 1996). Baldwin and Moses (1996) wondered whether these emotional signals might not best be interpreted as commands (e.g., "don't touch") rather than as active information seeking on the infant's part. During the second year, toddlers will often look to their companions *after* they have appraised a new object or situation, thereby suggesting that they are now using others' emotional reactions as information to assess the accuracy of their own judgments (Hornik & Gunnar, 1988).

empathy
the ability to experience the same emotions that someone else is experiencing.

Conversations about Emotions

Once toddlers begin to talk about emotions at 18 to 24 months, family conversations that center on emotional experiences can help them achieve a much richer understanding of their own and others' feelings (Jenkins et al., 2003). In fact, Judith Dunn and her associates (Dunn, Brown, & Beardsall, 1991; Herrara & Dunn, 1997) found that the more often 3-year-olds had discussed emotional experiences with other family members, the better they were at interpreting others' emotions and at settling disputes with friends when evaluated 3 years later in grade school. The ability to identify how others are feeling and to understand why they feel that way has important social consequences. Understanding the causes of others' emotions is an important contributor to **empathy,** which often motivates children to comfort or otherwise assist distressed companions. This may explain why parents talk just as much about positive emotions as about negative emotions to their 2- to 5-year-olds, although discussions about negative emotions center more heavily on their causes, their relationships to other mental states and goals, and on regulating issues (Lagattuta & Wellman, 2002).

Stephanie Rausser/Getty Images

Conversations that focus on the emotional experiences that family members have had promote emotional understanding, empathy, and social competencies in young children.

Later Milestones in Emotional Understanding

Before age 3, children are notoriously bad at identifying and labeling the emotional expressions posed by people in pictures or on puppets' faces (see Widen & Russell, 2003, for a review). However, the ability to recognize and interpret others' emotional displays steadily improves throughout childhood. By age 4 to 5 children can correctly infer whether a person is happy, angry, or sad from his or her expressive body movements (Boone & Cunningham, 1998). What's more, they increasingly recognize that a person's current emotional state (particularly negative emotions) may stem not from current events but rather from the person's thinking about past events (Lagattuta & Wellman, 2001). As grade school children gradually begin to rely more on personal, situational, and historical information to interpret emotions, they achieve several important breakthroughs in emotional understanding. By age 8 they recognize that many situations (e.g., the approach of a big dog) will elicit different emotional reactions (e.g., fear versus joy) from different individuals (Gnepp & Klayman, 1992). Six- to nine-year-olds are also beginning to understand that a person can experience more than one emotion (e.g., excitement and wariness) at the same time (Arsenio & Kramer, 1992; Brown & Dunn, 1996). These children also display some ability to integrate contrasting facial, behavioral, and situational cues to infer what emotions these cues reveal, such as they might witness in a fearful but eager child waiting in line for a roller-coaster ride (Hoffner & Badzinski, 1989).

Notice that these latter advances in emotional understanding emerge at about the same age that children can integrate more than one piece of information (e.g., height and width of a column of liquid) in Piagetian conservation tasks that we discussed in Chapter 7, and they may depend, in part, on the same underlying cognitive developments. Nevertheless, social experiences are also important. Jane Brown and Judith Dunn (1996), for example, found that 6-year-olds who show an early understanding of conflicting emotions had often discussed the causes of emotions with their parents earlier in childhood. Apparently, these discussions prepared them to analyze mixed feelings.

Emotions and Early Social Development

What role do emotions play in early social development? Clearly, a baby's displays of emotion serve a communicative function that is likely to affect the behavior of caregivers. For example, cries of distress summon close companions. Early suggestions of a smile or expressions of interest may convince caregivers that their baby is willing and even eager to strike up a social relationship with them. Later expressions of fear or sadness may indicate that the infant is insecure or feeling blue and needs some attention or comforting. Anger may imply that the infant wishes her companions to cease whatever they are doing that is upsetting her. Joy serves as a prompt for caregivers to prolong an ongoing interaction or perhaps signals the baby's willingness to accept new challenges. Infant emotions are adaptive in that they promote social contact and help caregivers to adjust their behavior to the infant's needs and goals. The emotional expressions of infancy help infants and their close companions get to know each other (Tronick, 1989).

An infant's emerging ability to recognize and interpret others' emotions is an important achievement that enables him to infer how he should be feeling or behaving in a variety of situations. The beauty of this social referencing is that children can quickly acquire knowledge in this way. For example, a sibling's joyful reaction to the family dog should indicate to a toddler that this ball of fur is a friend rather than an unspeakable monster. A mother's worried expression and accompanying vocal concern might immediately suggest that the knife in one's hand is an implement to be avoided. And given the frequency with which expressive caregivers direct an infant's attention to important aspects of the environment or display their feelings about an infant's appraisal of objects and events, it is likely that the information contained in their emotional displays will contribute in a major way to the child's understanding of the world in which he lives (Rosen, Adamson, & Bakeman, 1992).

Developmentalists who investigate these issues believe that achieving emotional competence is crucial to children's social competence, that is, their ability to achieve personal goals in social interactions while continuing to maintain positive relationships with others (Rubin, Bukowski, & Parker, 1998). Emotional competence has three components: *competent emotional expressivity,* which involves frequent expression of more positive emotions and relatively infrequent displays of negative ones; *competent emotional knowledge,* which involves the abilities to correctly identify other people's feelings and the factors responsible for those emotions; and *competent emotional regulation,* or the ability to adjust one's experience and expression of emotional arousal to an appropriate level of intensity to successfully achieve one's goals (Denham et al., 2003). Research has consistently revealed that each of these components of emotional competence is related to children's social competence. For example, children who express predominately positive affect and relatively little anger or sadness tend to be appraised more favorably by teachers and to establish more favorable relationships with peers than those who are angry, sad, or otherwise moody much of the time (Hubbard, 2001; Ladd, Birch, & Buhs, 1999; Rubin et al., 1998). Children who score high on tests of emotional understanding tend to be rated high in social competence by their teachers and to display social skills that enable them to easily make friends and establish positive relations with their classmates (Brown & Dunn, 1996; Dunn, Cutting & Fisher, 2002; Mostow et al., 2002). Finally, children who have difficulties appropriately regulating their emotions (particularly anger) are often rejected by peers (Rubin et al., 1998) and face such adjustment problems as overimpulsivity and a general lack of self-control, inappropriate aggression, anxiety, depression, and social withdrawal (Eisenberg et al., 2001; Gilliom et al., 2002; Maughan & Cicchetti, 2002). The Box below examines this type of research in more detail.

FOCUS ON RESEARCH

Assessing Emotional Competence in Young Children

© Masterfile

Early emotional competence has implications for children's later social abilities and social adjustment.

Susanne Denham and her associates (2003) conducted a longitudinal study in which they measured all three components of emotional competence in 3- to 4-year-old children. They were interested in determining which aspects of early emotional development are most clearly linked to children's emerging social abilities, both during the preschool period and later in kindergarten. *Emotional expressivity* was measured by time sampling: each 3- to 4-year-old child was observed over a series of 5-minute periods and the frequency of the child's display of positive or negative emotions was counted. *Emotional knowledge* was measured by asking children to name what emotion a puppet would be experiencing in eight common situations (such as after receiving an ice cream cone or after having a nightmare). Finally, *emotional self-regulation* was measured in two ways: mothers were asked how well their children could control their emotional expressions and the number of times children expressed an emotion they didn't mean to express was counted from the time-sampling measure of emotional expressivity described previously. These three measures of emotional competence (that is, emotional expressivity, emotional knowledge, and emotional self-regulation) were related to children's social competence when they were 3 to 4 years old and again when they were in kindergarten. Social competence was measured in two ways: teachers rated the children's cooperativeness and sensitivity to the feelings of peers, and the children were all asked to rate the likeability of the other children.

The results were complex but very informative. At age 3 to 4 years, children's emotional expressivity predicted both their emotional knowledge and emotional self-regulation. That is, children who expressed mostly positive emotions were generally more knowledgeable about emotions and were better at regulating their own expression of emotions than were children who expressed mostly negative emotions. Yet, only emotional self-regulation predicted children's social competence: children who were skilled at controlling the expression of their emotions were rated as more socially competent by day-care teachers and as more likable by their day-care classmates than were children who were less able to control their emotional expressions.

The picture changed by kindergarten. In kindergarten, both competent emotional expressivity (that is, displaying mostly positive emotions) and knowing a lot about emotions (that is, competent emotional knowledge) became strong predictors of social competence. In kindergarten, the ability to control the expression of emotions (that is, emotional self-regulation) became less important in social interactions.

What is so interesting about these results is not so much the particulars as the bigger picture: all three aspects of emotional competence *assessed early in life* have implications for children's emerging social abilities and, ultimately, for their patterns of social adjustment. Clearly, what children are learning early on about the desirability of expressing particular emotions, inhibiting or otherwise regulating less desirable feelings, the meaning of the emotions that other people express, and finally, how the children should respond to other people's emotional signals, are all crucial lessons that are apt to serve them well throughout childhood, adolescence, and the rest of their lives.

As adults, we realize that the emotions we experience and how we express those feelings contribute to how we see our selves, or our personality. Emotional competence also contributes to children's personalities. It is to this aspect of the development of the self that we now turn.

Temperament and Development

temperament
a person's characteristic modes of responding emotionally and behaviorally to environmental events, including such attributes as activity level, irritability, fearfulness, and sociability.

As parents and day-care providers well know, every baby has a distinct "personality." In trying to describe infant personalities, researchers have focused on aspects of **temperament,** which Mary Rothbart and John Bates (1998) define as "constitutionally based" individual differences in emotional, motor, and attentional reactivity and self-regulation" (p. 109) that many believe to be the emotional and behavioral building blocks of the adult personality. What kinds of emotional and behavioral variations? Although different researchers do not always define or measure temperament in precisely the same ways, we agree with those that argue that the following six dimensions provide a fairly good description of individual differences in infant temperament (Rothbart & Bates, 1998):

Fearful distress: wariness, distress, and withdrawal in new situations or in response to novel stimuli
Irritable distress: fussiness, crying, and showing distress when desires are frustrated (sometimes called frustration/anger)
Positive affect: frequency of smiling, laughing, willingness to approach others and to cooperate with them (called sociability by some researchers)
Activity level: amount of gross motor activity (e.g., kicking, crawling)
Attention span/persistence: length of time child orients to and focuses on objects or events of interest
Rhythmicity: regularity/predictability of bodily functions such as eating, sleeping, and bowel functioning

Notice, then, that infant temperament reflects two kinds of negative emotionality (fearfulness and irritability) as well as a single, general measure of positive affect. What's more, the first five of these six temperamental components are also useful for describing temperamental variations that preschool and older children display (Rothbart & Bates, 1998). Variations on some temperamental dimensions take some time to appear and are undoubtedly influenced by biological maturation and experience (Rothbart et al., 2001). For example, fearful distress does not appear until age 6 to 7 months, and variations in attention span, while certainly apparent early, become more noticeable later in the first year as the frontal lobes of the brain mature and babies become more capable of regulating attention.

Hereditary and Environmental Influences on Temperament

To many, the very term temperament implies a biological foundation for individual differences in behavior, a foundation that is genetically influenced and stable over time. But as we know, heredity and environment contribute in complex ways and interact with each other to produce most developmental outcomes. Temperament is no exception.

Hereditary Influences

Behavioral geneticists have looked for hereditary influences by comparing the temperamental similarities of pairs of identical and fraternal twins. By the middle of the first year identical twins are already more similar than fraternal twins are on most temperamental attributes, including activity level, demands for attention, irritability, and sociability

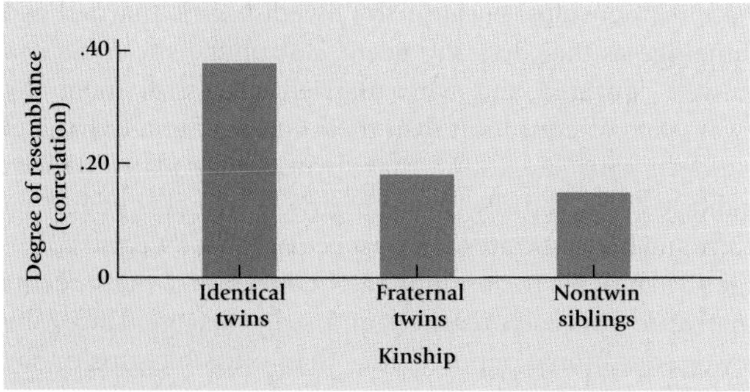

Figure 11.3 Average correlations in infant temperament among identical twins, fraternal twins, and nontwin siblings born at different times. *Based on Braungart et al., 1992; Emde et al., 1992.*

(Braungart et al., 1992; Emde et al., 1992) (see Figure 11.3). Although the heritability coefficients for most temperamental attributes are moderate at best throughout infancy and the preschool period (Goldsmith, Buss, & Lemery, 1997), it seems that many important components of temperament are genetically influenced.

Environmental Influences

The fact that temperamental attributes are only moderately heritable means that environment also influences children's temperaments. Which aspects of environment are most important? Recent research implies that the home environments that siblings share most clearly influence such *positive* aspects of temperament as smiling/sociability and soothability; yet shared environment contributes very little to children's activity levels and to *negative* attributes such as irritability and fearfulness. This is believed because siblings living together often barely resemble each other in these negative aspects of temperament, but siblings are often quite similar in positive aspects of temperament (Goldsmith, Buss, & Lemery, 1997; Goldsmith et al., 1999). Negatively toned temperamental attributes are shaped more by *nonshared environmental influences*—those aspects of environment that siblings do not share and that conspire to make them temperamentally *dissimilar.* This can easily happen if parents notice early behavioral differences among their children and adjust their parenting to each child. For example, if a mother observes that her infant son Dylan is more upset by strangers and unfamiliar settings than her 3-year-old daughter Gretchen was at Dylan's age, she may allow Dylan more freedom to avoid new experiences (that is, not push him to try new things or meet new people), thereby encouraging him to become ever more fearful of novel contexts he may later encounter, such as day care (Park et al., 1997).

Cultural Influences

Culture also affects certain aspects of temperament. For example, in the United States, children who are shy and reserved are at a social disadvantage. They run the risk of being neglected or even rejected by peers, which can lead to low self-esteem, depression, and a number of other adjustment problems. Furthermore, even if shy adolescents or young adults are otherwise well adjusted, they often fail to act boldly or assertively enough to take advantage of many opportunities, and they typically lag far behind bolder peers in getting married, having children, and firmly establishing themselves in a career (Caspi, Elder, & Bem, 1988).

In contrast, many Asian cultures value what Americans would call a shy and somewhat inhibited demeanor. In China, for example, children who are more reserved are perceived as socially mature by their teachers (Chen, Rubin, & Li, 1995) and are much more likely than active, assertive children to be popular with their peers—precisely the opposite pattern to what we see in the United States and Canada (Chen, Rubin, & Sun, 1992). The boisterous classroom behaviors that many Western children display on occasion (and that American teachers view as normal) are likely to be branded conduct disorders by teachers in Thailand, who expect their pupils to be reserved, respectful, and obedient (Weisz et al., 1995).

There are even differences among Western cultures in outcomes associated with shyness. Swedes, for example, view shyness somewhat more positively than Americans do and prefer shy, reserved behaviors to bold, assertive, or attention-seeking antics. Consequently, shyness is not really a disadvantage for Swedish men. Like shy American men, shy Swedish men married and had children later than their less shy counterparts; however, shyness did not constrain their careers in the same way it does for American men (Kerr, Lambert, & Bem, 1996). What about Swedish women? Shyness posed no problems for them in establishing intimate relationships, because shy Swedish girls married and had children at roughly the same age as their less shy peers. But unlike shy American women, who were generally well educated and who married successful men, shy Swedish women completed fewer years of education than their bolder counterparts and married men who made less money, thus suggesting that shyness may place them at some risk of economic disadvantage. Why did shy Swedish girls receive less education than less shy peers? Margaret Kerr and her associates (1996) speculate that Swedish teachers are more likely to encourage shy students to continue their education if the students are males. So, lacking the initiative to approach teachers and seek their guidance, shy Swedish girls end up having fewer educational opportunities than outgoing girls or shy boys do.

We see, then, that outcomes associated with shyness vary dramatically across cultures (and even within a culture, depending on one's gender). Clearly, some temperamental qualities fit better with a culture's specific values and traditions than others. In addition, because cultural traditions vary so widely, we can safely conclude that there is no one temperamental profile that is most adaptive in all cultures.

Stability of Temperament

How stable is early temperament over time? Is the fearful 8-month-old who is highly upset by a strange face likely to remain wary of strangers at 24 months and to shun new playmates as a 4-year-old? Longitudinal research indicates that several components of temperament—activity level, irritability, sociability, and fearfulness—are moderately stable through infancy, childhood, and sometimes even into the early adult years (Caspi & Silva, 1995; Eisenberg et al., 2004; Lemery et al., 1999; Pedlow et al., 1993). In fact, one longitudinal study in New Zealand found that several components of temperament measured at age 3 were not only moderately stable between ages 3 and 18, but also predicted individual differences in participants' antisocial tendencies and the quality of their personal and family relationships at ages 18 to 21 (Caspi & Silva, 1995; Henry et al., 1996; Newman et al., 1997). Findings such as these illustrate why many developmentalists consider temperament to be the cornerstone of the adult personality. However, not all individuals are so temperamentally stable.

behavioral inhibition
a temperamental attribute reflecting one's tendency to withdraw from unfamiliar people or situations.

Consider what Jerome Kagan and his associates found while conducting longitudinal studies of a temperamental attribute they call **behavioral inhibition,** the tendency to withdraw from unfamiliar people or situations (Kagan, 1992; Snidman et al., 1995). At 4 months inhibited infants are already fussing and showing heightened motor activity to such novel objects as a brightly colored mobile, and they often display intense physiological arousal (e.g., high heart rates) to situations that barely phase uninhibited infants. When tested at 21 months, toddlers classified as inhibited were rather shy and sometimes even fearful when they encountered unfamiliar people, toys, or settings whereas most uninhibited children responded quite adaptively to these events. And when retested at ages 4, 5½, and 7½, inhibited youngsters were still less sociable with strange adults and peers and more cautious than uninhibited children were about engaging in activities that involved an element of risk (e.g., walking a balance beam).

Behavioral inhibition is a moderately stable attribute that may have deep biological roots. Researchers have found that infants easily upset by novelty show greater electrical activity in the right cerebral hemisphere of the brain (the center for negative emotions) than in the left hemisphere, whereas infants who are less reactive show either the opposite pattern or no hemispheric differences in electrical activity (Fox et al., 2001; Fox, Bell, & Jones, 1992). In addition, family studies clearly indicate that behavioral inhibition is a genetically influenced attribute (DiLalla, Kagan, & Reznick, 1994; Robinson et al., 1992). Nevertheless, both Kagan and his associates (1998) and other researchers (Kerr et al., 1994; Pfeifer et al., 2002) found that children at the extremes of the continuum—the most highly inhibited and most highly uninhibited youngsters—were most likely to display such long-term stability, with most other children showing considerable fluctuation in their levels of inhibition over time. What these observations imply is that genetically influenced aspects of temperament are often modified by environmental influences. Interestingly, a similar conclusion emerges from Alexander Thomas and Stella Chess's classic longitudinal research on the stability of temperamental profiles from infancy to adulthood.

Early Temperamental Profiles and Later Development

easy temperament
temperamental profile in which the child quickly establishes regular routines, is generally good natured, and adapts easily to novelty.

difficult temperament
temperamental profile in which the child is irregular in daily routines and adapts slowly to new experiences, often responding negatively and intensely.

slow-to-warm-up temperament
temperamental profile in which the child is inactive and moody and displays mild passive resistance to new routines and experiences.

"goodness-of-fit" model
Thomas and Chess's notion that development is likely to be optimized when parents' child-rearing practices are sensitively adapted to the child's temperamental characteristics.

In their earliest reports Thomas and Chess (1977; Thomas, Chess, & Birch, 1970) noted that certain aspects of infant temperament tend to cluster in predictable ways, forming broader temperamental profiles. In fact, the majority of the 141 infants in their *New York Longitudinal Study* could be placed into one of three temperamental profiles:

- **Easy temperament** (40 percent of the sample): Easygoing children are even-tempered, typically in a positive mood, and quite open and adaptable to new experiences. Their habits are regular and predictable.
- **Difficult temperament** (10 percent of the sample): Difficult children are active, irritable, and irregular in their habits. They often react very vigorously to changes in routine and are very slow to adapt to new persons or situations.
- **Slow-to-warm-up temperament** (15 percent of the sample): These children are quite inactive, somewhat moody, and can be slow to adapt to new persons and situations. But, unlike the difficult child, they typically respond to novelty in mildly (rather than intensely) negative ways. For example, they may resist cuddling by looking away rather than by kicking or screaming.

The remaining children fit none of these profiles, showing their own unique patterns of temperamental attributes.

Bob Daemmrich/Stock Boston

Difficult children are likely to retain their difficult temperaments if parents are impatient and forceful with them.

Temperamental Profiles and Children's Adjustment

Apparently, these broader temperamental patterns may persist over time and influence a child's adjustment to a variety of settings later in life. For example, temperamentally difficult children are more likely than other children to have problems adjusting to school activities, and are often irritable and aggressive in their interactions with siblings and peers (Rubin et al., 2003; Stams, Juffer, & van IJzendoorn, 2002; Thomas, Chess, & Korn, 1982). About half of all children who are slow to warm up show a different kind of adjustment problem: their hesitancy to embrace new activities and challenges may cause them to be ignored or neglected by peers (Chess & Thomas, 1984).

Child Rearing and Temperament

Do those observations imply that early temperamental profiles are difficult to alter and largely determine our personalities and social adjustment? No, they do not! Thomas and Chess (1986; Chess & Thomas, 1984) found that early temperamental characteristics *sometimes do* and *sometimes do not* carry over into later life. In other words, temperament can change, and one factor that often determines whether it does change is the **goodness of fit** between the child's temperamental style and patterns of child rearing used by parents (see, for example, Porter & Hsu, 2003; Rubin et al., 2003).

Let's first consider a good fit between temperament and child rearing. Difficult infants and toddlers who fuss a lot and have trouble adapting to new routines often become less cranky and more adaptable over the long run if parents remain calm as they insist that their children comply with rules. It also helps if parents exercise restraint and allow them to respond to new routines at a more leisurely pace. Indeed, many difficult youngsters who experience such patient, sensitive, and yet demanding caregiving are no longer classifiable as temperamentally difficult or displaying problem behaviors later in childhood or adolescence (Bates et al., 1998; Chess & Thomas, 1984).

It is not always easy for parents to be patient and sensitive with a highly active, moody child who resists their bids for attention; in fact, many parents become extremely irritable, impatient, and punitive with difficult children (van den Boom, 1995). Unfortunately, these attitudes and behaviors constitute a poor fit with a difficult child, who is apt to become all the more fussy and resistant in response to the parent's forceful and punitive tactics. True to form, difficult infants and toddlers are especially likely to remain difficult and to display behavior problems later in life if their parents are often impatient, angry, demanding, and forceful (Chess & Thomas, 1984; Rubin et al., 2003).

Finally, as we noted previously, there is a great deal of variation across cultures in what qualifies as a desirable temperament and in the developmental outcomes that are associated with particular temperamental attributes.

So far, we have examined how children experience and express their emotions and how emotional expressiveness and other aspects of temperament form the cornerstone of adult personality. But what about the child's emotional ties with others? How do these intimate relationships develop? These are the issues we will examine next.

CONCEPT CHECK 11.1 Emotional Development and Temperament

Check your understanding of important processes in the development of emotions and children's temperaments by answering the following questions. Answers appear in the Appendix.

Matching: Identify the following environmental influences that contribute to temperamental attributes as described below:

a. shared environmental influences
b. nonshared environmental influences

1. ________ contribute most to positively toned temperamental attributes
2. ________ contribute most to negatively toned temperamental attributes

True or False: Identify whether the following statements are true or false.

3. (T)(F) Shyness or behavioral inhibition describes children who adapt well to unfamiliar people, settings, or toys.
4. (T)(F) Uninhibited children display temperamental attributes that are valued more highly in Asian than in Western societies.

Fill in the Blank: Complete the following phrases with the correct terms.

5. The infant's capability for ________ is thought to be necessary for the development of all complex emotions.
6. The infant's ________ are communicative signals that affect the behavior of caregivers.
7. The child's capability for ________ is necessary for the child to comply with emotional display rules.
8. Shandra would like her son, Alex, to grow up with a strong prosocial attitude, including concern and empathy for others. When she discovers that Alex has hit another boy in his preschool class, she strongly reprimands Alex by saying "Alex, it is wrong to hit! It hurts other people's feelings. You need to go over and apologize and give that boy a hug." This type of reaction from Shandra is likely to make Alex feel ________ but not ________.

Short Answer: Provide a brief answer to each of the following questions.

9. List and describe the three most common temperamental profiles exhibited by infants and children.

Essay: Provide a more detailed answer to the following question.

10. Describe the way infant temperament and parenting styles interact to produce positive developmental outcomes.

Attachment and Development

Returning to the experience I had with my own daughters: I was fortunate to be able to stay at home for the first 2 years of my daughters' lives, but when they turned 2 it was time for them to enter day care so that I could continue my education. I remember that first day: they happily walked into the day care and seemed interested in all the activity around them. But when they realized I was about to leave without them, they both started to wail and cling to me as if their world was about to end! I did leave them, and spent a while crying in the car. After a few minutes I snuck back in to check on them through the one-way mirror and saw that they had stopped crying and were playing happily. Within a few weeks, they were eager to go to day care and reserved their wailing tantrums for when it was time to come home from day care. I wondered whether I was a horrible mother. Why did my babies cry and carry on when I left them? And why did they eventually only cry when I came to pick them up? Looking at the literature, I discovered that all these tantrums were signs of secure attachments: first with me, and eventually also with their day-care providers. In this next section we will learn how these attachments form and what consequences they might have for later development.

Although babies can communicate many of their feelings right from the start, their social lives change rather dramatically as they become emotionally attached to their caregivers. What is an emotional **attachment?** John Bowlby (1969) uses the term to describe the strong affectional ties that we feel with the special people in our lives. According to Bowlby (1969), people who are securely attached take pleasure in their interactions and feel comforted by their partner's presence in times of stress or uncertainty. So 10-month-old Dala may reflect the attachment relationship he shares with his mother by reserving his biggest grins for her and by crying out to her or crawling in her direction whenever he is upset, discomforted, or afraid.

attachment
a close emotional relationship between two persons, characterized by mutual affection and a desire to maintain proximity.

Attachments as Reciprocal Relationships

Bowlby (1969) also stressed that parent/infant attachments are *reciprocal* relationships: Infants become attached to parents, and parents become attached to infants.

Parents clearly have an edge on infants when it comes to forming these intimate affectional ties. Even before their baby is born, they often display their readiness to become attached by talking blissfully about the baby, formulating grand plans for him or her, and expressing delight in such milestones as feeling the fetus kick or seeing his image in a sonogram (Grossman et al., 1980). And as we learned in Chapter 5, close contact with a newborn in the first few hours after birth can intensify positive feelings parents already have for their baby (Klaus & Kennell, 1982), particularly if they are younger, economically disadvantaged, and know very little about babies or infant care (Eyer, 1992). Yet, it is important to emphasize that genuine emotional attachments build slowly from parent-infant interactions that occur over the first several months and can become highly intimate, even when there is no early contact between parents and their newborn. The likelihood that a mother and her infant will become securely attached is just as high (or higher) in adoptive families as in nonadoptive ones (Stams, Juffer, & van Ijzendoorn, 2002; Singer et al., 1985) and in families formed through surrogacy arrangements (Golombok et al., 2004).

synchronized routines
generally harmonious interactions between two persons in which participants adjust their behavior in response to the partner's feelings and behaviors.

Ann Clark Beurskens

Young children and caregivers who are securely attached interact often and try to maintain proximity.

Establishment of Interactional Synchrony

One important contributor to the growth of attachments is the **synchronized routines** that caregivers and infants often establish over the first few months of a baby's life (Stern, 1977; Tronick, 1989). Infants normally begin gazing quite intently and showing more interest in their mothers' faces between 4 and 9 weeks of age (Lavelli & Fogel, 2002), and by 2 to 3 months are beginning to understand some simple social contingencies as well. Thus, if a mother smiles at her 3-month-old when the baby is alert and attentive, he will often become delighted, crack a big smile in return, and expect a meaningful response from Mom (Lavelli & Fogel, 2002; Legerstee & Varghese, 2001). When social expectancies are violated, as they are in the "still face" procedure when a parent is instructed to look sullen, 2- to 6-month-olds usually smile briefly at the parent to regain her attention before becoming distressed by her lack of responsiveness (Moore, Cohn, & Campbell, 2001). Even very young infants have come to expect some degree of "synchrony" between their own gestures and those of caregivers, and these expectancies are one reason that face-to-face play interactions with regular companions become increasingly coordinated and complex over the first several months (Stern, 1977).

These coordinated interactions, likened to dances, are most likely to develop if the caregiver attends carefully to her baby's state, provides playful stimulation when the baby is alert and attentive, and avoids pushing things when an overexcited or tired infant is fussy. Edward Tronick (1989, p. 112) described one very synchronous interaction that unfolded as a mother played peekaboo with her infant:

> . . . The infant abruptly turns away from his mother as the game reaches its "peek" of intensity and begins to suck on his thumb and stare into space with a dull facial expression. The mother stops playing and sits back watching. . . . After a few seconds the infant turns back to her with an inviting expression. The mother moves closer, smiles, and says in a high-pitched, exaggerated voice, "Oh, now you're back!" He smiles in response and vocalizes. As they finish crowing together, the infant reinserts his thumb and looks away. The mother again waits. [Soon] the infant turns . . . to her and they greet each other with big smiles.

Notice that much information is exchanged in this simple but synchronous interaction. By turning away and sucking, the excited infant is saying, "Hey, I need to slow down and regulate my emotional state." His mother tells him she understands by patiently awaiting his return. As he returns, mom tells him she's glad he's back, and he acknowledges that signal with a smile and an excited blurt. When the baby becomes overstimulated a minute or two later, his mother waits for him to calm once again, and he communicates his thanks by smiling wide for her when he turns back the second time.

Daniel Stern (1977) believes that synchronized interactions between infants and their caregivers may occur several times a day and are particularly important contributors to emotional attachments. As an infant continues to interact with a caregiver who is responsive to the infant's needs and desires, the infant learns what this person is like and how to regulate her attention (Keller et al., 1999). The caregiver also becomes better at interpreting the baby's signals and learns how to adjust her behavior to successfully capture and maintain his attention. As the caregiver and the infant practice their routines and become better "dance partners," their relationship becomes more satisfying for both parties and eventually blossoms into a strong reciprocal attachment (Isabella, 1993; Isabella & Belsky, 1991).

How Do Infants Become Attached?

Although many parents find themselves emotionally drawn to their infant very soon after their baby is born, an infant requires some time before she is developmentally ready to form a genuine attachment to another human being. Many theories have been proposed to explain how and why infants become emotionally involved with the people around them. Before we consider these theories, we will briefly discuss the phases that babies go through in becoming attached to a close companion.

The Growth of Primary Attachments

Many years ago, Rudolph Schaffer and Peggy Emerson (1964) studied the development of emotional attachments by following a group of Scottish infants from early infancy to 18 months of age. Once a month, mothers were interviewed to determine (1) how the infant responded when separated from close companions in seven situations (for example, being left in a crib, being left in the presence of strangers) and (2) the persons to whom the infant's separation responses were directed. A child was judged to be attached to someone if separation from that person reliably elicited a protest.

Schaffer and Emerson found that infants pass through the following phases as they develop close ties with their caregivers:

asocial phase (of attachment) approximately the first 6 weeks of life, in which infants respond in an equally favorable way to interesting social and nonsocial stimuli.

1. The Asocial Phase (birth to about 6 weeks). The very young infant is somewhat "asocial" in that many kinds of social or nonsocial stimuli produce a favorable reaction, and few produce any kind of protest. By the end of this period, infants are beginning to show a preference for social stimuli such as a smiling face.

phase of indiscriminate attachments period between 6 weeks and 6 to 7 months of age in which infants prefer social to nonsocial stimulation and are likely to protest whenever any adults puts them down or leaves them alone.

2. The Phase of Indiscriminate Attachments (about 6 weeks to 6 or 7 months). Now infants clearly enjoy human company but tend to be somewhat indiscriminate: they smile more at people than at other lifelike objects such as talking puppets (Ellsworth, Muir, & Hains, 1993) and are likely to fuss whenever *any* adult puts them down. Although 3- to 6-month-olds reserve their biggest grins for familiar companions (Watson et al., 1979) and are more quickly soothed by a regular caregiver, they seem to enjoy the attention they receive from just about anyone (including strangers).

phase of specific attachment period between 7 and 9 months of age when infants are attached to one close companion (usually the mother).

3. The Specific Attachments Phase (about 7 to 9 months). Between 7 and 9 months of age, infants begin to protest only when separated from one particular individual, usually the mother. Now able to crawl, infants often try to follow along behind their mothers to stay close and greet mothers warmly when they return. They also become somewhat wary of strangers. According to Schaffer and Emerson, these babies have established their first genuine attachments.

secure base use of a caregiver as a base from which to explore the environment and to which to return for emotional support.

The formation of a secure attachment has an important consequence: it promotes the development of exploratory behavior. Mary Ainsworth (1979) emphasizes that an attachment figure serves as a **secure base** for exploration: a point of safety from which an infant can feel free to venture away. Thus Juan, a securely attached infant visiting a neighbor's home with his mother, may be quite comfortable exploring the far corners of the living room so long as he can check back occasionally to see that Mom is still seated on the sofa. Should she disappear into another room, Juan may become wary and reluctant to explore. Paradoxical as it may seem, infants apparently need to rely on another person in order to feel confident about acting independently.

phase of multiple attachments period when infants are forming attachments to companions other than their primary attachment object.

4. The Phase of Multiple Attachments (about 9 to 18 months). Within weeks after forming their initial attachments, about half the infants in Schaffer and Emerson's study were becoming attached to other people such as fathers, siblings, grandparents, or perhaps even a regular babysitter. By 18 months of age, very few infants were attached to only one person, and some were attached to five or more.

Few signals attract as much attention as a baby's social smile.

Theories of Attachment

If you have ever had a kitten or a puppy, you may have noticed that pets often seem especially responsive and affectionate to the person who feeds them. Might the same be true of human infants? Developmentalists have long debated this very point, as we will see in examining four influential theories of attachment: psychoanalytic theory, learning theory, cognitive-developmental theory, and ethological theory.

Psychoanalytic Theory: I Love You Because You Feed Me. According to Freud, young infants are "oral" creatures who derive satisfaction from sucking and mouthing objects and should be attracted to any person who provides oral pleasure. Because it was usually mothers who fed them, it seemed logical to Freud that the mother would become the baby's primary object of security and affection, particularly if she was relaxed and generous in her feeding practices.

Erik Erikson also believed that a mother's feeding practices would influence the strength or security of her infant's attachments. However, he claimed that a mother's overall responsiveness to her child's needs is more important than feeding itself. According to Erikson, a caregiver who consistently responds to all an infant's needs fosters a sense of trust in other people, whereas unresponsive or inconsistent caregiving breeds mistrust. He adds that children who have learned not to trust caregivers during infancy may come to avoid close mutual-trust relationships throughout life.

Before we examine the research on feeding practices and attachments, we need to consider another viewpoint that assumes that feeding is important: learning theory.

Learning Theory: I Love You Because You Reward Me. For quite different reasons, some learning theorists also assumed that infants become attached to persons who feed them and gratify their needs. Feeding was thought to be particularly important for two reasons (Sears, 1963). First, it elicits positive responses from a contented infant (smiles, coos) that increase a caregiver's affection for the baby. Second, feeding is an occasion when mothers provide an infant with many comforts—food, warmth, tender touches, soft, reassuring vocalizations, changes in scenery, and even a dry diaper (if necessary)—all in one sitting.

secondary reinforcer
an initially neutral stimulus that acquires reinforcement value by virtue of its repeated association with other reinforcing stimuli.

Over time, then, an infant would come to associate his mother with pleasant or pleasurable sensations, so that the mother herself becomes a valuable commodity. Once the mother (or any other caregiver) has attained this status as a **secondary reinforcer,** the infant is attached, and he or she will now do whatever is necessary (smile, cry, coo, babble, or follow) in order to attract the caregiver's attention or to remain near this valuable and rewarding individual.

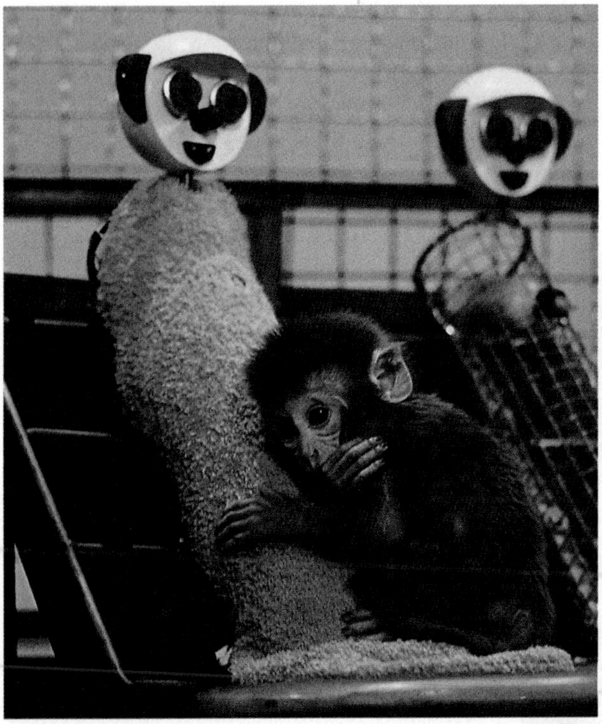
Martin Rogers/Stock Boston

The "wire" and "cloth" surrogate mothers used in Harlow's research. Infants became attached to the cloth mother even if it was the wire mother who fed them.

Just how important is feeding? In 1959, Harry Harlow and Robert Zimmerman reported the results of a study designed to compare the importance of feeding versus tactile stimulation for the development of attachments in infant monkeys. The monkeys were separated from their mothers in the first day of life and reared for the next 165 days by two surrogate mothers. As you can see in the photograph, each surrogate mother had a face and well-proportioned body constructed of wire. However, the body of one surrogate (the "cloth mother") was wrapped in foam rubber and covered with terry cloth. Half the infants were always fed by this warm, comfortable cloth mother, the remaining half were always fed by the rather uncomfortable "wire mother."

The research question was simple: Would these infants become attached to the "mother" who fed them, or would they instead prefer the soft, cuddly "cloth mother"? It was no contest! Even if their food had come from the "wire mother," infants spent time with "her" only while feeding and ran directly to the "cloth mother" whenever they were upset or afraid. So all infants became attached to the cloth mother, thereby implying that *contact comfort* is a more powerful contributor to attachment in monkeys than feeding or the reduction of hunger.

Apparently, feeding is not any more important to human infants than to baby monkeys. When Schaffer and Emerson (1964) asked mothers about the feeding schedules they used (regular interval versus demand feeding) and the age at which they weaned their infants, they found that the generosity of a mother's feeding practices simply did not predict the quality of her infant's attachment to her. In fact, for 39 percent of these infants, the person who usually fed, bathed, and changed them (typically the mother) was not even the child's primary attachment object!

Although it is now quite clear that feeding is not the primary contributor to attachments in either monkeys or humans, modern learning theorists continue to argue that reinforcement is the mechanism responsible for social attachments (Gewirtz & Petrovich, 1982). Their revised viewpoint, which is similar to that of Erik Erikson, is that infants will be attracted to any individual who is quick to respond to all their needs and who provides them with a variety of pleasant or rewarding experiences. Consistent with this viewpoint, Schaffer and Emerson (1964) found that the two aspects of a mother's behavior that predicted the character of her infant's attachment to her were her *responsiveness* to the infant's behavior and the total amount of *stimulation* that she provided. Mothers who responded reliably and appropriately to their infants' bids for attention and who often played with their babies had infants who were closely attached to them.

Cognitive-Developmental Theory: To Love You, I Must Know You Will Always Be There. Cognitive-developmental theory has little to say about which adults are most likely to appeal to infants, but it does remind us of the holistic character of development by suggesting that the ability to form attachments depends, in part, on the infant's level of cognitive development. Before an attachment can occur, the infant must be able to discriminate familiar companions from strangers. He must also recognize that familiar companions have a "permanence" about them (object permanence), for it would be difficult to form a stable relationship with a person who ceases to exist whenever she passes from view (Schaffer, 1971). So perhaps it is no accident that attachments first emerge at age 7 to 9 months—precisely the time when infants are entering Piaget's *fourth sensorimotor substage,* the point at which they first begin to search for and find objects that they've seen someone hide from them.

Barry Lester and his associates (1974) evaluated this hypothesis by giving 9-month-old infants a test of object permanence before exposing them to brief separations from their mothers, their fathers, and a stranger. They found that 9-month-olds who scored high in object permanence (substage 4 or above) only protested when separated from their mothers, whereas age-mates who scored lower (substage 3 or below) showed little evidence of *any* separation protest. Only the cognitively advanced 9-month-olds had formed a primary attachment (to their mothers), which implies that the timing of this important emotional milestone depends, in part, on the infant's level of cognitive development.

Ethological Theory: Perhaps I Was Born to Love. Ethologists proposed an interesting and influential explanation for emotional attachments that has strong evolutionary overtones. A major assumption of the ethological approach is that all species, including human beings, are born with a number of innate behavioral tendencies that have in some way contributed to the survival of the species over the course of evolution. John Bowlby (1969, 1980), who was originally a psychoanalyst, came to believe that many of these built-in behaviors are specifically designed to promote attachments between infants and their caregivers. Even the attachment relationship itself is said to have adaptive significance, serving to protect the young from predators and other natural calamities and to ensure that his needs are met. Ethologists argue that the long-range purpose of the primary attachment is to permit members of each successive generation to live long enough to reproduce, thereby enabling the species to survive.

Origins of the Ethological Viewpoint. The ethological theory of attachment was prompted by research with animals. In 1937, Konrad Lorenz reported that very young goslings followed almost any moving object—their mothers, a duck, or even a human

Figure 11.4 Infants of many species display the "kewpie doll effect," which makes them appear lovable and elicits caregivers' attention. *Adapted from "The Innate Forms of Possible Experience," by K. Z. Lorenz, 1943,* Zeitschrift fur Tierpsychologie, *5, 233–409.*

being, a behavior he labeled **imprinting.** Lorenz also noted that imprinting (1) is automatic—young fowl do not have to be taught to follow, (2) occurs only within a narrowly delimited critical period after the bird has hatched, and (3) is irreversible—once the bird begins to follow a particular object, it will remain attached to it.

Lorenz concluded that imprinting was an adaptive response. Young birds generally survive if they follow their mothers because they are led to food and afforded protection. Those that wander away may starve or be eaten by predators and thus fail to pass their genes to future generations. Over the course of many, many generations, the imprinting response eventually became an inborn, **preadapted characteristic** that attaches a young fowl to its mother.

Attachment in Humans. Although human infants do not imprint on their mothers in the same way that young fowl do, they seem to have inherited a number of attributes that help them to maintain contact with others and to elicit caregiving. Lorenz (1943), for example, suggested that a baby's **"kewpie doll"** appearance (that is, large forehead, chubby cheeks, and soft, rounded features (see Figure 11.4) makes the infant appear cute or lovable to caregivers. Thomas Alley (1981) agrees. Alley found that adults judged line drawings of infant faces (and profiles) to be "adorable"—much cuter than those of 2-, 3-, and 4-year-old children. So babyish facial features may help elicit the kinds of positive attention from others that promote social attachments. The more attractive the baby, the more favorably mothers and other companions respond to him or her (Barden et al., 1989; Langlois et al., 1995). Nevertheless, babies need not be adorable to foster close attachments, for a clear majority of unattractive infants end up securely attached to their caregivers (Speltz et al., 1997).

imprinting
an innate or instinctual form of learning in which the young of certain species will follow and become attached to moving objects (usually their mothers).

preadapted characteristic
an attribute that is a product of evolution and serves some function that increases the chances of survival for the individual and the species.

kewpie doll effect
the notion that infantlike facial features are perceived as cute and lovable and elicit favorable responses from others.

Not only do most infants have "cute" faces, but many of their inborn, reflexive responses have an endearing quality about them (Bowlby, 1969). For example, the rooting, sucking, and grasping reflexes may lead parents to believe that their infant enjoys being close to them. Smiling, which is initially a reflexive response to almost any pleasing stimulus, is a particularly potent signal to caregivers, as are cooing, excitable blurting, and spontaneous babbling (Keller & Scholmerich, 1987). An adult's typical response to a baby's smiles and positive vocalizations is to smile at (or vocalize to) the infant (Gewirtz & Petrovich, 1982; Keller & Scholmerich, 1987). From 3 to 6 months of age infants become more likely to emit raised cheek, open-mouth (or big) smiles in response to a smiling caregiver, as if they are signaling their willingness to share positive affect with her (Messinger, Fogel, & Dickson, 2001). Parents often interpret their baby's grins, laughs, and babbles as an indication that the child is contented and that they are effective caregivers. A smiling or babbling infant can reinforce caregiving activities and thereby increase the likelihood that parents or other nearby companions will want to attend to this happy little person in the future.

Finally, Bowlby insists that under normal circumstances adults are just as biologically predisposed to respond favorably to a baby's signals as their baby is to emit them. It is difficult, he claims, for parents to ignore an urgent cry or to fail to warm up to a baby's big grin. In sum, human infants and their caregivers are said to have evolved in ways that predispose them to respond favorably to each other and to form close attachments, thus enabling infants (and ultimately, the species) to survive.

Does this mean that attachments are automatic? Bowlby claims that secure attachments develop gradually as parents become more proficient at reading and reacting appropriately to the baby's signals and as the baby learns what his parents are like and how he might regulate their behavior. The process can easily go wrong, resulting in insecure attachments, as illustrated by the finding that an infant's preprogrammed signals (such as crying and cooing for attention) eventually stop if those signals fail to produce favorable reactions from an unresponsive companion, such as a depressed mother or an unhappily married father (Ainsworth et al., 1978).

While Bowlby believes that human beings are biologically *prepared* to form close attachments, he also stresses that secure emotional bonds will not develop unless each participant has learned how to respond appropriately to the behavior of the other.

Comparing the Four Theoretical Approaches. Although the four theories we have reviewed differ in many respects, each has something to offer. Clearly, feeding practices are not as important to human attachments as psychoanalysts originally thought; but it was Freud who stressed that we need to know more about mother-infant interactions if we hope to understand how babies form attachments. Erik Erikson and the learning theorists pursued Freud's early leads and concluded that caregivers do play an important role in the infant's emotional development. Presumably, infants are likely to view a responsive companion who provides many comforts as a trustworthy and rewarding individual who is worthy of affection. Ethologists can agree with this point of view, but they add that infants are *active participants* in the attachment process who emit innate responses that enable them to promote the very interactions from which attachments are likely to develop. Finally, cognitive theorists have contributed by showing that the timing of emotional attachments is related to the infant's level of cognitive development. So it makes little sense to conclude that only one of these theories is "correct" and to ignore the others, for each theory has helped us to understand how infants become attached to their most intimate companions.

Attachment-Related Fears of Infancy

At about the same time that infants are establishing close affectional ties to a caregiver, they often begin to display negative emotional reactions that may puzzle or perhaps even annoy their companions. In this section we will briefly look at two of the common fears of infancy—*stranger anxiety* and *separation anxiety.*

Stranger Anxiety. Nine-month-old Micah is sitting on the floor in the den when his mother leads a strange person into the room. The stranger suddenly walks closer, bends over, and says "Hi, Micah! How are you?" If Micah is like many 9-month-olds, he may stare at the stranger for a moment and then turn away, whimper, and crawl toward his mother.

stranger anxiety
a wary or fretful reaction that infants and toddlers often display when approached by an unfamiliar person.

This wary reaction to a stranger, or **stranger anxiety,** stands in marked contrast to the smiling, babbling, and other positive greetings that infants display when approached by a familiar companion. Most infants react positively to strangers until they form their first attachment, and then become apprehensive shortly thereafter (Schaffer & Emerson, 1964). Wary reactions to strangers, which are often mixed with signs of interest, peak at 8 to 10 months of age, and gradually decline in intensity over the second year (Sroufe, 1977). However, even an 8- to 10-month-old is not afraid of every strange face she sees and may occasionally react positively to strangers. In the Box on p. 442, we consider the circumstances under which stranger anxiety is most likely to occur and see how medical personnel and other child-care professionals might use this knowledge to head off outbreaks of fear and trembling in their offices.

Separation Anxiety. Many infants who have formed primary attachments also begin to display obvious signs of discomfort when separated from their mothers or other attachment objects. Ten-month-old Rashime, for example, is likely to cry when he sees his mother put on a coat as she prepares to go shopping, whereas 15-month-old Kenesha might even follow her mother to the door while whining and pleading not to be left behind. These reactions reflect the children's **separation anxiety.** Separation anxiety normally appears at 6 to 8 months of age, peaks at 14 to 18 months, and gradually becomes less frequent and less intense throughout infancy and the preschool period (Kagan, Kearsley, & Zelazo, 1978; Weinraub & Lewis, 1977). Grade school children and even adolescents may still show signs of anxiety and depression when separated for long periods from their loved ones (Thurber, 1995).

separation anxiety
a wary or fretful reaction that infants and toddlers often display when separated from the person(s) to whom they are attached.

APPLYING RESEARCH TO YOUR LIFE

Combating Stranger Anxiety: Some Helpful Hints for Caregivers, Doctors, and Child-Care Professionals

It is not at all unusual for toddlers visiting the doctor's office to break into tears and to cling tenaciously to their parents. Some youngsters who remember previous visits may be suffering from "shot anxiety" rather than stranger anxiety, but many are simply reacting fearfully to the approach of an intrusive physician who may poke, prod, and handle them in ways that are atypical and upsetting. Fortunately, there are steps that caregivers and medical personnel (or any other stranger) can take to make such encounters less terrifying for an infant or toddler. What can we suggest?

- *Keep familiar companions available.* Infants react much more negatively to strangers when they are separated from their mothers or other close companions. Indeed, most 6- to 12-month-olds are not particularly wary of an approaching stranger if they are sitting on their mother's lap; however, they frequently whimper and cry at the stranger's approach if seated only a few feet from their mothers (Morgan & Ricciuti, 1969; and see Bohlin & Hagekull, 1993). Clearly, doctors and nurses can expect a more constructive response from their youngest patients if they can avoid separating them from their caregivers.
- *Arrange for companions to respond positively to the stranger.* Stranger anxiety is less likely to occur if the caregiver issues a warm greeting to the stranger or uses a positive tone of voice when talking to the infant about the stranger (Feinman, 1992). These actions permit the child to engage in *social referencing* and to conclude that maybe the stranger really isn't all that scary if mom and dad seem to like him. It might not hurt, then, for medical personnel to strike up a pleasant conversation with the caregiver before directing their attention to the child.
- *Make the setting more "familiar."* Stranger anxiety occurs less frequently in familiar settings than in unfamiliar ones. For example, few 10-month-olds are especially wary of strangers at home, but most react negatively to strange companions when tested in an unfamiliar laboratory (Sroufe, Waters, & Matas, 1974). Although it may be unrealistic to advise modern physicians to make home visits, they could make at least one of their examination rooms more homelike for young children, perhaps by placing an attractive mobile in one corner and posters of cartoon characters on the wall, or by having a stuffed toy or two available for the child to play with. The infant's familiarity with a strange setting also makes a difference: Whereas the vast majority (90 percent) of 10-month-olds become upset if a stranger approaches them within a minute after being placed in an unfamiliar room, only about half will react negatively to the stranger when they have had 10 minutes to grow accustomed to this setting (Sroufe, Waters, & Matas, 1974). Perhaps trips to the doctor would become more tolerable for an infant or a toddler if medical personnel gave the child a few minutes to familiarize himself with the examination room before making their entrance.
- *Be a sensitive, unobtrusive stranger.* Not surprisingly, an infant's response to a stranger depends on the stranger's behavior (Sroufe, 1977). The meeting is likely to go best if the stranger initially keeps his or her distance and then approaches slowly while smiling, talking, and offering a familiar toy or suggesting a familiar activity (Bretherton, Stolberg, & Kreye, 1981; Sroufe, 1977). It also helps if the stranger, like any sensitive caregiver, takes his or her cues from the infant (Mangelsdorf, 1992). Babies prefer strangers they can control! Intrusive strangers who approach quickly and force themselves on the child (for example, by trying to pick infants up before they have time to adjust) probably get the response they deserve.
- *Try looking a little less strange to the child.* Stranger anxiety depends, in part, on the stranger's physical appearance. Jerome Kagan (1972) has argued that infants form mental representations, or *schemas,* for the faces that they encounter in daily life and are most likely to be afraid of people whose appearance is not easily assimilated into these existing schemas. So a doctor in a sterile white lab coat with a strange stethoscope around her neck (or a nurse with a pointed hat that may give her a "witchlike" look) can make infants and toddlers rather wary indeed! Pediatric professionals may not be able to alter various physical features (for example, a huge nose or a facial scar) that might make children wary; but they can and often do shed their strange instruments and white uniforms in favor of more "normal" attire that will help their youngest patients to recognize them as members of the human race.

Why Do Infants Fear Strangers and Separations?

Why do infants who are just beginning to experience the pleasures of love suddenly become wary of strangers and anxious when separated from their objects of affection? Let's consider two views that have received some support.

The Ethological Viewpoint. Ethologist John Bowlby (1973) claims that many situations that infants face qualify as natural clues to danger: they have been so frequently associated with danger throughout human evolutionary history that a fear or avoidance response has become "biologically programmed." Among the situations that infants may be programmed to fear, once they can readily discriminate familiar objects and events from unfamiliar ones, are strange faces (which, in earlier eras, may have been a predatory animal), strange settings, and the "strange circumstance" of being separated from familiar companions.

Consistent with this ethological viewpoint, infants show stronger reactions to strangers and separations in an unfamiliar laboratory than at home; presumably the "strangeness" of the laboratory magnifies the apprehension they ordinarily experience upon encountering a stranger or having to endure a separation. This ethological viewpoint also explains an interesting cross-cultural variation in separation anxiety: Infants from many nonindustrialized societies, who sleep with their mothers and are nearly always in close contact with them, begin to protest separations about 2 to 3 months earlier than Western infants do. Why? Because those infants are so rarely apart from their caregivers that almost any separation is a very "strange" and fear-provoking event for them (Ainsworth, 1967). (As co-sleeping with infants becomes more common in the United States and other industrialized countries, we may see a shift in this cross-cultural difference in separation anxieties.)

Ethological theory also explains why stranger and separation anxieties decline during the second year. Once infants begin to walk and can use their attachment objects as *secure bases* for exploration, they actively initiate separations, becoming much more tolerant of them and much less wary of other novel stimuli (including friendly strangers) that had previously been a source of concern (Ainsworth, 1989; Posada et al., 1995).

The Cognitive-Developmental Viewpoint. Cognitive theorists view both stranger anxiety and separation anxiety as natural outgrowths of the infant's perceptual and cognitive development. Jerome Kagan (1972, 1976) suggests that 6- to 10-month-olds have developed stable schemes for (1) the faces of familiar companions and (2) the fact that absent companions do return. Suddenly a strange face that is discrepant with the infants' schemes for caregivers now upsets children because they can't explain who this is or what has become of familiar caregivers. Kagan also proposes that 7- to 10-month-olds will *not* protest most separations at home because they have a pretty good idea where a caregiver has gone should he leave them in the living room and proceed to a familiar area, such as the kitchen. But should a caregiver violate this "familiar faces in familiar places" scheme by lifting his briefcase and walking out the front door, an infant cannot easily account for his whereabouts and will probably cry.

Indeed, infants observed at home are more likely to protest when caregivers depart through an unfamiliar doorway (such as the entry to the cellar) than through a familiar one (Littenberg, Tulkin, & Kagan, 1971). And 9-month-old infants who have played quietly during a separation soon become extremely upset after looking for their mother and discovering that she is not where they thought she was (Corter, Zucker, & Galligan, 1980). Clearly, these observations support Kagan's theory: Infants are most likely to protest separations from a caregiver when they are uncertain about her whereabouts.

In sum, stranger anxiety and separation anxiety are relatively complex emotional responses that stem, in part, from an infant's general apprehension of the unfamiliar (the ethological viewpoint), and her inability to explain who a stranger may be or what has become of familiar companions (cognitive-developmental viewpoint). Yet, it is important to note that infants vary dramatically in their responses to separations and strangers: some are almost indifferent to these events, whereas others act as if they are terrified. Why the variations? Developmentalists now believe that these differences in reactions often reflect individual differences in the quality, or security, of infant's attachment relationships. See Table 11.1 for an overview of theories of attachment.

TABLE 11.1 Each Theory of Attachment has a Different Perspective on the Basis of Attachment and Attachment Related Behaviors, and Together the Four Theories Help to Explain the Complexity of the Attachment Relationship.

Attachment Theory	Basis of Attachment Formation	Attachment Related Behaviors
Psychoanalytic Theory	Feeding and responsiveness to infant's needs	Caregiver's responsiveness to infant's hunger and other basic needs
Learning Theory	Caregivier becomes secondary reinforcer following basic learning principles	Feeding and responsiveness to infant's needs Providing pleasant and rewarding experience to infant
Cognitive Developmental Theory	Level of cognitive development	Infant discriminates between caregivers and strangers Infant attains object permanence, recognizing that caregivers continue to exist even when absent from view
Ethological Theory	Innate behavorial tendencies ensure attachment and attachment ensures survival of infants	Imprinting in animals Infants have characteristics that elicit attachment from caregivers

CONCEPT CHECK 11.2 Understanding Attachments and Theories of Attachment

Check your understanding of the development of attachments and important theories of attachment by answering the following questions. Answers appear in the Appendix.

Matching: Match the theory of attachment to the propositions that follow.

a. psychoanalytic theory
b. learning theory
c. cognitive developmental theory
d. ethological theory

1. _______ This theory proposes that infants are attached once the caregiver attains the status of a secondary reinforcer.
2. _______ This theory proposes that infants protest separations when they cannot account for the caregiver's whereabouts.
3. _______ This theory proposes that the caregiver's feeding practices determine the strength of infant attachments.

Multiple Choice: Select the theorist who made the arguments described below.

_____ 4. This theorist argued that the caregiver's responsiveness and the infant's feelings of trust were the primary determinants of attachment security.
a. Mary Ainsworth
b. John Bowlby
c. Erik Erikson
d. Konrad Lorenz

_____ 5. This theorist argued that strange faces and separations from attachment objects are natural clues to danger that infants are programmed to fear.
a. Mary Ainsworth
b. John Bowlby
c. Erik Erikson
d. Konrad Lorenz

_____ 6. This theorist argued that newborn creatures imprint upon their caregivers during a critical period in early development.
a. Mary Ainsworth
b. John Bowlby
c. Erik Erikson
d. Konrad Lorenz

Fill in the Blank: Complete the following statements with the correct concept or phrase.

7. _______ is an attachment-related fear that develops late in the infant's first year, peaking at 8 to 10 months of age, and then declines during the infant's second year. Making new people and new situations as familiar as possible is one way to combat this fear. Offering the infants toys is another way to combat this fear.
8. _______ help infants and caregivers develop a relationship by showing caregivers how to respond to the infants' emotions.

Short Answer: Provide brief answers to the following questions.

9. List in order the phases through which infants pass in their development of attachments.

Essay: Provide a detailed answer to the following question.

10. Describe the contributions of the infant and the contributions of the caregiver to the development of attachments.

TABLE 11.2 The Eight Episodes of the Strange Situation

Episode	Events	Potential attachment behaviors noted
1.	Experimenter introduces parent and baby to playroom and leaves.	
2.	Parent sits while baby plays.	Parent as a secure base
3.	Stranger enters, sits, and talks to parent.	Stranger anxiety
4.	Parent leaves, stranger offers comfort if the baby is upset.	Separation anxiety
5.	Parent returns, greets baby, and offers comfort if baby is upset. Stranger leaves.	Reunion behaviors
6.	Parent leaves room.	Separation anxiety
7.	Stranger enters and offers comfort.	Ability to be soothed by stranger
8.	Parent returns, greets baby, offers comfort if necessary, and tries to interest baby in toys.	Reunion behaviors

Note: Episodes two through eight last for 3 minutes each, although separation episodes may be cut short and reunion episodes may be expanded for babies who become extremely upset.
Source: Based on *Patterns of Attachment*, by M. D. S. Ainsworth, M. Blehar, E. Waters, & S. Wall, 1978. Copyright © 1978 by Lawrence Erlbaum Associates, Inc. Reprinted by permission.

Individual Differences in Attachment Quality

The attachment relationships that virtually all home-reared infants establish with their caregivers clearly differ in quality. Some infants are quite secure and relaxed around caregivers, whereas others seem highly anxious or uncertain about what to expect next. Why are some infants secure and others insecure in their attachment relationships? Does the security of a child's early attachments have any impact on later development? To answer these questions, researchers first had to find ways of measuring attachment quality.

Strange Situation
a series of eight separation and reunion episodes to which infants are exposed in order to determine the quality of their attachments.

Assessing Attachment Security. The most widely used technique for measuring the quality of attachments that 1- to 2-year-olds have established with their parents or other caregivers is Mary Ainsworth's **Strange Situation** (Ainsworth et al., 1978). The Strange Situation consists of a series of eight episodes (summarized in Table 11.2 that attempt to simulate (1) naturalistic caregiver–infant interactions in the presence of toys (to see if the infant uses the caregiver as a *secure base* from which to explore); (2) brief separations from the caregiver and encounters with strangers (which will often stress the infant); and (3) reunion episodes (to determine whether a stressed infant derives any comfort and reassurance from the caregiver and can once again become involved with toys). By recording and analyzing an infant's responses to these episodes—that is, exploratory activities, reactions to strangers and to separations, and, in particular, behaviors when reunited with the close companion—it is usually possible to characterize his or her attachment to the caregiver in one of four ways:

secure attachment
an infant-caregiver bond in which the child welcomes contact with a close companion and uses this person as a secure base from which to explore the environment.

resistant attachment
an insecure infant-caregiver bond, characterized by strong separation protest and a tendency of the child to remain near but resist contact initiated by the caregiver, particularly after a separation.

Secure Attachment. About 65 percent of 1-year-old North American infants fall into this category. The **securely attached** infant actively explores while alone with the mother and may be visibly upset by separations. The infant often greets the mother warmly when she returns and, if highly distressed, often seeks physical contact with her, which helps to alleviate that distress. The child is outgoing with strangers while the mother is present.

Resistant Attachment. About 10 percent of 1-year-olds show this type of "insecure" attachment. These infants try to stay close to their mother but explore very little while she is present. They become very distressed as the mother departs. But when she returns, the infants are ambivalent: They remain near her, although they seem angry at her for having left them and are likely to resist physical contact initiated by the mother. Resistant infants are quite wary of strangers, even when their mothers are present.

avoidant attachment
an insecure infant-caregiver bond, characterized by little separation protest and a tendency of the child to avoid or ignore the caregiver.

Avoidant Attachment. These infants (about 20 percent of 1-year-olds) also display an "insecure" attachment. They often show little distress when separated from the mother and will generally turn away from and may continue to ignore their mothers, even when their mothers try to gain their attention. Avoidant infants are often rather sociable with strangers but may sometimes avoid or ignore them in much the same way that they avoid or ignore their mothers.

disorganized/disoriented attachment
an insecure infant-caregiver bond, characterized by the infant's dazed appearance on reunion or a tendency to first seek and then abruptly avoid the caregiver.

Disorganized/Disoriented Attachment. This attachment pattern characterizes the 5 percent of American infants who are most stressed by the Strange Situation and who may be the most insecure (NICHD Early Child Care Research Network, 2001a). It appears to be a curious combination of the resistant and the avoidant patterns that reflects confusion about whether to approach or avoid the caregiver (Main & Solomon, 1990). When reunited with their mothers, these infants may act dazed and freeze, or they may move closer but then abruptly move away as the mother draws near, or they may show both patterns in different reunion episodes.

There is current controversy about whether attachment should be understood as existing in distinct types or categories, as those described above. Some researchers argue that an attachment style continuum would more accurately reflect the relationships between infants and their caregivers (e.g., Fraley & Spieker, 2003; and special issue of *Developmental Psychology*, 2003). Until this debate is resolved in the literature, we can best make sense of the vast amount of research on attachment by adopting those categories most often used in the developmental research (that is, the ones described above).

The Strange Situation is not as useful for characterizing the attachments of children much older than 2 who are becoming quite accustomed to (and less stressed by) brief separations and encounters with strangers (but see Moss et al., 2004). An alternative assessment of attachment quality—the **Attachment Q-set (AQS)**—has become quite popular. Appropriate for use with 1- to 5-year-olds, the Attachment Q-set requires an observer, usually a parent or trained observer, to sort a set of 90 descriptors of attachment-related behaviors (for example, "Child looks to caregiver for reassurance when wary"; "Child greets caregiver with big smiles. . . .") into categories ranging from "most like" to "least like" the child's behavior at home. The resulting profile represents how secure the child is with his or her caregiver (Waters et al., 1995). Trained observers' Q-set assessments for infants and toddlers are usually the same as Strange Situation attachment classifications for the children (Pederson & Moran, 1996; Vaughn & Waters, 1990). The ability to classify the attachment security of older preschool children in their natural environments makes the AQS a versatile alternative to the Strange Situation.

Attachment Q-set (AQS)
alternative method of assessing attachment security that is based on observations of the child's attachment-related behaviors at home; can be used with infants, toddlers, and preschool children.

Developmental psychologists have also found it useful to use individual differences in adults' attachment security to investigate their relationships and parenting behaviors (Adam, Gunnar, & Tanaka, 2004; Treboux, Crowell, & Waters, 2004). Attachment types are identified in adults with a questionnaire, the Adult Attachment Inventory, that assesses the quality of current and past relationships (George, Kaplan, & Main, 1985). Research investigating attachment styles in adults has found that married couples who share secure attachment styles are more satisfied with their relationships, self-confident, and experience lower conflict in their relationships than married couples who are insecure in their attachment styles (Treboux, Crowell, & Waters, 2004). In addition, mothers who have secure attachment styles are rated more positively in their parenting styles than those who have insecure attachment styles.

Cultural Variations in Attachment Classifications

The percentages of infants and toddlers who fall into the various attachment categories differ somewhat from culture to culture and seem to reflect cultural variations in child rearing. For example, parents in northern Germany deliberately encourage their infants to be independent and tend to discourage clingy close contact, perhaps explaining why more German than American babies show reunion behaviors characteristic of the avoidant attachment pattern (Grossmann et al., 1985). Furthermore, intense separation and stranger anxieties, which characterize resistant attachments, are much more common in cultures such as Japan, where caregivers rarely leave their infants with substitute caregivers. In Israel, where communally reared kibbutz children who sleep in infant houses without their parents being accessible to them at night are found to have more insecure attachment relationships than children who sleep at home with their mothers, and this is theoretically linked to mothers' emotional unavailability (Aviezer et al., 1999).

Western researchers generally interpret these findings as evidence that the meanings of attachment relationships and attachment security are culturally universal, and that cultural variations in attachment classifications simply illustrate how different patterns of caregiving across cultures lead to varying percentages of securely or insecurely attached infants (van Ijzendoorn & Sagi, 1999; Waters & Cummings, 2000). We agree with other researchers who argue that what qualifies as a secure (or an insecure) attachment varies from culture to culture.

In Japan, for example, mothers respond very differently to babies than Western mothers (Rothbaum, Pott, et al., 2000; Rothbaum, Weisz, et al., 2000). Compared to American mothers, Japanese mothers have much more close contact with their infants and strive to anticipate and satisfy all their babies' needs, rather than react to their needy babies' cries. Japanese mothers emphasize social routines more and exploration less than American mothers do, and they seek to promote the infant's **amae** (pronounced "ah-MY-ay")—a state of total dependence on the mother and a presumption of mother love and indulgence. Given these child-rearing practices, it is hardly surprising that Japanese babies are upset by separations and will cling to their mother on reunion. These are behaviors that cause many of them to be classified as insecurely attached when tested in the Strange Situation. The establishment of a healthy sense of amae is considered highly adaptive in Japan, a hallmark of attachment *security.* Amae is important because it sets the stage for the development of a culturally valued communal orientation (or symbiotic harmony): one in which Japanese children learn to become interdependent by accommodating to other's needs, cooperating, and working toward the accomplishment of group goals (Rothbaum, Weisz, et al., 2000). A secure attachment in Western societies is one in which infants have been encouraged to separate themselves from their watchful and protective caregivers to explore the environment, to become independent and autonomous, and to pursue mostly *individual* goals.

amae
Japanese concept; refers to an infant's feeling of total dependence on his or her mother and the presumption of mother's love and indulgence.

In sum, both the meaning and the long-range outcomes of "secure" attachments may vary from culture to culture and reflect important cultural values. What seems to be universal is that parents around the world prefer that their youngsters feel secure in their relationships with them, and most parents try to promote culturally valued forms of security (Posada et al., 1995, 1999; Rothbaum, Pott, et al., 2000).

Unfortunately, most of the research conducted to date has focused exclusively on caregiving provided by mothers and has largely ignored fathers. Let's take a closer look at fathers as caregivers and at the contributions that fathers can make to their infants' social and emotional development.

Keren Su/Stone/Getty Images

Although child-rearing traditions vary dramatically across cultures, secure attachments are more common than insecure attachments around the world.

Fathers as Caregivers

In 1975, Michael Lamb described fathers as the "forgotten contributors to child development." And he was right. Until the mid-1970s fathers were treated as biological necessities who played only a minor role in the social and emotional development of their infants and toddlers. One reason for overlooking or discounting the father's early contributions may have been that fathers spend less time interacting with babies than mothers (Belsky, Gilstrap, & Rovine, 1984; Parke, 1995). Nevertheless, fathers appear to be just as fascinated with their newborn infants as mothers are (Nichols, 1993), and they become increasingly involved with their babies over the first year of life (Belsky, Gilstrap, & Rovine, 1984), spending an average of nearly an hour a day interacting with their 9-month-olds (Ninio & Rinott, 1988). Fathers are most highly involved with their infants and hold more favorable attitudes about them when they are happily married (Belsky, 1996; Cox et al., 1989, 1992) and when their wives encourage them to become an important part of their babies' lives (DeLuccie, 1995; Palkovitz, 1984). (A happy marriage is also a key contributor to mothers' interactions and attachments with their infants, a point we will discuss further later in this chapter.)

Attachment. Many infants form secure attachments to their fathers during the latter half of the first year, particularly if the father has a positive attitude about parenting, spends considerable time with them, and is a sensitive caregiver (van IJzendoorn & De Wolff, 1997). How do fathers compare to mothers as companions? Research conducted in Australia, Israel, India, Italy, Japan, and the United States reveals that mothers and fathers in all these societies tend to play somewhat different roles in a baby's life. Mothers are more likely than fathers to hold their infants, to soothe and talk to them, to play traditional games such as peekaboo, and to care for their physical needs; fathers are more likely than mothers to provide playful physical stimulation and to initiate unusual or unpredictable games that infants often enjoy. Although most infants prefer their mothers' company when upset or afraid, fathers are often preferred as playmates (Lamb, 1997; Roopnarine et al., 1990).

However, the playmate role is but one of many that modern fathers fulfill, particularly if their wives are working and they must assume at least some of the caregiving burden (Grych & Clark, 1999; Pleck, 1997). And what kinds of caregivers do dads make? Many of them are (or soon become) rather skillful at virtually all phases of routine care (including diapering, bathing, and soothing a distressed infant). Moreover, once fathers become objects of affection they begin to serve as a secure base from which their babies will venture to explore the environment (Hwang, 1986; Lamb, 1997). So fathers are rather versatile companions who can assume any and all functions normally served by the other parent (of course, the same is true of mothers).

Fathers as Contributors to Emotional Security and Other Social Competencies. Although many infants form the same kind of attachment with their fathers that they establish with their mothers (Fox, Kimmerly, & Schafer, 1991; Rosen & Rothbalm, 1993), it is not at all unusual for a child to be securely attached to one parent and insecure with the other (van IJzendoorn & De Wolff, 1997). For example, when Mary Main and Donna Weston (1981) used the Strange Situation to measure the quality of 44 toddlers' attachments to their mothers and their fathers, they found that 12 toddlers were securely attached to both parents, 11 were secure with the mother but insecure with the father, 10 were insecure with the mother but secure with the father, and 11 were insecurely attached to both parents.

For many infants, fathers assume the role of special playmate.

What does the father add to a child's social and emotional development? One way to find out is to compare the social behavior of children who are securely attached to their fathers to those whose relationships with their fathers are insecure. Main and Weston did just that by exposing their four groups of toddlers to a friendly stranger in a clown outfit who spent several minutes trying to play with the child and then turned around and cried when a person at the door told the clown he would have to leave. As the clown went through his routine, the toddlers were each observed and rated for (1) the extent to which they were willing to establish a positive relationship with the clown (low ratings indicated that the infant was wary or distressed) and (2) signs of emotional conflict (that is, indications of psychological disturbance such as curling up in the fetal position on the floor or

Measure	Patterns of attachment: Securely attached to both parents	Secure with mother, insecure with father	Insecure with mother, secure with father	Insecurely attached to both parents
Social responsiveness	6.04	4.87	3.30	2.45
Emotional conflict	1.17	1.00	1.80	2.50

Note: Social responsiveness ratings could vary from 1 (wary, distressed) to 9 (happy, responsive). Conflict ratings could vary from 1 (no conflict) to 5 (very conflicted).
Source: Adapted from Main & Weston, 1981.

Figure 11.5 Average levels of social responsiveness and emotional conflict shown by infants who were either securely or insecurely attached to their mothers and fathers. Note: Social responsiveness ratings could vary from 1 (wary, distressed) to 9 (happy, responsive). Conflict ratings could vary from 1 (no conflict) to 5 (very conflicted). *Adapted from "The Quality of the Toddler's Relationship to Mother and to Father: Related to Conflict and the Readiness to Establish New Relationships," by M. Main & D. R. Weston, 1981,* Child Development, *52, 932–940. Copyright © 1981 by The Society for Research in Child Development, Inc. Adapted with permission.*

vocalizing in a "social" manner to a wall). Figure 11.5 shows the results of this stranger test. Note that toddlers who were securely attached to both parents were the most socially responsive group. Equally important is the finding that toddlers who were securely attached to at least one parent were more friendly toward the clown and less emotionally conflicted than those who had insecure relationships with both parents. Other recent research has shown that, compared to children who are securely attached to only one or neither parent, those who are secure with both parents are less anxious and socially withdrawn and make better adjustments to the challenges of attending school (Verschueren & Marcoen, 1999). Children who are secure with their fathers also display better emotional self-regulation, greater social competencies with peers, and lower levels of problem behaviors and delinquency throughout childhood and adolescence (Cabrera et al., 2000; Lieberman, Doyle, & Markiewicz, 1999). Indeed, the positive benefits of having a secure, supportive relationship with one's father often occur even if he may no longer be residing in the home (Black, Dubowitz, & Starr, 1999; Coley, 1998). So not only are fathers potentially important contributors to many (perhaps all) aspects of child development, but it seems that a secure attachment to one's father may help to buffer against the potentially harmful effects of an insecure mother-child attachment relationship (Main & Weston, 1981; Verschueren & Marcoen, 1999). Nevertheless, a secure attachment with *both* parents contributes the most to a child's development (Verschueren & Marcoen, 1999).

Factors That Influence Attachment Security

Among the many factors that seem to influence the kinds of attachments that infants establish are the quality of caregiving they receive, the character or emotional climate of their homes, and their own health conditions and temperaments. Much of what we know about the origins of secure and insecure attachments comes from research conducted in European and North American cultures, and most has focused on mothers as primary attachment objects. With this limitation in mind, let's see what researchers have learned about how Western infants become securely or insecurely attached.

Quality of Caregiving

Mary Ainsworth (1979) believes that the quality of an infant's attachment to his mother (or any other close companion) depends largely on the kind of attention he has received.

giving hypothesis
sworth's notion that the type of attachment that an infant develops with a particular caregiver depends primarily on the kind of caregiving he has received from that person.

According to this **caregiving hypothesis,** mothers of *securely attached* infants are thought to be sensitive, responsive caregivers from the very beginning. And apparently they are. A review of 66 studies found that mothers who display the characteristics described in Table 11.3 tend to have infants who form secure attachments with them (De Wolff & van IJzendoorn, 1997). So if a caregiver has a positive attitude toward her baby, is usually sensitive to his needs, has established interactional synchrony with him, and provides ample stimulation and emotional support, the infant often derives comfort and pleasure from their interactions and is likely to become securely attached.

Babies who show a *resistant* rather than secure pattern of attachment sometimes have irritable and unresponsive temperaments (Cassidy & Berlin, 1994; Waters, Vaughn, & Egeland, 1980); more often they have parents who are *inconsistent* in their caregiving—reacting enthusiastically or indifferently depending on their moods and being unresponsive a good deal of the time (Ainsworth, 1979; Isabella, 1993; Isabella & Belsky, 1991). The infant copes with this inconsistent caregiving by trying desperately, through clinging, crying, and other attachment behaviors, to obtain emotional support and comfort and then becomes angry and resentful when these efforts often fail.

There are at least two patterns of caregiving that place infants at risk of developing *avoidant* attachments. Ainsworth and others (for example, Isabella, 1993) find that some mothers of avoidant infants are often impatient with their babies and unresponsive to their signals, are likely to express negative feelings about their infants, and seem to derive little pleasure from close contact with them. Ainsworth (1979) believes that these mothers are rigid, self-centered people who are likely to reject their babies. In other cases, however, avoidant babies have overzealous parents who chatter endlessly and provide high levels of stimulation even when their babies do not want it (Belsky, Rovine, & Taylor, 1984; Isabella & Belsky, 1991). Infants may be responding quite adaptively by learning to avoid adults who seem to dislike their company or who bombard them with stimulation they cannot handle. Whereas resistant infants make vigorous attempts to gain emotional support, avoidant infants seem to have learned to do without it (Isabella, 1993).

Finally, Mary Main believes that infants who develop *disorganized/disoriented* attachments are often drawn to but also fearful of caregivers because of past episodes in which they were neglected or physically abused (Main & Soloman, 1990). The infant's approach/avoidance (or totally dazed demeanor) at reunion is quite understandable if she has experienced cycles of acceptance and abuse (or neglect) and doesn't know whether to approach the caregiver for comfort or to retreat from her to safety. Available research supports Main's theorizing: although disorganized/disoriented attachments are occasionally observed in any research sample, they seem to be the rule rather than the exception among groups of abused infants (Carlson, 1998; Carlson et al., 1989; True, Pisani, & Oumar, 2001). This curious mixture of approach and avoidance, coupled with sadness upon reunion, also characterizes many infants of severely depressed mothers, who may

TABLE 11.3 Aspects of Caregiving That Promote Secure Mother-Infant Attachments

Characteristic	Description
Sensitivity	Responding promptly and appropriately to the infant's signals
Positive attitude	Expressing positive affect and affection for the infant
Synchrony	Structuring smooth, reciprocal interactions with the infant
Mutuality	Structuring interactions in which mother and infant attend to the same thing
Support	Attending closely to and providing emotional support for the infant's activities
Stimulation	Frequently directing actions toward the infant

Note: These six aspects of caregiving are moderately correlated with each other.
Source: Based on "Sensitivity and Attachment: A Meta-Analysis on Parental Antecedents of Infant Attachment," by M. S. De Wolff and M. H. van IJzendoorn, 1997, *Child Development, 68,* 571–591.

be inclined to mistreat or neglect their babies (Lyons-Ruth et al., 1990; Murray et al., 1996; Teti et al., 1995).

Who Is at Risk of Becoming an Insensitive Caregiver? Several personal characteristics place parents at risk of displaying the insensitive patterns of parenting that contribute to insecure attachments. Insecure attachments of one kind or the other are typical of infants of clinically depressed caregivers (Radke-Yarrow et al., 1985; Kaplan, Dungan, & Zinse, 2004; Teti et al., 1995). Depressed parents often ignore babies' social signals and generally fail to establish satisfying and synchronous relationships with them. Infants often become angry at these caregivers' lack of responsiveness and may soon begin to match their depressive symptoms, even when interacting with other *nondepressed* adults (Campbell, Cohn, & Meyers, 1995; Field et al., 1988).

Another group of parents who are often insensitive caregivers are those who themselves felt unloved, neglected, or abused as children. These formerly mistreated caregivers often start out with the best intentions, vowing never to do to their children what was done to them, but they often expect their infants to be perfect and to love them right away. So when their babies are irritable, fussy, or inattentive (as all infants are at times), these emotionally insecure adults are likely to feel as if they are being rejected once again (Steele & Pollack, 1974). They may then back off or withdraw their own affection (Biringen, 1990; Crowell & Feldman, 1991), sometimes to the point of neglecting or even abusing their babies.

Caregivers whose pregnancies were unplanned and their babies unwanted can be particularly insensitive caregivers whose children fare rather poorly in all aspects of development. In one longitudinal study in Czechoslovakia (Matejcek, Dytrych, & Schuller, 1979), mothers who had been denied permission to abort an unwanted pregnancy were judged to be less closely attached to their children than a group of same-aged mothers of similar marital and socioeconomic status who had not requested an abortion. Although both the wanted and the unwanted children were physically healthy at birth, over the next 9 years the unwanted children were more frequently hospitalized, made lower grades in school, had less stable family lives and poorer relations with peers, and were generally more irritable than the children whose parents had wanted them. Follow-up observations in young adulthood tell much the same story: compared with their wanted peers, the formerly unwanted children were now much less satisfied with their marriages, jobs, friendships, and general mental health, having more often sought treatment for a variety of psychological disorders (David, 1992, 1994). Although this study is correlational rather than experimental, it suggests that parents are unlikely to be very sensitive or to foster the development of children they did not intend to raise.

Insensitive parenting is more likely to occur in families experiencing health-related, financial, or marital distress.

Ecological Constraints on Caregiving Sensitivity. Of course, parent-child interactions always take place in a broader ecological context that may influence how caregivers respond to their children. Insensitive parenting, for example, is much more likely among caregivers who are experiencing health-related, legal, or financial problems. It is hardly surprising that the incidence of insecure attachments is highest among poverty-stricken families that receive inadequate health care, or those who have to hold down multiple jobs leading to prolonged absences from their children, a point we will consider in more detail later in the chapter (Murray et al., 1996; NICHD Early Child Care Research Network, 1997; Rosenkrantz & Huston, 2004).

The quality of a caregiver's relationship with his or her spouse can also have a dramatic effect on parent-infant interactions. Consider that parents who were unhappily married *prior* to the birth of their child (1) are less sensitive caregivers after the baby is born, (2) express less favorable attitudes about their infants and the parenting role, and (3) establish less secure ties with their infants and toddlers, compared with other parents from similar socioeconomic backgrounds whose marriages are close and confiding (Cox et al., 1989; Howes & Markman, 1989). Happily married couples usually support each other's parenting efforts. This positive social support for parenting is especially important if the baby has already shown a tendency to be irritable and unresponsive. Jay Belsky (1981) found that newborns who are at risk for later emotional difficulties (as indicated by their poor performance on the Brazelton Neonatal Behavioral Assessment Scale, the test of physical and neurological difficulties discussed in Chapter 4) are likely to have nonsynchronous interactions with their parents *only when the parents are unhappily married.* So it seems that a stormy marriage is a major environmental hazard that can hinder or even prevent the establishment of secure emotional ties between parents and their infants.

What Can Be Done to Assist Insensitive Caregivers? Fortunately, there are ways of assisting at-risk parents to become more sensitive and responsive caregivers. The field of infant mental health (IMH) combines theory, research, and therapy from various fields such as developmental psychology, social work, education, and pediatric medicine to provide intervention and assistance to caregivers of very young infants to promote infants' healthy development (see Tomlin & Viehweg, 2003, for an overview of IMH.)

In one intervention, depressed poverty-stricken mothers were visited regularly by a professional, who first established a friendly, supportive relationship, and then taught them how to elicit more favorable responses from their babies and encouraged their participation in weekly parenting groups. Toddlers whose mothers received this support later scored higher on intelligence tests and were much more likely to be securely attached than those of other depressed mothers who hadn't participated in an intervention (Lyons-Ruth et al., 1990).

In another intervention in Holland, economically disadvantaged mothers whose babies were extremely irritable received a 3-month intervention designed to improve the mothers' sensitivity and responsiveness to their infants' difficult temperaments. Not only did these mothers become more sensitive caregivers, but their infants were more likely than those of comparable mothers who received no intervention to be securely attached at age 12 months and to remain more secure with their mothers at age $3\frac{1}{2}$ years (van den Boom, 1995). The intervention studies clearly indicate that caregiving sensitivity can be fostered and that it promotes secure attachments. But are there characteristics of the infants that contribute to the quality of the attachment relationship? Yes indeed, as we will examine next.

Infant Characteristics

Thus far, we have talked as if parents are totally responsible for the kind of attachments infants establish. But because it takes two people to form an attachment relationship, we might suspect that babies can also influence the quality of parent-infant emotional ties. Jerome Kagan (1984, 1989) argued that the Strange Situation really measures individual differences in infants' temperaments rather than the quality of their attachments. This idea grew from his observation that the percentages of 1-year-olds who have established *secure, resistant,* and *avoidant* attachments corresponds closely to the percentages of babies who fall into Thomas and Chess's *easy, difficult,* and *slow-to-warm-up* temperamental profiles (see Table 11.4). And the linkages make sense. A temperamentally difficult infant who actively resists changes in routine and is upset by novelty may become so distressed by the Strange Situation that he is unable to respond constructively to his mother's comforting and is thus classified as resistant. A friendly, easygoing child is apt to be classified as "securely attached," whereas one who is shy or "slow to warm up" may appear distant or detached in the Strange Situation and will probably be classified as avoidant. So Kagan's **temperament hypothesis** implies that infants, not caregivers, are the primary architects of their attachment classifications and that the attachment behaviors that a child displays reflect his or her own temperament.

temperament hypothesis
Kagan's view that the Strange Situation measures individual differences in infants' temperaments rather than the quality of their attachments.

TABLE 11.4 Percentage of 1-Year-Olds Who Can Be Classified as Temperamentally "Easy," "Difficult," and "Slow to Warm Up" Who Have Established Secure, Resistant, and Avoidant Attachments with Their Mothers

Temperamental profile	Percentage of "classifiable" infants	Attachment classification	Percentage of 1-year-olds
Easy	60	Secure	65
Difficult	15	Resistant	10
Slow to warm up	23	Avoidant	20

Source: Ainsworth, Blehar, Waters, & Wall, 1978; Thomas & Chess, 1977.

Does Temperament Explain Attachment Security? Although such components of temperament as irritability and negative emotionality reliably predict certain attachment behaviors (for example, intensity of separation protests) (Goldsmith & Alansky, 1987; Kochanska & Coy, 2002; Seifer et al., 1996), most experts view Kagan's temperament hypothesis as far too extreme. Consider, for example, that many infants are securely attached to one close companion and insecurely attached to another. This is a pattern that we would not expect to see if attachment classifications were merely reflections of the child's relatively stable temperamental characteristics (Goossens & van IJzendoorn, 1990; Sroufe, 1985).

In addition, we have already seen that when mothers of *temperamentally difficult* Dutch infants are trained to be more sensitive, the vast majority of their babies establish secure rather than insecure attachments, which indicates that sensitive caregiving is causally related to attachment quality (van den Boom, 1995). One review of 34 studies revealed that maternal characteristics that often predict insensitive parenting, such as illness, depression, and child maltreatment, were associated with a sharp increase in insecure attachments (see Figure 11.6). Child temperamental problems stemming from prematurity, illness, and other psychological disorders had virtually no impact on attachment quality (van IJzendoorn et al., 1992).

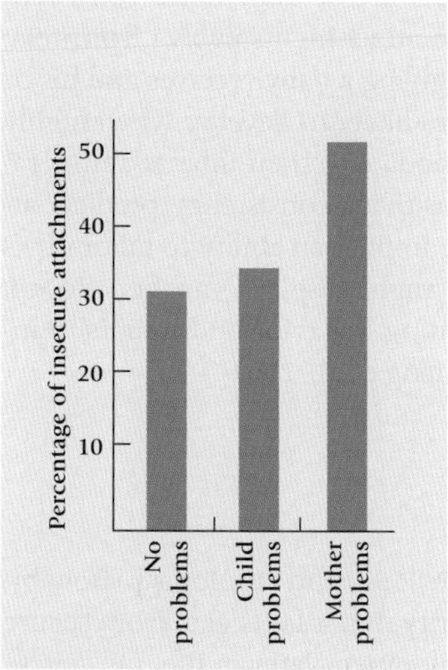

Figure 11.6 Comparing the impact of maternal and child problem behaviors on the incidence of insecure attachments. Maternal problems were associated with a sharp increase in insecure attachments, whereas child problems were not. *Based on "The Relative Effects of Maternal and Child Problems on the Quality of Attachment: A Meta-Analysis of Attachment in Clinical Samples," by M. H. van IJzendoorn, S. Goldberg, P. M. Kroonenberg, and O. J. Frenkel, 1992,* Child Development, *63, 840–858. Copyright © 1992 by the Society for Research in Child Development, Inc.*

Finally, a recent study of identical and same-sex fraternal twins revealed that 70 percent of the identical twin pairs and 64 percent of the fraternal twins established the same kind of attachments (that is, both twins secure or both insecure) with their caregiver (O'Connor & Croft, 2001). These findings have two important implications. First, because concordance in attachment classifications was not much higher for the identical twin pairs, it appears that genetic contributions to children's attachments (including the contribution of genetically influenced components of temperament) were modest. Second, because most twins were concordant in their attachment classifications, shared environmental influences (for example, interacting with the same sensitive or insensitive caregiver) must have contributed substantially to the resemblances in attachments that twin siblings displayed.

The Combined Influences of Caregiving and Temperament

Although the findings just cited seem to favor Ainsworth's caregiving hypothesis over Kagan's temperamental model, more recent research suggests a more complicated relationship among various factors (e.g., Seifer et al., 2004). One study clearly illustrates the important link between sensitive caregiving and secure attachments while also demonstrating how child temperament can sometimes contribute to the kinds of attachments infants form. Let's take a look.

Grazyna Kochanska (1998) sought to test an integrative theory of infant-caregiver attachments—one specifying that (1) quality of caregiving is most important in determining whether an infant's emerging attachments are secure or insecure, but (2) infant temperament is the better predictor of the type of insecurity infants display, should their attachments be insecure. Kochanska began by measuring quality of caregiving mothers provided (that is, maternal responsiveness to her infant and the synchrony of positive emotions between mother and infant) when their babies were 8 to 10 months and 13 to 15 months old. She also assessed the aspect of infant temperament know as fearfulness. Fearful children are prone to show strong distress in new and uncertain situations and are similar to those children that Kagan calls *behaviorally inhibited*. *Fearless* children, by contrast, are largely unperturbed by strange settings, people, or separations, and are similar to children that Kagan refers to as *behaviorally uninhibited*. Finally, Kochanska used the Strange Situation to assess the quality of infants' attachments to their mothers at age 13 to 15 months. Thus, she had data allowing her to determine whether caregiving or temperament contributed more strongly to the security and specific type of attachments that infants display.

The study produced two particularly interesting sets of results. First, as anticipated by the integrative theory, quality of caregiving (but not infant temperament) clearly predicted whether infants established secure or insecure attachments with their mothers, with positive, responsive parenting being associated with secure attachments. And yet, quality of caregiving did not predict the specific type of insecurity that infants with insecure attachments displayed.

What, then, predicted *type* of insecurity? Infant temperament did! As anticipated by the integrative theory and a knowledge of the fearlessness/fearfulness dimension, temperamentally fearful children who had insecure attachments were prone to display resistant attachments, whereas the insecure infants who were temperamentally fearless were more likely to display avoidant attachments.

Clearly, the findings imply that strong versions of both the caregiving and the temperament hypothesis are overstatements. In fact, the data are actually quite consistent with Thomas and Chess's goodness of fit model: secure attachments evolve from relationships in which there is a "good fit" between the caregiving a baby receives and his or her own temperament, whereas insecure attachments are likely to develop when highly stressed or otherwise inflexible caregivers fail to accommodate to their infants' temperamental qualities. Indeed, one reason why caregiver sensitivity consistency predicts attachment security is that the very notion of sensitive care implies an ability to tailor one's routines to whatever temperamental qualities a baby might display (van den Boom, 1995). Indeed, the intricate relationships between parenting behavior and infants' temperament and behavior continue into childhood (e.g., Chang et al., 2003).

Attachment and Later Development

Both psychoanalytic theorists (Erikson, 1963; Freud, 1905/1930) and ethologists (Bowlby, 1969) believe that the feelings of warmth, trust, and security that infants gain from secure attachments set the stage for healthy psychological development later in life. Of course one implication of this viewpoint is that insecure attachments may forecast less than optimal developmental outcomes in the years ahead.

Long-Term Correlates of Secure and Insecure Attachments

Although the existing data are somewhat limited in that they focus almost exclusively on infants' attachments to their mothers, it seems that infants who have established secure primary attachments are likely to display more favorable developmental outcomes. For example, infants who were securely attached at age 12 to 18 months are better problem solvers as 2-year-olds (Frankel & Bates, 1990), are more complex and creative in their symbolic play (Pipp, Easterbrooks, & Harmon, 1992), display more positive and fewer negative emotions (Kanchanska, 2001), and are more attractive to toddlers as playmates (Fagot, 1997; Jacobson & Wille, 1986) than those who were insecurely attached. In fact, infants whose primary attachments are disorganized/disoriented are at risk of becoming hostile and aggressive preschool and grade school children whom peers are likely to reject (Lyons-Ruth, Alpern, & Repacholi, 1993; Lyons-Ruth, Easterbrooks, & Cibelli, 1997).

Many longer-term studies of securely and insecurely attached children paint a similar picture. Everett Waters and his associates (Waters, Wippman, & Sroufe, 1979), for example, first measured the quality of children's attachments at 15 months of age and then observed these children in a nursery school setting at age 3½ years. Children who had been securely attached to their mothers at age 15 months were now social leaders in the nursery school: they often initiated play activities, were generally sensitive to the needs and feelings of other children, and were very popular with their peers. Observers described these children as curious, self-directed, and eager to learn. By contrast, children who had been insecurely attached at age 15 months were socially and emotionally withdrawn, were hesitant to engage other children in play activities, and were described by observers as less curious, less interested in learning, and much less forceful in pursuing their goals. A follow-up study when these children were 11 to 12 years and 15 to 16 years old revealed that those who had been securely attached still displayed better social skills, enjoyed better peer relations, and were more likely to have close friends than age-mates whose primary attachments had been insecure (Englund et al., 2000; Elicker, Englund, & Sroufe, 1992; Shulman, Elicker, & Sroufe, 1994). Studies with other samples consistently reveal that youngsters whose attachments to parents were or are currently insecure are more likely than those with secure attachments to be unenthused about mastering challenges (Moss & St-Laurent, 2001), to display poorer peer relations and to display deviant behaviors (for example disobedience at school) and other psychopathological symptoms throughout childhood and adolescence (Allen et al., 1998; Atkinson & Tardif, 2001; Carlson, 1998; DeMulder et al., 2000).

So it seems that children can be influenced by the quality of their attachments for many years to come. This is due, in part, to the fact that attachments are often stable over time. In middle-class samples, most children (84 percent in one American sample and 82 percent in a German sample) experienced the same kind of attachment relationships with their parents during the grade school years that they did in infancy (Main & Cassidy, 1988; Wartner et al., 1994). In fact, a sizable majority of adolescents and young adults from stable family backgrounds continue to display the same kinds of attachments that they had established in infancy with their parents (Hamilton, 2000; Waters et al., 2000).

Why Might Attachment Quality Forecast Later Outcomes?

Why is the quality of one's early attachments so often stable over time? How might attachments shape one's behavior and influence the character of one's future interpersonal relationships?

Attachments as Working Models of Self and Others. Ethologists John Bowlby (1980, 1988) and Inge Bretherton (1985, 1990) have proposed an interesting explanation for both the stability and the enduring effects of early attachment classifications. They believe that as infants interact with primary caregivers, they develop **internal working models**—that is, cognitive representations of *themselves* and *other people*—that are used to interpret events and to form expectations about the character of human relationships. Sensitive, responsive caregiving may lead the child to conclude that people are dependable (positive working model of others), whereas insensitive, neglectful, or abusive caregiving may lead to insecurity and a lack of trust (negative working model of others). This is very similar to Erik Erikson's earlier ideas about the importance of trust, but ethologists proceed one step further, arguing that infants also develop a working model of the self based largely on their ability to elicit attention and comfort *when they need it.* Therefore, an infant whose caregivers respond promptly and appropriately to her bids for attention is apt to believe that "I'm lovable" (positive working model of self), whereas one whose signals are ignored or misinterpreted may conclude that "I'm unworthy or loathful" (negative working model of self). Presumably, these two models

internal working models
cognitive representations of self, others, and relationships that infants construct from their interactions with caregivers.

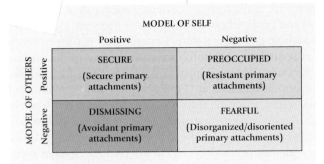

	MODEL OF SELF: Positive	MODEL OF SELF: Negative
MODEL OF OTHERS: Positive	SECURE (Secure primary attachments)	PREOCCUPIED (Resistant primary attachments)
MODEL OF OTHERS: Negative	DISMISSING (Avoidant primary attachments)	FEARFUL (Disorganized/disoriented primary attachments)

Figure 11.7 Four perspectives on close emotional relationships that evolve from the positive or negative "working models" of self and others that people construct from their experiences with intimate companions. *Adapted from "Attachment Styles among Young Adults: A Test of a Four-Category Model," by K. Bartholomew & L. M. Horowitz, 1991,* Journal of Personality and Social Psychology, *61, 226–244. Copyright © 1991 by the American Psychological Association. Adapted with permission.*

combine to influence the quality of the child's primary attachments and the expectations she has about future relationships. What kinds of expectations might she form?

A version of this working models theory appears in Figure 11.7. As shown, infants who construct positive working models of themselves and their caregivers are the ones who should (1) form secure primary attachments, (2) have the self-confidence to approach and to master new challenges, and (3) be inclined to establish secure, mutual-trust relationships with friends and spouses later in life (Waters & Cummings, 2000). A positive model of self coupled with a negative model of others (as might result when infants can successfully attract the attention of an insensitive, overintrusive caregiver) is thought to predispose the infant to form avoidant attachments and to "dismiss" the importance of close emotional bonds. A negative model of self and a positive model of others (as might result when infants sometimes can but often cannot attract the attention they need) should be associated with resistant attachments and a preoccupation with establishing secure emotional ties. Finally, a negative working model of both the self and others is thought to underlie disorganized/disoriented attachments and an emerging fear of being hurt (either physically or emotionally) in intimate relationships (Bartholomew & Horowitz, 1991).

Jay Belsky and his associates (Belsky, Spritz, & Crnic, 1996) demonstrated that children who were securely or insecurely attached as infants process information in ways that suggest that they have formed very different internal working models of self and others. Three-year-olds were treated to puppet shows dramatizing positive events such as getting a birthday present and negative events such as spilling juice. The researchers hypothesized that children who had been securely attached as infants would expect positive experiences in life and remember them especially well, whereas children with insecure attachment histories would expect and tend to recall the more negative events. Although the securely and insecurely attached children did not differ in their attention to positive and negative events, Figure 11.8 shows that the securely attached children did excel at remembering the positive events, whereas insecurely attached children were better at remembering the negative ones.

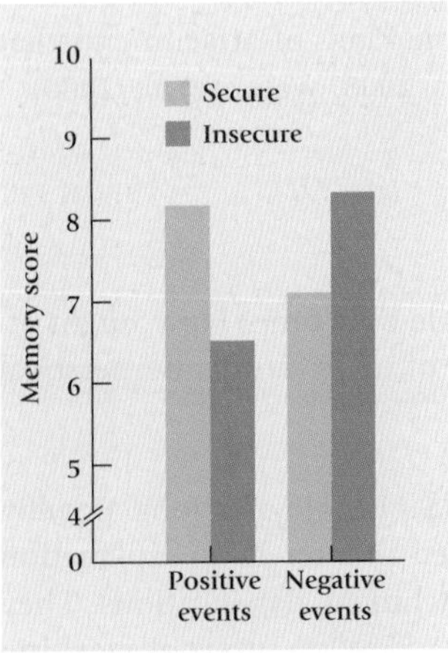

Figure 11.8 Because of differences in their internal working models, securely attached children are biased to remember positive experiences and insecurely attached children to remember negative experiences. *Based on Table 1, p. 113 in J. Belsky, B. Spritz, & K. Crnic, 1996, "Infant Attachment Security and Affective-Cognitive Information Processing at Age 3,"* Psychological Science, *7, 111–114. Reprinted by permission of Blackwell Publishing.*

Other research reveals that children with positive working models of both self and their caregivers are more likely than those whose working models are not so positive to display self-confidence and earn higher grades later in adolescence, develop better social skills and more positive representations of peers, and enjoy closer, more supportive friendships (Cassidy et al., 1996; Jacobsen & Hofmann, 1997; Verschueren & Marcoen, 1999). So Bowlby was on the right track in theorizing that differences in the internal working models that securely and insecurely attached persons form may have important implications for later development (Waters & Cummings, 2000).

Parents' Working Models and Attachment. Parents also have positive or negative working models of themselves and others based on their own life experiences. There are several methods to measure adults' working models, based either on a detailed analysis of their memories of childhood attachment experiences or on their current view of themselves, other people, and the character of interpersonal relationships (Bartholomew & Horowitz, 1991; Main & Goldwyn, 1994). Using these instruments, adults can be reliably cast into the classifications described earlier in Figure 11.7. Do their own working models influence the kinds of attachments their babies form?

Indeed they do. Peter Fonagy and his associates (Fonagy, Steele, & Steele, 1991), for example, found that English mothers' working models of attachment relationships measured before their babies were born accurately predicted about 75 percent of the time whether their infants would establish secure or insecure attachments with them. Similar results have now been reported in studies conducted in Canada, Germany, the Netherlands, and the

United States (Benoit & Parker, 1994; Das Eiden, Teti, & Corns, 1995; Steele, Steele, & Fonagy, 1996; van IJzendoorn, 1995), with an exact matching of working models occurring in 60 to 70 percent of the mother-infant pairs. One contributor to these working model "matches" is that mothers with the more positive working models are more likely to provide the kind of sensitive, responsive, and nonintrusive caregiving that fosters secure infant attachments (Aviezer et al., 1999; Slade et al., 1999; van Bakel & Riksen-Walraven, 2002). Another contributor is that mothers with secure attachment representations derive more joy and pleasure from interacting with their infants than do those whose attachment representations are insecure (Slade et al., 1999), and it appears that these two factors may contribute independently to the kinds of attachments infants form (Pederson et al., 1998).

This research suggests that cognitive representations of intimate relationships are often transmitted from generation to generation. Indeed, Bowlby (1988) proposed that once formed early in life, working models may stabilize, becoming an aspect of personality that continues to influence the character of one's close emotional ties throughout life.

Is Attachment History Destiny?

Although it appears that early working models can be long-lasting and that there are some clear advantages to having formed secure emotional attachments early in life, the future is not always so bleak for infants who are insecurely attached. A secure relationship with another person such as the father (or perhaps a grandparent or a day-care provider) can help to offset whatever undesirable consequences might otherwise result from an insecure attachment with the mother.

Let's also note that secure attachments may often become insecure should a mother return to work, deliver another baby that requires attention, or experience life stresses such as marital problems, depression, a major illness, or financial woes that drastically alter the ways that she and her infant respond to each other (Lewis, Feiring, & Rosenthal, 2000; Weinfield, Sroufe, & Egeland, 2000). One reason Bowlby used the term "working models" was to emphasize that a child's cognitive representations of self, others, and close emotional relationships are dynamic and can change (for better or for worse) based on later experiences with caregivers, close friends, romantic partners, or spouses.

In sum, secure attachment histories are no guarantee of positive adjustment later in life, nor are insecure early attachments a certain indicator of poor life outcomes. This does not mean we should underestimate the adaptive significance of secure early attachments, for children who have functioned adequately as infants but very poorly during the preschool period are more likely to recover and to display good social skills and self-confidence during the grade school years if their early attachment histories were secure rather than insecure (Sroufe, Egeland, & Kreutzer, 1990).

CONCEPT CHECK 11.3 Understanding Individual Differences in Attachment

Check your understanding of the individual differences in attachment by answering the following questions. Answers appear in the Appendix.

Matching: Match the descriptions of theories listed below with the following theoretical approaches to individual differences in attachment.

a. Ainsworth's caregiving hypothesis
b. Kagan's temperament hypothesis
c. Thomas & Chess's goodness-of-fit model
d. Kochanska's integrative theory

1. ________ This theory best summarizes how characteristics of infants and caregivers combine to influence attachment quality.
2. ________ This theory has difficulty explaining why an infant might be securely attached to one parent and insecurely attached to the other parent.
3. ________ This theory claims that temperament influences attachment classification only when caregiving does not foster a secure attachment.

CONTINUED

r False: Identify whether the following statements are true or false.

4. (T)(F) Dr. Lowenstein is a developmental psychologist who studies attachment between infants and their caregivers in various cultures around the world. Based on his research, Dr. Lowenstein concludes that the distributions of attachment classifications vary across cultures and often reflect cultural differences in child-rearing practices. Based on what you have learned about attachment, would you conclude that Dr. Lowenstein's hypothesis is true or false?
5. (T)(F) More infants around the world establish one of the three insecure types of attachment (resistant, avoidant, or disorganized/disoriented) than secure attachment patterns.

Fill in the Blank: Identify which attachment quality is described in each of the following statements.

6. An infant with a ________ attachment will greet the mother warmly and seek physical contact with her when he is distressed.
7. An infant with a ________ attachment will turn way from and ignore her mother, even when the mother tries to get the infant's attention.
8. An infant with a ________ attachment shows confusion about whether to approach or avoid her mother.
9. An infant with a ________ attachment may seem angry with her mother and resist physical contact initiated by her mother.

Essay: Provide a detailed answer to the following question.

10. Describe the developmental outcomes in childhood most commonly linked to infants who are securely and insecurely attached to their caregivers.

Working Moms, Day-Care, and Early Emotional Development

In recent years, an important question has arisen about the ways in which infants in our society spend their time. Should they be cared for at home by a parent, or can they pursue their developmental agendas just as well in a day-care setting? Now that more than 60 percent of all mothers work outside the home at least part time (National Research Council and Institute for Medicine, 2000), more and more young children are receiving alternative forms of care. According to the U.S. Department of Labor statistics, only 40 percent of infants and toddlers are cared for full-time by their parents, whereas 21 percent receive day-care from other relatives, 4 percent are cared for at home by a sitter, 14 percent receive care in day-care homes (typically run by a woman who cares for a few children in her own home during the day for payment), and 31 percent are enrolled in large day-care centers (the numbers add up to more than 100 percent because some children experience multiple forms of care at different times during the week) (Scarr, 1998).

Do infants who attend day-care homes or centers suffer in any way compared with those who stay at home with a parent? Research to date suggests that they usually do not (Ahnert et al., 2004; Ahnert, Rickert, & Lamb, 2000; NICHD Early Child Research Network, 1997, 2000, 2001a, 2001b, 2003a). In fact, we learned in Chapter 9 that high-quality day care promotes both the social responsiveness and the intellectual development of children from disadvantaged backgrounds who are otherwise at risk of experiencing behavior problems and developmental delays (Love, Harrison, & Sagi-Schwartz, 2003; Ramey & Ramey, 1998). Furthermore, a large, well-controlled longitudinal study of 1,153 children in alternative care revealed that neither the age at which children enter day care nor the amount of care they receive was related in any simple way to the security of their attachments to their mothers or their emotional well-being (NICHD Early Child Care Research Network, 1997). The one cause for concern in this large longitudinal study was that children who spent more time in alternative care throughout the first 4½ years of life were somewhat more aggressive and disobedient than those who had experienced less out of home care (NICHD, 2003a). These "amount of care" effects were not large and have not been found in other well-controlled studies (see Love, Harrison, & Sagi-Schwartz, 2003).

TABLE 11.5 Characteristics of High-Quality Infant and Toddler Day Care

Physical setting	The indoor environment is clean, well-lighted, and ventilated; outdoor play areas are fenced, spacious, and free of hazards; they include age-appropriate implements (slides, swings, sandbox, etc.).
Child:caregiver ratio	No more than three infants or four to six toddlers per adult caregiver.
Caregiver characteristics/ qualifications	Caregivers should have some training in child development and first aid; they should be warm, emotionally expressive, and responsive to children's bids for attention. Ideally, staffing is consistent so that infants and toddlers can form relationships (even attachment relationships) with their caregivers.
Toys/activities	Toys and activities are age appropriate; infants and toddlers are always supervised, even during free play indoors.
Family links	Parents are always welcome, and caregivers confer freely with them about their child's progress.
Licensing	Day-care setting is licensed by the state and (ideally) accredited by the National Family Day Care Program or the National Academy of Early Childhood Programs.

Unfortunately, this broad generalization does not tell the full story. Let's briefly consider two factors that are likely to influence how an infant or toddler adjusts to maternal employment and day care.

Quality of Alternative Care

Table 11.5 lists what experts now know to be the most important characteristics of high-quality day care for infants and toddlers (Burchinal et al., 2000; Howes, 1997). Unfortunately, the quality of alternative care in the United States is very uneven compared with that widely available in many Western European countries. Large numbers of American infants and toddlers are cared for by sitters who have little knowledge of or training in child development, or in unlicensed day-care homes that often fail to meet minimum health and safety standards (Scarr, 1998).

How important is high-quality care? Apparently there is far less risk that children will display insecure attachments (or any other adverse outcome) when children receive excellent day care, even when that care begins very early. Jerome Kagan and his associates (1978) found that the majority of infants who entered a high-quality, university-sponsored day-care program at age 3½ to 5½ months not only developed secure attachments to their mothers but were just as socially, emotionally, and intellectually mature over the first 2 years of life as children from similar backgrounds who had been cared for at home. Studies conducted in Sweden (where day care is government subsidized, closely monitored, and typically of high quality) report similar positive outcomes (Broberg et al., 1997). In addition, it seems that the earlier that Swedish infants enter high-quality day care, the better their cognitive, social, and emotional development appear 6 to 8 years later in elementary and middle school (Andersson, 1989, 1992). Studies of U.S. children in day-care centers of varying quality reveal that early entry into higher-quality day care is a reasonably good predictor of favorable social, emotional, and intellectual outcomes throughout the first 3 years of life (Burchinal et al., 2000; Howes, 1997; Loeb et al., 2004; Love, Harrison, & Sagi-Schwartz, 2003; NICHD Early Childcare Research Network, 2003b; Votruba-Drzal, 2004), with low-quality care being associated with poor outcomes.

Unfortunately, children who receive the poorest and most unstable day care are often those whose parents are living complex, stressful lives that may constrain their sensitivity as parents and their involvement in children's learning activities (Fuller, Holloway, & Liang, 1996; Howes, 1997). So a child's poor progress in day care may often stem as much

© Paul Conklin/PhotoEdit

High-quality day care have beneficial effects on children's social, emotional, and intellectual development.

from a disordered home life (in which parents are not all that involved with parenting) as from the less-than-optimal alternative care that he or she receives (NICHD Early Child Care Research Network, 1997, 1998a). Let's explore this idea further.

Parenting and Parents' Attitudes about Work

According to Lois Hoffman (1989), a mother's attitudes about working and child care may be as important to her child's social and emotional well-being as her actual employment status. Mothers tend to be much happier and more sensitive as caregivers when their employment status matches their attitudes about working (Harrison & Ungerer, 2002; NICHD Early Child Care Research Network, 1998b). So, if a woman wants to work, it may make little sense to pressure her into staying home to care for her child when she might be depressed, hostile, or otherwise unresponsive in that role.

Does it matter when a mother returns to work? Unfortunately, there is no simple answer to this question. Some researchers have found that infants may face a slightly elevated risk of insecure attachments (and, in one study, risk of lower scores on tests of school readiness at age 36 months) if their mothers returned to work within the first 9 months after giving birth (see, for example, Barglow, Vaughn, & Molitor, 1987; Belsky & Rovine, 1988; Brooks-Gunn, Han, & Waldfogel, 2002). Yet we must not read too much into these findings because most infants whose mothers return early to work still end up securely attached, particularly when their mothers are working because they want to and are, themselves, sensitive caregivers (Belsky & Rovine, 1988; Harrison & Ungerer, 2002).

Even when children receive less-than-optimal alternative care, their outcomes depend greatly on the parenting they receive (NICHD Early Child Care Research Network, 1997, 1998b, 2001a, 2001b, 2003a). Outcomes are likely to be better if a working mother has positive attitudes both about working and about being a mother (Belsky & Rovine, 1988; Crockenberg & Litman, 1991). It also helps immensely if her spouse approves of her working and supports her in her parenting role (Cabrera et al., 2000). Ultimately, parents' attitudes about parenting and the quality of care they provide at home have far more to do with an infant's development than the kind of alternative care he receives (Broberg et al., 1997; NICHD Early Child Care Research Network, 1997, 1998a, 2001a, 2001b).

What conclusions can we draw, then, about day care and children's emotional development? Considered together, the evidence suggests that (1) children who receive sensitive, responsive care at home are at little risk of poor emotional outcomes, and that (2) excellent day care helps buffer children against emotional insecurity (or other adverse outcomes) should the parenting they receive be far less than optimal. One way excellent day care may serve this protective function is by making children more socially and intellectually responsive, which may have the effect of making parents more sensitive and responsive to them (see Burchinal et al., 2000; NICHD Early Child Care Research Network, 1999). Taken together, the research suggests that day care is most likely to be associated with poor emotional (and other negative) outcomes should infants and toddlers face the dual risk of insensitive parenting and poor alternative care (NICHD Early Child Care Research Network, 1997).

What, then, might be done to help working parents establish and maintain more secure ties with their infants and toddlers and otherwise optimize their development? A national policy governing parental leave for child care is certainly one step in the right direction. In 1993, the U.S. Congress passed the *Family Medical and Leave Act*—a law guaranteeing workers in firms with 50 or more employees the right to take 12 weeks of

TABLE 11.6 Sample Parental-Leave Policies in Modern Industrialized Nations

Canada	Mothers receive 15 weeks of leave at 55% of pay. An additional 10 weeks of parental leave is available to either parent.
Finland	Mothers receive 18 weeks of leave at 70% pay. Additional parental leave of 26 weeks at 70% pay is available to either parent.
Germany	Mothers receive 14 weeks at 100% pay and up to 2½ years of additional leave at partial pay.
Sweden	Mothers receive 14 weeks of leave at 80% pay; the mother or father may take an additional 38 weeks of parental leave at 60% pay, and may extend leave benefits for yet another 6 months, receiving a similar fraction of pay.
United Kingdom	Mothers receive 6 weeks of 90% pay and 12 additional weeks in which they receive a flat-rate monetary stipend. Thirteen weeks of additional unpaid leave can be taken by either parent.
United States	Either parent may take up to 12 weeks of *unpaid* leave in firms of 50 or more employees.

From S. B. Kamerman (2000), "Parental love policies: An essential ingredient in early childhood education and care policies," *Social Policy Report,* Vol. 14, No. 2. Reprinted with permission.

unpaid leave to spend time with their infant, without jeopardizing their jobs. Note that this act (1) does not apply to nearly half of American workers, who are employed by firms with fewer than 50 employees (Kamerman, 2000), and (2) seems miserly compared with the often-generous parental-leave policies that many other industrialized societies have established (see Table 11.6).

An early report on the impact of maternal leave reveals that longer leaves are more beneficial than shorter ones. Specifically, American mothers who took 4-month leaves after the birth of their babies displayed less negative affect when interacting with their babies than did mothers whose leaves lasted only 2 months (Clark et al., 1997). The benefits of longer leaves were most noticeable among mothers who reported depressive symptoms or who had babies with difficult temperaments: these mothers were much more positively involved with their infants and more sensitive in their face-to-face interactions if their leave had lasted a full 4 months. Longer leaves may allow depressed mothers to become more confident as caregivers, while allowing more time for those with difficult infants to establish a "good fit" between their parenting and their baby's temperamental attributes. Unfortunately, many mothers cannot afford to take 4-month, unpaid leaves, thus prompting researchers and child advocates to recommend that the Family Medical and Leave Act of 1993 be revised to provide 4 to 6 months of leave with at least partial pay to employees in all firms, regardless of their size (Clark et al., 1997; Kamerman, 2000).

A workable national policy governing day care may be equally (or more) important. At present, middle-class families are the ones caught most directly in a day-care squeeze. Upper-income families have the resources to purchase excellent day care, and the compensatory education (or other subsidized alternative care) that many lower-income children receive is typically of higher quality than that which middle-class parents can afford to purchase (Scarr, 1998). Meanwhile parents from all social backgrounds must often struggle to find and keep competent sitters or other high-quality day-care placements, which are in short supply, due, in part, to the continuing reluctance of the U.S. government to subsidize day care for all citizens and carefully monitor its quality, as many European countries have done. Increasingly, employers are realizing that it is in their best interest to help workers obtain quality day care. According to Sandra Scarr (1998) many corporations vie each year to be on the *Working Woman* magazine list of the top 100 most family-friendly companies, and some larger employers have established day-care centers at the work site. Edward Zigler (Zigler & Finn-Stevenson, 1996) has suggested that public schools, which are already established institutions in all communities, could be a relatively economical way to provide day care for preschool children, with costs funded by a mix of federal, state, and local tax dollars and parental fees. In fact, Zigler has prompted more than 400 school systems in the United States to incorporate child care into their educational programs. These efforts by corporations and the public schools are not widespread, and until more options are available, most working parents in the United States will continue to face the very real challenge of finding good alternative care at a cost they can afford.

Applying Developmental Themes to Emotional Development, Temperament, and Attachment

Take a few minutes to review the chapter summary. Can you think of examples from this chapter that relate to our four developmental themes: the active child, nature and nurture interactions, quantitative and qualitative changes, and the holistic nature of development?

We have learned that children certainly play an active role in their emotional development and the formation of attachments. For example, children use social referencing by watching their caretakers' responses to novel situations to learn appropriate emotional responses in those new situations. Children learn to regulate the display of their emotions to comply with cultural display rules. And children form cognitive working models of social relationships that they may hold and apply to intimate relationships throughout their lives. But remember that children are active in their development in ways that don't involve conscious behaviors or choices. An excellent example of this is the effect that children's own temperament has on their development. For example, children's temperament and their innate characteristics play a role in the formation of the attachment relationship they develop with their caretakers.

This chapter also highlighted the nature and nurture interactions in development. We saw that hereditary influences and environmental influences interact to shape children's temperament and attachment relationships. For example, children's temperamental profiles contribute to the attachment relationship, as do their experiences of using their caretakers as secure bases for exploration. The caretakers' responses to reunions after separations also contribute to the relationship.

A very clear example of qualitative changes in development was provided by the stages of attachment that children move through as they develop. We saw that children move from an asocial phase, to a phase of indiscriminate attachments, to a phase of specific attachments, to a phase of multiple attachments. Although quantitative changes most likely underlie these qualitative changes, the differences in form and function in each phase make these true qualitative differences.

Finally, throughout this chapter we saw examples of the holistic nature of child development. For each of the emotional aspects of development that we considered, children's cognitive development was shown to play a contributory role in the child's emotional development. Furthermore, children's physical development contributed to emotional development in the ways that caretakers responded to the children's behaviors and appearance, and in the children's growing physical abilities that allowed them to explore and move away from caretakers, but still use the caretaker as a secure base because of their attachment relationships.

You may find many more examples of how our developmental themes were illustrated in this chapter. The important point to remember is that each of these themes plays a role in all of child development, including emotional development, temperament, and the formation of attachment relationships.

SUMMARY

Emotional Development

- At birth, babies display interest, distress, disgust, and contentment.
- Anger, sadness, surprise, and fear normally appear by the middle of the first year.
- Embarrassment, pride, guilt, and shame emerge in the second (or third) year, after children achieve self-recognition and self-evaluation.
- To socialize emotions, parents model positive emotions, attend carefully to their infants' pleasant feelings, and are less responsive to infants' negative emotional displays.
- Emotional self-regulation begins by the end of the first year.
- The ability to regulate emotions develops very slowly: grade school children gradually are able to comply with culturally defined **emotional display rules.**
- By 8 to 10 months of age, infants are capable of **social referencing.**
- The ability to identify and interpret others' emotions improves throughout childhood, aided by cognitive development and conversations about emotions.
- Infants' and children's emotional displays promote social contact with caregivers.
- Understanding others' emotions also helps children infer how to feel, think, or behave in uncertain situations.

Temperament and Development

- **Temperament** is a person's tendency to respond in predictable ways to environmental events.
- Temperament is influenced by genetic and environmental factors.
- Such components of temperament as activity level, irritability, sociability, and **behavioral inhibition** are moderately stable over time.
- Temperamental attributes often cluster in **easy, difficult,** and **slow-to-warm-up** profiles.
- Children with difficult and slow-to-warm-up temperaments are at greater risk of experiencing adjustment problems, depending on the **goodness of fit** between parenting and temperamental attributes.

Attachment

- Infants form affectional ties to their caregivers during the first year of life. These **attachments** are reciprocal relationships.
- Parents' initial bonding with their infant builds in strength as they gear their behavior to the infant's social signals and establish **synchronized routines.**
- How Do Infants Become Attached?
  - Infants pass through an **asocial phase** and a **phase of indiscriminate attachment** before forming their first true attachments at 7 to 9 months of age during the **phase of specific attachments.**
  - Attached infants use their attachment object as a **secure base** for exploration and eventually enter the **phase of multiple attachments.**
- Theories of Attachment
  - Early psychoanalytic and learning theories were discredited because feeding plays less of a role in human attachments than these models expected.
  - The cognitive-developmental notion that attachments depend on cognitive development has received some support.
  - Ethological theory, which argues that humans have **preadapted characteristics** that predispose them to form attachments, has become especially influential in recent years.
- Attachment-Related Fears of Infancy
  - **Stranger anxiety** and **separation anxiety** stem from infants' wariness of strange situations and their inability to explain who strangers are and the whereabouts of absent companions.
  - These two fears usually decline in the second year as toddlers mature intellectually and venture away from their secure bases to explore.
- Individual Differences in Attachment Quality
  - The **Strange Situation** is used to assess the quality of attachments in 1- to 2-year-olds.
  - The **Attachment Q-set** is an alternative test of attachment that can be used with older children.
  - Four attachment classifications have been identified: **secure, resistant, avoidant,** and **disorganized/disoriented.**
  - The distribution of attachment classifications varies across cultures and often reflects cultural differences in child-rearing practices.
  - More infants around the world establish secure attachments than any other pattern.
- Factors That Influence Attachment Security
  - Sensitive, responsive caregiving is associated with the development of secure attachments.
  - Inconsistent, neglectful, overintrusive, and abusive caregiving predict insecure attachments.
  - Infant characteristics and temperamental attributes may also influence attachment quality by affecting the character of caregiver-infant interactions.
  - Caregiving may determine whether attachments are secure or insecure and child temperament may determine the kind of insecurity displayed by a child who received insensitive caregiving.
- Attachment and Later Development
  - Secure attachment during infancy predicts intellectual curiosity and social competence later in childhood.

- Infants may form **internal working models** of themselves and others that are often stable over time and influence their reactions to people and challenges for years to come.
- Parents' working models correspond closely with those of their children and contribute to the attachments infants form.
- Children's working models can change: a secure attachment history is no guarantee of positive adjustment later in life, nor are insecure attachments a certain indication of poor life outcomes.

■ Working Moms, Day Care, and Early Emotional Development

- Separations from working parents and placement into day care do not prevent infants from establishing secure attachments provided that parents are sensitive and responsive caregivers when they are at home.

KEY TERMS

bonding 421
basic emotions 422
complex emotions 423
emotional display rules 424
emotional self-regulation 424
social referencing 427
empathy 427
temperament 430
behavioral inhibition 432
easy temperament 433
difficult temperament 433
slow-to-warm-up temperament 433
"goodness-of-fit" model 433
attachment 435
synchronized routines 435
asocial phase (of attachment) 437
phase of indiscriminate attachments 437
phase of specific attachment 437
secure base 437
phase of multiple attachments 437
secondary reinforcer 438
imprinting 440
preadapted characteristic 440
kewpie doll effect 440
stranger anxiety 441
separation anxiety 441
Strange Situation 445
secure attachment 445
resistant attachment 445
avoidant attachment 446
disorganized/disoriented attachment 446
Attachment Q-set (AQS) 446
amae 447
caregiving hypothesis 450
temperament hypothesis 452
internal working models 455

Bettmann/Corbis

CHAPTER

12 Development of the Self and Social Cognition

W*ho am I?*

> I'm a person who says what I think . . . not [one] who's going to say one thing and do the other. I'm really lucky. I've never [drunk or] done drugs, but I'm always high. I love life. I've got a lot of different business interests . . . a construction company, oil wells, land . . . I'm trying everything. I travel a lot . . . it's difficult to be traveling and in school at the same time. [People] perceive me as being unusual . . . very mysterious, and I hope they see me as being a competitor, because I do all my talking on the field.
>
> —Herschel Walker, former college student, Olympic bobsledder, and professional football star (as quoted by Blount, 1986)

self
the combination of physical and psychological attributes that is unique to each individual.

social cognition
thinking people display about the thoughts, feelings, motives, and behaviors of themselves and other people.

How would you answer the "Who am I?" question above? If you are like most adults, you would probably respond by mentioning some of your noteworthy personal characteristics (honesty, friendliness), some roles you play in life (student, hospital volunteer), your religious or moral views, and perhaps your political leanings. In doing so, you would be describing that elusive concept that psychologists call the **self.**

But when did your sense of self develop? Were you born with a sense of self, or did it develop over time with experience in the world? More generally, do babies have a sense of self at birth? We explore this issue in the first section of the chapter, as we trace the growth of the self-concept from infancy though adolescence. We will then consider how children and adolescents evaluate the self and construct a sense of *self-esteem*. Our focus next shifts to the development of one very important contributor to self-esteem, as we explore how children develop an interest (or disinterest) in achievement and form positive or negative academic self-concepts. We will then discuss a major developmental hurdle faced by adolescents: the need to establish a firm, future-oriented self-portrait, or *identity,* with which to approach the responsibilities of young adulthood. Finally, we will consider what developing children know about other people and interpersonal relationships and see that this aspect of **social cognition,** which parallels the development of the self-concept, illustrates the idea that personal (self) and social aspects of development are intertwined in complex ways.

Of course, we all develop conceptions of ourselves (and others) as males or females and as moral (or immoral) beings. Research on these topics is now so extensive that it merits chapters of its own (see Chapters 13 and 14). For now, let's return to the starting point and see how children come to know this entity we call the *self.*

Development of the Self-Concept

Some developmentalists (see Brown, 1998; Meltzoff, 1990) believe that even newborn infants have the capacity to distinguish the self from the surrounding environment. An interesting piece of evidence for this view is the finding that newborns become distressed at hearing a recording of another baby's cries but not on hearing a recording of their own

proprioceptive information
sensory information from the muscles, tendons, and joints that help one to locate the position of one's body (or body parts) in space.

cries, implying that a differentiation of self and others is possible at birth (Dondi, Simion, & Caltran, 1999). Newborns also anticipate the arrival of their own hands at their mouths and seem capable of using **proprioceptive feedback** from their own facial expressions to mimic at least some of the facial expressions their caregivers display. These kinds of observations suggested to Andrew Meltzoff (1990) that "the young infant possesses an embryonic body scheme. [Although] this body scheme develops [over time], it is present as a psychological primitive right from the earliest phases of infancy" (p. 160). Of course, the observations of imitation are subject to alternative interpretations (many believe them to be mere reflexes).

Other developmentalists believe that infants are born without a sense of self. Psychoanalyst Margaret Mahler (Mahler, Pine, & Bergman, 1975) likens the newborn to a "chick in an egg" who has no reason to differentiate the self from the surrounding environment. After all, every need that the child has is soon satisfied by his or her ever-present companions, who are simply "there" and have no identities of their own.

It is by no means an easy task to clearly establish when infants first become self-aware. In fact, the same findings from research on infants and their sense of self can be interpreted in different ways to support different hypotheses and we may never know the "truth" about whether infants are born with a sense of self. Because infants cannot *tell* us, we must use inference and interpretation to come to our own conclusions. This ambiguity is one of the reasons that research with infants is so fascinating, and one of the reasons that so many researchers continue to study infants, their developing sense of self, and countless other aspects of infant development. For now, let's take a look at what some researchers have concluded about infants' sense of differentiation from others and their self-recognition.

Self-Differentiation in Infancy

Despite the differing views on the emergence of self, almost everyone agrees that the first glimmerings of this capacity can be seen by at least the first 2 or 3 months of life (Samuels, 1986; Stern, 1995). Recall Piaget's (and others') descriptions of cognitive development early in infancy: during the first 2 months, babies exercise their reflexive schemes and repeat pleasurable acts centered on their own bodies (for example, sucking their thumbs and waving their arms). In other words, they are becoming acquainted with their own physical capabilities. We also learned in Chapter 6 that infants only 2 to 3 months old delight at producing interesting sights and sounds by kicking their legs or pulling their arms (when they are attached by strings to mobiles or to audiovisual machinery) (Lewis, Alessandri, & Sullivan, 1990; Rovee-Collier, 1995). Even an 8-week-old infant can recall how to produce these interesting events for 2 to 3 days; and if the strings are disconnected so she can no longer exert any control, she may pull or kick all the harder and become rather distressed (Lewis, Alessandri, & Sullivan, 1990; Sullivan, Lewis, & Alessandri, 1992). Thus it seems that 2-month-old infants may have some limited sense of **personal agency,** or understanding that *they* are responsible for at least some of the events that so fascinate them.

personal agency
recognition that one can be the cause of an event.

In sum, it is still an open question whether *newborns* can truly differentiate themselves from the surrounding environment. But even if they can't, it is likely that they learn the limits of their own bodies during the first month or two and differentiate this "physical self" from the external objects that they can control shortly thereafter (Samuels, 1986). So if a 2- to 6-month-old could talk, he might answer the "Who am I?" question by saying, "I am a looker, a chewer, a reacher, and a grabber who acts on objects and makes things happen."

Self-Recognition in Infancy

self-concept
one's perceptions of one's unique attributes or traits.

Once infants know that they *are* (that they exist independent of other entities), they are in a position to find out *who* or *what* they are (Harter, 1983), the basis of the **self-concept.**

When, for example, do infants recognize their own physical features and become able to tell themselves apart from other infants?

One way to answer these questions is to expose infants to a visual representation of the self (that is, a videotape or mirror reflection) and see how they respond to these images. Research of this type reveals that infants only 5 months old seem to treat their own faces as familiar social stimuli (Legerstee, Anderson & Schaffer, 1998; Rochat & Striano, 2002). For example, Marie Legerstee and her associates (1998) found that 5-month-olds who viewed moving images of themselves and an age-mate (on videotape) could clearly discriminate their own image from that of the peer, as indicated by their preference to gaze at the peer's face (which was presumably novel and interesting to them) rather than at their own (which was presumably familiar and, hence, less interesting). How might infants this young come to discriminate their own faces from those of other people? One explanation is that babies (in Western cultures, at least) often find themselves in front of mirrors, usually beside a caregiver who is playing a social game with them (Fogel, 1995; Stern, 1995). Such experiences may allow ample opportunity for infants to match their own movement-produced proprioceptive information with the actions of one of the figures in the mirror, thereby discriminating this "self" from an older social partner, whose movements do not correspond so closely with their own (Legerstee, Anderson, & Schaffer, 1998).

Over the next several months, infants become better able to discriminate visual representations of themselves and other people and perceive others as potential social partners. In one study (Rochat & Straiano, 2002), 9-month-olds saw either a video representation of themselves or of an adult who mimicked the actions the infant was performing. Not only did these 9-month-olds pay more attention to the mimicking adult than to their own images, but they were much more inclined to treat the adult as a "playmate" by smiling and trying to reengage this person when the video was paused and the mimicry stopped.

The remarkable feats that these young infants display may simply represent their powers of visual discrimination rather than any conscious awareness that the image in a mirror or on videotape is "me." How might we determine whether infants have truly constructed a firm *self*-image that is stable over time?

self-recognition
the ability to recognize oneself in a mirror or a photograph.

Michael Lewis and Jeanne Brooks-Gunn (1979) studied the development of **self-recognition** by asking mothers to surreptitiously apply a spot of rouge to their infants' noses (under the pretext of wiping the infants' faces) and then place the infants before a mirror. If infants have a scheme for their own faces and recognize their mirror images as themselves, they should soon notice the new red spot and reach for or wipe their *own* noses. When infants 9 to 24 months old were given this *rouge test,* the younger ones showed no self-recognition: they seemed to treat the image in the mirror as if it were "some other kid." Signs of self-recognition were observed among a few of the 15- to 17-month-olds, but only among the 18- to 24-month-olds did a majority of infants touch their own noses, apparently realizing that they had a strange mark on their faces. They knew exactly who that kid in the mirror was!

© Laura Dwight

Recognizing one's mirror image as "me" is a crucial milestone in the development of self.

Infants from nomadic tribes, who have no experience with mirrors, begin to display self-recognition on the rouge test at the same age as city-reared infants (Priel & deSchonen, 1986). And many 18- to 24-month-olds can even recognize themselves in current photographs and often use a personal pronoun ("me") or their own name to label their photographic image (Lewis & Brooks-Gunn, 1979). Children this young are not fully aware that the self is an entity that is stable over time. Not until age $3\frac{1}{2}$ will they retrieve a brightly colored sticker placed surreptitiously on their heads if their first glimpse of it comes after a 2- to 3-minute delay on videotape or in a photograph (Povinelli, Landau, & Perilloux, 1996). Apparently, 2- to 3-year-olds who display some self-recognition do not retrieve the sticker because their concept of self is to that of a

present self
early self-representation in which 2- and 3-year-olds recognize current representations of self but are unaware that past self-representations or self-relevant events have implications for the present.

extended self
more mature self-representation, emerging between ages 3½ and 5 years, in which children are able to integrate past, current, and unknown future self-representations into a notion of a "self" that endures over time.

present self and they don't yet appreciate that events that occurred in the past have implications for them now. By contrast, 4- and 5-year-olds quickly retrieve the sticker after a brief delay, but will not retrieve it if the videotape depicts events that happened a week earlier. These older preschoolers have developed the concept of **extended self:** they recognize that the self is stable over time and that (1) events that happened very recently have implications for the present, but (2) the sticker they see a week later on film is *not* still on their heads because this event happened to them a long time ago (Povinelli et al., 1999; Povinelli & Simon, 1998).

Contributors to Self-Recognition

Why do 18- to 24-month-olds suddenly recognize themselves in a mirror? Recall that this is precisely the age when toddlers are said to internalize their sensorimotor schemes to form mental images—at least one of which may be an image of their own facial features. Even children with Down syndrome can recognize themselves in a mirror if they have attained a mental age of 18 to 20 months (Hill & Tomlin, 1981). And once 3½- to 4-year-olds begin to encode noteworthy experiences as autobiographical memories, as we discussed in Chapter 8, they clearly realize that the self is a stable entity and that earlier events they can remember did indeed happen to *them* (Povinelli, Landau, & Perilloux, 1996).

Although a certain level of cognitive development may be necessary for self-recognition, social experiences are probably of equal importance. Gordon Gallup (1979) found that adolescent chimpanzees can easily recognize themselves in a mirror (as shown by the rouge test) unless they have been reared in complete social isolation. In contrast to normal chimps, social isolates react to their mirror images as if they were looking at another animal.

One social experience that contributes to self-awareness in humans is a secure attachment to a primary caregiver. Sandra Pipp and her associates (1992) administered a complex test of self-knowledge to 2- and 3-year-olds—a test assessing the child's awareness of his name and gender as well as tasks to assess self-recognition. As we see in Figure 12.1, securely attached 2-year-olds were outperforming their insecurely attached age-mates on the test, and differences in self-knowledge between secure and insecure 3-year-olds were even greater.

Parents also contribute to a child's expanding self-concept by providing descriptive information ("You're a big girl"; "You're such a smart boy") and by evaluating the child's behavior ("That's wrong Billy; big boys don't snatch their baby sister's toys"). Parents also talk with their children about noteworthy events they have shared together, such as a trip to the zoo or to Disney World. In these conversations, children are typically asked such questions as "Where did we go last week?" and "What was your favorite thing about the trip?" These interchanges help young children to organize their experiences into storyline narratives and to recall them as events that have personal significance—as things that happened to *me* (Farrant & Reese, 2000). And these autobiographical memories, which are initially co-constructed with the aid of an adult, help to illustrate that the self is stable over time, thus contributing to a growing sense of *extended self* (Povinelli & Simon, 1998).

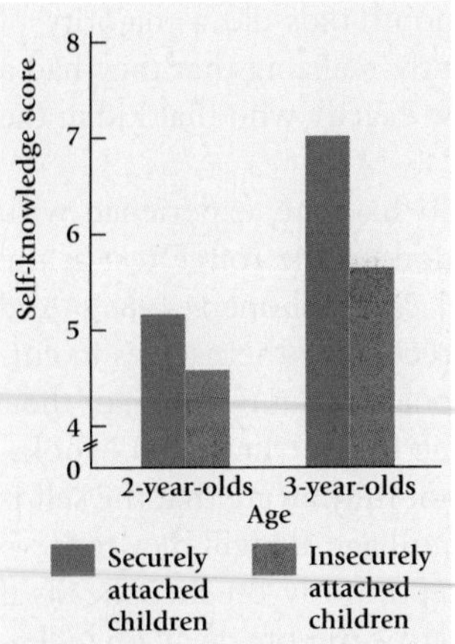

Figure 12.1 Average scores on a test of self-knowledge as a function of age and attachment quality.

There is also evidence that cultural differences in parenting styles influence toddlers' achievement of self-recognition. Heidi Keller and her colleagues (2004) contrasted parenting styles and self-recognition achievement in toddlers from three cultures that varied in their parenting styles. First they observed parenting styles used by mothers of 3-month-old infants. They were particularly interested in the extent to which mothers from the different cultures stressed autonomy, measured by frequency of eye-contact attempts with the infants, versus interdependence, measured by body contact with the infants. They expected these parenting styles to differ among the three cultures examined: the collectivist society of the Nso of Cameroon, the individualistic society of Greece, and the society of Costa Rica, which fell somewhere between the extremes of the other two cultures. Indeed, Keller and her colleagues found that the mothers from the three cultures did differ in the parenting styles with their 3-month-old infants, with the Nso mothers stressing interdependence, the Greek mothers stressing autonomy, and the Costa Rican mothers falling in between the other two. Next, the researchers tested the same children when they were between 18 and 20 months old to see if the toddlers had

TABLE 12.1 Proportion of Mothers Adopting Different Parenting Styles with 3-Month-Olds and the Proportion of Those Children Achieving Self-Recognition When They were 18 to 20 Months Old

		Culture		
		Nso	Costa Rica	Greece
Parenting style at 3 months old	Autonomous style	53.54%	59.91%	74.23%
	Interdependent style	100%	65.00%	31.30%
Toddlers' achievement at 18 to 20 months old	Not self-recognizer	96.8%	50%	31.80%
	Self-recognizer	3.2%	50%	68.20%

Adapted from Keller et al., 2004.

attained self-recognition (using the rouge test). As depicted in Table 12.1, toddlers whose mothers had stressed interdependence were not likely to recognize themselves in the rouge test, whereas toddlers whose mothers had stressed autonomy were much more likely to recognize themselves. In sum, it is clear that social experiences, including those relating to cultural differences in child-rearing practices, do influence the age at which children attain self-recognition.

Social and Emotional Consequences of Self-Recognition

The growth of self-recognition and an emerging awareness of oneself as a participant in *social* interactions pave the way for many new social and emotional competencies. For example, we saw in Chapter 11 that the ability to experience *self-conscious* emotions such as embarrassment depends on self-recognition. Toddlers who have reached this self-referential milestone soon become more outgoing and socially skilled. They now take great pleasure in imitating a playmate's activities (Asendorph, Warkentin, & Baudonniere, 1996) and occasionally even cooperate to achieve shared goals (as illustrated by one child's operating a handle so that another can retrieve toys from a container) (Brownell & Carriger, 1990).

Once toddlers display self-recognition, they also recognize the ways in which people differ and begin to categorize themselves on these dimensions—a classification called the **categorical self** (Stipek, Gralinski, & Kopp, 1990). Age, gender, and evaluative dimensions are the first social categories that toddlers incorporate into their self-concepts, as illustrated by such statements as "I big boy, not a baby" or "Jennie good girl."

categorical self
a person's classification of the self along socially significant dimensions such as age and sex.

Who Am I? Responses of Preschool Children

Toddlers who display self-recognition become much more socially skilled and can now cooperate to achieve shared goals.

Until very recently, developmentalists believed that the self-concepts of preschool children were concrete, physical, and nearly devoid of any *psychological* self-awareness. Why? Because when 3- to 5-year-olds are asked to describe themselves, they talk mostly about their physical attributes ("I have blue eyes"), their possessions ("I have a new bike"), or about *actions* of which they feel especially proud, such as catching a ball or turning cartwheels. Psychological descriptors such as "I'm happy," "I'm good at math," or "I like people" are rarely used by children this young (Damon & Hart, 1988; Keller, Ford, & Meachum, 1978).

Not everyone agrees that preschoolers' self-concepts are limited to observable characteristics. Rebecca Eder (1989, 1990) finds that when 3½- to 5-year-olds are asked to respond to contrasting forced-choice statements that require fewer verbal skills than open-ended "Who am I?" questions, they can quickly characterize themselves on *psychological* dimensions such as sociability (by choosing, for example, between such statements as "I like to play by myself" versus "I like to play with my friends"), athleticism, achievement orientation, argumentativeness, or intelligence. Furthermore, they characterize themselves differently on different dimensions, and these self-characterizations are stable over time (Eder, 1990). Although preschool children may not be consciously aware of what it means to be "sociable" or "athletic" or an "achiever," Eder's research implies that they have rudimentary psychological conceptions of self long before they can express this knowledge in trait-like terminology.

Jeffery W. Myers/Photo Network

Preschool children are already aware of their behavioral patterns and preferences are are using this information to form an early portrait of the self.

Conceptions of Self in Middle Childhood and Adolescence

As children get older, their self-descriptions gradually evolve from listings of their physical, behavioral, and other "external" attributes to sketches of their enduring *inner* qualities—that is, their traits, values, beliefs, and ideologies (Damon & Hart, 1988; Livesley & Bromley, 1973). This developmental shift toward a more abstract or "psychological" portrayal of self can be seen in the following three responses to the "Who am I?" question:

9-year-old: My name is Bruce C. I have brown eyes. I have brown hair. I love! sports. I have seven people in my family. I have great! eye site [*sic*]. I have lots! of friends. I live at . . . I have an uncle who is almost 7 feet tall. My teacher is Mrs. V. I play hockey! I'm almost the smartest boy in the class. I love! food . . . I love! school.

11½-year-old: My name is A. I'm a human being . . . a girl . . . a truthful person. I'm not pretty. I do so-so in my studies. I'm a very good cellist. I'm a little tall for my age. I like several boys . . . I'm old fashioned. I am a very good swimmer . . . I try to be helpful . . . Mostly I'm good, but I lose my temper. I'm not well liked by some girls and boys. I don't know if boys like me . . .

17-year-old: I am a human being . . . a girl . . . an individual . . . I am a Pisces. I am a moody person . . . an indecisive person . . . an ambitious person. I am a big curious person . . . I am lonely. I am an American (God help me). I am a Democrat. I am a liberal person. I am a radical. I am conservative. I am a pseudoliberal. I am an Atheist. I am not a classifiable person (that is, I don't want to be) (Montemayor & Eisen, 1977, pp. 317–318).

In addition to using more psychological terms to describe the self than grade-school children do, adolescents are becoming much more aware that they are not the same person in all situations—a fact that may puzzle or even annoy them. Susan Harter and Ann Monsour (1992) asked 13-, 15-, and 17-year-olds to describe themselves when they are with (1) parents, (2) friends, (3) romantic partners, and (4) teachers and classmates. Then each participant was asked to sort through the four self-descriptions, picking out any inconsistencies and indicating how confusing or upsetting they were. As we see in Figure 12.2, 13-year-olds reported few inconsistencies and were not bothered much by those they did detect. By contrast, 15-year-olds listed many inconsistent qualities and were often confused about them. One 15-year-old talked about her tendency to be happy with friends but depressed at home: "I really think of myself as happy—and want to be that way because I think that's my true self, but I get depressed with my family and it bugs me." (Harter & Monsour, 1992, p. 253). These 15-year-olds seemed to feel that there were several different selves inside them and were concerned about finding the "real me." Adolescents who are most upset over inconsistencies in their self-portrayals are those who put on false fronts, acting out of character in an attempt to improve their images or win the approval

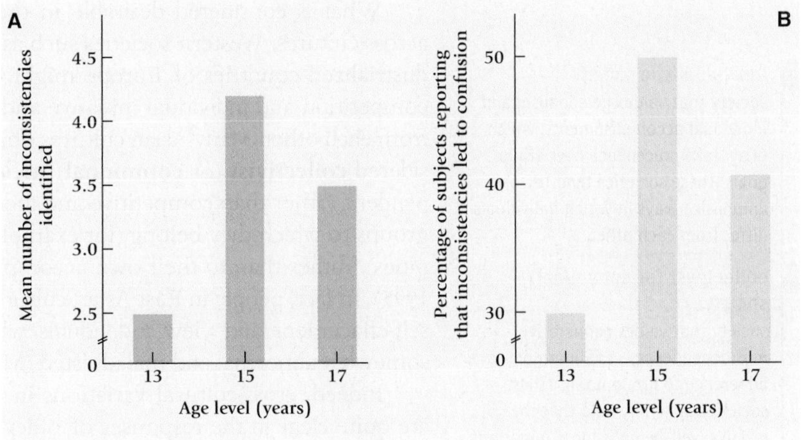

Figure 12.2 Average number of inconsistent attributes reported by 13-, 15-, and 17-year-olds (panel A) and the percentages of 13-, 15-, and 17-year-olds who said they were confused or "mixed up" by these inconsistencies in their self-reports (panel B). *Adapted from "Developmental Analysis of Conflict Caused by Opposing Attributes in the Adolescent Self-Portrait," by S. Harter & A. Monsour, 1992,* Developmental Psychology, 28, *251–260. Copyright © 1992 by the American Psychological Association. Adapted by permission.*

false self-behavior
acting in ways that do not reflect one's true self or the "true me."

of parents or peers. Those who most often display these **false self-behaviors** are the ones who feel least confident that they know who they truly are (Harter et al., 1996).

Inconsistent self-portrayals are less bothersome to older adolescents, who have often integrated them into a higher-order, more coherent view of themselves. A 17-year-old boy, for example, might conclude that it is perfectly understandable to be relaxed and confident in most situations but nervous on dates if one has not yet had much dating experience, or he might conclude that moodiness can explain his being cheerful with friends on some occasions but irritable on others. Harter and Monsour believe that cognitive development—specifically the formal-operational ability to compare abstract traits like "cheerful" and "irritable" and to ultimately integrate them into more general concepts like moodiness—is behind this change in self-perceptions.

In sum, one's self-concept becomes more psychological, more abstract, and more of a coherent, integrated self-portrait from childhood throughout adolescence. The adolescent becomes a sophisticated self-theorist who can reflect on and understand the workings of his or her personality.

There is one final important point: the overview of self-concept development presented here stems largely from research conducted in Western industrialized societies that value independence and view personal attributes as the hallmark of one's character. Might self-concept development follow a different path in children from different societies? Let's see.

Cultural Influences on the Self-Concept

Indicate the extent to which you agree or disagree with each of the items below, on the following scale:

1	2	3	4	5	6	7
Strongly Disagree						Strongly Agree

_______ 1. I have respect for authority figures with whom I interact.

_______ 2. I am comfortable with being singled out for praise or rewards.

_______ 3. My happiness depends on the happiness of those around me.

_______ 4. Speaking up in class is not a problem for me.

_______ 5. I should take my parents' advice into consideration when making education/career plans.

_______ 6. My identity independent of others is very important to me.

(Adapted from Singelis, 1994)

individualistic society
society that values personalism and individual accomplishments, which often take precedence over group goals. These societies tend to emphasize ways in which individuals differ from each other.

collectivist (or communal) society
society that values cooperative interdependence, social harmony, and adherence to group norms. These societies generally hold that the group's well-being is more important than that of the individual.

What is considered desirable in the way of a self-concept may vary dramatically across cultures. Western societies such as the United States, Canada, Australia, and the industrialized countries of Europe might be termed **individualistic societies:** they value competition and individual initiative and tend to emphasize ways in which people differ from each other. Many Asian cultures (for example, India, Japan, and China) could be considered **collectivist** (or **communal**) **societies:** people are more cooperative and interdependent rather than competitive and independent. Their identities are closely tied to the groups to which they belong (for example, families, religious organizations, and communities), rather than to their own accomplishments and personal characteristics (Triandis, 1995). In fact, people in East Asian cultures such as China, Korea, and Japan tend to value self-effacement and view individuals who are preoccupied with personal concerns as somewhat abnormal and maladjusted (Markus & Kitayama, 1994; Triandis, 1995).

Indeed, cross-cultural variations in the nature or content of people's self-concepts are quite clear in the responses of older American and Japanese adolescents to a "Who Am I?" questionnaire (Cousins, 1989). The questionnaire required them to first rate themselves on *personal/individualistic* attributes (for example, "I am honest"; "I am smart") and *social/relational* attributes (for example, "I'm a student"; "I'm a good son"). Then, participants were asked to place a check mark by the five responses that they viewed as most self-descriptive and central to their self-concepts.

The results of this study were quite clear. As shown in Figure 12.3, the majority of American students' core self-descriptors (59 percent) were personal/individualistic attributes, whereas these same attributes made up only 19 percent of the core self-descriptors of the Japanese students. On the other hand, Japanese students were much more inclined than American students to list social/relational attributes as especially noteworthy components of their self-concepts. In terms of developmental trends, older Japanese and Chinese adolescents are less inclined than preadolescents to make distinctions among people on the basis of individualistic attributes, whereas American participants become more inclined to make such distinctions as they grow older (Crystal et al., 1998). Finally, research reveals that Asian American adolescents, whose families often retain many collectivist values even after immigrating to the United States, tend to place more emphasis on their social identities and connections to other people than European American adolescents (Chao, 2001; Fuligni, Yip, & Tseng, 2002).

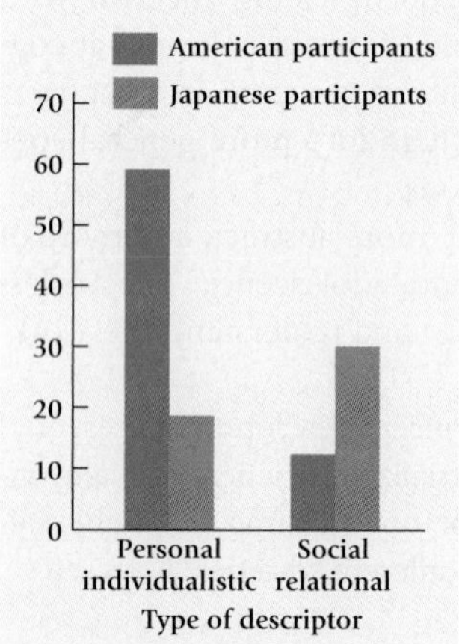

Figure 12.3 Average percentages of personal/individualistic and social/relational attributes listed as core dimensions of the self-concept by American and Japanese students who responded to a "Who Am I?" questionnaire.

Where do you stand on the individualist-collectivist continuum? If you are like most people from individualistic societies, you probably indicated greater agreement with items 2, 4, and 6 on the above scale (which tap independence and individualistic concerns), whereas people from collectivist societies usually find it easier to agree with items 1, 3, and 5 (which tap interdependence and communal concerns).

Clearly, the traditional values and beliefs of one's culture can dramatically influence the kinds of self-concepts that emerge. And as we will see throughout the remainder of the text, the distinctions between individualistic and collectivist cultures and value systems are important ones. These distinctions have implications for such aspects of self as the ways in which individuals look at and evaluate achievement behavior, aggression, altruism, and moral development, to name just a few.

Self-Esteem: The Evaluative Component of Self

self-esteem
one's evaluation of one's worth as a person based on an assessment of the qualities that make up the self-concept.

As children develop, they not only grow to understand more and more about themselves and construct more intricate self-portraits, but they also begin to evaluate the qualities that they perceive themselves as having. This evaluative aspect of self is called **self-esteem.** Children with high self-esteem are satisfied with the type of person they are; they recognize their strong points, can acknowledge their weaknesses (often hoping to overcome them), and generally feel quite positive about the characteristics and competencies they display. Children with low self-esteem view the self in a less favorable light, often choosing to dwell on perceived inadequacies rather than on any strengths they may happen to display (Brown, 1998).

Origins and Development of Self-Esteem

Children's evaluation of themselves and their competencies is a most important part of self that can influence all aspects of their conduct and their psychological well-being. How does self-esteem originate and when do children first establish a sense of self-worth?

These questions are not easy to answer, but Bowlby's (1988) working models theory (which we discussed in Chapter 11) provides some meaningful clues. The theory predicts that securely attached children, who presumably construct a positive working model of self and others, should soon begin to evaluate themselves more favorably than insecurely attached children, whose working models are not so positive. And apparently they do. In studies conducted in Belgium, 4- to 5-year-olds were asked questions about their worthiness, which they answered through a hand puppet (for example, "Do you [puppet] like to play with [this child]?; Is [this child] a good [bad] boy/girl?"). Children with secure ties to their mothers not only described themselves more favorably (through the puppet) than did children who were insecurely attached, but they were also rated as more socially skilled by their preschool teachers (Verschueren, Marcoen, & Schoefs, 1996). What's more, self-esteem was highest for those children who were securely attached to both their parents (Verschueren & Marcoen, 1999), and proved to be stable over time when reassessed at age 8 (Verschueren, Buyck, & Marcoen, 2001). So it seems that by age 4 or 5 (and possibly sooner) children have already established an early and meaningful sense of self-esteem—one that is influenced by their attachment history and is a reasonably accurate reflection of how their teachers evaluate their social competencies.

Components of Self-Esteem

When we adults think about self-esteem, a global appraisal of self comes to mind based on the strengths and weaknesses we display in several different life domains. The same is not true for children, who first evaluate their competencies separately in many different areas and only later integrate these impressions into an overall self-evaluation.

Susan Harter (1982, 1999) proposed a hierarchical model of childhood self-esteem (shown in Figure 12.4). To test her model, she asked children to complete a Self-Perception Scale on which they evaluated themselves in five domains: scholastic competence, social acceptance, physical appearance, athletic competence, and behavioral conduct. Children made self-appraisals by indicating the extent to which statements such as "Some kids are good at figuring out answers at school" (scholastic competence) and "Some kids are always chosen for games" (athletic competence) are true of themselves.

According to Harter, 4- to 7-year-olds might be accused of having inflated self-perceptions because they tend to rate themselves positively in all domains. Some researchers think that these very positive assessments reflect a desire to be liked or be good at various activities, rather than a firm sense of self-worth (Eccles et al., 1993; Harter & Pike, 1984). However, the self-appraisals of 4- to 7-year-olds are not totally unrealistic because they are modestly correlated with ratings teachers give them on the same competency domains (Marsh, Ellis, & Craven, 2002; Measelle et al., 1998).

Starting at about age 8, children's own competency appraisals begin to more closely reflect other people's evaluations of them (Harter, 1982; Marsh, Craven, & Debus, 1998). For example, ratings of social self-esteem are now confirmed by peers who

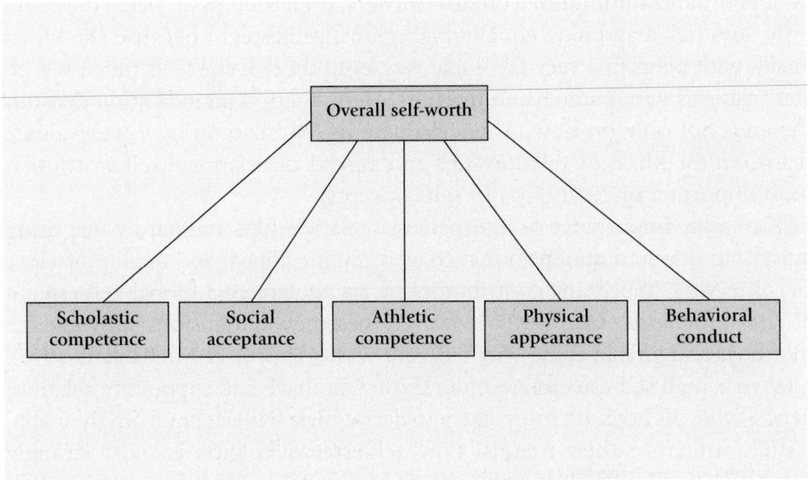

Figure 12.4 A multidimensional and hierarchical model of self-esteem. *Adapted from S. Harter (1996) "Historical roots in contemporary issues" in* Handbook of Self-Concept, *B. A. Bracken, Ed. Copyright © 1996 by John Wiley & Sons, Inc. Reprinted by permission.*

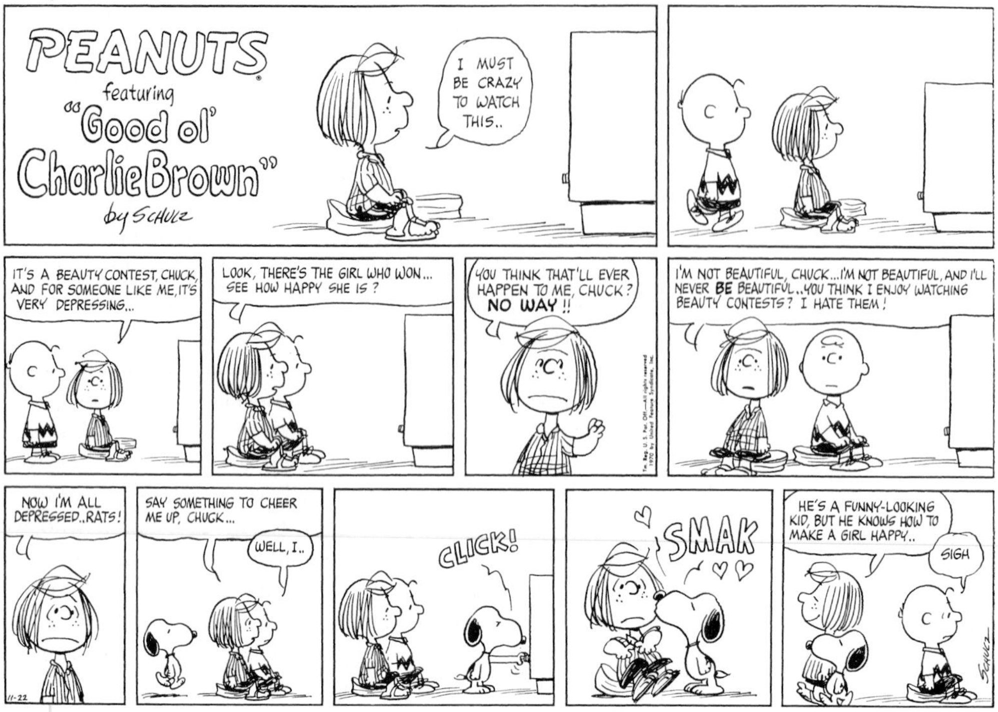

have been asked to rate their classmates' social competencies; and children with high athletic self-esteem are more frequently chosen for team sports and are rated higher in physical competence by gym teachers than classmates who feel physically inadequate. Taken together, these findings suggest that both self-knowledge and self-esteem may depend, to a large extent, on the way that others perceive and react to the child's behavior.

By early adolescence, one's perceptions of self-worth become increasingly centered on interpersonal relationships. Susan Harter and her associates (1998) coined the term **relational self-worth** to describe their finding that adolescents often begin to perceive their self-worth somewhat differently in different relational contexts (e.g., with parents, with teachers, with male classmates, and with female classmates). All these domains of relational self-worth contribute to one's global self-esteem, although one domain may be much more important for some teenagers than for others. For example, one adolescent may enjoy high global self-esteem because he views himself as especially bright and as receiving ample support and admiration from his teachers, even though his peers may consider him nerdy; another may enjoy equally high global self-esteem because she views her competencies with peers in a very favorable way, even though she feels much less efficacious in her relations with parents and teachers. Here, then, is an indication that our self-esteem depends not only on how others evaluate us, but also on how we evaluate ourselves (that is, on the kinds of relationships and aspects of relational self-worth that we view as most important or central to our self-concepts).

relational self-worth
feelings of self-esteem within a particular relationship context (for example, with parents, with male classmates); may differ across relationship contexts.

In adolescence, the quality of one's friendships becomes one of the strongest determinants of self-esteem.

Given the increasing importance of interpersonal relationships, it is hardly surprising that new relationship-oriented dimensions such as romantic appeal and quality of close friendships become very important contributors to an adolescent's global self-esteem (Masden et al., 1995; Richards et al., 1998). However, these new dimensions influence the self-appraisal of boys and girls in somewhat different ways (Thorne & Michaelieu, 1996). Girls who enjoy very high self-esteem are often those who have had supportive relationships with friends, whereas boys are more likely to derive high self-esteem from their ability to successfully influence their friends. Low self-esteem in girls is most strongly associated with a failure to win friends' approval, whereas a major contributor to low self-esteem in adolescent boys is a lack of romantic competence, as reflected by a failure to win or maintain the affection of girls.

Changes in Self-Esteem

How stable are one's feelings of self-worth? Is a child who enjoys high self-esteem as an 8-year-old likely to feel especially good about himself as an adolescent? Or is it more reasonable to assume that the stresses and strains of adolescence cause most teenagers to doubt themselves and their competencies, thereby undermining their self-esteem?

Erik Erikson (1963) favored the latter point of view, arguing that young adolescents who experience the many physical, cognitive, and social changes associated with puberty often become confused and show at least some erosion of self-esteem as they leave childhood behind and begin to search for stable adult identity. Longitudinal studies that assess children's and adolescents' perceptions of their competencies in particular domains (such as academics, social acceptance, physical skills/sports, and appearance), often find that children's and adolescents' views of their own competence gradually decline across the elementary, middle, and high school years (see Fredricks & Eccles, 2002, and Jacobs et al., 2002, for recent findings and reviews), with particularly noticeable dips for some domains (e.g., academics, sporting competence) early in adolescence (Cole et al., 2001). These declining competency beliefs may partially reflect the more realistic self-appraisals that older children provide as they discover that they may not be particularly skilled in one or more competency domains. So do most younger adolescents show the sudden confusion and erosion in self-esteem that Erikson anticipated?

Recent studies of large representative samples suggest that Erikson may have been correct in thinking that early adolescence is a time when many youngsters experience some erosion in self-worth. Richard Robins and his associates (2002), for example, surveyed the global self-esteem of more than 300,000 individuals between the ages of 9 and 90, reporting that the trends for both males and females was for self-esteem to show a meaningful decline between ages 9 and 20, followed by a recovery and gradual increase in self-worth from young adulthood to about age 65, when self-esteem begins to decline again among the elderly.

But before we conclude that adolescence is hazardous to our sense of self-worth, let's note the results of a recent meta-analysis of 50 studies of self-esteem across the life span. The analysis found that the temporal stability of self-esteem is lowest in childhood and early adolescence and becomes much stronger later in adolescence and early adulthood (Trzesniewski, Donnellan, & Robins, 2003). What these data imply is that there are tremendous individual variations in the ways children experience the transition to adolescence: many do show a loss of self-esteem, whereas many others may not fluctuate much, or even post gains in self-worth. Erosion of self-esteem is likely to be observed in those youth who are experiencing multiple stressors as they enter adolescence—those who are transitioning from elementary schools to more rigorous middle and high schools where they are the youngest and the least competent students, while also coping with pubertal changes, beginning to date, and perhaps dealing with family transitions such as a move to a new town or their parents' divorce, all at the same time (Gray-Little & Hafdahl, 2000; Simmons et al., 1987). Because girls mature faster than boys, they are more likely to be experiencing school transitions and pubertal changes at the same time. What's more, girls are more likely than boys to be dissatisfied with their bodies and physical appearance during the adolescent years (Leadbeater et al., 1999; Rosenblum & Lewis, 1999). Perhaps this helps to explain why more girls than boys become depressed during adolescence (Wichstrom, 1999; Stice & Bearman, 2001), and why adolescent girls tend to show more sizable drops in perceived self-worth than adolescent boys (Robins et al., 2002).

Don't misunderstand: most teenagers manage to cope rather well with whatever changes in self-esteem they may experience. And we should recall that despite some fluctuation (either up or down), self-esteem does show some meaningful temporal stability during the adolescent years (Trzesniewski, Donnellan, & Robins, 2003). So those who enter their teens with a reasonably favorable sense of self-worth are likely to exit adolescence with their self-esteem intact—and can look forward to a gradual increase in self-esteem as they successfully negotiate the developmental challenges of young adulthood (Robins et al., 2002).

Social Contributors to Self-Esteem

So biology and cognitive development are important contributors to our developing self-esteem. There are many social influences that contribute to the development of our self-esteem as well. Our home environments, our parents' interactions with us, our peers, and even the culture we live in all influence our self-esteem. Let's see how.

Parenting Styles

Parents can play a crucial role in shaping a child's self-esteem. As we noted in Chapter 11, the sensitivity of parenting early in childhood clearly influences whether infants and toddlers construct positive or negative working models of self. Furthermore, grade school children and adolescents with high self-esteem tend to have parents who are warm and supportive, set clear standards for them to live up to, and allow them a voice in making decisions that affect them personally (Coopersmith, 1967; Isberg et al., 1989; Lamborn et al., 1991). The link between high self-esteem and this nurturing-democratic parental style is much the same in Taiwan and Australia as it is in the United States and Canada (Scott, Scott, & McCabe, 1991). Although these child-rearing studies are correlational and we cannot be sure that warm, supportive parenting *causes* high self-esteem, it is easy to imagine such a causal process at work. Certainly, sending a message that "You're a good kid whom I trust to follow rules and make good decisions" is apt to promote higher self-esteem than more aloof or more controlling styles in which parents may be saying, in effect, "You are no good and a bad kid."

Peer Influences

social comparison
the process of defining and evaluating the self by comparing oneself to other people.

As early as age 4 or 5, children are beginning to recognize differences among themselves and their classmates as they use **social comparison** information to tell them whether they perform better or worse in various domains than their peers (Butler, 1998; Pomerantz et al., 1995). For example, they glance at each others' papers and say "How many did you miss?" or will make such statements as "I'm faster than you" after winning a race (Frey & Ruble, 1985). This kind of comparison increases and becomes more subtle with age (Pomerantz et al., 1995). It plays an important role in shaping children's perceived competencies and global self-esteem (Altermatt et al., 2002)—particularly in Western cultures where competition and individual accomplishments are stressed. This preoccupation with evaluating oneself in comparison with peers is not nearly as strong among communally reared kibbutz children in Israel, perhaps because cooperation and teamwork rather than individual accomplishments are so strongly emphasized there (Butler & Ruzany, 1993).

Peer influences on self-esteem become even more apparent during adolescence. Young adolescents who receive ample and balanced social support from both parents and peers tend to display high levels of self-esteem and few problem behaviors (DuBois et al., 2002b). And recall that some of the strongest contributions to adolescent self-appraisals are the quality of one's relationships with particularly close friends. In fact, when young adults reflect back on life experiences that were noteworthy to them and that may have influenced their self-esteem, they mention experiences with friends and romantic partners far more frequently than experiences with parents and family members (McLean & Thorne, 2003; Thorne & Michaelieu, 1996).

Culture, Ethnicity, and Self-Esteem

Children and adolescents from such collectivist societies as China, Japan, and Korea tend to report lower levels of global self-esteem than their age-mates from individualistic countries such as the United States, Canada, and Australia (Harter, 1999). Why is this? The differences seem to reflect the different emphases that collectivist and individualistic societies place on individual accomplishments and self-promotion. In Western societies, people often compete as they pursue individual objectives and take pride in (and even brag about) their individual accomplishments. People from collectivist societies are more interdependent than independent. They tend to value humility and self-effacement and to derive self-worth from contributing to the welfare of the groups (e.g., families, communities, classrooms, or even the larger society) to which they belong. In fact, acknowledging one's weaknesses and needs for self-improvement—admissions that may lower one's reported self-worth on traditional measures of self-esteem—can actually make children from collectivist societies feel *good* about themselves because these behaviors are likely to be viewed by others as evidence of appropriate humility and increased commitment to the group's welfare (Heine et al., 1999).

These differences in self-concept found among adolescents of different cultures can be traced back to differences in child-rearing practices among cultures (Wang, 2004; Wang, Leichtman, & Davies, 2000). Wang (2004) found that American and Chinese mothers differ in the way they help their toddlers and preschoolers develop their self-concepts, and cultural differences in self-concept that begin in preschool only grow wider with age. American children tend to emphasize the individualistic nature of their selves, whereas Chinese children tend to emphasize the relational nature of their selves, both in their reports of autobiographical memories and their own self-descriptions (Wang, 2004). These differences may be influenced by differences in the way American and Chinese mothers talk with their children about past events, as illustrated in this example of mothers talking with their 3-year-old children, reported by Wang and colleagues (2000):

American Mother-Child Dyad

MOTHER: Do you remember when we were at Nana's on vacation and we went down to the dock at Grandmommy's? You went swimming?

CHILD: Um-hum.

MOTHER: What did you do that was really neat?

CHILD: Jump off the dock.

MOTHER: Yeah. That was the first time you've ever done that.

CHILD: That was like a diving board.

MOTHER: You're right, it was. And where did Mommy have to stand?

CHILD: In the sandy spot.

MOTHER: In the sandy spot, right. Mommy said, "Wait, wait, wait! Don't jump 'til I get into my sandy spot!"

CHILD: Why?

MOTHER: 'Cause you remember how I told you all the leaves pile up on the bottom of the lake? And it makes it a little mushy. And so, you jumped off the dock and then what did you do?

CHILD: Swim

MOTHER: To . . .

CHILD: Nana.

MOTHER: Yeah. All by yourself with what on your back?

CHILD: Bubbles.

MOTHER: Yeah.

Chinese Mother-Child Dyad

MOTHER: That day, mom took you to take a big bus and go skiing in the park. What did you play at the place of skiing? What did you play?

CHILD: Played . . . Played the . . .

MOTHER: Sat on the ice ship, right?

CHILD: Yes. Then . . .

MOTHER: We two rowed together, right?

CHILD: Then . . . then . . .

MOTHER: Then we rowed and rowed, rowed round a couple of times, right?

CHILD: Um.

MOTHER: We rowed around a couple of times. Then you said, "Stop rowing. Let's go. Go home." Right?

CHILD: Um.

MOTHER: Then we took a bus to go home, right?

CHILD: Um.

Notice that the American mother focuses more on the child and the child's accomplishments than the Chinese mother, who is more leading and directive, and who focuses more on the group than the individual child. A lifetime of differences like this one would surely contribute to differences in the construction of self-concept across cultures.

CONCEPT CHECK 12.1 Understanding the Development of the Self

Check your understanding of important processes in the development of the self by answering the following questions. Answers appear in the Appendix.

Matching: Identify the following components of self that correspond to the descriptions below:

a. categorical self
b. self-concept
c. self-esteem

1. ________ the evaluative component of the self that is influenced by attachment history
2. ________ one's perceptions of one's unique attributes or traits
3. ________ early self-description along such socially significant dimensions as age and gender

True or False: Identify whether the following statements are true or false.

4. (T)(F) Parental warmth and responsiveness is a strong contributor to self-esteem beginning in adolescence.
5. (T)(F) Friendship quality promotes high self-esteem in childhood.

Multiple Choice: Select the best answer for the following question.

______ 6. Little Richie is just 1 month old. His mother has attached an attractive mobile to his crib. When she puts him in his crib, he begins to move his arms and legs and he watches the mobile with delight as it turns and plays a tune. One day the batteries in the mobile burn out and his movements no longer make the mobile turn and play its tune. Richie wiggles more vigorously and begins to cry. It appears that little Richie has attained the recognition that one can be the cause of an event, referred to by developmental psychologists as
a. self-recognition
b. personal agency
c. proprioceptive feedback
d. self-power

Short Answer: Provide a brief answer to each of the following questions.

7. Diagram Harter's hierarchical model of self-esteem.
8. Describe the "rouge test" and explain what different responses to the test tell us about the toddler who is being tested.

Essay: Provide a more detailed answer to the following question.

9. Outline the progression of young children's developing self-concept. In your answer, define self-recognition, the present self, and the extended self.

There are also ethnic differences in self-esteem among people in multicultural societies (e.g., Ward, 2004). Consider findings from the United States. Throughout elementary school, disadvantaged African American and Hispanic children, who are becoming aware of negative ethnic stereotypes and possibly even experiencing prejudice from some adults and peers, often express lower levels of self-esteem than their European American age-mates. By adolescence the picture changes somewhat. Older African American and Hispanic youth are likely to express about the same or even higher levels of self-esteem than European Americans (Gray-Little & Hafdahl, 2000; Twenge & Crocker, 2002). This is particularly true if they have ample social support from parents and have been encouraged to identify with and take pride in their ethnic group and its cultural traditions (Caldwell et al., 2002; Umana-Taylor et al., 2002).

One major aspect of self-esteem that has been studied in some depth is the development of children's academic self-concepts. What children think about their academic competency and the importance they assign to this aspect of their selves can have implications for their learning and development through the elementary and high school years. In the next section we will examine these aspects of children's developing sense of self.

Development of Achievement Motivation and Academic Self-Concepts

achievement motivation
a willingness to strive to succeed at challenging tasks and to meet high standards of accomplishment.

In Chapter 9, we learned that even though IQ predicts academic achievement, the relationship is far from perfect. Why? One reason is that children differ in **achievement motivation**—their willingness to strive to succeed at challenging tasks and to meet high standards of accomplishment. Although the meaning of achievement varies somewhat from society to society, one survey conducted in 30 cultures revealed that people around the world value personal attributes such as self-reliance, responsibility, and a willingness to work hard to attain important objectives (Fyans et al., 1983).

mastery motivation
an inborn motive to explore, understand, and control one's environment.

Many years ago, psychoanalyst Robert White (1959) proposed that from infancy onward, human beings are intrinsically motivated to "master" their environments—to have an effect on or to cope successfully with a world of people and objects. We see this **mastery motive** in action as we watch infants struggle to turn knobs, open cabinets, and operate toys—and then notice their pleasure when they succeed (Busch-Rossnagel, 1997).

But even though all babies may be curious, mastery-oriented beings, it is obvious that some children try harder than others to master their school assignments, music lessons, or the positions they play on the softball team. How do we explain these individual differences? Let's begin by tracing the development of achievement motivation early in life and then examining some of the factors that promote (or inhibit) its growth.

Early Origins of Achievement Motivation

How does a baby's mastery motivation evolve into a grade school child's achievement motivation? Deborah Stipek and her associates (Stipek, Recchia, & McClintic, 1992) have conducted a series of studies with 1- to 5-year-olds to find out when children develop the capacity to evaluate their accomplishments against performance standards—a capacity central to achievement motivation. In Stipek's research, children were observed as they undertook activities that had clear-cut achievement goals (for example, hammering pegs into pegboards, working puzzles, knocking down plastic pins with a bowling ball). Tasks were structured so that children either could or could not master them in order to observe their reactions to success or failure. Based on this research, Stipek and her colleagues suggest that children progress through three phases in learning to evaluate their performances in achievement situations, phases we will call joy in mastery, approval seeking, and use of standards.

Phase 1: Joy in Mastery

Before age 2, infants are visibly pleased to master challenges, displaying the mastery motivation White (1959) wrote about. However, they do not call other people's attention to their triumphs or otherwise seek recognition, and, rather than being bothered by failures, they simply shift goals and attempt to master other toys. They are not yet evaluating their outcomes in relation to performance standards that define success and failure.

Phase 2: Approval-Seeking

As they near age 2, toddlers begin to anticipate how others will evaluate their performances. They seek recognition when they master challenges and expect disapproval when they fail. For example, children as young as 2 who succeeded on a task often smiled, held their heads and chins up high, and made such statements as "I did it" as they called the experimenter's attention to their feats. Meanwhile, 2-year-olds who failed to master a challenge often turned away from the experimenter as though they hoped to avoid criticism. It seems, then, that 2-year-olds are already appraising their outcomes as mastery successes or failures and have already learned that they can expect approval after successes and disapproval after failures (see also Bullock & Lutkenhaus, 1988).

Phase 3: Use of Standards

An important breakthrough occurs around age 3 as children begin to react more independently to their successes and failures. They seem to have adopted objective standards for appraising their performance and are not as dependent on others to tell them when they have done well or poorly. These Phase-3 children seem capable of experiencing real *pride* (rather than mere pleasure) in their achievements and real *shame* (rather than mere disappointment) after failure (see also Lewis, Alessandri, & Sullivan, 1992; Lewis & Ramsay, 2002).

In sum, infants are guided by a mastery motive and take pleasure in their everyday accomplishments; 2-year-olds begin to anticipate others' approval or disapproval of their performances; and children 3 and older evaluate their accomplishments against performance standards and are capable of experiencing pride or shame depending on how successfully they match those standards.

© Bill Schild/Corbis

Many 3-year-olds are highly motivated to master challengees and can take pride in their accomplishments.

Achievement Motivation During Middle Childhood and Adolescence

In their pioneering studies of achievement motivation, David McClelland and his associates (1953) gave children and adolescents a series of four somewhat ambiguous pictures and asked them to write stories about them as part of a test of creative imagination. Assuming that people project their own motives into their stories, one can measure their achievement motivation by counting the number of achievement-related themes they mention. What kind of story would you tell about the scene portrayed in Figure 12.5? A person high in achievement motivation might respond by saying that the individual in the photo has been working for months on a new scientific breakthrough that will revolutionize the field of medicine, whereas a person low in achievement motivation might say that this worker is glad the day is over so that she can go home and relax. Early research revealed that children and adolescents who scored high in achievement motivation on this and other measures tended to receive better grades in school than those who scored low (McClelland et al., 1953). These findings prompted investigators to look more closely at parent-child interactions to determine how the home setting influences achievement motivation.

Robert Reichert/The Liaison Agency/Getty Images

Figure 12.5 Scenes like this one were used by David McClelland and his associates to measure achievement motivation.

Home Influences on Mastery Motivation and Achievement

Over the years, researchers have identified three especially potent home influences on children's mastery/achievement motivation and actual achievement behavior: the quality of the child's attachments, the character of the home environment, and the child-rearing practices that parents use—practices that can either foster or inhibit a child's will to achieve.

Quality of Attachment. We learned in Chapter 11 that children who were securely attached to primary caregivers at age 12 to 18 months are more likely than those who were insecurely attached to solve problems successfully as 2-year-olds. They were also more likely to display a strong sense of curiosity, self-reliance, and an eagerness to solve problems some 3 to 5 years later as they entered elementary school. And children whose attachments are secure on entering school tend to remain more self-assured and do better in school than their insecurely attached peers throughout middle childhood and adolescence—even when other factors known to affect academic achievement, such as IQ and social class, are held constant (Jacobsen & Hoffman, 1997). Securely attached youngsters are no more intellectually competent, on average, than their insecurely attached age-mates; they simply seem to be more eager to apply their competencies to the new challenges they encounter (Belsky, Garduque, & Hrncir, 1984). So children apparently need the "secure base" provided by a loving, responsive parent to feel comfortable about taking risks and seeking challenges.

The Home Environment. The young child's tendency to explore, acquire new skills, and solve problems also depends on the kind of challenges the home environment provides. In one study (van Doorninck et al., 1981), researchers visited the homes of 50 12-month-old infants from lower-income families and used the *HOME Inventory* to classify the child's early environment as intellectually stimulating or unstimulating (refer to our discussion of the HOME Inventory in Chapter 9 to review the criteria used to classify the home environment). Five to nine years later, the research team followed up on these children by looking at their standardized achievement test scores and the grades they had

TABLE 12.2 Relation between Quality of Home Environment at 12 Months of Age and Children's Grade-School Academic Achievement 5 to 9 Years Later

	Academic achievement	
Quality of home environment at age 12 months	Average or high (top 70%)	Low (bottom 30%)
Stimulating	20 children	10 children
Unstimulating	6 children	14 children

Source: Adapted from "The Relationship between twelve-month home stimulation and school achievement," by W. J. van Doornick, B. M. Caldwell, C. Wright, & W. K. Frankenberg, 1981, *Child Development, 52,* 1080–1083.

earned at school. As we see in Table 12.2, the quality of the home environment at 12 months of age predicted children's academic achievement several years later. Two out of three children from stimulating homes were performing quite well at school, whereas 70 percent of those from unstimulating homes were doing very poorly. Not only do stimulating home environments foster good grades among children from all ethnic groups and social classes, but they also promote an **intrinsic orientation to achievement**—a strong willingness to seek out and master challenges to satisfy *personal* needs for competence or mastery. It seems that the joy of discovery and problem solving is most likely to blossom in an intellectually stimulating home environment that provides many age-appropriate challenges and the encouragement to master them. Such an environment is described in the following section.

intrinsic achievement orientation a desire to achieve in order to satisfy one's *personal* needs for competence or mastery (as opposed to achieving for external incentives such as grades).

Child-Rearing and Achievement. In their book *The Achievement Motive,* McClelland and his associates (1953) proposed that parents who stress *independence training*—doing things on one's own—and who warmly reinforce such self-reliant behavior contribute in a positive way to achievement motivation. And research bears this out (Grolnick & Ryan, 1989; Winterbottom, 1958). However, it is important to note that successfully fostering autonomy and self-reliance requires far more than encouraging a child to accomplish objectives alone. Consistent with Vygotsky's viewpoint on the importance of collaborative learning, one longitudinal study found that 2-year-olds whose parents had carefully scaffolded their efforts, thereby allowing the youngsters to eventually master challenges that would have been impossible without such gentle parental guidance, were the children who felt most comfortable and most motivated in achievement contexts 1 year later, as 3-year-olds (Kelly, Brownell, & Campbell, 2000). What's more, direct *achievement training*—setting high standards and encouraging children to do things well—also fosters achievement motivation (Rosen & D'Andrade, 1959). Finally, patterns of praise, criticism, and punishment that accompany the child's accomplishments are also important: children who seek challenges and display high levels of achievement motivation have parents who praise their successes and are not overly critical of an occasional failure. Children who shy away from challenges and are low in achievement motivation have parents who are slow to acknowledge their successes (or who do so in a matter-of-fact way) and are inclined to criticize or punish failures (Burhans & Dweck, 1995; Kelly, Brownell, & Campbell, 2000; Teeven & McGhee, 1972).

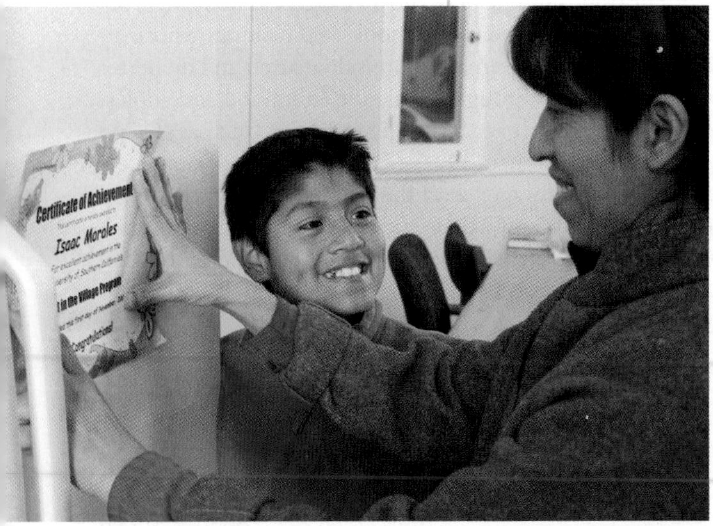

© Bill Aron/PhotoEdit

Parents who encourage achievement and who respond warmly to success are likely to raise mastery-oriented children who enjoy challenges.

We see, then, that parents of children high in achievement motivation possess three characteristics: (1) they are warm, accepting, and quick to praise their child's accomplishments; (2) they provide guidance and control by setting standards for their child to live up to and then monitoring her progress to ensure that she does; and (3) they permit their child some independence or autonomy, carefully scaffolding tasks for young children to allow them to succeed on their own and allowing older children a voice in deciding how best to master challenges and meet their expectations. Diana Baumrind calls this warm, firm, but democratic parenting an **authoritative parenting** style—a style that she and others have found to foster positive attitudes about achievement and considerable academic success among grade-school children and adolescents, both in Western societies (Glasgow et al., 1997; Lamborn et al., 1991; Steinberg, Elmen, & Mounts, 1989) and in Asia (Lin & Fu, 1990). If children are encouraged and supported in a positive manner as they tackle their schoolwork, they are likely to enjoy new challenges and feel confident of mastering them (McGrath & Repetti, 2000). On the other hand, parents can undermine a child's school performance and motivation to succeed if they (1) are uninvolved and offer little in the way of guidance or (2) are highly controlling and do such things as nag continually about homework, offer tangible bribes for good grades, or harp incessantly about bad ones (Ginsburg & Bronstein, 1993; Ng, Kenney-Bensen, & Pomerantz, 2004).

authoritative parenting
flexible, democratic style of parenting in which warm, accepting parents provide guidance and control while allowing the child some say in deciding how best to meet challenges and obligations.

Peer Group Influences

Peers are also an important source of influence on grade school children and adolescents—sometimes supporting and at other times undermining parents' efforts to encourage academic achievement. Peer pressures that interfere with academic achievement may be especially acute for many lower-income African American and Latino students. Such pressures may help explain why these students often lag behind Euro American and Asian American students in school achievement (Slaughter-Defoe et al., 1990; Tharp, 1989). Lawrence Steinberg and his colleagues (1992) found that African American and Latino peer groups in many low-income areas actively discourage academic achievement, and Euro and Asian American peer groups tend to value and encourage it. High-achieving African American students in some inner-city schools may run the risk of being rejected by their African American peers if their academic accomplishments cause them to be perceived as "acting white" (Ford & Harris, 1996; Fordham & Ogbu, 1986).

Other research finds that children whose parents value education highly and work hard to promote their achievement tend to associate with peers who share those values. In his study of Latino, East Asian, Filipino, and European immigrant families, Andrew Fuligni (1997) found that immigrant adolescents tended to make higher grades at school than native-born U.S. adolescents, despite the fact that their parents were not highly educated and often spoke little English at home. Why? Because the parents of these high achievers strongly endorsed the value of academics, a value that was clearly reinforced by the adolescents' friends, who often studied together with them, shared class notes, and encouraged them to do well in school. This kind of peer support for parental values also fosters the academic achievement of talented African American students (Ford & Harris, 1996) and preadolescents in Shanghai, China (Chen, Rubin, & Li, 1997). It is probably a strong contributor to the academic successes of students from *any* background. Clearly, it is easier for a student to remain focused on academic goals if parents and peers are not sending mixed messages about the value of those goals.

Cultural Influences

There are also cultural differences in achievement motivation and attitudes toward learning. For example, in contrast to American children who may display achievement motivation but also are quite tolerant of failures in performance, Chinese children display achievement motivation and view failures as personal failures and may be quite ashamed of such failures. Li (2004) found that such differences are evident as early as the preschool years. Li read stories about learning failures to 4-, 5-, and 6-year-old American and Chinese children. The children were then asked their opinions about the story character's failure and their responses were examined. Li found that these young children differed in their responses. The American preschoolers were more likely to view learning as a task to be accomplished and they were not critical of learning failures. In contrast, Chinese preschoolers were likely to view learning as a personal virtue to be attained and they were highly critical of failures in learning. These differences are evident in the following example: the preschoolers heard this story and were then asked questions about the character in the story.

> Little Bear watches her Mommy and Daddy catch fish. She really wants to learn how to catch fish by herself. She tries for a while, but she cannot catch any fish. Then she says to herself, "Forget it! I don't want to catch fish anymore!"

American 5-year-old girl's responses:

CHILD: She shouldn't have given up cause then she wouldn't have, um, done it. Um she could eat the fish that Mommy and Daddy caught, so um that she can get bigger and taller so that she can catch fish.

INTERVIEWER: You see, Daddy and Mommy each caught one fish. And they are kind of big, you know? So maybe they also need to eat the fish themselves. What will Little Bear do?

CHILD: She can, um, get get something else to practice on.

INTERVIEWER: Like what?

CHILD: Like a little stream.

INTERVIEWER: What?

CHILD: A stream fish live in.

INTERVIEWER: Do you like Little Bear?

CHILD: Yes.

INTERVIEWER: Why do you like her?

CHILD: Cause she is so furry and cute.

Chinese 5-year-old girl's responses:

CHILD: Daddy and Mommy divide their fish into several pieces, and they eat together.

INTERVIEWER: But do you see that Daddy and Mommy are big, and they each got one fish. Hm, they probably can't give their fish to Little Bear. What would she do next?

CHILD: Mommy keeps a small piece for herself, and she gives a big piece to Little Bear. Then they eat with their child, and they are happy.

INTERVIEWER: Do you like Little Bear?

CHILD: No.

INTERVIEWER: Why not?

CHILD: She does some thing and stops halfway; she's got three hearts and two minds [i.e., no concentration].

INTERVIEWER: What's wrong with having three hearts and two minds?

CHILD: You do this thing for a while, then you switch to another thing for a while. You don't even pay attention. You can't learn good, and that's not good.

Note that the girls in this example clearly differed in their views of learning and in evaluating Little Bear in this situation. The American girl saw Little Bear's attempts as worthy and she looked for other ways for Little Bear to accomplish her objective. The

Chinese girl saw Little Bear's attempts to learn as laudable, but she was very disapproving of Little Bear's giving up, seeing this as a personal failure. In sum, cultural differences in achievement motivation and views of learning are clear and evident even in very young children.

Beyond Achievement Motivation: Development of Achievement Attributions

Many contemporary researchers acknowledge that the concept of achievement motivation has some value, but they believe it is naive to presume that this one global motive will predict behavior in all achievement situations. Why? Because they have also discovered that children's achievement behavior and academic self-concepts depend very heavily on their **achievement attributions,** or how they interpret their successes and failures.

achievement attributions
causal explanations that one provides for his/her successes and failures.

Types of Achievement Attributions

Bernard Weiner (1974, 1986) found that adolescents and young adults tend to attribute their successes and failures to any of four possible causes: ability (or the lack thereof), effort, task difficulty, or luck (either good or bad). As shown in Table 12.3, two of these causes, ability and task difficulty are *stable* causes, which foster strong **achievement expectancies,** whereas effort and luck are *unstable,* or highly variable from situation to situation, and promote weaker expectancies. To illustrate, if you do poorly on a test and attribute your failure to a stable cause like low ability, you would likely feel less confident of future success (strong negative expectancy) than if you had attributed that failure to low effort, which you might overcome by studying harder next time. Notice also that two of the causes in Table 12.3, ability and effort, are internal causes (characteristics of the individual), whereas the other two, task difficulty and luck, are external causes (characteristics of the situation). Weiner proposes that the internality/externality of our achievement attributions affects how much we value our achievement outcomes. So, if we attribute an A on a test to an internal cause such as our high ability or hard work, we are more likely to value our success than if we attributed it to such external factors as blind luck or a ridiculously easy exam.

achievement expectancy
how well (or poorly) one expects to perform should she try to achieve a particular objective.

According to Weiner, it is adaptive to attribute our successes to high ability, for this internal and stable attribution causes us to value what we have accomplished and leads us to expect that we can repeat our success. It is more adaptive to attribute failures to low effort (rather than low ability) because effort is unstable and we are more likely to believe that we can do better in the future if we just try harder.

In sum, Weiner's attribution theory claims that two cognitive variables influence our willingness to work to achieve particular objectives within any given achievement domain. Presumably, the perceived locus of causality (that is, internality/externality) of an outcome affects how much we value that outcome, whereas our attributions about the

TABLE 12.3 Weiner's Classification of the Causes of Achievement Outcomes (and Examples of How You Might Explain a Terrible Test Grade)

	Locus of causality	
	Internal cause	**External cause**
Stable cause	*Ability* "I'm hopeless in math."	*Task difficulty* "That test was incredibly hard and much too long."
Unstable cause	*Effort* "I should have studied more instead of going out to the concert."	*Luck* "What luck! Every question seemed to be about information taught on the days of class I missed."

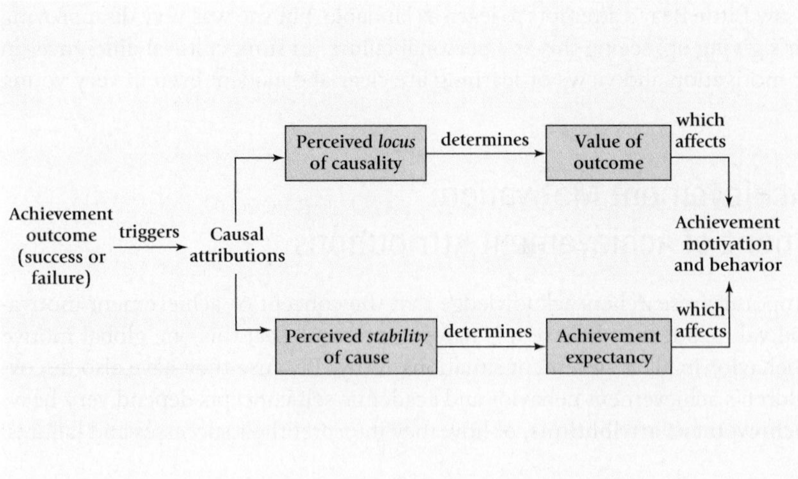

Figure 12.6 An overview of Weiner's attribution theory of achievement.

stability of the outcome affect our achievement expectancies. Together, these two cognitive judgments influence our willingness to undertake similar challenges in the future (see Figure 12.6 for an overview of Weiner's theory).

Age Differences in Achievement-Related Attributions

If it seems to you that Weiner's theory sounds a little too cognitive and abstract to explain the achievement attributions that young children display, you're right. Before age 7 or so, children tend to be unrealistic optimists who think they have the ability to succeed on almost any task, even those that they have repeatedly failed to master in the past (Stipek & Mac Iver, 1989). Preschool and primary grade teachers may contribute to this rosy optimism by setting mastery goals and by praising children more for their efforts than for the quality of their work, thus leading them to believe that they can accomplish much and "be smart" by working hard (Rosenholtz & Simpson, 1984; Stipek & Mac Iver, 1989). Young children seem to have an **incremental view of ability:** they believe that ability is changeable, not stable, and they can get smarter or become more capable through increased effort and lots of practice (Droege & Stipek, 1993; Dweck & Leggett, 1988; Heyman, Gee, & Giles, 2003).

incremental view of ability
belief that one's ability can be improved through increased effort and practice.

entity view of ability
belief that one's ability is a highly stable trait that is not influenced much by effort or practice.

When do children begin to distinguish ability from effort? When do they move toward an **entity view of ability**—a perspective that ability is a fixed or stable trait that is not influenced much by effort or practice? Eight- to twelve-year-olds begin to distinguish effort from ability (Nicholls & Miller, 1984). This is due, in part, to the changing character of their experiences at school. Teachers gradually place more and more emphasis on ability appraisals; they assign grades that reflect the quality of work that students perform rather than the amount of effort expended. All these performance evaluations are supplemented by such competitive activities as science fairs and spelling bees, which also place a premium on the quality rather than the quantity of students' work. Older grade-school children are often placed into "ability groups" based on the teacher's appraisal of their competencies (Rosenholtz & Simpson, 1984; Stipek & Mac Iver, 1989). These practices, coupled with children's increased use of social comparison to appraise their outcomes (Altermatt et al., 2002; Pomerantz et al., 1995), help to explain why older grade-school students begin to distinguish effort from ability and make the kind of causal attributions for their successes and failures that Weiner's theory anticipates.

The late elementary school period (fourth to sixth grades) is also the time when many students begin to value academic achievement less and to develop rather negative academic self-concepts, a trend that becomes even stronger during the middle school years (Butler, 1999; Eccles et al., 1993; Jacobs et al., 2002). As we are about to see, children's tendency to distinguish ability and effort and adopt an entity view of ability is a major contributor to these trends.

Dweck's Learned-Helplessness Theory

All children fail on occasion as they attempt to master challenges, but they don't all respond to failure in the same way. Building on Weiner's attribution theory, Carol Dweck and her colleagues have tried to understand why some children persist in the face of failure and ultimately achieve their objectives, whereas others who fail quickly give up. Their findings revealed that these two types of children explain their achievement outcomes in very different ways (Dweck, 2001; Dweck & Leggett, 1988).

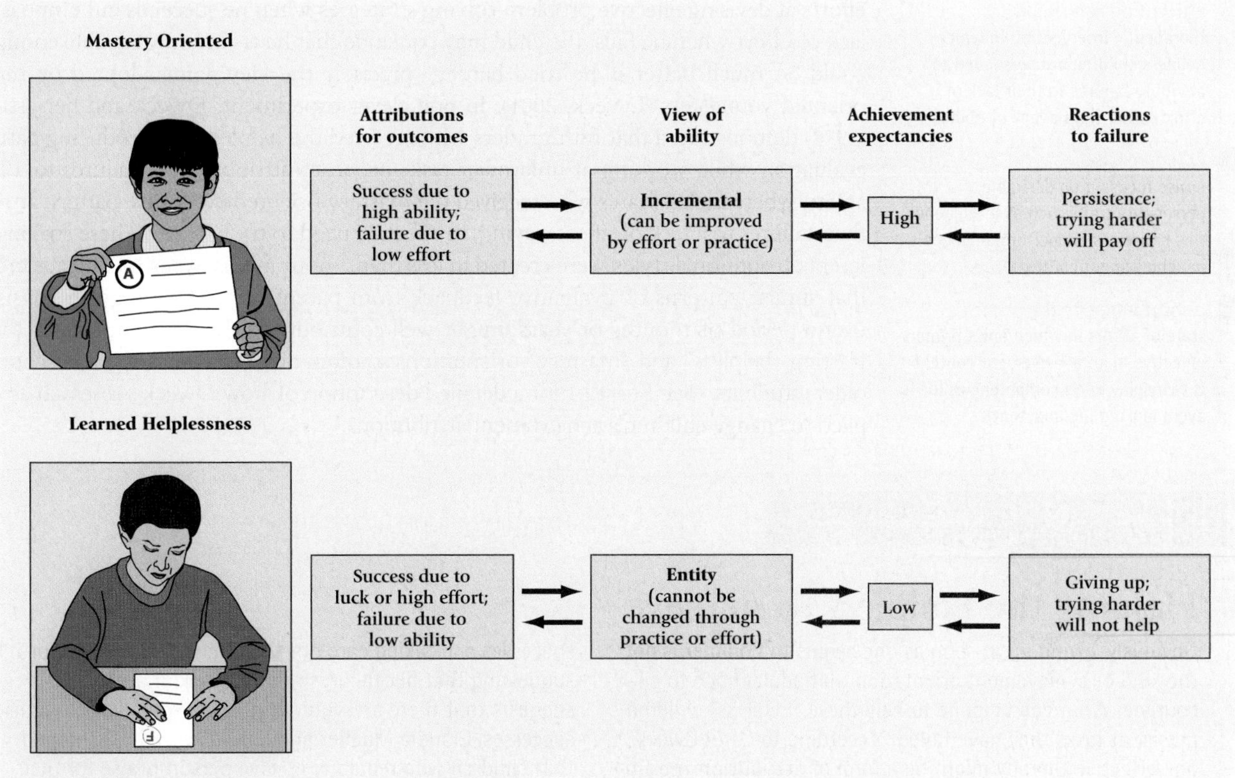

Figure 12.7 Characteristics of the mastery-oriented and learned helplessness achievement orientations.

mastery orientation
a tendency to persist at challenging tasks because of a belief that one has high ability and/or that earlier failures can be overcome by trying harder.

Some children are **mastery oriented:** they attribute their successes to their high ability but tend to externalize the blame for their failures ("That test was unfair"), or attribute them to unstable causes that they can easily overcome ("I'll do better if I try harder"). These students are called "mastery oriented" because they persist in the face of failure, believing that their increased effort will allow them to succeed. Although they see their ability as a reasonably stable attribute that doesn't fluctuate radically from day to day (which allows them to feel confident about repeating their successes), they still think that they can improve their competencies (an incremental viewpoint) by trying harder after a failure. So mastery-oriented youngsters are highly motivated to "master" new challenges, regardless of whether they have previously succeeded or failed at similar tasks (see Figure 12.7).

learned helplessness orientation
a tendency to give up or to stop trying after failing because these failures have been attributed to a lack of ability that one can do little about.

Other children often attribute their successes to the unstable factors of hard work or luck; they do not experience the pride and self-esteem that come from viewing themselves as highly competent. They often attribute their failures to a stable and internal factor—namely, their lack of ability—which causes them to form low expectations of future successes and give up. It appeared to Dweck as if these youngsters were displaying a **learned helplessness orientation:** if failures are attributed to a stable cause—lack of ability—that the child thinks he can do little about (an entity view of ability), he becomes frustrated and sees little reason to try to improve. So he stops trying and acts helpless (see also Pomerantz & Ruble, 1997). Unfortunately, even talented students may adopt this unhealthy attributional style, which, once established, tends to persist over time and eventually undermines their academic performances (Fincham, Hokada & Sanders, 1989; Phillips, 1984; Ziegert et al., 2001).

How Does Learned Helplessness Develop? According to Dweck (1978), parents and teachers may unwittingly foster the development of a helpless achievement orientation if they praise the child for working hard when he succeeds but criticize his lack of ability when he fails. Even 4- to 6-year-olds can begin to develop a helpless orientation if their failures are often punished or otherwise criticized in ways that cause them to doubt their abilities (Burhans & Dweck, 1995; Ziegert et al., 2001). If parents and teachers praise the child's

attribution retraining
therapeutic intervention in which helpless children are persuaded to attribute failures to their lack of effort rather than a lack of ability.

person praise
praise focusing on desirable personality traits such as intelligence; this praise fosters performance goals in achievement contexts.

performance goal
state of affairs in which one's primary objective in an achievement context is to display one's competencies (or to avoid looking incompetent).

efforts at devising effective problem-solving strategies when he succeeds but emphasize his lack of effort when he fails, the child may conclude that he is certainly capable enough and could do much better if he tried harder—precisely the viewpoint adopted by mastery-oriented youngsters (Dweck, 2001). In one clever experiment, Dweck and her associates (1978) demonstrated that fifth-graders who received the helplessness-producing pattern of evaluation while working at unfamiliar tasks began to attribute their failures to a lack of ability, whereas classmates who received the mastery-oriented evaluative pattern attributed their failures to a lack of effort, saying, in effect, "I need to try harder." These strikingly different attributional styles were created in less than 1 hour in this experiment, thus implying that similar patterns of evaluative feedback from parents or teachers, given consistently over a period of months or years, might well contribute to the development of the contrasting "helpless" and "mastery" orientations so often observed among grade-school (and older) students. (See Box 12.1 for a detailed description of how Dweck's research an be applied to change children's achievement attributions.)

APPLYING RESEARCH TO YOUR LIFE

Helping the Helpless to Achieve

Obviously, giving up as soon as one begins to flounder is not the kind of achievement orientation that adults hope to encourage. What can be done to help these "helpless" children persist at tasks they have failed? According to Carol Dweck, one effective therapy might be a form of **attribution retraining** in which children with a learned helplessness orientation are persuaded to attribute their failures to unstable causes—namely, insufficient effort—that they can do something about, rather than continuing to view their failures as stemming from their lack of ability, which is not so easy to change.

Dweck (1975) tested her hypothesis by exposing children who had become "helpless" after failing a series of tough math problems to either of two "therapies." Over a period of 25 therapy sessions, half the children received a *success-only* therapy in which they worked problems they could solve and received tokens for their successes. The other half received *attribution retraining:* they experienced nearly as many successes over the 25 sessions as did the children in the other group but were also told after each of several prearranged failures that they had not worked fast enough and should have tried harder. Thus, an explicit attempt was made to convince these youngsters that failures can reflect a lack of effort rather than a lack of ability. Did this therapy work? Yes, indeed! At the end of the experiment, "helpless" children in the attribution-retraining condition now performed much better on the tough math problems they had initially failed to solve. When they did fail a problem they usually attributed their outcome to a lack of effort and tried harder. Children in the success-only condition showed no such improvements, giving up once again after failing the original problems. Merely showing children who act helpless that they are capable of succeeding is not enough! To alleviate learned helplessness, one must teach children to respond more constructively to their failures by viewing these experiences as something they can overcome if they try harder.

Can we do better than this? Certainly we can by taking steps to prevent learned helplessness from developing. Parents and teachers can play a major part by praising a child's successes and taking care not to undermine her self-worth by suggesting that her failures reflect a lack of ability. Research suggests that there are right ways and wrong ways to praise successes. Claudia Mueller and Carol Dweck (1998) found that children who regularly receive **person praise** for their success, such as "you're really smart, intelligent," often become more interested in **performance goals** than in new learning when faced with novel challenges, as they seek to show how smart they are. A failure quickly undermines this performance goal, causing the child to give up and act helpless. How, then, are adults to praise a child's successes? Melissa Kamins and Carol Dweck (1999) found that children who receive **process-oriented praise** when they succeed—feedback that praises the effort they have expended at finding or formulating good problem-solving strategies—tend to adopt **learning goals.** They come to view task mastery rather than displaying their "smarts" as the most important objective when faced with new challenges. An initial failure at a new problem simply tells these youngsters that they need to devise a new strategy and keep working if they hope to achieve their learning goal, and they do just that rather than giving up and acting helpless (Kamins & Dweck, 1999).

Process-oriented rather than person-oriented praise for success appears to promote a mastery orientation and prevent learned helplessness. In addition, Dweck's distinction between adaptive learning goals and maladaptive performance goals implies that a little restructuring of classroom activities could go a long way toward preventing learned helplessness. Altering curricula to emphasize individual mastery and improving one's competencies should not only convince children to adopt learning goals (Dweck, 2001), but should be particularly helpful to slower learners (Butler, 1999; Stipek & Mac Iver, 1989). Such a focus on mastering new skills for their own sake should also persuade students to view initial failures as evidence that they need to change strategies and keep on working, rather than treating such missteps as "proof" that they have little ability and simply cannot master their assignments.

Who Am I to Be?: Forging an Identity

process-oriented praise
praise of effort expended to formulate good ideas and effective problem-solving strategies; this praise fosters learning goals in achievement contexts.

learning goal
state of affairs in which one's primary objective in an achievement context is to increase one's skills or abilities.

identity
a mature self-definition; a sense of who one is, where one is going in life, and how one fits into society.

identity crisis
Erikson's term for the uncertainty and discomfort that adolescents experience when they become confused about their present and future roles in life.

identity diffusion
identity status characterizing individuals who are not questioning who they are and have not yet committed themselves to an identity.

foreclosure
identity status characterizing individuals who have prematurely committed themselves to occupations or ideologies without really thinking about these commitments.

moratorium
identity status characterizing individuals who are currently experiencing an identity crisis and are actively exploring occupational and ideological positions in which to invest themselves.

identity achievement
identity status characterizing individuals who have carefully considered identity issues and have made firm commitments to an occupation and ideologies.

According to Erik Erikson (1963), the major developmental hurdle that adolescents face is establishing an **identity**—a firm and coherent sense of who they are, where they are heading, and where they fit into society. Forging an identity involves grappling with many important choices: What kind of career do I want? What religious, moral, and political values should I adopt? Who am I as a man or a woman, and as a sexual being? Just where do I fit into society? All this, of course, is a lot for teenagers to have on their minds, and Erikson used the term **identity crisis** to capture the sense of confusion, and even anxiety, that adolescents may feel as they think about who they are today and try to decide "What kind of self can (or should) I become?"

Can you recall a time during the teenage years when you were confused about who you were, what you should be, and what you were likely to become? Is it possible that you have not yet resolved these identity issues and are still seeking answers?

James Marcia (1980) has developed a structured interview that allows researchers to classify adolescents into one of four identity statuses—identity diffusion, foreclosure, moratorium, and identity achievement—based on whether or not they have explored various alternatives and made firm commitments to an occupation, a religious ideology, a sexual orientation, and a set of political values. These identity statuses are as follows:

Identity diffusion. Persons classified as "diffuse" have not yet thought about or resolved identity issues and have not yet charted future life directions. *Example:* "I haven't really thought much about religion, and I guess I don't know exactly what I believe."

Foreclosure. Persons classified as "foreclosed" are committed to an identity but have made this commitment without experiencing the "crisis" of deciding what really suits them best. *Example:* "My parents are Baptists and so I'm a Baptist; it's just the way I grew up."

Moratorium. Persons in this status are experiencing what Erikson called an identity crisis and are actively asking questions about life commitments and seeking answers. *Example:* "I'm evaluating my beliefs and hope that I will be able to decide what's right for me. I like many of the answers provided by my Catholic upbringing, but I'm skeptical about some teachings as well. I have been looking into Unitarianism to see if it might help me answer my questions."

Identity Achievement. Identity-achieved individuals have resolved identity issues by making *personal* commitments to particular goals, beliefs, and values. *Example:* "After a lot of soul-searching about my religion and other religions too, I finally know what I believe and what I don't."

Developmental Trends in Identity Formation

Although Erikson assumed that the identity crisis occurs in early adolescence and is often resolved by age 15 to 18, his age norms were overly optimistic. When Philip Meilman (1979) measured the identity statuses of males between the ages of 12 and 24, he observed a clear developmental progression. As shown in Figure 12.8, the vast majority of 12- to 18-year-olds were identity diffused or foreclosed, and not until age 21 or older had the majority of participants reached the moratorium status or achieved stable identities.

Is the identity formation process different for girls and women than it is for boys and men? In most respects, no (Archer, 1992; Kroger, 2000). Girls make progress toward achieving a clear sense of identity at about the same ages that boys do (Streitmatter, 1993). However, one intriguing sex difference has been observed: although today's college women are just as concerned about establishing a career identity as men are, they attach greater importance to the aspects of identity that center on sexuality, gender roles, and the issue of balancing family and career goals (Archer, 1992; Kroger, 2000).

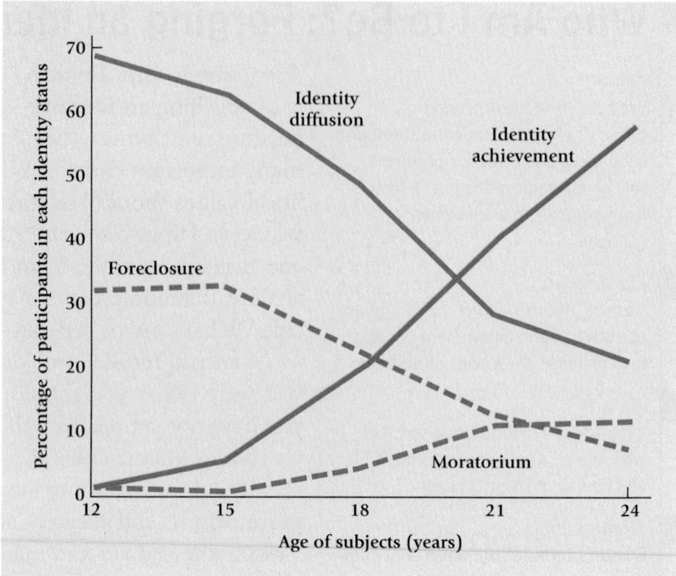

Figure 12.8 Percentages of participants in each of Marcia's four identity statuses as a function of age. Note that resolution of the identity crisis occurs much later than Erikson assumed: Only 4 percent of the 15-year-olds and 20 percent of the 18-year-olds had achieved a stable identity. *From "Cross-Sectional Age Changes in Ego Identity Status During Adolescence," by P. W. Meilman, 1979,* Developmental Psychology, 15, *230-231. Copyright © 1979 by the American Psychological Association. Reprinted by permission.*

Judging from the research on this topic, identity formation takes quite a bit of time. Not until late adolescence—during the college years—do many young men and women move from the diffusion or foreclosure status into the moratorium status and proceed to achieve a sense of identity (Kroger, 2000; Waterman, 1982). But this is by no means the end of the identity formation process. Many adults are *still* struggling with identity issues or have reopened the question of who they are after thinking they had all the answers earlier in life (Kroger, 1996). A divorce, for example, may cause a stay-at-home mother to rethink what it means to be a woman and re-raise questions about other aspects of her identity as well.

The process of achieving identity is quite uneven (Archer, 1982; Kroger, 2000). For example, Sally Archer (1982) assessed the identity statuses of sixth- to twelfth-graders in four domains: occupational choice, gender-role attitudes, religious beliefs, and political ideologies. Only 5 percent of her adolescents were in the same identity status in all four areas, with 95 percent being in two or even three statuses across the four domains. This demonstrates that adolescents can achieve a strong sense of identity in one area and still be searching in others.

How Painful Is Identity Formation?

Perhaps it is unfortunate that Erikson used the term *crisis* to describe the adolescent's active search for an identity (or identities), because adolescents in the moratorium status do not appear all that "stressed out." In fact, James Marcia and his associates (1993) find that these active identity-seekers feel much better about themselves and their futures than do age-mates in the diffusion and foreclosure statuses. Erikson was right in characterizing identity achievement as a very healthy and adaptive development: identity achievers do enjoy higher self-esteem and are less self-conscious or preoccupied with personal concerns than their counterparts in the other three identity statuses (Adams, Abraham, & Markstrom, 1987; O'Connor, 1995).

What may be most painful or crisislike about identity seeking is a long-term failure to establish one. Erikson believed that individuals without a clear identity eventually become depressed and lacking in self-confidence as they drift aimlessly, trapped in the diffusion status. They might heartily embrace what Erikson called a *negative identity,* becoming a "delinquent," or a "loser." Why? Because for these floundering souls, it is better to become everything that one is not supposed to be than to have no identity at all (Erikson, 1963). Research suggests that many adolescents stuck in the diffusion status are highly apathetic and express a sense of hopelessness about the future, sometimes even becoming suicidal (Chandler et al., 2003; Waterman & Archer, 1990). Others who enter high school with very low self-esteem often drift into delinquency and view their deviant self-image as having provided them with a boost in self-worth (Loeber & Stouthamer-Loeber, 1998; Wells, 1989). In this case it seems that a small minority of adolescents and young adults experience what might be termed an identity *crisis* after all.

Influences on Identity Formation

The adolescent's progress toward identity achievement is influenced by at least four factors: cognitive growth, parenting, schooling, and the broader social-cultural context.

Cognitive Influences

Cognitive development plays an important role in identity achievement. Adolescents who have achieved solid mastery of formal-operational thought and can reason logically about hypotheticals are better able to imagine and contemplate future identities. Consequently, they are more likely to raise and resolve identity issues than are age-mates who are less intellectually mature (Boyes & Chandler, 1992; Waterman, 1992).

Parenting Influences

The relationships that adolescents have with their parents can also affect their progress at forging an identity (Markstrom-Adams, 1992; Waterman, 1982). Adolescents in the diffusion status are more likely than those in other statuses to feel neglected or rejected by their parents and to be distant from them (Archer, 1994). Perhaps it is difficult to establish one's own identity without first having the opportunity to identify with respected parental figures and take on some of their desirable qualities. At the other extreme, adolescents in the identity foreclosure status are often extremely close to and sometimes fear rejection from relatively controlling parents (Berzonsky & Adams, 1999). Foreclosed adolescents may never question parental authority or feel any need to forge a separate identity.

Adolescents in the moratorium and identity achievement statuses appear to have a solid base of affection at home combined with considerable freedom to be individuals in their own right (Grotevant & Cooper, 1986, 1998). In family discussions, for example, these adolescents experience a sense of closeness and mutual respect while feeling free to disagree with their parents. We find the same loving and democratic style of parenting that fosters academic achievement and helps children gain a strong sense of self-esteem is also associated with healthy and adaptive identity outcomes in adolescence.

Scholastic Influences

Does attending college help one to forge an identity? The answer is yes—and no. Attending college does seem to push people toward setting career goals and making stable occupational commitments (Waterman, 1982). On the other hand, college students are often far behind their working peers in terms of establishing firm political and religious identities (Munro & Adams, 1977). In fact, some collegians regress from identity

APPLYING RESEARCH TO YOUR LIFE

Exploring Identity in an Online World

As our society becomes more and more saturated with media for children, developmentalists are beginning to explore the implications of media use for child development. For example, the Society for Research in Child Development published one of their Social Policy Reports on the effects of media on child development. It was titled *From Baby Einstein to Leapfrog, from Doom to the Sims, From Instant Messaging to Internet Chat Rooms: Public Interest in the Role of Interactive Media in Children's Lives* (Wartella, Caplovitz, & Lee, 2004).

One of the interesting aspects of media that Wartella and colleagues uncovered was that today's adolescents are using online activities to explore their identities in ways that were not possible before the Internet age. Today's youth talk about themselves online (Bers & Cassell, 2000). They use the potential anonymity of online exchanges to create alternative identities and enhance their self-esteem by creating more popular identities (Thomas, 2000) and by identifying with characters in online interactive gaming sites (McDonald & Kim, 2001). Teenagers also explore their identities by creating personal websites (Lenhart, Rainie, & Lewis, 2001). Indeed, using online activities to explore and change identities is a fairly common pursuit among teenagers today, as illustrated in the accompanying table.

Wartella and colleagues describe a myriad of ways that media influence child development, noting that the exploration of identity is just one aspect of this common activity. And although we can now document what children and adolescents are doing online, and speculate about how this might influence their identity explorations, it is up to future research to determine how these online identities relate to "real life" identities.

Percentage of teenagers who are active on the Internet who self-reported different indentity exploration activities in their online activity

Self-Reported Activities of Online Teens

56%	Have more than one account or screen name to use for different purposes
13%	Have a secret account or screen name to use when they don't want anyone to know they are online
24%	Have pretended to be a different person when they were online
33%	Have given false information about themselves to others online
15%	Have given false ages to access age-restricted websites (such as pornography)
24%	Have created their own websites
48%	Have used online activity to improve their friendships
32%	Have used online activity to make new friends

Adapted from lenhart, Raine, & Lewis, 2001.

© Colin Young-Wolff/PhotoEdit

Middle-school students and adolescents use websites to communicate with each other and explore their own identities.

achievement to the moratorium or even the diffusion status in certain areas—most notably religion. But let's not be too critical of the college environment, for, like college students, many adults later reopen the question of "who they are" when exposed to people or situations that challenge old viewpoints and offer new alternatives (Kroger, 2000).

Social-Cultural Influences

Finally, identity formation is strongly influenced by the broader social and historical context in which it occurs—a point that Erikson himself emphasized. (See the Box above for a discussion of identity exploration in the social and historical context of an "online world.") The very idea that adolescents should choose a personal identity after carefully exploring many options may well be peculiar to industrialized societies of the 20th cen-

TABLE 12.4 Ethnic Self-Identification

	Single Race Selected when Asked to Self-Identify a Single Race Category					
Race Based on Parents' Race	% Black	% White	% Asian	% Hispanic	% Other	% No Choice
Black/Asian	57	15	7	7	7	7
Black/Hispanice	56	7	1	25	7	4
Other/Asian	11	15	23	15	37	1
Asian/Hispanic	13	16	15	40	12	5
Other/Hispanic	9	9	2	46	33	0
Other/Black	61	1	3	4	20	1
Black/White	68	16	1	2	4	9
White/Asian	4	33	43	6	10	4
Other/White	5	62	1	8	25	0
White/Hispanic	3	38	1	52	1	5

Adapted from Hermann, 2004.
Based on a sample of 1,989 adolescents, the data show the percent of multiracial adolescents (based on their parents' races) who self-identified with each single race and those who refused to self-identify with a single race.

tury (Cote & Levine, 1988). As in past centuries, adolescents in many nonindustrialized societies today simply adopt the adult roles they are expected to adopt, without any soul-searching or experimentation: sons of farmers will become farmers; the children of fishermen become (or perhaps marry) fishermen, and so on. For many of the world's adolescents what Marcia calls identity foreclosure is probably the most adaptive route to adulthood. In addition, the specific life goals that these adolescents pursue are necessarily constrained somewhat by whatever options are available and valued in their society at any given point in time (Bosma & Kunnen, 2001; Fuligni & Zhang, 2004; Matsumoto, 2000; Tseng, 2004).

In sum, Western societies permit and expect adolescents to raise serious questions about the self and answer them. Erikson was right in claiming that the individual who achieves identity, regardless of the society in which he or she lives, is likely to be better off for it. Although Erikson recognized that identity issues can and do crop up later in life, even for those people who forge positive identities as adolescents, he quite rightly identified adolescence as a key time of life for defining who we are (and will likely become).

Identity Formation among Minority Youth

In addition to identity issues that confront all adolescents, members of ethnic minority groups must also decide upon the merits of establishing an ethnic identity—a personal identification with an ethnic group and its values and traditions (Hermann, 2004; Phinney, 1996). This is not always an easy task, and it is a very personal task. For example, Hermann (2004) found that multiracial adolescents differed widely in their stated racial identity when they were forced to choose a single racial category as a personal label (see Table 12.4). Some of these adolescents even refused to choose a single racial category to describe themselves.

As we saw earlier, some minority children may even identify at first with the culture's ethnic majority, apparently wanting to affiliate with the group that has the most status in society (Spencer & Markstrom-Adams, 1990). One Hispanic adolescent who had done this said, "I remember I would not say I was Hispanic. My friends . . . were White and

Oriental and I tried so hard to fit in with them" (Phinney & Rosenthal, 1992, p. 158). It is not that young children have no knowledge of their subcultural traditions. Mexican American preschoolers, for example, may learn such culturally relevant behaviors as giving a Chicano handshake; yet not until about age 8 are they likely to fully understand which ethnic labels apply to them, what they mean, or that one's ethnicity is a lifelong attribute (Bernal & Knight, 1997).

Forming a positive ethnic identity during adolescence seems to involve the same steps, or statuses, as forming a vocational or religious identity (Phinney, 1993). Young adolescents often say that they identify with their own ethnic group because their parents and other members of the group influenced them to do so (foreclosure status), or because that is what they are and they have not given the issue much thought (diffusion status). But between ages 16 and 19, many minority youths move into the moratorium or achievement phases of ethnic identity. One Mexican American girl describes her moratorium period this way: "I want to know what we do and how our culture is different from others. Going to festivals and cultural events helps me to learn more about my own culture and about myself" (Phinney, 1993, p. 70). Once ethnic identity is achieved, minority youth tend to display higher self-esteem, better academic adjustment, better relations with parents, and more favorable assessments of peers of other ethnicities than their counterparts who still merely label themselves as a minority and are still ethnically diffuse or foreclosed (Chavous et al., 2003; Phinney, 1996; Phinney, Ferguson, & Tate, 1997; Yip & Fuligni, 2002).

Questions regarding ethnic identity are sometimes triggered by the stresses associated with others' prejudicial comments or by being discriminated against because of one's ethnicity (see Caldwell et al., 2002; DuBois et al., 2002a; Ogbu, 1998). Minority youth also face thorny identity questions when they encounter conflicts between the values of their subculture and those of the majority culture. Members of their subcultural communities (especially peers) often discourage identity explorations that clash with the traditions of their own group. Virtually all North American minorities have a term for community members who are "too white" in orientation, be it the "apple" (red on the outside, white on the inside) for Native Americans, the Hispanic "coconut," the Asian "banana," or the African American "Oreo." Minority adolescents must resolve these value conflicts and decide for themselves what *they* are inside.

Mixed-ethnicity adolescents and cross-ethnic adoptees in white adoptive homes sometimes face even greater conflicts. These youngsters may feel pressured to choose between minority and white peer groups, thereby encountering social barriers to achieving an identity as *both* African American (for example) and white (DeBerry, Scarr, & Weinberg, 1996; Kerwin et al., 1993). About half the cross-ethnic adoptees in Scarr's classic Minnesota Transracial Adoption Study were showing some signs of social maladjustment at age 17. Although African American in appearance, many of these adoptees looked to whites as their primary reference group. Thus their maladjustment could reflect the fact that (1) they were not prepared to function effectively within the African American community, and (2) they were likely to face some prejudice and discrimination as a black person trying to fit into a white ecological niche (DeBerry, Scarr, & Weinberg, 1996). Yet a stronger identification with *either* a white or an African American reference group predicted better adjustment outcomes than did maintaining a more ethnically diffuse orientation. Here is another sign that establishing some kind of ethnic identity, or point of reference, is an adaptive developmental outcome for members of a minority group.

Forging a positive ethnic identity is an adaptive development for minority youths.

How can we help minority youths forge positive ethnic identities and achieve more favorable adjustment outcomes? Their parents can play a major role, starting in the preschool period, by (1) teaching them about their group's cultural traditions and fostering ethnic pride, (2) preparing them to deal constructively with the prejudices and value conflicts they may encounter, and (3) simply being warm and supportive confidants (Bernal & Knight, 1997; Caldwell et al., 2002; Caughy et al., 2002; Hughes & Chen, 1999). Schools and communities can also help by promoting a greater understanding and appreciation

CONCEPT CHECK 12.2 Establishing an Achievement Orientation and a Personal Identity

Check your understanding of the development of achievement attributions and orientations, and the development of a personal identity, by answering the following questions. Answers appear in the Appendix.

Matching: Match the type of parental, peer, or teacher feedback listed with the likely developmental outcome defined below.

a. process-orientated praise
b. negative peer influences
c. person praise
d. strong parental criticism of failure

1. ________ This is a strong contributor to academic underachievement among disadvantaged minorities.
2. ________ This is a correlate of low achievement motivation.
3. ________ This may promote adoption of performance goals (and a helpless orientation).
4. ________ This is likely to promote adoption of learning goals (and a mastery orientation).

True or False: Identify whether the following statement is true or false.

5. (T)(F) Jacob lives in a nonindustrialized, communal society. When asked what he plans to be when he grows up, Jacob answers, "Well certainly a carpenter like my father and grandfather." From this reply, we can assume that Jacob is in the stage of identity foreclosure with respect to his occupation and that he is on an adaptive route to identity formation.

Fill in the Blank: Complete the following statements with the correct concept or phrase.

6. The belief that one's ability can be improved through increased effort and practice is known as an ________ view of ability.
7. The belief that one's ability is a highly stable trait that is not influenced much by effort or practice is an ________ view of ability.

Short Answer: Provide brief answers to the following questions.

8. List Marcia's proposed identity statuses in the order in which most children progress through them on their way to establishing a personal identity.
9. Distinguish between "mastery orientation" and "learned helplessness." Define each concept and list potential learning outcomes of each.

Essay: Provide a detailed answer to the following question.

10. Diagram Weiner's classification of the causes of achievement outcomes. Include potential "loci of causality," "stability of causes," and likely attributions for success and failure for each classification.

of ethnic diversity starting early in the preschool years (Burnette, 1997), and by continuing their efforts to ensure that educational and economic opportunities are extended to all (Spencer & Markstrom-Adams, 1990).

The Other Side of Social Cognition: Knowing about Others

Being appropriately social requires us to interact with other people, and these interactions are more likely to be harmonious if we know what our social partners are thinking or feeling and can predict how they are likely to behave (Heyman & Gelman, 1998). Children's knowledge of other people—their descriptions of other's characteristics and the inferences they make about their companions' feelings, thoughts, and actions—become more accurate with age (Bartsch & London, 2000; Flavell & Miller, 1998). What kinds of information do children use to form impressions of others? How do these impressions change over time? And what skills do children acquire that might explain such changes in person perception? These are the issues we will now explore.

Age Trends in Person Perception

Children younger than 7 or 8 are likely to characterize people they know in the same concrete, observable terms that they use to describe the self (Livesley & Bromley, 1973; Ruble & Dweck, 1995) (see the Box on p. 499). Five-year-old Jenny, for example, said: "My daddy is big. He has hairy legs and eats mustard. Yuck! My daddy likes dogs—do you?" Not much of a personality profile there! When young children do use a psychological term to describe others, it is typically a very general attribute such as "He's *nice*" or "She's *mean*" that they may use more as a label for the person's recent behavior than as a description of the person's enduring qualities (Rholes & Ruble, 1984; Ruble & Dweck, 1995).

It's not that preschoolers have *no* appreciation for the inner qualities people display. As we noted earlier in the chapter, even 18-month-olds imitate the purposeful acts of humans but not mechanical toys, thus reflecting an awareness that human behaviors are guided by intentions (Meltzoff, 1995; Repacholi & Gopnik, 1997). By age 3 to 5, children are aware of how their closest peer companions typically behave in a variety of different situations (Eder, 1989). Kindergartners already know that their classmates differ in academic competencies and social skills. They reliably choose classmates who normally do well in school as teammates for academic competitions and those who are socially skilled as partners for play activities (Droege & Stipek, 1993). This suggests that 5- to 6- year-olds are becoming more aware of behavioral consistencies that their companions display. They are also beginning to make other kinds of "traitlike" inferences based on their emerging understanding of subjective mental states—such as desires and motives—that might explain other people's conduct. For example, 5-year-olds who hear stories about a child who has often shared and a second child who rarely has can correctly infer that the first child will be motivated to share in the future and is "generous," whereas the second child will be unmotivated to share and is "selfish" (Yuill & Pearson, 1998). Thus, 5-year-olds assume that individual differences in past behaviors imply different motives and different traits. Even 4-year-olds have some appreciation of traitlike labels and can use them to make appropriate psychological inferences. When told that a boy is "shy," for example, they know that he would prefer to use the swimming pool when there were few people

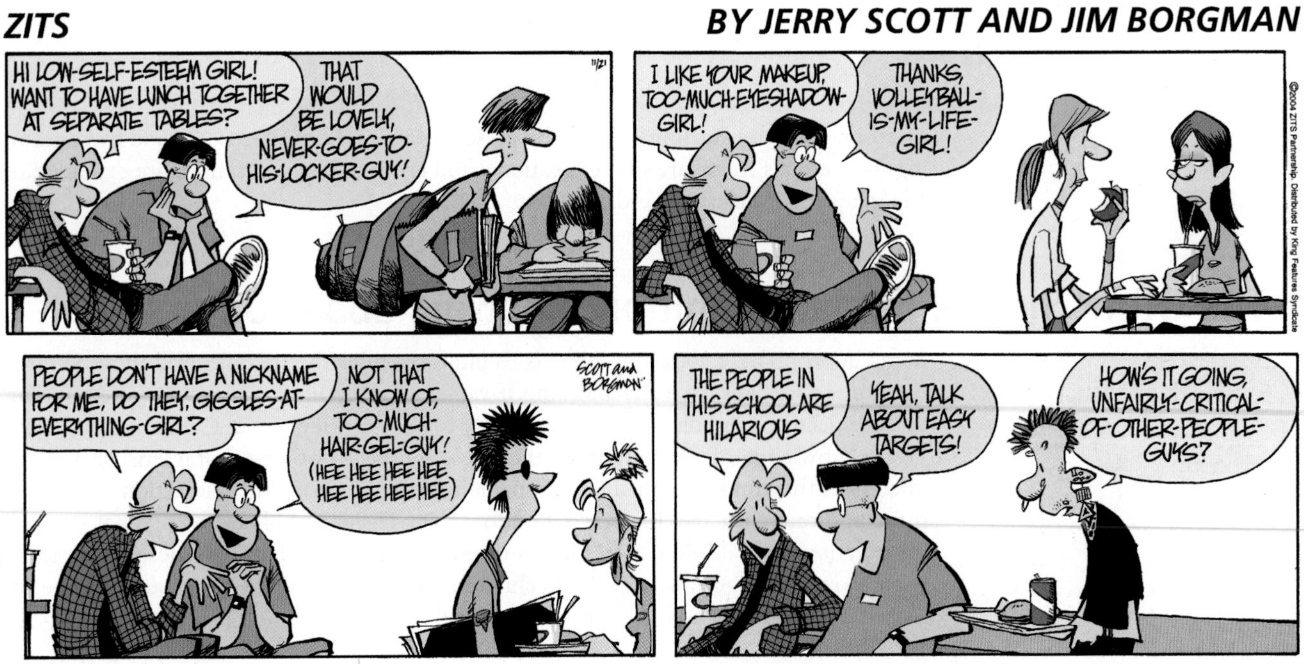

APPLYING RESEARCH TO YOUR LIFE

Racial Categorization and Racism in Young Children

Bob Daemmrich/The Image Works

Mixed-ethnicity discussion groups can foster an appreciation of diverse subcultural traditions and combat the formation of prejudicial attitudes.

Because toddlers and preschool children tend to define others in terms of their observable characteristics and to place people into categories, it may come as no surprise to learn that even 3- and 4-year-olds have formed ethnic categories and can apply labels such as *black* and *white* to different people or to photos of blacks and whites. Furthermore, studies conducted in Australia, Canada, and the United States reveal that by age 5, many white children have some knowledge of ethnic stereotypes (Bigler & Liben, 1993) and display at least some prejudicial attitudes toward blacks and Native Americans (Aboud, 2003; Black-Gutman & Hickson, 1996; Doyle & Aboud, 1993.)

Interestingly, parents often believe that their own children are largely oblivious to ethnic diversity and that prejudicial attitudes and behaviors in other children arise when their bigoted parents pass their own intolerant views to them (Burnette, 1997). However, research suggests otherwise. The ethnic attitudes of young children often bear little relationship to those of their parents or their friends (Aboud, 1988; Burnette, 1997). The origins of ethnic discrimination may be more cognitive than social, reflecting the tendency of egocentric youngsters to rigidly categorize people by skin color (and other physical correlates of ethnicity), and to strongly favor the group to which they belong, without necessarily being overtly hostile toward people of other ethnicities (Aboud, 2003; see also Bennett et al., 2004; Kowalski, 2003).

As children enter concrete operations and become more flexible in their thinking, prejudicial attitudes often decline in strength. This increased tolerance of 8- to 9-year-olds reflects their more realistic evaluation of ethnic groups in which outgroups are viewed more favorably and their own group somewhat less favorably than was true during the preschool years (Doyle & Aboud, 1993; Teichman, 2001).

Nevertheless, social forces can obviously play a role in maintaining or even intensifying racial prejudice. Daisa Black-Gutman and Fay Hickson (1996) found that Euro-Australian children's prejudice toward black Aborigines declined between ages 5 and 9, and then intensified at age 10 to 12, returning to the levels displayed by 5- to 6-year-olds! Since the 10- to 12-year-olds were no longer constrained by the egocentrism and rigid categorization schemes of a 5- or 6-year-old, their increased prejudice apparently reflected the influence of adult attitudes, namely the deep-seated animosity that many Euro-Australians feel toward black Aborigines. However, increases in prejudice during early adolescence may also reflect the fact that personal identity issues are becoming increasingly important; thus, praising the virtues of one's own group and the shortcomings of other groups is a way of solidifying one's group identity and enhancing self-worth (Kiesner et al., 2003; Teichman, 2001).

Developmentalists now believe that the best way to combat ethnic prejudice is for parents and teachers to talk openly about the merits of ethnic diversity and the harmful effects of prejudice, beginning in the preschool period when strong favoritism of one's own in-group and early indications of prejudice often take root (Burnette, 1997). One especially promising program in the public schools of western Massachusetts takes a three-pronged approach:

- *Teacher training.* Teachers receive a four-month course that defines ethnic prejudice, explores how educators and children display it, and provides guidance for handling it at school.
- *Youth groups.* Children of different ethnicities first meet for 7 weeks with ethnic peers to discuss the values and traditions of their own subcultures. Then participants meet for 7 more weeks in mixed-ethnicity groups to discuss their different perspectives and to devise strategies for getting along.
- *Parent groups.* Once a month, parents of program participants attend classes to learn more about ethnic prejudice and how to comfortably discuss diversity issues with their children.

This program is based on the proposition that the key to combating ethnic prejudice is to be honest about it with children rather than shunning the topic and trying to cover it up. Such strong measures may be essential because prejudicial attitudes, once established, are very difficult to change by limited interventions involving increased use of multicultural curricula and materials in the classroom (Bigler, 1999). As developmentalist Vonnie McLoyd (cited in Burnette, 1997, p. 33) has noted, "Racism is so deeply rooted that [overcoming it] is going to take hard work by open, honest, fair-minded people who are not easily discouraged."

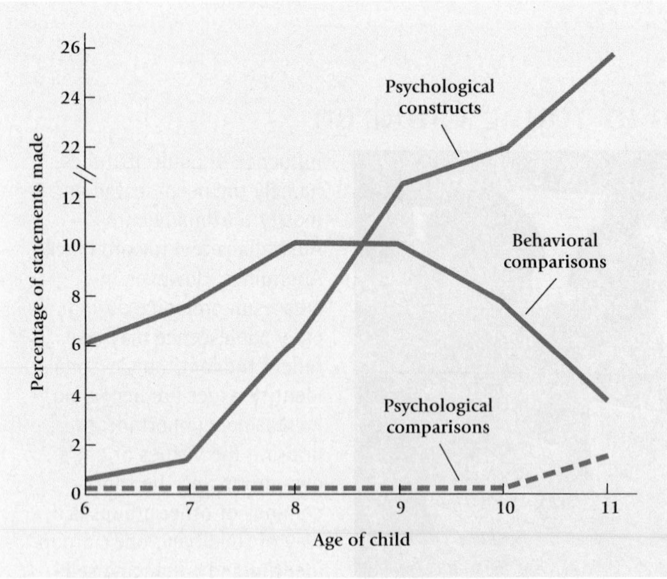

Figure 12.9 Percentages of descriptive statements classified as behavioral comparisons, psychological (traitlike) constructs, and psychological comparisons for children between ages 6 and 11. *From "The Development of Person Perception in Childhood and Adolescence: From Behavioral Comparison to Psychological Constructs to Psychological Comparisons," by C. Barenboim, 1981,* Child Development, *52, 129–144. Copyright © 1981 by The Society for Research in Child Development, Inc. Reprinted by permission.*

around and would be upset rather than pleased upon encountering the pool with a lot of people there (Heyman & Gelman, 1999).

If 4- to 6-year-olds are capable of thinking about traits in psychologically meaningful ways (Alvarez, Ruble, & Bolger, 2001; Lockhart, Chang, & Story, 2002), why do they use so few trait words to describe their companions? Probably because they are (1) less likely than older children to view traits as stable over time, thinking that they are subject to change (Heyman & Gelman, 1998), and (2) they are still using trait labels as adjectives to describe recent behaviors (for example, "that was *mean,* Vinceta") without fully understanding how to weave their emerging knowledge of traits into their everyday speech.

Between ages 7 and 16, children come to rely less and less on concrete attributes and more on psychological descriptors to characterize their friends and acquaintances. These changes are nicely illustrated in a program of research by Carl Barenboim (1981) who asked 6- to 11-year-olds to describe three persons they knew well. Rather than simply listing the behaviors that close companions display, 6- to 8-year-olds often compared others on noteworthy behavioral dimensions, making such statements as "Dominick runs faster than Jason" or "She draws the best pictures in our whole class." As shown in Figure 12.9, use of these **behavioral comparisons** increased between ages 6 and 8 and declined rapidly after age 9. One outgrowth of the behavioral comparison process is that children become increasingly aware of regularities in a companion's behavior and eventually begin to attribute them to stable **psychological constructs,** or traits, that the person is now presumed to have. So a 10-year-old who formerly described one of her acquaintances as drawing better than anyone in her class may now convey the same impression by saying that the acquaintance is "very artistic." Notice in reexamining Figure 12.9 that children's use of these psychological constructs increased rapidly between ages 8 and 11, the same period when behavioral comparisons became less common. Eventually, children begin to compare and contrast others on important psychological dimensions, making statements such as "Thomas is more shy than Rosemary" or "Devin is the most artistic person in our class." Although few 11-year-olds generate these **psychological comparisons** when describing others (see Figure 12.9), the majority of 12- to 16-year-olds in Barenboim's second study actively compared their associates on noteworthy psychological dimensions.

behavioral comparisons phase
the tendency to form impressions of others by comparing and contrasting their overt behaviors.

psychological constructs phase
tendency to base one's impressions of others on the stable traits these individuals are presumed to have.

psychological comparisons phase
tendency to form impressions of others by comparing and contrasting these individuals on abstract psychological dimensions.

By age 14 to 16, adolescents are not only aware of the *dispositional* similarities and dissimilarities that characterize their acquaintances, but they are also beginning to recognize that any number of *situational* factors (for example, illness, family strife) can cause a person to act "out of character" (Damon & Hart, 1988). By midadolescence, young people are becoming sophisticated "personality theorists" who are able to look both inside and outside a companion to explain her conduct and form coherent impressions of her character.

Theories of Social-Cognitive Development

Why do children progress from behavioral comparisons to psychological constructs to psychological comparisons? Why do their own self-concepts and their impressions of others become increasingly abstract and coherent over time? In addressing these issues, we will first examine two cognitive points of view before considering how social forces might contribute, both directly and indirectly, to the growth of social cognition.

Cognitive Theories of Social Cognition

The two cognitive theories that are most often used to explain developmental trends in social cognition are Piaget's cognitive-developmental approach and Robert Selman's role-taking analysis.

Cognitive-Developmental Theory. According to cognitive-developmental theorists, the ways that children think about the self and other people largely depend on their own levels of cognitive development. Recall that the thinking of 3- to 6-year-old "preoperational" children tends to center on the most salient perceptual aspects of stimuli and events. So it would hardly surprise a Piagetian to find that 3- to 6-year-olds describe their associates in very concrete, observable terms, mentioning their appearances and possessions, their likes and dislikes, and the actions they can perform.

The thinking of 7- to 10-year-olds will change in many ways as these youngsters enter Piaget's concrete-operational stage. Not only is egocentrism becoming less pronounced, but children are now *decentering* from their focus on the most obvious perceptual characteristics and beginning to recognize that certain properties of an object remain unchanged despite changes in the object's appearance (*conservation*). These emerging abilities to look beyond immediate appearances and infer underlying invariances might help to explain why 7- to 10-year-olds, who are actively comparing themselves with their peers, become more attuned to regularities in their own and others' conduct and use psychological constructs, or traits, to describe these patterns.

By ages 12 to 14, children are entering formal operations and are able to think more logically and systematically about abstractions. Although the concept of a psychological trait is itself an abstraction, it is one based on regularities in concrete, observable behaviors, perhaps explaining why *concrete* operators can think in these terms. However, a trait *dimension* is even more of a mental inference or abstraction that refers to few, if any, concrete, observable behaviors. The ability to think in dimensional terms and to reliably order people along a dimensional scale (as is necessary in making psychological comparisons) implies that a person is able to operate on abstract concepts—a formal-operational ability (O'Mahoney, 1989).

Although children begin to make behavioral comparisons at ages 6 to 8 and psychological comparisons at about age 12—precisely the times that Piaget's theory implies that they should—Robert Selman (1980) believes that there is one particular aspect of cognitive development that underlies a mature understanding of the self and other people: the growth of **role-taking** skills.

role taking
the ability to assume another person's perspective and understand his or her thoughts, feelings, and behaviors.

Selman's Role-Taking Theory. According to Selman (1980; Yeates & Selman, 1989), children gain much richer understandings of themselves and other people as they acquire the ability to discriminate their own perspectives from those of their companions and see the relationships between these potentially discrepant points of view. Selman believes that in order to "know" a person, one must be able to assume his perspective and understand his thoughts, feelings, motives, and intentions—in short, the internal factors that account for his behavior. If a child has not yet acquired these important role-taking skills, she may have little choice but to describe her acquaintances in terms of their external attributes—that is, their appearance, their activities, and the things they possess.

Selman has studied the development of role-taking skills by asking children to comment on a number of interpersonal dilemmas. Here is one example (from Selman, 1976, p. 302):

> Holly is an 8-year-old girl who likes to climb trees. She is the best tree climber in the neighborhood. One day while climbing down from a tall tree, she falls . . . but does not hurt herself. Her father sees her fall. He is upset and asks her to promise not to climb trees any more. Holly promises. Later that day, Holly and her friends meet Shawn. Shawn's kitten is caught in a tree and can't get down. Something has to be done right away or the kitten may fall. Holly is the only one who climbs trees well enough to reach the kitten and get it down but she remembers her promise to her father.

To assess how well a child understands the perspectives of Holly, her father, and Shawn, Selman asks: Does Holly know how Shawn feels about the kitten? How will Holly's father feel if he finds out she climbed the tree? What does Holly think her father will do if he finds out she climbed the tree? What would you do? Children's responses to these probes led Selman to conclude that role-taking skills develop in a stagelike manner, as shown in Table 12.5.

Notice in examining Table 12.5 that children progress from largely egocentric beings, who may be unaware of any perspective other than their own (stage 0), to sophisticated social-cognitive theorists, who can keep several perspectives in mind and compare each with the viewpoint "most people" would adopt (stage 4). Apparently these role-taking skills represent a true developmental sequence, because 40 of 41 boys who were repeatedly tested over a 5-year period showed a steady forward progression from stage to stage with no skipping of stages (Gurucharri & Selman, 1982). Perhaps the reason that these skills develop in one particular order is that they are closely related to Piaget's invariant sequence of cognitive stages (Keating & Clark, 1980): preoperational children are at Selman's first or second level of role taking (stage 0 or 1), whereas most concrete operators are at the third or fourth level (stage 2 or 3), and formal operators are about equally distributed between the fourth and fifth levels of role taking (stages 3 and 4).

Role Taking and Thinking about Relationships. As children acquire role-taking skills, their understanding of the meaning and character of human relationships

TABLE 12.5 Selman's Stages of Social Perspective Taking

Stage of role taking	Typical responses to the "Holly" dilemma
0. **Egocentric or undifferentiated perspective** (roughly 3 to 6 years) Children are unaware of any perspective other than their own. They assume that whatever they feel is right for Holly to do will be agreed on by others.	Children often assume that Holly will save the kitten. When asked how Holly's father will react to her transgression, these children think he will be "happy because he likes kittens." In other words, these children like kittens themselves, and they assume that Holly and her father also like kittens.
1. **Social-informational role taking** (roughly 6 to 8 years) Children now recognize that people can have perspectives that differ from their own but believe that this happens only because these individuals have received different information.	When asked whether Holly's father will be angry because she climbed the tree, the child may say, "If he didn't know why she climbed the tree, he would be angry. But if he knew why she did it, he would realize that she had a good reason."
2. **Self-reflective role taking** (roughly 8 to 10 years) Children now know that their own and others' points of view may conflict even if they have received the same information. They are now able to consider the other person's viewpoint. They also recognize that the other person can put himself in their shoes, so that they are now able to anticipate the person's reactions to their behavior. However, the child cannot consider his own perspective and that of another person at the same time.	If asked whether Holly will climb the tree, the child might say, "Yes. She knows that her father will understand why she did it." In so doing, the child is focusing on the father's consideration of Holly's perspective. But if asked whether the father would want Holly to climb the tree, the child usually says no, thereby indicating that he is now assuming the father's perspective and considering the father's concern for Holly's safety.
3. **Mutual role taking** (roughly 10 to 12 years) The child can now simultaneously consider her own and another person's points of view and recognize that the other person can do the same. The child can also assume the perspective of a disinterested third party and anticipate how each participant (self and other) will react to the viewpoint of his or her partner.	At this stage, a child might describe the outcome of the "Holly" dilemma by taking the perspective of a disinterested third party and indicating that she knows that both Holly and her father are thinking about what each other is thinking. For example, one child remarked: "Holly wanted to get the kitten because she likes kittens, but she knew that she wasn't supposed to climb trees. Holly's father knew that Holly had been told not to climb trees, but he couldn't have known about [the kitten]."
4. **Societal role taking** (roughly 12 to 15 and older) The adolescent now attempts to understand another person's perspective by comparing it with that of the social system in which he operates (that is, the view of the "generalized other"). In other words, the adolescent expects others to consider and typically assume perspectives on events that most people in their social group would take.	When asked if Holly should be punished for climbing the tree, the stage 4 adolescent is likely to say "No" and claim that the value of humane treatment of animals justifies Holly's act and that most fathers would recognize this point.

Source: Adapted from "Social Cognitive Understanding: A Guide to Educational and Clinical Experience," by R. L. Selman, 1976, in T. Likona (Ed.), *Moral Development and Behavior: Theory, Research, and Social Issues.*

begins to change. Consider what children of different ages say about the meaning of friendship.

Preschoolers at Selman's egocentric (level 0) stage think that virtually any pleasant interactions between themselves and available playmates will qualify those playmates as "friends." So 5-year-old Chang might describe Terry as a close friend simply because "He lives next door and plays games with me" (Damon, 1977).

Common activity continues to be the principal basis for friendship among 6- to 8-year-olds (Hartup, 1992). But because these youngsters have reached Selman's stage 1 and recognize that others may not always share their perspectives, they begin to view a friend as someone who *chooses* to "do nice things for me." Friendships are often one-way at this stage, for the child feels no strong pressure to reciprocate these considerations. And should a friend fail to serve the child's interests (for example, by turning down an invitation to camp out in the back yard), she may quickly become a "nonfriend."

Later, at Selman's stage 2, 8- to 10-year-olds show increasing concern for the needs of a friend and begin to see friendships as reciprocal relationships, based on mutual trust, in which two people exchange respect, kindness, and affection (Selman, 1980). No longer are common activities sufficient to brand someone a friend. As children appreciate how their own interests and perspectives and those of their peers can be similar or different, they insist that their friends be psychologically similar to themselves.

By early adolescence, many children have reached Selman's stage 3 or 4. Although they still view friends as psychologically similar people who like, trust, and assist each other, they have expanded their notions of the obligations of friendship to emphasize the exchange of intimate thoughts and feelings (Berndt & Perry, 1990). They increasingly expect their friends to stick up for them and be loyal, standing ready to provide close emotional support whenever they may need it (Berndt & Perry, 1990; Buhrmester, 1990). Perhaps because they rest on a firmer basis of intimacy and interpersonal understanding, the close friendships of older children and adolescents are viewed as more important and are more stable, or long-lasting, than those of younger children (Berndt, 1989; Berndt & Hoyle, 1985; Furman & Buhrmester, 1992).

With the growth of role-taking skills children's conceptions of friendship gradually change from the one-sided, self-centered view of friends as "people who benefit me" to a harmonious, reciprocal perspective in which each party truly understands the other, enjoys providing him or her with emotional support and other niceties, and expects these same considerations in return.

Disagreements among peers are important contributors to role-taking skills and the growth of interpersonal understanding.

Social Influences on Social-Cognitive Development

Some developmentalists have wondered whether the growth of children's self-awareness and their understanding of other people are as closely tied to cognitive development as cognitive theories suggest. Consider, for example, that even though children's role-taking abilities are related to their performances on Piagetian measures and IQ tests (Pellegrini, 1985), it is quite possible for a child to grow less egocentric and mature intellectually without becoming an especially skillful role-taker (Shantz, 1983). There must be other, *noncognitive* factors that contribute to the growth of role-taking skills and may even exert their own unique effects on children's social-cognitive development. Might social experiences play such a role? No less an authority than Jean Piaget thought so.

Social Experience as a Contributor to Role Taking. Many years ago, Piaget (1965) argued that playful interactions among grade school children promote the development of role-taking skills and mature social judgments. Piaget's view was that, by assuming different roles while playing together, young children become more aware of discrepancies between their own perspectives and those of their playmates. When conflicts arise in play, children must learn to coordinate their points of view with those of their companions (that is, compromise) in order for play to continue. So Piaget assumed that *equal-status contacts among peers* are an important contributor to social perspective-taking and the growth of interpersonal understanding.

Not only has research consistently supported Piaget's viewpoint, but it appears that some forms of peer contact may be better than others at fostering the growth of interpersonal understanding. Janice Nelson and Francis Aboud (1985) propose that disagreements among friends are particularly important because children tend to be more open and honest with their friends than with mere acquaintances and are more motivated to resolve disputes with friends. As a result, disagreeing friends should be more likely than disagreeing acquaintances to provide each other with the information needed to understand and appreciate their conflicting points of view. When 8- to 10-year-olds discuss an interpersonal issue on which they disagree, pairs of friends are much more critical of their partners than pairs of acquaintances are, but friends are also more likely to fully explain the rationales for their own points of view. Disagreeing friends display increases in social understanding after these discussions are over, whereas disagreeing acquaintances do not (Nelson & Aboud, 1985). So it seems that equal-status contacts among friends may be especially important for the growth of role-taking skills and interpersonal understanding.

Social Experience as a Direct Contributor to Person Perception. Social contacts with peers not only contribute indirectly to person perception by fostering the development of role-taking skills, but they are also a form of direct experience by which children

CONCEPT CHECK 12.3 Understanding Social Cognition

Check your understanding of the development of social cognition by answering the following questions. Answers appear in the Appendix.

Matching: Match the ages below to the following bases of friendship:

a. psychological similarities
b. common activities
c. loyalty and sharing of intimacies

1. ________ principal basis for friendships among 3- to 7-year-olds
2. ________ principal basis for friendships among 9- to 12-year-olds
3. ________ principal basis for friendships among adolescents

True or False: Identify whether the following statement is true or false.

4. (T)(F) Eva is asked to describe herself by answering the question "Who am I?" She replies, "I am a girl. I have brown hair. I have a bike. I have a sister." She's then asked to describe her sister and she replies, "Irene is a girl. She has lots of books. She is 5 years old." From these descriptions, we can assume that Eva is younger than 7 or 8 years old.

Fill in the Blank: Complete the following statements with the correct concept or phrase.

5. Impressions derived by noting and comparing the actions of one's peers are known as ________ .
6. Impressions stemming from dispositional similarities or differences in others are known as ________.
7. Impressions based on the traits that others are presumed to possess are known as ________.

Short Answer: Provide brief answers to the following questions.

8. List the stages in Selman's role-taking theory.
9. Describe the basic research design used by Selman to test his theory.

can learn what others are like. In other words, the more experience a child has with peers, the more motivated she should be to try to understand them, and the more practiced she should become at appraising the causes of their behavior (Higgins & Parsons, 1983).

Popularity is a convenient measure of social experience; that is, popular children interact more often with a wider variety of peers than do their less popular age-mates (LeMare & Rubin, 1987). If the amount of direct experience a child has with peers exerts its own unique influence on his or her social-cognitive judgments, then popular children should outperform less popular age mates on tests of social understanding, even when their role-taking skills are comparable. This is precisely what Jackie Gnepp (1989) found when she tested the ability of popular and less popular 8-year-olds to make appropriate traitlike inferences about an unfamiliar child from a small sample of the child's previous behaviors. Both social experience (as indexed by popularity) and cognitive competence (role-taking skills) contribute in their own ways to the development of children's understanding of other people.

Applying Developmental Themes to the Development of the Self and Social Cognition

The four development themes in this book (the active child, nature and nurture influences on development, quantitative and qualitative developmental change, and the holistic nature of child development) are prominent in this chapter. Have you identified examples to illustrate each theme as you have been reading the chapter? Let's take a look at a few examples.

The child as an active participant in his or her development is an important theme in the development of self and social cognition. We've seen that the child's cognitive development and social experiences gradually accumulate to stimulate the child's developing sense of self, self-esteem, achievement motivations, and social cognition. One theory we examined that stated this theme explicitly was Bowlby's theory of the development of self-esteem. Recall that according to Bowlby, infants who are securely attached to their caregivers form positive working models of the self and others. These working models form a basis for the origins of self-esteem.

The interaction of nature and nurture on development was illustrated by toddlers' acquisition of self-recognition in the second year of life. We saw that biological maturation and cognitive development, to a certain point, were necessary for self-recognition, but that without the experience of social interaction, self-recognition may be delayed (or never achieved in the case of chimpanzees).

We discussed several developmental achievements in the development of self (such as the phases of achievement motivation and the stages of identity development) and the development of social cognition (such as the stages of role-taking ability) that followed qualitative forms of developmental change. However, the majority of the developmental change we discussed throughout this chapter would better be described as following a quantitative form of change. Children's cognitive development and social experiences were seen to gradually accumulate to move children forward in their understandings of self and others.

Finally, the topics in this chapter were all relevant to the holistic nature of child development. Indeed, the very title of "social cognition" indicates that the child's social and cognitive attributes work together in development. Throughout the chapter nearly every developmental milestone was achieved through an integration of the child's cognitive development and social experiences.

SUMMARY

■ The development of **social cognition** deals with how children's understanding of the **self** and other people changes with age.

Development of the Self-Concept

■ Most developmentalists believe that infants come to distinguish themselves from the external environment over the first 2 to 6 months.
■ By 18 to 24 months of age, toddlers display true **self-recognition**—and a sense of a **present self,** which gradually evolves into a conception of **extended self,** or a self that is stable over time.
■ Toddlers also classify themselves along socially significant dimensions such as age and sex, forming **categorical self.**
■ The self-descriptions of 3- to 5-year-olds are typically very concrete, focusing mostly on their physical features, possessions, and the activities they can perform.
■ By about age 8, children begin to describe themselves in terms of their inner and enduring psychological attributes.
■ Adolescents have a more integrated and abstract self-concept that includes not only their dispositional qualities but also a knowledge of how these characteristics might interact with situational influences to affect their behavior.
■ Frequent displays of **false self-behaviors** can leave adolescents confused about who they really are.
■ Core aspects of self-concept tend to be personal characteristics among people in **individualistic societies,** but social/relational attributes among people in **collectivist (or communal) societies.**

Self-Esteem: The Evaluative Component of Self

■ **Self-esteem** begins as infants form positive or negative working models of self from their interactions with caregivers.
■ By age 8, children's self-evaluations become reflections of how others would evaluate their behavioral and social competencies.
■ In adolescence, feelings of **relational self-worth,** romantic appeal, and quality of close friendships become important contributors to global self-esteem.
■ Except for a temporary decline that some children experience with the transition to middle and high school, self-esteem is reasonably stable over time.
■ Warm, responsive, democratic parenting fosters self-esteem; aloof or controlling parenting styles undermine it.
■ Peers influence each other's self-esteem through **social comparison** during the grade school years.
■ For adolescents, the strongest determinants of self-worth are one's relationship with peers, close friends, and prospective romantic partners.

Development of Achievement Motivation and Academic Self-Concept

■ Infants display an inborn **mastery motive.**
■ Children differ in **achievement motivation**—their willingness to strive for success and master new challenges.
■ Infants who are securely attached and raised in a stimulating home environment are likely to develop strong achievement motivation.
■ Parents foster achievement motivation by encouraging their children to do things on their own and by focusing on a child's successes.
■ Peers may either foster or undermine parents' efforts to encourage academic achievement.
■ Academic self-concepts depend on children's **achievement attributions.**
■ **Mastery-oriented** children have very positive **achievement expectancies:** they attribute their successes to stable, internal causes, and their failures to unstable causes. They adopt an **incremental view of ability.**
■ **Helpless children** often stop trying after a failure because they display an **entity view of ability** and attribute their failures to a lack of ability.
■ Children who are often criticized for their lack of ability adopt **performance goals** rather than **learning goals** and are at risk of becoming helpless.
■ Helpless children can become more mastery-oriented if they are taught (through **attribution retraining**) that their failures can be attributed to unstable causes they can overcome by trying harder.

Who Am I to Be?: Forging an Identity

■ One task of adolescence is forming a stable **identity.**
■ From the **diffusion** and **foreclosure** statuses, many college-age youths progress to the **moratorium** status (where they are experimenting to find an identity) and ultimately to **identity achievement.**
■ Identity formation is an uneven process that often continues well into adulthood.
■ Identity achievement and moratorium are psychologically healthy statuses.
■ Adolescents stuck in the diffusion status often assume a *negative identity* and display poor psychological adjustment.
■ Healthy identity outcomes are fostered by cognitive development, by parents who encourage individual self-expression, and by a culture that expects adolescents to find their own niches.
■ For minority youth, achieving a positive *ethnic identity* fosters healthy identity outcomes.

The Other Side of Social Cognition: Knowing About Others

- Children younger than 7 or 8 generally describe friends and acquaintances in the same concrete observable terms that they use to describe the self.
- Grade school children become more attuned to regularities in their own and others' conduct (the **behavioral comparisons** phase), and later begin to rely on stable psychological constructs, or traits, to describe these patterns (the **psychological constructs** phase).
- Young adolescents' impressions of others become even more abstract as they begin to make **psychological comparisons** among their friends and acquaintances.
- By age 14 to 16, adolescents know that situational influences can cause a person to act "out of character."
- The growth of children's social-cognitive abilities is related to cognitive development in general and to the emergence of **role-taking** skills in particular.
- To truly "know" a person, one must be able to assume her perspective and understand her thoughts, feelings, motives, and intentions.
- *Social interactions*—particularly equal-status contacts with friends and peers—are crucial to social-cognitive development.
- Social interactions contribute indirectly by fostering the growth of role-taking skills.
- Social interactions contribute directly by providing the experiences children need to learn what others are like.

KEY TERMS

self 467
social cognition 467
proprioceptive feedback 468
personal agency 468
self-concept 468
self-recognition 469
present self 470
extended self 470
categorical self 471
false self-behavior 473
individualistic society 474
collectivistic (or communal) society 474
self-esteem 474
relational self-worth 476
social comparison 478
achievement motivation 481
mastery motivation 481
intrinsic achievement orientation 484
authoritative parenting 485
achievement attributions 487
achievement expectancies 487
incremental view of ability 488
entity view of ability 488
mastery orientation 489
learned helplessness orientation 489
attribution retraining 490
person praise 490
performance goal 490
process-oriented praise 491
learning goal 491
identity 491
identity crisis 491
identity diffusion 491
identity foreclosure 491
identity moratorium 491
identity achievement 491
behavioral comparisons phase 500
psychological constructs phase 500
psychological comparisons phase 500
role taking 501

MEDIA RESOURCES

The Human Development Book Companion Website

See the companion website http://www.thomsonedu.com/psychology/shaffer for flashcards, practice quiz questions, Internet links, updates, critical thinking exercises, discussion forums, games, and more

ThomsonNOW! http://www.thomsonedu.com
Go to this site for the link to ThomsonNOW, your one-stop shop. Take a pre-test for this chapter, and ThomsonNOW will generate a personalized study plan based on your test results. The study plan will identify the topics you need to review and direct you to online resources to help you master those topics. You can then take a post-test to help you determine the concepts you have mastered and what you will still need to work on.

© Cut and Deal Ltd/Alamy

CHAPTER 13 Sex Differences and Gender-Role Development

We all know that there are physical differences between men and women, girls and boys. But what about psychological differences? Is the popular book that says "Men are from Mars and Women are from Venus" true (Gray, 1992)? If so, where do these differences come from? Our biology? Our upbringing?

Throughout my teenage years and undergraduate training I (Katherine Kipp) believed that any psychological differences between men and women were purely due to differences in our upbringing or socialization. Speaking in Piagetian terms (as we learned in Chapter 7), I had a schema for sex differences and it excluded any notion of biological differences contributing to psychological differences. I held fast to this belief, distorting any evidence to the contrary (or "assimilating" as Piaget would say).

Then I had my children and my schema was changed forever. My daughters have very different activity levels, a biological difference that was evident in the womb, and one that characterizes a basic difference between boys (who have higher activity levels on average) and girls. From the beginning of their lives, this difference affected my daughters' development. Although I was a first-time parent (and so would think I would react to my daughters similarly), I found myself responding to them quite differently. Debby has a lower activity level and loved to be cuddled; Rachel has a higher activity level and liked to be thrown into the air! Their differences influenced their personalities and their interests. I remember trying to raise them in a gender-neutral environment, giving them both dolls and trucks for special occasions. To my wonder, within a few hours' time all the "boy" toys ended up in Rachel's room and all the "girl" toys ended up in Debby's.

Although the differences between my daughters were not sex differences, they helped me to understand that some differences between the sexes are indeed biological.

What is your opinion on psychological differences between the sexes? Are you ready to accommodate your scheme on this issue based on the research evidence we will present? Let's take a look, first by examining what differences actually exist between the sexes, and then examining theoretical explanations for those differences. See if your scheme changes as we go.

Gender-role socialization begins very early as parents provide their infants with "gender-appropriate" clothing, toys, and hairstyles.

Defining Sex and Gender

sex
a person's biological identity: their chromosomes, physical manifestations of their identity, and hormonal influences.

gender
a person's social and cultural identity as male or female.

Before we begin it may be helpful to address the issue of terminology, specifically the difference between the terms **sex** and **gender.** Distinguishing between these terms has been an issue of debate in psychology, and the debate is not yet settled (Deaux, 1993; Ruble & Martin, 1998). We will use the term *sex* to refer to a person's biological identity: his or her chromosomes, physical manifestations of identity, and hormonal influences. We will use the term *gender* to refer to a person's social and cultural identity as male or female. With this distinction in mind, let's now begin our discussion of sex differences and gender-role development.

How important is a child's gender to development? Many people would say, "Very important!" Often the first thing parents learn about their baby is his or her sex, and the question "Is it a boy or a girl?" is the very first one that most friends and relatives ask when proud new parents announce the birth of their baby (Intons-Peterson & Reddel, 1984). Indeed, the ramifications of this gender labeling are normally swift in coming and rather direct. In the hospital nursery or delivery room, parents often call an infant son things like "big guy" or "tiger," and they are likely to comment on the vigor of his cries, kicks, or grasps. Infant daughters are more likely to be labeled "sugar" or "sweetie" and described as soft, cuddly, and adorable (MacFarlane, 1977). A newborn infant is usually blessed with a name that identifies his or her sex, and in many Western societies boys are immediately adorned in blue and girls in pink. Mavis Hetherington and Ross Parke (1975, pp. 354–355) describe the predicament of a developmental psychologist who "did not want her observers to know whether they were watching boys or girls":

> Even in the first few days of life some infant girls were brought to the laboratory with pink bows tied to wisps of their hair or taped to their little bald heads . . . When another attempt at concealment of sex was made by asking mothers to dress their infants in overalls, girls appeared in pink and boys in blue overalls, and 'Would you believe overalls with ruffles?'

This gender socialization continues from early in infancy onward as parents provide their children with "gender-appropriate" clothing, toys, and hairstyles (Pomerleau et al., 1990). They also play differently with and expect different reactions from their young sons and daughters (Bornstein et al., 1999; Caldera, Huston, & O'Brien, 1989). For example, parents tend to subtly encourage play with same-sex-typed toys for their daughters and sons. They also play in closer proximity and with more verbal interaction when playing together with their daughters and feminine-sex-typed toys than with their sons and masculine-sex-typed-toys. So it is clear that a child's caregivers view gender as an important attribute that often influences how they respond to and care for him or her.

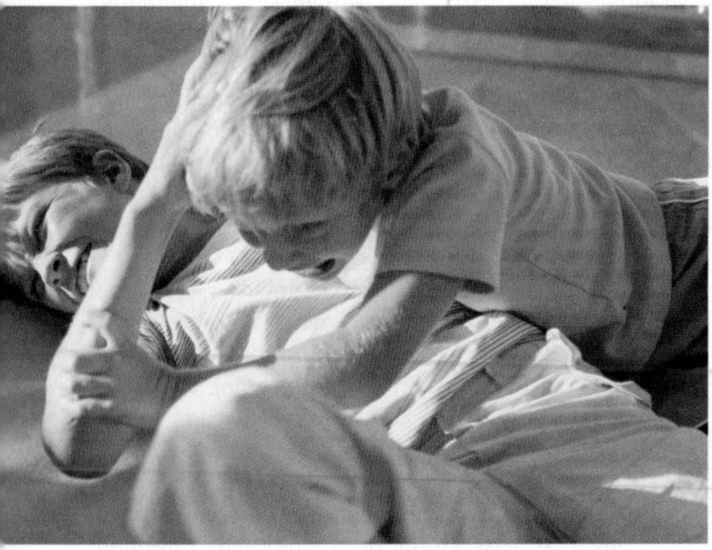

Rough-and-tumble play is more common among boys than among girls.

Why do people react differently to males and females? One explanation centers on the biological differences between the sexes. Recall that fathers determine the sex of their children. A zygote that receives an X chromosome from each parent is a genetic (XX) female that develops into a baby girl, whereas a zygote that receives a Y chromosome from the father is a genetic (XY) male that will normally assume the appearance of a baby boy. Could it be that this basic genetic difference between the sexes is ultimately responsible for *sex differences in behavior* that might explain why parents often do not treat their sons and daughters alike? We will explore this interesting idea in some detail in a later section of the chapter.

There is more to sex differences than biology. Virtually all societies expect males and females to behave differently and to assume different roles. In order to conform to these expectations, the child must understand that he is a boy or that she is a girl and must incorporate this information into his or her self-concept. In this chapter we will concentrate on the interesting topic of **gender typing**—the process by which children acquire not only a gender identity but also the motives, values, and behaviors considered appropriate in their culture for members of their biological sex.

gender typing
the process by which a child becomes aware of his or her gender and acquires motives, values, and behaviors considered appropriate for members of that sex.

We begin the chapter by summarizing what people generally believe to be true about sex differences in cognition, personality, and social behavior. As it turns out, some of these beliefs have an element of truth to them, although many others are best described as fictions or fables that have no basis in fact. We will then look at developmental trends in gender typing and see that youngsters are often well aware of gender-role stereotypes and are displaying gender-typed patterns of behavior long before they are old enough to go to kindergarten. And how do children learn so much about the sexes and gender roles at such an early age? We will address this issue by reviewing several influential theories that specify how biological forces, social experiences, and cognitive development might combine and interact to influence the gender-typing process. And after examining a perspective that asserts that traditional gender-roles have outlived their usefulness in today's modern society, the chapter concludes by considering how the constraining and potentially harmful effects of gender stereotypes might be reduced.

Categorizng Males and Females: Gender Role Standards

Most of us have learned a great deal about males and females by the time we enter college. In fact, if you and your classmates were asked to jot down 10 psychological dimensions on which men and women are thought to differ, it is likely that every member of the class could easily generate such a list. Here's a head start: Which gender is most likely to display emotions? to be tidy? to be competitive? to use harsh language?

A **gender-role standard** is a value, a motive, or a class of behavior that is considered more appropriate for members of one sex than the other. Taken together, a society's gender-role standards describe how males and females are expected to behave and reflect the stereotypes by which we categorize and respond to members of each sex.

gender-role standard
a behavior, value, or motive that members of a society consider more typical or appropriate for members of one sex.

The female's role as childbearer is largely responsible for the gender-role standards and stereotypes that have prevailed in many societies, including our own. Girls have typically been encouraged to assume an **expressive role** that involves being kind, nurturant, cooperative, and sensitive to the needs of others (Parsons, 1955). These psychological traits, it was assumed, would prepare girls to play the wife and mother roles, keep the family functioning, and raise children successfully. Boys have been encouraged to adopt an **instrumental role** that involves being dominant, assertive, independent, and competitive. These psychological traits, it was assumed, would prepare boys to play the role of a traditional husband and father, and face the tasks of providing for the family and protecting it from harm. Similar norms and role prescriptions are found in many, though certainly not all, societies (Williams & Best, 1990). In one ambitious project, Herbert Barry, Margaret Bacon, and Irving Child (1957) analyzed the gender-typing practices of 110 nonindustrialized societies, looking for sex differences in the socialization of five attributes: nurturance, obedience, responsibility, achievement, and self-reliance. As shown in Table 13.1, achievement and self-reliance were more strongly encouraged in young boys, whereas young girls were encouraged to become nurturant, responsible, and obedient.

expressive role
a social prescription, usually directed toward females, that one should be cooperative, kind, nurturant, and sensitive to the needs of others.

instrumental role
a social prescription, usually directed toward males, that one should be dominant, independent, assertive, competitive, and goal-oriented.

Children in modern industrialized societies also face strong gender-typing pressures, though not always to the same extent and in the same ways that children in nonindustrialized societies do. (An example of a difference among cultures in gender typing is that parents in many Western societies place roughly equal emphasis on achievement for sons and for daughters, thus *not* gender-typing achievement motivation; Lytton & Romney, 1991). Furthermore, the findings in Table 13.1 do not imply that self-reliance in girls is frowned on or that disobedience by young boys is acceptable. In fact, all five attributes that Barry and his colleagues studied are encouraged of *both* boys and girls, but with different emphases on different attributes depending on the sex of the child (Pomerantz &

TABLE 13.1 Sex Differences in the Socialization of Five Attributes in 110 Societies

	Percentage of societies in which socialization pressures were greater for:	
Attribute	**Boys**	**Girls**
Nurturance	0	82
Obedience	3	35
Responsibility	11	61
Achievement	87	3
Self-reliance	85	0

Note: The percentages for each attribute do not add to 100 because some of the societies did not place differential pressures on boys and girls with respect to that attribute. For example, 18% of the societies for which pertinent data were available did not differentiate between the sexes in the socialization of nurturance.

Source: Adapted from "A Cross-Cultural Survey of Some Sex Differences in Socialization," by H. Barry III, M. K. Bacon, & I. L. Child, 1957, *Journal of Abnormal and Social Psychology, 55,* 327–332.

Ruble, 1998; Zern, 1984). So it appears that the first goal of socialization is to encourage children to acquire those traits that will enable them to become well-behaved, contributing members of society. A second goal (but one that adults view as important nevertheless) is to "gender type" the child by stressing the importance of relationship-oriented (or expressive) attributes for girls and individualistic (or instrumental) attributes for boys.

Because cultural norms specify that girls should assume an expressive role and boys an instrumental role, we may be inclined to assume that girls and women actually display expressive traits and that boys and men possess instrumental traits (Broverman et al., 1972; Williams & Best, 1990). If you assume that these stereotypes have disappeared as attention to women's rights has increased and as more women have entered the labor force, think again. Although some change has occurred in the latter half of the 20th century in the direction of more egalitarian gender roles and norms (Boltin, Weeks, & Morris, 2000; Eagly, Wood, & Diekman, 2000), adolescents and young adults still endorse many traditional stereotypes about men and women (Bergen & Williams, 1991; Twenge, 1997). For example, college students in one study (Prentice & Carranza, 2002) insisted that women ought to be friendly, cheerful, compassionate, emotionally expressive, and patient. They thought women should not be stubborn, arrogant, intimidating, or domineering. They thought that men ought to be rational, ambitious, assertive, athletic, and leaders with strong personalities. They insisted that men should not be emotional, gullible, weak, or approval seeking. Might these beliefs about sex differences have any basis in fact? Let's see if they do.

Some Facts and Fictions about Sex Differences

The old French maxim "Vive la difference" reflects a fact that we all know to be true: males and females are anatomically different. Adult males are typically taller, heavier, and more muscular than adult females, whereas females may be hardier in the sense that they live longer. But although these physical variations are fairly obvious, the evidence for sex differences in psychological functioning is not as clear as most of us might think.

Actual Psychological Differences Between the Sexes

In a classic review of more than 1,500 studies comparing males and females, Eleanor Maccoby and Carol Jacklin (1974) concluded that few traditional gender stereotypes have any basis in fact. In fact, their review pointed to only four *small* but reliable differences between the sexes that were consistently supported by research. Here are their conclusions, with some updates and amendments.

Verbal Ability

Girls have greater verbal abilities than boys. Girls acquire language and develop verbal skills at an earlier age than boys (Bornstein & Haynes, 1998) and display a small but consistent verbal advantage on tests of reading comprehension and speech fluency throughout childhood and adolescence (Halpern, 1997, 2000; Hedges & Nowell, 1995). Females also outscore males on math tests that require verbal strategies (Gallagher, Levin & Cahalan, 2002) or are similar to verbal strategies (Halpern, 2004).

Visual/Spatial Abilities

visual/spatial abilities
the ability to mentally manipulate or otherwise draw inferences about pictorial information.

Boys outperform girls on tests of **visual/spatial abilities**—that is, the ability to draw inferences about or to otherwise mentally manipulate pictorial information (see Figure 13.1 for a visual/spatial task on which sex differences have been found). The male advantage in spatial abilities is not large, although it is detectable as early as age 4 and persists across the life span (Halpern, 2004; Levine et al., 1999; Voyer, Voyer, & Bryden, 1995).

Mathematical Ability

Beginning in adolescence, boys show a small but consistent advantage over girls on tests of *arithmetic reasoning* (Halpern, 1997, 2000; Hyde, Fennema, & Lamon, 1990). Girls actually exceed boys in computational skills (Halpern, 2004); but boys have acquired more mathematical problem-solving strategies that enable them to outperform girls on geometry and the mathematics portion of the Scholastic Assessment Test (SAT) (Byrnes & Takahira, 1993; Casey, 1996). The male advantage in mathematical problem solving is most apparent among high math achievers; more males than females are exceptionally talented in math (Stumpf & Stanley, 1996). And it seems that sex differences in visual/spatial abilities and the problem-solving strategies they support contribute to sex differences in arithmetic reasoning (Casey, Nuttal, & Pezaris, 1997).

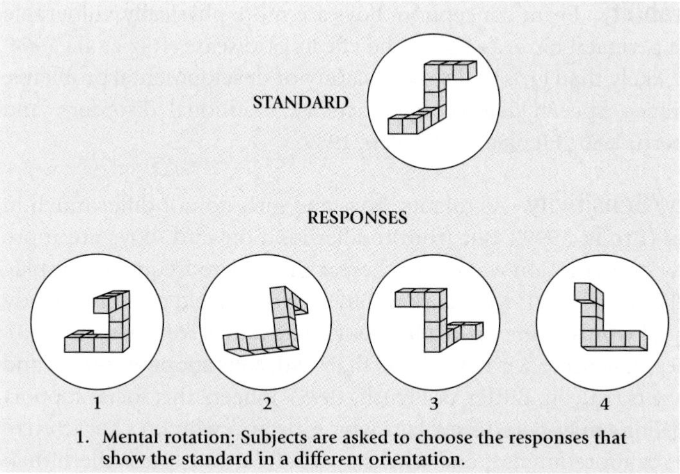
STANDARD
RESPONSES
1
2
3
4
1. Mental rotation: Subjects are asked to choose the responses that show the standard in a different orientation.

Figure 13.1 A spatial task for which sex differences in performance have been found. *From "Emergence and Characteristics of Sex Differences in Spatial Ability: A Meta-Analysis," by M. C. Linn & A. C. Petersen, 1985,* Child Development, 56, *1479–1498. Copyright © 1985 by the Society for Research in Child Development, Inc. Reprinted by permission.*

Aggression

Boys are more physically and verbally aggressive than girls, starting as early as age 2, and are about 10 times more likely than girls to be involved in antisocial behavior and violent crime during adolescence (U.S. Department of Justice, 1995). Girls are more likely than boys to display covert forms of hostility toward others by snubbing or ignoring them or by trying to undermine their relationships or social status (Crick, Casas & Mosher, 1997; Crick & Grotpeter, 1995).

Other Sex Differences

Critics were quick to challenge Maccoby and Jacklin's review, claiming that the procedures they used to gather and tabulate their results led them to underestimate the number of sex differences that actually exist (Block, 1976; Huston, 1983). More recent research, which often combines the results of several studies and provides a better estimate of the reliability of

By age 2½ to 3, children know that boys and girls prefer different kinds of activities, and they have already begun to play in gender-stereotyped ways.

sex-related differences, points to the following additional sex differences in personality and social behavior.

Activity Level. Even before they are born, boys are more physically active than girls (DiPietro et al., 1996), and they remain more active throughout childhood, especially when interacting with peers (Eaton & Enns, 1986; Eaton & Yu, 1989). The heightened activity that boys display may help to explain why they are more likely than girls to initiate and to be receptive to bouts of nonaggressive rough-and-tumble play (Pellegrini & Smith, 1998).

Fear, Timidity, and Risk-Taking. As early as the first year of life, girls appear to be more fearful or timid in uncertain situations than are boys. They are also more cautious and less assertive in these situations than are boys, taking far fewer risks than do boys (Christophersen, 1989; Feingold, 1994). However, girls and boys do not differ in patterns of *cognitive* impulsivity (such as quick, less accurate responding to ambiguous questions or problems) or reflective behavior (such as slower, more accurate responding to ambiguous questions or problems) (Buela-Casal et al., 2003).

Developmental Vulnerability. From conception, boys are more physically vulnerable than girls to prenatal and perinatal hazards and to the effects of disease (Raz et al., 1994, 1995). Boys are also more likely than girls to display a variety of developmental problems, including reading disabilities, speech defects, hyperactivity, emotional disorders, and mental retardation (Halpern, 1997; Henker & Whalen, 1989).

Emotional Expressivity/Sensitivity. As infants, boys and girls do not differ much in their displays of emotion (Brody, 1999). But from toddlerhood onward, boys are more likely than girls to display one emotion—anger—whereas girls more frequently display most other emotions (Fabes et al., 1991; Kochanska, 2001). Two-year-old girls are already using more emotion-related words than two-year-old boys (Cervantes & Callanan, 1998), and parents of preschoolers talk more with daughters than with sons about emotions and memorable emotional events (Kuebli, Butler, & Fivush, 1995). Indeed, this social support for reflecting on their feelings may help to explain why girls and women characterize their emotions as deeper, or more intense, and why they feel freer to express them than do boys and men (Diener, Sandvik, & Larson, 1985; Fischer et al., 2004; Fuchs & Thelen, 1988; Saarni, 1999; see also Chang et al., 2003).

The evidence for sex differences in nurturance and empathy is mixed. Girls and women consistently rate themselves (and are described by others) as more nurturant and empathic than boys and men (Cohen & Strayer, 1996; Feingold, 1994). Yet, boys often appear no less empathic or compassionate than girls when studied in naturalistic settings (Fabes, Eisenberg, & Miller, 1990; Zahn-Waxler et al., 1992). For example, boys display at least as much affection toward and concern for the welfare of their pets and older relatives as do girls (Melson, Peet, & Sparks, 1991).

Compliance. From early in the preschool period, girls are more compliant than boys with the requests and demands of parents, teachers, and other authority figures (Calicchia & Santostefano, 2004; Feingold, 1994; Maccoby, 1998). And when trying to persuade others to comply with them, girls are especially inclined to rely on tact and polite suggestions. Boys are nevertheless more likely than girls to resort to demanding or controlling strategies (Leaper, Tennenbaum, & Shaffer, 1999; Strough & Berg, 2000).

Conclusions. In reviewing the evidence for "real" sex differences, we must keep in mind that the data reflect *group averages* that may not characterize the behavior of any particular individual. For example, gender accounts for about 5 percent of the variation children display in overt aggressive behaviors (Hyde, 1984), so that the remaining 95 percent is due to other differences between people. The sex differences in verbal, spatial, and mathematical abilities that Maccoby and Jacklin identified are also small, are most apparent at the extremes (that is, very high or very low) ends of the ability distributions (Halpern, 1997, 2000), and may not be evident elsewhere (Stetsenko et al., 2000). For example, women do better on tests of mathematical ability in societies like Israel, where women have excellent opportunities in technical training and technical occupations (Baker & Jones, 1992). Findings such as these imply that most sex differences are not biologically inevitable and that cultural and other social influences play an important role in the development of differences between males and females (Halpern, 1997).

What, then, should we conclude about psychological differences between the sexes? Although contemporary scholars may quibble at times about which sex differences are real or meaningful (Eagly, 1995; Hyde & Plant, 1995) most developmentalists can agree on this: *Males and females are far more psychologically similar than they are different,* and even the most well-documented differences seem to be modest (see Figure 13.2). This means it is impossible to predict the aggressiveness, the mathematical skills, the activity level, or the emotional expressivity of any individual simply by knowing his or her gender. Only when group averages are computed do the sex differences emerge.

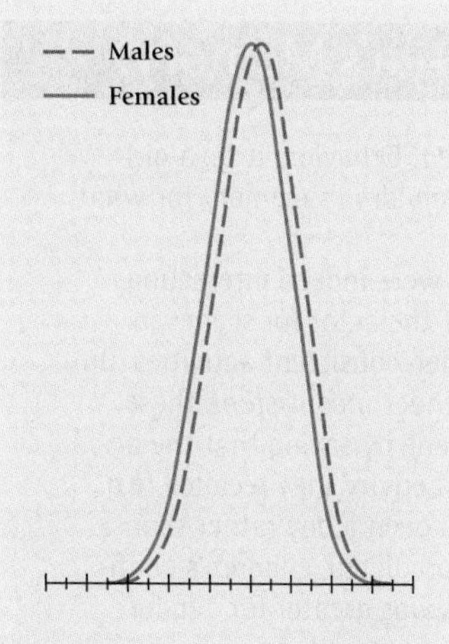

Figure 13.2 These two distributions of scores—one for males, one for females—give some idea of the size of the gap between the sexes in abilities for which sex differences are consistently found. Despite a small difference in average performance, the scores of males and females overlap considerably. *Adapted from "Gender Differences in Mathematics Performance: A Meta-Analysis," by J. S. Hyde, E. Fennema, & S. J. Lamon, 1990,* Psychological Bulletin, 107, *139–155. Copyright © 1990 by the American Psychological Association. Adapted by permission.*

Cultural Myths

Another conclusion that most developmentalists now endorse is Maccoby and Jacklin's (1974) proposition that many (perhaps most) gender-role stereotypes are "cultural myths" that have no basis in fact. Among the most widely accepted of these "myths" are the notions that females are more sociable, suggestible, illogical, and less analytical and achievement oriented than males.

Why do these and so many other inaccuracies persist? Maccoby and Jacklin (1974) propose that:

> a . . . likely explanation for the perpetuation of "myths" is the fact that stereotypes are such powerful things. An ancient truth is worth restating here: if a generalization about a group of people is believed, whenever a member of the group behaves in the expected way the observer notes it and his belief is confirmed and strengthened; when a member of the group behaves in a way that is not consistent with the observer's expectations, the instance is likely to pass unnoticed, and the observer's generalized belief is protected from disconfirmation . . . [This] well-documented [selective attention] . . . process . . . results in the perpetuation of myths that would otherwise die out under the impact of negative evidence (p. 355).

In other words, gender-role stereotypes are well-ingrained cognitive schemes that we use to interpret and often *distort* the behavior of males and females (Martin & Halverson,

1981) (see the Box below). People even use these schemas to classify the behavior of infants. In one study (Condry & Condry, 1976), college students watched a videotape of a 9-month-old child who was introduced as either a girl ("Dana") or a boy ("David"). As the students observed the child play, they were asked to interpret his/her reactions to toys such as a teddy bear or a jack-in-the-box. Impressions of the infant's behavior clearly depended on his or her presumed sex. For example, a strong reaction to the jack-in-the-box was labeled "anger" when the child was presumed to be a boy and "fear" when the child had been introduced as a girl (see also Burnham & Harris, 1992).

As it turns out, the persistence of unfounded or inaccurate gender-role stereotypes has important consequences for both boys and girls. Some of the more negative implications of these cultural myths are discussed in the following section.

Do Cultural Myths Contribute to Sex Differences in Ability (and Vocational Opportunity)?

In 1968 Phillip Goldberg asked college women to judge the merits of several scientific articles that were attributed to a male author ("John McKay") or to a female author ("Joan McKay"). Although these manuscripts were identical in every other respect, participants judged the articles written by a male to be of higher quality than those by a female.

These young women were reflecting a belief, common to people in many societies, that girls and women lack the potential to excel in either math and science courses or in occupations that require this training (Eccles et al., 2000; Tennenbaum & Leaper, 2002).

FOCUS ON RESEARCH — Do Gender Stereotypes Influence Children's Memory?

Maccoby and Jacklin (1974) proposed that, once people learn gender stereotypes, they are more likely to attend to and remember events that are consistent with these beliefs than events that would disconfirm them. Carol Martin and Charles Halverson (1981) agree, arguing that gender stereotypes are well-ingrained schemes or naive theories that people use to organize and represent experience. Once established, these gender schemes should have at least two important effects on a child's (or an adult's) cognitive processes: (1) an *organizational* effect on memory, such that information consistent with the scheme will be easier to remember than counterstereotypic events, and (2) a *distortion* effect, such that counterstereotypic information will tend to be remembered as much more consistent with one's gender scheme than the information really is. For example, it should be easier for people to remember that they saw a girl at the stove cooking (gender-consistent information) than a boy partaking in the same activity (gender-inconsistent information). And if people were to witness the latter event, they might distort what they had seen to make it more consistent with their stereotypes—perhaps by remembering the actor as a girl rather than a boy or by reconstructing the boy's activities as *fixing* the stove rather than cooking.

Martin and Halverson (1983) tested their hypotheses in an interesting study with 5- and 6-year-olds. During a first session, each child was shown 16 pictures, half of which depicted a child performing *gender-consistent* activities (for example, a boy playing with a truck) and half showing children displaying *gender-inconsistent* behaviors (e.g., a girl chopping wood). One week later, children's memory for what they had seen was assessed.

The results of this experiment were indeed interesting. Children easily recalled the sex of the actor for scenes in which actors had performed gender-consistent activities. But when the actor's behavior was gender *inconsistent*, these youngsters often distorted the scene by saying that the actor's sex was consistent with the activity they recalled (e.g., they were likely to say that it had been a boy rather than a girl who had chopped wood). As predicted, children's confidence about the sex of the actors was greater for gender-consistent scenes than for gender-inconsistent ones, suggesting that counterstereotypic information is harder to remember. But it was interesting to note that, when children actually distorted a gender-inconsistent scene, they were just as confident about the sex of the actor (which they recalled *incorrectly*) as they were for the gender-consistent scenes in which they correctly recalled the actor's sex. So it seems that children are likely to distort counterstereotypic information to be more consistent with their stereotypes and that these memory distortions are as "real" to them as stereotypical information that has not been distorted.

Why, then, do inaccurate gender stereotypes persist? Because we find disconfirming evidence harder to recall and, in fact, often distort that information in ways that will confirm our initial (and inaccurate) beliefs.

Kindergarten and first-grade girls already believe that they are not as good as boys are in arithmetic; and throughout the grade school years, children increasingly come to regard reading, art, and music as girls' domains and mathematics, athletics, and mechanical subjects as more appropriate for boys (Eccles, Jacobs & Harold, 1990; Eccles, Wigfield, Harold, & Blumenfeld, 1993; Eccles, Freeman-Doan, Jacobs, & Yoon, 2000; Entwisle and Baker, 1983). Furthermore, an examination of the percentages of male and female practitioners in various occupations reveals that women are overrepresented in fields that call for verbal ability (for example, library science and elementary education) and are seriously underrepresented in most other professions, particularly the sciences and other technical fields (for example, engineering) that require a math/science background (Eccles, Freeman-Doan, Jacobs, & Yoon, 2000; National Council for Research on Women, 2002), and those imbalances are also seen in Europe (Dewandre, 2002). How do we explain these dramatic sex differences? Are the small sex-related differences in verbal, mathematical, and visual/spatial performances responsible? Or alternatively, do gender-role stereotypes create a **self-fulfilling prophecy** that *promotes* sex differences in cognitive performance and steers boys and girls along different career paths? Today, many developmentalists favor the latter viewpoint. Let's take a closer look.

self-fulfilling prophecy
phenomenon whereby people cause others to act in accordance with the expectations they have about those others.

Home Influences

Parents may often contribute to sex differences in ability and self-perceptions by treating their sons and daughters differently. Jacquelynne Eccles and her colleagues (1990) have conducted a number of studies aimed at understanding why girls tend to shy away from math and science courses and are underrepresented in occupations that involve math and science. They find that parental expectations about sex differences in mathematical ability do become self-fulfilling prophecies. The plot goes something like this:

Parents, influenced by gender stereotypes, expect their sons to outperform their daughters in math. Even before their children have received any formal math instruction, mothers in the United States, Japan, and Taiwan express a belief that boys have more mathematical ability than girls (Lummis & Stevenson, 1990).

Parents attribute their sons' successes in math to *ability* but credit their daughters' successes to *hard work* (Parsons, Adler, & Kaczala, 1982). These attributions further reinforce the belief that girls lack mathematical talent and turn in respectable performances only through plodding effort.

Children begin to internalize their parent's views, so that boys feel self-confident whereas girls are somewhat more inclined to become anxious or depressed and to underestimate both their general academic abilities (Cole et al., 1999; Stetsenko et al., 2000), and in particular, their proficiencies in math (Fredricks & Eccles, 2002; Jacob & Eccles, 1992).

Thinking they lack ability, girls become less interested in math, less likely to take math courses, and less likely than boys to pursue career possibilities that involve math after high school (Benbow & Arjimand, 1990; Jacobs et al., 2002).

In short, parents who expect their daughters to have trouble with numbers may get what they expect. In their research, Eccles and her colleagues have ruled out the possibility that parents (and girls themselves) expect less of girls because girls actually do worse in math than boys do. The negative effects of low parental expectancies on girls' self-perceptions are evident even when boys and girls perform *equally well* on tests of math aptitude and attain similar grades in math (Eccles, Freeman-Doan, Jacobs, & Yoon, 2000; Fredricks & Eccles, 2002; Tennenbaum & Leaper, 2002). And the lower math expectancies that girls develop undoubtedly help to explain why fewer girls than boys "bounce back" to show good math performance should they begin to underachieve in math (Kowaleski-Jones & Duncan, 1999). Parental beliefs that girls excel in English and that boys excel in sports contribute to sex differences in interests and competencies in these areas as well (Eccles, Jacobs, & Harold, 1990).

Scholastic Influences

Teachers also have stereotyped beliefs about the relative abilities of boys and girls in particular subjects. Sixth-grade math instructors, for example, believe that boys have more ability in math but that girls try harder at it (Jussim & Eccles, 1992). And even though these teachers often reward girls' greater efforts by assigning them equal or higher grades than they give to boys (Jussim & Eccles, 1992), their message that girls must try harder to succeed in math may nonetheless convince many girls that their talents might be best directed toward other nonquantitative achievement domains for which they are better suited . . . like music or English.

In sum, unfounded beliefs about sex differences in cognitive abilities may indeed contribute to the small sex-related ability differences we have discussed and, ultimately, to the large underrepresentation of women in the sciences and other occupations requiring quantitative skills. Clearly, the chain of events that Eccles describes is not inevitable. In fact, girls whose parents are nontraditional in their gender-role attitudes and behaviors do not show the declines in math and science achievement that girls from more traditional families are likely to display (Updegraff, McHale, & Crouter, 1996).

Female underachievement in math and science remains a serious problem that has professionals from many disciplines calling for programs to educate parents, teachers, and counselors about the subtle ways that gender stereotypes can undermine the educational and occupational aspirations of talented female students (American Association of University Women, 1992; Benbow & Arjimand, 1990). Fortunately, there are some hopeful signs that times are changing. In a longitudinal study, Eccles and her colleagues (Fredricks & Eccles, 2002; Jacobs & Eccles, 1992) found that by 12th grade, girls valued mathematics as much as boys did and viewed themselves just as competent at it as boys (although the fact remained that both sexes showed declines in their perceived competencies and valuation of math across the high school years). And although women make up only 23 percent of the total science and engineering work force in the United States today, women in 1999 earned 40 percent of all law degrees in the United States, 30 percent of all medical degrees, and nearly 40 percent of all graduate degrees in science and engineering (Smith, 2000). The corresponding percentages for 1970 were about 9 percent for law, 5 percent for medicine, and 7 percent for science and engineering (Bianchi, 1995). So there is reason to suspect that many of the constraining stereotypes about women's competencies will eventually crumble as women, in ever-increasing numbers, enter politics, professional occupations, and the sciences, skilled trades, and virtually all other walks of life. To oppose such a trend is to waste a most valuable resource: the abilities and efforts of more than half the world's population.

Now let's examine the gender-typing process to see why it is that boys and girls may come to view themselves so differently and will often choose to assume different roles.

Developmental Trends in Gender Typing

gender identity
one's awareness of one's gender and its implications.

Gender-typing research has traditionally focused on three separate but interrelated topics: (1) the development of **gender identity,** or the knowledge that one is either a boy or a girl and that gender is an unchanging attribute, (2) the development of *gender-role stereotypes,* or ideas about what males and females are supposed to be like, and (3) the development of *gender-typed patterns of behavior*—that is, the child's tendency to favor same-sex activities over those normally associated with the other sex.

Development of the Gender Concept

The first step in the development of a gender identity is to discriminate males from females and to place oneself into one of these categories. Simple gender discriminations begin rather early. By 4 months of age, infants have already begun to match male and

Girls who often play with visual/spatial toys tend to perform better on tests of spatial ability.

female voices with faces in tests of intermodel perception (Walker-Andrews et al., 1991); and by the end of the first year, they can reliably discriminate still photographs of men and women (Leinbach & Fagot, 1993).

Between ages 2 and 3, children begin to tell us what they know about gender as they acquire and correctly use such labels as "mommy" and "daddy" and (slightly later) "boy" and "girl" (Leinbach & Fagot, 1986). By age 2½ to 3 almost all children can accurately label themselves as either boys or girls (Thompson, 1975), although it takes longer for them to grasp the fact that gender is a permanent attribute. Many 3- to 5-year-olds, for example, think that boys could become mommies or girls daddies if they really wanted to, or that a person who changes clothing and hairstyles can become a member of the other sex (Fagot, 1985b; Szkrybalo & Ruble, 1999). Children normally begin to understand that sex is an unchanging attribute between the ages of 5 and 7, so that most youngsters have a firm, future-oriented identity as a boy or a girl by the time they enter grade school.

Development of Gender-Role Stereotypes

Remarkable as it may seem, toddlers begin to acquire gender-role stereotypes at about the same time that they become aware of their basic identities as boys or girls (e.g., Gelman, Taylor, & Nguyen, 2004). Deanna Kuhn and her associates (1978) showed a male doll ("Michael") and a female doll ("Lisa") to 2½ to 3½-year-olds and then asked each child which of the two dolls would engage in sex-stereotyped activities such as cooking, sewing, playing with dolls, trucks, or trains, talking a lot, giving kisses, fighting, or climbing trees. Almost all the 2½-year-olds had some knowledge of gender-role stereotypes. For example, boys and girls agreed that girls talk a lot, never hit, often need help, like to play with dolls, and like to help their mothers with chores such as cooking and cleaning. By contrast, these young children felt that boys like to play with cars, help their fathers, and build things, and are apt to make statements such as "I can hit you." The 2- to 3-year-olds who know the most about gender stereotypes are those who can correctly label photographs of other children as boys and girls (Fagot, Leinbach, & O'Boyle, 1992).

Over the preschool and early grade-school years, children learn more and more about the toys, activities, and achievement domains considered appropriate for boys and for girls (Serbin, Powlishta, & Gulko, 1993; Welch-Ross & Schmidt, 1996). Eventually, grade school children draw sharp distinctions between the sexes on *psychological* dimensions, learning first the positive traits that characterize their own gender and the negative traits associated with the other sex (Serbin, Powlishta, & Gulko, 1993). By age 10 to 11, children's stereotyping of personality traits begins to rival that of adults. In one well-known cross-cultural study, Deborah Best and her colleagues (1977) found that fourth- and fifth-graders in England, Ireland, and the United States generally agreed that women were weak, emotional, soft-hearted, sophisticated, and affectionate, whereas men were ambitious, assertive, aggressive, dominating, and cruel. Later research revealed that these same personality dimensions (and many others) are reliably attributed to men and women by male and female participants from many countries around the world (Williams, Satterwhite, & Best, 1999).

Do children take gender stereotypes seriously and believe that they must conform to these prescriptions? Many 3- to 7-year-olds do; they often reason like little chauvinists, treating gender-role standards as blanket rules that are not to be violated (Biernat, 1991; Ruble & Martin, 1998). Consider the reaction of one 6-year-old to a boy named George who likes to play with dolls:

> *(Why do you think people tell George not to play with dolls?)* Well, he should only play with things that boys play with. The things that he is playing with now is girls' stuff . . . *(Can George play with Barbie dolls if he wants to?)* No sir! . . . *(What should George do?)* He should stop playing with girls' dolls and start playing with G.I. Joe. *(Why can a boy play with G.I. Joe and not a Barbie doll?)* Because if a boy is playing with a Barbie doll, then he's just going to get people teasing him . . . and if he tries to play more, to get girls to like him, then the girls won't like him either (Damon, 1977, p. 255; italics added).

Why are young children so rigid and intolerant of gender-role transgressions? Possibly because gender-related issues are very important to them between ages 3 and 7: after all, this is the time when they are firmly classifying themselves as boys or girls and beginning to suspect that they will *always be* boys and girls. Thus, they may exaggerate gender-role stereotypes to "get them cognitively clear" so that they can live up to their self-images (Maccoby, 1998).

By age 8 to 9, however, children are becoming more flexible and less chauvinistic in their thinking about gender (Blakemore, 2003; Levy, Taylor, & Gelman, 1995; McHale et al., 2001). Notice how 9-year-old James makes a clear distinction between moral rules that people are obligated to obey and gender-role standards that are customary but *nonobligatory.*

> *(What do you think his parents should do?)* They should . . . get him trucks and stuff, and see if he will play with those. *(What if . . . he kept on playing with dolls? Do you think they would punish him?)* No. *(How come?)* It's not really doing anything bad. *(Why isn't it bad?)* Because . . . if he was breaking a window, and he kept on doing that, they could punish him, because you're not supposed to break windows. But if you want to you can play with dolls. *(What's the difference? . . .)* Well, breaking windows you're not supposed to do. And if you play with dolls, you can, but boys usually don't (Damon, 1977, p. 263; italics added).

However, just because grade school children say that boys and girls can legitimately pursue cross-sex interests and activities does not necessarily imply that they *approve* of those who do. When asked about whether they could be friends with a boy who wears lipstick or a girl who plays football and to evaluate such gender-role transgressions, grade school children (and adults) were reasonably tolerant of violations by girls. However, participants (especially boys) came down hard on boys who behaved like girls, viewing these transgressions as almost as bad as violating a moral rule. Here, then, is an indication of the greater pressure placed on boys to conform to gender roles (Blakemore, 2003; Levy, Taylor, & Gelman, 1995).

Cultural Influences

Although 8- to 10-year-olds from Western individualistic societies are becoming more flexible in their thinking about many violations of gender stereotypes, the same pattern may not be apparent elsewhere. In Taiwan, a collectivist society with an emphasis on maintaining social harmony and living up to social expectations, children are strongly encouraged to accept and conform to appropriate gender-role prescriptions. As a result, Taiwanese 8- to 10-year-olds are less accepting of gender-role violations (particularly by boys) than their age-mates from a Western individualistic society (urban Israelis) (Lobel et al., 2001).

Adolescent Thinking about Gender Stereotypes

Thinking about the traits that males and females might display and the hobbies and occupations they might pursue becomes increasingly flexible during early adolescence, as children make the transition from elementary school to middle school. But soon thereafter, gender-role prescriptions once again become less flexible, with both boys and girls

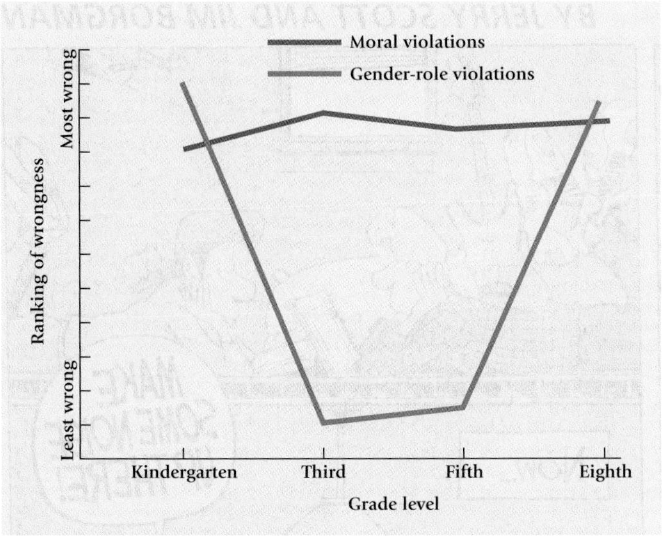

Figure 13.3 Children's rankings of the wrongness of gender-role transgressions (such as a boy's wearing nail polish) and violations of moral rules (such as pushing another child from a swing). Notice that children of all ages deplore immoral acts but that only kindergartners and adolescents view gender-role violations as wrong. Elementary school children come to think about gender-role standards in a more flexible way than they did earlier in life, but adolescents become concerned about the psychological implications of deviating from one's "proper" gender identity. *Adapted from "Children's Concepts of Cross-Gender Activities," by T. Stoddart & E. Turiel, 1985,* Child Development, *59, 793–814. Copyright © 1985 by the Society for Research in Child Development, Inc. Adapted by permission.*

showing a strong intolerance of cross-sex mannerisms displayed by either males or females (Alfieri, Ruble, & Higgins, 1996; Sigelman, Carr, & Begley, 1986; Signorella, Bigler & Liben, 1993; and see Figure 13.3 which graphically depicts this developmental change in children's feelings about gender-stereotyped behavior). How might we explain this second round of gender chauvinism?

Apparently, an adolescent's increasing intolerance of cross-sex mannerisms and behaviors is tied to a larger process of **gender intensification**—a magnification of sex differences that is associated with increased pressure to conform to gender roles as one reaches puberty (Galambos, Almeida, & Petersen, 1990; Hill and Lynch, 1983). Boys begin to see themselves as more masculine; girls emphasize their feminine side (McHale et al., 2001). Why might gender intensification occur? Parental influence is one contributor: as children enter adolescence, mothers become more involved in joint activities with daughters and fathers more involved with sons (Crouter, Manke, & McHale, 1995). However, peer influences may be even more important. Adolescents increasingly find that they must conform to traditional gender norms in order to succeed in the dating scene. A girl who was a tomboy and thought nothing of it may find during adolescence that she must dress and behave in more "feminine" ways to attract boys, and a boy may find that he is more popular if he projects a more sharply "masculine" image (Burn, O'Neil, & Nederend, 1996; Katz, 1979). Social pressures on adolescents to conform to traditional roles may even help explain why sex differences in cognitive abilities sometimes become more noticeable as children enter adolescence (Hill & Lynch, 1983; Roberts et al., 1990). Later in high school, teenagers become more comfortable with their identities as young men or women and more flexible once again in their thinking about gender (Urberg, 1979). Nevertheless, even adults may remain highly intolerant of males who blatantly disregard gender-role prescriptions (Levy, Taylor, & Gelman, 1995).

gender intensification
a magnification of sex differences early in adolescence; associated with increased pressure to conform to traditional gender roles.

Development of Gender-Typed Behavior

The most common method of assessing the "gender-appropriateness" of children's behavior is to observe whom and what they like to play with. Sex differences in toy preferences develop very early—even before the child has established a clear gender identity or can correctly label various toys as "boy things" or "girl things" (Blakemore, LaRue, & Olejnik, 1979; Fagot, Leinbach, & Hagan, 1986; Weinraub et al., 1984). Boys aged 14 to 22 months usually prefer trucks and cars to other objects, whereas girls of this age would rather play with dolls and soft toys (Smith & Daglish, 1977). In fact, 18- to 24-month-old toddlers often refuse to play with cross-sex toys, even when there are no other objects available for them to play with (Caldera, Huston, & O'Brien, 1989).

Gender Segregation

Children's preferences for same-sex playmates also develop very early. In nursery school, 2-year-old girls already prefer to play with other girls (La Freniere, Strayer, & Gauthier, 1984), and by age 3, boys are reliably selecting boys rather than girls as companions. This **gender segregation,** which has been observed in a variety of cultures (Leaper, 1994; Whiting & Edwards, 1988), becomes progressively stronger with each passing year. Four- and

gender segregation
children's tendency to associate with same-sex playmates and to think of the other sex as an outgroup.

Zits reprinted by permission of King Features Syndicate.

five-year-olds have already begun to actively *reject* playmates of the other sex (Ramsey, 1995), and by age 6½, children spend more than 10 times as much time with same-sex as with opposite-sex companions (Maccoby, 1998). When a young child does play with other-sex peers, there is usually at least one same-sex comrade present (Fabes, Martin, & Hanish, 2003). Grade school and preadolescent children generally find cross-gender contacts less pleasing and are likely to behave more negatively toward opposite-sex than same-sex peers (Underwood, Schockner, Hurley, 2001). Interestingly, even young children believe that it is wrong to exclude a child from such contexts as doll play or playing with trucks on the basis of gender (Killen et al., 2001) but they often do so anyway.

Alan Sroufe and his colleagues (1993) find that those 10- to 11-year-olds who insist most strongly on maintaining clear gender boundaries and who avoid consorting with the "enemy" tend to be viewed as socially competent and popular, whereas children who violate gender segregation rules tend to be much less popular and less well-adjusted. In fact, children who display a preference for cross-sex friendships are likely to be rejected by their peers (Kovacs, Parker, & Hoffman, 1996). However, gender boundaries and biases against other-sex companions decline in adolescence when the social and physiological events of puberty trigger an interest in members of the opposite sex, as depicted in the cartoon on this page (Bukowski, Sippola, & Newcomb, 2000; Serbin, Powlishta, & Gulko, 1993).

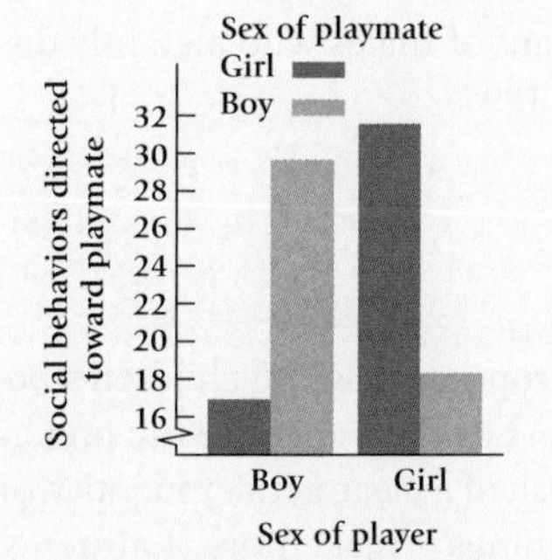

Figure 13.4 Two- to three-year-old toddlers already prefer playmates of their own sex. Boys are much more social with boys than with girls, whereas girls are more outgoing with girls than with boys.
Adapted from "Social Behavior at 33 Months in Same-Sex and Mixed-Sex Dyads," by C. N. Jacklin & E. E. Maccoby, 1978, Child Development, *49, 557–569. Copyright © 1978 by the Society for Research in Child Development, Inc. Adapted by permission.*

Why does gender segregation occur? Eleanor Maccoby (1998) believes that it largely reflects differences between boys' and girls' play styles—an incompatibility that may stem from boys' heightened levels of androgen, which fosters active, rambunctious behavior. In one study (Jacklin & Maccoby, 1978), an adult observer recorded how often pairs of same-sex and mixed-sex toddlers played together or played alone when placed in a playroom with several interesting toys. As we see in Figure 13.4, boys directed far more social responses to boys than to girls, whereas girls were more sociable with girls than with boys. Interactions between playmates in the same-sex pairings were lively and positive in character. In contrast, girls tended to withdraw from boys in the mixed-sex pairs. Boys were simply too boisterous and domineering to suit the taste of many girls, who prefer less roughhousing and would rather rely on polite negotiations rather than demands or shows of force when settling disputes with their playmates (Martin & Fabes, 2001; Moller & Serbin, 1996). In addition, girls are expected to play quietly and gently and

TABLE 13.2 Percentages of Boys and Girls Who Requested Popular "Masculine" and "Feminine" Items from Santa Claus

	Percentage of boys requesting	Percentage of girls requesting
Masculine items		
Vehicles	43.5	8.2
Sports equipment	25.1	15.1
Spatial/temporal toys (construction sets, clocks, and so on)	24.5	15.6
Feminine items		
Dolls (adult female)	.6	27.4
Dolls (babies)	.6	23.4
Domestic accessories	1.7	21.7

Source: Adapted from "Children, Gender and Social Structure: An Analysis of the Contents of Letters to Santa Claus," by J. G. Richardson & C. H. Simpson, 1982, *Child Development, 53,* 429–436. Copyright © 1982 by The Society for Research in Child Development, Inc. Adapted with permission.

are subject to criticism (by both boys and girls) should they become loud and rough like the boys (Blakemore, 2003).

Cognitive and social-cognitive development also contribute to the increasing gender segregation children display. Once preschoolers label themselves as boys or girls and begin to acquire gender stereotypes, they come to favor the group to which they belong and eventually view the other sex as a homogeneous out-group with many negative characteristics (Martin, 1994; Powlishta, 1995). In fact, children who hold the more stereotyped views of the sexes are most likely to maintain gender segregation in their own play activities and to make few if any opposite-sex friends (Kovacs, Parker, & Hoffman, 1996; Martin, 1994).

Sex Differences in Gender-Typed Behavior

Many cultures, including our own, assign greater status to the male gender-role (Turner & Gervai, 1995), and boys face stronger pressures than girls to adhere to gender-appropriate codes of conduct (Bussey & Bandura, 1992; Lobel & Menashri, 1993). Consider that fathers of baby girls are generally willing to offer a truck to their 12-month-old daughters, whereas fathers of baby boys are likely to withhold dolls from their sons (Snow, Jacklin, & Maccoby, 1983). And boys are quicker than girls to adopt gender-typed toy preferences. Judith Blakemore and her associates (1979), for example, found that 2-year-old boys clearly favor gender-appropriate toys whereas some 2-year-old girls may not. And by age 3 to 5, boys (1) are much more likely than girls to say that they dislike opposite-sex toys (Bussey & Bandura, 1992; Eisenberg, Murray, & Hite, 1982) and (2) may even prefer a girl playmate who likes "boy" toys to a boy playmate who prefers girls' activities (Alexander & Hines, 1994).

Between the ages of 4 and 10, both boys and girls are becoming more aware of what is expected of them and conforming to these cultural prescriptions (Huston, 1983). Yet, girls are more likely than boys to retain an interest in cross-sex toys, games, and activities. Consider what John Richardson and Carl Simpson (1982) found when recording the toy preferences of 750 5- to 9-year-olds as expressed in their letters to Santa Claus. Although most requests were clearly gender-typed, we see in Table 13.2 that more girls than boys were asking for "opposite sex" items. With respect to their actual gender-role preferences, young girls often wish they were boys, and nearly half of today's college women claim that they were tomboys when they were young (Burn, O'Neil, & Nederend, 1996). Yet it is unusual for a boy to wish he were a girl (Martin, 1990).

There are probably several reasons that girls are drawn to male activities and the masculine role during middle childhood. For one thing, they are becoming increasingly aware that masculine behavior is more highly valued, and perhaps it is only natural that girls would want to be what is "best" (or at least something other than a second-class citizen) (Frey & Ruble, 1992). Furthermore, girls are given much more leeway than boys are to partake in cross-sex activities; it is okay to be a "tomboy" but a sign of ridicule and rejection should a boy be labeled a "sissy" (Martin, 1990). Finally, fast-moving masculine games and "action" toys may simply be more interesting than the familiar household playthings and pastimes (dolls, dollhouses, dish sets, cleaning and caretaking utensils) often imposed on girls to encourage their adoption of a nurturant, expressive orientation.

In spite of their earlier interest in masculine activities, most girls come to prefer (or at least to comply with) many of the prescriptions for the feminine role by early adolescence. Why? Probably for biological, cognitive, and social reasons. Once they reach puberty and their bodies assume a more womanly appearance (*biological growth*), girls often feel the need to become more "feminine" if they hope to be attractive to members of the other sex (Burn, O'Neil, & Nederend, 1996; Katz, 1979). Furthermore, these young adolescents are also attaining formal operations and advanced role-taking skills (*cognitive growth*), which may help to explain why they become self-conscious about their changing body images (Von Wright, 1989), so concerned about other people's evaluation of them (Elkind, 1981), and thus, more inclined to conform to the *social* prescriptions of the female role.

Subcultural Variations in Gender Typing

Although not extensive, research on social-class and ethnic variations in gender typing reveals that (1) middle-class adolescents (but not children) hold more flexible gender-role attitudes than their low-socioeconomic-status peers (Bardwell, Cochran, & Walker, 1986; Canter & Ageton, 1984) and (2) African American children hold less stereotyped views of women than European American children do (Bardwell, Cochran, & Walker, 1986; see also Leaper, Tennenbaum, & Shaffer, 1999).

Researchers have attributed these social-class and ethnic variations in gender typing to differences in education and family life. For example, people from middle-class backgrounds typically have a wider array of educational and occupational options available to them, perhaps explaining why they eventually adopt more flexible attitudes about the roles that men and women should play. And a greater percentage of African American than European American children are living in single-parent homes and have mothers who are employed outside the house (U.S. Bureau of the Census, 2001). So the less stereotyped portrayal of women observed among African American youngsters may simply reflect the fact that their mothers are more likely than European American mothers to be assuming both instrumental (male) and expressive (female) functions in their own roles as a parent (Leaper, Tennenbaum, & Shaffer, 1999).

Finally, children raised in homes in which parents strive to promote egalitarian sex role attitudes are indeed less gender-stereotyped than children from traditional families in their *beliefs* about which activities and occupations are appropriate for males and females (Weisner & Wilson-Mitchell, 1990). Nevertheless, these children are quite aware of traditional gender stereotypes and are just as "gender-typed" in their toy and activity preferences as children from traditional families.

In sum, gender-role development proceeds at a remarkable pace (Ruble & Martin, 1998). By the time they enter school, children have long been aware of their basic gender identities, have acquired many, many stereotypes about how the sexes differ, and have come to prefer gender-appropriate activities and same-sex playmates. During middle childhood, their knowledge continues to expand as they learn more about gender-stereotyped *psychological* traits, and they become more flexible in their thinking about gender roles. Yet their *behavior,* especially if they are boys, becomes even more gender-typed, and they segregate themselves even more from the other sex. Now a most intriguing question: How does all this happen so fast?

CONCEPT CHECK 13.1 Understanding Sex Differences and Gender-Role Development

Check your understanding of important processes in the development of sex differences and gender roles by answering the following questions. Answers appear in the Appendix.

True or False: Identify whether the following statements are true or false.

1. (T)(F) Girls show a small but consistent advantage in reading comprehension, compared to boys.
2. (T)(F) Boys show a small but consistent advantage in visual/spatial ability, compared to girls.
3. (T)(F) Girls show a small but consistent advantage in achievement motivation, compared to boys.

Fill in the Blank: Complete the following phrases with the correct terms.

4. The process that seems responsible for young teenager's renewed intolerance of cross-sex mannerisms is known as ______.
5. Our ______ can cause us to distort or misinterpret gender-atypical behaviors that we observe.

Matching: Match the following concepts with the correct definitions below:

a. gender-role standard
b. gender segregation
c. variations in play styles

6. ______ A value, motive, or behavior considered more appropriate for members of one sex than the other.
7. ______ An attribute that some researchers believe to be responsible for gender segregation.
8. ______ An affiliative preference that becomes stronger with age across childhood.

Multiple Choice: Select the correct answer for each question.

______ 9. Juanita has a strong sense of herself as a girl, knowing that she will always be a girl regardless of her activities or what she becomes when she grows up. We can assume that Juanita has achieved
a. gender comprehension
b. gender intensification
c. gender identity

______ 10. Juan would like to play with dolls, but his father will not allow any dolls in the house. His father expects Juan to play with boys and to adopt a very manly gender identity. Juan will likely adopt such a gender identity because of the forces of
a. self-fulfilling prophecies
b. gender-role standards
c. gender intensification

Theories of Gender Typing and Gender-Role Development

Several theories have been proposed to account for sex differences and the development of gender roles. Some theories emphasize the role of biological differences between the sexes, whereas others emphasize social influences on children. Some emphasize how society influences children, others the choices children make as they try to understand gender and all its implications. Let's briefly examine two biologically oriented theories and then consider the more "social" approaches offered by psychoanalytic theory, social learning theory, cognitive-developmental theory, and gender schema theory.

Evolutionary Theory

Evolutionary psychologists (for example, Buss, 1995, 2000; Kenrick & Luce, 2000) contend that men and women faced different evolutionary pressures over the course of human history and that the natural selection process conspired to create fundamental differences among males and females that determined gender divisions of labor. In Chapter 2, for example, we noted how evolutionary theorists explain different mating strategies favored by men and women to preserve their genes. Males, who need only contribute sperm to produce offspring, can best ensure that their genes survive by mating with multiple partners and producing many children. Females must invest much more to achieve the same objective, taking 9 months from conception to the birth of each child and years to raise each to ensure that their genes survive. To successfully raise children, women presumably evolved in ways that would make them kind, gentle, and nurturant (expressive characteristics) and to prefer men who would display kindness toward them and would provide resources (food and protection) to help ensure children's survival. Men should become more competitive, assertive, and aggressive (instrumental traits) because these attributes should increase their chances of successfully attracting mates and procuring resources.

According to evolutionary theorists (Buss, 1995, 2000), males and females may be psychologically similar in many ways but should differ in any domain in which they have faced different adaptive problems throughout evolutionary history. Consider the male superiority in visual/spatial performance. Spatial skills are essential for hunting; few kills would be made if hunters could not anticipate the trajectory of their spears (or rocks, or arrows) with the path of a moving prey animal. Thus, the pressure to provide food necessary for survival might ensure that males, who were most often the hunter-providers, would develop greater spatial skills than females.

Children share this view that gender is closely linked to biological sex. Consider what Marianne Taylor (1996) found when she interviewed young children using the following story: "Once there was a baby named Chris . . . [who] went to live on a beautiful island . . . [where] there were only boys and men; Chris was the only girl. Chris lived a very happy life on this island, but she never saw another girl or woman" (Taylor, 1996, p. 1559). What would Chris be like?

When Taylor (1996) asked 4- to 10-year-olds to indicate Chris's toy preferences, occupational aspirations, and personality traits, 4- to 8-year-olds assigned stereotypically feminine attributes to her, despite the fact that she was raised in a masculinizing environment and never saw a girl or woman. In other words, preschool and young grade-school children display an *essentialist bias,* assuming that Chris's biological status as a girl will determine what she will become. Only the 9- to 10-year-olds in this study showed any awareness that Chris's masculinizing environment might influence her activities, aspirations, and personality characteristics.

Criticisms of the Evolutionary Approach

The evolutionary account of sex differences and gender typing has been roundly criticized. It applies mainly to sex differences that are consistent across cultures and largely ignores differences that are limited to particular cultures or historical periods (Blakemore et al., in preparation). What's more, proponents of the **social roles hypothesis** have argued that psychological sex differences do not reflect biologically evolved dispositions. Instead, they emerge because of variations in (1) roles that cultures *assign* to men and women (provider vs. homemaker, for example) and on (2) agreed upon socialization practices to promote traits in boys and girls (assertion vs. nurturance, for example) to properly enact these roles (Eagly, Wood, & Diekman, 2000). Even many biologically oriented theorists take a softer, less essentialist stance, arguing that biological and social influences interact to determine a person's behaviors and role preferences.

social roles hypothesis
the notion that psychological differences between the sexes and other gender-role stereotypes are created and maintained by differences in socially assigned roles that men and women play (rather than attributable to biologically evolved dispositions).

What biological differences between the sexes might be important? For one, males have a Y chromosome and, hence, some genes that all females lack. For another, the sexes clearly differ in hormonal balance, with males having higher concentrations of androgens (including testosterone) and lower levels of estrogen than females do. According to the best-known interactive theory of gender typing, these biological correlates of gender, in concert with important social influences, steer boys and girls toward different patterns of behavior and gender roles. Let's now consider this influential theory.

Money and Ehrhardt's Biosocial Theory of Gender Differentiation and Development

Money and Ehrhardt (1972) proposed that there are a number of critical events that affect a person's eventual preference for the masculine or the feminine gender role. The first critical event occurs at conception as the child inherits either an X or a Y chromosome from the father. Over the next 6 weeks, the developing embryo has only an undifferentiated gonad, and the sex chromosomes determine whether this structure becomes the male testes or the female ovaries. If a Y chromosome is present, the embryo develops testes; otherwise, ovaries form.

These newly formed gonads then determine the outcome of the second event. The testes of a male embryo secrete two hormones: *testosterone,* which stimulates the development of a male internal reproductive system, and *mullerian inhibiting substance* (MIS), which inhibits the development of female organs. In the absence of these hormones, the embryo develops the internal reproductive system of a female.

At a third critical point, 3 to 4 months after conception, secretion of testosterone by the testes normally leads to the growth of a penis and scrotum. If testosterone is absent (as in normal females) or if the male fetus has inherited a rare recessive disorder, called **testicular feminization syndrome (TFS),** that makes his body insensitive to male sex hormones, female external genitalia (labia and clitoris) form. Testosterone is also thought to alter the development of the brain and nervous system. For example, it signals the male brain to stop secreting hormones in a cyclical pattern so that males do not experience menstrual cycles at puberty.

testicular feminization syndrome (TFS)
a genetic anomaly in which a male fetus is insensitive to the effects of male sex hormones and will develop female external genitalia.

Once a child is born, *social* factors immediately come into play. Parents and other people label and begin to react to the child based on the appearance of his or her genitals. If one's genitals are abnormal so that he or she is mislabeled as a member of the other sex, this incorrect label can affect his or her future development. For example, if a biological male were consistently labeled and treated as a girl (as a boy with TFS syndrome and female external genitalia might be), he would, by about age 2½ to 3, acquire the gender identity (though not the biological characteristics) of a girl. Finally, biological factors enter the scene again at puberty when large quantities of hormones are released, stimulating the growth of the reproductive system, the appearance of secondary sex characteristics, and the development of sexual urges. These events, in combination with one's earlier self-concept as a male or a female, provide the basis for an adult gender identity and gender role preference (as depicted in Figure 13.5). But how much is nature and how much is nurture?

Evidence for Biological Influences on Gender-Role Development

How much influence *do* biological factors have on the behavior of males and females? To answer this question, we must consider what investigators have learned about genetic and hormonal influences.

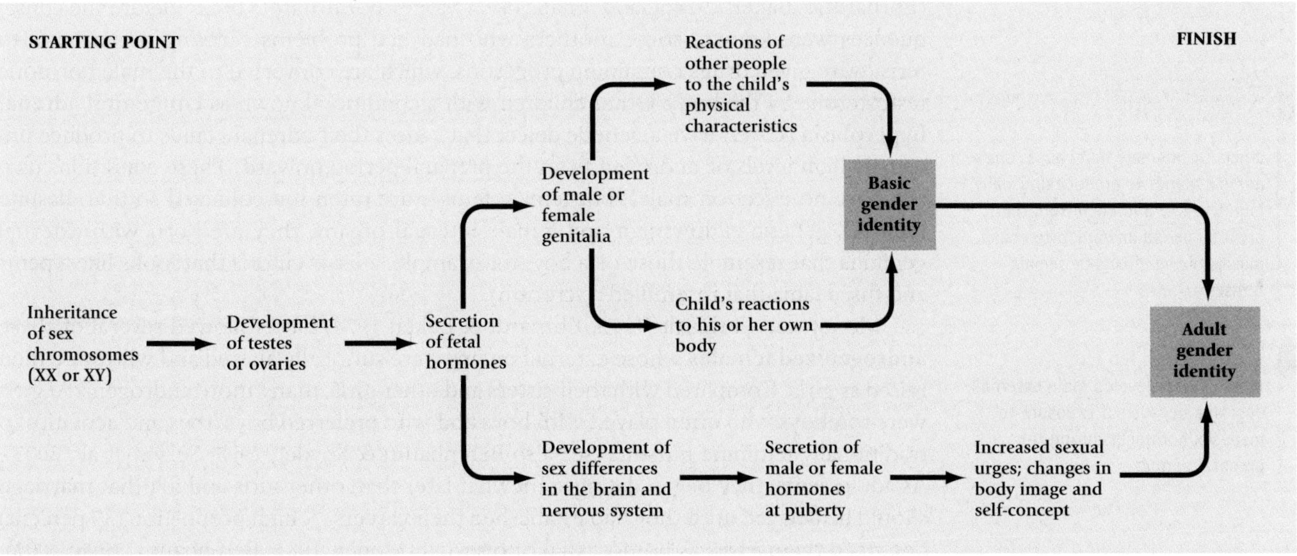

Figure 13.5 Critical events in Money and Ehrhardt's biosocial theory of sex typing. *From* Man and Women, Boy and Girl, *by J. Money & A. Ehrhardt, 1972. Copyright © 1972 by Johns Hopkins University Press. Reprinted by permission.*

Gender-role behaviors are often specific to one's culture. Like many Peruvian boys, this boy routinely washes clothes and attends to other household tasks.

Genetic Influences. Genetic factors may contribute to some sex differences in personality, cognitive abilities, and social behavior. Corrine Hutt (1972), for example, suspected that several of the developmental disorders more commonly seen among boys may be X-linked recessive traits (e.g., Fragile X Syndrome, muscular dystrophy, and hemophilia). (Recall from Chapter 3 that boys are more likely to display such traits because they have but one X chromosome and need only inherit one recessive gene to be affected.) Furthermore, **timing of puberty,** a biological variable regulated in part by our genotypes, has a slight effect on visual/spatial performances. Both boys and girls who mature *late* tend to outperform early maturers of their own sex on some visual/spatial tasks, allegedly because slow maturation promotes increasing specialization of the brain's right hemisphere, which serves spatial functions (see Newcombe & Dubas, 1987). However, later research indicates that the spatial performances of both boys and girls are more heavily influenced by their *previous involvement* in spatial activities and their *self-concepts* than by the timing of puberty (Levine et al., 1999; Newcombe & Dubas, 1987; Signorella, Jamison, & Krupa, 1989). Specifically, it appears that having a strong masculine self-concept and ample experience with spatial toys and activities fosters the growth of spatial skills in both boys and girls, whereas having restricted spatial experiences and a feminine self-concept seems to inhibit spatial abilities.

timing of puberty effect
the finding that people who reach puberty late perform better on visual/spatial tasks than those who mature early.

How closely are our masculine and feminine self-concepts related to the genes that we have inherited? Results from several behavioral genetics studies of adolescent twins suggest that genotype accounts for about 50 percent of the differences in people's masculine self-concepts but only 0 to 20 percent of the differences in their feminine self-concepts (review Chapter 3 for details on behavioral genetics studies; Loehlin, 1992; Mitchell, Baker, & Jacklin, 1989). So even though genes determine our biological sex and may have some influence on the outcome of gender typing, it appears that at least half the differences in people's masculine and feminine self-concepts is attributable to environmental influences.

Hormonal Influences. Biological influences on development are clearer in studies of children who have been exposed to the "wrong" hormones during the prenatal period (Ehrhardt & Baker, 1974; Gandelman, 1992; Money & Ehrhardt, 1972). Before the consequences were known, some mothers who had had problems carrying pregnancies to term were given drugs containing progestins, which are converted to the male hormone testosterone by the body. Other children with a condition known as **congenital adrenal hyperplasia (CAH)** have a genetic defect that causes their adrenal glands to produce unusually high levels of androgen from the prenatal period onward. These conditions usually have no effect on males; but female fetuses are often masculinized so that, despite their XX genetic endowment and female internal organs, they are born with external genitalia that resemble those of a boy (for example, a large clitoris that looks like a penis and fused labia that resembled a scrotum).

congenital adrenal hyperplasia (CAH)
a genetic anomaly that causes one's adrenal glands to produce unusually high levels of androgen from the prenatal period onward; often has masculinizing effects on female fetuses.

Money and Ehrhardt (1972; Ehrhardt & Baker, 1974) have followed several of these **androgenized females** whose external organs were surgically altered and who were then raised as girls. Compared with their sisters and other girls, many more androgenized girls were tomboys who often played with boys and who preferred boys' toys and activities to traditionally feminine pursuits (see also Berenbaum & Snyder, 1995; Servin et al., 2003). As adolescents, they began dating somewhat later than other girls and felt that marriage should be delayed until they had established their careers. A high proportion (37 percent) described themselves as homosexual or bisexual (Money, 1985; Berenbaum, 1998, 2002). Androgenized females also perform better than most girls and women on tests of spatial

androgenized females
females who develop male external genitalia because of exposure to male sex hormones during the prenatal period.

ability, further suggesting that early exposure to male hormones may have "masculinizing" effects on a female fetus's brain (Berenbaum, 1998, 2002; Resnick et al., 1986). Indeed, one Swedish study showed a dose-related effect: girls with more severe cases of CAH (and, thus, greater prenatal exposure to male sex hormones) showed the strongest interest in masculine toys and careers (Servin et al., 2003). Although a skeptic might wonder whether other family members had reacted to the girls' abnormal genitalia early in life, treating those girls more like boys, interviews with girls' parents suggested that they had not (Ehrhardt & Baker, 1974). Even normal variations in girls' exposure to testosterone (produced by their mothers) prior to their birth are associated with girls' play behavior at age 3½: Girls exposed to high-normal levels of testosterone before birth show stronger preferences for masculine toys and activities than do female age-mates exposed to lower levels of testosterone (Hines et al., 2002). So we must seriously consider the possibilities that (1) some differences between males and females may be hormonally mediated and (2) prenatal exposure to male sex hormones can influence the attitudes, interests, and activities of human females.

Evidence for Social-Labeling Influences

Although biological forces may steer boys and girls toward different activities and interests, Money and Ehrhardt (1972) insist that social-labeling influences are also important—so important, in fact, that they can modify or even *reverse* biological predispositions.

In the past, some androgenized girls were labeled boys at birth and raised as such until their abnormalities were detected. Money and Ehrhardt (1972) report that the discovery and correction of this condition (by surgery and gender reassignment) presents few if any adjustment problems, provided that the sex change occurs *before age 18 months.* But after age 3, gender reassignment is exceedingly difficult because these genetic females have experienced prolonged masculine gender typing and have already labeled themselves as boys. These data led Money and Ehrhardt to conclude that there is a "critical period" between 18 months and 3 years of age for the establishment of gender identity. It may be more accurate to call the first 3 years a *sensitive* period, for other investigators have claimed that it is possible to assume a new identity later in adolescence. Nevertheless, Money's findings indicate that early social labeling and gender role socialization can play a very prominent role in determining a child's gender identity and role preferences.

Cultural Influences. The fact that most societies encourage instrumental traits of males and expressive traits of females has led some theorists to conclude that traditional gender roles are part of the natural order of things—a product of our bioevolutionary history (Archer, 1996; Buss, 1995). Yet, there are sizable differences across cultures in what people expect of boys and girls (Whiting & Edwards, 1988). Consider Margaret Mead's (1935) classic study of three tribal societies in New Guinea. *Both* males and females among the Arapesh were taught to be cooperative, nonaggressive, and sensitive to the needs of others. This behavioral profile would be considered "expressive" or "feminine" in Western cultures. *Both* men and women of the Mundugumor tribe were expected to be assertive, aggressive, and emotionally unresponsive in their interpersonal relationships—a masculine pattern of behavior by Western standards. Finally, the Tchambuli displayed a pattern of gender-role development opposite to that of Western societies: males were passive, emotionally dependent, and socially sensitive, whereas females were dominant, independent, and assertive. So members of these three tribes developed in accordance with the gender roles that were *socially* prescribed by their culture—none of which matched the female / expressive, male / instrumental pattern seen in Western societies (as depicted in the photo on the previous page). Clearly, social forces contribute heavily to gender typing.

According to Freud, children become appropriately "masculine" or "feminine" by identifying with the same-sex parent.

psychobiosocial model
perspective on nature/nurture interactions specifying that specific early experiences affect the organization of the brain which, in turn, influences one's responsiveness to similar experiences in the future.

phallic stage
Freud's third stage of psychosexual development (from 3 to 6 years of age) in which children gratify the sex instinct by fondling their genitals and developing an incestuous desire for the parent of the other sex.

identification
Freud's term for the child's tendency to emulate another person, usually the same-sex parent.

castration anxiety
in Freud's theory, a young boy's fear that his father will castrate him as punishment for his rivalrous conduct.

Oedipus complex
Freud's term for the conflict that 3- to 6-year-old boys were said to experience when they develop an incestuous desire for their mothers and a jealous and hostile rivalry with their fathers.

Electra complex
female version of the Oedipus complex, in which a 3- to 6-year-old girl was thought to envy her father for possessing a penis and would choose him as a sex object in the hope that he would share with her this valuable organ that she lacked.

In sum, Money and Ehrhardt's biosocial theory stresses the importance of early biological developments that influence how parents and other social agents label a child at birth and that possibly also affect behavior more directly. However, the theory also holds that whether children are socialized as boys or girls strongly influences their gender-role development—in short, that biological and social forces *interact*. But how, exactly, do they interact?

A Psychobiosocial Viewpoint. Diane Halpern (1997) proposed a *psychobiosocial model* to explain how nature and nurture might jointly influence the development of gender-typed attributes. According to the model, prenatal exposure to male or female hormones influences the organization of male and female brains in ways that might make boys, for example, somewhat more receptive to spatial activities and girls somewhat more susceptible to quiet verbal exchanges. These heightened sensitivities, in concert with others' beliefs about the kinds of experiences most appropriate for boys and for girls, means that boys are likely to (and actually do) receive a richer array of spatial experiences than girls do, whereas girls will be exposed more often to verbal play activities (see Bornstein et al., 1999). Drawing on advances in the field of cognitive neuroscience, Halpern proposes that the different early experiences that boys and girls have will influence the neural pathways laid down in their immature and highly *plastic* (that is, changeable) brains. Although the genetic code imposes some constraints on brain development, it does not provide specific "wiring" instructions, and the precise architecture of the brain is heavily influenced by the experiences one has (Johnson, 1998). So according to Halpern (1997), boys who receive more early spatial experiences than girls do may develop a richer array of neural pathways in areas of the brain's right cerebral hemisphere that serve spatial functions which, in turn, may make them ever more receptive to spatial activities and to acquiring spatial skills. Girls may develop a richer array of neural interconnections in areas of the left cerebral hemisphere that serve verbal functions, thereby becoming ever more receptive to verbal activities and to acquiring verbal skills. From a psychobiosocial perspective, then, nature and nurture feed on each other and really cannot be separated. In Halpern's words ". . . biology and environment are as inseparable as conjoined twins who share a common heart" (p. 1097).

What both biosocial theory and the psychobiosocial model do *not* do is to specify the precise social processes that contribute most heavily to children's emerging gender identities and gender-typed patterns of behavior. Let's turn now to the social theories of gender typing, the first of which was Sigmund Freud's psychoanalytic approach.

By encouraging and engaging in counterstereotypic activities, parents may deter their children from developing rigid gender stereotypes.

Freud's Psychoanalytic Theory

Recall from Chapter 2 that Freud thought that sexuality (the sex instinct) was inborn. However, he believed that one's gender identity and preference for a gender role emerge during the **phallic stage** as children begin to emulate and to identify with their same-sex parent. Specifically, Freud claimed that a 3- to 6-year-old boy internalizes masculine attributes and behaviors when he is forced to **identify** with his father as a means of renouncing his incestuous desire for his mother, reducing his **castration anxiety,** and thus resolving his **Oedipus complex.** However, Freud believed that gender typing is more difficult for a young girl who lacks a penis, already feels castrated, and experiences no overriding fear that would compel her to identify with her mother and resolve her **Electra complex.** Why, then, would a girl ever develop a preference for the feminine role? Freud offered several suggestions, one of which was that the object of a girl's affection, her father, was likely to encourage her feminine behavior—an act that increases the attractiveness of the mother, who serves as the girl's model of femininity. So by trying to please her father (or to prepare for relationships with other males after she recognizes the implausibility of possessing her father), a girl is motivated to incorporate her mother's feminine attributes and eventually becomes gender typed (Freud, 1924/1961).

Although children are rapidly learning gender stereotypes and developing gender-typed playmate and activity preferences at roughly the ages Freud says they should, his psychoanalytic theory of gender typing has not fared well at all. Many 4- to 6-year-olds are so ignorant about differences between male and female genitalia that it is hard to see how most boys could fear castration or how most girls could feel castrated as Freud says they do (Bem, 1989; Katcher, 1955). Furthermore, Freud assumed that a boy's identification with his father is based on fear; but most researchers find that boys identify more strongly with fathers who are warm and nurturant rather than overly punitive and threatening (Hetherington & Frankie, 1967; Mussen & Rutherford, 1963). Finally, school-age children are not especially similar psychologically to their same-sex parents (Maccoby & Jacklin, 1974). Clearly, these findings are damaging to Freud's notion that children are inspired by fear to acquire gender-typed attributes by identifying with the same-sex parent.

Let's now consider the social learning interpretation of gender typing to see whether this approach looks any more promising.

Social Learning Theory

According to social learning theorists such as Albert Bandura (1989; Bussey & Bandura, 1992, 1999) children acquire their gender identities and gender-role preferences in two ways. First, through **direct tuition,** children are encouraged and rewarded for gender-appropriate behaviors and are punished or otherwise discouraged for behaviors considered more appropriate for members of the other sex. Second, through **observational learning,** children adopt the attitudes and behaviors of a variety of same-sex models.

direct tuition
teaching young children how to behave by reinforcing "appropriate" behaviors and by punishing or otherwise discouraging inappropriate conduct.

observational learning
learning that results from observing the behavior of others.

Direct Tuition of Gender Roles

Are parents actively involved in teaching boys how to be boys and girls how to be girls? Yes, indeed (Leaper, Anderson, & Sanders, 1998; Lytton & Romney, 1991), and their shaping of gender-typed behaviors begins rather early. Beverly Fagot and Mary Leinbach (1989), for example, found that parents are already encouraging gender-appropriate activities and discouraging cross-gender play during the second year of life, before children have acquired their basic gender identities or display clear preferences for male or female activities. By age 20 months to 24 months, daughters are consistently reinforced for dancing, dressing up (as women), following parents around, asking for help, and playing with dolls; and they are generally discouraged from manipulating objects, running, jumping, and climbing. Sons, on the other hand, are often reprimanded for such "feminine" behaviors as doll play or seeking help and are actively encouraged to play with masculine items such as blocks, trucks, and push-and-pull toys that require large muscle activity (Fagot, 1978).

Are children influenced by the "gender curriculum" their parents provide? They certainly are! Parents who show the clearest patterns of differential reinforcement have children who are relatively quick to (1) label themselves as boys or girls, (2) develop strong gender-typed toy and activity preferences, and (3) acquire an understanding of gender stereotypes (Fagot & Leinbach, 1989; Fagot, Leinbach, & O'Boyle, 1992). And fathers are even more likely than mothers to encourage "gender-typed" behaviors and to discourage behavior considered more appropriate for the other sex (Leve & Fagot, 1997; Lytton & Romney, 1991). So it seems that a child's earliest preferences for gender-typed toys and activities may well result from their parents' (particularly fathers') successful attempts to reinforce these interests.

Throughout the preschool period, parents become less and less inclined to carefully monitor and differentially reinforce their children's gender-typed activities (Fagot & Hagan, 1991; Lytton & Romney, 1991). Instead, many other factors conspire to maintain these gender-typed interests, including the behavior of siblings and same-sex peers (Beal, 1994; McHale, Crouter, & Tucker, 1999). Peer influences are especially powerful: Even before they have established their basic gender identities, 2-year-old boys often belittle or disrupt each other for playing with girl toys or with girls, and 2-year-old girls are quite critical of other girls who choose to play with boys (Fagot, 1985a). So peers are beginning to differentially reinforce gender-typed attitudes and behaviors even as parents become somewhat less likely to do so. Peers continue to reinforce this gender typing throughout childhood (Martin & Fabes, 2001).

Observational Learning

The second way children acquire many of their gender-typed attributes and interests, according to social learning theory (Bandura, 1989), is by observing and imitating a variety of same-sex models. The assumption is that boys will see which toys, activities, and behaviors are "for boys" and girls will learn which activities and behaviors are "for girls" by selectively attending to and imitating a variety of same-sex models, including peers, teachers, older siblings, and media personalities, as well as their mothers or their fathers (Fagot, Rodgers, & Leinbach, 2000).

Yet, there is some question just how important *same-sex* modeling influences are during the preschool period, for researchers often find that 3- to 6-year-olds learn much about typical patterns of both male and female behavior by carefully observing models of each sex (Leaper, 2000; Ruble & Martin, 1998). For example, children of employed mothers (who play the *masculine* instrumental role) or of fathers who routinely perform such *feminine* household tasks as cooking, cleaning, and child care are less aware of gender stereotypes than are children of more traditional parents (Serbin, Powlishta, & Gulko, 1993; Turner & Gervai, 1995). Similarly, boys with sisters and girls with brothers have less gender-typed activity preferences than children who have only same-sex siblings (Colley et al., 1996; Rust et al., 2000). What's more, John Masters and his associates (1979) found that preschool children are much more concerned about the sex-appropriateness of the *behavior* they are observing than the sex of the model who displays it. Four- to five-year-old boys, for example, will play with objects labeled "boys' toys" even after they have seen a girl playing with them. However, these youngsters are reluctant to play with "girls' toys" that boy models have played with earlier, and they think that other boys would also shun objects labeled as girls' toys (Martin, Eisenbud, & Rose, 1995). So children's toy choices are affected more by the labels attached to the toys than by the sex of the child who served as a model. But once they recognize that gender is an unchanging aspect of their personalities (at age 5 to 7), children do begin to attend more selectively to same-sex models and are now likely to avoid toys and activities that other-sex models seem to enjoy (Frey & Ruble, 1992; Ruble, Balaban, & Cooper, 1981).

Media Influences. Not only do children learn by observing other children and adult models with whom they interact, but they also learn about gender roles from reading stories and watching television. Although sexism in children's books has declined over the past 50 years, male characters are still more likely than female characters to engage in active, instrumental pursuits such as riding bikes or making things, whereas female characters are often depicted as passive and dependent individuals who spend much of their time playing quietly indoors and "creating problems that require masculine solutions" (Kortenhaus & Demarest, 1993; Turner-Bowker, 1996). It is similar in the world of television: Males are usually featured as the central characters who work at professions, make important decisions, respond to emergencies, and assume positions of leadership, whereas females are often portrayed as relatively passive and emotional creatures who manage a home or work at "feminine" occupations such as nursing (Signorielli & Kahlenberg, 2001). And, children are influenced by these highly traditional role portrayals, for those who watch a lot of television are more likely to prefer gender-typed activities and to hold highly stereotyped views of men and women than their classmates who watch little television (McGhee & Frueh, 1980; Signorielli & Lears, 1992).

In sum, there is a lot of evidence that differential reinforcement and observational learning contribute to gender-role development. However, social learning theorists have often portrayed children as passive pawns in the process: Parents, peers, and media characters show them what to do and reinforce them for doing it. Might this perspective miss something, namely the child's own contribution to gender-role socialization? Children do not always receive gender-stereotyped Christmas presents because their sexist parents force these objects upon them. Many parents who would rather buy gender-neutral or educational toys end up "giving in" to sons who beg for toy guns or daughters who want tea sets (Robinson & Morris, 1986).

Kohlberg's Cognitive-Developmental Theory

Lawrence Kohlberg (1966) proposed a cognitive theory of gender-typing that is quite different from the other theories we have considered and helps to explain why boys and girls adopt traditional gender roles even when their parents may not want them to. Kohlberg's major themes are:

- Gender-role development depends on cognitive development; children must acquire certain understandings about gender before they will be influenced by their social experiences.
- Children *actively socialize themselves;* they are not merely passive pawns of social influence.

According to both psychoanalytic theory and social learning theory, children first learn to do "boy" or "girl" things because their parents encourage these activities. Next, they come to identify with or habitually imitate same-sex models, thereby acquiring a stable gender identity. Kohlberg proposes the opposite. He argues that children *first* establish a stable gender identity and then *actively* seek out same-sex models and other information to learn how to act like a boy or a girl. To Kohlberg, it's not "I'm treated like a boy; therefore, I must be one" (social learning view). It's more like "Hey, I'm a boy; therefore, I'd better do everything I can do to find out how to behave like one" (cognitive-developmental view).

Kohlberg believes that children pass through the following three stages as they acquire a mature understanding of what it means to be a male or a female:

Basic gender identity. By age 3, children label themselves as boys or girls.

Gender stability. Later, gender is perceived as *stable over time.* Boys invariably grow up to become men and girls grow up to be women.

Gender consistency. The gender concept is complete when the child realizes that one's sex is also *stable across situations.* Five- to seven-year-olds who have reached this stage are no longer fooled by appearances. They know, for example, that one's gender cannot be altered by cross-dressing or taking up cross-sex activities.

basic gender identity
the stage of gender identity in which the child first labels the self as a boy or a girl.

gender stability
the stage of gender identity in which the child recognizes that gender is stable over time.

gender consistency
the stage of gender identity in which the child recognizes that a person's gender is invariant despite changes in the person's activities or appearance (also known as gender constancy).

When do children become motivated to socialize themselves—that is, to seek out same-sex models and learn how to act like males and females? According to Kohlberg, self-socialization begins only after children attain *gender consistency.* So for Kohlberg, a mature understanding of gender instigates true gender typing.

Studies conducted in more than 20 different cultures reveal that preschool children proceed through Kohlberg's three stages of gender identity in the sequence he describes and that attainment of gender consistency (or conservation of gender) is clearly associated with other relevant aspects of cognitive development, such as the conservation of liquids and mass (Marcus & Overton, 1978; Munroe, Shimmin & Munroe, 1984; Szkrybalo & Ruble, 1999). Furthermore, boys who have achieved gender consistency display more gender-stereotypic play preferences (Warin, 2000), begin to pay more attention to male than to female characters on television (Luecke-Aleksa et al., 1995), and favor novel toys that male models prefer rather than the ones that female models like—even when the toys they are passing on are the *more attractive toys* (Frey & Ruble, 1992). So children with a mature gender identity (especially boys) often play it safe and select the toy or activity that other members of their gender view as more appropriate for them.

Criticisms of Kohlberg's Theory

You may have already noticed the major problem with Kohlberg's theory: gender typing is well under way before the child acquires a mature gender identity. Recall that 2-year-old boys already prefer masculine toys before they have achieved a basic gender identity, and that 3-year-olds of each sex have learned many gender-role stereotypes and clearly prefer same-sex activities and playmates long before they begin to attend more selectively to same-sex models. Furthermore, gender reassignment is exceedingly difficult after children reach age 3 (Kohlberg's basic identity stage) and have *initially* categorized themselves as boys or girls. So Kohlberg overstates the case in arguing that a mature understanding of gender is necessary for gender typing to begin. As we are about to see, only a rudimentary understanding of gender is necessary before children acquire strong gender stereotypes and activity preferences.

Gender Schema Theory

Carol Martin and Charles Halverson (1981, 1987) proposed a somewhat different cognitive theory of gender typing (actually, an information-processing theory) that appears quite promising. Like Kohlberg, Martin and Halverson believe that children are highly motivated to acquire interests, values, and behaviors that are consistent with their "boy" or "girl" self-images. But unlike Kohlberg, they argue that this "self-socialization" begins as soon as the child acquires a basic gender identity at age 2½ or 3 and is well under way by age 6 to 7 when the child achieves gender consistency.

According to Martin and Halverson's gender schema theory, establishing a basic gender identity motivates a child to learn about the sexes and to incorporate this information into **gender schemas**—that is, organized sets of beliefs and expectations about males and females that influence the kinds of information attended to, elaborated, and remembered. First, children acquire a simple **"in-group/out-group" schema** that allows them to classify some objects, behaviors, and roles as "for boys" and others as "for girls" (for example, trucks are for boys, girls can cry but boys should not, and so on). This is the information that researchers normally tap when studying children's knowledge of gender stereotypes. This initial categorization of objects and activities clearly affects children's thinking. In one research program, 4- and 5-year-olds were shown unfamiliar gender-neutral toys (for example, spinning bells, a magnet stand), were told that these objects were either "for boys" or "for girls," and were asked whether they and other boys or girls would like them. Children clearly relied on the labels to guide their thinking. Boys, for example, liked "boy" objects better than girls did, and children assumed that other boys would also like these objects better than other girls would. Just the opposite pattern of reasoning was observed when these same objects were labeled as "for girls." Even highly attractive toys soon lost their appeal if they were labeled as for the other gender (Martin, Eisenbud, & Rose, 1995).

gender schemas
organized sets of beliefs and expectations about males and females that guide information processing.

"in-group/out-group" schema
one's general knowledge of the mannerisms, roles, activities, and behaviors that characterize males and females.

According to this theory, children also construct an **own-sex schema,** which consists of detailed information they will need to perform various gender-consistent behaviors. So a girl who has a basic gender identity might first learn that sewing is "for girls" and building model airplanes is "for boys." Then, because she is a girl and wants to act consistently with her own self-concept, she will gather a great deal of information about sewing to add to her own-sex schema, while largely ignoring information about building model airplanes (this sequence is depicted in Figure 13.6). To test this notion, 4- to 9-year-olds were given boxes of gender-neutral objects (for example, burglar alarms, pizza cutters) and told that these objects were either "boy" or "girl" items (Bradbard et al., 1986). As predicted, boys

own-sex schema
detailed knowledge or plans of action that enable a person to perform gender-consistent activities and to enact his or her gender role.

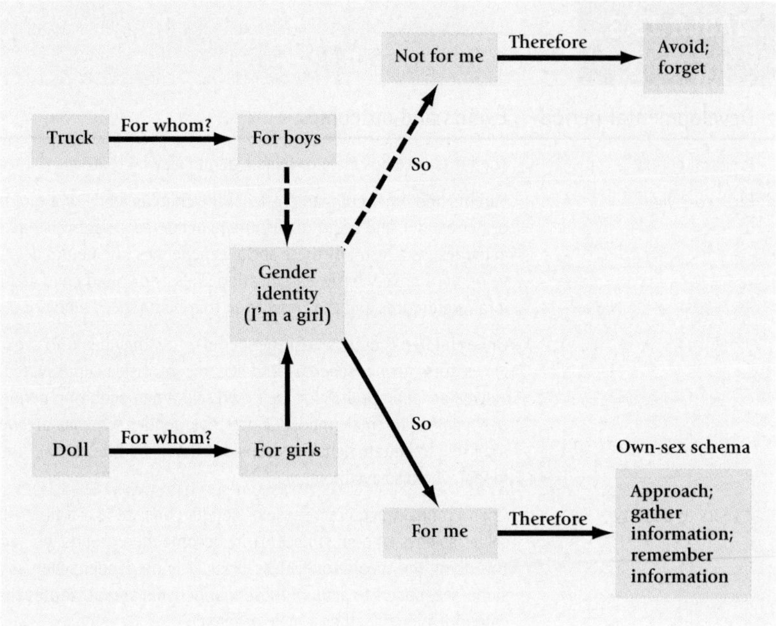

Figure 13.6 Gender schema theory in action. A young girl classifies new information according to an in-group/out-group schema as either "for boys" or "for girls." Information about boys' toys and activities is ignored, but information about toys and activities for girls is relevant to the self and so is added to an ever-larger own-sex schema. *Adapted from Martin & Halverson, 1987.*

subsequently explored "boy" items more than girls did, whereas girls explored more than boys when the objects were described as things girls enjoy. One week later, boys recalled much more in-depth information about "boy items" than girls did, whereas girls recalled more than boys about these very same objects if they had been labeled "girl" items. If children's information-gathering efforts are consistently guided by their own-sex schemas in this way, we can easily see how boys and girls might acquire very different stores of knowledge and develop different interests and competencies as they mature.

Once formed, gender schemas serve as scripts for processing social information. Recall from Chapter 8 that preschool children often have a difficult time recalling information that deviates from their scripted knowledge of everyday events. The same applies to gender-related knowledge: Children are likely to encode and remember information consistent with their gender schemas and to forget schema-inconsistent information or otherwise distort it so that it becomes more consistent with their stereotypes (Liben & Signorella, 1993; Martin & Halverson, 1983). This is especially true if they have reached age 6 to 7, when their own stereotyped knowledge and preferences have crystallized and are especially strong (Welch-Ross & Schmidt, 1996). Support for this idea was presented in the Box on p. 516; recall that children who heard stories in which actors performed gender-atypical behaviors (e.g., a girl chopping wood) tended to recall the action but to alter the scene to conform to their gender stereotypes (saying that a boy had been chopping). Surely these strong tendencies to forget or to distort counterstereotypic information help explain why unfounded beliefs about males and females are so slow to die.

In sum, Martin and Halverson's gender schema theory is an interesting perspective on the gender-typing process. Not only does this model describe how gender-role stereotypes might originate and persist over time, but it also indicates how these emerging gender schemas might contribute to the development of strong gender-role preferences and gender-typed behaviors long before a child may realize that gender is an unchanging attribute.

An Integrative Theory

Biological, social learning, cognitive-developmental, and gender schema perspectives have each contributed in important ways to our understanding of sex differences and gender-role development (Ruble & Martin, 1998). In fact, the processes that different theories emphasize seem to be especially important at different periods. Biological theories account for the major biological developments that occur before birth that induce people to label

TABLE 13.3 An Overview of the Gender-Typing Process from the Perspective of an Integrative Theorist

Developmental period	Events and outcomes	Pertinent theory(ies)
Prenatal period	The fetus develops male or female genitalia, which others will react to once the child is born.	Biosocial/psychobiosocial
Birth to 3 years	Parents and other companions label the child as a boy or a girl, frequently remind the child of his or her gender, and begin to encourage gender-consistent behavior while discouraging cross-sex activities. As a result of these social experiences, the neural developments they foster, and the development of very basic classification skills, the young child acquires some gender-typed behavioral preferences and the knowledge that he or she is a boy or a girl (basic gender identity).	Social learning (differential reinforcement) Psychobiosocial
3 to 6 years	Once children acquire a basic gender identity, they begin to seek information about sex differences, form gender schemas, and become intrinsically motivated to perform those acts that are viewed as "appropriate" for their own sex. When acquiring gender schemas, children attend to *both* male and female models. Once their gender schemas are well established, these youngsters are likely to imitate behaviors considered appropriate for their sex, regardless of the gender of the model who displays them.	Gender schema
7 years to puberty	Children finally acquire a sense of gender consistency—a firm, future-oriented image of themselves as boys who must necessarily become men or girls who will obviously become women. At this point, they begin to rely less exclusively on gender schemas and to look to the behavior of same-sex models to acquire those mannerisms and attributes that are consistent with their firm categorization of self as a male or female.	Cognitive-developmental (Kohlberg)
Puberty and beyond	The biological upheavals of adolescence, in conjunction with new social expectations (gender intensification), cause teenagers to reexamine their self-concepts, forming an adult gender identity.	Biosocial/psychobiosocial Social learning Gender schema Cognitive-developmental

the child as a boy or a girl and to treat him or her accordingly. The differential reinforcement process that social learning theorists emphasize seems to account rather well for early gender-typing: young children display gender-consistent behaviors largely because other people encourage these activities and will often discourage behaviors considered more appropriate for members of the other sex. As a result of this early socialization and the growth of categorization skills, 2½ to 3-year-olds acquire a basic gender identity and begin to form gender schemas which tell them (1) what boys and girls are like and (2) how they, as boys and girls, are supposed to think and act. And when they finally understand, at age 6 or 7, that their gender will never change, children begin to focus less exclusively on gender schemas and to pay more and more attention to same-sex models to decide which attitudes, activities, interests, and mannerisms are most appropriate for members of their own sex (Kohlberg's viewpoint). Of course, summarizing developments in an integrative model such as this one (see Table 13.3 for an overview) does not mean that biological forces play no further role after the child is born or that differential reinforcement ceases to affect development once the child acquires a basic gender identity. But an integrative theorist would emphasize that, from age 3 on, children are active *self-socializers* who will try very hard to acquire the masculine or feminine attributes that they view as consistent with their male or female self-images. This is why parents who hope to discourage their children from adopting traditional gender roles are often amazed that their sons and daughters seem to become little "sexists" all on their own.

One more point: All theories of gender-role development would agree that what children actually learn about being a male or a female depends greatly on what their society offers them in the way of a "gender curriculum." In other words, we must view gender-role development through an *ecological* lens and appreciate that there is nothing inevitable about the patterns of male and female development that we see in our society today. (Indeed, recall the gender-role reversals that Mead observed among the Tchambuli of New Guinea.) In another era, in another culture, the gender-typing process can produce very different kinds of boys and girls.

Should we in Western cultures be trying to raise different kinds of boys and girls? As we will see in our next section, some theorists would answer this question with a resounding "yes!"

CONCEPT CHECK 13.2 Understanding Theories of Gender-Role Development

Check your understanding of theories of gender-role development by answering the following questions. Answers appear in the Appendix.

True or False: Identify whether the following statements are true or false.

1. (T)(F) Halpern's psychobiological model explains why unfounded beliefs about males and females are likely to persist.
2. (T)(F) Kohlberg's cognitive-developmental theory cannot easily explain why gender reassignment usually fails with 3- to 5-year-olds.

Multiple Choice: Select the one best answer for each question.

_____ 3. _______ The starting point for self-socialization, according to Kohlberg's cognitive-developmental theory of gender-role development is
   a. gender consistency
   b. basic gender identity
   c. gender stability
   d. gender-role achievement

_____ 4. _______ The starting point for self-socialization, according to Martin and Halverson's gender schema theory is
   a. gender consistency
   b. basic gender identity
   c. gender stability
   d. gender-role achievement

Fill in the Blank: Complete the following statements with the correct theoretical perspective.

5. You are a developmental psychologist who believes that there is a critical period for gender typing between 18 months and 3 years. You also believe that biological and social factors interact to direct gender-role development. Based on your beliefs, you would most closely associate with _______ perspective.
6. You are a developmental psychologist who believes that early gender typing largely reflects the gender curriculum that parents provide. You also believe that siblings and playmates help to establish children's gender-roles. Based on your beliefs, others might label you a _______ psychologist.
7. You are a developmental psychologist who believes that children adopt gender roles by identifying with the same-sex parent. Based on your beliefs, others might label you a _______ psychologist.

Short Answer: Provide a brief answer to the following question.

8. List in order the phases through which children pass in their development of gender roles, according to Kohlberg's cognitive-developmental theory of gender-role development.

Essay: Provide a detailed answer to the following question.

9. Describe ways in which parents, peers, and the media influence gender-role development.

Psychological Androgyny: A Prescription for the 21st Century?

Throughout this chapter, we have used the term *gender-appropriate* to describe the mannerisms and behaviors that societies consider more suitable for members of one sex than the other. Today many developmentalists believe that these rigidly defined gender-role standards are actually harmful because they constrain the behavior of both males and females. Sandra Bem (1978), for example, has stated that her major purpose in studying gender roles is "to help free the human personality from the restrictive prison of sex-role stereotyping and to develop a conception of mental health that is free from culturally imposed definitions of masculinity and femininity."

For many years, psychologists assumed that masculinity and femininity were at opposite ends of a single dimension. If one possessed highly masculine traits, one must be very unfeminine; being highly feminine implied being unmasculine. Bem (1974) challenged this assumption by arguing that individuals of either sex can be characterized by psychological **androgyny**—that is, by a balancing or blending of desirable masculine-stereotyped traits (for example, being assertive, analytical, forceful, and independent) and desirable feminine-stereotyped traits (for example, being affectionate, compassionate, gentle, and understanding). In Bem's model, then, masculinity and femininity are *two*

androgyny
a psychological identity that includes both masculine and feminine characteristics or traits.

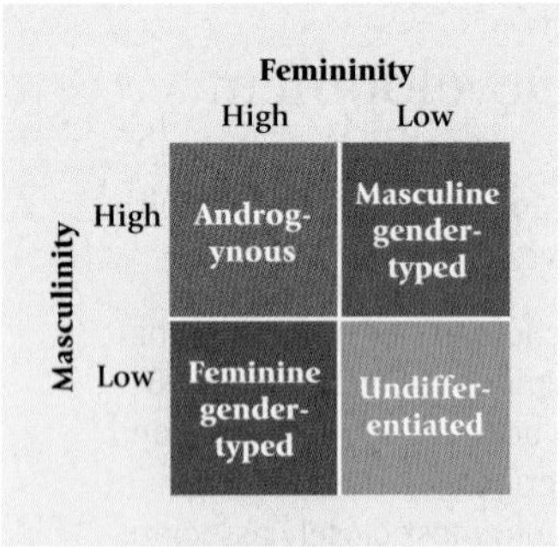

Figure 13.7 Categories of sex-role orientation based on viewing masculinity and femininity as separate dimensions of personality.

separate dimensions of personality. A male or female who has many desirable masculine-stereotyped traits and few feminine ones is defined as a *masculine gender-typed* person. One who has many feminine- and few masculine-stereotyped traits is said to be *feminine gender-typed*. The androgynous person possesses both masculine and feminine traits, whereas the *undifferentiated* individual lacks both of these kinds of attributes (these categories are depicted in Figure 13.7).

Do Androgynous People Really Exist?

Bem (1974) and other investigators (Spence & Helmreich, 1978) have developed self-perception inventories that contain both a masculinity (or instrumentality) scale and a femininity (or expressivity) scale. In one large sample of college students (Spence & Helmreich, 1978), roughly 33 percent of the test takers proved to be "masculine" men or "feminine" women, about 30 percent were androgynous, and the remaining individuals were either undifferentiated or "sex-reversed" (masculine gender-typed females or feminine gender-typed males). Janet Boldizar (1991) developed a similar gender-role inventory for grade school children (see Table 13.4 for sample items) and found that approximately 25 to 30 percent of third- through seventh-graders can be classified as androgynous. So androgynous individuals do exist, and in sizable numbers.

Are There Advantages to Being Androgynous?

When we consider the idea that a person can be both assertive and sensitive, both independent and understanding, we can't help but think that being androgynous is psychologically healthy. Is it? Bem (1975, 1978) demonstrated that androgynous men and women behave more flexibly than more traditionally gender-typed individuals. For example, androgynous people, like masculine gender-typed people, can display the "masculine" instrumental trait of independence by resisting social pressure to judge very unamusing cartoons as funny just because their companions do. Yet they are as likely as feminine gender-typed individuals to display the "feminine" expressive quality of nurturance by interacting positively with a baby. Androgynous people do seem to be more highly adaptable, able to adjust their behavior to the demands of the situation at hand

TABLE 13.4 Sample Items from a Gender-Role Inventory for Grade School Children

Personality trait	Item
Masculine	
Dominant	I can control a lot of the kids in my class.
Authoritative	I am a leader among my friends.
Self-sufficient	I can take care of myself.
Ambitious	I am willing to work hard to get what I want.
Masculine	I like to do what boys and men do.
Feminine	
Compassionate	I care about what happens to others.
Cheerful	I am a cheerful person.
Loyal	I am faithful to my friends.
Nurturant	I like babies and small children a lot.
Feminine	I like to do what girls and women do.

Format: The child is asked to respond to each item on a four-point scale, with options ranging from 1 = "not at all true of me" to 4 = "very true of me."

Source: Adapted from "Assessing Sex-Typing and Androgyny in Children: The Children's Sex-Role Inventory," by J. P. Boldizar, 1991, *Developmental Psychology, 27,* 505–515. Copyright © 1991 by the American Psychological Association. Adapted with permission.

(Harter et al., 1998; Morrison & Shaffer, 2003; Shaffer, Pegalis, & Cornell, 1992). Furthermore, androgynous children and adolescents appear to enjoy higher self-esteem and are perceived as more likable and better adjusted than their traditionally gender-typed peers (Allgood-Merten & Stockard, 1991; Boldizar, 1991; O'Heron & Orlofsky, 1990). It has also become clear that androgynous men can still feel quite masculine and androgynous women quite feminine even though they sometimes express traits traditionally associated with the other sex (Spence, 1993).

But before we conclude that androgyny is something for which everybody should strive, let's note that children who strive too hard and express too many of the traits considered more appropriate for members of the other sex are at risk of being rejected by peers and experiencing low self-esteem (Lobel, Slone, & Winch, 1997). What's more, it is the possession of "masculine" traits rather than androgyny per se that is most strongly associated with good adjustment and high self-esteem (Spence & Hall, 1996; Whitley, 1983). In their study of gender roles and adjustment outcomes among fourth- through eighth-graders, Susan Egan and David Perry (2001) found that well-adjusted boys and girls perceived themselves to be typical members of their own sex but also felt free to explore cross-gender options when they wanted to. Perhaps, then, one must first be secure in a gender-typical orientation in childhood, feeling like one of the guys and gals, before one can derive many benefits from cross-gender explorations later in life.

So it may be premature to conclude that one is better off in *all* respects to be androgynous rather than masculine or feminine in orientation. But given the behavioral flexibility that androgynous people display and the strong contribution that androgyny makes to children's global self-worth, we can safely assume that, as long as it is not overdone, it is probably adaptive and certainly not harmful for girls and women to become a little more "masculine," and for boys and men to become a little more feminine.

Applications: On Changing Gender Role Attitudes and Behavior

Today many people believe that the world would be a better place if sexism were eliminated and boys and girls were no longer steered toward adopting the confining "masculine" or "feminine" roles. In a nonsexist culture, women would no longer suffer from a lack of assertiveness and confidence in the world of work, and men would be freer to display their sensitive, nurturant sides that many now suppress in the interest of appearing "masculine." How might we reduce sexism and encourage children to be more flexible about the interests and attributes they might display?

Bem (1983, 1989) believes that parents must take an active role by (1) teaching their young children about genital anatomy as part of a larger lesson that one's biological sex is unimportant outside the domain of reproduction, and (2) delaying children's exposure to gender stereotypes by encouraging cross-sex as well as same-sex play and by dividing household chores more equitably (with fathers sometimes cooking and cleaning and mothers cutting grass or making repairs; see photo). If preschoolers come to think of sex as a purely biological attribute and often see themselves and their parents pursuing cross-sex interests and activities, they should be less inclined to construct the rigid gender stereotypes that might otherwise evolve in a highly sexist early environment. Research suggesting that androgynous parents tend to raise androgynous children is consistent with Bem's prescriptions for change (Orlofsky, 1979). So, too, are findings that children whose parents hold nontraditional attitudes toward gender roles or whose fathers routinely perform "feminine" household and child care tasks are less aware of gender stereotypes. These children are also less likely to display gender-typed interests and ability profiles, compared with youngsters whose parents are more traditional in their gender-role attitudes and behaviors (McHale, Crouter, & Tucker, 1999; Tennenbaum & Leaper, 2002; Turner & Gervai, 1995).

How might we reach children from more traditional backgrounds, who have already received thousands of gender-stereotyped messages from family members, television, and their peers? Apparently, interventions that simply show children the benefits of cross-gender cooperation or that praise them for playing with other-sex toys and play partners have no lasting effect: children soon retreat to same-sex play and continue to prefer same-sex peers after the interventions are over (Maccoby, 1998). One particularly ambitious program (Guttentag & Bray, 1976) exposed kindergarten, fifth-grade, and ninth-grade students to age-appropriate readings and activities designed to teach them about the capabilities of women and about the problems created by stereotyping and sexism. This program worked quite well with the younger children, particularly the girls, who often became outraged about what they learned about sexism. However, it actually had a boomerang effect among ninth-grade boys, who seemed to resist the new ideas they were being taught and actually expressed more stereotyped views after the training than before. And although ninth-grade girls took many of the lessons to heart, they still tended to cling to the idea that women should run the family and that men should be the primary breadwinners.

This study and others (see Katz & Walsh, 1991, for a review) suggest that efforts to change gender-role attitudes are more effective with younger children than with older ones and possibly with girls than with boys. It makes some sense that it is easier to alter children's thinking early on, before their stereotypes have become fully crystallized; and many researchers now favor *cognitive interventions* that either attack the stereotypes directly or remove constraints on children's thinking that permit them to construct these rigid gender schemas. As you can see in the Box on p. 541, these cognitive interventions can be quite effective indeed.

Finally, there is some evidence that programs designed to modify children's gender-stereotyped attitudes and behaviors may be more effective when the adult in charge is a man (Katz & Walsh, 1991). Why? Possibly because men normally make stronger distinctions between "gender-appropriate" and "gender-inappropriate" behaviors than women do; thus, men may be particularly noteworthy as *agents of change.* In other words, children may feel that cross-gender activities and aspirations are quite legitimate indeed if it is a man who encourages (or fails to discourage) these pursuits.

So new gender-role attitudes can be taught, although it remains to be seen whether such change persists and generalizes to new situations should these attitudes not be reinforced at home or in the culture at large. Sweden is one culture that has made a strong commitment to gender equality: men and women have the same opportunities to pursue traditionally masculine (or traditionally feminine) careers, and fathers and mothers are viewed as equally responsible for housework and child care. Swedish adolescents still value masculine attributes more highly than feminine characteristics. However, they are much less adamant about it than American adolescents are and they are much more inclined to view gender roles as acquired domains of expertise rather than biologically programmed duties (Intons-Peterson, 1988).

Although our society has not made the commitment to gender equality that Sweden has, it is slowly becoming more egalitarian, and some people believe that these changes are having an impact on children (Etaugh, Levine, & Mennella, 1984; Tennenbaum & Leaper, 2002).

Applying Developmental Themes to Sex Differences and Gender Role Development

The four developmental themes that we have been exploring in this book are the active child, nature and nurture interactions, qualitative and quantitative developmental changes, and the holistic nature of development. Once again we find that these themes have been highlighted in this chapter on sex differences and gender-role development.

The active child theme is perhaps best illustrated by the self-socialization processes that children go through as they develop their gender identities and gender roles. Children are not passive recipients of environmental influences or biological forces. Instead, they actively seek out information about appropriate behaviors and characteristics of

APPLYING RESEARCH TO YOUR LIFE

Combating Gender Stereotypes with Cognitive Interventions

During the preschool period when children are constructing gender schemas, their thinking tends to be intuitive and one-dimensional. As we have seen, children who encounter a violation of their gender schemas, learning of a boy who likes to cook, for example, are unlikely to process and retain this information. After all, their one-dimensional, intuitive thinking makes it extremely hard to separate the gender-typed activity (cooking) from the gender category (for girls). So the information doesn't compute and is likely to be distorted or forgotten.

Roger Sandler/The Liaison Agency/Getty Images

Interventions that show men and women participating side by side at traditionally "masculine" or traditionally "feminine" occupations can be highly effective at combating rigid gender stereotypes.

Rebecca Bigler and Lynn Liben (1990, 1992) have devised and compared two cognitive interventions aimed at reducing children's gender schematic thinking about the occupations that men and women might pursue. The 5- to 11-year-olds who participated in this research were assigned to one of three conditions:

Rule training. Through a series of problem-solving discussions, children were taught that (1) the most important considerations in deciding who would perform well at such traditionally masculine and feminine occupations as construction worker and beautician are the person's interests and willingness to learn, and (2) that the person's gender was irrelevant.

Classification training. Children were given multiple classification tasks that required them to sort objects into two categories at once (for example, men and women engaged in masculine and feminine activities). This training was designed to illustrate that objects can be classified in many ways—knowledge that would hopefully help children to see that occupations can be classified independently of the kinds of people who normally enact these roles.

Control group. Children were simply given lessons on the contributions of various occupations to the community.

Compared to children in the control group, those who either received rule-training or who improved in classification skills showed clear declines in occupational stereotyping. Furthermore, later tests of information processing provided further evidence for the weakening of children's stereotypes. Specifically, children who received rule-training or who had gained in classification skills after the classification training were much more likely than "control" children to remember counterstereotypic information in stories (for example, recalling that the garbage man in a story was actually a woman). It seems, then, that gender stereotypes can be modified by directly attacking their accuracy (rule-training) or by promoting the cognitive skills (classification-training) that help children to see the fallacies in their own rigid gender schemas.

Unfortunately, teachers may unwittingly foster gender-schematic thinking should they group children on the basis of gender and emphasize gender differences during the first few years of school. In a recent experiment, Bigler (1995) randomly assigned some 6- to 11-year-old summer school students to "gender classrooms" in which teachers created separate boy and girl bulletin boards, seated boys with boys and girls with girls, and often made statements that distinguished boys from girls (for example, "All the boys should be sitting down"; "All the girls put their bubble-makers in the air."). Other children were assigned to classrooms in which teachers were instructed to refer to their pupils only by name and to treat the entire class as a unit.

After only 4 weeks, children in the "gender classrooms" endorsed more gender stereotypes than those in control classrooms, particularly if they were one-dimensional thinkers who have trouble understanding that a person can belong to more than one social category at the same time. So it seems that teachers can help to combat gender stereotyping should they avoid grouping pupils on the basis of gender during the early grades, when young one-dimensional thinkers are otherwise prone to construct rigid gender schemas.

their gender and work to incorporate these attributes into their own identities. This was reflected in Kohlberg's cognitive-developmental theory of gender-role development and in Martin and Halverson's gender schema theory. Even the more biological theories of gender-role development concur that children are active in their gender-role acquisition.

Concerning developing gender identities and gender roles, we've seen several theories propose qualitative stages of developmental change, with children behaving and thinking differently across these stages (the hallmark of qualitative developmental change). For example, in Kohlberg's cognitive-developmental theory children pass through three qualitatively distinct stages on their way to developing a mature gender identity. The biological (both genetic and hormonal) forces that help shape gender also follow qualitative developmental changes as different developmental events help shape the child's biological gender and the child's reactions to those biological changes.

Perhaps the best example from this chapter of the interaction of nature and nurture in development is the interactive model of gender-role development. In that model we saw biological forces interact with social and interpersonal influences to help guide children to the development of mature gender identities. We should not forget, however, that the other theoretical perspectives on gender-role development also made room for both nature and nurture in influencing gender development.

Our final theme, the holistic nature of child development, is well illustrated by the interplay between cognitive, social, and biological changes in children's development, all working together to help children achieve gender identity. Indeed, a mature gender identity would not be possible without the influences of the child's cognitive function, his or her interactions with other children and adults, and the biological changes that underlie many of the initial changes in gender.

CONCEPT CHECK 13.3 Understanding Androgyny

Check your understanding of psychological androgyny by answering the following questions. Answers appear in the Appendix.

True or False: Identify whether the following statements are true or false.

1. (T)(F) It is always preferable for children to be androgynous in their gender role orientation.
2. (T)(F) Children can be taught to be less sexist in their orientation to self and others.

Fill in the Blank: Identify whether each of the following attributes would be "high" or "low."

3. Androgynous people are ________ in masculine traits and ________ in feminine traits.
4. Undifferentiated people are ________ in masculine traits and ________ in feminine traits.

Multiple Choice: Select the one best answer for the following question.

_____ 5. Historically, masculinity and femininity were viewed as existing on a single continuum. If you subscribe to this position, you would believe that
   a. individuals who are highly masculine could also be highly feminine
   b. individuals who are highly feminine could also be highly masculine
   c. individuals could be low in masculinity or femininity, but not both
   d. a very masculine person would necessarily have few feminine characteristics

Essay: Provide a detailed answer to the following question.

6. In some Islamic societies (for example, Iran), gender roles are much more sharply delineated than is true of Western societies such as our own. Do you think that there are any advantages to being psychologically androgynous in such a society?

SUMMARY

■ **Gender typing** is the process by which children acquire a gender identity and the motives, values, and behaviors considered appropriate in their society for members of their biological sex.

Categorizing Males and Females: Gender-Role Standards

■ A **gender-role standard** is a motive, value, or behavior considered more appropriate for members of one sex than the other.
■ Many societies are characterized by a gender-based division of labor in which females adopt an **expressive role** and males an **instrumental role.**

Some Facts and Fictions about Sex Differences

■ As a group, girls outperform boys in many assessments of verbal ability and are more emotionally expressive, compliant, and timid than boys are.
■ As a group, boys are more active and more physically and verbally aggressive than girls and tend to outperform girls on tests of arithmetic reasoning and **visual/spatial skills.**
■ These sex differences are small, refer only to group norms, and overall, males and females are far more psychologically similar than they are different.
■ Cultural myths of traditional gender-role stereotypes that are *not* true include ideas that females are more sociable, suggestible, and illogical and less analytical and achievement oriented than males.
■ The persistence of these "cultural myths" can create **self-fulfilling prophecies** that promote sex differences in cognitive performance and steer males and females along different career paths.

Developmental Trends in Gender Typing

■ By age 2½ to 3, children label themselves as boys or girls, a first step in the development of **gender identity.**
■ Between ages 5 and 7, they come to realize that gender is an unchanging aspect of self.
■ Children begin to learn gender-role stereotypes at about the same age that they display a basic gender identity.
■ By age 10 to 11, children's stereotyping of male and female personality traits is strong and these preteens view stereotypes as obligatory prescriptions.
■ Children become more flexible in their thinking about gender during middle childhood.
■ Children become somewhat more rigid once again during the adolescent period of **gender intensification.**
■ Many toddlers display gender-typed toy and activity preferences, even before reaching basic gender identity.
■ By age 3, children show **gender segregation** by preferring to spend time with same-sex playmates and developing clear prejudices against members of the other sex.
■ Boys face stronger gender-typing pressures than girls do and are quicker to develop gender-typed toy and activity preferences.

Theories of Gender-Typing and Gender-Role Development

■ According to **evolutionary theory,** males and females faced different evolutionary pressures over the course of human history and the natural selection process created fundamental differences between males and females.
■ Money and Ehrhardt's **biosocial theory** emphasizes biological developments that occur before birth and influence the way a child is socialized. Prenatal hormone differences may contribute to sex differences in play styles and aggression.
■ Nevertheless, social labeling and gender-role socialization play a crucial role in determining one's gender identity and role preferences.
■ Freud's theory that children become gender typed as they **identify** with the same-sex parent to resolve their **Oedipus** or **Electra complexes** has not been supported by research.
■ Consistent with social learning theory, children acquire gender-typed toy and activity preferences through **direct tuition. Observational learning** also contributes to gender typing as preschool children attend to models of *both sexes* and become increasingly aware of gender stereotypes.
■ Kohlberg's cognitive-developmental theory claims that children are self-socializers and must pass through **basic gender identity** and **gender stability** before reaching **gender consistency,** when they selectively attend to same-sex models and become gender typed. However, research suggests that gender typing begins much earlier than Kohlberg thought and measures of gender consistency do not predict the strength of gender typing.
■ According to Martin and Halverson's **gender schema theory,** children who have established a basic gender identity construct **"in-group/out-group"** and **own-sex gender schemas.** These schemas serve as scripts for processing gender-related information and developing gender roles. Schema-consistent information is gathered and retained, whereas schema-inconsistent information is ignored or distorted, thus perpetuating gender stereotypes that may have no basis in fact.
■ The best account of gender typing is an eclectic, integrative theory that recognizes that processes emphasized in biosocial, social learning, cognitive-developmental, and gender schema theories all contribute to gender-role development.

Psychological Androgyny: A Prescription for the Future?

■ The psychological attributes "masculinity" and "femininity" were historically considered to be at opposite ends of a single dimension. However, a newer perspective holds that masculinity and femininity are two separate dimensions and that the **androgynous** person is someone who possesses a fair number of masculine *and* feminine characteristics.

■ Research shows that androgynous people do exist, are relatively popular and well adjusted, and may be adaptable to a wider variety of environmental demands than people who are traditionally gender typed.

■ Parents and teachers (particularly males) may prevent rigid sex-typing by emphasizing that one's sex is largely irrelevant outside the domain of reproduction, by encouraging and modeling other-sex as well as same-sex activities, and by highlighting and discussing the many exceptions to any unfounded gender stereotypes that children may have acquired.

KEY TERMS

sex 510
gender 510
gender typing 511
gender-role standard 511
expressive role 511
instrumental role 511
visual/spatial abilities 513
self-fulfilling prophecy 517
gender identity 518
gender intensification 521
gender segregation 521
social roles hypothesis 526
testicular feminization syndrome (TFS) 527
timing of puberty effect 528
congenital adrenal hyperplasia (CAH) 528
androgenized females 528
psychobiosocial model 530
phallic stage 530
identification 530
castration anxiety 530
Oedipus complex 530
Electra complex 530
direct tuition 531
observational learning 531
basic gender identity 533
gender stability 533
gender consistency 533
gender schemas 534
"in-group/out-group" schema 534
own-sex schema 534
androgyny 537

MEDIA RESOURCES

The Human Development Book Companion Website

See the companion website http://www.thomsonedu.com/psychology/shaffer for flashcards, practice quiz questions, Internet links, updates, critical thinking exercises, discussion forums, games, and more

Thomson NOW! http://www.thomsonedu.com
Go to this site for the link to ThomsonNOW, your one-stop shop. Take a pre-test for this chapter, and ThomsonNOW will generate a personalized study plan based on your test results. The study plan will identify the topics you need to review and direct you to online resources to help you master those topics. You can then take a post-test to help you determine the concepts you have mastered and what you will still need to work on.

© Don Smetzer/Getty Images

CHAPTER 14 Aggression, Altruism, and Moral Development

What would *you* say is the most important aspect of a child's social development? When one sample of new parents encountered this item in a child-rearing survey conducted by one of our laboratory classes, 74 percent of them indicated that they hoped, above all, that their children would acquire a strong sense of *morality*—right and wrong—to guide their transactions with other people.

When then asked what sort of moral principles they hoped to instill, these new parents provided many answers. However, most of their responses fit into one of the following three categories:

- *Avoid hurting others.* Parents generally hoped their children could learn to become appropriately autonomous and to fulfill their needs without harming others. In fact, unprovoked and intentional acts of harmdoing—or aggression—was one class of behavior that most parents said they would try to suppress.
- *Prosocial concern.* Another value that many parents hoped to instill was a sense of altruism—that is, a selfless concern for the welfare of other people and a willingness to act on that concern. It is not at all unusual for parents to encourage such altruistic acts as sharing, comforting, or helping others while their children are still in diapers.
- *A personal commitment to abide by rules.* Finally, almost all of our survey respondents mentioned the importance of persuading children to comply with socially condoned rules of conduct and monitoring their behavior to ensure that these rules are followed. They felt that the ultimate goal of this moral socialization is to help the child acquire a set of personal values, or ethical principles, that will enable her to distinguish right from wrong and to do the "right" things, even when there may be no one else present to monitor and evaluate her conduct.

This chapter explores these three interrelated aspects of social development that people often consider when making judgments about one's character. We begin with the topic of aggression, asking how it develops and changes over time and then considering some of the ways that adults might effectively control such conduct. Our focus will then shift from harmdoing to altruism and prosocial behavior as we consider how young and reputedly selfish children might learn to make personal sacrifices to benefit others. Finally, we turn to the broader issue of moral development as we trace the child's evolution from a seemingly self-indulgent creature who appears to respect no rules to a moral philosopher of sorts who has internalized certain ethical principles to evaluate his own and others' conduct.

aggression
behavior performed with the intention of harming a living being who is motivated to avoid this treatment.

The Development of Aggression

What qualifies as **aggression?** According to the most widely accepted definition, an aggressive act is any form of behavior designed to harm or injure a living being who is motivated to avoid such treatment (Coie & Dodge, 1998). Notice that it is the actor's *intent* that defines an act as "aggressive," not the act's consequences. So this intentional definition would classify as aggressive all acts in which harm was intended but not done (for example, a violent kick that misses its target, an undetected snub) while excluding accidental harmdoing or rough-and-tumble play in which participants are enjoying themselves with no harmful intent.

hostile aggression
aggressive acts for which the perpetrator's major goal is to harm or injure a victim.

instrumental aggression
aggressive acts for which the perpetrator's major goal is to gain access to objects, space, or privileges.

Aggressive acts are often divided into two categories: **hostile aggression** and **instrumental aggression.** If a person's ultimate goal is to harm a victim, his or her behavior qualifies as hostile aggression. Instrumental aggression describes those situations in which one person harms another as a means to some other end. The same overt act could be classified as either hostile or instrumental aggression depending on the circumstances. If a young boy clobbered his sister and then teased her for crying, we might consider this hostile aggression. But these same actions could be labeled instrumentally aggressive (or a mixture of hostile and instrumental aggression) had the boy also grabbed a toy that his sister was using.

Origins of Aggression in Infancy

Although young infants get angry and may occasionally strike people, it is difficult to think of these actions as having an aggressive intent (Sullivan & Lewis, 2003). Piaget (1952) describes an incident in which he frustrated 7-month-old Laurent by placing his hand in front of an interesting object that Laurent was trying to reach. The boy then smacked Piaget's hand, as if it merely represented an obstruction that must be removed.

Within a short amount of time, this reaction changes. Marlene Caplan and her associates (1991) found that 1-year-old infants can be quite forceful with each other when one infant controls a toy that the other wants. Even when duplicate toys were available, 12-month-olds occasionally ignored these unused objects and tried to overpower a peer in order to control that child's toy. And the intimidators in these tussles appeared to be treating the other child as an *adversary* rather than an inanimate obstacle, implying that the seeds of instrumental aggression have been already sown by the end of the first year.

conflict
circumstances in which two (or more) persons have incompatible needs, desires, or goals.

Although 2-year-olds have just as many (or more) conflicts over toys as 1-year-olds do, they are more likely than 1-year-olds to resolve these disputes by negotiating and sharing than by fighting, particularly when toys are in short supply (Caplan et al., 1991). So early **conflicts** need not be training grounds for aggression and can even be adaptive, serving as a context in which infants, toddlers, and preschool children can learn to negotiate and achieve their aims without resorting to shows of force—especially when adults intervene and encourage harmonious means of conflict resolution (NICHD Early Child Care Research Network, 2001; Perlman & Ross, 1997). Japanese mothers are especially intolerant of harmdoing and encourage their children to suppress anger in the interest of promoting social harmony. As a result, Japanese preschoolers are already less angered by interpersonal conflicts and less likely to respond aggressively to them than are American children (Zahn-Waxler et al., 1996).

Elizabeth Crews

The squabbles of young children usually center around toys, candy, and other treasured resources and qualify as examples of instrumental aggression.

Developmental Trends in Aggression

The character of children's aggression changes dramatically with age. In her classic study of the development of aggression among preschoolers, Florence Goodenough (1931) asked mothers of 2- to 5-year-olds to keep diaries in which they recorded the details of their children's angry outbursts. In examining these data, Goodenough found that unfocused temper tantrums become less and less common between ages 2 and 3 as children began to physically retaliate (by hitting or kicking) when playmates frustrated or attacked them. However, physical aggression gradually declined between ages 3 and 5, only to be replaced by teasing, tattling, name-calling, and other forms of verbal aggression. What were these preschoolers squabbling about? Goodenough found that they fought most often over toys and other possessions, so that their aggression was usually *instrumental* in character.

A more recent study sought to characterize developmental change in physical aggression across the span from toddlerhood to middle childhood (NICHD Early Child Care

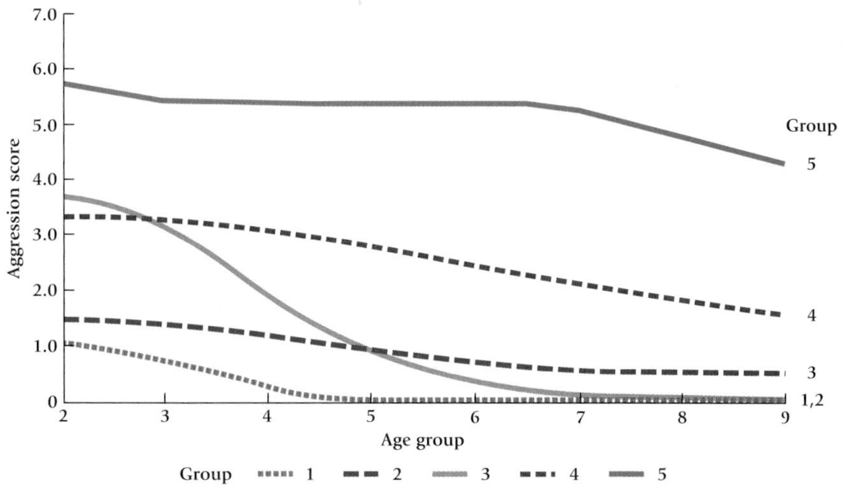

Figure 14.1 Trajectories of mother-rater aggression for children from age 2 to 9 years.
Adapted from NICHD Early Child Care Research Network, 2004.

Research Network, 2004). This study used mothers' reports of the children's levels of physical aggression, assessed each year from when their children were 2 years old to when they were 9 years old, and 1,195 children were included in the study. Consistent with Goodenough's findings, most of these children declined in physical aggression over the preschool years. This study also identified five different patterns of developmental change across toddlerhood and middle childhood, as depicted in Figure 14.1. The vast majority of the children (70 percent) were rated by their mothers as low in aggression across the entire study period. Other children (27 percent of the sample) were moderate in physical aggression during at least some point in the study, although these children did show some decline in physical aggression with age. Quite striking was a small group of children, only 3 percent of the sample, who displayed high levels of physical aggression that remained stable across the entire study period.

What can we conclude from these interesting findings? It appears that some level of physical aggression is relatively normal early in toddlerhood, but for most children this type of aggression is relatively rare by middle childhood. Only a small group of children appear to have problems with displays of physical aggression that remain relatively stable into middle childhood and which may be a cause for concern in their development (NICHD Early Child Care Research Network, 2004).

Thus, over the course of middle childhood, the overall incidence of physical and verbal aggression declines as children learn to settle most disputes in amicable ways (Loeber & Stouthamer-Loeber, 1998; Shaw et al., 2003). Yet, hostile aggression increases slightly, even as instrumental aggression becomes less common (Hartup, 1974). Why? Probably because older children are becoming better at recognizing when someone is trying to harm them, and they sometimes strike back against the harmdoer (Coie et al., 1991; Hartup, 1974). In fact, grade school children are reluctant to condemn this **retaliatory aggression,** often viewing "fighting back" as a normal (though not necessarily moral) response to provocation (Astor, 1994; Coie et al., 1991).

retaliatory aggression
aggressive acts elicited by real or imagined provocations.

Catherine Ursillo/Photo Researchers Inc.

As children mature, an increasing percentage of their aggressive acts qualify as examples of hostile aggression.

Sex Differences

Although the trends we've described hold for both boys and girls, data from more than 100 countries around the world reveal that boys and men are more physically and more verbally aggressive, on average, than are girls and women (Harris, 1992; Maccoby & Jacklin, 1974). As we noted in Chapter 13, boys' higher levels of male sex hormones—namely testosterone—may contribute to sex differences in aggression. Yet, recent studies reveal that very young boys are *not* more aggressive than girls (Hay, Castle, & Davies, 2000). Marlene Caplan and her associates (1991), for example, found that forceful, aggressive resolutions of disputes over toys were actually more numerous among 1-year-olds when the play groups were dominated by girls! Even at age 2, groups dominated by boys were more likely than those dominated by girls to negotiate and share when toys were scarce. It is not until age $2\frac{1}{2}$ to 3 that sex differences in aggression are reliable, and this is clearly enough time for gender-typing to have steered boys and girls in different directions (Fagot, Leinbach, & O'Boyle, 1992).

What social influences might conspire to make boys more aggressive than girls? For one, parents play rougher with boys than with girls and react more negatively to the aggressive behaviors of daughters than to those of sons (Mills & Rubin, 1990; Parke & Slaby, 1983). Furthermore, the guns, tanks, missile launchers, and other symbolic implements of destruction that boys often receive encourage the enactment of aggressive themes—and actually promote aggressive behavior (Feshbach, 1956; Watson & Peng, 1992). During the preschool years, children come to view aggression as a male attribute in their gender schemas; and by middle childhood, boys expect aggressive acts to provide them with more tangible benefits and to elicit less disapproval from either parents or peers than girls do (Hertzberger & Hall, 1993; Perry, Perry, & Weiss, 1989). So even though biological factors may contribute, it is clear that sex differences in aggression depend to no small extent on gender-typing and gender differences in social learning.

One final point: Some investigators today believe that boys may appear so much more aggressive than girls because researchers have focused on overt aggressive behaviors and have failed to consider *covertly* hostile acts that may be more common among girls than boys. The research in the following Box clearly supports this point of view.

FOCUS ON RESEARCH How Girls Are More Aggressive than Boys

Recently, Nicki Crick and Jennifer Grotpeter (1995) proposed that both boys and girls can be quite hostile and aggressive, but they display their aggression in very different ways. Boys, who often pursue competitive, instrumental goals, are likely to strike, insult, or display other *overt* forms of aggression toward others who displease them or who interfere with their objectives. Girls, by contrast, are more likely to focus on *expressive* or *relational* goals—on establishing close, intimate connections with others rather than attempting to compete with or dominate their associates. So Crick and Grotpeter proposed that girls' aggressive behavior would be more consistent with the *social* goals they pursue, consisting largely of covert forms of **relational aggression**—actions such as withdrawing acceptance from an adversary, excluding her from one's social network, or taking some sort of action (for example, spreading rumors) that might damage her friendships or general status in the peer group.

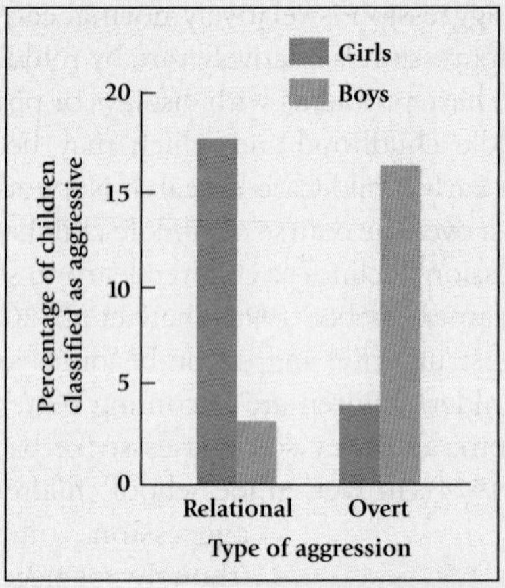

Percentage of girls and boys nominated by classmates as high in relationally manipulative behaviors and overt aggression (physical or verbal assaults) by a sample of third- through sixth-graders. Adapted from Crick & Grotpeter, 1995.

To test this hypothesis, third- through sixth-graders were asked to nominate classmates who often displayed (1) overtly aggressive acts (for example, hitting or insulting others) and (2) *relationally manipulative* acts (for example, withdrawing acceptance; snubbing or excluding others). As we see in the accompanying figure, far more boys than girls were viewed as high in overt aggression—a finding that replicates past research. However, far more girls than boys were perceived to be high in relational aggression. Clearly, such subtle or indirect expressions of hostility may be difficult at times for victims to detect, and may thus allow the perpetrator to behave aggressively while avoiding open conflict. Even 3- to 5-year-old girls are learning this lesson, for they are already more inclined than preschool boys are to try to exclude rather than hit a peer who provokes them (Crick, Casas, & Mosher, 1997; Crick et al., 1999), and to victimize certain peers in relationally manipulative ways (Crick, Casas, & Ku, 1999).

Do other children perceive these attempts to undermine a person's status or the quality of his or her personal relationships as clear examples of aggression? Crick and her associates (1996) addressed this issue by asking 9- to 12-year-olds to indicate the ways in which peers of each sex try to get back at or "to be mean to" someone who makes them mad. Overwhelmingly children said that boys will hit or insult their adversaries, whereas they felt that the most likely response for girls was to try to undermine an adversary's social standing. So children clearly do view these relationally manipulative acts as harmful and "aggressive"—a viewpoint that grows even stronger among adolescents (Galen & Underwood, 1997). Furthermore, girls who frequently display relational aggression are often lonely and are rejected by their peers in much the same way that boys high in overt aggression are at risk of poor peer relations (McNeilly-Choque et al., 1996; Tomada & Schneider, 1997).

In sum, boys and girls tend to express their hostilities in very different ways. Because most prior research on children's aggression has focused on physical and verbal assaults and has largely ignored relationally manipulative acts, it clearly underestimates girls' aggressive inclinations.

From Aggression to Antisocial Conduct

The incidence of fighting and other overt, easily detectable forms of aggression continue to decline from middle childhood throughout adolescence (Broidy et al., 2003; Loeber & Stouthamer-Loeber, 1998; Nagin & Tremblay, 1999), a trend that holds for both boys and girls (Stranger, Achenbach, & Verhulst, 1997). This does not necessarily mean that adolescents are becoming any better behaved. Juvenile arrests for assault and other forms of serious violence increase dramatically in late adolescence and early adulthood (Loeber & Farrington, 1998; Snyder, 2000; U.S. Department of Health and Human Services, 2001). **Relational aggression** in girls becomes more subtle and malicious during the adolescent years (Galen & Underwood, 1997), and teenage boys become more inclined to express their anger and frustrations *indirectly* through such acts as thefts, truancy, substance abuse, and sexual misconduct (Loeber & Stouthamer-Loeber, 1998; U.S. Department of Justice, 1995). So it seems that adolescents who are becoming less overtly aggressive may simply turn to other forms of antisocial conduct to express their discontents.

relational aggression
acts such as snubbing, exclusion, withdrawing acceptance, or spreading rumors that are aimed at damaging an adversary's self-esteem, friendships, or social status.

Is Aggressiveness a Stable Attribute?

Apparently aggression is a reasonably stable attribute. Not only are aggressive toddlers likely to become aggressive 5-year-olds (Cummings, Iannotti, & Zahn-Waxler, 1989; Rubin, Burgess, Dwyer, & Hastings, 2003), but longitudinal research (see Chapter 1 for a review of this research method) conducted in Finland, Iceland, New Zealand, and the United States reveals that the amount of moody, ill-tempered, and aggressive behavior that children display between ages 3 and 10 is a fairly good predictor of their aggressive or other antisocial inclinations later in life (Cillessen & Mayeux, 2004; Hart et al., 1997; Henry et al., 1996; Kokko & Pulkkinen, 2000; Newman et al., 1997). Rowell Huesmann and his associates (1984), for example, tracked one group of 600 participants for 22 years. As we see in Figure 14.2, highly aggressive 8-year-olds often became relatively hostile 30-year-olds who were likely to batter their spouses or children and to be convicted of criminal offenses.

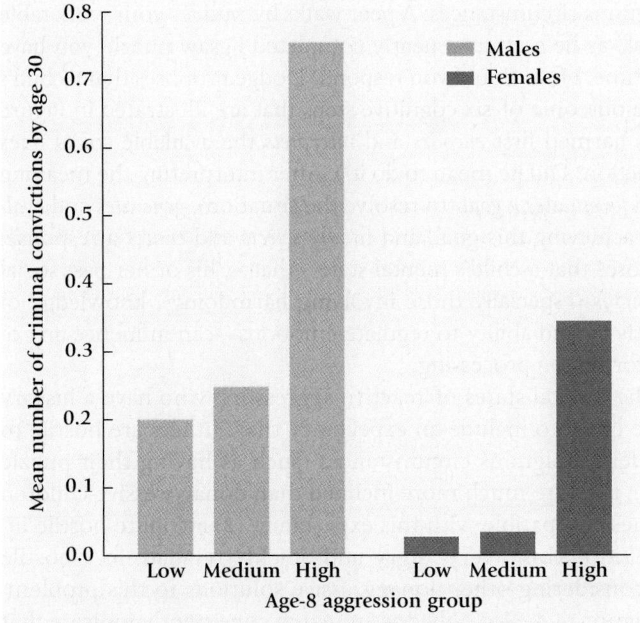

Figure 14.2 Aggression in childhood predicts criminal behavior in adulthood for both males and females. *From "Stability of Agression over Time and Generations," by L. R. Huesmann, L. D. Eron, M. M. Lefkowitz, & L. O. Walder, 1984,* Developmental Psychology, *20, 1125. Copyright © 1984 by the American Psychological Association. Reprinted by permission.*

These findings reflect group trends and do not necessarily imply that all highly aggressive children remain highly aggressive over time. In fact, one recent study found that only about 1 of 8 highly aggressive kindergarten boys remained highly aggressive as adolescents (Nagin & Tremblay, 1999). Other research has identified a set of individuals who were relatively tranquil as children but who become more aggressive and antisocial as adolescents (Aguilar et al., 2000; Brennan et al., 2003). Yet, we should not be surprised to find that aggression is a reasonably stable attribute for many individuals. Consider that children who are genetically predisposed to be temperamentally irritable may remain relatively aggressive over time because they regularly evoke negative reactions from other people, which may foster hostile, aggressive responses (see, for example, Eley, Lichtenstein, & Stevenson, 1999; O'Connor et al., 1998). And regardless of their genetic predispositions, other children may remain highly aggressive because they are raised in home environments that nurture and maintain aggressive habits (Coie & Dodge, 1998). Thus, there is a great deal of variability in the development of aggression when we consider the issue at the individual level. But what characteristics do these aggressive children and adolescents display?

Individual Differences in Aggressive Behavior

Children vary dramatically in their levels of aggression and only a small percentage can be described as chronically aggressive. Some researchers who have charted aggressive incidents among grade-school and high-school students find that a small minority of youngsters are involved in a large majority of the conflicts. Who is involved? In many groups, the participants are a handful of highly aggressive instigators and the 10 to 15 percent of their classmates who are regularly abused by these bullies (Olweus, 1984; Perry, Kusel, & Perry, 1988).

Recent research points to two kinds of highly aggressive children: proactive aggressors and reactive aggressors. Compared with nonaggressive youngsters, **proactive aggressors** are quite confident that aggression will "pay off" in tangible benefits (such as control of a disputed toy), and they are inclined to believe that they can enhance their self-esteem by dominating other children, who generally submit to them before any serious harm has been done (Crick & Dodge, 1996; Frick et al., 2003; Quiggle et al., 1992). So for proactive aggressors, shows of force are an instrumental strategy by which they achieve personal goals.

proactive aggressors
highly aggressive children who find aggressive acts easy to perform and who rely heavily on aggression as a means of solving social problems or achieving other personal objectives.

Reactive aggressors display high levels of hostile, retaliatory aggression. These youngsters are quite suspicious and wary of other people, often viewing them as belligerent adversaries who deserve to be dealt with in a forceful manner (Astor, 1994; Crick & Dodge, 1996; Hubbard et al., 2001; Hubbard et al., 2002).

reactive aggressors
children who display high levels of hostile, retaliatory aggression because they over-attribute hostile intents to others and can't control their anger long enough to seek nonaggressive solutions to social problems.

Interestingly, each of these groups of aggressive children displays distinct biases in their processing of social information that contribute to their high levels of aggressive behavior. Let's take a closer look.

Dodge's Social Information-Processing Theory of Aggression

Kenneth Dodge (1986; Crick & Dodge, 1994) has formulated a social information-processing model that seeks to explain how children come to favor aggressive or nonaggressive solutions to social problems. To illustrate, imagine that you are an 8-year-old who is harmed under ambiguous circumstances: A peer walks by, nudges your work table with his leg and says "Oops!" as he scatters a nearly completed jigsaw puzzle you have been working on for a long time. How would you respond? Dodge proposes that a child's response will depend on the outcome of six cognitive steps that are illustrated in Figure 14.3. The youngster who is harmed first *encodes* and *interprets* the available social cues (What is the harmdoer's reaction? Did he mean to do it?). After interpreting the meaning of these cues, the child then *formulates a goal* (to resolve the situation), *generates* and *evaluates* possible strategies for achieving this goal, and finally *selects* and *enacts* a response. Notice that the model proposes that a child's mental state—that is, his or her past social experiences, social expectancies (especially those involving harmdoing), knowledge of social rules, emotional reactivity, and ability to regulate emotions—can influence any of the model's six phases of information processing.

According to Dodge, the mental states of reactive aggressors, who have a history of bickering with peers, are likely to include an expectancy that "others are hostile to me." So when harmed under ambiguous circumstances (such as having their puzzle scattered by a careless peer), they are much more inclined than nonaggressive children to (1) search for and find cues compatible with this expectancy, (2) attribute hostile intent to the harmdoer, and (3) become very angry and quickly retaliate in a hostile manner without carefully considering other nonaggressive solutions to this problem. This cycle is illustrated in Figure 14.4. Not only does research consistently indicate that reactive aggressors over-attribute hostile intent to peers (Crick & Dodge, 1996; Dodge, 1980; Hubbard et al., 2001, Hubbard et al., 2002), but by virtue of their own hostile retaliations, these children have many negative experiences with teachers and peers (Trachtenberg & Viken, 1994), who come to dislike them, thereby reinforcing their expectancy that "others are hostile to me." Girls can be as reactively aggressive as boys,

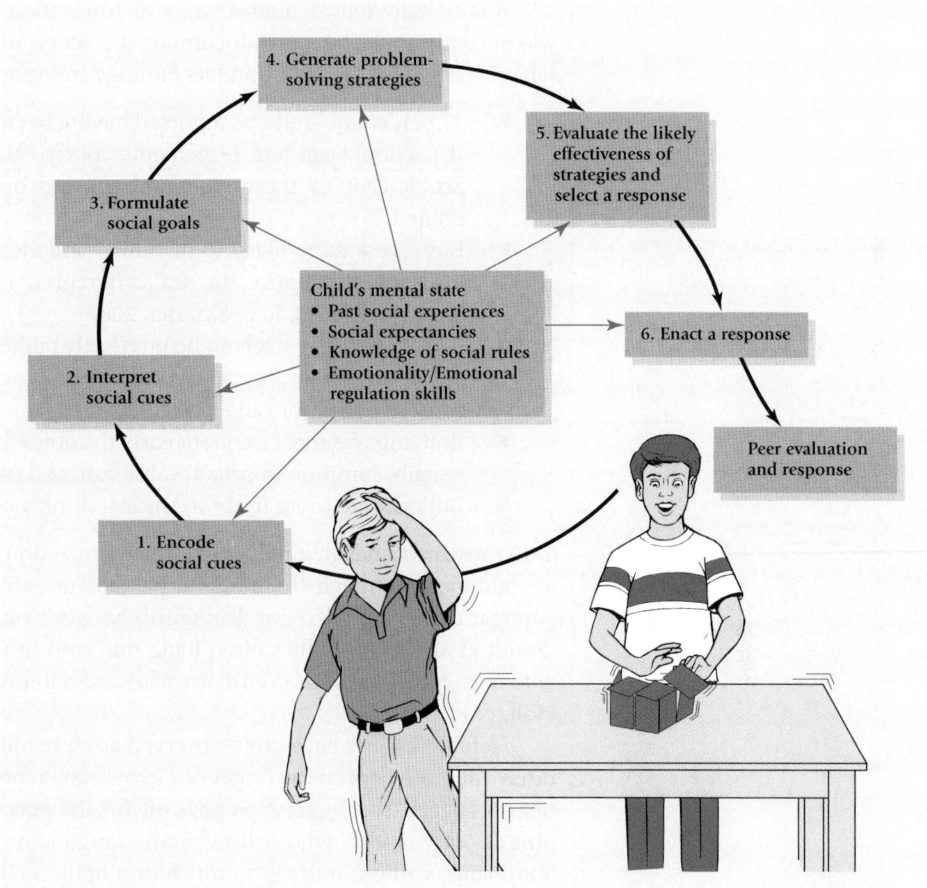

Figure 14.3 Dodge's social information-processing model of the steps children take when deciding how to respond to harmdoing or other social problems. The boy whose creation is destroyed by the other boy's nudging the table must first encode and interpret the social cues (i.e., did he mean it or was it accidental?) and then proceed through the remaining steps to formulate a response to this harmdoing. *Adapted from "A Review and Reformulation of Social Information Processing Mechanisms in Children's Social Adjustment," by N. R. Crick & K. A. Dodge,* Psychological Bulletin, 115, *74–101. Copyright © 1994 by the American Psychological Association. Adapted by permission.*

hostile attributional bias
tendency to view harm done under ambiguous circumstances as having stemmed from a hostile intent on the part of the harmdoer; characterizes reactive aggressors.

displaying the same kind of **hostile attributional bias** and a strong readiness to react aggressively to ambiguous harmdoing (Crick & Dodge, 1996; Crick, Grotpeter, & Bigbee, 2002; Guerra & Slaby, 1990).

Proactive aggressors display a different pattern of social information processing. Because these youngsters do not feel especially disliked (and may even have many friends) (LaFontana & Cillessen, 2002; Rodkin et al., 2000), they are not so inclined to quickly attribute hostile intent to a harmdoer. But this does not mean that the proactive aggressor is inclined to let the incident pass. In fact, these youngsters are likely to carefully formulate an instrumental goal (for example, I'll teach careless peers to be more careful around me) and to coolly and consciously decide that an aggressive response is likely to be most effective at achieving this aim. In fact, proactive aggressors are likely to display such positive emotions as happiness during aggressive encounters with peers (Arsenio, Cooperman, & Lover, 2000). Their mental states favor aggressive solutions to conflict because they expect positive outcomes to result from their use of force, and they feel quite capable about the prospect of dominating their adversaries (Crick & Dodge, 1996).

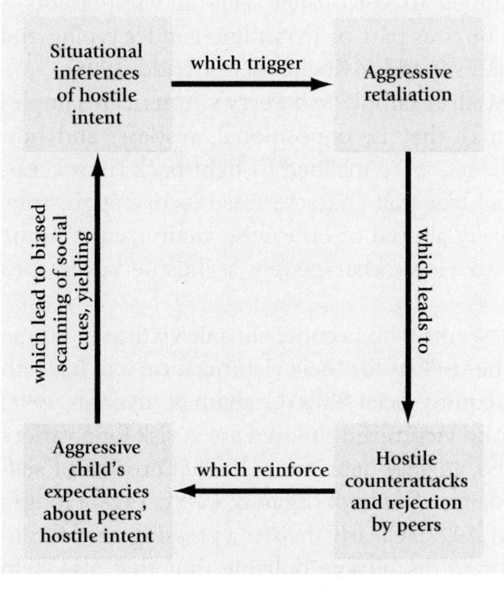

Figure 14.4 A social-cognitive model of the reactive aggressor's biased attributions about ambiguous harmdoing and their behavioral outcomes.

Perpetrators and Victims of Peer Aggression

Each of us has probably known at least one victimized peer—a youngster who repeatedly serves as a target for other children's hostile acts. Who are these children and who singles them out for abuse?

A nationally representative study of more than 15,000 sixth- through tenth-graders was recently undertaken to document the scope of bullying and victimization in U.S. schools (Nansel et al., 2001), and its findings are noteworthy:

- 17 percent of students reported having been bullied at least "sometimes" during the school year, and 19 percent reported bullying others at least "sometimes." Six percent of these students reported both being a bully and having been bullied.
- Boys were more likely to be bullies and victims than girls were (although other investigators report no sex differences in bullying and victimization (see Kochenderfer-Ladd & Skinner, 2002).
- Boys were more likely to be physically bullied, whereas girls were more likely to be verbally bullied or abused in psychological ways (e.g., socially excluded, victimized by rumors and malicious gossip).
- Bullying was most frequent early in adolescence (sixth to eighth grades) and was equally common in urban, suburban, and rural areas.
- Bullies were more likely to smoke, drink alcohol, and to be poor students.

Other research finds that bullying (and victimization) may be even more frequent earlier in childhood, although these higher percentages are hard to interpret because children younger than 9 often do not distinguish between bullying episodes and general fighting (Smith et al., 2000). Bullies often hang out with other aggressive peers like themselves, who may egg them on or even assist with and reinforce their bullying activities (Espelage, Holt, & Henkel, 2003).

Habitual bullies have often observed adult conflict and aggression at home but have rarely themselves been the target of aggression (Schwartz et al., 1997). Their home experiences suggest that aggression pays off for the perpetrator, and they come to view victims as "easy marks" who will surrender tangible resources or otherwise submit to their dominance without putting up much of a fight. So bullies appear to harass their victims for personal or instrumental reasons (Olweus, 1993) and are usually classifiable as proactive aggressors.

Although chronic victims are generally disliked by their peers (Boivin & Hymel, 1997), they are not at all alike. Most are **passive victims** who are socially withdrawn, sedentary, physically weak, and reluctant to fight back, and appear to do little (other than being "easy marks") to invite the hostilities they receive (Boulton, 1999; Olweus, 1993). Passively victimized boys often have had close, overprotective relationships with their mothers in which they have been encouraged to voice their fears and self-doubts—practices that are generally discouraged in boys as part of masculine gender typing and which are not well received by male classmates (Ladd & Kochenderfer-Ladd, 1998)

passive victims (of aggression)
socially withdrawn, anxious children with low self-esteem whom bullies torment, even though they appear to have done little to trigger such abuse.

A smaller number in both Olweus's Swedish sample and Perry's American samples could be described as **provocative victims**—that is, oppositional, restless, and hot-tempered individuals who often irritated peers, were inclined to fight back (unsuccessfully), and displayed the hostile attributional bias that characterizes reactive aggressors. Provocative victims have often been physically abused or otherwise victimized at home and have learned from their experiences to view other people as hostile adversaries (Schwartz et al., 1997).

provocative victims (of aggression)
restless, hot-tempered, and oppositional children who are victimized because they often irritate their peers.

Unfortunately, many children and adolescents who become chronic victims continue to be victimized, especially if they blame themselves for their victimization and have no friends to stick up for them and help them acquire social skills (Graham & Juvonen, 1998; Hodges et al., 1999; Schwartz et al., 2000). And victimized children are at risk for a variety of adjustment problems, including loneliness, anxiety, depression, further erosion of self-esteem, and a growing dislike for and avoidance of school (Egan & Perry, 1998; Hodges et al., 1999; Ladd, Kochenderfer & Coleman, 1997). Clearly there is a pressing need for interventions that not only take strong steps to discourage bullying, but that also help chronic victims to build self-esteem and develop the social skills and supportive friendships that will improve their social standing and make them less inviting targets for their tormentors (Egan & Perry, 1998; Hodges et al., 1999).

Popularity and Aggression

popularity
a social construction by children, with popular children being well-known and accepted by other (especially popular) children, and having high-status attributes such as attractiveness, athleticism, and desirable possessions.

At the other end of the spectrum are popular children, the high-status children and adolescents who are at the center of the social world in school and other children's groups. **Popularity** is defined by researchers as a social construction by children, with popular children being well-known and accepted by other children (especially other popular children) and having high-status attributes such as attractiveness, athleticism, and even highly desirable possessions (LaFontana & Cillesen, 2002; Lease, Kennedy, & Axelrod, 2002; Rose, Swenson, & Waller, 2004). Notice that what is lacking from this definition is being well liked! Popular children are not necessarily well liked, but they do maintain their high status in peer groups.

One way popular children build and maintain their popularity is through overt and relational aggression (Bagwell & Coie, 2004; Rose, Swenson, & Waller, 2004). A number of research studies have found positive correlations between children's and adolescents' popularity and their tendency to be aggressive, particularly in relational ways. That is, the popular children tend to ignore, exclude, threaten, and spread rumors about other children as a means to enhance their own popularity (e.g., Parkhurst & Hopmeyer, 1998; Rodkin et al., 2000; Xie et al., 2002). One study even found that popular boys were thought to start more fights and be more disruptive than other children (Rodkin et al., 2000).

Rose and her colleagues (2004) recently conducted a series of longitudinal studies to investigate whether popular children used aggression to become popular, or whether their secure position as popular children gave them the freedom to aggress against others without fear of sanction. They found that aggressive acts both preceded and followed from achieving the popular status. Rose and her colleagues noted that this translates into a difficult situation for parents and schools that wish to intervene with programs to reduce aggression. The high-status popular children are not likely to be noticed as the aggressors as easily as the class bullies who stand out for their overt aggression. Furthermore, popular adolescents are likely to serve as role models for aggression, so intervention programs would need to address the entire social culture, not just the popular aggressors!

Cultural and Subcultural Influences on Aggression

Cross-cultural and ethnographic studies consistently indicate that some societies and subcultures are more violent and aggressive than others. Peoples such as the Arapesh of New Guinea, the Lepchas of Sikkim, and the Pygmies of central Africa all use weapons to hunt but rarely show any kind of interpersonal aggression. When these peace-loving societies are invaded by outsiders, their members retreat to inaccessible regions rather than stand and fight (Gorer, 1968).

In marked contrast to these groups are the Gebusi of New Guinea, who teach their children to be combative and emotionally unresponsive to the needs of others and who show a murder rate that is more than 50 times higher than that of any industrialized nation (Scott, 1992). The United States is also an "aggressive" society. On a percentage basis, the incidence of rape, homicide, and assault is higher in the United States than in any other industrialized nation, and the United States ranks a close second to Spain (and far above third-place Canada) in the incidence of armed robbery (Wolff, Rutten, & Bayer, 1992).

Studies conducted in the United States and in England also point to social-class differences in aggression: Children and adolescents from the lower socioeconomic strata (SES), particularly males from larger urban areas, exhibit more aggressive behavior and higher levels of delinquency than their age-mates from the middle class (Loeber & Stouthamer-Loeber, 1998; Macmillan, McMorris, & Kruttschnitt, 2004; Tolan, Gorman-Smith, & Henry, 2003). These trends appear to be closely linked to social-class differences in child rearing. For example, parents from lower-income families are more likely than

Antisocial or deliquent conduct is rather common among teenagers whose parents fail to monitor their activities, whereabouts, and choice of friends.

middle-class parents to rely on physical punishment to discipline aggression and defiance, thereby *modeling aggression* even as they try to suppress it (Dodge, Pettit, & Bates, 1994). Low-SES parents are also more inclined to endorse aggressive solutions to conflict and to encourage their children to respond forcefully when provoked by peers (Dodge, Pettit, & Bates, 1994; Jagers, Bingham, & Hans, 1996)—practices that may foster the development of the hostile attributional bias that highly aggressive youngsters so often display. Finally, low-SES parents often live complex stressful lives that may make it difficult for them to manage or monitor their children's whereabouts, activities, and choice of friends. Unfortunately, this lack of parental monitoring is consistently associated with such aggressive or delinquent activities as fighting, sassing teachers, destroying property, drug use, and breaking rules outside the home (Barber, Olsen, & Shagle, 1994; Kilgore, Snyder, & Lentz, 2000).

In sum, a person's aggressive and antisocial inclinations depend, in part, on the extent to which the culture or subculture condones or fails to discourage such behavior. Yet not all people in pacifistic societies are kind, cooperative, and helpful, and the vast majority of people raised in relatively "aggressive" societies or subcultures are not especially prone to violence. Why are there such dramatic individual differences in aggression within a given culture or subculture? Gerald Patterson and his associates answer by claiming that highly aggressive children often live in homes that can be described as "breeding grounds" for hostile, antisocial conduct.

Coercive Home Environments: Breeding Grounds for Aggression

Patterson (1982; Patterson, Reid, & Dishion, 1992) has observed patterns of interaction among children and their parents in families that have at least one highly aggressive child. The aggressive children in Patterson's sample seemed "out of control"; they fought a lot at home and at school and were generally unruly and defiant. These families were then compared with other families of the same size and socioeconomic status that had no problem children.

Families as Social Systems

Patterson soon discovered that he could not explain "out of control" behavior by merely focusing on the child-rearing practices that parents used. Instead, it seemed that highly aggressive children lived in atypical family environments that were characterized by a social climate that *they had helped to create* (see, for example, Brennan et al., 2003; Frick et al., 2003, and Rubin et al., 2003). Unlike most homes, where people frequently display approval and affection, the highly aggressive problem child usually lived in a setting in which family members were constantly bickering with one another: They were reluctant to initiate conversations, and, when they did talk, they tended to needle, threaten, or otherwise irritate other family members rather than conversing amiably. Patterson called these settings **coercive home environments** because a high percentage of interactions centered on one family member's attempts to force another to stop irritating him or her. He also noted that **negative reinforcement** was important in maintaining these coercive interactions: When one family member makes life unpleasant for another, the second learns to whine, yell, scream, tease, or hit because these actions often force the antagonist to stop (and thus are reinforced).

coercive home environment
a home in which family members often annoy one another and use aggressive or otherwise antisocial tactics as a method of coping with these aversive experiences.

negative reinforcer
any stimulus whose removal or termination as the consequence of an act will increase the probability that the act will recur.

Mothers of problem children rarely use social approval as a means of behavior control, choosing instead to largely ignore prosocial conduct, to interpret many innocuous acts as antisocial, and rely almost exclusively on coercive tactics to deal with perceived misconduct (Nix et al., 1999; Strassberg, 1995). Perhaps the overwhelmingly negative treatment that these problem children receive at home (including parents' tendency to label ambiguous events as antisocial) helps to explain why they generally mistrust other people and display the hostile attributional bias so commonly observed among highly aggressive children (Dishion, 1990; Weiss et al., 1992). And ironically, children from highly coercive home environments eventually become resistant to punishment. They have learned to fight coercion with countercoercion and will often do so by defying the parent and repeating the very act that she is trying to suppress. Why? Because this is one of the few ways that the child can successfully command the attention of an adult who rarely offers praise or shows any signs of affection. No wonder Patterson calls these children "out of control"! Children from *noncoercive families* receive much more positive attention from siblings and parents, so that they don't have to irritate other family members to be noticed (Patterson, 1982).

So we see that the flow of influence in the family setting is *multidirectional:* Coercive interactions between parents and their children and the children themselves affect the behavior of all parties and contribute to the development of a hostile family environment—a true breeding ground for aggression (Brody et al., 2004; Caspi et al., 2004; Garcia et al., 2000). Unfortunately, these problem families may never break out of this destructive pattern of attacking and counterattacking one another unless they receive help.

Methods of Controlling Aggression in Young Children

What approaches might assist parents and teachers in suppressing the aggressive antics of young children so that antisocial solutions to conflict do not become habitual? Let's look at three general strategies that have achieved some success.

Creating Nonaggressive Environments

One simple but effective approach for reducing children's aggression is to create play areas that minimize the likelihood of conflict. For example, parents and teachers might remove (or refuse to buy) "aggressive" toys such as guns, tanks, and rubber knives, which are known to provoke aggression (Watson & Peng, 1992). Providing ample space for vigorous play also helps to eliminate the accidental bumps, shoves, and trips that often escalate into full-blown hostilities (Hartup, 1974). Finally, children are likely to play quite harmoniously if adults provide enough balls, slides, swings, and other toys to keep them from having to compete for scarce resources (Smith & Connolly, 1980).

Eliminating the Payoffs for Aggression

Researchers who study development now recognize that different forms of aggression may require different kinds of interventions (Crick & Dodge, 1996). Recall that proactive aggressors rely on forceful strategies because they are easy for them to enact and often enable these youngsters to achieve personal goals. An effective intervention for these children might teach them that aggression doesn't pay and that alternative prosocial responses, such as cooperation or sharing, are better ways to achieve their objectives.

Parents and teachers can reduce the incidence of proactive aggression by identifying and eliminating its reinforcing consequences and encouraging alternative means of achieving one's objectives. For example, if 4-year-old Juan were to hit his 3-year-old sister Rosita in order to take possession of a toy, Juan's mother could teach him that this instrumental aggression doesn't pay by simply returning the toy to Rosita and denying him his objective. However, this strategy wouldn't work if Juan is an insecure child who feels neglected and has attacked his sister in order to attract his mother's attention; under these circumstances, the mother would be reinforcing Juan's aggression if she attended to it at all! So what is she to do?

incompatible-response technique
a nonpunitive method of behavior modification in which adults ignore undesirable conduct while reinforcing acts that are incompatible with these responses.

time-out technique
a form of discipline in which children who misbehave are removed from the setting until they are prepared to act more appropriately.

One proven method that she might use is the **incompatible-response technique**—a strategy of ignoring all but the most serious of Juan's aggressive antics (thereby denying him an "attentional" reward) while reinforcing such acts as cooperation and sharing that are incompatible with aggression. Teachers who have tried this strategy find that it quickly produces an increase in children's prosocial conduct and a corresponding decrease in their hostilities (Brown & Elliot, 1965; Slaby & Crowley, 1977). And how might adults handle serious acts of harmdoing without "reinforcing" them with their attention? One effective approach is the **time-out technique** that Patterson favors, in which the adult removes the offender from the situation in which his aggression has been reinforced (for example, by sending him to his room until he is ready to behave appropriately). Although this approach may generate some resentment, the adult in charge is not physically abusing the child or serving as an aggressive model and is not likely to unwittingly reinforce the child who misbehaves as a means of attracting attention. The time-out procedure is most effective at controlling children's hostilities when adults also reinforce cooperative or helpful acts that are incompatible with aggression (Parke & Slaby, 1983).

Social-Cognitive Interventions

Whereas the previous methods for controlling aggression work best with young children, there are at least some methods for dealing with aggression in older children and adolescents. Hot-headed reactive aggressors may profit more from programs that teach them to control their anger and suppress their tendency to over-attribute hostile intentions to companions who displease them. Highly aggressive youngsters, particularly those high in reactive aggression, can profit from social-cognitive interventions that help them to (1) regulate their anger and (2) become more skilled at empathizing with and taking others' perspectives so that they will not be so likely to over-attribute hostile intentions to their peers (Crick & Dodge, 1996). In one study (Guerra & Slaby, 1990), a group of violent adolescent offenders were coached in such skills as (1) looking for nonhostile cues that might be associated with harmdoing, (2) controlling their anger, and (3) generating nonaggressive solutions to conflict. Not only did these violent offenders show dramatic improvements in their social problem-solving skills, but they also became less inclined to endorse beliefs supporting aggression and less aggressive in their interactions with authority figures and other adolescents.

CONCEPT CHECK 14.1 Understanding Aggression

Check your understanding of the development of aggression by answering the following questions. Answers appear in the Appendix.

Matching: Identify the following types of aggression in the statements below:

a. hostile aggression
b. instrumental aggression
c. relational aggression

1. ______ type of aggression for which girls exceed boys
2. ______ this kind of aggression is first to appear, often by age 12 months
3. ______ type of aggression that becomes more common with the growth of role-taking skills

True or False: Identify whether the following statements are true or false.

4. (T)(F) Reactive aggressors may often become the provocative victims of bullies.
5. (T)(F) Positive reinforcement is the process by which unpleasant interactions are maintained in coercive home environments.

Multiple Choice: Pick the best alternative to the following question.

______ 6. Linda is in the kitchen preparing dinner while her young children are playing in another room. After an hour of this, Linda hears a loud cry from Judy. She runs to the playroom and finds that George has hit Judy and taken the doll she was playing with. What would be the best method of handling this situation if Linda wanted to reduce George's aggressive antics?

a. Take the doll away from George and give him a slap on the wrist.
b. Give the doll back to Judy and give George a lecture about the reasons hitting is bad.
c. Give the doll back to Judy and send George to time-out until he is able to play nicely with Judy.
d. Give the doll back to Judy and take George into the kitchen where Linda can keep an eye on him.

Fill in the Blank: Complete the following statements with the correct concept or phrase.

7. In the "incompatible response technique," adults control aggression by ______ undesirable conduct and ______ acts that are incompatible with the undesirable conduct.
8. Researchers have found that there are two types of children who become the victims of bullies in childhood: ______ victims and ______ victims.

Short Answer: Provide a brief answer to the following question.

9. List the six steps in Dodge's social information-processing model of aggression.

Essay: Provide a more detailed answer to the following question.

10. Use what you have learned about coercive home environments, aggression, and methods of controlling aggression to design a program for preventing violence in the classroom.

Altruism: Development of the Prosocial Self

altruism
a selfless concern for the welfare of others that is expressed through prosocial acts such as sharing, cooperating, and helping.

As we noted in opening this chapter, most parents hope their children will acquire a sense of **altruism**—a genuine concern for the welfare of other people and a willingness to act on that concern. In fact, many parents encourage altruistic acts such as sharing, cooperating, or helping while their children are still in diapers! Experts in child development once would have claimed that these well-intentioned adults were wasting their time, for infants and toddlers were thought to be incapable of considering the needs of anyone other than themselves. But the experts were wrong!

Origins of Altruism

Long before children receive any formal moral or religious training, they may act in ways that resemble the prosocial behavior of older people. Twelve- to eighteen-month-olds, for example, occasionally offer toys to companions (Hay et al., 1991) and even attempt to

Robert Van Der Hilgt/Getty Images

Even toddlers can learn to show compassion toward distressed companions.

help their parents with such chores as sweeping or dusting or setting the table (Rheingold, 1982). And the prosocial conduct of very young children even has a certain "rationality" about it. For example, 2-year-olds are more likely to offer toys to a peer when playthings are scarce rather than plentiful (Hay et al., 1991).

Are toddlers capable of expressing sympathy and behaving compassionately toward their companions? Yes, indeed, and these displays of prosocial concern are not all that uncommon (Eisenberg & Fabes, 1998; Hoffman, 2000; Zahn-Waxler et al., 1992). Consider the reaction of 21-month-old John to his distressed playmate, Jerry, as recounted by John's mother:

> Today Jerry was kind of cranky; he just started . . . bawling and he wouldn't stop. John kept coming over and handing Jerry toys, trying to cheer him up. . . . He'd say things like "Here Jerry," and I said to John "Jerry's sad; he doesn't feel good; he had a shot today." John would look at me with his eyebrows wrinkled together like he really understood that Jerry was crying because he was unhappy . . . He went over and rubbed Jerry's arm and said "Nice Jerry," and continued to give him toys (Zahn-Waxler, Radke-Yarrow, & King, 1979, pp. 321–322).

Clearly, John was concerned about his little playmate and did what he could to make him feel better.

Although some toddlers often try to comfort distressed companions, others rarely do. These individual variations are due, in part, to temperamental variations. For example, 2-year-olds who are behaviorally inhibited are likely to become highly upset by others' distress and are more likely than uninhibited toddlers to turn away from a distressed acquaintance in an attempt to regulate their arousal (Young, Fox, & Zahn-Waxler, 1999).

affective explanations
discipline which focuses a child's attention on the harm or distress that his or her conduct has caused others.

Individual differences in early compassion also depend quite heavily on parents' reactions to occasions in which their toddler has harmed another child. Carolyn Zahn-Waxler and her associates (1979) found that mothers of less compassionate toddlers typically used coercive tactics such as verbal rebukes or physical punishment to discipline harmdoing. By contrast, mothers of highly compassionate toddlers frequently disciplined harmdoing with **affective explanations** that may foster sympathy (and perhaps some remorse) by helping children to see the relation between their own acts and the distress they have caused (for example, "You made Lamar cry; it's not nice to bite!").

© Mary Kate Denny/PhotoEdit

Preschool children must often be coaxed to share.

Developmental Trends in Altruism

Although many 2- to 3-year-olds show sympathy and compassion toward distressed companions, they are not particularly eager to make truly self-sacrificial responses, such as sharing a treasured toy with a peer. Sharing and other benevolent acts are more likely to occur if adults instruct a toddler to consider others' needs (Levitt et al., 1985), or if a peer actively elicits sharing through a request or a threat of some kind, such as "I won't be your friend if you won't gimme some" (Birch & Billman, 1986). But, on the whole, acts of *spontaneous* self-sacrifice in the interest of others are relatively infrequent among toddlers and young preschool children. Is this because toddlers are largely oblivious to others' needs and to the good they might do by sharing or helping their companions? Probably not, for at least one observational study in a nursery-school setting found that 2½- to 3½-year-olds often took pleasure in performing acts of kindness for others during pretend play; by contrast, 4- to 6-year-olds performed more real helping acts and rarely "play-acted" the role of an altruist (Bar-Tal, Raviv, & Goldberg, 1982).

Many studies conducted in cultures from around the world find that sharing, helping, and most other forms of prosocial conduct become more and more common from the early elementary school years onward (see, for example, Underwood & Moore, 1982;

Whiting & Edwards, 1988). Indeed, much of the research that we will examine seeks to explain why older children and adolescents tend to become more prosocially inclined. Before turning to this research, let's address one other issue developmentalists have pondered: Are there sex differences in altruism?

Sex Differences in Altruism

People commonly assume that girls are (or will become) more helpful, generous, and compassionate than boys. Truth or fiction? Perhaps this stereotype qualifies as a half-truth. Girls are often reported to help and to share more than boys, although the magnitude of this sex difference is not large (Eisenberg & Fabes, 1998). People believe that girls are more concerned about others' welfare, and girls often emit stronger facial and vocal expressions of sympathy than boys do (Hastings et al., 2000). But these findings are difficult to interpret because boys experience just as much physiological arousal upon encountering someone who is distressed as girls do (Eisenberg & Fabes, 1998). However, boys are often found to be less cooperative and more competitive than girls. For example, one recent study found that, by middle childhood, boys were more likely than girls to act so as to hinder another child's chances of winning a prize while playing a game, even when they, themselves, could easily earn the same prize without regard to how the other player performed (Roy & Benenson, 2002). Thus, it seems as if looking good or attaining status or dominance over others seems to be more important to boys than to girls.

Social-Cognitive and Affective Contributors to Altruism

Children with well-developed role-taking skills are often found to be more helpful or compassionate than poor role-takers, largely because they are better able to infer a companion's needs for assistance or comforting (Eisenberg, Zhou, & Koller, 2001; Shaffer, 2005). In fact, evidence for a causal link between affective and social perspective-taking (recognizing what another person is feeling, thinking, or intending) and altruism is quite clear in studies showing that children and adolescents who receive training to further these role-taking skills subsequently become more charitable, more cooperative, and more concerned about the needs of others when compared with age-mates who receive no training (Chalmers & Townsend, 1990; Iannotti, 1978). However, role taking is only one of several personal attributes that play a part in the development of altruistic behavior. Two especially important contributors are children's level of **prosocial moral reasoning** and their empathic reactions to the distress of other people.

prosocial moral reasoning
the thinking that people display when deciding whether to help, share with, or comfort others when these actions could prove costly to themselves.

Prosocial Moral Reasoning

Over the past 25 years, researchers have charted the development of children's reasoning about prosocial issues and its relationship to altruistic behavior. Nancy Eisenberg and her colleagues, for example, have presented children with stories in which the central character has to decide whether or not to help or comfort someone when the prosocial act would be personally costly. Here is one such story (Eisenberg-Berg & Hand, 1979):

> One day a girl named Mary was going to a friend's birthday party. On her way she saw a girl who had fallen down and hurt her leg. The girl asked Mary to go to her house and get her parents so that [they] could come and take her to a doctor. But if Mary did . . . , she would be late to the party and miss the ice-cream, cake, and all the games. What should Mary do?

Reasoning about these prosocial dilemmas may progress through as many as five levels between early childhood and adolescence. Preschoolers' responses are frequently self-serving: These youngsters often say that Mary should go to the party so as not to miss out on the goodies. But as children mature, they tend to become increasingly responsive to the needs and wishes of others; so much so that some high school students feel that they could no longer respect themselves were they to ignore the appeal of a person in need in order to pursue their own interests (Eisenberg, 1983; Eisenberg, Miller, Shell, McNally & Shea, 1991).

Does a child's or adolescent's level of prosocial moral reasoning predict his or her altruistic behavior? Apparently so. Preschoolers who have progressed beyond the hedonistic level of prosocial moral reasoning are more likely to help and to spontaneously share valuable commodities with their peers than are those who still reason in a self-serving way (Eisenberg-Berg & Hand, 1979; Miller et al., 1996). Studies of older participants tell a similar story. Mature moral reasoners among a high school sample often said they would help someone they disliked if that person really needed their help, whereas immature moral reasoners were apt to ignore the needs of a person they disliked (Eisenberg, 1983; Eisenberg, Miller, Shell, McNally & Shea, 1991). Finally, Eisenberg and her associates (1999) found in a 17-year longitudinal study that the children who showed more spontaneous sharing and were relatively mature in their levels of prosocial moral reasoning at ages 4 to 5 remained more helpful, more considerate of others, and reasoned more complexly about prosocial issues and social responsibility throughout childhood, adolescence, and into young adulthood. Thus, prosocial dispositions can be established early and often remain reasonably stable over time.

Empathy: An Important Affective Contributor to Altruism

Why are mature moral reasoners so sensitive to the needs of others—even disliked others? Eisenberg's view is that the child's growing ability to *empathize* with others contributes heavily to mature prosocial reasoning and to the development of a selfless concern for promoting the welfare of whomever might require one's assistance (Eisenberg et al., 1999; Eisenberg, Zhou, & Koller, 2001).

Empathy refers to a person's ability to experience the emotions of other people. According to Martin Hoffman (1981, 1993), empathy is a universal human response that has a neurological basis and can be either fostered or suppressed by environmental influences. Hoffman believes that empathic arousal eventually becomes an important mediator of altruism. Why else, Hoffman asks, would we set aside our own selfish motives to help other people or to avoid harming them unless we had the capacity to share their emotions and experience their distress?

Although infants and toddlers seem to recognize and often react to the distress of their companions (Zahn-Waxler et al., 1979, 1992), their responses are not always helpful ones. In fact, some young children experience *personal* distress upon witnessing the distress or misfortunes of others (this may be the predominant response early in life) and may ignore or turn away from a person in need in order to relieve their own discomfort (Young, Fox, & Zahn-Waxler, 1999). Other children (even some young ones) are more inclined to interpret their empathic arousal as concern for distressed others, and it is this **sympathetic empathic arousal,** rather than **self-oriented distress,** that should eventually come to promote altruism (Batson, 1991; Hoffman, 2000).

sympathetic empathic arousal
feelings of sympathy or compassion that may be elicited when we experience the emotions of (that is, empathize with) a distressed other; thought to become an important mediator of altruism.

self-oriented distress
feeling of *personal* discomfort or distress that may be elicited when we experience the emotions of (that is, empathize with) a distressed other; thought to inhibit altruism.

Socialization of Empathy. As we noted earlier when discussing the origins of compassion in toddlers, parents can help to promote sympathetic empathic arousal by (1) modeling empathic concern and (2) relying on affectively oriented forms of discipline that help young children to understand the harmful effects of any distress they may have caused others (Eisenberg, Fabes, Schaller, Carlo & Miller, 1991; Hastings et al., 2000; Zahn-Waxler, Radke-Yarrow, & King 1979; Zahn-Waxler et al., 1992). Interestingly, mothers who use more positive facial expressions while modeling sympathy and who explicitly verbalize their own sympathetic feelings have children who act more sympathetically (Zhou et al., 2002). This may be because the mother's positivity and her affective explanations help to counteract the negative reactions that young children may have to others' misfortunes, making them less inclined to interpret their own arousal as personal distress (Fabes et al., 1994).

Age Trends in the Empathy–Altruism Relationship. So what is the relationship between empathy and altruism? The answer depends, in part, on how empathy is measured and how old the research participants are. In studies that assess empathy by having children report their own feelings about the misfortunes of story characters, researchers have found little association between empathy and altruism. In studies assessing teacher ratings, children's empathic sensitivities and children's own facial expressions of emotion in response to others' misfortunes are better predictors of prosocial behavior (Chapman, Zahn-Waxler, Cooperman, & Iannotti, 1987; Eisenberg et al., 1990). Overall, the evidence for a link between empathy and altruism is modest at best for preschool and young grade-school children but stronger for preadolescents, adolescents, and adults (Underwood & Moore, 1982).

One possible explanation for these age trends is that it simply takes some time for children to become better at regulating negative emotionality and suppressing personal distress to others' misfortunes so that they can respond more sympathetically (Eisenberg, Fabes et al., 1998). Social-cognitive development plays an important part in this process, for younger children may lack the role-taking skills and insight about their own emotional experiences to fully understand and appreciate (1) why others are distressed and, thus, (2) why they are feeling aroused (Roberts & Strayer, 1996). For example, when kindergartners see a series of slides showing a boy becoming depressed after his dog runs away, they usually attribute his sadness to an external cause (the dog's disappearance) rather than to a more "personal" or internal one, such as the boy's longing for his pet (Hughes, Tingle, & Sawin, 1981). Kindergartners report that they feel sad after seeing the slides, but they usually provide egocentric explanations for their empathic arousal that seem to reflect *personal distress* (for example, "I might lose my dog"). However, 7- to 9-year-olds begin to associate their own empathic emotions with those of the story character as they put themselves in his place and infer the *psychological* basis for his sadness (for example, "I'm sad because he's sad . . . because, if he really liked the dog, then . . ."). So empathy may become a stronger contributor to altruism once children become better at inferring others' points of view (role taking) and understanding the causes of their own empathic emotions—causes that can help them to feel sympathy for distressed or needy companions (Eisenberg, Zhou, & Koller, 2001; Roberts & Strayer, 1996).

"felt responsibility" hypothesis the theory that empathy may promote altruism by causing one to reflect on altruistic norms and, thus, to feel some obligation to help distressed others.

© David Young-Wolff/PhotoEdit

As children mature and develop better role-taking skills, they are more likely to sympathize with distressed companions and to provide them with comfort or assistance.

The Felt-Responsibility Hypothesis. Now an important question: *How* exactly does empathy promote altruism? One possibility is that a child's *sympathetic* empathic arousal causes him to reflect on altruistic lessons he has learned—lessons such as the Golden Rule, the *norm of social responsibility* (that is, help others who need help), or even the knowledge that other people approve of helping behavior. As a result of this reflection, the child is likely to assume some personal *responsibility* for aiding a victim in distress and would now feel guilty for callously ignoring that obligation (Chapman et al., 1987; Williams & Bybee, 1994). Notice that this **"felt responsibility" hypothesis** is reflected in Eisenberg's higher levels of prosocial moral reasoning and may help to explain why the link between empathy and altruism becomes stronger with age. Because older children are likely to have learned (and internalized) more altruistic principles than younger children, they should have much more to reflect on as they experience empathic arousal. Consequently, they are more likely than younger children to feel responsible for helping a distressed person and to follow through by rendering the necessary assistance.

TABLE 14.1 Prosocial Behavior in Six Cultures: Percentages of Children in Each Culture Who Scored above the Median Altruism Score for the Cross-Cultural Sample as a Whole

Type of society	Percentage scoring high in altruism	Type of society	Percentage scoring high in altruism
Nonindustrialized		*Industrialized*	
Kenya	100	Okinawa	29
Mexico	73	India	25
Philippines	63	United States	8

Source: Based on Whiting & Whiting, 1975.

Cultural and Social Influences on Altruism

Are there certain experiences children have, in addition to just growing older and more cognitively mature, that help them to become more altruistic? Indeed there are! Research has found that certain cultural and social experiences relate to children's developing altruism. We will examine these next.

Cultural Influences

Cultures clearly differ in their endorsement or encouragement of altruism. In one interesting cross-cultural study, Beatrice and John Whiting (1975) observed the altruistic behavior of 3- to 10-year-olds in six cultures—Kenya, Mexico, the Philippines, Okinawa, India, and the United States. As we see in Table 14.1, the cultures in which children were most altruistic were the less industrialized societies—cultures in which people live in large families and children routinely contribute to the family welfare by processing food, preparing meals, fetching wood and water, or caring for younger brothers and sisters. Although children in Western industrialized societies are involved in relatively few family-maintenance activities, those who are assigned housework or other tasks that benefit family members are more prosocially inclined than age-mates whose responsibilities consist mainly of self-care routines, such as cleaning their own rooms (Grusec, Goodnow, & Cohen, 1996).

Another factor contributing to the low altruism scores of children from Western individualistic nations is the tremendous emphasis that these societies place on competition and on individual rather than group goals. Self-sacrificial, other-oriented behaviors are certainly condoned but are generally not obligatory. Children from collectivist societies and subcultures are taught to suppress individualism and to cooperate with others for the greater good of the group (Triandis, 1995). So for children in many of the world's collectivist societies, prosocial behavior does not have the same "discretionary" quality about it that is true of individualistic societies; instead, giving of oneself for the greater good of the group is as much an obligation as resolving not to break moral rules (Chen, 2000; Triandis, 1995).

In Western individualistic societies, children are taught that prosocial acts are laudable and that they should take credit for their self-sacrificial behaviors. By contrast, children in one collectivist society, the People's Republic of China, not only learn that prosocial conduct is necessary and an obligation, they are also taught to be modest, to avoid self-aggrandizement, and thus, not to seek praise or personal recognition for their own good deeds. How might these teachings affect Chinese children's thinking about prosocial issues? Would they truly seek to downplay their acts of kindness?

To address these issues, Kang Lee and associates (1997) conducted an interesting cross-cultural study in which 7-, 9-, and 11-year-old children from Canada and the

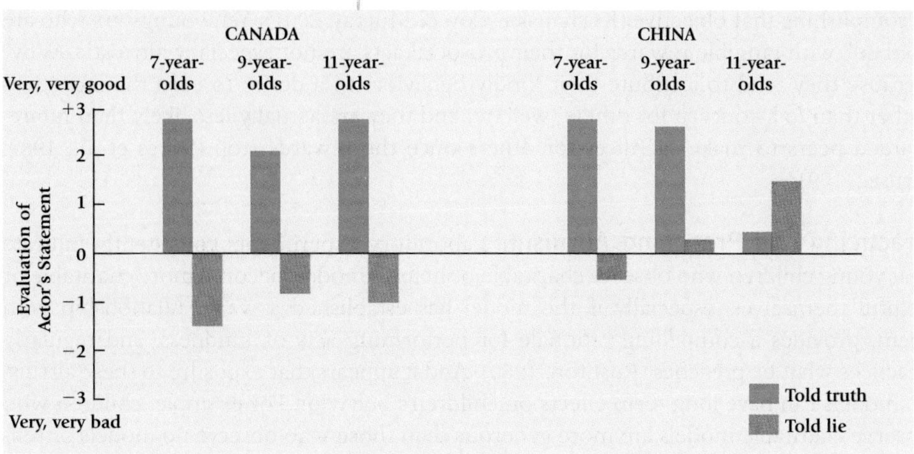

Figure 14.5 Rating by Canadian and Chinese children of actors who told the truth or lied about committing good deeds. *Adapted with permission from "Chinese and Canadian Children's Evaluation" by K. Lee in* Child Development, *68, 924–934. Copyright © 1997 by the Society for Research in Child Development.*

People's Republic of China evaluated four brief stories. To compare Canadian and Chinese children's thinking about prosocial issues, two stories involved a child who first carried out a good deed (for example, anonymously donating money to a classmate who otherwise could not go on a field trip) and who then either truthfully admitted this prosocial act or who lied about it (saying "I did not do it" when the teacher asked, "Do you know who is responsible for this act of kindness?"). For comparative purposes, children's thinking about antisocial conduct was also assessed. Each participant heard two stories in which the actor committed a misdeed (for example, injuring a classmate by knocking him down) and who then either truthfully admitted or lied about this act when questioned by a teacher. After hearing each story, participants evaluated the goodness or naughtiness of both the actor's behavior and his or her statement about the behavior.

There were no major cultural differences in evaluation of either the actor's antisocial conduct (which was considered very bad) or evaluations of the actor's statements about it. Both Chinese and Canadian children felt that it was very good for harmdoers to tell the truth about committing transgressions and very bad to lie about them. Similarly, both Chinese and Canadian children evaluated prosocial acts quite positively. However, their thinking about lying and telling the truth about prosocial conduct diverged sharply.

As Figure 14.5 illustrates, Canadian children at all three ages thought that altruists should readily admit (that is, tell the truth and take credit for) their good deeds and that denying responsibility for (lying about) them was bad (or perhaps stupid). By contrast, we see that as Chinese children grow older they increasingly come to view taking credit for prosocial acts in *less* positive terms and denying responsibility for them much *more* positively. In fact, the strong emphasis on self-effacement and modesty in Chinese culture eventually overrides children's reluctance to lie, so that Chinese children come to view acting modest about performing behavior expected of them to be more praiseworthy than boldly telling the truth and calling undue attention to acts that any good child should perform (Lee et al., 1997).

In sum, Lee's study clearly illustrates that the values that shape people's thinking about prosocial behavior (as well as the circumstances under which "little white lies" might be appropriate) can vary dramatically from culture to culture.

Social Influences

Although cultures may differ in the emphasis that they place on altruism, most people in most societies endorse the *norm of social responsibility*—the rule that one should help others who need help. Let's now consider some of the ways that adults might persuade young children to adopt this important value and to become more concerned about the welfare of other people.

Reinforcing Altruism. Many experiments (reviewed in Shaffer, 2005) reveal that likable and respected adults can promote children's prosocial behavior by verbally reinforcing their acts of kindness. Children are generally motivated to live up to the standards of people they admire, and praise that accompanies their kindly acts suggests that they are accomplishing that objective (Kochanska, Coy, & Murray, 2001). Yet, youngsters who are "bribed" with tangible rewards for their prosocial acts are not especially altruistic. Why? Because they tend to attribute their kindly behaviors to a desire to earn the incentives rather than to a concern for others' welfare, and they are actually less likely than nonrewarded peers to make sacrifices for others once the rewards stop (Fabes et al., 1989; Grusec, 1991).

Practicing and Preaching Altruism. Laboratory experiments consistently indicate that young children who observe charitable or helpful models become more charitable or helpful themselves, especially if the model has established a warm relationship with them, provides a compelling rationale for performing acts of kindness, and regularly practices what he preaches (Rushton, 1980). And it appears that exposure to these altruistic models can have long-term effects on children's behavior. For example, children who observe charitable models are more generous than those who observe no models or selfish models, even when they are not tested until 2 to 4 months later (Rice & Grusec, 1975; Rushton, 1980). So it seems that encounters with altruistic models help to promote the development of prosocial concern—a conclusion that is strongly reinforced in the child-rearing literature.

Who Raises Altruistic Children?

Studies of unusually charitable adults indicate that these "altruists" were raised by highly altruistic parents. For example, Christians who risked their lives to save Jews from the Nazis during World War II reported that they had had close ties to moralistic parents who always acted in accordance with their ethical principles (London, 1970). And interviews of White "freedom riders" from the U.S. civil rights movement of the 1960s reveal that "fully committed" activists (volunteers who gave up their homes and/or careers to work full-time for the cause) differed from "partially committed" (part-time) activists in two major ways: They had enjoyed warmer relations with their parents, and they had had parents who advocated altruism and backed up these exhortations by performing many kind and compassionate deeds. By contrast, parents of partially committed activists had often preached but rarely practiced altruism (Rosenhan, 1970; see also Clary & Snyder, 1991). Clearly, these findings are consistent with the laboratory evidence we have reviewed, which indicates that compassionate models who practice what they preach are especially effective at eliciting prosocial responses from young children.

Elizabeth Crews/The Image Works

Children who are committed to performing prosocial acts often have parents who have encouraged altruism and who have practiced what they preach.

Parental reactions to a child's harmdoing also play an important role in the development of altruism. Recall that mothers of less compassionate infants and toddlers react to harmdoing in punitive or forceful ways, whereas mothers of compassionate toddlers rely more heavily on nonpunitive, affective explanations in which they display sympathy as they persuade the child to accept personal responsibility for her harmdoing and urge her to direct some sort of comforting or helpful response toward the victim (Zahn-Waxler, Radke-Yarrow, & King, 1979; Zahn-Waxler et al., 1992). Research with older children paints a similar picture: Parents who continue to rely on rational, nonpunitive disciplinary techniques in which they regularly display sympathy and concern for others tend to raise children who are sympathetic and self-sacrificing, whereas frequent use of forceful and punitive discipline appears to inhibit altruism and lead to the development of self-centered values (Brody & Shaffer, 1982; Eisenberg et al., 1992; Hastings et al., 2000; Krevans & Gibbs, 1996).

Now let's turn to the broader issue of *moral development,* which encompasses both the growth of prosocial concern and the inhibition of hostile, antisocial impulses.

CONCEPT CHECK 14.2 Understanding the Development of Altruism

Check your understanding of the development of altruism by answering the following questions. Answers appear in the Appendix.

Matching: Match the type of arousal listed to the correct definition.

a. sympathetic empathic arousal
b. self-oriented distress

1. ________ This type of arousal is thought to inhibit altruism.
2. ________ This type of arousal is thought to promote altruism.

True or False: Identify whether the following statements are true or false.

3. (T)(F) Verbal reinforcement promotes children's prosocial conduct when given by a respected or admired adult.
4. (T)(F) Tangible incentives (like candy or a new toy) promote children's prosocial conduct when given by a respected or admired adult.
5. (T)(F) Brian wants to promote altruistic behavior in his children. He is careful to reward each act of altruism he observes and frequently lectures them on the importance of being kind to others. He is not particularly altruistic himself, however, and so he is not a model of altruistic behavior. His parenting style is rather cool and distant. Based on these characteristics, we can assume that Brian's children will behave altruistically even in the absence of an adult observer.

Fill in the Blank: Complete the following statements with the correct concept or phrase.

6. Eisenberg's first level of prosocial moral reasoning, the ________ level, is used by preschoolers and early elementary-school children.
7. A type of discipline that focuses a child's attention on the harm or distress that his conduct has caused others is called ________.

Essay: Provide a detailed answer to the following question.

8. Describe how the development of empathy contributes to the development of altruism in children.

Moral Development: Affective, Cognitive, and Behavioral Components

morality
a set of principles or ideals that help the individual to distinguish right from wrong, to act on this distinction, and to feel pride in virtuous conduct and guilt (or other unpleasant emotions) for conduct that violates one's standards.

internalization
the process of adopting the attributes or standards of other people—taking these standards as one's own.

As we develop, most of us arrive at a point at which we wish to behave responsibly and to think of ourselves (and be thought of by others) as *moral* individuals (Damon & Hart, 1992). What is **morality?** College students generally agree that morality implies a capacity to (a) distinguish right from wrong, (b) act on this distinction, and (c) experience pride in virtuous conduct and guilt or shame over acts that violate one's standards (Quinn, Houts, & Graesser, 1994; Shaffer, 1994). When asked to indicate the particular attributes that morally mature individuals display, adults in one Western society (Canada) generally agreed on six aspects of moral maturity (see Table 14.2).

Implicit in these consensual definitions is the idea that morally mature individuals do not submit to society's dictates because they expect tangible rewards for complying or fear punishments for transgressing. Rather, they eventually internalize moral principles that they have learned and conform to these ideals, even when authority figures are not present to enforce them. As we will see, virtually all contemporary theorists consider **internalization**—the shift from externally controlled actions to conduct that is governed by internal standards and principles—to be a most crucial milestone along the road to moral maturity.

How Developmentalists Look at Morality

Developmental theorizing and research have centered on the same three moral components that college students mention in their consensual definition of morality:

- An *affective,* or emotional, component that consists of the feelings (guilt, concern for others' feelings, and so on) that surround right or wrong actions and that motivate moral thoughts and actions.

TABLE 14.2 Six Dimensions of Character That Define Moral Maturity for Canadian Adults

Character dimension	Sample traits
1. Principled-idealistic	Has clear values; concerned about doing right; ethical; highly developed conscience; law abiding
2. Dependable-loyal	Responsible; loyal; reliable; faithful to spouse; honorable
3. Has integrity	Consistent; conscientious; rational; hard working
4. Caring-trustworthy	Honest; trustful; sincere; kind; considerate
5. Fair	Virtuous; fair; just
6. Confident	Strong; self-assured; self-confident

Source: Walker & Pitts, 1998.

- A *cognitive* component that centers on the way we conceptualize right and wrong and make decisions about how to behave.
- A *behavioral component* that reflects how we actually behave when we experience the temptation to lie, cheat, or violate other moral rules.

As it turns out, each of the three major theories of moral development has focused on a different component of morality. Psychoanalytic theorists emphasize the affective component, or powerful **moral affects.** They believe that children are motivated to act in accordance with their ethical principles in order to experience positive affects such as pride and to avoid such negative moral affects as guilt and shame. Cognitive-developmental theorists have concentrated on the cognitive aspects of morality, or **moral reasoning,** and have found that the ways children think about right and wrong may change rather dramatically as they mature. Finally, the research of social-learning and social information-processing theorists has helped us to understand how children learn to resist temptation and to practice **moral behavior,** suppressing actions such as lying, stealing, and cheating that violate moral norms.

moral affect
the emotional component of morality, including feelings such as guilt, shame, and pride in ethical conduct.

moral reasoning
the cognitive component of morality; the thinking that people display when deciding whether various acts are right or wrong.

moral behavior
the behavioral component of morality; actions that are consistent with one's moral standards in situations in which one is tempted to violate them.

In examining each of these theories and the research it has generated, we will look at relationships among moral affect, moral reasoning, and moral behavior. This information should help us to decide whether a person really has a unified moral character that is stable over time and across situations. We will then consider how various child-rearing practices may affect a child's moral development and attempt to integrate much of the information we have reviewed.

The Affective Component of Moral Development

In Chapter 2, we learned that psychoanalysts view the mature personality as having three components: An irrational *id* that seeks the immediate gratification of instinctual needs, a rational *ego* that formulates realistic plans for meeting these needs, and a moralistic superego (or conscience) that monitors the acceptability of the ego's thoughts and deeds. Freud claimed that infants and toddlers lack a superego and act on their selfish impulses unless parents control their behavior. But once the superego emerges, it was said to function as an *internal* censor that has the power to make a child feel proud of his virtuous conduct and guilty or shameful about committing moral transgressions. So children who are morally mature should generally resist temptation to violate moral norms in order to maintain self-esteem and avoid experiencing negative moral affects.

Freud's Theory of Oedipal Morality

According to Freud (1935/1960), the superego develops during the phallic stage (age 3 to 6), when children were said to experience an emotional conflict with the same-sex parent that stemmed from their incestuous desire for the other-sex parent. To resolve this *Oedipus complex,* a boy was said to identify with and pattern himself after his father, particularly if his father was a threatening figure who aroused fear. Not only does he learn his masculine role in this manner, but he also internalizes his father's moral standards. Similarly, a girl resolves her *Electra complex* by identifying with her mother and internalizing her mother's moral standards. However, Freud claimed that because girls do not experience the intense fear of castration that boys experience, they will develop weaker superegos than boys do.

Evaluating Freud's Theory

We might credit Freud for pointing out that moral emotions such as pride, shame, and guilt are potentially important determinants of ethical conduct and that the internalization of moral principles is a crucial step along the way to moral maturity. Yet the specifics of his theory are largely unsupported. For example, threatening and punitive parents do not raise children who are morally mature. Quite the contrary: parents who rely on harsh forms of discipline tend to have children who often misbehave and rarely express feelings of guilt, remorse, shame, or self-criticism (Brody & Shaffer, 1982; Kochanska, Coy, & Murray, 2001). Furthermore, there is simply no evidence that boys develop stronger superegos than girls. In fact, recent research indicates that, if anything, 3- to 5-year-old girls are less likely to break rules and are more likely to experience guilt when they think they've committed a transgression than are 3- to 5-year-old boys (Kochanska et al., 2002; Labile & Thompson, 2002). Finally, Freud's proposed age trends for moral development are actually quite pessimistic. As early as 13 to 15 months of age, some toddlers are already complying with some prohibitions in the absence of external surveillance (Kochanska, Tjebkes, & Forman, 1998). By age 2, more toddlers are beginning to show clear signs of distress when they violate rules (Kochanska, Casey, & Fukomoto, 1995; Kochanska et al., 2002), and they sometimes try to correct any mishaps they think they have caused—even when no one else is present to tell them to (Cole, Barnett, & Zahn-Waxler, 1992). These observations imply that the process of moral internalization may have already begun long before young children would have even experienced an Oedipus or Electra complex, much less have resolved it. So even though Freud's broader themes about the significance of moral emotions have some merit, perhaps it is time to lay his theory of **Oedipal morality** to rest.

Oedipal morality
Freud's theory that moral development occurs during the phallic period (ages 3 to 6) when children internalize the moral standards of the same-sex parent as they resolve their Oedipus or Electra conflicts.

Newer Ideas about the Early Development of the Conscience

In recent years, a number of investigators have taken a new look at the early development of "conscience" from a social-learning or socialization perspective (e.g., Kochanska, Coy, & Murray, 2001; Kochanska & Murray, 2000; Labile & Thompson, 2000, 2002) and their findings are quite revealing. It seems that children may begin to form a conscience as toddlers if they are securely attached to warm and responsive parents who have often cooperated with their wishes during joint play and have shared many positive emotional experiences with them. Within the context of a warm, **mutually responsive relationship** (rather than a fear-provoking one), toddlers are likely to display **committed compliance**—an orientation in which they are (1) highly motivated to embrace the parent's agenda and to comply with her rules and requests, (2) sensitive to a parent's emotional signals indicating whether they have done right or wrong, and (3) beginning to internalize those parental reactions to their triumphs and transgressions, coming to experience the pride, shame, and (later) guilt that will help them to evaluate and regulate their own conduct (Emde et al., 1991; Kochanska, 1997b; Labile & Thompson, 2000). By contrast,

mutually responsive orientation
parent-child relationship characterized by mutual responsiveness to each other's needs and goals and shared positive affect.

committed compliance
compliance based on the child's eagerness to cooperate with a responsive parent who has been willing to cooperate with him or her.

situational compliance
compliance based primarily on a parent's power to control the child's conduct.

aloof or insensitive parents who have shared few mutually enjoyable activities with a toddler are likely to promote **situational compliance**—generally nonoppositional behavior that stems more from parents' power to control the child's conduct than from the child's eagerness to cooperate or comply.

Evidence is rapidly emerging to support these newer ideas about early development of conscience. Consider, for example, that 2- to 2½-year-old toddlers who have mutually responsive relationships with mothers who resolve conflicts with them calmly and rationally are more likely to resist temptations to touch prohibited toys at age 3 (Labile & Thompson, 2002) and continue to show more signs of having a strong internalized conscience (e.g., a willingness to comply with rules when adults are not present, clear signs of guilt when they think they have transgressed) at ages 4½ to 6 than do age-mates whose earlier mother-toddler relationships had been less warm and mutually responsive (Kochanska & Murray, 2000). What's more, boys who show committed compliance to their mothers at 33 months soon come to view themselves as "good" or "moral" individuals (Kochanska, 2002), a finding which may help to explain why such children are more inclined to cooperate with other adult authority figures (e.g., fathers, day-care providers, experimenters) compared to those whose compliance with their mother is less consistent and more situational in nature (Feldman & Klein, 2003; Kochanska, Coy, & Murray, 2001).

The Cognitive Component of Moral Development

Cognitive developmentalists study morality by examining the development of *moral reasoning* that children display when deciding whether various acts are right or wrong. According to cognitive theorists, both cognitive growth and social experiences help children to develop progressively richer understandings of the meaning of rules, laws, and interpersonal obligations. As children acquire these new understandings, they are said to progress through an invariant sequence of moral stages, each of which evolves from and replaces its predecessor and represents a more advanced or "mature" perspective on moral issues. In this part of the chapter, we first examine Jean Piaget's early theory of moral development before turning to Lawrence Kohlberg's revision and extension of Piaget's approach.

Piaget's Theory of Moral Development

Piaget's (1932/1965) early work on children's moral judgments focused on two aspects of moral reasoning: respect for rules and conceptions of justice. He studied developing respect for rules by playing marbles with Swiss children between ages 5 and 13. As they played, Piaget asked questions such as "Where do these rules come from? Must everyone obey a rule? Can these rules be changed?" To study children's conceptions of justice, Piaget gave them moral-decision stories to ponder. Here is one example:

> *Story A.* A little boy who is called John is in his room. He is called to dinner. He goes into the dining room. But behind the door there was a chair, and on the chair there was a tray with 15 cups on it. John couldn't have known that there was all this behind the door. He goes in, the door knocks against the tray, bang go the 15 cups, and they all get broken.
>
> *Story B.* Once there was a little boy whose name was Henry. One day when his mother was out he tried to reach some jam in the cupboard. He climbed onto a chair and stretched out his arm. But the jam was too high up, and he couldn't reach it . . . While he was trying to get it, he knocked over a cup. The cup fell down and broke (Piaget, 1932/1965, p. 122).

Having heard the stories, participants were asked such questions as "Which child is naughtier? Why?" and "How should the naughtier child be punished?" Using these research techniques, Piaget formulated a stage theory of moral development that includes a premoral period and two moral stages.

The Premoral Period. According to Piaget, preschool children show little concern for or awareness of rules. In a game of marbles, these **premoral** children do not play systematically with the intent of winning. Instead, they seem to make up their own rules, and they think the point of the game is to take turns and have fun.

> **premoral period**
> in Piaget's theory, the first 5 years of life, when children are said to have little respect for or awareness of socially defined rules.

> **heteronomous morality**
> Piaget's first stage of moral development, in which children view the rules of authority figures as sacred and unalterable.

Heteronomous Morality. Between the ages of 5 and 10, the child develops a strong respect for rules as they enter Piaget's stage of **heteronomous morality** ("heteronomous" means "under the rule of another"). Children now believe that rules are laid down by powerful authority figures such as God, the police, or their parents, and they think that these regulations are sacred and unalterable. Try breaking the speed limit with a 6-year-old at your side and you may see what Piaget was talking about. Even if you are rushing to the hospital in a medical emergency, the young child may note that you are breaking a rule and consider your behavior unacceptable conduct that deserves to be punished. Heteronomous children think of rules as *moral absolutes.* They believe that there is a "right" side and a "wrong" side to any moral issue, and right always means following the rules.

Heteronomous children are also likely to judge the naughtiness of an act by its objective consequences rather than the actor's intent. For example, many 5- to 9-year-olds judged John, who broke 15 cups while performing a well-intentioned act, to be naughtier than Henry, who broke one cup while stealing jam.

Heteronomous children also favor *expiatory punishment*—punishment for its own sake with no concern for its relation to the nature of the forbidden act. So a 6-year-old might favor spanking a boy who had broken a window rather than making the boy pay for the window from his allowance. Furthermore, the heteronomous child believes in **immanent justice**—the idea that violations of social rules will invariably be punished in one way or another (see, for example, Dennis's warning to Joey in the cartoon on this page). Life for the heteronomous child is fair and just.

> **immanent justice**
> the notion that unacceptable conduct will invariably be punished and that justice is ever present in the world.

> **autonomous morality**
> Piaget's second stage of moral development, in which children realize that rules are arbitrary agreements that can be challenged and changed with the consent of the people they govern.

Autonomous Morality. By age 10 or 11, most children have reached Piaget's second moral stage—**autonomous morality.** Older, autonomous children now realize that social rules are arbitrary agreements that can be challenged and even changed with the consent of the people they govern. They also feel that rules can be violated in the service of human needs. Thus, a driver who speeds during a medical emergency is no longer considered immoral, even though she is breaking the law. Judgments of right and wrong now depend more on the actor's intent to deceive or to violate social rules rather than the objective consequences of the act itself. So 10-year-olds reliably say that Henry, who broke one cup while stealing some jam (bad intent), is naughtier than John, who broke 15 cups while coming to dinner (good or neutral intent).

"HEY, CAREFUL, JOEY! GOD SEES EVERYTHING WE DO, THEN HE GOES AN' TELLS SANTA CLAUS!"

When deciding how to punish transgressions, the morally autonomous child usually favors *reciprocal punishments*—that is, treatments that tailor punitive consequences to the "crime" so that the rule breaker will understand the implications of a transgression and perhaps be less likely to repeat it. So an autonomous child may decide that the boy who deliberately breaks a window should pay for it out of his allowance (and learn that windows cost money) rather than simply submitting to a spanking. Finally, autonomous youngsters no longer believe in immanent justice, because they have learned from experience that violations of social rules often go undetected and unpunished.

Moving from Heteronomous to Autonomous Morality. According to Piaget, both cognitive maturation and social experience play a role in the transition from heteronomous to autonomous morality. The cognitive advances that are necessary for this shift are a general decline in egocentrism and the development of role-taking skills that enable the child to view moral issues from several perspectives. The kind of social experience that Piaget considers important is equal status contact with peers. As we noted in Chapter 12, peers must learn to take each other's perspectives and resolve their disagreements in mutually beneficial ways, often without any adult intervention, if they are to play cooperatively or accomplish other group goals (Carpendale, 2000). So equal-status contacts with peers may lead to a more flexible, autonomous morality because they (1) lessen the child's respect for adult authority, (2) increase his or her self-respect and respect for peers, and (3) illustrate that rules are arbitrary agreements that can be changed with the consent of the people they govern.

And what role do parents play? Interestingly, Piaget claimed that unless parents relinquish some of their power, they may *slow* the progress of moral development by reinforcing the child's respect for rules and authority figures. If, for example, a parent enforces a demand with a threat or a statement such as "Do it because I told you to!," it is easy to see how the young child might conclude that rules are absolutes that derive their power from the parent's enforcement.

An Evaluation of Piaget's Theory

Many researchers in many cultures have replicated Piaget's findings when they rely on his research methods. For example, younger children around the world are more likely than older ones to display such aspects of heteronomous morality as a belief in immanent justice or a tendency to emphasize consequences more than intentions when judging how wrong an act is (Jose, 1990; Lapsley, 1996). In addition, the maturity of children's moral judgments is related to such indications of cognitive development as IQ and role-taking skills (Lapsley, 1996). There is even some support for Piaget's "peer participation" hypothesis: Popular children who often take part in peer-group activities and who assume positions of leadership tend to make mature moral judgments (Bear & Rys, 1994; Keasey, 1971).

Nevertheless, there is ample reason to believe that Piaget's theory clearly underestimates the moral capacities of preschool and grade school children. For example, there is evidence that modifications to Piaget's methods reveal hidden competencies in young children, and specifically that younger children do not ignore actors' intentions to the extent Piaget proposed (see the Box on the following page).

According to Piaget, heteronomous children think of rules as sacred and obligatory prescriptions that are laid down by respected authority figures and are not to be challenged. However, Elliot Turiel (1983) notes that children actually encounter two kinds of rules. **Moral rules** focus on the welfare and basic rights of individuals and include prescriptions against hitting, stealing, lying, cheating, or otherwise harming others or violating their rights. By contrast, **social-conventional rules** are determined by social consensus and regulate conduct in particular social situations. These standards are more like rules of social etiquette and include the rules of games as well as school rules that forbid snacking in class or using the restroom without permission. Do children treat these two kinds of rules as equivalent?

moral rules
standards of acceptable and unacceptable conduct that focus on the rights and privileges of individuals.

social-conventional rules
standards of conduct determined by social consensus that indicate what is appropriate within a particular social context.

Apparently not. Judith Smetana (1981, 1985; Smetana, Schlagman, & Adams, 1993; Yau & Smetana, 2003) finds that even 2½- to 3-year-olds consider moral transgressions such as hitting, stealing, and refusing to share to be much more serious and more deserving of punishment than social conventional violations such as snacking in class or not saying "please" when requesting a toy. When asked whether a violation would be okay if there were no rule against it, children said that moral transgressions are always wrong but social-conventional violations are okay in the absence of any explicit rule. Clearly parents view themselves as responsible for enforcing both moral and social-conventional rules. However, they attend more closely to moral violations and place much more emphasis on the harm such violations do to others (Nucci & Smetana, 1996; Turiel, 2002), perhaps explaining why children understand the need for and importance of moral prescriptions by age 2½ to 3—much sooner than Piaget had assumed they would.

Another example of Piaget's underestimations is evidence that 6- to 10-year-old heteronomous children are quite capable of challenging adult authority. They believe that

FOCUS ON RESEARCH

Updating Piaget's Methods to Find Hidden Competencies

Consider Piaget's claim that children younger than 9 or 10 judge acts as right or wrong based on the consequences that the acts produce rather than the intentions that guided them. Unfortunately, Piaget's moral-decision stories were flawed in that they (1) confounded intentions and consequences by asking whether a person who caused little harm with a bad intent was naughtier than one who caused a larger amount of harm while serving good intentions, and (2) made information about the consequences of an act much clearer than information about the actor's intentions.

Figure 1 *Example of drawings used by Nelson to convey an actor's intentions to preschool children.* Adapted from "Factors Influencing Young Children's Use of Motives and Outcomes as Moral Criteria," by S. A. Nelson, 1980, Child Development, 51, 823–829. Copyright © 1980 by the Society for Research in Child Development. Adapted by permission.

Sharon Nelson (1980) overcame these flaws in an interesting experiment with 3-year-olds. Each child listened to stories in which a character threw a ball to a playmate. The actor's motive was described as good (his friend had nothing to play with) or bad (the actor was mad at his friend), and the consequences of his act were either positive (the friend caught the ball and was happy to play with it) or negative (the ball hit the friend in the head and made him cry). To ensure that her 3-year-olds understood the actor's intentions, Nelson showed them drawings such as Figure 1, which depicts a negative intent.

Not surprisingly, the 3-year-olds in this study judged acts that had positive consequences more favorably than those that caused harm. However, as Figure 2 shows, they also judged the well-intentioned child who had wanted to play much more favorably than the child who intended to hurt his friend, regardless of the consequences of his actions. What's more, 3- to 5-year-olds clearly discriminate and react more negatively to blatant lies, in which a person presents false information with intent to deceive, from honest mistakes on the person's part (Siegal & Peterson, 1998). So even preschool children consider an actor's intentions when making moral judgments (Chandler, Sokel & Weinryb, 2000). In fact, young children often attempt to escape punishment through such intentional pleas as, "I didn't mean to, mommy!" But Piaget was right in one respect: Younger children do assign more weight to consequences and less weight to intentions than older children do, even though both younger and older children consider both sources of information when evaluating others' conduct (Lapsley, 1996; Zelazo, Helwig, & Lau, 1996).

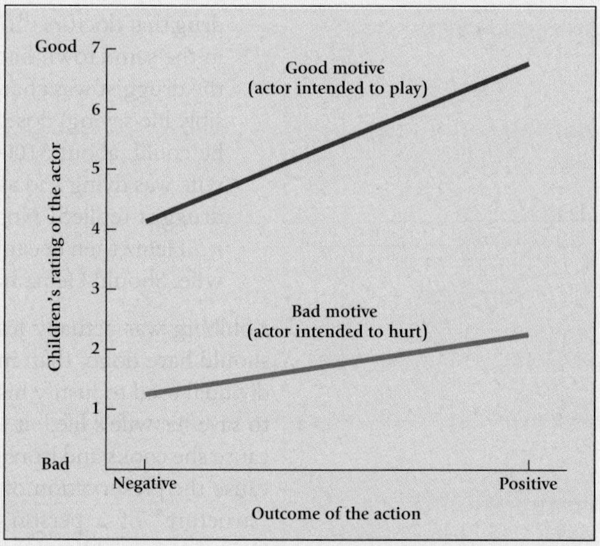

Figure 2 *Average ratings of an actor's behavior for actors who produced positive or negative outcomes while serving either good or bad intentions.* Adapted from Nelson, 1980.

parents are justified in enforcing rules against stealing and other moral transgressions; but they feel that a parent is clearly abusing authority should he arbitrarily make decisions that affect them or impose rules that restrict their choice of friends or leisure activities—areas that they perceive as either negotiable or under their own personal jurisdiction (Ardila-Ray & Killen, 2001; Yau & Smetana, 2003). In addition, they increasingly recognize that adult authority may be limited to certain contexts, acknowledging, for example, that teachers have a right to regulate smoking at school but not in the neighborhood (Smetana & Bitz, 1996). So 6- to 10-year-olds do have ideas about what constitutes legitimate authority, and those ideas are not based solely on an unwavering respect for the sanctity or wisdom of adults as Piaget had assumed (Kim, 1998; Yau & Smetana, 2003).

Finally, Piaget was right in claiming that parents and other adults can retard moral growth by exerting authority and relying on their greater power to enforce rules and regulations. Where he was wrong was in implying that most adults operate this way. Indeed, recent research demonstrates that when parents discuss real-life moral issues and present their own, more sophisticated reasoning in a gentle, supportive manner (rather than in a lecture-like format as a lesson to be learned), they typically foster rather than impede the growth of moral reasoning (Walker, Hennig, & Krettenauer, 2000).

Developmentalists are indebted to Piaget for suggesting that children's moral reasoning develops in stages that are closely tied to cognitive growth. Even today, his theory continues to stimulate research and new insights—including the findings above, which reveal that children younger than 10 are considerably more sophisticated in their moral reasoning than Piaget made them out to be. But is moral reasoning fully developed by age 10 to 11, as Piaget had assumed? Lawrence Kohlberg certainly didn't think so.

Kohlberg's Theory of Moral Development

Kohlberg (1963, 1984; Colby & Kohlberg, 1987) has refined and extended Piaget's theory of moral development by asking 10-, 13-, and 16-year-old boys to resolve a series of moral dilemmas. Each dilemma challenged the respondent by requiring him to choose between (1) obeying a rule, law, or authority figure and (2) taking some action that conflicted with these rules and commands while serving a human need. The following story is the best known of Kohlberg's moral dilemmas:

> In Europe, a woman was near death from a special kind of cancer. There was one drug that doctors thought might save her. It was a form of radium that a druggist in the same town had recently discovered. The drug was expensive to make, but the druggist was charging $2000, or 10 times the cost of the drug, for a small (possibly life-saving) dose. Heinz, the sick woman's husband, borrowed all the money he could, about $1000, or half of what he needed. He told the druggist that his wife was dying and asked him to sell the drug cheaper or to let him pay later. The druggist replied "No, I discovered the drug, and I'm going to make money from it." Heinz then became desperate and broke into the store to steal the drug for his wife. Should Heinz have done that?

Kohlberg was actually less interested in the respondent's decision (that is, what Heinz should have done) than in the underlying rationale, or "thought structures," that the individual used to justify his decision. So, if a participant says "Heinz should steal the drug to save his wife's life," it is necessary to determine why her life is so important. Is it because she cooks and irons for Heinz? Because it's a husband's duty to save his wife? Or because the preservation of life is among the highest of human values? To determine the "structure" of a person's moral reasoning, Kohlberg asked probing questions: Does Heinz have an obligation to steal the drug? If Heinz doesn't love his wife, should he steal it for her? Should Heinz steal the drug for a stranger? Is it important for people to do everything they can to save another life? Is it against the law to steal? Does that make it morally wrong? The purpose of these probes was to clarify how individual participants reasoned about obedience and authority on the one hand and about human needs, rights, and privileges on the other.

Through his use of these elaborate clinical interviews, Kohlberg's first discovery was that moral development extends far beyond Piaget's autonomous stage, becoming increasingly complex throughout adolescence and into young adulthood. Careful analyses of his participants' responses to several dilemmas led Kohlberg to conclude that moral growth progresses through an invariant sequence of three moral levels, each of which is composed of two distinct moral stages. According to Kohlberg, the order of these moral levels and stages is invariant because they depend on the development of certain cognitive abilities that evolve in an invariant sequence. Like Piaget, Kohlberg assumes that each succeeding stage evolves from and replaces its predecessor; once the individual has attained a higher stage of moral reasoning, he or she should never regress to earlier stages.

Before examining Kohlberg's moral stages, it is important to emphasize that each stage represents a particular perspective, or method of thinking about moral dilemmas, rather than a particular type of moral decision. Decisions are not very informative in themselves, because people at each moral stage might well endorse either course of action when resolving one of these ethical dilemmas. (However, participants at Kohlberg's highest moral level generally favor serving human needs over complying with rules or laws that would compromise others' welfare.)

The basic themes and defining characteristics of Kohlberg's three moral levels and six stages are as follows:

preconventional morality
Kohlberg's term for the first two stages of moral reasoning, in which moral judgments are based on the tangible punitive consequences (Stage 1) or rewarding consequences (Stage 2) of an act for the actor rather than on the relationship of that act to society's rules and customs.

Level 1: Preconventional Morality. Rules are truly external to the self rather than internalized. The child conforms to rules imposed by authority figures to avoid punishment or obtain personal rewards. Morality is self-serving: what is right is what one can get away with or what is personally satisfying.

Stage 1: Punishment-and-Obedience Orientation. The goodness or badness of an act depends on its consequences. The child obeys authorities to avoid punishment, but may not consider an act wrong if it is not detected and punished. The greater the harm done or the more severe the punishment, the more "bad" the act is.

Stage 2: Naive Hedonism. A person at this second stage conforms to rules in order to gain rewards or satisfy personal objectives. There is some concern for the perspective of others, but other-oriented behaviors are ultimately motivated by the hope of benefiting in return. "You scratch my back and I'll scratch yours" is the guiding philosophy.

conventional morality
Kohlberg's term for the third and fourth stages of moral reasoning, in which moral judgments are based on a desire to gain approval (Stage 3) or to uphold laws that maintain social order (Stage 4).

Level 2: Conventional Morality. The individual now strives to obey rules and social norms in order to win others' approval or to maintain social order. Social praise and the avoidance of blame have now replaced tangible rewards and punishments as motivators of ethical conduct. The perspectives of other people are clearly recognized and given careful consideration.

Stage 3: "Good Boy" or "Good Girl" Orientation. Moral behavior is that which pleases, helps, or is approved of by others. People are often judged by their intentions. "Meaning well" is valued and being "nice" is important.

Stage 4: Social-Order-Maintaining Morality. At this stage, the individual considers the perspectives of the generalized other—that is, the will of society as reflected in law. Now what is right is what conforms to the rules of *legal* authority. The reason for conforming is not a fear of punishment, but a belief that rules and laws maintain a social order that is worth preserving. Laws always transcend special interests.

postconventional morality
Kohlberg's term for the fifth and sixth stages of moral reasoning, in which moral judgments are based on social contracts and democratic law (Stage 5) or on universal principles of ethics and justice (Stage 6).

Level 3: Postconventional (or Principled) Morality. A person at this highest level of moral reasoning defines right and wrong in terms of broad principles of justice that could conflict with written laws or with the dictates of authority figures. Morally right and legally proper are not always one and the same.

Stage 5: The Social-Contract Orientation. At Stage 5, the individual views laws as instruments for expressing the will of the majority and furthering human welfare. Laws that accomplish these ends and are impartially applied are viewed as social contracts that one has an obligation to follow; but imposed laws that compromise human rights or dignity are considered unjust and worthy of challenge. Distinctions between what is legal and what is moral begin to appear in Stage 5 responses.

Stage 6: Morality of Individual Principles of Conscience. At this highest moral stage, the individual defines right and wrong on the basis of the self-chosen ethical principles of his or her own conscience. These principles are not concrete rules such as government laws. They are abstract moral guidelines or principles of universal justice (and respect for the rights of all human beings) that transcend any law or social contract that may conflict with them.

Stage 6 is Kohlberg's vision of ideal moral reasoning. But because it is so very rare and virtually no one functions consistently at this level, Kohlberg came to view it as a hypothetical construct—that is, the stage to which people would progress were they to develop beyond Stage 5. In fact, the later versions of Kohlberg's manual for scoring moral judgments no longer attempt to measure Stage 6 reasoning (Colby & Kohlberg, 1987).

Support for Kohlberg's Theory

Although Kohlberg believes that his stages form an invariant and universal sequence of moral growth that is closely tied to cognitive development, he also claims that cognitive growth, by itself, is not sufficient to guarantee moral development. In order to ever move beyond the preconventional level of moral reasoning, children must be exposed to persons or situations that introduce *cognitive disequilibria*—that is, conflicts between existing moral concepts and new ideas that force them to reevaluate their viewpoints. So, like Piaget, Kohlberg believes that both cognitive development and relevant social experiences underlie the growth of moral reasoning.

How much support is there for these ideas? Let's review the evidence, starting with data bearing on Kohlberg's invariant-sequence hypothesis.

Are Kohlberg's Stages an Invariant Sequence? If Kohlberg's stages represent a true developmental sequence, we should find a strong positive correlation between age and maturity of moral reasoning. This is precisely what researchers have found in studies conducted in the United States, Mexico, the Bahamas, Taiwan, Turkey, Honduras, India, Nigeria, and Kenya (Colby & Kohlberg, 1987). So it seems that Kohlberg's levels and stages of moral reasoning are "universal" structures that are age-related, just as we would expect them to be if they formed a developmental sequence. But do these studies establish that Kohlberg's stages form a fixed, or *invariant* sequence?

No, they do not! The problem is that participants at each age level were *different* people, and we cannot be certain that a 25-year-old at Stage 5 has progressed through the various moral levels and stages in the order specified by Kohlberg's theory.

The Longitudinal Evidence. Clearly, the most compelling evidence for Kohlberg's invariant-sequence hypothesis would be a demonstration that individual children progress through the moral stages in precisely the order that Kohlberg says they should. Ann Colby and her associates (1983) have conducted a 20-year longitudinal study of Kohlberg's original research participants, who were reinterviewed five times at 3- to 4-year intervals. As shown in Figure 14.6, moral reasoning developed very gradually, with use of preconventional reasoning (Stages 1 and 2) declining sharply in adolescence—the same period in which conventional reasoning (Stages 3 and 4) is on the rise. Conventional reasoning remained the dominant form of moral expression in adulthood, with very few participants ever moving beyond it to postconventional morality (Stage 5). But even so, participants proceeded through the stages they did attain in precisely the order Kohlberg predicted and

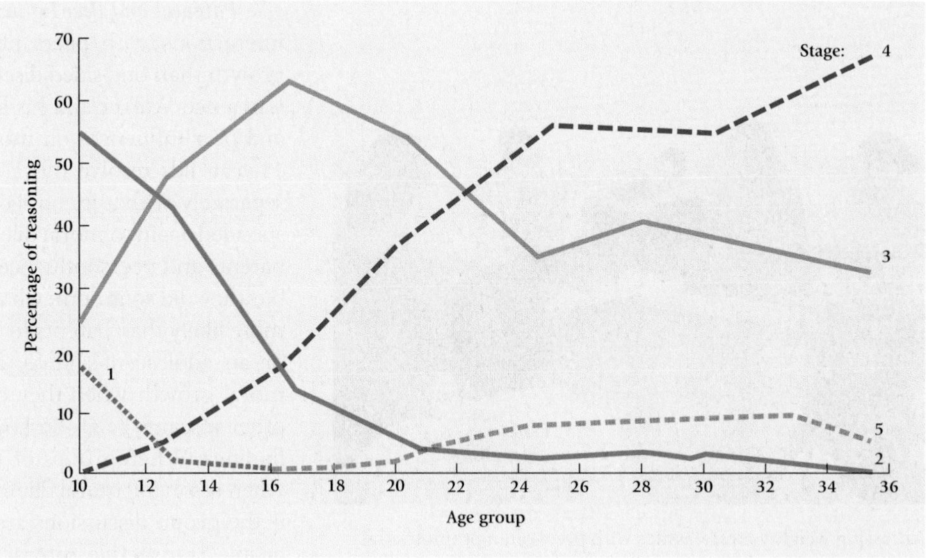

Figure 14.6 Use of Kohlberg's moral stages at ages 10 through 36 by male participants studied longitudinally over a 20-year period. *Adapted from "A Longitudinal Study of Moral Judgement," by A. Colby, L. Kohlberg, J. Gibbs, & M. Liberman, 1983,* Monographs of The Society for Research in Child Development, 48 *(Nos. 1–2, Serial No. 200). Copyright © 1983 by the Society for Research in Child Development, Inc. Adapted by permission.*

no one ever skipped a stage. Similar results have been reported in a 9-year longitudinal study of adolescents in Israel and a 12-year longitudinal project conducted in Turkey (Colby & Kohlberg, 1987). So Kohlberg's moral stages do seem to represent an invariant sequence (see also Rest, Thoma, & Edwards, 1997). Let's note, however, that people progress in an orderly fashion to their highest stage of reasoning and that Stage 3 or 4 is the end of this developmental journey for most individuals worldwide (Snarey, 1985).

Cognitive Prerequisites for Moral Growth. According to Kohlberg (1963), the young, preconventional child reasons about moral issues from an egocentric point of view. At Stage 1 the child thinks that certain acts are bad because they are punished. At Stage 2 the child shows a limited awareness of the needs, thoughts, and intentions of others but still judges self-serving acts as appropriate. However, conventional reasoning clearly requires some role-taking abilities. A person at Stage 3, for example, must necessarily recognize others' points of view before she will evaluate intentions that would win their approval as "good" or morally acceptable. Furthermore, Kohlberg proposed that postconventional moral reasoning requires formal operations. A Stage 5 individual who bases moral judgments on abstract principles must be able to reason abstractly rather than simply adhering to the rule of law or concrete moral norms.

These hypotheses have received ample support. Lawrence Walker (1980), for example, found that all 10- to 13-year-olds who had reached Kohlberg's Stage 3 ("good boy–good girl" morality) were quite proficient at mutual role-taking, although not all proficient role takers had reached Stage 3 in their moral reasoning. Similarly, Carolyn Tomlinson-Keasey and Charles Keasey (1974) and Deanne Kuhn and her associates (1977) found that (1) all participants who showed any evidence of postconventional (Stage 5) moral reasoning had reached formal operations but that (2) most formal operators had not reached Kohlberg's postconventional level of moral reasoning. What these findings imply is that role-taking skills are necessary but not sufficient for the development of conventional morality, and that formal operations are necessary but not sufficient for the emergence of postconventional morality. This pattern is precisely what Kohlberg had expected, as he viewed cognitive growth as only one prerequisite for moral development. The other prerequisite is *relevant social experience*—that is, exposure to persons or situations that force a person to reevaluate and alter his current moral perspectives.

Evidence for Kohlberg's Social-Experience Hypothesis. Does research support the proposition that social experience contributes to moral development? Yes, indeed, as the following research demonstrates.

© Mary Kate Denny/PhotoEdit

Discussing weighty ethical issues with peers often promotes the growth of moral reasoning.

transactive interactions
verbal exchanges in which individuals perform mental operations on the reasoning of their discussion partners.

Parental and Peer Influences. Like Piaget, Kohlberg felt that interactions with peers probably contribute more to moral growth than one-sided discussions with adult authority figures. Lawrence Walker and his associates (2000) compared parental and peer influences on moral development by having 11- and 15-year-olds resolve moral dilemmas with a parent and then separately with a friend. Four years later, these participants responded again to moral dilemmas. Earlier discussions with both parents and peers influenced participants' moral development, but they did so in somewhat different ways. Friends were much more likely than parents to challenge and disagree with a child's or an adolescent's ideas, and they contributed positively to moral growth when they did confront and challenge. Indeed, other research (e.g., Berkowitz & Gibbs, 1983) supports these findings. When groups of peers are asked to reach consensus when resolving moral dilemmas, moral growth typically results if the group discussions are characterized by explicit but nonhostile **transactive interactions**—exchanges in which discussants challenge each other and hash out their differences. These are important findings for they reinforce Kohlberg's idea that social experiences promote moral growth by introductory cognitive challenges to one's current reasoning.

By contrast, parents made bigger contributions to moral growth when they presented their reasoning in a positive, supportive way and asked gentle probing questions to see if their children or adolescents were understanding their viewpoints (Walker, Hennig, & Kettenauer, 2000). Direct confrontations by parents, however, did more harm than good, possibly because children and adolescents view a direct parental challenge as hostile criticism, which may make them defensive. The same kind of challenge is much less threatening when voiced by a social equal; in fact, adolescents may be especially inclined to listen carefully and accommodate to peers' positions because they are so highly motivated to establish and maintain good relations with peers. So Piaget and Kohlberg were right in calling attention to peers as agents of moral socialization, but they failed to appreciate that parents may also have much to contribute.

Advanced Education. Another kind of social experience that promotes moral growth is receiving an advanced education. Consistently, adults who go on to college and receive many years of education reason more complexly about moral issues than those who are less educated (Speicher, 1994), and differences in the moral reasoning between college students and their nonstudent peers become greater with each successive year of school that the college students complete (Rest & Thoma, 1985). Advanced education may foster moral growth in two ways: by (1) contributing to cognitive growth and (2) exposing students to diverse moral perspectives that produce cognitive conflict and soul-searching (Kohlberg, 1984; Mason & Gibbs, 1993).

Cultural Influences. Finally, simply living in a complex, diverse, and democratic society can stimulate moral development. Just as we learn the give-and-take of mutual perspective taking by discussing issues with our friends, we learn in a diverse democracy that the opinions of many groups must be weighed and that laws reflect a consensus of the citizens rather than the arbitrary rulings of a dictator. Cross-cultural studies suggest that postconventional moral reasoning emerges primarily in Western democracies and that people in rural villages in many nonindustrialized countries show no signs of it (Harkness, Edwards, & Super, 1981; Snarey & Keljo, 1991). People in these homogeneous communities may have less experience with the kinds of political conflicts and compromises that take place in a more diverse society and so may never have any need to question conventional moral standards. By adopting a contextual perspective on development, we can appreciate that the conventional (mostly Stage 3) reasoning typically displayed by adults in these societies—with its emphasis on cooperation and loyalty to the immediate social group—is adaptive and mature within their own collectivist social systems (Harkness, Edwards, & Super, 1981).

In sum, Kohlberg has described an invariant sequence of moral stages and has identified some of the cognitive factors and major environmental influences that determine how far an individual progresses in this sequence. Yet, critics have offered many reasons for suspecting that Kohlberg's theory is far from a complete account of moral development.

Criticisms of Kohlberg's Approach

Many of the criticisms of Kohlberg's theory have centered on the possibilities that it is biased against certain groups of people, that it underestimates the moral sophistication of young children, and that it says much about moral reasoning but little about moral affect and moral behavior.

Is Kohlberg's Theory Culturally Biased? Although research indicates that children and adolescents in many cultures proceed through the first three or four of Kohlberg's stages in order, we have seen that postconventional morality as Kohlberg defines it simply does not exist in some societies. Critics have charged that Kohlberg's highest stages reflect a Western ideal of justice and that his stage theory is therefore biased against people who live in non-Western societies or who do not value individualism and individual rights highly enough to want to challenge society's rules (Gibbs & Schnell, 1985; Shweder, Mahapatra, & Miller, 1990). People in collectivist societies that emphasize social harmony and place the good of the group ahead of the good of the individual may be viewed as conventional moral thinkers in Kohlberg's system but may actually have very sophisticated concepts of justice (Li, 2002; Snarey & Keljo, 1991; Shweder, 1997), including a strong respect for individual rights and such "democratic" principles as decision by majority rule (Helwig et al., 2003). Although there are some aspects of moral development that do seem to be common to all cultures, some research suggests that other aspects of moral growth can vary considerably from society to society.

Consider the differences in cultural and subcultural moral development revealed in research by Shweder and his colleagues. Is each of the following acts wrong? If so, how serious a violation is it?

- A young married woman is beaten black and blue by her husband after going to a movie without his permission despite having been warned not to do so again.
- A brother and sister decide to get married and have children.
- The day after his father died, the oldest son in a family has a haircut and eats chicken.

These are 3 of 39 acts presented by Richard Shweder, Manamahan Mahapatra, and Joan Miller (1987) to children ages 5 to 13 and adults in India and the United States. You may be surprised to learn that Hindu children and adults rated the son's having a haircut and eating chicken after his father's death as among the very most morally offensive of the 39 acts they rated, and the husband's beating of his disobedient wife as not wrong at all. American children and adults, of course, viewed wife beating as far more serious than breaking seemingly arbitrary rules about appropriate mourning behavior. Although Indians and Americans could agree that a few acts like brother-sister incest were serious moral violations, they did not agree on much else.

Furthermore, Indian children and adults viewed the Hindu ban against behavior disrespectful of one's dead father as a *universal moral rule;* they thought it would be best if everyone in the world followed it and strongly disagreed that it would be acceptable to change the rule if most people in their society wanted to change it. Hindus also believed that it is a serious moral offense for a widow to eat fish or wear brightly colored clothes or for a woman to cook food for her family during her menstrual period. To orthodox Hindus, rules against such behavior are required by natural law; they are not just arbitrary social conventions created by members of society. Hindus also regard it as morally

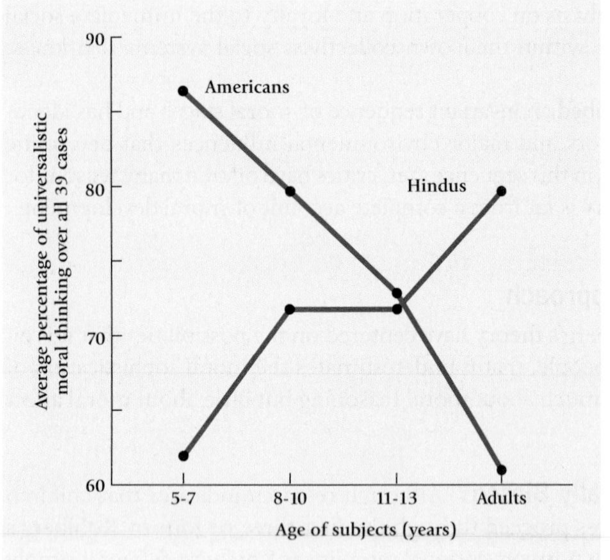

Figure 14.7 Universalistic moral thinking—the tendency to view rules of behavior as universally valid and unalterable—increases with age among Hindu children in India but decreases with age in the United States. The course of moral development is likely to be different in different societies. *Adapted from "Culture and Moral Development" by R. Shweder, M. Mahapatra, & J. G. Miller, 1987, in J. Kagan & S. Lamb (Eds.),* The Emergence of Morality in Young Children. *Copyright © 1987 University of Chicago Press. Adapted by permission.*

necessary for a man to beat his disobedient wife in order to uphold his obligations as head of the family.

What effects do cultural beliefs of this sort have on moral development? The developmental trend in moral thinking Shweder detected in India was very different from the developmental trend he observed in the United States, as Figure 14.7 shows. With age, Indian children saw more and more issues as matters of universal moral principle, whereas American children saw fewer and fewer issues in the same light (and more and more as matters of arbitrary social convention that can legitimately differ from society to society).

Based on these cross-cultural findings, Shweder calls into question Kohlberg's claims that all children everywhere construct similar moral codes at similar ages and that certain universal moral principals exist. Instead, he believes that culture defines exactly what is morally acceptable or unacceptable and then assists the young to adopt that conceptual framework. Indeed, we saw evidence of this very process earlier: Children from the collectivist People's Republic of China gradually adopt their society's communist-collectivist ideals of behaving prosocially and remaining modest or humble about it—to the point that they think it better to lie and deny personal responsibility for a good deed than to boldly claim responsibility or seek recognition for their acts of kindness.

Interestingly, there are also important *subcultural* influences on moral reasoning. For example, individuals who occupy a subordinate position within the societies (for example, Arab women and Brazilian children from the lower socioeconomic strata) are more inclined than age-mates of higher status to view themselves as having relatively few personal choices about how to behave and as under greater moral obligation to submit to authority (Nucci, Camino & Sapiro, 1996; Turiel & Wainryb, 2000).

Clearly, these findings challenge the cognitive-developmental position that all important aspects of moral growth are universal. Instead, they tend to support a *contextual* perspective on moral development by suggesting that children's moral judgments are shaped by the culture and subculture in which they live. In Canada, for example, one need not display a strong sense of religiosity or spiritualism to be considered morally mature (Walker & Pitts, 1998), whereas a strong sense of spiritualism and adherence to an "ethics of divinity" is of central importance to Hindus (Shweder, 1997). What then should we conclude about culture and moral reasoning? Perhaps children all over the world do think in more cognitively complex ways about issues of morality and justice as they get older, as Kohlberg claimed, but at the same time adopt different notions about what is right and what is wrong (or a personal choice versus a moral obligation) as Shweder and others claim.

Is Kohlberg's Theory Gender Biased? Critics have also charged that Kohlberg's theory, which was developed from data provided by male participants, does not adequately represent female moral reasoning. Carol Gilligan (1982, 1993), for example, pointed out that, in some early studies, women seemed to be the moral inferiors of men, typically reasoning at Kohlberg's Stage 3 while men usually reasoned at Stage 4. She argued that differential gender-typing causes boys and girls to adopt different moral orientations. The strong independence and assertiveness training that boys receive encourages them to view moral dilemmas as inevitable conflicts of interest between individuals that laws and other social conventions are designed to resolve. Gilligan calls this orientation the **morality of justice,** a perspective that approximates Stage 4 in Kohlberg's scheme. By contrast, girls are taught to be nurturant, empathic, and concerned about others—in short, to define their sense of "goodness" in terms of their interpersonal relationships. So for females, morality implies a

morality of justice
Gilligan's term for what she presumes to be the dominant moral orientation of males, focusing more on socially defined justice as administered through law than on compassionate concerns for human welfare.

morality of care
Gilligan's term for what she presumes to be the dominant moral orientation of females—an orientation focusing more on compassionate concerns for human welfare than on socially defined justice as administered through law.

sense of caring or compassionate concern for human welfare—a **morality of care** that approximates Stage 3 in Kohlberg's scheme. Gilligan argues that the morality of care that females adopt can become quite abstract or "principled," even though Kohlberg's scheme might place it at Stage 3 because of its focus on interpersonal obligations.

There is little support for Gilligan's claim that Kohlberg's theory is biased against women. Most studies indicate that women reason just as complexly about moral issues as men do when their answers are scored by Kohlberg's criteria (Jaffee & Hyde, 2000; Walker, 1995). Nor is there much evidence for sex differences in moral orientations: When reasoning about real-life dilemmas they have faced, *both* males and females raise issues of compassion and interpersonal responsibility about as often as or more often than they talk about issues of law, justice and individual rights (Walker, 1995; Wark & Krebs, 1996). What's more, young men and women view both justice-related and care-related attributes as central elements of moral maturity (Walker & Pitts, 1998; and review Table 14.2). So it has become quite clear that the justice and the care orientations are not sex-specific moralities, as Gilligan had claimed.

Gilligan's theory and the research designed to test it have broadened our view of morality by illustrating that both men and women often think about moral issues—especially real-life as opposed to hypothetical moral issues—in terms of their responsibilities for the welfare of other people. Kohlberg emphasized only one way, a very legalistic way, of thinking about right and wrong. There seems to be merit in tracing the development of *both* a morality of justice and a morality of care in *both* males and females (Brabeck, 1983; Gilligan, 1993).

Is Kohlberg's Theory Incomplete? Another common criticism of Kohlberg's theory is that it focuses too heavily on moral reasoning and neglects moral affect and behavior. Indeed, Kohlberg does largely ignore the role of such powerful emotions as pride, shame, guilt, and remorse that influence our moral thoughts and actions (Haan, Aerts, & Cooper, 1985; Hart & Chmiel, 1992). Yet, he did assume that mature moral reasoners should be more inclined to behave morally and that the relationship between moral reasoning and moral behavior would become stronger as individuals progress toward higher levels of moral understanding.

Does Moral Reasoning Predict Moral Conduct? Most of the available data are consistent with Kohlberg's viewpoint. With few exceptions (for example, Kochanska & Murray, 2000), most researchers have found that the moral judgments of young children do *not* predict their behavior in situations where they are induced to cheat or violate other moral norms (see Shaffer, 2005, for a review). However, studies of older grade-school children, adolescents, and young adults often find that individuals at higher stages of moral reasoning are more likely than those at lower stages to behave altruistically and conscientiously and are less likely to cheat or take part in delinquent or criminal activity (Judy & Nelson, 2000; Midlarsky et al., 1999; Rest, Thoma, & Edwards, 1997). Kohlberg (1975), for example, found that only 15 percent of college students who reasoned at the postconventional level actually cheated on a test when given an opportunity, compared with 55 percent of the "conventional" students and 70 percent of those at the preconventional level. Yet the relationship between stages of moral reasoning and moral behavior is only moderate at best (Bruggerman & Hart, 1996). Why? Because personal qualities other than moral reasoning, and many situational factors as well (for example, likelihood that transgressions will be punished or do harm to others), influence moral conduct in daily life. The process of moral growth may even contribute to inconsistencies between moral reasoning and moral behavior (e.g., Walker, 2000). Stephen Thoma and James Rest (1999) for example, propose that situational factors will have a stronger influence on moral decision making when a person is reexamining (and often rejecting) existing moral principles as she makes the transition from one moral stage to the next higher stage.

Does Kohlberg Underestimate Young Children? Finally, Kohlberg's focus on legalistic dilemmas that laws were designed to address caused him to overlook other "nonlegalistic" forms of moral reasoning that influence the behavior of grade school children.

Although children this young usually display preconventional moral reasoning on Kohlberg's legalistic dilemmas, they actually have some reasonably sophisticated standards of distributive justice.

We've seen, for example, that young elementary-school children do often consider the needs of others or do whatever they think people will approve of when resolving Eisenberg's prosocial moral dilemmas—even though these same youngsters are hopelessly mired in Stage 1 (or Stage 2) when tested on Kohlberg's dilemmas. Furthermore, 8- to 10-year-old Stage 1 reasoners have often developed some sophisticated notions about *distributive justice*—deciding what is a "fair and just" allocation of limited resources (toys, candies, etc.) among a group of deserving recipients (Damon, 1988; Sigelman & Waitzman, 1991)—reasoning not adequately represented in Kohlberg's theory. Interestingly, fear of punishment, deference to authority, and other legalistic themes that Kohlberg believes to characterize the moral judgments of 8- to 10-year-olds do not even appear in children's distributive-justice reasoning. So by focusing so heavily on legalistic concepts, Kohlberg has clearly underestimated the moral sophistication of grade school children.

In sum, Kohlberg's theory of moral development has many strengths; yet, there is also some merit to the criticisms. His theory does not fully capture the morality of people who live in non-Western societies or who choose to emphasize a morality of care rather than a morality of justice, and it clearly underestimates the moral reasoning of young children. And because Kohlberg concentrates so heavily on moral reasoning, we must rely on other perspectives to help us to understand how moral affect and moral behavior develop, and how thought, emotions, and behavior interact to make us the moral beings that most of us ultimately become.

The Behavioral Component of Moral Development

Social learning theorists such as Albert Bandura (1986, 1991) and Walter Mischel (1974) have been primarily interested in the behavioral component of morality—what we actually do when faced with temptation. They claim that moral behaviors are learned in the same way that other social behaviors are: through the operation of reinforcement and punishment and through observational learning. They also consider moral behavior to be strongly influenced by the specific situations in which people find themselves. It is not at all surprising, they say, to see a person behave morally in one situation but transgress in another situation, or to proclaim that nothing is more important than honesty but then lie or cheat.

How Consistent Are Moral Conduct and Moral Character?

The most extensive study of children's moral conduct is one of the oldest—the Character Education Inquiry reported by Hugh Hartshorne and Mark May (1928–1930). This 5-year project investigated the moral "character" of 10,000 children ages 8 to 16 by repeatedly tempting them to lie, cheat, or steal in a variety of situations. The most noteworthy finding of this massive investigation was that children tended *not* to be consistent in their moral behavior; a child's willingness to cheat in one situation did not predict his willingness to lie, cheat, or steal in other situations. Of particular interest was the finding that children who cheated in a particular setting were just as likely as those who did not to state that cheating is wrong. Hartshorne and May concluded that "honesty" is largely specific to the situation rather than a stable character trait.

Resisting temptation is a difficult feat for young children to accomplish, particularly when there is no one around to help the child exercise willpower.

However, more modern and sophisticated analyses of data from the Character Education Inquiry (Burton, 1963), as well as newer studies (Hoffman, 2000; Kochanska & Murray, 2000), have challenged Hartshorne and May's **doctrine of specificity,** finding that moral behaviors of a particular kind (for example, a child's willingness to cheat or not cheat on tests or to share or not share toys with playmates) are reasonably consistent over time and across situations. What's more, the correlations among measures of children's moral conduct, moral reasoning, and moral behavior become progressively stronger with age (Blasi, 1990; Kochanska et al., 2002). So there is some consistency or coherence to moral character after all, especially as we become more morally mature. Yet, we should never expect even the most morally mature individuals to be perfectly consistent across all situations, for one's willingness to lie, cheat, or violate other moral norms (or one's feelings and thoughts about doing so) may always depend to some extent on important contextual factors such as the importance of the goal that might be achieved by breaking a rule or the amount of encouragement from peers for deviant conduct (Burton, 1976).

Learning to Resist Temptation

From society's standpoint, one of the more important indexes of morality is the extent to which an individual is able to resist pressures to violate moral norms, even when the possibility of detection and punishment is remote (Hoffman, 1970). A person who resists temptation in the absence of external surveillance not only has learned a moral rule but is *internally* motivated to abide by that rule. How do children acquire moral standards, and what motivates them to obey these learned codes of conduct? Social-learning theorists have attempted to answer these questions by studying the effects of reinforcement, punishment, and social modeling on children's moral behavior.

Reinforcement as a Determinant of Moral Conduct

We have seen on several occasions that the frequency of many behaviors can be increased if these acts are reinforced. Moral behaviors are certainly no exception. When warm, accepting parents set clear and reasonable standards for their children and often praise them for behaving well, even toddlers are likely to meet their expectations and to display strong evidence of an internalized conscience by age 4 to 5 (Kochanska et al., 2002; Kochanska & Murray, 2000). Children are generally motivated to comply with the wishes of a warm, socially reinforcing adult, and the praise that accompanies their desirable conduct tells them that they are accomplishing that objective.

doctrine of specificity
a viewpoint shared by many social-learning theorists which holds that moral affect, moral reasoning, and moral behavior may depend as much or more on the situation one faces than on an internalized set of moral principles.

inhibitory control
an ability to display acceptable conduct by resisting the temptation to commit a forbidden act.

The Role of Punishment in Establishing Moral Prohibitions

Although reinforcing acceptable behaviors is an effective way to promote desirable conduct, adults often fail to recognize that a child has *resisted* a temptation and is deserving of praise. Yet, many adults are quick to punish moral transgressions. Is punishment an effective way to foster the development of **inhibitory controls?** The answer depends critically on the child's *interpretation* of these aversive experiences.

Investigating Resistance to Temptation. Ross Parke (1977) used the *forbidden toy paradigm* to study the effects of punishment on children's resistance to temptation.

During the first phase of a typical experiment, participants are punished (by hearing a noxious buzzer) whenever they touch an attractive toy; however, nothing happens when they play with unattractive toys. Once the child has learned the prohibition, the experimenter leaves and the child is surreptitiously observed to determine whether he or she plays with the forbidden toys.

In general, research suggests that firm (rather than mild) punishments, administered immediately (rather than later) and consistently by a warm (rather than an aloof) disciplinarian are most effective at inhibiting a child's undesirable conduct. Yet, Parke's most important discovery was that all forms of punishment became more effective if accompanied by a cognitive rationale that provides the transgressor with reasons for not performing a forbidden act.

Explaining the Effects of Cognitive Rationales. Why do rationales increase the effectiveness of punishment, even mild or delayed punishments that produce little moral restraint by themselves? Probably because rationales provide children with information specifying why the punished act is wrong and why they should feel guilty or shameful for repeating it. So when these youngsters think about committing the forbidden act in the future, they should experience a general uneasiness (stemming from previous disciplinary encounters), should be inclined to make an *internal attribution* for this arousal (for example, "I'd feel guilty if I caused others harm"; "I'd violate my positive self-image"), and should eventually become more likely to inhibit the forbidden act and to feel rather good about their "mature and responsible" conduct. By contrast, children who receive no rationales or who have heard reasoning that focuses their attention on the negative consequences that they can expect for future transgressions (for example, "You'll be spanked again if you do it") will experience just as much uneasiness when they think about committing the forbidden act. However, these youngsters should tend to make *external attributions* for their emotional arousal (for example, "I'm worried about getting caught and punished") that might make them comply with moral norms in the presence of authority figures but probably won't inhibit deviant conduct if there is no one around to detect their transgressions.

So fear of detection and punishment is not enough to persuade children to resist temptation in the absence of external surveillance. In order to establish truly internalized self-controls, adults must structure disciplinary encounters to include an appropriate rationale—one that informs the child why the prohibited act is wrong and why she should feel guilty or shameful about repeating it (Hoffman, 1988). Clearly, true self-restraint is largely under cognitive control; it depends more on what's in children's heads rather than on the amount of fear or uneasiness in their guts.

Moral Self-Concept Training. If making internal attributions about one's conduct truly promotes moral self-restraint, we should be able to convince children that they can resist temptations to violate moral norms because they are "good," "honest," or otherwise "responsible" persons (an internal attribution). This kind of moral self-concept training really does work. William Casey and Roger Burton (1982) found that 7- to 10-year-olds became much more honest while playing games if "honesty" was stressed and the players learned to remind themselves to follow the rules. Yet when honesty was not stressed, players often cheated. Furthermore, David Perry and his associates (1980) found that 9- to 10-year-olds who had been told that they were especially good at carrying out instructions and following rules (moral self-concept training) behaved very differently after succumbing to a nearly irresistible temptation (leaving a boring task to watch an exciting TV show) than did peers who had not been told they were especially good. Specifically, children who had heard positive attributions about themselves were more inclined than control participants to punish their own transgressions by giving back many of the valuable prize tokens they had been paid for working at the boring task. So it seems that labeling children as "good" or "honest" may not only increase the likelihood that they will resist temptations, but also contributes to children's feelings of guilt or remorse should they behave inappropriately and violate their positive self-images.

In sum, moral self-concept training, particularly when combined with praise for desirable conduct, can be a most effective alternative to punishment as a means of establishing inhibitory controls—one that should help convince the child that "I'm resisting temptation because *I* want to," and lead to the development of truly internalized controls rather than a response inhibition based on a fear of detection and punishment. Furthermore, this positive, nonpunitive approach should produce none of the undesirable side effects (for example, resentment) that often accompany punishment.

Social Modeling Influences on Moral Behavior

Might children be influenced by rule-following models who exhibit moral behaviors in a "passive" way by failing to commit forbidden acts? Indeed they may, as long as they are aware that the "passive" model is resisting the temptation to violate a rule. Joan Grusec and her associates (1979) found that a rule-following model can be particularly effective at inspiring children to behave in kind if the model clearly verbalizes that he is following a rule and states a rationale for not committing the deviant act. Furthermore, rule-following models whose rationales match the child's customary level of moral reasoning are more influential than models whose rationales are well beyond that level (Toner & Potts, 1981).

Finally, consider what Nace Toner and his associates (1978) found: 6- to 8-year-olds who were persuaded to serve as models of moral restraint for other children became more likely than age-mates who had not served as rule-following models to obey other rules during later tests of resistance to temptation. It was almost as if serving as a model produced a change in children's self-concepts, so that they now defined themselves as "people who follow rules." The implications for child-rearing are clear: perhaps parents could succeed in establishing inhibitory controls in their older children by appealing to their maturity and persuading them to serve as models of self-restraint for their younger brothers and sisters.

Who Raises Children Who Are Morally Mature?

Many years ago, Martin Hoffman (1970) reviewed the child-rearing literature to see whether the disciplinary techniques that parents actually use have any effect on the moral development of their children. Three major approaches were compared:

- **Love withdrawal:** withholding attention, affection, or approval after a child misbehaves or, in other words, creating anxiety over a loss of love.
- **Power assertion:** use of superior power to control the child's behavior (including techniques, such as forceful commands, physical restraint, spankings, and withdrawal of privileges, that may generate fear, anger, or resentment.
- **Induction:** explaining why a behavior is wrong and should be changed by emphasizing how it affects other people, often suggesting how the child might repair any harm done.

love withdrawal
a form of discipline in which an adult witholds attention, affection, or approval in order to modify or control a child's behavior.

power assertion
a form of discipline in which an adult relies on his or her superior power (for example, by administering spankings or withholding privileges) to modify or control a child's behavior.

induction
a nonpunitive form of discipline in which an adult explains why a child's behavior is wrong and should be changed by emphasizing its effects on others.

Suppose that little Tomeka has just terrorized the family dog by chasing him with a lit sparkler during a Fourth of July celebration. Using love withdrawal, a parent might say "How could you? Get away! I can't bear to look at you." Using power assertion, a parent might spank Tomeka or say "That's it! No movie for you this Saturday." Using induction, the parent might say "Tomeka, look how scared Pokey is. You could have set him on fire, and you know how sad we'd all be if he was burned." Induction, then, is a matter of providing rationales that focus special attention on the consequences of one's wrongdoing for other people (or dogs, as the case may be).

TABLE 14.3 Relationship between Parents' Use of Three Disciplinary Strategies and Children's Moral Development

	Type of discipline		
Direction of relationship between parents' use of a disciplinary strategy and children's moral maturity	Power assertion	Love withdrawal	Induction
+ (positive correlation)	7	8	38
− (negative correlation)	32	11	6

Note: Table entries represent the number of occasions on which a particular disciplinary technique was found to be associated (either positively or negatively) with a measure of children's moral affect, reasoning, or behavior.

Source: Adapted from "Contributions of Parents and Peers to Children's Moral Socialization," by G. H. Brody & D. R. Shaffer, 1982. *Developmental Review, 2,* 31–75. Copyright © Academic Press, Inc. Adapted by permission.

Although only a limited number of child-rearing studies had been conducted by 1970, their results suggested that (1) neither love withdrawal nor power assertion were particularly effective at promoting moral maturity, but that (2) induction seemed to foster the development of all three aspects of morality—moral emotions, moral reasoning, and moral behavior (Hoffman, 1970). Table 14.3 summarizes the relationships among the three patterns of parental discipline and various measures of children's moral maturity that emerged from a later review of the literature that included many more studies (Brody & Shaffer, 1982). Clearly, these data confirm Hoffman's conclusions: Parents who rely on inductive discipline tend to have children who are morally mature, whereas frequent use of power assertion is more often associated with moral immaturity than with moral maturity. The few cases in which induction was *not* associated with moral maturity all involved children under age 4. However, recent research indicates that reasoning-based discipline can be highly effective with 2- to 5-year-olds, reliably promoting sympathy and compassion for others as well as a willingness to comply with parental requests. By contrast, use of such high-intensity power-assertive tactics as becoming angry and physically restraining or spanking the child is already associated with and seems to promote noncompliance, defiance, and a lack of concern for others (Crockenberg & Litman, 1990; Kochanska et al., 2002; Kochanska & Murray, 2000; Labile & Thompson, 2000, 2002).

"IF YOU'RE TRYIN' TO GET SOMETHING INTO MY HEAD, YOU'RE WORKIN' ON THE WRONG END!"

Why is inductive discipline effective? Hoffman cites several reasons. First, it provides children with cognitive standards (or rationales) to evaluate their conduct. Second, this form of discipline helps children to sympathize with others (Krevans & Gibbs, 1996) and allows parents to talk about such moral affects as pride, guilt, and shame that are not easily discussed with a child who is made emotionally insecure by love withdrawal or angry by power-assertive techniques (see Labile & Thompson, 2000). Finally, parents who use inductive discipline are likely to explain to the child (1) what he or she should have done when tempted to violate a prohibition and (2) what he or she can now do to make up for a transgression. So induction may be an effective method of moral socialization because it calls attention to the cognitive, affective, and behavioral aspects of morality and may help the child to integrate them.

APPLYING RESEARCH TO YOUR LIFE

How Should I Discipline My Children?

Few if any parents are totally inductive, love oriented, or power assertive in their approach to discipline; most make at least some use of all three disciplinary techniques. Although parents classified as "inductive" rely heavily on reasoning, they occasionally take punitive measures whenever punishment is necessary to command the child's attention or to discipline repeated transgressions. So the style of parenting that Hoffman calls induction may be very similar to the "rationale + mild punishment" treatment that Parke (1977) found most effective in laboratory studies of resistance to temptation.

Several investigators have wondered whether Hoffman's conclusions about the effectiveness of inductive discipline might not be overstated. For example, inductive discipline used by white, middle-class mothers is consistently associated with measures of children's moral maturity; however, the same findings don't always hold for fathers or for parents from other socioeconomic backgrounds (Brody & Shaffer, 1982; Grusec & Goodnow, 1994). Furthermore, the positive association between parents' use of power-assertive discipline and children's aggressive, antisocial conduct seems to hold for European American but not for African American children (Deater-Deckard & Dodge, 1997; and see Walker-Barnes & Mason, 2000). Clearly more research is needed to establish how culturally specific Hoffman's ideas may be.

Other critics have raised the direction-of-effects issue: Does induction promote moral maturity or, rather, do morally mature children elicit more inductive forms of discipline from their parents? Because child-rearing studies are based on correlational data, either of these possibilities can explain Hoffman's findings. Hoffman (1975) responded by claiming that parents exert far more control over their children's behavior than children exert over parents. In other words, he believes that parental use of inductive discipline promotes moral maturity rather than the other way around. And there is some experimental support for Hoffman's claim in that induction is much more effective than other forms of discipline at persuading children to keep their promises and to comply with rules imposed by unfamiliar adults (Kuczynski, 1983).

Children can influence the discipline they receive. A child who acts out or defies his parents, for example, will often elicit more coercive (and less effective) forms of discipline in the future (Patterson, 1998; Stoolmiller, 2001). And although most youngsters may respond quite favorably to inductive discipline, it is becoming quite clear that there is no one discipline that works best for all children and that effective approaches are those that provide a "good fit" with the child's behaviors and other attributes (Grusec, Goodnow, & Kuczynski, 2000). To illustrate, Grazyna Kochanska (1997a) found that different strategies were necessary to promote moral internalization in children with different temperaments. Temperamentally fearful toddlers, who are anxious, socially inhibited, and prone to burst into tears when sharply reprimanded, seem to require gentle, inductive forms of discipline if they are to show signs of developing a strong conscience during the preschool years. But unlike most children, temperamentally impulsive and fearless toddlers are not sufficiently aroused by inductive discipline to learn moral lessons. These youngsters show more signs of developing an internalized conscience early in life if their parents have established warm, mutually responsive relationships with them that foster a strong desire to cooperate and maintain parental approval.

So, as effective as inductive discipline appears to be, it is not the best way to promote moral maturity in all children. However, Kochanska and associates (1996) did find that parents' heavy reliance on power assertion consistently inhibits moral internalization and represents a "poor fit" with children of all temperaments.

A Child's-Eye View of Discipline

What do children think about various disciplinary strategies? Do they feel (as many developmentalists do) that physical punishment and love withdrawal are ineffective methods of promoting moral restraint? Would they favor inductive techniques or perhaps prefer that their parents adopt more permissive attitudes about transgressions?

Michael Siegal and Jan Cowen (1984) addressed these issues by asking children and adolescents between the ages of 4 and 18 to listen to stories describing different kinds of misdeeds and to evaluate strategies that mothers had used to discipline these antics. Five kinds of transgressions were described: (1) simple disobedience (the child refusing to clean his room), (2) causing physical harm to others (the child punching a playmate), (3) causing physical harm to oneself (ignoring an order not to touch a hot stove), (4) causing psychological harm to others (making fun of a physically disabled person), and (5) causing physical damage (breaking a lamp while roughhousing). The four disciplinary techniques on which parents were said to have relied were *induction* (reasoning with the culprit by pointing out the harmful consequences of his or her actions), *physical punishment* (striking the child), *love withdrawal* (telling the child to stay away), and *permissive nonintervention* (ignoring the incident and assuming that the child would learn important lessons on his or her own). Each participant heard 20 stories that resulted from pairing each of the four disciplinary strategies with each of the five transgressions. After listening to or reading each story, the participant indicated whether the parent's approach to the problem was "very wrong," "wrong," "half right-half wrong," "right," or "very right."

The results were clear: Induction was the most preferred disciplinary strategy for participants of all ages (even preschoolers), and physical punishment was the next most favorably evaluated technique. So all participants seemed to favor a rational disciplinarian who relies heavily on reasoning that is occasionally backed by power assertion. By contrast, love withdrawal and permissiveness were favorably evaluated by no age group. However, the 4- to 9-year-olds in the sample favored *any* form of discipline, even love withdrawal, over a permissive attitude on the parent's part (which they viewed as "wrong" or "very wrong"). Apparently young children see the need for adults to step in and restrain their inappropriate conduct, for they were disturbed by stories in which youngsters were completely free to do their own thing.

In sum, the disciplinary style that children favor (induction backed by occasional use of power assertion) is the one most closely associated with measures of moral maturity in child-rearing studies and with resistance to temptation in the laboratory. Perhaps another reason that inductive discipline often promotes moral maturity is simply that many children view this approach as the "right" way to deal with transgressions, and they may be highly motivated to accept influence from a disciplinarian whose "world view" matches their own. By contrast, children who favor induction but are usually disciplined in other ways may see little justification for internalizing the values and exhortations of a disciplinarian whose very methods of inducing compliance seem unwise, unjust, and hardly worthy of their respect.

Integrating the Components of Moral Development

As we conclude this discussion of moral development in children and adolescents, we point out once again the distinct and separate nature of the theory and research on moral affect, reasoning, and behavior. It is almost as if these three domains address conceptually unrelated topics rather than sharing an inherent emphasis on the broad category of morality and its development. Although it makes sense to examine these areas separately (Dodge & Rabiner, 2004), we believe it is also important to remember and consider their shared bases in the construct of moral development. Indeed, there is some evidence that developmental researchers may be moving in that direction (Arsenio & Lemerise, 2004; Dodge & Rabiner, 2004; Nucci, 2004).

Consider, for example, Arsenio and Lemerise's social information-processing model of moral behavior, depicted in Figure 14.8. This model borrows from Dodge's (1986) social information-processing model of aggression, depicted in Figure 14.2. Notice that this model combines moral affect (or emotion), moral reasoning (or information-processing steps), and moral behavior (or action). Clearly, Arsenio and Lemerise propose the time has come to integrate these areas of research and theory. Although we agree with others who argue that we may never be able to totally integrate these domains (Dodge & Rabiner, 2004; Nucci, 2004), we agree with Arsenio and Lemerise that the future of the field of developmental psychology would benefit from a consideration of this integration.

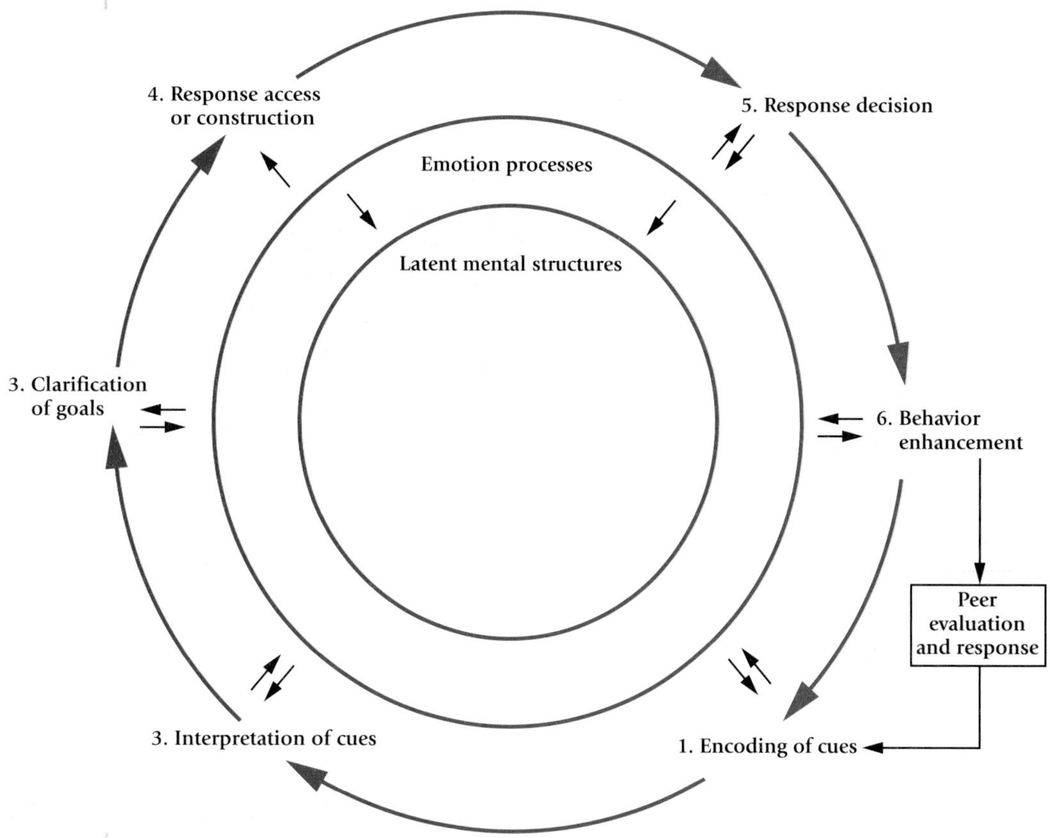

Figure 14.8 A simplified version of Arsenio and Lemerise's Social Information-Processing Model of Moral Behavior. *Adapted from "Aggression and moral development: Integrating social information processing and moral domain models," by W. F. Arsenio and E. A. Lemerise in* Child Development, *75, 987–1002. Reprinted by permission of Blackwell Publishing.*

CONCEPT CHECK 14.3 Understanding Moral Development

Check your understanding of moral development by answering the following questions. Answers appear in the Appendix.

Matching: Match the following concepts with the descriptive phrases below:

a. morality of care
b. peer interactions
c. role-taking skills

1. _______ Both Piaget and Kohlberg emphasize this *social* contributor to moral development.
2. _______ According to Gilligan, Kohlberg overlooks the growth of this moral aspect.
3. _______ This is a cognitive prerequisite for Kohlberg's conventional morality.

True or False: Identify whether the following statements are true or false.

4. (T)(F) Induction is the type of discipline consistently associated with moral *immaturity.*
5. (T)(F) Power assertion is the type of discipline to which most children, particularly fearful ones, respond best.
6. (T)(F) Love withdrawal is perhaps the most successful form of discipline for young children.

Fill in the Blank: Complete the following statements with the correct concept or phrase.

7. Gilligan proposed two types of morality, morality of _______ and morality of _______, and argued that Kohlberg's theory ignored the morality of _______.
8. Recent research correcting for some of the flaws in Piaget's research has revealed that Piaget tended to _______ the moral abilities of young children.

Short Answer: Provide a brief answer to the following question.

9. Examine the cartoon on the following page. To which stage of moral reasoning would the speaking child in the cartoon be assigned in Piaget's and Kohlberg's theories of moral development?

CONTINUED

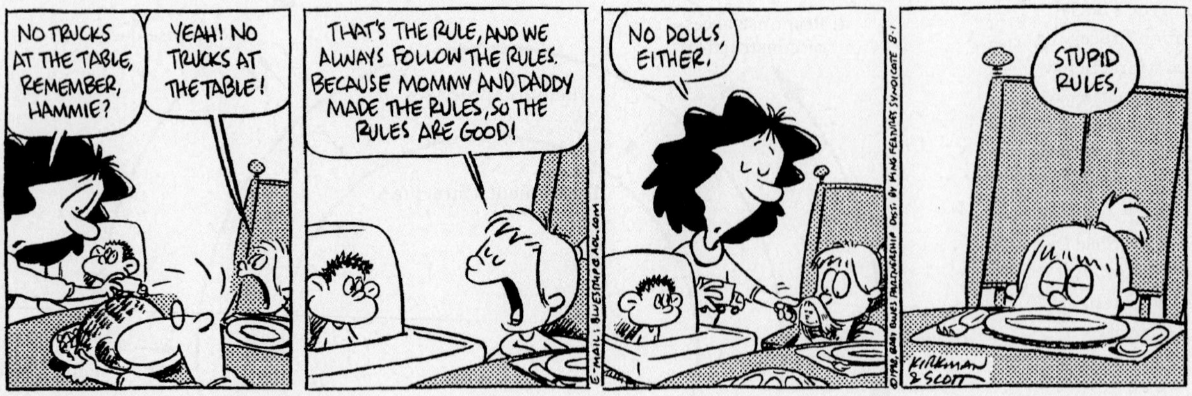

Essay: Provide a more detailed answer to the following question.

10. Describe the three components of moral development and provide a brief description of the type of research used to investigate each component.

Applying Developmental Themes to the Development of Aggression, Altruism, and Morality

This chapter covered a broad range of social development topics, including aggression, altruism, and morality. Our developmental themes (the active child, nature and nurture interactions, qualitative and quantitative developmental changes, and the holistic nature of child development) are evident throughout the topics we've covered. Let's take a look at how our themes relate to different social development topics with examples from this chapter.

The child's active participation in his or her development was illustrated by our discussion of proactive aggressors and proactive victims. These children think and behave in ways that serve to promote and maintain their status as aggressor or victim. But not all children are classified this way. An example of all children playing an active role in their development is Dodge's social information-processing model of aggression. Recall that this model proposes that all children are active in thinking about situations that may or may not lead them to behave aggressively, and that the cycle of information processing children use lead to the development of children's thinking about and acting out aggression.

Sex differences in aggressive behavior illustrate the combined influence of nature and nurture on development. We learned that sex differences in aggression are partly attributable to gender differences in testosterone (a biological or nature influence). But sex differences are also clearly dependent on gender-typing and gender differences in social learning (an environmental or nurture influence). Clearly, both nature and nurture combine to influence this aspect of social development!

The qualitative and quantitative nature of developmental change was of special significance in this chapter because each topic illustrated the complexity of qualitative/quantitative interactions and the fact that qualitative changes are often seen after a series of quantitative changes in behavior. For example, both moral reasoning and aggressive behavior change qualitatively as children progress through stages that differ in form or type from earlier stages. However, each of these different stages is achieved after a series of quantitative changes as children experience social interaction and cognitive development.

Finally, the holistic nature of child development was illustrated in each topic, as children's cognitive function was seen to derive from and contribute to their social experiences. This relationship was stated explicitly in Kohlberg's theory of moral reasoning. Recall that Kohlberg proposed that children progress through stages of moral reasoning in an invariant order and that their progression through stages is mediated both by their cognitive development and by their social interactions with peers. For Kohlberg, cognition and social interaction are inseparable in guiding moral development.

These are just a few examples of the way our developmental themes relate to the development of aggression, altruism, and morality. Perhaps you can identify additional examples. Clearly, our themes are important constructs that underlie our theory and understanding of these areas of social development in children and adolescents.

SUMMARY

The Development of Aggression

- Intentional acts of harmdoing, or **aggression,** are often divided into two categories: **hostile aggression** and **instrumental aggression.**
- Instrumental aggression appears by the end of the first year as infants have **conflicts** over toys and other possessions.
- During early childhood, aggression becomes less physical and increasingly verbal, and somewhat less instrumental and increasingly **retaliatory.**
- Boys are more overtly aggressive; girls are more **relationally aggressive.**
- Overt aggression declines with age, whereas more covert forms of antisocial conduct increase with age.
- Aggressiveness is a moderately stable attribute for both males and females.
- **Proactive aggressors** rely on aggression to satisfy personal objectives and are quite confident that aggression will "pay off" for them; they may become bullies.
- **Reactive aggressors** display a **hostile attributional bias** that causes them to over-attribute hostile intents to others and to retaliate in a hostile manner; they may become **provocative victims.**
- Most victims of bullies are **passive victims** whom bullies find easy to dominate.
- Aggressive inclinations depend, in part, on the cultural, subcultural, and family settings in which a child is raised.
- Children from a **coercive home environment** in which hostile behaviors are **negatively reinforced** are likely to become aggressive.
- The incidence of children's aggression can be reduced by taking care to create "nonaggressive" play environments, relying on control procedures such as **time-out** and the **incompatible-response technique,** and by implementing social-cognitive interventions.

Altruism: Development of the Prosocial Self

- Early indications of **altruism,** such as sharing toys and comforting distressed companions, appear in infancy and toddlerhood.
- Sharing, helping, and other forms of **prosocial conduct** become more and more common from the preschool period onward.
- The growth of altruistic concern is linked to the development of role-taking skills, **prosocial moral reasoning,** and **sympathetic empathic arousal.**
- Like aggression, a person's altruistic tendencies are influenced by his or her cultural and family environments.
- Parents can promote altruistic behavior by praising their child's kindly deeds, and by practicing themselves the prosocial lessons that they preach.
- Parents who discipline harmdoing with nonpunitive, affective explanations are likely to raise children who become sympathetic, self-sacrificing, and concerned about the welfare of others.

Moral Development: Affective, Cognitive, and Behavioral Components

- **Morality** implies a set of **internalized** principles or ideals that help the individual to distinguish right from wrong and to act on this distinction.
- The Affective Component of Moral Development:
  - According to Freud's theory of **Oedipal morality,** children internalize the moral standards of the same-sex parent during the phallic stage as they resolve their Oedipus or Electra complexes and form a conscience or superego.
  - Research has consistently discredited Freud's theory.
  - Newer research finds that the conscience forms earlier in toddlerhood in the context of a warm, **mutually responsive relationship.**
- The Cognitive Component of Moral Development:
  - In Jean Piaget's stage model of moral development children move from a **premoral period,** in which they allegedly respect no rules, to **heteronomous morality,** in which they view rules as moral absolutes and believe in **immanent justice,** and finally, to **autonomous morality,** in which they regard rules as flexible and justice as relative.

- Shortcomings of Piaget's research methods caused him to underestimate the moral sophistication of preschool and young grade-school children.
- Lawrence Kohlberg's theory views moral reasoning as progressing through an invariant sequence of three levels, **preconventional, conventional,** and **postconventional moralities,** each composed of two distinct stages.
- Research supports Kohlberg's stages and his proposals that cognitive development and social experiences with parents, peers, and other participants in higher education or democratic activities contribute to the growth of moral reasoning.
- Kohlberg's theory may not adequately describe the morality of people who live in non-Westernized societies or who emphasize a **morality of care** rather than a **morality of justice.**

- The Behavioral Component of Moral Development:
  - Social learning theorists explain how children learn to resist temptation and inhibit acts that violate moral norms.
  - Among the factors that promote the development of **inhibitory controls** are praise given for virtuous conduct, punishments that include appropriate rationales, and exposing children to (or having them serve as) models of moral restraint.
  - Other nonpunitive techniques such as moral self-concept training are also quite effective at promoting moral behavior.
  - Child-rearing studies consistently imply that use of **inductive discipline** promotes moral maturity, whereas **love withdrawal** has little effect, and **power-assertion** is associated with moral *immaturity.*
  - The effectiveness of induction may vary depending on the child's temperament.
  - Children generally prefer inductive discipline to other approaches, and most seem highly motivated to accept influence from an inductive adult whose methods they can respect.
- Integrating the Components of Moral Development
  - Although it may not be feasible to totally integrate the affective, cognitive, and behavioral components of moral development, a social information processing model of moral behavior may take the field in the direction of integration.

KEY TERMS

aggression 547
hostile aggression 548
instrumental aggression 548
conflict 548
retaliatory aggression 549
relational aggression 551
proactive aggressors 552
reactive aggressors 552
hostile attributional bias 553
passive victims (of aggression) 554
provocative victims (of aggression) 554
popularity 555
coercive home environment 556
negative reinforcer 556
incompatible-response technique 558
time-out technique 558
altruism 559
affective explanations 560
prosocial moral reasoning 561
sympathetic empathic arousal 562
self-oriented distress 562
"felt responsibility" hypothesis 563
morality 567
internalization 567
moral affect 568
moral reasoning 568
moral behavior 568
Oedipal morality 569
mutually responsive relationship 569
committed compliance 569
situational compliance 570
premoral period 571
heteronomous morality 571
immanent justice 571
autonomous morality 571
moral rules 572
social-conventional rules 572
preconventional morality 575
conventional morality 575
postconventional morality 575
transactive interactions 578
morality of justice 580
morality of care 581
doctrine of specificity 583
inhibitory control 583
love withdrawal 585
power assertion 585
induction 585

MEDIA RESOURCES

The Human Development Book Companion Website

See the companion website http://www.thomsonedu.com/psychology/shaffer for flashcards, practice quiz questions, Internet links, updates, critical thinking exercises, discussion forums, games, and more

Thomson™ NOW! http://www.thomsonedu.com
Go to this site for the link to ThomsonNOW, your one-stop shop. Take a pre-test for this chapter, and ThomsonNOW will generate a personalized study plan based on your test results. The study plan will identify the topics you need to review and direct you to online resources to help you master those topics. You can then take a post-test to help you determine the concepts you have mastered and what you will still need to work on.

Child and Adolescent Development CD-ROM

For more information about the concepts covered in this chapter, go to

Module III: Personality, Social-Emotional, and Moral development

- Moral Development
- Module III Media

Jack Hollingsworth/Getty Images

CHAPTER 15 The Context of Development I: The Family

In April of 1995, at the age of 95 and on the day after her own 75th wedding anniversary, Cora Shaffer attended the 50th wedding anniversary party of her eldest son (then aged 73). Also present at that gathering was Cora's other surviving child, 4 of her 8 grandchildren, 8 of her 11 great-grandchildren, and 9 of her 11 great-great grandchildren. Remarkably, Cora could easily recite the most notable dates (birthdays, wedding anniversaries) of all of her descendants and could give you a pretty fair account of the most notable current events (for example, recent occupational, educational, or personal attainments) of all these relatives as well. When I (Dave Shaffer) asked her how she managed to keep up with all the family doings, she laughed, said she had ample time for family matters since her retirement in 1985 (at age 85!), and quipped that "Alexander Graham Bell must have had folks like me in mind when he invented the telephone." And yet, this woman could also expound at length about the lives and times of departed relatives she had known, some of whom had been born in the early 1840s, before the telephone (or even the Pony Express) had been invented. Clearly, Cora Shaffer valued her ties to past, present, and future generations of Shaffers.

Most of us will never have the opportunity to know and care about as many generations of relatives as my grandmother did, but her emphasis on family ties is not at all unusual. More than 99 percent of children in the United States are raised in a family of one kind or another (U.S. Bureau of the Census, 2002), and the vast majority of children in all societies grow up in a home setting with at least one relative. So virtually all of us are bound to families. We are born into them, work our way toward adulthood in them, start our own as adults, and remain connected to them in old age. We are part of our families, and they are part of us.

Our focus in this chapter is on the family as a *social system*—an institution that both influences and is influenced by its young. What is a family and what functions do families serve? How does the birth of a child affect other family members? Are some patterns of parenting better than others? Does the family's cultural heritage and socioeconomic status affect parenting? How important are siblings in child development? How are children affected by the increasing diversity of family life we see today? These are some of the major issues that we will consider as we look at the important roles that families play in the development of children and adolescents.

Understanding the Family

From a developmental perspective, the most important function that families serve in all societies is to care for and socialize their young. **Socialization** refers to the process by which children acquire the beliefs, motives, values, and behaviors deemed significant and appropriate by older members of their society.

socialization
the process by which children acquire the beliefs, values, and behaviors considered desirable or appropriate by their culture or subculture.

Of course, families are only one of many institutions involved in the socialization process. As we will see in Chapter 16, such institutions as schools, religious groups, mass media, and children's groups (for example, Boy Scouts and Girl Scouts) frequently

Juan Silva/The Image Bank/Getty Images

supplement the training and emotional support functions served by families and promote healthy developmental outcomes (Brody, Stoneman, & Flor, 1996). Nevertheless, many children have limited exposure to people outside the **family** until they are placed in day care or nursery school or begin their formal schooling. So the family has a clear head start on other institutions when it comes to socializing a child. It is appropriate to think of the family as society's primary instrument of socialization.

The Family as a Social System

It is not easy to define the term family in a way that applies to all cultures, subcultures, or historical eras because there are so many different forms of family life (Coontz, 2000). By one definition, a family is "two or more persons related by birth, marriage, adoption, or choice" who have emotional ties and responsibilities to each other (Allen, Fine, & Demo, 2000, p. 1).

family
two or more persons, related by birth, marriage, adoption, or choice, who have emotional ties and responsibilities to each other.

When developmentalists began to study socialization in the 1940s and 1950s, they focused almost entirely on the mother-child relationship, operating under the assumption that mothers (and to a lesser extent fathers) were the agents who molded children's conduct and character (Ambert, 1992). However, modern family researchers have rejected this simple unidirectional model in favor of a more comprehensive "systems" approach—one that is similar to Urie Bonfenbrenner's ecological systems theory that we discussed in Chapter 1 (Bronfenbrenner & Morris, 1998). The systems approach recognizes that parents influence their children. But it also stresses that (1) children influence the behavior

"I guess we'd be considered a family. We're living together, we love each other, and we haven't eaten the children yet."

and child-rearing practices of their parents, and (2) that families are complex social systems—that is, networks of *reciprocal* relationships and alliances that are constantly evolving and are greatly affected by community and cultural influences.

family social system
the complex network of relationships, interactions, and patterns of influence that characterize a family with three or more members.

traditional nuclear family
a family unit consisting of a wife/mother, a husband/father, and their dependent child or children.

To say that a family is a **social system** means that the family, much like the human body, is a *holistic structure*. It consists of interrelated parts, each of which affects and is affected by every other part. Each part contributes to the functioning of the whole (Fingerman & Bermann, 2000).

To illustrate, let's consider the simplest of **traditional nuclear families,** consisting of a mother, a father, and a firstborn child. Even this man-woman-infant "system" is a complex entity (Belsky, 1981). An infant interacting with his or her mother is already involved in a process of *reciprocal influence*. This is evident when we notice that the infant's smile is likely to be greeted by the mother's smile or that a mother's concerned expression often makes her infant wary. And what happens when Dad arrives? As shown in Figure 15.1, the mother-infant dyad is suddenly transformed into a "'*family system*' [comprising] a husband-wife as well as mother-infant and father-infant relationships" (Belsky, 1981, p. 17).

One implication of viewing the family as a system is that interactions between any two family members are likely to be influenced by attitudes and behaviors of a third family member (e.g., Parke, 2004). For example, fathers influence the mother-infant relationship: happily married mothers who have close, supportive relationships with their husbands tend to interact much more patiently and sensitively with their infants than mothers who experience marital tension and feel that they are raising their children on their own (Cox et al., 1992; Cox et al., 1989). The infants of happily married mothers are therefore more likely to be securely attached (Doyle et al., 2000). Meanwhile, mothers influence the father-infant relationship: fathers tend to be more engaged and supportive with their children when their relations with their spouses are harmonious (Kitzmann, 2000). Overall, children fare best when couples coparent—that is, mutually support each other's parenting efforts and function as a cooperative (rather than an antagonistic) team (Leary & Katz, 2004; McHale et al., 2004). Unfortunately, effective **coparenting** is difficult for couples experiencing marital discord and other life stresses (Kitzmann, 2000; McHale, 1995; Vetere, 2004). (And in the United States, a 47 percent divorce rate indicates that many couples experience marital discord [U.S. Bureau of the Census, 2006]). Unhappy couples have disputes over child-rearing issues that can be particularly intense and harmful (Papp, Cummings, & Goeke-Morey, 2002). These negative interactions often forecast increases in childhood and adolescent adjustment problems over and above those attributable to other aspects of marital conflict (Mahoney, Jourilies, & Scavone, 1997).

coparenting
circumstance in which parents mutually support each other and function as a cooperative parenting team.

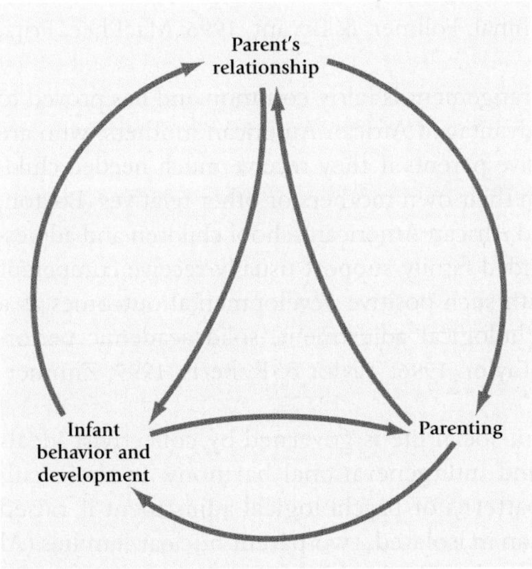

Figure 15.1 A model of the family as a social system. As implied in the diagram, a family is bigger than the sum of its parts. Parents affect infants, who affect each parent and the marital relationship. Of course, the marital relationship may affect the parenting that the infant receives, the infant's behavior, and so on. Clearly, families are complex social systems. *From "Early Human Experience: A Family Perspective," by J. Belsky, 1981,* Developmental Psychology, *17, 3–23. Copyright © 1981 by the American Psychological Association. Reprinted by permission.*

Of course, children also exert effects on their parents. A highly impulsive child who throws tantrums and shows little inclination to comply with requests may drive a mother to punitive coercive methods of discipline (a "child-to-mother" effect) (Stoolmiller, 2001), which, in turn, may make the child more defiant than ever (a "mother-to-child" effect) (Crockenberg & Litman, 1990; Donovan, Leavitt, & Walsh, 2000). The exasperated mother may then criticize her husband for his nonintervention, precipitating an unpleasant discussion about parental obligations and responsibilities (an effect of the child's impulsivity on the husband-wife relationship).

In short, every person and every relationship within the family affects every other person and relationship through pathways of influence illustrated in Figure 15.1 (and see Belsky & Fearon, 2004). We begin to see why it was rather naive to think we might understand how families influence children by concentrating exclusively on the mother-child relationship (Frascarolo et al., 2004).

Now think about how complex the family system becomes with the birth of a second child and the addition of sibling-sibling and sibling-parent relationships! Another level of complexity exists in families with twins, triplets, or other multiple-births (e.g., Feldman, Eidelman, & Rotenberg, 2004). Or consider the complexity of an **extended family** household, a practice in which parents and their children live with (or in very close proximity to) other relatives—grandparents or aunts, uncles, nieces, and nephews (Ruggles, 1994).

extended family
a group of blood relatives from more than one nuclear family (for example, grandparents, aunts, uncles, nieces, and nephews) who live together, forming a household.

Families Are Developing Systems

Not only are families complex social systems, they are dynamic, or changing, systems as well. Consider that every family member is a *developing* individual and that relationships between husband and wife, parent and child, and sibling and sibling will also change in ways that can influence the development of each family member (Klein & White, 1996). Many such changes are normal developmental changes, as when parents allow toddlers to do more things on their own as a means of encouraging autonomy and the development of individual initiative. Yet, a host of unplanned or unforeseen changes (such as the death of a sibling or the souring of the husband-wife relationship) can greatly affect family interactions and children's development. So the family is not only a system in which developmental change takes place; its dynamics also change with development of its members.

© David Young-Wolff/PhotoEdit

In extended families, children develop relationships with older generations.

The social systems perspective also emphasizes that all families are embedded within larger cultural and subcultural contexts and that the ecological niche a family occupies (for example, the family's religion, its socioeconomic status, and the values that prevail within a subculture, a community, or even a neighborhood) can affect family interactions and the development of a family's children (Bronfenbrenner & Morris, 1998; Taylor, Clayton, & Rowly, 2004). As we will see later in the chapter, economic hardship exerts a strong influence on parenting: parents often become depressed over their financial situation. This, in turn, can cause them to become less nurturant toward and involved with their children (Conger et al., 1992; Conger et al., 2002; Mistry et al., 2002). However, economically distressed parents who have close ties to a "community"—a church group, a volunteer organization, or a circle of close friends—experience far less stress and less disruption of their parenting routines (Burchinal, Follmer, & Bryant, 1996; MacPhee, Fritz, & Miller-Heyl, 1996).

For example, the extended family arrangement is fairly common and has proved to be highly adaptive for economically disadvantaged African American mothers, who are likely to become more sensitive, responsive parents if they receive much needed child-rearing assistance and social support from their own mothers or other relatives (Burton, 1990; Taylor, 2000). Indeed, disadvantaged African American school children and adolescents whose families receive ample extended family support usually receive competent parenting at home. This is associated with such positive developmental outcomes as a strong sense of self-reliance, good psychological adjustment, solid academic performance, and fewer behavioral problems (Taylor, 1996; Taylor & Roberts, 1995; Zimmerman, Salem, & Maton, 1995).

In some cultures, such as the Sudan, social life is governed by collectivist ideals stressing communal interdependence and intergenerational harmony. In these cultures children routinely display better patterns of psychological adjustment if raised in extended-family households rather than in isolated, two-parent nuclear families (Al Awad & Sonuga-Barke, 1992). So it seems that the healthiest family contexts for development will depend very heavily on both the needs of individual families and the values that families (within particular cultural and subcultural contexts) are trying to promote.

Clearly the broader social contexts that families experience can greatly affect the ways that family functions are carried out. And these broader social contexts are also constantly changing and developing. During the last half of the 20th century, several dramatic social changes have affected the makeup of the typical family and the character of family life in the United States. Drawing on U.S. census data and other surveys, Table 15.1 describes some of these changes.

TABLE 15.1 Changing Family Systems in the United States

Changes in Parents	More single adults	There are more single adults today than in the past.
Changes in Families		95% of adults do eventually marry.
	Postponed marriage	The age of first marriage has risen to 24 for women and 26 for men.
	Fewer children	The age of first child has increased from the past.
		The number of children in a family has decreased to 1.8 on average.
		Only 85% of married women ever have any children.
	Working mothers	63% of women with children under age 6 work outside the home (compared with 12% in 1950).
	More divorce	Divorce rates are increasing. Between 40% and 50% of recently married couples can expect to divorce.
		One million children each year are affected by their parents' divorce.
	More single-parent families	More children live in single-parent homes, partly because of the rise in divorce rates and partly because of a rise in never-married parents.
		In 1960, only 9% of children lived with a single parent, usually a widowed one.
		In 1998, 27% of children lived with a single parent, usually a divorced or never-married one.
		Father-headed single-parent families are more common than they used to be, accounting for 17% of all single-parent families.
	More remarriage	More adults are remarrying, forming blended or step-families.
		66% of divorced mothers and 75% of divorced fathers remarry.
		25% of American children will spend some time in a stepparent family.
	More multigenerational families	More children today know and spend time with their grandparents and great-grandparents.

Data compiled from: Bengston, 2001; Cabrera et al., 2000; Hetherington & Jodl, 1994; Hetherington et al., 1999; Meckler, 2002; U.S. Bureau of the Census, 2000, 2002.

Conclusions about Understanding Families

In sum, even the simplest of families is a true social system that is much bigger than the sum of its parts. Not only does each family member influence the behavior of every other, but the relationship between any two family members can affect the interactions and relationships of all other family members. And when we consider that family members develop, relationships change, and that all family dynamics are influenced by the broader social contexts in which families are embedded, it becomes quite clear that socialization within the family is best described not as a two-way street between parents and children, but as the busy intersection of many, many avenues of influence.

Because divorce and remarriage are so common, many children now live in blended (stepparent) families with stepsiblings.

What these changes tell us is that modern families are much more diverse than ever (Demo, Allen, & Fine, 2000). Our stereotyped image of the model family—the nuclear aggregation with a breadwinning father, a housewife mother, and at least two children—is just that: a stereotype. By one estimate, this "typical" family represented about 50 percent of American households in 1960, but only 12 percent in 1995 (Hernandez, 1997). Although families are no less influential today than they were in previous eras, we must broaden our image of them to include the many dual-career, single-parent, blended, and multigenerational families that exist today and are influencing the development of the *majority* of our children. Bear that in mind as we begin our excursion into family life, seeking to determine how families influence the development of their children.

CONCEPT CHECK 15.1 Understanding Families as Systems

Check your understanding of the family as a social system and the important differences in family structure and function by answering the following questions. Answers appear in the Appendix.

Fill in the Blank: Complete the following sentences with the correct terms.

1. A family consisting of a mother, father, and their children is called a(n) ________ by developmental psychologists.
2. In a(n) ________ parents and children live with the parents' parents or other relatives.
3. The process of helping children to accept the beliefs, values, and behaviors appropriate for their culture is called ________.

Multiple Choice: Select the correct answer for each question.

_____ 4. Janet and Eric have two children. They both try to be active parents for their children, and they try to support each other's parenting activities. Their mutual efforts are an example of
a. a social system
b. an extended family
c. coparenting
d. active child effects

Short Answer: Briefly answer the following question.

5. Diagram the directions of influence in a traditional nuclear family with one child, assuming a family systems perspective.

Parental Socialization During Childhood and Adolescence

In previous chapters, we considered the results of a large body of research aimed at understanding how parents might affect the social, emotional, and intellectual development of their infants and toddlers. Recall that this work was remarkably consistent: warm and sensitive parents who often talk to their infants and try to stimulate their curiosity are contributing to positive developmental outcomes. Their children are securely attached, willing to explore, sociable, and show signs of positive intellectual development. It also helps if *both* parents are sensitive, responsive caregivers who support each other in their roles as parents. Jay Belsky (1981) argued that parental warmth/sensitivity "is the most influential dimension of [parenting] in infancy. It not only fosters healthy psychological functioning during this developmental epoch, but also . . . lays the foundation on which future experience will build" [p. 8].

During the second year, parents continue to be caregivers and playmates. They also become more concerned with teaching children how to behave (or how *not* to behave) in a variety of situations (Fagot & Kavanaugh, 1993). According to Erik Erikson (1963), this is the period when socialization begins in earnest. Parents must now manage the child's budding autonomy in the hope of instilling a sense of social propriety and self-control. Meanwhile, they must take care not to undermine the child's curiosity, initiative, and feelings of personal competence.

Two Major Dimensions of Parenting

acceptance/responsiveness a dimension of parenting that describes the amount of responsiveness and affection that a parent displays toward a child.

demandingness/control a dimension of parenting that describes how restrictive and demanding parents are.

Two aspects of parenting are especially important throughout childhood and adolescence: parental **acceptance/responsiveness** and parental **demandingness/control** (sometimes called "permissiveness-restrictiveness") (e.g., Erikson, 1963; Maccoby & Martin, 1983).

Acceptance/responsiveness refers to the amount of support and affection that a parent displays. Parents classified as accepting and responsive often smile at, praise, and encourage their children. They express a great deal of warmth, even though they can

Charles Gullung/Getty Images

Warmth and affection are crucial components of effective parenting.

become quite critical when a child misbehaves. Less accepting and relatively unresponsive parents are often quick to criticize, belittle, punish, or ignore a child. They rarely communicate to children that they are valued or loved.

Demandingness/control refers to the amount of regulation or supervision parents undertake with their children. Controlling/demanding parents place limits on their children's freedom of expression by imposing many demands. They actively monitor their children's behavior to ensure that these rules are followed. Less controlling/demanding parents are much less restrictive. They make fewer demands and allow children considerable freedom to pursue their interests and make decisions about their own activities.

As we have seen throughout this book, warm, responsive parenting is consistently associated with such positive developmental outcomes as secure emotional attachments, a prosocial orientation, good peer relations, high self-esteem, and a strong sense of morality. Children generally want to please loving parents and so are motivated to do what is expected of them and learn what parents would like them to learn (Forman & Kochanska, 2001; Kochanska, 2002). At the other end of the continuum is a family setting in which one or both parents have treated the child as if he or she was unworthy of their attention and affection, a primary contributor to poor peer relations, clinical depression, and other adjustment problems later in life (Ge et al., 1996; MacKinnon-Lewis et al., 1997; Scaramella et al., 2002). Children simply do not thrive when they are often ignored or rejected.

Is it better for parents to be highly controlling; or rather, should they impose few restrictions and grant their children considerable autonomy? To answer these questions, we need to be more specific about the degrees of control that parents display and look carefully at patterns of parental acceptance.

authoritarian parenting
a restrictive pattern of parenting in which adults set many rules for their children, expect strict obedience, and rely on power rather than reason to elicit compliance.

authoritative parenting
flexible, democratic style of parenting in which warm, accepting parents provide guidance and control while allowing the child some say in deciding how best to meet challenges and obligations.

Four Patterns of Parenting

It turns out that the two major parenting dimensions are reasonably independent, so we find parents who display each of the few possible combinations of acceptance/responsiveness and control/demandingness shown in Figure 15.2. These four parenting styles are described as follows:

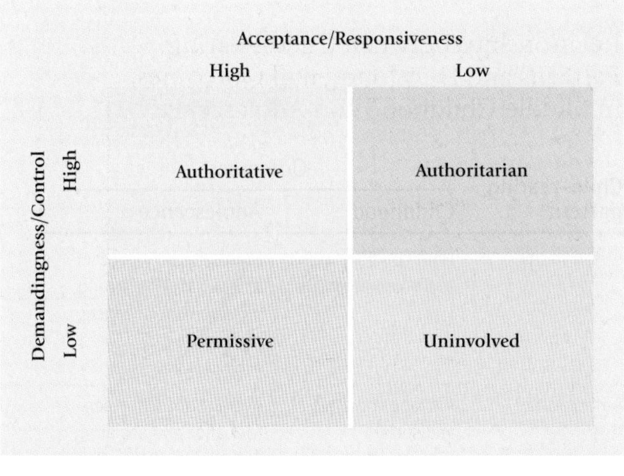

Figure 15.2 Two major dimensions of parenting. When we cross the two dimensions, we come up with four parenting styles: accepting/controlling (or "authoritative"); accepting/uncontrolling (or "permissive"); aloof/controlling (or "authoritarian"); and aloof/uncontrolling (or "uninvolved"). Which parenting style did your parents use? *From E. E. Maccoby & J. A. Martin (1983), Socialization in the context of the family: Parent-child interaction. In E. M. Hetherington (Ed.; P. H. Mussen, General Ed.),* Handbook of Child Psychology, *Vol. 4. Socialization, personality, and social development, pp. 1–101. New York: Wiley. Used by permission of John Wiley & Sons, Inc.*

Authoritarian Parenting

A very restrictive pattern of parenting in which adults impose many rules, expect strict obedience, and will rarely if ever explain to the child why it is necessary to comply with all these regulations. These parents will often rely on punitive, forceful tactics (such as power-assertion or love withdrawal) to gain compliance. Authoritarian parents are not sensitive to a child's differing viewpoints. Rather, they are domineering and expect the child to accept their word as law and respect their authority.

Authoritative Parenting

A controlling but flexible style in which parents make many reasonable demands of their children. They are careful to provide rationales for complying with the limits they set and will ensure that their children follow those guidelines. However, they are much more accepting of and responsive to their children's points of view than authoritarian parents. They will often seek their children's participation in family decision making. So, authoritative parents exercise control in a *rational, democratic* way that recognizes and respects their children's perspectives.

permissive parenting
a pattern of parenting in which otherwise accepting adults make few demands of their children and rarely attempt to control their behavior.

Permissive Parenting

An accepting but lax pattern of parenting in which adults make relatively few demands, permit their children to freely express their feelings and impulses, do not closely monitor their children's activities, and rarely exert firm control over their behavior.

uninvolved parenting
a pattern of parenting that is both aloof (or even hostile) and overpermissive, almost as if parents neither cared about their children nor about what they may become.

Uninvolved Parenting

An extremely lax and undemanding approach displayed by parents who have either *rejected* their children or are so overwhelmed with their own stresses and problems that they haven't much time or energy to devote to child rearing (Maccoby & Martin, 1983). These parents impose few rules and demands. They are uninvolved and insensitive to their children's needs.

These patterns of parenting are associated with various developmental outcomes, some good and some bad. One program of research that has investigated the relationships between parenting styles and child characteristics is described in the following Box. As that

FOCUS ON RESEARCH Parenting Styles and Developmental Outcomes

Perhaps the best-known research on parenting styles is Diana Baumrind's (1967, 1971) early studies of preschool children and their parents. Each child in Baumrind's sample was observed on several occasions in nursery school and at home. These data were used to rate the child on such behavioral dimensions as sociability, self-reliance, achievement, moodiness, and self-control. Parents were also interviewed and observed while interacting with their children at home. When Baumrind analyzed the parental data, she found that individual parents generally used one of three parenting styles shown in Figure 15.2 (none of the parents could be classified as "uninvolved").

When Baumrind (1967) linked these three parenting styles to the characteristics of the preschool children who were exposed to each style, she found that children of authoritative parents were developing rather well. They were cheerful, socially responsible, self-reliant, achievement oriented, and cooperative with adults and peers. Children of authoritarian parents were not doing so well. They tended to be moody and seemingly unhappy much of the time, easily annoyed and unfriendly, relatively aimless, and generally not very pleasant to be around. Finally, children of permissive parents were often impulsive and aggressive, especially if they were boys. They tended to be bossy and self-centered, lacking in self-control, and quite low in independence and achievement.

Do children of authoritarian or permissive parents eventually "outgrow" whatever shortcomings they displayed as preschoolers? Seeking to answer this question, Baumrind followed up on her child participants when they were 8 to 9 years old. As we see in the accompanying table, children of authoritative parents were still relatively high in both cognitive competencies (that is, showing originality in thinking, having high achievement motivation, liking intellectual challenges) and social skills (for example, being sociable and outgoing, participating actively and showing leadership in group activities), whereas children of authoritarian parents were generally average to below average in cognitive and social skills, and children of permissive parents were relatively unskilled in both areas. Indeed, the strengths of children exposed to authoritative parenting were still evident in adolescence: compared to teenagers raised by either permissive or authoritarian parents, those raised by authoritative parents were relatively confident, achievement oriented, and socially skilled, and they tended to stay clear of drug use and other problem behaviors (Baumrind, 1991). The link between authoritative parenting and positive developmental outcomes seems to hold for all racial and ethnic groups studied to date in the United States (Glasgow et al., 1997; Steinberg et al., 1994) and in a variety of different cultures as well (Chen et al., 1998; Scott, Scott, & McCabe, 1991).

Relationships between Child-Rearing Patterns and Developmental Outcomes in Middle Childhood and Adolescence

Child-rearing pattern	Outcomes: Childhood	Outcomes: Adolescence
Authoritative	High cognitive and social competencies	High self-esteem, excellent social skills, strong moral/prosocial concern, high academic achievement
Authoritarian	Average cognitive and social competencies	Average academic performance and social skills; more conforming than adolescents of permissive parents
Permissive	Low cognitive and social competencies	Poor self-control and academic performance; more drug use than adolescents of authoritative or authoritarian parents

Sources: Baumrind, 1977, 1991; Steinberg et al., 1994.

research clearly indicates, authoritative parenting is associated with many positive outcomes. The research is limited, however, because none of the participants in the samples exhibited uninvolved parenting. Research investigating parents who are uninvolved suggests that this may be the least successful style of parenting. For example, by age 3, children of uninvolved parents are already relatively high in aggression and such externalizing behaviors as temper tantrums (Miller et al., 1993). Furthermore, they tend to be disruptive and perform very poorly in the classroom later in childhood (Eckenrode, Laird, & Doris, 1993; Kilgore, Snyder, & Lentz, 2000). These children often become hostile, selfish, and rebellious adolescents who lack meaningful long-range goals and are prone to commit such antisocial and delinquent acts as alcohol and drug abuse, sexual misconduct, truancy, and a wide variety of criminal offenses (Kurdek & Fine, 1994; Patterson, Reid, & Dishion, 1992; Pettit et al., 2001). In effect, these youngsters have neglectful (or even "detached") parents whose actions (or lack thereof) seem to be saying "I don't care about you or about what you do"—a message that undoubtedly breeds resentment and willingness to strike back at these aloof, uncaring adversaries or at other authority figures.

Authoritative parenting is consistently associated with positive social, emotional, and intellectual outcomes. There are probably several reasons for this. First, authoritative parents are warm and accepting—they communicate a sense of caring concern that may motivate their children to comply with the directives they receive in a way that children of more aloof and demanding (authoritarian) parents are not. Then there is the issue of how control is exercised. Unlike the authoritarian parent who sets inflexible standards and dominates the child, allowing little if any freedom of expression, the authoritative parent exercises control in a rational way, carefully explaining his or her point of view, while also considering the child's viewpoint. Demands that come from a warm, accepting parent and that appear to be fair and reasonable rather than arbitrary and dictatorial are likely to elicit committed compliance rather than complaining or defiance (Kochanska, 2002). Finally, authoritative parents are careful to tailor their demands to the child's ability to regulate his or her own conduct. In other words, they set standards that children can realistically achieve and allow the child some freedom, or autonomy, in deciding how best to comply with these expectations. This kind of treatment carries a most important message—something like "You are a capable human being whom I trust to be self-reliant and accomplish important objectives." Of course, we've seen in earlier chapters that feedback of this sort fosters the growth of self-reliance, achievement motivation, and high self-esteem in childhood. It is the kind of support that adolescents need to feel comfortable about exploring various roles and ideologies to forge a personal identity. (See the Box on p. 604 for more details on parenting adolescents.)

In sum, it appears that authoritative parenting—warmth combined with moderate and rational parental control—is the parenting style most consistently associated with positive developmental outcomes. Children apparently need love *and* limits—a set of rules that help them to structure and evaluate their conduct. Without such guidance, they may not learn self-control and may become quite selfish, unruly, and lacking in clear achievement goals, particularly if their parents are also aloof or uncaring (Steinberg et al., 1994). But if they receive too much guidance and are hemmed in by inflexible restrictions, they may have few opportunities to become self-reliant and may lack confidence in their own decision-making abilities (Grolnick & Ryan, 1989; Steinberg et al., 1994).

Behavioral Control versus Psychological Control

Brian Barber and his associates (Barber, 1996; Barber, Olsen, & Shagle, 1994) raise another important issue about parental exercise of control that is not captured completely by classifying parents as authoritative, authoritarian, permissive, or uninvolved. They point out that parents may differ in their exercise of **behavioral control**—regulating the child's conduct through firm but reasonable discipline and monitoring his or her activities, such as withholding privileges, grounding, or taking away toys for misbehavior.

behavioral control
attempts to regulate a child's or an adolescent's conduct through firm discipline and monitoring of his or her conduct.

APPLYING RESEARCH TO YOUR LIFE

Renegotiating the Parent-Child Relationship During Adolescence

One of the most important developmental tasks that adolescents face is to achieve a mature and healthy sense of *autonomy*—the capacity to make one's own decisions and to manage life tasks without being overly dependent on other people. If adolescents are to "make it" as adults, they cannot be rushing home for loving hugs after every little setback. Nor can they continue to rely on parents to get them to work on time or to remind them of their duties and obligations.

So what happens within the family system as children mature and begin to act more autonomously? Sparks fly! In cultures as diverse as China and the United States, conflicts between parents and children about self-governance issues become much more common early in adolescence and gradually decline in frequency (though not necessarily in intensity) throughout the teenage years (Laursen, Coy, & Collins, 1998; Yau & Smetana, 1996; in press). These squabbles, which occur about equally as often in families that have immigrated from collectivist cultures as in European American homes (see Fuligni, 1998), are usually neither prolonged nor severe, often centering around such issues as the adolescent's physical appearance, her choice of friends, or her neglect of schoolwork and household chores. And much of the friction stems from the different perspectives that parents and adolescents adopt. Parents view conflicts through a moral or *social-conventional* lens, feeling that they have a responsibility to monitor and regulate their child's conduct, whereas the adolescent, locked in his quest for autonomy, views his nagging parents as infringing on *personal* rights and choices (Smetana & Daddis, 2002). As teenagers continue to assert themselves and parents slowly loosen the reins, the parent-child relationship normally evolves from an enterprise in which the parent was dominant to one in which parents and adolescents are on more equal footing (Steinberg, 2002). Yet, Asian American parents tend to exert their authority far longer than European American parents (Greenberger & Chen, 1996; Yau & Smetana, 1996), a practice that often bothers and may depress some Asian American adolescents (Greenberger & Chen, 1996; Zhou & Bangston, 1998).

Researchers once believed that the most adaptive route to establishing autonomy was for adolescents to separate from parents by cutting the emotional cords. Indeed, teenagers who perceive their relationships with parents to be very conflictual and nonsupportive do appear to be better adjusted when they distance themselves a bit from their families and can gain the support of a teacher, a "Big Brother," or another adult mentor from outside the home (Fuhrman & Holmbeck, 1995; Rhodes, Grossman, & Resch, 2000). Yet adolescents who are warmly received at home would be ill-advised to "cut the emotional cords." Securely attached adolescents feel freer to disagree with parents, take independent stands, and become autonomous, without worrying about losing parental warmth and affection (Allen et al., 2003). Those adolescents who are best adjusted overall have maintained a close attachment to the parents, even as they gained autonomy and prepared to leave the nest (Beyers & Goossens, 1999; Steinberg, 2002). So autonomy *and* attachment, or independence *and* interdependence, are most desirable.

Encouraging Autonomy

Adolescents are most likely to become appropriately autonomous, achievement-oriented, and otherwise well adjusted if their parents recognize and acknowledge their greater need for autonomy and gradually loosen the reins. A good deal of research indicates that parents should consistently enforce a well reasoned set of rules while involving their teenagers in discussions and decisions about self-governance issues, monitoring their comings and goings, going easy on the guilt trips (or other forms of psychological control), and continuing to be warm and supportive, even in the face of inevitable conflicts that arise (Barber & Harmon, 2002; Steinberg, 2002). Does this parenting style sound familiar? It should, for this winning combination of parental acceptance and a pattern of flexible **behavioral control** that is neither too lax nor overly restrictive is an *authoritative* approach that is consistently associated with healthy developmental outcomes in many contexts. Indeed, adolescents treated this way often interpret parents' questions about their activities and whereabouts as a sign of caring, thereby preventing parents from having to badger them or snoop in order to know what they are doing (Kerr & Stattin, 2000). It is mainly when parents resist a teenager's push for autonomy and become overly controlling or overly permissive and uninvolved that adolescents are likely to experience personal distress and rebel, volunteering little information about their activities and eventually getting into trouble (Barber & Harmon, 2002; Kerr & Stattin, 2000; Laird et al., 2003). Of course, we must remind ourselves that socialization within the family is a matter of reciprocal influence, and that it may be much easier for a parent to respond authoritatively to a responsible, levelheaded adolescent than to one who is rude, hostile, and unruly.

In sum, conflicts and power struggles are an almost inevitable consequence of an adolescent's quest for autonomy. Yet, most teenagers and their parents are able to resolve these differences while maintaining positive feelings for one another as they renegotiate their relationship so that it becomes more equal (Furman & Buhrmester, 1992). As a result, young autonomy seekers become more self-reliant while also developing a more "friendlike" attachment to their parents.

psychological control
attempts to regulate a child's or an adolescent's conduct by such psychological tactics as withholding affection and/or inducing shame or guilt.

They may also differ in exercise of **psychological control**—attempts to influence a child's or adolescent's behavior by such psychological means as withholding affection or inducing shame or guilt.

Based on research we've covered throughout the text, you can probably guess which form of control is associated with more positive developmental outcomes. Parents who rely on firm behavioral control without often resorting to psychological guilt trips tend to have well-behaved children and adolescents who do not become involved in deviant peer activities and generally stay out of trouble. Heavy use of psychological control (or high levels of *both* behavioral and psychological control) are often associated with such poor developmental outcomes as anxiety and depression, affiliation with deviant peers, and antisocial conduct in adolescence (Barnes et al., 2000; Galambos, Barker, & Almeida, 2003; Pettit et al., 2001). These outcomes may reflect the findings that parents who use behavioral control have generally displayed a pattern of supportive but firm guidance, whereas those who rely heavily on psychological control use harsh discipline and attempts to thwart the child's autonomy (Barber & Harmon, 2002; Pettit et al., 2001). It may be difficult, indeed, to feel very autonomous, self-confident, and self-reliant when psychologically controlling parents are often sending the message that "you are loathful or shameful for ignoring me and behaving inappropriately"—a message that may depress the child or push her away, often into the arms of a deviant peer group.

Parent Effects or Child Effects?

parental effects model
model of family influence in which parents (particularly mothers) are believed to influence their children rather than vice versa.

child effects model
model of family influence in which children are believed to influence their parents rather than vice versa.

Social-developmentalists have long been guided by a **parent effects model**, which assumes that influences in families run primarily one way, from parent to child. Proponents of this viewpoint would claim that authoritative parenting causes positive developmental outcomes. On the other hand, a **child effects model** of family influences claims that children have a major influence on their parents. Proponents of this viewpoint claim that authoritative parenting looks so adaptive because easygoing, manageable, and competent children enable their parents to become more authoritative.

Longitudinal studies of early parental control strategies used by mothers with their 1½- to 3-year-olds support the parental-effects hypothesis. Specifically, authoritative mothers who insisted that their children perform competent actions (or *do*'s) and who dealt firmly but patiently with noncompliance had toddlers who became more compliant over time and displayed few problem behaviors. Authoritarian mothers whose demands emphasized *don'ts* (don't touch, don't yell) and who used arbitrary, power-assertive control strategies had children who were less compliant and cooperative, and who displayed an increase in problem behaviors over time (Crockenberg & Litman, 1990; Kuczynski & Kochanska, 1995).

In support of the child effects model, it is also true that extremely stubborn and impulsive children who show little self-control do tend to elicit more coercive forms of parenting (Kuczynski & Kochanska, 1995; Stoolmiller, 2001). These children may eventually wear their parents out, causing them to become more lax, less affectionate, and possibly even hostile and uninvolved (Lytton, 1990; Stoolmiller, 2001).

transactional model
model of family influences in which parent and child are believed to influence each other reciprocally.

Today, most developmentalists favor a **transactional model** of family influence in which socialization is viewed as a matter of reciprocal influence (Collins et al., 2000; Papp, Goeke-Morey, & Cummings, 2004). Longitudinal studies generally imply that patterns of parenting influence children more than children influence parenting (Crockenberg & Litman, 1990; Scaramella et al., 2002; Wakschlag & Hans, 1999). Yet, the transactional model recognizes that (1) children can and often do affect their parents, for better or worse (Cook, 2001), and (2) we simply cannot take for granted, as John Watson (1928) proclaimed, that parents are almost solely responsible for determining whether their children turn out good or bad.

Social Class and Ethnic Variations in Child Rearing

Associations between authoritative parenting and healthy psychological development have been found in many cultures and subcultures. Yet, people from different social strata and ethnic backgrounds face different kinds of problems, pursue different goals, and adopt different values about what it takes to adapt to their environments. These ecological considerations often affect their approaches to child rearing. Let's take a look.

Social Class Differences in Child Rearing

Compared to middle-class parents, economically disadvantaged and working-class parents tend to (1) stress obedience and respect for authority; (2) be more restrictive and authoritarian, using more power-assertive discipline; (3) reason with their children less frequently; and (4) show less warmth and attention (Maccoby, 1980; McLoyd, 1998).

These class-linked differences in parenting have been observed in many cultures and across racial and ethnic groups in the United States (Maccoby, 1980). However, we should keep in mind that what we are talking about here are *group trends* rather than absolute contrasts: some middle-class parents are highly restrictive, power-assertive, and aloof in their approach to child rearing, whereas many economically disadvantaged and working-class parents are less restrictive, power-assertive, and more involved in child rearing (Kelly, Power, & Wimbush, 1992; Laosa, 1981).

Undoubtedly, many factors contribute to general trends in social-class differences in child rearing, and economic considerations seem to head the list. Vonnie McLoyd (1989, 1998), for example, claims that economic hardship creates its own psychological distress—a most pervasive discomfort about life's conditions that makes economically disadvantaged adults more edgy and irritable. These distressed adults are more vulnerable to all negative life events (including the daily hassles associated with child rearing). These conditions diminish their capacity to be warm, supportive parents who are highly involved in their children's lives (Parke et al., 2004).

Rand Conger and his associates (1992, 1995, 2002; see also Mistry et al., 2002) offered support for this "economic distress" hypothesis by finding clear links between family economic hardships, nonnurturant/uninvolved parenting, and poor child-rearing outcomes. The chain of events, shown in Figure 15.3, goes like this: parents who are experiencing economic pressure, or feeling that they cannot cope with their financial problems, tend to become depressed, which increases marital conflict. Marital conflict, in turn, disrupts each parent's ability to be a supportive, involved parent. Meanwhile, their children and adolescents often react negatively to the marital strife and the insensitive parenting they receive, experiencing a loss of *emotional security*. This contributes to such child and adolescent problems as low self-esteem, poor school performance, poor peer relations, and such problem behaviors as depression, hostility, and antisocial conduct (see Davies & Cummings, 1998). These child adjustment problems that nonnurtant/coercive parenting help to create may further exasperate parents, causing them to back away and become even less nurturant and involved in the lives of their children (Rueter & Conger, 1998; Vuchinich, Bank, & Patterson, 1992).

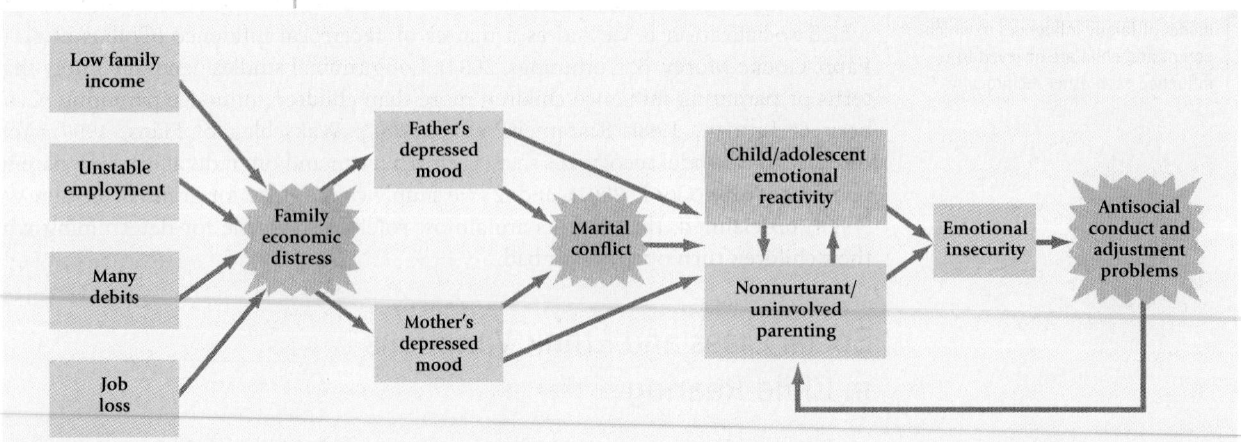

Figure 15.3 A model of the relationships among family economic distress, patterns of parenting, and child/adolescent adjustment. *Adapted from "A Family Process Model of Economic Hardship and Adjustment of Early Adolescent Boys," by R. D. Conger, K. J. Conger, G. H. Elder, Jr., F. O. Lorenz, R. L. Simons, & L. B. Whitbeck, 1992,* Child Development, 63, 526–541. *Copyright © 1992 by the Society for Research in Child Development, Inc.*

family distress model
Conger's model of how economic distress affects family dynamics and developmental outcomes.

Families living below the poverty line are especially inclined to experience all the maladaptive family dynamics outlined in Conger's **family distress model**, and the deeper the poverty and the longer it lasts, the less favorable the prognosis for developing children and adolescents (Duncan & Brooks-Gunn, 1997, 2000). Of course, we should keep in mind that many, many low-income adults are able to cope with their problems and parent quite effectively, particularly if their economic and/or marital distresses are not prolonged, they feel optimistic and highly efficacious about parenting, and they receive emotional and parenting support from kin, friends, and other adults living outside the home (Ackerman et al., 1999; Brody et al., 2002; Livner, Brooks-Gunn, & Kohen, 2002). However, it appears that Maccoby and McLoyd were quite correct in assuming that economic hardships are a very important contributor to the relatively aloof and coercive style of parenting often observed in low-income, economically distressed families.

Another explanation for the link between social class and parenting styles focuses on the skills needed by workers in white-collar and blue-collar jobs (Arnett, 1995; Kohn, 1979). A large percentage of lower-socioeconomic-status (SES) and working-class breadwinners are blue-collar workers who must please a supervisor and defer to his or her authority. So many lower-income parents may emphasize obedience and respect for authority because these are precisely the attributes they view as critical for success in the blue-collar economy. White-collar workers need different skills to succeed. Middle- and upper-class parents may reason and negotiate more with their children while emphasizing individual initiative, curiosity, and creativity because these are the skills, attributes, and abilities that matter in their own occupations as business executives, white-collar workers, or professionals (Greenberger, O'Neil, & Nagel, 1994). Nevertheless, as described in the Box on p. 608, affluence and upper-class standing are not always associated with positive developmental outcomes.

Ethnic Variations in Child Rearing

Parents of different ethnicities may also hold distinct child-rearing beliefs and values that are products of their cultural backgrounds or the ecological niches they occupy in society (MacPhee, Fritz, & Miller-Heyl, 1996; McLoyd & Smith, 2002). For example, Native American and Hispanic parents, whose cultural backgrounds are more collectivistic and stress communal rather than individual goals, are more inclined than European American parents to maintain close ties to a variety of relatives. They also insist that their children display calm, proper, and polite behaviors and a strong respect for authority figures (particularly fathers), rather than independence and competitiveness (Harwood, Schoelmerich, Ventura-Cook, Schulze, & Wilson, 1996; MacPhee et al., 1996). Mexican American parents who speak Spanish and are experiencing considerable **acculturation stress** are more controlling than are European American parents (Ispa et al., 2004). But this highly controlling form of parenting, when combined with warmth and emotional support, can be adaptive because it gives their children few options about how to behave with a new cultural setting that may seem unusual and highly confusing to them (Hill, Bush, & Roosa, 2003).

acculturation stress
anxiety or uneasiness that new residents may feel upon attempting to assimilate a new culture and its traditions.

Asian and Asian American parents also tend to stress self-discipline and interpersonal harmony. They are even more rigidly controlling than parents of other ethnicities (Greenberger & Chen, 1996; Uba, 1994). Yet, this authoritarian parenting style may mean something quite different for children of East Asian ancestry than for European Americans. Ruth Chao (1994, 2001) notes, for example, that Chinese and Chinese American children perform very well in school despite the fact that their parents are highly authoritarian. In Chinese culture, parents believe that strictness is the best way to express love for children and train them properly. Children accept longstanding cultural values specifying that they obey elders and honor their families. Chinese American adolescents are involved in more family maintenance activities than children of other ethnicities. They are generally adept at balancing these family responsibilities with academic demands and peer group activities at little cost to their mental health (Fuligni, Yip, & Tseng, 2002). Thus, an "authoritarian" style that may be too controlling to work well for European Americans appears highly effective indeed in China (and among Asian immigrant families in the United States).

FOCUS ON RESEARCH Developmental Surprises from Affluent Parents

Luthar and Latendresse (2005) point out that although developmentalists have been studying the effects of social class and parenting on child development since the 1970s, we have mostly ignored one social class: that of the affluent or upper-middle class. They saw this neglect and began a research program to study affluent children in the early 1990s (e.g., Luthar & Becker, 2002; Luthar & D'Avanzo, 1999; Luthar & Latendresse, in press). Since then they have collected data on three large groups of children of the affluent living in the suburban United States. What they found is quite disturbing. We tend to assume that affluent families provide the best for their children and therefore the children grow up in the best of circumstances. This simply is not true.

Luthar and Latendresse compared three groups of children of the affluent with control groups of children living in low-SES homes in urban areas of the United States (characteristics of their samples are described in the accompanying table). They also compared the affluent children to national norms on variables for which data was available.

Even though upper-middle-class and affluent parents are more likely to use authoritative parenting styles, their children are not faring well. These rich kids are more depressed and anxious than national averages. They are more likely to smoke, drink alcohol, and do drugs than national averages. And these negative developmental outcomes begin to surface as early as the seventh grade! All the advantages available to them, compared to low-SES urban children, do not seem to make much of a difference because they are not significantly different than the urban children to whom they were compared on most developmental outcomes.

Luthar and Latendresse point to several parenting variables that appear to contribute to these poor outcomes for affluent children. They include an intense pressure to succeed academically, coupled with an emotional and literal distance from their parents. That is, the affluent parents are not home for their kids much of the time, and when they are home they continue to be preoccupied with their high-powered jobs instead of spending quality time with their children. Surprisingly, there were few differences between the very affluent and the low-SES families in many aspects of family life, including the children's not feeling closeness to either of their parents, and the families not having many dinners together.

What's more, it turns out that even though the affluent kids theoretically have access to expensive treatment centers for their substance abuse and antisocial behaviors, and to therapy for their clinical depression and anxiety, they are not as likely to receive that help as are lower-SES children. Luthar and Latenderesse attribute this to parents' denial or embarrassment, with affluent parents wanting to keep family problems within the family rather than to seek available help.

Clearly, this program of research has revealed an important, but overlooked, population of needy children. As developmentalists, we must not neglect these kids and assume that financial success and authoritative parenting always provide the best environment for children's development.

Characteristics of affluent families from research program

Sample	Number of participants	Minority ethnicity in sample	Participants eligible for free or reduced lunch in school	Median annual family income in the area (from census data)	Adults with graduate or professional degrees in the area (from census data)
Affluent Group 1	264	18	1	$80,000–$102,000	24–37
Low SES Group 1	224	87	86	$35,000	5
Affluent Group 2	302	8	3	$120,000	33
Affluent Group 3	314	7	3	$125,000	33
Low SES Group 2	300	80	79	$27,000	6

Adapted from Luthar & Latendresse, 2005.

It is difficult to summarize the diversity of child-rearing practices that characterize African American families. Research suggests that urban African American mothers (particularly if they are single and less educated) are inclined to demand strict obedience from their children and use coercive forms of discipline to ensure obedience (Kelley, Power, & Wimbush, 1992; Ogbu, 1994). Were we to quickly assume (as researchers did for years) that one particular pattern of parenting (authoritative) is superior to all others, then we might be tempted to conclude that the "no-nonsense" parenting often seen in African American families is maladaptive. Yet, this coercive and controlling pattern of parenting may actually be *highly adaptive* for many young mothers who lack caregiving support if it protects children who reside in dangerous neighborhoods from becoming victims of crime (Ogbu, 1994), or from associating with antisocial peers (Mason et al., 1996). In fact, use of spanking and other tactics does not foster heightened aggression and antisocial

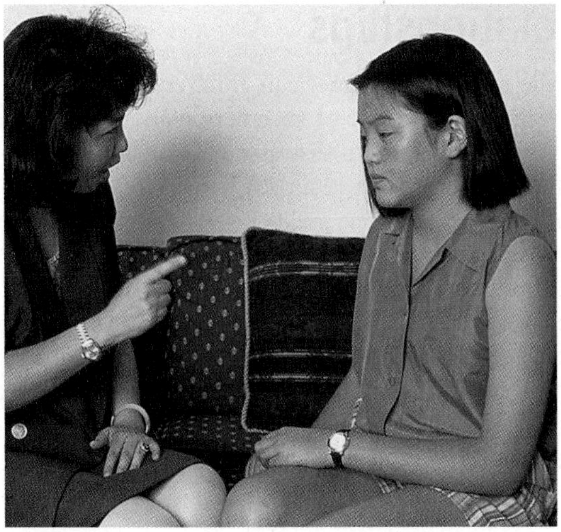
© Michael Newman/PhotoEdit

Asian Americans may be more authoritarian in parenting, but their children adapt well to this style.

conduct in African American youth in the same way it does for European Americans. It may be viewed by African American children as a sign of caring and concern rather than a symptom of parental hostility (Deater-Deckard & Dodge, 1997; Spieker et al., 1999). Furthermore, this no-nonsense parenting, which falls somewhere in between the authoritarian and authoritative styles, is adaptive in other ways, for African American children who are treated in this way tend to be cognitively and socially competent youngsters who display little anxiety, depression, or other internalizing disorders (Brody & Flor, 1998). They are also less inclined as adolescents to become (or to remain) involved in delinquent activities (Walker-Barnes & Mason, 2001).

Considering the findings we have reviewed, one must be careful *not* to assume that a "middle-class" pattern of authoritative parenting that seems to promote favorable outcomes in many contexts is necessarily the most adaptive pattern for all ecological niches. There simply is no single pattern of child rearing that is optimal for all cultures and subcultures. Louis Laosa (1981, p. 159) made this same point about 25 years ago, noting that "indigenous patterns of child care throughout the world represent largely successful adaptations to conditions of life that have long differed from one people to another. [Adults] are 'good [parents]' by the only relevant standards, those of their own culture."

CONCEPT CHECK 15.2 Understanding Parental Socialization

Check your understanding of the different styles of parenting, associated developmental outcomes, and social class and ethnic differences in parenting by answering the following questions. Answers appear in the Appendix.

True or False: Identify whether the following statements are true or false.

1. (T)(F) The authoritarian style of parenting is always the best for children's development.
2. (T)(F) Parents should rely on behavioral control rather than psychological control when socializing their children.
3. (T)(F) Longitudinal studies of $1\frac{1}{2}$- to 3-year-olds suggest that parents who use authoritarian styles have children who show an increase in problem behaviors over time.

Fill in the Blank: Complete the following sentences with the correct terms.

4. Lower-class parents are more likely to use ________ parenting styles.
5. Middle- and upper-class parents are more likely to use ________ parenting styles.
6. Asian American parents are more likely to use ________ parenting styles.

Multiple Choice: Select the correct answer for each question.

_____ 7. Which model of influence do most contemporary developmental psychologists adopt?
a. child effects model
b. parent effects model
c. interaction model
d. transactional model

_____ 8. Dr. Jones argues that authoritative parents are able to adopt this style because their children are easygoing and manageable. Dr. Jones is endorsing which model of family influence?
a. child effects model
b. parent effects model
c. interaction model
d. transactional model

_____ 9. Richard has lost his job and is worried about how to support his family of four children. He's found that he is having trouble getting along with his wife lately, and he just doesn't have the energy to devote to his children the way he used to. Richard's experience illustrates Conger's
a. authoritarian loss model
b. behavioral control model
c. economic distress model
d. transactional influence model

Short Answer: Briefly answer the following question.

10. Diagram the two dimensions of parenting and label the four parenting styles created when high and low levels of these dimensions are crossed.

The Influence of Siblings and Sibling Relationships

Although families are getting smaller, the majority of American children still grow up with at least one sibling, and there is certainly no shortage of speculation about the roles that brothers and sisters play in a child's life. Many parents, distressed by the fighting and bickering that their children display, often fear that such rivalrous behavior will undermine the growth of children's prosocial concern and their ability to get along with others. At the same time, a popular view is that only children are likely to be lonely, overindulged "brats" who would profit both socially and emotionally from having siblings to teach them that they are not nearly as "special" as they think (Falbo, 1992).

Although rivalries among siblings are certainly commonplace, we will see that siblings can play some very positive roles in a child's life, often serving as caregivers, teachers, playmates, and confidants. We will also see that only children may not be as disadvantaged by their lack of sibling relationships as people have commonly assumed.

Changes in the Family Systems When a New Baby Arrives

Judy Dunn and Carol Kendrick (1982; see also Dunn, 1993) have studied how firstborn children adapt to a new baby, and the account they provide is not an entirely cheerful

"I hope you kept the box it came in."

one. After the baby arrives, mothers typically devote less warm and playful attention to their older child. The older child may respond to this perceived "neglect" by becoming difficult and disruptive and less securely attached. These events are particularly likely if the older child is 2 years of age or older and can more readily appreciate that an "exclusive" relationship with caregivers has been undermined by the baby's birth (Teti et al., 1996). Thus, older children often resent losing the mother's attention, may harbor animosities toward the baby for stealing it, and their own difficult behavior may make matters worse by alienating their parents.

sibling rivalry
the spirit of competition, jealousy, and resentment that may arise between two or more siblings.

So, **sibling rivalry**—a spirit of competition, jealousy, or resentment between siblings—often begins as soon as a younger brother or sister arrives. How can it be minimized? The adjustment process is easier if the firstborn had secure relationships with both parents before the baby arrived and continues to enjoy close ties afterward (Dunn & Kendrick, 1982; Volling & Belsky, 1992). Parents are advised to continue to provide love and attention to their older children and maintain their normal routines as much as possible. It also helps to encourage older children to become aware of the baby's needs and assist in the care of their new brother or sister (Dunn & Kendrick, 1982; Howe & Ross, 1990).

Sibling Relationships Over the Course of Childhood

Fortunately, most older siblings adjust fairly quickly to having a new brother or sister, becoming much less anxious and less inclined to display the problem behaviors that they showed early on. But even in the best of sibling relationships, conflict is normal. Judy Dunn (1993) reports that the number of minor skirmishes between very young siblings can range as high as 56 per hour! These sibling squabbles tend to center heavily on personal possessions and scripts to be followed during pretend play (Howe et al., 2002; McGuire et al., 2000). The squabbles decline with age and are often resolved in constructive ways, particularly if siblings view their relationships as positive rather than negative (Ram & Ross, 2001). There are some reliable differences in the behavior of older and younger siblings, with older siblings often becoming more domineering and aggressive, and younger siblings more compliant (Abramovitch et al., 1986; Erel, Margolin, & John, 1998). At the same time, older siblings also initiate helpful, playful, and other prosocial behaviors, a finding that may reflect the pressure parents place on them to demonstrate their maturity by caring for a younger brother or sister (Brody, 1998).

In general, siblings are much more likely to get along if their parents get along (Dunn, 1993; Reese-Weber, 2000). Marital conflict and dissatisfaction is a very good predictor of jealousy and antagonistic sibling interactions. This is especially true if the older sibling has a shaky, insecure relationship with either or both parents, and if the parents rely heavily on power assertive discipline (Erel, Margolin, & John, 1998; Volling, McElwain, & Miller, 2002). Marital conflict may put children on edge emotionally and contribute directly to emotional insecurity (Davies & Cummings, 1998). Parental use of power assertion may communicate to a more powerful older sibling that forceful strategies are the way one deals with people (particularly smaller, less powerful ones) who displease them.

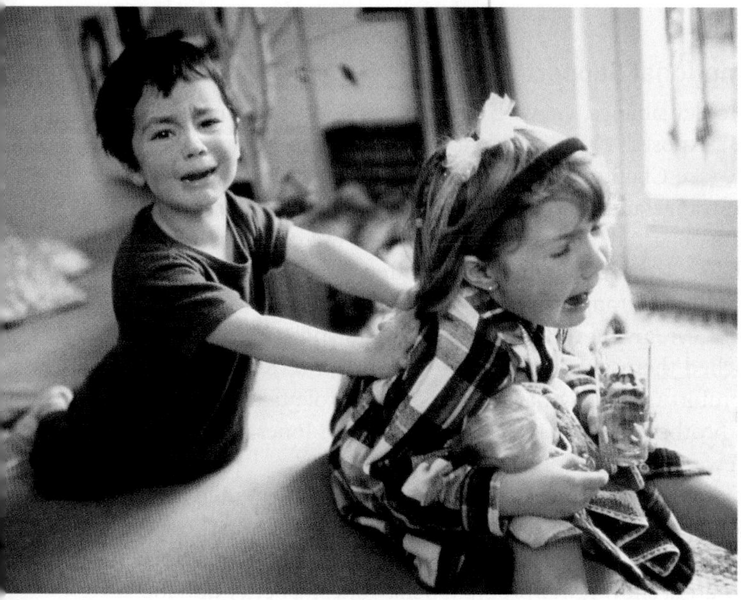
Ursula Markus/Photo Researchers Inc.

Coercive and rivalrous conduct between siblings is a normal aspect of family life.

Sibling relationships are friendlier if parents make an effort to monitor their children's activities. Unfortunately, normal conflicts among young, preschool children can escalate into serious incidents that become habitual if parents often let them pass without intervening (Kramer, Perozynski, &

Chung, 1999). In fact, intense, destructive sibling battles that occur against a backdrop of uninvolved parenting are a very strong predictor of aggressive, antisocial behavior outside the home (Garcia et al., 2000).

Finally, sibling relationships tend to be less conflictual when mothers and fathers respond warmly and sensitively to *all* their children and do not consistently favor one child over the other (Boyle et al., 2004; Brody, 1998; McHale et al., 2000). Younger siblings are particularly sensitive to unequal treatment, often reacting negatively and displaying adjustment problems if they perceive that the older sibling is favored by parents. It is not that older siblings are unaffected by differential treatment. Because they are older, they are usually better able to understand that siblings may have different needs and that unequal treatment may be justified, even if that means that parents may sometimes favor a younger sibling in certain respects (Kowal & Kramer, 1997).

But it is easy to overemphasize sibling rivalries. Grade school children tend to value their relationships with siblings, even though they have many conflicts with them (Furman & Buhrmester, 1985). Adolescents often view siblings as intimate associates—people to whom they can turn for companionship and emotional support, despite the fact that relations with them have often been stormy (Buhrmester & Furman, 1990; Furman & Buhrmester, 1992). So why do siblings value a relationship that has often been conflictual? The observational record provides one answer: Brothers and sisters often do nice things for one another and resolve disputes amicably, and these prosocial acts are typically much more common than hateful, rivalrous, or destructive conduct (see, for example, Abramovitch et al., 1986; Ram & Ross, 2001).

Positive Contributions of Sibling Relationships

What positive roles might siblings play in one another's lives? One important contribution that older siblings make is to provide *caretaking* services for younger brothers and sisters. A survey of child-rearing practices in 186 societies found that older children were the *principal* caregivers for infants and toddlers in 57 percent of the groups studied (Weisner & Gallimore, 1977). Even in industrialized societies such as the United States, older siblings (particularly girls) are often asked to look after their younger brothers and sisters (Brody, 1998). Of course, their role as caregivers provides older children with opportunities to influence their younger siblings in many ways, by serving as their teachers, playmates, and advocates, and as important sources of emotional support.

Siblings as Providers of Emotional Support

Do infants become attached to older siblings, viewing them as providers of security? To find out, Robert Stewart (1983) exposed 10- to 20-month-old infants to a variation of Ainsworth's "Strange Situation" (see Chapter 11). Each infant was left with a 4-year-old sibling in a strange room that a strange adult soon entered. The infants typically showed signs of distress as their mothers departed, and they were wary in the company of the stranger. Stewart noted that these distressed infants would often approach their older brother or sister, particularly when the stranger first appeared. And most 4-year-olds offered some sort of comforting or caregiving to their baby brothers and sisters, particularly if they were securely attached themselves to their mothers (Teti & Ablard, 1989). Older siblings are also more comforting if they have developed the role-taking skills to understand why their younger brother or sister is distressed (Garner, Jones, & Palmer, 1994; Howe & Rinaldi, 2004; Stewart & Marvin, 1984).

As they mature, siblings may frequently protect and confide in each other, often more than they confide in parents (Howe et al., 2000). Siblings may draw strength from the support older siblings provide. For example, children with severe medical problems and those with an alcoholic or mentally ill parent show fewer problem behaviors and better developmental outcomes when their relations with siblings are solid and supportive (Vandell, 2000). A secure tie to a sibling also helps to minimize the anxiety and adjustment problems

© Dennis MacDonald/PhotoEdit

Older siblings often serve as teachers for their younger brothers and sisters.

that grade school children often display if they are ignored or rejected by their peers (Brody & Murry, 2001; East & Rook, 1992; Stormshak et al., 1996).

Siblings as Models and Teachers

In addition to the caretaking and emotional support they may provide, older siblings often teach new skills to younger brothers and sisters, either by modeling these competencies or by providing direct instruction (Brody et al., 2003). Even toddlers are quite attentive to older siblings, often choosing to imitate their behaviors as they actively participate with siblings at play, infant care, and other household routines (Maynard, 2002; see also Downey & Condron, 2004).

Younger children tend to admire their older siblings, who continue to serve as important models and tutors throughout childhood (Buhrmester & Furman, 1990). Given a problem to master, children are likely to learn more when they have an older sibling available to guide them than when they have access to an equally competent older peer (Azmitia & Hesser, 1993). Why? Because (1) older siblings feel a greater responsibility to teach if the pupil is a younger *sibling,* (2) they provide more detailed instructions and encouragement than older peers do, and (3) younger children are more inclined to seek the older sibling's guidance. This kind of informal instruction clearly pays off: when older siblings play school with younger brothers and sisters, teaching them such lessons as the ABCs, younger siblings have an easier time learning to read (Norman-Jackson, 1982). What's more, older siblings who often tutor younger ones may profit as well, for they score higher on tests of academic aptitude than peers who have not had these tutoring experiences (Paulhus & Shaffer, 1981; Smith, 1990).

Characteristics of Only Children

Are "only" children who grow up without siblings the spoiled, selfish, overindulged brats that people often presume them to be? Hardly! Two major reviews of hundreds of pertinent studies found that only children are (1) relatively high, on average, in self-esteem and achievement motivation, (2) more obedient and slightly more intellectually competent than children with siblings, and (3) likely to establish very good relations with peers (Falbo, 1992; Falbo & Polit, 1986).

These findings do not mean that parents who prefer to have only one child are different from those who have more children. For example, in 1979 the People's Republic of China implemented a one-child family policy in an attempt to control its burgeoning population. So regardless of the number of children parents may have wanted, most Chinese couples, in urban areas at least, have been limited to one child. Contrary to the fears of many critics, there is no evidence that China's one-child policy has produced a generation of spoiled, self-centered brats. Only children in China closely resemble only children in Western countries, scoring slightly higher than children with siblings on measures of intelligence and academic achievement and showing few meaningful differences in personality (Jaio, Ji, & Jing, 1996; Wang et al., 2000). In fact, only children in China actually report *less* anxiety and depression than children with siblings, a finding that may reflect China's social condemnation of multichild families and only children's tendency to taunt children with siblings with such remarks as "You shouldn't be here" or "Your parents should have only one child" (Yang et al., 1995).

So evidence from very different cultural settings suggests that only children are hardly disadvantaged by having no brothers and sisters. Apparently, many singletons are able to gain through their friendships and peer alliances whatever they may miss by not having siblings at home.

Diversity in Family Life

As we noted earlier in the chapter, modern families are so diverse today that the *majority* of children are growing up in dual-career, single-parent, or blended families that may be very different from the two-parent, single breadwinner family with two or more children that people often think of as the "typical" family unit. So let's examine some of these variations in family life and the effects they may have on developing children.

Adoptive Families

If one member of the pair is infertile, couples who hope to become parents often seek to adopt a child. Most adoptive parents develop secure emotional ties to their genetically unrelated adoptees (Levy-Shiff, Goldschmidt, & Har-Even, 1991; Stams, Juffer, & van Ijzendoorn, 2002). The sensitivity of care that parents provide predicts children's attachment classifications for adoptees in the same way that it does for biologically related children. This implies that an adult's desire to be a parent is much more important to a child's development than the adult's genetic ties to the child (Golombok et al., 1995).

Nevertheless, when infants and children experience abuse, neglect, and rejection prior to adoption, they may develop insecure, disorganized, or disordered attachment styles. They then carry these attachment difficulties into their adoptive homes (Howe, 2001; Rutter, 2000; Juffer et al., 2005.) Negative relational effects from such early attachment difficulties are positively correlated with the duration of mistreatment (Rutter, 2000; Howe, 2001). That is, the longer an adoptee spends in an abusive and rejecting environment prior to adoption, the more intransigent the negative attachment behaviors that arise due to the abuse. However, interactions with caring and sensitive adoptive parents can increase the attachment security of such children (Neil et al., 2003). In fact, interventions that promote caregiver sensitivity have been shown to increase security among previously abused children in adoptive and foster care situations (Juffer et al., 2005).

Even if adoptees have not been abused prior to their adoption, it is important to note that because adoptive parents and their children share no genes, the rearing environments adoptive parents provide may not be as closely compatible with an adoptee's own genetic predispositions as they are for a biological child. These environmental incompatibilities are coupled with the fact that many adoptees have been neglected or abused prior to their adoptions, or have other special needs (Kirchner, 1998). These disadvantages may help to explain why adoptees display more learning difficulties, emotional problems, and higher rates of delinquency than their nonadopted peers later in childhood and adolescence (Miller et al., 1993; Sharma, McGue, & Benson, 1998.)

However, the vast majority of adopted children are quite well adjusted (Stams, Juffer, & van Ijzendoorn, 2002) and typically fare much better in adoptive homes than in foster care, where their foster parents may not be very invested in them or their long-range prospects (Brodzinsky, Smith, & Brodzinsky, 1998; Miller et al., 2000). Even transracially adopted children from lower socioeconomic backgrounds usually fare quite well intellectually and academically, and often display healthy patterns of psychosocial adjustment, when raised in supportive, relatively affluent middle-class adoptive homes (Brodzinsky et al., 1987; DeBerry, Scarr, & Weinberg, 1996; Sharma, McGue, & Benson, 1998). So adoption is a great arrangement for most adoptive parents and their children.

Adoption practices in the United States are changing from a confidential system, in which the identities of the birth mother and adoptive parents are withheld from each other, to a more open system that allows for varying amounts of direct or indirect contact between birth mothers and members of adoptive families. Because adoptees are often curious about their biological origins and may be upset about the prospect of never knowing their birth parents, more open arrangements may prove beneficial to them. Indeed, research conducted in the United States and a variety of other countries reveals that children are both more curious and more satisfied with information about their biological roots when they could share information or even have contact with their birth mothers (see Leon, 2002, for a review). What's more, information about and contact with biological relatives typically help adoptees see that their adoptive parents are their "true" mothers and fathers and to think of their birth parents as "birthgivers" (Leon, 2002). So there is little evidence that providing information about birth parents will confuse children about the meaning of adoption or undermine their self-esteem, as some critics of open adoption policies had feared.

Donor Insemination (DI) Families

donor insemination
process by which a fertile woman conceives with the aid of sperm from an unknown donor.

Rather than adoption, some infertile couples choose to have children through **donor insemination** (DI)—a process by which a fertile woman conceives with the aid of sperm from an unknown donor. Several concerns have been raised about the creation of families in this way. For example, Burns (1990) argued that stresses associated with the couple's infertility may lead to dysfunctional patterns of parenting. Moreover, children conceived in this way do not have genetic ties to their fathers, who may be more distant and less nurturant than genetically related fathers, thus having a negative impact on a DI child's emotional well-being and other developmental outcomes (Turner & Coyle, 2000). Are there reasons for concern about the development of DI children?

Apparently not. In a 12-year longitudinal study conducted in England, Susan Golombok and her colleagues (2002) compared the developmental progress of children raised in DI families to that of adopted children and children raised by two biological parents. They found that the DI children at age 12 showed no more behavioral problems and were as well adjusted on measures of emotional development, scholastic progress, and peer relations as their adoptive or naturally conceived peers. Mothers of DI children were found to be warmer and more sensitive to their children's needs than mothers of adoptive or naturally conceived children. And although fathers of DI families were less involved in disciplining their children, they were no less involved in other aspects of parenting and were judged just as close to their children as adoptive or biological fathers. Although this is only one study of a relatively small sample of DI families, it was carefully conducted and suggests that couples who truly want to be parents and are comfortable with donor insemination need not to be concerned about adverse developmental outcomes in a child of theirs conceived in this way.

Gay and Lesbian Families

In the United States, several million gay men and lesbian women are parents, most through previous heterosexual marriages, although some have adopted children or conceived through donor insemination (Chan, Raboy, & Patterson, 1998; Flaks et al., 1995). Historically, many courts have been so opposed to the prospect of lesbian women and gay men raising children that they have denied the petitions of homosexual parents in child custody hearings solely on the basis of these parents' sexual orientations. Among the concerns people have are that gay and lesbian parents may be less mentally healthy or that they will molest their children. Another concern is that the children are at risk of being stigmatized by peers because of their parents' sexual orientations. But perhaps the greatest concern is the fear that children raised by gay or lesbian parents are likely to become gay or lesbian themselves (Bailey et al., 1995).

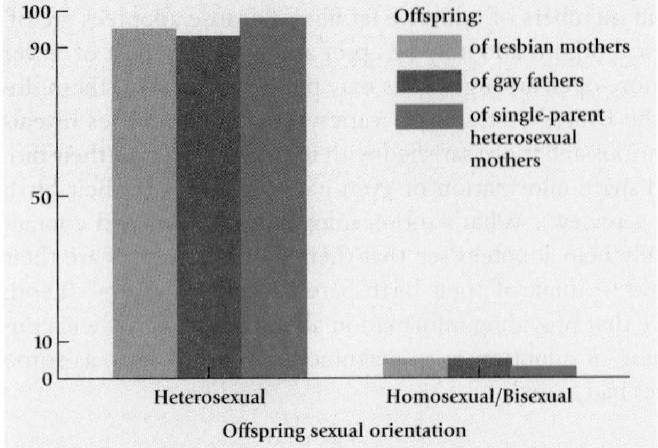

Figure 15.4 Sexual orientation of adult children raised by lesbian mothers, gay fathers, and single-parent heterosexual mothers. (Notice that children with homosexual parents are just as likely to display a heterosexual orientation as children raised by heterosexuals.) *Adapted from Bailey et al., 1995; Golombok & Tasker; 1996.*

Ample research suggests there is no basis for any of these speculations (MacCallum & Golombok, 2004; Wainright, Russell, & Patterson, 2004). As shown in Figure 15.4, more than 90 percent of adult children of lesbian mothers or gay fathers develop a heterosexual orientation—a figure that is not different from the percentages of heterosexuals raised by heterosexual parents. Furthermore, children of gay and lesbian parents are just as cognitively, emotionally, and morally mature, on average, and are otherwise as well adjusted as children of heterosexual parents (Chan, Raboy, & Patterson, 1998; Flaks et al., 1995; Golombok et al., 2003). And in respect to recent criticisms that children of gay and lesbian parents may be less appropriately gender typed (Stacey & Biblarz, 2001), Susan Golombok and her colleagues (2003) found only that boys from single-parent homes headed by mothers (the vast majority of whom were *heterosexual*) had less traditionally masculine activity preferences than boys raised by two parents, whether homosexual or heterosexual. Finally, gay fathers and lesbian mothers are every bit as knowledgeable about effective child rearing practices as heterosexual parents (Bigner & Jacobsen, 1989; Flaks et al., 1995), and partners of homosexual parents are usually attached to the children and assume caregiving responsibilities for their children.

In sum, there is no credible scientific evidence that would justify denying a person's rights of parenthood on the basis of his or her sexual orientation. Children raised in gay and lesbian families are virtually indistinguishable from those raised by heterosexual couples.

Family Conflict and Divorce

Earlier we noted that between 40 and 50 percent of today's marriages will end in divorce and more than half of all children born in the 1990s and 2000s will spend some time (about 5 years, on average) in a single-parent home—usually one headed by the mother (Hetherington, Bridges, & Insabella, 1998). What effects might a divorce have on developing children? As we address this issue, let's first note that divorce is *not* a singular life event. Instead, it represents a series of stressful experiences for the entire family that often begins with marital conflict before the actual separation and includes a multitude of life changes afterward. As Mavis Hetherington and Kathleen Camara (1984) see it, families must often cope with "the diminution of family resources, changes in residence, assumption of new roles and responsibilities, establishment of new patterns of [family] interaction, reorganization of routines . . . , and [possibly] the introduction of new relationships [that is, stepparent/child and stepsibling relationships] into the existing family" (p. 398).

Before the Divorce: Exposure to Marital Conflict

The period prior to divorce is often accompanied by a dramatic rise in family conflict that may include many heated verbal arguments and even physical violence between parents. How are children influenced by their exposure to marital conflict? A growing body of evidence indicates that they often become extremely distressed and that continuing conflict at home increases the likelihood that children will have hostile, aggressive interactions with siblings and peers (Cummings & Davies, 1994). Regular exposure to marital discord is a contributor to a number of other child and adolescent adjustment problems, including anxiety, depression, and externalizing conduct disorders (Davies & Cummings, 1998; Harold et al., 1997; Shaw, Winslow, & Flanagan, 1999). Marital discord can have *direct effects* on children and adolescents by putting them on edge emotionally and undermining the maturity of their behavior (Thompson, 2000). It can also have *indirect effects* by undermining parental acceptance/sensitivity and the quality of the parent-child relationship (Davies et al., 2003; Erel

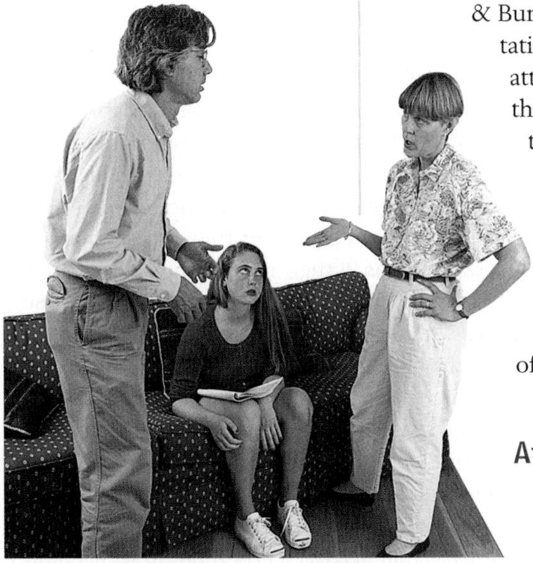

Youngsters who live in conflict-ridden nuclear families often suffer physically and emotionally. In the long run, children of divorce are usually better adjusted than those whose unhappily married parents stay together "for the sake of the children."

& Burman, 1995; Harold et al., 1997). Children with secure attachment representations cope somewhat better with parental conflict than those with insecure attachment representations (Davies & Forman, 2002). This may be because they feel less responsible for precipitating the conflict and/or less concerned that their parents will stop loving them (El-Sheikh & Harger, 2001; Grych et al., 2000; Grynch, Harold, & Miles, 2003). But conflict-ridden homes are not healthy contexts for child or adolescent development, and many family researchers now believe that children in strife-ridden homes will often fare better in the long run if their parents separate or divorce (Amato, Loomis, & Booth, 1995; Hetherington, Bridges, & Insabella, 1998). Nevertheless, divorce can be a highly unsettling life transition that often has its own effects on the well-being of all family members.

After the Divorce: Crisis and Reorganization

Most families going through a divorce experience a *crisis period* of a year or more in which the lives of all family members are seriously disrupted (Amato, 2000; Hetherington, Bridges, & Insabella, 1998). Typically, both parents experience emotional as well as practical difficulties. The mother, who obtains custody of any children in about 83 percent of divorcing families, may feel angry, depressed, lonely, or otherwise distressed, although often relieved as well. The father is also likely to be distressed, particularly if he did not seek the divorce and feels shut off from his children. Having just become single adults, both parents often feel isolated from former married friends and other bases of social support on which they relied when married. Divorced women with children usually face the added problem of getting by with less money—about 50 to 75 percent of the family income they had before, on average (Bianchi, Subaiya, & Kahn, 1997). And life may seem especially difficult if they must move to a lower-income neighborhood, and try to work and raise young children single-handedly (Emery & Forehand, 1994).

As you might expect, psychologically distressed adults do not make the best parents (Papp et al., 2004). Hetherington and her associates (Hetherington, Cox, & Cox, 1982; Hetherington & Kelly, 2002) found that custodial mothers, overwhelmed by responsibilities and by their own emotional reactions to divorce, often become edgy, impatient, and insensitive to their children's needs. As a result, they frequently begin to rely on coercive methods of child rearing. Divorced mothers often appear (to their children, at least) to have been transformed into more hostile, less caring parents (Fauber et al., 1990). Meanwhile, noncustodial fathers are likely to change in a different way, becoming somewhat overpermissive and indulging during visits with their children.

Children of divorce, who are often anxious, angry, or depressed by the family breakup, may react by becoming whiney and argumentative, disobedient, and disrespectful. Parent-child relationships during this crisis phase have been described as a vicious circle in which the child's emotional distress and problem behaviors and the adult's ineffective parenting styles feed on each other and make everyone's life unpleasant (Baldwin & Skinner, 1989). However, children's initial reactions to divorce vary somewhat as a function of their age and gender.

Younger, cognitively immature preschool and early grade-school children often display the most visible signs of distress as a divorce unfolds. They may not understand why their parents have divorced and are even inclined to feel guilty if they think they are somehow responsible for the breakup of their families (Hetherington, 1989). Older children and adolescents are better able to understand the personality conflicts and lack of caring that may lead distressed parents to divorce. However, they often remain highly distressed over their parent's divorce and may react by withdrawing from family members and becoming more involved in such undesirable activities as truancy, sexual misconduct, substance abuse, and other forms of delinquent behavior (Amato, 2000; Hetherington, Bridges, & Insabella, 1998). So even though they are better able to comprehend the reasons for the parents' divorce and to feel less responsible for having caused it, older children and adolescents seem to suffer no less than younger children (Hetherington & Clingempeel, 1992).

Although the finding is by no means universal, many investigators report that the impact of marital strife and divorce is more powerful and enduring for boys than for girls. Even before a divorce, boys are already displaying more overt behavioral problems than girls (Block, Block, & Gjerde, 1986, 1988). And at least two early longitudinal studies found that girls had largely recovered from their social and emotional disturbances 2 years after a divorce. However, boys, who had also improved dramatically over this same period, continued to show signs of emotional stress and problems in their relationships with parents, siblings, teachers, and peers (Hetherington, Cox, & Cox, 1982; Wallerstein & Kelly, 1980).

A word of caution on gender differences, however. Most early research focused on mother-headed families and *overt* problem behaviors that are easy to detect. Subsequent work suggests that boys may fare better when their fathers are the custodial parent (Amato & Keith, 1991; Clarke-Stewart & Hayward, 1996) and that girls in divorced families experience more *covert* distress than boys do, often becoming withdrawn or depressed rather than acting out their angers, fears, or frustrations (Chase-Lansdale, Cherlin, & Kiernan, 1995; Doherty & Needle, 1991). Also, a disproportionate number of girls from divorced families show precocious sexual activity early in adolescence and a persistent lack of self-confidence in their relationships with boys and men (Cherlin, Kiernan, & Chase-Lansdale, 1995; Ellis et al., 2003; Hetherington, Bridges, & Insabella, 1998). So divorce can strike hard at children of either gender, although it is likely to affect boys and girls in somewhat different ways.

Long-Term Reactions to Divorce

The vast majority of children and adolescents whose parents divorce eventually adjust to this family transition and display healthy patterns of psychological adjustment (Hetherington & Kelly, 2002). Nevertheless, even well-adjusted children of divorce may show some lingering after-effects. In one longitudinal study children from divorced families were still very negative in the assessment of the impact of divorce on their lives when interviewed more than 20 years after the divorce (Wallerstein & Lewis, as cited by Fernandez, 1997). A common source of dissatisfaction is a perceived loss of closeness with their parents, especially with fathers (Emery, 1999; Woodward, Fergusson, & Belsky, 2000). Another interesting long-term reaction is that adolescents from divorced families are more likely than those from nondivorced families to fear that their own marriages will be unhappy (Franklin, Janoff-Bulman, & Roberts, 1990). There may well be some basis for this concern, for adults whose parents divorced are more likely than adults from intact families to experience an unhappy marriage and a divorce themselves (Amato, 1996).

In sum, divorce tends to be a most unsettling and troubling life event—one that few children feel very positive about, even after 20 years have elapsed. But despite the gloomy portrait of divorce we have painted here, there are more encouraging messages. First, researchers are consistently finding that children in *stable,* single-parent (or stepparent) homes are usually better adjusted than those who remain in conflict-ridden two-parent families. In fact, many of the behavior problems that children display after a divorce are actually evident well *before* the divorce and may often be more closely related to long-standing family conflict than to the divorce itself (Amato & Booth, 1996; Shaw, Winslow, & Flanagan, 1999). Take away the marital discord and the breakdown in parenting often associated with divorce and the experience, while always stressful, need not always be damaging. So today's conventional wisdom holds that unhappily married couples who have unreconcilable differences might well *divorce* for the good of the children. That is, children are likely to benefit if the ending of a stormy marriage ultimately reduces the stress they experience and enables either or both parents to be more sensitive and responsive to their needs (Booth & Amato, 2001; Hetherington, Bridges, & Insabella, 1998). A second encouraging message is that not all divorcing families experience all the difficulties we have described. In fact, some adults and children manage this transition quite well and may even grow psychologically as a result of it.

CONCEPT CHECK 15.3 Understanding Sibling Influences and Diversity in Family Life

Check your understanding of the influences of siblings on child development and the influence of diverse family systems on child development by answering the following questions. Answers appear in the Appendix.

True or False: Identify whether the following statements are true or false.

1. (T)(F) Older siblings who tutor or instruct their younger siblings often benefit with increased academic aptitude.
2. (T)(F) Children who have no siblings are often developmentally disadvantaged compared to children who have siblings.
3. (T)(F) Conflict between siblings is a sign of a dysfunctional family and often predicts poor developmental outcomes for the children involved.
4. (T)(F) Research supports the conclusion that a parent's desire to be a parent is more important to a child's developmental outcome than the parent's genetic relationship to the child.

Fill in the Blank: Complete the following sentences with the correct terms.

5. When most adopted children are given the opportunity to meet their birth mothers, they come to believe that their adoptive mothers are their ________ mothers and their birth mothers are ________.
6. The process by which a fertile woman conceives a child with the aid of sperm from a donor is known as ________.
7. Contemporary wisdom suggests that unhappily married couples with irreconcilable differences should ________ for the good of their children.

Multiple Choice: Select the correct answer for each question.

_____ 8. Which one of the following is *not* a reason younger siblings learn more from an older sibling than from an equally competent older peer?

   a. Older siblings feel a greater responsibility to teach younger siblings than unrelated younger peers.
   b. Older siblings provide more detailed instructions than do older peers.
   c. Siblings often are better able to understand each other because they often develop a unique language that older peers do not understand.
   d. Younger siblings are more likely to accept instruction from older siblings than from older peers.

_____ 9. If possible, a child should be raised by heterosexual parents rather than homosexual parents because

   a. Children raised by homosexual parents are less cognitively mature.
   b. Children raised by homosexual parents are less socially mature.
   c. Children raised by homosexual parents are more likely to become homosexual themselves.
   d. None of the above. In fact, there is no scientific evidence to suggest any differences in child outcomes between homosexual and heterosexual parents.

Short Answer: Briefly answer the following question with the material you've learned from this chapter.

10. Describe several short-term and long-term effects of parents' divorce on the development of boys and girls.

Applying Developmental Themes to Family Life, Parenting, and Siblings

The four themes that we have been examining throughout this book (the active child, nature and nurture interactions, quantitative and qualitative changes, and the holistic nature of development) become harder to consider when we change our focus from the individual child to the context in which the child develops. That is our challenge as we stop to consider how these themes might play out in the family, in parenting, and in sibling relationships. But developmental psychologists are concerned with these themes in all aspects of development, and we can see their influence even when adopting a contextual perspective.

For example, in studying the family as a social system, developmentalists believe that each person in the system and each relationship between people in the system has an effect on the development of all other people and relationships within the system. Specifically, we saw that modern developmentalists adopt a transactional view of family effects, incorporating both parent-to-child effects and child-to-parent (or "active child") effects, as well as more complex interactions and directions of influence.

Much of the material we covered in this chapter focused on nurture effects in development: how the family environment, parenting styles, and sibling interactions affected children's development. It is true that when we delve into more social and contextual aspects of developmental psychology we see more influences of nurture on development. Nevertheless, there were also some hints of nature effects as well. For example, we discussed theoretical positions arguing that children's temperament might affect the parenting styles used by their parents. Conversely, we reviewed evidence that nature may not play a significant role in parenting when we found that, for adoptive and donor insemination parents, the desire to be a parent is a stronger force than a genetic relation between parent and child in providing positive parenting techniques and positive child development outcomes.

There was little in this chapter relating to quantitative and qualitative changes in development. We did review evidence that parenting styles and sibling relationships change as children become adolescents, but other developmental themes were more relevant to these topics.

Our final theme, the holistic nature of development, was predominant in this chapter. We saw that family systems, parenting styles, and sibling interactions all affect children's cognitive, social, and even biological development. In short, children thrive when the context of development (in terms of family life) is positive and supportive. This is the kind of research that can be used to make a real difference in the lives of children.

SUMMARY

■ **Socialization** is the process by which children acquire the beliefs, attitudes, values, and behaviors considered appropriate in their society.

Understanding of the Family

■ The **family** is the primary agent of socialization.

■ Whether a **traditional nuclear family** or an **extended family,** families are best viewed as **social systems.**

■ Children fare better when adult members of the family can effectively **coparent,** mutually supporting each other's parenting efforts.

■ Families are also developing social systems embedded in community and cultural contexts that affect how family functions are carried out.

Parental Socialization During Childhood and Adolescence

■ Parents differ along two broad child-rearing dimensions—**acceptance/responsiveness** and **demandingness/control.**

■ There are four styles of parenting: authoritative, authoritarian, permissive, and uninvolved.

■ Accepting and demanding (or **authoritative**) parents who appeal to reason in order to enforce their demands tend to raise highly competent, well-adjusted children.

■ Children of less accepting but highly demanding (or **authoritarian**) parents, and accepting but undemanding (or **permissive**) parents display somewhat less favorable developmental outcomes.

■ Children of unaccepting, unresponsive, and undemanding (or **uninvolved**) parents are often deficient in virtually all aspects of psychological functioning.

■ Recent research on parental control clearly favors use of **behavioral control** over **psychological control.**

■ Developmentalists believe that a complete account of family socialization involves reciprocal influences between parents and their children (transactional model).

Social Class and Ethnic Variations in Child Rearing

■ Parents from different cultures, subcultures, and social classes have different values, concerns, and outlooks on life that influence their child-rearing practices.

■ Parents from all social backgrounds emphasize the characteristics that contribute to *success as they know it* in their own ecological niches.

■ It is inappropriate to conclude that one particular style of parenting is somehow "better" or more competent than all others.

The Influence of Siblings and Sibling Relationships

■ **Sibling rivalry** is a normal aspect of family life that may begin as soon as a younger sibling arrives.
■ Siblings are likely to get along and do many nice things for one another, particularly if parents get along, encourage their children to resolve conflicts amicably, and do not consistently favor one child more than the other(s).
■ Siblings are typically viewed as intimate associates who can be counted on for support.
■ Older siblings frequently serve as caregivers, security objects, models, and teachers for their younger siblings, and they often profit themselves from the instruction and guidance they provide.
■ Sibling relationships are not essential for normal development, for only children are just as socially, emotionally, and intellectually competent (or slightly more so), on average, than children with siblings are.

Diversity in Family Life

■ Infertile couples and single adults who desire to be parents often adopt to start a family.
■ Adopted children are often more satisfied with their family lives in open adoption systems that permit them to learn about their biological roots.
■ Despite concerns raised about forming families in this way, children conceived through **donor insemination** are as well adjusted, on average, as children raised by two biological parents.
■ Gay and lesbian parents are just as effective as heterosexual parents are. Their children tend to be well adjusted and are overwhelmingly heterosexual in orientation.
■ Divorce represents a major transition in family life that is stressful and unsettling for children and their parents.
■ Children's initial reactions to divorce often include anger, fear, depression, and guilt.
■ Visible signs of distress after a divorce may be most apparent in younger children, and girls adjust better than boys to life in a single-parent, mother-headed home.
■ Children of divorce are usually better adjusted than those who remain in conflict-ridden two-parent families.

KEY TERMS

MEDIA RESOURCES

The Human Development Book Companion Website

See the companion website http://www.thomsonedu.com/psychology/shaffer for flashcards, practice quiz questions, Internet links, updates, critical thinking exercises, discussion forums, games, and more

Thomson™ NOW! http://www.thomsonedu.com
Go to this site for the link to ThomsonNOW, your one-stop shop. Take a pre-test for this chapter, and ThomsonNOW will generate a personalized study plan based on your test results. The study plan will identify the topics you need to review and direct you to online resources to help you master those topics. You can then take a post-test to help you determine the concepts you have mastered and what you will still need to work on.

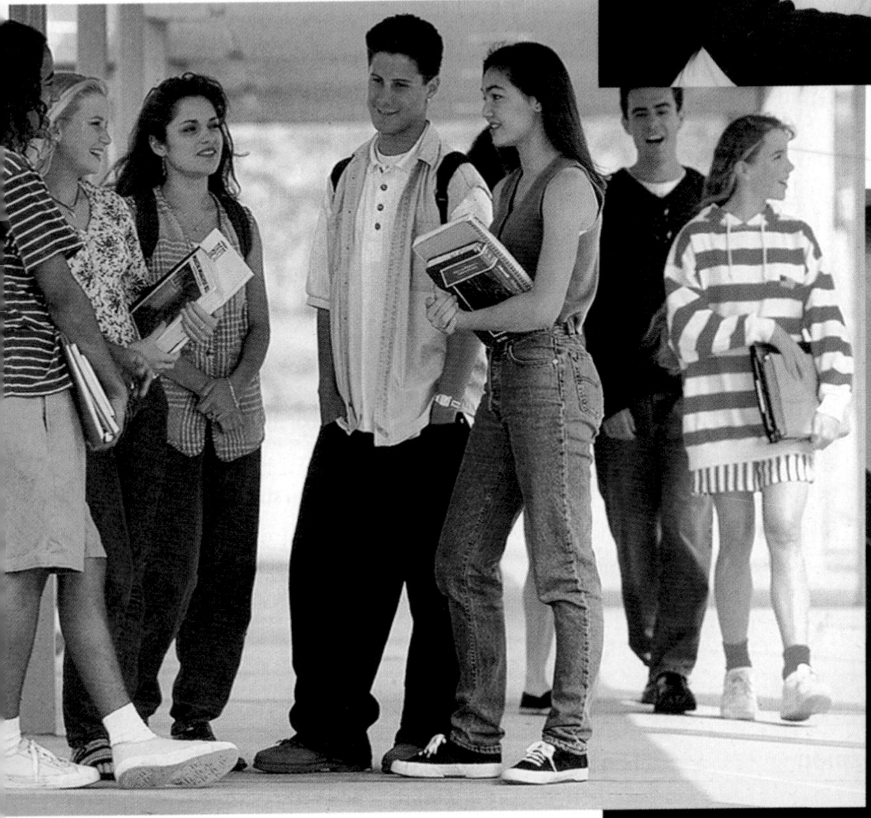

Clockwise from top left: © Thinkstock/Alamy, © Ellen Senisi/The Image Works, © Corbis, Bob Torrez/Getty Images

CHAPTER

16 The Context of Development II: Television, Computers, School, and Peers

In Chapter 15, we considered the family as an agent of socialization, looking at the ways that parents and siblings affect developing children. Although families have an enormous impact on their young, it is only a matter of time before other societal institutions begin to exert their influence. For example, infants, toddlers, and preschool children are often exposed to alternative caregivers and a host of new playmates when their working parents place them in day care or nursery school. Even those toddlers who remain at home soon begin to learn about a world beyond the family once they develop an interest in television. And by age 6 to 7, virtually all children in Western societies go to elementary school, a setting that requires them to interact with other little people who are similar to themselves and to adjust to rules and practices that may be very dissimilar to those they follow at home.

So as they mature, children become increasingly familiar with the outside world and spend much less time under the watchful eyes of their parents. How do these experiences affect their lives? This is the issue to which we will now turn as we consider the impact of four **extrafamilial influences** on development: television, computers, schools, and the society of one's peers.

extrafamilial influences
social agencies other than the family that influence a child's or an adolescent's cognitive, social, and emotional development.

The Effects of Television on Child Development

It seems almost incomprehensible that the average American of only 50 years ago had never seen a television. Now more than 98 percent of American homes have one or more TV sets, and children between the ages of 3 and 11 watch an average of 3 to 4 hours of TV a day (Bianchi & Robinson, 1997; Comstock, 1993). As we see in Figure 16.1, TV viewing begins in infancy, increases until about age 11, and then declines somewhat during adolescence—a trend that holds in Australia, Canada, and several European countries, as well as in the United States. By age 18, a child will have spent more time watching television than in any other single activity except sleeping (Liebert & Sprafkin, 1988). Boys watch more TV than girls do, and ethnic minority children living in poverty are especially likely to be heavy viewers (Huston et al., 1999; Signorielli, 1991). Is all this time in front of the TV damaging to children's cognitive, social, and emotional development, as many critics have feared?

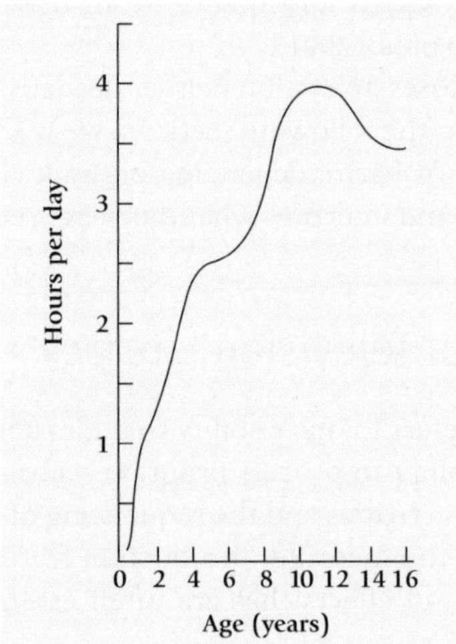

Figure 16.1 Average number of hours per day that American children and adolescents spend watching television. *From* The Early Windows: Effects of Television on Children and Youth, *3rd ed., by R. M. Liebert & J. Sprafkin, 1988. Copyright © 1988. Reprinted by permission of Allyn & Bacon.*

ZITS reprinted by permission of King Features Syndicate.

One way to assess the impact of television is to see whether children who have access to the TV differ systematically from those who live in remote areas not served by television. One such study of Canadian children gave some cause for concern. Prior to the introduction of television to the isolated town Notel, children living there tested higher in creativity and reading proficiency than did age-mates in comparable Canadian towns served by television. Two to four years after television was introduced, the children of Notel showed declines in their reading skills and creativity (to levels shown by peers in other towns). They also showed declines in community involvement, and dramatic increases in aggression and gender stereotyping (Corteen & Williams, 1986; Harrison & Williams, 1986).

Although sobering, these findings may be somewhat misleading. Other investigators report that the biggest impact of the coming of television is that children substitute TV viewing for such other leisure activities as listening to the radio, reading comics, or going to movies (Huston & Wright, 1998; Liebert & Sprafkin, 1988). There are also seasonal variations: children watch more TV in the winter months when the weather is bad and they have nothing better to do (McHale, Crouter, & Tucker, 2001). And as long as TV viewing is not excessive, children exposed to TV show no significant cognitive or academic deficiencies and spend no less time playing with peers (Huston et al., 1999; Liebert & Sprafkin, 1988). In fact, one review of the literature found that children may actually learn a great deal of useful information from television, particularly educational programming (Anderson et al., 2001).

So in moderate doses, television neither deadens young minds nor impairs children's social development. In the following sections, we will see that this medium does have the potential to do good or harm, depending on *what* children are watching and children's ability to understand and interpret what they have seen.

Development of Television Literacy

television literacy
one's ability to understand how information is conveyed in television programming and to interpret this information properly.

Television literacy refers to one's ability to understand how information is conveyed on TV. It involves the ability to process program *content,* so that one can construct a story line from characters' activities and the sequencing of scenes. It also involves an ability to interpret the *form* of the message—production features such as zooms, cuts, fade-outs, split-screens, and sound effects that are often essential to understanding a program's content.

© Bob Daemmrich/PhotoEdit

Prior to age 8 or 9, children process program content in a piecemeal fashion. They are likely to be captivated by zooms, cuts, fast-paced action, loud music, and children's (or cartoon characters') voices. They often direct their attention elsewhere during slower scenes that contain adults and quiet dialogue (Schmidt, Anderson, & Collins, 1999). Consequently, preschool children are often unable to understand the chain of events leading from the beginning to the end of a story from watching a TV show. Even 6-year-olds have trouble recalling a coherent story line. These children tend to remember the actions that characters perform rather than the motives or goals that characters pursue and the events that shaped these goals (McKenna & Ossoff, 1998; van den Broek, Lorch, & Thurlow, 1996). In addition, children younger than 7 do not fully grasp the fictional nature of television, often believing that characters retain their roles (and scripted characteristics) in real life (Wright et al., 1994). And even though 8-year-olds may know that TV programming is fiction, they may still view it as an accurate portrayal of everyday events (Wright et al., 1995).

Comprehension of TV programming increases sharply from middle childhood throughout adolescence. Experience watching TV helps children to properly interpret the zooms, fade-outs, musical scores, and other production features that assist viewers in inferring characters' motives and connecting nonadjacent scenes. Older children and adolescents are increasingly able to draw inferences about scenes that are widely separated in time (van den Broek, 1997). So if a character were to act nice and gain someone's trust in order to deceive him later, a 10-year-old may eventually recognize the character's deceptive intent and evaluate him negatively. A 6-year-old, who focuses more on concrete behaviors than on subtle intentions, will often brand this con artist as a "nice guy" and is likely to evaluate his later self-serving acts much more positively (van den Broek, Lorch, & Thurlow, 1996).

Some Potentially Undesirable Effects of Television

Does their strong focus on actions and general lack of television literacy increase the likelihood that younger children will imitate the particularly vivid behaviors that TV characters display? Yes, indeed; and whether these imitations are beneficial or harmful depends critically on *what* children happen to be viewing.

Effects of Televised Violence

As early as 1954, complaints raised by parents, teachers, and experts in child development prompted Senator Estes Kefauver, then chairman of the Senate Subcommittee on Juvenile Delinquency, to question the need for violence in television programming. The National Television Violence Study, a 2-year survey of the frequency, nature, and context of TV violence, reveals that American television programming is incredibly violent (Mediascope, 1996; Seppa, 1997). Fifty-eight percent of programs broadcast between 6 a.m. and 11 p.m. contained repeated acts of overt aggression, and 73 percent contained violence in which the perpetrator neither displayed any remorse nor received any penalty or criticism. The most violent TV programs are those intended for children, especially cartoons, and nearly 40 percent of the violence on TV is initiated by such violent heroes as "The Mighty Morphin Power Rangers," who are portrayed as attractive role models for children (Seppa, 1997). Nearly two-thirds of the violent incidents in children's programming

FOCUS ON RESEARCH Do *The Mighty Morphin Power Rangers* Promote Children's Aggression?

In the 1990s, one of the most popular and most violent TV shows for children was *The Mighty Morphin Power Ranger*—a program that aired five to six times a week in many markets and contained in excess of 200 violent acts per hour. The *Power Rangers* were a racially diverse group of adolescents who were ordered by Zordon, their elderly leader, to transform, or "morph," into superheroes to battle monsters sent to earth by an evil Asian woman bent on taking control of the planet. Violence occurred not only in battles between the forces of good and evil but in non-battle scenes in which the adolescent heroes practiced martial arts on each other. According to the National Coalition on Television Violence, *Power Rangers* was the most violent TV program for children that it has ever studied (Kiesewetter, 1993)—and most of its violence is *hostile*, being intended to harm or to kill another character. Do unedited versions of this immensely popular program increase the likelihood of aggression among its young viewers as they play in their *natural* environment?

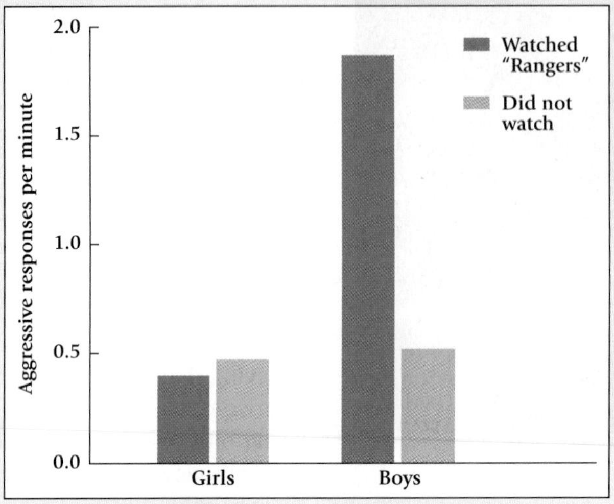

Average number of aggressive responses per minute in the free play of girls and boys who either had or had not watched an episode of The Mighty Morphin Power Rangers. Adapted from Boyatzis, Matillo, & Nesbitt, 1995.

Chris Boyatzis and associates (1995) sought to answer this question in an interesting experiment with 5- to 7-year-olds. Half of the children in this study had been randomly assigned to watch a randomly selected, unedited episode of *The Mighty Morphin Power Rangers* at school, whereas the remaining children in a control group engaged in other activities and did not view the program. After the program had been shown, children in the experimental group were each observed for a set length of time as they played in their classrooms, and instances of aggressive behavior (for example, physical and verbal aggression, taking objects by force) were recorded. Their behavior was then compared to that of children in the control group, who had not viewed the program.

The dramatic results appear in the accompanying graph. Notice that watching *Power Rangers* had no effect on the girls, probably because the majority of the *Rangers* are boys and young boys may have identified more strongly with the *Rangers* than young girls did. However, we see that boys who had watched the show committed seven times the number of aggressive acts during free play as the boys who had not watched this episode.

Here, then, is dramatic evidence that exposure to an unedited and *randomly selected* episode of a violent children's show featuring male characters dramatically increases the likelihood of aggression among young male playmates in the *natural environment.* Furthermore, it is worth emphasizing that the boys who became more aggressive had been *randomly assigned* to watch *Power Rangers* and were not merely the most aggressive boys in their classes.

Later research suggests that a lack of TV literacy may have contributed strongly to these results, for children younger than 8 or 9 tend not to recall any prosocial causes the *Power Rangers* are pursuing and usually say "the fights" when asked what they do remember (McKenna & Ossoff, 1998). The Boyatzis and associates (1995) experiment may have somewhat overdramatized the impact of *Power Rangers* on young boys by observing their play immediately after they viewed the show. Nevertheless, the results certainly imply that repeated exposure of young, non-TV-literate audiences to this popular and highly accessible program can and probably does increase the frequency of aggressive peer interactions in the natural environment and may lead children (particularly boys) to favor aggressive solutions to conflict as well.

are couched in humor. And, as the above Box illustrates, boys who watch an unedited and highly violent program *designed for children* do subsequently become more aggressive with their peers in their natural environments. Let's take a closer look at this issue.

Does TV Violence Instigate Aggression? It has been argued that the often-comical violence portrayed in children's programming is unlikely to affect the behavior of young viewers. Yet hundreds of experimental studies and correlational surveys suggest otherwise. Simply stated, children and adolescents who watch a lot of televised violence tend to be more hostile and aggressive than their classmates who watch little violence. This positive relationship between exposure to TV violence and aggressive behavior in naturalistic

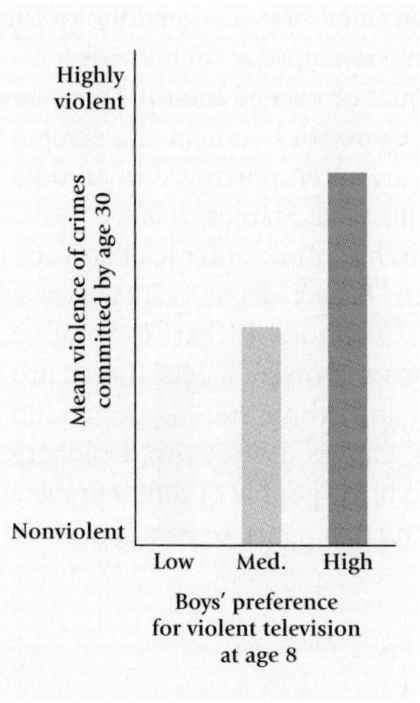

Figure 16.2 Relationship between boys' preference for violent TV programming at age 8 and mean violence of crimes committed by age 30. *Adapted from "Psychological Processes Promoting the Relation Between Exposure to Media Violence and Aggressive Behavior by the Viewer," by L. R. Huesmann, 1986,* Journal of Social Issues, *42, No. 3, 125–139. Copyright © 1986 by the* Journal of Social Issues. *Adapted by permission.*

mean-world belief
a belief, fostered by televised violence, that the world is a more dangerous and frightening place than is actually the case.

desensitization hypothesis
the notion that people who watch a lot of media violence will become less aroused by aggression and more tolerant of violent and aggressive acts.

settings has been documented over and over with preschool, grade school, high school, and adult participants in the United States and with grade school boys and girls in Australia, Canada, Finland, Great Britain, Israel, and Poland (Bushman & Husemann, 2001; Geen, 1998). Furthermore, longitudinal studies suggest that the link between TV violence and aggression is *reciprocal:* watching TV violence increases children's aggressive tendencies, which stimulates interest in violent programs, which promotes further aggression (Eron, 1982; Huesmann, Lagerspitz, & Eron, 1984). Although longitudinal surveys are correlational research and do *not* demonstrate causality, their results are at least consistent with the argument that early exposure to a heavy diet of televised violence can lead to the development of hostile, antisocial habits that persist over time. For example, when Rowell Huesmann (1986) followed up on boys from an earlier study when they were 30 years old, he found that their earlier preferences for violent television at age 8 predicted not only their aggressiveness as adults, but their involvement in serious criminal activities as well (see Figure 16.2).

Other Effects of Televised Violence. Even if children do not act out the aggression that they observe on television, they may be influenced by it in other ways. For example, a steady diet of televised violence can instill **mean-world beliefs**—a tendency to view the world as a violent place inhabited by people who typically rely on aggressive solutions to their interpersonal problems (Huesmann et al., 2003; Huston & Wright, 1998; Slaby et al., 1995). In fact, 7- to 9-year-olds who show the strongest preferences for violent television are the ones most likely to believe that violent shows are an accurate portrayal of everyday life.

In a similar vein, prolonged exposure to televised violence can desensitize children—that is, make them less emotionally upset by violent acts and more willing to tolerate them in real life. Margaret Thomas and her colleagues (1977; Drabman & Thomas, 1974) tested this **desensitization hypothesis** with 8- to 10-year-olds. Each child watched either a violent detective show or a nonviolent but exciting sporting event while hooked up to a physiograph that recorded his or her emotional reactions. Then the child was told to watch over two kindergartners, visible in the next room on a TV monitor, and to come to get the experimenter should anything go wrong. A prepared film then showed the two kindergartners getting into an intense battle that escalated until the screen went blank. Children who had earlier watched the violent program were now less physiologically aroused by the fight they observed and were more inclined to tolerate it (by being much slower to intervene) than the children who had watched an equally arousing but nonviolent sporting event. Apparently TV violence can desensitize viewers to real-world instances of aggression (see also Huesmann et al., 2003).

Michael Newman/PhotoEdit

Heavy exposure to media violence may blunt children's emotional reactions to real-life aggression and convince them that the world is a violent place populated mainly by hostile and aggressive people.

Television as a Source of Social Stereotypes

Another unfortunate effect that television may have on children is to reinforce a variety of potentially harmful social stereotypes (Huston & Wright, 1998). In Chapter 13, for example, we noted that gender-role stereotyping is common on television and that children who watch a lot of commercial TV are likely to hold more traditional views of men and women than their classmates who watch little television. Television might instead be used to counter gender stereotypes. Early attempts to accomplish this aim by showing males performing competently at traditionally feminine activities and females excelling at traditionally masculine pursuits are enjoying some limited success (Johnston & Ettema, 1982; Rosenwasser, Lingenfelter, & Harrington, 1989). However, these programs would undoubtedly be more effective if they were combined with the kinds of cognitive training procedures that undermine the inflexible and erroneous beliefs on which gender stereotypes rest (Bigler & Liben, 1990, 1992).

Stereotyped views of minorities are also common on television. Largely due to the influence of the civil rights movement, African Americans now appear on television in a much wider range of occupations, and their numbers equal or exceed their proportions in the population. However, Latinos and other ethnic minorities remain underrepresented. And when non-Black minorities do appear, they are often portrayed in an unfavorable light, cast as villains or victims (Liebert & Sprafkin, 1988; Staples, 2000).

Although the evidence is limited, it seems that children's ethnic and racial attitudes are influenced by televised portrayals of minority groups. Earlier depictions of African Americans as comical, inept, or lazy led to negative racial attitudes (Liebert & Sprafkin, 1988), whereas positive portrayals of minorities in cartoons and on such educational programs as *Sesame Street* appear to reduce children's racial and ethnic stereotypes and increase their likelihood of having ethnically diverse friends (Graves, 1993; Gorn, Goldberg, & Kanungo, 1976). Apparently television has the power to bring people of different racial and ethnic backgrounds closer together or to drive them further apart, depending on the ways in which these social groups are depicted.

Children's Reactions to Commercial Messages

In the United States, the average child is exposed to nearly 20,000 television commercials each year, many of which are for toys, fast foods, and sugary treats that parents may not want their children to have. Young children are inclined to ask for things that they have seen on television, and conflicts may arise when parents refuse to buy these things (Atkin, 1978; Kunkel & Roberts, 1991). Young children may be so persistent because they rarely understand the manipulative intent of commercials to sell products. Young children often regard commercials like public service announcements that are intended to be helpful and informative (Liebert & Sprafkin, 1988). By age 9 to 11, most children realize that commercials are designed to persuade and sell. By age 13 to 14, they have acquired a healthy skepticism about advertising and product claims (Linn, de Benedictis, & Delucchi, 1982; Robertson & Rossiter, 1974). Nevertheless, even adolescents are often persuaded by the commercials they see, particularly if the commercial features a celebrity or if the appeals are deceptive and misleading (Cialdini, 2001; Huston et al., 1992).

Is it any wonder, then, that many parents are concerned about the impact of commercials on their children? Children's commercials often push products that are unsafe or of poor nutritional value. Also, the many commercials for over-the-counter drugs and glamorous depictions of alcohol use could lead children to underestimate the consequences of such risky behaviors as drinking, self-medication, and drug use (Tinsley, 1992). The National Foundation to Improve Television, an organization of parents that monitors and works to improve children's television, considers the potentially harmful influence of TV commercials to be an even greater problem than televised violence!

Television Viewing and Children's Health

Heavy TV viewing can also contribute in subtle ways to undermining children's health and well-being. You have probably heard one of the many recent reports that the American public is becoming **obese**—a medical term that is applied to people who are 20 percent or more over their ideal weight for their height, age, and sex. Obesity is clearly a threat to physical health—having been implicated as a major contributor to heart disease, high blood pressure, and diabetes—and rates of obesity have been increasing among all age groups, even young children (Dwyer & Stone, 2000). There are many contributors to obesity, with hereditary predispositions and poor eating habits being most heavily cited. However, it is also true that many people are obese because they do not get sufficient exercise to burn the calories they've consumed (Cowley, 2001).

obese
a medical term describing individuals who are at least 20 percent above the ideal weight for their height, age, and sex.

Unfortunately, television viewing is an inherently sedentary activity that is less likely to assist children to burn excess calories than physically active play or even performing household chores. Interestingly, one of the strongest predictors of *future* obesity is the amount of time children spend watching television (Anderson et al., 2001; Cowley, 2001),

TABLE 16.1 Strategies for Regulating the Effects of TV on Children's Development

Goal	Strategies
Reduce the amount of TV viewing	Work together to keep a time chart of your child's activities, including TV viewing, homework, and play with friends. Then, discuss what you believe to be a balanced set of activities.
	Set a weekly viewing limit. Rule out TV at certain times (before breakfast or on school nights).
	Don't locate a television set in your child's room.
	Remember that if you watch a lot of TV, chances are your child will also.
Limit the effects of violent TV	Judge the amount of violence in the shows your children view by watching several episodes.
	View TV together and discuss the violence with your child. Talk about why the violence happened and how painful it is. Ask the child how conflicts can be solved without violence.
	Explain to your child how violence on an entertainment program is "faked."
	Restrict violent videos.
	Encourage your child to watch programs with characters that cooperate, help and care for each other. These programs have been shown to have a positive influence on children.
Counteract negative values portrayed on TV	Ask your child to compare what is shown on the screen with real life.
	Discuss with your child what is real and what is make-believe on TV.
	Explain to your child the values you hold about sex, alcohol, and drugs.
	If you own a VCR or DVD player, begin a selective video library specifically for children.
	Before subscribing to cable television, be aware of the variety and types of programming seen on it. Many of these easily accessed channels are for adult viewing only. Ask for a parental "lock out" device from the cable company that will allow you to select channels for your child.
Deal with the effects of TV advertising	Tell your child that advertising is used to sell products to as many viewers as possible.
	Put advertising disclaimers into words children understand.
	On shopping trips, let your child see that advertising claims are often exaggerated. Toys that look big, fast, and exciting on TV may be disappointingly small, slow, and unexciting close up.

Adapted from Murray, J. P., & Lonnborg, B. (2005). *Children and television: Using TV sensibly.* Kansas State University Agricultural Experiment Station and Cooperative Extension Service.

with young couch potatoes who watch more than 5 hours a day being most at risk of actually coming to resemble a potato (Gortmaker et al., 1996). Aside from restricting children's physical activity, television viewing also promotes poor eating habits. Not only do children tend to snack while passively watching TV, but the foods they see advertised (and may be snacking on) are mostly high-calorie products containing lots of fat and sugar and few beneficial nutrients (Tinsley, 1992).

Reducing the Harmful Effects of Television Exposure

How might concerned parents control the harmful effects of television? Table 16.1 lists several effective strategies recommended by experts. One particularly important tactic is for parents to monitor children's home viewing habits to limit their exposure to highly violent or offensive programs, while trying to interest them in programs with prosocial or educational themes.

Although each of the guidelines in Table 16.1 is an excellent one, a couple of comments are in order. First, the effectiveness of lock-out provisions to control what the TV can broadcast was weakened from the start. Producers of violent programming managed to ensure that the content-based rating system for television programming reflects age-guideline ratings rather than a more detailed system that would allow parents to make lock-out decisions based on a program's sexual or violent content (Huesmann et al., 2003). Unfortunately, the recent voluntary content guidelines that have arisen are not used by all networks and are poorly understood by parents (Bushman & Cantor, 2003).

Second, the suggestion that parents help their young non-TV-literate viewers to evaluate what they are watching is particularly important. One reason that younger children are so responsive to aggressive models on TV is that they don't always interpret the violence they see in the same way adults do. Children often miss subtleties such as an aggressor's antisocial motives and intentions or the unpleasant consequences that perpetrators may suffer as a result of their aggressive acts (Collins, Sobol, & Westby, 1981; Slaby et al., 1995). Young children's tendency to strongly identify with aggressive heroes whose violence is socially reinforced makes them even more susceptible to the instigating effects of TV violence—a fact that parents need to know (Huesmann et al., 2003). When adults highlight the information children miss while strongly disapproving of a perpetrator's (or hero's) conduct, young viewers gain a much better understanding of media violence and are less affected by what they have seen. This is particularly true if the adult commentator also suggests how these perpetrators might have approached their problems in a more constructive way (see also Collins, 1983; Liebert & Sprafkin, 1988). Unfortunately, this may be an underutilized strategy, for as Michele St. Peters and her associates (1991) have noted, parent/child co-viewing at home most often occurs *not* during action/adventure shows or other highly violent fare, but during the evening news, sporting events, or prime-time dramas—programming that is not particularly captivating for young children.

Television as an Educational Tool

Thus far, we've cast a wary eye at television, talking mostly about its capacity to do harm. Yet, TV could become a most effective way of teaching a number of valuable lessons if only its content were altered to convey such information. Let's examine some of the evidence to support this claim.

Educational Television and Children's Prosocial Behavior

Many TV programs—especially offerings such as *Sesame Street* and *Mister Roger's Neighborhood*—are designed, in part, to teach prosocial activities such as cooperation, sharing, and comforting distressed friends. One major review of the literature found that young children who often watch prosocial programming become more prosocially inclined (Hearold, 1986). However, it is important to note that these programs may have few if any *lasting* benefits unless an adult monitors the programs and encourages children to rehearse and enact the prosocial lessons they have learned (Friedrich & Stein, 1975; Friedrich-Cofer et al., 1979). Young children are more likely to process and enact any prosocial lessons that are portrayed when the program is free of violent acts that otherwise compete for their attention. Despite these important qualifications, it seems that the positive effects of prosocial programming greatly outweigh the negatives (Hearold, 1986), especially if adults encourage children to pay close attention to episodes that emphasize constructive methods of resolving interpersonal conflicts.

Television as a Contributor to Cognitive Development

Researchers have been slow to explore television's potential for fostering the adaptive capabilities of very young children, owing perhaps to the limited cognitive and verbal skills of infants and toddlers. Yet, there are some early research findings worth considering. For example, we learned in Chapter 11 that 12-month-old infants are capable of *social referencing* from television, learning to avoid an apparently dangerous object that frightened an adult actor (Mumme & Fernald, 2003). What's more, Georgene Troseth (2003)

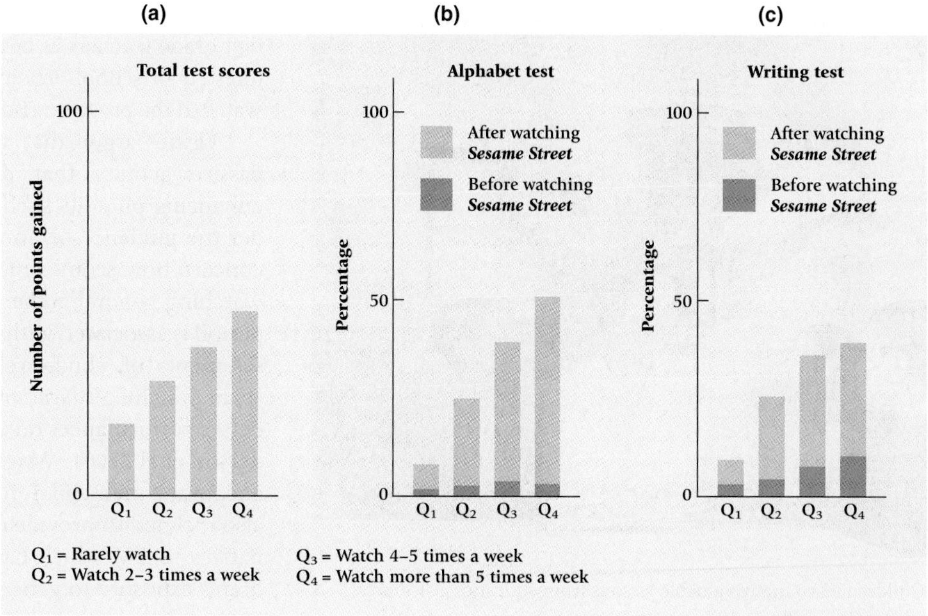

Figure 16.3 Relationship between amount of viewing of *Sesame Street* and children's abilities: (a) improvement in total test scores for children grouped into different quartiles according to amount of viewing; (b) percentage of children who recited the alphabet correctly, grouped according to quartiles of amount of viewing; (c) percentage of children who wrote their first names correctly, grouped according to quartiles of amount of viewing. *From* The Early Windows: Effects of Television on Children and Youth, *3rd ed., by R. M. Liebert & J. Sprafkin, 1988. Copyright © 1988. Reprinted by permission of Allyn & Bacon.*

demonstrated that 2-year-olds who had often seen their own image on TV were able to find a toy that an adult on video had hidden in an adjoining room—a remarkable feat of symbolic problem-solving not normally seen until age 2½ to 3. Apparently, these 2-year-olds had learned from seeing themselves (and other family members) on TV that televised information can be informative about the real world; thus, they used what they saw on television to find the hidden toy.

This research is still very new and limited. It remains to be seen exactly how television might be used in a practical way to foster very young children's adaptive capabilities. However, attempts to exploit the potential of television for optimizing the development of preschool children have a long history.

In 1968 the U.S. government and a number of private foundations provided funds to create *Children's Television Workshop (CTW),* an organization committed to producing TV programs that would hold children's interest and foster their intellectual development. CTW's first production, *Sesame Street,* became the world's most popular children's series—seen an average of three times a week by about half of America's preschool children and broadcast to nearly 50 other countries around the world (Liebert & Sprafkin, 1988). Targeted at 3- to 5-year-olds, *Sesame Street* attempts to foster important cognitive skills such as counting, recognizing and discriminating numbers and letters, ordering and classifying objects, and solving simple problems. It was hoped that children from disadvantaged backgrounds would be much better prepared for school after viewing this programming on a regular basis.

During the first season that *Sesame Street* was broadcast, its impact was measured by the Educational Testing Service. About 950 3- to 5-year-olds from five areas of the United States took a pretest that measured their cognitive skills and determined what they knew about letters, numbers, and geometric forms. At the end of the season, they took this test again to see what they had learned. When the data were analyzed, it was clear that *Sesame Street* was achieving its objectives. As shown in Figure 16.3, children who watched *Sesame Street* the most (groups Q3 and Q4, who watched 4 or more times a week) showed the biggest improvements in their total test scores (panel a), their scores on the alphabet test (panel b), and their ability to write their names (panel c). The 3-year-olds posted bigger gains than the 5-year-olds, probably because the younger children knew less to begin with.

The results of a second similar study that included only urban disadvantaged preschoolers paralleled those of the original study (Bogatz & Ball, 1972), and others have found that regular exposure to *Sesame Street* is associated with impressive gains in preschoolers' vocabularies and prereading skills as well (Rice et al., 1990). Finally, disadvantaged children who had

Children learn many valuable lessons from educational TV programs such as *Sesame Street*.

been heavy viewers of *Sesame Street* were later rated by their first-grade teachers as better prepared for school and more interested in school activities than classmates who had rarely watched the program (Bogatz & Ball, 1972).

Critics argue that viewing educational television is a passive activity that displaces more valuable, growth-enhancing pursuits such as reading and active learning under the guidance of an adult (Singer & Singer, 1990). This concern now seems unfounded. Although more time spent watching general audience programs during the preschool period is associated with poor performances on cognitive assessments of children's readiness for school, more time spent watching *educational* programming is associated with better performances on these same school-related skills (Anderson et al., 2001; Wright et al., 2001). In fact, parents who encourage their children to watch educational programs are also inclined to provide other educational activities as alternatives to TV, which have the effect of limiting their children's exposure to general audience programming (Huston et al., 1999).

It was also once feared that *Sesame Street* might actually widen the intellectual gap between disadvantaged children and their middle-class peers if the middle-class youngsters were more likely to watch the program (Cook et al., 1975). Later research showed that children from disadvantaged backgrounds watch *Sesame Street* about as often as their advantaged peers (Pinon, Huston, & Wright, 1989) and they learn just as much from it (Rice et al., 1990). So viewing *Sesame Street* appears to be a potentially valuable experience for *all* preschool children—and a true educational bargain that only costs about a penny a day per viewer (Palmer, 1984). The formidable task is to convince more parents that *Sesame Street* (and other educational programs) are valuable resources that they and their children should not be missing (Larson, 2001).

Child Development in the Computer Age

Like television, the computer is a modern technology that has the potential to influence children's learning and lifestyles. But in what ways? Most educators today believe that the computer is an effective supplement to classroom instruction that helps children to learn more and to have more fun learning. By 1996, over 98 percent of American public schools were using computers as instructional tools, and by 2003, more than 60% of American homes had computers and more than 50% of American homes had internet access (U.S. Bureau of the Census, 1997; Day, Janus, & Davis, 2003). So computers are now widely accessible. But, do they really help children to learn, think, or create? Is there a danger that young "hackers" will become so enamored of computer technology and so reclusive or socially unskilled that they risk being ostracized by their peers?

Computers in the Classroom

computer-assisted instruction (CAI)
Use of computers to teach new concepts and practice academic skills.

The results of hundreds of studies confirm that classroom use of computers produces many, many benefits. For example, elementary school students do learn more and report that they enjoy school more when they receive at least some **computer-assisted instruction (CAI)** (Clements & Nastasi, 1992; Collis, 1996; Lepper & Gurtner, 1989). Many CAI programs are simply drills that start at a child's current skill level and present increasingly difficult problems, often with hints or clues when progress breaks down.

Bob Daemmrich/Stock Boston

Learning by computer is an effective complement to classroom instruction and an experience that can teach young children to collaborate.

More elaborate forms of CAI are guided tutorials that rely less on drill and more on the *discovery* of important concepts and principles in the context of highly motivating games. Regular use of drill programs during the early grades does seem to improve children's basic reading and math skills—particularly for disadvantaged students and low achievers (Clements & Nastasi, 1992; Fletcher-Flinn & Gravatt, 1995; Lepper & Gurtner, 1989). However, the benefits of CAI are greatest when children receive at least some exposure to the highly involving guided tutorial games as well as simple drills.

Aside from their drill function, computers are also *tools* that can further children's basic writing and communication skills (Clements, 1995). Once children can read and write, using computer word-processing programs eliminates much of the drudgery of handwriting and increases the likelihood that children will revise, edit, and polish their writing (Clements & Nastasi, 1992). For older children and adolescents, computer-prompted metacognitive strategies, using spreadsheet and note-organizing software programs (Pea, 1985), also help students to think about what they wish to say and to organize their thoughts into more coherent essays (Lepper & Gurtner, 1989).

Finally, teaching students to *program* (and thus *control*) a computer can foster mastery motivation and self-efficacy. It also promotes novel modes of thinking that are unlikely to emerge from computer-assisted academic drills. For example, Douglas Clements (1991, 1995) trained first- and third-graders in Logo, a computer language that allows children to translate drawings they've made into input statements so that they can reproduce their creations on the computer monitor. Although Clements's "Logo" children performed no better on achievement tests than age-mates who participated in the more usual kinds of computer-assisted academic exercises, Logo users scored higher on tests of Piagetian concrete-operational abilities, mathematical problem-solving strategies, and creativity (Clements, 1995; Nastasi & Clements, 1994). And because children must detect errors and debug their Logo programs to get them to work, programming promotes thinking about one's own thinking and is associated with gains in metacognitive knowledge (Clements, 1990).

Concerns about Computers

What are the danger signs of exposing children to computer technology? Three concerns are raised most often.

Concerns about Video Games

An example of a video game that parents would probably be concerned about their children playing is:

> *Grand Theft Auto: Vice City:* A video game in which participants ramp up their scores by having sex with a prostitute and gain additional points by killing her. The game includes scenes in which blood splatters out of a woman's body as the player beats her to death (National Institute on Media and the Family, as cited in Associated Press, 2002b).

One national survey revealed that 80 percent of U.S. adolescents spend 2 or more hours a week playing computer video games (Williams, 1998), and game playing is the predominant computer activity for grade school children (Subrahmanyam et al., 2000). It is not

that this activity necessarily diverts children from schoolwork and peer activities, as many parents have assumed; time spent playing at the computer is usually a substitute for other leisure activities, most notably TV viewing (Huston et al., 1999). Nevertheless, critics have feared that heavy exposure to such popular and incredibly violent video games such as *Alien Intruder* and *Mortal Kombat* can instigate aggression and cultivate aggressive habits in the same ways that televised violence does.

The critics' concerns are valid ones. At least three surveys of fourth- to twelfth-graders found moderate positive correlations between the amount of time spent playing video games and real-world aggressive behaviors (Dill & Dill, 1998). The experimental evidence is even more revealing: One study of third- and fourth-graders (Kirsch, 1998) and another study of college students (Anderson & Dill, 2000) found that participants randomly assigned to play violent video games later displayed a strong bias to react aggressively toward events that could be interpreted either aggressively or nonaggressively and significantly more aggressive behavior than the participants who had played nonviolent video games (see also Bushman & Anderson, 2002). And because violent game players are *actively* involved in planning and performing aggressive acts and are *reinforced* for their successful symbolic violence, it has been argued that the aggression-instigating effects of violent video games is probably far greater than that of violent television programming, in which children are only passively exposed to aggression and violence (Anderson & Dill, 2000). Clearly, these findings imply that parents should be at least as concerned about what their children are playing on-screen as they are about what children watch.

Concerns about Social Inequalities

Other critics argued that the computer revolution may leave some groups of children behind, lacking in skills required in our increasingly computer-dependent society. For example, children from economically disadvantaged families may be exposed to computers at school but are less likely to have them at home (Becker, 2000; Rocheleau, 1995). At one time, boys were far more likely than girls to take an interest in computers and to sign up for computer camps. Why? Probably because computers were often viewed as involving mathematics, a traditionally masculine subject, and many available computer games were designed to appeal to boys (Lepper, 1985; Ogletree & Williams, 1990). This gender gap has essentially closed in the United States (Subrahmanyam et al., 2000), largely due to the increasing use of computers to socialize with chat mates and to foster cooperative classroom learning activities that girls typically enjoy (Collis, 1996; Rocheleau, 1995).

Concerns about Internet Exposure

The proliferation of home computers and Internet services means that millions of children and adolescents around the world now have unsupervised access to the World Wide Web. Clearly, exposure to information available on the Web can be a boon to students researching topics pertinent to their school assignments. Nevertheless, many parents and teachers are alarmed about potentially negative Web influences. For example, children and adolescents chatting with acquaintances online have been drawn into cybersexual relationships and, occasionally, to meetings with and exploitation by their adult chat-mates (Curry, 2000; Donnerstein & Smith, 2001). Furthermore, the Web is (or has been) an important recruiting tool for such dangerous cults as *Heaven's Gate,* as well as hate organizations such as the *Ku Klux Klan* (Downing, 2003). So there are reasons to suspect that unrestricted Web access could prove harmful to some children and adolescents, and additional research aimed at estimating those risks is sorely needed.

Like television, then, computers may prove to be either a positive or a negative force on development, depending on how they are used. Outcomes may be negative if a young person's primary uses of the machine are to fritter away study time chatting about undesirable topics on line, or to hole up by himself, zapping mutant aliens from space. But the news may be positive for youngsters who use computers to learn, to create, and to collaborate amicably with siblings and peers.

CONCEPT CHECK 16.1 Understanding Socialization and the Media

Check your understanding of the effects of television and computers on socialization and child development by answering the following questions. Answers appear in the Appendix.

True or False: Identify whether the following statements are true or false.

1. (T)(F) Children who watch a great deal of television develop *television literacy* early in childhood, by around age 5 or 6.
2. (T)(F) Television viewing is much more harmful than beneficial for young children and parents should make every effort to keep their children from watching TV.

Fill in the Blank: Complete the following sentences with the correct terms.

3. Watching violent TV can instill in children a ________, or a tendency to view the world as a violent place where people use violence to solve their problems.
4. Another danger for children watching violent TV is that they can become ________ to violence, eventually considering violence to be an everyday and uneventful occurrence.
5. A danger of watching too much TV, whatever the content, is that it may contribute to a child's development of the physical problem of ________, either in childhood or later in adulthood.

CONTINUED

Multiple Choice: Select the correct answer for each question.

_____ 6. Which of the following are *not* examples of research findings demonstrating that watching TV can contribute to cognitive development?
   a. A 3-year-old can distinguish between friendly and evil characters based on the story line of a TV program.
   b. A 12-month-old can use a TV for social referencing.
   c. A 2-year-old with experience seeing herself on TV can use the TV as a symbol for finding a hidden toy.

_____ 7. Computers have been in schools to teach children through a variety of methods, including all of the following *except:*
   a. computer-aided instruction based on simple skill drills
   b. computer-aided instruction based on discovery games
   c. word-processing for developing writing and editing skills
   d. computer-aided basic math computations (like multiplication) so that the child's efforts can be devoted to high-level conceptual math problems

_____ 8. Some critics are concerned about children's use of computers. Among their concerns are all of the following *except:*
   a. children's use of violent and offensive video games
   b. concerns that use of computers may exaggerate social inequalities among groups of children who have access to computers and those who do not have access to computers
   c. concerns about the unmonitored use of the Internet and the offensive and dangerous materials available to children on the Internet
   d. concerns about the excessive us of chat programs by children to socialize with classmates in an impersonal climate

Short Answer: Briefly answer the following questions.

9. Discuss some of the methods parents can use to help control the amount and effects of TV violence their children view. Also describe some of the problems inherent in these methods.
10. Sheri is considering buying a computer with Internet access for her third-grade daughter. Discuss some of the concerns Sheri might face and how she might address these concerns while still giving her daughter the opportunities available with a computer and Internet access at home.

School as a Socialization Agent

Of all the formal institutions that children encounter away from home, few have as much opportunity to influence their development as the schools they attend. Obviously, students acquire a great deal of knowledge and many academic skills at school. But schooling also promotes cognitive and metacognitive growth by teaching children a variety of rules, strategies, and problem-solving skills (including an ability to concentrate and an appreciation for abstraction). These are skills that children can apply to many different kinds of information (Ceci, 1991). Consider what Frederick Morrison and his associates (1995, 1997) found when comparing the cognitive performance of children who had just made the age cutoff for entering first grade with that of children who had just missed the cutoff and had spent the year in kindergarten. When tested at the end of the school year, the youngest first-graders outperformed the nearly identically aged kindergartners in reading, memory, language, and arithmetic skills. In another study, U.S. schoolchildren on an extended-year (210 day) calendar tested higher in academic achievement and general cognitive competencies in the fall of the next school year than did peers who were equally competent at the beginning of the study but who had attended school on a normal 180-day calendar (Frazier & Morrison, 1998). Finally, Janellen Huttenlocker and her associates (1998) tracked kindergartners' and first-graders' cognitive development at 6-month intervals and found that growth was significantly greater during the October to April period of heavy schooling than during the April to October period, when children spent less time in school. Clearly, intellectual development is influenced, in part, by attending school.

informal curriculum
noncurricular objectives of schooling such as teaching children to cooperate, to respect authority, to obey rules, and to become good citizens.

In addition to the cognitive and academic challenges they provide, schools expose children to an **informal curriculum:** Students are expected to obey rules, cooperate with their classmates, respect authority, and become good citizens. And much of the influence that peers have on developing children occurs in the context of school-related activities and depends critically on the type of school that a child attends and the quality of a child's school experiences (Brody et al., 2002). So it is quite proper to think of the school as an agent of socialization that is likely to affect children's social and emotional development as well as imparting knowledge and helping to prepare students for a job and economic self-sufficiency.

The vast majority of children in our society now begin their schooling well before age 6—attending kindergarten as 5-year-olds and, in many cases, going to nursery school or day care before that (National Center for Educational Statistics, 1995). Is this a healthy trend? As we will see in the Box on p. 638, there are advantages as well as some possible disadvantages associated with early entry into a school-like environment.

Determinants of Effective Schooling

effective schools
schools that are generally successful at achieving curricular and noncurricular objectives, regardless of the racial, ethnic, or socioeconomic background of the student population.

One of the first questions that parents often ask when searching for a residence in a new town is "Where should we live so that our children will get the best education?" This concern reflects the common belief that some schools are "better" or "more effective" than others. But are they?

Michael Rutter (1983) certainly thinks so. According to Rutter, **effective schools** are those that promote academic achievement, social skills, polite and attentive behavior, positive attitudes toward learning, low absenteeism, continuation of education beyond the age at which attendance is mandatory, and acquisition of skills that enable students to find and hold a job. Rutter argues that some schools are more successful than others at accomplishing these objectives, regardless of the students' racial, ethnic, or socioeconomic backgrounds. Let's examine the evidence for this claim.

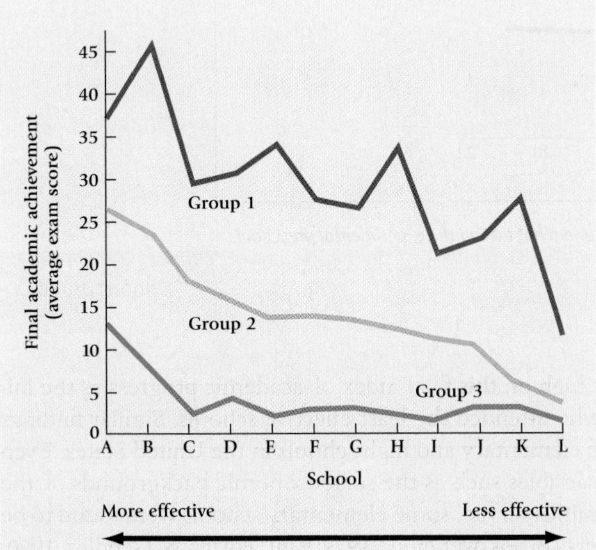

Figure 16.4 Average level of academic achievement in secondary school as a function of initial achievement at the time of entry (Groups 1–3) and the school that pupils were attending (Schools A–L). Note that pupils in all three groups performed at higher levels on this final academic assessment if they attended the more effective schools. Furthermore, students in Group 2 performed like Group 1 students in the more effective schools but like Group 3 students in the least effective schools. *Reprinted by permission of the publisher from* Fifteen Thousand Hours: Secondary Schools and Their Effects on Children, *by Michael Rutter, Barbara Maughan, Peter Mortimore, & Janet Ouston, Cambridge, Mass.: Harvard University Press. Copyright © 1980 by Nuffield Provincial Hospitals Trust.*

In one study, Rutter and his associates (1979) conducted extensive interviews and observations in 12 high schools serving lower- to lower-middle-income populations in London, England. As the students entered these schools, they were given a battery of achievement tests to measure their prior academic accomplishments. At the end of high school, students took another major exam to assess their academic progress. Other information, such as attendance records and teacher ratings of classroom behavior, was also available. When the data were analyzed, Rutter found that the 12 schools clearly differed in "effectiveness": students from the "better" schools exhibited fewer problem behaviors, attended school more regularly, and made more academic progress than students from the less effective schools. We get some idea of the importance of these "schooling effects" from Figure 16.4. The "groups" on the graph refer to the pupils' academic accomplishments at the time they entered high school (Group 3, low achievers; Group 1, high achievers). The first thing to notice is the downward trends of the three groups across the graph from the most effective to the least effective schools. This means that in all three groups, students attending the "more effective" schools outperformed those in the "less effective" schools on the final assessment of academic achievement. Next compare the scores of Group 1 at school A to the scores of Group 3 at School L. This shows that the initially poor students (Group 3) who attended the "better"

APPLYING RESEARCH TO YOUR LIFE

Should Preschoolers Attend School?

Over the past 10 years, the popular media has let it be known that infants and toddlers are quite capable of learning and that such enrichment activities as reading to babies or exposing them to music can stimulate brain development and intellectual growth (e.g., Kulman, 1997). Many parents have bought heavily into this idea and embrace programs such as Bookstart, which claims to help parents promote preliteracy skills in 6- to 9-month-old infants (Hall, 2001)! And already many preschoolers spend 4- to 8-hour days in day-care settings and nursery schools that have a strong academic emphasis. Is this beneficial?

David Elkind (1987), author of *Miseducation: Preschoolers at Risk,* certainly doesn't think so. He argues that the current push for earlier and earlier education may be going too far (see also Bruer, 1999). He argues that many young children today are not given enough time simply to be children—to play and socialize as they choose. Elkind even worries that children may lose their self-initiative and enjoyment of learning if their lives are orchestrated by parents who incessantly push them to achieve.

Several recent studies (e.g., Hart et al., 1998; Marcon, 1999; Stipek et al., 1995; Valeski & Stipek, 2001) seem to confirm Elkind's concerns. Three- to six-year-olds in academically oriented preschools or kindergartens sometimes display an initial advantage in such basic academic competencies as a knowledge of letters and reading skills but often lose it by the end of kindergarten. What's more, students in these highly structured academically oriented programs proved to be less creative, more stressed and more anxious about tests, less prideful about their successes, less confident about succeeding in the future, and generally less enthused about school than children who attended preschool or kindergarten programs that emphasized child-centered social agendas and flexible, hands-on, discovery-

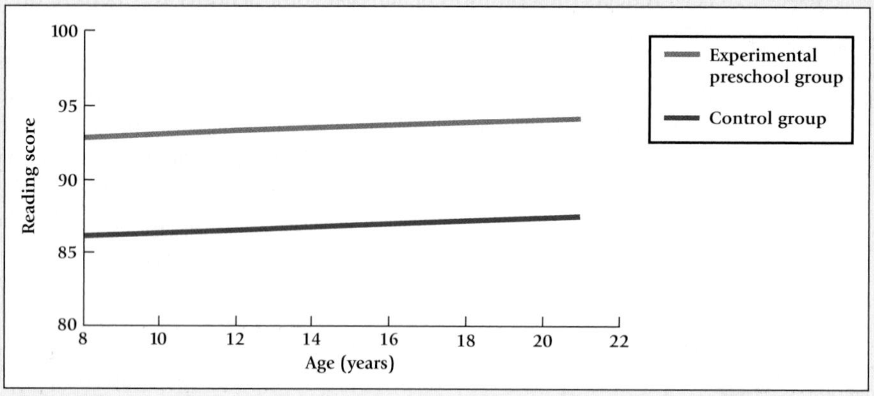

Figure 1 *Reading achievement scores for children who did or did not attend the experimental preschool.*
Adapted from Campbell et al., 2001.

CONTINUED

schools ended up scoring just as high on this final index of academic progress as the initially good (Group 1) students who attended the least effective schools. Similar findings were obtained in large studies of elementary and high schools in the United States. Even after controlling for important variables such as the socioeconomic backgrounds of the students and the type of communities served, some elementary schools were found to be much more "effective" than others (Brookover et al., 1979; Hill, Foster, & Gendler, 1990; see also Eccles & Roeser, 2005).

Factors That Contribute to Effective Schooling

So the school that children attend can make a difference. A large body of research has investigated factors that contribute to effective schools and communities for promoting positive child development. Let's review some of the factors that have been found to make a difference.

Composition of the Student Body. To some extent, the "effectiveness" of a school is a function of what it has to work with. On average, academic achievement is lowest in schools with a preponderance of economically disadvantaged students (Lee, Loeb, &

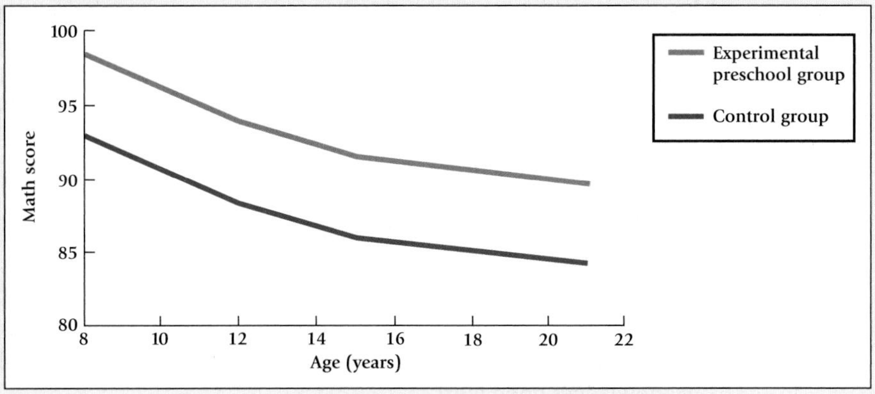

Figure 2 *Math achievement scores for children who did or did not attend the experimental preschool.*
Adapted from Campbell et al., 2001.

based learning. So there seem to be dangers in overemphasizing academics during the preschool period after all.

On the other hand, preschool programs that offer a healthy mix of play and child-initiated discovery learning can be very beneficial to young children, especially to disadvantaged children (Stipek, 2002). Although most children who attend preschool classes are no more or less intellectually advanced than those who remain at home, *disadvantaged* preschoolers who attend child-centered programs designed to prepare them for school do display more cognitive growth and achieve more later success in school than other disadvantaged youngsters who do no attend these programs (Campbell et al., 2001; Reynolds & Temple, 1998). This is due, in part, to increasing involvement by parents in the program participants' education (Reynolds & Robertson, 2003). And there is evidence that these gains are maintained over time as well. As shown in the accompanying graphs, disadvantaged children who attended an experimental preschool program scored higher on tests of reading and math achievement than a control group of equally disadvantaged children who did not attend the program. This difference was maintained throughout childhood and into young adulthood. Clearly, when the preschool programs are high quality, there can be long-term benefits for disadvantaged children.

So as long as preschool programs allow plenty of time for play and for skill building in the context of group social interactions, they can help children from all social backgrounds acquire social and communication skills, as well as an appreciation of rules and routines, that will smooth the transition from individual learning at home to group learning in an elementary school classroom (Zigler & Finn-Stevenson, 1993).

Lubeck, 1998; Rutter, 1983), and it appears that *any* child is likely to make more progress if taught in a school with a higher concentration of highly motivated, intellectually capable peers. However, this *does not* mean that a school is only as good as the students it serves, for many schools that draw heavily from disadvantaged minority populations are highly effective at motivating students and preparing them for jobs or higher education (Reynolds, 1992).

School Climate. Students' perceptions of school climate, including how safe they feel and how much support and encouragement they feel from school personnel, also affects the schools' effectiveness (Loukas & Robinson, 2004; Taylor & Lopez, 2005a). When children feel safe and encouraged, they are more engaged in school and this helps them to achieve academically and socially (Eccles & Roeser, 2005; Taylor & Lopez, 2005b).

The Scholastic Atmosphere of Successful Schools. So what is it about the learning environment of some schools that allows them to accomplish so much? Reviews of the literature (Eccles & Roeser, 2005; National Research Council and Institute of Medicine, 2004; Phillips, 1997; Reynolds, 1992; Rutter, 1983) point to the following values and practices that characterize effective schools:

Academic Emphasis. Effective schools have a clear focus on academic goals. Children are regularly assigned homework, which is checked, corrected, and discussed with them.

Challenging, Developmentally Appropriate Curricula. Content that children can relate to because it emphasizes their culture and history, as well as the developmental issues they are currently facing, promotes achievement-related behaviors, such as effort, attention, attendance, and appropriate classroom behavior (Eccles, Wigfield, & Schiefele, 1998; Jackson & Davis, 2000; Lee & Smith, 2001). Conversely, content that does not challenge children or adolescents, or that they don't feel they can personally relate to, leads to poor school performance and alienation from the school society (Eccles & Roeser, 2005; Jackson & Davis, 2000).

Classroom Management. In effective schools, teachers waste little time getting activities started or dealing with distracting disciplinary problems. Lessons begin and end on time. Pupils are told exactly what is expected of them and receive clear and unambiguous feedback about their academic performance. The classroom atmosphere is comfortable; all students are actively encouraged to work to the best of their abilities, and ample praise acknowledges good work.

Discipline. In effective schools, the staff is firm in enforcing rules and does so on the spot rather than sending offenders off to the principal's office. Rarely do instructors resort to physical sanctions (slapping or spanking), which contribute to truancy, defiance, and a tense classroom atmosphere. At the same time, well-behaved children and adolescents who are given leeway in making their own decisions at school experience a strong sense of self-efficacy, and this supports academic success (Deci & Ryan, 2000; Ryan & Deci, 2000a, 2000b; Grolnick et al., 2002).

Teamwork. Effective schools have faculties that work as a team, jointly planning curricular objectives and monitoring student progress, under the guidance of a principal who provides active, energetic leadership.

In sum, the effective school environment is a *comfortable* but *businesslike* setting in which academic successes are expected and students are *motivated* to learn (Midgley, 2002; Phillips, 1997; Rutter, 1983). Effective teachers are like authoritative parents—caring and concerned but firm and controlling (Wentzel, 2002). Research consistently indicates that children and adolescents from many social backgrounds prefer authoritative instruction and are more likely to thrive when treated this way than students taught by more authoritarian or more permissive teachers (Arnold, McWilliams, & Arnold, 1998; Wentzel, 2002).

Finally, one can hardly emphasize strongly enough just how important effective schooling can be for economically disadvantaged students who are not only at risk of academic underachievement but may be living in neighborhoods or in family settings that place them at risk of displaying conduct problems, internalizing disorders (e.g., anxiety, depression), and other antisocial behaviors (Eccles & Gootman, 2002; Eccles & Templeton, 2002). Gene Brody and his colleagues (Brody et al., 2002), for example, found that teachers who create an effective classroom environment help low-income, at-risk 7- to -15-year-olds from single-parent homes to cope with stresses they experience, keep on track at school, and avoid the internalizing and externalizing disorders commonly observed among such populations. This protective stabilizing effect of effective schooling was quite clear in this study, even when the parenting that children received was compromised (that is, low in warmth and involved-supervision). Deborah O'Donnell and her colleagues (2002) found that high-risk adolescents living in violent neighborhoods are less subject to deviant peer influences and less involved in substance abuse and other antisocial conduct when they receive the support and encouragement of teachers in effective schools (see also Meehan, Hughes, & Cavell, 2003). Findings such as these clearly illustrate just how important effective schooling can be in the socialization process, contributing substantially to positive social and emotional (as well as positive academic) outcomes.

The "Goodness of Fit" between Students and Schools

It is important to recognize that characteristics of the student and of the school environment often interact to affect student outcomes—a phenomenon Lee Cronbach and

aptitude-treatment interaction (ATI)
phenomenon whereby characteristics of the student and of the school environment interact to affect student outcomes, such that any given educational practice may be effective with some students but not with others.

Richard Snow (1977) call **aptitude-treatment interaction (ATI).** Over the years, much educational research has been based on the assumption that a particular teaching method, philosophy of education, or organizational system will prove superior for all students, regardless of their abilities, personalities, and cultural backgrounds. This assumption is often wrong. Instead, many approaches to education are highly effective with *some* kinds of students but quite ineffective with others. The secret to being effective is to find an appropriate fit between learners and educational practices.

For example, teachers tend to get the most out of high-ability, middle-class students by moving at a quick pace and insisting on high standards of performance—that is, by challenging these students. Low-ability and disadvantaged students often respond more favorably to a teacher who motivates them by being warm and encouraging rather than intrusive and demanding (Good & Brophy, 1994; Sacks & Mergendoller, 1997).

Sensitivity to students' cultural traditions is also important. European American students come from cultures that stress individual learning, perhaps making them especially well-suited for the individual mastery expectations that are emphasized in traditional classrooms. But the traditional classroom doesn't work for everyone. Ethnic Hawaiians and students from other cultures that stress cooperation and collaborative approaches to learning often founder in traditional classrooms. They pay little attention to the teacher or their lessons and spend a lot of time seeking the attention of classmates—behaviors that are perceived by teachers as reflecting their lack of interest in school (Tharp, 1989). When instruction is made more culturally compatible for these children by having teachers circulate among small groups, instructing and encouraging group members to pull together and assist each other to achieve learning objectives, Hawaiian children become much more enthusiastic about school and achieve much more as well (see Figure 16.5).

Unfortunately, young adolescents from any social background may begin to lose interest in academics should they experience a mismatch between their school environments and their changing developmental needs. In sum, the "goodness of fit" between students and their classroom environments is a crucial aspect of effective schooling. Education that is carefully tailored to students' cultural backgrounds, personal characteristics, and developmental needs is much more likely to succeed.

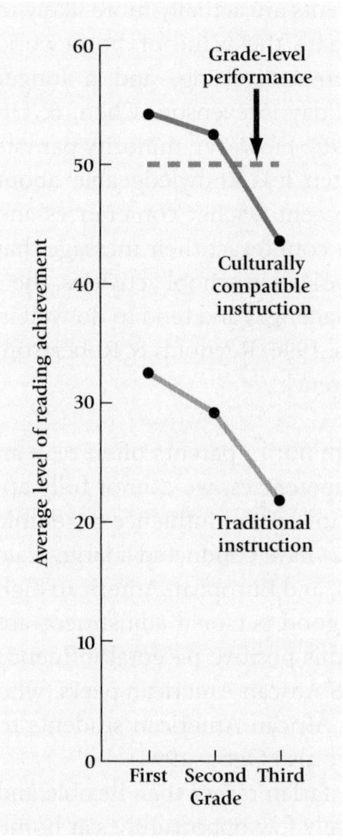

Figure 16.5 Reading achievement of ethnic Hawaiian first- through third-grade students who received traditional or culturally compatible classroom instruction. The students who received culturally compatible instruction read at grade level, whereas those receiving traditional instruction read far below grade level. *Adapted from* Rousing Minds to Life: Teaching, Learning, and Schooling in Social Context, *by R. G. Tharp & R. Gallimore, 1988, p. 116. Cambridge, England: Cambridge University Press. Adapted with the permission of Cambridge University Press.*

Do Our Schools Meet the Needs of All Our Children?

Public education in the United States arose not so much from a desire to educate a work force (most 19th-century workers were farmers or unskilled laborers who required little education) as from the need to "Americanize" a nation of immigrants—to bring them into the mainstream of American society (Rudolph, 1965). So our public schools have traditionally been majority-culture, middle-class institutions staffed by white instructors who promote middle-class values.

However, more and more of the students educated in our public schools come from non-white social backgrounds; in fact, a majority of students in California's public schools now belong to various "minority" groups (Garcia, 1993). How well are minority students being served by our schools?

Educational Experiences of Ethnic Minorities

African American, Latino, and Native American children tend to earn poorer grades in school and make lower scores on standardized achievement tests than their European American classmates. They are also more likely to be disciplined, to be "held back" in a grade, and to drop out before completing high school (Associated Press, 2002a; Dusek, 1991; U.S. Bureau of the Census, 2001). Asian Americans (particularly recent immigrants) tend to outperform European American students at school (Fuligni, 1997; Slaughter-Defoe et al., 1990). These ethnic differences in academic achievement are still found even after group differences in socioeconomic status are controlled, and they are not merely

Robert E. Daemmrich/Getty Images

Children are more likely to do well in school if their parents value education and are interested and involved in school activities.

the product of group differences in intellectual ability (Alexander & Entwisle, 1988; Pungello et al., 1996; Sue & Okazaki, 1990). Why, then, do such differences exist?

Parental Attitudes and Involvement. Let's first note that underachieving minority students do not have difficulty at school because their parents devalue education. African American and Latino American parents stress the importance of education at least as much as European American parents do (Galper, Wigfield, & Seefeldt, 1997; Steinberg, Dornbusch, & Brown, 1992). Minority parents are actually more likely to appreciate the value of homework, competency testing, and a longer school day (Stevenson, Chen, & Uttal, 1990). However, minority parents are often less knowledgeable about and less involved in such school-sponsored activities as parent-teacher conferences and PTA meetings, and this lack of participation may partially counteract their message that school is important. When minority parents *are* highly involved in school activities, their children feel more confident about mastering academic challenges and tend to do well in school (Connell, Spencer, & Aber, 1994; Luster & McAdoo, 1996; Reynolds & Robertson, 2003). So active parental involvement can make a big difference.

Interfacing Parent and Peer Influences. Although minority parents often play an important role in fostering their children's scholastic competencies, we cannot fully appreciate their contribution without also understanding how peers influence academic achievement. Lawrence Steinberg and his colleagues (1992) have conducted a large-scale study of school achievement among African, Latino, Asian, and European American high school students. They found that academic success and good personal adjustment are usually associated with *authoritative parenting.* However, this positive parental influence on academic achievement may be undermined by low-SES African American peers, who often devalue academic achievement and pressure many African American students to choose between academic success and peer acceptance (see also Ogbu, 1994).

Latino parents tend to be strict and somewhat authoritarian rather than flexible and authoritative. As a result, Latino students may have relatively few opportunities at home to act autonomously and acquire decision-making skills that would serve them well in school (Steinberg, Dornbusch, & Brown, 1992). Furthermore, Latino students from low-income areas also tend to associate with peers who do not strongly value academics and who may undercut their parents' efforts to promote academic achievement. On the other hand, European American students are more likely than either African American or Latino students to have *both* authoritative parents and peer support for education working in their favor.

High-achieving Asian American students often experience restrictive, authoritarian parenting at home. However, this highly controlling pattern, coupled with a very strong emphasis on education and the very high achievement standards that many Asian American parents set for their children, actually fosters academic success. Why? Because Asian American children are also taught from a very early age to be respectful and to obey their elders, who have a duty to train them to be socially responsible and competent human beings (Chao, 1994, 2001; Zhou & Bankston, 1998). Given this kind of socialization in Asian American homes, it is hardly surprising that the Asian American peer group strongly endorses education and encourages academic success (Fuligni, 1997). The result? Asian American students typically spend more hours studying, often with their supportive friends, than other students do, which undoubtedly accounts for much of their academic success (Fuligni, 1997; Steinberg, Dornbusch, & Brown, 1992).

Teacher Expectancies. Finally, we must consider another hypothesis about ethnic differences in school achievement: the possibility that underachievement by some minority students is rooted in subtle stereotyping on the part of teachers. According to social stereotypes, Asian Americans are expected to be bright and hardworking, whereas African Americans and Latino students from low-income neighborhoods are expected to perform poorly in school. And teachers are hardly immune to these stereotypes. Minority students often feel that white teachers do not understand them and that they could do better in school were they given more respect and understanding (Ford & Harris, 1996). Consistent with this viewpoint, teachers in one study were asked to select from a checklist those attributes that best described their lower-income minority pupils. Teachers consistently selected adjectives such as *lazy, fun-loving,* and *rebellious,* thus implying that they did not expect much of these students (Gottlieb, 1966). Teacher expectancy effects on academic achievement are largest in the early grades, particularly in classrooms where high- and low-expectancy students reliably receive differential treatment (Kuklinski & Weinstein, 2000, 2001).

In sum, parents' values and styles of parenting, peers' level of support for academic achievement, and teacher expectancies probably all contribute to ethnic differences in school achievement. Some theorists believe that children from lower-income minority subcultures are at an immediate disadvantage when they enter a middle-class scholastic setting and that schools must change dramatically if they are to motivate and better educate these children. Researchers have known for years that underachieving ethnic minorities fare better at school if the experiences that they have in class or read about in their textbooks include more information about people of their ethnicity (Kagan & Zahn, 1995; Stevenson, Chen, & Uttal, 1990), and this knowledge is part of the rationale behind recent efforts to make school experiences more culturally relevant for these youngsters. Among the positive changes that we see today are more effective bilingual education programs designed to meet the needs of children from the over 100 distinct language groups in the United States (Winsler et al., 1999), and multicultural education programs designed to bring the perspectives of many cultural and subcultural groups into the classroom so that all students feel more welcome there (Banks, 1993; Burnette, 1997).

Education and Developmental Transitions

For some time now, educators have been concerned about a number of undesirable changes that often occur when students make the transition from elementary school to junior high school: loss of self-esteem and interest in school, declining grades, and increased troublemaking, to name a few (Eccles et al., 1996; Seidman et al., 1994). Why is this a treacherous move?

One reason the transition is difficult is because young adolescents, particularly girls, are often experiencing major physical and psychological changes at the same time they are required to change schools. Roberta Simmons and Dale Blyth (1987), for example, found that girls who were reaching puberty as they were making the transition from sixth-grade in an elementary school to seventh-grade in a junior high school were more likely to experience drops in self-esteem and other negative changes than girls who remained in a kindergarten through eighth-grade (K–8) school during this vulnerable period. Adolescents at greatest risk of academic and emotional difficulties are those who must also cope with other life transitions, such as family turmoil or a change in residence, about the time they change schools (Flanagan & Eccles, 1993). Might more adolescents remain interested in academics and show better adjustment outcomes if they weren't forced to change schools at the precise time they are experiencing the many other changes often associated with puberty? This has been part of the rationale for the devel-

Moving from small, close-knit elementary schools to highly bureaucratic and impersonal secondary schools is stressful to adolescents, many of whom lose interest in academics and become more susceptible to peer group influences.

opment of *middle schools,* serving grades six through eight, which are now more common than junior high schools in the United States (Braddock & McPartland, 1993).

Yet Jacquelynne Eccles and her colleagues (Eccles, Lord, & Midgley, 1991; Roeser & Eccles, 1998) report that students do not necessarily find the transition to middle school any easier than the transition to junior high school. This led them to suspect that it is not as important *when* adolescents make a school change as *what* their new school is like. Specifically, they proposed a "goodness of fit" hypothesis stating that the transition to a new school is likely to be especially difficult when that school, whether a junior high or middle school, is poorly matched to adolescents' developmental needs.

What "mismatches" might be involved? Consider that the transition from elementary school to a middle or junior high school often involves going from a small school with close student-teacher ties, a good deal of choice regarding learning activities, and gentle discipline to a larger, more bureaucratized environment where student-teacher relationships are impersonal, good grades are emphasized but harder to come by, opportunities for choice in learning activities are limited, and discipline is rigid—all this at a time when adolescents are seeking *more* rather than less autonomy (Andermann & Midgley, 1997).

Eccles and others have demonstrated that the "fit" between developmental needs and school environments is indeed an important influence on adolescent adjustment to school. In one study (Mac Iver & Reuman, 1988), the transition to junior high brought about a decline in intrinsic interest in learning mainly among students who wanted more involvement in classroom decisions but ended up with fewer such opportunities than they had in elementary school. A second study illustrates just how important a good fit between student and schools can be: Students experienced negative changes in their attitudes toward mathematics if their transition to junior high resulted in less personal and supportive relations with math teachers; but for those few students whose transition to junior high involved gaining more supportive teachers than they had in elementary school, interest in academics actually *increased* (Midgley, Feldlaufer, & Eccles, 1989). Finally, students in a third study fared better psychologically and academically when they felt that their school encouraged all students to do their best (learning goals) than when competition for grades (that is, performance goals) were emphasized (Roeser & Eccles, 1998).

The message? Declines in academic motivation and performance are not inevitable as students move from elementary to secondary schools. These declines occur primarily when the fit between student and school environment goes from good to poor. How might we improve the fit? Parents can help by recognizing how difficult school transitions can be and communicating this understanding to their teens. One study found that adolescents whose parents were in tune with their developmental needs and who fostered autonomy in decision making generally adjusted well to the transition to junior high and posted *gains* in self-esteem (Lord, Eccles, & McCarthy, 1994). Teachers can also help by stressing mastery goals rather than grades and by seeking parents' opinions about scholastic matters and keeping them involved during this transitional period—a time when collaborative relations between parents and teachers normally declines and adolescents often feel that they are facing the stresses of this new, impersonal academic setting with little social support (Eccles & Harold, 1993). Indeed, specially designed programs to provide these supports for young adolescents do help them to adjust to school transitions and reduce the odds that they will drop out of school (Smith, 1997).

How Well-Educated Are Our Children? A Cross-Cultural Comparison

How successful are our schools at imparting academic skills to their pupils? Large surveys of the reading, writing, and mathematical achievement of 9- to 17-year-old American students reveal that most of them do learn to read during the elementary school years and have acquired such mathematical proficiencies as basic computational skills and graph reading abilities by the time they finish high school (Dossey et al., 1988; National Education Goals Panel, 1992). Yet, only about one American student in four could be described as truly proficient in reading and mathematics achievement, and American children do not write very well (National Assessment of Educational Progress, as cited in Greene, 1997). Are these findings cause for concern?

Many educators think so (Short & Talley, 1997; Tirozzi & Uro, 1997), especially in view of the results of several cross-national surveys of children's academic achievement—studies indicating that the average scores obtained by American schoolchildren in mathematics, science, and verbal skills are consistently lower, and sometimes much lower, than those made by students in many other industrialized nations (National Education Goals Panel, 1992; Stevenson, Chen, & Lee, 1993).

Cross-cultural research conducted by Harold Stevenson and his colleagues (Chen & Stevenson, 1995; Stevenson, Lee, & Stigler, 1986, Stevenson, Chen, & Lee, 1993) leaves no doubt that schoolchildren in Taiwan, the People's Republic of China, and Japan outperform students in the United States in math, reading, and other school subjects. The gap in math performance is especially striking; in testings of fifth-graders, for example, only 4 percent of Chinese children and 10 percent of Japanese students had scores on a math achievement test as low as those of the average American child (Stevenson, Chen, & Lee, 1993). Achievement differences of this sort are evident from the time children enter school and grow larger each year as children progress from first to fifth to eleventh grade (Geary et al., 1996; Stevenson, Chen, & Lee, 1993). Why do these differences exist, and what can they tell us about improving American education?

The problem is not that American students are any less intelligent, for they enter school performing just as well on IQ tests as their Asian counterparts (Stevenson et al., 1985), and they score at least as well as Japanese and Chinese students on general information tests covering material *not* typically covered in school (Stevenson, Chen, & Lee, 1993). In Chapter 8, we touched on some linguistic and instructional supports that help East Asian children to acquire mathematical knowledge. Yet, most of the achievement gap between American and Asian students seems to reflect cultural differences in educational attitudes and practices. For example:

Classroom Instruction

Asian students spend more time being educated than American students do. Elementary school teachers in Asian countries devote more class time to core academic subjects: For example, two to three times as many hours a week are spent on math instruction. The Asian classroom is a comfortable but businesslike setting where little time is wasted; Asian students spend about 95 percent of their time on "on-task" activities such as listening to the teacher and completing assignments, whereas American students spend only about 80 percent of their time "on task" (Stigler, Lee, & Stevenson, 1987). Asian students also attend school for more hours per day and more days per year (often attending half the day on Saturdays) than American students do (Fuligni & Stevenson, 1995; Stevenson, Lee, & Stigler, 1986).

Fujifotos/The Image Works

Children in traditional Asian classrooms are required to stay in their seats working on assignments or paying close attention to their teacher.

Parental Involvement

Asian parents are strongly committed to the educational process. They hold higher achievement expectancies for their children than American parents do, and even though their children are excelling by American standards, Asian parents are much less likely than American parents to be satisfied with their children's current academic performance (Chen & Stevenson, 1995; Stevenson, Chen, & Lee, 1993). Asian parents think that homework is more important than American parents do, and they also receive frequent communications from their children's teachers in notebooks that children carry to and from school each day. These communications enable Asian parents to keep close tabs on how their children are progressing and to follow teachers' suggestions about how they can encourage and assist their children at home (Stevenson & Lee, 1990). By contrast, communications between U.S. parents and teachers are often limited to brief annual parent-teacher conferences.

Student Involvement

Not only do Asian students spend more days in class and more class time on academic assignments than American children do, but they are assigned and complete more homework as well (Stevenson, Chen, & Lee, 1993). During the high school years, Asian students continue to devote more time to scholastic activities and spend much less time working, dating, or socializing with friends than American students do (Fuligni & Stevenson, 1995). Much of the socializing that Asian students undertake with peers centers around academics (e.g., studying together), and academic achievement is an important contributor to social adjustment and popularity in Asian peer groups (Chen, Chang, & He, 2003).

A Strong Emphasis on Effort

A major reason that Asian students apply themselves so diligently to academic activities is that their parents, teachers, and they themselves share the strong belief that *all* youngsters have the potential to master their studies if they work hard enough. Their American counterparts are more inclined to believe that academic success reflects other factors such as the quality of the child's teachers (see Figure 16.6) or one's intelligence (Chen & Stevenson, 1995; Stevenson, Chen, & Lee, 1993). Asian students face especially strong pressures to excel in the classroom because their prospects for obtaining a college education largely depend on the results of a competitive exam taken in high school. Their strong belief that effort will ultimately pay off in better learning (and higher test scores) helps to explain why Asian youngsters are no more anxious about school or otherwise psychologically maladjusted than American students are (Chen, Chang, & He, 2003; Chen & Stevenson, 1995; Crystal et al., 1994).

So the formula for more effective education may not be so mysterious after all, judging from the success of the Chinese and Japanese educational systems. The secret is to get teachers, students, and parents working together to make education a top priority, to set high achievement goals, and to invest the day-by-day effort required to attain those objectives. In response to evidence that American schools are being outclassed by those in other countries, many states and local school districts have taken up the challenge of improving American education. How? By strengthening curricula, tightening standards for teacher certification, raising standards for graduation and promotion from grade to grade, implementing alternative academic calendars to shorten summer vacations and increase student retention of previously learned material, mandating smaller classes in the primary grades, and, most importantly, seeking ways to involve parents as partners with teachers, at both the elementary and secondary school levels, to create more supportive learning environments and foster higher academic achievement (Gonzalez, 2000; Tirozzi & Uro, 1997; U.S. Department of Education, 1996). These educational reformers are well aware that improving the scholastic and vocational preparation of American's youth is crucial if Americans are to maintain a leadership role in an ever-changing and ever more competitive world.

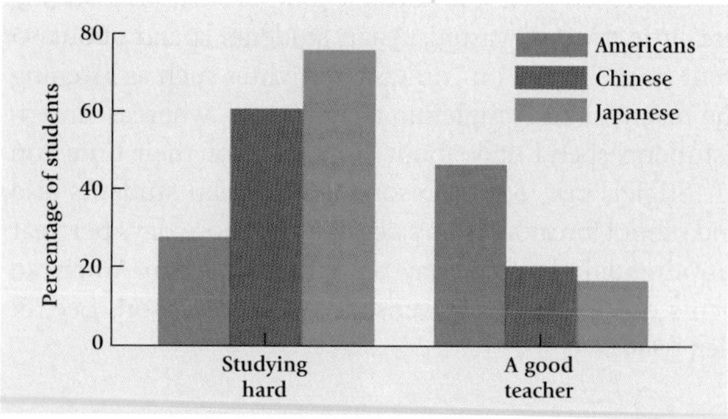

Figure 16.6 Percentages of Chinese, Japanese, and American high school students who picked "studying hard" or having "a good teacher" as the most important factor influencing their performance in mathematics. *Adapted from "Motivation and Mathematics Achievement: A Comparative Study of Asian-American, Caucasian-American, and East Asian high school students," by C. Chen & H. W. Stevenson, 1995,* Child Development, *66, 1215–1234. Copyright © 1995 by the Society for Research in Child Development, Inc. Adapted by permission.*

CONCEPT CHECK 16.2 Understanding Schools as Agents of Socialization

Check your understanding of schools as agents of socialization and the effects of schools on child development by answering the following questions. Answers appear in the Appendix.

True or False: Identify whether the following statements are true or false.

1. (T)(F) Children's perception of school climate, meaning how safe they feel at school and how much nurturance and encouragement they feel from teachers, is one aspect of effective schooling.
2. (T)(F) In general, traditional classrooms with an emphasis on individual work and achievement and with student attention directed to the teacher, is the best format for effective schooling for children from all cultural backgrounds.

Fill in the Blank: Complete the following sentences with the correct terms.

3. American school systems may not be meeting the educational needs of ______ in our culture.
4. American school transitions (from elementary to junior high, for example) may not be meeting the ______ needs of children in our culture.

Multiple Choice: Select the correct answer for each question.

______ 5. The training that schools provide that teaches children to obey rules and authority, cooperate with peers, and generally become good citizens is called
   a. the social curriculum
   b. the socialization curriculum
   c. the citizen curriculum
   d. the informal curriculum

______ 6. Which of the following was *not* proposed as one of the reasons American school children perform so much more poorly than Asian school children on standardized tests of reading and math?
   a. A stronger emphasis on independent learning and discovery learning in Asian school cultures.
   b. Asian children spending more time in school *and* more time "on task" when they are in school.
   c. Both parents *and* peers in Asian cultures are more concerned with academics and achievement than American parents and peers.
   d. Asian cultures tend to emphasize effort in the pursuit of academic success, whereas American cultures tend to emphasize intelligence and school quality as determinants of academic success.

______ 7. Mrs. Phurtile has fraternal twin boys, Andy and Zack, who were born on the cutoff date assigned for the local school system for entry into school. By the time the boys were 5 years old, it was clear that although they were both normally intelligent, Zack was delayed in his social development compared to Andy and other 5-year-olds. Because of this, Mrs. Phurtile decided to enroll Andy in school at 5 but delay Zack for school entry until he was 6. What would you expect to find in comparing the twins' academic process when they turned 7 years old?
   a. Because they are the same age, their academic progress would be roughly equivalent at this young age.
   b. Because Zack was able to delay school for a year and make progress on his social development, his cognitive development would also have shown gains and he would be more advanced on cognitive competency tests than Andy.
   c. Because Andy attended more school, he would be more advanced than Zack on cognitive competency tests, even though they were the same age.

Short Answer: Briefly answer the following question.

8. List and describe four qualities of "effective" schools.

Peers as Agents of Socialization

Throughout the text, we have focused on adults as socializing agents. In their various roles as parents, teachers, coaches, scoutmasters, and religious leaders, adults represent the authority, power, and expertise of a society. However, some theorists, Jean Piaget among them, believe that peers may contribute as much or even more to a child's or an adolescent's development as adults do (Harris, 1998, 2000; Youniss, McLellan, & Strouse, 1994). They argue that there are "two social worlds of childhood," one involving adult/child transactions and the other involving the society of children's peers. These social systems influence development in different ways.

By the time they enter school, most children spend the majority of their leisure time in the company of peers. What roles might peers play in a child's or an adolescent's development? We will see in the pages that follow that peers clearly have the potential to affect each other in many positive ways.

Who or What Is a Peer and What Functions Do Peers Serve?

peers
two or more persons who are operating at similar levels of behavioral complexity.

Developmentalists think of **peers** as "social equals" or as individuals who, for the moment at least, are operating at similar levels of behavioral complexity (Lewis & Rosenblum, 1975). According to this activity-based definition, children who differ somewhat in age are still considered "peers" as long as they can adjust their behaviors to suit one another's capabilities as they pursue common interests or goals.

Both older and younger children benefit from mixed-age interactions.

© Jeff Greenberg/PhotoEdit

Peers as Equal-Status Contacts

We gain some idea why peer contacts among peers may be important by contrasting them to contacts with parents. A child's interactions with parents are lopsided: Because parents have more power than children do, children are in a subordinate position and must often defer to adult authority. On the other hand, peers typically have equal status and power and must learn to appreciate each other's perspectives, negotiate and compromise, and cooperate with each other if they hope to get along or achieve joint goals. Thus, *equal-status* contacts with peers likely contribute to the development of social competencies that are difficult to acquire in the unequal interactions with parents and other adults.

Interaction among children of different ages is also important for development (Hartup, 1983). Although cross-age interactions tend to be somewhat unbalanced, with one child (typically the elder) having more power than the other, these interactions help children to develop social competencies. One cross-cultural survey found that the presence of younger peers fostered the development of compassion, caregiving, assertiveness, and leadership skills in older children (Whiting & Edwards, 1988; see also Kowalski et al., 2004). At the same time, younger children benefited from mixed-age interactions by acquiring a variety of new skills from older playmates and by learning how to seek assistance from and defer gracefully to these more powerful peers. Older children usually took charge in mixed-age interactions and adjusted their behavior to the competencies of their younger peers. Even 2-year-olds show such powers of leadership and accommodation, for they are more inclined to take the initiative and display simpler and more repetitive play routines when paired with an 18-month-old toddler than with an age-mate (Brownell, 1990).

Frequency of Peer Contacts

Between the ages of 2 and 12, children spend more and more time with peers and less and less time with adults. This trend is

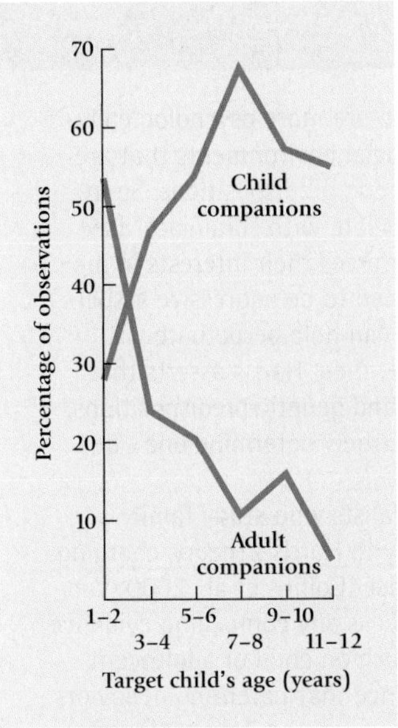

Figure 16.7 Developmental changes in children's companionship with adults and other children. *Adapted from "Age Segregation in Children's Social Interactions," by S. Ellis, B. Rogoff, & C. C. Cromer, 1981.* Developmental Psychology, *17, 399–407. Copyright © 1981 by the American Psychological Association. Adapted by permission.*

illustrated in Figure 16.7, which summarizes what Sherri Ellis and her colleagues (1981) found while observing 436 children playing in their homes and around the neighborhood. This study revealed that children of all ages spent less time with age-mates (defined as children whose ages were within a year of their own) than with children who were more than a year older or younger than they were. This illustrates the idea that peers are "social equals" rather than only age-mates.

Another finding of this study is a familiar one: Even 1- to 2-year-olds played more often with same-sex peers than with other-sex peers, and this gender segregation increased with age. Once in their sex-segregated worlds, boys and girls experience different kinds of social relationships. Boys tend to form "packs," whereas girls form "pairs." That is, a boy often plays competitive games or team sports in groups, whereas a girl more often establishes a longer and more cooperative relationship with one playmate (Benenson, Apostoleris, & Parnass, 1997; Fabes, Martin, & Hanish, 2003).

Overall, then, children spend an increasing amount of time with peers, and those peers are typically *same*-sex children who are only *roughly similar* in age but who enjoy the same kinds of gender-typed activities.

How Important Are Peer Influences?

To this point, we have argued that peer interactions may foster many social and personal competencies that are not acquired within parent-child relationships. Just how important are these peer influences? As described in the Box on p. 650, some researchers believe that peer influences are more important than parental influences in child development. One review of more than 30 studies revealed that children who had been rejected by their peers during grade school are much more likely than those who had good peer relations to drop out of school, become involved in delinquent or criminal activities, and display serious psychological difficulties later in adolescence and young adulthood (Parker & Asher, 1987; Parker et al., 1995; see also Ladd & Troop-Gordon, 2003). So merely having contact with peer associates is not enough to ensure positive developmental outcomes; getting along with peers is important, too.

In sum, peers are meaningful agents of socialization, and the task of becoming *appropriately* sociable with peers is an important developmental hurdle. In our next section, we will focus on the growth of peer sociability and on some of the factors that influence how appropriately (or inappropriately) sociable a child turns out to be.

The Development of Peer Sociability

sociability
a person's willingness to engage others in social interaction and to seek their attention or approval.

Sociability is a term that describes a person's willingness to engage others in social interaction and to seek their attention or approval. In Chapter 11, we learned that even young infants are sociable creatures: months before forming their first attachments, they are already smiling, cooing, or otherwise attracting the attention of caregivers and are likely to protest whenever *any* adult puts them down or walks off and leaves them alone. But are young infants so sociable with other infants?

Peer Sociability in Infancy and Toddlerhood

Babies show an interest in other babies from the first months of life, and they begin to interact by about the middle of the first year. By then, infants often smile or babble at their tiny peers. They vocalize, offer toys, and gesture to one another (Vandell & Mueller, 1995; Vandell, Wilson, & Buchanan, 1980). However, many of these friendly gestures go unnoticed and are not returned by the fellow baby.

FOCUS ON RESEARCH Are Peers More Important than Parents?

One of the more controversial ideas to emerge in recent years is Judith Harris's (1995, 1998, 2000) notion that peers are far more important as socialization agents than are parents. Specifically, Harris claims that:

- Developmentalists have long assumed that correlations between parenting practices and child outcomes are due to parental influences (that is, socialization) within the family when, in fact, they are largely due to genes shared by parents and their children.
- Any influence that parents do have is limited to children's behavior at home; such influence is strongest for young children and rarely affects their behaviors away from home.
- Because adaptive social learning is specific to particular contexts, peers are more important than parents in socializing children for the world outside the home.

Harris states that "Children would develop into the same sort of adults if we left their lives outside the home unchanged and left them in their schools and neighborhoods—but switched all the parents around" (Harris, 1998, p. 359). To make her point, she notes that immigrant children quickly acquire a new language and new cultural traditions from peers, even when their parents come from a very different culture and speak a different language.

Harris's ideas were heavily influenced by some of the behavioral genetics research that we discussed in Chapter 3. She argues that research claiming that certain parenting styles (e.g, authoritative parenting) foster adaptive outcomes fails to control for important genetic influences. For example, if certain parents are genetically predisposed to parent authoritatively, their children may turn out well not because of the parenting they receive but because they may share genes that foster adaptive development with their parents. Harris correctly notes that siblings raised by the same parents often turn out differently. Why? Because, she argues, they have different genes and genetically influenced attributes that elicit different responses from parents. In effect, parents are said to react to preexisting genetic differences among their children rather than to parent in ways that would create individual differences in developmental outcomes (Reiss et al., 2000).

Harris goes on to argue that peer socialization makes children from different families alike. As they spend more time with peers and figure out the social groups (based on age, sex, and interest patterns) to which they belong, children increasingly want to be like other members of these groups. Thus, they carefully attend to other children and adopt the attitudes, speech patterns, dress codes, and patterns of behavior that prevail within their peer groups. They eventually begin to associate with peers who are more psychologically similar to themselves, creating social environments that are largely compatible with their genetic predispositions. So intellectually inclined children associate with "brainiacs" (see Iervolino et al., 2002), which reinforces their interests in intellectual pursuits. Children inclined to be aggressive associate with aggressive peers, which can help perpetuate aggressive inclinations. Over time, then, Harris asserts that parenting practices matter little and genetic predispositions, in concert with peer influences, largely determine one's developmental outcomes.

Not surprisingly, developmentalists who study family processes have reacted negatively to Harris's theory, charging that she greatly overstates her case (Collins et al., 2000; Vandell, 2000). They claim that she lacks any compelling evidence that peers are the primary influence on child or adolescent development. There is solid evidence that parenting behaviors do matter, even when genetic influences are taken into account. For example, we learned in Chapter 3 that identical twins will show different patterns of development to the extent that they are treated differently by their parents (Asbury et al., 2003). Because these identical twins have identical genes, the differences they display have to be attributable (in part at least) to different parenting. And recall from Chapter 11 that the caregiving sensitivity (or lack of it) of adoptive parents largely determines whether their adopted children form secure or insecure attachments with them (Stams, Juffer, & van Ijzendoorn, 2002). Again, this reflects a true parental influence because adoptive parents share no genes with their adopted children. Indeed, parents of temperamentally difficult infants can be helped to become more sensitive, responsive caregivers and improvements in caregiver sensitivity are *causally related* to the security of attachments their infants form. Finally, we saw in the last chapter that parents not only influence their children's ability to interact amicably with peers but that their parenting practices also influence the kinds of peers with whom their children are likely to associate.

In sum, Harris is correct in asserting that (1) both genes and peers contribute substantially to our social and personality development and (2) developmentalists have often overestimated the role of parenting in shaping child and adolescent outcomes. However, she is wrong in concluding that patterns of parenting don't matter. As we've seen throughout the text, *both* parents and peers—as well as siblings, teachers, and other socialization agents operating within specific cultural or subcultural contexts—all contribute substantially to human development (Collins et al., 2000; Vandell, 2000).

Between 12 and 18 months of age, toddlers begin to react more to each other's behavior, often engaging in more complex exchanges in which they appear to take turns. Here is one example:

> Larry sits on the floor and Bernie turns and looks toward him. Bernie waves his hand and says "da," still looking at Larry. He repeats the vocalization three more

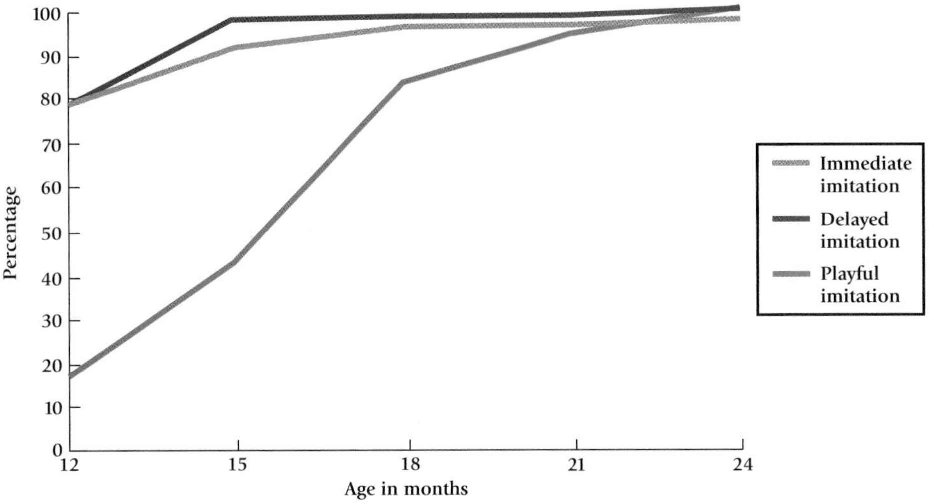

Figure 16.8 The percentage of toddlers showing evidence of immediate imitation, delayed imitation, and playful imitation across the second year of life. *From "Multiple motivations for imitation in infancy," by M. Nielsen and V. Slaughter in* Models and Mechanisms of Imitation and Social Learning in Robots, Humans, and Animals: Behavioural, Social and Communicative Dimensions, *K. Dautenhahn and C.L. Nehaniv (eds.), 2006, Cambridge University Press.*

> times before Larry laughs, Bernie vocalizes again and Larry laughs again. This same sequence is repeated twelve more times before Bernie . . . walks off (Mueller & Lucas, 1975, p. 241).

There is some debate about whether these "action/reaction" episodes qualify as true social interactions, because 12- to 18-month-olds often treat peers as particularly responsive "toys." They act as if they can control the "toys" by making them look, gesture, smile and laugh (Brownell, 1986).

By 18 months of age, however, toddlers are beginning to display *coordinated interactions* with age-mates that are clearly social. They now take great delight in imitating each other (Asendorpf, 2002; Nielsen & Dissanayake, 2003; Suddendorf & Whiten, 2001). They even gaze and smile at their partners as they make their imitation into social games (Eckerman & Stein, 1990; Howes & Matheson, 1992). It appears that this playful imitation requires social and cognitive skills not typically developed until the middle of the second year. As Figure 16.8 illustrates, 12- and 15-month-old infants are mostly capable of immediate and delayed imitation, but it is not until 18- to 24-months that most infants engage in playful, reciprocal imitation (Nielsen & Dissanayake, 2003; Nielsen & Slaughter, in press).

social skills
thoughts, actions, and emotional regulatory activities that enable children to achieve personal or social goals while maintaining harmony with their social partners.

By age 20 to 24 months, toddlers' play has a strong verbal component. Playmates often describe their activities to each other ("I fall down!" "Me too, I fall down") or attempt to direct the role that their playmate should assume ("You go in playhouse") (Eckerman & Didow, 1996). This coordinated social speech makes it easier for 2- to 2½-year-olds to assume *complementary roles,* such as chaser or chasee in a game of tag. These older toddlers also cooperate to achieve a shared goal, as illustrated by one child's operating a handle, so that his playmate can retrieve attractive toys from a container (Brownell & Carriger, 1990).

Both social and cognitive developments contribute to the growth of peer sociability over the first two years. Regarding social development, in Chapter 11, we learned that toddlers who are securely attached to their caregivers are generally more outgoing and even more "popular" as playmates than those who are insecurely attached. This implies that the sensitive, responsive caregiving that securely attached infants receive contributes in a positive way to development of **social skills** necessary for social interaction (see also Englund et al., 2000). Regarding cognitive developments that contribute to social interaction, 18- to 24-month-olds begin to display truly coordinated, reciprocal interactions at precisely the time that they first recognize themselves in a mirror and can tell the difference between photographs of themselves and those of peers (see Chapter 12). This may be no accident. Celia Brownell and Michael Carriger (1990) propose that toddlers must first realize that both they and their peers are independent, intentional actors who can

Laura Dwight/Corbis

With age, toddlers' interactions with one another become increasingly skilled and reciprocal.

make things happen before they are likely to play complementary games or try to coordinate their actions to accomplish a goal. In their research, Browneell & Carriger found that toddlers who cooperated successfully to achieve a goal scored higher on a test of self–other differentiation than their less cooperative age-mates. This is strong evidence that early interactive skills may depend heavily on social-cognitive development.

Sociability during the Preschool Period

Between the ages of 2 and 5, children become more outgoing and also direct their social gestures to a wider audience. Observational studies find that 2- to 3-year-olds are more likely than older children to remain near an adult and to seek physical affection. The sociable behaviors of 4- to 5-year-olds normally consist of playful bids for attention or approval that are directed at *peers* rather than adults (Harper & Huie, 1985; Hartup, 1983).

As preschool children become more peer oriented, the character of their interactions changes as well. In a classic study, Mildred Parten (1932) observed 2- to 4½-year-olds during free-play periods at nursery school, looking for developmental changes in the *social complexity* of peer interactions. She classified preschoolers' play activities into five categories, arranged from least to most socially complex:

nonsocial activity
onlooker behavior and solitary play.

onlooker play
children linger around other children, watching them play, but making no attempts to join in the play.

parallel play
largely noninteractive play in which players are in close proximity but do not often attempt to influence each other.

associative play
form of social discourse in which children pursue their own interests but will swap toys or comment on each other's activities.

cooperative play
true social play in which children cooperate or assume reciprocal roles while pursing shared goals.

Nonsocial activity. Children watch other children play or they engage in their own solitary play and largely ignore what other children are doing.

Onlooker play. Children linger around other children, watching them play, but making no attempts to join in the play.

Parallel play. Children play side by side but interact with each other very little and do not try to influence the behavior of other children.

Associative play. Children now share toys and swap materials, but each child is focused mostly on his or her own play and they do not cooperate with each other to achieve shared goals.

Cooperative play. Children now act out make-believe themes, assume reciprocal roles in their play together, and collaborate to achieve shared goals.

Parten found that solitary and parallel play declined with age, whereas associative and cooperative play became more common. However, all five kinds of play were observed among children of *all* ages. Even a nonsocial activity like solitary play need not be considered "immature" if the child is doing something constructive such as drawing pictures or completing a puzzle (Hartup, 1983).

Remember that Parten was focused on *social* complexity in her observations of the development of play. Given her findings, could it be that the "maturity" of preschool play depends as much (or more) on its *cognitive complexity* as on its social or nonsocial character? To test this idea, Carolee Howes and Catherine Matheson (1992) conducted a longitudinal study in which the play activities of a group of 1- to 2-year-olds were observed at 6-month intervals for 3 years. They found that play became more and more cognitively complex with age, as described by the six-category sequence in Table 16.2. They also found a clear relationship between the cognitive complexity of a child's play and the child's social competence with peers: children whose play was more complex at any given age were rated as more outgoing and prosocially inclined, and as less aggressive and withdrawn, at the next observation period 6 months later. So it seems that the *cognitive complexity* of a child's play (particularly pretend play) is a reliable predictor of his or her future social competencies with peers (see also Doyle et al., 1992; Rubin, Fein, & Vandenberg, 1983; Rubin, Bukowski, & Parker, 1998).

Functions of Play in Early Childhood. Although cognitively complex forms of social pretend play become more frequent with age in all cultures, the forms of preschoolers' play is influenced by cultural values and teaches young children different cultural values (Goencue, Mistry, & Mosier, 2000). For example, Farver, Kim, & Lee-Shin (2000) compared the pretend play of American and Korean preschoolers. They found that American preschoolers act out themes of danger, whereas Korean preschoolers act out themes of family roles and everyday activities. American children played up their individual exploits

TABLE 16.2 Changes in the Cognitive Complexity of Play Activities from Infancy through the Preschool Period

Play type	Age of appearance	Description
Parallel play	6–12 months	Two children perform similar activities without paying any attention to each other.
Parallel aware play	By age 1	Children engage in parallel play while occasionally looking at each other or monitoring each other's activities.
Simple pretend play	1–1½ years	Children engage in similar activities while talking, smiling, sharing toys, or otherwise interacting.
Complementary and reciprocal play	1½–2 years	Children display action-based role reversals in social games such as run-and-chase or peekaboo.
Cooperative social pretend play	2½–3 years	Children play complementary *nonliteral*, or "pretend," roles (for example, mommy and baby), but without any planning or discussion about the meaning of these roles or about the form that the play will take.
Complex social pretend play	3½–4 years	Children actively *plan* their pretend play. They name and explicitly assign roles for each player and propose a play script, and may stop playing to modify the script if play breaks down.

Source: Adapted from "Sequences in the Development of Competent Play with Peers: Social and Social Pretend Play," by C. Howes & C. C. Matheson, 1992, *Developmental Psychology, 28,* 961–974. Copyright © 1992 the American Psychological Association. Adapted by permission.

and bossed others around, whereas Korean children were more quietly attentive to their partner's activities and more inclined to cooperate. Thus, children from an individualistic culture (Americans) used play to teach them their identities as individuals, whereas children from a collectivist culture (Korea) used play to keep their own egos and emotions under control to promote group harmony.

Regardless of the cultural variations in forms of pretend play, these activities serve at least three critical functions, according to Howes and Matheson (1992). First, pretend play helps children learn ways of communicating effectively with their social equals. Second, pretend play provides opportunities for younger children to learn to compromise as they negotiate the roles they will take in their play and the rules that guide these pretend episodes. Third, pretend play is a context that allows children to display feelings that may bother them. This provides them with opportunities to (1) better understand their own (or their partner's) emotional crises, (2) receive social support from (or provide it to) playmates, and (3) develop a sense of trust and close emotional ties to these playmates. So pretend play may be a major contributor to the growth of communication skills, emotional understanding, social perspective-taking, and an enhanced capacity for caring. Viewed in this way, it is hardly surprising that preschoolers who are good at pretend play tend to be popular with their peers (Farver, Kim, & Lee-Shin, 2000; Rubin, Bukowski, & Parker, 1998).

The content of a young child's pretend play can also point to emotional disturbances that may require adult intervention. For example, preschoolers who persist in immature forms of solitary play (such as wandering around aimlessly and not attempting to join in groups at play) are at risk of displaying problem behaviors (such as extreme shyness and anxiety disorders) later that could cause them to be rejected by peers (Coplan, 2000; Coplan et al., 2001; Gazelle et al., 2005). And those who often enact violent fantasy themes are also heading for trouble: they tend to display a lot of anger and aggressive behavior and little prosocial conduct (Dunn & Hughes, 2001). Thus, early play may provide indications of which preschool children might profit from social-skills training that is designed to improve their prospects of being accepted by peers.

Peer Sociability in Middle Childhood and Adolescence

Peer interactions become increasingly sophisticated throughout the grade school years. Cooperative forms of complex pretend play become more commonplace, and, by age 6 to 10, children become enthusiastic participants in games (such as T-Ball and Monopoly) that are governed by formal sets of rules (Hartup, 1983; Piaget, 1965).

peer group
a confederation of peers that interact regularly, defines a sense of membership, and formulates norms that specify how members are supposed to look, think, act.

Another very noticeable way that peer interactions change during middle childhood is that contacts among 6- to 10-year-olds often occur in what psychologists call **peer groups.** A peer group is a group of children who (1) interact on a regular basis, (2) provide a sense of belonging, (3) formulate *norms* that specify how members are supposed to dress, think, and behave, and (4) develop a hierarchical organization (for example, leader and other roles) that helps group members to work together toward shared goals. So between ages 6 and 10, the peer groups become a social context in which children can discover the value of teamwork, develop a sense of commitment and loyalty to shared goals, and learn other important lessons about how social organizations work (Hartup, 1983; Sherif et al., 1961).

cliques
a small group of friends that interacts frequently.

By early adolescence, youngsters spend more time with peers than with parents, siblings, or any other agent of socialization (Berndt, 1996; Larson & Richards, 1991). Early adolescents typically form **cliques,** which usually consist of four to eight *same-sex* members who share similar values and activity preferences. By midadolescence, boy cliques and girl cliques begin to interact more frequently, eventually forming *heterosexual cliques* (Dunphy, 1963; Richards et al., 1998). Once formed, cliques often develop distinct and colorful dress codes, dialects, and behaviors that set the cliques apart and help clique members establish a firm sense of belongingness, or a group identity (Cairns et al., 1995).

crowds
a large, reputationally based peer group made up of individuals and cliques that share similar norms, interests, and values.

Often several cliques with similar norms and values will form into larger, more loosely organized groups known as **crowds** (Connolly, Furman, & Konarski, 2000). Crowds do not replace cliques; membership in a crowd is based on reputation, and individual members within a particular clique may even belong to different crowds (Urberg et al., 1995). Crowds are defined by the attitudes and activities their members share. They come into play mainly as a mechanism for defining an adolescent's niche within the larger social structure of a high school. Crowds usually come together for such social activities as parties, trips to the football game, and so on. The names may vary, but most schools have crowds of "suck-ups," "preps," "jocks," "stoners," "goths," and "rednecks." Each crowd consists of a loose grouping of cliques that are similar to one another in some fundamental way and different from adolescents in other crowds (Brown, Mory, & Kinney, 1994; La Greca, Prinstein, & Fetter, 2001). And everyone in the high school seems to recognize these differences: "[the suck-ups] all wear glasses and "kiss up" to teachers." (Brown, Mory, & Kinney, 1994, p. 128); "the [rednecks] goof off a lot more than the jocks do, but they don't come to school stoned like the [stoners] do" (p. 133). Peer cliques and crowds may be universal group structures among high school students. Although the names may vary, crowds similar to those identified in primarily European American high schools are also found in majority African American high schools (Hughes, 2001), and student cliques (and presumably crowds) with very different interests and values have been identified among 10th-graders in Shanghai, China, as well (Chen, Chang, & He, 2003).

Martin Rogers/Stone

Young adolescents spend more time socializing with their peers than with their parents or siblings. Much time is spent with small numbers of same-sex associates who genuinely like each other and prefer similar activities. These same-sex cliques often evolve into mixed-sex (heterosexual) cliques by midadolescence.

Cliques and crowds permit adolescents to express their values and try out new roles as they begin to forge an identity apart from their families. They also pave the way for the establishment of romantic relationships (Brown, 1990; Connolly, Furman, & Konarski, 2000; Davies & Windle, 2000; Dunphy, 1963). Gender segregation usually breaks down early in adolescence as members of boys' and girls' cliques begin to interact. Same-sex cliques provide what amounts to a "secure base" for exploring ways to behave with members of the other sex; talking to girls when your buddies are there is far less threatening than doing so on your own. And as heterosexual cliques and crowds take shape, adolescents are likely to have many opportunities to get to know members of the other sex in casual social situations, without having to be intimate. Eventually, strong cross-sex friendships develop and couples form, often double-dating or spending time with a small number of other couples (Feiring, 1996). From this point on, crowds often begin to disintegrate, having served their purposes of helping adolescents to establish a social identity and bringing the boys and girls together (Brown, 1990; Dunphy, 1963).

Peer Acceptance and Popularity

peer acceptance
a measure of a person's likability (or dislikability) in the eyes of the peers.

sociometric techniques
procedures that ask children to identify those peers whom they like or dislike or to rate peers for their desirability as companions; used to measure children's peer acceptance (or nonacceptance).

Perhaps no other aspect of children's social lives has received more attention than **peer acceptance:** The extent to which a child is viewed by peers as a worthy or likable companion. Typically, researchers assess peer acceptance through self-report instruments called **sociometric techniques** (Jiang & Cillessen, 2005). In a sociometric survey, children might be asked to nominate several classmates whom they like and several whom they dislike. Another method is to ask children to rate every other child in the group on a 5-point likeability scale (ranging from "really like to play with" to "really don't like to play with" (Cillessen & Bukowski, 2000; DeRosier & Thomas, 2003; Terry & Coie, 1991). Sociometric results suggest that sociometric status (based on liking) and peer popularity (based on who is perceived as "popular") are somewhat different constructs, and children don't necessarily like popular children (Cillessen, 2004; LaFontana & Cillessen, 2002). Even 3- to 5-year-olds can respond appropriately to sociometric surveys (Denham et al., 1990); and the choices (or ratings) that children make correspond reasonably well to teacher ratings of peer popularity. This suggests that sociometric surveys provide *valid* assessments of children's social standing in their peer groups (Hymel, 1983).

popular children
children who are liked by many members of their peer group and disliked by very few.

rejected children
children who are disliked by many peers and liked by few.

neglected children
children who receive few nominations as either a liked or a disliked individual from members of their peer group.

controversial children
children who receive many nominations as a liked and many as a disliked individual.

average-status children
children who receive a average number of nominations as a liked and/or a disliked individual from members of their peer group.

When sociometric data are analyzed, it is usually possible to classify each child into one of the following categories: **popular children,** who are liked by many peers and disliked by few; **rejected children,** who are disliked by many peers and liked by a few; **neglected children,** who receive very few nominations as a liked or a disliked companion and who seem almost invisible to their peers; and **controversial children,** who are liked by many peers but disliked by many others. Together, these four types of children make up about two-thirds of the children in a typical elementary school classroom. The remaining one-third are **average-status children,** who are liked (or disliked) by a moderate number of peers (Coie, Dodge, & Coppotelli, 1982).

Notice that both neglected children and rejected children are low in acceptance and are not well received by their peers. Yet it is not nearly so bad to be ignored by other children as to be rejected by them. Neglected children do not feel as lonely as rejected children do (Cassidy & Asher, 1992; Crick & Ladd, 1993). Neglected children are also much more likely than rejected children to achieve a more favorable sociometric status if they enter a new class at school or a new play group (Coie & Dodge, 1983). Furthermore, rejected children are the ones who face the greater risk of displaying deviant, antisocial

Calvin and Hobbes © Waterson. Reprinted by permission of Universal Press Syndicate.

behavior and other serious adjustment problems later in life (Dodge & Pettit, 2003; Parker & Asher, 1987).

Why Are Children Accepted, Neglected, or Rejected by Peers?

At several points throughout the text, we have discussed factors that seem to contribute to children's popularity with peers. By way of brief review:

Parenting Styles. Warm, sensitive, and authoritative parents who rely on reasoning rather than power to guide and control children's conduct tend to raise children who are *liked* by adults and peers. On the other hand, highly authoritarian or uninvolved parents who rely heavily on power-assertion as a control tactic often have children who are surly, uncooperative, and aggressive, and are actively *disliked* by peers (Baumrind, 1977, 1991).

Temperamental Characteristics. Certain aspects of children's temperaments are correlated with and contribute to their sociometic statuses. This influence is most likely bidirectional, meaning that temperaments influence peer relations and peer relations influence children's temperaments (e.g, Caldwell et al., 2004). As we learned in Chapter 11, difficult children who are often irritable and impulsive are at risk for having negative interactions with peers that could cause them to become rejected. In addition, relatively passive children who are behaviorally inhibited or slow to warm up are at risk (in Western societies, at least) of being neglected or even rejected by peers (see also Gazelle et al., 2005).

Cognitive Skills. Popular children tend to have well-developed role-taking skills (LeMare & Rubin, 1987). Popular, average-status, and neglected youngsters also tend to perform better academically and to score higher on IQ tests than rejected children and adolescents do (Bukowski et al., 1993; Chen, Chang, & He, 2003; Chen, Rubin, & Li, 1997; Wentzel & Asher, 1995).

Social Behaviors. Several studies of preschool, elementary, and middle-school (young adolescent) children report that children's behavior is related to their sociometric standings. *Popular* children are observed to be relatively calm, outgoing, friendly, and supportive companions who can successfully initiate and maintain interactions and can resolve disputes in a friendly way (Coie, Dodge, & Kupersmidt, 1990; Denham et al., 1990; Ladd, Price, & Hart, 1988). In both the United States and China, these "sociometric stars" are generally warm, cooperative, and compassionate individuals who display many prosocial behaviors and are seldom disruptive or aggressive (Chen, Chang, & He, 2000; Rubin, Bukowski, & Parker, 1998).

Neglected children often appear shy or withdrawn. They are not very talkative; they make fewer attempts than children of average status to enter play groups; and they seldom call attention to themselves (Coie, Dodge, & Kupersmidt, 1990; Harrist et al., 1997). Nevertheless, these neglected children are no less socially skilled than children of average status. They also are not more lonely or more distressed about the character of their social relationships (Cassidy & Asher, 1992; Wentzel & Asher, 1995). Their withdrawn behavior appears to stem more from their own social anxieties and their beliefs that they are not socially skilled than from any active ostracism or exclusion by their peer groups (Cassidy & Asher, 1992; Younger & Daniels, 1992).

There are at least two categories of *rejected* children, each with a distinct behavioral profile. **Rejected-aggressive children** often alienate peers by using forceful *proactive* means to dominate them or their resources. These disruptive braggarts tend to be uncooperative and critical of peer group activities and to display very low levels of prosocial behavior (Newcomb Bukowski, & Pattee, 1993; Parkhurst & Asher, 1992). Rejected-aggressive children overestimate their social standing, often saying that they are liked just as well as, or better than, most children (Zakriski & Coie, 1996). These are the children

rejected-aggressive children
a subgroup of rejected children who display high levels of hostility and aggression in their interactions with peers.

who display the greatest risk of becoming chronically hostile (Haselager et al., 2002). They also display externalizing conduct disorders and criminal acts of violence later in adolescence and adulthood (Parker et al., 1995; Rubin, Bukowski, & Parker, 1998).

rejected-withdrawn children
a subgroup of rejected children who are often passive, socially anxious, socially unskilled, and insensitive to peer-group expectations.

Rejected-withdrawn children, on the other hand, are typically socially awkward companions who display many unusual, immature behaviors, are insensitive to peer group expectations, and may become hostile and *react* aggressively to any criticism by peers. Unlike rejected-aggressive children, they are well aware that other children do not like them and they eventually begin to withdraw as peers actively exclude them from their activities (Gazelle et al., 2005; Gazelle & Ladd, 2003; Harrist et al., 1997; Hymel, Bowker, & Woody, 1993; Zakriski & Coie, 1996). These rejected-withdrawn children feel especially lonely and are at risk of experiencing low self-esteem, depression, and other internalizing disorders (Hymel, Bowker, & Woody, 1993; Rabiner, Keane, & MacKinnon-Lewis, 1993). Because of their unusual behaviors, hypersensitivity to criticism, and lack of close friends to stick up for them, they are particularly inviting targets for abuse at the hands of bullies (Hodges et al., 1999; Ladd & Burgess, 1999).

Do popular children become popular because they are friendly, cooperative, and nonaggressive? Or is it that children become friendlier, more cooperative, and less aggressive after achieving their popularity? One way to test these competing hypotheses is to observe children in play groups or classes with *unfamiliar* peers to see whether the behaviors they display predict their eventual status in the peer group. Several studies of this type have been conducted (Coie & Kupersmidt, 1983; Dodge, 1983; Dodge et al., 1990; Gazelle et al., 2005; Ladd, Price, & Hart, 1988; Ladd, Birch, & Buhs, 1999) and the results are reasonably consistent: the patterns of behavior that children display do predict the statuses they will achieve with their peers. Children who are ultimately accepted by unfamiliar peers are effective at initiating social interactions and at responding positively to others' bids for attention. When they want to join a group activity, for example, these socially skilled, *soon-to-be-accepted* children first watch and attempt to understand what is going on, and then comment constructively about the proceedings as they blend smoothly into the group. On the other hand, children who are ultimately *rejected* are pushy and self-serving. They often criticize or disrupt group activities and may even threaten reprisals if they are not allowed to join in. Other children who end up being *neglected* by their peers tend to hover around the edges of a group, initiating few interactions and shying away from other children's bids for attention.

Jeff I. Greenberg/Photo Researchers Inc.

Neglected children are often shy and hover on the fringes of a group, making few attempts to enter it.

In sum, peer popularity is affected by many factors. It may help to have a pleasant temperament, and academic skills, but it is even more important to display good social-cognitive skills and to behave in socially competent ways. Definitions of desirable social behavior, of course, may vary from culture to culture and change over time (Chen, Cen, Li & He, 2005). The ingredients of popularity also change with age. Aggression is generally associated with unfavorable peer statuses at any age. However, during preadolescence and early adolescence at least *some* "tough" boys who view themselves as cool, popular, and antisocial do become popular with male classmates and attractive to girls (Bukowski, Sippola, & Newcomb, 2000; LaFontana & Cillessen, 2002; Rodkin et al., 2000). Another example of age differences in popularity relates to how a child interacts with children of the other gender. Establishing close relationships with members of the other sex suddenly enhances popularity during adolescence. Frequent consorting with "the enemy" violates norms of gender segregation during childhood and *detracts* from one's popularity (Kovacs, Parker, & Hoffman, 1996; Sroufe et al., 1993). In short, contextual factors clearly influence who is popular and who is not.

CONCEPT CHECK 16.3 Understanding Peers as Agents of Socialization

Check your understanding of the effects of peers as agents of socialization and peer relations in children's development by answering the following questions. Answers appear in the Appendix.

True or False: Identify whether the following statements are true or false.

1. (T)(F) Children as young as 2 years old have been found to change their play routines (as compared to their play with older toddlers) to accommodate younger toddlers' abilities.
2. (T)(F) Social development is more important than cognitive development in the growth of peer sociability over the toddler years.

Fill in the Blank: Complete the following sentences with the correct terms.

3. Children playing side by side but not interacting with each other and not trying to influence each other's behavior are engaged in ________ play.
4. When Parten studied the development of social play, she found that ________ and ________ play declined with age over the preschool years and ________ and ________ play became more common over the preschool years.
5. Brett often alienates his classmates by using forceful proactive aggression to control them and by being especially critical and mean to them. Brett thinks that he is liked by most everyone, but sociometric surveys would probably classify him as a ________ child.

Multiple Choice: Select the correct answer for each question.

_____ 6. As discussed in the chapter, pretend play in early childhood has many beneficial functions, including all of the following *except:*
   a. providing an opportunity for children to better understand emotional crises
   b. developing social support among playmates
   c. teaching cultural values to young children
   d. helping children develop better motor skills and promoting their physical development

_____ 7. Early adolescents often form groups of four to eight same-sex peers who share similar values and activity preferences. These groups are known as
   a. peer groups
   b. cliques
   c. crowds
   d. gangs

_____ 8. Dr. Frendlee is a psychologist who would like to help children in elementary school who are having difficulty getting along with other children. He plans to use sociometric surveys to identify the children who need help. He knows that the results of other research have found that young children can complete these surveys and that the results of the surveys are very similar to results from teacher ratings of children's popularity. What might we expect Dr. Frendlee to do to identify children who need help making friends?
   a. Dr. Frendlee plans to also use observational techniques to identify children who need help because the surveys are not really reliable.
   b. Dr. Frendlee plans to use only the surveys because he is confident that the results will be valid, based on previous research.
   c. Dr. Frendlee plans to use only the surveys because he is confident that the results will be reliable, based on previous research.
   d. Dr. Frendlee plans to use only teacher reports of children's popularity because he is convinced that the sociometric surveys completed by classmates will not be a good method for identifying children who need help.

Short Answer: Briefly answer the following questions.

9. List and describe the five categories of peer acceptance typically revealed by sociometric techniques used with children.
10. Contrast the levels of play based on social complexity (with preschoolers) with the categories of play based on cognitive complexity (again, with preschoolers).

Applying Developmental Themes to Extrafamilial Contextual Forces in Child Development

As in the last chapter, our focus here has been on how the context in which a child develops affects developmental outcomes. In this chapter we examined extrafamilial contextual forces, specifically the media, schooling, and peers, as influences on a child's development. Do our developmental themes, which admittedly are more focused on the child than on the context of development, apply even here? Indeed they do. Developmental psychologists are interested in the active child, nature and nurture interactions, qualitative and quantitative changes, and the holistic nature of child development as these themes relate to all contextual aspects of child development. Let's examine a few examples from the chapter that relate to these themes.

In examining the effects of television and computers on child development, we saw evidence that the child's active choices in his or her exposure to these technologies do influence his or her later behavior and views of the world. These choices may not be conscious, just as a child's choice of peer groups and school environment may not be conscious, but the child's temperament and experiences do help direct the child in these extrafamilial contexts and the contexts then influence the child's further development. We also saw evidence of the active child when we examined children's peer relationships. A child's temperament and social behavior are strong influences on the types of relationships a child experiences within his or her peer group.

It might seem that the nature and nurture interactions are lopsided when we focus on the context of development, or the effects of experience (and nurture) on development. However, even here the child's nature does have an influence and the two forces do interact. The examples we cited above when discussing the active child can also be applied to the theme of nature and nurture interactions. Another example from the chapter was the finding that boys were more likely to react aggressively after watching an aggressive TV show than were girls. This may have something to do with gender differences in nature, or it may be an effect of gender differences in nurture. In the Box on p. 650 we discussed the controversial issue of nature and nurture effects on child development in the context of peers influences versus parental influences. We discussed some theorists' views that genetic influences and environmental influences (in the form of peer group interactions) are more important in child development than are socialization effects from parenting. Not all theorists agree (indeed, probably the majority of developmental psychologists do not agree with the extreme position here), but it does give us an occasion to consider the nature and nurture interactions theme in the context of extrafamilial influences.

Qualitative and quantitative changes were also evident in the material we covered in this chapter. One striking example is the qualitative changes that children go through as they become adolescents, and the difficulties they sometimes experience in this transition when it is coupled with a school transition. We also noted qualitative changes in play behavior as children progressed from toddlerhood to childhood, and noted that these qualitative changes were both a function of increases in the child's social abilities and in cognitive abilities. Perhaps quantitative changes in social and cognitive complexity underlie the qualitative changes in form of play across childhood. We also described qualitative changes in peer relationships across toddlerhood, childhood, and adolescence. So, even as the extrafamilial influences are providing a context for development, the child's development changes in quantitative and qualitative form within those contexts.

Finally, we consider the theme of the holistic nature of development. Some examples that we have already mentioned also fit here. For instance, social and cognitive development both interact to influence children's play and peer relations. Also, children's biological development as they make the transition from childhood to adolescence clearly influences their social adjustment. Perhaps it is easiest to see the holistic nature of child development when examining it from a contextual perspective. Clearly, all aspects of child development interact with the familial and extrafamilial contexts to influence the course and eventual outcome of child development.

SUMMARY

- In addition to studying the effects of family, parents, and siblings on child development, developmentalists study **extrafamilial influences** on socialization and child development, including the effects of television, computers, schooling, and peers.

The Effects of Television on Child Development

- Although children watch a lot of TV and it can influence their behavior, research suggests that watching TV in moderation is not likely to impair children's cognitive growth, academic achievement, or peer relations.
- Cognitive development and experience watching television leads to increases in **television literacy** during middle childhood and adolescence.
- Televised violence can instigate aggressive behavior, instill **mean-world beliefs,** and **desensitize** children to aggression.
- TV also presents stereotypes that influence children's beliefs about ethnicity, race, and gender.
- Children are easily manipulated by TV commercials.
- On the positive side, children learn prosocial lessons and put them into practice after watching acts of kindness on TV.
- Educational programs such as *Sesame Street* have been quite successful at fostering basic cognitive skills, particularly when children watch with an adult who discusses the material with them and helps them to apply what they have learned.

Child Development in the Computer Age

- Children benefit, both intellectually and socially, from their use of computers.
- **Computer-assisted instruction** (**CAI**) often improves children's basic academic skills, especially when basic drills are supplemented by discovery programs that are presented as games.
- Word-processing programs foster the growth of writing skills; and computer programming facilitates cognitive and metacognitive development.
- Despite the advantages associated with children's use of computers, critics fear that:
  - disadvantaged children and girls may reap fewer of these benefits
  - violent computer games may instigate aggression
  - harm may result from children's unrestricted access to the Internet and the World Wide Web.

The School as a Socialization Agent

- Schools influence many aspects of development:
  - Formal school curricula teach academic knowledge.
  - Schooling promotes cognitive and metacognitive development by teaching rules and problem-solving strategies that can be applied to many different kinds of information.
  - Schools' **informal curricula** teach children skills that help them to become good citizens.
- Experimental research demonstrates that children who attend school, or who attend more school than others, post reliable cognitive gains from that schooling.
- "Effective" schools produce positive outcomes such as low absenteeism, an enthusiastic attitude about learning, academic achievement, occupational skills, and socially desirable patterns of behavior.
- Research suggests the following characteristics that make schools "effective":
  - students who are highly motivated and intellectually competent
  - a positive, safe school climate
  - an effective "goodness of fit" between students and schools
  - a scholastic atmosphere stressing:
    - an academic emphasis
    - challenging, developmentally appropriate curricula
    - authoritative classroom management and discipline
    - teamwork
- Research suggests that American schools are not meeting the needs of all American children, particularly ethnic minorities and children making the transition between school levels.
  - Racial and ethnic differences in academic achievement can often be traced to parental and peer influences and to teacher expectancies.
  - Children making the transition between elementary and secondary schools need special attention to their changing developmental needs and support from parents and teachers.
- Cross-national surveys of academic achievement clearly brand American students as "underachievers," especially in math and science.
- The achievement gap that exists between American schoolchildren and those in other industrialized societies centers around cultural differences in:
  - educational attitudes
  - educational practices
  - the involvement of both parents and students in the learning process

Peers as Agents of Socialization

- Peer relationships are a second social world for children—a world of equal-status interactions that is very different from the social interactions children have with adults.

- **Peers** are social equals (not necessarily the same age), who behave at similar levels of social and cognitive complexity.
- Contacts with peers increase dramatically with age, and during the preschool or early elementary-school years, the "peer group" consists mainly of *same-sex* children of somewhat *different ages.*
- **Sociability** and the form of social interactions changes across development:
  - By age 18 to 24 months, toddlers' sociable interactions become complex and coordinated as they reliably imitate each other, assume complementary roles in simple social games, and occasionally coordinate their actions to achieve shared goals.
  - During the preschool years, **nonsocial activities** and **parallel play** become less common, whereas the **social skills** that foster **associative play** and **cooperative play** become more common.
  - During middle childhood, more peer interactions occur in **peer groups**—groups of children who associate regularly, define a sense of group membership, and formulate norms that specify how group members are supposed to behave.
  - Early adolescents spend even more time with peers—particularly with their closest friends in small **cliques,** and in larger groups of like-minded cliques, known as **crowds.**
    - Cliques and crowds help adolescents forge an identity apart from their families and pave the way for the establishment of dating relationships.
- Children clearly differ in **peer acceptance**—the extent to which other children like or dislike them.
  - Using **sociometric techniques,** developmentalists find that there are five categories of peer acceptance:
    - **popular children:** liked by many and disliked by few
    - **rejected children:** disliked by many and liked by few
    - **controversial children:** liked by many and disliked by many
    - **neglected children:** seldom nominated by others as likable or dislikable
    - **average-status children:** those who are liked or disliked by a moderate number of peers
- Social status with peers is related to a child's temperament, cognitive skills, and the parenting style she or he has experienced.
- The strongest predictor of peer acceptance is a child's pattern of social behavior:
  - Popular children are generally warm, cooperative, and compassionate peers who display many prosocial behaviors and are rarely disruptive or aggressive.
  - Neglected children often have adequate social skills, but they experience social anxieties that cause them to appear shy and to hover at the edge of peer-group activities.
  - Rejected children display many unpleasant and annoying behaviors and few prosocial ones.
    - **Rejected-aggressive** children are hostile, impulsive, highly, uncooperative, and aggressive.
    - **Rejected-withdrawn** children are socially awkward and immature companions who are hypersensitive to criticism and actively isolate themselves from peers.

KEY TERMS

extrafamilial influences 623
television literacy 624
mean-world beliefs 627
desensitization hypothesis 627
obese 628
computer-assisted instruction (CAI) 632
informal curriculum 637
effective schools 637
aptitude-treatment interaction (ATI) 641
peers 648
sociability 649
social skills 651
nonsocial activity 652
onlooker play 652
parallel play 652
associative play 652
cooperative play 652
peer groups 654
cliques 654
crowds 654
peer acceptance 655
sociometric techniques 655
popular children 655
rejected children 655
neglected children 655
controversial children 655
average-status children 655
rejected-aggressive children 656
rejected-withdrawn children 657

Appendix | Answers to Concept Checks

CHAPTER 1

Concept Check 1.1

1. *d:* the product of both maturation and learning
2. *d: all* of the above might be considered developmentalists
3. *d:* all of the above
4. *b:* Development is marked by plasticity.
5. normative deviant; ideographic development
6. Hobbes—original sin—passive
7. Rousseau—innate purity—active
8. Locke—blank slate—passive

Concept Check 1.2

1. *b.* Her measure was not valid.
2. *c.* scientific method
3. *b.* interrater reliability
4. *d.* the clinical method
5. *d.* structured observation
6. *a.* structured interview
7. *e.* psychophysiological methods
8. *c.* naturalistic observation
9. *b.* ethnography

Concept Check 1.3

1. *b.* It is subject to the cross-generational problem.
2. *a.* It does not evaluate individual differences in development.
3. *d.* It may cause developmental changes that would not occur naturally and which may not be long lasting.
4. selective attrition
5. cohort
6. the researcher
7. *b.* longitudinal design
8. *a.* cross-sectional design
9. *d.* microgenetic design

CHAPTER 2

Concept Check 2.1

1. Your view on the nature vs. nurture issue is:

a. nature

b. both

c. nurture

2. Your view on the active vs. passive issue is:

a. active

b. passive

3. Your view on the continuity vs. discontinuity issue is:

a. discontinuity

b. continuity

4. Your view on the holistic vs. distinct aspects of development is:

a. distinct

b. holistic

5. *b*
6. *c*
7. *a*
8. *a.* nature
9. *a.* the active child
10. *b.* discontinuous development

Concept Check 2.2

1. *a.* conscious drives and motivations
2. *b.* Erikson's
3. *c.* begin to train their children at birth and do not coddle their children in order to instill good habits in the children
4. *c.* a consequence that *strengthens* a response and *increases* the likelihood that it will recur
5. *a.* the freely emitted response that produces a result to influence learning
6. *b.* the consequence that *suppresses* a response and *decreases* the likelihood that it will recur
7. True
8. True

Concept Check 2.3

1. *c.* ethology
2. *a.* Piaget's cognitive-developmental theory
3. *d.* ecological systems theory
4. *b.* information processing theory
5. *e.* Vygotsky's sociocultural theory
6. assimilation; accommodation
7. sensitive periods

CHAPTER 3

Concept Check 3.1

1. *d.* genotype; phenotype
2. *a.* gene is to chromosome
3. *b.* mitosis
4. *c.* autosomes; sex chromosomes
5. *a.* the fertilization of two different ova by two different sperm
6. (1) inside the cell; (2) outside the cell; (3) outside the individual: experience-expectant; (4) outside the individual: experience-dependent

8. zero probability
9. Both children have a 100 percent probability of being color-blind.

Concept Check 3.2

1. *c.* abnormal contact between mother and child during postnatal development
2. *c.* both chromosomal and genetic abnormalities
3. *a.* pedigree
4. *c.* chorionic villus sampling
5. F
6. T

Concept Check 3.3

1. *b.* bred rats and tested their maze-running abilities
2. *c.* identical twins; fraternal twins
3. *c.* anorexia nervosa
4. *b.* range of reaction
5. F
6. T
7. T

CHAPTER 4

Concept Check 4.1

1. *c.* implantation
2. *b.* placenta
3. *a.* embryo
4. *c.* blindness, deafness, mental retardation
5. *a.* eye and brain damage; late-pregnancy miscarriage
6. *b.* missing or malformed arms and legs
7. fetal alcohol effects; fetal alcohol syndrome
8. amniocentesis; chorionic villus sampling
9. Y; indifferent gonad
10. diethylstilbestrol (DES)

Concept Check 4.2

1. *c.* postpartum depression
2. *b.* anoxia
3. *c.* respiratory distress syndrome
4. second
5. Brazelton Neonatal Assessment Scale; brain damage
6. obstetrical forceps; vacuum extractor
7. *b*
8. *a*

CHAPTER 5

Concept Check 5.1

1. *c.* autostimulation
2. *b.* Have the baby tested for the SIDS virus by a pediatrician.
3. *c.* Crying diminishes rapidly over the first 2 weeks of life as the baby's brain matures.

4. *e.* alert activity

5. *f.* crying

6. *a.* regular sleep

7. sensation

8. perception

9. primitive

10. survival

Concept Check 5.2

1. *a.* 0 to 2 months

2. *b.* the visual cliff

3. *c.* intermodal perception

4. poor

5. very well

6. quite sensitive

7. *a.* the preference method

8. *d.* the high-amplitude sucking method

Concept Check 5.3

1. T

2. F

3. T

4. *c.* conditioned stimulus

5. *a.* operant conditioning

6. *c.* operant conditioning

7. *c.* infant imitation

8. *a.* newborn imitation

9. *b.* deferred imitation

CHAPTER 6

Concept Check 6.1

1. *b.* the cephalocaudal trend

2. *c.* the lymphoid system

3. *b.* neurons

4. *a.* plasticity

5. *b.* with its right ear facing outward

6. F

7. T

8. F

9. T

Concept Check 6.2

1. F

2. T

3. T

4. F

5. F

6. *b.* the experiential viewpoint

7. c

8. *a.* pincer grasp

9. *b*

10. *c*

Concept Check 6.3

1. T

2. F

3. *b*

4. *d*

5. *c*

6. *a*

7. *d*

8. *c*

9. *c*

CHAPTER 7

Concept Check 7.1

1. *d.* the changing of a current scheme in order to incorporate new information

2. *b.* individual seeking to stabilize his or her cognitive structures

3. *a.* agrees with Piaget and is a stage theorist

4. *d.* intelligence

5. *c.* cognitive equilibration

6. *f.* assimilation

7. *b.* constructivist

8. *a.* schemes

9. *e.* organization

Concept Check 7.2

1. *d.* are able to comprehend the world around them through their actions on it

2. *b.* assimilation

3. *a.* object permanence

4. *a.* knowledge that objects have an existence in space and time independent of one's perceptions of and action on them

5. *c.* A-not-B error

6. *f.* primary circular reactions

7. *a.* invariant developmental sequence

8. *e.* theory theories

9. *b.* coordination of secondary circular reactions

10. *d.* neo-nativism

Concept Check 7.3

1. *c.* egocentrism

2. *c.* symbolic, intuitive, and egocentric thinking

3. *d.* perceptual centration

4. *c.* theory of mind

5. *d.* theory of mind

6. *a.* representational insight

7. *c.* conservation

8. *f.* hypothetico-deductive reasoning

9. *b.* animism

10. *e.* horizontal décalage

Concept Check 7.4

1. *d.* prenatal development

2. *a.* the number words used in Chinese and English

3. *c.* Vygotsky's perspective, that private speech serves as a cognitive self-guidance system for young children.

4. *b.* zone of proximal development

5. *d.* ontogenetic development

6. *f.* guided participation

7. *e.* microgenetic development

8. *c.* scaffolding

9. *a.* tools of intellectual adaptation

CHAPTER 8

Concept Check 8.1

1. *c.* short-term store (STS)

2. *f.* multistore model

3. *b.* sensory register

4. *a.* metacognition

5. *e.* long-term store (LTS)

6. *d.* executive control processes

Concept Check 8.2

1. *b.* utilization deficiency

2. *d.* Compared to older children, young children prefer to operate on the gist end of the trace continuum; older children and adults prefer to operate on the verbatim end of the trace continuum.

3. *a.* Siegler's adaptive strategy choice model

4. *a.* memory span

5. *e.* a fuzzy representation of information that preserves the central content but few precise details

6. *c.* explicit cognition

7. *f.* a failure to spontaneously generate and use known strategies that could improve learning and memory

8. *d.* span of apprehension

9. *b.* implicit cognition

Concept Check 8.3

1. *a.* Parents teach their children specific memory strategies, such as organization and rehearsal.

2. *c.* clustering (organization)

3. *b.* infantile amnesia

4. *d.* organization

5. *c.* script

6. *f.* mnemonics

7. *a.* autobiographical memory

8. *b.* metamemory

9. *e.* retrieval

Concept Check 8.4

1. *c*

2. *d*

CHAPTER 9

Concept Check 9.1

1. *b.* the psychometric approach

2. *c.* the theory of multiple intelligences

3. *a.* the triarchic theory

4. *b.* comparing the child's performance to other children of his or her own age

5. *c.* has deficits reflecting a combination of low genetic potential and an unstimulating rearing environment

6. *d.* poor predictors of later IQ, probably because infant tests and later IQ tests tap different abilities

7. *c.* crystallized intelligence

Concept Check 9.2

1. *a.* heredity in intellectual performance

2. *d.* Level II abilities

3. *c.* IQs have risen in the entire population

4. *d.* tacit/practical intelligence

5. *c.* encourage rote memorization

6. F

7. T

Concept Check 9.3

1. *b.* prepare low-income children for elementary school

2. *b.* low-income infants at risk for mental retardation

3. *b.* parental involvement in the program

4. *a.* creative

5. T
6. T
7. F

CHAPTER 10

Concept Check 10.1

1. *b.* phonology
2. *a.* morphology
3. *d.* semantics
4. *e.* syntax
5. *c.* pragmatics
6. *d.* Children sift language they hear through a biological device in their brains.
7. *a.* his Broca's area
8. *b.* examples and support of the development of the universal grammar
9. *d.* I'm a nativist!

Concept Check 10.2

1. overextensions
2. syntactic bootstrapping
3. holophrase
4. *a.* the naming explosion
5. *b.* develop with maturation of the brain and vocal organs
6. *c.* fulfill the infant's requests
7. *b.* the birth order hypothesis

Concept Check 10.3

1. *a.* "What is mommy reading?"
2. *b.* use many passives in their own uttered sentences
3. *d.* phonological awareness
4. *d.* Noticing siblings' comprehension errors makes the speaker aware of the need to express ideas clearly.
5. F
6. T

CHAPTER 11

Concept Check 11.1

1. *a.* shared environmental influences
2. *b.* nonshared environmental influences
3. F
4. T
5. self-recognition or self-evaluation
6. emotional expressions
7. emotional self-regulation
8. guilty; shameful
9. easy, difficult, and slow-to-warm-up

Concept Check 11.2

1. *b.* learning theory
2. *c.* cognitive developmental theory
3. *a.* psychoanalytic theory
4. *c.* Erik Erikson
5. *b.* John Bowlby
6. *d.* Konrad Lorenz
7. stranger anxiety
8. synchronized routines
9. (1) asocial phase; (2) phase of indiscriminate attachments; (3) phase of specific attachments; (4) phase of multiple attachments

Concept Check 11.3

1. *c.* Thomas & Chess's goodness-of-fit model
2. *b.* Kagan's temperament hypothesis
3. *d.* Kochanska's integrative theory
4. T
5. F (most infants are securely attached)
6. secure
7. avoidant
8. disorganized/disoriented
9. resistant

CHAPTER 12

Concept Check 12.1

1. *c.* self-esteem
2. *b.* self-concept
3. *a.* categorical self
4. F
5. F
6. *b.* personal agency
7. See Figure 12.4.
8. In the rouge test, a small spot of color is placed on the toddler's nose, and then the toddler looks in the mirror. If the toddler touches his own nose, it suggests self-recognition; if the toddler does not touch his own nose, or touches the mirror image, it suggests that the toddler does not recognize his image.

Concept Check 12.2

1. *b.* negative peer influences
2. *d.* strong parental criticism of failure
3. *c.* person praise
4. *a.* process-oriented praise
5. T
6. incremental
7. entity
8. identity diffusion; foreclosure; moratorium; identity achievement
9. Mastery orientation is the tendency to persist at challenging tasks because of a belief that one has high ability or that earlier failure can be overcome by trying harder; it results in persistence in the face of failure. Learned helplessness is a tendency to give up or to stop trying after failing because these failures are attributed to a lack of ability that one can do little about.

Concept Check 12.3

1. *b.* common activities
2. *a.* psychological similarities
3. *c.* loyalty and sharing of intimacies
4. T
5. behavioral comparisons
6. psychological comparisons
7. psychological constraints
8. egocentric or undifferentiated; social-informational role taking; self-reflective role taking; mutual role taking; societal role taking
9. Selman asked children of different ages to listen to a story in which multiple people approached a situation from multiple perspectives. He asked the children to identify each character's perspective and explain how they would react in the story.

CHAPTER 13

Concept Check 13.1

1. T
2. T
3. F
4. gender intensification
5. gender-role stereotypes
6. *a.* gender-role standard
7. *c.* variations in play styles
8. *b.* gender segregation
9. *c.* gender identity
10. *a.* self-fulfilling prophecies

Concept Check 13.2

1. T
2. F
3. *a.* gender consistency
4. *b.* basic gender identity
5. Money and Erhardt's biosocial theory
6. social learning theory
7. Freudian
8. (1) basic gender identity; (2) gender stability; (3) gender consistency

Concept Check 13.3

1. F
2. T
3. high; high
4. low; low
5. *d.* a very masculine person would necessarily have few feminine characteristics

CHAPTER 14

Concept Check 14.1

1. *c.* relational aggression
2. *b.* instrumental aggression
3. *a.* hostile aggression
4. T
5. F
6. *c.* Give the doll back to Judy and send George to time-out until he is able to play nicely with Judy.
7. ignoring; reinforcing
8. passive; provocative
9. (1) encode social cues; (2) interpret social cues; (3) formulate social goals; (4) generate problem-solving strategies; (5) evaluate the likely effectiveness of strategies and select a response; (6) enact a response

Concept Check 14.2

1. *b.* self-oriented distress
2. *a.* sympathetic empathic arousal
3. T
4. F
5. F
6. hedonistic
7. affective explanations

Concept Check 14.3

1. *b.* peer interactions
2. *a.* morality of care
3. *c.* role-taking skills

4. F

5. F

6. F

7. justice; care; care

8. underestimate

9. In Piaget's theory, the stage of moral realism, or heteronomous morality. In Kohlberg's theory, Stage 1 (punishment and obedience orientation) of Level 1 (preconventional morality).

CHAPTER 15

Concept Check 15.1

1. nuclear family
2. extended family
3. socialization
4. *c.* coparenting
5. This diagram is presented in Figure 15.1.

Concept Check 15.2

1. F
2. F
3. T
4. authoritarian
5. authoritative
6. authoritarian
7. *d.* transactional model
8. *a.* child effects model
9. *c.* economic distress model
10. This diagram is illustrated in Figure 15.2.

Concept Check 15.3

1. T
2. F
3. F
4. T
5. true mothers; birthgivers
6. donor insemination
7. divorce
8. *c.* Siblings often are better able to understand each other because they often develop a unique language that older peers do not understand.
9. *d.* Children raised by homosexual parents are more likely to become homosexual themselves.

CHAPTER 16

Concept Check 16.1

1. F
2. F
3. mean-world beliefs
4. desensitize
5. obesity
6. *a.* A 3-year-old can distinguish between friendly and evil characters based on the story line of a TV program.
7. *d.* computer-aided basic math computations (like multiplication) so that the child's efforts can be devoted to high-level conceptual math problems
8. *d.* concerns about the excessive us of chat programs by children to socialize with classmates in an impersonal climate

Concept Check 16.2

1. T
2. F
3. ethnic minorities
4. developmental
5. *d.* the informal curriculum
6. *a.* A stronger emphasis on independent learning and discovery learning in Asian school cultures.
7. *c.* Because Andy attended more school, he would be more advanced than Zack on cognitive competency tests, even though they were the same age.

Concept Check 16.3

1. T
2. F
3. parallel
4. solitary and parallel; associative and cooperative
5. rejected aggressive
6. *d.* helping children develop better motor skills and promoting their physical development
7. *b.* cliques
8. *b.* Dr. Frendlee plans to use only the surveys because he is confident that the results will be valid, based on previous research.

Glossary

acceptance/responsiveness: a dimension of parenting that describes the amount of responsiveness and affection that a parent displays toward a child.

accommodation: Piaget's term for the process by which children modify their existing schemes in order to incorporate or adapt to new experiences.

acculturation stress: anxiety or uneasiness that new residents may feel upon attempting to assimilate a new culture and its traditions.

achievement attributions: causal explanations that one provides for his/her successes and failures.

achievement expectancy: how well (or poorly) one expects to perform should she try to achieve a particular objective.

achievement motivation: a willingness to strive to succeed at challenging tasks and to meet high standards of accomplishment.

acquired immune deficiency syndrome (AIDS): a viral disease that can be transmitted from a mother to her fetus or neonate and that results in a weakening of the body's immune system and, ultimately, death.

active genotype/environment correlations: the notion that our genotypes affect the types of environments that we prefer and seek out.

activity/passivity issue: a debate among developmental theorists about whether children are active contributors to their own development or, rather, passive recipients of environmental influence.

adaptation: an inborn tendency to adjust to the demands of the environment.

adaptive strategy choice model: Siegler's model to describe how strategies change over time; the view that multiple strategies exist within a child's cognitive repertoire at any one time, with these strategies competing with one another for use.

adolescent growth spurt: the rapid increase in physical growth that marks the beginning of adolescence.

adoption design: study in which adoptees are compared with their biological relatives and their adoptive relatives to estimate the heritability of an attribute, or attributes.

affective explanations: discipline which focuses a child's attention on the harm or distress that his or her conduct has caused others.

age of viability: a point between the 22nd and 28th prenatal weeks when survival outside the uterus is possible.

aggression: behavior performed with the intention of harming a living being who is motivated to avoid this treatment.

alleles: alternative forms of a gene that can appear at a particular site on a chromosome.

alternative birth center: a hospital birthing room or other independent facility that provides a homelike atmosphere for childbirth but still makes medical technology available.

altruism: a selfless concern for the welfare of others that is expressed through prosocial acts such as sharing, cooperating, and helping.

amae: Japanese concept; refers to an infant's feeling of total dependence on his or her mother and the presumption of mother's love and indulgence.

amniocentesis: a method of extracting amniotic fluid from a pregnant woman so that fetal body cells within the fluid can be tested for chromosomal abnormalities and other genetic defects.

amnion: a watertight membrane that surrounds the developing embryo, serving to regulate its temperature and to cushion it against injuries.

analogical reasoning: reasoning that involves using something one knows already to help reason about something not known yet.

androgenized females: females who develop male external genitalia because of exposure to male sex hormones during the prenatal period.

androgyny: a psychological identity that includes both masculine and feminine characteristics or traits.

anencephaly: a birth defect in which the brain and neural tube fail to develop (or develop incompletely) and the skull does not close.

animism: attributing life and lifelike qualities to inanimate objects.

anorexia nervosa: a life-threatening eating disorder characterized by self-starvation and a compulsive fear of getting fat.

A-not-B error: tendency of 8- to 12-month-olds to search for a hidden object where they previously found it even after they have seen it moved to a new location.

anoxia: a lack of sufficient oxygen to the brain; may result in neurological damage or death.

Apgar test: a quick assessment of the newborn's heart rate, respiration, color, muscle tone, and reflexes that is used to gauge perinatal stress and to determine whether a neonate requires immediate medical assistance.

aphasia: a loss of one or more language functions.

appearance/reality distinction: ability to keep the true properties or characteristics of an object in mind despite the deceptive appearance the object has assumed; notably lacking among young children during the preconceptual period.

aptitude-treatment interaction (ATI): phenomenon whereby characteristics of the student and of the school environment interact to affect student outcomes, such that any given educational practice may be effective with some students but not with others.

asocial phase (of attachment): approximately the first 6 weeks of life, in which infants respond in an equally favorable way to interesting social and nonsocial stimuli.

assimilation: Piaget's term for the process by which children interpret new experiences by incorporating them into their existing schemes.

associative play: form of social discourse in which children pursue their own interests but will swap toys or comment on each other's activities.

attachment: a close emotional relationship between two persons, characterized by mutual affection and a desire to maintain proximity.

Attachment Q-set (AQS): alternative method of assessing attachment security that is based on observations of the child's attachment-related behaviors at home; can be used with infants, toddlers, and preschool children.

attention span: capacity for sustaining attention to a particular stimulus or activity.

attention-deficit hyperactivity disorder (ADHD): an attentional disorder involving distractibility, hyperactivity, and impulsive behavior that often leads to academic difficulties, poor self-esteem, and social or emotional problems.

attribution retraining: therapeutic intervention in which helpless children are persuaded to attribute failures to their lack of effort rather than a lack of ability.

authoritarian parenting: a restrictive pattern of parenting in which adults set many rules for their children, expect strict obedience, and rely on power rather than reason to elicit compliance.

authoritative parenting: flexible, democratic style of parenting in which warm, accepting parents provide guidance and control while allowing the child some say in deciding how best to meet challenges and obligations.

autobiographical memory: memory for important experiences or events that have happened to us.

autonomous morality: Piaget's second stage of moral development, in which children realize that rules are arbitrary agreements that can be challenged and changed with the consent of the people they govern.

autosomes: the 22 pairs of human chromosomes that are identical in males and females.

average-status children: children who receive a average number of nominations as a liked and/or a disliked individual from members of their peer group.

avoidant attachment: an insecure infant-caregiver bond, characterized by little separation protest and a tendency of the child to avoid or ignore the caregiver.

babbles: vowel/consonant combinations that infants begin to produce at about 4 to 6 months of age.

baby biography: a detailed record of an infant's growth and development over a period of time.

basic emotions: the set of emotions present at birth or emerging early in the first year that some theorists believe to be biologically programmed.

basic gender identity: the stage of gender identity in which the child first labels the self as a boy or a girl.

behavioral comparisons phase: the tendency to form impressions of others by comparing and contrasting their overt behaviors.

behavioral control: attempts to regulate a child's or an adolescent's conduct through firm discipline and monitoring of his or her conduct.

behavioral genetics: the scientific study of how genotype interacts with environment to determine behavioral attributes such as intelligence, personality, and mental health.

behavioral inhibition: a temperamental attribute reflecting one's tendency to withdraw from unfamiliar people or situations.

behaviorism: a school of thinking in psychology that holds that conclusions about human development should be based on controlled observations of overt behavior rather than speculation about unconscious motives or other unobservable phenomena; the philosophical underpinning for the early theories of learning.

belief-desire reasoning: the process whereby we explain and predict what people do based on what we understand their desires and beliefs to be.

benefits-to-risks ratio: a comparison of the possible benefits of a study for advancing knowledge and optimizing life conditions versus its costs to participants in terms of inconvenience and possible harm.

bipolar disorder: a psychological disorder characterized by extreme fluctuations in mood.

blastocyst: name given to the ball of cells formed when the fertilized egg first begins to divide.

bonding: the strong affectionate ties that parents may feel toward their infant; some theorists believe that the strongest bonding occurs shortly after birth, during a sensitive period.

bound morphemes: morphemes that cannot stand alone but that modify the meaning of free morphemes (for example, the *-ed* attached to English verbs to indicate past tense).
brain growth spurt: the period between the seventh prenatal month and 2 years of age when more than half of the child's eventual brain weight is added.
breech birth: a delivery in which the fetus emerges feet first or buttocks first rather than head first.
Broca's area: structure located in the frontal lobe of the left hemisphere of the cerebral cortex that controls language production.
bulimia: a life-threatening eating disorder characterized by recurrent eating binges followed by such purging activities as heavy use of laxatives or vomiting.
canalization: genetic restriction of phenotype to a small number of developmental outcomes; a highly canalized attribute is one for which genes channel development along predetermined pathways, so that the environment has little effect on the phenotype that emerges.
cardinality: principle specifying that the last number in a counting sequence specifies the number of items in a set.
caregiving hypothesis: Ainsworth's notion that the type of attachment that an infant develops with a particular caregiver depends primarily on the kind of caregiving he has received from that person.
carrier: a heterozygous individual who displays no sign of a recessive allele in his or her own phenotype but can pass this gene to offspring.
case study: a research method in which the investigator gathers extensive information about the life of an individual and then tests developmental hypotheses by analyzing the events of the person's life history.
castration anxiety: in Freud's theory, a young boy's fear that his father will castrate him as punishment for his rivalrous conduct.
catch-up growth: a period of accelerated growth in which children who have experienced growth deficits grow very rapidly to "catch up to" the growth trajectory that they are genetically programmed to follow.
categorical self: a person's classification of the self along socially significant dimensions such as age and sex.
centration (centered thinking): in Piaget's theory, the tendency of preoperational children to attend to one aspect of a situation to the exclusion of others; contrast with *decentration*.
cephalocaudal development: a sequence of physical maturation and growth that proceeds from the head (cephalic region) to the tail (or caudal region).
cerebral cortex: the outer layer of the brain's cerebrum that is involved in voluntary body movements, perception, and higher intellectual functions such as learning, thinking, and speaking.
cerebral lateralization: the specialization of brain functions in the left and the right cerebral hemispheres.
cerebrum: the highest brain center; includes both hemispheres of the brain and the fibers that connect them.
cesarean section: surgical delivery of a baby through an incision made in the mother's abdomen and uterus.
child effects model: model of family influence in which children are believed to influence their parents rather than vice versa.
chorion: a membrane that becomes attached to the uterine tissues to gather nourishment for the embryo.
chorionic villus sampling (CVS): an alternative to amniocentesis in which fetal cells are extracted from the chorion for prenatal tests. CVS can be performed earlier in pregnancy than is possible with amniocentesis.
chromosome: a threadlike structure made up of genes; in humans there are 46 chromosomes in the nucleus of each body cell.
chronosystem: in ecological systems theory, changes in the individual or the environment that occur over time and influence the direction development takes.
classical conditioning: a type of learning in which an initially neutral stimulus is repeatedly paired with a meaningful nonneutral stimulus so that the neutral stimulus comes to elicit the response originally made only to the nonneutral stimulus.
cleft lip: a congenital disorder in which the upper lip has a vertical (or pair of vertical) openings or grooves.
cleft palate: a congenital disorder in which the roof of the mouth does not close properly during embryonic development, resulting in an opening or groove in the roof of the mouth.
clinical method: a type of interview in which a participant's response to each successive question (or problem) determines what the investigator will ask next.
cliques: a small group of friends that interacts frequently.
codominance: condition in which two heterozygous but equally powerful alleles produce a phenotype in which both genes are fully and equally expressed.
coercive home environment: a home in which family members often annoy one another and use aggressive or otherwise antisocial tactics as a method of coping with these aversive experiences.
cognition: the activity of knowing and the processes through which knowledge is acquired.
cognitive development: age-related changes that occur in mental activities such as attending, perceiving, learning, thinking, and remembering.
cognitive equilibrium: Piaget's term for the state of affairs in which there is a balanced, or harmonious, relationship between one's thought processes and the environment.
cognitive self-guidance system: in Vygotsky's theory, the use of private speech to guide problem-solving behavior.
cohort: a group of people of the same age who are exposed to similar cultural environments and historical events as they are growing up.
cohort effect: age-related difference among cohorts that is attributable to cultural/historical differences in cohorts' growing-up experiences rather than to true developmental change.
collectivist (or communal) society: society that values cooperative interdependence, social harmony, and adherence to group norms. These societies generally hold that the group's well-being is more important than that of the individual.
committed compliance: compliance based on the child's eagerness to cooperate with a responsive parent who has been willing to cooperate with him or her.
communication: the process by which one organism transmits information to and influences another.
compensatory interventions: special educational programs designed to further the cognitive growth and scholastic achievements of disadvantaged children.
complex emotions: self-conscious or self-evaluative emotions that emerge in the second year and depend, in part, on cognitive development.
computer-assisted instruction (CAI): use of computers to teach new concepts and practice academic skills.
conception: the moment of fertilization, when a sperm penetrates an ovum, forming a zygote.
concordance rate: the percentage of cases in which a particular attribute is present for one member of a twin pair if it is present for the other.
concrete-operational period: Piaget's third stage of cognitive development, lasting from about age 7 to age 11, when children are acquiring cognitive operations and thinking more logically about real objects and experiences.
conditioned response (CR): a learned response to a stimulus that was not originally capable of producing the response.
conditioned stimulus (CS): an initially neutral stimulus that comes to elicit a particular response after being paired with a UCS that always elicits the response.
confidentiality: the right of participants to concealment of their identity with respect to the data that they provide.
conflict: circumstances in which two (or more) persons have incompatible needs, desires, or goals.
confounding variable: some factor other than the independent variable that, if not controlled by the experimenter, could explain any differences across treatment conditions in participants' performance on the dependent variable.
congenital adrenal hyperplasia (CAH): a genetic anomaly that causes one's adrenal glands to produce unusually high levels of androgen from the prenatal period onward; often has masculinizing effects on female fetuses.
congenital defect: a problem that is present (though not necessarily apparent) at birth; such defects may stem from genetic and prenatal influences or from complications of the birth process.
conservation: the recognition that the properties of an object or substance do not change when its appearance is altered in some superficial way.
constructivist: one who gains knowledge by acting or otherwise operating on objects and events to discover their properties.
context-independent learning: learning that has no immediate relevance to the present context, as is done in modern schools; acquiring knowledge for knowledge's sake.
contextual model: view of children as active entities whose developmental paths represent a continuous, dynamic interplay between internal forces (nature) and external influences (nurture).
continuity/discontinuity issue: a debate among theorists about whether developmental changes are quantitative and continuous, or qualitative and discontinuous (i.e., stagelike).
controversial children: children who receive many nominations as a liked and many as a disliked individual.
conventional morality: Kohlberg's term for the third and fourth stages of moral reasoning, in which moral judgments are based on a desire to gain approval (Stage 3) or to uphold laws that maintain social order (Stage 4).
convergent thinking: thinking that requires one to come up with a single correct answer to a problem; what IQ tests measure.
cooperative play: true social play in which children cooperate or assume reciprocal roles while pursing shared goals.
coordination of secondary circular reactions: fourth substage of Piaget's sensorimotor stage; infants begin to coordinate two or more actions to achieve simple objectives. This is the first sign of goal-directed behavior.
coos: vowel-like sounds that young infants repeat over and over during periods of contentment.
coparenting: circumstance in which parents mutually support each other and function as a cooperative parenting team.
corpus callosum: the bundle of neural fibers that connects the two hemispheres of the brain and transmits information from one hemisphere to the other.
correlation coefficient: a numerical index, ranging from -1.00 to $+1.00$, of the strength and direction of the relationship between two variables.
correlational design: a type of research design that indicates the strength of associations among variables; though correlated variables are systematically related, these relationships are not necessarily causal.
creativity: the ability to generate novel ideas or works that are useful and valued by others.
creoles: languages that develop when pidgins are transformed into grammatically complex "true" languages.
cross-cultural comparison: a study that compares the behavior and/or development of people from different cultural or subcultural backgrounds.
cross-generational problem: the fact that long-term changes in the environment may limit conclusions of a longitudinal project to that generation of children who were growing up while the study was in progress.
crossing-over: a process in which genetic material is exchanged between pairs of chromosomes during meiosis.
cross-sectional design: a research design in which subjects from different age groups are studied at the same point in time.
crowds: a large, reputationally based peer group made up of individuals and cliques that share similar norms, interests, and values.
crystallized intelligence: the ability to understand relations or solve problems that depend on knowledge acquired from schooling and other cultural influences.
cued recall: a recollection that is prompted by a cue associated with the setting in which the recalled event originally occurred.
cultural bias: the situation that arises when one cultural or subcultural group is more familiar with test items than another group and therefore has an unfair advantage.

cultural test bias hypothesis: the notion that IQ tests and testing procedures have a built-in, middle-class bias that explains the substandard performance of children from lower-class and minority subcultures.
culture fair tests: intelligence tests constructed to minimize any irrelevant cultural biases in test content that could influence test performance.
cumulative-deficit hypothesis: the notion that impoverished environments inhibit intellectual growth and that these inhibiting effects accumulate over time.
decentration: in Piaget's theory, the ability of concrete operational children to consider multiple aspects of a stimulus or situation; contrast with *centration*.
deferred imitation: the ability to reproduce a modeled activity that has been witnessed at some point in the past.
demandingness/control: a dimension of parenting that describes how restrictive and demanding parents are.
deoxyribonucleic acid (DNA): long, double-stranded molecules that make up chromosomes.
dependent variable: the aspect of behavior that is measured in an experiment and assumed to be under the control of the independent variable.
deprivation dwarfism: a childhood growth disorder that is triggered by emotional deprivation and characterized by decreased production of GH, slow growth, and small stature.
desensitization hypothesis: the notion that people who watch a lot of media violence will become less aroused by aggression and more tolerant of violent and aggressive acts.
development: systematic continuities and changes in the individual over the course of life.
developmental continuities: ways in which we remain stable over time or continue to reflect our past.
developmental psychology: branch of psychology devoted to identifying and explaining the continuities and changes that individuals display over time.
developmental quotient (DQ): a numerical measure of an infant's performance on a developmental schedule relative to the performance of other infants of the same age.
developmental stage: a distinct phase within a larger sequence of development; a period characterized by a particular set of abilities, motives, behaviors, or emotions that occur together and form a coherent pattern.
developmentalist: any scholar, regardless of discipline, who seeks to understand the developmental process (e.g., psychologists, biologists, sociologists, anthropologists, educators).
deviation IQ score: an intelligence test score that reflects how well or poorly a person performs compared with others of the same age.
diethylstilbestrol (DES): a synthetic hormone, formerly prescribed to prevent miscarriage, that can produce cervical cancer in female offspring and genital-tract abnormalities in males.
difficult temperament: temperamental profile in which the child is irregular in daily routines and adapts slowly to new experiences, often responding negatively and intensely.
direct tuition: teaching young children how to behave by reinforcing "appropriate" behaviors and by punishing or otherwise discouraging inappropriate conduct.
disequilibriums: imbalances or contradictions between one's thought processes and environmental events. On the other hand, **equilibrium** refers to a balanced, harmonious relationship between one's cognitive structures and the environment.
dishabituation: increase in responsiveness that occurs when stimulation changes.
disorganized/disoriented attachment: an insecure infant-caregiver bond, characterized by the infant's dazed appearance on reunion or a tendency to first seek and then abruptly avoid the caregiver.
divergent thinking: thinking that requires a variety of ideas or solutions to a problem when there is no one correct answer.
dizygotic (fraternal) twins: twins that result when a mother releases two ova at roughly the same time and each is fertilized by a different sperm, producing two zygotes that are genetically different.
doctrine of specificity: a viewpoint shared by many social-learning theorists which holds that moral affect, moral reasoning, and moral behavior may depend as much or more on the situation one faces than on an internalized set of moral principles.
dominant allele: a relatively powerful gene that is expressed phenotypically and masks the effect of a less powerful gene.
donor insemination: process by which a fertile woman conceives with the aid of sperm from an unknown donor.
double standard: the view that sexual behavior that is appropriate for members of one gender is less appropriate for the other.
Down syndrome: a chromosomal abnormality (also known as trisomy-21) caused by the presence of an extra 21st chromosome; people with this syndrome have a distinctive physical appearance and are moderately to severely retarded.
dual representation (dual encoding): the ability to represent an object simultaneously as an object itself and as a representation of something else.
dynamic assessment: an approach to assessing intelligence that evaluates how well individuals learn new material when an examiner provides them with competent instruction.
dynamical systems theory: a theory that views motor skills as active reorganizations of previously mastered capabilities that are undertaken to find more effective ways of exploring the environment or satisfying other objectives.
easy temperament: temperamental profile in which the child quickly establishes regular routines, is generally good natured, and adapts easily to novelty.
eclectics: those who borrow from many theories in their attempts to predict and explain human development.
ecological systems theory: Bronfenbrenner's model emphasizing that the developing person is embedded in a series of environmental systems that interact with one another and with the person to influence development.
ecological validity: state of affairs in which the findings of one's research are an accurate representation of processes that occur in the natural environment.
effective schools: schools that are generally successful at achieving curricular and noncurricular objectives, regardless of the racial, ethnic, or socioeconomic background of the student population.
ego: psychoanalytic term for the rational component of the personality.
egocentric speech: Piaget's term for the subset of a young child's utterances that are nonsocial—that is, neither directed to others nor expressed in ways that listeners might understand.
egocentrism: the tendency to view the world from one's own perspective while failing to recognize that others may have different points of view.
Electra complex: female version of the Oedipus complex, in which a 3- to 6-year-old girl was thought to envy her father for possessing a penis and would choose him as a sex object in the hope that he would share with her this valuable organ that she lacked.
embryo: name given to the prenatal organism from the third through the eighth week after conception.
emotional bonding: term used to describe the strong affectionate ties that parents may feel toward their infant; some theorists believe that the strongest bonding occurs shortly after birth, during a sensitive period.
emotional display rules: culturally defined rules specifying which emotions should or should not be expressed under which circumstances.
emotional self-regulation: strategies for managing emotions or adjusting emotional arousal to an appropriate level of intensity.
empathic concern: a measure of the extent to which an individual recognizes the needs of others and is concerned about their welfare.
empathy: the ability to experience the same emotions that someone else is experiencing, or in more advanced forms, the ability to understand another person's emotional state or psychological experience.
encoding: the process by which external stimulation is converted to a mental representation.
engrossment: paternal analogue of maternal emotional bonding; term used to describe fathers' fascination with their neonates, including their desire to touch, hold, caress, and talk to the newborn baby.
entity view of ability: belief that one's ability is a highly stable trait that is not influenced much by effort or practice.
environmental determinism: the notion that children are passive creatures who are molded by their environments.
environmental hypothesis: the notion that groups differ in IQ because the environments in which they are raised are not equally conducive to intellectual growth.
estrogen: female sex hormone, produced by the ovaries, that is responsible for female sexual maturation.
ethnography: method in which the researcher seeks to understand the unique values, traditions, and social processes of a culture or subculture by living with its members and making extensive observations and notes.
ethology: the study of the bioevolutionary bases of behavior and development.
event memory: long-term memory for events.
evocative genotype/environment correlations: the notion that our heritable attributes affect others' behavior toward us and thus influence the social environment in which development takes place.
evoked potential: a change in patterning of the brain waves which indicates that an individual detects (senses) a stimulus.
executive control processes: the processes involved in regulating attention and in determining what to do with information just gathered or retrieved from long-term memory.
exosystem: social systems that children and adolescents do not directly experience but that may nonetheless influence their development; the third of Bronfenbrenner's environmental layers or contexts.
expansions: responding to a child's ungrammatical utterance with a grammatically improved form of that statement.
experimental control: steps taken by an experimenter to ensure that all extraneous factors that could influence the dependent variable are roughly equivalent in each experimental condition; these precautions must be taken before an experimenter can be reasonably certain that observed changes in the dependent variable were caused by the manipulation of the independent variable.
experimental design: a research design in which the investigator introduces some change in the participant's environment and then measures the effect of that change on the participant's behavior.
explicit cognition: thinking and thought processes of which we are consciously aware.
expressive role: a social prescription, usually directed toward females, that one should be cooperative, kind, nurturant, and sensitive to the needs of others.
expressive style: early linguistic style in which toddlers use language mainly to call attention to their own and others' feelings and to regulate social interactions.
extended family: a group of blood relatives from more than one nuclear family (for example, grandparents, aunts, uncles, nieces, and nephews) who live together, forming a household.
extended self: more mature self-representation, emerging between ages 3½ and 5 years, in which children are able to integrate past, current, and unknown future self-representations into a notion of a "self" that endures over time.
extrafamilial influences: social agencies other than the family that influence a child's or an adolescent's cognitive, social, and emotional development.
factor analysis: a statistical procedure for identifying clusters of tests or test items (called factors) that are highly correlated with one another and unrelated to other test items.
false self-behavior: acting in ways that do not reflect one's true self or the "true me."
false-belief task: a type of task used in theory-of-mind studies, in which the child must infer that another person does not possess knowledge that he or she possesses (that is, that other person holds a belief that is false).

falsifiability: a criterion for evaluating the scientific merit of theories. A theory is falsifiable when it is capable of generating predictions that could be disconfirmed.
family: two or more persons, related by birth, marriage, adoption, or choice, who have emotional ties and responsibilities to each other.
family distress model: Conger's model of how economic distress affects family dynamics and developmental outcomes.
family social system: the complex network of relationships, interactions, and patterns of influence that characterize a family with three or more members.
fast mapping: process of acquiring a word after hearing it applied to its referent on a small number of occasions.
"felt responsibility" hypothesis: the theory that empathy may promote altruism by causing one to reflect on altruistic norms and, thus, to feel some obligation to help distressed others.
fetal alcohol effects (FAE): a group of mild congenital problems that are sometimes observed in children of mothers who drink sparingly to moderately during pregnancy.
fetal alcohol syndrome (FAS): a group of serious congenital problems commonly observed in the offspring of mothers who abuse alcohol during pregnancy.
fetus: name given to the prenatal organism from the ninth week of pregnancy until birth.
field experiment: an experiment that takes place in a naturalistic setting such as home, school, or a playground.
first stage of labor: the period of the birth process lasting from the first regular uterine contractions until the cervix is fully dilated.
fixation: arrested development at a particular psychosexual stage which can prevent movement to higher stages.
fluid intelligence: the ability to perceive relationships and solve relational problems of the type that are not taught and are relatively free of cultural influences.
Flynn effect: systematic increase in IQ scores observed over the 20th century.
folic acid: B-complex vitamin that helps to prevent defects of the central nervous system.
foreclosure: identity status characterizing individuals who have prematurely committed themselves to occupations or ideologies without really thinking about these commitments.
formal operations: Piaget's fourth and final stage of cognitive development, from age 11 or 12 and beyond, when the individual begins to think more rationally and systematically about abstract concepts and hypothetical events.
fragile-X syndrome: abnormality of the X chromosome caused by a defective gene and associated with mild to severe mental retardation, particularly when the defective gene is passed from mother to child.
free morphemes: morphemes that can stand alone as a word (for example, *cat, go, yellow*).
free recall: a recollection that is not prompted by specific cues or prompts.
fuzzy-trace theory: theory proposed by Brainerd and Reyna that postulates that people encode experiences on a continuum from literal, verbatim traces to fuzzy, gistlike traces.
g: Spearman's abbreviation for *neogenesis,* which, roughly translated, means one's ability to understand relations (or general mental ability).
gender: a person's social and cultural identity as male or female.
gender consistency: the stage of gender identity in which the child recognizes that a person's gender is invariant despite changes in the person's activities or appearance (also known as gender constancy).
gender identity: one's awareness of one's gender and its implications.
gender intensification: a magnification of sex differences early in adolescence; associated with increased pressure to conform to traditional gender roles.
gender schemas: organized sets of beliefs and expectations about males and females that guide information processing.
gender segregation: children's tendency to associate with same-sex playmates and to think of the other sex as an outgroup.
gender stability: the stage of gender identity in which the child recognizes that gender is stable over time.
gender typing: the process by which a child becomes aware of his or her gender and acquires motives, values, and behaviors considered appropriate for members of that sex.
gender-role standard: a behavior, value, or motive that members of a society consider more typical or appropriate for members of one sex.
genes: hereditary blueprints for development that are transmitted unchanged from generation to generation.
genetic counseling: a service designed to inform prospective parents about genetic diseases and to help them determine the likelihood that they would transmit such disorders to their children.
genetic epistemology: the experimental study of the development of knowledge, developed by Piaget.
genetic hypothesis: the notion that group differences in IQ are hereditary.
genital herpes: a sexually transmitted disease that can infect infants at birth, causing blindness, brain damage, or even death.
genotype: the genetic endowment that an individual inherits.
germline gene therapy: a procedure, not yet perfected or approved for use with humans, in which harmful genes would be repaired or replaced with healthy ones, thereby permanently correctly a genetic defect.
giftedness: the possession of unusually high intellectual potential or other special talents.
gist: a fuzzy representation of information that preserves the central content but few precise details.
glia: nerve cells that nourish neurons and encase them in insulating sheaths of myelin.
"goodness-of-fit" model: Thomas and Chess's notion that development is likely to be optimized when parents' child-rearing practices are sensitively adapted to the child's temperamental characteristics.
grammatical morphemes: prefixes, suffixes, prepositions, and auxiliary verbs that modify the meaning of words and sentences.
growth hormone (GH): the pituitary hormone that stimulates the rapid growth and development of body cells; primarily responsible for the adolescent growth spurt.
guided participation: adult-child interactions in which children's cognitions and modes of thinking are shaped as they participate with or observe adults engaged in culturally relevant activities.
habits: well-learned associations between stimuli and responses that represent the stable aspects of one's personality.
habituation: a decrease in one's response to a stimulus that has become familiar through repetition.
Head Start: a large-scale preschool educational program designed to provide children from low-income families with a variety of social and intellectual experiences that might better prepare them for school.
heritability: the amount of variability in a trait that is attributable to hereditary factors.
heritability coefficient: a numerical estimate, ranging from .00 to +1.00, of the amount of variation in an attribute that is due to hereditary factors.
heteronomous morality: Piaget's first stage of moral development, in which children view the rules of authority figures as sacred and unalterable.
heterozygous: having inherited two alleles for an attribute that have different effects.
heuristic value: a criterion for evaluating the scientific merit of theories. A heuristic theory is one that continues to stimulate new research and new discoveries.
hierarchical model of intelligence: model of the structure of intelligence in which a broad, general ability factor is at the top of the hierarchy, with a number of specialized ability factors nested underneath.
high-amplitude sucking method: a method of assessing infants' perceptual capabilities that capitalizes on the ability of infants to make interesting events last by varying the rate at which they suck on a special pacifier.
holistic perspective: a unified view of the developmental process that emphasizes the important interrelationships among the physical, mental, social, and emotional aspects of human development.
holophrase: a single-word utterance that represents an entire sentence's worth of meaning.
holophrase period: the period when the child's speech consists of one-word utterances, some of which are thought to be holophrases.
HOME inventory: a measure of the amount and type of intellectual stimulation provided by a child's home environment.
homozygous: having inherited two alleles for an attribute that are identical in their effects.
horizontal décalage: Piaget's term for a child's uneven cognitive performance; an inability to solve certain problems even though one can solve similar problems requiring the same mental operations.
hostile aggression: aggressive acts for which the perpetrator's major goal is to harm or injure a victim.
hostile attributional bias: tendency to view harm done under ambiguous circumstances as having stemmed from a hostile intent on the part of the harmdoer; characterizes reactive aggressors.
Huntington's disease: a genetic disease, caused by a dominant allele, that typically appears later in life and causes the nervous system to degenerate.
hypothesis: a theoretical prediction about some aspect of experience.
hypothetico-deductive reasoning: in Piaget's theory, a formal operational ability to think hypothetically.
id: psychoanalytic term for the inborn component of the personality that is driven by the instincts.
identification: Freud's term for the child's tendency to emulate another person, usually the same-sex parent.
identity: a mature self-definition; a sense of who one is, where one is going in life, and how one fits into society.
identity achievement: identity status characterizing individuals who have carefully considered identity issues and have made firm commitments to an occupation and ideologies.
identity crisis: Erikson's term for the uncertainty and discomfort that adolescents experience when they become confused about their present and future roles in life.
identity diffusion: identity status characterizing individuals who are not questioning who they are and have not yet committed themselves to an identity.
identity training: an attempt to promote conservation by teaching nonconservers to recognize that a transformed object or substance is the same object or substance, regardless of its new appearance.
ideographic development: individual variations in the rate, extent, or direction of development.
immanent justice: the notion that unacceptable conduct will invariably be punished and that justice is ever present in the world.
implantation: the burrowing of the blastocyst into the lining of the uterus.
implicit cognition: thought that occurs without awareness that one is thinking.
imprinting: an innate or instinctual form of learning in which the young of certain species will follow and become attached to moving objects (usually their mothers).
incompatible-response technique: a nonpunitive method of behavior modification in which adults ignore undesirable conduct while reinforcing acts that are incompatible with these responses.
incremental view of ability: belief that one's ability can be improved through increased effort and practice.
independent assortment: the principle stating that each pair of chromosomes segregates independently of all other chromosome pairs during meiosis.
independent variable: the aspect of the environment that an experimenter modifies or manipulates in order to measure its impact on behavior.
individualistic society: society that values personalism and individual accomplishments, which often take precedence over group goals. These societies tend to emphasize ways in which individuals differ from each other.
induction: a nonpunitive form of discipline in which an adult explains why a child's behavior is wrong and should be changed by emphasizing its effects on others.
inductive reasoning: the type of thinking that scientists display, where hypotheses are generated and then systematically tested in experiments.

infantile amnesia: a lack of memory for the early years of one's life.
informal curriculum: noncurricular objectives of schooling such as teaching children to cooperate, to respect authority, to obey rules, and to become good citizens.
information-processing theory: a perspective that views the human mind as a continuously developing, symbol-manipulating system, similar to a computer, into which information flows, is operated on, and is converted to output (answers, inferences, and solutions to problems).
informed consent: the right of research participants to receive an explanation, in language they can understand, of all aspects of research that may affect their willingness to participate.
"in-group/out-group" schema: one's general knowledge of the mannerisms, roles, activities, and behaviors that characterize males and females.
inhibition: the ability to prevent ourselves from executing some cognitive or behavioral response.
inhibitory control: an ability to display acceptable conduct by resisting the temptation to commit a forbidden act.
innate purity: the idea that infants are born with an intuitive sense of right and wrong that is often misdirected by the demands and restrictions of society.
inner experimentation: in the sixth substage of Piaget's sensorimotor stage, the ability to solve simple problems on a mental, or symbolic, level without having to rely on trial-and-error experimentation.
instinct: an inborn biological force that motivates a particular response or class of responses.
instrumental aggression: aggressive acts for which the perpetrator's major goal is to gain access to objects, space, or privileges.
instrumental role: a social prescription, usually directed toward males, that one should be dominant, independent, assertive, competitive, and goal-oriented.
intelligence: in Piaget's theory, a basic life function that enables an organism to adapt to its environment.
intelligence quotient (IQ): a numerical measure of a person's performance on an intelligence test relative to the performance of other examinees.
interactionist theory: the notion that biological factors and environmental influences interact to determine the course of language development.
intermodal perception: the ability to use one sensory modality to identify a stimulus or pattern of stimuli that is already familiar through another modality.
internal working models: cognitive representations of self, others, and relationships that infants construct from their interactions with caregivers.
internalization: the process of adopting the attributes or standards of other people—taking these standards as one's own.
intrinsic achievement orientation: a desire to achieve in order to satisfy one's *personal* needs for competence or mastery (as opposed to achieving for external incentives such as grades).
introversion/extroversion: the opposite poles of a personality dimension: introverts are shy, anxious around others, and tend to withdraw from social situations; extroverts are highly sociable and enjoy being with others.
invariant developmental sequence: a series of developments that occur in one particular order because each development in the sequence is a prerequisite for those appearing later.
investment theory of creativity: recent theory specifying that the ability to invest in innovative projects and to generate creative solutions depends on a convergence of creative resources, namely background knowledge, intellectual abilities, personality characteristics, motivation, and environmental support/encouragement.
iron deficiency anemia: a listlessness caused by too little iron in the diet that makes children inattentive and may retard physical and intellectual development.
kewpie doll effect: the notion that infantlike facial features are perceived as cute and lovable and elicit favorable responses from others.
kinship: the extent to which two individuals have genes in common.
knowledge base: one's existing information about a topic or content area.
kwashiorkor: a growth-retarding disease affecting children who receive enough calories but little if any protein.
language: a small number of individually meaningless symbols (sounds, letters, gestures) that can be combined according to agreed-on rules to produce an infinite number of messages.
language acquisition device (LAD): Chomsky's term for the innate knowledge of grammar that humans were said to possess—knowledge that might enable young children to infer the rules governing others' speech and to use these rules to produce language.
language-making capacity (LMC): a hypothesized set of specialized linguistic processing skills that enable children to analyze speech and to detect phonological, semantic, and syntactical relationships.
lanugo: fine hair covering the fetus's body which helps vernix stick to the skin.
learned helplessness orientation: a tendency to give up or to stop trying after failing because these failures have been attributed to a lack of ability that one can do little about.
learning: a relatively permanent change in behavior (or behavioral potential) that results from one's experiences or practice.
learning goal: state of affairs in which one's primary objective in an achievement context is to increase one's skills or abilities.
learning to learn: improvements in performance on novel problems as a result of acquiring a new rule or strategy from the earlier solution of similar problems.
Level I abilities: Jensen's term for lower-level intellectual abilities (such as attention and short-term memory) that are important for simple association learning.
Level II abilities: Jensen's term for higher-level cognitive skills that are involved in abstract reasoning and problem solving.
lexical contrast constraint: notion that young children make inferences about word meanings by contrasting new words with words they already know.
linguistic universal: an aspect of language development that all children share.
longitudinal design: a research design in which one group of subjects is studied repeatedly over a period of months or years.
long-term store (LTS): third information-processing store, in which information that has been examined and interpreted is permanently stored for future use.
love withdrawal: a form of discipline in which an adult witholds attention, affection, or approval in order to modify or control a child's behavior.
macrosystem: the larger cultural or subcultural context in which development occurs; Bronfenbrenner's outermost environmental layer or context.
marasmus: a growth-retarding disease affecting infants who receive insufficient protein and too few calories.
mastery motivation: an inborn motive to explore, understand, and control one's environment.
mastery orientation: a tendency to persist at challenging tasks because of a belief that one has high ability and/or that earlier failures can be overcome by trying harder.
maturation: developmental changes in the body or behavior that result from the aging process rather than from learning, injury, illness, or some other life experience.
mean-world belief: a belief, fostered by televised violence, that the world is a more dangerous and frightening place than is actually the case.
mechanistic model: view of children as passive entities whose developmental paths are primarily determined by external (environmental) influences.
meiosis: the process in which a germ cell divides, producing gametes (sperm or ova) that each contain half of the parent cell's original complement of chromosomes; in humans, the products of meiosis contain 23 chromosomes.
memory span: a general measure of the amount of information that can be held in the short-term store.
menarche: the first occurrence of menstruation.
mental age (MA): a measure of intellectual development that reflects the level of age-graded problems a child is able to solve.
mental retardation: significant sub-average intellectual functioning associated with impairments in adaptive behavior in everyday life.
mental seriation: a cognitive operation that allows one to mentally order a set of stimuli along a quantifiable dimension such as height or weight.
mesosystem: the interconnections among an individual's immediate settings or Microsystems; the second of Bronfenbrenner's environmental layers or contexts.
metacognition: one's knowledge about cognition and about the regulation of cognitive activities.
metalinguistic awareness: a knowledge of language and its properties; an understanding that language can be used for purposes other than communicating.
metamemory: one's knowledge about memory and memory processes.
microgenetic design: a research design in which participants are studied intensively over a short period of time as developmental changes occur; attempts to specify how or why those changes occur.
microgenetic development: changes that occur over relatively brief periods of time, in seconds, minutes, or days, as opposed to larger-scale changes, as conventionally studied in ontogenetic development.
microsystem: the immediate settings (including role relationships and activities) that the person actually encounters; the innermost of Bronfenbrenner's environmental layers or contexts.
mitosis: the process in which a cell duplicates its chromosomes and then divides into two genetically identical daughter cells.
mnemonics (memory strategies): effortful techniques used to improve memory, including rehearsal, organization, and elaboration.
monozygotic (identical) twins: twins who develop from a single zygote that later divides to form two genetically identical individuals.
moral affect: the emotional component of morality, including feelings such as guilt, shame, and pride in ethical conduct.
moral behavior: the behavioral component of morality; actions that are consistent with one's moral standards in situations in which one is tempted to violate them.
moral reasoning: the cognitive component of morality; the thinking that people display when deciding whether various acts are right or wrong.
moral rules: standards of acceptable and unacceptable conduct that focus on the rights and privileges of individuals.
morality: a set of principles or ideals that help the individual to distinguish right from wrong, to act on this distinction, and to feel pride in virtuous conduct and guilt (or other unpleasant emotions) for conduct that violates one's standards.
morality of care: Gilligan's term for what she presumes to be the dominant moral orientation of females—an orientation focusing more on compassionate concerns for human welfare than on socially defined justice as administered through law.
morality of justice: Gilligan's term for what she presumes to be the dominant moral orientation of males, focusing more on socially defined justice as administered through law than on compassionate concerns for human welfare.
moratorium: identity status characterizing individuals who are currently experiencing an identity crisis and are actively exploring occupational and ideological positions in which to invest themselves.
morphemes: smallest meaningful language units.
morphological knowledge: one's knowledge of the meaning of morphemes that make up words.
morphology: rules governing the formation of meaningful words from sounds.
motherese: the short, simple, high-pitched (and often repetitive) sentences that adults use when talking with young children (also called **child-directed speech**).
multimodal motherese: older companion's use of information that is exaggerated and synchronized across two or more senses to call an infant's attention to the referent of a spoken word.

multistore model: information-processing model that depicts information as flowing through three processing units (or stores): the sensory store, the short-term store (STS), and the long-term store (LTS).
mutation: a change in the chemical structure or arrangement of one or more genes that has the effect of producing a new phenotype.
mutual exclusivity constraint: notion that young children will assume that each object has but one label and that different words refer to separate and non-overlapping categories.
mutually responsive orientation: parent-child relationship characterized by mutual responsiveness to each other's needs and goals and shared positive affect.
myelinization: the process by which neurons are enclosed in waxy myelin sheaths that will facilitate the transmission of neural impulses.
naming explosion: term used to describe the dramatic increase in the pace at which infants acquire new words in the latter half of the second year; so named because many of the new words acquired are the names of objects.
natural, or prepared, childbirth: a delivery in which physical and psychological preparations for the birth are stressed and medical assistance is minimized.
natural (or quasi) experiment: a study in which the investigator measures the impact of some naturally occurring event that is assumed to affect people's lives.
natural selection: an evolutionary process, proposed by Charles Darwin, stating that individuals with characteristics that promote adaptation to the environment will survive, reproduce, and pass these adaptive characteristics to offspring; those lacking these adaptive characteristics will eventually die out.
naturalistic observation: a method in which the scientist tests hypotheses by observing people as they engage in everyday activities in their natural habitats (for example, at home, at school, or on the playground).
nature/nurture issue: the debate among developmental theorists about the relative importance of biological predispositions (nature) and environmental influences (nurture) as determinants of human development.
negative reinforcer: any stimulus whose removal or termination as the consequence of an act will increase the probability that the act will recur.
neglected children: children who receive few nominations as either a liked or a disliked individual from members of their peer group.
Neonatal Behavior Assessment Scale (NBAS): a test that assesses a neonate's neurological integrity and responsiveness to environmental stimuli.
neonate: a newborn infant from birth to approximately 1 month of age
neo-nativism: the idea that much cognitive knowledge, such as object concept, is innate, requiring little in the way of specific experiences to be expressed, and that there are biological constraints, in that the mind/brain is designed to process certain types of information in certain ways.
neural tube: the primitive spinal cord that develops from the ectoderm and becomes the central nervous system.
neurons: nerve cells that receive and transmit neural impulses.
neurotic disorder: an irrational pattern of thinking or behavior that a person may use to contend with stress or to avoid anxiety.
nonorganic failure to thrive: an infant growth disorder, caused by lack of attention and affection, that causes growth to slow dramatically or stop.
nonrepresentative sample: a subgroup that differs in important ways from the larger group (or population) to which it belongs.
nonshared environmental influence (NSE): an environmental influence that people living together do not share, which should make these individuals different from one another.
nonsocial activity: onlooker behavior and solitary play.
normal distribution: a symmetrical, bell-shaped curve that describes the variability of certain characteristics within a population; most people fall at or near the average score, with relatively few at the extremes of the distribution.
normative development: developmental changes that characterize most or all members of a species; typical patterns of development.
obese: a medical term describing individuals who are at least 20 percent above the ideal weight for their height, age, and sex.
object permanence: the realization that objects continue to exist when they are no longer visible or detectable through the other senses.
object scope constraint: the notion that young children will assume that a new word applied to an object refers to the whole object rather than to parts of the object or to object attributes (for example, its color).
observational learning: learning that results from observing the behavior of others.
observer influence: tendency of participants to react to an observer's presence by behaving in unusual ways.
Oedipal morality: Freud's theory that moral development occurs during the phallic period (ages 3 to 6) when children internalize the moral standards of the same-sex parent as they resolve their Oedipus or Electra conflicts.
Oedipus complex: Freud's term for the conflict that 3- to 6-year-old boys were said to experience when they develop an incestuous desire for their mothers and a jealous and hostile rivalry with their fathers.
onlooker play: children linger around other children, watching them play, but making no attempts to join in the play.
ontogenetic development: development of the individual over his or her lifetime.
operant: the initially voluntary act that becomes more or less probable of occurring depending on the consequence that it produces.
operant conditioning: a form of learning in which freely emitted acts (or operants) become either more or less probable depending on the consequences they produce.
operant learning: a form of learning in which voluntary acts (or operants) become either more or less probable, depending on the consequences they produce.
organismic model: view of children as active entities whose developmental paths are primarily determined by forces from within themselves.
organization: a strategy for remembering that involves grouping or classifying stimuli into meaningful (or manageable) clusters that are easier to retain.
original sin: the idea that children are inherently negative creatures who must be taught to rechannel their selfish interests into socially acceptable outlets.
otitis media: common bacterial infection of the middle ear that produces mild to moderate hearing loss.
overextension: the young child's tendency to use relatively specific words to refer to a broader set of objects, actions, or events than adults do (for example, using the word *car* to refer to all motor vehicles).
overregularization: the overgeneralization of grammatical rules to irregular cases where the rules do not apply (for example, saying *mouses* rather than *mice*).
own-sex schema: detailed knowledge or plans of action that enable a person to perform gender-consistent activities and to enact his or her gender role.
parallel play: largely noninteractive play in which players are in close proximity but do not often attempt to influence each other.
parental effects model: model of family influence in which parents (particularly mothers) are believed to influence their children rather than vice versa.
parsimony: a criterion for evaluating the scientific merit of theories; a parsimonious theory is one that uses relatively few explanatory principles to explain a broad set of observations.
passive genotype/environment correlations: the notion that the rearing environments that biological parents provide are influenced by the parents' own genes, and hence are correlated with the child's own genotype.
passive victims (of aggression): socially withdrawn, anxious children with low self-esteem whom bullies torment, even though they appear to have done little to trigger such abuse.
peer acceptance: a measure of a person's likability (or dislikability) in the eyes of the peers.
peer group: a confederation of peers that interact regularly, defines a sense of membership, and formulates norms that specify how members are supposed to look, think, act.
peers: two or more persons who are operating at similar levels of behavioral complexity.
perception: the process by which we categorize and interpret sensory input.
perceptual learning: changes in one's ability to extract information from sensory stimulation that occur as a result of experience.
performance goal: state of affairs in which one's primary objective in an achievement context is to display one's competencies (or to avoid looking incompetent).
perinatal environment: perinatal refers to the time around birth, both before and after birth; perinatal environment refers to the environment surrounding birth.
period of the embryo: second phase of prenatal development, lasting from the third through the eighth prenatal week, during which the major organs and anatomical structures take shape.
period of the fetus: third phase of prenatal development, lasting from the ninth prenatal week until birth; during this period, all major organ systems begin to function and the fetus grows rapidly.
period of the zygote: first phase of prenatal development, lasting from conception until the developing organism becomes firmly attached to the wall of the uterus.
permissive parenting: a pattern of parenting in which otherwise accepting adults make few demands of their children and rarely attempt to control their behavior.
person praise: praise focusing on desirable personality traits such as intelligence; this praise fosters performance goals in achievement contexts.
personal agency: recognition that one can be the cause of an event.
phallic stage: Freud's third stage of psychosexual development (from 3 to 6 years of age) in which children gratify the sex instinct by fondling their genitals and developing an incestuous desire for the parent of the other sex.
phase of indiscriminate attachments: period between 6 weeks and 6 to 7 months of age in which infants prefer social to nonsocial stimulation and are likely to protest whenever any adults puts them down or leaves them alone.
phase of multiple attachments: period when infants are forming attachments to companions other than their primary attachment object.
phase of specific attachment: period between 7 and 9 months of age when infants are attached to one close companion (usually the mother).
phenotype: the ways in which a person's genotype is expressed in observable or measurable characteristics.
phenylketonuria (PKU): a genetic disease in which the child is unable to metabolize phenylalanine; if left untreated, it soon causes hyperactivity and mental retardation.
phonemes: smallest meaningful sound units that make up a spoken language.
phonology: the sound system of a language and the rules for combining these sounds to produce meaningful units of speech.
phylogenetic development: development over evolutionary time.
physically active play: moderate to vigorous play activities such as running, jumping, climbing, play fighting, or game playing that raise a child's metabolic rate far above resting levels.
pidgins: structurally simple communication systems that arise when people who share no common language come into constant contact.
pincer grasp: a grasp in which the thumb is used in opposition to the fingers, enabling an infant to become more dexterous at lifting and fondling objects.
pituitary: a "master gland" located at the base of the brain that regulates the endocrine glands and produces growth hormone.
placenta: an organ, formed from the lining of the uterus and the chorion, that provides for respiration and nourishment of the unborn child and the elimination of its metabolic wastes.

plasticity: capacity for change; a developmental state that has the potential to be shaped by experience.
polygenic trait: a characteristic that is influenced by the action of many genes rather than a single pair.
popular children: children who are liked by many members of their peer group and disliked by very few.
popularity: a social construction by children, with popular children being well-known and accepted by other (especially popular) children, and having high-status attributes such as attractiveness, athleticism, and desirable possessions.
postconventional morality: Kohlberg's term for the fifth and sixth stages of moral reasoning, in which moral judgments are based on social contracts and democratic law (Stage 5) or on universal principles of ethics and justice (Stage 6).
postpartum depression: strong feelings of sadness, resentment, and despair that may appear shortly after childbirth and can linger for months.
power assertion: a form of discipline in which an adult relies on his or her superior power (for example, by administering spankings or withholding privileges) to modify or control a child's behavior.
practice effect: changes in participants' natural responses as a result of repeated testing.
pragmatics: principles that underlie the effective and appropriate use of language in social contexts.
preadapted characteristic: an attribute that is a product of evolution and serves some function that increases the chances of survival for the individual and the species.
preconventional morality: Kohlberg's term for the first two stages of moral reasoning, in which moral judgments are based on the tangible punitive consequences (Stage 1) or rewarding consequences (Stage 2) of an act for the actor rather than on the relationship of that act to society's rules and customs.
preference method: a method used to gain information about infants' perceptual abilities by presenting two (or more) stimuli and observing which stimulus the infant prefers.
prelinguistic phase: the period before children utter their first meaningful words.
premoral period: in Piaget's theory, the first 5 years of life, when children are said to have little respect for or awareness of socially defined rules.
prenatal development: development that occurs between the moment of conception and the beginning of the birth process.
preoperational period: Piaget's second stage of cognitive development, lasting from about age 2 to age 7, when children are thinking at a symbolic level but are not yet using cognitive operations.
present self: early self-representation in which 2- and 3-year-olds recognize current representations of self but are unaware that past self-representations or self-relevant events have implications for the present.
preterm babies: infants born more than three weeks before their normal due dates.
primary circular reactions: second substage of Piaget's sensorimotor stage; a pleasurable response, centered on the infant's own body, that is discovered by chance and performed over and over.
primary mental abilities: seven mental abilities, identified by factor analysis, that Thurstone believed to represent the structure of intelligence.
private speech: Vygotsky's term for the subset of a child's verbal utterances that serve a self-communicative function and guide the child's thinking.
proactive aggressors: highly aggressive children who find aggressive acts easy to perform and who rely heavily on aggression as a means of solving social problems or achieving other personal objectives.
processing constraints: cognitive biases or tendencies that lead infants and toddlers to favor certain interpretations of the meaning of new words over other interpretations.
process-oriented praise: praise of effort expended to formulate good ideas and effective problem-solving strategies; this praise fosters learning goals in achievement contexts.
production deficiency: a failure to spontaneously generate and use known strategies that could improve learning and memory.
productive language: that which the individual is capable of expressing (producing) in his or her own speech.
proprioceptive information: sensory information from the muscles, tendons, and joints that help one to locate the position of one's body (or body parts) in space.
prosocial moral reasoning: the thinking that people display when deciding whether to help, share with, or comfort others when these actions could prove costly to themselves.
protection from harm: the right of research participants to be protected from physical or psychological harm.
provocative victims (of aggression): restless, hot-tempered, and oppositional children who are victimized because they often irritate their peers.
proximodistal development: a sequence of physical maturation and growth that proceeds from the center of the body (the proximal region) to the extremities (distal regions).
psychobiosocial model: perspective on nature/nurture interactions specifying that specific early experiences affect the organization of the brain which, in turn, influences one's responsiveness to similar experiences in the future.
psycholinguists: those who study the structure and development of children's language.
psychological comparisons phase: tendency to form impressions of others by comparing and contrasting these individuals on abstract psychological dimensions.
psychological constructs phase: tendency to base one's impressions of others on the stable traits these individuals are presumed to have.
psychological control: attempts to regulate a child's or an adolescent's conduct by such psychological tactics as withholding affection and/or inducing shame or guilt.
psychometric approach: a theoretical perspective that portrays intelligence as a trait (or set of traits) on which individuals differ; psychometric theorists are responsible for the development of standardized intelligence tests.
psychophysiological methods: methods that measure the relationships between physiological processes and aspects of children's physical, cognitive, social, or emotional behavior/development.
psychosexual theory: Freud's theory that states that maturation of the sex instinct underlies stages of personality development, and that the manner in which parents manage children's instinctual impulses determines the traits that children display.
psychosocial theory: Erikson's revision of Freud's theory that emphasizes sociocultural (rather than sexual) determinants of development and posits a series of eight psychosocial conflicts that people must resolve successfully to display healthy psychological adjustment.
puberty: the point at which a person reaches sexual maturity and is physically capable of fathering or conceiving a child.
punisher: any consequence of an act that suppresses that act and/or decreases the probability that it will recur.
qualitative change: changes in kind that make individuals fundamentally different than they were before; the transformation of a prelinguistic infant into a language user is viewed by many as a qualitative change in communication skills.
quantitative change: incremental change in degree without sudden transformations; for example, some view the small yearly increases in height and weight that 2- to 11-year-olds display as quantitative developmental changes.
random assignment: a control technique in which participants are assigned to experimental conditions through an unbiased procedure so that the members of the groups are not systematically different from one another.
range of reaction principle: the idea that genotype sets limits on the range of possible phenotypes that a person might display in response to different environments.
reactive aggressors: children who display high levels of hostile, retaliatory aggression because they over-attribute hostile intents to others and can't control their anger long enough to seek nonaggressive solutions to social problems.
reasoning: a particular type of problem solving that involves making inferences.
recasts: responding to a child's ungrammatical utterance with a nonrepetitive statement that is grammatically correct.
receptive language: that which the individual comprehends when listening to others' speech.
recessive allele: a less powerful gene that is not expressed phenotypically when paired with a dominant allele.
reciprocal determinism: the notion that the flow of influence between children and their environments is a two-way street; the environment may affect the child, but the child's behavior also influences the environment.
referential communication skills: abilities to generate clear verbal messages, to recognize when others' messages are unclear, and to clarify any unclear messages one transmits or receives.
referential style: early linguistic style in which toddlers use language mainly to label objects.
reflex activity: first substage of Piaget's sensorimotor stage; infants' actions are confined to exercising innate reflexes, assimilating new objects into these reflexive schemes, and accommodating their reflexes to these novel objects.
rehearsal: a strategy for remembering that involves repeating the items one is trying to retain.
reinforcer: any consequence of an act that increases the probability that the act will recur.
rejected-aggressive children: a subgroup of rejected children who display high levels of hostility and aggression in their interactions with peers.
rejected children: children who are disliked by many peers and liked by few.
rejected-withdrawn children: a subgroup of rejected children who are often passive, socially anxious, socially unskilled, and insensitive to peer-group expectations.
relational aggression: acts such as snubbing, exclusion, withdrawing acceptance, or spreading rumors that are aimed at damaging an adversary's self-esteem, friendships, or social status.
relational primacy hypothesis: the hypothesis that analogical reasoning is available in infancy.
relational self-worth: feelings of self-esteem within a particular relationship context (for example, with parents, with male classmates); may differ across relationship contexts.
reliability: the extent to which a measuring instrument yields consistent results, both over time and across observers.
representational insight: the knowledge that an entity can stand for (represent) something other than itself.
repression: a type of motivated forgetting in which anxiety-provoking thoughts and conflicts are forced out of conscious awareness.
resistant attachment: an insecure infant-caregiver bond, characterized by strong separation protest and a tendency of the child to remain near but resist contact initiated by the caregiver, particularly after a separation.
respiratory distress syndrome: a serious condition in which a preterm infant breathes very irregularly and is at risk of dying (also called hyaline membrane disease).
retaliatory aggression: aggressive acts elicited by real or imagined provocations.
retrieval: class of strategies aimed at getting information out of the long-term store.
reversibility: the ability to reverse, or negate an action by mentally performing the opposite action (negation).
RH factor: a blood protein that, when present in a fetus but not the mother, can cause the mother to produce antibodies. These antibodies may then attack the red blood cells of subsequent fetuses who have the protein in their blood.
rites of passage: rituals that signify the passage from one period of life to another (for example, puberty rites).
role taking: the ability to assume another person's perspective and understand his or her thoughts, feelings, and behaviors.
rubella (German measles): a disease that has little effect on a mother but may cause a number of serious birth defects in unborn children who are exposed in the first 3 to 4 months of pregnancy.
s: Spearman's term for mental abilities that are specific to particular tests.

scaffolding: process by which an expert, when instructing a novice, responds contingently to the novice's behavior in a learning situation, so that the novice gradually increases his or her understanding of a problem.

scheme: an organized pattern of thought or action that a child constructs to make sense of some aspect of his or her experience; Piaget sometimes uses the term cognitive structures as a synonym for schemes.

schizophrenia: a serious form of mental illness characterized by disturbances in logical thinking, emotional expression, and interpersonal behavior.

scientific method: the use of objective and replicable methods to gather data for the purpose of testing a theory or hypothesis. It dictates that, above all, investigators must be *objective* and must allow their data to decide the merits of their thinking.

script: a general representation of the typical sequencing of events (i.e., what occurs and when) in some familiar context.

second stage of labor: the period of the birth process during which the fetus moves through the birth canal and emerges from the mother's body (also called the delivery).

secondary circular reactions: third substage of Piaget's sensorimotor stage; a pleasurable response, centered on an external object, that is discovered by chance and performed over and over.

secondary reinforcer: an initially neutral stimulus that acquires reinforcement value by virtue of its repeated association with other reinforcing stimuli.

secular trend: a trend in industrialized societies toward earlier maturation and greater body size now than in the past.

secure attachment: an infant-caregiver bond in which the child welcomes contact with a close companion and uses this person as a secure base from which to explore the environment.

secure base: use of a caregiver as a base from which to explore the environment and to which to return for emotional support.

selective attention: capacity to focus on task-relevant aspects of experience while ignoring irrelevant or distracting information.

selective attrition: nonrandom loss of participants during a study which results in a nonrepresentative sample.

selective breeding experiment: a method of studying genetic influences by determining whether traits can be bred in animals through selective mating.

self: the combination of physical and psychological attributes that is unique to each individual.

self-concept: one's perceptions of one's unique attributes or traits.

self-esteem: one's evaluation of one's worth as a person based on an assessment of the qualities that make up the self-concept.

self-fulfilling prophecy: phenomenon whereby people cause others to act in accordance with the expectations they have about those others.

self-oriented distress: feeling of *personal* discomfort or distress that may be elicited when we experience the emotions of (that is, empathize with) a distressed other; thought to inhibit altruism.

self-recognition: the ability to recognize oneself in a mirror or a photograph.

semantics: the expressed meaning of words and sentences.

sensation: detection of stimuli by the sensory receptors and transmission of this information to the brain.

sensitive period: period of time that is optimal for the development of particular capacities, or behaviors, and in which the individual is particularly sensitive to environmental influences that would foster these attributes.

sensitive-period hypothesis (of language acquisition): the notion that human beings are most proficient at language learning before they reach puberty.

sensorimotor period: Piaget's first intellectual stage, from birth to 2 years, when infants are relying on behavioral schemes as a means of exploring and understanding the environment.

sensory store (or sensory register): first information-processing store, in which stimuli are noticed and are briefly available for further processing.

separation anxiety: a wary or fretful reaction that infants and toddlers often display when separated from the person(s) to whom they are attached.

sequential design: a research design in which subjects from different age groups are studied repeatedly over a period of months or years.

sex: a person's biological identity: their chromosomes, physical manifestations of their identity, and hormonal influences.

sex-linked characteristic: an attribute determined by a recessive gene that appears on the X chromosome; more likely to characterize males.

sexuality: aspect of self referring to one's erotic thoughts, actions, and orientation.

shared environmental influence (SE): an environmental influence that people living together share which should make these individuals similar to one another.

short-term store (STS): second information-processing store, in which stimuli are retained for several seconds and operated on (also called working memory).

sibling rivalry: the spirit of competition, jealousy, and resentment that may arise between two or more siblings.

sickle-cell anemia: a genetic blood disease that causes red blood cells to assume an unusual sickled shape and to become inefficient at distributing oxygen.

simple dominant-recessive inheritance: a pattern of inheritance in which one allele dominates another so that only its phenotype is expressed.

situational compliance: compliance based primarily on a parent's power to control the child's conduct.

size constancy: the tendency to perceive an object as the same size from different distances despite changes in the size of its retinal image.

skeletal age: a measure of physical maturation based on the child's level of skeletal development.

slow-to-warm-up temperament: temperamental profile in which the child is inactive and moody and displays mild passive resistance to new routines and experiences.

small-for-date babies: infants whose birth weight is far below normal, even when born close to their normal due dates.

sociability: a person's willingness to engage others in social interaction and to seek their attention or approval.

social cognition: thinking people display about the thoughts, feelings, motives, and behaviors of themselves and other people.

social comparison: the process of defining and evaluating the self by comparing oneself to other people.

social-conventional rules: standards of conduct determined by social consensus that indicate what is appropriate within a particular social context.

social referencing: the use of others' emotional expressions to infer the meaning of otherwise ambiguous situations.

social roles hypothesis: the notion that psychological differences between the sexes and other gender-role stereotypes are created and maintained by differences in *socially assigned* roles that men and women play (rather than attributable to biologically evolved dispositions).

social skills: thoughts, actions, and emotional regulatory activities that enable children to achieve personal or social goals while maintaining harmony with their social partners.

socialization: the process by which children acquire the beliefs, values, and behaviors considered desirable or appropriate by their culture or subculture.

sociocultural theory: Vygotsky's perspective on cognitive development, in which children acquire their culture's values, beliefs, and problem-solving strategies through collaborative dialogues with more knowledgeable members of society.

sociohistorical development: changes that have occurred in one's culture and the values, norms, and technologies such a history has generated.

sociolinguistic knowledge: culturally specific rules specifying how language should be structured and used in particular social contexts.

sociometric techniques: procedures that ask children to identify those peers whom they like or dislike or to rate peers for their desirability as companions; used to measure children's peer acceptance (or nonacceptance).

span of apprehension: the number of items that people can keep in mind at any one time, or the amount of information that people can attend to at a single time without operating mentally to store this information.

spina bifida: a bulging of the spinal cord through a gap in the spinal column.

Stanford-Binet Intelligence Scale: modern descendent of the first successful intelligence test that measures general intelligence and four factors: verbal reasoning, quantitative reasoning, spatial reasoning, and short-term memory.

Strange Situation: a series of eight separation and reunion episodes to which infants are exposed in order to determine the quality of their attachments.

stranger anxiety: a wary or fretful reaction that infants and toddlers often display when approached by an unfamiliar person.

strategic memory: processes involved as one consciously attempts to retain or retrieve information.

strategies: goal-directed and deliberately implemented mental operations used to facilitate task performance.

structured interview or structured questionnaire: a technique in which all participants are asked the same questions in precisely the same order so that the responses of different participants can be compared.

structured observation: an observational method in which the investigator cues the behavior of interest and observes participants' responses in a laboratory.

structure-of-intellect model: Guilford's factor-analytic model of intelligence, which proposes that there are 180 distinct mental abilities.

sudden infant death syndrome (SIDS): the unexplained death of a sleeping infant who suddenly stops breathing (also called *crib death*).

superego: psychoanalytic term for the component of the personality that consists of one's internalized moral standards.

symbolic function: the ability to use symbols (for example, images and words) to represent objects and experiences.

sympathetic empathic arousal: feelings of sympathy or compassion that may be elicited when we experience the emotions of (that is, empathize with) a distressed other; thought to become an important mediator of altruism.

synapse: the connective space (juncture) between one nerve cell (neuron) and another.

synaptogenesis: formation of connections (synapses) among neurons.

synchronized routines: generally harmonious interactions between two persons in which participants adjust their behavior in response to the partner's feelings and behaviors.

syntactical bootstrapping: notion that young children make inferences about the meaning of words by analyzing the way words are used in sentences and inferring whether they refer to objects (nouns), actions (verbs), or attributes (adjectives).

syntax: the structure of a language; the rules specifying how words and grammatical markers are to be combined to produce meaningful sentences.

syphilis: a common sexually transmitted disease that may cross the placental barrier in the middle and later stages of pregnancy, causing miscarriage or serious birth defects.

tabula rasa: the idea that the mind of an infant is a "blank slate" and that all knowledge, abilities, behaviors, and motives are acquired through experience.

tacit (or practical) intelligence: ability to size up everyday problems and solve them; only modestly related to IQ.

telegraphic speech: early sentences that consist of content words and omit the less meaningful parts of speech, such as articles, prepositions, pronouns, and auxiliary verbs.

television literacy: one's ability to understand how information is conveyed in television programming and to interpret this information properly.

temperament: a person's characteristic modes of responding emotionally and behaviorally to environmental events, including such attributes as activity level, irritability, fearfulness, and sociability.

temperament hypothesis: Kagan's view that the Strange Situation measures individual differences in infants' temperaments rather than the quality of their attachments.

teratogens: external agents such as viruses, drugs, chemicals, and radiation that can harm a developing embryo or fetus.

tertiary circular reactions: fifth substage of Piaget's sensorimotor stage; an exploratory scheme in which the infant devises a new method of acting on objects to reproduce interesting results.

test norms: standards of normal performance on psychometric instruments that are based on the average scores and the range of scores obtained by a large, representative sample of test takers.

testicular feminization syndrome (TFS): a genetic anomaly in which a male fetus is insensitive to the effects of male sex hormones and will develop female external genitalia.

testosterone: male sex hormone, produced by the testes, that is responsible for male sexual maturation.

thalidomide: a mild tranquilizer that, taken early in pregnancy, can produce a variety of malformations of the limbs, eyes, ears, and heart.

theory: a set of concepts and propositions designed to organize, describe, and explain an existing set of observations.

theory of mind: a person's concepts of mental activity; used to refer to how children conceptualize mental activity and how they attribute intention to and predict the behavior of others; see also belief-desire reasoning.

theory of multiple intelligences: Gardner's theory that humans display as many as nine distinct kinds of intelligence, each linked to a particular area of the brain, and several of which are not measured by IQ tests.

theory theories: theories of cognitive development that combine neo-nativism and constructivism, proposing that cognitive development progresses by children generating, testing, and changing theories about the physical and social world.

third stage of labor: expulsion of the placenta (afterbirth).

three-stratum theory of intelligence: Carroll's hierarchical model of intelligence with *g* at the top of the hierarchy, eight broad abilities at the second level, or stratum, and narrower domains of each second-stratum ability at the third stratum.

thyroxine: a hormone produced by the thyroid gland; essential for normal growth of the brain and the body.

time-out technique: a form of discipline in which children who misbehave are removed from the setting until they are prepared to act more appropriately.

time-sampling: a procedure in which the investigator records the frequencies with which individuals display particular behaviors during the brief time intervals each is observed.

timing of puberty effect: the finding that people who reach puberty late perform better on visual/spatial tasks than those who mature early.

tools of intellectual adaptation: Vygotsky's term for methods of thinking and problem-solving strategies that children internalize from their interactions with more competent members of society.

toxoplasmosis: disease caused by a parasite found in raw meat and cat feces; can cause birth defects if transmitted to an embryo in the first trimester and miscarriage later in pregnancy.

traditional nuclear family: a family unit consisting of a wife/mother, a husband/father, and their dependent child or children.

transactional model: model of family influences in which parent and child are believed to influence each other reciprocally.

transactive interactions: verbal exchanges in which individuals perform mental operations on the reasoning of their discussion partners.

transformational grammar: rules of syntax that allow one to transform declarative statements into questions, negatives, imperatives, and other kinds of sentences.

transitivity: the ability to recognize relations among elements in a serial order (for example, if $A > B$ and $B > C$, then $A > C$).

triarchic theory: a recent information-processing theory of intelligence that emphasizes three aspects of intelligent behavior not normally tapped by IQ tests: the *context* of the action; the person's *experience* with the task (or situation); and the *information-processing strategies* the person applies to the task (or situation).

twin design: study in which sets of twins that differ in zygosity (kinship) are compared to determine the heritability of an attribute.

two-generation intervention: interventions with goals to both stimulate children's intellectual development through preschool day care/education and to assist parents to move out of poverty.

two-way bilingual education: programs in which English-speaking (or other majority-language) children and children who have limited proficiency in that language are instructed half of the day in their primary language and the other half in a second language.

ulnar grasp: an early manipulatory skill in which an infant grasps objects by pressing the fingers against the palm.

ultrasound: method of detecting gross physical abnormalities by scanning the womb with sound waves, thereby producing a visual outline of the fetus.

umbilical cord: a soft tube containing blood vessels that connects the embryo to the placenta.

unconditioned stimulus (UCS): a stimulus that elicits a particular response without any prior learning.

unconscious motives: Freud's term for feelings, experiences, and conflicts that influence a person's thinking and behavior, but lie outside the person's awareness.

underextension: the young child's tendency to use general words to refer to a smaller set of objects, actions, or events than adults do (for example, using *candy* to refer only to mints).

uninvolved parenting: a pattern of parenting that is both aloof (or even hostile) and overpermissive, almost as if parents neither cared about their children nor about what they may become.

universal grammar: in nativist theories of language acquisition, the basic rules of grammar that characterize all languages.

utilization deficiency: a failure to benefit from effective strategies that one has spontaneously produced; thought to occur in the early phases of strategy acquisition when executing the strategy requires much mental effort.

validity: the extent to which a measuring instrument accurately reflects what the researchers intended to measure.

vernix: white cheesy substance that covers the fetus to protect the skin from chapping.

visual acuity: a person's ability to see small objects and fine detail.

visual cliff: an elevated platform that creates an illusion of depth, used to test the depth perception of infants.

visual contrast: the amount of light/dark transition in a visual stimulus.

visual/spatial abilities: the ability to mentally manipulate or otherwise draw inferences about pictorial information.

vitamin/mineral deficiency: a form of malnutrition in which the diet provides sufficient protein and calories but is lacking in one or more substances that promote normal growth.

vocables: unique patterns of sound that a prelinguistic infant uses to represent objects, actions, or events.

Wechsler Intelligence Scale for Children (WISC-IV): widely used individual intelligence test that includes a measure of general intelligence and both verbal and performance intelligence.

Wernicke's area: structure located in the temporal lobe of the left hemisphere of the cerebral cortex that is responsible for interpreting speech.

X chromosome: the longer of the two sex chromosomes; normal females have two X chromosomes, whereas normal males have but one.

Y chromosome: the shorter of the two sex chromosomes; normal males have one Y chromosome, whereas females have none.

zone of proximal development: Vygotsky's term for the range of tasks that are too complex to be mastered alone but can be accomplished with guidance and encouragement from a more skillful partner.

zygote: a single cell formed at conception from the union of a sperm and an ovum.

References

Abbassi, V. (1998). Growth and normal puberty, *Pediatrics, 102,* 507–511.

Abel, E. L. (1981). Behavioral teratology of alcohol. *Psychological Bulletin, 90,* 564–581.

Abel, E. L. (1998). *Fetal alcohol abuse syndrome.* New York: Plenum.

Abma, J. C., & Mott, F. L. (1991). Substance use and prenatal care during pregnancy among young women. *Family Planning Perspectives, 23,* 117–122, 128.

Aboud, F. E. (1988). *Children and prejudice.* New York: Blackwell.

Aboud, F. E. (2003). The formation of in-group favoritism and out-group prejudice in young children: Are they distinct attitudes? *Developmental Psychology, 39,* 48–60.

Abramovitch, R., Corter, C., Pepler, D. J., & Stanhope, L. (1986). Sibling and peer interaction: A final follow-up and a comparison. *Child Development, 57,* 217–229.

Abravanel, E., & Sigafoos, A. D. (1984). Exploring the presence of imitation during early infancy. *Child Development, 55,* 381–392.

Achenbach, T. M., Phares, V., Howell, C. T., Rauh, V. A., & Nurcombe, B. (1990). Seven-year outcome of the Vermont Intervention Program for low-birthweight infants. *Child Development, 61,* 1672–1681.

Ackerman, B. P. (1993). Children's understanding of the speaker's meaning in referential communication. *Journal of Experimental Child Psychology, 55,* 56–86.

Ackerman, B. P., Schoff, K., Levinson, K., Youngstrom, E., & Izard, C. E. (1999). The relatives between cluster indexes of risk and promotion and the problem behaviors of 6- and 7-year-old children from economically disadvantaged families. *Developmental Psychology, 35,* 1355–1366.

Ackerman, B. P., Szymanski, J., & Silver, D. (1990). Children's use of common ground in interpreting ambiguous referential utterances. *Developmental Psychology, 26,* 234–245.

Ackerman, M. C. (2002). Benefits of sports participation for adolescent girls. *Dissertation Abstract International: The Sciences and Engineering, 63,* 2618.

Ackerman, P. L., Bowen, K. R., Beier, M. E., & Kanfer, R. (2001). Determinants of Individual Differences and Gender Differences in Knowledge. *Journal of Educational Psychology, 93,* 797–825.

Ackermann-Liebrich, U., Voegeli, T., Gunter-Witt, K., Kunz, I., Zullig, M., Schlindler, C., & Maurer, M. (1996). Home versus hospital deliveries: Follow up study of matched pairs for procedures and outcome. *British Medical Journal, 313,* 1313–1318.

Acredolo, L. P., & Goodwyn, S. W. (1990). Sign language in babies: The significance of symbolic gesturing for understanding language development. In R. Vasta (Ed.), *Annals of child development* (Vol. 7) (pp. 1–42). Greenwich, CT: JAI Press.

Adam, E. K., Gunnar, M., & Tanaka, A. (2004). Adult attachment, parent emotion, and observed parenting behavior: Mediator and moderator models. *Child Development, 74,* 110–112.

Adams, G. R., Abraham, K. G., & Markstrom, C. A. (1987). The relations among identity development, self-consciousness, and self-focusing during middle and late adolescence. *Developmental Psychology, 23,* 292–297.

Adams, R. J., & Courage, M. L. (1998). Human newborn color vision: Measurement with chromatic stimuli varying in excitation purity. *Journal of Experimental Child Psychology, 67,* 22–34.

Adams, T. P. Gullotta, & R. Montemayor (Eds.), *Adolescent identity formation* (Advances in Adolescent Development, Vol. 4). Newbury Park, CA: Sage.

Adamson, L. B., Bakeman, R., & Deckner, D. F. (2004). The development of symbol-infused joint engagement. *Child Development, 75,* 1171–1187.

Adey, P. S., & Shayer, M. (1992). Accelerating the development of formal thinking in middle and high school students: II. Postproject effects on science achievement. *Journal of Research in Science Teaching, 29,* 81–92.

Adler, A. (1964). *Problems of neurosis.* New York: Harper & Row. (Original work published 1929.)

Adolph, K. E., Eppler, M. A., & Gibson, E. J. (1993). Crawling versus walking infants' perception of affordances for locomotion over sloping surfaces. *Child Development, 64,* 1158–1174.

Adolph, K. E., Vereijken, B., & Denny, M. A. (1998). Learning to crawl. *Child Development, 69,* 1299–1312.

Aguiar, A., & Baillargeon, R. (1998). Eight-and-a-half-month-old infants' reasoning about containment events. *Child Development, 69,* 636–653.

Aguilar, B., Sroufe, L. A., Egeland, B., & Carlson, E. (2000). Distinguishing the life-course- persistent and adolescent-limited antisocial behavior types: From birth to 16 years. *Development and Psychopathology, 12,* 109–132.

Ahnert, L., Gunnar, M. R., Lamb, M. E., & Barthel, M. (2004). Transition to child care: Associations with infant-mother attachment, infant negative emotion, and cortisol elevations. *Child Development, 75,* 639–650.

Ahnert, L., Rickert, H., & Lamb, M. E. (2000). Shared caregiving: Comparisons between home and child-care settings. *Developmental Psychology, 36,* 339–351.

Ainsworth, M. D. S. (1967). *Infancy in Uganda: Infant care and the growth of love.* Baltimore: Johns Hopkins University Press.

Ainsworth, M. D. S. (1979). Attachment as related to mother-infant interaction. In J. S. Rosenblatt, R. A. Hinde, C. Beer, & M. Busnel (Eds.), *Advances in the study of behavior* (Vol. 9). New York: Academic Press.

Ainsworth, M. D. S. (1989). Attachments beyond infancy. *American Psychologist, 44,* 709–716.

Ainsworth, M. D. S., Bell, S. M., & Stayton, D. J. (1972). Individual differences in the development of some attachment behaviors. *Merrill–Palmer Quarterly, 18,* 123–143.

Ainsworth, M. D. S., Blehar, M., Waters, E., & Wall, S. (1978). *Patterns of attachment.* Hillsdale, NJ: Erlbaum.

Akhtar, N. (2004). Nativist versus constructivist goals in studying child language. *Journal of Child Language, 31,* 459–462.

Akhtar, N., Carpenter, M., & Tomasello, M. (1996). The role of discourse novelty in early word learning. *Child Development, 67,* 635–645.

Al Awad, A. M. H., & Sonuga-Barke, E. J. S. (1992). Childhood problems in a Sudanese city: A comparison of extended and nuclear families. *Child Development, 63,* 906–914.

Albert, R. S. (1994). The achievement of eminence: A longitudinal study of exceptionally gifted boys and their families. In R. F. Subotnik & K. D. Arnold (Eds.), *Beyond Terman: Contemporary studies of giftedness and talent* (pp. 282–315). Norwood, NJ: Ablex.

Alessandri, S. M., & Lewis, M. (1996). Differences in pride and shame in maltreated and non-maltreated toddlers. *Child Development, 67,* 1857–1869.

Alessandri, S. M., Bendersky, M., & Lewis, M. (1998). Cognitive functioning in 8- to 18-month-old drug-exposed infants. *Developmental Psychology, 34,* 565–573.

Alessandri, S. M., Sullivan, M. W., Imaizumi, S., & Lewis, M. (1993). Learning and emotional responsivity in cocaine–exposed infants. *Developmental Psychology, 29,* 989–997.

Alexander, G. M., & Hines, M. (1994). Gender labels and play styles: Their relative contribution to children's selection of playmates. *Child Development, 65,* 869–879.

Alexander, K. L., & Entwisle, D. R. (1988). Achievement in the first two years of school: Patterns and processes. *Monographs of the Society for Research in Child Development, 53*(2, Serial No. 218).

Alfieri, T., Ruble, D. N., & Higgins, E. T. (1996). Gender stereotypes during adolescence: Developmental changes and the transition to junior high school. *Developmental Psychology, 32,* 1129–1137.

Allen, J. P., McElhaney, K. B., Land, D. J., Kupermin, G. P., Moore, C. W., O'Beirne-Kelly, H., & Kilmer, S. L. (2003). A secure base in adolescence: Markers of attachment security in the mother–adolescent relationship. *Child Development, 74,* 292–307.

Allen, J. P., Moore, C., Kuperminc, G., & Bell, K. (1998). Attachment and adolescent psychosocial functioning. *Child Development, 69,* 1406–1419.

Allen, J. P., Philliber, S., Herrling, S., & Kuperminc, G. P. (1997). Preventing teen pregnancy and academic failure: Experimental evaluation of a developmentally based approach. *Child Development, 68,* 729–742.

Allen, K. R., Fine, M. A., & Demo, D. H. (2000). An overview of family diversity: controversies, questions, and values. In D. H. Demo, K. R. Allen & M. A. Fine (Eds.), *Handbook of family diversity.* New York: Oxford University Press.

Allen, M. C., & Capute, A. J. (1986). Assessment of early auditory and visual abilities of extremely premature infants. *Developmental Medicine and Child Neurology, 28,* 458–466.

Allen, S. E. M., & Crego, M. B. (1996). Early passive acquisition in Inuktitut. *Journal of Child Language, 23,* 129–156.

Alley, T. R. (1981). Head shape and the perception of cuteness. *Developmental Psychology, 17,* 650–654.

Allgood-Merten, B., & Stockard, J. (1991). Sex role identity and self-esteem: A comparison of children and adolescents. *Sex Roles, 25,* 129–139.

Allin, M., Henderson, M., Suckling, J., Nosarti, C., Rushe, T., Fearon, P., Stewart, A. L., Bullmore, E. T., Rifkin, L., & Murray, R. (2004). The effects of very low birthweight on brain structure in adulthood. *Developmental Medicine & Child Neurology, 46,* 46–54.

Altermatt, E. R., Pomerantz, E. M., Ruble, D. N., Frey, K. S., & Grenlich, F. K. (2002). Predicting changes in children's self-perceptions of academic competence: A naturalistic examination of evaluative discourse among classmates. *Developmental Psychology, 38,* 903–917.

Alvarez, J. M., Ruble, D. N., & Bolger, N. (2001). Trait understanding or evaluative reasoning: An analysis of children's behavioral predictions. *Child Development, 72,* 1409–1425.

Amabile, T. M. (1983). *The social psychology of creativity.* New York: Springer-Verlag.

Amato, P. R. (1996). Explaining the intergenerational transmission of divorce. *Journal of Marriage and the Family, 58,* 628–640.

Amato, P. R. (2000). The consequences of divorce for adults and children. *Journal of Marriage and Family, 62,* 1269–1287.

Amato, P. R., & Booth, A. (1996). A prospective study of divorce and parent–child relationships. *Journal of Marriage and the Family, 58,* 356–365.

Amato, P. R., & Keith, B. (1991). Parental divorce and the well-being of children: A meta-analysis. *Psychological Bulletin, 110,* 26–46.

Amato, P. R., Loomis, L. S., & Booth, A. (1995). Parental divorce, marital conflict, and offspring well-being during early childhood. *Social Forces, 73,* 895–915.

Ambert, A. (1992). *The effect of children on parents.* New York: Haworth.

Amend, B. (1992). *Fox Trot: en masse.* Kansas City, MO: Andrews & McMeel Publishing.

American Academy of Pediatrics (2000). Changing concepts of Sudden Infant Death Syndrome: Implications for infant sleeping environment and sleep position (RE8946). *Pediatrics, 105,* 650–656.

American Association of University Women (1992). *How schools shortchange girls: A study of major findings on girls and education.* Washington, DC: American Association of University Women Educational Foundation.

American Association on Mental Retardation (1992). *Mental retardation: Definition, classification, and systems of support* (9th ed.). Washington, DC: Author.

American Psychiatric Association (1994). *Diagnostic and statistical manual of mental disorders* (4th ed.). Washington, DC: American Psychiatric Association.

American Psychiatric Association (2000). *Diagnostic and statistical manual of mental disorders* (4th ed. text rev.). Washington, DC: Author.

Amiel-Tison, C., Cabrol, D., Denver, R., Jarreau, P., Papiernik, E., & Piassa, P. V. (2004). Fetal adaptation to stress: Part I: acceleration of fetal maturation and earlier birth triggered by placental insufficiency in humans. *Early Human Development, 78,* 15–27.

Anastasi, A. (1958). Heredity, environment, and the question "How?" *Psychological Review.*

Andermann, E. M., & Midgley, C. (1997). Changes in achievement goal orientation, perceived academic competence, and grades across the transition to middle level schools. *Contemporary Educational Psychology, 22,* 269–298.

Anderson, C. A., & Bushman, B. J. (2002). Human aggression. *Annual Review of Psychology, 53,* 27–52.

Anderson, C. A., & Dill, K. E. (2000). Video games and aggressive thoughts, feelings, and behavior in the laboratory and in life. *Journal of Personality and Social Psychology, 78,* 772–790.

Anderson, D. R., Huston, A. C., Schmitt, K. L., Linebarger, D. L., & Wright, J. C. (2001). Early childhood television viewing and adolescent behavior. *Monographs of the Society of the Research in Child Development, 66,* (1, Serial No. 264).

Anderson, J. B. (2005). Improving Latin America's school quality: Which special interventions work? *Comparative Education Review, 49,* 205–229.

Andersson, B. (1989). Effects of public day-care: A longitudinal study. *Child Development, 60,* 857–866.

Andersson, B. (1992). Effects of day-care on cognitive and socioemotional competence of thirteen-year-old Swedish schoolchildren. *Child Development, 63,* 20–36.

Anglin, J. M. (1993). Vocabulary development: A morphological analysis. *Monographs of the Society for Research in Child Development, 58*(10, Serial No. 238).

Angulo-Kinzler, R. M. (2001). Exploration and selection of intralimb coordination pattern in three-month-old infants. *Journal of Motor Behavior, 33,* 363–376.

Angulo-Kinzler, R. M., Ulrich, B., & Thelen, E. (2002). Three-month-old infants can select specific leg motor solutions. *Motor Control, 6,* 52–68.

Anthony, J. L., & Francis, D. J. (2005). Development of phonological awareness. *Current Directions in Psychological Science, 14,* 255–259.

Anthony, L. G., Anthony, B. J., Glanville, D. N., Naiman, D. Q., Waanders, C., & Shaffer, S. (2005). The relationships between parenting stress, parenting behaviour and preschoolers' social competence and behaviour problems in the classroom. *Infant & Child Development, 14,* 133–154.

Apgar, V., & Beck, J. (1974). *Is my baby all right?* New York: Pocket Books.

Archer, J. (1996). Sex differences in social behavior: Are the social role and evolutionary explanations compatible? *American Psychologist, 51,* 909–917.

Archer, S. L. (1982). The lower age boundaries of identity development. *Child Development, 53,* 1551–1556.

Archer, S. L. (1994). *Interventions for adolescent identity development.* Thousand Oaks, CA: Sage.

Ardila-Ray, A., & Killen, M. (***2001). Columbian preschool children's judgments about autonomy and conflict resolution in the classroom setting. *International Journal of Behavioral Development, 25,* 246–255.

Arendt, R. E., Noland, J. S., Short, E. J., & Singer, L. T. (2004a). Prenatal drug exposure and mental retardation. *International Review of Research in Mental Retardation, 29,* 31–61.

Arendt, R. E., Short, E. J., Singer, L. T., Minnes, S., Hewitt, J., Flynn, S., Carlson, L., Min, M. O., Klein, N., & Flannery, D. (2004b). Children prenatally exposed to cocaine: developmental outcomes and environmental risks at seven years of age. *Journal of Developmentala & Behavioral Pediatrics, 25,* 83–90.

Aries, P. (1962). *Centuries of childhood.* New York: Knopf.

Arnett, J. J. (1995). Broad and narrow socialization: The family in the context of a cultural theory. *Journal of Marriage and the Family, 57,* 617–628.

Arnold, D. H., McWilliams, L., & Arnold, E. H. (1998). Teacher discipline and child misbehavior in day care: Untangling causality with correlational data. *Developmental Psychology, 34,* 267–287.

Aro, H., & Taipale, V. (1987). The impact of timing of puberty on psychosomatic symptoms among fourteen- to sixteen-year-old Finnish girls. *Child Development, 58,* 261–268.

Aronson, E., & Rosenbloom, S. (1971). Space perception within a common auditory-visual space. *Science, 172,* 1161–1163.

Arsenio, W. F., Cooperman, S., & Lover, A. (2000). Affective predictors of preschoolers' aggression and peer acceptance: Direct and indirect effects. *Developmental Psychology, 36,* 438–448.

Arsenio, W. F., & Kramer, R. (1992). Victimizers and their victims: Children's conceptions of mixed emotional consequences of moral transgressions. *Child Development, 63,* 915–927.

Arsenio, W. F., & Lemerise, E. A. (2004). Aggression and moral development: Integrating social information processing and moral domain models. *Child Development, 75,* 987–1002.

Arterberry, M., Yonas, A., & Bensen, A. S. (1989). Self-produced locomotion and the development of responsiveness to linear perspective and texture gradients. *Developmental Psychology, 25,* 976–982.

Asbjørnsen, A., Obrzut, J., Boliek, C., Myking, E., Holmefjord, A., Reisæter, S., Klausen, O., & Møller, P. (2005). Impaired auditory attention skills following middle-ear infections. *Child Neuropsychology, 11,* 121–133.

Asbury, K., Dunn, J., Pike, A., & Plomin, R. (2003). Nonshared environmental influences on individual differences in early behavioral development: A monozygotic twin differences study. *Child Development, 74,* 933–943.

Asendorpf, J. B. (2002). Self awareness, other awareness, and secondary representation. In A. Meltzoff & W. Prinz (Eds.), *The imitative mind: Development, evolution, and brain bases* (pp. 63–73). Cambridge, UK: Cambridge University Press.

Asendorpf, J. B., Warkentin, V., & Baudonniere, P. (1996). Self-awareness and other awareness II: Mirror self-recognition, social contingency awareness, and synchronic imitation. *Developmental Psychology, 32,* 313–321.

Asher, O. (2002). The effects of alcohol and illicit drugs on the human embryo and fetus. *Israel Journal of Psychiatry & Related Sciences, 39*(2), 120–132.

Askin, D. F., & Diehl-Jones, B. (2001). Cocaine: effects of in utero exposure on the fetus and neonate. *Journal of Perinatal and Neonatal Nursing, 14,* 83–103.

Aslin, R. N. (1987). Visual and auditory development in infancy. In J. D. Osofsky (Ed.), *Handbook of infant development* (2nd ed.). New York: Wiley.

Aslin, R. N., Pisoni, D. B., & Jusczyk, P. W. (1983). Auditory development and speech perception in infancy. In M. M. Haith & J. J. Campos (Eds.), *Handbook of child psychology: Vol. 2. Infancy and developmental psychobiology.* New York: Wiley.

Associated Press (1999, January 10). TV sex rampant, critics say. *Atlanta Constitution,* p. D1, D3.

Associated Press (2002a, October 11). Hispanic dropout rate soars. *Athens Banner Herald,* p. D6.

Associated Press (2002b, December 21). Video game warning. *Athens Banner Herald,* p. C1.

Astin, A. W., Korn, W. S., Sax, L. J., & Mahoney, K. M. (1994). *The American freshman: National norms for fall, 1994.* Los Angeles, CA: Higher Education Research Institute, University of California at Los Angeles.

Astington, J. W., & Jenkins, J. M. (1995). Theory of mind development and social understanding. *Cognition and Emotion, 9,* 151–165.

Astor, R. A. (1994). Children's moral reasoning about family and peer violence: The role of provocation and retribution. *Child Development, 65,* 1054–1067.

Atkin, C. (1978). Observation of parent–child interaction in supermarket decision-making. *Journal of Marketing, 42,* 41–45.

Atkinson, L., Scott, B., Chisholm, V., Blackwell, J., Dickens, S., Tam, F., & Goldberg, S. (1995). Cognitive coping, affective stress, and material sensitivity: Mothers of children with Down Syndrome. *Developmental Psychology, 31,* 668–676.

Atkinson, R. C., & Shiffrin, R. M. (1968). Human memory: A proposed system andits control processes. In K. W. Spence & J. T. Spence (Eds.), *The psychology of learning and motivation: Advances in research and theory* (Vol. 2, pp. 90–195). Orlando, FL: Academic Press.

Austin, S. Bryn, Ziyadeh, Najat, Kahn, Jessica A., Camargo Jr., Carlos A., Colditz, Graham A., & Field, Alison E. (2004). Sexual orientation, weight concerns, and eating-disordered behaviors in adolescent girls and boys. *Journal of the American Academy of Child & Adolescent, 43,* 1115–1123.

Autti-Rämö, I., Autti, T., Korkman, M., Kettunen, S., Salonen, & Oili, V. (2002). MRI findings in children with school problems who had been exposed prenatally to alcohol. *Developmental Medicine & Child Neurology, 44,* 98–106.

Aviezer, D., Sagi, A., Joels, T., & Ziv, Y. (1999). Emotional availability and attachment representations in kibbutz infants and their mothers. *Developmental Psychology, 35,* 811–821.

Axia, G., Bonichini, S., & Benini, F. (1999). Attention and reaction to distress in infancy: A longitudinal study. *Developmental Psychology, 35,* 500–504.

Azmitia, M. (1992). Expertise, private speech, and the development of self-regulation. In R. M. Diaz & L. E. Berk (Eds.), *Private speech: From social interaction to self-regulation.* Hillsdale, NJ: Erlbaum.

Azmitia, M., & Hesser, J. (1993). Why siblings are important agents of cognitive development: A comparison of siblings and peers. *Child Development, 64,* 430–444.

Backschneider, A. G., Shatz, M., & Gelman, S. A. (1993). Preschoolers' ability to distinguish living kinds as a function of regrowth. *Child Development, 64,* 1242–1257.

Bagwell, C. L., & Coie, J. D. (2004). The best friendships of aggressive boys: Relational quality, conflict management, and rule-breaking behavior. *Journal of Experimental Child Psychology, 88,* 5–24.

Bahrick, L. E. (2000). Increasing specificity in the development of intermodal perception. In D. Muir & A. Slater (Eds.), *Infant development: The essential readings* (pp. 119–136). Malden, MA: Blackwell Publishers.

Bahrick, L. E., & Lickliter, R. (2000). Intersensory redundancy guides attentional selectivity and perceptual learning in infancy. *Developmental Psychology, 36,* 190–201.

Bahrick, L. E., Lickliter, R., & Flom, R. (2004). Intersensory redundancy guides the development of selective attention, perception, and cognition in infancy. *Current Directons in Psychological Science, 13,* 99–102.

Bahrick, L. E., Netto, D., & Hernandez-Reif, M. (1998). Intermodal perception of adult and child faces and voices by infants. *Child Development, 69,* 1263–1275.

Bailey, D. B., & Symons, F. J. (2001). Critical periods: Reflections and future directions. In D. B. Bailey, J. T. Bruer, F. J. Symons, & J. W. Lichtman (Eds.), *Critical thinking about critical periods.* Baltimore, MD: Paul H. Brookes Publishing.

Bailey, J. M., & Dunne, M. P., & Martin, N. G. (2000). Genetic and environmental influences on sexual orientation and its correlates in an Australian twin sample. *Journal of Personality and Social Psychology, 78,* 524–536.

Bailey, J. M., & Pillard, R. C. (1991). A genetic study of the male sexual orientation. *Archives of General Psychiatry, 48,* 1089–1096.

Bailey, J. M., Bobrow, D., Wolfe, M., & Mikach, S. (1995). Sexual orientation of adult sons of gay fathers. *Developmental Psychology, 31,* 124–129.

Bailey, J. M., Pillard, R. C., Neale, M. C., & Agyei, Y. (1993). Heritable factors influence sexual orientation in women. *Archives of General Psychiatry, 50,* 217–223.

Baillargeon, R. (1987). Object permanence in 3½- and 4½-month-old infants. *Developmental Psychology, 23,* 655–664.

Baillargeon, R. (2004). Infants' physical world. *Current Directions on Psychological Science, 13,* 89–94.

Baillargeon, R., & De Vos, J. (1991). Object permanence in young infants: Further evidence. *Child Development, 62,* 1227–1246.

Baillargeon, R., & Graber, M. (1988). Evidence of location memory in 8-month-old infants in a nonsearch AB task. *Developmental Psychology, 24,* 502–511.

Baillargeon, R., Kotovsky, L., & Needham, A. (1995). The acquisition of physical knowledge in infancy. In G. Lewis, D. Premack, & D. Sperber (Eds.), *Casual understandings in cognition and culture.* Oxford: Oxford University Press.

Bainbridge, J., Meyers, M., Tanaka, S., & Waldfogel, J. (2005). Who gets an early education? Family income and the enrollment of three- to five-year-olds from 1968 to 2000. *Social Science Quarterly, 86,* 724–745.

Baker, D. P. (1992). Compared to Japan the U.S. is a low achiever—really. *Educational Research, 22,* 18–20.

Baker, D. P., & Jones, D. P. (1992). Opportunity and performance: A socio-logical explanation for gender differences in academic mathematics. In J. Wrigley (Ed.), *Education and gender equality.* London: The Falmer Press.

Baker, R. L., & Mednick, B. R. (1984). *Influences on human development: A longitudinal perspective.* Boston: Kluwer Nijhoff.

Baker-Ward, L., Ornstein, P. A., & Holden, D. J. (1984). The expression of memorization in early childhood. *Journal of Experimental Child Psychology, 37,* 555–575.

Baldwin, D. A., & Moses, L. J. (1996). The ontogeny of social information gathering. *Child Development, 67,* 1915–1939.

Baldwin, D. A., Markman, E. M., Bill, B., Desjardins, R. N., Irwin, J. M., & Tidball, G. (1996). Infants' reliance on social criteria for establishing word–object relations. *Child Development, 67,* 3135–3153.

Baldwin, D. V., & Skinner, M. L. (1989). Structural model for antisocial behavior: Generalization to single-mother families. *Developmental Psychology, 25,* 45–50.

Baltes, P. B., Reese, H. W., & Lipsitt, L. P. (1980). Life-span developmental psychology. *Annual Review of Psychology, 31,* 65–110.

Bamberg, M. (2004). Form and functions of 'slut bashing' in male identity constructions in 15-year-olds. *Human Development, 47,* 331–353.

Bandura, A. (1965). Influence of models' reinforcement contingencies on the acquisition of imitative responses. *Journal of Personality and Social Psychology, 1,* 589–595.

Bandura, A. (1971). *Psychological modeling.* New York: Lieber-Atherton.

Bandura, A. (1977). *Social learning theory.* Englewood Cliffs, NJ: Prentice-Hall.

Bandura, A. (1986). *Social foundations of thought and action. A social cognitive theory.* Englewood Cliffs, NJ: Prentice-Hall.

Bandura, A. (1989). Social cognitive theory. In R. Vista (Ed.), *Annals of child development* (Vol. 6) (pp. 1–60). Greenwich, CT: JAI Press.

Bandura, A. (1991). Social cognitive theory of moral thought and action. In Kurtines, W. M., & Gewirtz, J. L. (Eds.), *Handbook of moral behavior and development* (Vol. 1) (pp. 45–103). Hillsdale, NJ: Erlbaum.

Bandura, A. (1992). Perceived self-efficacy in cognitive development and functioning. *Educational Psychologist, 28,* 117–148.

Bandura, A. (2001). Social cognitive theory: An agentic perspective. *Annual Review of Psychology, 52,* 1–26.

Bandura, A., Caprara, G. V., Barbaranelli, C., Gerbino, M., & Pastorelli, C. (2003). Role of affective self-regulatory efficacy in diverse spheres of psychosocial functioning. *Child Development, 74,* 769–782.

Banks, J. A. (1993). Multicultural education: Historical development, dimensions, and practice. *Review of Educational Research, 19,* 3–49.

Banks, M. S., & Ginsburg, A. P. (1985). Infant visual preferences: A review and new theoretical treatment. In H. W. Reese (Ed.), *Advances in child development and behavior* (Vol. 19, pp. 207–246). Orlando, FL: Academic Press.

Banks, M. S., & Salapatek, P. (1983). Infant visual perception. In M. M. Haith & J. J. Campos (Eds.), *Handbook of child psychology.* Vol. 2: *Infancy and developmental psychobiology* (4th ed., pp. 436–571). New York: Wiley.

Barber, B. K. (1996). Parental psychological control: Revisiting a neglected construct. *Child Development, 67,* 3296–3319.

Barber, B. K., Harmon, E. (2002). Violating the self: Parental psychological control of children and adolescents. In B. K. Barber (Ed.), *Intrusive parenting: How psychological control affects children and adolescents* (pp. 15–52). Washington, DC: American Psychological Association.

Barber, B. K., Olsen, J. E., & Shagle, S. C. (1994). Associations between parental psychological and behavioral control and youth internalized and externalized behaviors. *Child Development, 65,* 1120–1136.

Barber, B. K., Olsen, J. E., & Shagle, S. C. (1994). Associations between parental psychological and behavioral control and youth internalized and externalized behaviors. *Child Development, 65,* 1120–1136.

Barden, R. C., Ford, M. E., Jensen, A. G., Rogers-Salyer, M., & Salyer, K. E. (1989). Effects of craniofacial deformity in infancy on the quality of mother-infant interactions. *Child Development, 60,* 819–824.

Bardwell, J. R., Cochran, S. W., & Walker, S. (1986). Relation of parental education, race, and gender to sex-role stereotyping in five-year-old kindergartners. *Sex Roles, 15,* 275–281.

Barenboim, C. (1981). The development of person perception in childhood and adolescence: From behavioral comparisons to psychological constructs to psychological comparisons. *Child Development, 52,* 129–144.

Barglow, P., Vaughn, B. E., & Molitor, N. (1987). Effects of maternal absence due to employment on the quality of infant-mother attachment in a low-risk sample. *Child Development, 58,* 945.954.

Barker, D. J. P. (1994). *Mothers, babies, and disease in later life.* London: BMJ Publishing Group.

Barkley, R. A. (1997). Behavioral inhibition, sustained attention, and executive functions. Constructing a unifying theory of ADHD. *Psychological Bulletin, 121,* 65–94.

Barnard, K. E., & Bee, H. L. (1983). The impact of temporally patterned stimulation on the development of preterm infants. *Child Development, 54,* 1156–1167.

Barnes, G. M., Reifman, A. S., Farrell, M. P., & Dintcheff, B. A. (2000). The effects of parenting on the development of adolescents-alcohol misuse: A six-wave latent growth model. *Journal of Marriage and the Family, 62,* 175–186.

Barnett, W. S. (1995). Long-term effects of early childhood programs on cognitive and school outcomes. *The Future of Children, 5* (No. 3, Winter).

Barnett, W. S., & Hustedt, J. T. (2005). Head Start's lasting benefits. *Infants & Young Children: An Interdisciplinary Journal of Special Care Practices, 18,* 16–24.

Baron, I. S. (2005). Test review: Wechsler Intelligence Scale for Children—Fourth Edition (WISC–IV). *Child Neuropsychology, 11,* 475–479.

Baron, N. S. (1992). *Growing up with language: How children learn to talk.* Reading, MA: Addison-Wesley.

Baron-Cohen (in press). The Empathizing System: a revision of the 1994 model of the Mindreading System. To appear in B. J. Ellis & D. F. Bjorklund (Eds.), *Origins of the social mind: Evolutionary psychology and child development.* New York: Guilford.

Baron-Cohen, S. (1995). *Mindblindness: An essay on autism and theory of mind.* Cambridge, MA: MIT Press.

Baron-Cohen, S., Wheelwright, S., Stone, V., & Rutherford, M. (1999). A mathematician, a physicist and a computer scientist with Asperger syndrome: Performance on folk psychology and folk physics tests. *Neurocase, 5,* 475–483.

Baroni, M. R., & Axia, G. (1989). Children's meta-pragmatic abilities and the identification of polite and impolite requests. *First Language, 9,* 285–297.

Barr, H. M., Stressguth, A. P., Darby, B. L., & Sampson, P. D. (1990). Prenatal exposure to alcohol, caffeine, tobacco, and aspirin: Effects on fine and gross motor performance in 4- year-old children. *Developmental Psychology, 26,* 339–348.

Barr, R., & Hayne, H. (1999). Developmental changes in imitation from television during infancy. *Child Development, 70,* 1067–1081.

Barrett, D. E., & Frank, D. A. (1987). *The effects of undernutrition on children's behavior.* New York: Gordon and Breach.

Barry, H., III, Bacon, M. K., & Child, I. L. (1957). A cross-cultural survey of some sex differences in socialization. *Journal of Abnormal and Social Psychology, 55,* 327–332.

Barry, R. J., Clarke, A., McCarthy, R., & Selikowitz, M. (2002). EEG coherence in attention-deficit/hyperactivity disorder: A comparative study of two DSM–IV types. *Clinical Neurophysiology, 113,* 579–585.

Barry, R. J., Clarke, A., McCarthy, R., Selikowitz, M., Johnstone, S., & Rushby, J. (2004). Age and gender effects in EEG coherence: 1. Developmental trends in children. *Clinical Neurophysiology, 115,* 2252–2258.

Barry, R. J., Clarke, A., McCarthy, R., Selikowitz, M., Johnstone, S., Hsu, C.-I., Bond, D., Wallace, M. J., & Magee, C. (2005). Age and gender effects in EEG Coherence: II. Boys with attention deficit/hyperactivity disorder. *Clinical Neurophysiology, 116,* 977–984.

Bar-Tal, D., Raviv, A., & Goldberg, M. (1982). Helping behavior among preschool children: An observational study. *Child Development, 53,* 396–402.

Bartholomew, K., & Horowitz, L. M. (1991). Attachment styles among young adults: A test of a four-category model. *Journal of Personality and Social Psychology, 61,* 226–244.

Barton, M. E., & Tomasello, M. (1991). Joint attention and conversation in mother–infant sibling triads. *Child Development, 62,* 517–529.

Bartsch, K., & London, K. (2000). Children's use of mental state information in selecting persuasive arguments. *Developmental Psychology, 36,* 352–365.

Bastra, L., Hadders-Algra, M., & Neeleman, J. (2003). Effect of antenatal exposure to maternal smoking on behavioural problems and academic achievement in childhood: prospective evidence for a Dutch birth cohort. *Early Human Development, 73,* 21–33.

Bates, E. (1999). On the nature of language. In R. Levi-Montalcini, D. Baltimore, R. Dulbecco, & F. Jacob (Series Eds.), & E. Bizzi, P. Calissano, & V. Volterra (Vol. Eds.), *Frontiere della biologia* [Frontiers of biology], *The brain of homo sapiens.* Rome: Giovanni Trecanni.

Bates, E., O'Connell, B., & Shore, C. (1987). Language and communication in infancy. In J. D. Osofsky (Ed.), *Handbook of infant development,* (2nd ed.). New York: Wiley.

Bates, E., Thal, D., Whitsell, K., Fenson, L., & Oakes, L. (1989). Integrating language and gesture in infancy. *Developmental Psychology, 25,* 1004–1019.

Bates, J. E., Pettit, G. S., Dodge, K. A., & Ridge, B. (1998). Interaction of temperamental resistance to control and restrictive parenting in the development of externalizing behavior. *Developmental Psychology, 34,* 982–995.

Batson, C. D. (1991). *The altruism question: Toward a social-psychological answer.* Hillsdale, NJ: Erlbaum.

Bauer, P. J. (2004). Getting explicit memory off the ground: Steps toward construction of a neuro-developmental account of changes in the first two years of life. *Developmental Review, 24,* 347–373.

Bauer, P. J., Wenner, J. A., & Kroupina, M. G. (2002). Making the past present: Later verbal accessibility of early memories. *Journal of Cognition and Development, 3,* 21–47.

Bauer, P. J., Wenner, J. A., Dropik, P. L., & Wewerka, S. S. (2000). Parameters of remembering and forgetting in the transition from infancy to early childhood. *Monographs of the Society for Research in Child Development, 65* (Serial No. 263).

Baumrind, D. (1967). Child care practices anteceding three patterns of preschool behavior. *Genetic Psychology Monographs, 75,* 43–88.

Baumrind, D. (1971). Current patterns of parental authority. *Developmental Psychology Monographs, 4* (1, Part 2).

Baumrind, D. (1977, March). *Socialization determinants of personal agency.* Paper presented at the biennial meeting of the Society for Research in Child Development, New Orleans.

Baumrind, D. (1991). Effective parenting during the early adolescent transition. In P. A. Cowan & M. Hetherington (Ed.s), *Family transitions.* Hillsdale, NJ: Erlbaum.

Baumrind, D. (1995). Commentary on sexual orientation: Research and social policy implications. *Developmental Psychology, 31,* 130–136.

Bayley, N. (1969). *Bayley Scales of Infant Development.* New York: Psychological Corporation.

Bayley, N. (1993). *Bayley Scales of Infant Development* (2nd ed.). San Antonio, TX: Psychological Corporation.

Beal, C. R. (1990). Development of knowledge about the role of inference in text comprehension. *Child Development, 61,* 1011–1023.

Beal, C. R. (1994). *Boys and girls: The development of gender roles.* New York: McGraw-Hill.

Beal, C. R., & Belgrad, S. L. (1990). The development of message evaluation skills in young children. *Child Development, 61,* 705–712.

Bear, G. G., & Rys, G. S. (1994). Moral reasoning, classroom behavior, and sociometric status among elementary school children. *Developmental Psychology, 30,* 633–638.

Beard, R., & Chapple, J. (1995). An evaluation of maternity services. In B. P. Sachs, R. Beard, E. Papiernik, & C. Russell (Eds.), *Reproductive health care for women and babies* (pp. 246–262). New York: Oxford University Press.

Beato-Fernández, L., Rodríguez-Cano, T., Belmonte-Llario, A., Martínez-Delgado, C. (2004). Risk factors for eating disorders in adolescents. *European Child & Adolescent Psychiatry, 13,* 287–294.

Becker, H. J. (2000). Who's wired and who's not: Children's access to and use of computer technology. *The Future of Children, 10,* 44–75.

Begley, S. (2000). Designer babies. In K. L. Freiberg (Ed.), *Human development 00/01* (28th ed., pp. 8–9). Guilford, CT: Dushkin/McGraw–Hill.

Begley, S. (2001). Decoding the human body. In K. H. Freiberg (Ed)., *Human Development 01/02* (29th ed., pp. 8–12). Guildford, CT: McGraw–Hill/Duskin.

Beidelman, T. O. (1971). *The Kaguru: A matrilineal people of East Africa.* New York: Holt, Rinehart & Winston.

Beilin, H. (1992). Piaget's enduring contribution to developmental psychology. *Developmental Psychology, 28,* 191–204.

Bell, A. P., Weinberg, M. S., & Hammersmith, S. K. (1981). *Sexual preference: Its development in men and women.* Bloomington, IN: Indiana University Press.

Bell, M. A., & Fox, N. A. (1992). The relations between frontal brain electrical activity and cognitive development during infancy. *Child Development, 63,* 1142–1163.

Bell, R. Q. (1979). Parent, child, and reciprocal influences. *American Psychologist, 34,* 821–826.

Bellugi, U. (1988). The acquisition of a spatial language. In F. S. Kessel (Ed.), *The development of language and language researchers: Essays in honor of Roger Brown.* Hillsdale, NJ: Erlbaum.

Belsky, J. (1981). Early human experience: A family perspective. *Developmental Psychology, 17,* 3–23.

Belsky, J. (1993). Etiology of child maltreatment: A developmental ecological analysis, *Psychological Bulletin, 114,* 413–434.

Belsky, J. (1996). Parent, infant, and social-contextual antecedents of father-son attachment security. *Developmental Psychology, 32,* 905–913.

Belsky, J., & Fearon, R. M. (2004). Exploring marriage-parenting typologies and their contextual antecedents and developmental sequelae. *Development & Psychopathology, 16,* 501–523.

Belsky, J., & Rovine, M. (1988). Nonmaternal care in the first year of life and the security of infant-parent attachment. *Child Development, 59,* 157–167.

Belsky, J., Garduque, L., & Hrncir, E. (1984). Assessing performance, competence, and executive capacity in infant play: Relations to home environment and security of attachment. *Developmental Psychology, 20,* 406–417.

Belsky, J., Gilstrap, B., & Rovine, M. (1984). The Pennsylvania Infant and Family Development Project I: Stability and change in mother-infant and father-infant interaction in a family setting. *Child Development, 55,* 692–705.

Belsky, J., Rosenberger, K., & Crnic, K. (1995). Maternal personality, marital quality, social support, and infant temperament: Their significance for mother-infant attachment in human families. In C. Pryce, R. Martin, & D. Skuse (Eds.), *Motherhood in human and nonhuman primates* (pp. 115–124). Basel, Switzerland: Kruger.

Belsky, J., Rovine, M., & Taylor, D. G. (1984). The Pennsylvania Infant and Family Development Project, III: The origins of individual differences in infant-mother attachment—maternal and infant contributions. *Child Development, 55,* 718–728.

Belsky, J., Spritz, B., & Crnic, K. (1996). Infant attachment security and affective-cognitive information processing at age 3. *Psychological Science, 7,* 111–114.

Bem, S. L. (1974). The measurement of psychological androgyny. *Journal of Consulting and Clinical Psychology, 42,* 155–162.

Bem, S. L. (1975). Sex-role adaptability: One consequence of psychological androgyny. *Journal of Personality and Social Psychology, 31,* 634–643.

Bem, S. L. (1978). Beyond androgyny: Some presumptuous prescriptions for a liberated sexual identity. In J. A. Sherman & F. L. Denmark (Eds.), *The psychology of women: Future directions in research.* New York: Psychological Dimensions.

Bem, S. L. (1983). Gender schema theory and its implications for child development: Raising gender aschematic children in a gender-schematic society. *Signs: Journal of Women in Culture and Society, 8,* 598–616.

Bem, S. L. (1989). Genital knowledge and gender constancy in preschool children. *Child Development, 60,* 649–662.

Benasich, A. A., & Brooks-Gunn, J. (1996). Maternal attitudes and knowledge of child-rearing: Associations with family and child outcomes. *Child Development, 67,* 1186–1205.

Benbow, C. P., & Arjimand, O. (1990). Predictors of high academic achievement in mathematics and science by mathematically talented students: A longitudinal study. *Journal of Educational Psychology, 82,* 430–441.

Bendersky, M., & Lewis, M. (1994). Environmental risk, biological risk, and developmental outcome. *Developmental Psychology, 30,* 484–494.

Benedict, H. (1979). Early lexical development: Comprehension and production. *Journal of Child Language, 6,* 183–200.

Benenson, J., Markovits, H., Roy, R., & Denko, P. (2003). Behavioral rules underlying learning to share: Effects of development and context. *International Journal of Behavioral Development, 27,* 116–121.

Benenson, J. F., Apostoleris, N. H., & Parnass, J. (1997). Age and sex differences in dyadic and group interaction. *Developmental Psychology, 33,* 538–543.

Bennett, M., Karakozov, R., Kipiani, G., Lyons, E., Pavlenko, V., & Riazanova, T. (2004). Young children's evaluations of the ingroup and of outgroups: A multi-national study. *Social Development, 13,* 124–141.

Benoit, D., & Parker, K. C. H. (1994). Stability and transmission of attachment across three generations. *Child Development, 65,* 1444–1456.

Benson, M. J. (2004). After the adolescent pregnancy: Parents, teens, and families. *Child and Adolescent Social Work Journal, 21,* 435–455.

Berenbaum, S. A. (1998). How hormones affect behavioral and neural development: Introduction to the special issue on gonadal hormones and sex differences in behavior. *Developmental Neuropsychology, 14,* 175–196.

Berenbaum, S. A. (2002). Prenatal androgen and sexual differentiation of behavior. In E. A. Eugster & O. H. Pescovitz (Eds.), *Developmental Endrocrinology: From research to clinical practice* (pp. 293–311). Totowa, NJ: Humana Press.

Berenbaum, S. A., & Snyder, A. (1995). Early hormonal influences on childhood sex-typed activity and playmate preferences: Implications for the development of sexual orientation. *Developmental Psychology, 31,* 31–42.

Berg, W. K., & Berg, K. M. (1987). Psychophysiologic development in infancy: State, startle, and attention. In J. Osofsky (Ed.), *Handbook of infant development* (2nd ed.).

Bergen, D. J., & Williams, J. E. (1991). Sex stereotypes in the United States revisited: 1972–1988. *Sex Roles, 24,* 413–424.

Bering, J. M., & Bjorklund, D. F. (2004). The natural emergence of afterlife reasoning as a developmental regularity. *Developmental Psychology, 40,* 217–233.

Bering, J. M., Hernández-Blasi, C., & Bjorklund, D. F. (in press). The development of "afterlife" beliefs in religiously and secularly schooled children. *British Journal of Developmental Psychology.*

Berk, L. E. (1992). Children's private speech: An overview of theory and the status of research. In R. M. Diaz & L. E. Berk (Eds.), *Private speech: From social interaction to self-regulation.* Hillsdale, NJ: Erlbaum.

Berk, L. E., & Spuhl, S. T. (1995). Maternal intervention, private speech, and task performance in preschool children. *Early Childhood Research Quarterly, 10,* 145–169.

Berkey, C. S., Wang, X., Dockery, D. W., & Ferris, B. G. (1994). Adolescent height growth of U.S. children. *Annals of Human Biology, 21,* 435–442.

Berko, J. (1958). The child's learning of English morphology. *Word, 14,* 150–177.

Berkowitz, M. W., & Gibbs, J. C. (1983). Measuring the developmental features of moral discussion. *Merrill-Palmer Quarterly, 29,* 399–410.

Bermejo, V. (1996). Cardinality development and counting. *Developmental Psychology, 22,* 263–268.

Bernal, M. E., & Knight, G. P. (1997). Ethnic identity of Latino children. In J. G. Garcia & M. C. Zea (Eds.), *Psychological intervention and research with Latino populations.* Boston: Allyn & Bacon.

Berndt, T. J. (1989). Friendships in childhood and adolescence. In W. Damon (Ed.), *Child development today and tomorrow.* San Francisco: Jossey-Bass.

Berndt, T. J. (1996). Friendships quality affects adolescents' self-esteem and social behavior. In W. M. Bukowski, A. F. Newcombe, & W. W. Hartup (Eds.) *The company they keep: Friendship during childhood and adolescence* (pp. 346–365). New York: Cambridge University Press.

Berndt, T. J., & Hoyle, S. G. (1985). Stability and change in childhood and adolescent friendships. *Developmental Psychology, 21,* 1007–1015.

Berndt, T. J., & Perry, T. B. (1990). Distinctive features and effects of early adolescent friendships. In R. Montemayor, G. R. Adams, & T. P. Gulotta (Eds.), *From childhood to adolescence: A transitional period.* Newbury Park, CA: Sage.

Berne, Samuel A. (2003). The primitive survival reflexes. *Journal of Optometric Vision Development, 34,* 83–85.

Berrueta-Clement, J. R., Schweinhart, L. J., Barnett, S. W., Epstein, A. S., & Weikart, D. P. (1984). *Changed lives: The effects of the Perry Preschool Program on youths through age 19.* Ypsilanti, MI: High/ScopePress.

Berry, J. W., Poortinga, Y. H., Segall, M., & Dasen, P. R. (1992). *Cross-cultural psychology: Research and applications.* Cambridge, England: Cambridge University Press.

Bers, M. U., & Cassell, J. (2000). Children as designers of interactive storytellers: "Let me tell you a story about myself . . ." In K. Dautenhanhn (Ed.), *Human cognition and social agent technology* (pp. 61–83). Philadelphia: John Benjamins.

Bertenthal, B. I. (1993, March). *Emerging trends in perceptual development.* Paper presented at the biennial meeting of the Society for Research in Child Development, New Orleans, LA.

Bertenthal, B. I., & Campos, J. J. (1987). New directions in the study of early experience. *Child Development, 58,* 560–567.

Bertenthal, B. I., & Longo, M. R. (2002). Advancing Our Understanding of Early Perceptual and Cognitive Development. *Human Development, 45,* 434–441.

Berzonsky, M. D., & Adams, G. R. (1999). Reevaluating the identity status paradigm: Still useful after 35 years. *Developmental Review, 19,* 557–590.

Best, C. C., & McRoberts, G. W. (2003). Infant Perception of Non-Native Consonant Contrasts that Adults Assimilate in Different Ways. *Language & Speech, 46,* 183–216.

Best, D. L., Williams, J. E., Cloud, J. M., Davis, S. W., Robertson, L. S., Edwards, J. R., Giles, H., & Fowlkes, J. (1977). Development of sex-trait stereotypes among young children in the United States, England, and Ireland. *Child Development, 48,* 1375–1384.

Beyers, W., Goossens, L. (1999). Emotional autonomy, psychosocial adjustment, and parenting: Interactions, moderating, and mediating effects. *Journal of Adolescence, 22,* 753–769.

Bialystok, E. (1986). Factors in the growth of linguistic awareness. *Child Development, 57,* 498–510.

Bialystok, E. (1988). Levels of bilingualism and levels of metalinguistic awareness. *Developmental Psychology, 24,* 560–567.

Bialystok, E. (1999). Cognitive complexity and attentional control in the bilingual mind. *Child Development, 70,* 636–644.

Bialystok, E., Shenfield, T., & Codd, J. (2000). Languages, scripts, and the environment: Factors in developing concepts of print. *Developmental Psychology, 36,* 66–76.

Bianchi, S. M. (1995). The changing economic roles of women and men. In R. Farly (Ed.), *State of the Union: America in the 1990s.* New York: Russell Sage.

Bianchi, S. M., & Robinson, J. (1997). What did you do today? Children's use of time, family composition, and the acquisition of social capital. *Journal of Marriage and the Family, 59,* 332–344.

Bianchi, S. M., Subaiya, L., & Kahn, J. (1997, March). *Economic well-being of husbands and wives after marital disruption.* Paper presented at the annual meeting of the Population Association of America, Washington, DC.

Bickerton, D. (1983). Creole languages. *Scientific American, 249,* 116–122.

Bickerton, D. (1984). The language bioprogram hypothesis. *Behavioral and Brain Sciences, 7,* 173–221.

Bierman, K.L., & Furman, W. (1984). The effects of social skills training and peer involvement on the social adjustment of preadolescents. *Child Development, 55,* 157–162.

Biernat, M. (1991). Gender stereotypes and the relationship between masculinity and femininity: A developmental analysis. *Journal of Personality and Social Psychology, 61,* 351–365.

Bigler, R. S. (1995). The role of classification skill in moderating environmental influences on children's gender stereotyping: A study of the functional use of gender in the classroom. *Child Development, 66,* 1072–1087.

Bigler, R. S. (1999). The use of multicultural criteria and materials to counter racism in children. *Journal of Social Issues, 5,* 687–705.

Bigler, R. S., & Liben, L. S. (1990). The role of attitudes and interventions in gender-schematic processing. *Child Development, 61,* 1440–1452.

Bigler, R. S., & Liben, L. S. (1992). Cognitive mechanisms in children's gender stereotyping: Theoretical and educational implications of a cognitive-based intervention. *Child Development, 63,* 1351–1363.

Bigler, R. S., & Liben, L. S. (1993). A cognitive-developmental approach to racial stereotyping and reconstructive memory in Euro-American children. *Child Development, 64,* 1507–1518.

Bigner, J. J., & Jacobsen, R. B. (1989). Parenting behaviors of homosexual and heterosexual fathers. *Journal of Homosexuality, 18,* 173–186.

Bijeljac-Babic, R., Bertoncini, J., & Mahler, J. (1993). How do 4-day-old infants categorize multisyllabic utterances? *Developmental Psychology, 29,* 711–721.

Bingham, C. R., & Crockett, L. J. (1996). Longitudinal adjustment patterns of boys and girls experiencing early, middle, and later sexual intercourse. *Developmental Psychology, 32,* 647–658.

Birch, L. L. (1990). Development of food acceptance patterns. *Developmental Psychology, 26,* 515–519.

Birch, L. L., & Billman, J. (1986). Preschool children's food sharing with friends and acquaintances. *Child Development, 57,* 387–395.

Birch, L. L., Marlin, D. W., & Rotter, J. (1984). Eating as the "means" activity in a contingency: Effects on young children's food preference. *Child Development, 55,* 431–439.

Biringen, Z. (1990). Direct observation of maternal sensitivity and dyadic interactions in the home: Relations to maternal thinking. *Developmental Psychology, 26,* 278–284.

Biringen, Z., Emde, R. N., Campos, J. J., & Appelbaum, M. I. (1995). Affective reorganization in the infant, the mother, and the dyad: The role of upright locomotion and its timing. *Child Development, 66,* 499–514.

Bisanz, J., & Lefevre, J. (1990). Strategic and nonstrategic processing in the development of mathematical cognition. In D. F. Bjorklund (Ed.), *Children's Strategies: Contemporary views of cognitive development.* Erlbaum: Hillsdale, NJ.

Bishop, D. (1988). Language development after focal brain damage. In D. Bishop & K. Mogford (Eds.), *Language development in exceptional circumstances.* Edinburgh: Churchill Livingstone.

Bivens, J. A., & Berk, L. E. (1990). A longitudinal study of the development of elementary school children's private speech. *Merrill–Palmer Quarterly, 36,* 443–463.

Bjorklund, D. F. (1987). How age changes in knowledge base contribute to the development of children's memory: An interpretive review. *Developmental Review, 7,* 93–130.

Bjorklund, D. F. (2000). *Children's thinking: Developmental function and individual differences* (3rd ed.). Belmont, CA: Wadsworth.

Bjorklund, D. F. (2005). *Children's thinking: Cognitive development and individual differences* (4th ed.). Belmont, CA: Wadsworth.

Bjorklund, D. F., & Bjorklund, B. R. (1985). Organization versus item effects of an elaborated knowledge base on children's memory. *Developmental Psychology, 21,* 1120–1131.

Bjorklund, D. F., & Bjorklund, B. R. (1992). *Looking at children: An introduction to child development.* Pacific Grove, CA: Brooks/Cole.

Bjorklund, D. F., & Douglas, R N. (1997). The development of memory strategies. In N. Cowan (Ed.), *The development of memory in childhood.* London: London University College Press.

Bjorklund, D. F., & Harnishfeger, K. K. (1990). Children's strategies: Their definition and origins. In D. F. Bjorklund (Ed.), *Children's strategies: Contemporary views of cognitive development* (pp. 309–323). Hillsdale, NJ: Erlbaum.

Bjorklund, D. F., & Pellegrini, A. D. (2002). *The origins of human nature: Evolutionary developmental psychology.* Washington, DC: American Psychological Association.

Bjorklund, D. F., & Rosenblum, K. E. (2001). Children's use of multiple and variable addition strategies in a game context. *Developmental Science, 3,* 225–242.

Bjorklund, D. F., & Schwartz, R. (1996). The adaptive nature of developmental immaturity: Implications for language acquisition and language disabilities. In M. Smith & J. Damico (Eds.), *Childhood language disorders.* New York: Thieme Medical.

Bjorklund, D. F., Brown, R. D., & Bjorklund, B. R. (2001). Children's eyewitness memory: Changing reports and changing representations. In P. Graf & N. Ohta (Eds.), *Lifespan memory development.* Cambridge, MA: MIT Press.

Bjorklund, D. F., Miller, P. H., Coyle, T. R., & Slawinski, J. L. (1997). Instructing children to use memory strategies: Evidence of utilization deficiencies in memory training studies. *Developmental Review, 17,* 411–442.

Bjorklund, D. F., Schneider, W., Cassel, W. S., & Ashley, E. (1994). Training and extension of a memory strategy: Evidence for utilization deficiencies in the acquisition of an organizational strategy in high- and low-IQ children. *Child Development, 65,* 951–965.

Black, M. M., & Rollins, H. A. (1982). The effects of instructional variables on young children's organization and free recall. *Journal of Experimental Child Psychology, 31,* 1–19.

Black, M. M., Dubowitz, H., & Starr, R. H., Jr. (1999). African-American fathers in low-income urban families: Development, behavior, and home environment of their three-year-old children. *Child Development, 70,* 967–978.

Black, M. M., Dubowitz, H., & Starr, R. H., Jr. (2000). African-Americans in low-income urban families: Development, behavior and home environment of their three-year-old children. *Child Development, 70,* 967–978.

Black-Gutman, D., & Hickson, F. (1996). The relationship between racial attitudes and social-cognitive development in children: An Australian study. *Developmental Psychology, 32,* 448–456.

Blake, J., & Boysson-Bardies, B. de (1992). Patterns in babbling: a cross-linguistic study. *Journal of Child Language, 19,* 51–74.

Blake, K. V., Evans, S. F., Beilin, L. J., Landau, L. I., Stanley, F. J., et al. (2000). Maternal cigarette smoking during pregnancy, low birth weight and subsequent blood pressure in early childhood. *Early Human Development, 57,* 137–147.

Blakemore, J. E. O. (2003). Children's beliefs about violating gender norms: Boys shouldn't look like girls, and girls shouldn't act like boys. *Sex Roles, 48,* 411–419.

Blakemore, J. E. O., LaRue, A. A., & Olejnik, A. B. (1979). Sex-appropriate toy preference and the ability to conceptualize toys as sex-role related. *Developmental Psychology, 15,* 339–340.

Blasi, A. (1990). Kohlberg's theory and moral motivation. In D. Schrader (Ed.), *New Directions for child development* (No. 47) (pp. 51–57). San Francisco: Jossey-Bass.

Blass, E. M. (1997). Infant formula quiets crying human newborns. *Developmental and Behavioral Pediatrics, 18,* 162–165.

Blass, E. M., & Ciaramitaro, V. (1994). A new look at some old mechanisms in human newborns: Taste and tactile determinants of state, affect, and action. *Monographs of the Society for Research in Child Development, 59,* 1–81.

Blizzard, R. M. (1990). Psychosocial short stature. In F. Lifshitz (Ed.), *Pediatric Endrocrinology* (pp. 77–91). New York: Marcel Dekker.

Block, J. H. (1976). Issues, problems, and pitfalls in assessing sex differences: A critical review of *The psychology of sex differences. Merrill-Palmer Quarterly, 27,* 283–308.

Block, J. H., Block, J., & Gjerde, P. F. (1986). The personality of children prior to divorce: A prospective study. *Child Development, 57,* 827–840.

Block, J. H., Block, J., & Gjerde, P. F. (1988). Parental functioning and the home environment of families of divorce: Prospective and current analyses. *Journal of the American Academy of Child and Adolescent Psychiatry, 27,* 207–213.

Bloom, L. (1970). *Language development: Form and function in emerging grammars.* Cambridge, MA: M.I.T. Press.

Bloom, L. (1973). *One word at a time: The use of single word utterances before syntax.* The Hague: Mouton.

Bloom, L., Hood, L., & Lightbown, P. (1974). Imitation in language development: If, when and why. *Cognitive Psychology, 6,* 380–420.

Bloom, L., Margulis, C., Tinker, E., & Fujita, N. (1996). Early conversations and word learning: Contributions from child and adult. *Child Development, 67,* 3154–3175.

Blöte, A. W., Resing, W. C. M., Mazer, P., & Van Noort, D. A. (1999). Young children's organizational strategies on a same–different task: A microgenetic study and a training study. *Journal of Experimental Child Psychology, 74,* 21–43.

Blount, R. (1986, May 4). "I'm about five years ahead of my age." *Atlanta Journal and Constitution,* pp. C17–C20.

Boake, C. (2002). From the Binet-Simon to the Wechsler-Bellevue: Tracing the history of Intelligence Testing. *Journal of Clinical & Experimental Neuropsychology, 24,* 383–405.

Bochner, S., & Jones, J. (2003). *Child language development: Learning to talk.* London: Whurr Publishers, Ltd.

Bogatz, G. A., & Ball, S. (1972). *The second year of Sesame Street: A continuing evaluation.* Princeton, NJ: Educational Testing Service.

Bohannon, J. N., MacWhinney, B., & Snow, C. (1990). No negative evidence revisited: Beyond learnability or who has to prove what to whom. *Developmental Psychology, 26,* 221–226.

Bohannon, J. N., & Stanowicz, L. (1988). The issue of negative evidence: Adult responses to children's language errors. *Developmental Psychology, 24,* 684–689.

Bohannon, J. N., III, & Bonvillian, J. D. (1997). Theoretical approaches to language acquisition. In J. K. Gleason (Ed.), *The development of language* (4th ed.). Boston: Allyn & Bacon.

Bohannon, J. N., III, Padgett, R. J., Nelson, K. E., & Mark, M. (1996). Useful evidence on negative evidence. *Developmental Psychology, 32,* 551–555.

Bohlin, G., & Hagekull, B. (1993). Stranger wariness and sociability in the early years. *Infant Behavior and Development, 16,* 53–67.

Boismier, J. D. (1977). Visual stimulation and the wake-sleep behavior in human neonates. *Developmental Psychobiology, 10,* 219–227.

Boivin, M., & Hymel, S. (1997). Peer experiences and social self-perceptions: A sequential model. *Developmental Psychology, 33,* 135–145.

Boland, A. M., Haden, C. A., & Ornstein, P. A., (2003). Boosting children's memory by training mothers in the use of an elaborative conversational style as an event unfolds. *Journal of Cognition and Development, 4,* 39–65.

Boldizar, J. P. (1991). Assessing sex-typing and androgyny in children: The children's sex-role inventory. *Developmental Psychology, 27,* 505–515.

Boloh, Y., & Champaud, C. (1993). The past conditional verb form in French children: The role of semantics in late grammatical development. *Journal of Child Language, 20,* 169–189.

Boone, R. T., & Cunningham, J. G. (1998). Children's decoding of emotion in expressive body movement: The development of cue attunement. *Developmental Psychology, 34,* 1007–1016.

Booth, A., & Amato, P. R. (2001). Parental predivorce relations and offspring postdivorce well-being. *Journal of Marriage and the Family, 63,* 197–212.

Bornstein, M. H. (1992). Perception across the life span. In M. H. Bornstein & M. E. Lamb (Eds.), *Developmental psychology: An advanced textbook* (pp. 155–209). Hillsdale, NJ: Erlbaum.

Bornstein, M. H., & Haynes, O. M. (1998). Vocabulary competence in early childhood: Measurement, latent construct, and predictive validity. *Child Development, 69,* 654–674.

Bornstein, M. H., & Lamb, M. E. (Eds.). (2005). *Developmental science: An advanced textbook* (5th ed.). Mahwah, NJ: Lawrence Erlbaum Associates.

Bornstein, M. H., Cote, L. R., Maital, S., Painter, K., Sung-Yun Park, Pascual, L., Pêcheux, M.-G., Ruel, J., Venuti, P., & Vyt, A. (2004). Cross-linguistic analysis of vocabulary in young children: Spanish, Dutch, French, Hebrew, Italian, Korean, and American English. *Child Development, 75,* 1115–1139.

Bornstein, M. H., Haynes, O. M., O'Reilly, A. W., & Painter, K. M. (1996). Solitary and collaborative pretense play in early childhood: Sources of individual variation in the development of representational competence. *Child Development, 67,* 2910–2929.

Bornstein, M. H., Haynes, O. M., Pascual, L., Painter, K. M., & Galperin, C. (1999). Play in two societies: Pervasiveness of process, specificity of structure. *Child Development, 70,* 317–331.

Bornstein, M. H., Kessen, W., & Weiskopf, S. (1976). Color vision and hue categorization in young human infants. *Journal of Experimental Psychology: Human Perception and Performance, 2,* 115–129.

Borstlemann, L. J. (1983). Children before psychology: Ideas about children from antiquity to the late 1800s. In P. H. Mussen (Ed.), *Handbook of child psychology* (Vol. 1). New York: Wiley.

Bosma, H. A., & Kunnen, E. S. (2001). Determinants and mechanisms of ego identity development: A review and synthesis. *Developmental Review, 21,* 39–66.

Botkin, D. R., Weeks, M. O. N., & Morris, J. E. (2000). Changing marriage role expectations: 1991–1996. *Sex Roles, 42,* 933–942.

Bouchard, T. J., Jr., & McGue, M. (1981). Family studies of intelligence: A review. *Science, 212,* 1055–1059.

Bouchard, T. J., Jr., Lykken, D. T., McGue, M., Segal, N. L., & Tellegen, A. (1990). Sources of human psychological differences: The Minnesota study of twins reared apart. *Science, 250,* 223–228.

Boulton, M. J. (1999). Concurrent and longitudinal relations between children's playground behavior and social preferences, victimization, and bullying. *Child Development, 70,* 944–954.

Bower, B. (2000). Looking for the brain's g force. *Science News, 158,* 72.

Bower, B. (2003). Essence of G. *Science News, 163,* 92–93.

Bower, T. G. R. (1982). *Development in infancy.* New York: W. H. Freeman.

Bower, T. G. R., Broughton, J. M., & Moore, M. K. (1970). The coordination of vision and tactile input in infancy. *Perception and Psychophysics, 8,* 51–53.

Bowlby, J. (1969). *Attachment and loss.* Vol. 1: *Attachment.* London: Hogarth Press.

Bowlby, J. (1973). *Attachment and loss.* Vol. 2: *Separation: Anxiety and anger.* London: Hogarth Press.

Bowlby, J. (1980). *Attachment and loss.* Vol. 3: *Loss, sadness, and depression.* New York: Basic Books.

Bowlby, J. (1988). *A secure base: Clinical applications of attachment theory.* London: Routledge.

Boyatzis, C. J., Matillo, G. M., & Nesbitt, K. M. (1995). Effects of the "Mighty Morphin Power Rangers" on children's aggression with peers. *Child Study Journal, 25,* 44–55.

Boyes, M. C., & Chandler, M. (1992). Cognitive development, epistemic doubt, and identity formation in adolescence. *Journal of Youth and Adolescence, 21,* 277–304.

Boykin, A. W. (1994). Harvesting talent and culture: African-American children and educational reform. In R. Rossi (Ed.), *Schools and students at risk* (pp. 116–138) New York: Teachers College Press.

Boyle, M. H., Jenkins, J. M., Cairney, J., Duku, E., & Racine, Y. (2004). Differential-maternal parenting behavior: Estimating within- and between-family effects on children. *Child Development, 75,* 1457–1476.

Brabeck, M. (1983). Moral judgment: Theory and research on differences between males and females. *Developmental Review, 3,* 274–291.

Brackbill, Y., McManus, K., & Woodward, L. (1985). *Medication in maternity: Infant exposure and maternal information.* Ann Arbor: University of Michigan Press.

Bradbard, M. R., Martin, C. L., Endsley, R. C., & Halverson, C. F. (1986). Influence of sex stereotypes on children's exploration and memory: A competence versus performance distinction. *Developmental Psychology, 22,* 481–486.

Braddock, J. H. II, & McPartland, J. M. (1993). Education of early adolescents. *Review of Educational Research, 19,* 135–170.

Bradley, R. H., & Caldwell, B. M. (1982). The consistency of the home environment and its relationship to child development. *International Journal of Behavioral Development, 5,* 445–465.

Bradley, R. H., & Caldwell, B. M. (1984). 174 children: A study of the relationship between home environment and cognitive development during the first 5 years. In A. W. Gottfried (Ed.), *Home environment and early cognitive development: Longitudinal research.* Orlando, FL: Academic Press.

Bradley, R. H., Burchinal, M. R., & Casey, P. H. (2001). Early intervention: The moderating role of the home environment. *Applied Developmental Science, 5,* 2–8.

Bradley, R. H., Caldwell, B. M., & Rock, S. L. (1988). Home environment and school performance: A ten-year follow-up and examination of three models of environmental action. *Child Development, 59,* 852–867.

Bradley, R. H., Caldwell, B. M., Rock, S. L., Ramey, C. T., Barnard, K. E., Gray, C., Hammond, M. A., Mitchell, S., Gottfried, A. W., Siegel, L., & Johnson, D. L. (1989). Home environment and cognitive development in the first 3 years of life: A collaborative study involving six sites and three ethnic groups in North America. *Developmental Psychology, 25,* 217–235.

Bradley, R. H., Whiteside, L., Mundfrom, D. J., Casey, P. H., Kelleher, K. J., & Pope, S. K. (1994). Contribution of early intervention and early caregiving experiences to resilience of low birthweight premature children living in poverty. *Journal of Clinical Child Psychology, 23,* 425–434.

Brainerd, C. F. (1996). Piaget: A centennial celebration. *Psychological Science, 7,* 191–195.

Brainerd, C. J., & Gordon, L. L. (1994). Development of verbatim and gist memory for numbers. *Developmental Psychology, 30,* 163–177.

Brainerd, C. J., & Kingma, J. (1985). On the independence of short-term memory and working memory in cognitive development. *Cognitive Psychology, 17,* 210–247.

Brainerd, C. J., & Reyna, V. F. (2001). Fuzzy-trace theory: Dual processes in memory, reasoning, and cognitive neuroscience. In H. W. Reese (Ed.), *Advances in Child Development and Behavior.* San Diego: Academic Press.

Brainerd, C. J., Reyna, V. F. (2004). Fuzzy-race theory and memory development. *Developmental Review, 24,* 396–439.

Braungart, J. M., Fulker, D. W., & Plomin, R. (1992). Genetic mediation of the homeenvironment during infancy: A sibling adoption study of the HOME. *Developmental Psychology, 28,* 1048–1055.

Braungart, J. M., Plomin, R., DeFries, J. C., & Fulker, D. W. (1992). Genetic influence on tester-rated infant temperament as assessed by Bayley's Infant Behavior Record: Nonadoptive and adoptive siblings and twins. *Developmental Psychology, 28,* 40–47.

Brazelton, T. B. (1979). Behavioral competence of the newborn infant. *Seminars in Perinatology, 3,* 35–44.

Brendgen, M., Vitaro, F., Bukowski, W. M., Doyle, A. B., & Markiewcz, D. (2001). Developmental profiles of peer social preferences over the course of elementary school: Associations with trajectories of externalizing and internalizing behavior. *Developmental Psychology, 37,* 308–320.

Brennan, P. A., Hall, J., Bor, W., Najaman, J. M., & Williams, G. (2003). Integrating biological and social processes in relation to early-onset persistent aggression in boys and girls. *Developmental Psychology, 39,* 309–323.

Bretherton, I. (1985). Attachment theory: Retrospect and prospect. In I. Bretherton & E. Waters (Eds.), Growing points of attachment theory and research. *Monographs of the Society for Research in Child Development, 50* (Nos. 1–2, Serial No. 209).

Bretherton, I. (1990). Open communication and internal working models: Their role in the development of attachment relationships. In R. A. Thompson (Ed.), Socioemotional development. *Nebraska Symposium on Motivation* (Vol. 36). Lincoln: University of Nebraska Press.

Bretherton, I., Stolberg, U., & Kreye, M. (1981). Engaging strangers in proximal interaction: Infants' social initiative. *Developmental Psychology, 17,* 746–755.

Bridges, L. J., & Grolnick, W. J. (1995). The development of emotional self-regulation in infancy and early childhood. In N. Eisenberg (Ed.,), *Social development: Vol. 15. Review of personality and social psychology.* Thousand Oaks, CA: Sage.

Britt, G. C., & Myers, B. J. (1994). The effects of the Brazelton intervention. *Infant Mental Health Journal, 15,* 278–292.

Broberg, A. G., Wessels, H., Lamb, M. E., & Hwang, C. P. (1997). Effects of day care on the cognitive development of 8-year-olds: A longitudinal study. *Developmental Psychology, 33,* 62–69.

Brockington, I. (1996). *Motherhood and mental health.* Oxford, England: Oxford University Press.

Brody, G. H. (1998). Sibling relationship quality: Its causes and consequences. *Annual Review of Psychology, 49,* 1–14.

Brody, G. H. (2004). Siblings' direct and indirect contributions to child development. *Current Directions in Psychological Science, 13,* 124–126.

Brody, G. H., & Flor, D. L. (1998). Maternal resources, parenting practices, and child competence in rural single-parent African American families. *Child Development, 69,* 803–816.

Brody, G. H., & Murry, V. M. (2001). Sibling socialization of competence in rural, single-parent African American families. *Journal of Marriage and the Family, 63,* 996–1008.

Brody, G. H., & Shaffer, D. R. (1982). Contributions of parents and peers to children's moral socialization. *Developmental Review, 2,* 31–75.

Brody, G. H., Dorsy, D., Forehand, R., & Armistead, L. (2002). Unique and protective contributions of parenting and classroom processes in the adjustment of African American children living in single parent homes. *Child Development, 73,* 274–286.

Brody, G. H., Kim, S., Murray, V. M., & Brown, A. C. (2004). Protective longitudinal paths linking child competence to behavioral problems among African American siblings. *Child Development, 75,* 455–467.

Brody, G. H., Kim, S., Murry, V. B., & Brown, A. C. (2003). Longitudinal direct and indirect pathways linking older sibling competencies to the development of younger sibling competence. *Developmental Psychology, 39,* 618–628.

Brody, G. H., Murry, V. M., Kim, S., & Brown, A. C. (2002). Longitudinal pathways to competence and psychological adjustment among African American children living in rural single-parent households. *Child Development, 73,* 1505–1516.

Brody, G. H., Stoneman, Z., & Flor, D. (1996). Parental religiosity, family processes, and youth competence in rural, two-parent African-American families. *Developmental Psychology, 32,* 696–706.

Brody, L. R. (1999). *Gender, emotion, and the family.* Cambridge, MA: Harvard University Press.

Brody, N. (1992). *Intelligence* (2nd ed.). San Diego: Academic Press.

Brody, N. (1997). Intelligence, schooling, and society. *American Psychologist, 52,* 1046–1050.

Brodzinsky, D. M., Radice, C., Huffman, L., & Merkler, K. (1987). Prevalence of clinically significant symptomatology in nonclinical samples of adopted and nonadopted children. *Journal of Clinical Child Psychology, 16,* 350–356.

Brodzinsky, D. M., Smith, D. W., & Brodzinsky, A. B. (1998). *Children's adjustment to adoption: Developmental and clinical issues.* London: Sage.

Broidy, L. M., Nagin, D. S., Tremblay, R. E., Bates, J. E., Brane, B., Dodge, K. A., Ferguson, D., Horwood, J. L., Loeber, R., Laird, R., Lynam, D. R., Moffitt, T. E., Pettit, G. S., & Vitaro, F. (2003). Developmental trajectories of childhood disruptive behaviors and adolescent delinquency: A six-site, cross-national study. *Developmental Psychology, 39,* 222–245.

Broman, K. W., Murray, J. C., Sheffield, V. C., White, R. L., & Weber, J. L. (1998). Comprehensive Human Genetic Maps: Individual and Sex-Specific Variation in Recombination. *American Journal of Human Genetics, 63,* 861–869.

Bronfenbrenner, U. (1977). Toward an experimental ecology of human development. *American Psychologist, 32,* 513–531.

Bronfenbrenner, U. (1979). *The ecology of human development.* Cambridge, MA: Harvard University Press.

Bronfenbrenner, U. (1989). Ecological systems theory. In R. Vasta (Ed.) *Annals of child development: Theories of child development: Revised formulations and current issues* (Vol. 6, pp. 187–251). Greenwich, CT: JAI Press.

Bronfenbrenner, U. (1993). The ecology of cognitive development: Research models and fugitive findings. In R. H. Wozniak & K. W. Fisher (Eds.), *Development in context* (pp. 3–44). Hillsdale, NJ: Erlbaum.

Bronfenbrenner, U. (1995). The bioecological model from a life course perspective: Reflections of a participant observer. In P. Moen, G. H. Elder, Jr., & K. Luscher (Eds.), *Examining lives in context* (pp. 599–618). Washington, DC: American Psychological Association.

Bronfenbrenner, U. (2005). *Making human beings human.* Thousand Oaks, CA: Sage.

Bronfenbrenner, U., & Ceci, S. J. (1994). Nature-nurture reconceptualized in developmental perspective: A bioecological model. *Psychological Review, 101,* 568–586.

Bronfenbrenner, U., & Morris, P. (2006). The ecology of developmental processes. In W. Damon & R. M. Lerner (Series Eds.,) and R. M. Lerner (Vol. Ed.) *Handbook of child psychology* (6th ed.), Vol 1. New York: Wiley.

Brookes, H., Slater, A., Quinn, P. C., Lewkowicz, D. J., Hayes, R., & Brown, E. (2001). Three-month-old infants learn arbitrary auditory-visual pairings between voices and faces. *Infant and Child Development, 10,* 75–82.

Brookover, W., Beady, C., Flood, P., Schweitzer, J., & Wisenbaker, J. (1979). *School social systems and student achievement: Schools can make a difference.* New York: Praeger.

Brooks, P. J. (2004). Grammatical competence is not a psychologically valid construct. *Journal of Child Language, 31,* 467–470.

Brooks, P. J., & Tomasello, M. (1999). Young children learn to produce passives with nonce verbs. *Developmental Psychology, 35,* 29–44.

Brooks-Gunn, J., & Warren, M. P. (1988). The psychological significance of secondary sexual characteristics in nine- to eleven-year-old girls. *Child Development, 59,* 1061–1069.

Brooks-Gunn, J., Han, W., & Waldfogel, J. (2002). Maternal employment and child cognitive outcomes in the first three years of life. The NICHD study of early child care. *Child Development, 73,* 1052–1072.

Brooks-Gunn, J., Klebanov, P. K., & Duncan, G. J. (1996). Ethnic differences in children's intelligence test scores: Role of economic deprivation, home environment, and maternal characteristics. *Child Development, 67,* 396–408.

Brooks-Gunn, J., Klebanov, P. K., Liaw, F., & Spiker, D. (1993). Enhancing the development of low birthweight, premature infants: Changes in cognition and behavior over the first three years. *Child Development, 64,* 736–753.

Brooks-Gunn, J., Klebanov, P. K., Smith, J., Duncan, G., & Kyunghee, L. (2003). The black–white test score gap in young children: Contributions of test and family characteristics. *Applied Developmental Science, 7,* 239–42.

Broverman, I. K., Vogel, S. R., Clarkson, F. E., & Rosenkrantz, P. S. (1972). Sex-role stereotypes: A current appraisal. *Journal of Social Issues, 28,* 59–78.

Brown, A. L., & Kane, M. J. (1988). Preschool children can learn to transfer: learning to learn and learning by example. *Cognitive Psychology, 20,* 493–523.

Brown, A. L., Kane, M. J., & Long, C. (1989). Analogical transfer in young children: Analogies as tools for communication and exposition. *Applied Cognitive Psychology, 3,* 275–293.

Brown, A. M. (1990). Development of visual sensitivity to light and color vision in human infants: A critical review. *Vision Research, 30,* 1159–1188.

Brown, A. S., Cohen, P., Greenwald, S., & Susser, E. (2000). Nonaffective psychosis after prenatal exposure to rubella. *American Journal of Psychiatry, 157,* 438–443.

Brown, B. (1999). Optimizing expression of the common human genome for child development. *Current Directions in Psychological Science, 8,* 37–41.

Brown, B. B. (1990). Peer groups. In S. Feldman & G. Elliott (Eds.), *At the threshold: The developing adolescent.* Cambridge, MA: Cambridge University Press.

Brown, B. B., Mory, M. S., & Kinney, D. (1994). Casting adolescent crowds in a relational perspective: Caricature, channel, and context. In R. Montemayor, G. R., Adams, & T.P. Gulotta (Eds.), *Personal relationships during adolescence.* Thousand Oaks, CA: Sage

Brown, J. D. (1998). *The self.* New York: McGraw-Hill.

Brown, J. L. (1964). States in newborn infants. *Morrill-Palmer Quarterly, 10,* 313–327.

Brown, J. R., & Dunn, J. (1996). Continuities in emotion understanding from three to six years. *Child Development, 67,* 789–802.

Brown, P., & Elliot, R. (1965). Control of aggression in a nursery school class. *Journal of Experimental Child Psychology, 2,* 103–107.

Brown, R. (1973). *A first language: The early stages.* Cambridge, MA: Harvard University Press.

Brown, R., Cazden, C., & Bellugi, U. (1969). The child's grammar from I–III. In J. P. Hill (Ed.), *Minnesota Symposia on Child Psychology* (Vol. 2). Minneapolis: University of Minnesota Press.

Brown, R. T. (2000). Adolescent sexuality at the dawn of the 21st century. *Adolescent Medicine, 11,* 19–34.

Brownell, C. A. (1986). Convergent developments: Cognitive-developmental correlates of growth in infant/toddler peer skills. *Child Development, 57,* 275–286.

Brownell, C. A. (1990). Peer social skills in toddlers: Competencies and constraints illustrated by same-age and mixed-age interaction. *Child Development, 61,* 838–848.

Brownell, C. A., & Carriger, M. S. (1990). Changes in cooperation and self/other differentiation during the second year. *Child Development, 61,* 1164–1174.

Bruck, M., Ceci, S. J., & Hembrooke, H. (1998). Reliability and credibility of young children's reports: From research to policy and practice. *American Psychologist, 53,* 136–151.

Bruck, M., Ceci, S. J., Francoeur, E., & Renick, A. (1995). Anatomically detailed dolls do not facilitate preschoolers' reports of a pediatric examination involving genital touching. *Journal of Experimental Psychology: Applied, 1,* 95–109.

Bruer, J. T. (1999). *The myth of the first three years: A new understanding of early brain development and lifelong learning.* New York: Free Press.

Bruer, J. T. (2001). A critical and sensitive period primer. In D. B. Bailey, J. T. Bruer, F. J. Symons, & J. W. Lichtman (Eds.), *Critical thinking about critical periods.* Baltimore, MD: Paul H. Brookes Publishing.

Bruggerman, E. L., & Hart, K. J. (1996). Cheating, lying, and moral reasoning by religious and secular high school students. *Journal of Educational Research, 89,* 340–344.

Bruner, J. S. (1983). *Child's talk: Learning to use language.* New York: Norton.

Buchanan, C. M., Eccles, J. S., & Becker, J. B. (1992). Are adolescents the victims of raging hormones: Evidence for activational effects of hormones on moods and behavior at adolescence. *Psychological Bulletin, 111,* 62–107.

Buela-Casal, G., Carretero-Dios, H., Delos-Santos-Roig, M., & Bermudez, M. P. (2003). Psychometric properties of a Spanish adaptation of the Matching Familiar Figures Test (MFFT–20). *European Journal of Psychological Assessment, 19,* 151–159.

Buhrmester, D. (1990). Intimacy of friendship, interpersonal competence, and adjustment during preadolescence and adolescence. *Child Development, 61,* 1101–1111.

Buhrmester, D., & Furman, W. (1990). Perceptions of sibling relationships during middle childhood and adolescence. *Child Development, 61,* 1387–1398.

Bukowski, W. M., Gauze, C., Hoza, B., & Newcomb, A. F. (1993). Differences and consistency between same-sex and other-sex peer relationships during early adolescence. *Developmental Psychology, 29,* 253–263.

Bukowski, W. M., Sippola, L. K., & Newcomb, A. F. (2000). Variations in patterns of attraction to same- and other-sex peers during early adolescence. *Developmental Psychology, 36,* 147–154.

Bull, R., & Johnston, R. S. (1997). Children's arithmetical difficulties: Contributions from processing speed, item identification, and short-term memory. *Journal of Experimental Child Psychology, 65,* 1–24.

Bullock, M. (1985). Animism in childhood thinking: A new look at an old question. *Developmental Psychology, 21,* 217–225.

Bullock, M., & Lutkenhaus, P. (1988). The development of volitional behavior in the toddler years. *Child Development, 59,* 664–674.

Burchinal, M. R., Follmer, A., & Bryant, D. M. (1996). The relations of maternal social support and family structure with maternal responsiveness and child outcomes among African-American families. *Developmental Psychology, 32,* 1073–1083.

Burchinal, M. R., Roberts, J. E., Hooper, S., & Zeisel, S. A. (2000). Cumulative risk and early cognitive development: A comparison of statistical risk models. *Developmental Psychology, 36,* 793–807.

Burchinal, M. R., Roberts, J. E., Riggins, R., Jr., Ziesel, S. A., Neebe, E., & Bryant, D. (2000). Relating quality of center-based care to early cognitive and language development longitudinally. *Child Development, 71,* 339–357.

Burhans, K. K., & Dweck, C. S. (1995). Helplessness in early childhood: The role of contingent worth. *Child Development, 66,* 1719–1738.

Burn, S., O'Neil, A. K., & Nederend, S. (1996). Childhood tomboyishness and adult androgeny. *Sex Roles, 34,* 419–428.

Burnette, E. (1997). Talking openly about race thwarts racism in children. *Monitor of the American Psychological Association, 28*(6), 33.

Burnham, D. K., & Harris, M. B. (1992). Effects of real gender and labeled gender on adults' perceptions of infants. *Journal of Genetic Psychology, 153,* 165–183.

Burns, G. W., & Bottino, P. J. (1989). *The science of genetics* (6th ed.). New York: Macmillan.

Burns, L. H. (1990). An exploratory study of perceptions of parenting after infertility. *Family Systems Medicine, 8,* 177–189.

Burns, N. R., & Nettelbeck, T. (2003). Inspection time in the structure of cognitive abilities: Where does IT fit? *Intelligence, 31,* 237–255.

Burns, Y., O'Callaghan, McDonell, B., & Rogers, Y. (2004). Movement and motor development in ELBW infants at 1 year is related to cognitive and motor abilities at 4 years. *Early Human Development, 80,* 19–29.

Burton, L. M. (1990). Teenage childrearing as an alternative life-course strategy in multigenerational black families. *Human Nature, 1,* 123–143.

Burton, R. V. (1963). The generality of honesty reconsidered. *Psychological Review, 70,* 481–499.

Burton, R. V. (1976). Honesty and dishonesty. In T. Lickona (Ed.), *Moral development and behavior.* New York: Holt, Rinehart & Winston.

Busch-Rossnagel, N. A. (1997). Mastery motivation in toddlers. *Infants and Young Children, 9,* 1–11.

Bushman, B. J., & Anderson, C. R. (2002). Violent video games and hostile expectancies: A test for general aggression model. *Personality and Social Psychology Bulletin, 28,* 1679–1686.

Bushman, B. J., & Cantor, J. (2003). Media ratings for violence and sex: Implications for policymakers and parents. *American Psychologists, 58,* 130–141.

Bushman, B., & Husemann, L. R. (2001). Effects of televised violence on aggression. In D. Singer & J. Singer (Eds.), *Handbook of children and the media* (pp. 223–254). Thousand Oaks, CA: Sage.

Bushnell, E. W., & Boudreau, J. P. (1993). Motor development and the mind: The potential role of motor abilities as a determinant of aspects of perceptual development. *Child Development, 64,* 1005–1021.

Bushnell, I.W.R., & Sai, F. Z. (1989). Neonatal recognition of the mother's face. *British Journal of Developmental Psychology, 7,* 3–15.

Buss, A. H., & Plomin, R. (1984). *Temperament: Early developing personality traits.* Hillsdale, NJ: Erlbaum.

Buss, D. M. (1995). Psychological sex differences: Origins through sexual selection. *American Psychologist, 50,* 164–168.

Buss, D. M. (2000). Evolutionary psychology. In A. Kazdin (Ed.), *Encyclopedia of psychology.* Washington, DC, & New York: American Psychological Association and Oxford University Press.

Buss, K. A., & Goldsmith, H. H. (1998). Fear and anger regulation in infancy: Effects on temporal dynamics of affective expression. *Child Development, 69,* 359–374.

Bussell, D. A., Neiderhiser, J. M., Pike, A., Plomin, R., Simmens, S., Howe, G. W., Hetherington, E. M., Carroll, E., & Reiss, D. (1999). Adolescents' relationships to siblings and mothers: A multivariate genetic analysis. *Developmental Psychology, 35,* 1248–1259.

Bussey, K. (1999). Children's categorization and evaluation of different kinds of lies and truths. *Child Development, 70,* 1338–1347.

Bussey, K., & Bandura, A. (1992). Self-regulatory mechanisms governing gender development. *Child Development, 63,* 1236–1250.

Bussey, K., & Bandura, A. (1999). Social cognitive theory of gender development and differentiation. *Psychological Review, 106,* 676–713.

Butcher, C., & Goldin-Meadow, S. (2000). Gesture and the transition from one- to two-word speech: When hand and mouth come together. In D. McNeill (Ed.), *Language and gesture: Window into thought and action.* Cambridge, England: Cambridge University Press.

Butler, R. (1998). Age trends in the use of social and temporal comparison for self–evaluation: Examination of a novel developmental hypothesis. *Child Development, 69,* 1054–1073.

Butler, R. (1999). Information seeking and achievement motivation in middle childhood and adolescence: The role of conceptions of ability. *Developmental Psychology, 35,* 146–163.

Butler, R., & Ruzany, N. (1993). Age and socialization effects on the development of social comparison motives and normative ability assessment in kibbutz and urban children. *Child Development, 64,* 532–543.

Butterfield, E. C., & Siperstein, G. N. (1972). Influence of contingent auditory stimulation on non-nutritional suckle. In J. F. Bosma (Ed.), *Third symposium on oral sensation and perception: The mouth of the infant.* Springfield, IL: Charles C. Thomas.

Byrnes, J. P., & Fox, N. A. (1998). The educational relevance of research in cognitive neuroscience. *Educational Psychology Review, 10,* 297–342.

Byrnes, J. P., & Takahira, S. (1993). Explaining gender differences on SAT-math items. *Developmental Psychology, 29,* 805–810.

Cabaniss, M. L. (1996). Amniocentesis. In J. A. Kuller, N. C. Cheschier, & R. C. Cefalo (Eds.), *Prenatal diagnosis and reproductive genetics* (pp. 136–144). St. Louis: Mosby.

Cabrera, N. J., Tamis-LeMonda, C.S., Bradley, R. H., Hofferth, S., & Lamb, M.E. (2000). Fatherhood in the twenty-first century. *Child Development, 71,* 127–136.

Cairns, R. B., Leung, M., Buchanan, L., & Cairns, B. D. (1995). Friendships and social networks in childhood and adolescence: Fluidity, reliability, and interrelations. *Child Development, 66,* 1330–1345.

Caldera, Y. M., Huston, A. C., & O'Brien, M. (1989). Social interactions and play patterns of parents and toddlers with feminine, masculine, and neutral toys. *Child Development, 60,* 70–76.

Caldwell, B. M., & Bradley, R. H. (1984). *Manual for the home observation for measurement of the environment.* Little Rock: University of Arkansas Press.

Caldwell, C. H., Zimmerman, M. A., Bernat, D. H., Sellers, R. M., & Notaro, P. C. (2002). Racial identity, maternal support, and psychological distress among African American adolescents. *Child Development, 73,* 1322–1336.

Caldwell, M. S., Rudolph, K. D., Troop-Gordon, W., & Kim, D. (2004). Reciprocal influences among relational self-views, social disengagement, and peer status during early adolescence. *Child Development, 75,* 1140–1154.

Caldwell, P. (1996). Child survival: Physical vulnerability and resilience in adversity in the European past and the contemporary third world. *Social Science and Medicine, 43,* 609–619.

Calicchia, J. A., & Santostefano, S. (2004). The assessment of interrogative suggestibility in adolescents: Modalities, gender, and cognitive control. *North American Journal of Psychology, 6,* 1–12.

Callanan, M. A., & Sabbagh, M. A. (2004). Multiple labels for objects in conversations with young children: Parents' language and children's developing expectations about word meanings. *Developmental Psychology, 40,* 746–763.

Cameron-Faulkner, T., Lieven, E., & Tomasello, M. (2003). A construction based analysis of child directed speech. *Cognitive Science,* 843–873.

Campbell, F. A., & Ramey, C. T. (1994). Effects of early intervention on intellectual andacademic achievement: A follow-up study of children from low-income families. *Child Development, 65,* 684–698.

Campbell, F. A., & Ramey, C. T. (1995). Cognitive and school outcomes for high-risk African American students at middle adolescence: Positive effects of early intervention. *American Educational Research Journal, 32,* 743–772.

Campbell, F. A., Pungello, E. P., Miller-Johnson, S., Burchinal, M., & Ramey, C. T. (2001). The development of cognitive and academic abilities: Growth curves from an early childhood education experiment. *Developmental Psychology, 37,* 231–242.

Campbell, R., & Sais, E. (1995). Accelerated metalinguistic (phonological) awareness in bilingual children. *British Journal of Developmental Psychology, 13,* 61–68.

Campbell, S. B., Cohn, J. F., & Meyers, T. (1995). Depression in first-time mothers: Mother–infant interaction and depression chronicity. *Developmental Psychology, 31,* 349–357.

Campbell, S. B., Cohn, J. F., Flanagan, C., Popper, S., & Meyers, T. (1992). Course and correlates of postpartum depression during the transition to parenthood. *Development and Psychopathology, 4,* 29–47.

Campos, J. J., Bertenthal, B. I., & Kermoian, R. (1992). Early experience and emotional development: The emergence of wariness of heights. *Psychological Science, 3,* 61–64.

Campos, J. J., Frankel, C. B., & Camras, L. (2004). On the nature of emotion regulation. *Child Development, 75,* 377–394.

Campos, J. J., Langer, A., & Krowitz, A. (1970). Cardiac responses on the visual cliff in prelocomotor human infants. *Science, 170,* 196–197.

Campos, R. G. (1989). Soothing pain-elicited distress in infants with swaddling and pacifiers. *Child Development, 60,* 781–792.

Camras, L. A., Oster, H., Campos, J. J., Miyake, K., & Bradshaw, D. (1992). Japanese and American infants' responses to arm restraint. *Developmental Psychology, 28,* 578–583.

Canfield, R. L., & Smith, E. G. (1996). Number-based expectations and sequential enumeration by 5-month-old infants. *Developmental Psychology, 32,* 269–279.

Canpolat, B. I., Orsel, S., Akdemir, A., & Ozbay, M. H. (2005). The relationship between dieting and body image, body ideal, self-perception, and body mass index in Turkish adolescents. *International Journal of Eating Disorders, 37,* 150–155.

Canter, R. J., & Ageton, S. S. (1984). The epidemiology of adolescent sex-role attitudes. *Sex Roles, 11,* 657–676.

Cantwell, D. P. (1996). Attention deficit disorder: A review of the past 10 years. *Journal of the American Academy of the Child and Adolescent Psychiatry, 35,* 978–987.

Capaldi, D. M., Dishion, T. J., Stoolmiller, M., & Yoerger, K. (2001). Aggression toward female partners by at-risk young men: The contribution of male adolescent friendships. *Developmental Psychology, 37,* 61–73.

Caplan, M., Vespo, J., Pedersen, J., & Hay, D. F. (1991). Conflict and its resolution in small groups of one- and two-year-olds. *Child Development, 62,* 1513–1524.

Caputo, D. V., & Mandell, W. (1970). Consequences of low birth weight. *Developmental Psychology, 3,* 363–383.

Carlson, E. A. (1998). A prospective longitudinal study of attachment disorganization / disorientation. *Child Development, 69,* 1107–1128.

Carlson, S. M., Moses, L. J., & Claxton, L. J. (2004). Individual differences in executive functioning and theory of mind: An investigation of inhibitory control and planning ability. *Journal of Experimental Child Psychology, 87,* 299–319.

Carlson, S. M., Moses, L. J., & Hix, H. R. (1998). The role of inhibitory processes in young children's difficulties with deception and false belief. *Child Development, 69,* 672–691.

Carlson, V., Cicchetti, D., Barnett, D., & Braunwald, K. (1989). Disorganized / disoriented attachment relationships in maltreated infants. *Developmental Psychology, 25,* 525–531.

Carpendale, J. I. M. (2000). Kohlberg and Piaget on stages of moral reasoning. *Developmental Review, 20,* 181–205.

Carpenter, T. P., & Moser, J. M. (1982). The development of addition and subtraction problem-solving skills. In T. P. Carpenter, J. M. Moser, & T. A. Romberg (Eds.), *Addition and subtraction: A cognitive perspective.* Hillsdale, NJ: Erlbaum.

Carr, J. (1995). *Down syndrome: Children growing up.* Cambridge, UK: Cambridge University Press.

Carraher, T. N., Carraher, D., & Schliemann, A. D. (1985). Mathematics in the streets and in the schools. *British Journal of Developmental Psychology, 3,* 21–29.

Carrington, D. (1995). Infections. In M. J. Whittle & J. M. Connor (Eds.), *Prenatal diagnosis in obstetric practice* (2nd. ed., pp. 100–113). Oxford, England: Blackwell.

Carroll, J. B. (1993). *Human cognitive abilities: A survey of factor-analytic studies.* Cambridge, England: University of Cambridge Press.

Carroll, L. (1988). Concern with AIDS and the sexual behavior of college students. *Journal of Marriage and the Family, 50,* 405–411.

Carver, L. J., & Bauer, P. J. (1999). When the event is more than the sum of its parts: Individual differences in 9-month-olds' long-term ordered recall. *Memory, 7,* 147–174.

Casasola, M. (2005). When less is more: How infants learn to form an abstract categorical representation of support. *Child Development, 76,* 279–290.

Casasola, M., & Cohen, L. B. (2000). Infants' association of linguistic labels with causal actions. *Developmental Psychology, 36,* 155–168.

Case, R. (1992). *The mind's staircase: Exploring the conceptual underpinnings of children's thought and knowledge.* Hillsdale, NJ: Erlbaum.

Case, R., & Okamoto, Y. (1996). The role of central conceptual structures in the development of children's thought. *Monographs of the Society for Research in Child Development, 61,* (1–2, Serial No. 246).

Casey, M. B. (1996). Understanding individual differences in spatial ability within females: A nature / nurture interactions framework. *Developmental Review, 16,* 241–260.

Casey, M. B., Nuttall, R. L., & Pezaris, E. (1997). Mediators of gender differences in mathematics college entrance test scores: A comparison of spatial skills with internalized beliefs and anxieties. *Developmental Psychology, 33,* 669–680.

Casey, W. M., & Burton, R. V. (1982). Training children to be consistently honest through verbal self-instructions. *Child Development, 53,* 911–919.

Caspi, A., & Silva, P. A. (1995). Temperamental qualities at age three predict personality traits in young adulthood: Longitudinal evidence from a birth cohort. *Child Development, 66,* 486–498.

Caspi, A., Elder, G. H., Jr., & Bem, D. J. (1988). Moving away from the world: Life-course patterns of shy children. *Developmental Psychology, 24,* 824–831.

Caspi, A., Lynam, D., Moffitt, T. E., & Silva, P. A. (1993). Unraveling girls' delinquency: Biological, dispositional, and contextual contributors to adolescent misbehavior. *Developmental Psychology, 29,* 19–30.

Caspi, A., Moffitt, T. E., Morgan, J., Rutter, M., Taylor, A., Arseneault, L., Tully, L., Jacobs, C., Kim-Cohen, J., & Polo-Tomas, M. (2004). Maternal expressed emotion predicts children's antisocial behavior problems: Using monozygotic-twin differences to identify environmental effects on behavioral development. *Developmental Psychology, 40,* 149–161.

Cassel, W. S., & Bjorklund, D. F. (1995). Developmental patterns of eyewitness memory and suggestibility: An ecologically based short-term longitudinal study. *Law & Human Behavior, 19,* 507–532.

Cassidy, J., & Asher, S. R. (1992). Loneliness and peer relations in young children. *Child Development, 63,* 350–365.

Cassidy, J., & Berlin, L. J. (1994). The insecure/ambivalent pattern of attachment: Theory and research. *Child Development, 65,* 971–991.

Cassidy, J., Aikins, J. W., & Chernoff, J. J. (2003). Children's peer selection: Experimental examination of the role of self-perceptions. *Developmental Psychology, 39,* 495–508.

Cassidy, J., Kirsh, S. J., Scolton, K. L., & Parke, R. D. (1996). Attachment and representations of peer relationships. *Developmental Psychology, 32,* 892–904.

Cassidy, K. W. (1998). Preschoolers' use of desires to solve theory of mind problems in a pretense context. *Developmental Psychology, 34,* 503–511.

Casteel, M. A. (1993). Effects of inference necessity and reading goal on children's inferential generation. *Developmental Psychology, 29,* 346–357.

Cates, W., Jr. (1995). Sexually transmitted diseases. In B. P. Sachs, R. Beard, E. Papiernik, & C. Russell (Eds.), *Reproductive health care for women and babies* (pp. 57–84). New York: Oxford University Press.

Cattell, R. B. (1963). Theory of fluid and crystallized intelligence: A critical experiment. *Journal of Educational Psychology, 54,* 1–22.

Cauffman, E., & Steinberg, L. S. (1996). Interactive effects of menarcheal status and dating on dieting and disordered eating among adolescent girls. *Developmental Psychology, 32,* 631–635.

Caughy, M. O. (1996). Health and environmental effects on the academic readiness of school age children. *Developmental Psychology, 32,* 515–522.

Caughy, M. O., O'Campo, P. J., Randolph, S. M., & Nickerson, K. (2002). The influences of racial socialization practices on the cognitive and behavioral competencies of African American preschoolers. *Child Development, 73,* 1611–1625.

Cavanaugh, J. C., & Perlmutter, M. (1982). Metamemory: A critical examination. *Child Development, 53,* 11–28.

Ceci, S. J. (1991). How much does schooling influence general intelligence and its cognitive components? A reassessment of the evidence. *Developmental Psychology, 27,* 703–722.

Ceci, S. J., & Bruck, M. (1998). Children's testimony: Applied and basic issues. In I. E. Sigel & K. A. Renninger (Vol. Eds.) *Child psychology in practice,* Vol. 4. In W. Damon (Gen. Ed.), *Handbook of child psychology.* New York: Wiley.

Ceci, S. J., & Williams, W. W. (1997). Schooling, intelligence, and income. *American Psychologist, 52,* 1051–1058.

Ceci, S. J., Loftus, E. F., Leichtman, M., & Bruck, M. (1994). The role of source misattributions in the creation of false beliefs among preschoolers. *International Journal of Clinical and Experimental Hypnosis, 62,* 304–320.

Cefalo, R. C. (1996). Prevention of neural tube defects. In J. A. Kuller, N. C. Cheschier, & R. C. Cefalo (Eds.), *Prenatal diagnosis and reproductive genetics* (pp. 2–9). St. Louis: Mosby.

Cernoch, J. M., & Porter, R. H. (1985). Recognition of maternal axillary odors by infants. *Child Development, 56,* 1593–1598.

Cervantes, C. A., & Callanan, M. A. (1998). Labels and explanations in mother-child emotion talk: Age and gender differentiation. *Developmental Psychology, 34,* 88–98.

Chalmers, J. B., & Townsend, M. A. R. (1990). The effects of training in social perspective taking on socially maladjusted girls. *Child Development, 61,* 178–190.

Chan, R. W., Raboy, B., & Patterson, C. J. (1998). Psychosocial adjustment among children conceived via donor insemination by lesbian and heterosexual mothers. *Child Development, 69,* 443–457.

Chandler, M. J., Lalonde, C. E., Sokol, B. W., & Hallett, D. (2003). Personal persistence, identity development, and suicide. *Monographs of the Society for Research in Child Development, 68* (No. 2, Serial No. 273).

Chandler, M., Sokol, B. W., & Wainryb, C. (2000). Beliefs and truth and beliefs about rightness. *Child Development, 71,* 91–97.

Chandler, S., & Field, P. A. (1997). Becoming a father: First-time fathers' experience of labor and delivery. *Journal of Nurse-Midwifery, 42,* 17–24.

Chang, L., Schwartz, D., Dodge, K. A., & McBride-Chang, C. (2003). Harsh parenting in relation to child emotion regulation and aggression. *Journal of Family Psychology, 17,* 598–606.

Chao, R. (2001). Extending research on the consequences of parenting style for Chinese Americans and European Americans. *Child Development, 72,* 1832–1843.

Chao, R. K. (1994). Beyond parental control and authoritarian parenting style: Understanding Chinese parenting through the cultural notion of training. *Child Development, 65,* 1111–1119.

Chao, R. K. (2001). Extending research on the consequences of parenting style for Chinese Americans and European American. *Child Development, 72,* 1832–1843.

Chapman, M., & Lindenberger, U. (1988). Functions, operations, and decalage in the development of transitivity. *Developmental Psychology, 24,* 542–551.

Chapman, M., Zahn-Waxler, C., Cooperman, G., & Iannotti, R. J. (1987). Empathy and responsibility in the motivation of children's helping. *Developmental Psychology, 23,* 140–145.

Charlesworth, W. R. (1992). Darwin and developmental psychology: Past and present. *Developmental Psychology, 28,* 5–16.

Chase-Lansdale, P. L., Cherlin, A. J., & Kiernan, K. E. (1995). The long-term effects of parental divorce on the mental health of young adults: A developmental perspective. *Child Development, 66,* 1614–1634.

Chavkin, W. (1995). Substance abuse in pregnancy. In B. P. Sachs, R. Beard, E. Papiernik, & C. Russell (Eds.), *Reproductive health care for women and babies* (pp. 305–321). New York: Oxford University Press.

Chavous, T. M., Bernat, D. H., Schmeelk-Cone, K., Caldwell, C. H., Kohn-Wood, L., & Zimmerman, M. A. (2003). Racial identity and academic attainment among African American adolescents. *Child Development, 74,* 1076–1090.

Chen, C., & Stevenson, H. W. (1995). Motivation and mathematics achievement: a comparative study of Asian-American, Caucasian-American, and East Asian high school students. *Child Development, 66,* 1215–1234.

Chen, C., Li, D., Li, Z., Li, B., & Liu, M. (2000). Sociable and prosocial dimensions of social competence in Chinese children: Unique contributions to social, academic, and psychological adjustment. *Developmental Psychology, 36,* 302–314.

Chen, X. (2000). Growing up in a collectivist culture: Socialization and socioemotional development in Chinese children. In A. L. Comunian & U. P. Gielen (Eds.), *Human development in cross-culture perspective.* Padua, Italy: Cedam.

Chen, X., Cen, G., Li, D, & He, Y. (2005). Social functioning and adjustment in Chinese children: The imprint of historical time. *Child Development, 76,* 182–195.

Chen, X., Chang, L., & He, Y. (2003). The peer group as a context: Mediating and moderating effects on relations between academic achievement and social functioning in Chinese children. *Child Development, 74,* 710–727.

Chen, X., Hastings, P. D., Rubin, X. H., Sen, G., & Stewart, S. L. (1998). Child-rearing attitudes and behavioral inhibition in Chinese and Canadian toddlers: A cross-cultural study. *Developmental Psychology, 34,* 677–686.

Chen, X., Rubin, K. H., & Li, D. (1997). Relation between academic achievement and social adjustment: Evidence from Chinese children. *Developmental Psychology, 33,* 518–525.

Chen, X., Rubin, K. H., & Li, Z. (1995). Social functioning and adjustment in Chinese children: A longitudinal study. *Developmental Psychology, 31,* 531–539.

Chen, X., Rubin, K. H., & Sun, Y. (1992). Social reputation in Chinese and Canadian children: A cross–cultural study. *Child Development, 63,* 1336–1343.

Chen, X., Rubin, K. M., & Li, D. (1997). Relation between academic achievement and social adjustment: Evidence from Chinese children. *Developmental Psychology, 33,* 518–525.

Chen, Z., & Klahr, D. (1999). All other things being equal: Acquisition and transfer of the control of variables strategy. *Child Development, 70,* 1098–1120.

Chen, Z., Sanchez, R. P., & Campbell, T. (1997). From beyond to within their grasp: The rudiments of analogical problem solving in 10- and 13-month olds. *Developmental Psychology, 33,* 790–801.

Cherlin, A. J., Kiernan, K. E., & Chase-Lansdale, P. L. (1995). Parental divorce in childhood and demographic outcomes in young adulthood. *Demography, 32,* 299–318.

Cheschier, N. C. (1996). Overview of obstetric sonography. In J. A. Kuller, N. C. Cheschier, R. C., & Cefalo (Eds.), *Prenatal diagnosis and reproductive genetics.* St. Louis: Mosby.

Chess, S., & Thomas, R. (1984). *Origins and evolution of behavior disorders.* New York: Brunner/Mazel.

Chi, M. H. T. (1978). Knowledge structures and memory development. In R. S. Siegler (Ed.), *Children's thinking: What develops?* (pp. 73–96). Hillsdale, NJ: Erlbaum.

Chomitz, V. R., Cheung, L. W. Y., & Lieberman, E. (2000). The role of lifestyle in preventing low birth weight. In K. L. Freiberg (Ed.), *Human development 00/01* (28th ed., pp. 18–28). Guilford, CT: Dushkin/McGraw-Hill.

Chomsky, N. (1959). A review of B. F. Skinner's *Verbal Behavior. Language, 35,* 26–129.

Chomsky, N. (1968). *Language and mind.* San Diego, CA: Harcourt Brace Jovanovich.

Christopherson, E. R. (1989). Injury control. *American Psychologist, 44,* 237–241.

Chuah, Y. M. L., & Maybery, M. T. (1999). Verbal and spatial short-term memory: Common sources of developmental change? *Journal of Experimental Child Psychology, 73,* 7–44.

Cialdini, R. B. (2001). *Influence: Science and practice* (4th ed.). Boston: Allyn & Bacon.

Ciliska, D., Mastilli, P., Pioeg, J., Hayward, S., Brunton, G., & Underwood, J. (2001). The effectiveness of home visiting as a delivery strategy for public health nursing interventions to clients in the prenatal and post-natal period: A systematic review. *Primary Health Care Research and Development, 2,* 41–54.

Cillessen, A. H. N. (2004). From censure to reinforcement: Developmental changes in the association between aggression and social status. *Child Development, 75,* 147–163.

Cillessen, A. H. N., & Bukowski, W. M. (Eds.) (2000). *New directions for child and adolescent development: No. 88: Recent advances in the measurement of acceptance and rejection in the peer system.* San Francisco, CA: Jossey-Bass.

Cillessen, A. H. N., & Mayeux, L. (2004). From censure to reinforcement: Developmental changes in the association between aggression and social status. *Child Development, 75,* 147–163.

Clahsen, H., Hadler, M., & Weyerts, H. (2004). Speeded production of inflected words in children and adults. *Journal of Child Language, 31,* 683–712.

Clark, E. V. (1973). What's in a word? On the child's acquisition of semantics in his first language. In T. E. Moore (Ed.), *Cognitive development and the acquisition of language.* Orlando, FL: Academic Press.

Clark, H. H., & Clark, E. V. (1977). *Psychology and language: An introduction to psycholinguistics.* San Diego, CA: Harcourt Brace Jovanovich.

Clark, K. E., & Ladd, G. W. (2000). Connectedness and autonomy support in parent-child relationships: Links to children's socioemotional orientation and peer relationships. *Developmental Psychology, 36,* 485–498.

Clarke, R., Hyde, J. S., Essex, J., & Klein, M. H. (1997). Length of maternity leave and quality of mother-infant interactions. *Child Development, 68,* 364–383.

Clarke-Stewart, K. A., & Hayward, C. (1996). Advantages of father custody and contact for the psychological well-being of school-age children. *Journal of Applied Developmental Psychology, 17,* 239–270.

Clarkson, M. G., & Berg, W. K. (1983). Cardiac orienting and vowel discrimination in newborns: Crucial stimulus parameters. *Child Development, 54,* 162–171.

Clary, E. G., & Snyder, M. (1991). A functional analysis of altruism and prosocial behavior: The case of volunteerism. *Review of Personality and Social Psychology, 12,* 119–148.

Clausen, J. A. (1975). The social meaning of differential physical maturation. In D. E. Drugastin & G. H. Elder (Eds.), *Adolescence in the life cycle.* New York: Halsted Press.

Clearfield, M. W. (2004). The role of crawling and walking experience in infant spatial memory. *Journal of Experimental Child Psychology, 89,* 214–241.

Clements, D. H. (1990). Metacomponential development in a Logo programming environment. *Journal of Educational Psychology, 82,* 141–149.

Clements, D. H. (1991). Enhancement of creativity in computer environments. *American Educational Research Journal, 28,* 173–187.

Clements, D. H. (1995). Teaching creativity with computers. *Educational Psychology Review, 7,* 141–161.

Clements, D. H., & Nastasi, B. K. (1992). Computers and early childhood education. In M. Gettinger, S. N. Elliott, & T. R. Kratochwill (Eds.), *Advances in school psychology: Preschool and early childhood treatment directions.* Hillsdale, NJ: Erlbaum.

Clifton, R. K., Muir, D. W., Ashmead, D. H., & Clarkson, M. G. (1993). Is visually guided reaching in early infancy a myth? *Child Development, 64,* 1099–1110.

Cnattingius, S. (2004). The epidemiology of smoking during pregnancy: Smoking prevalence, maternal characteristics, and pregnancy outcomes. *Nicotine & Tobacco Research, 6,* S125–S140.

Cnattingius, S., Hultman, C. M., Dahl, M., & Sparén, P. (1999). Very preterm birth, birth trauma, and the risk of anorexia nervosa among young girls. *Archives of General Psychiatry, 56,* 634–638.

Coates, B., & Hartup, W. W. (1969). Age and verbalization in observational learning. *Developmental Psychology, 1,* 556–562.

Cognitive-ability testing? *American Psychologist, 47,* 1083–1101.

Cohen, D., & Strayer, J. (1996). Empathy in conduct disordered and comparison youth. *Developmental Psychology, 32,* 988–998.

Cohen, M. (1996). Preschooler's practical thinking and problem solving: The acquisition of an optimal solution. *Cognitive Development, 11,* 357–373.

Cohen, S., & Williamson, G. M. (1991). Stress and infectious disease in humans. *Psychological Bulletin, 109,* 5–24.

Coie, J. D., & Dodge, K. A. (1983). Continuities and changes in children's social status: A five–year longitudinal study. *Merrill-Palmer Quarterly, 19,* 261–282.

Coie, J. D., & Dodge, K. A. (1998). Aggression and antisocial behavior. In N. Eisenberg (Ed), W. Damon (Series Ed.), *Handbook of child psychology: Vol. 3, Social, emotional, and personality development* (pp. 779–862). New York: Wiley.

Coie, J. D., & Kupersmidt, J. B. (1983). A behavioral analysis of emerging social status in boys' groups. *Child Development, 54,* 1400–1416.

Coie, J. D., Dodge, K. A., & Coppotelli, H. (1982). Dimensions and types of social status: A cross-age perspective. *Developmental Psychology, 18,* 557–570.

Coie, J. D., Dodge, K. A., & Kupersmidt, J. B. (1990). Peer group behavior and social status. In S. R. Asher & J. D. Coie (Eds.), *Peer rejection in childhood.* Cambridge, England: Cambridge University Press.

Coie, J. D., Dodge, K. A., Terry, R., & Wright, V. (1991). The role of aggression in peer relations: An analysis of aggression episodes in boys' play groups. *Child Development, 62,* 812–826.

Colby, A., & Kohlberg, L. (1987). *The measurement of moral judgment* (Vol. 1): *Theoretical foundations and research validation.* Cambridge: Cambridge University Press.

Colby, A., Kohlberg, L., Gibbs, J., & Lieberman, M. (1983). A longitudinal study of moral judgment. *Monographs of the Society for Research in Child Development, 48* (Nos. 1–2, Serial No. 200).

Cole, D. A., Martin, J. M., Peeke, L. A., Seroczynski, A. D., & Fier, J. (1999). Children's over- and underestimation of academic competence: A longitudinal study of gender differences, depression, and anxiety. *Child Development, 70,* 459–473.

Cole, D. A., Maxwell, S. E., Martin, J. M., Peake, L. G. Scoroczynski, A. D., Tram, J. M., Hoffman, K. B., Ruiz, M. D., Jicquez, F., & Maschman, T. (2001). The development of multiple domains of child and adolescent self-concept: A cohort sequential longitudinal design. *Child Development, 72,* 1723–1746.

Cole, M. (1990). Cognitive development and formal schooling: The evidence from cross-cultural research. In L. C. Moll (Ed.), *Vygotsky and education.* New York: Cambridge University Press.

Cole, M. (2005). Culture in development. In M. H. Bornstein & M. E. Lamb, *Developmental science: An advanced textbook* (5th ed.). Mahwah, NJ: Lawrence Erlbaum Associates.

Cole, M., & Scribner, S. (1977). Cross-cultural studies of memory and cognition. In R. V. Kail & J. W. Hagen (Eds.), *Perspectives on the development of memory and cognition.* Hillsdale, NJ: Erlbaum.

Cole, P. M., & Tamang, B. L. (1998). Nepali Children's ideas about emotional displays in hypothetical challenges. *Developmental Psychology, 34,* 640–646.

Cole, P. M., Barrett, K. C., & Zahn-Waxler, C. (1992). Emotion displays in two-year-olds during mishaps. *Child Development, 63,* 314–324.

Cole, P. M., Martin, S. E., & Dennis, T. A. (2004). Emotion regulation as a scientific construct: Methodological challenges and directions for child development research. *Child Development, 75,* 317–333.

Coleman, L., & Coleman, J. (2002). The measurement of puberty: A review. *Journal of Adolescence, 25,* 535.

Coley, R. L. (1998). Children's socialization experiences and functioning in single-mother households: The importance of fathers and other men. *Child Development, 69,* 219–230.

Coley, R. L., & Chase-Lansdale, P. L. (1998). Adolescent pregnancy and parenthood: Recent evidence and future directions. *American Psychologist, 53,* 152–166.

Colley, A., Griffiths, D., Hugh, M., Landers, K., & Jaggli, N. (1996). Childhood play and adolescent leisure preferences: Associations with gender typing and the presence of siblings. *Sex Roles, 35,* 233–245.

Collie, R., & Hayne, R. (1999). Deferred imitation by 6- and 9-month-old infants: More evidence for declarative memory. *Developmental Psychobiology, 35,* 83–90.

Collins, W. A. (1983). Interpretation and inference in children's television viewing. In J. R. Bryant & D. R. Anderson (Eds.), *Children's understanding of television: Research on attention and comprehension.* New York: Academic Press.

Collins, W. A., Maccoby, E. E., Steinberg, L., Hetherington, E. M., & Bornstein, M. H. (2000). Contemporary research on parenting: The case for nature and nurture. *American Psychologist, 55,* 218–232.

Collins, W. A., Sobol, B. L., & Westby, S. (1981). Effects of adult commentary on children's comprehension and inferences about a televised aggressive portrayal. *Child Development, 52,* 158–163.

Collis, B. A. (1996). *Children and computers at school.* Mahwah, NJ: Erlbaum.

Colombo, J., & Horowtiz, F. D. (1987). Behavioral state as a lead variable in neonatal research. *Merrill-Palmer Quarterly, 33,* 423–437.

Colton, P., Olmsted, M., Daneman, D., Rydall, A., & Rodin, G. (2004). *Diabetes Care, 27,* 1654–1659.

Columbo, J. (1993). *Infant cognition: Predicting later intellectual functioning.* Newbury Park, CA: Sage.

Colwell, M. J., Mize, J., Pettit, G. S., & Laird, R. D. (2002). Contextual determinants of mothers' interventions in young children's peer interactions. *Developmental Psychology, 38,* 492–502.

Comstock, G. A. (1993). The medium and society: The role of television in American life. In G. L. Berry & J. K. Asamen (Eds.), *Children and television: Images in a changing sociocultural world* (pp. 117–131). Newbury Park, CA: Sage.

Condry, J., & Condry, S. (1976). Sex differences: A study in the eye of the beholder. *Child Development, 47,* 812–819.

Conger, R. D., Conger, K. J., Elder, G. H., Jr., Lonren, F. O., Simons, R. L., & Whitbeck, L. B. (1992). A family process model of economic hardship and adjustment of early adolescent boys. *Child Development, 63,* 527–541.

Conger, R. D., Patterson, G. R., & Ge, X. (1995). It takes two to replicate: A mediational model for the impact of parents' stress on adolescent adjustment. *Child Development, 66,* 80–97.

Conger, R. D., Wallace, L. B., Sun, Y., Simons, R. L., McLoyd, V., & Brody, G. H. (2002). Economic pressure in African American families: A replication and extension of the family stress model. *Developmental Psychology, 38,* 179–193.

Connell, J. P., Spencer, M. B., & Aber, J. L. (1994). Educational risk and resilience in African–American youth: Context, self, action, and outcomes in school. *Child Development, 65,* 493–506.

Connolly, J., Furman, W., & Konarski, R. (2000). The role of peers in the emergence of heterosexual romantic relationships in adolescence. *Child Development, 71,* 1395–1408.

Connor, J. M. (1995). Prenatal diagnosis of single-gene disorders by DNA analysis. In M. J. Whittle & J. M. Connor (Eds.), *Prenatal diagnosis in obstetric practice* (2nd ed., pp. 86–99). Oxford, England: Blackwell.

Cook, T. D., Appleton, H., Conner, R. F., Shaffer, A., Tabkin, G., & Weber, J. S. (1975). *Sesame Street revisited.* New York: Russell Sage Foundation.

Cook, W. L. (2001). Interpersonal influence in the family systems: A social relations model analysis. *Child Development, 72,* 1179–1197.

Cook-Darzens, S., Doyen, C., Falissard, B., & Mouren, M.-C. (2005). Self-perceived family functioning in 40 French families of anorexic adolescents: Implications for therapy. *European Eating Disorders Review, 13,* 223–236.

Cooke, R., & Sawyer, S. M. (2004). Eating disorders in adolescence: An approach to diagnosis and management. *Australian Family Physician, 33,* 27–31.

Coon, H., Fulker, D. W., DeFries, J. C., & Plomin, R. (1990). Home environment and cognitive ability of 7-year-old children in the Colorado Adoption Project: Genetic and environmental etiologies. *Developmental Psychology, 26,* 459–468.

Coontz, S. (2000). Historical perspective on family diversity. In D. H. Demo, K. R. Allen, & M. A. Fine (Eds.), *Handbook of family diversity.* New York: Oxford University Press.

Cooper, R. P., & Aslin, R. N. (1990). Preference for infant-directed speech in the first month after birth. *Child Development, 61,* 1585–1595.

Coopersmith, S. (1967). *The antecedents of self-esteem.* New York: W. H. Freeman.

Coplan, R. J. (2000). Assessing nonsocial play in early childhood: Conceptual and methodological approaches. In K. Gitlin-Weiner, A Sandgrund, & C. Schaefer, (Eds.), *Play diagnosis and assessment* (2nd ed.) (pp. 563–598). New York: Wiley.

Coplan, R. J., Gauinski-Molina, M., Lagace-Sequin, D. G., & Wichman, C. (2001). When girls versus boys play alone: Nonsocial play and adjustment in kindergarten. *Developmental Psychology, 27,* 464–474.

Corah, N. L., Anthony, E. J., Painter, P., Stern, J. A., & Thurston, D. (1965). Effects of perinatal anoxia after seven years. *Psychological Monographs, 79* (3, Whole No. 596).

Corbin, C. (1973). *A textbook of motor development.* Dubuque, IA: William C. Brown.

Corcoran, J. (2001). Multi-systemic influences on the family functioning of teens attending pregnancy prevention programs. *Child & Adolescent Social Work Journal, 18,* 37–49.

Coren, S., Porac, C., & Duncan, P. (1981). Lateral preference behaviors in preschool children and young adults. *Child Development, 52,* 443–450.

Cormier, C., Shin, H-E., Caen, L., Rosenberg, J. S., Bering, J. M., Hernández Blasi, C., & Bjorklund, D. F. (April 2004). *Developmental regularities in reasoning about the psychology of sleep.* Paper presented at the Conference on Human Development, Washington, DC.

Cornelius, M. D., Goldschmidt, L., Day, N. L., & Larkby, C. (2002). Alcohol, tobacco and marijuana use among pregnant teenagers: 6-year follow-up of offspring growth effects. *Neurotoxicology & Teratology, 24,* 703–710.

Corsini, R. J. (ed.) (1994). *Encyclopedia of Psychology, vol.1.* (p. 474) New York: John Wiley & Sons.

Corteen, R. S., & Williams, T. (1986). Television and reading skills. In T. Williams (Ed.), *The impact of television: A natural experiment in three communities.* Orlando, FL: Academic Press.

Corter, C. M., Zucker, K. J., & Galligan, R. F. (1980). Patterns in the infant's search for mother during brief separation. *Developmental Psychology, 16,* 62–69.

Cote, J. E., & Levine, C. (1988). A critical examination of the ego identity status paradigm. *Developmental Review, 8,* 147–184.

Courage, M. L., Edison, S. C., & Howe, M. L. (2005). Variability in the early development of visual self-recognition. *Infant Behavior & Development, 27,* 509–532.

Cousins, S. D. (1989). Culture and self-perception in Japan and the United States. *Journal of Personality and Social Psychology, 56,* 124–131.

Covington, D. L., Justason, B. J., & Wright, L. N. (2001). Severity, manifestations, and consequences of violence among pregnant adolescents. *Journal of Adolescent Health, 28,* 55–61.

Cowan, N., Nugent, L. D., Elliott, E. M., Ponomarev, I., & Saults, J. S. (1999). The role of attention in the development of short-term memory: Age differences in the verbal span of apprehension. *Child Development, 70,* 1082–1097.

Cowley, G. (2001). Generation XXL. In K. L. Freiberg (Ed.), *Human development 01/02* (29th ed.) (pp. 120–121). Guilford, CT: Duskin/McGraw-Hill.

Cox, B. C., Ornstein, P. A., Naus, M. J., Maxfield, D., & Zimler, J. (1989). Children's concurrent use of rehearsal and organizational strategies. *Developmental Psychology, 25,* 619–627.

Cox, C. M. (1926). *Genetic studies of genius. Vol. 2: The early mental traits of three hundred geniuses.* Stanford, CA: Stanford University Press.

Cox, D., & Waters, H. S. (1986). Sex differences in the use of organization strategies: A developmental analysis. *Journal of Experimental Child Psychology, 41,* 18–37.

Cox, M. J., Owen, M. T., Henderson, V. K., & Margand, N. A. (1992). Prediction of infant–father and infant–mother attachment. *Developmental Psychology, 28,* 474–483.

Cox, M. J., Owen, M. T., Lewis, J. M., & Henderson, V. K. (1989). Marriage, adult adjustment, and early parenting. *Child Development, 60,* 1015–1024.

Coyle, T. R. (2001). Factor analysis of variability measures in eight independent samples of children and adults. *Journal of Experimental Child Psychology, 78,* 330–358.

Coyle, T. R., & Bjorklund, D. F. (1997). Age differences in, and consequences of, multiple–and variable strategy use on a multitrial sort-recall task. *Developmental Psychology, 33,* 372–380.

Craton, L. G. (1996). The development of perceptual completion abilities: Infants' perception of stationary partially occluded objects. *Child Development, 67,* 890–904.

Crews, F. (1996). The verdict on Freud [Review of *Freud evaluated: The completed arc*]. *Psychological Science, 7,* 63–68.

Crick, N. R. (1996). The role of overt aggression, relational aggression, and prosocial behavior in the prediction of children's future social adjustment. *Child Development, 67,* 2317–2327.

Crick, N. R., Casas, J. F., & Ku, H. (1999). Relational and physical forms of peer victimization in preschool. *Developmental Psychology, 35,* 376–385.

Crick, N. R., Casas, J. F., & Mosher, M. (1997). Relational and overt aggression in preschool. *Developmental Psychology, 33,* 579–588.

Crick, N. R., & Dodge, K. A. (1994). A review and reformulation of social information processing mechanisms in children's social adjustment. *Psychological Bulletin, 115,* 74–101.

Crick, N. R., & Dodge, K. A. (1996). Social information-processing mechanisms in reactive and proactive aggression. *Child Development, 67,* 993–1002.

Crick, N. R., & Grotpeter, J. K. (1995). Relational aggression, gender, and social–psychological adjustment. *Child Development, 66,* 710–722.

Crick, N. R., Grotpeter, J.K., & Bigbee, M. A. (2002). Relationally and physically aggressive children's intent attributions and feelings of distress for relational and instrumental peer provocations. *Child Development, 73,* 1134–1142.

Crick, N. R., & Ladd, G. W. (1993). Children's perceptions of their peer experiences: Attributions, loneliness, social anxiety, and social avoidance. *Developmental Psychology, 29,* 244–254.

Crick, N. R., Werner, N. E., Casas, J. F., O'Brien, K. M., Nelson, D. A., Grotpeter, J. K., & Markon, K. (1999). Childhood aggression and gender: A new look at an old problem. In D. Bernstein (Ed.), *Nebraska Symposium on Motivation: Vol. 45.* Lincoln: University of Nebraska Press.

Criss, M. M., Pettit, G. S., Bates, J. E., Dodge, K. A., & Lapp, A. L. (2002). Family adversity, positive peer relationships, and children's externalizing behavior: A longitudinal perspective on risk and resilience. *Child Development, 73,* 1220–1237.

Crockenberg, S., & Litman, C. (1990). Autonomy as competence in 2-year-olds: Maternal correlates of child defiance, compliance, and self-assertion. *Developmental Psychology, 26,* 961–971.

Crockenberg, S., & Litman, C. (1991). Effects of maternal employment on maternal and two-year-old child behavior. *Child Development, 61,* 930–953.

Cronbach, L. J., & Snow, R. E. (1977). *Aptitude and instructional methods: A handbook for research on interactions.* New York: Irvington.

Crook, C. K. (1978). Taste perception in the newborn infant. *Infant Behavior and Development, 1,* 52–69.

Crosnoe, R., & Elder, G. H., Jr. (2002). Adolescent twins and emotional distress: The interrelated influence of nonshared environment and social structure. *Child Development, 73,* 1761–1774.

Crouter, A. C., Manke, B. A., & McHale, S. M. (1995). The family context of gender intensification in early adolescence. *Child Development, 66,* 317–329.

Crowell, J. A., & Feldman, S. S. (1991). Mothers' working models of attachment relationships and mother and child behavior during separation and reunion. *Developmental Psychology, 27,* 597–605.

Crowley, K., & Siegler, R. S. (1993). Flexible strategy use in young children's tic-tac-toe. *Cognitive Science, 17,* 531–561.

Crystal, D. S., Chen, C., Fuligni, A. J., Stevenson, H. W., Hsu, C., Ko, H., Kitamura, S., & Kimura, S. (1994). Psychological maladjustment and academic achievement: A cross-cultural study of Japanese, Chinese, and American high school students. *Child Development, 65,* 738–753.

Crystal, D. S., Watanabe, H., Weinfert, K., & Wu, C. (1998). Concepts of human differences: A comparison of American, Japanese, and Chinese children and adolescents. *Developmental Psychology, 34,* 714–722.

Cummings, E. M., & Davies, P. T. (1994). *Children and marital conflict: The impact of family dispute and resolution.* New York: Guilford Press.

Cummings, E. M., Iannotti, R. J., & Zahn-Waxler, C. (1989). Aggression between peers in early childhood: Individual continuity and developmental change. *Child Development, 60,* 887–895.

Cunningham, H. (1996). The history of childhood. In C. P. Hwang, M. E. Lamb, & I. E. Sigel (Eds.), *Images of childhood.* Mahwah, NJ: Erlbaum.

Curry, L. M. (2000). Net provides new expression for sexual offenders. *Monitor on Psychology, 31,* 21.

Curtiss, S. (1977). *Genie: a psycholinguistic study of a modern-day "wild child."* New York: Academic Press.

Curtiss, S. (1988). *The case of Chelsea: A new test case of the critical period for language acquisition.* Unpublished manuscript. University of California, Los Angeles.

D'Apolito, K., & Hepworth, J. T. (2001). Prominence of withdrawal symptoms in polydrug-exposed infants. *Journal of Perimatal & Neonatal Nursing, 14,* 46–61.

Damast, A. M., Tamis-LeMonda, C. S., & Bornstein, M. H. (1996). Mother-child play: Sequential interactions and the relation between maternal beliefs and behaviors. *Child Development, 67,* 1752–1766.

Damon, W. (1977). *The social world of the child.* San Francisco: Jossey-Bass.

Damon, W. (1988). *The moral child.* New York: Free Press.

Damon, W., & Hart, D. (1988). *Self-understanding in childhood and adolescence.* New York: Cambridge University Press.

Damon, W., & Hart, D. (1992). Self-understanding and its role in social and moral development. In M. H. Bornstein & M. E. Lamb (Eds.), *Developmental psychology: An advanced textbook.* Hillsdale, NJ: Erlbaum.

Daniels, D. (1986). Differential experiences of siblings in the same family as predictors of adolescent sibling personality differences. *Journal of Personality and Social Psychology, 51,* 339–346.

Daniels, D., & Plomin, R. (1985). Differential experience of siblings in the same family. *Developmental Psychology, 21,* 747–760.

Darling, C. A., Davidson, J. K., & Passarello, L. C. (1992). The mystique of first intercourse among college youth: The role of partners, contraceptive practices, and psychological reactions. *Journal of Youth and Adolescence, 21,* 97–117.

Darlington, R. B. (1991). The long-term effects of model preschool programs. In L. Okagaki & R. J. Sternberg (Eds.), *Directors of development. Influences on the development of children's thinking.* Hillsdale, NJ: Erlbaum.

Darwin, C. A. (1877). A biographical sketch of an infant. *Mind, 2,* 285–294.

Das Eiden, R., Teti, D. M., & Corns, K. M. (1995). Maternal working models of attachment, marital adjustment, and the parent–child relationship. *Child Development, 66,* 1504–1518.

Dasen, P. R. (1977). *Piagetian psychology: Cross-cultural contributions.* New York: Gardner Press.

David, H. P. (1992). Born unwanted: Long-term developmental effects of denied abortion. *Journal of Social Issues, 48,* 163–181.

David, H. P. (1994). Reproductive rights and reproductive behavior: Clash or convergence of private values and public policies. *American Psychologist, 49,* 343–349.

Davies, P. T., & Cummings, E. M. (1998). Exploring children's emotional insecurity as a mediator of the link between marital relations and child adjustment. *Child Development, 69,* 124–139.

Davies, P. T., & Forman, E. M. (2002). Children's patterns of preserving emotional security in the interparental subsystem. *Child Development, 73,* 1880–1903.

Davies, P. T., & Windle, M. (2000). Middle adolescents' dating pathways and psychological adjustment. *Merrill-Palmer Quarterly, 46,* 90–118.

Davies, P. T., Harold, G. T., Goeke-Morley, M. C., & Cummings, E. M. (2003). Child emotional security and interpersonal conflict. *Monographs of the Society for Research in Child Development, 67,* (3, Serial No. 270).

Davis, B. L., & MacNeilage, P. F. (2000). Prosodic correlates of stress in babbling: An acoustical study. *Child Development, 71,* 1258–1270.

Davis, T. L. (1995). Gender differences in masking negative emotions: Ability or motivation. *Developmental Psychology, 31,* 660–667.

Day, J. C., Janus, A., & Davis, J. (2003). Computer and internet use in the United States: 2003. *US Census Bureau, Current Population Study.* http://www.census.gov/prod/2005pubs/p23-208.pdf.

Day, N. L., Leech, S. L., Richardson, G. A., Cornelius, M. D., Robles, N., & Larkby, C. (2002). Prenatal alcohol exposure predicts continued deficits in offspring size at 14 years of age. *Alcoholism: Clinical & Experimental Research, 26,* 1584–1591.

Day, R. H. (1987). Visual size constancy in infancy. In B. E. McKenzie & R.H. Day (Eds.), *Perceptual development in early infancy: Problems and issues.* Hillsdale, NJ: Erlbaum.

Day, R. H., & McKenzie, B. E. (1981). Infant perception of the invariant size of approaching and receding objects. *Developmental Psychology, 17,* 670–677.

de Gaston, J. P., Jensen, L., & Weed, S. (1995). A closer look at adolescent sexual activity. *Journal of Youth and Adolescence, 24,* 465–479.

de Haan, M., & Nelson, C. A. (1999). Brain activity differentiates face and object processing in 6-month-old infants. *Developmental Psychology, 35,* 1113–1121.

De Lisi, R., & Staudt, J. (1980). Individual differences in college students' performance on formal operations tasks. *Journal of Applied Developmental Psychology, 1,* 163–174.

de Villiers, J. G., & de Villiers, P. A. (1973). A cross-sectional study of the acquisition of grammatical morphemes in child speech. *Journal of Psycholinguistic Research, 2,* 267–278.

de Villiers, P. A., & de Villiers, J. G. (1979). *Early language.* Cambridge, MA: Harvard University Press.

de Villiers, P. A., & de Villiers, J. G. (1992). Language development. In M. H. Bornstein & M. E. Lamb (Eds.), *Developmental psychology: An advanced textbook* (3rd ed.). Hillsdale, NJ: Erlbaum.

De Wolff, M. S., & van IJzendoorn, M. H. (1997). Sensitivity and attachment: A meta-analysis on parental antecedents of infant attachment. *Child Development, 66,* 571–591.

Deater-Deckard, K., & Dodge, K. A. (1997). Externalizing behavior problems and discipline revisited: Nonlinear effects and variation by culture, context, and gender. *Psychological Inquiry, 8,* 161–175.

Deater-Deckard, K., & O'Connor, T. G. (2000). Parent-child mutuality in early childhood: Two behavioral genetic studies. *Developmental Psychology, 36,* 561–570.

Deaux, K. (1993). Sorry, wrong number—A reply to Gentile's call: Sex or gender? *Psychological Science, 4,* 125–126.

DeBerry, K. M., Scarr, S., & Weinberg, R. (1996). Family racial socialization and ecological competence: Longitudinal assessments of African-American transracial adoptees. *Child Development, 67,* 2375–2399.

DeCasper, A. J., & Fifer, W. P. (1980). Of human bonding: Newborns prefer their mothers' voices. *Science, 208,* 1174–1176.

DeCasper, A. J., & Spence, M. J. (1986). Prenatal maternal speech influences newborns' perception of speech sounds. *Infant Behavior & Development, 9,* 133–150.

DeCasper, A. J., & Spence, M. J. (1991). Auditorially mediated behavior during the perinatal period: A cognitive view. In M. J. S. Weiss & P. R. Zelazo (Eds.), *Newborn attention: Biological constraints and the influence of experience.* Norwood, NJ: Ablex.

DeCasper, A. J., Lecanuet, J.-P., Busnel, M.-C., & Granier-Deferre, C. (1994). Fetal reactions to recurrent maternal speech. *Infant Behavior & Development, 17,* 159–164.

Deci, E. L, & Ryan, R. M. (2000). The "what" and "why" of goal pursuits: Human needs and the self-determination of behavior. *Psychological Inquiry, 11,* 227–268.

DeGarmo, D. S., Forgatch, M. S., & Martinez, C. R., Jr. (1999). Parenting of divorced mothers as a link between social status and boys' academic outcomes: Unpacking the effects of socioeconomic status. *Child Development, 70,* 1231–1245.

Delaney-Black, V., Covington, C., Templin, T., Kershaw, T., Nordstrom-Klee, B., Ager, J., Clark, N., Surendran, A., Martier, S., & Sokol, R. J. (2000). Expressive language development of children exposed to cocaine prenatally: Literature review and report of a prospective cohort study. *Journal of Communication Disorders, 33,* 463–481.

DelCampo, D. S., & DelCampo, R. L. (2000). *Taking sides: Clashing views on controversial issues in childhood and society* (3rd ed.). Guilford, CT: Dushkin/McGraw-Hill.

DeLoache, J. S. (1986). Memory in very young children: Exploitation of cues to the location of a hidden object. *Cognitive Development, 1,* 123–138

DeLoache, J. S. (1987). Rapid change in the symbolic functioning of very young children. *Science, 238,* 1556–1557.

DeLoache, J. S. (2000). Dual representation and young children's use of scale models. *Child Development, 71,* 329–338.

DeLoache, J. S., Miller, K. F., & Pierroutsakos, S. L. (1998). Reasoning and problem solving. In D. Kuhn & R. S. Siegler (Vol. Eds.), *Cognitive, language, and perceptual development, Vol. 2.* In B. Damon (Gen. Ed.), *Handbook of child psychology.* New York: Wiley.

DeLuccie, M. F. (1995). Mothers as gatekeepers: A model of maternal mediators of father involvement. *Journal of Genetic Psychology, 156,* 115–131.

DeMarie, D., & Ferron, H. J. (2003). Capacity, strategies, and metamemory: Tests of a three-factor model of memory development. *Journal of Experimental Child Psychology, 84,* 167–193.

deMause, L. (1974). The evolution of childhood. In L. deMause (Ed.), *The history of childhood.* New York: Harper & Row.

Demo, D. H., Allen, K. R., & Fine, M. A. (2000). *Handbook of family diversity.* New York: Oxford University Press.

Dempster, F. N. (1981). Memory span: Sources of individual and developmental differences. *Psychological Bulletin, 89,* 63–100.

Dempster, F. N. (1993). Resistance to interference: Developmental changes in a basic processing mechanism. In M. L. Howe & R. Pasnak (Eds.), *Emerging themes in cognitive development. Vol. 1: Foundations.* New York: Springer-Verlag.

DeMulder, E. K., Denham, S., Schmidt, M., & Mitchell, J. (2000). Q-sort assessment of attachment security during the preschool years: Links from home to school. *Developmental Psychology, 36,* 274–282.

Denham, S. A., Blair, K. A., DeMulder, E., Leviatas, J., Sawyer, K. Auerbach-Major, S., & Queenan, P. (2003). Preschool emotional competence: Pathway to social competence. *Child Development, 74,* 238–256.

Denham, S. A., McKinley, M., Couchoud, E. A., & Holt, R. (1990). Emotional and behavioral predictors of preschool peer ratings. *Child Development, 61,* 1145–1152.

Denning, C. R., Kagan, B. M., Mueller, D. H., & Neu, H. C. (1991). The CF gene—one year later. *Cystic Fibrosis Currents, 6,* 1–19.

Dennis, W. (1960). Causes of retardation among institutional children: Iran. *Journal of Genetic Psychology, 96,* 47–59.

DeRosier, M. E., & Thomas, J. M. (2003). Strengthening sociometric prediction: Scientific advances in the assessment of children's peer relations. *Child Development, 74,* 1379–1392.

Despert, J. L. (1965). *The emotionally disturbed child: Then and now.* New York: Brunner/Mazel. *Developmental Psychology,* 21,872–877.

DeVries, R. (1969). Constancy of generic identity in the years three to six. *Monographs of the Society for Research in Child Development, 34* (Serial No. 127).

Dewandre, N. (2002). European strategies for promoting women in science. *Science, 295,* 278–279.

Dews, S., Winner, E., Kaplan, J., Rosenblatt, E., Hunt, M., Lim, K., McGovern, A., Qualter, A., & Smarsh, B. (1996). Children's understanding of the meaning and functions of verbal irony. *Child Development, 67,* 3071–3085.

Dewsbury, D. A. (1992). Comparative psychology and ethology: A reassessment. *American Psychologist, 47,* 208–215.

Diamond, A. (1985). Development of the ability to use recall to guide action, as indicated by the infant's performance on AB. *Child Development, 56,* 868–883.

Diamond, A. (1991). Frontal lobe involvement in cognitive changes during the first year of life. In K. R. Gibson & A. C. Petersen (Eds.), *Brain maturation and cognitive development: Comparative and cross-cultural perspectives.* New York: Aldine de Gruyter.

Diamond, A. (1995). Evidence of robust recognition memory in early life even when assessed by reaching behavior. *Journal of Experimental Child Psychology, 59,* 419–456.

Diamond, A., & Taylor, C. (1996). Development of an aspect of executive control: Development of the abilities to remember what I said and to "Do as I say, not as I do." *Developmental Psychobiology, 29,* 315–324.

Diamond, L. M. (2000). Sexual identity, attractions, and behavior among young sexual-minority women over a 2-year period. *Developmental Psychology, 36,* 241–250.

Diamond, M., & Sigmundson, H. K. (1997). Sex reassignment at birth: Long-term review and clinical implications. *Archives of Pediatric and Adolescent Medicine, 151,* 298–304.

Diaz, J. (1997). *How drugs influence behavior: A neuro-behavioral approach.* Upper Saddle River, NJ: Prentice-Hall.

Diaz, R. M. (1983). Thought and two languages: The impact of bilingualism on cognitive development. In E. W. Gordon (Ed.), *Review of research in education* (Vol. 10). Washington, DC: American Educational Research Association.

Diaz, R. M. (1985). Bilingual cognitive development: Addressing three gaps in recent research. *Child Development, 56,* 1376–1388.

Dick, D. M., & Rose, R. J. (2002). Behavior genetics: What's new? What's next? *Current Directions in Psychological Science, 11,* 70–74.

Dick, D. M., Rose, R. J., Viken, R. J., & Kaprio, J. (2000). Pubertal timing and substance use between and within families across late adolescence. *Developmental Psychology, 36,* 180–189.

Dick-Read, G. (1972). *Childbirth without fear: The original approach to natural childbirth.* New York: Harper & Row. (Original work published 1933.)

Diener, E., Sandvik, E., & Larsen, R. J. (1985). Age and sex effects for emotional intensity. *Developmental Psychology, 21,* 542–546.

Diesendruck, G., & Markson, L. (2001). Children's avoidance of lexical overlap: A pragmatic account. *Developmental Psychology, 37,* 630–641.

DiLalla, L. F., Kagan, J., & Reznick, J. S. (1994). Genetic etiology of behavioral inhibition among 2-year-old children. *Infant Behavior and Development, 17,* 405–412.

Dill, K. E., & Dill, J. C. (1998). Video game violence: A review of the empirical literature. *Aggression and Violent Behavior: A Review Journal, 3,* 407–428.

DiPietro, J. (2004). The role of prenatal maternal stress in child development. *Current Directions in Psychological Science, 13,* 71–74.

DiPietro, J., Costigan, K. A., & Gurewitsch, E. D. (2003). Fetal response to induced maternal stress. *Early Human Development, 74,* 125–138.

DiPietro, J. A., Hodgson, D. M., Costigan, K. A., Hilton, S. C., & Johnson, T. R. B. (1996). Fetal neurobehavioral development. *Child Development, 67,* 2553–2567.

Dishion, T. J. (1990). The family ecology of boys' peer relations in middle childhood. *Child Development, 61,* 874–892.

Dishion, T. J., & Owen, L. D. (2002). A longitudinal analysis of friendships and substance use: Bidirectional influence from adolescence to adulthood. *Developmental Psychology, 38,* 480–491.

Disney, E. R. (2002). The impact of prenatal alcohol or tobacco exposure on later ADHD or CD in offspring. *Dissertaion Abstracts International: Section B: The Sciences and Engineering, 62,* 5369.

Dittman, R. W., Kappes, M. E., & Kappes, M. H. (1992).Sexual behavior in adolescent and adult females with congenital adrenal hyperplasia. *Psychoneuroendocrinology, 17,* 153–170.

Dixon, R. A., & Lerner, R. M. (1992). A history of systems in developmental psychology. In M. H. Bornstein & M. E. Lamb (Eds.), *Developmental psychology: An advanced textbook.* Hillsdale, NJ: Erlbaum.

Dodge, K. A. (1980). Social cognition and children's aggressive behavior. *Child Development, 51,* 162–170.

Dodge, K. A. (1983). Behavioral antecedents of peer social status. *Child Development, 54,* 1386–1399.

Dodge, K. A. (1986). A social information processing model of social competence in children. In M. Perlmutter (Ed.), *Minnesota symposia on child psychology* (Vol. 18). Hillsdale, NJ: Erlbaum.

Dodge, K. A., & Pettit, G. S. (2003). A biopsychosocial model of the development of chronic conduct problems in adolescence. *Developmental Psychology, 39,* 349–371.

Dodge, K. A., Coie, J. D., Pettit, G. S., & Price, J. M. (1990). Peer status and aggression in boys' groups: Developmental and contextual analyses. *Child Development, 61,* 1289–1309.

Dodge, K. A., Pettit, G. S., & Bates, J. E. (1994). Socialization mediators of the relation between socioeconomic status and child conduct problems. *Child Development, 65,* 649–665.

Dodge, K. A., & Rabiner, D. L. (2004). Returning to roots: On social information processing and moral development. *Child Development, 75,* 1003–1008.

Doherty, W. J., & Needle, R. H. (1991). Psychological adjustment and substance abuse among adolescents before and after a parental divorce. *Child Development, 62,* 328–337.

Dolgin, K. G., & Behrend, D. A. (1984). Children's knowledge about animates and inanimates. *Child Development, 55,* 1646–1650.

Dollberg, S., Seigman, D. S., Armon, Y., Stevenson, D. K., & Gale, R. (1996). Adverse perinatal outcome in the older primipara. *Journal of Perinatology, 16,* 93–97.

Dominey, P. F. (2005). Emergence of grammatical constructions: evidence from simulation and grounded agent experiments. *Connection Science, 17,* 289–306.

Domjan, M. (1993). *Principles of learning and behavior* (3rd ed.). Pacific Grove, CA: Brooks/Cole.

Dondi, M., Simion, F., & Caltran, G. (1999). Can newborns discriminate between their own cry and the cry of another newborn infant? *Developmental Psychology, 35,* 418–426.

Donnerstein, E., & Smith, S. (2001). Sex in the media: Theory, influence, and solutions. In D. Singer & J. Singer (Eds.), *Handbook of children and the media.* Thousand Oaks, CA: Sage.

Donovan, W. L., Leavitt, L. A., & Walsh, R. O. (2000). Maternal illusory control predicts socialization strategies and toddler compliance. *Developmental Psychology,* 36, 402–411.

Dossey, J. A., Mullis, I. V. S., Lindquist, M. M., & Chambers, D. L. (1988). *The Mathematics Report Card: Are we measuring up?* Princeton, NJ: Educational Testing Service.

Dougherty, T. M., & Haith, M. M. (1997). Infant expectations and reaction time as predictors of childhood speed of processing and IQ. *Developmental Psychology, 33,* 146–155.

Downer, J. T., & Mendez, J. L. (2005). *Early Education and Development, 16,* 317–340.

Downey, D. B., & Condron, D. J. (2004). Playing well with others in kindergarten: The benefit of siblings at home. *Journal of Marriage & Family, 66,* 333–350.

Downing, L. L. (2003). *Fragile realities: Conversion and commitment in cults and other powerful groups:* State University of New York at Oneonta.

Doyle, A. B., & Aboud, F. E. (1993). A longitudinal study of white children's racial prejudice as a social-cognitive development. *Merrill–Palmer Quarterly, 41,* 209–228.

Doyle, A. B., Doehring, P., Tessier, O., de Lorimier, S., & Shapiro, S. (1992). Transitions in children's play: A sequential analysis of states preceding and following social pretense. *Developmental Psychology, 28,* 137–144.

Doyle, A. B., Markiewicz, D., Brendgen, M., Lieberman, M., & Voss, K. (2000). Child attachment security and self-concept: Associations with mother and father attachment style and marital quality. *Merrill-Palmer Quarterly, 46,* 514–539.

Drabman, R. S., & Thomas, M. H. (1974). Does media violence increase children's toleration of real-life aggression? *Developmental Psychology, 10,* 418–421.

Drebitko, C. N., Sadler, L. S., Leventhal, J. M., Daley, A. M., & Reynolds, H. (2005). Adolescent girls with negative pregnancy tests. *Journal of Pediatric & Adolescent Gynecology, 18,* 261–267.

Dreyer, P. H. (1982). *Sexuality during adolescence.* In B. B. Wolman (Ed.), Handbook of developmental psychology. New York: Wiley.

Droege, K. L., & Stipek, D. J. (1993). Children's use of dispositions to predict classmates' behavior. *Developmental Psychology, 29,* 646–654.

Drotar, D. (1992). Personality development, problem solving, and behavior problems among preschool children with early histories of nonorganic failure-to-thrive. *Developmental and Behavioral Pediatrics, 13,* 266–273.

Drummey, A. B., & Newcombe, N. (1995). Remembering versus knowing the past: Children's explicit and implicit memory. *Journal of Experimental Child Psychology, 59,* 549–565.

Dubas, J. S., Graber, J. A., & Petersen, A. C. (1991). The effects of pubertal development on achievement during adolescence. *American Journal of Education, 99,* 444–460.

Dube, E. F. (1982). Literacy, cultural familiarity, and "intelligence" as determinants of story recall. In U. Neisser (Ed.), *Memory observed: Remembering in natural contexts.* San Francisco: W. H. Freeman.

Dubé, E. M., & Savin-Williams, R. C. (1999). Sexual identity development among ethnic sexual-minority male youths. *Developmental Psychology, 35,* 1389–1398.

Dubois, D. L., Burk-Braxton, C., Swanson, L. P., Tevendale, H. D., Lockerd, E. M., & Moran, B. L. (2002). Getting by with a little help from self and others: Self-esteem and social support as resources during early adolescence. *Developmental Psychology, 38,* 822–839.

Dubois, D. L., Burk-Braxton, C., Swenson, L. P., Tevendale, H. D., & Hardesty, J. L. (2002a). Race and gender influences on adjustment in early adolescence: Investigation of an integrative model. *Child Development, 73,* 1573–1592.

Dubois, D. L., Burk-Braxton, L., Swenson, L. P., Tevendale, H. D., Lockerd, E. M., & Moran, B. L. (2002b). Getting by with a little help from self and others: Self-esteem and social support as resources during early adolescence. *Developmental Psychology, 38,* 822–839.

Duch, H. (2005). Redefining parent involvement in Head Start: A two-generation approach. *Early Child Development & Care, 175,* 23–35.

Duke, P. M., Carlsmith, J. M., Jennings, D., Martin, J. A., Dornbusch, S. M., Gross, R. T., & Siegel Gorelick, B. (1982). Educational correlates of early and late sexual maturation in adolescence. *Journal of Pediatrics, 100,* 633–637.

Duncan, G. J., & Brooks-Gunn, J. (1997). *Consequences of growing up poor.* New York: Russell Sale Foundation.

Duncan, G. J., & Brooks-Gunn, J. (1997). *Growing up poor: Consequences across the life span.* New York: Russell Sage Foundation.

Duncan, G. J., & Brooks-Gunn, J. (2000). Family poverty, welfare reform, and child development. *Child Development, 71,* 188–196.

Duncan, G. J., Brooks-Gunn, J., & Klebanov, P. K. (1994). Economic deprivation and early childhood development. *Child Development, 65,* 296–318.

Dunn, J. (1993). *Young children's close relationships: Beyond attachment.* Newbury Park, CA: Sage.

Dunn, J. (1994). Changing minds and changing relationships. In C. Lewis & P. Mitchel (Eds.), Children's early understanding of mind: Origins and development (pp. 297–310). Hove: Erlbaum.

Dunn, J., Brown, J., & Beardsall, L. (1991). Family talk about feeling states and children's later understanding of children's emotions. *Developmental Psychology, 27,* 448–455.

Dunn, J., Brown, J. R., & Maguire, M. (1995). The development of children's moral sensibility: Individual differences and emotion understanding. *Developmental Psychology, 31,* 649–659.

Dunn, J., Cutting, A. L., & Fisher, N. (2002). Old friends, new friends: Predictors on children's perspective on their friends at school. *Child Development, 73,* 621–635.

Dunn, J., & Hughes, C. (2001). "I got some swords and you're dead": Violent fantasy, antisocial behavior, friendship, and moral sensibility in young children. *Child Development, 72,* 491–505.

Dunn, J., & Kendrick, C. (1982). *Siblings: Love, envy, and understanding.* Cambridge, MA: Harvard University Press.

Dunn, J., & Plomin, R. (1990). *Separate lives: Why siblings are so different.* New York: Basic Books.

Dunn, K. (June 2002). Cloning Trevor. *The Atlantic Monthly.*

Dunphy, D. C. (1963). The social structure of urban adolescent peer groups. *Sociometry, 26,* 230–246.

Dusek, J. B. (1991). *Adolescent development and behavior* (2nd ed.). Englewood Cliffs, NJ: Prentice-Hall.

Dweck, C. S. (1975). The role of expectations and attributions in the alleviation of learned helplessness. *Journal of Personality and Social Psychology, 31,* 674–685.

Dweck, C. S. (1978). Achievement. In M. E. Lamb (Ed.), *Social and personality development* (pp. 114–130). New York: Holt, Rinehart, and Winston.

Dweck, C. S. (2000). Caution—praise can be dangerous. In K. L. Freiberg (Ed.,) *Human development 00/01* (28th ed.) (pp. 117–121). Guilford, CT: Duskin/McGraw-Hill.

Dweck, C. S. (2001). Caution—praise can be dangerous. In K. L. Frieberg (Ed.), *Human development 01/02* (29th ed.) (pp. 105–109). Guilford, CT: Dushkin/McGraw-Hill.

Dweck, C. S., & Leggett, E. L. (1988). A social-cognitive approach to motivation and personality. *Psychological Review, 95,* 256–273.

Dweck, C. S., Davidson, W., Nelson, S., & Enna, B. (1978). Sex differences in learned helplessness: II. The contingencies of evaluative feedback in the classroom, and III. An experimental analysis. *Developmental Psychology, 14,* 268–276.

Dwyer, J. T., & Stone, J. E. (2000). Prevalence of marked overweight and obesity in a multiethnic pediatric population: Findings from the Child and Adolescent Trial for Cardiovascular Health (CATCH) study. *Journal of American Dietetic Association, 100,* 1149–1155.

Dwyer, T., Ponsonby, A. L. B., Newman, N. M., & Gibbons, L. E. (1991). Prospective Cohort study of prone sleeping position and sudden infant death syndrome. *Lancet, 337,* 1244–1247.

Dyer, K. F. (1977). The trend of male–female performance differential in athletics, swimming, and cycling 1948–1976. *Journal of Biosocial Science, 9,* 325–338.

Eagly, A. H. (1995). The science and politics of comparing men and women. *American Psychologist, 50,* 145–158.

Eagly, A. H., Wood, W., & Diekman, A. B. (2000). Social role theory of sex differences and similarities: A current appraisal. In T. Eckes & H. M. Trautner (Eds.), *The developmental social psychology of gender* (pp. 123–174). Mahwah, NJ: Erlbaum.

East, P. L. (1996). The younger sisters of childbearing adolescents: Their attitudes, expectations, and behaviors. *Child Development, 67,* 267–282.

East, P. L., & Jacobson, L. J. (2001). The younger siblings of teenage mothers: A follow-up of their pregnancy risk. *Developmental Psychology, 37,* 254–264.

East, P. L., & Rook, K. S. (1992). Compensatory patterns of support among children's peer relationships: A test using school friends, nonschool friends, and siblings. *Developmental Psychology, 28,* 163–172.

Eaton, W. O., & Enns, L. R. (1986). Sex differences in human motor activity level. *Psychological Bulletin, 100,* 19–28.

Eaton, W. O., & Yu, A. P. (1989). Are sex differences in child motor activity level a function of sex differences in maturational status? *Child Development, 60,* 1005–1011.

Ebeling, K. S., & Gelman, S. A. (1988). Coordination of size standards by young children. *Child Development, 59,* 888–896.

Ebeling, K. S., & Gelman, S. A. (1994). Children's use of context in interpreting "big" and "little." *Child Development, 65,* 1178–1192.

Eccles, J. S., & Gootman, J. A. (Eds.). (2002). *Community programs to promote youth development.* Washington, DC: National Academy Press.

Eccles, J. S., & Harold, R. D. (1993). Parent-school involvement during the early adolescent years. *Teachers College Record, 94,* 568–587.

Eccles, J. S., & Roeser, R. W. (2005). School and community influences on human development. In M. H. Bornstein & M. E. Lamb (Eds.), *Developmental Science: An advanced textbook* (5th ed.) (pp. 513–555). Mahwah, NJ: Lawrence Erlbaum Associates.

Eccles, J. S., & Templeton, J. (2002). Extracurricular and other after-school activities for youth. In W. S. Secada (Ed.), *Review of educational research, Vol. 26,* pp 113–180. Washington, DC: American Educational Research Association Press.

Eccles, J. S., Flanagan, C., Lord, S., & Midgley, C. (1996). Schools, families, and early adolescents: What are we doing wrong and what can we do instead? *Journal of Developmental and Behavioral Pediatrics, 17,* 267–276.

Eccles, J. S., Freeman-Doan, C., Jacobs, J., & Yoon, K. S. (2000). Gender-role socialization in the family: A longitudinal approach. In T. Eckes & H. M. Trautner (Eds.), *The developmental social psychology of gender* (pp. 333–360).

Eccles, J. S., Jacobs, J. E., & Harold, R. D. (1990). Gender role stereotypes, expectancy effects, and parents' socialization of gender differences. *Journal of Social Issues, 46,* 183–201.

Eccles, J. S., Lord, S., & Midgley, C. (1991). What are we doing to early adolescents? The impact of educational contexts on early adolescents. *American Journal of Education, 99,* 521–542.

Eccles, J. S., Wigfield, A., & Schiefele, U. (1998). Motivation. In N. Eisenberg (Ed.), *Handbook of child psychology, Vol. 3* (5th ed.) (pp. 1017–1095). New York: Wiley.

Eccles, J., Wigfield, A., Harold, R. D., & Blumenfeld, P. (1993). Age and gender differences in children's task perceptions during elementary school. *Child Development, 64,* 830–847.

Eckenrode, J., Laird, M., & Doris, J. (1993). School performance and disciplinary problems among abused and neglected children. *Developmental Psychology, 29,* 53–62.

Eckerman, C. O., & Didow, S. M. (1996). Nonverbal imitation and toddlers' mastery of verbal means of achieving coordinated action. *Developmental Psychology, 32,* 141–152.

Eckerman, C. O., & Stein, M. R. (1990). How imitation begets imitation and toddlers' generation of games. *Developmental Psychology, 26,* 370–378.

Eckerman, C.O., Hsu, H. C., Molitor, A., Leung, E. H. L., & Goldstein. R. F. (1999). Infant arousal as an en-face exchange with a new partner: Effects of prematurity and perinatal biological risk. *Developmental Psychology, 35,* 282–293.

Ecklund-Flores, L., & Turkewitz, G. (1996). Asymmetric headturning to speech and nonspeech in human newborns. *Developmental Psychology, 29,* 205–217.

Eder, R. A. (1989). The emergent personalogist: The structure and content of 3½-, 5½-, and 7½-year-olds' concepts of themselves and other persons. *Child Development, 60,* 1218–1228.

Eder, R. A. (1990). Uncovering young children's psychological selves: Individual and developmental differences. *Child Development, 61,* 849–863.

Egan, S. K., & Perry, D. G. (1998). Does low self-regard invite victimization? *Developmental Psychology, 34,* 299–309.

Egan, S. K., & Perry, D. G. (2001). Gender identity: A multidimensional analysis with implications for psychosocial adjustment. *Developmental Psychology, 37,* 451–463.

Ehrhardt, A. A., & Baker, S. W. (1974). Fetal androgens, human central nervous system differentiation, and behavioral sex differences. In R. C. Friedman, R. M. Rickard, & R. L. Van de Wiele (Eds.), *Sex differences in behavior.* New York: Wiley.

Eichorn, D. H. (1979). Physical development: Current foci of research. In J. D. Osofsky (Ed.), *Handbook of infant development.* New York: Wiley.

Eidin, R. D. (2001). Maternal substance abuse and mother-infant feeding interactions. *Infant Mental Health Journal, 22,* 487–512.

Eilers, R. E., & Oller, D. K. (1994). Infant vocalizations and the early diagnosis of severe hearing impairment. *Journal of Pediatrics, 124,* 199–203.

Eimas, P. D. (1975a). Auditory and phonetic cues for speech: Discrimination of the (r–l) distinction by young infants. *Perception and Psychophysics, 18,* 341–347.

Eimas, P. D. (1975b). Speech perception in early infancy. In L. B. Cohen & P. Salapatek (Eds.), *Infant perception: From sensation to cognition.* Orlando, FL: Academic Press.

Eimas, P. D. (1985). The perception of speech in early infancy. *Scientific American, 252,* 46–52.

Eisele, J., & Lust, B. (1996). Knowledge about pronouns: A developmental study using a truth value judgment task. *Child Development, 67,* 3086–3100.

Eisenberg, M. E., Neumark-Sztainer, D., Story, M., & Perry, C. (2005). The role of social norms and friends' influences on unhealthy weight-control behaviors among adolescent girls. *Social Science & Medicine, 60,* 1165–1173.

Eisenberg, M. E., Olson, R. E., Newmark-Sztainer, D., Story, M., & Bearinger, L. H. (2004). Correlations between family meals and psychosocial well-being among adolescents. *Archives of Pediatric Adolescent Medicine, 158,* 792–796.

Eisenberg, N. (1983). Children's differentiations among potential recipients of aid. *Child Development, 54,* 594–602.

Eisenberg, N., & Fabes, R. A. (1998). Prosocial development. In W. Damon (Series Ed.) & N. Eisenberg (Vol. Ed.) *Handbook of child psychology: Vol. 3: Social, emotional, and personality development* (5th ed.) (pp. 701–778). New York: Wiley.

Eisenberg, N., Cumberland, A., Spinrad, T. L., Fabes, R. A., Shepard, S. A., Reiser, M., Murphy, B. C., Losoya, S. H., & Gutherie, I. K. (2001). The relations of regulation and emotionality to children's externalizing and internalizing problem behavior. *Child Development, 72,* 1112–1134.

Eisenberg, N., Fabes, R. A., Carlo, G., Troyer, D., Speer, A. L., Karbon, M., & Switzer, G. (1992). The relations of maternal practices and characteristics to children's vicarious emotional responsiveness. *Child Development, 63,* 583–602.

Eisenberg, N., Fabes, R. A., Miller, P. A., Shell, R., Shea, C., & May-Plumlee, T. (1990). Preschoolers' vicarious emotional responding and their situational and dispositional prosocial behavior. *Merrill-Palmer Quarterly, 36,* 507–529.

Eisenberg, N., Fabes, R. A., Schaller, M., Carlo, G., & Miller, P. A. (1991). The relations of parental characteristics and practices in children's vicarious emotional responding. *Child Development, 62,* 1393–1408.

Eisenberg, N., Fabes, R. A., Shepard, S. A., Murphy, B. C., Jones, S., & Guthrie, I. K. (1998). Contemporaneous and longitudinal prediction of children's sympathy from dispositional regulation and emotionality. *Developmental Psychology, 34,* 910–924.

Eisenberg, N., Guthrie, I. K., Murphy, B. C., Shepard, S. A., Cumberland, A., & Carlo G. (1999). Consistency and development of prosocial dispositions. *Child Development, 70,* 1360–1372.

Eisenberg, N., Miller, P. A., Shell, R., McNalley, S., & Shea, C. (1991). Prosocial development in adolescence: A longitudinal study. *Developmental Psychology, 27,* 849–857.

Eisenberg, N., Murray, E., & Hite, T. (1982). Children's reasoning regarding sex-typed toy choices. *Child Development, 53,* 81–86.

Eisenberg, N., Spinrad, T. L., Fabes, R. A., Reiser, M., Cumberland, A., Shepard, S. A., Valiente, C., Losoya, S. H., Guthrie, I. K., & Thompson, M. (2004). The relations of effortful control and impulsivity to children's resiliency and adjustment. *Child Development, 75,* 25–46.

Eisenberg, N., Zhou, Q., & Koller, S. (2001). Brazilian adolescent's prosocial moral judgment and behavior: Relations to sympathy, perspective-taking, gender-role orientation, and demographic characteristics. *Child Development, 72,* 518–534.

Eisenberg, N., Zhou, Q., Losoya, S. H., Fabes, R. A., Shepard, S. A., Murphy, B.C., Reiser, M., Guthrie, I. K., & Cumberland, A. (2003). The relations of parenting, effortful control, and ego control to children's emotional expressivity. *Child Development, 74,* 875–895.

Eisenberg-Berg, N., & Hand, M. (1979). The relationship of preschoolers' reasoning about prosocial moral conflicts to prosocial behavior. *Child Development, 50,* 356–363.

Eisler, I. (2005). The empirical and theoretical base of family therapy and multiple family day therapy for adolescent anorexia nervosa. *Journal of Family Therapy, 27,*104–131.

Elder, G. H., Liker, J. K., & Cross, C. E. (1984). Parent-child behavior in the Great Depression: Life course and intergenerational influences. In P. B. Baltes & O. G. Brim (Eds.), *Life-span development and behavior* (Vol. 6). New York: Academic Press.

Eldred, L., & Chaisson, R. (1996). The clinical course of HIV infection in women. In R. R. Faden & N. E. Kass (Eds.), *HIV, AIDS, and childbearing* (pp. 15–30). New York: Oxford University Press.

Eley, T. C., Lichtenstein, P., & Stevenson, J. (1999). Sex differences in the etiology of aggressive and nonaggressive antisocial behavior: Results from two twin studies. *Child Development, 70,* 155–168.

El-Haddad, M., Desai, M., Gayle, D., & Ross, M. G. (2004). In utero development of fetal thirst and appetite: potential for programming. *Journal of the Society for Gynecologic Investigation, 11,* 123–131.

Elicker, J., Englund, M., & Stroufe, L. A. (1992). Predicting peer competence and relationships in childhood from early parent-child relationships. In R. D. Parke & G. W. Ladd (Eds.), *Family-peer relationships: Models of linkage.* Hillsdale, NJ: Erlbaum.

Elkind, D. (1977). Giant in the nursery—Jean Piaget. In E. M. Hetherington & R. D. Parke (Eds.), *Contemporary readings in child psychology.* New York: McGraw-Hill.

Elkind, D. (1987). *Miseducation: Preschoolers at risk.* New York: Knopf.

Elkind, D. (1981). *Children and adolescents: Interactive essays on Jean Piaget* (3rd ed.). New York: McGraw-Hill.

Elkind, D. (2001). Authority of the brain. *Pediatrics, 107,* 964–966.

Ellis, B. J., & Bjorklund, D. F. (Eds.) (2005). *Origins of the social mind: Evolutionary psychology and child development.* New York: Guilford.

Ellis, B. J., & Garber, J. (2000). Psychosocial antecedents of variation in girls' pubertal timing: Maternal depression, stepfather presence, and marital and family stress. *Child Development, 71,* 485–501.

Ellis, B. J., Bates, J. E., Dodge, K. A., Fergusson, D. M., Horwood, L. J., Pettit, G. S., & Woodward L. (2003). Does father absence place daughters at special risk for early sexual activity and teenage pregnancy? *Child Development, 74,* 801–821.

Ellis, S., Rogoff, B., & Cromer, C. C. (1981). Age segregation in children's social interactions. *Developmental Psychology, 17,* 399–407.

Ellsworth, C. P., Muir, D. W., & Hains, S. M. J. (1993). Social competence and person–object differentiation: An analysis of the still-face effect. *Developmental Psychology, 29,* 63–73.

El-Sheikh, M., & Harger, J. (2001). Appraisals of marital conflict and children's adjustment, health, and physiological reactivity. *Development Psychology, 37,* 875–885.

Emde, R. N., Biringen, Z., Clyman, R. B., & Oppenheim, D. (1991). The moral self of infancy: Affective core and procedural knowledge. *Developmental Review, 11,* 251–270.

Emde, R. N., Plomin, R., Robinson, J., Corley, R., DeFries, J., Fulker, D. W., Reznick, J. S., Campos, J., Kagan, J., & Zahn-Waxler, C. (1992). Temperament, emotion, and cognition at fourteen months: The MacArthur longitudinal twin study. *Child Development, 63,* 1437–1455.

Emery, R. E. (1999). Post divorce family life for children: An overview of research and some implications for policy. In R.A. Thompson & P.R. Amato (Eds.), *The post divorce family: Children, parenting, and society.* Thousand Oaks, CA: Sage.

Emery, R. E., & Forehand, R. (1994). Parental divorce and children's well-being: A focus on resilience. In R. J. Haggerty, L. R. Sherrod, N. Garmezy, & M. Rutter (Eds.), *Stress, risk, and resilience in children and adolescents* (pp. 64–99). New York: Cambridge University Press.

Englund, M. M., Levy, A. K., Hyson, D. M., & Sroufe, L. A. (2000). Adolescents' social competence: Effectiveness in a group setting. *Child Development, 71,* 1049–1060.

Entwisle, D. R., & Baker, D. P. (1983). Gender and young children's expectations for performance in arithmetic. *Developmental Psychology, 19,* 200–209.

Epstein, L. H., McCurley, J., Wing, R. R., & Valoski, A. (1990). Five-year follow-up of family based treatments for childhood obesity. *Journal of Consulting and Clinical Psychology, 58,* 661–664.

Epstein, L. H., Wing, R. R., Koeske, R., & Valoski, A. (1987). Long-term effects of family-based treatment of childhood obesity. *Journal of Consulting and Clinical Psychology, 55,* 91–95.

Erel, O., & Burman, B. (1995). Interrelatedness of marital relations and parent-child relations: A meta-analytic review. *Psychological Bulletin, 118,* 108–132.

Erel, O., Margolin, G., & John, R. S. (1998). Observed sibling interaction: Links with the marital and the mother–child relationship. *Developmental Psychology, 34,* 288–298.

Erikson, E. H. (1963). *Childhood and society* (2nd ed.). New York: Norton.

Erikson, E. H. (1982). *The life cycle completed. A review.* New York: Norton.

Eron, L. D. (1982). Parent–child interaction, television violence, and aggression of children. *American Psychologist, 37,* 197–211.

Espelage, D. L., Holt, M. K., & Henkel, R. R. (2003). Examination of peer-group contextual effects on aggression during early adolescence. *Child Development, 74,* 205–220.

Espy, K. A., Molfese, V. J., & DiLalla, L. F. (2001). Effects of environmental measures on intelligence in young children: Growth curve modeling of longitudinal data. *Merrill-Palmer Quarterly, 47,* 42–73.

Esters, I. G., & Ittenbach, R. F. (1999). Contemporary theories and assessments of intelligence: A primer. *Professional School Counseling, 2,* 1096–2409.

Etaugh, C., Levine, D., & Mennella, A. (1984). Development of sex biases in children: 40 years later. *Sex Roles, 10,* 911–922.

Evans, D. W., & Gray, F. L. (2000). Compulsive-like behavior in individuals with Down Syndrome: Its relation to mental age level, adaptive and maladaptive behavior. *Child Development, 71,* 288–300.

Evans, G. W., Maxwell, L. E., & Hart, B. (1999). Parental language and verbal responsiveness to children in crowded homes. *Developmental Psychology, 35,* 1020–1023.

Eyer, D. E. (1992). *Mother-infant bonding: A scientific fiction.* New Haven, CT: Yale University Press.

Fabes, R. A., Eisenberg, N., & Miller, P. A. (1990). Maternal correlates of children's vicarious emotional responsiveness. *Developmental Psychology, 26,* 639–648.

Fabes, R. A., Eisenberg, N., Karbon, M., Bernzweig, J., Speer, A. L., & Carlo, G. (1994). Socialization of children's vicarious emotional responding and prosocial behavior: Relations with mothers' perceptions of children's emotional reactivity. *Developmental Psychology, 30,* 44–55.

Fabes, R. A., Eisenberg, N., Nyman, M., & Michaelieu, Q. (1991). Young children's appraisals of others' spontaneous emotional reactions. *Developmental Psychology, 27,* 858–866.

Fabes, R. A., Fultz, J., Eisenberg, N., May-Plumlee, T., & Christopher, F. S. (1989). Effects of rewards on children's prosocial motivation: A socialization study. *Developmental Psychology, 25,* 509–515.

Fabes, R. A., Martin, C. L., & Hanish, L. D. (2003). Young children's play qualities in same-, other-, and mixed-sex peer groups. *Child Development, 74,* 921–933.

Fabes, R. A., Martin, C. L., Hanish, L. D., & Updegraff, K. A. (2000). Criteria for evaluating the significance of developmental research in the twenty-first century: Force and counterforce. *Child Developmental, 71,* 212–221.

Faden, R. R., & Kass, N. E. (1996). *HIV, AIDS, and childbearing.* New York: Oxford University Press.

Fagan, J. F. (2000). A theory of intelligence as processing: Implications for society. *Psychology, Public Policy, and Law, 6,* 168–179.

Fagan, J. F., III. (1973). Infants' delayed recognition memory and forgetting. *Journal of Experimental Child Psychology, 16,* 424–450.

Fagan, J. F., III. (1974). Infant recognition memory: The effects of length of familiarization and type of discrimination task. *Child Development, 45,* 351–356.

Fagan, J. F., III. (1984). Infant memory: History, current trends, and relations to cognitive psychology. In M. Moscovitch (Ed.), *Infant memory: Its relation to normal and pathological memory in humans and other animals.* New York: Plenum.

Fagot, B. I. (1978). The influence of sex of child on parental reactions to toddler children. *Child Development, 49,* 459–465.

Fagot, B. I. (1985a). Beyond the reinforcement principle: Another step toward understanding sex-role development. *Developmental Psychology, 21,* 1097–1104.

Fagot, B. I. (1985b). Changes in thinking about early sex-role development. *Developmental Review, 5,* 83–98.

Fagot, B. I. (1997). Attachment, parenting, and peer interactions of toddler children. *Developmental Psychology, 33,* 489–499.

Fagot, B. I., & Gauvain, M. (1997). Mother–child problem solving: Continuity through the early childhood years. *Developmental Psychology, 33,* 480–488.

Fagot, B. I., & Hagan, R. I. (1991). Observations of parent reactions to sex-stereotyped behaviors: Age and sex effects. *Child Development, 62,* 617–628.

Fagot, B. I., & Kavanaugh, K. (1993). Parenting during the second year: Effects of children's age, sex, and attachment classification. *Child Development, 64,* 258–271.

Fagot, B. I., & Leinbach, M. D. (1989). The young child's gender schema: Environmental input, internal organization. *Child Development, 60,* 663–672.

Fagot, B. I., Leinbach, M. D., & Hagan, R. (1986). Gender labeling and the adoption of sex-typed behaviors. *Developmental Psychology, 22,* 440–443.

Fagot, B. I., Leinbach, M. D., & O'Boyle, C. (1992). Gender labeling, gender stereotyping, and parenting behaviors. *Developmental Psychology, 28,* 225–230.

Fagot, B. I., Pears, K. C., Capaldi, D. M., & Leve, C. S. (1998). Becoming an adolescent father: Precursors and parenting. *Developmental Psychology, 34,* 1209–1219.

Fagot, B. I., Rodgers, C. S., & Leinbach, M. D. (2000). Theories of gender socialization. In T. Eckes & H. M. Trautner (Eds.), *The developmental social psychology of gender* (pp. 65–89). Mahwah, NJ: Erlbaum.

Falbo, T. (1992). Social norms and the one-child family: Clinical and policy implications. In F. Boer & J. Dunn (Eds.), *Children's sibling relationships* (pp. 71–82). Hillsdale, NJ: Erlbaum.

Falbo, T., & Polit, D. F. (1986). Quantitative review of the only child literature: Research evidence and theory development. *Psychological Bulletin, 100,* 176–189.

Fantz, R. L. (1961). The origin of form perception. *Scientific American, 204,* 66–72.

Fantz, R. L. (1963). Pattern vision in newborn infants. *Science, 140,* 296–297.

Farrant, K., & Reese, E. (2000). Maternal style and children's participation in reminiscing: Stepping stones to children's autobiographical memory development. *Journal of Cognition and Development, 1,* 193–225.

Farver, J. A. M., Kim, Y. K., & Lee-Shin, Y. (2000). Within cultural differences: Examining individual differences in Korean American and European American preschoolers' social pretend play. *Journal of Cross-Cultural Psychology, 31,* 583–602.

Fauber, R., Forehand, R., Thomas, A. M., & Wierson, M. (1990). A mediational model of the impact of marital conflict on adolescent adjustment in intact and divorced families: The role of disrupted parenting. *Child Development, 61,* 1112–1123.

Faust, M. S. (1960). Developmental maturity as a determinant of prestige in adolescent girls. *Child Development, 31,* 173–184.

Fein, G. G. (1986). The affective psychology of play. In A. W. Gottfried & C. C. Brown (Eds.), *Play interactions. The contributions of play material and parental involvement to children's development.* Lexington, MA: Lexington Books.

Feingold, A. (1994). Gender differences in personality: A meta-analysis. *Psychological Bulletin, 116,* 429–456.

Feinman, S. (1992). *Social referencing and the social construction of reality in infancy.* New York: Plenum.

Feiring, C. (1996). Concepts of romance in 15-year-old adolescents. *Journal of Research on Adolescence, 6,* 181–200.

Feist, G. J., & Barron, F. (2003). Predicting creativity from early to late adulthood: Intellect, potential, and personality. *Journal of Research in Personality, 37,* 62–88.

Feldhusen, J. F. (2002). Creativity: The knowledge base and children. *High Ability Studies, 13,* 179–183.

Feldhusen, J. F., & Goh, B. E. (1995). Assessing and accessing creativity: An interpretive review of theory, research, and development. *Creativity Research Journal, 8,* 231–247.

Feldman, D. H. (1982). A developmental framework for research with gifted children. In D. H. Feldman (Ed.), *New directions for child development: No. 17. Developmental approaches to giftedness and creativity.* San Francisco: Jossey-Bass.

Feldman, D. H., & Goldsmith, L. T. (1991). *Nature's gambit.* New York: Teacher's College Press.

Feldman, R., & Eidelman, A. (2003). Skin-to-skin contact (Kangaroo Care) accelerates autonomic and neurobehavioural maturation in preterm infants. *Developmental Medicine and Child Neurology, 45,* 274–282.

Feldman, R., & Klein, P. S. (2003). Toddler's self-regulated compliance to mothers, caregivers, and fathers: Implications for theories of socialization. *Developmental Psychology, 39,* 680–692.

Feldman, R., Eidelman, A. I., & Rotenberg, N. (2004). Parenting stress, infant emotion regulation, maternal sensitivity, and the cognitive development of triplets: A model for parent and child influences in a unique ecology. *Child Development, 75,* 1774–1791.

Feldmann, J., & Middleman, A. B. (2002). Adolescent sexuality and sexual behavior. *Current Opinion in Obstetrics & Gynecology,* 489–493.

Fentress, J. C., & McLeod, P. J. (1986). Motor patterns in development. In E. M. Blass (Ed.), *Handbook of behavioral neurobiology.* Vol. 8: *Developmental psychology and developmental neurobiology.* New York: Plenum.

Ferber, S. G., Feldman, R., Kohelet, D., Kuint, J., Dollberg, S., Arbel, E., & Weller, A. (2005). Massage therapy facilitates mother-infant interaction in premature infants. *Infant behavior and Development, 28,* 74–82.

Ferguson, C. A. (1977). Learning to produce: The earliest stages of phonological development in the child. In F D. Minifie & L. L. Lloyd (Eds.), *Communication and cognitive abilities: Early behavioral assessment.* Baltimore: University Park Press.

Fergusson, D. M., & Woodward, L. J. (2000). Teenage pregnancy and female educational underachievement: A prospective study of a New Zealand birth cohort. *Journal of Marriage and the Family, 62,* 147–161.

Fernald, A. (1989). Intonation and communicative intent in mothers' speech to infants: Is the melody the message? *Child Development, 60,* 1497–1510.

Fernald, A. (1993). Approval and disapproval: Infant responsiveness to vocal affect in familiar and unfamiliar languages. *Child Development, 64,* 657–674.

Fernald, A., & Morikawa, H. (1993). Common themes and cultural variations in Japanese and American mothers' speech to infants. *Child Development, 64,* 637–656.

Fernandez, E. (1997, June 3). The grim legacy of divorce. *The Atlanta Constitution,* p. F5.

Ferreria, F., & Morrison, F. J. (1994). Children's metalinguistic knowledge of syntactical constituents: Effects of age and schooling. *Developmental Psychology, 30,* 663–678.

Feshbach, S. (1956). The catharsis hypothesis and some consequences of interaction with aggressive and neutral play objects. *Journal of Personality, 24,* 449–461.

Feuerstein, R., Feurstein, R., & Gross, S. (1997). The learning potential assessment device. In D. P. Flanagan, J. Genshaft, & P. L. Harrison (Eds.), *Contemporary intellectual assessment: Theories, tests, and issues.* New York: Guilford.

Fichter, M. M. (2005). Anorexic and bulimic eating disorders. *Der Nervenarzt, 76,* 1141–53.

Field, D. (1981). Can preschool children really learn to conserve? *Child Development, 52,* 326–334.

Field, T. M. (1995). *Touch in early development.* Mahwah, NJ: Erlbaum.

Field, T. M., Healy, B., Goldstein, S., Perry, S., Bendell, D., Schanberg, S., Zimmerman, E. A., & Kuhn, C. (1988). Infants of depressed mothers show "depressed" behavior even with nondepressed adults. *Child Development, 59,* 1569–1579.

Field, T. M., Schanberg, S. M., Scafidi, F., Bauer, C. R., Vega-Lahr, N., Garcia, R., Nystrom, J., & Kuhn, C. M. (1986). Effects of tactile/kinesthetic stimulation on preterm neonates. *Pediatrics, 77,* 654–658.

Field, T. M., Woodson, R., Greenberg, R., & Cohen, D. (1982). Discrimination and imitation of facial expressions by neonates. *Science, 218,* 179–181.

Fielding-Barnsley, R., & Purdie, N. (2005). Teachers' attitude to and knowledge of metalinguistics in the process of learning to read. *Asia-Pacific Journal of Teacher Education, 33,* 65–76.

Fields, D., Sandweiss, R., & Sandweiss, R. (1998). *Twins.* Philadelphia, PA: Running Press Book Publishers.

Fincham, F. D., Hokoda, A., & Sanders, R., Jr. (1989). Learned helplessness, test anxiety, and academic achievement: A longitudinal analysis. *Child Development, 60,* 138–145.

Fingerman, K. L., & Bermann, E. (2000). Applications of family systems theory to the study of adulthood. *International Journal of Aging and Human Development, 51,* 5–19.

Fischer, A. H., Rodriguez Mosquera, P. M., vanVianen, A. E. M., & Manstead, A. S. R. (2004). Gender and cultural differences in emotion. *Emotion, 4,* 87–94.

Fischer, K. W. (1980). A theory of cognitive development: The control and construction of hierarchies of skills. *Psychological Review, 87,* 477–531.

Fischer, K. W., & Bidell, T. (1998). Dynamic development of psychological structures in action and thought. In R. M. Lerner (Ed.), *Theoretical models of human development,* Vol. 1, of W. Damon (Gen. Ed.), *Handbook of child psychology.* New York: Wiley.

Fischer, K. W., & Rose, S. P. (1995, Fall). Concurrent cycles in the dynamic development of the brain and behavior. *SRCD Newsletter,* pp. 3–4, 15–16.

Fisher, C. B., Higgins-D'Alessandro, A., Rau, J. B., Kuther, T. L., & Belanger, S. (1996). Referring and reporting research participants at risk: Views from urban adolescents. *Child Development, 67,* 2086–2100.

Fisher, C., & Tokura, H. (1996). Acoustic cues to grammatical structure in infant-directed speech: Cross-linguistic evidence. *Child Development, 67,* 3192–3218.

Fisher, E. P. (1992). The impact of play on development: A meta-analysis. *Play and Culture, 5,* 159–181.

Fisher, J. A., & Birch, L. L. (1995). 3–5-year-old children's fat preferences and fat consumption are related to parental adiposity. *Journal of the American Dietetic Association, 95,* 759–764.

Fivush, R., & Hamond, N. R. (1989). Time and again: Effects of repetition and retention interval on 2-year-olds' event recall. *Journal of Experimental Child Psychology, 47,* 259–273.

Fivush, R., & Hamond, N. R. (1990). Autobiographical memory across the preschool years: Toward reconceptualizing childhood amnesia. In R. Fivush & J. A. Hudson (Eds.), *Knowing and remembering in young children*. New York: Cambridge University Press.

Fivush, R., & Nelson, K. (2004). Culture and language in the emergence of autobiographical memory. *Psychological Science, 15*, 573–577.

Fivush, R., Kuebli, J., & Clubb, P. A. (1992). The structure of events and event representations: A developmental analysis. *Child Development, 63*, 188–201.

Flaks, D. K., Ficher, I., Masterpasqua, F., & Joseph, G. (1995). Lesbians choosing motherhood: A comparative study of lesbian and heterosexual parents and their children. *Developmental Psychology, 31*, 105–114.

Flanagan, C. A., & Eccles, J. S. (1993). Changes in parents' work status and adolescents' adjustment to school. *Child Development, 64*, 246–257.

Flavell, J. H. (1963). *The developmental psychology of Jean Piaget*. New York: Van Nostrand Reinhold.

Flavell, J. H. (1999). Cognitive development: Children's knowledge about the mind. In J. T. Spence, J. M. Darley, & D. J. Foss (Eds.), *Annual review of psychology* (pp. 21–45). Palo Alto, CA: Annual Reviews.

Flavell, J. H., & Miller, P. H. (1998). Social cognition. In W. Damon (Series Ed.) & D. Kuhn and R. Siegler (Vol. Eds.), *Handbook of child psychology: Vol. 2, Cognition, perception, and language* (5th ed.) (pp. 851–898). New York: Wiley.

Flavell, J. H., Beach, D. R., & Chinsky, J. H. (1966). Spontaneous verbal rehearsal in a memory task as a function of age. *Child Development, 37*, 283–299.

Flavell, J. H., Everett, B. H., Croft, K., & Flavell, E. R. (1981). Young children's knowledge about visual perception: Further evidence for the level 1–level 2 distinction. *Developmental Psychology, 17*, 99–103.

Flavell, J. H., Flavell, E. R., & Green, F. L. (1983). Development of the appearance–reality distinction. *Cognitive Psychology, 15*, 95–120.

Flavell, J. H., Green, F. L., & Flavell, E. R. (1986). Development of knowledge about the appearance–reality distinction. *Monographs of the Society for Research in Child Development, 51*, (Serial No. 212).

Flavell, J. H., Green, F. L., & Flavell, E. R. (1989). Young children's ability to differentiate appearance–reality and level 2 perspectives in the tactile modality. *Child Development, 60*, 201–213.

Flavell, J. H., Green, F. L., & Flavell, E. R. (1995). The development of children's knowledge about attentional focus. *Developmental Psychology, 31*, 706–712

Flavell, J. H., Green, F. L., & Flavell, E. R. (1998). The mind has a mind of its own: Developing knowledge about mental uncontrollability. *Cognitive Development, 13*, 127–138.

Flavell, J. H., Green, F. L., & Flavell, E. R. (2000). Development of children's awareness of their own thoughts. *Journal of Cognition and Development, 1*, 97–122.

Flavell, J. H., Green, F. L., Flavell, E. R., & Lin, N. T. (1999). Development of children's knowledge about unconsciousness. *Child Development, 70*, 396–412.

Flavell, J. H., Miller, P. H., & Miller, S. A. (1993). *Cognitive development* (3rd ed.). Englewood Cliffs, NJ: Prentice-Hall.

Fleminger, S. (2005). A model for the treatment of eating disorders of adolescents in a specialized centre in The Netherlands. *Journal of Family Therapy, 27*, 147–157.

Fletcher-Flinn, C. M., & Gravatt, B. (1995). The efficacy of computer-assisted instruction (CAI): A meta-analysis. *Journal of Educational Computing Research, 12*, 219–242.

Flieller, A. (1999). Comparison of the development of formal thought in adolescent cohorts aged 10 to 15 years (1967–1996 and 1972–1993). *Developmental Psychology, 35*, 1048–1058.

Flynn, E., O'Malley, & Wood, D. (2004). A longitudinal, microgenetic study of the emergence of false belief understanding and inhibition skills. *Developmental Science, 7*, 103–115.

Flynn, J. R. (1987). Massive IQ gains in 14 nations: What IQ tests really measure. *Psychological Bulletin, 101*, 171–191.

Flynn, J. R. (1991). *Asian-Americans: Achievement beyond IQ*. Hillsdale, NJ: Erlbaum.

Flynn, J. R. (1996). What environmental factors affect intelligence: The relevance of IQ gains over time. In D. K. Detterman (Ed.), *Current topics in human intelligence: Vol. 5. The environment*. Norwood: NJ: Ablex.

Fogel, A. (1995). Relational narratives of the prelinguistic self. In P. Rochat (Ed.) *The self in infancy: Theory and research* (pp. 117–139). Amsterdam: North Holland-Elsevier.

Folven, R. J., & Bonvillian, J. D. (1991). The transition for nonreferential to referential language in children acquiring American Sign Language. *Developmental Psychology, 27*, 806–816.

Fonagy, P., Steele, H., & Steele, M. (1991). Maternal representations of attachment during pregnancy predict the organization of infant–mother attachment at one year of age. *Child Development, 62*, 891–905.

Ford, C. S., & Beach, F. A. (1951). *Patterns of sexual behavior*. New York: Harper & Row.

Ford, D. Y., & Harris, J. J., III (1996). Perceptions and attitudes of black students toward school, achievement, and other educational variables. *Child Development, 67*, 1141–1152.

Fordham, S., & Ogbu, J. (1986). Black students' school success: Coping with the "burden of 'acting white.'" *Urban Review, 18*, 176–206.

Forman, D. R., & Kochanska, G. (2001). Viewing imitation as child responsiveness: A link between teaching and discipline domains of socialization. *Developmental Psychology, 37*, 198–206.

Forrest, J. D., & Singh, S. (1990). The sexual and reproductive behavior of American women, 1982–1988. *Family Planning Perspectives, 22*, 206–214.

Foster, M. A., Lambert, R., Abbott-Shim, M., McCarty, F., & Franze, S. (2005). A model of home learning environment and social risk factors in relation to children's emergent literacy and social outcomes. *Early Childhood Research Quarterly, 20*, 13–36.

Foster, Z., Byron, E., Reyes-Garcia, V., Huanca, T., Vadez, V., Apaza, L., Perez, E., Tanner, S., Gutierrez, Y., Sandstrom, B., Yakhedts, A., Osborn, C., Godoy, R. A., & Leonard, W. R. (2005). Physical growth and nutritional status of Tsimane' Amerindian children of lowland Bolivia. *American Journal of Physical Anthropology, 126*, 343–351.

Fowles, E. R., & Gabrielson, M. (2005). First trimester predictors of diet and birth outcomes in low-income pregnant women. *Journal of Community Health Nursing, 22*, 117–130.

Fox, N. A., & Fitzgerald, H. E. (1990). Autonomic function in infancy. *Merrill-Palmer Quarterly, 36*, 27–51.

Fox, N. A., Bell, M. A., & Jones, N. A. (1992). Individual differences in response to stress and cerebral asymmetry. *Developmental Neuropsychology, 8*, 161–184.

Fox, N. A., Henderson, H. A., Rubin, K. H., Calkins, S. D., & Schmidt, L. A. (2001). Continuity and discontinuity of behavioral inhibition and exuberance: Psychophysiological and behavioral influences across the first four years of life. *Child Development, 72*, 1–21.

Fox, N. A., Kimmerly, N. L., & Schafer, W. D. (1991). Attachment to mother/attachment to father: A meta-analysis. *Child Development, 62*, 210–225.

Fox, N. A., Rubin, K. H., Calkins, S. D., Marshall, T. R., Coplan, R. J., Porges, S. W., Long, J. M., & Stewart, S. (1995). Frontal activation asymmetry and social competence at four years of age. *Child Development, 66*, 1770–1784.

Fraley, R. C., & Spieker, S. J. (2003). Are infant attachment patterns continuously or categorically distributed? A taxometric analysis of Strange Situation behavior. *Developmental Psychology, 39*, 387–404.

Francis, N. (2005). Research findings on early first language attrition: Implications for the discussion on critical periods in language acquisition. *Language Learning, 55*, 491–531.

Franco, P., Schliwowski, H., Dramaiz, M., & Kuhn, A. (1998). Polysomnographic study of the autonomic nervous system in potential victims of sudden infant death syndrome. *Clinical Autonomic Research, 8*, 243–249.

Frank, D. A., Brown, J., Johnson, S., & Cabral, H. (2002). Forgotten fathers: An exploratory study of mothers' report of drug and alcohol problems among fathers of urban newborns. *Neurotoxicology & Teratology, 24*, 339–347.

Frankel, K. A., & Bates, J. E. (1990). Mother-toddler problem-solving: Antecedents in attachment, home behavior, and temperament. *Child Development, 61*, 810–819.

Franklin, K. M., Janoff-Bulman, R., & Roberts, J. E. (1990). Long-term impact of parental divorce on optimism and trust: Changes in general assumptions or narrow beliefs? *Journal of Personality and Social Personality, 59*, 743–755.

Frascarolo, F., Favez, N., Carneiro, C., & Fivaz-Depeursinge, E. (2004). Hierarchy of interactive functions in father-mother-baby three-way games. *Infant & Child Development, 13*, 301–322.

Frazier, J. A., & Morrison, F. J. (1998). The influence of extended-year schooling on the growth of achievement and perceived competence in early elementary school. *Child Development, 69*, 495–517.

Fredricks, J. A., & Eccles, J. S. (2002). Children's competence and value beliefs from childhood through adolescence: Growth trajectories in two male sex-typed domains. *Developmental Psychology, 38*, 519–533.

Freedman, D. G. (1979). Ethnic differences in babies. *Human Nature, 2*, 36–43.

Freiberg, K., Tually, K., & Crassini, B. (2001). Use of an auditory looming task to test infants' sensitivity to sound pressure level as an auditory distance cue. *British Journal of Psychology, 19*, 1–10.

Freud, S. (1930). *Three contributions to the theory of sex*. New York: Nervous and Mental Disease Publishing Co. (Original work published 1905.)

Freud, S. (1933). *New introductory lectures in psychoanalysis*. New York: Norton.

Freud, S. (1960). *A general introduction to psychoanalysis*. New York: Washington Square Press. (Original work published 1935.)

Freud, S. (1961). Some physical consequences of the anatomical distinction between the sexes. In J. Strachey (Ed.), *The standard edition of the complete psychological works of Sigmund Freud* (Vol. 19). London: Hogarth Press. (Originally published 1924.)

Freud, S. (1964). An outline of psychoanalysis. In J. Strachey (Ed. and Trans.), *The standard edition of the complete psychological works of Sigmund Freud* (Vol. 23). London: Hogarth Press. (Original work published 1940.)

Freund, L. S. (1990). Maternal regulation of children's problem-solving behavior and its impact on children's performance. *Child Development, 61*, 113–126.

Frey, K. S., & Ruble, D. N. (1985). What children say when the teacher is not around: Conflicting goals in social comparison and performance assessment in the classroom. *Journal of Personality and Social Psychology, 48*, 550–562.

Frey, K. S., & Ruble, D. N. (1992). Gender constancy and the cost of sex–typed behavior: A test of the conflict hypothesis. *Developmental Psychology, 28*, 714–721.

Frick, J. E. (1999, July). *Reducing the risk of sudden infant death syndrome*. Paper presented at Athens, Georgia, Maternity Fair.

Frick, P. J., Cornell, A. H., Bodin, S. D., Dane, H. E., Barry, C. T., & Loney, B. R. (2003). Callous-unemotional traits and developmental pathways to severe conduct disorders. *Developmental Psychology, 39*, 246–260.

Fried, P. A. (1993). Prenatal exposure to tobacco and marijuana: Effects during pregnancy, infancy, and early childhood. *Clinical Obstetrics and Gynecology, 36*, 319–337.

Fried, P. A. (2002). Conceptual issues in behavioral teratology and their application in determining long-term sequelae of prenatal marihuana exposure. *Journal of Child Psychology & Psychiatry, 43*, 81–102.

Friedman, H. S., Tucker, J. S., Schwartz, J. E., Tomlinson-Keasey, C., Martin, L. R., Wingard, D. L., & Criqui, M. H. (1995). Psychosocial and behavioral predictors of longevity: The aging and death of the "termites." *American Psychologist, 50*, 69–78.

Friedman, J. M., & Polifka, J. E. (1996). *The effects of drugs on the fetus and nursing infant*. Baltimore: Johns Hopkins University Press.

Friedman, M. S., Silvestre, A. J., Gold, M. A., Markovic, N., Savin-Williams, R. C., Huggins, J., & Sell, R. L. (2004). Adolescents define sexual orientation and suggest ways to measure it. *Journal of Adolescence, 27*, 303–317.

Friedrich, L. K., & Stein, A. H. (1975). Prosocial television and young children: The effects of verbal labeling and role-playing on learning and behavior. *Child Development, 46,* 27–38.

Friedrich-Cofer, L. K., Huston-Stein, A., Kipnis, D. M., Susman, E. J., & Clewett, A. S. (1979). Environmental enhancement of prosocial television content: Effects on interpersonal behavior. *Developmental Psychology, 15,* 637–646.

Friel-Patti, S., & Finitzo, T. (1990). Language learning in a prospective study of otitis media with effusion in the first two years of life. *Journal of Speech and Hearing Research, 33,* 188–194.

Friend, K. B., Goodwin, M. S., & Lipsitt, L. P. (2004). Alcohol use and sudden infant death syndrome. *Developmental Review, 24,* 235–252.

Frisby, C. L., & Braden, J. P. (1992). Feuerstein's dynamic assessment approach: A semantic, logical, and empirical critique. *Journal of Special Education, 26,* 281–301.

Frodi, A. (1985). When empathy fails: Aversive infant crying and child abuse. In B. M. Lester & C. F. Z. Boukydis (Eds.), *Infant crying: Theoretical and research perspectives* (pp. 263–277). New York: Plenum.

Frost, J. (2000). From 'Epi' through 'Meta' to Mastery. The balance of meaning and skill in early reading instruction. *Scandinavian Journal of Educational Research, 44,* 125–144.

Frost, J. J., & Forrest, J. D. (1995). Understanding the impact of effective teenage pregnancy prevention programs. *Family Planning Perspectives, 27,* 188–195.

Fry, C. L. (1996). Age, aging, and culture. In R. H. Binstock & L. K. George (Eds.), *Handbook of aging and the social sciences* (4th ed.). San Diego: Academic.

Fuchs, D., & Thelan, M. H. (1988). Children's expected interpersonal consequences of communicating their affective state and reported likelihood of expression. *Child Development, 59,* 1314–1322.

Fuhrman, T., & Holmbeck, G. N. (1995). A contextual-moderator analysis of emotional anatomy and adjustment in adolescence. *Child Development, 66,* 793–811.

Fukuda, M., Fukuda, K., Shimizu, T., Andersen, C. Y., & Byskov, A. G. (2002). Parental periconceptional smoking and male:female ratio of newborn infants. *Lancet, 359,* 1407–1408.

Fuligni, A. J. (1997). The academic achievement of adolescents from immigrant families: The roles of family background, attitudes, and behavior. *Child Development, 68,* 351–363.

Fuligni, A. J. (1998). Authority, autonomy, and parent–adolescent conflict and cohesion: A study of adolescents from Mexican, Chinese, Filipino, and European backgrounds. *Developmental Psychology, 34,* 782–792.

Fuligni, A. J., & Pedersen, S. (2002). Family obligation and the transition to young adulthood. *Developmental Psychology, 38,* 856–868.

Fuligni, A. J., & Stevenson, H. W. (1995). Time use and mathematics achievement among American, Chinese, and Japanese high school students. *Child Development, 66,* 830–842.

Fuligni, A. J., Yip, T., & Tseng, V. (2002). The impact of family obligation on the daily activities and psychological well-being of Chinese American adolescents. *Child Development, 73,* 302–314.

Fuligni, A. J., & Zhang, W. (2004). Attitudes toward family obligation among adolescents in contemporary urban and rural China. *Child Development, 75,* 180–192.

Fuller, B., Holloway, S. D., & Liang, X. (1996). Family selection of child-care centers: The influence of household support, ethnicity, and parental practices. *Child Development, 67,* 3320–3337.

Fullerton, J. T., & Severino, R. (1992). In-hospital care for low-risk childbirth: Comparison with results from the National Birth Center Study. *Journal of Nurse Midwifery, 37,* 331–340.

Furman, W., & Buhrmester, D. (1985). Children's perceptions of the qualities of sibling relationships. *Child Development, 56,* 448–461.

Furman, W., & Buhrmester, D. (1992). Age and sex differences in perceptions of networks of personal relationships. *Child Development, 63,* 103–115.

Fuson, K. C. (1988). *Children's counting and concepts of number.* New York: Springer-Verlag.

Fuson, K. C. (1992). Research on learning and teaching addition and subtraction of whole numbers. In G. Leinhardt, R. T. Putnam, & R. A. Hattrup (Eds.). *The analysis of arithmetic for mathematics teaching.* Hillsdale, NJ: Erlbaum.

Fuson, K. C., & Kwon, Y. (1992). Korean children's understanding of multidigit addition and subtraction. *Child Development, 63,* 491–506.

Fyans, L. J., Jr., Salili, F., Maehr, M. L., & Desai, K. A. (1983). A cross-cultural exploration into the meaning of achievement. *Journal of Personality and Social Psychology, 44,* 1000–1013.

Gaddis, A., & Brooks-Gunn, J. (1985). The male experience of pubertal change. *Journal of Youth and Adolescence, 14,* 61–69.

Galambos, N. L., Almeida, D. M., & Petersen, A. C. (1990). Masculinity, femininity, and sex role attitudes in early adolescence: Exploring gender intensification. *Child Development, 61,* 1905–1914.

Galambos, N. L., Barker, E. T., & Almeida, D. M. (2003). Parents do matter: Trajectories of change in externalizing and internalizing problems in early adolescence. *Child Development, 74,* 578–594.

Galambos, S. J., & Goldin-Meadow, S. (1990). The effects of learning two languages on levels of metalinguistic awareness. *Cognition, 34,* 1–56.

Gale, C. R., O'Callaghan, F. J., Godfrey, K. M., Law, C. M., & Martyn, C. N. (2004). Critical periods of brain growth and cognitive function in children. *Brain, 127,* 321–329.

Galen, B. R., & Underwood, M. K. (1997). A developmental investigation of social aggression among children. *Developmental Psychology, 33,* 589–600.

Gallagher, A., Levin, J., & Cahalan, C. (2002). *GRE research: Cognitive patterns of gender differences on mathematics admissions tests (ETS Report No. 02–19).* Princeton, NJ: Educational Testing Service.

Gallagher, J. M., & Easley, J. A., Jr. (1978). *Knowledge and development* (Vol.2). *Piaget and education.* New York: Plenum.

Gallahue, D. L. (1989). *Understanding motor development* (2nd ed.). Carmel, ID: Benchmark Press.

Gallistel, C. R., & Gelman, R. (1992). Preverbal and verbal counting and computation. *Cognition, 44,* 43–74.

Galloway, J. C., & Thelen, E. (2004). Feet first: Object exploration in young infants. *Infant Behavior and Development, 27,* 107–113.

Gallup, G. G., Jr. (1979). Self-recognition in chimpanzees and man: A developmental and comparative perspective. In M. Lewis & L. A. Rosenblum (Eds.), *Genesis of behavior. Vol. 2: The child and its family.* New York: Plenum.

Galper, A., Wigfield, A., & Seefeldt, C. (1997). Head Start parents' beliefs about their children's abilities, task values, and performances on different activities. *Child Development, 68,* 897–907.

Galupo, M. P., & St. John, S. (2001). Benefits of cross-sexual orientation friendships among adolescent females. *Journal of Adolescence, 24,* 83–93.

Galuska, D. A., Serdula, M., Pamuck, E., Siegel, P. Z., & Byers, T. (1996). Trends in overweight among U.S. adults from 1987 to 1993: A multistate telephone survey. *American Journal of Public Health, 86,* 1729–1735.

Ganchrow, J. R., Steiner, J. E., & Daher, M. (1983). Neonatal facial expressions to different qualities and intensities of gustatory stimuli. *Infant Behavior and Development, 6,* 189–200.

Gandelman, R. (1992). *Psychobiology of behavioral development.* New York: Oxford University Press.

Ganger, J., & Brent, M. R. (2004). Reexamining the vocabulary spurt. *Developmental Psychology, 40,* 621–632.

Garcia, E. E. (1993). Language, culture, and education. *Review of Educational Research, 19,* 51–98.

Garcia, M. M., Shaw, D. S., Winslow, E. B., & Yaggi, K. E. (2000). Destructive sibling conflict and the development of conduct problems in young boys. *Developmental Psychology,* 36, 44–53.

Garcia Coll, C., Bearer, E., & Lerner, R. M. (Eds.). (2003). *Nature and nurture: The complex interplay of genetic and environmental influences on human behavior and development.* Mahwah, NJ: Lawrence Erlbaum Associates.

Gardner, H. (1983). *Frames of mind: The theory of multiple intelligences.* New York: Basic Books.

Gardner, H. (1993). *Creating minds.* New York: Basic Books.

Gardner, H. (1999). Are there additional intelligences? The case for naturalist, spiritual, and existential intelligences. In J. Kane (Ed.), *Education, information, and transformation.* Englewood Cliffs, NJ: Prentice-Hall.

Gardner, L. J. (1972). Deprivation dwarfism. *Scientific American, 227,* 76–82.

Garner, P. W., & Power, T. G. (1996). Preschoolers' emotional control in the disappointment paradigm and its relation to temperament, emotional knowledge, and family expressiveness. *Child Development, 67,* 1406–1419.

Garner, P. W., Jones, D. C., & Palmer, D. J. (1994). Social-cognitive correlates of preschool children's sibling caregiving behavior. *Developmental Psychology, 30,* 905–911.

Garnets, L., & Kimmel, D. (1991). Lesbian and gay male dimensions of the psychological study of human diversity. In J. D. Goodchilds (Ed.), *Psychological perspectives on human diversity in America.* Washington, DC: American Psychological Association.

Garrett, P., Ng'andu, N., & Ferron, J. (1994). Poverty experiences of young children and the quality of their home environments. *Child Development, 65,* 331–345.

Garton, A. F., & Pratt, C. (1990). Children's pragmatic judgments of direct and indirect requests. *First Language, 10,* 51–59.

Gaulin, S. J. C., & McBurney, D. H. (2001). *Psychology: An evolutionary approach.* Upper Saddle River, NJ: Prentice-Hall.

Gauvain, M. (2001). *The social context of cognitive development.* New York: Guildford Press.

Gay, J., & Cole, M. (1967). *The new mathematics and an old culture.* New York: Holt, Rinehart & Winston.

Gazelle, H., & Ladd, G. W. (2003). Anxious solitude and peer exclusion: A diathesis-stress model of internalizing trajectories in childhood. *Child Development, 74,* 247–258.

Gazelle, H., Putaliaz, M., Li, Y., Grimes, C. L., Kupersmidt, J. B., & Coie, J. D. (2005). Anxious solitude across contexts: Girls' interactions with familiar and unfamiliar peers. *Child Development, 76,* 227–246.

Ge, X., Best, K. M., Conger, R. D., & Simons, R. L. (1996). Parenting behaviors and the occurrence and co-occurrence of adolescent depressive symptoms and conduct problems. *Developmental Psychology, 32,* 717–731.

Ge, X., Conger, R. D., & Elder, G. H., Jr. (1996). Coming of age too early: Pubertal influences on girls' vulnerability to psychological distress. *Child Development, 67,* 3386–3400.

Ge, X., Conger, R. D., & Elder, G. H., Jr. (2001). Pubertal transition, stressful life events, and the emergence of gender differences in adolescent depressive symptoms. *Developmental Psychology, 37,* 404–417.

Geary, D. C. (1995). Reflections on evolution and culture in children's cognition. *American Psychologist, 50,* 24–37.

Geary, D. C., & Bjorklund, D. F. (2000). Evolutionary developmental psychology. *Child Development, 71,* 57–65.

Geary, D. C., & Burlingham-Dubre, M. (1989). External validation of the strategy choice model for addition. *Journal of Experimental Child Psychology, 47,* 175–192.

Geary, D. C., & Widaman, K. F. (1992). Numerical cognition: On convergence of componential and psychometric models. *Intelligence, 16,* 47–80.

Geary, D. C., Bow-Thomas, C. C., Fan, L., & Siegler, R. S. (1993). Even before formal instruction, Chinese children outperform American children in mental arithmetic. *Cognitive Development, 8,* 517–529.

Geary, D. C., Bow-Thomas, C. C., Fan, L., & Siegler, R. S. (1996). Development of arithmetic competencies in Chinese and American children: Influence of age, language, and schooling. *Child Development, 67,* 2022–2044.

Geary, D. C., Brown, S. C., & Samaranayake, V. A. (1991). Cognitive addition: A short longitudinal study of strategy choice and speed of processing differences in normal and mathematically disabled children. *Developmental Psychology, 27,* 787–797.

Geary, D. C., Fan, L., & Bow-Thomas, C. C. (1992). Numerical cognition: Loci of ability differences comparing children from China and the United States. *Psychological Science, 3,* 180–185.

Geary, D. C., Hoard, M. K., Byrd-Craven, J., & DeSoto, M. C. (2004). Strategy choice in simple and complex addition: Contributions of working memory and counting knowledge for children with mathematical disability. *Journal of Experimental Child Psychology, 88,* 121–151.

Geary, D. C., Salthouse, T. A., Chen, P., & Fan, L. (1996). Are East Asian versus American differences in arithmetical ability a recent phenomenon? *Developmental Psychology, 32,* 254–262.

Geen, R. G. (1998). Aggression and antisocial behavior. In D. T. Gilbert, S. T. Fiske, & G. Lindzey (Eds.) *Handbook of social psychology* (Vol. 2) (pp. 317–356). New York: McGraw.

Geisel, J. (2003). Folic acid and neural tube deficits in pregnancy. *Journal of Perinatal and Neonatal Nursing, 17,* 268–280.

Gelman, R. (1969). Conservation acquisition: A problem of learning to attend to relevant attributes. *Journal of Experimental Child Psychology, 7,* 167–187.

Gelman, R., & Baillargeon, R. (1983). A review of Piagetian concepts. In P. H. Mussen (Ed.), *Handbook of child psychology: Vol. 3. Cognitive development.* New York: Wiley.

Gelman, R., & Shatz, M. (1977). Appropriate speech adjustments: The operation of conversational constraints on talk to two-year-olds. In M. Lewis & L. A. Rosenblum (Eds.), *Interaction, conversation, and the development of language.* New York: Wiley.

Gelman, R., & Williams, E. M. (1998). Enabling constraints for cognitive development and learning: Domain-specificity and epigenesis. In D. Kuhn & R. S. Siegler (Eds.), *Cognition, perception, and language,* Vol. 2, of W. Damon (Gen. Ed.), *Handbook of child psychology.* New York: Wiley.

Gelman, S. A., & Ebeling, K. S. (1989). Children's use of nonegocentric standards in judgments of functional size. *Child Development, 60,* 920–932.

Gelman, S. A., Taylor, M. G., & Nguyen, S. P. (2004). Mother–child conversations about gender. *Monographs of the Society for Research on Child Development, 69* (1).

Gelman, S. H., & Gottfried, G. M. (1996). Children's causal explanations of animate and inanimate motion. *Child Development, 67,* 1970–1987.

George, M., Kaplan, N., & Main, M. (1985). *The Adult Attachment Interview.* Unpublished manuscript. University of California, Berkeley.

Gergely, G., Bekkering, H., & Kiraly, I. (2002). Ratial imitation in preverbal infants. *Nature, 415,* 255–259.

Gerken, L., & McIntosh, B. J. (1993). Interplay of function morphemes and prosody in early language. *Developmental Psychology, 24,* 448–457.

Gerken, L., Landau, B., & Remez, R. E. (1990). Function morphemes in young children's speech perception and production. *Developmental Psychology, 26,* 204–216.

Gerlinghoff, M., & Backmund, H. (2004). Eating disorders in childhood and adolescence. Anorexia nervosa, bulimia nervosa, binge eating disorder. *Bundesgesundheitsblatt, Gesundheitsforschung, Gesundheitsschutz, 47,* 246–250.

Gershkoff-Stowe, L., & Smith, L. B. (1997). A curvilinear trend in naming errors as a function of early vocabulary growth. *Cognitive Psychology, 34,* 37–71.

Gesell, A. (1933). Maturation and the patterning of behavior. In C. Murchison (Ed.), *A handbook of child psychology.* Worcester, MA: Clark University Press.

Gesell, A., & Thompson, H. (1929). Learning and growth in identical twins: An experimental study by the method of co-twin control. *Genetic Psychology Monographs, 6,* 1–123.

Getzels, J. W., & Jackson, P. W. (1962). *Creativity and intelligence: Explorations with gifted children.* New York: Wiley.

Gewirtz, J. L., & Pelaez-Nogueras, M. (1992). Skinner, B. F.: Legacy to human infant behavior and development. *American Psychologist, 47,* 1411–1422.

Gewirtz, J. L., & Petrovich, S. B. (1982). Early social and attachment learning in the frame of organic and cultural evolution. In T. M. Field, A. Huston, H. C. Quay, L. Troll, & G. E. Finley (Eds.), *Review of human development.* New York: Wiley.

Gewolb, I. H., Fishman, D., Qureshi, M., & Vice, F. L. (2004). Coordination of suck-swallow-respiration in infants born to mothers with drug-abuse problems. *Developmental and Child Neurology, 46,* 700–706.

Ghatala, E. S., Levin, J. R., Pressley, M., & Goodwin, D. (1986). A componential analysis of the effects of derived and supplied strategy-utility information on children's strategy selections. *Journal of Experimental Child Psychology, 41,* 76–92.

Ghim, H. (1990). Evidence for perceptual organization in infants: Perception of subjective contours by young infants. *Infant Behavior and Development, 13,* 221–248.

Gibbs, J. C., & Schnell, S. V. (1985). Moral development "versus" socialization. A critique. *American Psychologist, 40,* 1071–1080.

Gibson, D., & Harris, A. (1988). Aggregated early intervention effects for Down's syndrome persons: patterning and longevity of benefits. *Journal of Mental Deficiency Research, 32,* 1–17.

Gibson, E. J. (1969). *Principles of perceptual learning and development.* East Norwalk, CT: Appleton-Century-Crofts.

Gibson, E. J., & Walk, R. D. (1960). The "visual cliff." *Scientific American, 202,* 64–71.

Gibson, E. J., & Walker, A. S. (1984). Development of knowledge of visual-tactile affordances of substance. *Child Development, 55,* 453–460.

Gilbert, N. (1997). *Combatting child abuse: International perspectives and trends.* New York: Oxford University Press.

Giles, J. W., & Heyman, G. D. (2004). Conceptions of aggression and withdrawal in early childhood. *Infant & Child Development, 13,* 407–421.

Gill, N. J., & Beazley, R. P. (1993). Grade 6 students benefit from learning about AIDS. *Canadian Journal of Public Health, 84,* (Suppl. 1), 524–527.

Gilligan, C. (1982). *In a different voice: Psychological theory and women's development.* Cambridge, MA: Harvard University Press.

Gilligan, C. (1993). Adolescent development reconsidered. In A. Garrod (Ed.), *Approaches to moral development: New research and emerging themes.* New York: Teachers College Press.

Gilliom, M., Shaw, D. S., Beck, J. E., Schonberg, M. A., & Lukon, J. L. (2001). Anger regulation in disadvantaged preschool boys: Strategies, antecedents, and the development of self-control. *Developmental Psychology, 38,* 222–235.

Gilmore, R. O., Baker, T. J., Grobman, K. H. (2004). Stability in young infants' discrimination of optic flow. *Developmental Psychology, 40,* 259–270.

Gilmore, R. O., & Rettke, H. R. (2003). Four-month-olds' discrimination of self-motion information from optic flow. *Infancy, 4,* 177–200.

Ginsburg, G. S., & Bronstein, P. (1993). Family factors related to children's intrinsic/extrinsic motivational orientation and academic performance. *Child Development, 64,* 1461–1474.

Ginsburg, H. J., & Opper, S. (1988). *Piaget's theory of intellectual development* (3rd ed.). Englewood Cliffs, NJ: Prentice Hall.

Glaser, D. (2000). Child abuse and neglect and the brain: A review. *Journal of Child Psychology & Psychiatry & Allied Disciplines, 41,* 97–117.

Glasgow, K. L., Dornbusch, S. M., Troyer, L., Steinberg, L., & Ritter, P. L. (1997). Parenting styles, adolescents' attributions, and educational outcomes in nine heterogeneous high schools. *Child Development, 68,* 507–529.

Gleitman, L. R. (1990). The structural sources of verb meanings. *Language Acquisition, 1,* 3–55.

Glover, V., O'Connor, T. G., Heron, J., & Golding, J. (2004). Antenatal maternal anxiety is linked with atypical handedness in the child. *Early Human Development, 79,* 107–129.

Glover, V., O'Connor, Thomas G., Heron, J., Golding, J., & the ALSPAC Study team (2004). A maternal anxiety is linked with atypical handedness in the child. *Early Human Development, 79,* 107–118.

Gnepp, J. (1989). Personalized inferences of emotions and appraisals: Component processes and correlates. *Developmental Psychology, 25,* 277–288.

Gnepp, J., & Klayman, J. (1992). Recognition of uncertainty in emotional inferences: Reasoning about emotionally equivocal situations. *Developmental Psychology, 28,* 145–158.

Goëb, J. L., Azcona, B., Troussier, F., Malka, J., Giniès, J. L., & Duverger, P. (2005). Food avoidance emotional disorder in 3- to 10-year-old children: A clinical reality. *Archives de pédiatrie: organe officiel de la Sociéte française, 12,* 1419–1423.

Goencue, A., Mistry, J., & Mosier, C. (2000). Cultural variations in the play of toddlers. *International Journal of Behavioral Development, 24,* 321–329.

Gogate, L. J., & Bahrick, L. E. (2000). A study of multimodal motherese: The role of temporal synchrony between verbal labels and gestures. *Child Development, 71,* 878–894.

Goldberg, A. E., (2004). But do we need universal grammar? Comment on Lidz et al. (2003). *Cognition, 94,* 77–84.

Goldberg, P. (1968). Are women prejudiced against women? *Trans/Action, 5,* 28–30.

Goldberg, S. (1983). Parent-infant bonding: Another look. *Child Development, 54,* 1355–1382.

Golden, M., Birns, B., Bridger, W., & Moss, A. (1971). Social class differentiation in cognitive development among black preschool children. *Child Development, 42,* 37–46.

Goldenberg, R. L. (1995). Small for gestational age infants. In B. P. Sachs, R. Beard, E. Papiernik, & C. Russell (Eds.), *Reproductive health care for women and babies* (pp. 391–399). New York: Oxford University Press.

Goldfield, E. C. (1989). Transition from rocking to crawling: Postural constraints on infant movement. *Developmental Psychology, 25,* 913–919.

Goldin-Meadow, S. (2000). Beyond words: The importance of gestures to researchers and learners. *Child Development, 71,* 231–239.

Goldin-Meadow, S., & Mylander, C. (1984). Gestural communication in deaf children: The effects and noneffects of parental input on early language development. *Monographs of the Society for Research in Child Development, 49* (Serial No. 207).

Goldschmidt, L., Richardson, G. A., Cornelius, M. D., & Day, N. L. (2004). Prenatal marijuana and alcohol exposure and academic achievement at age 10. *Neurotoxicology & Teratology, 26,* 521–532.

Goldsmith, H. H., & Alansky, J. A. (1987). Maternal and infant temperamental predictors of attachment: A meta-analytic review. *Journal of Consulting and Clinical Psychology, 55,* 805–816.

Goldsmith, H. H., Buss, K. A., & Lemery, K. S. (1997). Toddler and childhood temperament: Expanded content, stronger genetic evidence, new evidence for the importance of environment. *Developmental Psychology, 33,* 891–905.

Goldsmith, H. H., Lemery, K. S., Buss, K. A., & Campos, J. J. (1999). Genetic analysis of focal aspects of infant temperament. *Developmental Psychology, 35,* 972–985.

Golin, E. S. (1960). Developmental studies of visual recognition of incomplete objects. *Perceptual and Motor Skills, 11,* 289–298.

Golinkoff, R. M., Jacquet, R. C., Hirsh-Pasek, K., & Nandakumer, R. (1996). Lexical principles may underlie the learning of verbs. *Child Development, 67,* 3101–3119.

Golomb, C., & Galasso, L. (1995). Make believe and reality: Explorations of the imaginary realm. *Developmental Psychology, 31,* 800–810.

Golombok, S., & Tasker, F. (1996). Do parents influence the sexual orientation of their children: Findings from a longitudinal study of lesbian families. *Developmental Psychology, 32,* 3–11.

Golombok, S., Cook, R., Bish, A., & Murray, C. (1995). Families created by new reproductive technologies: Quality of parenting and social and emotional development of the children. *Child Development, 66,* 285–298.

Golombok, S., MacCallum, F., Goodman, E., & Rutter, M. (2002). Families with children conceived by donor insemination: A follow-up at age twelve. *Child Development, 73,* 952–968.

Golombok, S., Murray, C., Jadva, V., MacCallum, F., & Lycett, E. (2004). Families created through surrogacy arrangements: Parent–child relationships in the 1st year of life. *Developmental Psychology, 40,* 400–411.

Golombok, S., Perry, B., Burston, A., Murray, C., Mooney-Somers, J., Stevens, M., & Golding, J. (2003). Children with lesbian parents: A community study. *Developmental Psychology, 39,* 20–33.

Gonzalez, E. (2000, February 27). Reform bill draws mixed reactions. *Athens Daily News,* C1, C6.

Good, T. L., & Brophy, J. E. (1994). *Looking in classrooms* (6th ed.), New York: Harper Collins.

Goodenough, F. L. (1931). *Anger in young children.* Minneapolis: University of Minnesota Press.

Goodman, G. S., Quas, J. A., Batterman-Faunce, J. M., Riddlesberger, & Kuhn, J. (1994). Predictors of accurate and inaccurate memories of traumatic events experiences in childhood. *Consciousness and Cognition, 3,* 269–294.

Goodman, J. C., McDonough, L., & Brown, N. B. (1998). The role of semantic context and memory in the acquisition of novel nouns. *Child Development, 69,* 1330–1344.

Goodwyn, S. W., & Acredolo, L. P. (1993). Symbolic gesture versus word: Is there a modality advantage for onset of symbol use. *Child Development, 64,* 688–701.

Goossens, F. A., & van IJzendoorn, M. H. (1990). Quality of infants' attachments to professional caregivers: Relation to infant–parent attachment and day-care characteristics. *Child Development, 61,* 832–837.

Gopnik, A., & Choi, S. (1995). *Beyond names for things: Children's acquisition of verbs.* Hillsdale, NJ: Erlbaum.

Gopnik, A., & Meltzoff, A. N. (1987). Language and thought in the young child: Early semantic developments and their relationships to object permanence, means–ends understanding, and categorization. In K. Nelson & A. Van Kleeck (Eds.), *Children's language* (Vol. 6). Hillsdale, NJ: Erlbaum.

Gopnik, A., & Meltzoff, A. N. (1997). *Words, thoughts, and theories.* Cambridge, MA: MIT Press.

Gordon, C. M. (2003). Normal bone sccretion and effects of nutritional disorders in childhood. *Journal of Women's Health, 12,* 137–143.

Gordon, C. M., Goodman, E., Emans, S. J., et al. (2002). Physiologic regulators of bone turnover in young women with anorexia nervosa. *Journal of Pediatrics, 141,* 64–70.

Gordon, P. (1990). Learnability and feedback. *Developmental Psychology, 26,* 217–220.

Gorer, G. (1968). Man has no "killer" instinct. In M. F. A. Montague (Ed.), *Man and aggression.* New York: Oxford University Press.

Gormley. W. T., Jr. (2005). The universal pre-K bandwagon. *Phi Delta Kappan, 87,* 246–249.

Gorn, G. J., Goldberg, M. E., & Kanungo, R. N. (1976). The role of educational television in changing the intergroup attitudes of children. *Child Development, 47,* 277–280.

Gortmaker, S. L., Must, A., Sobol, A. M., Peterson, K., Colditz, G. A., & Dietz, W. H. (1996). Television viewing as a cause of increasing obesity among children in the Unites States, 1986–1990. *Archives of Pediatrics and Adolescent Medicine, 150,* 356–362.

Gosden, C., Nicolaides, K., & Whitting, V. (1994). *Is my baby all right?: A guide for expectant parents.* Oxford, England: Oxford University Press.

Goswami, U. (1995). Transitive relational mapping in three- and four-year-olds: The analogy of Goldilocks and the Three Bears. *Child Development, 66,* 877–892.

Goswami, U. (1996). Analogical reasoning and cognitive development. In H. W. Reese (Ed.), *Advances in child development and behavior* (Vol. 26). San Diego: Academic.

Goswami, U. (2003). Inductive and deductive reasoning. In U. Goswami (Ed.), *Blackwell handbook of childhood cognitive development.* Malden, MA: Blackwell Publishing.

Goswami, U., & Brown, A. L. (1990). Higher-order structure and relational reasoning: Contrasting analogical and thematic relations. *Cognition, 36,* 207–226.

Gotlib, I. H., Whiffen, V. E., Wallace, P. M., & Mount, J. (1991). Prospective investigation of postpartum depression: Factors involved in onset and recovery. *Journal of Abnormal Psychology, 100,* 122–132.

Gottesman, I. I. (1963). Genetic aspects of intelligent behavior. In N. Ellis (Ed.), *Handbook of mental deficiency.* New York: McGraw-Hill.

Gottesman, I. I. (1991). *Schizophrenia genesis: The origins of madness.* New York: W. H. Freeman.

Gottfried, A. E., Fleming, J. S., & Gottfried, A. W. (1998). Role of cognitively stimulating home environment in children's academic intrinsic motivation: A longitudinal study. *Child Development, 69,* 1448–1460.

Gottfried, A. W., Gottfried, A. E., Bathurst, K., & Guerin, D. W. (1994). *Gifted IQS: Early developmental aspects: The Fullerton Longitudinal Study.* New York: Plenum.

Gottlieb, D. (1966). Teaching and students: The views of Negro and white teachers. *Sociology of Education, 37,* 344–353.

Gottlieb, G. (1991). Experiential canalization of behavioral development: Results. *Developmental Psychology, 27,* 35–39.

Gottlieb, G. (1991b). Experiential canalization of behavioral development. Theory and commentary. *Developmental Psychology, 27,* 4–13.

Gottlieb, G. (1996). Commentary: A systems view of psychobiological development. In D. Magnusson (Ed.), *The lifespan development of individuals: Behavioral, neurobiological, and psychosocial perspectives. A synthesis.* Cambridge, England: Cambridge University Press.

Gottlieb, G. (2003). Normally occurring environmental and behavioral influences on gene activity. In C. Garcia Coll, E. Bearer, & R. M. Lerner (Eds.), *Nature and nurture: The complex interplay of genetic and environmental influences on human behavior and development.* Mahwah, NJ: Lawrence Erlbaum Associates.

Graber, J. A., Brooks-Gunn, J. Paikoff, R. L., & Warren, M. P. (1994). Prediction of eating problems: An 8-year study of adolescent girls. *Developmental Psychology, 30,* 823–834.

Graber, J., & Bastiani, A. (2001). Psychosocial change at puberty and beyond: Understanding adolescent sexuality and sexual orientation. In A. Augelli and G. Patterson (Eds.), *Lesbian, gay and bi-sexual identities and youth: Psychological perspectives.* London: Oxford Press.

Graham, S., & Juvonen, J. (1998). Self-blame and peer victimization in middle school: An attributional analysis. *Developmental Psychology, 34,* 587–599.

Grandjean, P., Weihe, P., Burse, V. W., Needham, L. L., Storr-Hansen, I., Heinszow, B., et al. (2001). Neurobehavioral deficits associated with PCB in 7-year-old children prenatally exposed to seafood neurotoxicants. *Neurotoxicology and Teratology, 23,* 305–317.

Grantham-McGregor, S. (1995). A review of studies of the effects of severe malnutrition on mental development. *Journal of Nutrition Supplement, 125,* 22335–22385.

Grantham-McGregor, S., Powell, C., Walker, S., Chang, S., & Fletcher, P. (1994). The long-term follow-up of severely malnourished children who participated in an intervention program. *Child Development, 65,* 428–439.

Graves, S. B. (1993). Television, the portrayal of African Americans, and the development of children's attitudes. In G. L. Berry & J. K. Asamen (Eds.), *Children and television: Images in a changing sociocultural world* (pp. 179–190).

Gray, J. (1992). *Men are from Mars, Women are from Venus: The classic guide to understanding the opposite sex.* New York: Harper-Collins Publishers.

Gray, J. R., Chabris, C. F., & Braver, T. S. (2003). Neural mechanisms of general fluid intelligence. *Nature Neuroscience, 6,* 316–322.

Gray, S. W., & Klaus, R. A. (1970). The early training project: A seventh-year report. *Child Development, 41,* 909–924.

Gray-Little, B., & Hafdahl, A. R. (2000). Factors influencing racial comparisons of self-esteem: A quantitative review. *Psychological Bulletin, 126,* 26–54.

Green, J. A., Gustafson, G. E., & McGhie, A. C. (1998). Changes in infants' cries as a function of time in a cry bout. *Child Development, 69,* 271–280.

Green, R. (1987). *The "sissy boy syndrome" and the development of homosexuality.* New Haven, CT: Yale University Press.

Greenberg, M., & Morris, N. (1974). Engrossment: The newborn's impact upon the father. *American Journal of Orthopsychiatry, 44,* 520–531.

Greenberg, M. T., Lengua, L. J., Coie, J. D., Pinderhughes, E. E., & The Conduct Problems Prevention Research Group (1999). Predicting developmental outcomes at school entry using a multiple-risk model: Four American communities. *Developmental Psychology, 35,* 403–417.

Greenberger, A., & Chen, C. (1996). Perceived family relationships and depressed mood in early and late adolescence: A comparison of European and Asian Americans. *Developmental Psychology, 32,* 707–716.

Greenberger, E., & Chen, C. (1996). Perceived family relationships and depressed mood in early and late adolescence: A comparison of European and Asian Americans. *Developmental Psychology, 32,* 707–716.

Greenberger, E., O'Neil, R., & Nagel, S. K. (1994). Linking workplace and homeplace: Relations between the nature of adults' work and their parenting behavior. *Developmental Psychology, 30,* 990–1002.

Greene, R. (1997, February 28). U.S. students scores getting better, but few performing above basic level. *The Atlanta Constitution,* p. C3.

Greenfield, P. M., & Smith, J. H. (1976). *The structure of communication in early language development.* New York: Academic.

Greenhoot, A. F., Ornstein, P. A., Gordon, B. N., & Baker-Ward, L. (1999). Acting out the details of a pediatric check-up: The impact of interview condition and behavioral style on children's memory reports. *Child Development, 70,* 363–380.

Greenough, W. T., & Black, J. E. (1992). Induction of brain structure by experience: Substrates for cognitive development. In M. R. Gunnar & C. A. Nelson (Eds.), *Minnesota symposia on child psychology* (pp. 155–200). Hillsdale, NJ: Erlbaum.

Greenough, W. T., Black, J. E., & Wallace, C. S. (1987). Experience and brain development. *Child Development, 58,* 539–559.

Greenough, W. T., Black, J. E., & Wallace, C. S. (2002). Experience and brain development. In M. H. Johnson, Y. Munakata, & R. Gilmore (Eds.), *Brain development and cognition: A reader* (2nd ed., pp. 186–216). Oxford: Blackwell Publishing.

Greif, E. B., & Ulman, K. J. (1982). The psychological impact of menarche on early adolescent females: A review of the literature. *Child Development, 53,* 1413–1430.

Greig, A., & Taylor, J. (2004). *Doing research with children.* London: SAGE Publications.

Groark, C. J., Muhamedrahimov, R. J., Palmov, O., Nikiforova, N. V., & McCall, R. B. (2005). Improvements in early care in Russian orphanages and their relationship to observed behaviors. *Infant Mental Health Journal, 26,* 96–109.

Grolnick, W. S., & Ryan, R. M. (1989). Parent styles associated with self-regulation and competence in school. *Journal of Educational Psychology, 81,* 143–154.

Grolnick, W. S., Bridges, L. J., & Connell, J. P. (1996). Emotion regulation in two-year-olds: Strategies and emotional expression in four contexts. *Child Development, 67,* 928–941.

Grolnick, W. S., Gurland, S. T., Jacob, K. F., & Decourcey, W. (2002). The development of self-determination in middle childhood and adolescence. In A. Wigfield & J. S. Eccles (Eds.), *Development of achievement motivation* (pp. 147–171). San Diego: Academic Press.

Groome, L. J., Swiber, M. J., Atterbury, J. L., Bentz, L. S., & Holland, S. B. (1997). Similarities and differences in behavioral state organization during sleep periods in the perinatal infant before and after birth. *Child Development, 68,* 1–11.

Gross, A. L., & Ballif, B. (1991). Children's understanding of emotion from facial expressions and situations: A review. *Developmental Review, 11,* 368–398.

Grossmann, K., Grossmann, K. E., Spangler, S., Suess, G., & Unzner, L. (1985). Maternal sensitivity and newborn responses as related to quality of attachment in Northern Germany. In I. Bretherton & E. Waters, Growing points of attachment theory. *Monographs of the Society for Research in Child Development, 50,* (1–2, Serial No. 209).

Grotevent, H. D., & Cooper, C. R. (1986). Individuation in family relations: A perspective on individual differences in the development of identity and role-taking skills in adolescence. *Human Development, 29,* 82–100.

Grotevant, H. D., & Cooper, C. R. (1998). Individuality and connectedness in adolescent development. In E. Skoe & A. vonder Lippe (Eds.), *Personality development in adolescence: A cross-national and life span perspective.* London: Routledge.

Gruber, H. (1982). On the hypothesized relation between giftedness and creativity. In D. H. Feldman (Ed.), *New directions for child development: No. 17. Developmental approaches to giftedness and creativity.* San Francisco: Jossey-Bass.

Grumbach, M. M., & Styne, D. M. (2003). Puberty: Ontogeny, neuroendocrinology, physiology, and disorders. In P. R. Larson (Ed.), *Williams textbook of endocrinology* (10th ed., pp. 1115–1200). St. Louis, MO: Saunders.

Grusec, J. E. (1991). Socializing concern for others in the home. *Developmental Psychology, 27,* 338–342.

Grusec, J. E. (1992). Social learning theory and developmental psychology: The legacies of Robert Sears and Albert Bandura. *Developmental Psychology, 28,* 776–786.

Grusec, J. E., & Goodnow, J. J. (1994). Impact of parental discipline methods on the child's internalization of values: A reconceptualization of current points of view. *Developmental Psychology, 30,* 4–19.

Grusec, J. E., Goodnow, J. J., & Cohen, L. (1996). Household work and the development of concern for others. *Developmental Psychology, 32,* 999–1007.

Grusec, J. E., Goodnow, J. J., & Kuczynski, L. (2000). New directions in analyses of parenting contributions to children's acquisitions of values. *Child Development, 71,* 205–211.

Grusec, J. E., Kuczynski, L., Rushton, J. P., & Simutis, Z. (1979). Learning resistance to temptation through observation. *Developmental Psychology, 15,* 233–240.

Grych, J. H., & Clark, R. (1999). Maternal employment and development of the father–infant relationship in the first year. *Developmental Psychology, 35,* 893–903.

Grych, J. H., Fincham, F. D., Jouriles, E. N., & McDonald, R. (2000). Interparental conflict and child adjustment: Testing the mediational role of appraisals in the cognitive-contextual framework. *Child Development, 71,* 1648–1661.

Grych, J. H., Harold, G. T., & Miles, C. J. (2003). A prospective investigation of appraisals as mediators of the link between interpersonal conflict and child adjustment. *Child Development, 74,* 1176–1193.

Gude, N. M., Roberts, C. T., Kalionis, B., & King, R. (2004). Growth and function of the normal human placenta. *Thrombosis Research, 114,* 397–408.

Guerra, N. G., & Slaby, R. G. (1990). Cognitive mediators of aggression in adolescent offenders: 2. Intervention. *Developmental Psychology, 26,* 269–277.

Guilford, J. P. (1967). *The nature of human intelligence.* New York: McGraw-Hill.

Guilford, J. P. (1988). Some changes in the structure-of-the-intellect model. *Educational and Psychological Measurement, 40,* 1–4.

Gullota, T. P., Adams, G. R., & Alexander, S. J. (1986). *Today's marriages and families: A wellness approach.* Monterey, CA: Brooks/Cole.

Gunderson, V., & Sackett, G. P. (1982). Paternal effects on reproductive outcome and developmental risk. In M. E. Lamb & A. L. Brown (Eds.), *Advances in developmental psychology* (Vol. 2). Hillsdale, NJ: Erlbaum.

Gunnar, M. R., Malone, S., Vance, G., & Fisch, R. O. (1985). Coping with aversive stimulation in the neonatal period: Quiet sleep and plasma cortisol levels during recovery from circumcision. *Child Development, 56,* 824–834.

Guo, Y. L., Lai, T. J., Chen, S. J., & Hsu, C. C. (1995). Gender-related decrease in Raven's progressive matrices scores in children prenatally exposed to polychlorinated biphenyls and related contaminants. *Bulletin of Environmental Contamination and Toxicology, 55,* 8–13.

Gurucharri, C., & Selman, R. L. (1982). The development of interpersonal understanding during childhood, preadolescence, and adolescence: A longitudinal follow-up study. *Child Development, 53,* 924–927.

Gusella, J., Clark, S., & Van Roosmalen, E. (2004). Body image self-evaluation colouring lens: comparing the ornamental and instrumental views of adolescent girls with eating disorders. *European Eating Disorders Review,* 12, 223–229.

Guttentag, M., & Bray, H. (1976). *Undoing sex stereotypes. Research and resources for educators.* New York: McGraw-Hill.

Guttentag, R. E., Ornstein, P. A., & Seimans, L. (1987). Children's spontaneous rehearsal: Transitions in strategy acquisition. *Cognitive Development, 2,* 307–326.

Guzell, J. R., & Vernon-Feagans, L. (2004). Parental perceived control over caregiving and its relationship to parent–infant interaction. *Child Development, 75,* 134–146.

Gzesh, S. M., & Surber, C. F. (1985). Visual perspective-taking skills in children. *Child Development, 56,* 1204–1213.

Haan, N., Aerts, E., & Cooper, B. A. B. (1985). *On moral grounds. The search for practical morality.* New York: New York University Press.

Haden, C. A., Haine, R. A., & Fivush, R. (1997). Developing narrative structure in parent–child reminiscing across the preschool years. *Developmental Psychology, 33,* 295–307.

Hagerman, R. J. (1996). Biomedical advances in developmental psychology: The case of Fragile X syndrome. *Developmental Psychology, 32,* 416–424.

Hagerman, R. J., & Cronister, A. (1996). *Fragile X syndrome: Diagnosis, treatment, and research* (2nd ed.). Baltimore: Johns Hopkins University Press.

Haight, W. L., Wang, X-l, Fung, H. H-t., Williams, K., & Mintz, J. (1999). Universal, developmental, and variable aspects of young children's play: A cross-cultural comparison of pretending at home. *Child Development, 70,* 1477–1488.

Hajdu, K., and Golbus, M. S. (1993). Stem cell transplantation. *Western Journal of Medicine, 159,* 356–359.

Hakuta, K. (1988). Why bilinguals? In F. S. Kessel (Ed.), *The development of language and language researchers: Essays in honor of Roger Brown.* Hillsdale, NJ: Erlbaum.

Hakuta, K., & Garcia, E. E. (1989). Bilingualism and education. *American Psychologist, 44,* 374–379.

Hala, S., & Chandler, M. (1996). The role of strategic planning in accessing false-belief understanding. *Child Development, 67,* 2948–2966.

Hall, D. G., & Waxman, S. R. (1993). Assumptions about word meaning: Individuation and basic-level kinds. *Child Development, 64,* 1550–1570.

Hall, D. G., Quantz, D. H., & Persoage, K. A. (2000). Preschoolers' use of form class cues in word learning. *Developmental Psychology, 36,* 449–462.

Hall, E. (2001). Babies, books, and "impact": Problems and possibilities in the evaluation of a Bookstart project. *Educational Review, 53,* 57–64.

Hall, G. S. (1891). The contents of children's minds on entering school. *Pedagogical Seminary, 1,* 139–173.

Hall, G. S. (1904). *Adolescence.* New York: Appleton-Century-Crofts.

Halpern, C. T., Udry, J. R., Campbell, B., & Suchindran, C. (1999). Effects of body fat on weight concerns, dating, and sexual activity: A longitudinal analysis of black and white adolescent girls. *Developmental Psychology, 35,* 721–736.

Halpern, D. F. (1997). Sex differences in intelligence: Implications for education. *American Psychologist, 52,* 1091–1102.

Halpern, D. F. (2000). *Sex differences in cognitive abilities* (3rd ed.). Mahwah, NJ: Erlbaum.

Halpern, D. F. (2004). A cognitive-process taxonomy for sex differences in cognitive abilities. *Current Directions in Psychological Science, 13,* 135–139.

Halpern, L. F., MacLean, W. E., Jr., & Baumeister, A. A. (1995). Infant sleep-wake characteristics: Relation to neurological status and prediction of developmental outcome, *Developmental Review, 15,* 255–291.

Halter, R., Kelsberg, G., Nashelsky, J., & Krist, A. (2004). Is antibiotic prophylaxis effective for recurrent acute otitis media? *Journal of Family Practice,* 53, 99–101.

Halverson, H. M. (1931). An experimental study of prehension in infants by means of systematic cinema records. *Genetic Psychology Monographs, 10,* 107–286.

Halvorsen, A. A., & Heyerdahl, S. (2004). Good outcome of adolescent onset anorexia nervosa after systematic treatment. *European Child & Adolescent Psychiatry, 13,* 295–306.

Hamilton, C. E. (2000). Continuity and discontinuity of attachment from infancy through adolescence. *Child Development, 71,* 690–694.

Hamond, N. R., & Fivush, R. (1991). Memories of Mickey Mouse: Young children recount their trip to Disney world. *Cognitive Development, 6,* 433–448.

Hampton, M. R., Smith, P., Jeffery, B., & McWatters, B. (2002). Sexual experience, contraception, and STI prevention among high school students: Results from a Canadian urban centre. *Canadian Journal of Human Sexuality, 10,* 111–116.

Hanlon, H. W., Thatcher, R. W., & Cline, M. J. (1999). Gender differences in the development of EEG coherence in normal children. *Developmental Neuropsychology, 16,* 479–507.

Hans, S., & Jeremy, R. (2001). Postneonatal mental and motor development of infants exposed in utero to opiod drugs. *Infant Mental Health Journal, 22,* 300–316.

Harding, J. E., & McCowan, L. M. E. (2003). Perinatal predictors of growth patterns to 18 months in children born small for gestational age. *Early Human Development, 74,* 13–26.

Hardy, J. B., Astone, N. M., Brooks-Gunn, J., Shapiro, S., & Miller, T. L. (1998). Like mother, like child: Intergenerational patterns of age at first birth and associations with childhood and adolescent characteristics and outcomes in the second generation. *Developmental Psychology, 34,* 1220–1232.

Harkness, S., Edwards, C. P., & Super, C. M. (1981). Social roles and moral reasoning: A case study in a rural African community. *Developmental Psychology, 17,* 595–603.

Harley, K., & Reese, E. (1999). Origins of autobiographical memory. *Developmental Psychology, 35,* 1338–1348.

Harlow, H. F., & Zimmerman, R. R. (1959). Affectional responses in the infant monkey. *Science, 130,* 421–432.

Harnishfeger, K. K. (1995). The development of cognitive inhibition: Theories, definitions, and research evidence. In F. Dempster & C. Brainerd (Eds.), *New perspectives on interference and inhibition in cognition* (pp. 176–204). New York: Academic Press.

Harnishfeger, K. K., & Bjorklund, D. F. (1990). Children's strategies: A brief history. In D. F. Bjorklund (Ed.), *Children's strategies: Contemporary views of cognitive development* (pp. 1–22). Hillsdale, NJ: Erlbaum.

Harnishfeger, K. K., & Bjorklund, D. F. (1994). The development of inhibition mechanisms and their relation to individual differences in children's cognitions. *Learning and Individual Differences, 6,* 331–355.

Harnishfeger, K. K., & Pope, R. S. (1996). Intending to forget: The development of cognitive inhibition in directed forgetting. *Journal of Experimental Child Psychology, 62,* 292–315.

Harold, G. T., Fincham, F. D., Osborne, L. M., & Conger, R. D. (1997). Mom and dad are at it again: Adolescent perceptions of marital conflict and adolescent psychological distress. *Developmental Psychology, 33,* 333–350.

Harper, L. V., & Huie, K. S. (1985). The effects of prior group experience, age, and familiarity on the quality and organization of preschoolers' social relationships. *Child Development, 56,* 704–717.

Harrington, D. M., Block, J. H., & Block, J. (1987). Testing aspects of Carl Rogers's theory of creative environments in young adolescents. *Journal of Personality and Social Psychology, 52,* 851–856.

Harris, J. R. (1998). *The nurture assumption: Why children turn out the way they do.* New York: Free Press.

Harris, J. R. (2000). Socialization, personality, development, and the child's environments: A comment on Vandell (2000). *Developmental Psychology, 36,* 711–723.

Harris, M. (1992). *Language experience and early language development: From input to uptake.* Hove, UK: Erlbaum.

Harris, M. J. (1995). Where is the child's environment? A group socialization theory of development. *Psychological Review, 102,* 458–489.

Harris, N. B. (1992). Sex, race, and the experiences of aggression. *Aggressive Behavior, 18,* 201–217.

Harris, P. L. (1989). *Children and emotion: The development of psychological understanding.* Oxford, England: Basil-Blackwell.

Harris, P. L., Kavanaugh, R. D., & Meredith, M. C. (1994). Young children's comprehension of pretend episodes: The integration of successive actions. *Child Development, 65,* 16–30.

Harrison, L. F., & Williams, T. (1986). Television and cognitive development. In T. Williams (Ed.), *The impact of television: A natural experiment in three communities.* Orlando, FL: Academic.

Harrison, L. J., & Ungerer, J. A. (2002). Maternal employment and mother–infant attachment security at 12 months postpartum. *Development Psychology, 38,* 758–773.

Harrist, A. W., Zaia, A. F., Bates, J. E., Dodge, K. A., & Pettit, G. S. (1997). Subtypes of social withdrawal in early childhood: Sociometric status and social-cognitive differences across four years. *Child Development, 68,* 278–294.

Hart B., & Risley, T. R. (1995). *Meaningful differences in the everyday experience of young American children.* Baltimore: Paul H. Brookes.

Hart, C. H., Burts, D. C., Durland, M. A., Charlesworth, R. DeWolf, M., & Fleege, P.O. (1998). Stress behaviors and activity type participation of preschoolers in more or less developmentally appropriate classrooms: SES and sex differences. *Journal of Research in Childhood Education,* in press.

Hart, D., & Chmiel, S. (1992). Influence of defense mechanisms on moral judgment development: A longitudinal study. *Developmental Psychology, 28,* 722–730.

Hart, D., Hofmann, V., Edelstein, W., & Keller, M. (1997). The relation of childhood personality types to adolescent behavior and development: A longitudinal study of Icelandic children. *Developmental Psychology, 33,* 195–205.

Hart, E. L., Lahey, B. B., Loeber, R., Applegate, B., & Frick, P. J. (1995). Developmental change in attention-deficit hyperactivity disorder in boys: A four-year longitudinal study. *Journal of Abnormal Child Psychology, 23,* 729–749.

Hart, S. N. (1991). From property to person status: Historical perspective on children's rights. *American Psychologist, 46,* 53–59.

Harter, S. (1982). The perceived competence scale for children. *Child Development, 53,* 87–97.

Harter, S. (1983). Developmental perspectives on the self-system. In P. H. Mussen (Ed.), *Handbook of child psychology.* Vol. 4: *Socialization, personality, and social development.* New York: Wiley.

Harter, S. (1999). *The cognitive and social construction of the developing self.* New York: Guilford.

Harter, S., & Monsour, A. (1992). Developmental analysis of conflict caused by opposing attributes in the adolescent self-portrait. *Developmental Psychology, 28,* 251–260.

Harter, S., & Pike, R. (1984). The pictorial scale of perceived competence and social acceptance for young children. *Child Development, 55,* 1969–1982.

Harter, S., & Whitesell, N. (1989). Developmental changes in children's understanding of simple, multiple, and blended emotion concepts. In C. Saarni & P. Harris (Eds.), *Children's understanding of emotion.* Cambridge, England: Cambridge University Press.

Harter, S., Marold, D. B., Whitesell, N. R., & Cobbs, G. (1996). A model of the effects of perceived parent and peer support on adolescent false self behavior. *Child Development, 67,* 360–374.

Harter, S., Waters, P., & Whitsell, N. R. (1998). Relational self-worth: Differences in perceived worth as a person across interpersonal contexts. *Child Development, 69,* 756–766.

Harter, S., Waters, P. L., Whitesell, N. R., & Kastelic, D. (1998). Level of voice among female and male high school students: Relational context, support, and gender orientation. *Developmental Psychology, 34,* 892–901.

Hartshorne, H., & May, M. S. (1928–1930). *Studies in the nature of character.* Vol. 1: *Studies in deceit.* Vol. 2: *Studies in self control.* Vol. 3: *Studies in the organization of character.* New York: Macmillan.

Hartung, B., & Sweeney, K. (1991). Why adult children return home. *Social Science Journal, 28,* 467–480.

Hartup, W. W. (1974). Aggression in childhood: Developmental perspectives. *American Psychologist, 29,* 336–341.

Hartup, W. W. (1983). Peer relations. In P. H. Mussen (Ed.), *Handbook of Child psychology. Vol. 4: Socialization, personality, and social development* (pp. 103–196). New York: Wiley.

Hartup, W. W. (1992). Friendships and their developmental significance. In H. McGurk (Ed.), *Childhood social development: Contemporary perspectives.* Hove, England: Erlbaum.

Harvey, S., Jarrell, J., Brant, R., Stainton, C., & Rach, D. (1996). A randomized, controlled trial of nurse-midwifery care. *Birth, 23,* 128–135.

Harwood, R. L., Schoelmerich, A., Ventura-Cook, E., Schulze, P. A., & Wilson, S. P. (1996). Culture and class influences on Anglo and Puerto Rican mothers' beliefs regarding lon-term socialization goals and child behavior. *Child Development, 67,* 2446–2461.

Haselager, G. J. T., Cillessen, A. H. N., Van Lieshout, C. F. M., Riksen-Walraven, J. M. A., & Hartup, W. W. (2002). Heterogeneity among peer-rejected boys across middle childhood: Developmental pathways of social behavior. *Developmental Psychology, 38,* 446–456.

Haskett, M. E., & Kistner, J. A. (1991). Social interactions and peer perceptions of young physically abused children. *Child Development, 62,* 979–990.

Hasselhorn, M. (1992). Task dependency and the role of category typicality and metamemory in the development of an organizational strategy. *Child Development, 63,* 202–214.

Hasselhorn, M. (1995). Beyond production deficiency and utilization inefficiency: Mechanisms of the emergence of strategic categorization in episodic memory tasks. In F. E. Weinert & W. Schneider (Eds.), *Memory performance and competencies: Issues in growth and development.* Hillsdale, NJ: Erlbaum.

Hastings, P. D., Zahn-Waxler, C. Z., Robinson, J., Usher, B., & Bridges, D. (2000). The development of concern for others in children with behavior problems. *Developmental Psychology, 36,* 531–546.

Haug, K., Irgens, L. M., Skjaerven, R., Markestad, T., Baste, V., & Schreuder (2000). Maternal smoking and birthweight: effect of modification of period maternal age and paternal smoking. *Acta Obstet Gyncol Scand, 79,* 485–489.

Hausenblas, H. A., & Carron, A. V. (1999). Eating disorder indices and athletes: An integration. *Journal of Sport and Exercise Psychology, 21,* 230–258.

Hauser-Cram, P., Warfield, M. E., Shonkoff, J. P., Krauss, M. W., Upshur, C. C., & Sayer, A. (1999). Family influences on adaptive development in young children with Down syndrome. *Child Development, 70,* 979–989.

Hay, D. F., Caplan, M., Castle, J., & Stimson, C. A. (1991). Does sharing become increasingly "rational" in the second year of life? *Developmental Psychology, 27,* 987–993.

Hay, D. F., Castle, J., & Davies, L. (2000). Toddlers' use of force against familiar peers: A precursor of serious aggression? *Child Development, 71,* 457–467.

Hayden, C. A., Haine, R. R., & Fivush, R. (1997). Developing narrative structure in parent-child reminiscing across the preschool years. *Developmental Psychology, 33,* 295–307.

Hayes, B. K., & Hennessy, R. (1996). The nature and development of nonverbal implicit memory. *Journal of Experimental Child Psychology, 63,* 22–43.

Hayne, H., & Rovee-Collier, C. (1995). The organization of reactivated memory in infancy. *Child Development, 66,* 893–906.

Haywood, H. C. (2001). What is dynamic 'testing'? *Issues in Education, 7,* 201–210.

Hearold, S. (1986). A synthesis of 1043 effects of television on social behavior. In G. Comstock (Ed.), *Public communications and behavior: Volume I* (pp. 65–133). New York: Academic Press.

Heath, S. B. (1989). Oral and literate traditions among black Americans living in poverty. *American Psychologist, 44,* 367–373.

Hebb, D. O. (1980). *Essay on mind.* Hillsdale, NJ: Erlbaum.

Hedges, L. V., & Nowell, A. (1995, July 7). Sex differences in mental test scores, variability,and numbers of high-scoring individuals. *Science, 269,* 41–45.

Hefford, N. A., & Keef, S. P. (2004). *Journal of Educational Computing Research, 30,* 69–86.

Heine, S. J., Lehman, D. R., Markus, H. R., & Kitayama, S. (1999). Is there a universal need for positive self-regard? *Psychological Review, 106,* 766–794.

Heinonen, O. P., Slone, D., & Shapiro, S. (1977). *Birth defects and drugs in pregnancy.* Littleton, MA: Publishing Sciences Group.

Helms, J. E. (1997). The triple quandary of race, culture, and social class in standardized cognitive ability testing. In D. P. Flanagan, J. Genshaft, & P. L. Harrison (Eds.), *Contemporary intellectual assessment: Theories, tests, and issues.* New York: Guilford.

Helms-Lorenz, M., Van de Vijver, F. J. R., & Poortinga, Y. H. (2003). Cross-cultural differences in cognitive performance and Spearman's hypothesis: g or c? *Intelligence,* 31, 9–30.

Helwig, C. C., Arnold, M., Dingliang, T., & Boyd, D. (2003). Chinese adolescents' reasoning about democratic and authority-based decision making in peer, family, and school context. *Child Development, 74,* 783–800.

Hendler, M., & Weisberg, P. (1992). Conservation acquisition, maintenance, and generalization by mentally retarded children using equality-rule training. *Journal of Experimental Child Psychology, 54,* 258–276.

Hendrick, B. (1994, June 7). Teen sexual activity increases, as does kids' use of condoms. *Atlanta Constitution,* p. A1, A6.

Hendrick, V., & Altshuler, L. L. (1999). Biological determinants of postpartum depression. In. L. J. Miller (Ed.), *Postpartum mood disorders* (pp. 65–82). Washington, DC: American Psychiatric Press.

Henker, B., & Whalen, C. K. (1989). Hyperactivity and attention deficits. *American Psychologist, 44,* 216–223.

Hennessey, B. A., & Amabile, T. M. (1988). The conditions of creativity. In R. J. Sternberg (Ed.), *The nature of creativity. Contemporary psychological perspectives.* Cambridge, England: Cambridge University Press.

Henry, B., Caspi, A., Moffitt, T. E., & Silva, P. A. (1996). Temperamental and familial predictors of violent and nonviolent criminal convictions: Age 3 to age 18. *Developmental Psychology, 32,* 614–623.

Hepp, U., Milos, G., & Braun-Scharm, H. (2004). Gender identity disorder and anorexia nervosa in male monozygotic twins. *International Journal of Eating Disorders, 35,* 239–243.

Herba, C., & Phillips, M. (2004). Development of facial expression recognition from childhood to adolescence: Behavioural and neurological perspectives. *Journal of Child Psychology & Psychiatry & Allied Disciplines, 45,* 1185–1199.

Herbert, J., & Hayne, H. (2000). Memory retrieval by 18–30-month-olds: Age related changes in representational flexibility. *Developmental Psychology, 36,* 473–484.

Herkowitz, J. (1978). Sex-role expectations and motor behavior of the young child. In M. V. Ridenour (Ed.), *Motor development: Issues and applications.* Princeton, NJ: Princeton Book Company.

Herman-Giddens, M. E., Slora, E. J., Wasserman, R. C., Bourdony, C. J., Bhapkar, M. V., Koch, G. G., & Hasemeier, C. M. (1997). Secondary sexual characteristics and menses in young girls seen in office practice: A study from the Pediatric Research in Office Settings Network. *Pediatrics, 99,* 505–512.

Hermann, M. (2004). Forced to choose: Some determinants of racial identification in multiracial adolescents. *Child Development, 75,* 730–748.

Hernández Blasi, C., & Bjorklund, D. F. (2003). Evolutionary developmental psychology: A new tool for better understanding human ontogeny. *Human Development, 46,* 259–281.

Hernandez, D. J. (1997). Child development and the social demography of childhood. *Child Development, 68,* 149–169.

Herpertz-Dahlmann, B., Muller, B., Herpertz, S., Heussen, N., Hiebebrand, J., & Remschmidt, R. (2001). Prospective 10-year follow-up in adolescent anorexia nervosa—course, outcome, psychiatric comorbidity and psycho-social adaptation. *Journal of Child Psychology and Psychiatry, 42,* 603–612.

Herrera, C., & Dunn, J. (1997). Early experiences with family conflict: Implications for arguments with a close friend. *Developmental Psychology, 33,* 869–881.

Herrnstein, R. J., & Murray, C. (1994). *The bell curve: Intelligence and class structure in American life.* New York: The Free Press.

Herschkowitz, N. (2000). Neurological bases of behavioral development in infancy. *Brain and Development, 22,* 411–416.

Hershberger, S. L., & D'Augelli, A. R. (1995). The impact of victimization on the mental health and suicidality of lesbian, gay, and bisexual youths. *Developmental Psychology, 31,* 65–74.

Hertzberger, S. D., & Hall, J. A. (1993). Consequences of retaliatory aggression against siblings and peers: Urban minority children's expectations. *Child Development, 64,* 1773–1785.

Hetherington, E. M. (1989). Coping with family transitions: Winners, losers, and survivors. *Child Development, 60,* 1–14.

Hetherington, E. M., & Camara, K. A. (1984). Families in transition: The processes of dissolution and reconstitution. In R. D. Parke (Ed.), *Review of child development research.* Vol. 7: *The family.* Chicago: University of Chicago Press.

Hetherington, E. M., & Clingempeel, W. G. (1992). Coping with marital transitions. *Monographs of the Society for Research in Child Development, 57* (2–3, Serial No. 227).

Hetherington, E. M., & Frankie, G. (1967). Effect of parental dominance, warmth, and conflict on imitation in children. *Journal of Personality and Social Psychology, 6,* 119–125.

Hetherington, E. M., & Kelly, J. (2002). *For better or for worse: Divorce reconsidered.* New York: W.W. Norton.

Hetherington, E. M., & Parke, R. D. (1975). *Child psychology: A contemporary viewpoint.* New York: McGraw-Hill.

Hetherington, E. M., Bridges, M., & Insabella, G. M. (1998). What matters? What does not? Five perspectives on the association between marital transitions and children's adjustment. *American Psychologist, 53,* 167–184.

Hetherington, E. M., Cox, M., & Cox, R. (1982). Effects of divorce on parents and children. In M. E. Lamb (Ed.), *Nontraditional families.* Hillsdale, NJ: Erlbaum.

Hewlett, B. S., Lamb, M. E., Shannon, D., Leyendecker, B., & Scholmerich, A., (1998). Culture and early infancy among central African foragers and farmers. *Developmental Psychology, 34,* 653–661.

Heyman, G. D., & Gelman, S. A. (1998). Young children use motive information to make trait inferences. *Developmental Psychology, 34,* 310–321.

Heyman, G. D., & Gelman, S. A. (1999). The use of trait labels in making psychological inferences. *Child Development, 70,* 604–619.

Heyman, G. D., Gee, C. L., & Giles, J. W. (2003). Preschool children's reasoning about ability. *Child Development, 74,* 516–534.

Higgins, C. I., Campos, J. J., & Kermoian, R. (1996). Effect of self-produced locomotion on infant postural compensation to optic flow. *Developmental Psychology, 32,* 836–841.

Higgins, E. T. (1987). Self-discrepancy: A theory relating self and affect. *Psychological Review, 94,* 319–340.

Higgins, E. T., & Parsons, J. E. (1983). Stages as subcultures: Social-cognitive development and the social life of the child. In E. T. Higgins, W. W. Hartup, & D. N. Ruble (Eds.), *Social cognition and social development: A sociocultural perspective.* New York: Cambridge University Press.

Hill, A. E. (1997, May 13). Doctors debate circumcision for infants. *Atlanta Constitution,* B3.

Hill, J. L., Brooks-Gunn, J., & Waldfogel, J. (2003). Sustained effects of high participation in an early intervention for low-birth-weight premature infants. *Developmental Psychology, 39,* 730–736.

Hill, J. P., & Lynch, M. E. (1983). The intensification of gender-related role expectations during early adolescence. In J. Brooks-Gunn & A. C. Petersen (Eds.), *Girls at puberty. Biological and psychosocial perspectives.* New York: Plenum.

Hill, N. E., Bush, K. R., & Roosa, M. W. (2003). Parenting and family socialization strategies and children's mental health: Low-income Mexican American and Euro American mothers and children. *Child Development, 74,* 189–204.

Hill, P. T., Foster, G. E., & Gendler, T. (1990). *High schools with character: Alternatives to bureaucracy.* Santa Monica, CA: Rand Corporation.

Hill, S. D., & Tomlin, C. (1981). Self-recognition in retarded children. *Child Development, 53,* 1320–1329.

Hinde, R. A. (1989). Ethological and relationships approaches. In R. Vasta (Ed.), *Annals of child development: Vol. 6. Theories of child development: Revised formulations and current issues.* Greenwich, CT: JAI Press.

Hines, M., Golombok, S., Rust, J., Johnston, K. J., Golding, J., & the Avon Longitudinal Study of Parents and Children Study Team (2002). Testosterone during pregnancy and gender role behavior of preschool children: A longitudinal, population study. *Child Development, 73,* 1678–1687.

Hinshaw, S. P., Zupan, B. A., Simmel, C., Nigg, J. T., & Melnick, S. (1997). Peer status in boys with attention-deficit hyperactivity disorder: Predictions from overt and covert antisocial behavior, social isolation, and authoritative parenting beliefs. *Child Development, 68,* 880–896.

Hirsh-Pasek, K., Kemler Nelson, D. G., Jusczyk, P. W., Cassidy, K. W., Druss, B., & Kennedy, L. (1987). Clauses are perceptual units for young infants. *Cognition, 26,* 269–286.

Hobbes, T. (1904). *Leviathan.* Cambridge: Cambridge University Press. (Original work published 1651.)

Hodges, E. V. E., Boivin, M., Vitaro, E., & Bukowski, W. M. (1999). The power of friendship: Protection against an escalating cycle of peer victimization. *Developmental Psychology, 35,* 94–104.

Hodges, E. V. E., Finnegan, R. A., & Perry, D. G. (1999). Skewed autonomy-relatedness in preadolescents' conceptions of their relationships with mother, father, and best friend. *Child Development, 70,* 737–748.

Hoff, E., & Naigles, L. (2002). How children use input to acquire a lexicon. *Child Development,* 418–434.

Hoff-Ginsberg, E. (1997). *Language development.* Pacific Grove, CA: Brooks/Cole.

Hoffman, L. W. (1989). Effects of maternal employment in the two-parent family. *American Psychologist, 44,* 283–292.

Hoffman, L. W. (1991). The influence of family environment on personality: Accounting for sibling differences. *Psychological Bulletin, 108,* 187–203.

Hoffman, L. W. (1994). Commentary on Plomin, R. (1994): A proof and a disproof questioned. *Social Development, 3,* 60–63.

Hoffman, M. L. (1970). Moral development. In P. H. Mussen (Ed.), *Carmichael's manual of child psychology* (Vol. 2). New York: Wiley.

Hoffman, M. L. (1975). Moral internalization, parental power, and the nature of parent-child interaction. *Developmental Psychology, 11,* 228–239.

Hoffman, M. L. (1981). Is altruism part of human nature? *Journal of Personality and Social Psychology, 40,* 121–127.

Hoffman, M. L. (1988). Moral development. In M. H. Bornstein & M. E. Lamb (Eds.), *Developmental Psychology: An advanced textbook* (2nd ed.) (pp. 497–548). Hillsdale, NJ: Erlbaum.

Hoffman, M. L. (1993). Empathy, social cognition, and moral education. In A. Garrod (Ed.), *Approaches to moral development: New research and emerging themes.* New York: Teachers College Press.

Hoffman, M. L. (2000). *Empathy and moral development: Implications for caring and justice.* Cambridge, England: Cambridge University Press.

Hoffner, C., & Badzinski, D. M. (1989). Children's integration of facial and situational cues to emotion. *Child Development, 60,* 411–422.

Hofsten, C. Von. (1984). Developmental changes in the organization of prereaching movements. *Developmental Psychology, 20,* 378–388.

Holahan, C. K., & Sears, R. R. (1995). *The gifted group in later maturity.* Stanford, CA: Stanford University Press.

Holden, G. W. (1988). Adults' thinking about a child rearing problem: Effects of experience, parental status, and gender. *Child Development, 59,* 1623–1632.

Holmang, A. (2001). Perinatal origin of adult diseases. *Scandinavian Cardiovascular Journal, 35,* 179–185.

Holodynski, M. (2004). The miniaturization of expression in the development of emotional self-regulation. *Developmental Psychology, 40,* 16–28.

Holodynski, M., & Friedlmeier, W. (in press). *The development of emotions and emotion regulation.* New York: Kluwer Academic/Plenum Press.

Holtkamp, K., Herpertz-Dahlmann, B., Vloet, T., & Hagenah, U. (2005). Group psychoeducation for parents of adolescents with eating disorders: The Aachen Program. *Eating Disorders, 13,* 381–390.

Homish, G. G. (2004). Antenatal psychosocial risk and protective factors associated with postpartum comorbid depressive symptomatology and alcohol use. *Dissertation Abstracts International: Section B: The Sciences & Engineering, 64,* 3184.

Honzik, M. P. (1983). Measuring mental abilities in infancy. The value and limitations. In M. Lewis (Ed.), *Origins of intelligence. Infancy and early childhood* (2nd ed.). New York: Plenum.

Honzik, M. P., Macfarlane, J. W., & Allen, L. (1948). The stability of mental test performance between two and eighteen years. *Journal of Experimental Education, 17,* 309–324.

Hoozemans, D. A., Schats, R., Lambalk, C. B., Homburg, R., & Hompes, P. G. A. (2004). Human embryo implantation: Current knowledge and clinical implications in assisted reproductive technology. *Reproductive BioMedicine Online, 9,* 692–716.

Hopkins, B. (1991). Facilitating early motor development: An intracultural study of West Indian mothers and their infants living in Britain. In J. K. Nugent, B. M. Lester, & T. B. Brazelton (Eds.), *The cultural context of infancy: Vol. 2. Multicultural and interdisciplinary approaches to parent-infant relations.* Norwood, NJ: Ablex.

Hopwood, N. J., Kelch, R. P., Hale, P. M., Mendes, T. M., Foster, C. M., & Beitins, Z. (1990). The onset of human puberty: Biological and environmental factors. In J. Bancroft & J. M. Reinisch (Eds.), *Adolescence and puberty.* New York: Oxford University Press.

Horn, J. L., & Noll, J. (1997). Human cognitive capabilities: G_fG_c theory. In D. P. Flanagan, J. Genshaft, & P. L. Harrison (Eds.), *Contemporary intellectual assessment: Theories, tests, and issues.* New York: Guilford.

Horney, K. (1967). *Feminine psychology.* New York: Norton. (Original work published 1923–1937.)

Hornik, R., & Gunnar, M. R. (1988). A descriptive analysis of social referencing. *Child Development, 59,* 626–634.

Horowitz, F. D. (1992). John B. Watson's legacy: Learning and environment. *Developmental Psychology, 28,* 360–367.

Houston-Price, C., & Nakai, S. (2004). Distinguishing novelty and familiarity effects in infant preference procedures. *Infant and Child Development, 13,* 341–348.

Howard, Robert W. (2005). Objective evidence of rising population ability: a detailed examination of longitudinal chess data. *Personality & Individual Differences, 38,* 347–363.

Howe, D. (2001). Age at placement, adoption experience and adult adopted people's contact with their adoptive and birth mothers: An attachment perspective. *Attachment and Human Development, 3,* 222–237.

Howe, M. L. (2003). Memories from the cradle. *Current Directions in Psychological Science, 12,* 62–65.

Howe, M. L., & Courage, M. L. (1993). On resolving the enigma of infantile amnesia. *Psychological Bulletin, 113,* 305–326.

Howe, N., & Rinaldi, C. M. (2004). 'You be the big sister': Maternal–preschooler internal state discourse, perspective-taking, and sibling caretaking. *Infant & Child Development, 13,* 217–234.

Howe, N., & Ross, H. S. (1990). Socialization, perspective-taking, and the sibling relationship. *Developmental Psychology, 26,* 160–165.

Howe, N., Aquan-Assee, J., Bukowski, W. M., Rinaldi, C. M., & Lehoux, P. M. (2000). Sibling self-disclosure in early adolescence. *Merrill-Palmer Quarterly, 46,* 653–671.

Howe, N., Rinaldi, C. M., Jennings, M., & Petrakos, H. (2002). "No! The lambs can stay out because they got cozies": Constructive and destructive sibling conflict, pretend play, and social understanding. *Child Development, 73,* 1460–1473.

Howes, C. (1997). Children's experiences in center-based child care as a function of teacher background and adult:child ratio. *Merrill-Palmer Quarterly, 43,* 404–425.

Howes, C., & Matheson, C. C. (1992). Sequences in the development of competent play with peers: Social and social pretend play. *Developmental Psychology, 28,* 961–974.

Howes, C., Droege, K., & Matheson, C. C. (1994). Play and communicative processes within long-term and short-term friendship dyads. *Journal of Social and Personal Relationships, 11,* 401–410.

Howes, P., & Markman, H. J. (1989). Marital quality and child functioning: A longitudinal investigation. *Child Development, 60,* 1044–1051.

Hubbard, J. A. (2001). Emotion expression processes in children's peer interaction: The role of peer rejection, aggression, and gender. *Child Development, 72,* 1426–1438.

Hubbard, J. A., Dodge, K. A., Cillessen, A. H. N., Coie, J. D., & Schwartz, D. (2001). The dyadic nature of boys' social information processing in boys' reactive and proactive aggression. *Journal of Personality and Social Psychology, 80,* 268–280.

Hubbard, J. A., Smithmyer, C. M., Ramsden, S. R., Parker, E. H., Flanagan, K. D., Dearing, K. P., Relyea, N., & Simons, R. F. (2002). Observational, physiological, and self-report measures of children's anger: Relations to reactive versus proactive aggression. *Child Development, 73,* 1101–1118.

Hudson, J. A. (1990). Constructive processing in children's event memory. *Developmental Psychology, 26,* 180–187.

Huesmann, L. R. (1986). Psychological processes promoting the relation between exposure to media violence and aggressive behavior by the viewer. *Journal of Social Issues, 42,* 125–139.

Huesmann, L. R., Eron, L. D., Lefkowitz, M. M., & Walder, L. O. (1984). Stability of aggression over time and generations. *Developmental Psychology, 20,* 1120–1134.

Huesmann, L. R., Lagerspitz, K., & Eron, L. D. (1984). Intervening variables in the TV violence–aggression relation: Evidence from two countries. *Developmental Psychology, 20,* 746–775.

Huesmann, L. R., Moise-Titus, J., Pokolski, C., & Eron, L. L. (2003). Longitudinal relations between children's exposure to TV violence and their aggressive and violent behavior in young adulthood: 1977–1992. *Developmental Psychology, 39,* 201–221.

Hughes, C., & Cutting, A. L. (1999). Nature, nurture, and individual differences in early understanding of mind. *Psychological Science, 10,* 429–432.

Hughes, C., & Dunn, J. (1999). Understanding of mind and emotion: Longitudinal associations with mental-state talk between young friends. *Developmental Psychology, 34,* 1026–1037.

Hughes, D., & Chen, L. (1999). The nature of parents' race-related communications to children: A developmental perspective. In L. Balter & C. S. Tamis-LeMonda (Eds.), *Child Psychology: A handbook of contemporary issues* (pp. 467–490). Philadelphia: Psychology Press/Taylor & Francis.

Hughes, P. (2001). *Crowd structures in African American student bodies.* Unpublished data, University of Georgia.

Hughes, R., Jr., Tingle, B. A., & Sawin, D. B. (1981). Development of empathic understanding in children. *Child Development, 52,* 122–128.

Humphreys, L. G., Rich, S. A., & Davey, T. C. (1985). A Piagetian test of general intelligence.

Hunter, J. E., & Hunter, R. F. (1984). Validity and utility of alternative predictors of job performance. *Psychological Bulletin, 96,* 72–98.

Hunter, S. K., & Yankowitz, J. (1996). Medical fetal therapy. In J. A. Kuller, N.C. Cheschier, & R. C. Cefalo (Eds.), *Prenatal diagnosis and reproductive genetics.* St. Louis: Mosby.

Huotilainen, M., Kujala, A., Hotakainen, M., Parkkonen, L., Taula, S., Simola, J., Neonen, J., Karjalianen, M., & Naatanen R. (2005). Short-term memory functions of the human fetus recorded with magnetoencephalography. *Neuroreport: For Rapid Communication of Neuroscience Research, 16,* 81–84.

Hura, S. L., & Echols, C. H. (1996). The role of stress and articulatory difficulty in children's early productions. *Developmental Psychology, 32,* 165–176.

Hussong, A. M., Zucker, R. A., Wong, M. M., Fitzgerald, H. E., & Puttler, L. I. (2005). Social competence in children of alcoholic parents over time. *Developmental Psychology, 41,* 747–759.

Huston, A. C. (1983). Sex-typing. In P. H. Mussen (Ed.), *Handbook of child psychology: Vol. 4. Socialization, personality, and social development* (4th ed.) (pp. 387–467). New York: Wiley.

Huston, A. C., & Wright, J. C. (1998). Mass media and children's development. In W. Damon (Series ed.), I. Sigel & A. Renniger (Vol. eds.), *Handbook of Child Psychology, Vol. 4* (5th ed.) (pp. 999–1058). New York: Wiley.

Huston, A. C., Donnerstein, E., Fairchild, H., Feshbach, N. D., Katz, P. A., Murray, J. P., Rubinstein, E. A., Wilcox, B. L., & Zuckerman, D. (1992). *Big world, small screen.* Lincoln, NE: University of Nebraska Press.

Huston, A. C., Wright, J. C., Marquis, J., & Green S. B. (1999). How children spend their time: Television and other activities. *Developmental Psychology, 35,* 912–925.

Hutt, C. (1972). *Males and females.* Baltimore: Penguin Books.

Huttenlocher, P. R. (1994). Synaptogenesis, synapse elimination, and neural plasticity in the human cerebral cortex. In C. A. Nelson (Ed.), *Threats to optimal development: Integrating biological, psychological, and social risk factors: Minnesota symposia on child psychology* (vol. 27, pp. 35–54). Hillsdale, NJ: Erlbaum.

Huttenlocker, J., Levine, S., & Vevea, J. (1998). Environmental input and cognitive growth: A study using time-period comparisons. *Child Development, 69,* 1012–1098.

Hutton, N. (1996). Health prospects for children born to HIV-infected women. In R. R. Faden & N. E. Kass (Eds.), *HIV, AIDS, and childbearing* (pp. 63–77). New York: Oxford University Press.

Hwang, C. P. (1986). Behavior of Swedish primary and secondary caretaking fathers in relation to mother's presence. *Developmental Psychology, 22,* 749–751.

Hyde, J. S. (1984). How large are sex differences in aggression? A developmental meta-analysis. *Developmental Psychology, 20,* 722–736.

Hyde, J. S., & Plant, E. A. (1995). Magnitude of psychological gender differences: Another side to the story. *American Psychologist, 50,* 159–161.

Hyde, J. S., Fennema, E., & Lamon, S. J. (1990). Gender differences in mathematics performance: A meta-analysis. *Psychological Bulletin, 107,* 139–155.

Hymel, S. (1983). Preschool children's peer relations: Issues in sociometric assessment. *Merrill-Palmer Quarterly, 19,* 237–260.

Hymel, S., Bowker, A., & Woody, E. (1993). Aggressive versus withdrawn unpopular children: Variations in peer and self-perceptions in multiple domains. *Child Development, 64,* 879–896.

Iannotti, R. J. (1978). Effect of role-taking experiences on role-taking, empathy, altruism, and aggression. *Developmental Psychology, 14,* 119–124.

Ibáñez, L., Ferrer, A., Marcos, M. V., Hierro, F. R., & de Zegher, F. (2000). Early puberty: Rapid progression and reduced final height in girls with low birth weight. *Pediatrics, 106,* E72.

Iervolino, A. C., Pike, A., Manke, B., Reiss, D., Hetherington, E. M., & Plomin, R. (2002). Genetic and environmental influences on adolescent peer socialization: Evidence from two genetically sensitive designs. *Child Development, 73,* 162–174.

Ingersoll, E. W., & Thoman, E. B. (1999). Sleep/wake states of preterm infants: Stability, developmental change, diurnal variation, and relation with caregiving activity. *Child Development, 70,* 1–10.

Ingram, D. (1986). Phonological development: Production. In P. Fletcher & M. Garman (Eds.), *Language acquisition* (2nd ed.). Cambridge: Cambridge University Press.

Ingram, D. (1989). *First language acquisition: Method, description, and explanation.* Cambridge: Cambridge University Press.

Inhelder, B., & Piaget, J. (1958). *The growth of logical thinking from childhood to adolescence.* New York: Basic Books.

Institute of Medicine (1999). *Reducing the odds.* Washington, DC: National Academy of Sciences.

Intons-Peterson, M. J. (1988). *Gender concepts of Swedish and American youth.* Hillsdale, NJ: Erlbaum.

Intons-Peterson, M. J., & Reddel, M. (1984). What do people ask about a neonate? *Developmental Psychology, 20,* 358–359.

Isabella, R. A. (1993). Origins of attachment: Maternal interactive behavior across the first year. *Child Development,* 605–621.

Isabella, R. A., & Belsky, J. (1991). Interactional synchrony and the origins of infant–mother attachment. *Child Development, 62,* 373–384.

Isberg, R. S., Hauser, S. T., Jacobson, A. M., Powers, S. I., Noam, G., Weiss-Perry, B., & Follansbee, D. (1989). Parental contexts of adolescent self-esteem: A developmental perspective. *Journal of Youth and Adolescence, 18,* 1–23.

Ismail, M. A. (1993). Maternal-fetal infections. In C. Lin, M. S. Verp, & R. E. Sabbagha (Eds.), *The high-risk fetus: Pathophysiology, diagnosis, management.* New York: Springer-Verlag.

Ispa, J. M., Fine, M. A., Halgunseth, L. C., Harper, S., Robinson, J., Boyce, L., Brooks-Gunn, J., & Brady-Smith, C. (2004). Maternal intrusiveness, maternal warmth, and mother–toddler relationship outcomes: Variations across low-income ethnic and acculturation groups. *Child Development, 75,* 1613–1631.

Iverson, J. M., & Fagan, M. K. (2004). Infant vocal–motor coordination: Precursor to the gesture–speech system? *Child Development, 75,* 1053–1066.

Iyasu, S., Randall, L. L., Welty, T. K., Hsia, J., Kinney, H. C., Mandell, F., McClain, M., Randall, B., Habbe, D., Wilson, H., & Willinger, M. (2002). Risk factors for sudden infant death syndrome among Northern Plains Indians. *JAMA: Journal of the American Medical Association, 288,* 2717–2723.

Izard, C. E. (1982). *Measuring emotions in infants and children.* New York: Cambridge University Press.

Izard, C. E. (1993). Four systems for emotion activation: Cognitive and noncognitive processes. *Psychological Review, 100,* 68–90.

Izard, C. E., Fantauzzo, C. A., Castle, J. M., Haynes. O. M., Rayias, M. F., & Putnam, P. H. (1995). The ontogeny and significance of infants' facial expressions in the first 9 months of life. *Developmental Psychology, 31,* 997–1013.

Jaccard, J., Dittus, P. J., & Gordon, V. V. (1998). Parent-adolescent congruency in reports of adolescent sexual behavior and in communications about sexual behavior. *Child Development, 69,* 247–261.

Jacklin, C. N., & Maccoby, E. E. (1978). Social behavior at 33 months in same-sex and mixed-sex dyads. *Child Development, 49,* 557–569.

Jackson, A., Kutnick, P., & Kington, A. (2001). Principles and practical grouping for the use of drill and practice programs. *Journal of Computer Assisted Learning, 17,* 130–141.

Jackson, A. P., Brooks-Gunn, J., Hwang, C., & Glassman, M. (2000). Single mothers in low-wage jobs: Financial strain, parenting, and preschoolers' outcomes. *Child Development, 71,* 1409–1423.

Jackson, A. W., & Davis, G. A. (2000). *Turning points 2000: Educating adolescents in the 21st century.* New York: Teachers College Press.

Jackson, J. L., & Jacobson, S. W (1999). Drinking moderately and pregnancy. *Alcohol Research and Health, 23,* 25–31.

Jackson, J. L., Jacobson, S. W., Padgett, R., Brumitt, G. A., & Billings, R. L. (1992). Effects of PCB exposure and infant information processing ability. *Developmental Psychology, 28,* 297–306.

Jacobs, J. E., & Eccles, J. S. (1992). The impact of mothers' gender-role stereotypic beliefs on mothers' and children's ability perceptions. *Journal of Personality and Social Psychology, 63,* 932–944.

Jacobs, J. E., Lanza, S., Osgood, D. W., Eccles, J. S., & Wigfield, A. (2002). Changes in children's self-competence and values: Gender and domain differences across grades one through twelve. *Child Development, 73,* 509–527.

Jacobsen, T., & Hofmann, V. (1997). Children's attachment representations: Longitudinal relations to school behavior and academic competency in middle childhood and adolescence. *Developmental Psychology, 33,* 703–710.

Jacobson, J. L., & Jacobson, S. W. (1996). Methodological considerations in behavioral toxicology in infants and children. *Developmental Psychology, 32,* 390–403.

Jacobson, J. L., & Wille, D. E. (1986). The influence of attachment pattern on developmental changes in peer interaction from the toddler to the preschool period. *Child Development, 57,* 338–347.

Jacobson, J. L., Jacobson, S. W., Fein, G. G., Schwartz, P. M., & Dowler, J. K. (1984). Prenatal exposure to an environmental toxin: A test of the multiple effects model. *Developmental Psychology, 20,* 523–532.

Jacobson, J. L., Jacobson, S. W., & Humphrey, H. E. (1990). Effects of in utero exposure to polychlorinated biphenyls and related contaminants on cognitive functioning in young children. *Journal of Pediatrics, 116,* 38–45.

Jacobson, J. L., Jacobson, S. W., Padgett, R. J., & Brumitt, G. A. (1992). Effects of prenatal PCB exposure on cognitive processing efficiency and sustained attention. *Developmental Psychology, 28,* 297–306.

Jacobson, J. L., Jacobson, S. W., Sokol, R. J., Martier, S. S., Ager, J. W., & Kaplan-Estrin, M. G. (1993). Teratogenic effects of alcohol on infant development. *Alcoholism: Clinical and Experimental Research, 17,* 174–183.

Jacobson, S. W., Fein, G. G., Jacobson, J. L., Schwartz, P. M., & Dowler, J. (1985). The effect of intrauterine PCB exposure on visual recognition memory, *Child Development, 56,* 853–860.

Jaffee, S., & Hyde, J. S. (2000). Gender differences in moral orientation: A meta-analysis. *Psychological Bulletin, 126,* 703–726.

Jagers, R. J., Bingham, K., & Hans, S. L. (1996). Socialization and social judgments among inner-city African-American kindergarteners. *Child Development, 67,* 140–150.

Jaio, S., Ji, G., & Jing, Q. (1996). Cognitive development of Chinese urban only children and children with siblings. *Child Development, 67,* 387–395.

James, S. J., Pogribna, M., Porgribna, I. P., Melnyk, S., Hine, R. J., Gibson, J. B., Vi, P., Tafoya, D. L., Swenson, D. H., Wilson, V. L., & Gaylor, D. W. (2000). Abnormal folate metabolism and mutation in the methylene tetrahydrofolate reductase gene may be maternal risk factors for Down syndrome. *American Journal of Clinical Nutrition, 70,* 495–501.

Janowsky, J. S., & Finlay, B. L. (1986). The outcome of perinatal brain damage: The role of normal neuron loss and axon retraction. *Developmental Medicine and Child Neurology, 28,* 375–389.

Jarrold, C., Butler, D. W., Cottingham, E. M., & Jimenez, F. (2000). Linking theory of mind and central coherence bias in autism and in the general population. *Developmental Psychology, 36,* 126–138.

Jay, J. (2005). Crystallized intelligence versus fluid intelligence. *Psychiatry: Interpersonal & Biological Processes, 68,* 9–13.

Jeffery, R., & Jeffery, P. M. (1993). Traditional birth attendants in rural northern India: The social organization of childbearing. In S. Lindenbaum & M. Lock (Eds.), *Knowledge, power, and practice: The anthropology of medicine and everyday life.* Berkeley, CA: University of California Press.

Jeffreys, A. J., & Neuman, R. (2002). Reciprocal crossover asymmetry and meiotic drive in a human recombination hot spot. *Nature Genetics, 31,* 267–271.

Jeffreys, A. J., Richie, A., & Neumann, R. (2000). High resolution analysis of halotype diversity and meiotic crossover in the human TAP2 recombination hot spot. *Human Molecular Genetics, 9,* 725–733.

Jenkins, J. M., Turrell, S. L., Kogushi, Y., Lollis, S., & Ross, H. S. (2003). A longitudinal investigation of the dynamics of mental state talk in families. *Child Development, 74,* 905–920.

Jensen, A. R. (1969). How much can we boost IQ and scholastic achievement? *Harvard Educational Review, 39,* 1–123.

Jensen, A. R. (1980). *Bias in mental testing.* New York: Free Press.

Jensen, A. R. (1985). The nature of black–white difference on various psychometric tests: Spearman's hypothesis. *Behavioral and Brain Sciences, 8,* 193–263.

Jensen, A. R. (1998). *The g factor: The science of mental ability.* Westport, CT: Praeger.

Jensen, P. S., Mrazek, D., Knapp, P. K., Steinberg, L., Pfeffer, C., Schwalter, J., & Shapiro, T. (1997). Evolution and revolution in child psychiatry: ADHD as a disorder of adaptation. *Journal of the American Academy of Child & Adolescent Psychiatry, 36,* 1672–1681.

Jerger, S., & Damian, M. F. (2005). What's in a name? Typicality and relatedness effects in children. *Journal of Experimental Child Psychology, 92,* 46–75.

Jiang, X. L., & Cillessen, A. H. N. (2005). Stability of continuous measures of sociometric status: A meta-analysis. *Developmental Review, 25,* 1–25.

Johnsen, E. P. (1991). Searching for the social and cognitive outcomes of children's play: A selective second look. *Play and Culture, 4,* 201–213.

Johnson, C. J., Pick, H. L., Siegel, G. M., Cicciarelli, A. W., & Garber, S. R. (1981). Effects of interpersonal distance on children's vocal intensity. *Child Development, 52,* 721–723.

Johnson, C. N., & Wellman, H. M. (1980). Children's developing understanding of mental verbs: Remember, know, and guess. *Child Development, 51,* 1095–1102.

Johnson, D. E. (2000). Long-term medical issues in international adoptees. *Pediatric Annals, 29,* 234–241.

Johnson, D. W., & Johnson, R. T. (1987). *Learning together and alone: Cooperative, competitive, and individualistic learning* (2nd ed.). Englewood Cliffs, NJ: Prentice Hall.

Johnson, D. W., & Johnson, R. T. (1989). *Cooperation and competition: Theory and research.* Edina, MN: Interaction.

Johnson, H., & Smith, L. B. (1981). Children's inferential abilities in the context of reading to understand. *Child Development, 52,* 1216–1223.

Johnson, J., & Newport, E. (1989). Critical period effects in second language learning: The influence of maturational state on the acquisition of English as a second language. *Cognitive Psychology, 21,* 60–99.

Johnson, M. H. (1998). The neural basis of cognitive development. In D. Kuhn & R. S. Siegler (Vol. Eds.), *Cognition, perception, and language* (Vol. 2). In W. Damon (Gen. Ed.), *Handbook of child psychology* (5th ed). New York: Wiley.

Johnson, M. H. (2000). Functional brain development in infants: Elements of an interactive specialization framework. *Child Development, 71,* 75–81.

Johnson, M. H. (2005). *Developmental cognitive neuroscience* (2nd ed.). Malden, MA: Blackwell Publishing.

Johnson, M. H., Dziurawiec, S., Ellis, H., & Morton, J. (1991). Newborns' preferential tracking of face-like stimuli and its subsequent decline. *Cognition, 40,* 1–19.

Johnson, S. P. (2001). Visual development in human infants: Binding features, surfaces, and objects. *Visual Cognition, 8,* 565–579.

Johnson, S. P., & Aslin, R. N. (1995). Perception of object unity in 2-month-old infants. *Developmental Psychology, 31,* 739–745.

Johnson, S. P., & Mason, U. (2002). Perception of kinetic illusory contours by two-month-old infants. *Child Development, 73,* 22–35.

Johnson, S. P., & Richard, N. (2000). Infants' perception of transparency. *Developmental Psychology, 36,* 808–816.

Johnson, S. P., Bremner, J. G., Slater, A. M., Mason, U. C., & Foster, K. (2002). Young infant's perception of unity and form in occlusion displays. *Journal of Experimental Child Psychology, 81,* 358–374.

Johnson, W., & Bouchard, T. J. (2005). The structure of human intelligence: It is verbal, perceptual, and image rotation (VPR), not fluid and crystallized. *Intelligence, 33,* 393–416.

Johnson, W., Emde, R. N., Pannabecker, B., Stenberg, C., & Davis, M. (1982). Maternal perception of infant emotion from birth through 18 months. *Infant Behavior and Development, 5,* 313–322.

Johnston, J., & Ettema, J. S. (1982). *Positive images.* Newbury Park, CA: Sage.

Jones, D. C., Abbey, B. B., & Cumberland, A. (1998). The development of display role knowledge: Linkage with family expressiveness and social competence. *Child Development, 69,* 1209–1222.

Jones, D. S., Byers, R. H., Bush, T. J., Oxtoby, M. J., & Rogers, M. F. (1992). Epidemiology of transfusion-associated acquired immunodeficiency syndrome in children in the United States, 1981 through 1989. *Pediatrics, 89,* 123–127.

Jones, K. L., Smith, D. W., Ulleland, C. N., & Streissguth, A. P. (1973). Pattern of malformation in offspring of chronic alcoholic mothers. *Lancet, 1,* 1267–1271.

Jones, L. B., Rothbart, M. K., & Posner, M. I. (2003). Development of executive attention in preschool children. *Developmental Science, 6,* 498–504.

Jones, M. C. (1965). Psychological correlates of somatic development. *Child Development, 36,* 899–911.

Jones, M. C., & Bayley, N. (1950). Physical maturing among boys as related to behavior. *Journal of Educational Psychology, 41,* 129–148.

Jones, S. S. (1996). Imitation or exploration: Young infant's matching of adults' oral gestures. *Child Development, 67,* 1952–1969.

Jordan, N. C., Hanich, L. B., & Kaplan, D. (2003). A longitudinal study of mathematical competencies in children with specific mathematics difficulties versus children with comorbid mathematics and reading difficulties. *Child Development, 74,* 834–850.

Jose, P. M. (1990). Just world reasoning in children's immanent justice arguments. *Child Development, 61,* 1024–1033.

Jourdain, G., Ngo-Giang-Huong, N., Coeur, S. L., Bowonwatanuwong, C., Kantipong, P., Leechanachai, P., Ariyadej, S., Leenasirimakul, P., Hammer, S., & Lallemant, M. (2004). Intrapartum exposure to Nevirapine and subsequent maternal responses to Nevirapine-based antiretroviral therapy. *New England Journal of Medicine, 351,* 229–240.

Judy, B., & Nelson, E. S. (2000). Relations between parents, peers, morality, and theft in an adolescent sample. *High School Journal, 83,* 31–42.

Juffer, F., Bakermans-Kranenburg, M. J., & van Ijzendoorn. (2005). The importance of parenting in the development of disorganized attachment: Evidence from a preventive intervention study in adoptive families. *Journal of Child Psychology and Psychiatry, 46,* 263–274.

Jung, T. T. K., Alper, C. M., Roberts, J. E., Casselbrant, M. L., Eriksson, P. O., Gravel, J. S., Hellström, S. O., Hunter, L. L., Paradise, J. L., Park, S. K., Spratley, J., Tos, M., & Wallace, I. (2005). Otitis media: Complications and sequelae. *Annals of Otology, Rhinology & Laryngology, January,* 140–160.

Jusczyk, P. W. (1995). Language acquisition: Speech sounds and phonological development. In J. L. Miller & P. D. Eimas (Eds.), *Handbook of perception and cognition: Vol. 11. Speech, language, and communication* (pp. 263–301). Orlando, FL: Academic Press.

Jusczyk, P. W., Cutler, A., & Redanz, N. J. (1993). Infants' preference for the predominant stress patterns of English words. *Child Development, 64,* 675–687.

Jussim, L., & Eccles, J. S. (1992). Teacher expectations II: Construction and reflection of student achievement. *Journal of Personality and Social Psychology, 63,* 947–961.

Justice, E. M., Baker-Ward, L., Gupta, S., & Jannings, L. R. (1997). Means to the goal of remembering: Developmental changes in awareness of strategy use–performance relations. *Journal of Experimental Child Psychology, 65,* 293–314.

Kagan, J. (1972). Do infants think? *Scientific American, 226,* 74–82.

Kagan, J. (1976). Emergent themes in human development. *American Scientist, 64,* 186–196.

Kagan, J. (1984). *The nature of the child.* New York: Basic Books.

Kagan, J. (1989). *Unstable ideas: Temperament, cognition, and self.* Cambridge, MA: Cambridge University Press.

Kagan, J. (1991). Continuity and discontinuity. In S. E. Brauth, W. S. Hall, & R. J. Dooling (Eds.), *Plasticity of development.* Cambridge, MA: Bradford Books, MIT Press.

Kagan, J. (1992). Behavior, biology, and the meaning of temperamental constructs. *Pediatrics, 90,* 510–513.

Kagan, J., & Moss, H. A. (1962). *Birth to maturity.* New York: Wiley.

Kagan, J., Kearsley, R. B., & Zelazo, P. R. (1978). *Infancy: Its place in human development.* Cambridge, MA: Harvard University Press.

Kagan, J., Snidman, N., & Areus, D. (1998). Childhood derivatives of high and low reactivity in infancy. *Child Development, 69,* 1483–1493.

Kagan, S., & Zahn, G. L. (1975). Field dependence and the school achievement gap between Anglo-American and Mexican-American children. *Journal of Educational Psychology, 67,* 643–650.

Kahn, A., Groswasser, J., Franco, P., Scaillet, S., Sasaguchi, T., Kelmason, I., & Dan, B. (2003). Sudden infant deaths: Stress, arousal and SIDS. *Early Human Development, 75,* S147–S166.

Kail, R. (1991). Processing time declines exponentially during childhood and adolescence. *Developmental Psychology, 27,* 259–266.

Kail, R. (1992). Processing speed, speech rate, and memory. *Developmental Psychology, 28,* 899–904.

Kail, R. (1997). Processing time, imagery, and spatial memory. *Journal of Experimental Child Psychology, 64,* 67–78.

Kail, R. V., & Salthouse, T. A. (1994). Processing speed as a mental capacity. *Acta Psychologica, 86,* 199–225.

Kaiser-Marcus, L. A. (2004). Birth characteristics of methadone exposed infants with and without comorbid alcohol exposure. *Dissertation Abstracts International: Section B: The Sciences and Engineering, 65,* 1051.

Kaitz, M., Meschulach-Sarfaty, O., Auerbach, J., & Eidelman, A. (1988). A reexamination of newborns' ability to imitate facial expressions. *Developmental Psychology, 24,* 3–7.

Kamerman, S. B. (2000). Parental leave policies: An essential ingredient in early childhood education and care policies. *Social Policy Report* (Vol. 14, No. 2). Ann Arbor: Society for Research in Child Development.

Kamins, M. L., & Dweck, C. S. (1999). Person versus process praise and criticism: Implications for contingent self-worth and coping. *Developmental Psychology, 35,* 835–847.

Kaplan, P. S., Dungan, J. K., & Zinser, M. C. (2004). Infants of chronically depressed mothers learn in response to male, but not female, infant-directed speech. *Developmental Psychology, 40,* 140–148.

Kaplan, P. S., Jung, P. C., Ryther, J. S., & Zarlengo-Strouse, P. (1996). Infant-directed versus adult-directed speech as signals for faces, *Developmental Psychology, 32,* 880–891.

Kaprio, J., Rimpela, A., Winter, T., Viken, R. J., Rimpela, M., & Rose, R. J. (1995). Common genetic influence on BMI and age at monarche. *Human Biology, 67,* 739–753.

Karmiloff-Smith, A. (1992). *Beyond modularity: A developmental perspective on cognitive science.* Cambridge, MA: MIT Press.

Karoly, L. A., Greenwood, P. W., Everingham, S. S., Houbé, J., Kilburn, M. R., Rydell, C. P., Sanders, M., & Chiesa, J. (1998). *Investing in our children: What we know and don't know about the costs and benefits of early childhood interventions.* RAND Distribution Services.

Katcher, A. (1955). The discrimination of sex differences by young children. *Journal of Genetic Psychology, 87,* 131–143.

Katz, G. S., Cohn, J. F., & Moore, C. A. (1996). A combination of vocal, dynamic and summary features discriminates between three pragmatic categories of infant-directed speech. *Child Development, 67,* 205–217.

Katz, P. A. (1979). The development of female identity. *Sex Roles, 5,* 155–178.

Katz, P. A., & Walsh, P. V. (1991). Modification of children's gender-stereo-typed behavior. *Child Development, 62,* 338–351.

Kaufman, A. S., & Kaufman, N. L. (1983). *Kaufman Assessment Battery for Children: Interpretive manual.* Circle Pines, MN: American Guidance Service.

Kaufman, A. S., Kamphaus, R. W., & Kaufman, N. L. (1985). New directions in intelligence testing: The Kaufman Assessment Battery for Children (K–ABC). In B. B. Wolman (Ed.), *Handbook of intelligence.* New York: Wiley.

Kavšek, M. (2004). Infant perception of object unity in static displays. *International Journal of Behavioral Development, 28,* 538–545.

Kaye, K., & Marcus, J. (1981). Infant imitation: The sensory-motor agenda. *Developmental Psychology, 17,* 258–265.

Kazdin, A. E. (1995). *Conduct disorders in childhood and adolescence* (2nd ed.). Thousand Oaks, CA: Sage.

Kean, A. W. G. (1937). The history of the criminal liability of children. *Law Quarterly Review, 3,* 364–370.

Kearins, J. M. (1981). Visual-spatial memory in Australian aboriginal children of desert regions. *Cognitive Psychology, 13,* 434–460.

Keasey, C. B. (1971). Social participation as a factor in the moral development of preadolescents. *Developmental Psychology, 5,* 216–220.

Keating, D., & Clark, L. V. (1980). Development of physical and social reasoning in adolescence. *Developmental Psychology, 16,* 23–30.

Kee, D. W. (1994). Developmental differences in associative memory: Strategy use, mental effort, and knowledge-access interactions. In H. W. Reese (Ed.), *Advances in child development and behavior* (Vol. 25). New York: Academic Press.

Keith, J. (1985). Age in anthropological research. In R. H. Binstock & E. Shanus (Eds.), *Handbook of aging and the social sciences* (2nd ed.). New York: Van Nostrand Reinhold.

Keller, A., Ford, L. H., Jr., & Meachum, J. A. (1978). Dimensions of self-concept in preschool children. *Developmental Psychology, 14,* 483–489.

Keller, H., & Scholmerich, A. (1987). Infant vocalizations and parental reactions during the first four months of life. *Developmental Psychology, 23,* 62–67.

Keller, H., Lohaus, A., Volker, S., Cappenberg, M., & Chasiotis, A. (1999). Temporal contingency as an independent component of parenting behavior. *Child Development, 70,* 474–485.

Keller, H., Yovsi, R., Borke, J., Kartner, J., Jensen, H., & Papaligoura, Z. (2004). Developmental consequences of early parenting experiences: Self-recognition and self-regulation in three cultural communities. *Child Development, 75,* 1745–1760.

Kelley, E., Jones, G., & Fein, D. (2004). Intellectual and neuropsychological assessment. In G. Goldstein, S. R. Beers, & M. Hersen (Eds.), *Comprehensive handbook of psychological assessment* (pp. 191–215).

Kelley, M. L., Power, T. G., & Wimbush, D. D. (1992). Determinants of disciplinary practices in low-income Black mothers. *Child Development, 63,* 573–582.

Kelley-Buchanan, C. (1988). *Peace of mind during pregnancy: An A–Z guide to the substances that could affect your unborn baby.* New York: Facts on File Publications.

Kellman, P. J., & Banks, M. S. (1998). Infant visual perception. In D. Kuhn & R. S. Siegler (Vol. Eds.), *Cognitive, language, and perceptual development* (Vol. 2). In W. Damon (Gen. Ed.), *Handbook of child psychology.* New York: Wiley.

Kellman, P. J., & Spelke, E. S. (1983). Perception of partly occluded objects in infancy. *Cognitive Psychology, 15,* 483–524.

Kellman, P. J., Spelke, E. S., & Short, K. R. (1986). Infant perception of object unity from translatory motion in depth and vertical translation. *Child Development, 57,* 72–86.

Kelly, A. M., Wall, M., Eisenberg, M. E., Story, M., & Newmark-Sztainer, D. (2005). Adolescent girls with high body satisfaction: Who are they and what can they teach us? *Journal of Adolescent Health, 37,* 391–396.

Kelly, S. A., Brownell, C. A., & Campbell, S. E. (2000). Mastery motivation and self-evaluative affect in toddlers: Longitudinal relations with maternal behavior. *Child Development, 71,* 1061–1071.

Kemperman, G., & Gage, F. H. (1999, May). New nerve cells for the adult brain. *Scientific American,* 48–53.

Kennedy, D. N., Makris, N., Herbert, M. R., Takahashi, T., & Caviness, V. S. (2002). Basic principles of MRI and morphometry studies of human brain development. *Developmental Science, 5,* 268–279.

Kennell, J. H., Voos, D. K., & Klaus, M. H. (1979). Parent-infant bonding. In J. D. Osofsky (Ed.), *Handbook of infant development.* New York: Wiley.

Kenrick, D. T. (2001). Evolutionary psychology, cognitive science, and dynamical systems: Building an integrative paradigm. *Current Directions in Psychological Science, 10,* 13–18.

Kenrick, D. T., & Luce, C. I. (2000). An evolutionary life-history model of gender differences and similarities. In T. Eckes & H. M. Trautner (Eds.), *The developmental social psychology of gender* (pp. 35–63). Mahwah, NJ: Erlbaum.

Keough, J., & Sugden, D. (1985). Movement skill development. New York: MacMillan.

Kermoian, R., & Campos, J. J. (1988). Locomotor experience: A facilitator of spatial cognitive development. *Child Development, 59,* 908–917.

Kerr, M., & Stattin, H. (2000). What parents know, how they know it and several forms of adolescent adjustment: Further support for a reinterpretation of monitoring. *Developmental Psychology, 36,* 366–380.

Kerr, M., Lambert, W. W., & Bem, D. J. (1996). Life course sequelae of childhood shyneed in Sweden: Comparison with the United States. *Developmental Psychology, 32,* 1100–1105.

Kerr, M., Lambert, W. W. Stattin, H., & Klackbengerg-Larsson, I. (1994). Stability of inhibition in a Swedish longitudinal sample. *Child Development, 65,* 138–146.

Kerwin, C., Ponterotto, J. G., Jackson, B. L., & Harris, A. (1993). Racial identity in biracial children: A qualitative investigation. *Journal of Counseling Psychology, 40,* 221–231.

Kesmodel, U., Wisborg, K., Olsen, S., Henriksen, T., Brink, S., & Jorgen, N. (2002). Moderate alcohol intake in pregnancy and the risk of spontaneous abortion. *Alcohol & Alcoholism, 37,* 87–92.

Kessel, B. (1995). Reproductive cycles in women: Quality of life impact. In B. P. Sachs, R. Beard, E. Papiernik, & C. Russell (Eds.), *Reproductive health care for women and babies* (pp. 18–39). New York: Oxford University Press.

Kessen, W. (1965). *The child.* New York: Wiley.

Kett, J. F. (1979). *Rites of passage: Adolescence in America, 1790 to the present.* New York: Basic Books.

Kiesewetter, J. (1993, Dec 17). Top kids show also ranks as most violent. *The Cincinnati Enquirer,* A1.

Kiesner, J., Maass, A., Cadinu, M., & Vallese, I. (2003). Risk factors for ethnic prejudice during early adolescence. *Social Development, 12,* 288–308.

Kilgore, K., Snyder, J., & Lentz, C. (2000). The contribution of parental discipline, parental monitoring, and school risk to early-onset conduct problems in African American boys and girls. *Developmental Psychology, 36,* 835–845.

Killen, M., Pisacane, K., Lee-Kim, J., & Ardila-Rey, A. (2001). Fairness or stereotypes? Young children's priorities when evaluating group exclusion and inclusion. *Developmental Psychology, 37,* 587–596.

Kim, J. M. (1998). Korean children's concepts of adult and peer authority and moral reasoning. *Developmental Psychology, 34,* 947–955.

Kim, K. H. S., Relkin, N. R., Lee, K., & Hirsch, J., et al. (1997). Distinct cortical areas associated with native and second languages. *Nature, 388,* 171–174.

Kimura, D. (1992). Sex differences in the brain. *Scientific American, 267,* 119–125.

Kinney, H. C., Filiano, J. J., Sleeper, L. A., & White, W. F. (1995). Decreased muscarinic receptor binding in the arcuate nucleus in sudden infant death syndrome. *Science, 269,* 1446–1460.

Kinsbourne, M. (1989). Mechanisms and development of hemisphere specialization in children. In C. R. Reynolds & E. Fletcher-Janzen (Eds.), *Handbook of clinical child neuropsychology.* New York: Plenum Press.

Kirchner, J. (1998, January 25). State making adoption process easier. Associated Press, as reported in the *Athens Banner Herald,* p. 4A.

Kirsch, S. J. (1998). Seeing the world through Mortal Kombat-colored glasses: Violent video games and the development of a short-term hostile attribution bias. *Childhood, 5,* 177–184.

Kisilevsky, B. S., & Muir, D. W. (1984). Neonatal habituation and dishabituation to tactile stimulation during sleep. *Developmental Psychology, 20,* 367–373.

Kitzinger, C., & Wilkinson, S. (1995). Transitions from heterosexuality to lesbianism: The discursive production of lesbian identities. *Developmental Psychology, 31,* 95–104.

Kitzmann, K. M. (2000). Effects of marital conflict on subsequent triadic family interactions and parenting. *Developmental Psychology, 36,* 3–14.

Klahr, D. (1992). Information-processing approaches to cognitive development. In M. H. Bernstein & M. E. Lamb (Eds.), *Developmental psychology: An advanced textbook* (3rd ed., pp. 273–335). Hillsdale, NJ: Erlbaum.

Klahr, D., & MacWhinney, B. (1998). Information processing. In D. Kuhn & R. S. Siegler (Eds.), *Cognitive, language, and perceptual development,* Vol. 2. In B. Damon (General Editor), *Handbook of child psychology.* New York: Wiley.

Klaus, M. H., & Kennell, J. H. (1976). *Maternal-infant bonding.* St. Louis, MO: Mosby.

Klaus, M. H., & Kennell, J. H. (1982). *Parent-infant bonding.* St. Louis, MO: Mosby.

Klebanov, P. K., Brooks-Gunn, J., McCarton, C., & McCormick, M. C. (1998). The contribution of neighborhood and family income to developmental test scores over the first three years of life. *Child Development, 69,* 1420–1436.

Klein, D. M., & White, J. M. (1996). *Family theories: An introduction.* Thousand Oaks, CA: Sage.

Klineberg, O. (1963). Negro–white differences in intelligence test performance: A new look at an old problem. *American Psychologist, 18,* 198–203.

Klinnert, M. D., Emde, R. N., Butterfield, P., & Campos, J. J. (1986). Social referencing: The infant's use of emotional signals from a friendly adult with mother present. *Developmental Psychology, 22,* 427–432.

Kobasigawa, A. (1974). Utilization of retrieval cues by children in recall. *Child Development, 45,* 127–134.

Kochanska, G. (1991). Socialization and temperament in the development of guilt and conscience. *Child Development, 62,* 1379–1392.

Kochanska, G. (1997a). Multiple pathways to conscience for children with different temperaments: From toddlerhood to age 5. *Developmental Psychology, 33,* 228–240.

Kochanska, G. (1997b). Mutually responsive orientation between mothers and their young children: Implications for early socialization. *Child Development, 68,* 94–112.

Kochanska, G. (1998). Mother–child relationships, child fearfulness, and emerging attachment: A short-term longitudinal study. *Developmental Psychology, 34,* 480–490.

Kochanska, G. (2001). Emotional development in children with different attachment histories: The first three years. *Child Development, 72,* 474–490.

Kochanska, G. (2002). Committed compliance, moral self, and internalization: A mediational model. *Developmental Psychology, 38,* 339–351.

Kochanska, G., & Coy, K. C. (2000). Child emotionality and maternal responsiveness as predictors of reunion behaviors in the Strange Situation: Links mediated and unmediated by separation distress. *Child Development, 73,* 228–240.

Kochanska, G., & Murray, K. T. (2000). Mother–child mutually responsive orientation and conscience development: From toddler to early school age. *Child Development, 71,* 417–431.

Kochanska, G., Casey, R. J., & Fukumoto, A. (1995). Toddlers' sensitivity to standard violations. *Child Development, 66,* 643–656.

Kochanska, G., Coy, K. C., & Murray, K. T. (2001). The development of self-regulation in the first four years of life. *Child Development, 72,* 1091–1111.

Kochanska, G., Green, J. N., Lin, M., & Nichols, K. E. (2002). Guilt in young children: Development, determinants, and relations with a broader system of standards. *Child Development, 73,* 461–482.

Kochanska, G., Murray, K., Jacques, T. Y., Koenig, A. L., & Vandegeest, K. A. (1996). Inhibitory control in young children and its role in emerging internalization. *Child Development, 67,* 490–507.

Kochanska, G., Padavich, D. L., & Koenig, A. L. (1996). Children's narratives about hypothetical moral dilemmas and objective measures of their conscience: Mutual relations and socialization antecedents. *Child Development, 67,* 1420–1436.

Kochanska, G., Tjebkes, T. L., & Forman, D. R. (1998). Children's emerging regulation of conduct: Restraint, compliance, and internalization from infancy to the second year. *Child Development, 69,* 1378–1389.

Kochenderfer-Ladd, B., & Skinner, K. (2002). Children's coping strategies: Moderators of the effects of peer victimization? *Developmental Psychology, 38,* 267–278.

Koff, E., & Rierdan, J. (1995). Early adolescent girls' understanding of menstruation. *Women and Health, 22,* 1–19.

Kohlberg, L. (1963). The development of children's orientations toward a moral order: I. Sequence in the development of moral thought. *Vita Humana, 6,* 11–33.

Kohlberg, L. (1966). A cognitive-developmental analysis of children's sex-role concepts and attitudes. In E. E. Maccoby (Ed.), *The development of sex differences.* Stanford, CA: Stanford University Press.

Kohlberg, L. (1984). *Essays on moral development: Vol. 2. The psychology of moral development.* San Francisco: Harper & Row.

Kohler, L., & Rigby, M. (2003). Indicators of children's development: Considerations when constructing a set of national Child Health Indicators for the European Union. *Child Care, Health & Development, 29,* 551–558.

Kohn, M. L. (1979). The effects of social class on parental values and practices. In D. Reiss & H. A. Hoffman (Eds.), *The American family: Dying or developing?* (pp. 49–68). New York: Plenum.

Kokko, K., & Pulkkinen, L. (2000). Aggression in childhood and long-term unemployment in adulthood: A cycle of maladaptation and some protective factors. *Developmental Psychology, 36,* 463–472.

Kolata, G. B. (1986). Obese children: A growing problem. *Science, 232,* 20–21.

Kolb, B., & Fantie, B. (1989). Development of the child's brain and behavior. In C. R. Reynolds & E. Fletcher-Janzen (Eds.), *Handbook of clinical child neuropsychology.* New York: Plenum Press.

Koniak-Griffin, D., & Turner-Pluta, C. (2001). Health risks and psychosocial outcomes of early childbearing: A review of the literature. *Journal of Perianatal and Neonatal Nursing, 15,* 1–17.

Kopp, C., & Kahler, S. R. (1989). Risk in infancy. *American Psychologist, 44,* 224–230.

Kopp, C. B. (1989). Regulation of distress and negative emotions: A developmental view. *Developmental Psychology, 25,* 343–354.

Korner, A. F. (1972). State as a variable, as obstacle and as mediator of stimulation in infant research. *Merrill-Palmer Quarterly, 18,* 77–94.

Korner, A. F. (1996). Reliable individual differences in preterm infants' excitation management. *Child Development, 67,* 1793–1805.

Kortenhaus, C. M., & Demarest, J. (1993). Gender role stereotyping in children's literature: An update. *Sex Roles, 28,* 219–232.

Kostanski, M., Fisher, A., & Gullone, E., et al. (2004). Current conceptualisation of body image dissatisfaction: Have we got it wrong? *Journal of Child Psychology and Psychiatry, 45,* 1317–1325.

Kovacs, D. M., Parker, J. G., & Hoffman, L. W. (1996). Behavioral, affective, and social correlates of involvement in cross-sex friendship in elementary school. *Child Development, 67,* 2269–2286.

Kowal, A., & Kramer, L. (1997). Children's understanding of parental differential treatment. *Child Development, 68,* 113–126.

Kowaleski-Jones, L., & Duncan, G. J. (1999). The structure of achievement and behavior across middle childhood. *Child Development, 70,* 930–943.

Kowalski, H. S., Wyver, S. R., Masselos, G., & De Lacey, P. (2004). Toddlers' emerging symbolic play: A first-born advantage? *Early Child Development & Care, 174,* 389–400.

Kowalski, K. (2003). The emergence of ethnic and racial attitudes in preschool-aged children. *The Journal of Social Psychology, 143,* 677–691.

Kramarski, B., & Gutman, M. (2006). How can self-regulated learning be supported in mathematical E-learning environments? *Journal of Computer Assisted Learning, 22,* 24–33.

Kramer, L. Perozynski, L. A., & Chung, T. (1999). Parental responses to sibling conflict: The effects of development and parent gender. *Child Development, 70,* 1401–1414.

Krauss, R. M., & Glucksberg, S. (1977). Social and nonsocial speech. *Scientific American, 236,* 100–105.

Krautter, T., & Lock, J. (2004). Is manualized family-based treatment for adolescent anorexia nervosa acceptable to patients? Patient satisfaction at the end of treatment. *Journal of Family Therapy, 26,* 66–82.

Kreutzer, M. A., Leonard, C., & Flavell, J. H. (1975). An interview study of children's knowledge about memory. *Monographs of the Society for Research in Child Development, 40,* (1, Serial No. 159).

Krevans, J., & Gibbs, J. C. (1996). Parents' use of inductive discipline: Relations to children's empathy and prosocial behavior. *Child Development, 67,* 3263–3277.

Kroger, J. (1996). Identity, regression, and development. *Journal of Adolescence, 19,* 203–222.

Kroger, J. (2000). *Identity development: Adolescence through adulthood.* Thousand Oaks, CA: Sage.

Kroll, J. (1977). The concept of childhood in the Middle Ages. *Journal of the History of the Behavioral Sciences, 13,* 384–393.

Kuczynski, L. (1983). Reasoning, prohibitions, and motivations for compliance. *Developmental Psychology, 19,* 126–134.

Kuczynski, L., & Kochanska, G. (1995). Function and content of maternal demands: Developmental significance of early demands for competent action. *Child Development, 66,* 616–628.

Kuebli, J., Butler, S., & Fivush, R. (1995). Mother–child talk about past emotions: Relations of maternal language and child gender over time. *Cognition and Emotion, 9,* 265–283.

Kuhana-Kalman, R., & Walker-Andrews, A. S. (2001). The role of person familiarity in young infants' perceptions of emotional expressions. *Child Development, 72,* 352–369.

Kuhl, P. K., Andruski, J. E., Christovich, I. A., Christovich, L. A., Kozhevnikova, E. V., Ryskina, V. L., Stolyarova, E. I., Sundberg, U., & Lacerda, F. (1997). Cross-language analysis of phonetic units in language addressed to infants. *Science, 277,* 684–686.

Kuhn, D. (1992). Cognitive development. In M. H. Bornstein & M. E. Lamb (Eds.), *Developmental psychology: An advanced textbook* (3rd ed.). Hillsdale, NJ: Erlbaum.

Kuhn, D., Amsel, E., & O'Loughlin, M. (1988). *The development of scientific thinking skills.* San Diego: Academic.

Kuhn, D., Kohlberg, L., Langer, J., & Haan, N. (1977). The development of formal operations in logical and moral judgment. *Genetic Psychology Monographs, 95,* 97–188.

Kuhn, D., Nash, S. C., & Brucken, L. (1978). Sex-role concepts of two- and three-year-olds. *Child Development, 49,* 445–451.

Kuklina, E., Ramakrishnan, U., Stein, A. D, Barnhart, H. H., & Martorelit, R. (2004). Growth and diet quality are associated with the attainment of walking in rural Guatemalan infants. *Journal of Nutrition, 134,* 3296–3300,

Kuklinski, M. R., & Weinstein, R. S. (2000). The stability of teacher expectations and perceived differential teacher treatment. *Learning Environmental Research, 3*(1), 1–34.

Kuklinski, M. R., & Weinstein, R. S. (2001). Classroom and developmental differences in a path model of teacher expectancy effects. *Child Development, 72,* 1554–1578.

Kuller, J. A. (1996). Chorionic villus sampling. In J. A. Kuller, N. C. Cheschier, & R. C. Cefalo (Eds.), *Prenatal diagnosis and reproductive genetics* (pp. 145–158). St. Louis: Mosby.

Kulman, L. (1997, March 10). The prescription for smart kids. *U.S. News and World Report,* p. 10.

Kunkel, D., & Roberts, D. (1991). Young minds and marketplace value: Issues in children's advertising. *Journal of Social Issues, 47*(1), 57–72.

Kupersmidt, J., & Dodge, K. A. (Eds.). (2004). *Children's peer relations: From development to intervention.* Washington, DC: American Psychological Association.

Kurdek, L. A., & Fine, M. A. (1994). Family acceptance and family control as predictors of adjustment in young adolescents: Linear, curvilinear, or interactive effects? *Child Development, 65,* 1137–1146.

Kurtz, B. E. (1990). Cultural influences on children's cognitive and meta-cognitive development. In W. Schneider & F. E. Weinert (Eds.), *Interactions among aptitude, strategies, and knowledge in cognitive performance.* Hillsdale, NJ: Erlbaum.

La Freniere, P., Strayer, F. F., & Gauthier, R. (1984). The emergence of same-sex affiliative preferences among preschool peers: A developmental ethological perspective. *Child Development, 55,* 1958–1965.

La Greca, A. M., Prinstein, M. J., & Fetter, M. D. (2001). Adolescent peer crowd affiliation: Linkages with health-risk behaviors and close friendships. *Journal of Pediatric Psychology, 26,* 131–143.

Labile, D. J., & Thompson, R. A. (2000). Mother–child discourse, attachment security, shared positive affect, and early conscience development. *Child Development, 71,* 1424–1440.

Labile, D. J., & Thompson, R. A. (2002). Mother–child conflict in the early toddler years: Lessons in emotion, morality, and relationships. *Child Development, 73,* 1187–1203.

Laboratory of Comparative Human Cognition (1983). Culture and cognitive development. In W. Kessen (Ed.), *Handbook of child psychology: Vol. 1: History, theory, and methods* (4th ed.). New York: Wiley.

Ladd, G. W., & Kochenderfer-Ladd, B. (1998). Parenting behaviors and parent–child relationships: Correlates of peer victimization in kindergarten. *Developmental Psychology, 34,* 1450–1458.

Ladd, G. W., & Troop-Gordon, W. (2003). The role of chronic peer difficulties in the development of children's psychological adjustment problems. *Child Development, 74,* 1344–1367.

Ladd, G. W., Birch, S. H., & Buhs, E. S. (1999). Children's social and scholastic lives in kindergarten: Related spheres of influence? *Child Development, 70,* 1373–1400.

Ladd, G. W., Burgess, K. B. (1999). Charting the relationship trajectories of aggressive, withdrawn, and aggressive/withdrawn children during early grade school. *Child Development, 70,* 910–929.

Ladd, G. W., Kochenderfer, B. J., & Coleman, C. C. (1997). Classroom peer acceptance, friendship, and victimization: Distinct relational systems that contribute uniquely to children's school adjustment. *Child Development, 68,* 1181–1197.

Ladd, G. W., Price, J. M., & Hart, C. H. (1988). Predicting preschoolers' play status from their playground behaviors. *Child Development, 59,* 986–992.

LaFontana, K. M., & Cillessen, A. H. N. (2002). Children's perceptions of popular and unpopular peers: A multimethod assessment. *Developmental Psychology, 38,* 635–647.

Lagattuta, K. H., & Wellman, H. M. (2002). Differences in early parent-child conversations about negative versus positive emotions: Implications for the development of psychological understanding. *Developmental Psychology, 38,* 564–580.

Lagattuta, K. H., & Wellman, H. M. (2001). Thinking about the past: Early knowledge about links between past experience, thinking, and emotion. *Child Development, 72,* 82–102.

Laird, R. D., Pettit, G. S., Bates, J. E., & Dodge, K. A. (2003). Parents' monitoring relevant knowledge and adolescents' delinquent behavior: Evidence of correlated developmental changed and reciprocal influences. *Developmental Psychology, 74,* 752–768.

Lamaze, F. (1958). *Painless childbirth: Psychoprophylactic method.* London: Burke.

Lamb, M. E. (1997). *The role of the father in child development* (3rd ed.). New York: Wiley.

Lamb, N. E., Sherman, S. L., & Hassold, T. J. (2005). Effect of meiotic recombination of the production of aneuploid gametes in humans. *Cytogenetic and Genome Research, 111,* 250–255.

Lamb, N. E., Yu, K., Shaffer, J. Feingold, E., & Sherman, S. L. (2005). An association between maternal age and meiotic recombination. *American Journal of Human Genetics, 76,* 91–99.

Lamb, T., & Yang, J. F. (2000). Could different directions of infant stepping be controlled by the same locomotor central pattern generator? *Journal of Neurophysiology, 83,* 2814–2824.

Lamborn, S. D., Mounts, N. S., Steinberg, L., & Dornbusch, S. M. (1991). Patterns of competence and adjustment among adolescents from authoritative, authoritarian, indulgent, and neglectful families. *Child Development, 62,* 1049–1065.

Lampl, M., Veldhuis, J. D., & Johnson, M. L. (1992). Saltation and stasis: A model of human growth. *Science, 258,* 801–803.

Lange, G., & Pierce, S. H. (1992). Memory-strategy learning and maintenance in preschool children. *Developmental Psychology, 28,* 453–462.

Langlois, J. H., Ritter, J. M., Casey, R. J., & Sawin, D. B. (1995). Infant attractiveness predicts maternal behaviors and attitudes. *Developmental Psychology, 31,* 464–472.

Lanza, E. (1992). Can bilingual 2-year-olds code-switch? *Journal of Child Language, 19,* 633–658.

Laosa, L. M. (1981). Maternal behavior: Sociocultural diversity in modes of family interaction. In R. W. Henderson (Ed.), *Parent–child interaction: Theory, research, and prospects.* Orlando, FL: Academic Press.

Lapsley, D. K. (1996). *Moral psychology.* Boulder, CO: Westview.

Larivée, S., Narmandeau, S., & Parent, S. (2000). The French connection: Some contributions of French-language research in the post–Piagetian era. *Child Development, 71,* 823–839.

Larroque, B., Kaminski, M., & Lelong, N. (1993). Effects on birth weight of alcohol and caffeine consumption during pregnancy. *American Journal of Epidemiology, 137,* 941–950.

Larsen, K. E. (2004). Prenatal negative affect states and reproductive health outcomes: The mediating role of health behaviors. *Dissertation Abstracts International: Section B: The Sciences & Engineering, 64,* 3573.

Larson, R. (2001). Commentary. In D. R. Anderson, A. C. Huston, K. L. Schmitt, D. L. Lingarger, & J. C. Wright. Early childhood television viewing and adolescent behavior. *Monographs of the Society for Research in Child Development, 66* (1, Serial No. 264).

Larson, R. W., & Richards, M. H. (1991). Daily companionship in late childhood and early adolescence: Changing developmental contexts. *Child Development, 62,* 284–300.

Lasser, J., & Tharinger, D. (2003). Visibility management in school and beyond: A qualitative study of gay, lesbian, bisexual youth. *Journal of Adolescence, 26,* 233–244.

Laumann, E. O., Gagnon, J. H., Michael, R. T., & Michaels, S. (1994). *The social organization of sexuality: Sexual practices in the United States.* Chicago: University of Chicago Press.

Laursen, B., Coy, K. C., & Collins, W. A. (1998). Reconsidering changes in parent–child conflict across adolescence: A meta-analysis. *Child Development, 69,* 817–832.

LaVelli, M., & Fogel, A. (2002). Developmental changes in mother–infant face-to-face communication: Birth to 3 months. *Developmental Psychology, 38,* 288–305.

Lazar, I., & Darlington, R. (1982). Lasting effects of early education: A report from the Consortium for Longitudinal Studies. *Monographs of the Society for Research in Child Development, 47* (2–3, Serial No. 195).

Leadbeater, B. J., Kuperminc, G. P., Blatt, S. J., & Herzog, C. (1999). A multivariate model of gender differences in adolescents' internalizing and externalizing problems. *Developmental Psychology, 35,* 1268–1282.

Leaper, C. (1994). Exploring the consequences of gender segregation on social relationships. In C. Leaper (Ed.), W. Damon (Series Ed.), *New directions for child development: Vol. 65. Childhood gender segregation: Causes and consequences* (pp. 67–86). San Francisco: Jossey-Bass.

Leaper, C. (2000). Gender, affiliation, assertion, and the interactive context of parent child play. *Developmental Psychology, 36,* 381–393.

Leaper, C., Anderson, K. J., & Sanders, P. (1998). Moderators of gender effects on parents' talk to their children. *Developmental Psychology, 34,* 3–27.

Leaper, C., Tennenbaum, H. R., & Shaffer, T. G. (1999). Communication patterns in African American girls and boys from low-income urban backgrounds. *Child Development, 70,* 1489–1503.

Leary, A., & Katz, L. F. (2004). Coparenting, family-level processes, and peer outcomes: The moderating role of vagal tone. *Development & Psychopathology, 16,* 593–608.

Lease, A. M., Kennedy, C. A., & Axelrod, J. L. (2002). Children's social constructions of popularity. *Social Development, 11,* 87–109.

Leboyer, F. (1975). *Birth without violence.* New York: Knopf.

Leckowicz, D. J. (2004). Perception of serial order in infants. *Developmental Science, 7,* 175–184.

Lee, K., Cameron, C. A., Xu, F., & Board, J. (1997). Chinese and Canadian children's evaluation of lying and truth-telling: Similarities and differences in the context of pro- and antisocial behaviors. *Child Development, 68,* 924–934.

Lee, V. E., & Smith, J. (2001). *Restructuring high schools for equity and excellence: What works.* New York: Teachers College Press.

Lee, V. E., Loeb, S., & Lubeck, S. (1998). Contextual effects of pre-kindergarten classrooms for disadvantaged children on cognitive development: The case of Chapter 1. *Child Development, 69,* 479–494.

Leekam, S. R., Lopez, B., & Moore, C. (2000). Attention and joint attention in preschool children with autism. *Developmental Psychology, 36,* 261–273.

Leese, H. J. (1994). Early human embryo development. *Journal of Biological Education, 28,* 6–13.

Legerstee, M., Anderson, D., & Schaffer, A. (1998). Five- and eight-month-olds recognize their faces and voices as familiar social stimuli. *Child Development, 69,* 37–50.

Legerstee, M., & Varghese, J. (2001). The role of maternal affect mirroring on social expectancies in three-month-old infants. *Child Development, 72,* 1301–1313.

Lehman, E. B., McKinley-Pace, M. J., Wilson, J. A., Savsky, M. D., & Woodson, M. E. (1997). Direct and indirect measures of intentional forgetting in children and adults: Evidence for retrieval inhibition and reinstatement. *Journal of Experimental Child Psychology, 64,* 295–316.

Lehman, S. J., & Joerner, S. S. (2005). Adolescent women's sports involvement and sexual behavior/health: A process-level investigation. *Journal of Youth & Adolescence, 33,* 443–455.

Leinbach, M. D., & Fagot, B. I. (1986). Acquisition of gender labeling: A test for toddlers. *Sex Roles, 15,* 655–666.

Leinbach, M. D., & Fagot, B. I. (1993). Categorical habituation to male and female faces: Gender schematic processing in infancy. *Infant Behavior and Development, 16,* 317–322.

LeMare, L. J., & Rubin, K. H. (1987). Perspective taking and peer interaction: Structural and developmental analyses. *Child Development, 58,* 306–315.

Lemerise, E. A., & Arsenio, W. F. (2000). An integrated model of emotion processes and cognition in social information processing. *Child Development, 71,* 107–118.

Lemery, K. S., Goldsmith, H. H., Klinnert, M.D., & Mrazek, D. A. (1999). Developmental models of infant and childhood temperament. *Developmental Psychology, 35,* 189–204.

Lemonick, M. D. (2001). The genome is mapped. Now what? In K. L. Freiberg (Ed.), *Human development, 01/02* (29th ed.) (pp. 13–17). Guildford, CT: McGraw-Hill/Duskin.

Lenhart, A., Rainie, L., & Lewis, O. (2001). *Teenage life online: The rise of the instant-message generation and the Internet's impact on friendships and family relationships.* Washington, DC: Pew Internet & American Life Project. Retrieved January 6, 2005, from http://www.pewinternet.org/pdfs/PIP_Teens_Report.pdf.

Lenneberg, E. H. (1967). *Biological foundations of language.* New York: Wiley.

Leon, I. G. (2002). Adoption losses: Naturally occurring or socially constructed? *Child Development, 73,* 652–663.

Lepper, M. R. (1985). Microcomputers in education: Motivation and social issues. *American Psychologist, 40,* 1–18.

Lepper, M. R., & Gurtner, J. (1989). Children and computers: Approaching the twenty-first century. *American Psychologist, 44,* 170–178.

Lerner, R. M. (1991). Changing organism-context relations as the basic process of development: A developmental contextual perspective. *Developmental Psychology, 27,* 27–32.

Lerner, R. M. (1996). Relative plasticity, integration, temporality, and diversity in human development: A developmental contextual perspective about theory, process, and method. *Developmental Psychology, 32,* 781–786.

Lerner, R. M. (2002). *Concepts and theories of human development.* Mahway, NJ: Lawrence Erlbaum Associates.

Lerner, R. M., & von Eye, A. (1992). Sociobiology and human development: Arguments and evidence. *Human Development, 35,* 12–33.

Lerner, R. M., Fisher, C. B., & Weinberg, R. A. (2000). Toward a science of and for the people: Promoting civil society through the application of developmental science. *Child Development, 71,* 11–20.

Lesch, E., & Kruger, L.-M. (2005). Mothers, daughters and sexual agency in one low-income South African community. *Social Science and Medicine, 61,* 1072–1082.

Lester, B. M. (1984). A biosocial model of infant crying. In L. P. Lipsitt (Ed.), *Advances in infancy research.* Norwood, NJ: Ablex.

Lester, B. M., Corwin, M. J., Sepkoski, C., Seifer, R., Peucker, M., McLaughlin, S., & Golub, H. L. (1991). Neurobehavioral syndromes in cocaine-exposed newborn infants. *Child Development, 62,* 694–705.

Lester, B. M., Hoffman, J., & Brazelton, T. B. (1985). The rhythmic structure of mother-infant interactions in term and preterm infants. *Child Development, 56,* 15–27.

Lester, B. M., Kotelchuck, M., Spelke, E., Sellers, M. J., & Klein, R. E. (1974). Separation protest in Guatemalan infants: Cross-cultural and cognitive findings. *Developmental Psychology, 10,* 79–85.

LeVay, S. (1996). *Queer science: The use and abuse of research into homosexuality.* Cambridge, MA: MIT Press.

Leve, L. D., & Fagot, B. I. (1997). Gender-role socialization and discipline processes in one- and two-parent families. *Sex Roles, 36,* 1–21.

Levin, I., & Druyan, S. (1993). When sociocognitive transaction among peers fails: The case of misconceptions in science. *Child Development, 64,* 1571–1591.

LeVine, R. A., Dixon, S., LeVine, S., Richman, A., Liederman, P. H., Keefer, C. H., & Brazelton, T. B. (1994). *Child care and culture: Lessons from Africa.* New York: Cambridge University Press.

Levine, S. C., Huttenlocher, J., Taylor, A., & Langrock, A. (1999). Early sex differences in spatial skill. *Developmental Psychology, 35,* 940–949.

Leviton, A. (1993). Coffee, caffeine, and reproductive hazards in humans. In S. Garattini (Ed.), *Monographs of the Mario Negri Institute for Pharmacological Research, Milan: Caffeine, Coffee, and Health* (pp. 348–358). New York: Raven Press.

Levitt, M. J., Weber, R. A., Clark, M. C., & McDonnell, P. (1985). Reciprocity of exchange in toddler sharing behavior. *Developmental Psychology, 21,* 122–123.

Levy, F., Hay, D. A., McStephen, M., Wood, C., & Waldman, I. (1997). Attention-deficit hyperactivity disorder: A category or a continuum? Genetic analysis of a large-scale twin study. *Journal of the American Academy of Child and Adolescent Psychiatry, 36,* 737–744.

Levy, G. D., Taylor, M. G., & Gelman, S. A. (1995). Traditional and evaluative aspects of flexibility in gender roles, social conventions, moral rules, and physical laws. *Child Development, 66,* 515–531.

Levy, Y. (1999). Early metalinguistic competence: Speech monitoring and repair behavior. *Developmental Psychology, 35,* 822–834.

Levy-Shiff, R., Goldschmidt, I., & Har-Evan, D. (1991). Transition to parenthood in adoptive families. *Developmental Psychology, 16,* 425–432.

Levy-Shiff, R., Goldschmidt, I., & Har-Even, D. (1991). Transition to parenthood in adoptive families. *Developmental Psychology, 27,* 131–140.

Lewin, L. M., Hops, H., Davis, B., & Dishion, T. J. (1993). Multimethod comparison of similarity in school adjustment of siblings and unrelated children. *Developmental Psychology, 24,* 963–969.

Lewis, B. A., Singer, L. T., Short, E., Minnes, S., Arendt, R., Weishampel, P., Klein, N., & Min, M. O. (2004). Four-year language outcomes of children exposed to cocaine in utero. *Neurotoxicology & Teratology, 26,* 617–628.

Lewis, C., Freeman, N. H., Kyriakidou, C., Maridaki-Kassotaki, K., & Berridge, D. M. (1996). Social influences on false belief access: Specific sibling influences or general apprenticeship? *Child Development, 67,* 2930–2947.

Lewis, L. B., Antone, C., & Johnson, J. S. (1999). Effects of prosodic stress and serial position on syllable omission in first words. *Developmental Psychology, 35,* 45–59.

Lewis, M., & Brooks-Gunn, J. (1979). *Social cognition and the acquisition of self.* New York: Plenum Press.

Lewis, M., & Ramsay, D. (2002). Cortisol response to embarrassment and shame. *Child Development, 73,* 1034–1045.

Lewis, M., & Ramsay, D. S. (1999). Effect of maternal soothing on infant stress response. *Child Development, 20,* 11–20.

Lewis, M., & Rosenblum, M. A. (1975). *Friendship and peer relations.* New York: Wiley.

Lewis, M., Alessandri, S. M., & Sullivan, M. W. (1990). Violation of expectancy, loss of control, and anger expressions in young infants. *Developmental Psychology, 26,* 745–751.

Lewis, M., Alessandri, S. M., & Sullivan, M. W. (1992). Differences in shame and pride as a function of children's gender and task difficulty. *Child Development, 63,* 630–638.

Lewis, M., Feiring, C., & Rosenthal, S. (2000). Attachment over time. *Child Development, 71,* 707–720.

Lewis, M., Stanger, C., & Sullivan, M. W. (1989). Deception in 3-year-olds. *Developmental Psychology, 24,* 434–440.

Lewis, M. D. (2000). The promise of dynamic systems approaches for an integrated account of human development. *Child Development, 71,* 36–43.

Lewontin, R. C. (1976). Race and intelligence. In N. J. Block & G. Dworkin (Eds.), *The IQ Controversy.* New York: Pantheon.

Leyens, J. P., Parke, R. D., Camino, L., & Berkowitz, L. (1975). Effects of movie violence on aggression in a field setting as a function of group dominance and cohesion. *Journal of Personality and Social Psychology, 32,* 346–360.

Li, J. (2002). Learning models in different culture. In J. Bempechat & J. G. Elliot (Eds.), Learning in culture and context. *New Directions for Child Development* (No. 96) (pp. 45–63). San Francisco: Jossey-Bass.

Li, J. (2004). Learning as a task or a virtue: U.S. and Chinese preschoolers explain learning. *Developmental Psychology, 40,* 595–605.

Liben, L. S., & Signorella, M. L. (1993). Gender-schematic processing in children: The role of initial interpretations of stimuli. *Developmental Psychology, 29,* 141–149.

Lichtenberger, E. O. (2005). General measures of cognition for the preschool child. *Mental Retardation & Developmental Disabilities Research Reviews, 11,* 197–208.

Lidz, J., & Gleitman, L. R. (2004). Argument structure and the child's contribution to language learning. *Trends in Cognitive Sciences, 8,* 157–161.

Lidz, J., Gleitman, H., & Gleitman, L. (2003). Understanding how input matters: Verb learning and the footprint of universal grammar. *Cognition, 87,* 151–178.

Lieberman, M., Doyle, A. B., & Markiewicz, D. (1999). Developmental patterns of security of attachment to mother and father in late childhood and early adolescence: Association with peer relations. *Child Development, 70,* 202–213.

Liebert, R. M., & Baron, R. A. (1972). Some immediate effects of televised violence on children's behavior. *Developmental Psychology, 6,* 469–475.

Liebert, R. M., & Sprafkin, J. N. (1988). *The early window: Effects of television on children and youth* (3rd ed.). New York: Pergamon Press.

Lieven, E. V. M. (1994). Crosslinguistic and crosscultural aspects of language addressed to children. In C. Gallaway & B. J. Richards (Eds.), *Input and interaction in language acquisition.* Cambridge, England: Cambridge University Press.

Lillard, A. S. (1993). Pretend play skills and the child's theory of mind. *Child Development, 64,* 348–371.

Lin, C. (1993). Breech presentation. In C. Lin, M. S. Verp, & R. E. Sabbagha (Eds.), *The high risk fetus: Pathophysiology, diagnosis, management.* New York: Springer-Verlag.

Lin, C. C., & Fu, V. R. (1990). A comparison of child-rearing practices among Chinese, immigrant Chinese, and Caucasian-American parents. *Child Development, 61,* 429–433.

Lindberg, M. A., Keiffer, J., & Thomas, S. W. (2000). Eyewitness testimony for physical abuse as a function of personal experience, development, and focus of study. *Journal of Applied Developmental Psychology, 21,* 555–591.

Linn, M. C., de Benedictis, T., & Delucchi, K. (1982). Adolescent reasoning about advertisements: Preliminary investigations. *Child Development, 53,* 1599–1613.

Linnet, K. M., Dalsgaard, S., Obel, C., Wisborg, K., Henriksen, T. B., Rodriquez, A., Kotimaa, A., Moilanen, I., Thomsen, P. H., Olsen, J., & Jarvelin, M. (2003). Maternal lifestyle factors in pregnancy risk of Attention Deficit Hyperactivity Disorder and associated behaviors: Review of the current evidence. *American Journal of Psychiatry, 160,* 1028–1040.

Lipsitt, L. (2003). Crib death: a biobehavioral phenomenon? *Current Directions in Psychological Science, 12,* 164–176.

Lipsitt, L. P., & Kaye, H. (1964). Conditioned sucking in the human newborn. *Psychonomic Science, 1,* 29–30.

Littenberg, R., Tulkin, S., & Kagan, J. (1971). Cognitive components of separation anxiety. *Developmental Psychology, 4,* 387–388.

Little, A. H., Lipsitt, L. P., & Rovee-Collier, C. K. (1984). Classical conditioning and retention of the infant's eyelid response: Effects of age and interstimulus interval. *Journal of Experimental Child Psychology, 37,* 512–524.

Little, J., Cardy, A., Arslan, Gilmour, M., & Mossey, P. A. (2004). Smoking and orofacial clefts: A United Kingdom-based case-control study. *Cleft Palate-Craniofacial Journal, 41,* 381–386.

Littschwager, J. C., & Markman, E. M. (1994). Sixteen- and 24-month-olds' use of mutual exclusivity as a default assumption in second-label learning. *Developmental Psychology, 30,* 955–968.

Livesley, W. J., & Bromley, D. B. (1973). *Person perception in childhood and adolescence.* London: Wiley.

Livner, M. R., Brooks-Gunn, J., & Kohen, D. E. (2002). Family processes as pathways from income to young children's development. *Developmental Psychology, 38,* 719–734.

Livson, N., & Peskin, H. (1980). Perspectives on adolescence from longitudinal research. In J. Adelson (Ed.), *Handbook of adolescent psychology* (pp. 47–98). New York: Wiley.

Lobel, M. (1994). Conceptualizations, measurement, and effects of prenatal maternal stress on birth outcomes. *Journal of Behavioral Medicine, 17,* 225–272.

Lobel, T., & Menashri, J. (1993). Relations of conceptions of gender-role transgressions and gender constancy to gender-typed toy preferences. *Developmental Psychology, 29,* 150–155.

Lobel, T., Slone, M., & Winch, G. (1997). Masculinity, popularity, and self-esteem among Israeli preadolescent girls. *Sex Roles, 36,* 395–408.

Lobel, T. E., Gruber, R., Govrin, N., & Mashraki-Pedhatzur, S. (2001). Children's gender related inferences and judgments: A cross-cultural study. *Developmental Psychology, 37,* 839–846.

Locke, J. (1913). *Some thoughts concerning education.* Sections 38 and 40. London: Cambridge University Press. (Original work published 1690.)

Locke, J. L. (1997). A theory of neurolinguistic development. *Brain and Language, 58,* 265–326.

Lockhart, K. L., Chang, B., & Story, T. (2002). Young children's beliefs about the stability of traits: Protective optimism. *Child Development, 73,* 1408–1430.

Loeb, S., Fuller, B., Kagan, S. L., & Carrol, B. (2004). Child care in poor communities: Early learning effects of type, quality, and stability. *Child Development, 75,* 47–65.

Loeber, R., & Farrington, D. P. (1998). *Serious and violent juvenile offenders: Risk factors and successful interventions.* Thousand Oaks, CA: Sage.

Loeber, R., & Stouthamer-Loeber, M. (1998). Development of juvenile aggression and violence: Some common misconceptions and controversies. *American Psychologist, 53,* 242–259.

Loehlin, J. C. (1985). Fitting heredity-environment models jointly to twin and adoption data from the California Psychological Inventory. *Behavior Genetics, 15,* 199–221.

Loehlin, J. C. (1992). *Genes and environment in personality development* (Individual Differences and Development Series, Vol. 2). Newbury Park, CA: Sage.

Loehlin, J. C., & Nichols, R. C. (1976). *Heredity, environment, and personality.* Austin: University of Texas Press.

Loehlin, J. C., Lindzey, G., & Spuhler, J. N. (1975). *Race differences in intelligence.* New York: W. H. Freeman.

Loftus, E. F., & Pickrell, J. E. (1995). The formation of false memories. *Psychiatric Annals, 25,* 720–725.

London, P. (1970). The rescuers: Motivational hypotheses about Christians who saved Jews from the Nazis. In J. Macaulay & L. Berkowitz (Eds.), *Altruism and helping behavior.* Orlando, FL: Academic Press.

Lorber, J. (1986). Dismantling Noah's ark. *Sex Roles, 14,* 567–580.

Lord, S. E., Eccles, J. S., & McCarthy, K. A. (1994). Surviving the junior high school transition: Family processes and self–perceptions as protective and risk factors. *Journal of Early Adolescence, 14,* 162–199.

Lore, D. (2000, December, 19). Choices grow for treating attention deficit. *Atlanta Constitution,* p. F4.

Lorenz, K. Z. (1937). The companion in the bird's world. *Auk, 54,* 245–273.

Lorenz, K. Z. (1943). The innate forms of possible experience. *Zeitschrift fur Tierpsychologie, 5,* 233–409.

Lorsbach, T. C., Katz, G. A., & Cupak, A. J. (1998). Developmental differences in the ability to inhibit the initial misinterpretation of garden path passages. *Journal of Experimental Child Psychology, 71,* 275–296.

Loukas, A., & Robinson, S. (2004). Examining the moderating role of perceived school climate in early adolescent adjustment. *Journal of Research on Adolescence, 14,* 209–233.

Love, J. M., Harrison, L., Sagi-Schwartz, A., et al. (2003). Child care quality matters: How conclusions may vary with context. *Child Development, 74,* 1021–1033.

Love, J. M., Kisker, E. E., Ross, C., Raikes, H., Constantine, J., Boller, K., Brooks-Gunn, J., Chazan-Cohen, R., Tarullo, L. B., Brady-Smith, C., Fuligni, Sidle, A., Schochet, P. Z., Paulsell, D., & Vogel, C. (2005). *Developmental Psychology, 41,* 885–901.

Lowy, J. (2000, February 24). U.S. teen pregnancy rate still high. *Atlanta Constitution,* p. E2.

Lozoff, B. (1989). Nutrition and behavior. *American Psychologist, 44,* 231–236.

Lozoff, B., Klein, N. K., Nelson, E. C., McClish, D. K., Manuel, M., & Chacon, M. E. (1998). Behavior of infants with iron-deficiency anemia. *Child Development, 68,* 24–36.

Lubart, T. I., & Sternberg, R. J. (1995). An investment approach to creativity: Theory and data. In S. M. Smith, T. B. Ward, & R. A. Finke (Eds.), *The creative cognition approach* (pp. 269–302). Cambridge, MA: MIT Press.

Luecke-Aleksa, D., Anderson, D. R., Collins, P. A., & Schmitt, K. L. (1995). Gender constancy and television viewing. *Developmental Psychology, 31,* 773–780.

Lummis, M., & Stevenson, H. W. (1990). Gender differences in beliefs and achievement: A cross-cultural study. *Developmental Psychology, 26,* 254–263.

Luna, B., Garver, K. E., Urban, T. A., Lazar, N. A., & Sweeney, J. A. (2004). Maturation of cognitive processes from late childhood to adulthood. *Child Development, 75,* 1357–1372.

Luster, T., & Dubow, E. (1992). Home environment and maternal intelligence as predictors of verbal intelligence: A comparison of preschool and school-age children. *Merrill-Palmer Quarterly, 38,* 151–175.

Luster, T., & McAdoo, H. (1996). Family and child influences on educational attainment: A secondary analysis of the High/Scope Perry preschool data. *Developmental Psychology, 32,* 26–39.

Luthar, S. S., & Becker, B. E. (2002). Privileged but Pressured: A study of affluent youth. *Child Development, 73,* 1593–1610.

Luthar, S. S., & D'Avanzo, K. (1999). Contextual factors in substance use: A study of suburban and inner-city adolescents. *Development and Psychopathology, 11,* 845–867.

Luthar, S. S., & Latendresse, S. J. (2005). Children of the affluent: Challenges to well-being. *Current Directions in Psychological Science, 14,* 49–53.

Luthar, S. S., & Latendresse, S. J. (in press). Comparable "risks" at the SES extremes: Pre–adolescents' perceptions of parenting. *Development and Psychopathology.*

Lynch, M. P., Eilers, R. E., Oller, D. K., & Urbano, R. C. (1990). Innateness, experience, and music perception. *Psychological Science, 1,* 272–276.

Lynn, A., Ashley, T., & Hassold, T. (2004). Variation in Human Meiotic Recombination. *American Review of Genomics and Human Genetics, 5,* 317–349.

Lynn, R. (1997). Direct evidence for a genetic basis for black–white differences in IQ. *American Psychologist, 52,* 73–74.

Lyons-Ruth, K., Alpern, L., & Repacholi, B. (1993). Disorganized infant attachment classification and maternal psychosocial problems as predictors of hostile-aggressive behavior in the preschool classroom. *Child Development, 64,* 572–585.

Lyons-Ruth, K., Connell, D. B., Grunebaum, H. U., & Botein, S. (1990). Infants at social risk: Maternal depression and family support services as mediators of infant development and security of attachment. *Child Development, 61,* 85–98.

Lyons-Ruth, K., Easterbrooks, M. A., & Cibelli, C. D. (1997). Infant attachment strategies, infant mental lag, and maternal depressive symptoms: Predictors of internalizing and externalizing problems at age 7. *Developmental Psychology, 33,* 681–692.

Lytton, H. (1990). Child and parent effects in boys' conduct disorder: A reinterpretation. *Developmental Psychology, 26,* 683–697.

Lytton, H., & Romney, D. M. (1991). Parents' differential socialization of boys and girls: A meta-analysis. *Psychological Bulletin, 109,* 267–296.

Mac Iver, D., & Reuman, D. A. (1988, April). *Decision-making in the classroom and early adolescents' valuing of mathematics.* Paper presented at the annual meeting of the American Educational Research Association, New Orleans, LA.

MacCallum, F., & Golombok, S. (2004). Children raised in fatherless families from infancy: A follow-up of children of lesbian and single heterosexual mothers at early adolescence. *Journal of Child Psychology & Psychiatry, 45,* 1407–1419.

Maccoby, E. E. (1980). *Social development.* San Diego, CA: Harcourt Brace Jovanovich.

Maccoby, E. E. (1998). *The two sexes: Growing up apart, coming together.* Cambridge, MA: Harvard University Press.

Maccoby, E. E., & Jacklin, C. N. (1974). *The psychology of sex differences.* Stanford, CA: Stanford University Press.

Maccoby, E. E., & Martin, J. A. (1983). Socialization in the context of the family: Parent–child interaction. In E. M. Hetherington (Ed.), P. H. Mussen (General Ed.), *Handbook of child psychology:* Vol. 4. *Socialization, personality, and social development* (4th ed.). New York: Wiley.

MacFarlane, A. (1977). *The psychology of childbirth.* Cambridge, MA: Harvard University Press.

MacGregor, S. N., & Chasnoff, I. J. (1993). Substance abuse in pregnancy. In C. Lin, M. S. Verp, & R. E. Sabbagha (Eds.), *The high-risk fetus: Pathophysiology, diagnosis, management.* New York: Springer-Verlag.

MacKinnon-Lewis, C., Starnes, R., Volling, B., & Johnson, S. (1997). Perceptions of parenting as predictors of boys' sibling and peer relations. *Developmental Psychology, 33,* 1024–1031.

Macmillan, R., McMorris, B. J., & Kruttschnitt, C. (2004). Linked lives: Stability and change in maternal circumstances and trajectories of antisocial behavior in children. *Child Development, 75,* 205–220.

MacNeilage, P. F., Davis, B. L., Kinney, A., & Matyear, C. L. (2000). The motor core of speech: A comparison of serial organization patterns in infants and languages. *Child Development, 71,* 153–163.

MacPhee, D., Fritz, J., & Miller-Heyl, J. (1996). Ethnic variations in personal social networks and parenting. *Child Development, 67,* 3278–3295.

MacPhee, D., Ramey, C. T., & Yeates, K. O. (1984). Home environment and early cognitive development: Implications for intervention. In A. W. Gottfried (Ed.), *Home environment and early cognition development. Longitudinal research.* Orlando, FL: Academic Press.

MacWhinney, B. (2004). A multiple process solution to the logical problem of language acquisition. *Journal of Child Language, 31,* 883–914.

Madison, L. S., Madison, J. K., & Adubato, S. A. (1986). Infant behavior and development in relation to fetal movement and habituation. *Child Development, 57,* 1475–1482.

Magnusson, D. (1995). Individual development: A holistic, integrated model. In P. Moen, G. H. Elder, Jr., & K. Luscher (Eds.), *Examining lives in context: Perspectives on the ecology of human development.* Washington, DC: American Psychological Association.

Mahler, M. S., Pine, F., & Bergman, A. (1975). *The psychological birth of the infant.* New York: Basic Books.

Mahoney, A., Jourilies, E. N., & Scavone, J. (1997). Marital adjustment and marital discard over childrearing, and child problems: Moderating effects of child age. *Journal of Clinical Child Psychology, 26,* 415–423.

Main, M., & Cassidy, J. (1988). Categories of response to reunion with the parent at age 6: Predictable from infant attachment classifications and stable over a 1-month period. *Developmental Psychology, 24,* 415–426.

Main, M., & Goldwyn, R. (1994). *Interview-based adult attachment classifications: Related to infant-mother and infant-father attachment.* Unpublished manuscript, University of California, Berkeley.

Main, M., & Solomon, J. (1990). Procedures for identifying infants as disorganized/disoriented during the Ainsworth Strange Situation. In M. T. Greenberg, D. Cicchetti, & E. M. Cummings (Eds.), *Attachment in the preschool years: Theory, research, and intervention.* Chicago: University of Chicago Press.

Main, M., & Weston, D. R. (1981). The quality of the toddler's relationship to mother and to father: Related to conflict and the readiness to establish new relationships. *Child Development, 52,* 932–940.

Malas, M. A., Aslankoç, R., Üngör, B., Sulak, O., & Candir, Ö. (2004). The development of large intestine during the fetal period. *Early Human Development, 78,* 1–13.

Malatesta, C. Z., & Haviland, J. M. (1982). Learning display rules: The socialization of emotion expression in infancy. *Child Development, 53,* 991–1003.

Malatesta, C. Z., Grigoryev, P., Lamb, C., Albin, M., & Culver, C. (1986). Emotional socialization and expressive development in preterm and full-term infants. *Child Development, 57,* 316–330.

Malcom, N. L. (2003). Constructing female athleticism: A study of girls' recreational softball. *American Behavioral Scientist, 46,* 1387–1404.

Malina, R. M. (1990). Physical growth and performance during the transitional years (9–16). In R. Montemayer, G. R. Adams, & T. P. Gullotta (Eds.), *From childhood to adolescence: A transitional period?* (pp. 41–62). Newbury Park, CA: Sage.

Mandel, D. R., Jusczyk, P. W., & Pisoni, D. B. (1995). Infants' recognition of sound patterns of their own names. *Psychological Science, 5,* 314–317.

Mandler, J. (2004). Thought before language. *Trends in Cognitive Sciences, 8,* 508–513.

Mandler, J. M. (2000). Perceptual and conceptual processes in infancy. *Journal of Cognition and Development, 1,* 3–36.

Mangelsdorf, S. C. (1992). Developmental changes in infant–stranger interaction. *Infant Behavior and Development, 15,* 191–208.

Mangelsdorf, S. C., Plunkett, J. W., Dedrick, C. F., Berlin, M., Meisels, S. J., McHale, J. L., & Dichtellmiller, M. (1996). Attachment security in very low birth weight infants. *Developmental Psychology, 32,* 914–920.

Mangelsdorf, S. C., Shapiro, J. R., & Marzolf, D. (1995). Developmental and temperamental differences in emotion regulation in infancy. *Child Development, 66,* 1817–1828.

Manlove, J. M., Mariner, C., & Papillo, A. R. (2000). Subsequent fertility among teen mothers: Longitudinal analyses of recent national data. *Journal of Marriage and the Family, 62,* 430–448.

Maratsos, M. (2000). More overregularizations after all: New data and discussion on Marcus, Pinker, Ullman, Hollander, Rosen & Xu. *Journal of Child Language, 27,* 183–212.

Marcia, J. E. (1980). Identity in adolescence. In J. Adelson (Ed.), *Handbook of adolescent psychology.* New York: Wiley.

Marcia, J. E., Waterman, A. S., Matteson, D., Archer, S. C., & Orlofsky, J. L. (1993). *Ego identity: A handbook for psychosocial research.* New York: Springer-Verlag.

Marcon, R. A. (1999). Differential impact of preschool models on developmental and early learning of inner-city children: A three-cohort study. *Developmental Psychology, 35,* 358–375.

Marcus, D. E., & Overton, W. F. (1978). The development of cognitive gender constancy and sex-role preferences. *Child Development, 49,* 434–444.

Marcus, G. F., Pinker, S., Ullman, M., Hollander, M., Rosen, T. J., & Xu, F. (1992). Overregularization in language acquisition. *Monographs of the Society for Research in Child Development, 57,* (4, Serial No. 228).

Marean, G. C., Werner, L. A., & Kuhl, P. K. (1992). Vowel categorization by very young infants. *Developmental Psychology, 28,* 396–405.

Marini, Z., & Case, R. (1994). The development of abstract reasoning about the physical and social world. *Child Development, 65,* 147–159.

Markovitch, S., & Zelazo, P. D. (1999). The A-not-B error: Results from a logistic meta-analysis. *Child Development, 70,* 1297–1313.

Markovits, H., & Dumas, C. (1999). Developmental patterns in the understanding of social and physical transitivity. *Journal of Experimental Child Psychology, 73,* 95–114.

Markovits, H., Benenson, J. F., & Kramer, D. L. (2003). Children and adolescents' internal models of food-sharing behavior include complex evaluations of contextual factors. *Child Development, 74,* 1697–1708.

Markstrom-Adams, C. (1992). A consideration of intervening factors in adolescent identity formation. In G. R. Adams, T. P. Gullotta, & R. Montemayer (Eds.), *Adolescent identity formation* (Advances in Adolescent Development, Vol. 4). Newbury Park, CA: Sage.

Markus, H., & Kitayama, S. (1994). A collective fear of the collective: Implications for selves and theories of selves. *Personality and Social Psychology Bulletin, 20,* 568–579.

Marlier, L., Schall, B., & Soussignan, R. (1998). Neonatal responsiveness to the odor of amniotic and lacteal fluids: A test of perinatal chemosensory continuity. *Child Development, 69,* 611–623.

Marsh, H. W., Craven, R., & Debus, R. (1998). Structure, stability, and development of children's self-concepts: A multicohort-multioccasion study. *Child Development, 69,* 1030–1052.

Marsh, H. W., Ellis, L. A., & Craven, R. G. (2002). How do preschool children feel about themselves? Unraveling the measurement and multidimensional self-concept structure. *Developmental Psychology, 38,* 376–393.

Marshall, W. A. (1977). *Human growth and its disorders.* Orlando, FL: Academic Press.

Martin, C. L. (1990). Attitudes and expectations about children with non-traditional gender roles. *Sex Roles, 22,* 151–165.

Martin, C. L. (1994). Cognitive influences on the development and maintenance of gender segregation. *New directions for Child Development, 65,* 35–51.

Martin, C. L., & Fabes, R. A. (2001). The stability and consequences of young children's same-sex peer interactions. *Developmental Psychology, 37,* 431–446.

Martin, C. L., & Halverson, C. F., Jr. (1981). A schematic processing model of sex typing and stereotyping in children. *Child Development, 52,* 1119–1134.

Martin, C. L., & Halverson, C. F., Jr. (1983). The effects of sex-typing schemas on young children's memory. *Child Development, 54,* 563–574.

Martin, C. L., & Halverson, C. F., Jr. (1987). The roles of cognition in sex-roles and sex-typing. In D. B. Carter (Ed.), *Current conceptions of sex roles and sex-typing: Theory and Research.* New York: Praeger.

Martin, C. L., Eisenbud, L., & Rose, H. (1995). Children's gender-based reasoning about toys. *Child Development, 66,* 1453–1471.

Martin, G. B., & Clark, R. D., III. (1982). Distress crying in neonates: Species and peer specificity. *Developmental Psychology, 18,* 3–9.

Martin, R. C. (2003). Language processing: Functional organization and neuroanatomical basis. *Annual Review of Psychology,* 55–89.

Martin, S. L., Clark, K. A., Lynch, S. R., Kupper, L. L., & Cilenti, D. (1999). Violence in the lives of pregnant teenage women: Associations with multiple substance use. *American Journal of Drug & Alcohol Abuse, 25,* 425–440.

Martorell, R. (1980). Interrelationships between diet, infectious disease, and nutritional status. In L. S. Green & F. E. Johnston (Eds.), *Social and biological predictors of nutritional status, physical growth, and neurological development.* New York: Academic Press.

Marx, M. H., & Henderson, B. B. (1996). A fuzzy trace analysis of categorical inferences and instantial associations as a function of retention interval. *Cognitive Development, 11,* 551–569.

Masataka, N. (1992). Early ontogeny of vocal behavior of Japanese infants in response to maternal speech. *Child Development, 63,* 1177–1185.

Masataka, N. (1996). Perception of motherese in a signed language by 6-month-old deaf infants. *Developmental Psychology, 32,* 874–879.

Masataka, N. (1998). Perception of motherese in Japanese Sign Language by 6-month-old hearing infants. *Developmental Psychology, 34,* 241–246.

Masden, A. S., Coatsworth, J. D., Neeman, J., Gest, J. D., Tellegen, A., & Garmezy, N. (1995). The structure and coherence of competence from childhood through adolescence. *Child Development, 66,* 1635–1659.

Mason, C. A., Cauce, A. M., Gonzales, N., & Hiraga, Y. (1996). Neither too sweet nor too sour: Problem peers, maternal control, and problem behavior in African-American adolescents. *Child Development, 67,* 2115–2130.

Mason, M. G., & Gibbs, J. C. (1993). Social perspective taking and moral judgment among college students. *Journal of Adolescent Research, 8,* 109–123.

Masters, J. C., Ford, M. E., Arend, R., Grotevant, H. D., & Clark, L. V. (1979). Modeling and labeling as integrated determinants of children's sex-typed imitative behavior. *Child Development, 50,* 364–371.

Matejcek, Z., Dytrych, Z., & Schuller, V. (1979). The Prague study of children born from unwanted pregnancies. *International Journal of Mental Health, 7,* 63–74.

Matias, R., & Cohn, J. F. (1993). Are Max-specified infant facial expressions during face-to-face interaction consistent with differential emotions theory? *Developmental Psychology, 29,* 524–531.

Matlin, M. W., & Foley, H. J. (1997). *Sensation and perception* (4th ed.). Boston: Allyn & Bacon.

Matsumoto, D. (1990). Cultural similarities and differences in display rules. *Motivation and Emotion, 14,* 195–214.

Matsumoto, D. (2000). *Culture and psychology* (2nd ed.). Belmont, CA: Wadsworth.

Matthews, K. A., Batson, C. D., Horn, J., & Rosenman, R. H. (1981). "Principles in his nature which interest him in the fortune of others": The heritability of empathic concern for others. *Journal of Personality, 49,* 237–247.

Mattson, S. N., Calarco, K. E., Chambers, C. D., & Jones, K. L. (2002). Interaction of maternal smoking and other in-pregnancy exposures: Analytic considerations. *Neurotoxicology and Teratology, 24,* 359–367.

Maughan, A., & Cicchetti, D. (2002). Impact of child maltreatment and interadult violence on children's emotional regulation abilities and socioemotional adjustment. *Child Development, 73,* 1525–1542.

Maurer, D., Stager, C. L., & Mondloch, C. J. (1999). Cross-modal transfer of shape is difficult to demonstrate in 1-month-olds. *Child Development, 70,* 1047–1057.

Mayberry, R. I. (1994). The importance of childhood to language acquisition: Evidence from American Sign Language. In J. C. Goodman & H. C. Nusbalm (Eds.), *The development of speech perception: The transition from speech sounds to spoken words.* Cambridge, MA: MIT Press.

Mayberry, R. I., & Nicoladis, E. (2000). Gesture reflects language development: Evidence from bilingual children. *Current Directions in Psychological Science, 9,* 192–196.

Maynard, A. E. (2002). Cultural teaching: The development of teaching skills in Maya sibling interactions. *Child Development, 73,* 969–982.

McCabe, M. P., & Ricciardelli, L. A. (2004a). Body image dissatisfaction among males across the lifespan: A review of past literature. *Journal of Psychosomatic Research, 56,* 675–685.

McCabe, M. P., & Ricciardelli, L. A. (2004b). A longitudinal study of pubertal timing and extreme body change behaviors among adolescent boys and girls. *Adolescence, 39,* 145–166.

McCall, R. B. (1977). Challenges to a science of developmental psychology. *Child Development, 48,* 333–344.

McCall, R. B., Applebaum, M. I., & Hogarty, P. S. (1973). Developmental changes in mental test performance. *Monographs of the Society for Research in Child Development, 38,* (3, Serial No. 150).

McCall, R. B., & Carriger, M. S. (1993). A meta-analysis of infant habituation and recognition memory performance as predictors of later IQ. *Child Development, 64,* 57–79.

McCall, R. B., & Groark, C. J. (2000). The future of applied developmental research and public policy. *Child Development, 71,* 197–204.

McCartney, K., Harris, M. J., & Bernieri, F. (1990). Growing up and growing apart: A developmental meta-analysis of twin studies. *Psychological Bulletin, 107,* 236–237.

McCarton, C. M., Brooks-Gunn, J., Wallace, I. F., Bauer, C. R., Bennett, F. C., Bernbaum, J. C., Broyles, S., Casey, P. H., McCormick, M. C., Scott, D. T., Tyson, J., Tonascia, J., & Meinhart, C. L. (1997). Results at age 8 years of early intervention for low-birth-weight premature infants. *Journal of the American Medical Association, 277,* 126–132.

McCarty, M. E., & Ashmead, D. H. (1999). Visual control of reaching and grasping in infants. *Developmental Psychology, 35,* 620–631.

McClelland, D. C., Atkinson, J. W., Clark, R. A., & Lowell, E. L. (1953). *The achievement motive.* East Norwalk, CT: Appleton-Century-Crofts.

McCormick, D. P., Chonmaitree, T., Pittman, C., Saeed, K., Friedman, N. R., Uchida, T., & Baldwin, C. D. (2005). Nonsevere acute otitis media: A clinical trial comparing outcomes of watchful waiting versus immediate antibiotic treatment. *Pediatrics, 115,* 1455–1465.

McCreary, D., & Sasse, D. K. (2000). An exploration of the drive for muscularity in adolescent boys and girls. *Journal of American College Health, 48,* 297–305.

McCubbin, J. A., Lawson, E. J., Cox, S., Shermin, J. J., Norton, J. A., & Read, J. A. (1996). Prenatal maternal blood pressure response to stress predicts birth weight and gestational age: A preliminary study. *American Journal of Obstetrics and Gynecology, 175,* 706–712.

McCulloch, A. U. (2001). Teenage childbearing in Great Britain and the spatial concentration of poverty households. *Journal of Epidemiology & Community Health, 55,* 16–23.

McDonald, D. G., & Kim, H. (2001). When I die, I feel small: Electronic game characters and the social self. *Journal of Broadcasting & Electronic Media, 45,* 241–258.

McDonough, L. (2002). Basic-level nouns: First learned but misunderstood. *Journal of Child Language, 29,* 357–377.

McGhee, P. E. (1976). Children's appreciation of humor: A test of the cognitive congruency principle. *Child Development, 47,* 420–426.

McGhee, P. E. (1979). *Humor: Its origins and development.* San Francisco: W. H. Freeman.

McGhee, P. E., & Frueh, T. (1980). Television viewing and the learning of sex-role stereotypes. *Sex Roles, 6,* 179–188.

McGhee-Bidlack, B. (1991). The development of noun definitions: a meta-linguistic analysis. *Journal of Child Languages, 18,* 417–434.

McGilly, K., & Siegler, R. S. (1990). The influence of encoding strategic knowledge on children's choices among serial recall strategies. *Developmental Psychology, 26,* 931–941.

McGrath, E. P., & Repetti, R. L. (2000). Mothers' and fathers' attitudes toward their children's academic performance and children's perceptions of their academic competence. *Journal of Youth and Adolescence, 29,* 713–723.

McGraw, M. B. (1935). *Growth: A study of Johnny and Jimmy.* East Norwalk, CT: Appleton-Century-Crofts.

McGuire, S., Manke, G., Eftekhari, A., & Dunn, J. (2000). Children's perception of sibling conflict during middle childhood. Issues and sibling (dis) similarity. *Social Development, 9,* 173–190.

McHale, J. P. (1995). Coparenting and triadic interactions during infancy: The roles of marital distress and child gender. *Developmental Psychology, 31,* 985–996.

McHale, J. P., Kazali, C., Rotman, T., Talbot, J., Carleton, M., & Lieberson, R. (2004). The transition to coparenthood: Parents' prebirth expectations and early coparental adjustment at 3 months postpartum. *Development & Psychopathology, 16,* 711–733.

McHale, S. M., Crouter, A. C., & Tucker, C. J. (1999). Family context and gender role socialization in middle childhood: Comparing girls to boys and sisters to brothers. *Child Development, 70,* 990–1004.

McHale, S. M., Crouter, A. C., & Tucker, C. J. (2001). Free-time activities in middle childhood: Links with adjustment in early adolescence. *Child Development, 72,* 1764–1778.

McHale, S. M., Updegraff, K. A., Helms-Erikson, H., & Crouter, A. C. (2001). Sibling influences on gender development in middle childhood and early adolescence: A longitudinal study. *Developmental Psychology, 37,* 115–125.

McHale, S. M., Updegraff, K. A., Jackson-Newsom, J., Tucker, C. J., & Crouter, A. C. (2000). When does parents' differential treatment have negative implications for siblings. *Social Development, 9,* 149–172.

McKee, C., & McDaniel, D. (2004). Multiple influences on children's language performance. *Journal of Child Language, 31,* 489–492.

McKenna, M. A. J. (1997, May 2). U.S., Georgia get welcome news on teenagers and sex. *Atlanta Constitution,* p. D1.

McKenna, M. W., & Ossoff, E. P. (1998). Age differences in children's comprehension of a popular television program. *Child Study Journal, 28,* 53–68.

McKusick, V. A. (1995). *Mendelian inheritance in Man* (10th ed.). Baltimore: Johns Hopkins University Press.

McLean, K. C., & Thorne, A. (2003). Late adolescents self-defining memories about relationships. *Developmental Psychology, 39,* 635–645.

McLoyd, V. C. (1989). Socialization and development in a changing economy: The effects of paternal job and income loss on children. *American Psychologist, 44,* 293–302.

McLoyd, V. C. (1990). The impact of economic hardship on Black families and children: Psychological distress, parenting, and socioemotional development. *Child Development, 61,* 311–346.

McLoyd, V. C. (1998). Socioeconomic disadvantage and child development. *American Psychologist, 53,* 185–204.

McLoyd, V. C., & Smith, J. (2002). Physical discipline and behavior problems in African American, European American, and Hispanic children: Emotional support as a moderator. *Journal of Marriage and the Family, 64,* 40–53.

McMahon, M. J., & Katz, V. L. (1996). Clinical teratology. In J. A. Kuller, N. C. Cheschier, & R. C. Cefalo (Eds.), *Prenatal diagnosis and reproductive genetics* (pp. 207–217). St. Louis: Mosby.

McNeill, D. (1970). *The acquisition of language.* New York: Harper & Row.

McNeilly-Choque, M. K., Hart, C. H., Robinson, C. C., Nelson, L. J., & Olsen, S. F. (1996). Overt and relational aggression on the playground: Correspondence among different informants. *Journal of Research in Childhood Education, 11,* 47–67.

Mead, M. (1935). *Sex and temperament in three primitive societies.* New York: William Morrow.

Measelle, J. R., Albow, J. C., Cowan, P., & Cowan, C. P. (1998). Assessing young children's views of their academic, social, and emotional lives: An evaluation of the self-perception scales of the Berkeley Puppet Interview. *Child Development, 69,* 1556–1576.

Mediascope, Inc. (1996). *National Television Violence Study: Executive summary 1994–1995.* Studio City, CA: Author.

Meehan, B. T., Hughes, J. N., & Cavell, T. A. (2003). Teacher–student relationships as compensatory resources for aggressive children. *Child Development, 74,* 1145–1157.

Mehan, H., Villaneueva, I., Hubbard, L., & Lintz, A. (1996). *Constructing school success: The consequences of untracking low-achievement students.* New York: Cambridge University Press.

Mehl-Madrona, L. E. (2004). The importance of psychosocial variables in predicting low birth weight. *Journal of Prenatal & Perinatal Psychology & Health, 18,* 255–264.

Mehlman, M. J., & Botkin, J. R. (1998). *Access to the genome: The challenge to equality.* Washington, DC: Georgetown University Press.

Meier, R. P. (1991). Language acquisition by deaf children. *American Scientist, 79,* 69–70.

Meilman, P. W. (1979). Cross-sectional age changes in ego identity status during adolescence. *Developmental Psychology, 15,* 230–231.

Melson, G. F., Peet, S., & Sparks, C. (1991). Children's attachments to their pets: Links to socioemotional development. *Children's Environmental Quarterly, 8,* 55–65.

Meltzoff, A. N. (1988a). Infant imitation after a 1-week delay: Long-term memory for novel acts and multiple stimuli. *Developmental Psychology, 24,* 470–476.

Meltzoff, A. N. (1988b). Imitation of televised models by infants. *Child Development, 59,* 1221–1229.

Meltzoff, A. N. (1988c). Infant imitation after a 1-week delay: Long-term memory for novel acts and multiple stimuli. *Developmental Psychology, 24,* 470–476.

Meltzoff, A. N. (1988d). Infant imitation and memory: Nine-month-olds in immediate and deferred tests. *Child Development, 59,* 217–225.

Meltzoff, A. N. (1990a). Foundations for developing a concept of self: The role of imitation in relating self to other and the value of social mirroring, social modeling, and self-practice in infancy. In D. Cicchetti & M. Beeghly (Eds.), *The self in transition: Infancy to childhood* (pp. 139–164). Chicago: University of Chicago Press.

Meltzoff, A. N. (1990b). Towards a developmental cognitive science: The implications of cross-modal matching and imitation for the development of memory in infancy. A. Diamond (Ed.), *The development and neural bases of higher cognitive functions,* Vol. 608, *Annals of the New York Academy of Sciences.*

Meltzoff, A. N. (1995a). Understanding the intentions of others: Re-enactment of intended acts by 18-month-old children. *Developmental Psychology, 31,* 838–850.

Meltzoff, A. N. (1995b). What infant memory tells us about infantile amnesia: Long-term recall and deferred imitation. *Journal of Experimental Child Psychology, 59,* 497–515.

Meltzoff, A. N., & Moore, M. K. (1977). Imitation of facial and manual gestures by human neonates. *Science, 198,* 75–78.

Meltzoff, A. N., & Moore, M. K. (1992). Early imitation within a functional framework: The importance of person, identity, movement, and development. *Infant Behavior and Development, 15,* 479–505.

Merewood, A. (2000). Sperm under seige. In K. L. Freiberg (Ed.), *Human development 00/01* (28th ed., pp. 41–45). Guilford, CT: Dushkin/McGraw-Hill.

Mervis, C. B., & Johnson, K. E. (1991). Acquisition of the plural morpheme: A case study. *Developmental Psychology, 27,* 222–235.

Mervis, C. B., Golinkoff, R. M., & Bertrand, J. (1994). Two-year-olds readily learn multiple labels for the same basic-level category. *Child Development, 65,* 1163–1177.

Meschke, L. L., Bartholomae, S., & Zentall, S. R. (2002). *Journal of Adolescent Health, 31,* 264–279.

Messinger, D. S., Fogel, A., & Dickson, K. L. (2001). All smiles are positive but some smiles are more positive than others. *Developmental Psychology, 37,* 642–653.

Meulemans, T., Van der Linden, M., & Perruchet, P. (1998). Implicit sequence learning in children. *Journal of Experimental Child Psychology, 69,* 199–221.

Meyer-Bahlberg, H. F. L., Ehrhardt, A. A., Rosen, L. R., Gruen, R. S., Veridiano, N. P., Vann, F. H., & Neuwalder, H. F. (1995). Prenatal estrogens and the development of homosexual orientation. *Developmental Psychology, 31,* 12–21.

Michaud, P.-A. (2003). Prevention and health promotion in school and community settings: A commentary on the international perspective. *Journal of Adolescent Health, 33,* 219–225.

Midgley, C. (2002). *Goals, goal structures, and patterns of adaptive learning.* Mahwah, NJ: Lawrence Ealbaum Associates.

Midgley, C., Feldlaufer, H., & Eccles, J. S. (1989). Student/teacher relations and attitudes toward mathematics before and after the transition to junior high school. *Child Development, 60,* 981–992.

Midlarsky, E., Kahana, E., Corley, R., Nemeroff, R., & Schonbar, R. A. (1999). Altruistic moral judgment among older adults. *International Journal of Aging and Human Development, 49,* 27–41.

Millberger, S., Biederman, J., Faraone, S. V., Chen, L., & Jones, J. (1996). Is maternal smoking during pregnancy a risk factor for attention deficit hyperactivity disorder n children? *American Journal of Psychiatry, 153,* 1138–1142.

Miller, B. C., Fan, X., Christenson, M., Grotevant, H. D., & Van Dulmen, M. (2000). Comparisons of adopted and nonadopted adolescents in a large, nationally representative sample. *Child Development, 71,* 533–541.

Miller, C. L., Miceli, P. J., Whitman, T. L., & Borkowski, J. G. (1996). Cognitive readiness to parent and intellectual–emotional development in children of adolescent mothers. *Developmental Psychology, 32,* 533–541.

Miller, G. V. (1995). *The gay male's odyssey in the corporate world.* Binghamton, NY: Haworth Press.

Miller, J. L., & Eimas, P. D. (1996). Internal structure of voicing categories in early infancy. *Perception and Psychophysics, 58,* 1157–1167.

Miller, J. L., Sonies, B. C., & Macedonia, C. (2003). Emergence of oroparyngeal, laryngeal and swallowing activity in the developing fetal upper aerodigestive tract: An ultrasound evaluation. *Early Human Development, 71,* 61–87.

Miller, K. F., Smith, C. M., Zhu, J., & Zhang, H. (1995). Preschool origins of cross-national differences in mathematical competence. *Psychological Science, 6,* 56–60.

Miller, L. T., & Vernon, P. A. (1997). Developmental changes in speed of information processing in young children. *Developmental Psychology, 33,* 549–554.

Miller, N. B., Cowan, P. A., Cowan, C. P., Hetherington, E. M., & Clingempeel, W. G. (1993). Externalizing in preschoolers and early adolescents: A cross-study replication of a family model. *Developmental Psychology, 29,* 3–18.

Miller, P. A., Eisenberg, N., Fabes, R. A., & Shell, R. (1996). Relations of moral reasoning and vicarious emotion to young children's prosocial behavior toward peers and adults. *Developmental Psychology, 32,* 210–219.

Miller, P. H. (2000). How best to utilize a deficiency. *Child Development, 71,* 1013–1017.

Miller, P. H. (2002). *Theories of developmental psychology* (4th ed.). New York: Worth Publishers.

Miller, P. H., & Seier, W. L. (1994). Strategy utilization deficiencies in children. In H. W. Reese (Ed.), *Advances in child development and behavior,* Vol. 25. New York: Academic Press.

Miller, P. H., & Weiss, M. G. (1981). Children's attention allocation, understanding of attention, and performance on the incidental learning task. *Child Development, 52,* 1183–1190.

Miller, P. H., & Weiss, M. G. (1982). Children's and adults' knowledge about what variables affect selective attention. *Child Development, 53,* 543–549.

Miller, S. A. (1997). *Developmental research methods* (2nd ed.). Englewood Cliffs, NJ: Prentice-Hall.

Mills, J. L. (2001). Food fortification to prevent neural tube defects. *JAMA: Journal of the American Medical Association, 285,* 3022–3024.

Mills, R. S. L., & Rubin, K. H. (1990). Parental beliefs about problematic social behaviors in early childhood. *Child Development, 61,* 138–151.

Minton, H. L., & Schneider, F. W. (1980). *Differential psychology.* Pacific Grove: Brooks/Cole.

Mischel, W. (1974). Processes in the delay of gratification. In L. Berkowitz (Ed.), *Advances in experimental social psychology* (Vol. 7). New York: Academic.

Mistry, J. (1997). The development of remembering in cultural context. In N. Cowan (Ed.), *The development of memory in childhood* (pp. 343–368). London: London University College Press.

Mistry, R. S., Vandwater, E. A., Huston, A. C., & McLoyd, V. C. (2002). Economic well-being and children's social adjustment: The role of family process in an ethnically diverse low-income sample. *Child Development, 73,* 935–951.

Mitchell, J. E., Baker, L. A., & Jacklin, C. N. (1989). Masculinity and femininity in twin children: Genetic and environmental factors. *Child Development, 60,* 1475–1485.

Mitchell, P. (1997). *Introduction to theory of mind: Children, autism, and apes.* London: Arnold.

Miura, I. T., Okamoto, Y., Vlahovic-Stetic, V., Kim, C. C., & Han, J. H. (1999). Language supports for children's understanding of numerical fractions: A cross-national comparison. *Journal of Experimental Child Psychology, 74,* 356–365.

Mix, K. S., Huttenlocher, J., & Levine, S. C. (2002). Multiple cues for quantification in infancy: Is number one of them? *Psychological Bulletin, 128,* 278–294.

Miyawaki, K., Strange, W., Verbrugge, R., Liberman, A. M., Jenkins, J. J., & Fujimura, D. (1975). An effect of linguistic experience: The discrimination of [r] and [l] by native speakers of Japanese and English. *Perception and Psychophysics, 18,* 331–340.

Mize, J., & Ladd, G. W. (1990). A cognitive-social learning approach to social skill training with low-status preschool children. *Developmental Psychology, 26,* 388–397.

Moely, B. E., Santulli, K. A., & Obach, M. S. (1995). Strategy instruction, metacognition, and motivation in the elementary school classroom. In F. E. Weinert & W. Schneider (Eds.), *Memory performance and competencies: Issues in growth and development.* Hillsdale, NJ: Erlbaum.

Moerk, E. L. (1989). The LAD was a lady and the tasks were ill-defined. *Developmental Review, 9,* 21–57.

Molfese, D. L. (1977). Infant cerebral asymmetry. In S. J. Segalowitz & F.A. Gruber (Eds.), *Language development and neurological theory.* Orlando, FL: Academic Press.

Molina, B. S. G., & Chassin, L. (1996). The parent-adolescent relationship at puberty: Hispanic ethnicity and parental alcoholism as moderators. *Developmental Psychology, 32,* 675–686.

Moller, L. C., & Serbin, L. A. (1996). Antecedents of toddler gender segregation: Cognitive consonance, gender-typed toy preferences and behavioral compatibility. *Sex Roles, 35,* 445–460.

Monass, J. A., & Engelhard, J. A., Jr. (1990). Home environment and the competitiveness of accomplished individuals in four talent fields. *Developmental Psychology, 26,* 264–268.

Money, J. (1985). Pediatric sexology and hermaphrodism. *Journal of Sex and Marital Therapy, 11,* 139–156.

Money, J. (1988). *Gay, straight, and in-between: The sexology of erotic orientation.* New York: Oxford University Press.

Money, J., & Ehrhardt, A. (1972). *Man and woman, boy and girl.* Baltimore: Johns Hopkins University Press.

Montemayor, R., & Eisen, M. (1977). The development of self-conceptions from childhood to adolescence. *Developmental Psychology, 13,* 314–319.

Moon, C., Cooper, R. P., & Fifer, W. P. (1993). Two-day-olds prefer their native language. *Infant Behavior and Development, 16,* 495–500.

Moore, C., Angelopoulos, M., & Bennett, P. (1999). Word learning in the context of referential and salience cues. *Developmental Psychology, 35,* 60–68.

Moore, E. G. J. (1986). Family socialization and the IQ test performance of traditionally and transracially adopted black children. *Developmental Psychology, 22,* 317–326.

Moore, G. A., Cohn, J. F., & Campbell, S. B. (2001). Infant affective responses to mothers still face at 6 months differentially predict externalizing and internalizing behaviors at 18 months. *Developmental Psychology, 37,* 706–714.

Moore, K. L., & Persaud, T. V. N. (1993). *Before we are born: Essentials of embryology and birth defects* (4th ed.). Philadelphia: Saunders.

Moore, S. M. (1995). Girls' understanding and social constructions of menarche. *Journal of Adolescence, 18,* 87–104.

Moore, V., & Davies, M. (2002). Nutrition before birth, programming and the perpetuation of social inequalities in health. *Asia Pacific Journal of Clinical Nutrition, 11,* S529–S536.

Morgan, G. A., & Ricciuti, H. N. (1969). Infants' responses to strangers during the first year. In B. M. Foss (Ed.), *Determinants of infant behavior* (Vol. 4). London: Methuen.

Morgan, J. L., & Saffran, J. R. (1995). Emerging integration of sequential and suprasegmental information in preverbal speech segmentation. *Child Development, 66,* 911–936.

Morrison, F. J., Griffith, E. M., & Alberts, D. M. (1997). Native-nurture in the classroom: Entrance age, school readiness, and learning in children. *Developmental Psychology, 33,* 254–262.

Morrison, F. J., Smith, L., & Dow-Ehrensberger, M. (1995). Education and cognitive development: A natural experiment. *Developmental Psychology, 31,* 789–799.

Morrison, M. M., & Shaffer, D. R. (2003). Gender-role congruence and self-referencing as determinants of advertising effectiveness. *Sex Roles, 49,* 265–275.

Moshman, D. (1998). Cognitive development beyond childhood. In D. Kuhn & R. S. Siegler (Vol. Eds.), *Cognitive, language, and perceptual development,* Vol. 2. In B. Damon (General Editor), *Handbook of child psychology.* New York: Wiley.

Moss, E., & St-Laurent, D. (2001). Attachment at school age and academic performance. *Developmental Psychology, 37,* 863–874.

Moss, E., Bureau, J., Cyr, C., Mongeau, C., & St-Laurent, D. (2004). Correlates of attachment at age 3: Construct validity of the preschool attachment classification system. *Developmental Psychology, 40,* 323–334.

Mostow, A. J., Izard, C. E., Fine, S., & Trentacosta, J. (2002). Modeling emotional, cognitive, and behavioral predictors of peer acceptance. *Child Development, 73,* 1775–1787.

Mueller, C. M., & Dweck, C. S. (1998). Praise for intelligence can undermine children's motivation and performance. *Journal of Personality and Social Psychology, 75,* 33–52.

Mueller, E., & Lucas T. (1975). A developmental analysis of peer interactions among toddlers. In M. Lewis & L. Rosenblum (Eds.). *Friendship and peer relations.* New York: Wiley.

Muir-Broaddus, J. E. (1995). Gifted underachievers: Insights from the characteristics of strategic functioning associated with giftedness and achievement. *Learning and Individual Differences, 7,* 189–206.

Mumford, M. D., & Gustafson, S. B. (1988). Creativity syndrome: Integration, application, and innovation. *Psychological Bulletin, 103,* 27–43.

Mumme, D. L., & Fernald, A. (2003). The infant as onlooker: Learning from emotional reactions observed in a television scenario. *Child Development, 74,* 221–237.

Mumme, D. L., Fernald, A., & Herrera, C. (1996). Infants' responses to facial and vocal emotional signals in a social referencing paradigm. *Child Development, 67,* 3219–3237.

Munro, G., & Adams, G. R. (1977). Ego-identity formation in college students and working youth. *Developmental Psychology, 13,* 523–524.

Munroe, R. H., Shimmin, H. S., & Munroe, R. L. (1984). Gender understanding and sex-role preferences in four cultures. *Developmental Psychology, 20,* 673–682.

Murray, A. D., Dolby, R. M., Nation, R. L., & Thomas, D. B. (1981). Effects of epidural anesthesia on newborns and their mothers. *Child Development, 52,* 71–82.

Murray, L., Fiori-Cowley, A., Hooper, R., & Cooper, P. (1996). The impact of postnatal depression and associated adversity on early mother–infant interactions and later infant outcome. *Child Development, 67,* 2512–2526.

Mussen, P. H., & Rutherford, E. (1963). Parent-child relations and parental personality in relation to young children's sex-role preferences. *Child Development, 34,* 589–607.

Musso, M., Moro, A., Glauche, V., Rijntjes, M., Reichenbach, J., Büchel, C., & Weiller, C. (2003). Broca's area and the language instinct. *Nature Neuroscience, 6,* 774–781.

Mustanski, B. S. (2002). A critical review of recent biological research on human sexual orientation. *Annual Review of Sex Research, 13,* 89–141.

Mustanski, B. S., & Bailey, J. M. (2003). A therapist's guide to the genetics of human sexual orientation. *Sexual & Relationship Therapy, 18,* 429–436.

Mustanski, B. S., Viken, R., Pulkkinen, L., & Rose, R. J. (2004). Genetic and environmental influences on pubertal development: Longitudinal data from Finnish twins at ages 11 and 14. *Developmental Psychology, 40,* 1188–1198.

Nagin, D., & Tremblay, R. E. (1999). Trajectories of boys' physical aggression, opposition, and hyperactivity on the path to physically violent and nonviolent juvenile delinquency. *Child Development, 70,* 1181–1196.

Naigles, L. G. (1990). Children use syntax to learn verb meanings. *Journal of Child Language, 17,* 357–374.

Naigles, L. G., & Gelman, S. A. (1995). Overextensions in comprehension and production revisited: Preferential looking in a study of dog, cat, and cow. *Journal of Child Language, 22,* 19–46.

Naigles, L. G., & Hoff-Ginsberg, E. (1995). Input to verb learning: Evidence for the plausibility of syntactic bootstrapping. *Developmental Psychology, 31,* 827–837.

Nanez, J., & Yonas, A. (1994). Effects of luminance and texture motion on infant defensive reactions to optical collision. *Infant Behavior and Development, 17,* 165–174.

Nansel, T. R., Overpeck, M., Pella, R. S., Ruan, W. J., Simons-Morton, B., & Scheidt, P. (2001). Bullying behaviors among U.S. Youths: Prevalence and association with psychosocial adjustment. *Journal of the American Medical Association, 285,* 2094–2100.

Nastasi, B. K., & Clements, D. H. (1994). Effectance motivation, perceived scholastic competence, and higher-order thinking in two cooperative computer environments. *Journal of Educational Computing Research, 10,* 249–275.

National Center for Educational Statistics (1995). *Digest of educational statistics.* Washington, DC: U.S. Government Printing Office.

National Council for Research on Women (2002). *Balancing the equation: Where are women and girls in science, engineering, and technology?* New York: Author.

National Education Goals Panel (1992). *The National Education Goals Report, 1992.* Washington, DC: U.S. Department of Education.

National Research Council and Institute for Medicine (2000). *From neurons to neighborhoods: The science of child Development.* Washington, DC: National Academy of Science Press.

National Research Council and Institute of Medicine (2004). *Engaging Schools.* Washington DC: National Academies Press.

Navarro, J., Marchena, E., Alcalde, C., & Ruiz, G. (2004). Stimulus control with computer assisted learning. *Journal of Behavioral Education, 13,* 83–91.

Neil, E., Beek, M., & Schofield, G. (2003). Thinking about and managing contact in permanent placements: The differences and similarities between adoptive parents and foster carers. *Clinical Child Psychology & Psychiatry, 8,* 401–418.

Neimark, E. D. (1979). Current status of formal operations research. *Human Development, 22,* 60–67.

Neimark, J. (2000). Nature's clones. In K. L. Freiberg (Ed.), *Human development 00/01* (28th ed., pp. 10–17). Guilford, CT: Dushkin/McGraw–Hill.

Neiss, M., & Rowe, D. C. (2000). Parental education and child's verbal IQ in adoptive and biological families in the National Longitudinal Study of Adolescent Health. *Behavior Genetics, 30,* 487–495.

Neisser, U. (1997). Never a dull moment. *American Psychologist, 52,* 79–81.

Neisser, U. (1998). *The rising curve: Long-term gains in IQ and related measures.* Washington, DC: American Psychological Association.

Neisser, U., Boodoo, G., Bouchard, T. J., Jr., Boykin, A. W., Brody, N., Ceci, S. J., Halpern, D. F., Loehlin. J. C., Perloff, R., Sternberg, R. J., & Urbina, S. (1996). Intelligence: Knowns and unknowns. *American Psychologist, 51,* 77–101.

Nelson, C. A. (1987). The recognition of facial expressions in the first two years of life: Mechanisms of development. *Child Development, 58,* 889–909.

Nelson, C. A. (1995). The ontogeny of human memory: A cognitive neuroscience perspective. *Developmental Psychology, 31,* 723–738.

Nelson, C. A. (1997). The neurobiological basis of early memory development. In N. Cowan (Ed.), *The development of memory in childhood.* Hove East Sussex, UK: Psychology Press.

Nelson, C. A., & Bloom, F. E. (1997). Child development and neuroscience. *Child Development, 68,* 970–987.

Nelson, J., & Aboud, F. E. (1985). The resolution of social conflict among friends. *Child Development, 56,* 1009–1017.

Nelson, K. (1973). Structure and strategy in learning to talk. *Monographs of the Society for Research in Child Development, 38* (Serial No. 149).

Nelson, K. (1981). Individual differences in language development: Implications for development and language. *Developmental Psychology, 17,* 170–187.

Nelson, K. (1996). *Language in cognitive development: The emergence of the mediated mind.* New York: Cambridge University Press.

Nelson, K. B. (1995). Cerebral palsy. In B. F. Sachs, R. Beard, E. Papiernik, & C. Russell (Eds.), *Reproductive health care for women and babies* (pp. 400–419). New York: Oxford University Press.

Nelson, S. A. (1980). Factors influencing young children's use of motives and outcomes as moral criteria. *Child Development, 51,* 823–829.

Nesmith, J., & McKenna, M. A. J. (2000, June 29). Genetic code map a milestone: But hurdles remain to conquer disease. *Atlanta Constitution,* pp. A1, A5.

Neumark-Sztainer, D., et al. (2005). In "Does Early Dieting Increase the Risk of Obesity and Eating Disorders?" *Eating Disorders Review, 16,* 7–8.

Neumark-Sztainer, D., Hannan, P. J., Story, M., & Perry, C. L. (2004). Weight-control behaviors among adolescent girls and boys: Implications for dietary intake. *Journal of the American Dietetic Association, 104,* 913–20.

Neumark-Sztainer, D., Wall, M., Story, M., & Fulkerson, J. A. (2004). Are family meal patterns associated with disordered eating behaviors among adolescents? *The Journal of Adolescent Health, 35,* 350–359.

Neville, H. J., Coffey, S. A., Lawson, D. S., Fischer, A., Emmorey, K., & Bellugi, U. (1997). Neural systems mediating American Sign Language: Effects of sensory experience and age of acquisition. *Brain and Language, 57,* 285–308.

Newcomb, A. F., Bukowski, W. M., & Pattee, L. (1993). Children's peer relations: A meta-analytic review of popular, rejected, neglected, controversial, and average sociometric status. *Psychological Bulletin, 113,* 99–128.

Newcombe, N., & Dubas, J. S. (1987). Individual differences in cognitive ability: Are they related to timing of puberty? In R. M. Lerner & T. T. Foch (Eds.), *Biological-psychosocial interactions in early adolescence: A life-span perspective.* Hillsdale, NJ: Erlbaum.

Newcombe, N., & Fox, N. A. (1994). Infantile amnesia: Through a glass darkly. *Child Development, 65,* 31–40.

Newcombe, N., & Huttenlocher, J. (1992). Children's early ability to solve perspective-taking problems. *Developmental Psychology, 28,* 635–643.

Newman, D. L., Caspi, A., Moffitt, T. E., & Silva, P. A. (1997). Antecedents of adult interpersonal functioning: Effects of individual differences in age 3 temperament. *Developmental Psychology, 33,* 206–217.

Newman, R. (2005). The cocktail party effect in infants revisited: Listening to one's name in noise. *Developmental Psychology, 41*, 352–362.

Newport, E. L. (1991). Contrasting conceptions of the critical period for language. In S. Carey & R. Gelman (Eds.), *The epigenesis of mind: Essays on biology and cognition* (pp. 111–130). Hillsdale, NJ: Erlbaum.

Ng, F. F., Kenney-Benson, G. A., & Pomerantz, E. M. (2004). Children's achievement moderates the effects of mothers' use of control and autonomy support. *Child Development, 75*, 764–780.

NICHD Early Child Care Research Network (1997). The effects of infant child care on mother–infant attachment security: Results of the NICHD study of early child care. *Child Development, 68*, 860–879.

NICHD Early Child Care Research Network (1998a.) Early child care and self-control, compliance, and problem behavior at twenty-four and thirty-six months. *Child Development, 69*, 1145–1170.

NICHD Early Child Care Research Network (1998b). Relations between family predictors and child outcomes: Are they weaker for children in child care? *Developmental Psychology, 34*, 1119–1128.

NICHD Early Child Care Research Network (1999). Child care and mother–child interaction in the first 3 years of life. *Developmental Psychology, 35*, 1399–1413.

NICHD Early Child Care Research Network (2000). The relation of child care to cognitive and language development. *Child Development, 71*, 960–980.

NICHD Early Child Care Research Network (2001a). Child care and children's peer interaction at 24 and 36 months: The NICHD study of early child care. *Child Development, 72*, 1478–1500.

NICHD Early Child Care Research Network (2001b). Child-care and family predictors of preschool attachment and stability from infancy. *Developmental Psychology, 37*, 847–862.

NICHD Early Child Care Research Network (2003a). Does amount of time spent in child care predict socioemotional adjustment during the transition to kindergarten? *Child Development, 74*, 976–1005.

NICHD Early Child Care Research Network (2003b). Does quality of child care affect child outcomes at age 4½ *Developmental Psychology, 39*, 451–469.

NICHD Early Child Care Research Network (2004). Trajectories of physical aggression from toddlerhood to middle childhood. *Monographs of the Society for Research in Child Development, 69, Serial No. 278.*

Nicholls, J. G., & Miller, A. T. (1984). Reasoning about the ability of self and others: A developmental study. *Child Development, 55*, 1990–1999.

Nichols, M. R. (1993). Parental perspectives on the childbirth experience. *Maternal-Child Nursing Journal, 21*, 99–108.

Nicoladis, E., Mayberry, R. I., & Genesee, F. (1999). Gesture and early bilingual development. *Developmental Psychology, 35*, 514–526.

Nielsen, M., & Dissanayake, C. (2003). A longitudinal study of immediate, deferred, and synchronic imitation through the scond year. *The Interdisciplinary Journal of Artifical Intelligence and the Simulation of Behaviour, 1*, 305–318.

Nielsen, M., & Slaughter, V. (in press). Multiple motivations for imitation in infancy. In K. Dautenhahn & C. L. Nehaniv (Eds.), *Models and mechanisms of imitation and social learning in robots, humans, and animals: Behavioural, social and communicative dimensions.* Cambridge, UK: Cambridge University Press.

Nieto, J. A. (2004, July). Children and adolescents as sexual beings: Cross-cultural perspectives. *Child & Adolescent Psychiatric Clinics of North America, 13*, 461–477.

Nilsson, K., & Hägglöf, B. (2005). Long-term follow-up of adolescent onset anorexia nervosa in northern Sweden. *European Eating Disorders Review, 13*, 89–100.

Ninio, A., & Rinott, N. (1988). Fathers' involvement in the care of their infants and their attributions of cognitive competence to infants. *Child Development, 59*, 652–663.

Nittrouer, S., & Burton, L. T. (2005). The role of early language experience in the development of speech perception and phonological processing abilities: Evidence from 5-year-olds with histories of otitis media with effusion and low socioeconomic status. *Journal of Communication Disorders, 38*, 29–63.

Nix, R. L., Pinderhughes, E. E., Dodge, K. A., Bates, J. E., Pettit, G. S., & McFadyen-Ketchum, S. A. (1999). The relation between mothers' hostile attribution tendencies and children's externalizing behavior problems: The mediating role of mothers' harsh discipline practices. *Child Development, 70*, 896–909.

Norman-Jackson, J. (1982). Family interactions, language development, and primary reading achievement of Black children in families of low income. *Child Development, 53*, 349–358.

Nowak, M. A., Komarova, N. L., & Niyogi, P. (2002). Computational and evolutionary aspects of language. *Nature, 417*, 611–617.

Nucci, L. (2004). Finding commonalities: Social information processing and domain theory in the study of aggression. *Child Development, 75*, 1009–1012.

Nucci, L., & Smetana, J. G. (1996). Mothers' concepts of young children's areas of personal freedom. *Child Development, 67*, 1870–1886.

Nucci, L., Camino, C., & Sapiro, C. M. (1996). Social class effects on northeastern Brazilian children's conceptions of areas of personal choice and social regulation. *Child Development, 67*, 1223–1242.

Nugent, J. K., Lester, B. M., & Brazelton, T. B. (1989). *Biology, culture, and development* (Vol. 1). Norwood, NJ: Eribaum.

O'Conner, B. P. (1995). Identity development and perceived parental behavior as sources of adolescent egocentrism. *Journal of Youth and Adolescence, 24*, 205–227.

O'Conner, T. G., Rutter, M., Beckett, C., Kleaveney, L., Kreppner, J. M., & the English and Romanian Adoptees Study Team (2000). The effects of global severe privation on cognitive competence: Extension and longitudinal follow-up. *Child Development, 71*, 376–390.

O'Connor, M. J. (2001). Prenatal alcohol exposure and infant negative affect as precursors of depressive features in children. *Infant Mental Health Journal, 22*, 291–300.

O'Connor, N., & Hermelin, B. (1991). Talents and preoccupations in idiot-savants. *Psychological Medicine, 21*, 959–964.

O'Connor, T. G., & Croft, C. M. (2001). A twin study of attachment in preschool children. *Child Development, 72*, 1501–1511.

O'Connor, T. G., Deater-Deckard, K., Fulker, D., Rutter, M., & Plomin, R. (1998). Genotype-environment correlations in late childhood and early adolescence: Antisocial behavior problems and coercive parenting. *Developmental Psychology, 34*, 970–981.

O'Dempsey, T. J. D. (1988). Traditional belief and practice among the Pokot people of Kenya with particular reference to mother and child health: 2. Mother and child health. *Annals of Tropical Paediatrics, 8*, 125.

O'Donnell, D. A., Schwab-Stone, M. E., & Muyeed, A. Z. (2002). Multidimensional resilience in urban children exposed to community violence. *Child Development, 73*, 1265–1282.

O'Heron, C. A., & Orlofsky, J. L. (1990). Stereotypic and nonstereotypic sex role trait and behavior orientations, gender identity, and psychological adjustment. *Journal of Personality and Social Psychology, 58*, 134–143.

O'Mahoney, J. F. (1989). Development of thinking about things and people: Social and nonsocial cognition during adolescence. *Journal of Genetic Psychology, 150*, 217–224.

O'Neill, D. K. (1996). Two-year-old children's sensitivity to a parent's knowledge state when making requests. *Child Development, 67*, 654–667.

O'Reilly, A. W., & Bornstein, M. H. (1993). Caregiver-child interaction in play. In M. H. Bornstein & A. W. O'Reilly (Eds.), *The role of play in the development of thought* (New Directions for Child Development, No. 59). San Francisco: Jossey-Bass.

O'Sullivan, J. T. (1996). Children's metamemory about the influence of conceptual relations on recall. *Journal of Experimental Child Psychology, 62*, 1–29

O'Sullivan, J. T. (1997). Effort, interest, & recall: Beliefs and behaviors of preschoolers. *Journal of Experimental Child Psychology, 65*, 43–67.

Ochs, E. (1982). Talking to children in western Samoa. *Language in Society, 11*, 77–104.

Ogbu, J. U. (1994). From cultural differences to differences in cultural frames of reference. In P. M. Greenfield & R. R. Cocking (Eds.), *Cross-cultural roots of minority child development* (pp. 365–391). Hillsdale, NJ: Erlbaum.

Ogbu, J. W. (1988). Black education: A cultural-ecological perspective. In H. P. McAdoo (Ed.), *Black families.* Beverly Hills: Sage.

Ogletree, S. M., & Williams, S. W. (1990). Sex and sex-typing effects on computer attitudes and aptitude. *Sex Roles, 23*, 703–712.

Okon, D. M., Greene, A. L., & Smith, J. E. (2003). Family interactions predict intraindividual symptom variation for adolescents with bulimia. *International Journal of Eating Disorders, 34*, 450–457.

Olivares, J. L., Vázquez, M., Fleta, J., Moreno, L. A., Pérez-González, J. M., & Bueno, M. (2005). Cardiac findings in adolescents with anorexia nervosa at diagnosis and after weight restoration. *European Journal of Pediatrics, 164*, 383–386.

Oller, D. K., & Eilers, R. E. (1988). The role of audition in infant babbling. *Child Development, 59*, 441–449.

Oller, J. W., Jr. (2005). Common ground between form and content: The pragmatic solution to the bootstrapping problem. *Modern Language Journal, 89*(1), 92–114.

Olvera-Ezzell, N., Power, T. G., & Cousins, J. H. (1990). Maternal socialization of children's eating habits: Strategies used by obese Mexican-American mothers. *Child Development, 61*, 395–400.

Olweus, D. (1984). Aggressors and their victims: Bullying at school. In H. Frude & H. Gault (Eds.), *Disruptive behaviors in schools* (pp. 57–76). New York: Wiley.

Olweus, D. (1993). *Bullying at school.* Oxford: Blackwell.

Opfer, J. E., & Gelman, S. A. (2001). Children's and adults' models of teleological action: The development of biology-based models. *Child Development, 72*, 1367–1381.

Orlofsky, J. L. (1979). Parental antecedents of sex-role orientation in college men and women. *Sex Roles, 5*, 495–512.

Ornstein, P. A., Gordon, B. N., & Larus, D. M. (1992). Children's memory for a personally experienced event: Implications for testimony. *Applied Developmental Psychology, 6*, 49–60.

Ornstein, P. A., Haden, C. A., & Hedrick, A. M. (2004). Learning to remember: Social-communicative exchanges and the development of children's memory skills. *Developmental Review*, 24, 374–396.

Ornstein, P. A., Naus, M. J., & Liberty, C. (1975). Rehearsal and organizational processes in children's memory. *Child Development, 46*, 818–830.

Osborne, M. L., Kistner, J. A., & Helgamo, B. (1993). Developmental progression in children's knowledge of AIDS: Implications for educational and attitudinal change. *Journal of Pediatric Psychology, 18*, 177–192.

Oster, A. (2005). The effect of introducing computers on children's problem-solving skills in science. *British Journal of Educational Technology, 36*, 907–909.

Ou, S.-R. (2005). Pathways of long-term effects of an early intervention program on educational attainment: Findings from the Chicago longitudinal study. *Journal of Applied Developmental Psychology, 26*, 578–611.

Overton, W. F. (1984). World views and their influence on psychological theory and research: Kuhn-Lakotes-Lunden. In H. W. Reese (Ed.), *Advances in child development and behavior* (Vol. 18). New York: Academic.

Oviatt, S. L. (1980). The emerging ability to comprehend language: An experimental approach. *Child Development, 51*, 97–106.

Oyen, A.-S., & Bebko, J. M. (1996). The effects of computer games and lesson context on children's mnemonic strategies. *Journal of Experimental Child Psychology, 62*, 173–189.

Ozwa, Y., Takashima, S., & Tada, H. (2003). Beta 2-Adrenergic receptor subtype alternations in the brainstem in the sudden infant death syndrome. *Early Human Development, 75*, S129–138.

Paarlberg, K. M., Vingerhoets, A. J. J. M., Passchier, J. Dekker, G. A., & van Giegn, H. P. (1995). Psychosocial factors and pregnancy outcome: A review with emphasis on methodological issues. *Journal of Psychosomatic Research, 39*, 563–595.

Padilla, Y. C., & Reichman, N. E. (2001). Low birthweight: Do unwed fathers help? *Children & Youth Services Review, 23*, 427–452.

Paikoff, R. L., & Brooks-Gunn, J. (1991). Do parent-child relationships change at puberty? *Psychological Bulletin, 110*, 47–66.

Paknawin-Mock, J., Jarvis, L., Jahari, A. B., Husaini, M. A., & Pollitt, E. (2000). Community-level determinants of child growth in an Indonesian tea plantation. *European Journal of Clinical Nutrition, 54,* S28–S42.

Palinscar, A. S., Brown, A. L., & Campione, J. C. (1993). First-grade dialogues for knowledge acquisition and use. In E. A. Forman, N. Minilk, & C. A. Stone (Eds.), *Contexts for learning.* New York: Oxford University Press.

Palkovitz, R. (1984). Parental attitudes and fathers' interactions with their 5-month-old infants. *Developmental Psychology, 20,* 1054–1060.

Palkovitz, R. (1985). Fathers' birth attendance, early contact, and extended contact with their newborns: A critical review. *Child Development, 56,* 392–406.

Palmer, C. F. (1989). The discriminating nature of infants' exploratory actions. *Developmental Psychology, 25,* 885–893.

Palmer, D. C., (2000). Chomsky's nativism: A critical review. *Analysis of Verbal Behavior, 17,* 39–50.

Palmer, E. L. (1984). Providing quality television for America's children. In J. P. Murray & G. Salomon (Eds.), *The future of children's television.* Boys Town, NE: Boys Town Center.

Pan, B. A., & Gleason, J. K. (1997). Semantic development: Learning the meaning of words. In J. K. Gleason (Ed.). *The development of language* (4th ed.). Boston: Allyn & Bacon.

Panigraphy, A., Filiano, J. J., Sleeper, L. A., et al. (1997). Decreased karinate binding in the arcuate nucleus of the sudden infant death syndrome. *Journal of Neuropathological Experimental Neurology, 56,* 1253–1261.

Panksepp, J. (1998). Attention deficit hyperactivity disorders, psychostimulants, and intolerance of childhood playfulness: A tragedy in the making? *Current Directions in Psychological Science, 7,* 91–98.

Papiernik, E. (1995). Prevention of preterm birth in France. In B. P. Sachs, R. Beard, E. Papiernik, & C. Russell (Eds.), *Reproductive health care for women and babies* (pp. 322–347). New York: Oxford University Press.

Papousek, H. (1967). Experimental studies of appetitional behavior in human newborns and infants. In H. W. Stevenson, E. H. Hess, & H. L. Rheingold (Eds.), *Early behavior: Comparative and developmental approaches.* New York: Wiley.

Papp, L. M., Cummings, E. M., & Goeke-Morey, M. C. (2002). Marital conflicts in the home when children are present versus absent. *Developmental Psychology, 38,* 774–783.

Papp, L. M., Goeke-Morey, M. C., & Cummings, E. M. (2004). Mothers' and fathers' psychological symptoms and marital functioning: Examination of direct and interactive links with child adjustment. *Journal of Child & Family Studies, 13,* 469–482.

Park, S., Belsky, J., Putnam, S., & Cynic, K. (1997). Infant emotionality, parenting, and 3-year inhibition: Exploring stability and lawful discontinuity in a male sample. *Developmental Psychology, 33,* 218–227.

Parke, R. D. (1977). Some effects of punishment on children's behavior—revisited. In E. M. Hetherington & R. D. Parke (Eds.), *Contemporary readings in child psychology.* New York: McGraw-Hill.

Parke, R. D. (1995). Fathers and families. In M. Bornstein (Ed.), *Handbook of parenting* (Vol. 3, pp. 27–63). Hillsdale, NJ: Erlbaum.

Parke, R. D. (2004). Development in the family. *Annual Review of Psychology, 55,* 365–399.

Parke, R. D., & Slaby, R. G. (1983). The development of aggression. In P. H. Mussen (Ed.), *Handbook of child psychology.* Vol. 4: *Socialization, personality, and social development* (4th ed.) (pp. 547–641). New York: Wiley.

Parke, R. D., Coltrane, S., Duffy, S., Buriel, R., Dennis, J., Powers, J., French, S., & Widaman, K. F. (2004). Economic stress, parenting, and child adjustment in Mexican American and European American families. *Child Development, 75,* 1632–1656.

Parker, J. G., & Asher, S. R. (1987). Peer relations and later adjustment: Are low-accepted children "at risk"? *Psychological Bulletin, 102,* 357–389.

Parker, J. G., Rubin, K. H., Price, J., & DeRosier, E. (1995). Peer relationships, child development, and adjustment. A developmental psychopathology perspective. In D. Cicchetti & E. Cohen (Eds.), *Developmental Psychopathology: Vol. 2 Risk, disorder, and adaptation* (pp. 96–161). New York: Wiley.

Parkhurst, J. T., & Asher, S. R. (1992). Peer rejection in middle school: Subgroup differences in behavior, loneliness, and interpersonal concerns. *Developmental Psychology, 28,* 231–241.

Parkhurst, J. T., & Hopmeyer, A. (1998). Sociometric popularity and peer-perceived popularity: Two distinct dimensions of peer status. *Journal of Early Adolescence, 18,* 125–144.

Parsons, J. E., Adler, T. F., & Kaczala, C. M. (1982). Socialization of achievement attitudes and beliefs: Parental influences. *Child Development, 53,* 310–321.

Parsons, T. (1955). Family structure and the socialization of the child. In T. Parsons & R. F. Bales (Eds.), *Family socialization and interaction processes.* New York: Free Press.

Parten, M. (1932). Social participation among preschool children. *Journal of Abnormal and Social Psychology, 27,* 243–269.

Pascual-Leone, J. (2000). Is the French connection neo-Piagetian? Not nearly enough! *Child Development, 71,* 843–845.

Passingham, R. E. (1982). *The human primate.* Oxford: W H. Freeman.

Passolunghi, M. C., & Siegl, L. S. (2004). Working memory and access to numerical information in children with disability in mathematics. *Journal of Experimental Child Psychology, 88,* 348–367.

Patel, D. R., Greydanus, D. E., Pratt, H. D., & Phillips, E. L. (2003). Eating disorders in adolescent athletes. *Journal of Adolescent Research, 18,* 280–296.

Patel, N., Power, T. G., & Bhavnagri, N. P. (1996). Socialization values and practices of Indian immigrant parents: Correlates of modernity and acculturation. *Child Development, 67,* 303–313.

Patterson, C. J. (1995). Sexual orientation and human development: An overview. *Developmental Psychology, 31,* 3–11.

Patterson, C. J., Kupersmidt, J. B., & Vaden, N. A. (1990). Income level, gender, ethnicity, and household composition as predictors of children's school-based competence. *Child Development, 61,* 485–494.

Patterson, G. R. (1982). *Coercive family processes.* Eugene, OR: Castilia Press.

Patterson, G. R. (1998). Continuities—A search for casual mechanisms: Comment on the special section. *Developmental Psychology, 34,* 1263–1268.

Patterson, G. R., Reid, J. B., & Dishion, T. J. (1992). *Antisocial boys.* Eugene, OR: Castalia Publishing.

Paul, J. P. (1993). Childhood cross-gender behavior and adult homosexuality: The resurgence of biological models of sexuality. *Journal of Homosexuality, 24,* 41–54.

Paulhus, D., & Shaffer, D. R. (1981). Sex differences in the impact of number of older and number of younger siblings on scholastic aptitude. *Social Psychology Quarterly, 44,* 363–368.

Pea, R. D. (1985). Beyond Amplification: Using the computer to reorganize mental functioning. *Educational Psychologist, 20,* 167–183.

Pedaste, M., & Sarapuu, T. (2006). Developing an effective support system for inquiry learning in a web-based environment. *Journal of Computer Assisted Learning, 22,* 47–62.

Pederson, D. R., & Moran, G. (1996). Expressions of the attachment relationship outside of the Strange Situation. *Child Development, 67,* 915–929.

Pederson, D. R., Gleason, K. E., Moran, G., & Bento, S. (1998). Maternal attachment representations, maternal sensitivity, and the mother–infant attachment relationship. *Developmental Psychology, 34,* 925–933.

Pedlow, R., Sanson, A., Prior, M., & Oberklaid, F. (1993). Stability of maternally reported temperament from infancy to 8 years. *Developmental Psychology, 29,* 998–1007.

Pegg, J. E., Werker, J. F., & McLeod, P. J. (1992). Preference for infant-directed over adult-directed speech: Evidence from 7-week-old infants. *Infant Behavior and Development, 15,* 325–345.

Pelham, W. E., Jr., Carlson, C., Sams, S. E., Vallano, G., Dixon, M. J., & Hoza, B. (1993). Separate and combined effects of methylphenidate and behavior modification on boys with attention deficit-hyperactivity disorder in the classroom. *Journal of Consulting and Clinical Psychology, 61,* 506–515.

Pellegrini, A. D. (1996). *Observing children in their natural worlds: A methodological primer.* Mahwah, NJ: Erlbaum.

Pellegrini, A. D., & Bjorklund, D. F. (2004). The ontogeny and phylogeny of children's object and fantasy play. *Human Nature, 15,* 23–43.

Pellegrini, A. D., & Smith, P. K. (1998). Physical activity play: The nature and function of a neglected aspect of play. *Child Development, 69,* 577–598.

Pellegrini, D. S. (1985). Social cognition and competence in middle childhood. *Child Development, 56,* 253–264.

Pelphrey, K. A., Reznick, J. S., Goldman, B. D., Sasson, N., Morrow, J., Donahue, A., & Hodgson, K. (2004). Development of visuospatial short-term memory in the second half of the 1st year. *Developmental Psychology, 40,* 836–851.

Peña, E., Bedore, L. M., & Rappazzo, C. (2003). Comparison of Spanish, English, and bilingual children's performance across semantic tasks. *Language, Speech, and Hearing Services in Schools, 34,* 5–16.

Penner, S. G. (1987). Parental responses to grammatical and ungrammatical child utterances. *Child Development, 58,* 376–384.

Pennington, B. F. (2001). Genetic methods. In C. A. Nelson & M. Luciana (Eds.), *Handbook of developmental cognitive neuroscience* (pp. 149–158). Cambridge, MA: MIT Press.

Perez, M., Joiner, T. E., Jr., & Lewinsohn, P. (2004). Is major depressive disorder or dysthymia more strongly associated with bulimia nervosa? *International Journal of Eating Disorders, 36,* 55–61.

Perez-Granados, D. R., & Callanan, M. A. (1997). Conversations with mothers and siblings: Young children's semantic and conceptual development, *Developmental Psychology, 33,* 120–134.

Perlman, M., & Ross, H. S. (1997). The benefits of parent intervention in children's disputes: An examination of concurrent changes in children's fighting styles. *Child Development, 68,* 690–700.

Perry, D. G., Kusel, S. J., & Perry, L. C. (1988). Victims of peer aggression. *Developmental Psychology, 24,* 807–814.

Perry, D. G., Perry, L. C., & Weiss, R. J. (1989). Sex differences in the consequences that children anticipate for aggression. *Developmental Psychology, 25,* 312–319.

Perry, D. G., Perry, L. C., Bussey, K., English, D., & Arnold, G. (1980). Processes of attribution and children's self-punishment following misbehavior. *Child Development, 51,* 545–551.

Peskin, J. (1992). Ruse and representations: On children's ability to conceal information. *Developmental Psychology, 28,* 84–89.

Peterson, G. H., Mehl, L. E., & Liederman, P. H. (1979). The role of some birth-related variables in father attachment. *American Journal of Orthopsychiatry, 49,* 330–338.

Petitto, L. A., & Marentette, P. F. (1991). Babbling in the manual mode: Evidence for the ontogeny of language. *Science, 251,* 1493–1496.

Petretic, P. A., & Tweney, R. D. (1977). Does comprehension precede production? The development of children's responses to telegraphic sentences of varying grammatical adequacy. *Journal of Child Language, 4,* 201–209.

Pettit, G. S., Laird, R. D., Dodge, K. A., Bates, J. E., & Criss, M. M. (2001). Antecedents and behavior-problem outcomes of parental monitoring and psychological control in early adolescence. *Child Development, 72,* 583–598.

Pezdek, K., & Hodge, D. (1999). Planting false childhood memories in children: The role of event plausibility. *Child Development, 70,* 887–895.

Pezdek, K., & Taylor, J. (2000). Discriminating between accounts of true and false events. In D. F. Bjorklund (Ed.), *Research and theory in false-memory creation in children and adults.* Mahwah, NJ: Erlbaum.

Pfeifer, M., Goldsmith, H. H., Davidson, R. J., & Rickman, M. (2002). Continuity and change in inhibited and uninhibited children. *Child Development, 73,* 1474–1485.

Phillips, D. (1984). The illusion of incompetence among academically competent children. *Child Development, 55,* 2000–2016.

Phillips, D. I. (2004). Fetal programming of the neuroendocrine response to stress: Links between low birth weight and the metabolic syndrome. *Endocrine Research, 30,* 819–827.

Phillips, M. (1997). What makes schools effective? A comparison of the relationships of communitarian climate and academic climate to mathematics achievement and attendance during middle school. *American Educational Research Journal, 34,* 633–662.

Philpott, R. H. (1995). Maternal health care in the developing world. In B. P. Sachs, R. Beard, E. Papiernik, & C. Russell (Eds.), *Reproductive health care for women and babies* (pp. 226–245). New York: Oxford University Press.

Phinney, J. S. (1993). A three-stage model of ethnic identity development in adolescence. In M. E. Bernal & G. P. Knight (Eds.), *Ethnic identity: Formation and transmission among Hispanics and other minorities.* Albany, NY: State University of New York Press.

Phinney, J. S. (1996). When we talk about American ethnic groups, what do we mean? *American Psychologist, 51,* 918–927.

Phinney, J. S., & Rosenthal, D. A. (1992). Ethnic identity in adolescence: Process, context, and outcome. In G. R. Adams, T. P. Gullotta, & R. Montemayor (Eds.), *Adolescent identity formation* (Advances in Adolescent Development, Vol. 4). Newbury Park, CA: Sage.

Phinney, J. S., Ferguson, D. L., & Tate, J. D. (1997). Intergroup attitudes among ethnic minority adolescents: A causal model. *Child Development, 68,* 955–969.

Phipps, M. G., Sowers, M., & Demonner, S. M. (2002). The Risk for Infant Mortality among Adolescent Childbearing Groups. *Journal of Women's Health, 11,* 889–897.

Piacentini, J., & Hynd, G. (1988). Language after dominant hemispherectomy: Are plasticity of function and equipotentiality viable concepts? *Clinical Psychology Review, 8,* 595–609.

Piaget, J. (1926). *The language and thought of the child.* New York: Harcourt, Bruce & World.

Piaget, J. (1950). *The psychology of intelligence.* San Diego, CA: Harcourt Brace Jovanovich.

Piaget, J. (1951). *Play, dreams, and imitation in childhood.* New York: Norton.

Piaget, J. (1952). *The origins of intelligence in children.* New York: International Universities Press.

Piaget, J. (1954). *The construction of reality in the child.* New York: Basic Books.

Piaget, J. (1960). *Psychology of intelligence.* Paterson, NJ: Littlefield, Adams.

Piaget, J. (1962). *Play, dreams, and imitation in childhood.* New York: Norton.

Piaget, J. (1965). *The moral judgment of the child.* New York: Free Press. (Original work published 1932.)

Piaget, J. (1970a, May). A conversation with Jean Piaget. *Psychology Today,* pp. 25–32.

Piaget, J. (1970b). Piaget's theory. In P. H. Mussen (Ed.), *Carmichael's manual of child psychology* (Vol. 1). New York: Wiley.

Piaget, J. (1971). *Science of education and the psychology of the child.* New York: Viking Press.

Piaget, J. (1972). Intellectual evolution from adolescence to adulthood. *Human Development, 15,* 1–12.

Piaget, J. (1976). *To understand is to invent: The future of education.* New York: Penguin.

Piaget, J., & Inhelder, B. (1969). *The psychology of the child.* New York: Basic Books.

Pichichero, M. E., & Casey, J. R. (2005). Acute otitis media: Making sense of recent guidelines on antimicrobial treatment. *Journal of Family Practice, 54,* 313–322.

Pickens, J. (1994). Perception of auditory-visual distance relations by 5-month-old infants. *Developmental Psychology, 30,* 537–544.

Pike, A., McGuire, S., Hetherington, E. M., Reiss, D., & Plomin, R. (1996). Family environment and adolescent depressive symptoms and antisocial behavior: A multivariate genetic analysis. *Developmental Psychology, 32,* 590–603.

Pillow, B. H. (1988). Young children's understanding of attentional limits. *Child Development, 59,* 31–46.

Pine, J. M. (1995). Variation in vocabulary development as a function of birth order. *Child Development, 66,* 272–281.

Pineda-Krch, M., & Redfield, R. J. (2005). Persistence and loss of meiotic recombination hotspots. *Genetics, 169,* 2319–2333.

Pinker, S. (1991). Rules of language. *Science, 253,* 530–535.

Pinon, M., Huston, A. C., & Wright, J. C. (1989). Family ecology and child characteristics that predict young children's educational television viewing. *Child Development, 60,* 846–856.

Pinyerd, B., & Zipf, W. B. (2005). Puberty-timing is everything. *Journal of Pediatric Nursing, 20,* 75–82.

Pipe, M.-E., Lamb, M. E., Orbach, Y., & Esplin, P. W. (2004). Recent research on children's testimony about experienced and witnessed events. *Developmental Review, 24,* 440–468.

Pipp, S., Easterbrooks, M. A., & Harmon, R. J. (1992). The relation between attachment and knowledge of self and mother in one- to three-year-old infants. *Child Development, 63,* 738–750.

Plagemann, A. (2004). Fetal programming and functional teratogenesis: On epigenetic mechanisms and prevention of perinatally acquired lasting health risks. *Journal of Perinatal Medicine, 32,* 297–306.

Pleck, J. H. (1997). Paternal involvement: Levels, sources, and consequences. In M.E. Lamb (Ed.), *The role of the father in child development* (3rd ed.) (pp. 66–103). New York: Wiley.

Plomin, R. (1990). *Nature and nurture: An introduction to behavior genetics.* Pacific Grove, CA: Brooks/Cole.

Plomin, R., & Rende, R. (1991). Human behavioral genetics. *Annual Review of Psychology, 42,* 161–190.

Plomin, R., DeFries, J. C., & Loehlin, J. C. (1977). Genotype-environment interaction and correlation in the analysis of human behavior. *Psychological Bulletin, 84,* 309–322.

Plomin, R., DeFries, J. C., McClearn, G. E., & McGuffin, P. (2001). *Behavioral genetics* (4th. ed.). New York: Worth.

Plomin, R., DeFries, J. C., McClearn, G. E., & Rutter, M. (1997). *Behavioral genetics* (3rd ed.). New York: W. H. Freeman.

Plomin, R., Owen, M. J. Y., & McGuffin, P. (1994). The genetic basis of complex human behaviors. *Science, 264,* 1733–1739.

Plomin, R., Reiss, D., Hetherington, E. M., & Howe, G. W. (1994). Nature and nurture: Genetic contributions to measures of the family environment. *Developmental Psychology, 30,* 32–43.

Plomin, R., & Rutter, M. (1998). Child development, molecular genetics, and what to do with genes once they are found. *Child Development, 69,* 1223–1242.

Plumert, J. M., & Nichols-Whitehead, P. (1996). Parental scaffolding of young children's spatial communication. *Developmental Psychology, 32,* 523–532.

Plumert, J. M., Ewert, K., & Spear, S. J. (1995). The early development of children's communication about nested spatial relations. *Child Development, 66,* 959–969.

Polak, A., & Harris, P. L. (1999). Deception by young children following noncompliance. *Developmental Psychology, 35,* 561–568.

Pollitt, E. (1994). Poverty and child development: Relevance of research in developing countries to the United States. *Child Development, 65,* 283–295.

Pollitt, E., Golub, M., Gorman, K., Grantham-McGregor, S., Levitsky, D., Schurch, B. Strupp, B., & Wachs, T. (1996). *A reconceptualization of the effects of undernutrition on children's biological, psychosocial, and behavioral development.* SRCD Social Policy Report (Vol. 10, No. 5). Ann Arbor, MI: Society for Research in Child Development.

Pomerantz, E. M., & Ruble, D. N. (1997). Distinguishing multiple dimensions and conceptions of ability: Implications for self-evaluation. *Child Development, 68,* 1165–1180.

Pomerantz, E. M., & Ruble, D. N. (1998). The role of maternal control in the development of sex differences in child self-evaluative factors. *Child Development, 69,* 458–478.

Pomerantz, E. M., Ruble, D. N., Frey, K. S., & Grenlich, F. (1995). Meeting goals and confronting conflict: Children's changing perceptions of social comparison. *Child Development, 66,* 723–738.

Pomerleau, A., Bolduc, D., Malcuit, G., & Cossette, L. (1990). Pink or blue: Environmental gender stereotypes in the first two years of life. *Sex Roles, 22,* 359–367.

Poole, D., & White, L. (1995). Tell me again and again: Stability and change in the repeated testimonies of children and adults. In. M. S. Zaragoza, J. R. Graham, C. N. Gordon, R. Hirschman, & Y. S. Ben Porath (Eds.), *Memory and testimony in the child witness.* Newbury Park, CA: Sage.

Poole, D. A., & Lamb, M. E. (1998). *Investigative interviews of children: A guide of helping professionals.* Washington, DC: American Psychological Association.

Poole, D. A., & Lindsay, D. S. (1995). Interviewing preschoolers: Effects of nonsuggestive techniques, parental coaching and leading questions on reports of nonexperienced events. *Journal of Experimental Child Psychology, 60,* 129–154.

Porter, C. L., & Hsu, H. (2003). First-time mothers' perceptions of efficacy during the transition to motherhood: Links to infant temperament. *Journal of Family Psychology, 17,* 54–64.

Porter, F. L., Porges, S. W., & Marshall, R. E. (1988). Newborn pain cries and vagal tone: Parallel changes in response to circumcision. *Child Development, 59,* 495–505.

Porter, R. H., Makin, J. W., Davis, L. B., & Christensen, K. M. (1992). Breast-fed infants respond to olfactory clues from their own mother and unfamiliar lactating females. *Infant Behavior and Development, 15,* 85–93.

Posada, G., Carbonell, O. A., Alzate, G., & Plata, S. J. (2004). Through Colombian lenses: ethnographic and conventional analyses of maternal care and their associations with secure base behavior. *Developmental Psychology, 40,* 508–518.

Posada, G., Gao, Y., Wu, F., Posada, R., Tascon, M., Schoelmerich, A., Sagi, A., Kondo-Ikemura, K., Haaland, W., & Synnevang, B. (1995). The secure base phenomenon across cultures: Children's behavior, mothers' preferences, and experts' concepts. In E. Waters, B. E. Vaughn, G. Posada, & K. Kondo-Ikemura (Eds.), Caregiving, cultural, and cognitive perspectives on secure-base behavior and working models: New growing points of attachment theory and research. *Monographs of the Society for Research in Child Development, 60* (2-3, Serial No. 244).

Posada, G., Jacobs, A., Carbonell, O. A., Alzate, G., Bustamante, M. R., & Arenas, A. (1999). Maternal care and attachment security in ordinary and emergency contexts. *Developmental Psychology, 35,* 1379–1388.

Povinelli, D. J., & Simon, B. B. (1998). Young children's reactions to briefly versus extremely delayed images of the self: Emergence of the autobiographical stance. *Developmental Psychology, 34,* 188–194.

Povinelli, D. J, Landau, A. M., Theall, L. A., Clark, B. R., & Castile, C. M. (1999). Development of young children's understanding that the recent past is causally bound to the present. *Developmental Psychology, 35,* 1426–1439.

Povinelli, D. J., Landau, K. R., & Perilloux, H. K. (1996). Self-recognition in young children using delayed versus live feedback: Evidence of a developmental asynchrony. *Child Development, 67,* 1540–1554.

Powlishta, K. K. (1995). Intergroup processes in childhood: Social categorization and sex role development. *Developmental Psychology, 31,* 781–788.

Pratt, K. C. (1954). The neonate. In L. Carmichael (Ed.), *Manual of child psychology.* New York: Wiley.

Prentice, D. A., & Carranza, E. (2002). What women and men should be, shouldn't be, are allowed to be, and don't have to be: The contents of prescriptive gender stereotypes. *Psychology of Women Quarterly, 26,* 269–281.

Presnell, K., Bearman, S., & Stice, E. (2004). Risk factors for body dissatisfaction in adolescent boys and girls: A prospective study. *International Journal of Eating Disorders, 36,* 389–401.

Pressley, M., & Woloshyn, V. (1995). *Cognitive strategy instruction that really improves children's academic performance* (2nd ed.). Cambridge, MA: Brookline Books.

Previc, F. H. (1991). A general theory concerning the prenatal origins of cerebral lateralization in humans. *Psychological Review, 98,* 299–334.

Priel, B., & Besser, A. (2002). Perceptions of early relationships during transition to motherhood: The mediating role of social support. *Infant Mental Health Journal, 23,* 343–361.

Priel, B., & deSchonen, S. (1986). Self-recognition: A study of a population without mirrors. *Journal of Experimental Child Psychology, 41,* 237–250.

Pungello, E. P., Kupersmidt, J. B., Burchinal, M. R., & Patterson, C.J. (1996). Environmental risk factors and children's achievement from middle childhood to early adolescence. *Developmental Psychology, 32,* 755–767.

Putallaz, M., & Bierman, K. L. (Eds.) (2004). Aggression, antisocial behavior, and violence among girls: A developmental perspective. In K. A. Dodge & M. P. (Series Eds.), *Duke series in child development and public policy.* New York: Guildford Press.

Putallaz, M., Kupersmidt, J. B., Coie, J. D., McKnight, K., & Grimes, C. L. (2004). A behavioral analysis of girls' aggression and victimization. In M. Putallaz & K. L. Bierman (Eds.), Aggression, antisocial behavior, and violence among girls: A developmental perspective. In K. A. Dodge & M. P. (Series Eds.), *Duke series in child development and public policy.* New York: Guildford Press.

Quay, L. C. (1971). Language dialect, reinforcement, and the intelligence-test performance of Negro children. *Child Development, 42,* 5–15.

Quiggle, N. L., Garber, J., Panak, W. F., & Dodge, K. A. (1992). Social information processing in aggressive and depressed children. *Child Development, 63,* 1305–1320.

Quinn, R. A., Houts, A. C., & Graesser, A. C. (1994). Naturalistic conceptions of morality: A question-answering approach. *Journal of Personality, 62,* 260–267.

Rabiner, D. L., Keane, S. P., & MacKinnon-Lewis, C. (1993). Children's beliefs about familiar and unfamiliar peers in relation to their sociometric status. *Developmental Psychology, 29,* 236–243.

Radke-Yarrow, M., Cummings, E. M., Kuczynski, L., & Chapman, M. (1985). Patterns of attachment in two- and three-year-olds in normal families and families with parental depression. *Child Development, 56,* 884–893.

Rahman, Q., & Wilson, G. (2003). Born gay? The psychobiology of human sexual orientation. *Personality and Individual Differences, 34,* 1337–1382.

Raikes, H. H., Summers, J. A., & Roggman, L. A. (2005). *Fathering: A Journal of Theory, Research, & Practice about Men as Fathers, 3,* 29–58.

Rakic, P. (1991). Plasticity of cortical development. In S. E. Brauth, W. S. Hall, & R. J. Dooling (Eds.), *Plasticity of development.* Cambridge, MA: Bradford/MIT Press.

Ram, A., & Ross, H. S. (2001). Problem solving, contention, and struggle: How siblings resolve a conflict of interest. *Child Development, 72,* 1710–1722.

Ramey, C. T., & Ramey, S. L. (1998). Early intervention and early experience. *American Psychologist, 53,* 109–120.

Ramos-Ford, V., & Gardner, H. (1997). Giftedness from a multiple intelligences perspective. In N. Conangelo & G. A. Davis (Eds.), *Handbook of gifted education* (2nd ed.) (pp. 54–66). Boston: Allyn & Bacon.

Ramsey, P. G. (1995). Changing social dynamics in early childhood classrooms. *Child Development, 66,* 764–773.

Rapoport, J. L., Castellanos, F. X., Gogate, N., Janson, K., Kohler, S., & Nelson, P. (2001). Imaging normal and abnormal brain development: New perspectives for child psychiatry. *Australian & New Zealand Journal of Psychiatry, 35,* 272–282.

Ray, S. L. (2004). Eating disorders in adolescent males. *Professional School Counseling, 8,* 98–101.

Raz, S., Goldstein, R., Hopkins, T. L., Lauterbach, M. D., Shah, F., Porter, C. L., Riggs, W. W., Magill, L. H., & Sander, C. J. (1994). Sex differences in early vulnerability to cerebral injury and their neurobehavioral implications. *Psychobiology, 22,* 244–253.

Raz, S., Lauterbach, M. D., Hopkins, T. L., Glogowski, B. K., Porter, C. L., Riggs, W. W., & Sander, C. J. (1995). A female advantage in cognitive recovery from early cerebral insult. *Developmental Psychology, 31,* 958–966.

Reed, T. E. (1997). "The genetic hypothesis": It was not tested but it could have been. *American Psychologist, 52,* 77–78.

Reeder, K. (1981). How young children learn to do things with words. In P. S. Dale & D. Ingram (Eds.), *Child language—an international perspective.* Baltimore: University Park Press.

Reese, E., & Cox, A. (1999). Quality of adult book reading affects children's emergent literacy. *Developmental Psychology, 35,* 20–28.

Reese, E., Haden, C., & Fivush, R. (1993). Mother–child conversations about the past: Relationships of style and memory over time. *Cognitive Development, 8,* 403–430.

Reese-Weber, M. (2000). Middle and late adolescent's conflict resolution skills with siblings: Association with interparental and parent–adolescent conflict resolution. *Journal of Youth and Adolescence, 29,* 697–711.

Reich, P. A. (1986). *Language development.* Englewood Cliffs, NJ: Prentice-Hall.

Reichman, N. E. (2005). Low birth weight and school readiness. *Future of Children, 15,* 91–116.

Reijonen, J. H., Pratt, H. D., Patel, D. R., & Greydanus, D. E (2003). Eating disorders in the adolescent population: An overview. *Journal of Adolescent Research, 18,* 209–222.

Reiss, D., Neiderhiser, J. M., Hetherington, E. M., & Plomin, R. (2000). *The relationship code: Deciphering genetic and social influences on adolescent development.* Cambridge, MA: Harvard University Press.

Remley, A. (1988, October). The great parental value shift: From obedience to independence. *Psychology Today, 56–59.*

Repacholi, B. M. (1998). Infants' use of attentional cues to identify the referent of another person's emotional expression. *Developmental Psychology, 34,* 1017–1025.

Repacholi, B. M., & Gopnik, A. (1997). Early reasoning about desires: Evidence from 14- and 18-month-olds. *Developmental Psychology, 33,* 12–21.

Resing, W. C. M. (2001). Beyond Binet. *Issues in Education, 7, 225–235.*

Resnick, S. M., Berenbaum, S. A., Gottesman, I. I., & Bouchard, T. J. (1986). Early hormonal influences on cognitive functioning in congenital adrenal hyperplasia. *Developmental Psychology, 22,* 191–198.

Rest, J. R., & Thoma, S. J. (1985). Relation of moral judgment development to formal education. *Developmental Psychology, 21,* 709–714.

Rest, J. R., Thoma, S. J., & Edwards, L. (1997). Designing and validating a measure of moral judgment: Stage preference and stage consistency approaches. *Journal of Educational Psychology, 89,* 5–28.

Revelle, G. L., Wellman, H. M., & Karabenick, J. D. (1985). Comprehension monitoring in preschool children. *Child Development, 56,* 654–663.

Reynolds, A. J., & Robertson, D. L. (2003). School-based early intervention and later child maltreatment in the Chicago Longitudinal Study. *Child Development, 74,* 3–26.

Reynolds, A. J., & Temple, J. A. (1988). Extended early childhood intervention and school achievement: Age thirteen findings from the Chicago Longitudinal Study. *Child Development, 69,* 231–246.

Reynolds, D. (1992). School effectiveness and school improvement: An updated review of the British literature. In D. Reynolds & P. Cuttance (Eds.), *School effectiveness: Research, policy, and practice.* London, England: Cassell.

Reynolds, E. H. (2002). Benefits and risks of folic acid to the nervous system. *Journal of Neurology & Psychiatry, 72, 567–571.*

Reznick, J. S., & Goldfield, B. A. (1992). Rapid change in lexical development in comprehension and production. *Developmental Psychology, 28,* 406–413.

Rheingold, H. L. (1982). Little children's participation in the work of adults, a nascent prosocial behavior. *Child Development, 53,* 114–125.

Rheingold, H. L., & Adams, J. L. (1980). The significance of speech to newborns. *Developmental Psychology, 16,* 397–403.

Rhodes, J. E., Grossman, J. B., & Resch, N. L. (2000). Agents of change: Pathways through which relationships influence adolescent's academic adjustment. *Child Development, 71,* 1662–1671.

Rholes, W. S., & Ruble, D. N. (1984). Children's understanding of dispositional characteristics of others. *Child Development, 55,* 550–560.

Rice, C., Koinis, D., Sullivan, K., Tager-Flusberg, & Winner, E. (1997). When 3-year-olds pass the appearance–reality test. *Developmental Psychology, 33,* 54–61.

Rice, M. E., & Grusec, J. E. (1975). Saying and doing: Effects on observer performance. *Journal of Personality and Social Psychology, 32,* 584–593.

Rice, M. L., Huston, A. C., Truglio, R., & Wright, J. (1990). Words from "Sesame Street": Learning vocabulary while viewing. *Developmental Psychology, 26,* 421–428.

Richards, J. E. (1997). Effects of attention on infant's preference for briefly exposed visual stimuli in the paired-comparison recognition-memory paradigm. *Developmental Psychology, 32,* 22–31.

Richards, M. H., Boxer, A. M., Petersen, A. C., & Albrecht, R. (1990). Relation of weight to body image in pubertal girls and boys from two communities. *Developmental Psychology, 26,* 313–321.

Richards, M. H., Crowe, P. A., Larson, R., & Swarr, A. (1998). Developmental patterns and gender differences in the experience of peer companionship during adolescence. *Child Development, 69,* 154–163.

Richardson, J. G., & Simpson, C. H. (1982). Children, gender, and social structure: An analysis of the contents of letters to Santa Claus. *Child Development, 53,* 429–436.

Richardson, T. M., & Benbow, C. P. (1990). Long-term effects of acceleration on the social-emotional adjustment of mathematically precocious youths. *Journal of Educational Psychology, 82,* 464–470.

Richman, E. L., & Shaffer, D. R. (2000). "If you let me play sports": How might sport participation influence the self-esteem of adolescent females? *Psychology of Women Quarterly, 24,* 189–199.

Riesen, A. H. (1947). The development of visual perception in man and chimpanzee. *Science, 106,* 107–108.

Riesen, A. H., Chow, K. L., Semmes, J., & Nissen, H. W. (1951). Chimpanzee vision after four conditions of light deprivation. *American Psychologist, 6,* 282.

Rieser, J., Yonas, A., & Wilkner, K. (1976). Radial localization of odors by human newborns. *Child Development, 47,* 856–859.

Rittle-Johnson, B., & Siegler, R. S. (1999). Learning to spell: Variability, choice, and change in children's strategy use. *Child Development, 70,* 332–348.

Roberts, L. R., Sarigiani, P. A., Petersen, A. C., & Newman, J. L. (1990). Gender differences in the relationship between achievement and self-image during early adolescence. *Journal of Early Adolescence, 10,* 159–175.

Roberts, W., & Strayer, J. (1996). Empathy, emotional expressiveness, and prosocial behavior. *Child Development, 67,* 449–470.

Robertson, T. S., & Rossiter, J. R. (1974). Children and commercial persuasion: An attribution theory analysis. *Journal of Consumer Research, 1,* 13–20.

Robin, D. J., Berthier, N. E., & Clifton, R. K. (1996). Infants' predictive reaching for moving objects in the dark. *Developmental Psychology, 32,* 824–835.

Robins, R. W., Trzesniewski, K. H., Tracey, J. L., Gosling, S. D., & Potter, J. (2002). Global self-esteem across the life span. *Psychology and Aging, 17,* 423–434.

Robinson, A., Bender, B. G., & Linden, M. G. (1992). Prenatal diagnosis of sex chromosome abnormalities. In A. Milunsky (Ed.), *Genetic disorders and the fetus: Diagnosis, prevention, and treatment.* Baltimore: Johns Hopkins University Press.

Robinson, B. F., & Mervis, C. B. (1998). Disentangling early language development: Modeling lexical and grammatical acquisition using an extension of case-study methodology. *Developmental Psychology, 34,* 363–375.

Robinson, C. C., & Morris, J. T. (1986). The gender-stereotyped nature of Christmas toys received by 36-, 48-, and 60-month-old children: A comparison between nonrequested vs. requested toys. *Sex Roles, 15,* 21–32.

Robinson, I., Ziss, K., Ganza, B., Katz, S., & Robinson, E. (1991). Twenty years of sexual revolution, 1965–1985: An update. *Journal of Marriage and the Family, 53,* 216–220.

Robinson, J. L., Kagan, J., Reznick, J. S., & Corley, R. (1992). The heritability of inhibited and uninhibited behavior. A twin study. *Developmental Psychology, 28,* 1030–1037.

Rochat, P. (1989). Object manipulation and exploration in 2- to 5-month-old infants. *Developmental Psychology, 25,* 871–884.

Rochat, P., & Goubet, N. (1995). Development of sitting and reaching in 5- to 6-month-old infants. *Infant Behavior and Development, 18,* 53–68.

Rochat, P., & Striano, T. (2002). Who's in the mirror? Self–other discrimination in specular images by four- and nine-month-old infants. *Child Development, 73,* 35–46.

Rochat, P., Querido, J. G., & Striano, T. (1999). Emerging sensitivity to the timing and structure of protoconversation in early infancy. *Developmental Psychology, 35,* 950–957.

Roche, A. F. (1981). The adipocyte-number hypothesis. *Child Development, 52,* 31–43.

Rocheleau, B. (1995). Computer use by school-age children: Trends, patterns, and predictors. *Journal of Educational Computing Research, 12,* 1–17.

Rock, A. M. L., & Trainor, L. J. (1999). Distinctive messages in infant-directed lullabies and play songs. *Developmental Psychology, 35,* 527–535.

Rodgers, J. L., & Rowe, D. C. (1988). Influence of siblings on adolescent sexual behavior. *Developmental Psychology, 24,* 722–728.

Rodkin, P. C., Farmer, T. W., Pearl, R., & Van Acker, R. (2000). Heterogencity of popular boys: Antisocial and prosocial configurations. *Developmental Psychology, 36,* 14–24.

Rodning, C., Beckwith, L., & Howard, J. (1991). Quality of attachment and home environments in children prenatally exposed to PCP and cocaine. *Development and Psychopathology, 3,* 351–366.

Rodriguez, J. L., Diaz, R. M., Duran, D., & Espinosa, L. (1995). The impact of bilingual preschool education on the language development of Spanish-speaking children. *Early Childhood Research Quarterly, 10,* 475–490.

Rodriguez-Fornells, A., Münte, T. F., & Clahsen, H. (2002). Morphological priming in Spanish verb forms: An ERP repetition priming study. *Journal of Cognitive Neuroscience, 14,* 443–454.

Roe, V. A. (2004). Living with genital Herpes: How effective is antiviral therapy? *Journal of Perinatal & Neonatal Nursing, 18,* 206–216.

Roeleveld, N., Zielhuis, G. A., & Gabreels, F. (1997). The prevalence of mental retardation: A critical review of present literature. *Developmental Medicine and Child Neurology, 39,* 125–132.

Roeser, R. W., & Eccles, J. S. (1998). Adolescents' perceptions of middle school: Relation to longitudinal changes in academic and psychological adjustment. *Journal of Research in Adolescence, 8,* 123–158.

Rogoff, B. (1990). *Apprenticeship in thinking: Cognitive development in social context.* New York: Oxford University Press.

Rogoff, B. (1998). Cognition as a collaborative process. In D. Kuhn & R. S. Siegler (Eds.), *Cognition language, and perceptual development,* Vol. 2, In B. Damon (Gen. Ed), *Handbook of child psychology* New York: Wiley.

Rogoff, B. (2002). How can we study cultural aspects of human development? *Human Development, 45,* 387–389.

Rogoff, B. (2003). *The cultural nature of human development.* New York: Oxford University Press.

Rogoff, B., & Waddell, K. J. (1982). Memory for information organized in a scene by children from two cultures. *Child Development, 53,* 1224–1228.

Rogoff, B., Mistry, J., Goncu, A., & Mosier, C. (1993). Guided participation in cultural activity by toddlers and caregivers. *Monographs of the Society for Research in Child Development, 58* (8, Serial No. 236).

Roid, G. H. (2003). *Stanford Binet Intelligence Scales, Fifth Edition.* Itasca, IL: Riverside Publishing.

Roithmaier, A., Kiess, W., Kopecky, M., Fuhrmann, G., & Butenandt, O. (1988). Psychosozialer Minderwuchs. *Monatschift fur Kinderheilkunde, 133,* 760–763.

Roland, M. G. M., Cole, T. J., & Whitehead, R. G. (1977). A quantitative study into the role of infection in determining nutritional status in Gambian village children. *British Journal of Nutrition, 37,* 441–450.

Romney, D. M., & Pyryt, M. C. (1999). Guilford's concept of social intelligence revisited. *High Ability Studies, 10,* 137–142.

Roopnarine, J. L., Talukder, E., Jain, D., Joshi, P., & Srivastave, P. (1990). Characteristics of holding, patterns of play, and social behaviors between parents and infants in New Delhi, India. *Developmental Psychology, 26,* 667–673.

Rose, A. J., Swenson, L. P., & Waller, E. M. (2004). Overt and relational aggression and perceived popularity: Developmental differences in concurrent and prospective relations. *Developmental Psychology, 40,* 378–387.

Rose, S. A. (1988). Shape recognition in infancy: Visual integration of sequential information. *Child Development, 59,* 1161–1176.

Rose, S. A., & Feldman, J. F. (1995). Prediction of IQ and specific cognitive abilities from infancy measures. *Developmental Psychology, 31,* 685–696.

Rose, S. A., & Feldman, J. F. (1996). Memory and processing speed in preterm children at eleven years: A comparison with full-terms. *Child Development, 67,* 2005–2021.

Rose, S. A., Feldman, J. F., & Janowski, J. J. (2004). Infant visual recognition memory. *Developmental Review, 24,* 74–100.

Rose, S. A., Feldman, J. F., Wallace, I. F., & McCarton, C. (1989). Infant visual attention: Relation to birth status and developmental outcome during the first 5 years. *Developmental Psychology, 25,* 560–576.

Rose, S. A., Gottfried, A. W., & Bridger, W. H. (1981). Cross-modal transfer in 6-month-old infants. *Developmental Psychology, 17,* 661–669.

Rose, S., Feldman, J., & Jankowski, J. J. (2002). Processing speed in the 1st year of life: A longitudinal study of preterm and full-term infants. *Developmental Psychology, 38,* 895–902.

Rosen, B. C., & D'Andrade, R. (1959). The psychosocial origins of achievement motivation. *Sociometry, 22,* 185–218.

Rosen, J. C., Tracey, B., & Howell, D. (1990). Life stress, psychological symptoms, and weight reducing behavior in adolescent girls: A prospective analysis. *International Journal of Eating Disorders, 9,* 17–26.

Rosen, K. S., & Rothbaum, F. (1993). Quality of parental caregiving and security of attachment. *Developmental Psychology, 29,* 358–367.

Rosen, W. D., Adamson, L. B., & Bakeman, R. (1992). An experimental investigation of infant social referencing: Mothers' messages and gender differences. *Developmental Psychology, 28,* 1172–1178.

Rosenblum, G. D., & Lewis, M. (1999). The relations among body image, physical attractiveness, and body mass in adolescents. *Child Development, 70,* 50–64.

Rosenfeld, R. M. (2004). Otitis, antibiotics, and the greater good. *Pediatrics, 114,* 1333–1335.

Rosenhan, D. L. (1970). The natural socialization of altruistic autonomy. In J. L. Macaulay & L. Berkowitz (Eds.), *Altruism and helping behavior.* New York: Academic Press.

Rosenholtz, S. J., & Simpson, C. (1984). The formation of ability conceptions: Developmental trend or social construction? *Review of Educational Research, 54,* 31–63.

Rosenkrantz Aronson, S., & Huston, A. C. (2004). The mother–infant relationship in single, cohabitating, and married families: A case for marriage? *Journal of Family Psychology, 18,* 5–18.

Rosenthal, M. K. (1982). Vocal dialogues in the neonatal period. *Developmental Psychology, 18,* 17–21.

Rosenwasser, S. M., Lingenfelter, M., & Harrington, A. F. (1989). Non-traditional gender role portrayals and children's gender role perceptions. *Journal of Applied Developmental Psychology, 10,* 97–105.

Rosenzweig, M. R. (1984). Experience, memory, and the brain. *American Psychologist, 39,* 365–376.

Ross, H. S., & Lollis, S. P. (1987). Communication within infant social games. *Developmental Psychology, 23,* 241–248.

Ross, M. G., & Nijland, M. J. M. (1998). Development of ingestive behavior. *American Journal of Physiology: Regulatory, Integrative & Comparative Physiology,* 43, 894.

Ross, R. T., Begab, M. J., Dondis, E. H., Giampiccolo, J. S., Jr., & Meyers, C. E. (1985). *Lives of the mentally retarded. A forty-year follow-up study.* Stanford, CA: Stanford University Press.

Ross-Sheehy, S., Oakes, L. M., & Luck, S. J. (2003). The development of visual short-term memory capacity in infants. *Child Development, 74,* 1807–1822.

Roth, F. P., Speece, D. L., & Cooper, D. H. (2002). A longitudinal analysis of the connection between oral language and early reading. *Journal of Educational Research, 95,* 259–262.

Rothbart, M. K., & Bates, J. E. (1998). Temperament. In W. Damon (Series Ed.), & N. Eisenberg (Vol. Ed.), *Handbook of child psychology: Vol. 3 Social, emotional, and personality development* (5th ed.) (pp. 105–176), New York: Wiley.

Rothbart, M. K., Ahadi, S. A., Hershey, K. L., & Fisher, P. (2001). Investigators of temperament at three to seven years: The Children's Behavior Questionnaire. *Child Development, 72,* 1394–1408.

Rothbaum, F., Pott, M., Azuma, H., Miyake, K., & Weisz, J. (2000). The development of close relationships in Japan and the United States: Paths of symbiotic harmony and generative tension. *Child Development, 71,* 1121–1142.

Rothbaum, F., Weisz, J., Pott, M., Miyake, K., & Morelli, G. (2000). Attachment and culture: Security in the United States and Japan. *American Psychologist, 35,* 1093–1104.

Rothberg, A. D., & Lits, B. (1991). Psychosocial support for maternal stress during pregnancy: Effect on birth weight. *American Journal of Obstetrics and Gynecology, 165,* 403–407.

Rousseau, J. J. (1955). *Emile.* New York: Dutton. (Original work published 1762.)

Rovee-Collier, C. (1995). Time windows in cognitive development. *Developmental Psychology, 31,* 147–169.

Rovee-Collier, C. (1999). The development of infant memory. *Current Directions in Psychological Science, 8,* 80–85.

Rovee-Collier, C. K. (1997). Dissociations in infant memory: Retention without remembering. In J. D. Osofsky (Ed.), *Handbook of infant development* (2nd. ed.). New York: Wiley.

Rowe, D. C. (1994). *The limits of family influence: Genes, experience, and behavior.* New York: Guilford.

Rowe, D. C., & Plomin, R. (1981). The importance of nonshared (E_1) environmental influences in behavioral development. *Developmental Psychology, 17,* 517–531.

Rowe, D. C., & Rodgers, J. (2005). Under the skin: On the impartial treatment of genetic and environmental hypotheses of racial differences. *American Psychologist, 60,* 60–70.

Roy, R., & Benenson, J. F. (2002). Sex and contextual effects on children's use of interference competition. *Developmental Psychology, 38,* 306–312.

Royden, C. S., Crowell, J. A., & Banks, M. S. (1994). Estimating heading during eye movements. *Vision Research, 34,* 3197–3214.

Rubin, K. H., Bukowski, W. M., & Parker, J. G. (1998). Peer interactions, relationships, and groups. In W. Damon (Series Ed.) and N. Eisenberg (Vol. Ed.), *Handbook of child psychology. Vol. 3. Social, emotional, and personality development* (5th ed.) (pp. 619–700). New York: Wiley.

Rubin, K. H., Burgess, K. B., Dwyer, K. M., & Hastings, P. D. (2003). Predicting preschoolers' externalizing behaviors from toddler temperament, conflict, and maternal negativity. *Developmental Psychology, 39,* 164–176.

Rubin, K. H., Fein, G., & Vandenberg, B. (1983). Play. In E. M. Hetherington (Ed.), *Handbook of child psychology.* Vol. 4: *Socialization, personality, and social development* (pp. 693–744). New York: Wiley.

Rubin, K. H., Hastings, P., Chen, X., Stewart, S., & McNichol, K. (1998). Interpersonal and maternal correlates of aggression, conflict, and externalizing problems in toddlers. *Child Development, 69,* 1614–1629.

Ruble, D. N., & Dweck, C. S. (1995). Self-conceptions, person conceptions, and their development. In N. Eisenberg (Ed.), *Social development.* Thousand Oaks, CA: Sage.

Ruble, D. N., & Martin, C. L. (1998). Gender development. In N. Eisenberg (Vol. Ed.), & W. Damon (Series Ed.), *Handbook of child psychology: Vol. 3 Social, emotional, and personality development.* (5th ed.) (pp. 933–1016). New York: Wiley.

Ruble, D. N., Balaban, T., & Cooper, J. (1981). Gender constancy and the effects of sex-typed televised toy commercials. *Child Development, 52,* 667–673.

Rucibwa, N., Modeste, N., Mongtomery, S., & Fox, C. (2003). Exploring family factors and sexual behaviors in a group of black and Hispanic adolescent males. *American Journal of Health Behaviors, 27,* 63–74.

Rudolph, F. (1965). *Essays on early education in the republic.* Cambridge, MA: Harvard University Press.

Rueter, M. A., & Conger, R. D. (1998). Reciprocal influences between parenting and adolescent problem-solving behavior. *Developmental Psychology, 34,* 1470–1482.

Ruff, H. A., & Capozzoli, M. (2003). Development of attention and distractibility in the first 4 years of life. *Developmental Psychology, 39,* 877–890.

Ruff, H. A., Capozzoli, M., & Weisberg, R. (1998). Age, individuality, and context as factors in sustained visual attention during the preschool years. *Developmental Psychology, 34,* 454–464.

Ruffman, T., Perner, J., Naito, M., Parkin, L., & Clements, W. A. (1998). Older (but not younger) siblings facilitate false belief understanding. *Developmental Psychology, 34,* 161–174.

Ruffman, T. K., & Olson, D. R. (1989). Children's ascriptions of knowledge to others. *Developmental Psychology, 25*, 601–606.

Ruffman, T. K., Olson, D. R., Ash, T., & Keenan, T. (1993). The ABCs of deception: Do young children understand deception in the same way as adults? *Developmental Psychology, 29*, 74–87.

Ruggles, S. (1994). The origins of African American family structure. *American Sociological Review, 59*, 136–151.

Runco, M. A. (1992). Children's divergent thinking and creative ideation. *Developmental Review, 12*, 233–264.

Rushton, J. P. (1980). *Altruism, socialization and society.* Englewood Cliffs, NJ: Prentice-Hall.

Rushton, J. P. (1999). *Race, evolution, and behavior.* New Brunswick, NJ: Transaction Publishers.

Russell, J., Mauthner, N., Sharpe, S., & Tidswell, T. (1991). The "windows tasks" as a measure of strategic deception in preschoolers and autistic subjects. *British Journal of Developmental Psychology, 9*, 331–349.

Rust, J., Golombok, S., Hines, M., Johnston, K., & Golding, J. (2000). The role of brothers and sisters in the gender development of preschool children. *Journal of Experimental Child Psychology, 77*, 292–303.

Rutter, D. R., & Durkin, K. (1987). Turn-taking in mother–infant interaction: An examination of vocalizations and gaze. *Developmental Psychology, 23*, 54–61.

Rutter, M. (1979). Protective factors in children's responses to stress and disadvantage. In M. W. Kent & J. E. Rolf (Eds.), *Primary prevention of psychopathology. Vol. 3: Social competence in children.* Hanover, NH: University Press of New England.

Rutter, M. (1981). *Maternal deprivation revisited* (2nd ed.). New York: Penguin Books.

Rutter, M. (1983). School effects on pupil progress: Research findings and policy implications. *Child Development, 54*, 1–29.

Rutter, M. (2000). Resilience reconsidered: Conceptual considerations, empirical findings, and policy implications. In J. P Shonkoff & S. J. Meisels (Eds.), *Handbook of early childhood intervention* (2nd Ed.), New York: Cambridge University Press.

Rutter, M., Maughan, B., Mortimore, P., Ouston, J., & Smith, A. (1979). *Fifteen thousand hours: Secondary schools and their effects on children.* Cambridge, MA: Harvard University Press.

Ryan, R. M., & Deci, E. L. (2000a). Self-determination theory and the facilitation of intrinsic motivation, social development, and well-being. *American Psychologist, 55*, 68–78.

Ryan, R. M., & Deci, E. L. (2000b). When rewards compete with nature: The undermining of intrinsic motivation and self-regulation. In C. Sansone & J. M. Harackiewicz (Eds.), *Intrinsic and extrinsic motivation: The search for optimal moivation and performance* (pp. 13–54). San Diego: Academic Press.

Saarni, C. (1990). Emotional competence: How emotions and relationships become integrated. In R. A. Thompson (Ed.), Socioemotional development. *Nebraska Symposium on Motivation* (Vol. 36). Lincoln, NE: University of Nebraska Press.

Saarni, C. (1999). *The development of emotional competence.* New York: Guilford.

Sabbagh, M. A., & Callanan, M. A. (1998). Metarepresentation in action: 3-, 4- and 5-year-olds' developing theories of mind in parent-child conversations. *Developmental Psychology, 34*, 491–502.

Sabbagh, M. A., & Taylor, M. (2000). Neural correlates of theory-of-mind reasoning: An event-related potential study. *Psychological Science, 11*, 46–50.

Sacks, C. H., & Mergendoller, J. R. (1997). The relationship between teachers' theoretical orientation toward reading and student outcomes in kindergarten children with different initial reading abilities. *American Educational Research Journal, 34*, 721–739.

Sacks, O. (1993, December 27). *A neurologist's notebook: An anthropologist on Mars. The New Yorker,* 106–125

Sadler, T. W. (1996). Embryology and experimental teratology. In J. A. Kuller, N. C. Cheschier, & R. C. Cefalo (Eds.), *Prenatal diagnosis and reproductive genetics* (pp. 218–226). St. Louis, MO: Mosby.

Saenger, P. (2003). Precocious puberty: McCune-Albright syndrome and beyond. *Journal of Pediatrics, 143*, 9–10.

Saffran, J. R., & Thiessen, E. D. (2003). Pattern induction by infant language learners. *Developmental Psychology, 39*, 484–494.

Sagi, A., & Hoffman, M. L. (1976). Empathic distress in newborns. *Developmental Psychology, 12*, 175–176.

Sahni, R., Schulze, K. F., Stefanski, M., Myers, M. M., & Fifer, W. P. (1995). Methodological issues in coding sleep states in immature infants. *Developmental Psychobiology, 28*, 85–101.

Sai, F. Z. (1990). The origins of human face perception by very young infants. Ph.D. Thesis, University of Glasgow, Scotland, UK.

Sai, F. Z. (2005). The role of the mother's voice in developing mother's face preference: evidence for intermodal perception at birth. *Infant and Child Development, 14*, 29–50.

Saigal, S., Hoult, L. A., Streiner, D. L., Stoskopf, F. L., & Rosenbaum, P. L. (2000). School difficulties at adolescence in a regional cohort of children who were extremely low birth weight. *Pediatrics, 105*, 325–331.

Saklofske, D. H., Gorsuch, R. L., Weiss, L. G., Zhu, J., & Patterson, C. A. (2005). General ability index for the WAIS-III: Canadian norms. *Canadian Journal of Behavioural Science, 37*, 44–48.

Salle, B. L., Rauch, F., Travers, R., Bouvier, R., & Glorieux, F. H. (2002). Human fetal bone development: Histomorphometric evaluation of the proximal femoral metaphysis. *BONE*, 30, 823–829.

Sallout, B., & Walker, M. (2003). The fetal origin of adult diseases. *Journal of Obstetrics and Gynecology, 23*, 555–560.

Sameroff, A. J., & Chandler, M. J. (1975). Reproductive risk and the continuum of caretaking casualty. In F. D. Horowitz, M. Hetherington, S. Scarr-Salapatek, & G. Siegel (Eds.), *Review of child development research* (Vol. 4). Chicago: University of Chicago Press.

Sameroff, A. J., Seifer, R., Baldwin, A., & Baldwin, C. (1993). Stability of intelligence from preschool to adolescence: The influence of social and family risk factors. *Child Development, 64*, 80–97.

Samuels, C. (1986). Bases for the infant's development of self-awareness. *Human Development, 29*, 36–48.

Samuelson, L. K. (2002). Statistical regularities in vocabulary guide language acquisition in connectionist models and 15–20-month-olds. *Developmental Psychology, 38*, 1016–1037.

Samuelson, L. K., & Smith, L. B. (2000). Grounding development in cognitive processes. *Child Development, 71*, 98–106.

Sansavini, A., Bertocini, J., & Giovanelli, G. (1997). Newborns discriminate the rhythm of multisyllabic stressed words. *Developmental Psychology, 33*, 3–11.

Satcher, C. (2001). The Surgeon General's call to action to promote sexual health and responsible sexual behavior. Washington, DC: U.S. Department of Health and Human Services.

Savage-Rumbaugh, E. S., Murphy, J., Sevcik, R. A., Brakke, K. E., Williams, S. L., & Rumbaugh, D. M. (1993). Language comprehension in ape and child. *Monographs of the Society for Research in Child Development, 58*(3–4, Serial No. 233).

Savin-Williams, R. C. (1995). An exploratory study of pubertal maturation timing and self-esteem among gay and bisexual male youths. *Developmental Psychology, 31*, 1100–1110.

Savin-Williams, R. C. (2001). A critique of research on sexual-minority youths. *Journal of Adolescence, 24*, 5–13.

Savin-Williams, R. C. (2001b). Suicide attempts among sexual-minority youths: Population and measurement issues. *Journal of Consulting and Clinical Psychology, 69*, 983–991.

Savin-Williams, R. C., & Small, S. A. (1986). The timing of puberty and its relationship to adolescent and parent perceptions of family interactions. *Developmental Psychology, 32*, 342–347.

Sawaguchi, T., Patricia, F., Kadhim, H., Groswasser, J., Sottiaux, M., Nishida, H., & Kahn, A. (2003a). The correlation between ubiquitin in the brainstem and sleep apnea in SIDS victims. *Early Human Development, 75*, S75–S86.

Sawaguchi, T., Patricia, F., Kadhim, H., Groswasser, J., Sottiaux, M., Nishida, H., & Kahn, A. (2003b). The presence of TATA-binding protein in the brainstem, correlated with sleep apnea in SIDS victims. *Early Human Development, 75*, S109–S118.

Sawaguchi, T., Patricia, F., Kadhim, H., Groswasser, J., Sottiaux, M., Nishida, H., & Kahn, A. (2003c). Correlation between the Ki-67 antigen in the brainstem and physiological data on sleep apnea in SIDS victims. *Early Human Development, 75*. S119–S127.

Sawaguchi, T., Patricia, F., Kadhim, H., Groswasser, J., Sottiaux, M., Nishida, H., & Kahn, A. (2003d). The correlation between serotonergic neurons in the brainstem and sleep apnea in SIDS victims. *Early Human Development, 75*, S31–S40.

Sawaguchi, T., Patricia, F., Kadhim, H., Groswasser, J., Sottiaux, M., Nishida, H., & Kahn, A. (2003e). The correlation between microtubule-associated protein 2 in the brainstem of SIDS victims and physiological data on sleep apnea. *Early Human Development, 75*. S87–S97.

Sawaguchi, T., Patricia, F., Kadhim, H., Groswasser, J., Sottiaux, M., Nishida, H., & Kahn, A. (2003f). The relationship between neuronal plasticity and serotonergic neurons in the brainstem of SIDS victims. *Early Human Development, 75*, S139–S146.

Sawaguchi, T., Patricia, F., Kadhim, H., Groswasser, J., Sottiaux, M., Nishida, H., & Kahn, A. (2003g). The presence of TATA-binding protein in the brainstem, correlated with sleep apnea in SIDS victims. *Early Human Development, 75*, S109–S118.

Sawaguchi, T., Patricia, F., Kadhim, H., Groswasser, J., Sottiaux, M., Nishida, H., & Kahn, A. (2003h). Pathological data on apoptosis in the brainstem and physiological data on sleep apnea in SIDS victims. *Early Human Development, 75*, S13–S20.

Sawaguchi, T., Patricia, F., Kadhim, H., Groswasser, J., Sottiaux, M., Nishida, H., & Kahn, A. (2003i). Clinicopathological correlation between brainstem gliosis using GFAP as a marker and sleep apnea in the sudden infant death syndrome, *Early Human Development, 75*. S3–S11.

Sawaguchi, T., Patricia, F., Kadhim, H., Groswasser, J., Sottiaux, M., Nishida, H., & Kahn, A. (2003j). Catecholaminergic neurons in the brain-stem and sleep apnea in SIDS victims. *Early Human Development, 75*, S41–S50.

Sawaguchi, T., Patricia, F., Kadhim, H., Groswasser, J., Sottiaux, M., Nishida, H., & Kahn, A. (2003k). Serotonergic receptors in the midbrain correlated with physiological data on sleep apnea in SIDS victims. *Early Human Development, 75*. S65–S74.

Sawaguchi, T., Patricia, F., Kadhim, H., Groswasser, J., Sottiaux, M., Nishida, H., & Kahn, A. (2003l). Substance P in the midbrains of SIDS victims and its correlation with sleep apnea. *Early Human Development, 75*, S51–S59.

Sawaguchi, T., Patricia, F., Kadhim, H., Groswasser, J., Sottiaux, M., Nishida, H., & Kahn, A. (2003m). The correlation between tau protein in the brain-stem and sleep apnea in SIDS victims. *Early Human Development, 75*, S99–S107.

Sawaguchi, T., Patricia, F., Kadhim, H., Groswasser, J., Sottiaux, M., Nishida, H., & Kahn, A. (2003n). Partial arousal deficiency in SIDS victims and noradrenergic neuronal plasticity. *Early Human Development, 75*, S61–S64.

Sawaguchi, T., Patricia, F., Kadhim, H., Groswasser, J., Sottiaux, M., Nishida, H., & Kahn, A. (2003o). Investigation into the correlation in SIDS victims between Alzheimer precursor protein A4 in the brain-stem and sleep apnea in SIDS victims. *Early Human Development, 75*, S21–S30.

Saxton, M. (1997). The contrast theory of negative input. *Journal of Child Language, 24*, 139–161.

Scafidi, F. A., Field, T. M., Schanberg, S. M., Bauer, C. R., Vega-Lahr, N., Garcia, R., Poirier, J., Nystrom, G., & Kuhn, C. M. (1986). Effects of tactile/kinesthetic stimulation on the clinical course and sleep/wake behavior pattern of preterm neonates. *Infant Behavior and Development, 9*, 91–105.

Scafidi, F. A., Field, T. M., Schanberg, S. M., Bauer, C. R., Vega-Lahr, N., Garcia, R., Poirer, J., Nystrom, G., & Kuhn, C. M. (1990). Massage stimulates growth in preterm infants: A replication. *Infant Behavior and Development, 13*, 167–188.

Scaramella, L. V., Conger, R. D., Simons, R. L., & Whitbeck, L. B. (1998). Predicting risk for pregnancy by late adolescence: A social-contextual perspective. *Developmental Psychology, 34*, 1233–1245.

Scaramella, L. V., Conger, R. D., Spoth, R., & Simons, R. L. (2002). Evoluation of a social contextual model of delinquency: A cross-study replication. *Child Development, 73,* 175–195.

Scarr, S. (1992). Developmental theories for the 1990s: Development and individual differences. *Child Development, 63,* 1–19.

Scarr, S. (1998). American child care today. *American Psychologist, 53,* 95–198.

Scarr, S., & McCartney, K. (1983). How people make their own environments: A theory of genotype/environment effects. *Child Development, 54,* 424–435.

Scarr, S., & Weinberg, R. A. (1978). The influence of family background on intellectual attainment. *American Sociological Review, 43,* 674–692.

Scarr, S., & Weinberg, R. A. (1983). The Minnesota adoption studies: Genetic differences and malleability. *Child Development, 54,* 260–267.

Scarr, S., Pakstis, A. J., Katz, S. H., & Barker, W. (1977). The absence of a relationship between degree of white ancestry and intellectual skills within a black population. *Human Genetics, 39,* 69–86.

Schaefer, G., & Plummert, K. (1998). Rapid word learning by 15-month-olds under tightly controlled conditions. *Child Development, 69,* 309–320.

Schaffer, H. R. (1971). *The growth of sociability.* Baltimore: Penguin Books.

Schaffer, H. R. (1977). *Mothering.* Cambridge, MA: Harvard University Press.

Schaffer, H. R., & Emerson, P. E. (1964). The development of social attachments in infancy. *Monographs of the Society for Research in Child Development, 29* (3, Serial No. 94).

Schaie, K. W. (1990). Intellectual development in adulthood. In E. J. Birren & K. W. Schaie (Eds.), *The handbook of the psychology of aging* (3rd ed.). San Diego, CA: Academic Press.

Schalet, A. T. (2000). Raging hormones, regulated love: adolescent sexuality and the constitution of the modern individual in the United States and the Netherlands. *Body & Society, 6,* 75–105.

Schalock, R. L., Holl, C., Elliott, B., & Ross, I. (1992). A longitudinal follow-up of graduates from a rural special education program. *Learning Disability Quarterly, 15,* 29–38.

Schauble, L. (1990). Belief revision in children: The role of prior knowledge and strategies for generating evidence. *Journal of Experimental Child Psychology, 49,* 31–57.

Schieffelin, B. B. (1986). *How Kaluli children learn what to say, what to do, and how to feel.* New York: Cambridge University Press.

Schiff-Myers, N. (1988). Hearing children of deaf parents. In D. Bishop & K. Mogford (Eds.), *Language development in exceptional circumstances.* Edinburgh: Churchill Livingstone.

Schlegel, A., & Barry, H., III. (1991). *Adolescence: An anthropological inquiry.* New York: Free Press.

Schliemann, A. D. (1992). Mathematical concepts in and out of school in Brazil: From developmental psychology to better teaching. *Newsletter of the International Society for the Study of Behavioral Development* (Serial No. 22, No. 2), 1–3.

Schmid, L. A. (2000). The influence of psychosocial factors on newborn birth outcomes. *Dissertation Abstracts International: Section B: The Sciences & Engineering, 60,* 3578.

Schmidt, K. L., Anderson, D. R., & Collins, P. A. (1999). Form and content: Looking at visual features of television. *Developmental Psychology, 35,* 1156–1167.

Schmuckler, M. A., & Li, N. S. (1998). Looming responses to obstacles and apertures: The role of accretion and deletion of background texture. *Psychological Science, 9,* 49–52.

Schmuckler, M. A., & Tsang-Tong, H.Y. (2000). The role of visual and body movement information in infant search. *Developmental Psychology, 36,* 499–510.

Schneider, B. H., Atkinson, L., & Tardif, C. (2001). Child–parent attachment and children's peer relations: A quantitative review. *Developmental Psychology, 37,* 85–100.

Schneider, M. L., Roughton, E. C., Koehler, A. J., & Lubach, G. R. (1999). Growth and development following prenatal stress exposure in primates: An examination of ontogenetic vulnerability. *Child Development, 70,* 263–274.

Schneider, W., & Bjorklund, D. F. (1998). Memory. In D. Kuhn & R. S. Siegler (Eds.), *Cognitive, language, and perceptual development,* Vol. 2. In B. Damon (General Editor), *Handbook of child psychology.* New York: Wiley.

Schneider, W., & Bjorklund, D. F. (2003). Memory and knowledge development. In J. Valsiner & K. Connolly (Eds.). *Handbook of developmental psychology.* London: Sage.

Schneider, W., & Pressley, M. (1997). *Memory development between 2 and 20* (2nd. ed.). Mahwah, NJ: Erlbaum.

Schneider, W., Bjorklund, D. F., & Maier-Brückner, W. (1996). The effects of expertise and IQ on children's memory: When knowledge is, and when it is not enough. *International Journal of Behavioral Development, 19,* 773–796.

Schneider, W., Gruber, H., Gold, A., & Opwis, K. (1993). Chess expertise and memory for chess positions in children and adults. *Journal of Experimental Child Psychology, 56,* 328–349.

Schneider, W., Körkel, J., & Weinert, F. E. (1989). Domain-specific knowledge and memory performance: A comparison of high- and low-aptitude children. *Journal of Educational Psychology, 81,* 306–312.

Schneider, W., Kuspert, P., Roth, E., & Visé, M. (1997). Short- and long-term effects of training in phonological awareness in kindergarten: Evidence from two German studies. *Journal of Experimental Child Psychology, 66,* 311–340.

Schoneberger, T. (2002). A departure from cognitivism: Implications of Chomsky's second revolution in linguistics. *Analysis of Verbal Behavior, 17,* 57–73.

Schor, C. M. (1985). Development of steropsis depends upon contrast sensitivity and spatial tuning. *Journal of the American Optometric Association, 56,* 628–635.

Schuetze, P., & Zeskind, P. S. (2001). Relation between maternal cigarette smoking during pregnancy and behavioral and physiological measures of autonomic regulation in neonates. *Infancy, 2,* 371–383.

Schulman, J. D., & Black, S. H. (1993). Genetics of some common inherited diseases. In R. G. Edwards (Ed.), *Preconception and preimplantation diagnosis of human genetic disease.* Cambridge, England: Cambridge University Press.

Schuster, D. T. (1990). Fulfillment of potential, life satisfaction, and competence: Comparing four cohorts of gifted women at midlife. *Journal of Educational Psychology, 82,* 471–478.

Schwanenflugel, P. J., Henderson, R. L., & Fabricius, W. V. (1998). Developing organization of mental verbs and theory of mind in middle childhood: Evidence from extension. *Developmental Psychology, 34,* 512–524.

Schwartz, D., Dodge, K. A., Pettit, G. S., & Bates, J. E. (1997). The early socialization of aggressive victims of bullying. *Child Development, 68,* 665–675.

Schwartz, D., Dodge, K.A., Pettit, G. S., & Bates, J. E., & the Conduct Problems Prevention Research Group (2000). Friendship as a moderating factor in the pathway between early harsh home environment and later victimization in the peer group. *Developmental Psychology, 36,* 646–662.

Schwebel, D. C., & Plumert, J. M. (1999). Longitudinal and concurrent relations among temperament, ability estimation, and accident proneness. *Child Development, 70,* 700–712.

Schwebel, D. C., Plumert, J. M., & Pick, H. L. (2000). Integrating basic and applied developmental research: A new model for the twenty-first century. *Child Development, 71,* 222–230.

Scott, J. P. (1992). Aggression: Functions and control in social systems. *Aggressive Behavior, 18,* 1–20.

Scott, W. A., Scott, R., & McCabe, M. (1991). Family relationships and children's personality: A cross-cultural, cross-source comparison. *British Journal of Social Psychology, 30,* 1–20.

Sears, R. R. (1963). Dependency motivation. In M. Jones (Ed.), *Nebraska Symposium on Motivation* (Vol. 11). Lincoln, NE: University of Nebraska Press.

Segal, N. L. (1997). Behavioral aspects of intergenerational cloning: What twins tell us. *Jurimetrics, 28,* 57–67.

Segal, U. A. (1991). Cultural variables in Asian Indian families. *Families in society: The Journal of Contemporary Human Services, 72,* 233–242.

Seidenfeld, M. E., Sosin, E., & Rickert, V. I. (2004). Nutrition and eating disorders in adolescents. *The Mount Sinai Journal of Medicine, 71,* 155–61.

Seidman, E., Allen, L., Aber, J. L., Mitchell, C., & Feinman, J. (1994). The impact of school transitions in early adolescence on the self-system and perceived social context of poor urban youth. *Child Development, 65,* 507–522.

Seifer, R., LaGasse, L. L., Lester, B., Bauer, C. R., Shankaran, S., Bada, H. S., Wright, L. L., Smeriglio, V. L., & Liu, J. (2004). Attachment status in children prenatally exposed to cocaine and other substances. *Child Development, 75,* 850–868.

Seifer, R., Schiller, M., Sameroff, A. J., Resnick, S., & Riordan, K. (1996). Attachment, maternal sensitivity, and infant temperament during the first year of life. *Developmental Psychology, 32,* 12–25.

Seitz, V., & Apfel, N. H. (1994a). Effects of a school for pregnant students on the incidence of low-birthweight deliveries. *Child Development, 65,* 666–676.

Seitz, V., & Apfel, N. H. (1994b). Parent-focused intervention: Diffusion effects on siblings. *Child Development, 65,* 677–683.

Seitz, V., Rosenbaum, L. K., & Apfel, N. H. (1985). Effects of family support intervention: A ten-year follow-up. *Child Development, 56,* 376–391.

Sellers, A. H., Burns, W. J., & Guyrke, J. (2002). Differences in young children's IQs on the Wechsler Preschool and Primary Scale of Intelligence–Revised as a function of stratification variables. *Applied Neuropsychology, 9,* 65–73.

Selman, R. L. (1976). Social-cognitive understanding: A guide to educational and clinical practice. In T. Lickona (Ed.), *Moral development and behavior: Theory, research, and social issues.* New York: Holt, Rinehart and Winston.

Selman, R. L. (1980). *The growth of interpersonal understanding.* Orlando, FL: Academic Press.

Seppa, N. (1997). Children's TV remains steeped in violence. *Monitor on Psychology, 28*(6), 36.

Serbin, L. A., Powlishta, K. K., & Gulko, J. (1993). The development of sex typing in middle childhood. *Monographs of the Society for Research in Child Development, 58*(2, Serial No. 232).

Servin, A., Nordenstrom, A., Larsson, A., & Bohlin, G. (2003). Prenatal androgens and gender-typed behavior: A study of girls with mild and severe forms of congenital adrenal hyperplasia. *Developmental Psychology, 39,* 440–450.

Shafer, H. H., & Kuller, J. A. (1996). Increased maternal age and prior anenploid conception. In J. A. Kuller, N. C. Cheschier, & R. C. Cefalo (Eds.), *Prenatal diagnosis and reproductive genetics* (pp. 23–28). St. Louis: Mosby.

Shaffer, D. R. (1973). *Children's responses to a hypothetical proposition.* Unpublished manuscript, Kent State University.

Shaffer, D. R. (1994). Do naturalistic conceptions of morality provide any [novel] answers? *Journal of Personality, 62,* 263–268.

Shaffer, D. R. (2005). *Social and personality development* (5th ed.). Belmont, CA: Wadsworth.

Shaffer, D. R., Pegalis, L. J., & Cornell, D. P. (1992). Gender and self-disclosure revisited: Personal and contextual variations in self-disclosure to same-sex acquaintances. *Journal of Social Psychology, 132,* 307–315.

Shakib, S. (2003). Female basketball participation. *American Behavioral Scientist, 46,* 1405–1423.

Shannon, R. L. (2004). Eating disorders in adolescent males. *Professional School Counseling, 8,* 98–101.

Shantz, C. U. (1983). Social cognition. In P. H. Mussen (Ed.), *Handbook of child psychology.* Vol. 3: *Cognitive development.* New York: Wiley.

Shaoying, G., & Danling, P., (2004). A review of the research on the critical period in second language acquisition. *Psychological Science (China), 27,* 711–714.

Sharma, A. R., McGue, M. K., & Benson, P. L. (1998). The psychological adjustment of United States adopted adolescents and their nonadopted siblings. *Child Development, 69,* 791–802.

Shatz, M. (1983). Communication. In P. H. Mussen (Ed.), *Handbook of child psychology* (Vol. 3). New York: Wiley.

Shatz, M. (1994). Theory of mind and the development of sociolinguistic intelligence in early childhood. In C. Lewis & P. Mitchell (Eds.), *Children's early understanding of the mind* (pp. 311–329). Hillsdale, NJ: Erlbaum.

Shatz, M., & Gelman, R. (1973). The development of communication skills: Modifications in the speech of young children as a function of listener. *Monographs of the Society for Research in Child Development, 38* (Serial No. 152).

Shaw, D. S., Gilliom, M., Ingoldsby, E. M., & Nagin, D. S. (2003). Trajectories leading to school-age conduct problem. *Developmental Psychology, 39,* 189–200.

Shaw, D. S., Winslow, E. E., & Flanagan, C. (1999). A prospective study of the effects of marital status and family relations on young children's adjustment among African American and European American families. *Child Development, 70,* 742–755.

Shearer, B. (2004). Multiple intelligences theory after 20 years. *Teachers College Record, 106,* 2–16.

Shears, J., & Robinson, J. (2005). Fathering attitudes and practices: Influences on children's development. *Child Care in Practice, 11,* 63–79.

Sheingold, K., & Tenney, Y. J. (1982). Memory for a salient childhood event. In U. Neisser (Ed.), *Memory observed: Remembering in natural contexts.* San Francisco: W. H. Freeman.

Sheldon, K. M., & Kasser, T. (2001). Getting older, getting better? Personal strivings and psychological maturity across the life span. *Developmental psychology, 37,* 491–501.

Sherif, M., Harvey, O. J., White, B. J., Hood, W. R., & Sherif, C. W. (1961). *Intergroup conflict and cooperation: The Robber's Cave experiment.* Norman: University of Oklahoma Press.

Shirley, M. M. (1933). *The first two years: A study of 25 babies. Vol. 1: Postural and locomotor development.* Minneapolis: University of Minnesota Press.

Shisana, O., & Simbayi, L. (2002). South African national HIV prevalence, behavioural risks and mass media household survey, HSRC. Cape Town: HSRC.

Short, R. J., & Talley, R. C. (1997). Rethinking psychology and the schools: Implications of recent national policy. *American Psychologist, 52,* 234–240.

Shulman, S., Elicker, J., & Sroufe, A. (1994). Stages of friendship growth in preadolescence as related to attachment history. *Journal of Social and Personal Relationships, 11,* 341–361.

Shultz, T. R. (2003). *Computational developmental psychology.* Boston, MA: Massachusetts Institute of Technology.

Shultz, T. R., & Robillard, J. (1980). The development of linguistic humor in children: Incongruity through rule violation. In P. E. McGhee & A. J. Chapman (Eds.), *Children's humor.* Chichester, England: Wiley.

Shure, M. B. (1989). Interpersonal competence training. In W. Damon (Ed.), *Child development today and tomorrow.* San Francisco: Jossey-Bass.

Shurkin, J. N. (1992). *Terman's kids. The groundbreaking study of how the gifted grow up.* Boston: Little, Brown.

Shwe, H. I., & Markman, E. M. (1997). Young children's appreciation of the mental impact of their communicative signals. *Developmental Psychology, 33,* 630–636.

Shweder, R. A. (1997, April). Varieties of moral intelligence: Autonomy community, divinity. In L. A. Jensen (Chair), *Shweder's ethics of autonomy, community, and divinity: Theory and research.* Symposium presented at the biennial meeting of the Society for Research in Child Development, Washington, DC.

Shweder, R. A., Mahapatra, M., & Miller, J. G. (1987). Culture and moral development. In J. Kagan & S. Lamb (Eds.), *The Emergence of morality in young children,* (pp. 1–83). Chicago: University of Chicago Press.

Shweder, R. A., Mahapatra, M., & Miller, J. G. (1990). Culture and moral development. In J. W. Stigler, R. A. Shweder, & G. Herdt (Eds.), *Cultural psychology. Essays on comparative human development.* Cambridge, UK: Cambridge University Press.

Siegal, M., & Cowen, J. (1984). Appraisals of intervention: The mother's versus the culprit's behavior as determinants of children's evaluations of discipline techniques. *Child Development, 55,* 1760–1766.

Siegal, M., & Peterson, C. C. (1998). Preschoolers' understanding of lies and innocent and negligent mistakes. *Developmental Psychology, 34,* 332–341.

Siegler, R. S. (1991). *Children's thinking* (2nd ed.). Englewood Cliffs, NJ: Prentice Hall.

Siegler, R. S. (1996a). A grand theory of development. In R. Case, Y. Okamoto & Associates, The role of central conceptual structures in the development of children's thought. *Monographs of the Society for Research in Child Development, 61* (1–2, Serial No. 246).

Siegler, R. S. (1996b). *Emerging minds: The process of change in children's thinking.* New York: Oxford University Press.

Siegler, R. S. (2000). The rebirth of learning. *Child Development, 71,* 26–35.

Siegler, R. S., & Alibali, M. W. (2005). *Children's Thinking* (4th ed.). Upper Saddle River, NJ: Prentice Hall.

Siegler, R. S., & Jenkins, E. A. (1989). *How children discover new strategies.* Hillsdale, NJ: Erlbaum.

Siegler, R. S., & Munakata, Y. (1993, Winter). Beyond the immaculate transition: Advances in the understanding of change. *Newsletter of the Society for Research in Child Development.*

Siegler, R. S., & Svetina, M. (2002). A microgenetic/cross-sectional study of matrix completion: Comparing short-term and long-term change. *Child Development, 73,* 793–809.

Sigelman, C. K., & Rider, E. (2003). *Life-span human development* (4th ed.). Belmont, CA: Wadsworth.

Sigelman, C. K., & Waitzman, K. A. (1991). The development of distributive justice orientations: Contextual influences on children's resource allocations. *Child Development, 62,* 1367–1378.

Sigelman, C. K., Carr, M. B., & Begley, N. L. (1986). Developmental changes in the influence of sex-role stereotypes on person perception. *Child Study Journal, 16,* 191–205.

Sigelman, C. K., Derenowski, E., Woods, T., Mukai, T., Alfred-Livo, L., Durazo, O., & Maddock, A. (1996). Mexican-American and Anglo-American children's responsiveness to a theory-centered AIDS education program. *Child Development, 67,* 253–266.

Sigelman, C. K., Miller, T. E., & Whitworth, L. A. (1986). The early development of stigmatizing reactions to physical differences. *Journal of Applied Developmental Psychology, 7,* 17–32.

Signorella, M. L., Bigler, R. S., & Liben, L. S. (1993). Developmental differences in children's gender schemata about others: A meta-analytic review. *Developmental Review, 13,* 147–183.

Signorella, M. L., Jamison, W., & Krupa, M. H. (1989). Predicting spatial performance from gender stereotyping in activity preferences and in self-concept. *Developmental Psychology, 25,* 89–95.

Signorielli, N. (1991). *A sourcebook on children and television.* Westport, CT: Greenwood Press.

Signorielli, N., & Kahlenberg, S. (2001). Television's world of work in the nineties. *Journal of Broadcasting & Electronic Media, 45,* 4–22.

Signorielli, N., & Lears, M. (1992). Children, television, and conceptions about chores: Attitudes and behaviors. *Sex Roles, 27,* 157–170.

Sim, L., & Zeman, J. (2004). Emotion awareness and identification skills in adolescent girls with bulimia nervosa. *Journal of Clinical Child & Adolescent Psychology, 33,* 760–771.

Simcock, G., & Hayne, H. (2002). Breaking the barrier? Children fail to translate their preverbal memories into language. *Psychological Science, 13,* 225–231.

Simmons, R. G., & Blyth, D. A. (1987). *Moving into adolescence: The impact of pubertal change in school context.* New York: Aldine de Gruyter.

Simmons, R. G., Burgeson, R., Carlton-Ford, S., & Blyth, D. A. (1987). The impact of cumulative change in early adolescence. *Child Development, 58,* 1220–1234.

Simon, T. J., Hespos, S. J., & Rochat, P. (1995). Do infants understand simple arithmetic? A replication of Wynn (1992). *Cognitive Development, 10,* 253–269.

Simonoff, E., Bolton, P., & Rutter, M. (1996). Mental retardation: Genetic findings, clinical implications, and research agenda. *Journal of Child Psychology and Psychiatry and Allied Disciplines, 37,* 259–280.

Simonton, D. K. (1994). Individual differences, developmental changes, and social context. *Behavioral and Brain Sciences, 17,* 552–553.

Simonton, D. K. (2000). Creativity: Cognitive, personal, developmental, and social aspects. *American Psychologist, 55,* 151–158.

Simpson, J. L. (1993). Genetic causes of spontaneous abortion. In C. Lin, M. S. Verp, & R. E. Sabbagha (Eds.), *The high-risk fetus: Pathophysiology, diagnosis, management.* New York: Springer-Verlag.

Simpson, K. R., & Creehan, P. A. (1996). *Perinatal nursing.* Philadelphia: Lippincott-Raven.

Singelis, T. M. (1994). The measurement of independent and interdependent self-construals. *Personality and Social Psychology Bulletin, 20,* 580–591.

Singer, D. G., & Singer, J. L. (1990). *The house of make-believe: Children's play and the developing imagination.* Cambridge, MA: Harvard University Press.

Singer, L. M., Brodzinsky, D. M., Ramsay, D., Steir, M., & Waters, E. (1985). Mother-infant attachments in adoptive families. *Child Development, 56,* 1543–1551.

Singer, L. T., Arendt, R., Minnes, S., Farkas, K., Salvator, A., Kirchner, H. L., & Kliegman, R. (2002). Cognitive and motor outcomes of cocaine-exposed infants. *JAMA: Journal of the American Medical Association, 287,* 1952–1961.

Singer, L. T., Arendt, R., Minnes, S., Salvator, A., Siegel, A. C., & Lewis, B. A. (2001). Developing language skills of cocaine-exposed infants. *Pediatrics, 10,* 1057–1065.

Singer, L. T., Minnes, S., Short, E., Arendt, R., Farkas, K., Lewis, B., Klein, N., Russ, S., Min, M. O. L., & Kirchner, H. L. (2004). Cognitive outcomes of preschool children with prenatal cocaine exposure. *JAMA: Journal of the American Medical Association, 29,* 2448–2456.

Singer, L. T., Salvator, A., Arendt, R., Minnes, S., Farkas, K., & Kliegman, R. (2002b). Effects of cocaine/polydrug exposure and maternal psychological distress on infant birth outcomes. *Neurotoxicology and Teratolgy, 24,* 127–136.

Singleton, C. (2001). An evaluation of Wordshark in the classroom. *British Journal of Educational Technology, 32,* 317–330.

Skinner, B. F. (1953). *Science and human behavior.* New York: Macmillan.

Skinner, B. F. (1957). *Verbal behavior.* East Norwalk, CT: Appleton-Century-Crofts.

Skodak, M., & Skeels, H. M. (1949). A final follow-up study of children in adoptive homes. *Journal of Genetic Psychology, 75,* 85–125.

Skouteris, H., McKenzie, B. E., & Day, R. H. (1992). Integration of sequential information for shape perception by infants: A developmental study. *Child Development, 63,* 1164–1176.

Slaby, R. G., & Crowley, C. G. (1977). Modification of cooperation and aggression through teacher attention to children's speech. *Journal of Experimental Child Psychology, 23,* 442–458.

Slaby, R. G., Roedell, W. C., Arezzo, D., & Hendrix, K. (1995). *Early violence prevention.* Washington, DC: National Association for the Education of Young Children.

Slade, A. (1987). A longitudinal study of maternal involvement and symbolic play during the toddler period. *Child Development, 58,* 367–375.

Slade, A., Belsky, J., Aber, J. L., & Phelps, J. L. (1999). Mothers' representation of their relationships with their toddlers: Links to adult attachment and observed mothering. *Developmental Psychology, 35,* 611–619.

Slater, A., Morrison, V., Somers, M., Mattock, A., Brown, E., & Taylor, D. (1990). Newborn and older infants' perception of partly occluded objects. *Infant Behavior and Development, 13,* 33–49.

Slaughter-Defoe, D. T., Nakagawa, K., Takanishi, R., & Johnson, D. J. (1990). Toward cultural/ecological perspectives on schooling and achievement in African- and Asian-American children. *Child Development, 61,* 363–383.

Sleek, S. (1994). Bilingualism enhances student growth. *Monitor of the American Psychological Association, 25*(4), 48–49.

Slobin, D. I. (1979). *Psycholinguistics.* Glenview, IL: Scott, Foresman.

Slobin, D. I. (1985). Crosslinguistic evidence for the language making capacity. In D. I. Slobin (Ed.), *The crosslinguistic study of language acquisition, Vol. 2: Theoretical issues.* Hillsdale, NJ: Erlbaum.

Smetana, J. G. (1981). Preschool children's conceptions of moral and social rules. *Child Development, 52,* 1333–1336.

Smetana, J. G. (1985). Preschool children's conceptions of transgressions: Effects of varying moral and conventional domain-related attributes. *Developmental Psychology, 21,* 18–29.

Smetana, J. G., & Bitz, B. (1996). Adolescents' conceptions of teachers' authority and their relations to rule violations at school. *Child Development, 67,* 1153–1172.

Smetana, J. G., & Daddis, C. (2002). Domain-specific antecedents of parental psychological control and monitoring: The role of parenting beliefs and practices. *Child Development, 73,* 563–580.

Smetana, J. G., & Gaines, C. (1999). Adolescent-parent conflict in middle-class African American families. *Child Development, 70,* 1447–1463.

Smetana, J. G., Schlagman, N., & Adams, P. W. (1993). Preschool children's judgments about hypothetical and actual transgressions. *Child Development, 64,* 202–214.

Smith, B. A., & Blass, E. M. (1996). Taste-mediated calming in premature, preterm, and full term infants. *Developmental Psychology, 32,* 1084–1089.

Smith, D. (2000). Women and minorities make gains in science and engineering education. *Monitor on Psychology, 31*(10), 32.

Smith, F. T. (1997). *Obesity in childhood.* New York: Basic Books.

Smith, J. B. (1997). Effects of eighth-grade transition programs on high school retention and experiences. *Journal of Educational Research, 90,* 144–152.

Smith, L. H., Guthrie, B. J., & Oakley, D. J. (2005). Studying adolescent male sexuality: Where are we? *Journal of Youth and Adolescence, 34,* 361–377.

Smith, P. K., & Connolly, K. J. (1980). *The ecology of preschool behavior.* New York: Cambridge University Press.

Smith, P. K., & Daglish, L. (1977). Sex differences in parent and infant behavior in the home. *Child Development, 48,* 1250–1254.

Smith, P. K., Cowie, H., Olafsson, R. F., & Liefooghe, A. P. D. (2000). Definitions of bullying: A comparison of terms used, and age and gender differences, in a fourteen-country international comparison. *Child Development, 73,* 1119–1133.

Smith, T. W. (1990). Academic achievement and teaching younger siblings. *Social Psychology Quarterly, 53,* 352–363.

Smoll, F. L., & Schutz, R. W. (1990). Quantifying gender differences in physical performance: A developmental perspective. *Developmental Psychology, 26,* 360–369.

Snarey, J. R. (1985). Cross-cultural universality of social-moral development: A critical review of Kohlbergian research. *Psychological Bulletin, 97,* 202–232.

Snarey, J. R., & Keljo, K. (1991). In a gemeinschaft voice: The cross-cultural expansion of moral development theory. In W. M. Kurtines & J. L. Gewirtz (Eds.), *Handbook of moral behavior and development* (Vol. 1) (pp. 395–424). Hillsdale, NJ: Erlbaum.

Snidman, N., Kagan, J., Riordan, L., & Shannon, D. C. (1995). Cardiac function and behavioral reactivity. *Psychophysiology, 32,* 199–207.

Snow, C. E., & Ferguson, C. A. (Eds.). (1977). *Talking to children.* Cambridge: Cambridge University Press.

Snow, M. E., Jacklin, C. N., & Maccoby, E. E. (1983). Sex-of-child differences in father-child interaction at one year of age. *Child Development, 54,* 227–232.

Snyder, H. N. (2000). *Special analyses of FBI serious violent crimes data.* Pittsburgh, PA: National Center for Juvenile Justice.

Socha, T. J., & Socha, D, M. (1994). Children's task-group communication. In L. R. Frey (Ed.), *Group communication in context: Studies of natural groups.* Hillsdale, NJ: Erlbaum.

Sodian, B., Taylor, C., Harris, P. L., & Perner, J. (1991). Early deception and the child's theory of mind: False trails and genuine markers. *Child Development, 62,* 468–483.

Soken, N. H., & Pick, A. D. (1999). Infants' perception of dynamic affective expressions: Do infants distinguish specific expressions? *Child Development, 70,* 1275–1282.

Sokolov, J. L. (1993). A local contingency analysis of the fine-tuning hypothesis. *Developmental Psychology, 29,* 1008–1023.

Somsen, R. J. M., van't Klooster, B. J., van der Molen, M. W., van Leeuwen, H. M. P., & Licht, R. (1997). Growth spurts in brain maturation during middle childhood as indexed by EEG power spectra. *Biological Psychology, 44,* 187–209.

Sondergaard, C., Henriksen, T. B., Obel, C., & Wisborg, K. (2002). Smoking during pregnancy and infantile colic. *Journal of the American Academy of Child & Adolescent Psychiatry, 41,* 147.

Sonnenschein, S. (1986). Development of referential communication skills: How familiarity with a listener affects a speaker's production of redundant messages. *Developmental Psychology, 22,* 549–555.

Sonnenschein, S. (1988). The development of referential communication: Speaking to different listeners. *Child Development, 59,* 694–702.

South, S. J., & Baumer, E. P. (2000). Deciphering community and race effects on adolescent premarital childbearing. *Social Forces, 78,* 1379–1408.

Souza, I., Pinheiro, M. A., Denardin, D., Mattos, P., & Rohde, L. A. (2004). Attention-Deficit/Hyperactivity Disorder and comorbidity in Brazil: Comparisons between two referred samples. *European Child & Adolescent Psychiatry,13,* 243–248.

Sowell, E. R., Thompson, P. M., Holmes, C. J., Jernigan, T. L., & Toga, A. W. (1999). In vivo evidence for post-adolescent brain maturation in frontal and striatal regions. *Nature Neuroscience, 2,* 859–862.

Spearman, C. (1927). *The abilities of man.* New York: Macmillan.

Speicher, B. (1994). Family patterns of moral judgment during adolescence and early adulthood. *Developmental Psychology, 30,* 624–632.

Spelke, E. S. (1991). Physical knowledge in infancy: Reflections on Piaget's theory. In S. Carey & R. Gelman (Eds.), *Epigenesis of mind: Essays in biology and knowledge.* Hillsdale, NJ: Erlbaum.

Spelke, E. S., & Newcomb, E. L. (1998). Nativism, empiricism, and the development of knowledge. In R. Learner (Ed.), *Theories of development, Vol. 1,* of W. Damon (Gen. Ed.), *Handbook of child psychology,* New York: Wiley.

Spelke, E. S., Breinlinger, K., Macomber, J., & Jacobson, K. (1992). Origins of knowledge. *Psychological Review, 99,* 605–632.

Speltz, M. L., Endriga, M. C., Fisher, P. A., & Mason, C. A. (1997). Early predictors of attachment in infants with cleft lip/or palate. *Child Development, 68,* 12–25.

Spence, J. T. (1993). Gender-related traits and gender ideology: Evidence for a multifactorial theory. *Journal of Personality and Social Psychology, 64,* 624–635.

Spence, J. T., & Hall, S. K. (1996). Children's gender-related self-perceptions, activity preferences, and occupational stereotypes: A test of three models of gender constructs. *Sex Roles, 35,* 659–691.

Spence, J. T., & Helmreich, R. L. (1978). *Masculinity and femininity: Their psychological dimensions, correlates, and antecedents.* Austin, TX: University of Texas Press.

Spence, M. J. (1996). Young infants' long-term auditory memory: Evidence for changes in preference as a function of delay. *Developmental Psychobiology, 29,* 685–695.

Spencer, J. P., & Thelen, E. (2000). Spatially specific changes in infants' muscle coactivity as they learn to reach. *Infancy, 1,* 275–302.

Spencer, J. P., Vereijken, B., Diedrich, F. J., & Thelen, E. (2000). Posture and the emergence of manual skills. *Developmental Science, 3,* 216–232.

Spencer, J., Zimet, G., Aslsma, M., & Orr, D. (2002). Self-esteem as a predictor of initiation of coitus in early adolescents. *Pediatrics, 109,* 581–584.

Spencer, M. B., & Markstrom-Adams, C. (1990). Identity processes among racial and ethnic minority children in America. *Child Development, 61,* 290–310.

Spencer, P. E. (1996). The association between language and symbolic play at two years: Evidence from deaf toddlers. *Child Development, 67,* 867–876.

Spieker, S. J., Larson, N. C., Lewis, S. M., Keller, T. E., & Gilchrist, L. (1999). Developmental trajectories of disruptive behavior problems in preschool children of adolescent mothers. *Child Development, 70,* 443–458.

Spiker, D., Ferguson, J., & Brooks-Gunn, J. (1993). Enhancing maternal interactive behavior and child social competence in low birthweight, premature infants. *Child Development, 64,* 754–768.

Spitz, R. A. (1945). Hospitalism: An inquiry into the genesis of psychiatric conditions in early childhood. In A. Freud (Ed.), *The psychoanalytic study of the child* (Vol. 1). New York: International Universities Press.

Spreen, O., Risser, A. H., & Edgell, D. (1995). *Developmental neuropsychology.* New York: Oxford University Press.

Sprigle, J. E., & Schaefer, L. (1985). Longitudinal evaluation of the effects of two compensatory preschool programs on fourth- through sixth-grade students. *Developmental Psychology, 21,* 702–708.

Springen K. (2001). The state of the art of pregnancy. In K. L. Freiberg (Ed.), *Human development, 01/02* (29th ed.) (pp. 18–20). Guildford, CT: McGraw-Hill/Duskin.

Sroufe, L. A. (1977). Wariness of strangers and the study of infant development. *Child Development, 48,* 1184–1199.

Sroufe, L. A. (1985). Attachment classification from the perspective of infant–caregiver relationships and infant temperament. *Child Development, 56,* 1–14.

Sroufe, L. A. (1997). Psychopathology as an outcome of development. *Development and Psychopathology, 9,* 251–268.

Sroufe, L. A., Bennett, C., Englund, M., Urban, J., & Shulman, S. (1993). The significance of gender boundaries in preadolescence: Contemporary correlates and antecedents of boundary violation and maintenance. *Child Development, 64,* 455–466.

Sroufe, L. A., Egeland, B., & Kreutzer, T. (1990). The fate of early experience following developmental change: Longitudinal approaches to individual adaptation in childhood. *Child Development, 61,* 1363–1373.

Sroufe, L. A., Waters, E., & Matas, L. (1974). Contextual determinants of infant affectional response. In M. Lewis & L. A. Rosenblum (Eds.), *The origins of fear.* New York: Wiley.

St. James-Roberts, I., & Plewis, I. (1996). Individual differences, daily fluctuations, and developmental changes in amounts of infant waking, fussing, crying, feeding, and sleeping. *Child Development, 67,* 2527–2540.

St. Peters, M., Fitch, M., Huston, A. C., Wright. J. C., & Eakins, D. J. (1991). Television and families: What do young children watch with their parents? *Child Development, 62,* 1409–1423.

Stacey, J., & Biblarz, T. (2001). (How) Does the sexual orientation of parents matter? *American Sociological Review, 6,* 159–183.

Stack, D. M., & Muir, D. W. (1992). Adult tactile stimulation during face-to-face interactions modulates five-month-olds' affect and attention. *Child Development, 63,* 1509–1525.

Staffieri, J. R. (1967). A study of social stereotype of body image in children. *Journal of Personality and Social Psychology, 7,* 101–104.

Stams, G. J. M., Juffer, F., & van Ijzendoorn, M. H. (2002). Maternal sensitivity, infant attachment, and temperament in early childhood predict adjustment in middle childhood: The case of adopted children and their biologically unrelated parents. *Developmental Psychology, 38,* 806–821.

Stanford, J. N., & McCabe, M. (2005). Evaluation of a body image prevention programme for adolescent boys. *European Eating Disorders Review, 13,* 360–370.

Stanger, C., Achenbach, T. M., & Verhulst, F. C. (1997). Accelerated longitudinal comparisons of aggressive versus delinquent syndromes. *Development and Psychopathology, 9,* 43–58.

Staples, G. B. (2000, November 15). Television in black and white: Report on the Children Now survey on ethnic representation in television programming. *Atlanta Constitution,* pp. D1–2.

Stattin, H., & Magnusson, D. (1990). *Paths through life: Vol. 2. Pubertal maturation in female development.* Hillsdale, NJ: Erlbaum.

Steele, B. F., & Pollack, C. B. (1974). A psychiatric study of parents who abuse infants and small children. In R. E. Helfer & C. H. Kempe (Eds.), *The battered child.* Chicago: University of Chicago Press.

Steele, C. M. (1997). A threat in the air. How stereotypes shape intellectual identity and performance. *American Psychologist, 52,* 613–629.

Steele, C. M., & Aronson, J. (1995). Stereotype threat and the intellectual test performance of African Americans. *Journal of Personality and Social Psychology, 69,* 797–811.

Steele, H., Steele, M., & Fonagy, P. (1996). Associations among attachment classifications of mothers, fathers, and their infants. *Child Development, 67,* 541–555.

Stein, J. H., & Reiser, L. W. (1994). A study of white middle-class adolescent boys' responses to "semenarche" (the first ejaculation). *Journal of Youth and Adolescence, 23,* 373–384.

Steinberg, L. (1981). Transformations in family relations at puberty. *Developmental Psychology, 17,* 833–840.

Steinberg, L. (1988). Reciprocal relation between parent-child distance and puberal maturation. *Developmental Psychology, 24,* 122–128.

Steinberg, L. (2002). *Adolescence* (6th ed.). Boston: McGraw-Hill.

Steinberg, L., Dornbusch, S. M., & Brown, B. B. (1992). Ethnic differences in adolescent achievement: An ecological perspective. *American Psychologist, 47,* 723–729.

Steinberg, L., Elmen, J. D., & Mounts, N. S. (1989). Authoritative parenting, psychosocial maturity, and academic success among adolescents. *Child Development, 60,* 1424–1436.

Steinberg, L., Lamborn, S. D., Darling, N., Mounts, N. S., & Dornbusch, S. M. (1994). Over-time changes in adjustment and competence among adolescents from authoritative, authoritarian, indulgent, and neglectful families. *Child Development, 65,* 754–770.

Steinberg, S. (1996). Childbearing research: A transcultural review. *Social Science and Medicine, 43,* 1765–1784.

Steiner, J. E. (1979). Human facial expressions in response to taste and smell stimulation. In H. W. Reese & L. P. Lipsitt (Eds.), *Advances in child development and behavior* (Vol. 13). Orlando, FL: Academic Press.

Stern, D. (1977). *The first relationship: Infant and mother.* Cambridge, MA: Harvard University Press.

Stern, D. N. (1995). Self/other differentiation in the domain of intimate socio-affective interaction: Some considerations. In P. Rochat (Ed.), *The self in infancy: Theory and research* (pp. 419–429). Amsterdam: North Holland-Elsevier.

Stern, W. (1912). *Die psychologischen methoden der intelligenzprufung.* Liepzig: Barth.

Sternberg, R. J. (1985). *Beyond IQ. A triarchic theory of human intelligence.* Cambridge: Cambridge University Press.

Sternberg, R. J. (1991). Theory-based testing of intellectual abilities: Rationale for the triarchic abilities test. In H.A. H. Rowe (Ed.), *Intelligence: Reconceptualization and measurement.* Hillsdale, NJ: Erlbaum.

Sternberg, R. J. (1995). Investing in creativity: Many happy returns. *Educational Leadership, 53,* 80–84.

Sternberg, R. J. (1997). The concept of intelligence and its role in lifelong learning and success. *American Psychologist, 52,* 1030–1037.

Sternberg, R. J. (2001). What is the common thread of creativity?: Its dialectical relation to intelligence and wisdom. *American Psychologist, 56*(4), 360–362.

Sternberg, R. J. (2003). Our research program validating the triarchic theory of successful intelligence: Reply to Gottfredson. *Intelligence, 31,* 399–414.

Sternberg, R. J., & Grigorenko, E. L. (2001a). All testing is dynamic testing. *Issues in Education, 7,* 138–371.

Sternberg, R. J., & Grigorenko, E. L. (2001b). Guilford's structure of intellect model and model of creativity: Contributions and limitations. *Creativity Research Journal, 13,* 309–316.

Sternberg, R. J., & Lubart, T. I. (1996). Investing in creativity. *American Psychologist, 51,* 677–688.

Sternberg, R. J., Wagner, R. K., Williams, W. M., & Horvath, J. A. (1995). Testing common sense. *American Psychologist, 50,* 912–927.

Stetsenko, A., Little, T. D., Gordeeva, T., Grasshof, M., & Oettingen, G. (2000). Gender effects in children's beliefs about school performance: A cross-cultural study. *Child Development, 71,* 517–527.

Stevens, C. P. (2000). Relationships between perinatal hypoxic-ischemic risk and motor skill performance at early school age. *Dissertation Abstracts International: Section B: The Sciences & Engineering, 60,* 4254.

Stevenson, H. W., & Lee, S. Y. (1990). Contents of achievement: A study of American, Chinese, and Japanese children. *Monographs of the Society for Research in Child Development, 55* (1–2, Serial No. 221).

Stevenson, H. W., Chen, C., & Lee, S. (1993). Mathematics achievement of Chinese, Japanese, and American children: Ten years later. *Science, 259,* 53–58.

Stevenson, H. W., Chen, C., & Uttal, D. H. (1990). Beliefs and achievement: A study of Black, White, and Hispanic children. *Child Development, 61,* 508–523.

Stevenson, H. W., Lee, S. Y., & Stigler, J. W. (1986). Mathematics achievement of Chinese, Japanese, and American children. *Science, 231,* 693–699.

Stevenson, H. W., Stigler, J. W., Lee, S. Y., Lucker, G. W., Litamura, S., & Hsu, C. (1985). Cognitive performance and academic achievement of Japanese, Chinese, and American children. *Child Development, 56,* 718–734.

Stewart, J. M. (2004). The fundamental difference between child and adult language acquisition: A longitudinal, naturalistic study of parameter resetting in Swedish interlanguage. *Dissertation Abstracts International Section A: Humanities and Social Sciences, 65,* 491.

Stewart, R. B. (1983). Sibling attachment relationships: Child–infant interactions in the strange situation. *Developmental Psychology, 19,* 192–199.

Stewart, R. B., & Marvin, R. S. (1984). Sibling relations: The role of conceptual perspective-taking in the ontogeny of sibling caregiving. *Child Development, 55,* 1322–1332.

Stice, E. (2001). A prospective test of the dual-pathway model of bulimic pathology: Mediating effects of dieting and negative affect. *Journal of Abnormal Psychology, 110,* 124–135.

Stice, E. (2002). Risk and maintenance factors for eating pathology: A meta-analytic review. *Psychological Bulletin, 128,* 825–849.

Stice, E., & Bearman, S. K. (2001). Body-image and eating disturbances prospectively predict increases in depressive symptoms in adolescent girls: A growth curve analysis. *Developmental Psychology, 73,* 597–607.

Stice, E., & Whitenton, K. (2002). Risk factors for body dissatisfaction in adolescent girls: A longitudinal investigation. *Developmental Psychology, 38,* 669–679.

Stice, E., Presnell, K., & Bearman, S. K. (2001). Relation of early menarche to depression, eating disorders, substance abuse, and comorbid psychopathology among adolescent girls. *Developmental Psychology, 37,* 608–619.

Stigler, J. W., Lee, S. Y., & Stevenson, H. W. (1987). Mathematics class-rooms in Japan, Taiwan, and the United States. *Child Development, 58,* 1272–1285.

Stiles, J. (2000). Neural plasticity and cognitive development. *Developmental Neuropsychology, 18,* 237–273.

Stipek, D. (2002). At what age should children enter kindergarten? A question for policy makers and parents. *Society for Research in Child Development Social Policy Report, 16,* Number 2.

Stipek, D., & Mac Iver, D. (1989). Developmental change in children's assessment of intellectual competence. *Child Development, 60,* 521–538.

Stipek, D., Feiler, R., Daniels, D., & Milbern, S. (1995). Effects of different instructional approaches on young children's achievement and motivation. *Child Development, 66,* 209–233.

Stipek, D., Gralinski, H., & Kopp, C. (1990). Self-concept development in the toddler years. *Developmental Psychology, 26,* 972–977.

Stipek, D., Recchia, S., & McClintic, S. (1992). Self-evaluation in young children. *Monographs of the Society for Research in Child Development, 57* (1, Serial No. 226).

Stipek, D. J., Recchia, S., & McClintic, S. (1992). Self-evaluation in young children. *Monographs of the Society for Research in Child Development, 57* (1, Serial No. 226).

Stirnimann, F., & Stirniman, W. (1940). The footgrasp reflex of the newborn and nursing; its diagnostic significance. *Annales Paediatrici, 154,* 249–264.

Stoddart, T., & Turiel, E. (1985). Children's concepts of cross-gender activities. *Child Development, 59,* 793–814.

Stoelhorst, G., Rijken, M., Martens, S. E., van Zwieten, P., Feenstra, Zwinderman, A., Wit, J.-M., & Veen, S. (2003). Developmental outcome at 18 and 24 months of age in very preterm children: A cohort study from 1996 to 1997. *Early Human Development, 72,* 83–96.

Stoffman, N., Schwartz, B., Austin, S. B., Grace, E., & Gordon, C. M. (2005). Influence of bone density results on adolescents with anorexia nervosa. *International Journal of Eating Disorders, 37,* 250–255.

Stoolmiller, M. (2001). Synergistic interaction of child manageability problems and parental-discipline tactics in predicting future growth in externalizing behavior for boys. *Developmental Psychology, 37,* 814–825.

Stormshak, E. A., Bellanti, C. J., Bierman, K. L., and the Conduct Problems Prevention Research Group (1996). The quality of sibling relationships and the development of social competence and behavioral control in aggressive children. *Developmental Psychology, 32,* 79–89.

Strachan, T., & Read, A. P. (1996). *Human molecular genetics.* New York: Wiley.

Stranger, C., Achenbach, T. M., & Verhulst, F. C. (1997). Accelerated longitudinal comparisons of aggressive versus delinquent syndromes. *Development and Psychopathology, 9,* 43–58.

Strassberg, Z. (1995). Social information processing in compliance situations by mothers of behavior-problem boys. *Child Development, 66,* 376–389.

Stratton, K., Howe, C., & Battaglia, F. (1996). *Fetal alcohol syndrome: Diagnosis, epidemiology, prevention, and treatment.* Washington, DC: National Academy Press.

Strauss, M. S., & Curtis, L. E. (1981). Infant perception of numerosity. *Child Development, 52,* 1146–1152.

Streissguth, A. P., Bookstein, F. L., Sampson, P. D., & Barr, H. M. (1993). *The enduring effects of prenatal alcohol exposure on child development.* Ann Arbor, MI: University of Michigan Press.

Streitmatter, J. (1993). Gender differences in identity development: An examination of longitudinal data. *Adolescence, 28,* 55–66.

Streri, A., & Spelke, E. S. (1988). Haptic perception of objects in infancy. *Cognitive Psychology, 20,* 1–23.

Stricker, J. M., Miltenberger, R. G., Garlinghouse, M. A., Deaver, C. M., & Anderson, C. A. (2001). Evaluation of an awareness enhancement device for the treatment of thumb sucking in children. *Journal of Applied Behavior Analysis, 34,* 77–80.

Strigini, P., Sansone, R., Carobbi, S., & Pierluigi, M. (1990). Radiation and Down's syndrome. *Nature, 347,* 717.

Strough, J., & Berg, C. A. (2000). Goals as a mediator of high-affiliation dyadic conversations. *Developmental Psychology, 36,* 117–125.

Stumpf, H., & Stanley, J. C. (1996). Gender-related differences on the College Board's Advanced Placement and Achievement Tests, 1982–1992. *Journal of Educational Psychology, 88,* 353–364.

Stunkard, A. J., Harris, J. R., Pedersen, N., & McClearn, G. E. (1990). The body-mass index of twins who have been reared apart. *New England Journal of Medicine, 322,* 1483–1487.

Stuss, D. T. (1992). Biological and psychological development of executive functions. *Brain & Cognition, 20,* 8–23.

Subotnik, R. F., Karp, D. E., & Morgan, E. R. (1989). High IQ children at midlife: An investigation into the generalizability of Terman's genetic studies of genius. *Roeper Review, 11,* 139–144.

Subrahmanyam, K., Kraut, K. E., Greenfield, P. M., & Gross, E. F. (2000). The impact of home computer use on children's activities and development. *The Future of Children, 10,* 123–144.

Suddendorf, T., & Whiten, A. (2001). Mental evolution and development: Evidence for secondary representation in children, great apes, and other animals. *Psychological Bulletin, 127,* 629–650.

Sudhalter, V., & Braine, M. D. S. (1985). How does comprehension of passives develop? A comparison of actional and experiential verbs. *Journal of Child Language, 12,* 455–470.

Sue, S., & Okazaki, S. (1990). Asian-American educational achievements: A phenomenon in search of explanation. *American Psychologist, 45,* 913–920.

Sullivan, H. S. (1953). *The interpersonal theory of psychiatry.* New York: Norton.

Sullivan, M. W., & Lewis, M. (2003). Contextual determinants of anger and other negative expressions in young infants. *Developmental Psychology, 39,* 693–705.

Sullivan, M. W., Lewis, M., & Alessandri, S. M. (1992). Cross-age stability in emotional expressions during learning and extinction. *Developmental Psychology, 28,* 58–63.

Super, C. M., Herrera, M. G., & Mora, J. O. (1990). Long-term effects of food supplementation and psychosocial intervention on the physical growth of Columbian infants at risk of malnutrition. *Child Development, 61,* 29–49.

Susser, M., & Stein, Z. (1994). Timing in prenatal nutrition: A reprise of the Dutch Famine Study. *Nutrition Reviews, 52,* 84–94.

Suzuki, L. A., & Valencia, R. R. (1997). Race-ethnicity and measured intelligence: Educational implications. *American Psychologist, 52,* 1103–1114.

Swarr, A. E., & Richards, M. H. (1996). Longitudinal effects of adolescent girls' pubertal development, perceptions of pubertal timing, and parental relations on eating problems. *Developmental Psychology, 32,* 636–646.

Swenne, I. (2004). Weight requirements for return of menstruations in teenage girls with eating disorders, weight loss and secondary amenorrhoea. *Acta Paediatrica, 93,* 1449–1455.

Szkrybalo, J., & Ruble, D. N. (1999). "God made me a girl": Sex-category constancy judgments and explanations revisited. *Developmental Psychology, 35,* 392–402.

Tamis-LeMonda, C. S., & Bornstein, M. H. (1989). Habituation and maternal encouragement of attention as predictors of toddler language, play, and representational competence. *Child Development, 60,* 738–751.

Tamis-LeMonda, C. S., Bornstein, M. H., & Baumwell, L. (2001). Maternal responsiveness and children's achievement of language milestones. *Child Development, 72,* 748–767.

Tangney, J. P., & Dearing, R. (2002). *Shame and guilt.* New York: Guilford Press.

Tanner, J. M. (1978). *Education and physical growth* (2nd ed.). London: Hodder and Stroughton.

Tanner, J. M. (1990). *Foetus into man* (2nd ed.). Cambridge, MA: Harvard University Press.

Tanner, J. M. (1998). Sequence, tempo, and individual variation in growth and development of boys and girls aged twelve to sixteen. In R. E. Muuss & H. D. Porton (Eds.), *Adolescent behavior and society: A book of readings* (pp. 34–46). New York: McGraw-Hill.

Tardif, T., Gelman, S. A., & Xu, F. (1999). Putting the "noun bias" in context: A comparison of English and Mandarin. *Child Development, 70,* 620–635.

Taylor, H. G., Klein, N., Minich, N. M., & Hack, M. (2000). Middle-school-age outcomes in children with very low birth weight. *Child Development, 71,* 1495–1511.

Taylor, L. C., Clayton, J. D., & Rowley, S. J. (2004). Academic socialization: Understanding parental influences on children's school-related development in the early years. *Review of General Psychology, 8,* 163–178.

Taylor, M. G. (1996). The development of children's beliefs about social and biological aspects of gender differences. *Child Development, 67,* 1555–1571.

Taylor, M., & Carlson, S. M. (1997). The relation between individual differences in fantasy and theory of mind. *Child Development, 68,* 436–455.

Taylor, M., & Gelman, S. A. (1988). Adjectives and nouns: Children's strategies for learning new words. *Child Development, 59,* 411–419.

Taylor, M., & Gelman, S. A. (1989). Incorporating new words into the lexicon: Preliminary evidence for language hierarchies in two-year-old children. *Child Development, 60,* 625–636.

Taylor, R. D. (1996). Adolescents' perceptions of kinship support and family management practices: Association with adolescent adjustment in African-American families. *Developmental Psychology, 32,* 687–695.

Taylor, R. D., & Lopez, E. I. (2005a). Family management practice, school achievement, and problem behavior in African American adolescents: Mediating processes. *Journal of Applied Developmental Psychology, 26,* 39–49.

Taylor, R. D., & Lopez, E. I. (2005b). Perceived school experiences, school engagement, and achievement among African-American adolescents. *Society for Research in Child Development,* Atlanta, GA.

Taylor, R. D., & Roberts, D. (1995). Kinship support and maternal and adolescent well-being in economically disadvantaged African-American families. *Child Development, 66,* 1585–1597.

Taylor, R. L. (2000). Diversity within African American families. In D. H. Demo, K. R. Allen, & M. A. Fine (Eds.), *Handbook of family diversity.* New York: Oxford University Press.

Teasdale, T. W., & Owen, D. R. (2005). A long-term rise and recent decline in intelligence test performance: The Flynn Effect in reverse. *Personality & Individual Differences, 39,* 837–843.

Teele, D. W., Klein, J. O., Chase, C., et al., and the Greater Boston Otitis Media Study Group (1990). Otitis media in infancy and intellectual ability, school achievement, speech, and language at age 7 years. *Journal of Infectious Disease, 162,* 685–694.

Teeven, R. C., & McGhee, P. E. (1972). Childhood development of fear of failure motivation. *Journal of Personality and Social Psychology, 21,* 345–348.

Teichman, Y. (2001). The development of Israeli children's images of Jews and Arabs and their expression in human figure drawings. *Developmental Psychology, 37,* 749–761.

Tennenbaum, H. R., & Leaper, C. (2002). Are parents' gender schemas related to their children's gender-related cognitions. *Developmental Psychology, 38,* 615–630.

Terman, L. M. (1954). The discovery and encouragement of exceptional talent. *American Psychologist, 9,* 221–238.

Terman, L. M., & Oden, M. H. (1959). *The gifted group at mid-life.* Stanford, CA: Stanford University Press.

Terry, R., & Coie, J. D. (1991). A comparison of methods for defining sociometric status among children. *Developmental Psychology, 27,* 867–880.

Teti, D. M., & Ablard, K. E. (1989). Security of attachment and infant-sibling relationships: A laboratory study. *Child Development, 60,* 1519–1528.

Teti, D. M., & Gelfand, D. M., Messinger, D. S., & Isabella, R. (1995). Maternal depression and the quality of early attachment: An examination of infants, preschoolers, and their mothers. *Developmental Psychology, 31,* 364–376.

Teti, D. M., Sakin, J. W., Kucera, E., Corns, K. M., & Das Eiden, R. (1996). And baby makes four: Predictors of attachment security among preschool-age first-borns during the transition to siblinghood. *Child Development, 67,* 579–596.

Tharp, R. G. (1989). Psychocultural variables and constants: Effects on teaching and learning in schools. *American Psychologist, 44,* 349–359.

Thatcher, R. W. (1992). Cyclic cortical reorganization during early childhood. *Brain and Cognition, 20,* 24–50.

Thatcher, R. W. (1994). Cyclic cortical reorganization: Origins of human cognitive development. In: G. Dawson & K. Fischer (Eds.), *Human behavior and the developing brain* (pp. 232–266). New York: The Guildford Press.

Thatcher, R. W., Walker, R., & Giudice, S. (1987). Human cerebral hemispheres develop at different rates and ages. *Science, 236,* 1110–1113.

Thelen, E., & Fisher, D. M. (1982). Newborn stepping: An explanation for a disappearing reflex. *Developmental Psychology, 18,* 760–775.

Thelen, E. (1984). Learning to walk: Ecological demands and phylogenetic constraints. In L. P. Lipsitt & C. Rovee-Collier (Eds.), *Advances in infancy research* (Vol. 3). Norwood, NJ: Ablex.

Thelen, E. (1986). Treadmill-elicited stepping in seven-month-old infants. *Child Development, 57,* 1498–1506.

Thelen, E. (1994). Three-month-old infants can learn task-specific patterns of interlimb coordination. *Psychological Science, 5,* 280–285.

Thelen, E. (1995). Motor development: A new synthesis. *American Psychologist, 50,* 79–95.

Thelen, E., & Smith, L. B. (1998). Dynamic systems theories. In R. M. Lerner (Vol. Ed.), *Theoretical models of human development,* Vol. 1. In W. Damon (Gen. Ed.), *Handbook of child psychology.* New York: Wiley.

Thelen, E., Corbetta, D., Kamm, K., Spencer, J. P., Schneider, K., & Zernicke, R. F. (1993). The transition to reaching: Mapping intention and intrinsic dynamics. *Child Development, 64,* 1058–1098.

Thelen, E., Fisher, D. M., & Ridley-Johnson, R. (2002). The relationship between physical growth and a newborn reflex. *Infant Behavior and Development, 23,* 72–85.

Therion, J. M., Worwa, C. T., Mattia, F. R., & deRegnier, O. (2004). Altered pathways for auditory discrimination and recognition memory in preterm infants. *Developmental Medicine & Child Neurology, 46,* 816–814.

Thiessen, E. D., Hill, E. A., & Saffran, J. R. (2005). Infant-directed speech facilitates word segmentation. *Infancy, 7,* 53–71.

Thoma, S. J., & Rest, J. R. (1999). The relationship between moral decision making and patterns of consolidation and transition in moral judgment development. *Developmental Psychology, 35,* 323–334.

Thoman, E. B. (1990). Sleeping and waking states in infants: A functional perspective. *Neuroscience and Behavioral Review, 14,* 93–107.

Thoman, E. B., & Ingersoll, E. W. (1993). Learning in premature infants. *Developmental Psychology, 28,* 692–700.

Thoman, E. B., & Whitney, M. P. (1989). Sleep states of infants monitored in the home: Individual differences, developmental trends, and origins of diurnal cyclicity. *Infant Behavior and Development, 12,* 59–75.

Thomas, A. (2000). Textual constructions of children's online identities. *CyberPsychology & Behavior, 3*(4), 665–672.

Thomas, A., & Chess, S. (1977). *Temperament and development.* New York: Brunner/Mazel.

Thomas, A., & Chess, S. (1986). The New York longitudinal study: From infancy to early adult life. In R. Plomin & J. Dunn (Eds.). *The study of temperament: Changes, continuities, and challenges.* Hillsdale, NJ: Erlbaum.

Thomas. A., Chess, S., & Birch, H. G. (1970). The origin of personality. *Scientific American, 223,* 102–109.

Thomas, D., Campos, J. J., Shucard, D. W., Ramsay, D. S., & Shucard, J. (1981). Semantic comprehension in infancy: a signal detection approach. *Child Development, 52,* 798–803.

Thomas, J. R., & French, K. E. (1985). Gender differences across age in motor performance: A meta-analysis. *Psychological Bulletin, 98,* 260–282.

Thomas, M. H., Horton, R. W., Lippincott, E. C., & Drabman, R. S. (1977). Desensitization to portrayals of real-life aggression as a function of exposure to television violence. *Journal of Personality and Social Psychology, 35,* 450–458.

Thompson, D. E., & Russell, J. (2004). The ghost condition: Imitation vs. emulation in young children's observational learning. *Developmental Psychology, 40,* 882–889.

Thompson, J. K., & Stice, E. (2001). Thin-ideal internalization: Mounting evidence for a new risk factor for body-image disturbance and eating pathology. *Current Directions in Psychological Science, 10,* 181–183.

Thompson, R. A. (1990). Vulnerability in research: A developmental perspective on research risk. *Child Development, 61,* 1–16.

Thompson, R. A. (1994). Emotion regulation: A theme in search of definition. In N. A. Fox (Ed.), The development of emotion regulation: Biological and behavioral considerations. *Monographs of the Society for Research in Child Development, 59* (Nos. 2–3, Serial No. 240).

Thompson, R. A. (1998). Early sociopersonality development. In N. Eisenberg (Ed.), W. Damon (Series Ed.), *Handbook of child psychology: Vol. 3: Social, emotional, and personality development* (5th ed.). New York: Wiley.

Thompson, R. A. (2000). The legacy of early attachments. *Child Development, 71,* 145–152.

Thompson, R. F. (1993). *The brain: A neuroscience primer* (2nd ed.). New York: W.H. Freeman.

Thompson, R. R. (2000). The legacy of early attachments. *Child Development, 71,* 145–152.

Thompson, S. K. (1975). Gender labels and early sex-role development. *Child Development, 46,* 339–347.

Thorndike, R. L., Hagen, E. P., & Sattler, J. M. (1986). *The Stanford-Binet Intelligence Scale* (4th ed.). Chicago: Riverside Publishing.

Thorndike, R. M. (1997). The early history of intelligence testing. In D. P. Flanagan, J. L. Genshaft, & P. L. Morrison (Eds.), *Contemporary intellectual assessment: Theories, tests, and issues.* New York: Guilford.

Thorne, A., & Michaelieu, Q. (1996). Situating adolescent gender and self-esteem with personal memories. *Child Development, 67,* 1374–1390.

Thorne, B. (1993). *Gender play: Girls and boys in school.* New Brunswick, NJ: Rutgers University Press.

Thurber, C. A. (1995). The experience and expression of homesickness in preadolescent and adolescent boys. *Child Development, 66,* 1162–1178.

Thurstone, L. L. (1938). *Primary mental abilities.* Chicago: University of Chicago Press.

Tigner, R. B., & Tigner, S. S. (2000). Triarchic theories of intelligence: Aristotle and Sternberg. *History of Psychology, 3,* 168–176.

Tinsley, B. J. (1992). Multiple influences on the acquisition and socialization of children's health attitudes and behavior: An integrative review. *Child Development, 63,* 1043–1069.

Tirozzi, G. N., & Uro, G. (1997). Education reform in the United States: National policy in support of local efforts for school improvement. *American Psychologist, 52,* 241–249.

Tolan, P. H., Gorman-Smith, D., & Henry, D. B. (2003). The developmental ecology of urban males' youth violence. *Developmental Psychology, 39,* 274–291.

Tolman, D. L., Striepe, M. I., & Harmon, T. (2003). Gender matters: Constructing a model of adolescent sexual health. *Journal of Sex Research, 40,* 4–12.

Tomada, G., & Schneider, B. H. (1997). Relational aggression, gender, and peer acceptance: Invariance across culture, stability over time, and concordance among informants. *Developmental Psychology, 33,* 601–609.

Tomasello, M. (1995). Language is not an instinct. *Cognitive Development, 10,* 131–156.

Tomasello, M. (2003). *Constructing a language: A usage-based theory of language acquisition.* Harvard University Press, 2003.

Tomasello, M., & Camaioni, L. (1997). A comparison of the gestural communication of apes and human infants. *Human Development, 40,* 7–24.

Tomasello, M., & Haberl, K. (2003). Understanding attention: 12- and 18-month-olds know what is new for other persons. *Developmental Psychology, 39,* 906–912.

Tomasello, M., Conti-Ramsden, G., & Ewert, B. (1990). Young children's conversations with their mothers and fathers: Differences in breakdown and repair. *Journal of Child Language, 17,* 115–130.

Tomlin, A. M., & Viehweg, S. A. (2003). Infant mental health: Making a difference. *Professional psychology: Research and Practice, 34,* 617–625.

Tomlinson-Keasey, C., & Keasey, C. B. (1974). The mediating role of cognitive development in moral judgment. *Child Development, 45,* 291–298.

Tomlinson-Keasey, C., & Little, T. D. (1990). Predicting educational attainment, occupational achievement, intellectual skill, and personal adjustment among gifted men and women. *Journal of Educational Psychology, 82,* 442–455.

Toner, I. J., & Potts, R. (1981). Effect of modeled rationales on moral behavior, moral choice, and level of moral judgment in children. *Journal of Psychology, 107,* 153–162.

Toner, I. J., Moore, L. P., & Ashley, P. K. (1978). The effect of serving as a model of self-control on subsequent resistance to deviation in children. *Journal of Experimental Child Psychology, 26,* 85–91.

Toro, J., Castro, J., Gila, A., & Pombo, C. (2005). Assessment of sociocultural influences on the body shape model in adolescent males with anorexia nervosa. *European Eating Disorders Review, 13,* 351–359.

Toro, J., Gila, A., Castro, J., Pombo, C., & Guete, O. (2004). Body image, risk factors for eating disorders and sociocultural influences in Spanish adolescents. *Eating and Weight Disorders, 10,* 91–97.

Torrance, E. P. (1988). The nature of creativity as manifest in its testing. In R. J. Sternberg (Ed.), *The nature of creativity: Contemporary psychological perspectives.* Cambridge, UK: Cambridge University Press.

Trabasso, T. (1975). Representation, memory, and reasoning: How do we make transitive inferences? In A. D. Pick (Ed.), *Minnesota symposia on child psychology* (Vol. 9). Minneapolis: University of Minnesota Press.

Trachtenberg, S., & Viken, R. J. (1994). Aggressive boys in the classroom: Biased attributions or shared perceptions. *Child Development, 65,* 829–835.

Treboux, D., Crowell, J. A., & Waters, E. (2004). When "new" meets "old": Configurations of adult attachment representations and their implications for marital functioning. *Developmental Psychology, 40,* 295–314.

Triandis, H. C. (1995). *Individualism and collectivism.* Boulder, CO: Westview Press.

Tronick, E. Z. (1989). Emotions and emotional communications in infants. *American Psychologist, 44,* 112–119.

Tronick, E. Z., Messinger, D. S., Weinberg, M. K., Lester, B. M., LaGasse, L., Seifer, R., Bauer, C. R., Shankaran, S., Bada, H., Wright, L. L., Poole, K., & Liu, J. (2005). Cocaine exposure is associated with subtle compromises of infants' and mothers' social-emotional behavior and dyadic features of their interaction in the face-to-face still-face paradigm. *Developmental Psychology, 41,* 711–722.

Tronick, E. Z., Thomas, R. B., & Daltabuit, M. (1994). The Quecha Manta pouch: A caregiving practice for buffering the Peruvian infant against multiple stresses of high altitude. *Child Development, 65,* 1005–1013.

Troseth, G. (2003). TV guide: Two-year-old children can learn to use video as a source of information. *Developmental Psychology, 39,* 140–150.

True, M. M., Pisani, L., & Oumar, F. (2001). Mother–infant attachment among the Dogon of Mali. *Child Development, 72,* 1451–1466.

Tryon, R. C. (1940). Genetic differences in maze learning in rats. *Yearbook of the National Society for Studies in Education, 39,* 111–119.

Trzesniewski, K. H., Donnellan, M. B., & Robins, R. W. (2003). Stability of self-esteem across the life span. *Journal of Personality & Social Psychology, 84,* 205–220.

Tseng, V. (2004). Family interdependence and academic adjustment in college: Youth from immigrant and U.S.-born families. *Child Development, 75,* 966–983.

Tudge, J. R. H. (1992). Processes and consequences of peer collaboration: A Vygotskian analysis. *Child Development, 63,* 1364–1379.

Tuladhar, R., Harding, R., Cranage, S.M., Adamson, T. M., & Horne, R. S. C. (2003). Effects of sleep position, sleep state and age on heart rate responses following provoked arousal in term infants. *Early Human Development, 71,* 157–169.

Tulkin, S. R., & Konner, M. J. (1973). Alternative conceptions of intellectual functioning. *Human Development, 16,* 33–52.

Turiel, E. (1983). *The development of social knowledge: Morality and convention.* Cambridge, England: Cambridge University Press.

Turiel, E. (2002). *The culture of morality: Social development, context, and conflict.* Cambridge, England: Cambridge University Press.

Turiel, E., & Wainryb, C. (2000). Social life in culture: Judgments, conflict, and subversion. *Child Development, 71,* 250–256.

Turkheimer, E. (1991). Individual and group differences in adoption studies of IQ. *Psychological Bulletin, 110,* 392–405.

Turkheimer, E. (2000). Three laws of behavior genetics and what they mean. *Current Directions in Psychological Science, 9,* 160–164.

Turner, A. J., & Coyle, A. (2000). What does it mean to be a donor offspring? The identity experiences of adults conceived by donor insemination and the implications of counseling and therapy. *Human Reproduction, 15,* 2041–2051.

Turner, P. J., & Gervai, J. (1995). A multidimensional study of gender typing in preschool children and their parents: Personality, attitudes, preferences, behavior, and cultural differences. *Developmental Psychology, 31,* 759–772.

Turner-Bowker, D. M. (1996). Gender stereotyped descriptions in children's picture books: Does "curious Jane" exist in the literature? *Sex Roles, 35,* 461–488.

Twenge, J. M. (1997). Changes in masculine and feminine traits over time: A meta-analysis. *Sex Roles, 36,* 305–325.

Twenge, J. M., & Crocker, J. (2002). Race and self-esteem: Meta-analysis comparing Whites, Blacks, Hispanics, Asians, and American Indians and comment on Gray-Little and Hafdahl (2000). *Psychological Bulletin, 128,* 371–408.

Tyson, P., & Tyson, R. L. (1990). *Psychoanalytic theories of development: An integration.* New Haven, CT: Yale University Press.

U.S. Bureau of the Census (1997). *Statistical abstract of the United States* (117th ed.). Washington, DC: U.S. Government Printing Office.

U.S. Bureau of the Census (1999). *Historical poverty tables.* Available at http: / / www.census.gov / hhes / poverty / histpov / hstpov8.html.

U.S. Bureau of the Census (2001). Statistical Abstract of the United States (121st ed). Washington, DC: U.S. Government Printing Office.

U.S. Bureau of the Census (2002). *Statistical abstract of the United States* (122nd ed.). Washington, DC: U.S. Government Printing Office.

U.S. Department of Education (1996). *Report to Congress: Goals 2000: Increasing student achievement through state and local initiatives.* Washington, DC: U.S. Government Printing Office.

U.S. Department of Health and Human Services (2001). *Youth violence: A report to the Surgeon General.* Rockville, MD: U.S. Public Health Service, Office of the Surgeon General.

U.S. Department of Justice (1995). *Crime in the United States.* Washington, DC: U.S. Government Printing Office.

Uba, L. (1994). *Asian Americans: Personality patterns, identity, and mental health.* New York: The Guilford Press.

Udry, J. R. (1990). Hormonal and social determinants of adolescent sexual initiation. In J. Bancroft & J. M. Reinisch (Eds.), *Adolescence and puberty* (pp. 70–87). New York: Oxford University Press.

Uller, C., Carey, S., Huntley-Fenner, G., & Klatt, L. (1999). What representations might underlie infant numerical knowledge? *Cognitive Development, 14,* 1–36.

Umana-Taylor, A., Diversi, M., & Fine, M. (2002). Ethnic identity and self-esteem among Latino adolscents: Distinctions among Latino populations. *Journal of Adolescent Research, 17,* 303–327.

Underwood, B., & Moore, B. (1982). Perspective-taking and altruism. *Psychological Bulletin, 91,* 143–173.

Underwood, M. K., Coie, J. D., & Herbsman, C. R. (1992). Display rules for anger and aggression in school-age children. *Child Development, 63,* 366–380.

Underwood, M. K., Hurley, J. C., Johnson, C. A., & Mosley, J. E. (1999). An experimental observational study of children's responses to peer provocation: Developmental and gender differences in middle childhood. *Child Development, 70,* 1428–1446.

Underwood, M. K., Schockner, A. E., & Hurley, J. C. (2001). Children's response to same- and other-gender peers: An experimental investigation with 8-, 10-, and 12-year-olds. *Developmental Psychology, 37,* 362–372.

Uniform Crime Reports for the United States, *1997. Federal Bureau of Investigation. Washington, DC: U.S. Government Printing Office.*

Updegraff, K., McHale, S. M., & Crouter, A. C. (1996). Gender roles in marriage: What do they mean for girls' and boys' school achievement? *Journal of Youth and Adolescence, 25,* 73–88.

Urberg, K. A. (1979). Sex-role conceptualization in adolescents and adults. *Developmental Psychology, 15,* 90–92.

Urberg, K. A., Degirmencioglu, S. M., Tolson, J. M., & Halliday-Scher, K. (1995). The structure of adolescent peer networks. *Developmental Psychology, 31,* 540–547.

Usher, J. A., & Neisser, U. (1993). Childhood amnesia and the beginnings of memory for four early life events. *Journal of Experimental Psychology: General, 122,* 155–165.

Uttal, D., Schreiber, J. C., & DeLoache, J. S. (1995). Waiting to use a symbol: The effects of delay on children's use of models. *Child Development, 66,* 1875–1889.

Vaish, A., & Strian, T. (2004). Is visual reference necessary? Contributions of facial versus vocal cues in 12-month-olds. *Developmental Science, 7,* 261–269.

Valdez-Menchaca, M. C., & Whitehurst, G. J. (1992). Accelerating language development through picture book reading: A systematic extension to Mexican day care. *Developmental Psychology, 28,* 1106–1114.

Valenzuela, M. (1990). Attachment in chronically underweight young children. *Child Development, 61,* 1984–1996.

Valenzuela, M. (1997). Maternal sensitivity in a developing society: The context of urban poverty and infant chronic undernutrition. *Developmental Psychology, 33,* 845–855.

Valeski, T. N., & Stipek, D. J. (2001). Young children's feelings about school. *Child Development, 72,* 1198–1213.

Valian, V., Hoeffner, J., & Aubry, S. (1996). Young children's imitation of sentence subjects: Evidence of processing limitations. *Developmental Psychology, 32,* 153–164.

Valiente, C., Fabes, R. A., Eisenberg, N., & Spinrad, T. L. (2004). The relations of parental expressivity and support to children's coping with daily stress. *Journal of Family Psychology, 18,* 97–106.

van Bakel, H. J. A., & Riksen-Walraven, M. (2002). Parenting and development of one-year-olds: Links with parental, contextual, and child characteristics. *Child Development, 73,* 256–273.

Van de Vijver, F., & Tanzer, N. K. (2004). Bias and equivalence in cross-cultural assessment: An overview. *European Review of Applied Psychology/Revue Européenne de Psychologie Appliquée, 54,* 119–135.

van den Boom, D. C. (1995). Do first-year intervention efforts endure? Follow-up during toddlerhood of a sample of Dutch irritable infants. *Child Development, 66,* 1798–1816.

van den Broek, P. (1989). Causal reasoning and inference making in judging the importance of story statements. *Child Development, 60,* 286–297.

van den Broek, P., Lorch, E. P., & Thurlow, R. (1996). Children's and adults' memory for television stories: The role of causal factors, story-grammar categories, and hierarchial level. *Child Development, 67,* 3010–3028.

van den Broek, P. W. (1997). Discovering the element of the universe: The development of event comprehension from childhood to adulthood. In P. van den Broek, P. Bauer, & T. Bourg (Eds.), *Developmental spans in event comprehension: Bridging fictional and actual events* (pp. 321–342). Mahwah, NJ: Erlbaum.

Van der Bergh, B. R. H., & Marcoen, A. (2004). High antenatal maternal anxiety is related to ADHD symptoms, externalizing problems, and anxiety in 8- and 9-year-olds. *Child Development, 75,* 1085–1097.

van Doorninck, W. J., Caldwell, B. M., Wright, C., & Frankenberg, W. K. (1981). The relationship between twelve-month home stimulation and school achievement. *Child Development, 52,* 1080–1083.

van IJzendoorn, M. H. (1995). Adult attachment representations, parental Responsiveness, and infant attachment: A meta-analysis on the predictive validity of the Adult Attachment Interview. *Psychological Bulletin, 117,* 387–403.

van IJzendoorn, M. H., & De Wolff, M. S. (1997). In search of the absent father—meta-analysis of infant–father attachment: A rejoinder to our discussants. *Child Development, 68,* 604–609.

van Ijzendoorn, M. H., & Sagi, A. (1999). Cross-cultural patterns of attachment: Universal and contextual dimensions. In J. Cassidy & P. R. Shaver (Eds.), *Handbook of Attachment: Theory, research, and clinical applications* (pp. 713–734). New York: Guilford Press.

van IJzendoorn, M. H., Goldberg, S., Kroonenberg, P. M., & Frenkel, O. J. (1992). The relative effects of maternal and child problems on the quality of attachment: A meta-analysis of attachment in clinical samples. *Child Development, 63,* 840–858.

Vandell, D. L. (2000). Parents, peer groups, and other socializing influences. *Developmental Psychology, 36,* 699–710.

Vandell, D. L., & Mueller, E. C. (1995). Peer play and friendships during the first two years. In H. C. Smith, A. J. Chapman, & J. R. Smith (Eds.), *Friendship and social relations in children* (pp. 181–208). New Brunswick, NJ: Transaction.

Vandell, D. L., Wilson, K. S., & Buchanan, N. R. (1980). Peer interaction in the first year of life: An examination of its structure, content, and sensitivity to toys. *Child Development, 51,* 481–488.

Vaughn, B. E., & Waters, E. (1990). Attachment behavior at home and in the lab: Q-sort observations and Strange Situation classifications of 1-year-olds. *Child Development, 61,* 1965–1973.

Vaughn, B. E., Bradley, C. F., Joffe, L. S., Seifer, R., & Barglow, P. (1987). Maternal characteristics measured prenatally are predictive of ratings of temperamental "difficulty" on the Carey Infant Temperament Questionnaire. *Developmental Psychology, 23,* 152–161.

Veddovi, M., Gibson, F., Kenny, D. Bowen, J., & Starte, D. (2004). Preterm behavior, maternal adjustment, and competencies in the newborn period: What influence do they have at 12 months postnatal age? *Infant Mental Health Journal, 25,* 580–600.

Vernon-Feagans, L., Manlove, E. E., & Volling, B. L. (1996). Otitis media and the social behavior of day-care-attending children. *Child Development, 67,* 1528–1539.

Verp, M. S. (1993a). Environmental causes of pregnancy loss and malformations. In C. Lin, M. S. Verp, & R. E. Sabbagha (Eds.), *The high-risk fetus: Pathophysiology, diagnosis, management.* New York: Springer-Verlag.

Verp, M. S. (1993b). Genetic counseling and screening. In C. Lin, M. S. Verp, & R. E. Sabbagha (Eds.), *The high-risk fetus: Pathophysiology, diagnosis, management.* New York: Springer-Verlag.

Verschueren, K., & Marcoen, A. (1999). Representation of self and socioemotional competence in kindergarteners: Differential and combined effects of attachment to mother and to father. *Child Development, 70,* 183–201.

Verschueren, K., Buyck, P., & Marcoen, A. (2001). Self–representations and socioemotional competence in young children: A 3-year-longitudinal study. *Developmental Psychology, 37,* 126–134.

Verschueren, K., Marcoen, A., & Schoefs, V. (1996). The internal working model of self, attachment, and competence in five-year-olds. *Child Development, 67,* 2493–2511.

Vetere, A. (2004). Editorial: Are we continuing to neglect fathers? *Clinical Child Psychology & Psychiatry, 9,* 323–326.

Vibeke, M., & Slinning, K. (2001). Children prenatally exposed to substances: gender-related differences in outcome from infancy to 3 years of age. *Infant Mental Health Journal, 22,* 334–51.

Vihman, M. M., Kay, E., Boysson-Bardies, B. de., Durand, C., & Sundberg, U. (1994). External sources of individual differences? A cross-linguistic analysis of the phonetics of mothers' speech to 1-year-old children. *Developmental Psychology, 30,* 651–662.

Vincent, A. S., Decker, B. P., & Mumford, M. D. (2002). Divergent thinking, intelligence, and expertise: A test of alternative models. *Creativity Research Journal, 14,* 163–178.

Vinter, A. (1986). The role of movement in eliciting early imitation. *Child Development, 57,* 66–71.

Vinter, A., & Perruchet, P. (2000). Implicit learning in children is not related to age: Evidence from drawing. *Child Development, 71,* 1223–1240.

Vobejda, B. (1991, September 15). The future deferred. Longer road from adolescence to adulthood often leads back through parents' home. *The Washington Post,* pp. A1–A29.

Volling, B. L., & Belsky, J. (1992). The contribution of mother–child and father–child relationships to the quality of sibling interaction: A longitudinal study. *Child Development, 63,* 1209–1222.

Volling, B. L., McElwain, N. L., & Miller, A. L. (2002). Emotion regulation in context: The jealousy complex between young siblings and its relations with child and family characteristics. *Child Development, 73,* 581–600.

Von Wright, M. R. (1989). Body image satisfaction in adolescent boys and girls: A longitudinal study. *Journal of Youth and Adolescence, 18,* 71–83.

Vorhees, C. V., & Mollnow, E. (1987). Behavioral teratogenesis: Long-term influences on behavior from early exposure to environmental agents. In J. D. Osofsky (Ed.), *Handbook of infant development* (2nd ed., pp. 913–971). New York: Wiley.

Votruba-Drzal, E., Coley, R. L., & Chase-Lansdale, P. L. (2004). Child care and low-income children's development: Direct and moderated effects. *Child Development, 75,* 296–312.

Voyer, D., Voyer, S., & Bryden, M. P. (1995). Magnitude of sex differences in spatial abilities: a meta-analysis and consideration of critical variables. *Psychological Bulletin, 117,* 250–270.

Vreman-de Olde, C., & de Jong, T. (2006). Scaffolding learners in designing investigation assignments for a computer simulation. *Journal of Computer Assisted Learning, 22,* 63–73.

Vreugenhil, H. J. I., Mulder, P. G. H., Emmen, H. H., & Weisglas-Kuperus, N. (2004). Effects of perinatal exposure to PCBs on neuropsychological functions in the Rotterdam cohort at 9 years of age. *Neuropsychology, 18,* 185–193.

Vuchinich, S., Bank, L., & Patterson, G. R. (1992). Parenting, peers, and the stability of antisocial behavior in preadolescent boys. *Developmental Psychology, 28,* 510–521.

Vuorela, P., Sarkola, T., Alfthan, H., & Halmesmaki, E. (2002). Hepatocyte growth factor, epidermal growth factor, and placenta growth factor concentrations in peripheral blood of pregnant women with alcohol abuse. *Alcoholism: Clinical and Experimental Research, 26,* 682–687.

Vygotsky, L. S. (1962). *Thought and language* (E. Hanfmann & G. Vakar, Eds. & Trans.). Cambridge, MA: MIT Press. (Original work published 1934.)

Vygotsky, L. S. (1978). *Mind in society: The development of higher mental processes.* (M. Cole, V. John-Steiner, S. Scribner, & E. Souberman, Eds.). Cambridge, MA: Harvard University Press. (Original work published in 1930, 1933, 1935.)

Wachs, T. D. (1992). *The nature of nurture.* Newbury Park, CA: Sage.

Waddington, C. H. (1966). *Principles of development and differentiation.* New York: Macmillan.

Wagner, R. K., Torgesen, J. K., Rashotte, C. A., Hecht, S. A., Barker, T. A., Burgess, S. R., Donahue, J., & Garon, T. (1997). Changing relations between phonological processing abilities and word-level reading as children develop from beginning to skilled readers: A 5-year longitudinal study. *Developmental Psychology, 33,* 468–479.

Wainright, J. L., Russell, S. T., & Patterson, C. J. (2004). Psychosocial adjustment, school outcomes, and romantic relationships of adolescents with same-sex parents. *Child Development, 75,* 1886–1898.

Wakschlag, L. S., & Hans, S. L. (1999). Relation of maternal responsiveness during infancy to the development of behavior problems in high-risk youths. *Developmental Psychology, 35,* 569–579.

Wald, E. R. (2005). To treat or not to treat. *Pediatrics, 115,* 1087–1089.

Walden, T. A., & Baxter, A. (1989). The effect of context and age on social referencing. *Child Development, 60,* 1511–1518.

Waldman, I. D., Weinberg, K. A., & Scarr, S. (1994). Racial-group differences in IQ in the Minnesota Transracial Adoption Study: A reply to Levin and Lynn. *Intelligence, 19,* 29–44.

Walker, J. S. (2000). Choosing biases, using power, and practicing resistance: Moral development in a world without certainty. *Human Development, 43,* 135–156.

Walker, L. J. (1980). Cognitive and perspective-taking prerequisites for moral development. *Child Development, 51,* 131–139.

Walker, L. J. (1995). Sexism in Kohlberg's moral psychology? In W. M. Kurtines & J. L. Gewirtz (Eds.), *Moral development: An introduction* (pp. 83–107). Boston: Allyn & Bacon.

Walker, L. J., & Pitts, R. C. (1998). Naturalistic conceptions of moral maturity. *Developmental Psychology, 34,* 403–419.

Walker, L. J., Hennig, K. H., & Kettenauer, T. (2000). Parent and peer contexts for children's moral reasoning development. *Child Development, 71,* 1033–1048.

Walker-Andrews, A. S., Bahrick, L. E., Raglioni, S. S., & Diaz, I. (1991). Infants' bimodal perception of gender. *Ecological Psychology, 3,* 55–75.

Walker-Andrews, A. S., & Lennon, E. M. (1985). Auditory-visual perception of changing distance by human infants. *Child Development, 56,* 544–548.

Walker-Barnes, C. J., & Mason, C. A. (2001). Ethnic differences in the effect of parenting on gang involvement and gang delinquency: A longitudinal, hierarchical linear modeling perspective. *Child Development, 72,* 1814–1831.

Wallach, M. A. (1985). Creativity testing and giftedness. In F. D. Horowitz & M. O'Brien (Eds.), *The gifted and talented. Developmental perspectives.* Washington, DC: American Psychological Association.

Wallach, M. A., & Kogan, N. (1965). *Thinking in young children.* New York: Holt, Rinehart & Winston.

Wallerstein, J. S., & Kelly, J. B. (1980). *Surviving the breakup: How children and parents cope with divorce.* New York: Basic Books.

Walters, A. S. (1997). Survey of 500 adolescents' discoveries about the facts of life. Unpublished data, University of Georgia.

Wang, D., Kato, N., Jnaba, Y., Tango, T., Yoshida, Y., Kusaka, Y., et al. (2000). Physical and personality traits of preschool children in Fuzhou, China: Only one child vs. sibling. *Child: Care, Health, and Development, 26,* 49–60.

Wang, Q. (2004). The emergence of cultural self-constructs: Autobiographical memory and self-description in European American and Chinese children. *Developmental Psychology, 40,* 3–15.

Wang, Q., Leichtman, M. D., & Davies, K. (2000). Sharing memories and telling stories: American and Chinese mothers and their 3-year-olds. *Memory, 8,* 159–177.

Wang, X., Dow-Edwards, D., Anderson, V., Minkoff, H., & Hurd, Y. (2004). In utero marijuana exposure associated with abnormal amygdala dopamin D-sub-2 gene expression in the human fetus. *Biological Psychiatry, 56,* 909–915.

Ward, L. M. (2004). Wading through the stereotypes: Positive and negative associations between media use and Black adolescents' conceptions of self. *Developmental Psychology, 40,* 284–294.

Ward, S. L., & Overton, W. F. (1990). Semantic familiarity, relevance, and the development of deductive reasoning. *Developmental Psychology, 26,* 488–493.

Warin, J. (2000). The attainment of self-consistency through gender in young children. *Sex Roles, 42,* 209–231.

Wark, G. R., & Krebs, D. L. (1996). Gender and dilemma differences in real-life moral judgments. *Developmental Psychology, 32,* 220–230.

Warren, W. H., Morris, M. W., & Kalish, M. (1988). Perception of translational heading from optic flow. *Performance, 14,* 646–660.

Warren-Leubecker, A., & Bohannon, J. N., III (1989). Pragmatics: Language in social contexts. In J. Berko Gleason (Ed.), *The development of language* (2nd ed.). Columbus, OH: Merrill.

Wartella, E., Caplovitz, A. G., & Lee, J. H. (2004). From Baby Einstein to Leapfrog, from Doom to The Sims, from instant messaging to Internet chat rooms: Public interest in the role of interactive media in children's lives. *Social Policy Report: Giving Child and Youth Development Knowledge Away, 28,* 3–11.

Wartner, U. G., Grossmann, K., Fremmer-Bombik, E., & Suess, G. (1994). Attachment patterns at age six in south Germany: Predictability from infancy and implications for preschool behavior. *Child Development, 65,* 1014–1027.

Waterman, A. S. (1982). Identity development from adolescence to adulthood: An extension of theory and a review of research. *Developmental Psychology, 18,* 341–358.

Waterman, A. S. (1992). Identity as an aspect of optimal psychological functioning. In G. R. Adams, T. P. Gullotta, & R. Montemayor (Eds.), *Adolescent identity formation* (Advances in Adolescent Development, Vol. 4). Newbury Park, CA: Sage.

Waterman, A. S., & Archer, S. L. (1990). A life-span perspective on identity formation: Developments in form, function, and process. In P. B. Baltes, D. L. Featterman, & R. M. Lerner (Eds.), *Life-span development and behavior: Vol. 10.* Hillsdale, NJ: Erlbaum.

Waters, E., & Cummings, E. M. (2000). A secure base from which to explore close relationships. *Child Development, 71,* 164–172.

Waters, E., Merrick, S., Treboux, D., Crowell, J., & Albersheim, L. (2000). Attachment security in infancy and early adulthood: A twenty-year longitudinal study. *Child Development, 51,* 208–216.

Waters, E., Vaughn, B. E., & Egeland, B. R. (1980). Individual differences in mother–infant attachment relationships at age one: Antecedents in neonatal behavior in an urban, economically disadvantaged sample. *Child Development, 51,* 208–216.

Waters, E., Vaughn, B. E., Posada, G., & Kondo-Ikemura, K. (1995). Caregiving, cultural, and cognitive perspectives on secure-base behavior and working models: New growing points of attachment theory and research. *Monographs of the Society for Research in Child Development, 60* (2–3, Serial No. 244).

Waters, E., Wippman, J., & Sroufe, L. A. (1979). Attachment, positive affect, and competence in the peer group: Two studies in construct validation. *Child Development, 50,* 821–829.

Watkins, W. E., & Pollitt, E. (1999). Iron deficiency and cognition among school-age children. In S. Grantham McGregor (Ed.), *Recent advances in research on the effects of health and nutrition on children's development and school achievement in the Third World.* Pan American Health Organization.

Watson, J. B. (1913). Psychology as the behaviorist views it. *Psychological Review, 20,* 158–177.

Watson, J. B. (1925). *Behaviorism.* New York: Norton.

Watson, J. B. (1928). *Psychological care of infant and child.* New York: Norton.

Watson, J. B., & Raynor, R. (1920). Conditioned emotional reactions. *Journal of Experimental Psychology, 3,* 1–14.

Watson, J. S., Hayes, L. A., Vietze, P., & Becker, J. (1979). Discriminative infant smiling to orientations of talking faces of mother and stranger. *Journal of Experimental Child Psychology, 28,* 92–99.

Watson, M. W., & Peng, Y. (1992). The relation between toy gun play and children's aggressive behavior. *Early Education and Development, 3,* 370–389.

Waxman, S. R., & Hatch, T. (1992). Beyond the basics: Preschool children label objects flexibly at multiple hierarchical levels. *Journal of Child Language, 19,* 153–166.

Waxman, S. R., & Markow, D. B. (1998). Object properties and object kind: Twenty-one-month-old infants' extension of novel adjectives. *Child Development, 69,* 1313–1329.

Waxman, S. R., & Senghas, A. (1992). Relations among word meanings in early lexical development. *Developmental Psychology, 28,* 862–873.

Weakliem, D., McQuillan, J., & Schauer, T. (1995). Toward meritocracy? Changing social-class differences in intellectual ability. *Sociology of Education, 68,* 271–286.

Wechsler, D. (1989). *Manual for the Wechsler Preschool and Primary Scale of Intelligence Revised.* New York: Psychological Corporation.

Wechsler, D. (1991). *Manual, WISC–III: Wechsler Intelligence Scale for Children-Third Edition.* San Antonio, TX: Psychological Corporation.

Weerth, C., Hees, Y., & Buitelaar, J. K. (2003). Prenatal maternal cortisol levels and infant behavior during the first 5 months. *Early Human Development, 74,* 139–151.

Weinberg, M. K., Tronick, E. A., Cohn, J. F., & Olson, K. L. (1999). Gender differences in emotional expressivity and self-regulation during early infancy. *Developmental Psychology, 35,* 175–188.

Weinberg, R. A. (2002, June). Of clones and clowns. *The Atlantic Monthly.*

Weinberg, R. A., Scarr, S., & Waldman, I. D. (1992). The Minnesota transracial adoption study: A follow-up of IQ test performance at adolescence. *Intelligence, 16,* 117–135.

Weindrich, D., Jennen-Steinmetz, C., Laucht, M., & Schmidt, M. H. (2003). Late sequelae of low birthweight: mediators of poor school performance at 11 years. *Developmental Medicine and Child Neurology, 45,* 463–470.

Weiner, B. (1974). *Achievement and attribution theory.* Morristown, NJ: General Learning Press.

Weiner, B. (1986). *An attributional theory of motivation and emotion.* New York: Springer-Verlag.

Weinraub, M., & Lewis, M. (1977). The determinants of children's responses to separation. *Monographs of the Society for Research in Child Development, 42* (4, Serial No. 172).

Weinraub, M., Clemens, L. P., Sockloff, A., Ethridge, T., Gracely, E., & Myers, B. (1984). The development of sex-role stereotypes in the third year: Relationships to gender labeling, gender identity, sex-typed toy preferences, and family characteristics. *Child Development, 55,* 1493–1503.

Weisfeld, G. B., & Woodward, L. (2004). Current evolutionary perspectives on adolescent romantic relations and sexuality. *Journal of the American Academy of Child & Adolescent Psychiatry, 43,* 11–19.

Weisner, T. S., & Gallimore, R. (1977). My brother's keeper: Child and sibling caretaking. *Current Anthropology, 18,* 169–190.

Weisner, T. S., & Wilson-Mitchell, J. E. (1990). Nonconventional family lifestyles and sex typing in six-year-olds. *Child Development, 61,* 1915–1933.

Weiss, B., Dodge, K. A., Bates, J. E., & Pettit, G. S. (1992). Some consequences of early harsh discipline: Child aggression and a maladaptive social information processing style. *Child Development, 63,* 1321–1335.

Weisz, J. R., Chaiyasit, W., Weiss, B., Eastman, K. L., & Jackson, E. W. (1995). A multimethod study of problem behavior among Thai and American children in school: Teacher reports versus direct observations. *Child Development, 66,* 402–415.

Welch-Ross, M. K., & Schmidt, C. R. (1996). Gender-schema development and children's constructive story memory: Evidence for a developmental model. *Child Development, 67,* 820–835.

Welles, C. E. (2005). Breaking the silence surrounding female adolescent sexual desire. *Women & Therapy, 28,* 31–45.

Wellman, H. M. (1990). *The child's theory of mind.* Cambridge, MA: MIT Press.

Wellman, H. M., & Lempers, J. D. (1977). The naturalistic communicative abilities of two-year-olds. *Child Development, 48,* 1052–1057.

Wellman, H. M., & Liu, D. (2004). Scaling theory-of-mind tasks. *Child Development, 75,* 523–541.

Wellman, H. M., & Woolley, J. (1990). From simple desires to ordinary beliefs: The early development of everyday psychology. *Cognition, 35,* 245–275.

Wellman, H. M., Cross, D., & Watson, J. (2001). Meta-analysis of theory-of-mind development: The truth about false belief. *Child Development, 72,* 655–684.

Wellman, H. M., Hollander, M., & Schult, C. A. (1996). Young children's understanding of thought bubbles and of thoughts. *Child Development, 67,* 768–788.

Wells, L. E. (1989). Self-enhancement through delinquency: A conditional test of self-derogation theory. *Journal of Research in Crime and Delinquency, 26,* 226–252.

Wenar, C., & Kerig, P. (2006). *Developmental psychopathology: From infancy through adolescence* (5th ed.). New York: McGraw-Hill.

Wender, P. H. (1995). *Attention-deficit hyperactivity disorder in adults.* New York: Oxford University Press.

Wendland-Carro, J., Piccinini, C. A., & Millar, W. S. (1999). The role of early intervention on enhancing the quality of mother-infant interaction. *Child Development, 70,* 713–721.

Wentzel, K. R. (2002). Are effective teachers like good parents? Teaching styles and student achievement in early adolescence. *Child Development, 73,* 278–301.

Wentzel, K. R., & Asher, S. R. (1995). The academic lives of neglected, rejected, popular, and controversial children. *Child Development, 66,* 754–763.

Werker, J. F., & Desjardins, R. N. (1995). Listening to speech in the first year of life: Experimental influences on phoneme perception. *Current Directions in Psychological Science, 4,* 76–81.

Werner, E. E., & Smith, R. S. (1992). *Overcoming the odds: High risk children from birth to adulthood.* Ithaca, NY: Cornell University Press.

Wertsch, J. V., & Tulviste, P. (1992). L. S. Vygotsky and contemporary developmental psychology. *Developmental Psychology, 28,* 548–557.

Whiffen, V. E. (1992). Is postpartum depression a distinct diagnosis? *Clinical Psychology Review, 12,* 485–508.

Whipp, B. J., & Ward, S. A. (1992). Will woman soon outrun men? *Nature, 355,* 25.

Whitaker, D. J., & Miller, K. S. (1999). Parent-adolescent discussion about sex and condoms: Input of peer influences on sexual risk behavior. *Journal of Adolescent Research, 15,* 251–272.

Whitall, J., & Getchell, N. (1995). From walking to running: Applying a dynamical systems approach to the development of locomotor skills. *Child Development, 66,* 1541–1553.

White, R. W. (1959). Motivation reconsidered: The concept of competence. *Psychological Review, 66,* 297–333.

White, S. H. (1992). G. Stanley Hall: From philosophy to developmental psychology. *Developmental Psychology, 28,* 25–34.

White, S. H. (2000). Conceptual foundations of IQ testing. *Psychology, Public Policy, and Law, 6,* 33–43.

Whitehurst, G. J., & Lonigan, C. J. (1998). Child development and emergent literacy. *Child Development, 69,* 848–872.

Whitehurst, G. J., & Valdez-Menchaca, M. C. (1988). What is the role of reinforcement in early language acquisition? *Child Development, 59,* 430–440.

Whitehurst, G. J., & Vasta, R. (1975). Is language acquired through imitation. *Journal of Psycholinguistic Research, 4,* 37–59.

Whitehurst, G. J., Falco, F. L., Lonigan, C. J., Fischel, J. E., DeBaryshe, B. D., Valdez Menchaca, M. C., & Caulfield, M. (1988). Accelerating language development through picture book reading. *Child Development, 59,* 552–559.

Whiting, B. B., & Edwards, C. P. (1988). *Children of different worlds: The formation of social behavior.* Cambridge, MA: Harvard University Press.

Whiting, B. B., & Whiting, J. W. M. (1975). *Children of six cultures.* Cambridge, MA: Harvard University Press.

Whitley, B. E., Jr. (1983). Sex-role orientation and self-esteem: A critical meta-analytic review. *Journal of Personality and Social Psychology, 44,* 765–778.

Whittle, M. J., & Connor, J. M. (1995). *Prenatal diagnosis in obstetric practice* (2nd ed.). Oxford, UK: Blackwell.

Wichstrom, L. (1999). The emergence of gender difference in depressed mood during adolescence: The role of intensified gender socialization. *Developmental Psychology, 35,* 232–245.

Widen, S. C., & Russell, J. A. (2003). A closer look at preschoolers' freely produced labels for facial expressions. *Developmental Psychology, 39,* 114–128.

Wiesner, M., & Ittel, A. (2002). Relations of pubertal timing and depressive symptoms to substance use in early adolescence. *Journal of Early Adolescence, 22,* 5–23.

Wiggam, A. E. (1923). *The new decalogue of science.* Indianapolis: Bobbs-Merrill.

Wilcock, A., Kobayashi, L., & Murray, I. (1997). Twenty-five years of obstetric patient satisfaction in North America: A review of the literature. *Journal of Perinatal and Neonatal Nursing, 10,* 36–47.

Wilcox, A. J., Baird, D. D., Weinberg, C. R., & Associates (1995). Fertility in men exposed prenatally to diethylstilbestrol. *New England Journal of Medicine, 332,* 1411–1416.

Wilcoxon, J. S., & Redei, E. (2004). Prenatal programming of adult thyroid function by alcohol and thyroid hormones. *American Journal of Physiology: Endocrinoloy and Metabolism, 50,* 318–327.

Wile, J., & Arechiga, M. (1999). Sociocultural aspects of postpartum depression. In L. J. Miller (Ed.), *Postpartum mood disorders* (pp. 83–98). Washington, DC: American Psychiatric Press.

Wilkinson, K. M., & Mazzitelli, K. (2003). The effect of 'missing' information on children's retention of fast-mapped labels. *Journal of Child Language, 30,* 47–73.

Wille, D. (1991). Relation of preterm birth with quality of infant-mother attachment at one year. *Infant Behavior and Development, 14,* 227–240.

Willems, E. P., & Alexander, J. L. (1982). The naturalistic perspective in research. In B. B. Wolman (Ed.), *Handbook of developmental psychology.* Englewood Cliffs, NJ: Prentice Hall.

Willford, J. A., Richardson, G. A., Leech, S. L., & Day, N. L. (2004). Verbal and visuospatial learning and memory function in children with moderate prenatal alcohol exposure. *Alcoholism: Clinical & Experimental Research, 28,* 497–507.

Williams, B. (1998; January 19). Stricter controls on Internet access sorely needed, parents fear. *Atlanta Constitution,* pp. A1, A15.

Williams, B. R., Ponesse, J. S., Schachar, R. J., Loyan, G. D., & Tannock, R. (1999). Development of inhibitory control across the life span. *Developmental Psychology, 35,* 205–213.

Williams, C., & Bybee, J. (1994). What do children feel guilty about? Developmental and gender differences. *Developmental Psychology, 30,* 617–623.

Williams, J. E., & Best, D. L. (1990). *Measuring sex stereotypes: A multination study* (rev. ed.). Newbury Park, CA: Sage.

Williams, J. E., Bennett, S. M., & Best, D. L. (1975). Awareness and expression of sex stereotypes in young children. *Developmental Psychology, 11,* 635–642.

Williams, J. E., Satterwhite, R. C., & Best, D. L. (1999). Pancultural gender stereotypes revisited: The five factor model. *Sex Roles, 40,* 513–525.

Wilson, R. S. (1978). Synchronies in mental development: An epigenetic perspective. *Science, 202,* 939–948.

Wilson, R. S. (1983). The Louisville twin study: Developmental synchronies in behavior. *Child Development, 54,* 298–316.

Wilson, R. S. (1985). Risk and resilience in early mental development. *Developmental Psychology, 21,* 795–805.

Wilson, S. (2003). Lexically specific constructions in the acquisition of inflection in English. *Journal of Child Language, 30,* 75–115.

Wilson, S. P., & Kipp, K. (1998). The development of efficient inhibition: Evidence from directed-forgetting tasks. *Developmental Review, 18,* 86–123.

Winick, M. (1976). *Malnutrition and brain development.* New York: Oxford University Press.

Winner, E. (1997). Exceptionally high intelligence and schooling. *American Psychologist, 52,* 1070–1081.

Winner, E. (2000). The origins and ends of giftedness. *American Psychologist, 55,* 159–169.

Winsler, A. (2003). Overt and covert verbal problem-solving strategies: Developmental trends in use, awareness, and relations with task performance in children age 5 to 17. *Child Development, 74,* 659–678.

Winsler, A., Diáz, R. M., Espinosa, L., & Rodriguez, J. L. (1999). When learning a second language does not mean losing the first: Bilingual language development in low-income, Spanish-speaking children attending bilingual preschool. *Child Development, 70,* 349–362.

Winterbottom, M. (1958). The relation of need for achievement to learning experiences in independence and mastery. In J. Atkinson (Ed.), *Motives in fantasy, action, and society.* Princeton, NJ: Van Nostrand.

Witelson, S. F. (1987). Neurobiological aspects of language in children. *Child Development, 58,* 653–688.

Wolff, M., Rutten, P., & Bayer, A. F., III (1992). *Where we stand: Can America make it in the race for health, wealth, and happiness?* New York: Bantam Books.

Wong Filmore, L. (1991). When learning a second language means losing the first. *Early Childhood Research Quarterly, 6,* 323–346.

Woo, E. (1995, December 11). Can racial stereotypes psych out students? *Los Angeles Times,* D1.

Wood, D., Bruner, J. S., & Ross, G. (1976). The role of tutoring in problem-solving. *Journal of Child Psychology and Psychiatry, 17,* 89–100.

Woods, S. (2004). Untreated recovery from eating disorders. *Adolescence, 39,* 361–371.

Woodward, A. L., Markman, E. M., & Fitzsimmons, C. M. (1994). Rapid word learning in 13-and 18-month-olds. *Developmental Psychology, 30,* 553–566.

Woodward, L., Fergusson, D. M., & Belsky, J. (2000). Timing of parental separation and attachment to parents in adolescence: Results of a prospective study from birth to age 16. *Journal of Marriage and the Family, 62,* 162–174.

Wright, J. C., Huston, A. C., Murphy, K. C., St. Peters, M., Pinon, M., Scantlin, R., & Kotler, J. (2001). The relations of early television viewing to school readiness and vocabulary of children from low-income families: The Early Window Project. *Child Development, 72,* 1347–1366.

Wright, J. C., Huston, A. C., Reitz, A. L., & Piemyat, S. (1994). Young children's perception of television reality: Determinants and developmental differences. *Developmental Psychology, 30,* 229–239.

Wright, J. C., Huston, A. C., Truglio, R., Fitch, M. Smith, E., & Piemyat, S. (1995). Occupational portrayals on television: Children's role schemata, career aspirations, and perceptions of reality. *Child Development, 66,* 1706–1718.

Wyman, P. A., Cowen, E. L., Work, W. C., Hoyt-Myers, L., Magnus, K. B., & Fagen, D. B. (1999). Caregiving and developmental factors differentiating young, at-risk urban children showing resilient versus stress-affected outcomes: A replication and extension. *Child Development, 70,* 645–659.

Wynn, K. (1992). Addition and subtraction by human infants. *Nature, 358,* 749–750.

Xie, H., Swift, D. J., Cairns, R. B., & Cairns, B. D. (2002). Aggressive behaviors in social interaction and developmental adaptation: A narrative analysis of interpersonal conflicts during early adolescence. *Social Development, 11,* 205–224.

Yang, B., Ollendick, T. H., Dong, Q., Xia, Y., & Lin, L. (1995). Only children and children with siblings in the People's Republic of China: Levels of fear, anxiety, and depression. *Child Development, 66,* 1301–1311.

Yang, C. D. (2004). Universal grammar, statistics or both? *Trends in Cognitive Sciences, 8,* 451–456.

Yankowitz, J. (1996). Surgical fetal therapy. In J. A. Kuller, N. C. Cheschier, & R. C. Cefalo (Eds.), *Prenatal diagnosis and reproductive genetics* (pp. 181–187). St. Louis: Mosby.

Yau, J., & Smetana, J. G. (1996). Adolescent–parent conflict among Chinese adolescents in Hong Kong. *Child Development, 67,* 1262–1275.

Yau, J., & Smetana, J. G. (2003). Conceptions of moral, social-conventional, and personal events among Chinese preschoolers in Hong Kong. *Child Development, 74,* 647–658.

Yau, J., & Smetana, J. G. (in press). Adolescent–parent conflict in Hong Kong and Shenzhen: A comparison of youth in two cultural contexts. *International Journal of Behavioral Development.*

Yazigi, R. A., Odem, R. R., & Polakoski, K. L. (1991). Demonstration of specific binding of cocaine to human spermatoza. *Journal of the American Medical Association, 266,* 1956–1959.

Yeates, K. O., & Selman, R. L. (1989). Social competence in the schools: Toward an integrative developmental model for intervention. *Developmental Review, 9,* 64–100.

Yeates, K. O., MacPhee, D., Campbell, F. A., & Ramey, C. T. (1983). Maternal IQ and home environment as determinants of early childhood intellectual competence: A developmental analysis. *Developmental Psychology, 19,* 731–739.

Yip, T., & Fuligni, A. J. (2002). Daily variation in ethnic identity, ethnic behaviors, and psychological well-being among American adolescents of Chinese descent. *Child Development, 73,* 1557–1572.

Yonas, A., Arterberry, M., & Granrud, C. E. (1987). Space perception in infancy. In R. A. Vasta (Ed.) *Annals of child development.* Greenwich, CT: JAI Press.

Yonas, A., Cleaves, W., & Pettersen, L. (1978). Development of sensitivity to pictorial depth. *Science, 200,* 77–79.

Young, S. K., Fox, N. A., & Zahn-Waxler, C. (1999). The relations between temperament and empathy in 2-year-olds. *Developmental Psychology, 35,* 1189–1197.

Youngblade, L. M., & Dunn, J. (1995). Individual differences in young children's pretend play with mother and sibling: Links to relationships and understanding other people's feelings and beliefs. *Child Development, 66,* 1472–1492.

Younger, A. J., & Daniels, T. M. (1992). Children's reasons for nominating their peers as withdrawn: Passive withdrawal versus active isolation. *Developmental Psychology, 28,* 955–960.

Youniss, J., McLellan, J. A., & Strouse, D. (1994). "We're popular, but we're not snobs": Adolescent's describe their crowds. In R. Montemayor, G. R. Adams, & T. P. Gullotta (Eds.), *Personal relationships in adolescence: Vol. 6: Advances in adolescent development.* Thousand Oaks, CA: Sage.

Yuill, N., & Pearson, A. (1998). The development of bases for trait attribution: Children's understanding of traits as casual mechanisms based on desires. *Developmental Psychology, 34,* 574–586.

Yussen, S. R., & Bird, J. E. (1979). The development of metacognitive awareness in memory, communication, and attention. *Journal of Experimental Child Psychology, 28,* 28, 300–313.

Zahn-Waxler, C., Friedman, R. J., Cole, P. M., Mizuta, I., & Himura, N. (1996). Japanese and United States preschool children's responses to conflict and distress. *Child Development, 67,* 2462–2477.

Zahn-Waxler, C., Radke-Yarrow, M., & King, R. A. (1979). Child rearing and children's prosocial initiations toward victims of distress. *Child Development, 50,* 319–330.

Zahn-Waxler, C., Radke-Yarrow, M., Wagner, E., & Chapman, M. (1992). Development of concern for others. *Developmental Psychology, 28,* 126–136.

Zahn-Waxler, C., Robinson, J. L., & Emde, R. N. (1992). The development of empathy in twins. *Developmental Psychology, 28,* 1038–1047.

Zakriski, A. L., & Coie, J. D. (1996). A comparison of aggressive-rejected and nonaggressive-rejected children's interpretations of self-directed and other-directed rejection. *Child Development, 67,* 1048–1070.

Zamuner, T. (2002). Input-based phonological acquisition. *Dissertation Abstracts International Section A: Humanities and Social Sciences, 62,* 3032.

Zani, B. (1991). Male and female patterns in the discovery of sexuality during adolescence. *Journal of Adolescence, 14,* 163–178.

Zelazo, N. A., Zelazo, P. R., Cohen, K. M., & Zelazo, P. D. (1993). Specificity of practice effects in elementary neuromotor patterns. *Developmental Psychology, 29,* 686–691.

Zelazo, P. D., Helwig, C. C., & Lau, A. (1996). Intention, act, and outcome in behavioral prediction and moral judgment. *Child Development, 67,* 2478–2492.

Zelazo, P. R., Zelazo, N. A., & Kolb, S. (1972). "Walking" in the newborn. *Science, 176,* 314–315.

Zeman, J., & Garber, J. (1996). Display rules for anger, sadness, and pain: It depends on who is watching. *Child Development, 67,* 957–973.

Zeman, J., & Shipman, K. (1997). Social-contextual influences on expectancies for managing anger and sadness: The transition from middle childhood to adolescence. *Developmental Psychology, 33,* 917–924.

Zern, D. S. (1984). Relationships among selected child-rearing variables in a cross-cultural sample of 110 societies. *Developmental Psychology, 20,* 683–690.

Zeskind, P. S. (1980). Adult responses to the cries of low- and high-risk infants. *Infant Behavior and Development, 3,* 167–177.

Zeskind, P. S., & Ramey, C. T. (1981). Preventing intellectual and interactional sequelae of fetal malnutrition: A longitudinal, transactional, and synergistic approach to development. *Child Development, 52,* 213–218.

Zeskind, P. S., Klein, L., & Marshall, T. R. (1992). Adults' perceptions of experimental modifications of durations of pauses and expiratory sounds in infant crying. *Developmental Psychology, 28,* 1153–1162.

Zeskind, P. S., Sale, J., Maio, M. L., Hungtington, L., & Weiseman, J. R. (1985). Adult perceptions of pain and hunger cries: A synchrony of arousal. *Child Development, 56,* 549–554.

Zhang, L. (2005). Prenatal hypoxia and cardiac programming. *Journal of the Society for Gynecologic Investigation, 12,* 12–14.

Zhou, M., & Bankston, C. I. (1998). *Growing up American: How Vietnamese children adapt to life in the United States.* New York: Russell Sage.

Zhou, Q., Eisenberg, N., Losoya, S. H., Fabes, R. A., Reiser, M., Guthrie, I. K., Murphy, B. C., Cumberland, A. J., & Shepard, S. A. (2002). The relations of parental warmth and positive expressiveness to children's empathy-related responding and social functioning: A longitudinal study. *Child Development, 73,* 893–915.

Ziegert, D. I., Kistner, J. A., Castro, R., & Robertson, B. (2001). Longitudinal study of young children's responses to challenging achievement situations. *Child Development, 72,* 609–624.

Zigler, E. F., & Finn Stevenson, M. (1996). Funding child care and public education. *The Future of Children, 6,* 104–121.

Zigler, E. F., & Finn Stevenson, M. F. (1993). *Children in a changing world: Development and social issues.* Pacific Grove, CA: Brooks/Cole.

Zigler, E. F., Abelson, W. D., Trickett, P. K., & Seitz, V. (1982). Is an intervention program necessary to improve economically disadvantaged children's IQ scores? *Child Development, 53,* 340–348.

Zimmerman, M. A., Salem, D. A., & Maton, K. I. (1995). Family structure and psychosocial correlates among urban African-American adolescent males. *Child Development, 66,* 1598–1613.

Credits

This page constitutes an extension of the copyright page. We have made every effort to trace the ownership of all copyrighted material and to secure permission from copyright holders. In the event of any question arising as to the use of any material, we will be pleased to make the necessary corrections in future printings. Thanks are due to the following authors, publishers, and agents for permission to use the material indicated.

Chapter 1. 1: Nicholas Prior/Getty Images. **3:** © Michael Newman/PhotoEdit. **4:** center left, © Elizabeth Crews; bottom left, © Elizabeth Crews. **5:** © Elizabeth Crews. **6:** © Elizabeth Crews. **7:** © Elizabeth Crews. **9:** bottom left, Hulton Archive/Getty Images; top left, Julia Margaret Cameron/Getty Images; center left, ©Corbis/Bettmann. **15:** © Mary Kate Denny/PhotoEdit. **16:** © Corbis. **18:** Vanderlei Almeida/AFP/Getty Images. **27:** Jeffrey Aaronson/Network Aspen. **32:** center left, Andrew Olney/Getty Images; top left, Lambert/Hulton Archive/Getty Images. **36:** Frank Pedrick/The Image Works.

Chapter 2. 42: Lori Adamski Peek/Getty Images. **50:** © Corbis/Bettmann. **52:** © Corbis/Bettmann. **53:** Courtesy of Professor Benjamin Harris. **54:** Nina Leen/Time & Life Pictures/Getty Images. **55:** Courtesy of Albert Bandura. **57:** Courtesy of Albert Bandura. **60:** Yves de Braine/Black Star. **61:** © Myrleen Ferguson Cate/PhotoEdit. **65:** Nina Leen/Time Life Pictures/Getty Images. **68:** © - LWA-Dann Tardif/Corbis. **69:** © Cornell University.

Chapter 3. 78: James Porto/Getty Images. **85:** top left, Barbara Penoyar/Getty Images; bottom right, Science Source/Photo Researchers Inc.; bottom left, Science Source/Photo Researchers, Inc. **88:** Science Source/Photo Researchers, Inc. **93:** Petit Format/Photo Researchers, Inc. **97:** Dr. Najeeb Layyous/Photo Researchers, Inc. **107:** Alan Carey/The Image Works. **110:** Koki lino/Getty Images. **112:** Robert Burroughs.

Chapter 4. 118: © Ralph Hutchings/Visuals Unlimited. **120:** © Eurelios/Phototake. **122:** Neil Harding/Getty Images. **123:** Nestle/Petit Format/Photo Researchers, Inc. **124:** bottom center and bottom right, Lennart Nilsson/Albert Bonniers Forlag AB/A CHILD IS BORN. **130:** Alistair Berg/FSP/ The Liaison Agency. **131:** George Steinmetz. **144:** David Sams/Stock Boston. **146:** Tom Tucker/Science Source/Photo Researchers, Inc. **148:** Jeff Persons/Stock Boston. **152:** Getty Images.

Chapter 5. 158: ©Anna Zuckerman-Vdovenko/PhotoEdit. **161:** bottom left, Cuhna/Petit Format/Photo Researchers, Inc.; bottom right © Spencer Grant/PhotoEdit. **165:** Jean-Gerard Sidaner/Photo Researchers, Inc. **167:** David Linton. **168:** © Journal-Courier/Steve Warmowski/The Image Works. **169:** top left, Anthony DeCasper; bottom left, © Bill Aron/PhotoEdit. **170:** © Joel Gordon. **173:** Steve McAlister/Getty Images. **178:** © Mark Richards/PhotoEdit. **180:** Bruce Plotkin/The Image Works. **184:** Panel series of photos from Casasola, M. (2005). When less is more: How infants learn to form an abstract categorical representation of support. *Child Development 76*, 279–290. **187:** Courtesy of Carolyn Rovee-Collier/Rutgers University. **188:** From A. N. Meltzoff & M. K. Moore (1977). "Imitation of facial and manual gestures by human neonates" *Science, 198*, 75–78. **189:** Peter Chapman.

Chapter 6. 194: Anne Ackermann/Getty Images. **197:** © Tony Freeman/PhotoEdit. **199:** © Novastock/PhotoEdit. **207:** H. Bruhat/The Liasion Agency. **209:** top center, Bruce Plotkin/The Image Works; bottom left, John & Eva Momatiuk/The Image Works. **210:** © Michelle D. Bridwell/PhotoEdit. **211:** Bob Daemmrich/Stock Boston. **213:** © Smiley N. Pool/Dallas Morning News/Corbis. **215:** Bob Daemmrich/Stock Boston. **218:** © Tony Freeman/PhotoEdit. **222:** © Barbara Stitzer/PhotoEdit. **229:** © Jennie Woodcock/Corbis. **233:** Jean Michel Turpin/Liaison/Getty Images.

Chapter 7. 242: Veer/Michael Malyszko/Getty Images. **244:** Elizabeth Crews/The Image Works. **248:** © Myrleen Ferguson Cate/PhotoEdit. **250:** Jean-Claude Le Jeune/Stock Boston. **256:** © Jeff Greenberg/PhotoEdit. **259:** Courtesy of Rheta de Vries. **264:** © Myrleen Ferguson Cate/PhotoEdit. **269:** © Dana White/PhotoEdit. **274:** Archives of the History of American Psychology, University of Akron. **278:** Bob Daemmrich/Stock Boston. **283:** © Myrleen Ferguson Cate/PhotoEdit.

Chapter 8. **290:** Photo Alto Photography / Veer.com. **291:** Roy Botterell / Getty Images. **296:** © Laura Dwight Corbis. **312:** Elizabeth Crews / The Image Works. **315:** Mark Burnett / Photo Researchers, Inc. **316:** © David Young-Wolff / PhotoEdit. **318:** © Cassy Cohen / PhotoEdit. **325:** Elizabeth Crews. **327:** David Wells / The Image Works. **328:** © David Young-Wolff / PhotoEdit.

Chapter 9. **336:** © Joel Gordon. **338:** © Corbis / Bettmann. **342:** Cameramann / The Image Works. **350:** Alan S.Weiner / The Liaison Agency / Getty Images. **353:** Nancy Stone / The Chicago Tribune. **360:** Bob Daemmrich / The Image Works. **369:** © Tony Freeman / PhotoEdit. **372:** Ken Cavanagh / Photo Researchers, Inc. **373:** Paul Conklin / Gail Meese Photography.

Chapter 10. **378:** © Corbis. **379:** Tom McHugh / Photo Researchers, Inc. **383:** © Corbis / Bettmann. **393:** David Grossman / Photo Researchers, Inc. **395:** © Tony Freeman / PhotoEdit. **396:** Elizabeth Crews. **402:** © Richard T. Nowitz / Corbis. **406:** Lawrence Migdale / Stock Boston. **408:** Frank Siteman / Stone / Getty Images. **410:** Joseph Nettis / Stock Boston. **412:** © Myrleen Ferguson Cate / PhotoEdit. **414:** Ann Clark Beurskens.

Chapter 11. **420:** Hoby Finn / PhotoDisc / Getty Images. **422:** Courtesy of Carroll E. Izard, University of Delaware. **426:** Elyse Lewin / Getty Images. **427:** Stephanie Rausser / Getty Images. **429:** © Masterfile. **433:** Bob Daemmrich / Stock Boston. **435:** Ann Clark Beurskens. **437:** © Ronnie Kaufman / Corbis. **438:** Martin Rogers / Stock Boston. **440:** © David Young-Wolff / PhotoEdit. **447:** Keren Su / Getty Images. **448:** © Robert Brenner / PhotoEdit. **451:** © Michael Newman / PhotoEdit. **460:** © Paul Conklin / PhotoEdit.

Chapter 12. **466:** © Bettmann / Corbis. **469:** © Laura Dwight. **470:** Bob Daemmrich / Stock Boston. **472:** Jeffery W. Myers / Photo Network. **476:** Jeffrey Greenberg / Photo Researchers, Inc. **482:** © Bill Schild / Corbis. **483:** Robert Reichert / The Liaison Agency / Getty Images. **484:** © Bill Aron / PhotoEdit. **494:** © Colin Young-Wolff / PhotoEdit. **496:** © Jonathan Nourok / PhotoEdit. **499:** Bob Daemmrich / The Image Works. **503:** © Robert Brenner / PhotoEdit.

Chapter 13. **508:** © Cut and Deal Ltd / Alamy. **509:** © Corbis. **510:** © Grace / zefa / Corbis. **514:** J. Kramer / The Image Works. **514:** Lawrence Migdale / Photo Researchers, Inc. **519:** Elizabeth Crews / The Image Works. **528:** Rick Smolan / Stock Boston. **529:** © David Young-Wolff / PhotoEdit. **530:** bottom left, © Laura Dwight / Corbis. **541:** Roger Sandier / The Liaison Agency / Getty Images.

Chapter 14. **546:** Don Smetzer / Getty Images. **548:** © Elizabeth Crews. **549:** Catherine Ursillo / Photo Researchers, Inc. **556:** © Janine Wiedel Photolibrary / Alamy. **560:** top left, Robert Van Der Hilgt / Getty Images; bottom left, © Mary Kate Denny / PhotoEdit. **563:** © David Young-Wolff / PhotoEdit. **566:** bottom left, Elizabeth Crews / The Image Works. **578:** © Mary Kate Denny / PhotoEdit. **582:** © Bob Krist / Corbis. **583:** Phil Boorman / Getty Images.

Chapter 15. **594:** Jack Hollingsworth / Getty Images. **596:** Juan Silva / The Image Bank / Getty Images. **598:** © David Young-Wolff / PhotoEdit. **599:** © Michael Newman / PhotoEdit. **601:** Charles Gullung / Getty Images. **609:** © Michael Newman / PhotoEdit. **611:** Ursula Markus / Photo Researchers, Inc. **613:** © Dennis MacDonald / PhotoEdit. **617:** © Michael Newman / PhotoEdit.

Chapter 16. **622:** bottom left, Bob Torrez / Getty Images; bottom right, © Corbis; top right, © Ellen Senisi / The Image Works; top left, © Thinkstock / Alamy. **625:** © Bob Daemmrich / PhotoEdit. **627:** © Michael Newman / PhotoEdit. **632:** © Everett Collection, Inc. **633:** Bob Daemmrich / Stock Boston. **642:** Robert E. Daemmrich / Getty Images. **644:** Bob Daemmrich / The Image Works. **645:** Fujifotos / The Image Works. **648:** © Jeff Greenberg / PhotoEdit. **651:** © Laura Dwight / Corbis. **654:** Martin Rogers / Stone / Getty Images. **657:** Jeff I. Greenberg / Photo Researchers, Inc.

Name Index

G

Subject Index

D